Witness Neuroscience Firsthand

 Macmillan Education **LaunchPad**Solo **NEUROSCIENCE**

Available at www.macmillanhighered.com/launchpadsolo/neurotk

The 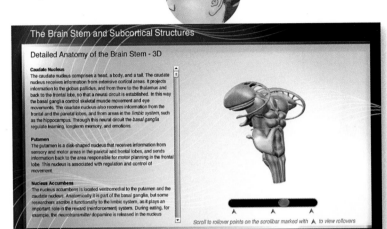 Macmillan Education **LaunchPad**Solo for Neuroscience is a powerful web-based tool for learning the core concepts of behavioral neuroscience—by witnessing them firsthand. These thirty interactive tutorials allow students to see the nervous system in action via dynamic illustrations, animations, and models that demystify the neural mechanisms behind behavior. Each activity is accompanied by a set of carefully crafted multiple choice questions for assessment that is easy to assign and instantly graded. Based on Worth Publishers' groundbreaking *Foundations of Behavioral Neuroscience CD-ROM*, the Macmillan Education **LaunchPad**Solo for Neuroscience is a valuable accompaniment to any course.

TOPICS AND ACTIVITIES

Neural Communication

Structure of a Neuron

The Membrane Potential

Conduction of the Action Potential

Synaptic Transmission

Neural Integration

Central Nervous System

Subdivisions of the Central Nervous System

Subcortical Structures

Sensory Systems–Vision

Sensory Systems–Audition

Sensory Systems–Somatosenses

Sensory Systems–Olfaction

Motor System

Limbic System

Language

The Cortex

Brain Stem

The Spinal Cord

Visual System

The Eye

Retina

Optic Chiasm

Lateral Geniculate Nucleus

Superior Colliculus

Primary Visual Cortex

Higher Order Visual Areas

Control of Movement

Organization of the Motor Systems

Muscle and Receptor Anatomy

Muscle Contraction

Spinal Reflexes

Descending Motor Tracts

Primary Motor Cortex

Higher Order Motor Cortex

Basal Ganglia

Cerebellum

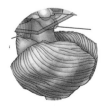

Fundamentals of
HUMAN NEUROPSYCHOLOGY

SEVENTH EDITION

BRYAN KOLB & **IAN Q. WHISHAW**

University of Lethbridge

WORTH
PUBLISHERS

A Macmillan Education Imprint
New York

Publisher: Rachel Losh
Senior Acquisitions Editor: Daniel DeBonis
Development Editor: Barbara Brooks
Assistant Editor: Nadina Persaud
Editorial Assistant: Katie Pachnos
Executive Marketing Manager: Katherine Nurre
Executive Media Editor: Rachel Comerford
Director of Editing, Design, and Media Production for the Sciences
    and Social Sciences: Tracey Kuehn
Managing Editor: Lisa Kinne
Project Editors: Enrico Bruno, Andrew Roney, and Janice Stangel
Production Manager: Sarah Segal
Associate Media Editor: Anthony Casciano
Photo Editor: Cecilia Varas
Photo Researcher: Richard Fox
Art Director: Diana Blume
Interior Designer: Tamara Newnam
Cover Designer: Kevin Kall
Art Manager: Matthew McAdams
Illustrations: Dragonfly Media
Composition: Northeastern Graphic, Inc.
Printing and Binding: King Printing Co., Inc.
Cover Art: *Orla* by Cian McLoughlin

Library of Congress Preassigned Control Number: 2014946473

ISBN-10: 1-4292-8295-9
ISBN-13: 978-1-4292-8295-6

Printed in the United States of America

Seventh Printing

Worth Publishers
41 Madison Avenue
New York, NY 10010
www.worthpublishers.com

To all the students whose interest in how the brain produces
the mind and controls behavior makes this book possible.

ABOUT THE AUTHORS

Bryan Kolb received his Ph.D. from The Pennsylvania State University and conducted postdoctoral work at the University of Western Ontario and the Montreal Neurological Institute. In 1976 he moved to the University of Lethbridge, Alberta, where he is a professor of neuroscience and holds a Board of Governors Chair in Neuroscience. His current research examines how perinatal factors—including tactile stimulation, psychoactive drugs, stress, and injury—modify the developing cerebral cortex and how these changes are related to behavior. Kolb is a fellow of the Royal Society of Canada, the Canadian Psychological Association (CPA), the American Psychological Association, and the Association of Psychological Science. Currently a senior fellow of the Child Brain Development program of the Canadian Institute for Advanced Research, he is a recipient of the Hebb Prize from the CPA and from the Canadian Society for Brain, Behaviour, and Cognitive Science (CSBBCS). He has received honorary doctorates from the University of British Columbia, Thompson Rivers University, and Concordia University. He is a recipient of the Ingrid Speaker Gold Medal for research, the distinguished teaching medal from the University of Lethbridge, and the Key to the City of Lethbridge. He and his wife train and show horses in Western riding performance events.

Ian Q. Whishaw received his Ph.D. from Western University and is a professor of neuroscience at the University of Lethbridge. He has held visiting appointments at the University of Texas, the University of Michigan, the University of Cambridge, and the University of Strasbourg. He is a fellow of Clair Hall, Cambridge, the Canadian Psychological Association, the American Psychological Association, and the Royal Society of Canada. He is a recipient of the Canadian Humane Society Bronze Medal for bravery, the Ingrid Speaker Gold Medal for research, the distinguished teaching medal from the University of Lethbridge, and the Donald O. Hebb Prize. He has received the Key to the City of Lethbridge and has honorary doctorates from Thompson Rivers University and the University of Lethbridge. His research addresses the neural basis of skilled movement and the neural basis of brain disease. The Institute for Scientific Information includes him in its list of most-cited neuroscientists. His hobby is training and showing horses for Western performance events.

BRIEF CONTENTS

CONTENTS

Coverage links neuropsychological theory and assessment

PREFACE

Looking back to 1980, when *Fundamentals of Human Neuropsychology*'s first edition appeared, reminds us that in the 1970s, human neuropsychology did not yet exist as a unified body of knowledge about the human brain. The field had coalesced around hunches and inferences based on laboratory studies of monkeys, cats, and rats as well as on scattered studies of humans with assorted brain injuries. Over the past 40 years, as neuropsychology expanded, cognitive and social neuroscience have emerged as disciplines. Advances in and ever-more incisive use of noninvasive neuroimaging and abundant research innovations all have improved our understanding of brain anatomy.

Studies of nonhuman species remain central to human neuropsychology's core principles, especially in understanding the structure and connectivity of the primate brain, but are more focused on mechanisms than behavioral phenomena. Many researchers may share a bias that functional neuroimaging can replace studying brain-injured humans and laboratory animals. To others, this seems unlikely given the complexity of brain processes and the nature of subtraction methods used in imaging. The two approaches have become complementary, and this seventh edition reflects their intellectual evolution:

- *Neuroimaging has led the renaissance in understanding neural networks and appreciating the brain's connectome.* In this edition, we have expanded Chapter 7, Imaging the Brain's Activity, both to include new methods and to consider the pros and cons of different techniques in light of their relevant uses and costs (see Section 7.5). Coverage of dynamic neural networks appears throughout the book, especially in Chapters 10, 16 to 22, and 27.

- *Epigenetics explains how our behaviors change our brains.* We introduce basic genetics and epigenetic principles in Section 2.3 and highlight both factors throughout the book to reflect the expanding emphasis on epigenetics as a factor in cerebral organization.

- *Neuropsychological assessment is vital for evaluating patients with focal brain injuries.* One unexpected consequence of the cognitive neuroscience revolution is a declining appreciation for neuropsychological theory and clinical focus. In this new edition, we employ the venerable maze as a graphic icon (shown at right) to identify for the reader particular discussions, cases, tables, and figures that link theory and assessment throughout the book.

Content and Structure

Fundamentals differs from other textbooks of psychology, cognitive neuroscience, or neuroscience. In our experience, students find it helpful to see the brain from two organizational perspectives, anatomical and behavioral.

- We continue to provide the requisite basic background—about history, evolution, genetics and epigenetics, anatomy, physiology, pharmacology, and methodology—in Part I, Chapters 1 to 7.

- Equally fundamental to understanding subsequent material, Part II, Chapters 8 to 12, outlines the general organization and functions of the cerebral cortex.

- Part III, Chapters 13 to 17, focuses on the anatomically defined cortical regions. Understanding the organization of the cerebral cortex is central to appreciating how the brain functions to produce the complex processes that underlie complex behaviors.

- The psychological constructs presented in Part IV, Chapters 18 to 22, including language, memory, social behavior and affect, spatial behavior, and attention and consciousness, emerge from the neuronal networks explored in Part III. Shifting from anatomy to psychological processes naturally means revisiting material from earlier parts, but this time in the context of psychological theory rather than anatomy.

- Part V, Chapters 23 to 28, considers brain development and plasticity and includes more-detailed discussions of brain disorders introduced earlier in the book. Chapters on neurological and psychiatric disorders and on neuropsychological assessment continue the book's emphasis on approaching human brain functions from an interdisciplinary perspective.

We have updated all of the chapters and the glossary that follows, both to correspond to new material that reflects the changing face of neuropsychology and to include some unexpected topics—neuroeconomics in Section 22.4 and micronutrients in Section 27.9 are two. Maintaining a manageable length meant sacrificing some detail that may have been prominent in previous editions, sometimes reaching back to the first edition.

To address the challenge inherent in using a comprehensive text and to facilitate access to information, we added section numbers to each chapter's main headings. Readers can easily locate interrelated material relevant across several topics, refresh their knowledge, or jump ahead to learn more.

Acknowledgments

As in the past, we must sincerely thank many people who have contributed to the development of this edition. We are particularly indebted to colleagues from around the world who have been so supportive and have strongly encouraged us to include their favorite topics. We have done so wherever possible.

We also thank the reviewers solicited by our editors on the sixth edition of *Fundamentals*. Their anonymous comments contributed varied perspectives and valuable points of consensus that helped us shape the new edition.

Julie Alvarez
Tulane University

Marlene Behrmann
Carnegie Mellon University

Edward Castañeda
The University of Texas at El Paso

Pauline Dibbets
Maastricht University

Peter Donovick
The State University of New York at Binghamton

Amanda Higley
Point Loma Nazarene University

Jamie Lillie
Argosy University, Schaumburg

Salvatore Massa
Marist College

Taryn Myers
Virginia Wesleyan College

Martin Paczynski
George Mason University

Rosie Reid
Dublin Business School

Tony Robertson
Vancouver Island University

Joe Wayand
Walsh University

Robin Wellington
St. John's University

The staff at Worth Publishers and W. H. Freeman and Company are amazing and have made this task far more enjoyable than it would be without them. These folks include our sponsoring editor, Daniel DeBonis, assistant editor Nadina Persaud, and editorial assistant Katie Pachnos; our project editors, Enrico Bruno, Andrew Roney, and Janice Stangel; and our production manager, Sarah Segal. Our thanks to art director Diana Blume and interior designer Tamara Newnam for a fresh, inviting, accessible new book design, and to Kevin Kall for a striking cover.

Once again, Cecilia Varas coordinated photo research, ably assisted by researcher Richard Fox. They found photographs and other illustrative materials that we would not have found on our own. We remain indebted to art manager Matt McAdams and the artists at Dragonfly Media for their excellent work in expanding the illustration program and to Kate Scully and her team at Northeastern Graphic for their talents in translating the manuscript onto the page.

Our manuscript editor, Martha Solonche, has contributed to the book's clarity and consistency and proofreader Kate Daly to its accuracy. And as in the past, our gratitude to Barbara Brooks, our development editor, knows no bounds. She has provided a strong guiding hand to our thinking and organization and has done so with humor and a commitment to excellence that shows its stamp all over the book. Thank you, Barbara, for reminding us that the book is for students, not senior investigators, and thus requires us to write simply and clearly, and for keeping us abreast of topical news items that we might otherwise not encounter in our reading of the field's diverse literature.

Once again, errors remain solely attributable to us. In a field that has expanded so dramatically since our first edition, we hope that readers continue to acquire a breadth of knowledge in the ever-expanding world of human neuropsychology. Finally, we thank our students, who have motivated us to continue the journey of *Fundamentals of Human Neuropsychology* for nearly 40 years. Seeing the faces of students light up when they begin to understand how the marvelous brain can produce cognition and behavior continues to be rewarding and is what this endeavor is all about. Once again, we must thank our wives for putting up with us when we were distracted by deadlines and may not always have been our "usual" selves.

Bryan Kolb and Ian Q. Whishaw

MEDIA AND SUPPLEMENTS

Fundamentals of Human Neuropsychology, Seventh Edition, features a variety of supplemental materials for students and teachers of the text. For more information about any of the items below, please visit Macmillan's online catalog at http://www.macmillanhighered.com.

Available at www.macmillanhighered.com/launchpadsolo/neurotk

LaunchPad Solo is a powerful Web-based tool for learning the core concepts of behavioral neuroscience—by witnessing them firsthand. These 30 interactive tutorials allow students to see the nervous system in action via dynamic illustrations, animations, and models that demystify the neural mechanisms behind behavior. These interactive simulations enhance students' understanding of complex biological mechanisms, and carefully crafted multiple-choice questions make it easy to assign and assess each activity. Based on Worth Publishers' groundbreaking *Foundations of Behavioral Neuroscience* CD-ROM, LaunchPad Solo is a valuable accompaniment to any biopsychology course.

Topics and Activities

Neural Communication
- Structure of a Neuron
- The Membrane Potential
- Conduction of the Action Potential
- Synaptic Transmission
- Neural Integration

Central Nervous System
- Subdivisions of the Central Nervous System
- Subcortical Structures
- Sensory Systems—Vision
- Sensory Systems—Audition
- Sensory Systems—Somatosenses
- Sensory Systems—Olfaction
- Motor System
- Limbic System
- Language
- The Cortex
- Brain Stem and Subcortical Structures
- The Spinal Cord

Visual System
- The Eye
- Retina
- Optic Chiasm
- Lateral Geniculate Nucleus
- Superior Colliculus
- Primary Visual Cortex
- Higher Order Visual Areas

Control of Movement
- Organization of the Motor Systems
- Muscle and Receptor Anatomy
- Muscle Contraction
- Spinal Reflexes
- Descending Motor Tracts
- Primary Motor Cortex
- Higher Order Motor Cortex
- Basal Ganglia
- Cerebellum

> *Fundamentals of Human Neuropsychology*, Seventh Edition, can be ordered with LaunchPad Solo at no additional cost by using the following ISBNs.
>
> Hardcover Text & LaunchPad Solo Access Card
>
> ISBN-10: 1-3190-1715-0 / ISBN-13: 978-1-3190-1715-6

CourseSmart e-Book A complete electronic version of *Fundamentals of Human Neuropsychology*, Seventh Edition, can be previewed and purchased at **www.coursesmart.com**. Students can choose to view the CourseSmart e-Book online or download it to a personal computer or a portable media player such as a smartphone or iPad. This flexible, easy-to-use format makes the text more portable than ever before!

Psychology and the Real World: Essays Illustrating Fundamental Contributions to Society, Second Edition, is a superb collection of essays by major researchers that describes their landmark studies. Published in association with the not-for-profit FABBS Foundation, this engaging reader includes Bruce McEwen's work on the neurobiology of stress and adaptation, Elizabeth Loftus's own reflections on her study of false memories, and Jeremy Wolfe on his study of visual search. The new edition also features the new essay, "Can the Mind Be Read in the Brain Waves?" by Emanual Donchin, among many others. A portion of all proceeds is donated to FABBS to support societies of cognitive, psychological, behavioral, and brain sciences.

Revised! Test Bank Prepared by Tony Robertson of Vancouver Island University and Robin Wellington of St. John's University, the revised test bank includes over 50 questions per chapter including multiple-choice and short-answer questions. Each item is keyed to the page in the textbook on which the answer can be found. All of the questions have been thoroughly reviewed and edited for accuracy and clarity.

PowerPoint Slide Sets For download on the book's catalog page (http://www.macmillanhighered.com/Catalog/product/fundamentalsofhumanneuropsychology-seventhedition-kolb/instructorresources) we offer two sets of PowerPoint © presentations. For each chapter, there is a set that includes chapter art and illustrations and a final lecture presentation set that merges detailed chapter outlines with text illustrations and artwork from the book. Each set can be used directly or customized to fit your needs.

Course Management Aids The various resources for this textbook are available in the appropriate format for users of Blackboard, WebCT, Angel, Desire2Learn, and other systems. For more information, please visit our Web site at **www.macmillanhighered.com/lms.**

1 The Development of Neuropsychology

| PORTRAIT | Living with Traumatic Brain Injury |

L.D., an aspiring golfer, had worked as a cook. Following brain damage, the lawyers negotiating his case puzzled over how L.D. continued to excel at golf but at the same time was unable to return to his former work as a cook.

Four years earlier, when he was 21, L.D. had been invited to participate in a sports promotion at a pub. He became ill and was helped onto a balcony by a pub employee. On the balcony, he slipped out of the employee's grasp and fell down five flights of stairs, striking his head against the stairs and wall. He was taken, unconscious, to the emergency ward of the local hospital, where his concussion was assessed on the Glasgow Coma Scale rating as 3, the lowest score on a scale from 3 to 15.

A computed tomography (CT) scan revealed bleeding and swelling on the right side of L.D.'s brain. A neurosurgeon performed a craniotomy (skull removal) over his right frontal cortex to relieve pressure and remove blood. A subsequent CT scan revealed further bleeding on the left side of his brain, and a second craniotomy was performed.

When discharged from the hospital 6 weeks later, L.D.'s recall of the events consisted only of remembering that he had entered the pub and then becoming

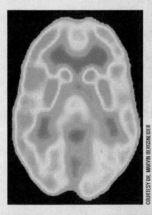
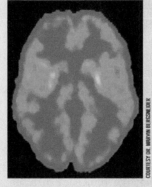

COURTESY DR. MARVIN BERGSNEIDER

aware that he was in a hospital 3 weeks later. L.D. was unable to return to work because he found the multitasking involved in preparing meals too difficult. He was seeking compensation from the company that had hosted the sports promotion and from the pub where he had been injured.

We found that L.D. became frustrated and annoyed when attempting to cook. He had lost his sense of smell and taste and was not interested in socializing. He and his girlfriend had ended their 4-year relationship. We administered a comprehensive neuropsychological examination, and his scores on most tests were typical, except for tests of verbal memory and attention. Magnetic resonance imaging (MRI), a brain-scanning method that can reveal the brain's structure in detail, showed some diffuse damage to both sides of his brain. The accompanying positron emission tomography (PET) images contrast blood flow in a healthy brain (top) to blood flow in patients like L.D. (bottom).

Based on previous patients with traumatic brain injuries and behavioral and brain symptoms similar to L.D.'s, we recommended compensation, which L.D. did receive, in addition to assistance in finding work less demanding than cooking. He was able to live on his own and successfully returned to playing golf.

According to National Institute of Neurological Disorders and Stroke estimates, 1.7 million U.S. residents receive medical attention each year after suffering **traumatic brain injury** (TBI), a wound to the brain that results from a blow to the head (detailed in Section 26.3, including *concussion*, the common term for mild TBI). TBI is a contributing factor in 30% of deaths due to accidents and can result from head blows while playing sports, from falls, and from vehicle accidents. While also the most common cause of discharge from military service

(Gubata et al., 2013), TBI most frequently occurs in children under the age of 6, young adults, and those over age 65. The number of people who endure TBI each year but do not report an injury is not known.

L.D. is not unusual in that, in his own view and in the view of acquaintances, he has mainly recovered, but lingering problems prevent him from resuming his former level of employment. L.D. is also not unusual in that he puzzles both friends and experts with his ability to do some things well while being unable to do other things that appear less difficult. Finally, L.D. is not unusual in that the diffuse brain injury revealed by brain-scanning methods (see Chapter 7) does not predict his abilities and disabilities well.

Neuropsychological testing is required to confirm that he has enduring cognitive deficits and to identify those deficits. L.D.'s poor scores on tests of memory and attention are associated with his difficulty in everyday problem solving, a mental skill referred to as *executive function*. Thus, L.D. can play golf at a high level because it requires that he execute only one act at a time, but he cannot prepare a meal, which requires him to multitask.

This book's objective is to describe **neuropsychology**, the scientific study of the relations between brain function and behavior. Neuropsychology draws information from many disciplines—anatomy, biology, biophysics, ethology, pharmacology, physiology, physiological psychology, and philosophy among them. Neuropsychological investigations into the brain–behavior relationship can identify impairments in behavior that result from brain trauma and from diseases that affect the brain.

Neuropsychology is strongly influenced by two experimental and theoretical investigations into brain function: the **brain theory**, which states that the brain is the source of behavior; and the **neuron theory**, the idea that the unit of brain structure and function is the **neuron**, or nerve cell. This chapter traces the development of these two theories and introduces neuropsychology's major principles, which have emerged from investigating brain function and which we apply in subsequent chapters.

1.1 The Brain Theory

People knew what the brain looked like long before they had any idea of what it did. Early in human history, hunters must have noticed that all animals have brains and that the brains of different animals, including humans, although varying greatly in size, look quite similar. Over the past 2000 years, anatomists have produced drawings of the brain, named its distinctive parts, and developed methods to describe the functions of those parts.

What Is the Brain?

Brain is an Old English word for the tissue found within the skull (cranium). **Figure 1.1**A shows a human brain as oriented in the skull of an upright human. Just as your body is symmetrical, having two arms and two legs, so is your brain. Its two almost symmetrical halves are called **hemispheres**, one on the left side of the body and the other on the right, as shown in the frontal view. If you make your right hand into a fist and hold it up with the thumb pointing toward the front, the fist can represent the brain's left hemisphere as positioned within the skull (Figure 1.1B).

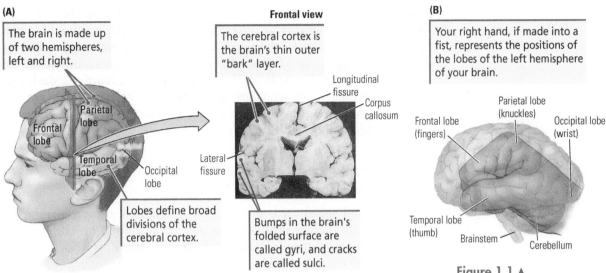

(A)

The brain is made up of two hemispheres, left and right.

Parietal lobe

Frontal lobe

Temporal lobe

Occipital lobe

Lobes define broad divisions of the cerebral cortex.

Frontal view

The cerebral cortex is the brain's thin outer "bark" layer.

Longitudinal fissure

Corpus callosum

Lateral fissure

Bumps in the brain's folded surface are called gyri, and cracks are called sulci.

(B)

Your right hand, if made into a fist, represents the positions of the lobes of the left hemisphere of your brain.

Parietal lobe (knuckles)

Frontal lobe (fingers)

Occipital lobe (wrist)

Temporal lobe (thumb)

Brainstem

Cerebellum

Figure 1.1 ▲

The Human Brain (A) The human brain, as oriented in the head. The visible part of the intact brain is the cerebral cortex, a thin sheet of tissue folded many times and fitting snugly inside the skull. (B) Your right fist can serve as a guide to the orientation of the brain and its cerebral lobes. (Photograph: Arthur Glauberman/ Science Source.)

The brain's basic plan is that of a tube filled with salty fluid called **cerebrospinal fluid** (CSF), which cushions the brain and assists in removing metabolic waste. Parts of the tube's covering have bulged outward and folded, forming the more complicated-looking surface structures that initially catch the eye in Figure 1.1A. The brain's most conspicuous outer feature is the crinkled tissue that has expanded from the front of the tube to such an extent that it folds over and covers much of the rest of the brain (Figure 1.1A at right). This outer layer is the **cerebral cortex** (usually referred to as just the cortex). The word *cortex*, meaning "bark" in Latin, is apt, because the cortex's folded appearance resembles the bark of a tree and because, as bark covers a tree, cortical tissue covers most of the rest of the brain.

The folds, or bumps, in the cortex are called **gyri** (*gyrus* is Greek for "circle"), and the creases between them are called **sulci** (*sulcus* is Greek for "trench"). Some large sulci are called fissures: the **longitudinal fissure**, shown in the Figure 1.1 frontal view, divides the two hemispheres, and the **lateral fissure** divides each hemisphere into halves. (In our fist analogy, the lateral fissure is the crease separating the thumb from the other fingers.) Pathways called *commissures*, the largest of which is the **corpus callosum**, connect the brain's hemispheres.

The cortex of each hemisphere forms four lobes, each named after the skull bones beneath which they lie. The **temporal lobe** is located below the lateral fissure at approximately the same place as the thumb on your upraised fist (Figure 1.1B). Lying immediately above the temporal lobe is the **frontal lobe**, so called because it is located at the front of the brain beneath the frontal bones. The **parietal lobe** is located behind the frontal lobe, and the **occipital lobe** constitutes the area at the back of each hemisphere.

The cerebral cortex constitutes most of the **forebrain**, so named because it develops from the front part of the neural tube that makes up an embryo's primitive brain. The remaining "tube" underlying the cortex is the **brainstem**. The brainstem is in turn connected to the **spinal cord**, which descends down the back within the vertebral column. To visualize the relations among these parts of the brain, again imagine your upraised fist: the folded fingers represent the cortex, the heel of the hand represents the brainstem, and the arm represents the spinal cord.

This three-part brain is conceptually useful evolutionarily, anatomically, and functionally. Evolutionarily, animals with only spinal cords preceded those with brainstems, which preceded those with forebrains. Anatomically, in prenatal development, the spinal cord forms before the brainstem, which forms before the forebrain. Functionally, the forebrain mediates cognitive functions; the brainstem mediates regulatory functions such as eating, drinking, and moving; and the spinal cord conveys sensory information into the brain and sends commands from the brain to the muscles to move.

How Does the Brain Relate to the Rest of the Nervous System?

The brains and spinal cords of mammals are encased in protective bones: the skull protects the brain, and vertebrae protect the spinal cord. Together, the brain and spinal cord are called the **central nervous system**, or CNS. The CNS is connected to the rest of the body through nerve fibers.

Some fibers carry information away from the CNS; others bring information into it. These nerve fibers constitute the **peripheral nervous system**, or PNS. One distinguishing feature between the central and peripheral nervous systems is that PNS tissue will regrow after damage, whereas the CNS does not regenerate lost tissue. Thus the long-term prospect for L.D. is that he will show little further recovery in higher brain functions such as planning, but his golf game may improve.

Nerve fibers that bring information to the CNS are extensively connected to sensory receptors on the body's surface and to muscles, enabling the brain to sense the world and to react. This subdivision of the PNS is called the **somatic nervous system** (SNS). Organized into **sensory pathways**, collections of fibers carry messages for specific senses, such as hearing, vision, and touch. Sensory pathways carry information collected on one side of the body mainly to the cortex in the *opposite* hemisphere. The brain uses this information to construct perceptions of the world, memories of past events, and expectations about the future.

Motor pathways are groups of nerve fibers that connect the brain and spinal cord to the body's muscles through the SNS. Movements produced by motor pathways include the eye movements that you are using to read this book, the hand movements that you make while turning or scrolling through the pages, and your body's posture as you read. The parts of the cortex that produce movement mainly send information out via motor pathways to muscles on the opposite side of the body. Thus, one hemisphere uses muscles on the opposite side of the body to produce movement.

Sensory and motor pathways also influence the muscles of your internal organs—the beating of your heart, contractions of your stomach, raising and lowering of your diaphragm to inflate and deflate your lungs. The pathways that control these organs are a subdivision of the PNS called the **autonomic nervous system** (ANS). **Figure 1.2** diagrams these major divisions of the human nervous system.

Figure 1.2 ▼

Major Divisions of the Human Nervous System
The brain and spinal cord together make up the CNS. All the nerve processes radiating from it and the neurons outside it connect to the sensory receptors and muscles in the SNS and to internal organs in the ANS. This constitutes the peripheral nervous system (PNS).

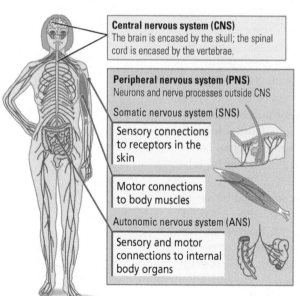

Central nervous system (CNS)
The brain is encased by the skull; the spinal cord is encased by the vertebrae.

Peripheral nervous system (PNS)
Neurons and nerve processes outside CNS

Somatic nervous system (SNS)

Sensory connections to receptors in the skin

Motor connections to body muscles

Autonomic nervous system (ANS)

Sensory and motor connections to internal body organs

◎ 1.2 Perspectives on the Brain and Behavior

The central topic in neuropsychology is how brain and behavior are related. We begin with three classic theories—mentalism, dualism, and materialism—representative of the many attempts scientists and philosophers have made to relate brain and behavior. Then we explain why contemporary brain investigators subscribe to the materialist view. In reviewing these theories, you will recognize that some "commonsense" ideas you might have about behavior are derived from one or another of these perspectives (Finger, 1994).

Aristotle: Mentalism

The Greek philosopher Aristotle (384–322 B.C.E.) was the first person to develop a formal theory of behavior. He proposed that a nonmaterial *psyche* is responsible for human thoughts, perceptions, and emotions and for such processes as imagination, opinion, desire, pleasure, pain, memory, and reason.

The psyche is independent of the body but in Aristotle's view, works through the heart to produce action. As in Aristotle's time, heart metaphors serve to this day to describe our behavior: "put your heart into it" and "she wore her heart on her sleeve" are but two. Aristotle's view that this nonmaterial psyche governs behavior was adopted by Christianity in its concept of the soul and has been widely disseminated throughout the world. *Mind* is an Anglo-Saxon word for memory, and, when "psyche" was translated into English, it became *mind*.

The philosophical position that a person's mind is responsible for behavior is called *mentalism*, meaning "of the mind." Mentalism still influences modern neuropsychology: many terms—sensation, perception, attention, imagination, emotion, memory, and volition among them—are still employed as labels for patterns of behavior. (Scan some of the chapter titles in this book.) Mentalism also influences people's ideas about how the brain might work, because the mind was proposed to be nonmaterial and so have no "working parts." We still use the term *mind* to describe our perceptions of ourselves as having unitary consciousness despite recognizing that the brain is composed of many parts, and as we describe in Section 1.3, has many separate functions.

Descartes: Dualism

René Descartes (1596–1650), a French anatomist and philosopher, wrote what could be considered the first neuropsychology text in 1684. In it he gave the brain a prominent role. Descartes was impressed by machines made in his time, such as those encased in certain statues on display for public amusement in the water gardens of Paris. When a passerby stopped in front of one particular statue, for example, his or her weight depressed a lever under the sidewalk, causing the statue to move and spray water at the person's face. Descartes proposed that the body is like these machines. It is material and thus clearly has spatial extent, and it responds mechanically and reflexively to events that impinge on it (**Figure 1.3**).

Described as nonmaterial and without spatial extent, the mind, as Descartes saw it, was different from the body. The body

Figure 1.3 ▼

Descartes's Concept of Reflex Action In this mechanistic depiction, heat from the flame causes a thread in the nerve to be pulled, releasing ventricular fluid through an opened pore. The fluid flows through the nerve, causing not only the foot to withdraw but the eyes and head to turn to look at it, the hands to advance, and the whole body to bend to protect it. Descartes ascribed to reflexes behaviors that today are considered too complex to be reflexive, whereas he did not conceive of behavior described as reflexive today. (From Descartes, 1664. Print Collector/Getty Images.)

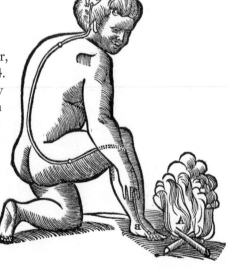

operated on principles similar to those of a machine, but the mind decided what movements the machine should make. Descartes located the site of action of the mind in the *pineal body*, a small structure high in the brainstem. His choice was based on the logic that the pineal body is the only structure in the nervous system not composed of two bilaterally symmetrical halves and moreover that it is located close to the ventricles. His idea was that the mind, working through the pineal body, controlled valves that allowed CSF to flow from the ventricles through nerves to muscles, filling them and making them move.

For Descartes, the cortex was not functioning neural tissue but merely a covering for the pineal body. People later argued against Descartes's hypothesis by pointing out that no obvious changes in behavior occur when the pineal body is damaged. Today, the pineal body, now called the *pineal gland*, is known to influence daily and seasonal biorhythms. And the cortex became central to understanding behavior as scientists began to discover that it performs the functions Descartes attributed to a nonmaterial mind.

Descartes's position that mind and body are separate but can interact is called **dualism**, to indicate that behavior is caused by two things. Dualism originated a quandary known as the **mind–body problem**: for Descartes, a person is capable of consciousness and rationality only because of having a mind, but how can a nonmaterial mind produce movements in a material body?

To understand the mind–body problem, consider that for the mind to affect the body, it must expend energy, adding new energy to the material world. The spontaneous creation of new energy violates a fundamental law of physics, the law of conservation of matter and energy. Thus, dualists who argue that mind and body interact causally cannot explain how.

Other dualists avoid this problem by reasoning either that the mind and body function in parallel, without interacting, or that the body can affect the mind but the mind cannot affect the body. These dualist positions allow for both a body and a mind by sidestepping the problem of violating the laws of physics.

Descartes's theory also spawned unforeseen and unfortunate consequences. In proposing his dualistic theory of brain function, Descartes also proposed that animals do not have minds and therefore are only machinelike, that the mind develops with language in children, and that mental disease impairs rational processes of the mind. Some of his followers justified the inhumane treatment of animals, children, and the mentally ill on the grounds that they did not have minds: an animal did not have a mind, a child developed a mind only at about 7 years of age when able to talk and reason, and the mentally ill had "lost their minds." Likewise misunderstanding Descartes's position, some people still argue that the study of animals cannot be a source of useful insight into human neuropsychology.

Descartes himself, however, was not so dogmatic. He was kind to his dog, Monsieur Grat. He suggested that whether animals had minds could be tested experimentally. He proposed that the key indications of the presence of a mind are the use of language and reason. He suggested that, if it could be demonstrated that animals could speak or reason, then such demonstration would indicate that they have minds. Exciting lines of research in modern experimental neuropsychology, demonstrated throughout this book, are directed toward the comparative study of animals and humans with respect to language and reason.

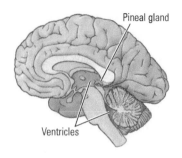

Pineal gland

Ventricles

Darwin: Materialism

By the mid-nineteenth century, our contemporary perspective of **materialism** was taking shape. The idea is that rational behavior can be fully explained by the workings of the nervous system. No need to refer to a nonmaterial mind. Materialism has its roots in the evolutionary theories of two English naturalists, Alfred Russel Wallace (1823–1913) and Charles Darwin (1809–1892).

Evolution by Natural Selection

Darwin and Wallace looked carefully at the structures of plants and animals and at animal behavior. Despite the diversity of living organisms, the two were struck by their many similarities. For example, the skeleton, muscles, internal organs, and nervous systems of humans, monkeys, and other mammals are similar. These observations support the idea that living things must be related, an idea widely held even before Wallace and Darwin. More importantly, these same observations led to the idea that the similarities could be explained if all animals had evolved from a common ancestor.

Darwin elaborated his theory in *On the Origin of Species by Means of Natural Selection, or the Preservation of Favored Races in the Struggle for Life*, originally published in 1859. He argued that all organisms, both living and extinct, are descended from an ancestor that lived in the remote past. Animals have similar traits because those traits are passed from parents to their offspring. The nervous system is one such trait, an adaptation that emerged only once in animal evolution. Consequently, the nervous systems of living animals are similar because they are descendants of that first nervous system. Those animals with brains likewise are related, because all animals with brains descend from the first animal to evolve a brain.

Natural selection is Darwin's theory for explaining how new species evolve and how they change over time. A **species** is a group of organisms that can breed among themselves but usually not with members of other species. Individual organisms within a species vary in their **phenotype**, the traits we can see or measure. Some are big, some are small, some are fat, some are fast, some are light colored, some have large teeth. Individual organisms whose traits best help them to survive in their environment are likely to leave more offspring that feature those traits.

Natural Selection and Heritable Factors

Beginning about 1857, Gregor Mendel (1822–1884), an Austrian monk, experimented with plant traits, such as the flower color and height of pea plants, and determined that such traits are due to heritable factors we now call *genes* (elaborated in Section 2.3). Thus, the unequal ability of individual organisms to survive and reproduce is related to the different genes they inherit from their parents and pass on to their offspring.

Mendel realized that the environment plays a role in how genes express traits: planting tall peas in poor soil reduces their height. Likewise, experience affects gene expression: children who lack educational opportunities may not adapt as well in society as children who attend school. The science that studies differences in *gene expression* related to environment and experience is **epigenetics** (see Section 2.3). Epigenetic factors do not change the genes individuals inherit, but they do affect whether a gene is active—turned on or off—and in this way influence an individual's phenotypic traits.

‣Environment and experience play an important role in how animals adapt and learn. Adaptation and learning are in turn enabled by the brain's ability to form new connections and pathways. This **neuroplasticity** is the nervous system's potential for physical or chemical change that enhances its adaptability to environmental change and its ability to compensate for injury. Epigeneticists are especially involved in describing how genes express the brain's plastic changes under the influence of environment and experience.

Contemporary Perspectives

As a scientific theory, contemporary brain theory is both materialistic and neutral with respect to beliefs, including religious beliefs. Science is not a belief system but rather a set of procedures designed to allow investigators to confirm answers to questions independently. Behavioral scientists, both those with and those without religious beliefs, use the scientific method to examine relations between the brain and behavior and to *replicate* (repeat) others' work on brain–behavior relationships. Today, when neuroscientists use the term *mind*, most are not referring to a nonmaterial entity but using it as shorthand for the collective functions of the brain.

◎ 1.3 Brain Function: Insights from Brain Injury

You may have heard statements such as, "Most people use only 10% of their brains" or "He put his entire mind to the problem." Both statements arise from early suggestions that people with brain damage often get along quite well. Nevertheless, most people who endure brain damage will tell you that some behavior is lost and some survives, as it did for L.D., whose case begins this chapter. Our understanding of brain function has its origins in individuals with brain damage. We now describe some fascinating neuropsychological concepts that have emerged from studying such individuals.

Localization of Function

The first general theory to propose that different parts of the brain have different functions was developed in the early 1800s by German anatomist Franz Josef Gall (1758–1828) and his partner Johann Casper Spurzheim (1776–1832) (Critchley, 1965). Gall and Spurzheim proposed that the cortex and its gyri were functioning parts of the brain and not just coverings for the pineal body. They supported their position by showing through dissection that the brain's most distinctive motor pathway, the *corticospinal* (cortex to spinal cord) *tract*, leads from the cortex of each hemisphere to the spinal cord on the opposite side of the body. Thus, they suggested, the cortex sends instructions to the spinal cord to command muscles to move. They also recognized that the two symmetrical hemispheres of the brain are connected by the corpus callosum and can thus interact.

Gall's ideas about behavior began with an observation made in his youth. Reportedly, he observed that students with good memories had large, protruding eyes and surmised that a well-developed memory area of the cortex located behind the eyes would cause them to protrude. Thus, he developed his hypothesis, called **localization of function**, that a different, specific brain area controls each kind of behavior.

Gall and Spurzheim furthered this idea by collecting instances of individual differences that they related to other prominent features of the head and skull. They proposed that a bump on the skull indicated a well-developed underlying cortical gyrus and therefore a greater capacity for a particular behavior; a depression in the same area indicated an underdeveloped gyrus and a concomitantly reduced faculty.

Thus, just as a person with a good memory had protruding eyes, a person with a high degree of musical ability, artistic talent, sense of color, combativeness, or mathematical skill would have large bumps in other areas of the skull. **Figure 1.4** shows where Gall and Spurzheim located the trait of amativeness (sexiness). A person with a bump there would be predicted to have a strong sex drive, whereas a person low in this trait would have a depression in the same region.

Gall and Spurzheim identified a long list of behavioral traits borrowed from the English or Scottish psychology of the time. They assigned each trait to a particular part of the skull and, by inference, to the underlying brain part. Spurzheim called this study of the relation between the skull's surface features and a person's mental faculties **phrenology** (*phren* is a Greek word for "mind"). **Figure 1.5** shows the resulting phrenological map that he and Gall devised.

Some people seized on phrenology as a means of making personality assessments. They developed a method called *cranioscopy*, in which a device was placed around the skull to measure its bumps and depressions. These measures were then correlated with the phrenological map to determine the person's likely behavioral traits. The faculties described in phrenology—characteristics such as faith, self-love, and veneration—are impossible to define and to quantify objectively. Phrenologists also failed to recognize that the superficial features on the skull reveal little about the underlying brain. Gall's notion of localization of function, although inaccurate scientifically, laid the conceptual foundation for modern views of functional localization, beginning with the localization of language.

Among his many observations, Gall gave the first account of a case in which frontal-lobe brain damage was followed by loss of the ability to speak. The patient was a soldier whose brain was pierced by a sword driven through his eye. Note that, on the phrenological map in Figure 1.5, language is located below the eye. Gall gave the

(A)

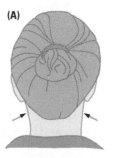

(B)

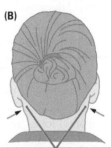

Gall correlated bumps in the region of the cerebellum with the brain's "amativeness" center.

Figure 1.4 ◄

Gall's Theory Depressions (A) and bumps (B) on the skull indicate the size of the underlying area of brain and thus, when correlated with personality traits, indicate the part of the brain controlling the trait. While examining a patient (who because of her behavior became known as "Gall's Passionate Widow"), Gall found a bump at the back of her neck that he thought located the center for "amativeness" in the cerebellum. (Research from Olin, 1910.)

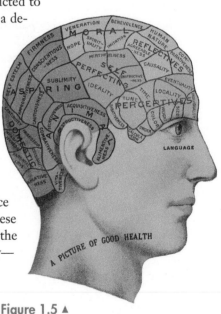

Figure 1.5 ▲

Phrenology Bust Originally, Gall's system identified putative locations for 27 faculties. As the study of phrenology expanded, the number of faculties increased. Language, indicated at the front of the brain, below the eye, actually derived from one of Gall's case studies. A soldier had received a knife wound that penetrated the frontal lobe of his left hemisphere through the eye. The soldier lost the ability to speak. (Mary Evans Picture Library/Image Works.)

observation no special emphasis, thinking it merely a confirmation of his theory. The case subsequently came to factor in discoveries concerning the brain's role in language.

Lateralization of Function

A now legendary chain of observations and speculations led to confirmation that language is both localized in the brain and **lateralized**, that is, located on one side of the brain. This discovery led to the principle of lateralization of function, that one cerebral hemisphere can perform a function not shared by the other (Benton, 1964). We begin on February 21, 1825, as French physician Jean Baptiste Bouillaud (1796–1881) read a paper before the Royal Academy of Medicine in France. Bouillaud argued from clinical studies that certain functions are localized in the cortex and, specifically, that speech is localized in the frontal lobes, in accordance with Gall's theory.

Observing that acts such as writing, drawing, painting, and fencing are carried out with the right hand, Bouillaud also suggested that the part of the brain that controls them might be the left hemisphere. Physicians had long recognized that damage to a hemisphere of the brain impairs movement of the opposite side of the body. A few years later, in 1836, Marc Dax (1770–1837) presented a paper in Montpellier, France, discussing a series of clinical cases demonstrating that disorders of speech were constantly associated with lesions of the left hemisphere. Dax's manuscript received little attention, however, and was not published until 1865, by his son.

Ernest Auburtin (1825–1893), Bouillaud's son-in-law, supported Bouillaud's cause. At a meeting of the Anthropological Society of Paris in 1861, he reported the case of a patient who lost the ability to speak when pressure was applied to his exposed frontal lobe. Auburtin also described another patient, ending with a promise that other scientists interpreted as a challenge:

> For a long time during my service with M. Bouillaud I studied a patient, named Bache, who had lost his speech but understood everything said to him and replied with signs in a very intelligent manner to all questions put to him. . . . I saw him again recently and his disease has progressed; slight paralysis has appeared but his intelligence is still unimpaired, and speech is wholly abolished. Without a doubt this man will soon die. Based on the symptoms that he presents we have diagnosed softening of the anterior lobes. If, at autopsy, these lobes are found to be intact, I shall renounce the ideas that I have just expounded to you. (Stookey, 1954)

Paul Broca, founder of the Society, heard Auburtin's challenge. Five days later he received a patient, a Monsieur Leborgne, who had lost his speech and was able to say only "tan" and utter an oath. The right side of his body was paralyzed, but he seemed intelligent and typical in other respects. Broca recalled Auburtin's challenge and invited him to examine Tan, as the patient came to be called.

Together they agreed that, if Auburtin was right, Tan should have a frontal lesion. Tan died on April 17, 1861, and the next day Broca (1960) submitted his findings to the Anthropological Society. (This submission is claimed to be the fastest publication ever made in science.) Auburtin was correct: the left frontal lobe was the focus of Tan's lesion. By 1863, Broca had collected eight more cases similar to Tan's, all with a frontal lobe lesion in the left hemisphere (Broca, 1865).

As a result of his studies, Broca located speech in the third convolution (gyrus) of the frontal lobe on the left side of the brain (**Figure 1.6**A). By demonstrating that speech is located only in one hemisphere, Broca discovered the brain property of functional lateralization. Because speech is thought central to human consciousness, the left hemisphere is frequently referred to as the dominant hemisphere to recognize its special role in language (Joynt, 1964). In recognition of Broca's contribution, the anterior speech region of the brain is called **Broca's area**, and the syndrome that results from its damage is called **Broca's aphasia** (from the Greek *a*, for "not," and *phasia*, for "speech").

An interesting footnote: Broca examined Tan's brain (Figure 1.6B) only by inspecting its surface. His anatomical analysis was criticized by French anatomist Pierre Marie (1906), who reexamined the preserved brains of Broca's first two patients, Tan and Monsieur Lelong, 25 years after Broca's death. Marie pointed out in his article, "The Third Left Frontal Convolution Plays No Particular Role in the Function of Language," that Lelong's brain showed general nonspecific atrophy, common in senility, and that Tan had additional extensive damage in his posterior cortex that may have accounted for his aphasia.

Broca was aware of Tan's posterior damage but concluded that, whereas it contributed to his death, the anterior damage had occurred earlier, producing his aphasia. Broca's view on localization and his discovery of lateralization became dogma in neuropsychology for the next 100 years, but a dogma tempered by Pierre Marie's criticism.

A Lateralized Language Model

German anatomist Carl Wernicke (1848–1904) created the first model of how the brain produces language in 1874. Wernicke was aware that the part of the cortex into which the sensory pathway from the ear projects—the auditory cortex—is located in the temporal lobe behind Broca's area. He therefore suspected a relation between hearing and speech functioning, and he described cases in which aphasic patients had lesions in this auditory area of the temporal lobe.

These patients displayed no opposite-side paralysis. (Broca's aphasia is frequently associated with paralysis of the right arm and leg, as described for Tan.) They could speak fluently, but what they said was confused and made little sense. (Broca's patients could not articulate, but they seemed to understand the meaning of words.) Although Wernicke's patients could hear, they could neither understand nor repeat what was said to them. Wernicke's syndrome is sometimes called *temporal-lobe aphasia* or **fluent aphasia**, to emphasize that the person can say words, but is more frequently called **Wernicke's aphasia**. The associated region of the temporal lobe is called **Wernicke's area**.

Wernicke's model of language organization in the left hemisphere is illustrated in **Figure 1.7**A. He proposed that auditory information travels to the temporal lobes from the auditory receptors in the ears. In Wernicke's area, sounds are processed into auditory images or ideas of objects and stored. From

(A)

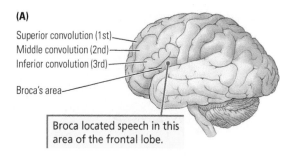

Superior convolution (1st)
Middle convolution (2nd)
Inferior convolution (3rd)

Broca's area

Broca located speech in this area of the frontal lobe.

(B)

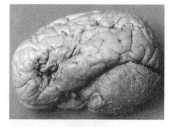

Figure 1.6 ▲

Lateralization of Language (A) Broca's area is located in the posterior third of the inferior, or third, convolution (gyrus) of the frontal lobe in the left hemisphere. (B) Photograph of the left hemisphere of the brain of Leborgne ("Tan"), Broca's first aphasic patient. (Part B, Paul Broca's historic cases: High resolution MR imaging of the brains of Leborgne and Lelong, from N. F. Dronkers, O. Plaisant, M. T. Iba-Zizen, and E. A. Cabanis, *Brain*, Oxford University Press, May 1, 2007.)

(A) Wernicke's original model

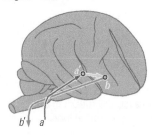

(B) Contemporary version of Wernicke's model

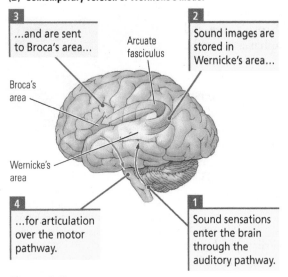

3
...and are sent to Broca's area...

2
Sound images are stored in Wernicke's area...

Arcuate fasciculus

Broca's area

Wernicke's area

4
...for articulation over the motor pathway.

1
Sound sensations enter the brain through the auditory pathway.

Figure 1.7 ▲

Organization of Language in the Brain

(A) In Wernicke's 1874 model, sounds enter the brain through the auditory pathway (*a*). Sound images stored in Wernicke's auditory area (*a'*) are sent to Broca's word area (*b*) for articulation through the motor pathway (*b'*). Lesions along this route *a–a'–b–b'*) could produce different types of aphasia, depending on their location. Curiously, Wernicke drew all his language models on the right hemisphere even though he believed that the left hemisphere is the dominant hemisphere for language, and he drew the brain of an ape, which, Wernicke knew, cannot speak. (B) A contemporary rendition of Wernicke's model. (Part A research from Wernicke, 1874.)

Wernicke's area, auditory ideas flow through a pathway, the *arcuate fasciculus* (from the Latin *arc*, for "bow," and *fasciculus*, for "band of tissue," because the pathway arcs around the lateral fissure, as shown in Figure 1.7B). The pathway leads to Broca's area, where representations of speech movements are stored, and may link brain regions related to intelligence (see Figure 16.17). To produce the appropriate sounds, neural instructions are sent from Broca's area to muscles that control mouth movements.

According to Wernicke's model, if the temporal lobe is damaged, speech movements are preserved in Broca's area, but the speech makes no sense because the person cannot monitor words. Damage to Broca's area produces a loss of speech movements without the loss of sound images, and therefore Broca's aphasia is not accompanied by a loss of understanding.

Disconnection

From his model, Wernicke also predicted a new language disorder but never saw such a case. He suggested that, if the arcuate fibers connecting the two speech areas were cut, disconnecting the areas but without inflicting damage on either one, a speech deficit that Wernicke described as **conduction aphasia** would result. In this condition, speech sounds and movements are retained, but speech is impaired because it cannot be conducted from one region to the other. The patient would be unable to repeat what is heard. After Wernicke's prediction was subsequently confirmed, American neurologist Norman Geschwind (1974) updated the speech model (Figure 1.7B) in what is now referred to as the Wernicke-Geschwind model.

Wernicke's idea of disconnection offered investigators a completely new way of viewing symptoms of brain damage by proposing that, although different brain regions have different functions, they are interdependent: to work, they must interact. Just as a washed-out bridge prevents traffic from moving from one side of a river to the other and therefore prevents people from performing complex activities such as commercial transactions or emergency response services, cutting connecting pathways prevents two brain regions from communicating and performing complex functions.

Using this same reasoning, in 1892 French neurologist Joseph Dejerine (1849–1917) described a case in which the loss of the ability to read (**alexia**, meaning "word blindness," from the Greek *lexia*, for "word") resulted from a disconnection between the brain's visual area and Wernicke's area. Similarly, Wernicke's student Hugo Liepmann (1863–1925) showed that an inability to make sequences of movements (**apraxia**, from the Greek *praxis*, for "movement") results from the disconnection of motor areas from sensory areas.

Disconnection is important in neuropsychology, first because it predicts that complex behaviors are built up in assembly-line fashion as information collected by sensory systems enters the brain and traverses different structures before producing an overt response. Second, disconnecting brain structures by cutting connecting pathways can impair those structures in ways that resemble damage to the structures themselves. Chapter 17 elaborates these ideas.

Neuroplasticity

In the nineteenth century, the work of French physiologist Pierre Flourens (1794–1867) and, later, the German physiologist Friedrich L. Goltz (1834–1902) once again challenged the idea that brain functions are localized (Flourens, 1960; Goltz, 1960). Both men created animal models of human clinical cases by removing small regions of cortex. Both expected that the animals would lose specific functions. Flourens found instead that with the passage of time, his animals recovered from their initial impairments to the point that they seemed to behave typically. Thus, an impaired pigeon that would not initially eat or fly with time recovered both abilities.

More dramatically, Goltz removed almost the entire cortex and a good deal of underlying brain tissue from three dogs that he studied for 57 days, 92 days, and 18 months, respectively, until each dog died. The dog that survived for 18 months was more active than a typical dog. Its periods of sleep and waking were shorter than normal, but it still panted when warm and shivered when cold. It walked well on uneven ground and was able to regain its balance when it slipped. If placed in an abnormal posture, it corrected its position.

After hurting a hind limb on one occasion, this dog trotted on three legs, holding up the injured limb. It was able to orient to touches or pinches on its body and to snap at the object that touched it, although its orientations were not very accurate. If offered meat soaked in milk or meat soaked in bitter quinine, it accepted the first and rejected the second. It responded to light and sounds, although its response thresholds were elevated; that is, its senses were not as acute as those typical of a dog. Although impaired, its recovered abilities clearly suggested that the remaining brainstem could substitute for the cortex.

These early experiments actually built the foundation for neuropsychology's emphases on recovery of function and on promoting recovery by rehabilitation after brain damage, even in extreme circumstances, as illustrated in the Snapshot. Neuropsychologists recognize that, although all function may not be recovered after injury, the brain's plasticity can be harnessed to produce significant functional improvements.

Hierarchical Organization

The experiments that Flourens and Goltz conducted made a strong argument against localization of function and even cast doubt on the role of the cortex in behavior. Removing the cortex did not appear to eliminate any function completely, though it seemed to reduce all functions somewhat.

An explanation for the apparent disconnect between experiments that support functional localization and those that observe recovery of function is **hierarchical organization**. English neurologist John Hughlings-Jackson (1835–1911) proposed this principle of cerebral organization in which information is processed serially and organized as a functional hierarchy (1931). Each successively higher level controls more-complex aspects of behavior and does so via the lower levels.

SNAPSHOT | The Dilemma in Relating Behavior and Consciousness

In his 2007 paper, "Consciousness Without a Cerebral Cortex: A Challenge for Neuroscience and Medicine," Bjorn Merker reviewed the difficulty in determining what is unconscious and what is conscious behavior. Consider three contrasting cases.

Case 1: Marie "Terri" Schiavo, a 26-year-old woman from St. Petersburg, Florida, collapsed in her home in 1990 and experienced respiratory and cardiac arrest. Terri was completely unresponsive, comatose for 3 weeks, and although she did become more responsive, her typical conscious behavior did not return. Terri was diagnosed as being in a **persistent vegetative state** (PVS): she was alive but unable to communicate or to function independently at even the most basic level because the damage to her brain was so extensive that no recovery could be expected.

In 1998, Terri's husband and guardian, Michael Schiavo, petitioned the courts to remove her gastric feeding tube, maintaining that she would not wish to live with such severe impairment. Terri's parents, Robert and Mary Schindler, were opposed, citing their belief that Terri's behavior signaled that she was consciously aware and fighting to recover. Amid a storm of national controversy, Michael Schiavo prevailed. Terri's feeding tube was removed, and she died 13 days later, on March 31, 2005, at the age of 41.

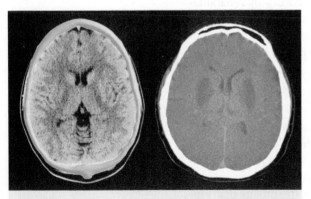

CT scan of a healthy adult brain (left) and a comatose brain (right). (Left: Du Cane Medical Imaging Ltd./Science Source; right: Zephyr/Science Source.)

Case 2: Giacino and colleagues (2012) described a 38-year-old man who lingered in a **minimally conscious state** (MCS) for more than 6 years after an assault. He was occasionally able to utter single words and make a few movements but could not feed himself. As part of a **clinical trial** (a consensual experiment directed toward developing a treatment), the researchers implanted thin wire electrodes into the man's brainstem and applied mild electrical stimulation for 12 hours each day. (Section 7.2 details this process of *deep brain stimulation*.) The patient's behavior improved dramatically: he could follow commands, feed himself, and even watch television.

Case 3. Using MRI, Adrian Owen (2013) recorded the brain's electrical or metabolic activity to determine whether patients who have been in a vegetative state for years can answer questions. For example, patients are asked to attempt to move a hand or a foot, whether they are in pain, whether their brother's child is called Thomas, or to imagine playing tennis. As determined from control participants, characteristic changes in brain activity signal the patients' answers.

Not only do such tests indicate level of consciousness but conscious patients also can learn to use their brain activity to control a robot or other *brain–computer interface* (BCI) and therefore communicate and interact. As detailed in the opening Portrait of Chapter 9, BCIs engage the brain's electrical signals to direct computer-controlled devices. Such innovations in neuroscience are aiding both in assessing the level of consciousness of patients in apparent vegetative or minimally conscious states and in assisting those patients who are conscious to communicate and exert control over their lives.

Giacino, J., J. J. Fins, A. Machado, and N. D. Schiff. Central thalamic deep brain stimulation to promote recovery from chronic posttraumatic minimally conscious state: Challenges and opportunities. *Neuromodulation* 15:339–349, 2012.

Merker, B. Consciousness without a cerebral cortex: A challenge for neuroscience and medicine. *Behavioural and Brain Sciences* 30:63–134, 2007.

Owen, A. M. Detecting consciousness: A unique role for neuroimaging. *Annual Review of Psychology* 64:109–133, 2013.

Often, Hughlings-Jackson described the nervous system as having three levels—the spinal cord, the brainstem, and the forebrain—that had developed successively in evolution. But equally often, he assigned no particular anatomical area to a given level. Hughlings-Jackson suggested that diseases or damage that affects the highest levels of the brain hierarchy would produce *dissolution*, the reverse of evolution: animals would still have a behavioral repertoire, but the behaviors would be simpler, more typical of an animal that had not yet evolved the missing brain structure.

This description fits the symptoms displayed by Goltz's dogs. Hughlings-Jackson's theory gave rise to the idea that functions are not simply represented in one location in the brain but are re-represented in the neocortex, in the brainstem, and in the spinal cord, as elaborated in Section 10.3. Thus, understanding a function such as walking requires understanding what each level of organization contributes to that behavior.

Multiple Memory Systems

People usually describe memory as unitary—as for example, "I have a poor memory." But the conclusion from more than six decades of study is that many memory systems operate within the brain. Contemporary research on memory began in 1953, when neurosurgeon William B. Scoville removed parts of the temporal lobes from the left and right hemispheres of patient H.M. to treat his **epilepsy**, a condition characterized by recurrent seizures associated with disturbance of consciousness. The surgery stopped the epilepsy but left H.M. with a severe memory problem: **amnesia**, partial or total loss of memory (Scoville and Milner, 1957).

H.M. was studied for more than 50 years, and more scientific papers have been written about his case than that of any other neuropsychological patient (Corkin, 2000). His case, detailed throughout Chapter 18, reveals that rather than a single memory structure in the brain, a number of neural structures encode memories separately and in parallel. H.M. appeared to have retained memories from before the surgery but was unable to form new memories that endured for more than a few seconds to minutes. Nevertheless, he could acquire motor skills but could not remember having done so. Thus, H.M. and L.D., whose case opens this chapter, both demonstrate that the neural structures for learning motor skills and those for remembering that one has those skills are separate.

The study of amnesia suggests that when people have a memorable experience, they encode different parts of the experience in different parts of the brain concurrently. Spatial location is stored in one brain region, emotional content in another, events comprising the experience in still another region, and so on. In fact, nowhere in the brain do all the aspects of the experience come together to form "the memory."

How does the brain tie single and varied sensory and motor events together into a unified perception or behavior, or a memory? This **binding problem** extends from perceptive to motor to cognitive processes, the different parts of which are mediated by different neural structures. The essence of the puzzle: although the brain analyzes sensory events through multiple parallel channels that do not converge on a single brain region, we perceive a unified experience, such as a memory. We recall a single memory of an event when in fact we have many separate memories, each stored in a different region of the brain.

Two Brains

In the early 1960s, to prevent the spread of intractable epileptic seizures from one hemisphere to the other in a number of patients, two neurosurgeons, Joseph Bogen and Phillip Vogel, cut the corpus callosum and the smaller commissures that connect the two cortical hemispheres. Essentially, the surgeries made two brains from one. The surgery was effective in reducing the seizures and in improving the lives of these split-brain patients. Roger W. Sperry conducted a series of studies on them that provided a new view of how each hemisphere functions.

By taking advantage of the anatomy of sensory pathways that project preferentially to the opposite hemisphere, Sperry presented information separately to these split-brain patients' left and right hemispheres. Although mute, the right hemisphere was found to comprehend words spoken aloud, read printed words, point to corresponding objects or pictures in an array, and match presented objects or pictures correctly from spoken to printed words and vice versa. (Sections 11.2 and 17.4 expand on split-brain phenomena.)

In his Nobel lecture, Sperry (1981) concluded that each hemisphere possesses complementary self-awareness and social consciousness and that much of internal mental life, especially in the right hemisphere, is inaccessible to analysis using spoken language. Sperry proposed that a neuropsychology that does not accept the existence of a private mental life and relies solely on quantitative, objective measurement of behavior cannot fully understand a brain in which inner experience itself is causal in expressing overt behavior.

Conscious and Unconscious Neural Streams

In February 1988, near Milan, Italy, D.F. was poisoned by carbon monoxide (CO) emitted by a faulty space heater. As the CO replaced the oxygen in her blood, D.F.'s brain was deprived of oxygen, and she sank into a coma. When she recovered consciousness in the hospital, D.F. was alert, could speak and understand, but could see nothing. The diagnosis of her *cortical blindness* resulted from damage to the visual cortex at the back of the occipital lobe rather than to any problem with her eyes.

D.F. eventually regained some vision: she could see color and even identify what objects were made of by their color. Her deficit was **visual form agnosia**: she could not see the shapes of objects nor recognize objects visually by their shape. D.F.'s visual acuity was normal, but she could not distinguish vertical lines from horizontal lines. She could not recognize objects or drawings of objects. She could draw objects from memory but could not recognize the objects she had drawn.

One day in a clinical setting in St. Andrews, Scotland, Scottish neuropsychologist David Milner and Canadian neuropsychologist Melvyn Goodale observed that D.F. accurately reached for and grasped a pencil that they offered her. Nevertheless, she could not see the pencil or tell whether its orientation was horizontal or vertical. D.F.'s ability to perform this act presented a paradox. How could she reach out to grasp the pencil when, at the same time, she could not tell the neuropsychologists what she saw?

In further tests, D.F. demonstrated that she could shape her hand correctly to grasp many objects that she could not recognize, and even step over objects that she could not see. In sum, D.F. appears able to see if she is required to move to perform an action; otherwise, she is blind to the form of objects. (D.F.'s case is featured in Section 13.4.)

D.F.'s visual agnosia stands in contrast to the deficits displayed by patients whose visual **ataxia** (*taxis*, meaning "to move toward") leads them to make errors in reaching for objects while still being able to describe the objects accurately. The brain lesions in agnosia patients such as D.F. occur in neural structures that constitute a pathway, called the **ventral stream**, from the visual cortex to the temporal lobe for object identification. Brain lesions in patients with optic ataxia are in neural structures that form a pathway from the visual cortex to the parietal cortex called the **dorsal stream** to guide action relative to objects (**Figure 1.8**).

Goodale and Milner (2004) proposed that the ventral stream mediates actions controlled by conscious visual perception, whereas the dorsal stream mediates actions controlled by unconscious visual processes. Although we believe that we are consciously guiding our visual actions, much of what vision does for us lies outside our conscious visual experience and essentially uses computations that are robotic in nature. Thus, vision, like language and memory, is not unitary.

It follows that other sensory systems are not unitary but rather consist of separate pathways that mediate unconscious or conscious actions. Nevertheless, we experience a seamless, binding interaction between conscious and unconscious action. We see the world, and ourselves, as whole, so much so that subsequent to brain damage, such as L.D.'s traumatic brain injury described in the chapter's Portrait, people may not be aware of their behavioral deficits. The paradox posed by the discovery of conscious and unconscious vision is that in its goal to account for our conscious behavior, neuropsychology must also identify and account for our unconscious behavior.

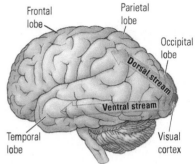

Figure 1.8 ▲

Neural Streams The dorsal and ventral streams mediate vision for action and for recognition, respectively.

1.4 The Neuron Theory

Alongside the *brain theory*, the idea that the brain is responsible for all behavior, the second major source of findings that influences modern neuropsychology is the *neuron theory*, the idea that the unit of brain structure and function is the nerve cell. In this section, we introduce the three aspects of the neuron theory: (1) neurons are discrete, autonomous cells that interact but are not physically connected; (2) neurons send electrical signals that have a chemical basis; and (3) neurons use chemical signals to communicate with one another.

Nervous System Cells

The nervous system is composed of two classes of cells, neurons and **glia** (from the Greek word for "glue"). Neurons produce our behavior and mediate the brain's plasticity, allowing us to learn and adapt. Glial cells help the neurons out, holding them together (some *do* act as glue) and providing other support functions, such as delivering nutrients and removing waste. The human nervous system contains about 85 billion neurons and 86 billion glial cells (Azevedo et al., 2009).

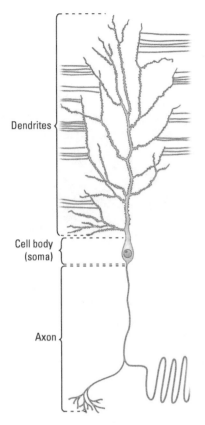

Figure 1.9 ▲

Major Parts of a Neuron

Figure 1.9 shows the three basic parts of a neuron. The core region is called the **cell body**, or **soma** (Greek for "body" and the root of words such as "somatic"). Most of a neuron's branching extensions are called **dendrites** (Latin for "branch"), but the main "root" is called the **axon** (Greek for "axle"). A neuron has only one axon, but most neurons have many dendrites. As you will see, some have so many dendrites that they resemble garden hedges.

The dendrites and axon are extensions of the neuron's cell body, enlarging the cell's surface area to increase its interactions with other cells. Dendrites can be several millimeters long, but the axon can extend as long as a meter, as do those in the motor pathway that extends from the cortex to the spinal cord. In the giraffe, these same corticospinal axons are many meters long.

Understanding how billions of cells, many with long, complex extensions, produce behavior is a formidable task. Just imagine what the first anatomists with their crude microscopes thought when they began to make out some of the brain's structural details. Through the development of powerful microscopes and techniques for selectively highlighting structures, good descriptions of neurons emerged in the nineteenth century. More-recent technological advances have revealed how neurons work, how they receive information on their dendrites, and how their axons influence other neurons, all detailed in Chapters 4 and 5.

Identifying the Neuron

The earliest anatomists who sought to examine the substructure of the nervous system found a gelatinous white substance, almost a goo. Eventually, they discovered that when preserved and "fixed" by immersion in formaldehyde, which changes the structure of brain protein, the goo could be made firm, cut into thin sections, then examined under a microscope. Using just this procedure, Amunts and colleagues (2013) created "BigBrain," a high-resolution, three-dimensional atlas and the most detailed reconstruction of the human brain ever made (see Section 10.2). To create BigBrain, technicians sliced the brain of a 65-year-old female into over 7000 sections (**Figure 1.10**).

Early theorists, including Descartes, described nerves as hollow, fluid-containing tubes (recall Figure 1.3). However, later in the 1600s, when the first cellular anatomist, Anton van Leeuwenhoek (1632–1723), examined nerves using a primitive microscope, he found no such thing. As microscopes improved, the nerve came into ever-sharper focus, eventually leading to the recognition that cells are its basic structural units, just as they are in the rest of the body.

This finding came from exciting developments in visualizing cells—staining, which allows different parts of the nervous system and of cells to be distinguished. Various dyes used for staining cloth in the German textile industry were applied to thinly cut brain tissue with various results. By interacting with different chemical elements in the cell, some selectively stained the soma, some

Figure 1.10 ▲

Constructing BigBrain One at a time, ultrathin sections of brain are cut, slid onto a conveyor belt, and collated for staining, scanning, and digital reassembly as the BigBrain atlas, the most detailed three-dimensional model of the human brain in existence. (K. Amunts et al., *Science,* 2013.)

stained the nucleus, and some stained the axons. The most amazing cell stain came from the application of photographic chemicals to nervous system tissue.

In 1875, Italian anatomist Camillo Golgi (1843–1926) impregnated tissue with silver nitrate (one substance responsible for forming the images in black-and-white photographs) and found that a few cells in their entirety—cell body, dendrites, and axons—became encrusted with silver. This technique allowed the entire neuron and all its processes to be visualized for the first time. Golgi never described what led him to his remarkable discovery.

Spanish anatomist Santiago Ramón y Cajal (1852–1934) used Golgi's silver-staining technique to examine the brains of chicks at various ages and produced beautiful drawings of neurons at different stages of growth (1937). He was able to see a neuron develop from a simple cell body with few extensions to a highly complex cell with many extensions (**Figure 1.11**). But he never saw connections from cell to cell.

Golgi and Cajal interpreted their observations differently. Golgi proposed that neurons are interconnected and form a net, thus providing the basis for a holistic mind. Cajal proposed that neurons are autonomous, providing the basis for functional localization. Their acrimonious debate is manifest in their Nobel speeches in 1906, Golgi supporting his nerve net and Cajal supporting his neuron hypothesis. For the most part, images produced by electron microscopes later in the twentieth century support the neuron theory that Cajal hypothesized.

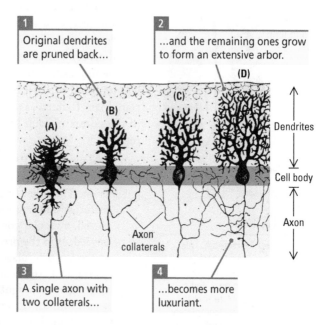

Figure 1.11 ▲

Neuron Growth Successive phases (A–D) in the development of a type of neuron called a Purkinje cell as drawn by Ramón y Cajal (1937) illustrates the garden-hedge analogy.

◎ Relating Electrical Activity in Neurons to Behavior

Insights into how neurons work began in the eighteenth century with Italian physicist Luigi Galvani's (1737–1798) finding that electrical stimulation delivered by wires to a frog's nerve causes muscle contractions. The idea for this experiment came from Galvani's observation that frogs' legs hanging from metal wire in a market twitched during an electrical storm. Subsequently, many studies considered how electrical conduction through the body might relate to information flow in neurons (Brazier, 1959).

A most interesting experiment demonstrating that information flow in the brain has an electrical basis comes from studies in 1870 by Gustav Theodor Fritsch (1838–1929) and Eduard Hitzig (1838–1907). Their technique consisted of placing a thin, insulated wire, an *electrode*, onto or into the cortex and passing a weak electrical current through the wire's uninsulated tip, thus exciting the tissue near it (Fritsch and Hitzig, 1960). Hitzig may have derived the idea of electrically stimulating the cortex from an observation he had made while dressing the head wound of a soldier during the Prussian war: mechanical irritation of the soldier's brain on one side caused twitching in the limbs on the opposite side.

Fritsch and Hitzig performed successful experiments with a rabbit and then a dog. They showed that stimulating the cortex electrically produces movement.

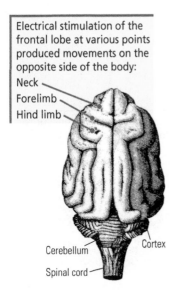

Electrical stimulation of the frontal lobe at various points produced movements on the opposite side of the body:

Neck
Forelimb
Hind limb

Cerebellum
Cortex
Spinal cord

Figure 1.12 ▲

Localizing Function This 1870 drawing from Fritsch and Hitzig (1960) shows the dorsal view, looking down on a dog's brain from above. Note that the dog's cortex does not completely cover the brainstem, and so the cerebellum is visible.

Furthermore, not only was the cortex excitable, it was selectively excitable. Stimulation of the frontal lobe produced movements on the opposite side of the body, whereas stimulation of the parietal lobe produced no movement. Stimulation of restricted parts of the frontal lobe elicited movement of particular body parts—for example, neck, forelimb, and hind limb (**Figure 1.12**)—suggesting that the cortex forms topographic neural–spatial representations of the body's different parts. The study of this **topographic organization** in many brain functions remains a central focus of research to this day.

The first experiment describing the electrical stimulation of a human cortex was reported in 1874 by Roberts Bartholow (1831–1904), a Cincinnati physician. Mary Rafferty, a patient in his care, had a cranial defect that exposed a part of the cortex in each hemisphere. The following extract is from Bartholow's report:

> Observation 3. Passed an insulated needle into the left posterior lobe so that the non-insulated portion rested entirely in the substance of the brain. The other insulated needle was placed in contact with the dura mater, within one-fourth of an inch of the first. When the circuit was closed, muscular contraction in the right upper and lower extremities ensued, as in the preceding observations. Faint but visible contraction of the left orbicularis palpebrarum [eyelid], and dilation of the pupils, also ensued. Mary complained of a very strong and unpleasant feeling of tingling in both right extremities, especially in the right arm, which she seized with the opposite hand and rubbed vigorously. Notwithstanding the very evident pain from which she suffered, she smiled as if much amused. (Bartholow, 1874)

Bartholow's publication caused a public outcry, and he was forced to leave Cincinnati. Nevertheless, he had demonstrated that the electrical-stimulation technique can be used with a conscious person, who can then report the subjective sensations produced by the stimulation. (The pain that Rafferty reported was not caused by stimulation of pain receptors in the brain—because there are none—but was probably evoked by a part of the brain that normally receives pain messages from other parts of the body.)

In the twentieth century, the scientific community established ethical standards for research on human and nonhuman subjects, and brain stimulation has become a standard part of many neurosurgical procedures, including improving the functioning of MCS patients as described in the Snapshot on page 14. Experiments can also be conducted without resorting to practices such as placing electrodes into the brains of conscious humans. By using *transcranial magnetic stimulation (TMS)*, for example, researchers induce electrical activation in the brain by passing a magnetized coil across the skull (see Section 7.2). This noninvasive technique allows investigators to study how the typical brain produces behavior and which parts participate in particular actions.

◉ Connections Between Neurons As the Basis of Learning

In his book, *The War of the Soups and the Sparks*, neuropsychologist Elliott Valenstein (2005) recounts the remarkable events and debates about how neurons influence one another. In the early twentieth century at Cambridge University in England, Alan Hodgkin and Andrew Huxley investigated how neurons conduct information. They were awarded the Nobel Prize in Physiology in 1963 for their work, which explained that neurons generate brief electrical charges that are conveyed along the neuron's axon, as detailed in Section 4.2.

A puzzle remained: How does one neuron influence the next one? The "Soups" proposed that neurons release chemicals to influence the activity of other neurons and muscles. The "Sparks" proposed that electrical impulses simply travel from one neuron to the next.

Charles Scott Sherrington (1857–1952), an English physiologist, had examined how nerves connect to muscles (1906). At first he suggested that no continuous connection exists. He applied an unpleasant stimulation to a dog's paw, measured how long it took the dog to withdraw its foot, and compared that rate with the speed at which messages were known to travel along axons. According to Sherrington's calculations, the dog took 5 milliseconds too long to respond. Sherrington theorized that neurons are separated by junctions and that additional time is required for the message to get across the junction, which he called a *synapse* (from the Greek word for "clasp").

Otto Loewi (1953) eventually demonstrated that chemicals carry the message across the synapse. His decisive and simple experiment, detailed in the opening Portrait of Chapter 5, consisted of electrically stimulating a nerve to the heart of a frog while washing fluid over it and collecting the fluid. When he poured the fluid on the same heart or a second heart, its beating changed in the same way that the electrical stimulation had changed the first heart's beating rate.

The general assumption that developed in response to Loewi's discovery was that a synapse releases chemicals to influence the adjacent cell. On the basis of this principle, Canadian neuropsychologist Donald Hebb (1949) proposed a learning theory: when individual cells are activated at the same time, they establish connecting synapses or strengthen existing ones and thus become a functional unit.

Hebb proposed that new or strengthened connections, sometimes called *Hebb* or *plastic synapses*, are the structural bases of memory. He also proposed that families of neurons thus connected form **cell assemblies** to represent units of behavior, such as an idea, and cell assemblies linked together could underlie thinking and consciousness.

We now accept that the brain is plastic and that one aspect of plasticity is change: the changes constantly occurring at each of the brain's billions of synapses. Although we retain our identity over a lifetime, that identity is housed in a dynamic structure. Consider that each day, as you muse, daydream, remember, and interact with others, you are both reinforcing the activity of millions of existing synapses and creating new synapses. We are always a work in progress.

1.5 Contributions to Neuropsychology from Allied Fields

Neuropsychology's standing as a distinct scientific discipline draws on numerous contributions from allied fields: neurosurgery; **psychometrics**—the science of measuring human mental abilities—and statistical analysis; and technological advances that allow us to observe the living brain.

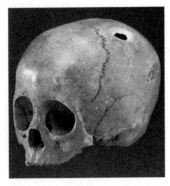

(A)

Figure 1.13 ▲

The Original Neurosurgery (A) A 4000-year-old trephined human skull excavated from Jericho. (B) Today, in the Zulu Nation of southern Africa, shamans carry a model skull indicating locations where holes should be made to relieve pressure on the brains of warriors who have suffered brain trauma in battle. (Part A, Photo by SSPL/Getty Images; part B, Obed Zilwa/AP.)

(B)

Neurosurgery

As Wilder Penfield and Herbert Jasper (1954) noted, anthropologists have found evidence of brain surgery dating to prehistoric times (**Figure 1.13**A). Neolithic skulls that show postsurgical healing have been found in Europe. The early Incas of Peru left similar skulls behind. These ancient peoples likely found surgery to have a beneficial effect, perhaps by reducing pressure within the skull when an injured brain began to swell.

Hippocrates gave written directions for **trephining** (cutting a circular hole in the skull) on the side of the head opposite the site of an injury as a therapeutic intervention to relieve pressure from a swelling brain. Between the thirteenth and nineteenth centuries, many attempts to relieve various symptoms with surgery, some quite successful, were documented. TBI and its treatment have a long history, and the trephination procedure continues to be employed to this day (Figure 1.13B). Recall from the chapter-opening Portrait that a neurosurgeon performed a craniotomy (skull removal) over L.D.'s right frontal cortex after a CT scan revealed bleeding and swelling there.

The modern era in neurosurgery began with the introduction of antisepsis, anesthesia, and the principle of functional localization. In the 1880s, many surgeons reported success with operations for treating brain abscesses, tumors, and epilepsy-producing scars. Later, the *stereotaxic device* that holds the head in a fixed position for surgery was developed (**Figure 1.14**). Advances in local anesthetics allowed patients to remain awake during surgery and contribute to its success by providing information about the effects of localized brain stimulation.

Neurosurgery's advancement as a practical solution to some brain abnormalities in humans had an enormous influence on neuropsychology. The surgeon would draw a map of the lesion, sometimes after stimulating the surrounding tissue electrically to discover the exact extent of damage. As a result, correlations were obtained between focal lesions in the brain and the changes in behavior that resulted from those lesions. Neuropsychological tests developed to assess behavioral changes then established a methodology for evaluating brain and behavior more generally (see Chapter 28).

Information about behavior obtained from patients who have undergone neurosurgery contributes to diagnosing the causes of problems in other patients. For example, if tissue removal from the temporal lobes is found to be related to subsequent memory problems (recall H.M.'s amnesia), then people who develop memory problems also might have injury or disease of the temporal lobes.

Figure 1.14 ▶

Contemporary Neurosurgery A human patient held in a stereotaxic device for brain surgery. The device immobilizes the head by means of bars placed in the ear canals and under the front teeth to allow the precise positioning of electrodes, determined in conjunction with a brain atlas. (Michael English, M.D./Custom Medical Stock.)

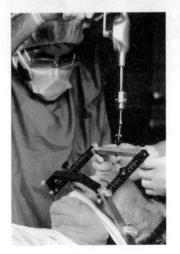

Psychometrics and Statistical Evaluation

On superficial examination, the brains of different people look very similar, but they must be functionally very different to account for vast differences in ability and behavior. Charles Darwin's cousin, Francis Galton (1822–1911), conducted the first systematic study (1891) of the cause of such individual differences. Galton paid participants three pennies to allow him to measure their physical features, perceptions, and reaction times. His goal: finding individual differences that could explain variations in intelligence. To Galton's surprise, the perceptual and reaction time differences that he measured did not distinguish the people he was predisposed to think average from those he thought intellectually gifted.

Galton's elegant innovation was to apply to his results the statistical methods of Adolphe Quetelet (1796–1874), a Belgian statistician (Quetelet, 1842). Galton ranked his participants on a frequency distribution graph, the so-called "bell curve," showing that, on almost every factor measured, some people perform exceptionally well, some perform exceptionally poorly, and most fall somewhere in between. This innovation was essential for developing modern psychological tests.

French biologist Alfred Binet (1857–1911) devised a solution to Galton's problem of identifying intelligence (1903). The French minister of public instruction commissioned Binet to develop tests to identify children who required special instruction. The tests that he developed in collaboration with Theodore Simon (1872–1961) were derived empirically by administering questions to 50 typical 3- to 11-year-old children and to some children and adults who displayed learning disabilities.

The Binet-Simon scale was revised in 1908. Unsatisfactory tests were deleted, new tests were added, and the student population was increased to 300 children aged 3 to 13 years. From the tests, a mental level was calculated based on a score attained by 80% to 90% of typical children of a particular age. In 1916 in the United States, Lewis Terman (1877–1956) produced a version of the Stanford-Binet test in which the **intelligence quotient** (IQ)—mental age divided by chronological age times 100—was first used (Terman and Merrill, 1937). Terman set the average intelligence level to equal an IQ score of 100.

Neuropsychologists have adapted subtests such as those that comprise the Stanford-Binet, each of which measures abilities such as mathematical reasoning and memory, as instruments for measuring many aspects of brain function. Donald Hebb first gave IQ tests to brain-damaged people in Montreal, Canada, with the resultant surprising discovery that lesions in the frontal lobes—since Gall's time considered the center of highest intelligence—did not decrease IQ scores (Hebb and Penfield, 1940)! (Recall that L.D.'s frontal-lobe injuries impaired his executive function but not his intelligence.) Lesions to other brain areas not formerly implicated in "intelligence" did reduce IQ scores. This counterintuitive finding revealed the tests' utility for assessing the location of brain damage and effectively created a bond of common interest between neurology and neuropsychology.

Neuropsychological tests described throughout this book are objectively scored and standardized using statistical procedures. Although certain applications of "mental testing" are open to criticism, even harsh critics concede that such tests do have appropriate uses in neuropsychology (Gould, 1981). Most importantly, tests can identify behavioral changes and aid in understanding the effects of brain damage, even such diffuse brain damage as L.D. suffered.

Brain Imaging

Early in neuropsychology's history, relations between the brain and behavior could be made only at autopsy. Investigators such as French physician Jean-Martin Charcot (1825–1893), the director of a mental institution housing thousands of women patients, developed a method of collecting symptoms and relating them to brain pathology after death (1889). Although this took time, one of his many discoveries was that *multiple sclerosis (MS)*, a degenerative disease characterized by a loss of sensory and motor function, results from hardening (*sclerosis* means "hardening") of nerve-fiber pathways in the spinal cord (see Section 4.3 Snapshot).

Today, brain imaging allows a rapid correlation between symptoms and brain pathology and is an essential diagnostic tool as well. A variety of computer-assisted brain-imaging methods can reconstruct two- and three-dimensional images of the brain. Images can describe regional differences in structure or function, electrical activity, cell density, or chemical activity (such as the amount of glucose a cell is using or the amount of oxygen it is consuming). The principal imaging methods, detailed in Section 7.4 and illustrated in **Figure 1.15**A–D, are as follows:

- **Computed tomography** (CT) scanning passes X-rays through the head. X-rays are absorbed less by fluid than by brain cells and less by brain cells than by bone. Brain injury can be visualized, because dead cells in the injured area produce a darker image on the scan than do healthy, living brain cells that contain less water. A computer can generate a three-dimensional image of the brain and thus a three-dimensional image of the injured region.

(A) CT scan

(B) PET scan

(C) MRI scan

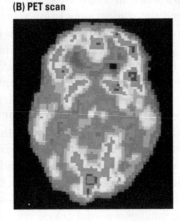

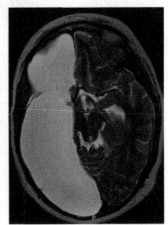

Figure 1.15 ▲

Brain-imaging Techniques Viewed from above: (A) CT scan showing effects of stroke on the right side of the brain and (B) PET scan of blood flow in a typical brain. Areas of strongest flow appear red; those of weakest flow appear blue. (C) MRI showing a brain after removal of the left hemisphere. (D) Color overlaid on a DTI tractography of temporal lobe auditory circuits, orange in the left hemisphere and purple in right hemisphere. (Part A, Canadian Stroke Network; part B, Hank Morgan/Science Source; part C, Dr. George Jallo/Johns Hopkins Hospital; part D, Loui, P., Li, H. C., Hohmann, A., & Schlaug, G. Enhanced Connectivity in Absolute Pitch Musicians: A Model of Hyperconnectivity. *Journal of Cognitive Neuroscience* 23(4):1015-1026, 2011, © 2011 Massachusetts Institute of Technology.)

(D) DTI tractography

- **Positron emission tomography** (PET) entails injecting radioactive substances that decay in minutes into the bloodstream to reach the brain. As the radioactivity decays, it gives off photons, allowing a computer to draw their location on a two- or three-dimensional reconstruction of the brain. For example, if a radioactive form of oxygen is administered, more active parts of the brain that use more oxygen can be identified and correlated with the behavior in which a test subject is engaging. Damaged brain areas use less oxygen. PET is also useful for studying blood flow in brain areas engaged in typical behaviors such as speaking, reading, and writing.

- **Magnetic resonance imaging** (MRI) calculates the location of moving molecules by detecting the electrical charge their movement generates. Because brain tissue varies in its concentration of molecules (for example, in nerve fibers versus cell bodies), MRI can use regional differences to reveal excellent brain images. MRI can also determine the relative concentrations of oxygen and carbon dioxide and so can be used to determine regional differences in brain activity. Thus, brain function (*functional MRI*, or *fMRI*) can be imaged and superimposed on brain anatomy (MRI).

- **Diffusion tensor imaging** (DTI) is an MRI method that detects the directional movements of water molecules to create virtual images of the brain's nerve fiber pathways. Using *DTI tractography*, the Human Connectome Project is pursuing the goal of mapping the human brain's connectivity. The project also seeks to reveal how connections form during development and how they change with aging and brain injury (Johansen-Berg, 2013).

The strengths of brain imaging procedures vary, as detailed in Section 7.5. CT scans can be obtained quickly and cheaply. PET can image many chemicals; thus, diseases characterized by chemical changes can be imaged. The high resolution of MRIs can create lifelike images of the brain and provide excellent detail of brain areas active during particular behaviors.

In sum, brain imaging not only can reveal dead tissue formerly accessible only at autopsy but also can identify active brain regions with a moment-to-moment resolution. Imaging has greatly expanded the kinds of studies that neuropsychologists can conduct to study function, both in injured and in uninjured brains. From MRI images of many hundreds of participants, scientists are producing a functional atlas of the human brain, a task phrenology attempted but failed to achieve.

SUMMARY

This first chapter sketches the history of neuropsychology by examining its two formative theories: (1) the brain is the source of behavior and (2) the neuron is its functional unit. The chapter also summarizes how major ideas about brain functions originated. The history that led to the current science of neuropsychology is long, and the major advances presented here selective. Taken in context, these advances result from countless small discoveries that tend to cap a long period of investigation by many people.

1.1 The Brain Theory

The brain's nearly symmetrical left and right cerebral hemispheres feature a folded outer layer, the neocortex, which is divided into four lobes: temporal, frontal, parietal, and occipital. The brain and spinal cord together make up the central nervous system. All the nerve fibers radiating out beyond the CNS as well as all the neurons outside the brain and spinal cord form the peripheral nervous system. Sensory pathways in the PNS carry information toward the CNS; motor pathways carry instructions from the CNS out to the body's muscles and tissues.

1.2 Perspectives on the Brain and Behavior

Mentalism views behavior as the product of an intangible entity called the mind. Dualism is the notion that the mind acts through the brain to produce "higher" functions such as language and rational behavior, whereas the brain alone is responsible for those "lower" functions we share in common with other animals. Materialism, the view that all behavior—language and reasoning included—can be fully accounted for by brain function, guides contemporary research in neuroscience.

1.3 Brain Function: Insights from Brain Injury

Examining the behavior of individual patients who have suffered brain damage due to illness, injury, or surgery yields insights into brain function. Major principles include *functional hierarchy*: functions are not represented in a sole location in the brain but are rather re-represented in the neocortex, in the brainstem, and in the spinal cord; *localization*: different brain regions have different functions; *lateralization*: the left and right hemispheres have different functions, some conscious and some unconscious; and *multiple memory* systems: different brain regions produce a stunning variety of forms and types of memory. Studying individual patients also establishes landmarks for treatments based on neuroplasticity and recovering function: even after losing a brain region induces severe behavioral impairment, significant recovery is possible.

1.4 The Neuron Theory

The brain is composed of nerve cells that serve as its functional units. Neurons send electrical signals along their dendrites and axons by chemical means and exchange information by secreting chemical messages at their synapses. Neurons are plastic: they can change many aspects of their functioning, thus mediating learning.

1.5 Contributions to Neuropsychology from Allied Fields

Studies of human neurosurgical patients with well-localized brain lesions, improvements in the statistical tools used to develop and interpret behavioral tests, and ever-evolving brain imaging techniques all provide new ways of evaluating and improving neuropsychological theories and practice.

References

Amunts, K., C. Lepage, L. Borgeat, H. Mohlberg, T. Dickscheid, M-E. Rousseau, S. Bludau, P-L. Bazin, L. B. Lewis, A-M. Oros-Peusquens, N. J. Shah, T. Lippert, K. Zilles, and A. C. Evans. BigBrain: An ultrahigh-resolution 3D human brain model. *Science* 340:1472–1475, June 21, 2013.

Azevedo, F. A. C., L. R. B. Carvalho, L. T. Grinberg, J. M. Farfel, R. E. L. Ferretti, R. E. P. Leite, W. Jacob Filho, R. Lent, and S. Herculano-Houzel. Equal numbers of neuronal and nonneuronal cells make the human brain an isometrically scaled-up primate brain. *Journal of Comparative Neurology* 513(5):532–541, 2009.

Bartholow, R. Experimental investigation into the functions of the human brain. *American Journal of Medical Sciences* 67:305–313, 1874.

Benton, A. L. Contributions to aphasia before Broca. *Cortex* 1:314–327, 1964.

Binet, A. *Etude expérimentale de l'intelligence.* Paris: Librairie C. Reinwald, 1903.

Brazier, M. A. B. The historical development of neurophysiology. In J. Field, H. W. Magoun, and V. E. Hall, Eds. *Handbook of Physiology*, vol. 1. Washington, D.C.: American Physiological Society, 1959.

Broca, P. Sur le siège de la faculté du langage articulé. *Bulletin of the Society of Anthropology* 6:377–396, 1865.

Broca, P. Remarks on the seat of the faculty of articulate language, followed by an observation of aphemia. In G. von

Bonin, Ed. *The Cerebral Cortex.* Springfield, Ill.: Charles C Thomas, 1960.

Charcot, J. M. *Clinical lectures on diseases of the nervous system* [*Leçons sur les maladies du système nerveux*] (Thomas Savill, Trans., Ed.). London: The New Sydenham Society, 1889.

Corkin, S. What's new with the amnesic patient H.M.? *Nature Reviews Neuroscience* 3(2):153–160, 2000.

Critchley, M. Neurology's debt to F. J. Gall (1758–1828). *British Medical Journal* 2:775–781, 1965.

Darwin, C. *On the Origin of Species by the Means of Natural Selection, or the Preservation of Favored Races in the Struggle for Life.* New York: New American Library, 1985. (Original publication 1859)

Descartes, R. *Traite de l'homme.* Paris: Angot, 1664.

Finger, S. *Origins of Neuroscience.* New York: Oxford University Press, 1994.

Flourens, P. Investigations of the properties and the functions of the various parts which compose the cerebral mass. In G. von Bonin, Ed. *The Cerebral Cortex.* Springfield, Ill.: Charles C Thomas, 1960.

Fritsch, G., and E. Hitzig. On the electrical excitability of the cerebrum. In G. von Bonin, Ed. *The Cerebral Cortex.* Springfield, Ill.: Charles C Thomas, 1960.

Galton, F. *Hereditary Genius.* New York: D. Appleton and Co., 1891.

Geschwind, N. *Selected Papers on Language and Brain.* Dordrecht, Holland, and Boston: D. Reidel, 1974.

Goltz, F. On the functions of the hemispheres. In G. von Bonin, Ed. *The Cerebral Cortex*. Springfield, Ill.: Charles C Thomas, 1960.

Goodale, M. A., and D. A. Milner. *Sight Unseen: An Exploration of Conscious and Unconscious Vision*. Oxford, U.K.: Oxford University Press, 2004.

Gould, S. J. *The Mismeasure of Man*. New York: Norton, 1981.

Gubata M. E., E. R. Packnett, C. D. Blandford, A. L. Piccirillo, D. W. Niebuhr, and D. N. Cowan. Trends in the epidemiology of disability related to traumatic brain injury in the US Army and Marine Corps: 2005 to 2010. *Journal of Head Trauma and Rehabilitation* (1):65–75, 2014.

Hebb, D. O. *The Organization of Behavior: A Neuropsychological Theory*. New York: Wiley, 1949.

Hebb, D. O., and W. Penfield. Human behavior after extensive bilateral removals from the frontal lobes. *Archives of Neurology and Psychiatry* 44:421–438, 1940.

Hughlings-Jackson, J. *Selected Writings of John Hughlings-Jackson*, J. Taylor, Ed., vols. 1 and 2. London: Hodder, 1931.

Johansen-Berg, H. Human connectomics—What will the future demand? *NeuroImage* 80:541–544, 2013.

Joynt, R. Paul Pierre Broca: His contribution to the knowledge of aphasia. *Cortex* 1:206–213, 1964.

Loewi, O. *From the Workshop of Discoveries*. Westbrooke Circle, Lawrence, Kansas: University of Kansas Press, 1953.

Marie, P. The third left frontal convolution plays no special role in the function of language. *Semaine Médicale* 26:241–247. Reprinted in *Pierre Marie's Papers on Speech Disorders*, M. F. Cole and M. Cole, Eds. New York: Hafner, 1906, 1971.

Olin, C. H. *Phrenology*. Philadelphia: Penn Publishing, 1910.

Penfield, W., and H. Jasper. *Epilepsy and the Functional Anatomy of the Human Brain*. Boston: Little, Brown, 1954.

Quetelet, A. M. *On Man and the Development of His Faculties*. Edinburgh: William and Robert Chambers, 1842.

Ramón y Cajal, S. *Recollections of My Life*, E. Horne Craigie, Trans., with assistance from J. Cano. Cambridge, Mass.: MIT Press, 1937, 1989.

Scoville, W. B., and B. Milner. Loss of recent memory after bilateral hippocampal lesions. *Journal of Neuropsychiatry and Clinical Neuroscience* 20(1):11–21, 1957.

Sherrington, C. S. *The Integrative Action of the Nervous System*. Cambridge, U.K.: Cambridge University Press, 1906.

Sperry, R. W. Some Effects of Disconnecting the Cerebral Hemispheres. Nobel Lecture, December 8, 1981.

Stookey, B. A note on the early history of cerebral localization. *Bulletin of the New York Academy of Medicine* 30:559–578, 1954.

Terman, L.M., and M. A. Merrill. *Measuring Intelligence*. Boston: Houghton Mifflin, 1937.

Valenstein, E. S. *The War of the Soups and the Sparks*. New York: Columbia University Press, 2005.

Wernicke, C. *Der aphasische Symptomenkomplex*. Breslau, Poland: M. Cohn and Weigert, 1874.

2 Research on the Origins of the Human Brain and Behavior

Evolving a Capacity for Language

Does human language have antecedents in nonhuman animals? Many species that lack a forebrain, including fishes and frogs, are capable of elaborate vocalizations, which are still more elaborate in species that do have a forebrain, such as birds, whales, and primates.

Language is not solely vocal, however. We communicate using our bodies, including hand gestures, both spontaneously and in signing. We also recognize communicative intentions in the motor activities of other animals, including our pets.

In 1969, Beatrice and Alan Gardner taught American Sign Language (ASL or Ameslan) to a chimpanzee named Washoe. Their experiment provided evidence that nonverbal forms of language might have preceded verbal language (Gardner and Gardner, 1969).

Sue Savage-Rumbaugh and her coworkers (Gillespie-Lynch et al., 2013) then taught a pygmy chimpanzee named Malatta a symbolic language called Yerkish. (The pygmy chimpanzee, or *bonobo*, is a species thought to be an even closer relative of humans than the common chimp.) Malatta's son, Kanzi, accompanied his mother to class, and though not specifically trained, learned more Yerkish than his mother.

Kanzi, pictured here all grown up, also understands human speech. Jared Taglialatela and coworkers have found that Kanzi makes many sounds associated with their meanings, or semantic context; makes various peeps associated with specific foods; and makes sounds such as a raspberry or extended grunt in specific contexts to attract attention. Chimps learn these joint attention-getting signals from their mothers (Hopkins and Taglialatela, 2012).

Imaging of chimps' brain blood flow associated with the use of "chimpanzeeish" indicates that the same brain regions activated when humans use language are also activated when chimpanzees use language. Finding antecedents in animal vocalizations, gestures, and the importance of parent–child teaching, along with similarities in brain activity, all support the idea that human language has antecedents in nonhuman animals.

Kanzi is a member of the primate order, a group of animal families that includes lemurs, tarsiers, monkeys, and apes—including humans. All primates diverged from a common ancestor. The primate order is shown in **Figure 2.1** as a **cladogram**, a branching chart that shows the relative time sequence of the origin of various closely related groups of animals. Each branch point distinguishes animals that evolved before that time point from animals positioned after it by one or more physical or behavioral traits. All apes, for example, can raise their arms to brachiate (swing through the trees). No primate preceding the ape can do so.

Primates' color vision and enhanced depth perception allow them to guide their hand movements. Female primates usually produce only one infant per pregnancy, and they spend a great deal more time caring for their young than

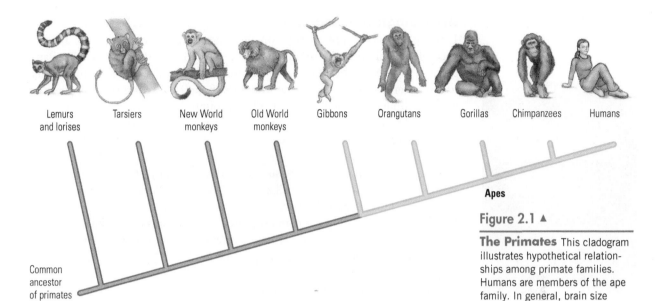

| Lemurs and lorises | Tarsiers | New World monkeys | Old World monkeys | Gibbons | Orangutans | Gorillas | Chimpanzees | Humans |

Apes

Figure 2.1 ▲

The Primates This cladogram illustrates hypothetical relationships among primate families. Humans are members of the ape family. In general, brain size increases from left to right across the groupings, with humans having the largest brains in the family.

most other animals do. In the past 5 million to 8 million years, our humanlike ancestors acquired characteristics that distinguished them from other apes. These **hominids** were taller, bipedal, had long legs, and were such great travelers that their descendants, including all human species, living and extinct, have populated every continent.

Changes in hominid hand structure allowed skilled tool use. Changes in tooth structure and a reduced jaw size facilitated consuming a more varied diet. The hominid brain underwent an unmatched evolution in size, increasing to more than three times its original volume. Important clues to understanding the modern human brain come from considering the evolutionary forces that sculpted it, how investigators describe its function by studying the nervous systems of other animals, and the interplay of genetic makeup, environment, and epigenetic factors.

2.1 Human Origins and the Origins of Larger Brains

The evolution of humans, from an ancestral ape species to present-day humans, or *Homo sapiens*, is not linear. Even as recently as 20,000 to 40,000 years ago, numerous human species coexisted, including modern humans, Neanderthals in Europe, Denisovans in Siberia, *Homo floresiensis* on the island of Flores in Indonesia, and perhaps other species yet to be discovered. Today our species is the sole survivor.

Research on Hominid Evolution

Scientists attempt to reconstruct the story of human evolution using three general lines of research: archeological; biochemical, genetic, and epigenetic; and behavioral.

Figure 2.2 ▲

Neanderthal Woman This facial reconstruction by Elisabeth Daynes was created from a casting of the skull. The female, given the name Pierrette, died a violent death between the ages of 17 and 20. Discovered in western France in 1979, the 36,000-year-old remains were lying near tools from the Neanderthal period. (Philippe Plailly & Atelier Daynes/ Science Source.)

Archeological Research

Using morphological reconstruction, investigators can approximate the appearance of a hominid body, often from only skeletal remains, to reveal similarities and differences between other hominids and us. Fossils of Neanderthals, named after Neander, Germany, where their skulls were found, were the first ancestral humans to be discovered. This accounts in part for why Neanderthals have maintained preeminence among modern human ancestors. Contrary to the original assumption that Neanderthal were brutish, reconstructions such as that shown in **Figure 2.2** demonstrate how similar to us they really were.

Neanderthals used tools very similar to those used by *Homo sapiens* living at that time. They also lived in similar family groups, made music, cared for their elders, and buried their dead. From these archeological insights we can infer that Neanderthals probably communicated using language and held religious beliefs. Contemporary genetic evidence shows that modern European humans interbred with Neanderthals and acquired from them genes that helped them adapt to the cold, to novel diseases, and possibly favored genes for light skin that better absorbs vitamin D (Zhang et al., 2011).

Biochemical, Genetic, and Epigenetic Research

As detailed in Section 4.1, genes direct the body's cells to produce protein molecules composed of long chains of amino acids. The amino acid sequence of a cellular protein in one species can be compared to that in another species. A change in one amino acid may occur, on average, about once every million years, and so the differences between proteins provide a molecular clock that can be used to compare the relative ages of different species.

For example, geological evidence says Old World and New World monkeys diverged from each other 30 million years ago. Their 24 differences in albumin amino acids gives one amino acid change every 1.25 million years. Applying this rate change to apes shows that chimpanzees and humans diverged between 5 million years and 8 million years ago.

Species relatedness is also determined by comparing **deoxyribonucleic acid** (DNA), the genetic material in the nucleus of the cell. Each gene is a long chain of *nucleotide bases*, the constituent molecules of the genetic code (see Section 4.1). Through mutations, the sequence of bases can change to some extent and still leave a functional gene. Signatures of modern humans and chimpanzees suggest that they share 99% of their genes and are each other's closest living relatives. Therefore, chimps and humans have a recent common ancestor, and the 1% genetic difference produces huge differences between the two species.

As describing the **genome**, the full set of a species' genes, has progressed, it has become clear that the complement of genes among diverse species is surprisingly similar. Nevertheless, gene expression and its timing contribute to diversity. *Epigenetics*, the science that studies differences in gene expression related to environment and experience, contributes to understanding similarities and differences among ourselves and other animal species.

Behavioral Research

Comparative behavioral research can shed light on the origins of many human behavioral traits. Ethologist Jane Goodall's (1986) behavioral studies of chimpanzees paint a picture of a species so similar to humans that one has the impression of looking into a mirror. Chimps occupy large territories that the males defend as a group. The males wage war and kill neighbors to expand their territories.

Chimps are travelers, ambulating along the ground at a rate that humans must appreciate, for distances of 8 kilometers or more a day. They are omnivores, eating vegetation, fruit, and insects, and hunt cooperatively to catch monkeys, pigs, and other mammals. They live in complex social groups within which family relations are important both for the individual chimpanzee and for the group structure. They have rich manual, facial, and vocal communication, and they construct and use tools for defense and to obtain food and water. These few among countless similarities in chimp and human behavior reinforce the genetic evidence that chimps and humans have a common ancestor.

In the Gallup (1970) mirror test, a chimpanzee points to a dot that has been placed on its forehead, demonstrating self-recognition, a cognitive ability displayed by higher primates. (Cognitive Evolution Group, University of Louisiana/The Povinelli Group, LLC.)

Evolution of the Human Brain and Behavior

Physical similarities among humans, apes, and monkeys extend to their brains. We now consider the relation between brain size and behavior across different species and survey leading hypotheses for how the human brain enlarged as the nervous system became more complex.

Australopithecus: Our Distant Ancestor

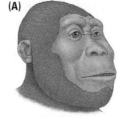

(A)

One of our hominid ancestors is probably *Australopithecus* (from the Latin word *austral*, meaning "southern," and the Greek word *pithekos*, meaning "ape"). **Figure 2.3** reconstructs the animal's face and body. The many *Australopithecus* species that are now known walked upright and used tools (Pickering et al., 2011). Scientists have deduced their upright posture from the

Australopithecus

shape of their back, pelvic, knee, and foot bones and from a set of fossilized footprints that a family of australopiths left behind, walking through freshly fallen volcanic ash some 3.8 million years ago. The footprints feature the impressions of a well-developed arch and an unrotated big toe, more like human feet than those of other apes. Evidence for tool use is implied in the structure of their hands (Pickering et al., 2011).

The First Humans

The oldest fossils designated as genus *Homo* (human) are those found by Mary and Louis Leakey in the Olduvai Gorge in Tanzania in 1964, dated to about 2 million years old. The primates that left these skeletal remains strongly resembled *Australopithecus* but more closely resembled modern humans in one important respect: they made simple stone tools. The Leakeys named the species *Homo habilis* ("handy human") to signify that its members were toolmakers.

The first humans whose populations spread widely beyond Africa migrated into Europe and into Asia. This species was *Homo erectus* ("upright human"), so named because of the mistaken notion that its predecessor, *H. habilis*, had a stooped posture. *Homo erectus* first shows up in the fossil record about 1.6 million years ago. As shown in **Figure 2.4**, its brain was bigger than that of any preceding hominid, overlapping in size the measurements of present-day human brains.

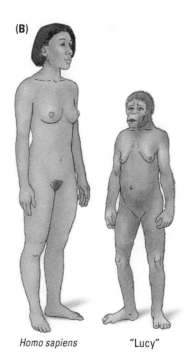

(B)

Homo sapiens   "Lucy"

Figure 2.3 ▲

Australopithecus (A) This hominid walked upright with hands free, as do modern humans, but its brain was about one-third the size of a modern human's brain—the size of a modern-day nonhuman ape. (B) Human and *Australopithecus* figures compared on the basis of the most complete *Australopithecus* skeleton yet found, a young female about 1 meter tall who lived 3 million years ago, popularly known as Lucy.

Figure 2.4 ▶

Increases in Hominid Brain Size The brain of *Australopithicus* was about the same size as that of living non-human apes, but succeeding members of the human lineage display a steady increase in brain size. Note also the increasing tool complexity across *Homo* species. (Data from Johanson and Edey, 1981.)

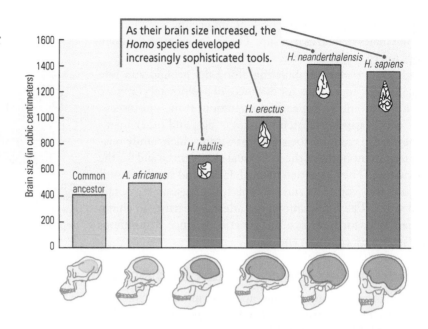

Modern humans, *Homo sapiens*, appeared in Africa within about the past 200,000 years. Until about 30,000 years ago in Europe and 18,000 ago in Asia, they coexisted and interbred with other hominid species. We do not know how *H. sapiens* completely replaced other human species. Perhaps they had advantages in toolmaking, language use, or social organization.

Relating Brain Size and Behavior

Scientists who study brain evolution propose that changes in brain size and complexity in different species enable more complex behavior to evolve. Having a large brain clearly has been adaptive for humans, but many animals have large brains. Whales' and elephants' gross brain sizes are much larger than ours. Of course, whales and elephants are much larger than humans overall. How is relative brain size measured, and what does it signify?

The two main ways of estimating relative brain size are to compare brain size to body size and to count brain cells. Consider the small roundworm, *Caenorhabditis elegans*, a favorite research species among neuroscientists. *C. elegans* has 959 cells. Of these, 302 are neurons. In contrast, the blue whale—the largest animal that has ever lived, weighing as much as 200 tons—has a brain weighing 15,000 grams. As a percentage of cell number, 30% of *C. elegans* is nervous system, whereas in terms of body weight, less than 0.01% of the blue whale is nervous system.

Estimating Relative Brain–Body Size Versus Counting Brain Cells

To sum up the idea that species exhibiting more-complex behaviors must possess relatively larger brains than species whose behaviors are less complex, Harry Jerison (1973) developed an index of brain size that compares the brains of different species relative to their differing body sizes. He calculated that as body size increases, brain size increases at about two-thirds the increase in body weight.

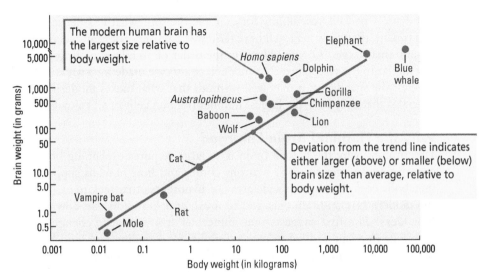

Figure 2.5 ◄

Brain-to-Body Size Ratios of Common Mammals A wide range of body and brain sizes is represented logarithmically on this graph. Average brain size relative to body weight falls along the diagonal trend line, where you find the cat. (Data from Jerison, 1973.)

Using the ratio of actual brain size to expected size for a typical mammal of a particular body size, Jerison developed a quantitative measure, the **encephalization quotient** (EQ). The farther an animal's brain falls below trend line in **Figure 2.5**, the smaller its EQ. The higher an animal's brain lies above the trend line, the larger its EQ.

Notice that the cat's brain is average, the rat's brain a little smaller (lower EQ), and the elephant's brain a little larger (higher EQ) than the ratio predicts. A modern human brain, located farther above the line than any other animal, has the highest EQ. The dolphin's relative brain size is almost as large as the human's. **Table 2.1** shows the brain size and EQs of some common mammals, including monkeys, apes, and humans. The nearly threefold increase in brain size from chimpanzees (EQ 2.5) to modern humans (EQ 7.3) is dramatic.

Countering Jerison's rationale, Suzana Herculano-Houzel (Fonseca-Azevedo et al., 2012) argues that body size and brain size can evolve independently. For example, a gorilla is as large as a modern human but has a smaller brain. The gorilla has specialized in having a large body, while humans have specialized in having both a large body and a large brain. Herculano-Houzel proposes that a more useful estimate of brain ability is a count of neurons, the brain's functional units.

Using a method that involves dissolving the soma of brain neurons, then collecting and counting the cell nuclei with a counting machine, Herculano-Houzel has measured both the packing density and cell number in a variety of species, including primates. The packing density of cells in the primate lineage is constant, and therefore a count of neurons provides an accurate comparative measure of primate species differences. Applied to hominoid brains, *Australopithicus* had about 50 to 60 billion neurons, *Homo habilis* about 60 billion, *Homo erectus* about 75 to 90 billion, and modern humans have about 86 billion neurons.

In terms of cell counts then, what makes us modern humans special is that we have so many. Although similar neuron counts in other animal species with large EQs have not been made, Herculano-Houzel speculates that if their neurons are

Table 2.1 Brain sizes of species most commonly studied in neuropsychology

Species	Brain Volume (ml)	Encephalization Quotient
Rat	2.3	0.40
Cat	25.3	1.01
Rhesus monkey	106.4	2.09
Chimpanzee	440.0	2.48
Human	1350.0	7.30

not densely packed, resembling for example the somewhat less-dense packing of a rodent, then they may well have far fewer neurons. For example, dolphins, despite their large EQ, would have in the order of 30 billion neurons, a number similar to the chimpanzee's. Once cell counts are made for a wider range of species, she speculates, it may well turn out that what makes modern humans special is that they have the largest number of brain cells of all animals.

Why the Hominid Brain Enlarged

Determining why the human brain is so large requires explaining both what adaptive advantages so many neurons confer and how humans support their metabolic cost. Among the wide array of hypotheses that seek to explain why the modern human brain enlarged so much and so rapidly, we now examine four ideas. The first suggests that numerous drastic climate changes forced hominids to adapt and led to more-complex food-finding and food-handling behavior. A second hypothesis contends that the primate lifestyle favors an increasingly complex nervous system that humans capitalized upon. A third links brain growth to brain cooling, and the fourth proposes that a slowed maturation rate favors larger brains.

Climate and the Evolving Hominid Brain
Climate changes have driven many physical changes in hominids, including changes in the brain, and even the emergence of human culture. Evidence suggests that each new hominid species appeared after climate changes devastated old environments and created new ones.

▲ Africa's Great Rift Valley cut off ape species living in a wetter climate to the west from species to the east, which evolved into hominids adapted to a drier climate.

About 8 million years ago, a massive tectonic event (deformation of Earth's crust) produced the Great Rift Valley, which runs through the eastern part of Africa from south to north. The reshaped landmass left a wet jungle climate to the west and a much drier savannah climate to the east. To the west, the apes continued unchanged in their former habitat. But the fossil record shows that in the drier eastern region, apes evolved rapidly into upright hominids in response to the selective environmental pressures that formed their new home. The changed environment encouraged many adaptations that included bipedalism, increased body size, and increased brain size.

Just before *Homo habilis* appeared 2 million years ago, the African climate rapidly grew even drier, with spreading grasslands and even fewer trees. Anthropologists speculate that the hominids that evolved into *H. habilis* adapted to this new habitat by scavenging the dead of the large herds of grazing animals that then roamed the open grasslands. The appearance of *Homo erectus* 1 million years ago may have been associated with further climate change: a rapid cooling that lowered sea levels (by trapping more water as ice) and opened up land bridges into Europe and Asia. At the same time, *H. erectus* upgraded their hunting skills and the quality of their tools for killing, skinning, and butchering animals.

Other climatic changes track the disappearance of other members of the human family. For example, warming in Europe as recently as 30,000 years ago probably contributed to modern humans migrating to the continent and to the Neanderthals' disappearance.

What makes modern humans special? Anthropologist Rick Potts (2010) suggests that *Homo sapiens* has evolved to adapt to change itself and that this adaptability has allowed us to populate almost every climatic region on Earth. Potts cautions that modern humans have been around only a short time relative to the million years that *H. erectus* survived: our adaptability has yet to be severely tested.

The Primate Lifestyle British anthropologist Robin Dunbar (1998) argues that a primate's social group size, a cornerstone of its lifestyle, is correlated with brain size. His conclusion: the average group size of about 150 favored by modern humans explains their large brains. He cites as evidence that 150 represents the estimated size of hunter-gather groups and the average size of many contemporary institutions—a company in the military, for instance—and coincidentally, the number of people that each of us can gossip about.

Consider how group size might enhance how primates forage for food. Foraging is important for all animals, but some foraging activities are simple; others are complex. Eating grass or vegetation is an individual pursuit: an animal need only munch and move on. Vegetation eaters such as gorillas do not have especially large brains. In contrast, apes that eat fruit, such as chimpanzees and humans, have relatively large brains.

Katharine Milton (2003) documented the relation between fruit foraging and larger brains by examining the feeding behavior and brain size of two South American (New World) monkeys of the same body size. She found that the spider monkey obtains nearly three-quarters of its nutrients from eating fruit and has a brain twice as large as that of the howler monkey, which obtains less than half its nutrients from fruit.

What is so special about eating fruit that favors a larger brain? Good sensory skills, such as color vision, are needed to recognize ripe fruit in a tree, and good motor skills are required to reach and manipulate it. Good spatial skills are needed to navigate to trees that contain fruit. Good memory skills are required to remember where fruit trees are, when the fruit will be ripe, and from which trees the fruit has already been eaten.

Fruit eaters must be prepared to deal with competitors, including members of their own species, who also want the fruit. To keep track of ripening fruit, having friends who can help search benefits a fruit eater, so successful fruit-eating animals have complex social relations and means of communicating with others of their species. Having a parent who can teach fruit-finding skills is helpful to a fruit eater, so being both a good learner and a good teacher is useful.

The payoff in eating fruit is its excellent nutritional value for nourishing a large, energy-dependent brain that uses more than 20% of the body's resources. We humans exploited and elaborated fruit-eating skills to obtain other temporary and perishable types of food as we scavenged, hunted, and gathered. These new food-getting efforts also required cooperation in navigating long distances and in recognizing a variety of food sources. At the same time, food getting required making tools for digging it up, killing animals, cutting skin, and breaking bones.

Karina Fonseca-Azevedo and Suzana Herculano-Houzel (2012) suggest that a unique contribution to hominid brain development is food cooking. The energy consumed by a single neuron is similar in all animals, so primates with abundant neurons are challenged to support their metabolic costs. Gorillas must

(A) Spider monkey

(B) Howler monkey

▲ Katharine Milton examined the feeding behavior and brain size of two New World monkeys equal in body size. The spider monkey, whose brain weighs in at 107 g, obtains 72% of its nutrients from fruit. Fruit constitutes only 42% of the howler monkey's diet, and its brain weighs 50 g. (Top: P. A. Souders/Corbis; bottom: K. Schafer/Corbis.)

spend up to 8 hours of each day foraging and eating vegetation. Chimps and early hominids with a more varied diet could support more neurons, but that required that they spend most of their waking time foraging.

The use of fire by *Homo erectus* and later hominids allowed for cooking, which predigests food and thus maximizes caloric gain to the point that much less time need be devoted to foraging. Finally, a high degree of male–male, female–female, and male–female cooperation among hominids in food gathering and cooking would have further supported the evolution of a larger brain.

Changes in Hominid Physiology   One adaptation that may have given a special boost to greater brain size in our human ancestors was changes in the morphology (form) of the skull. Dean Falk (1990) developed the "radiator hypothesis" from her car mechanic's remark that, to increase the size of a car's engine, you also have to increase the size of the radiator that cools it. Falk reasoned that, if the brain's radiator, the circulating blood, adapted into a more-effective cooling system, brain size could increase.

Brain cooling is so important because the brain's metabolic activity generates a great deal of heat and is at risk of overheating under conditions of exercise or heat stress. Falk argued that, unlike australopith skulls, *Homo* skulls contain holes through which cranial blood vessels pass. These holes suggest that, compared to earlier hominids, *Homo* species had a much more widely dispersed blood flow from the brain, which would have greatly enhanced brain cooling.

A second adaptation, identified by Hansell Stedman and his colleagues (2004), stems from a genetic mutation associated with marked size reductions in individual facial-muscle fibers and entire masticatory muscles. The Stedman team speculates that smaller masticatory muscles in turn led to smaller, more-delicate bones in the head. Smaller bones in turn allowed for changes in diet and access to more energy-rich food.

Neoteny   In the slowing of maturation, a process called neoteny, juvenile stages of predecessors become the adult features of descendants. Many anatomical features link us with the juvenile stages of other primates, including a small face, vaulted cranium, unrotated big toe, upright posture, and primary distribution of hair on the head, armpits, and pubic areas. Because the head of a human infant is large relative to body size, neoteny has also led to adults with proportionally larger bodies and larger skulls to house larger brains.

The shape of a baby chimpanzee's head is more similar to the shape of an adult human's head than to an adult chimpanzee's head (**Figure 2.6**). Adult humans also retain some behaviors of primate infants, including play, exploration, and intense interest in novelty and learning. Neoteny is common in the animal world. Flightless birds are neotenic adult birds, domesticated dogs are neotenic wolves, and sheep are neotenic goats. One aspect of neoteny related to human brain development is that slowing down human maturation would have allowed more time for body and brain size to increase (McKinney, 1998).

Among a number of views about what promotes neoteny, one is that at times of abundant resources, less physiologically and behaviorally mature individual organisms can successfully reproduce, yielding offspring that share this trait. This "babies having babies" situation could lead to a population in which individual members have immature physical features and behavioral traits while at

Figure 2.6 ▼

Neoteny The shape of an adult human's head more closely resembles that of a juvenile chimpanzee's head (top) than that of an adult chimp's head (bottom), leading to the hypothesis that we humans may be neotenic descendants of our more ape-like common ancestors. (Top: PHOTO 24/Getty Images, bottom: FLPA/SuperStock.)

the same time are sexually mature. Another view is that, at times of food insufficiency, maturation and reproduction are slowed, allowing a longer time for development.

The Meaning of Human Brain-Size Comparisons

In *The Descent of Man*, Charles Darwin detailed the following paradox:

> No one, I presume, doubts the large proportion which the size of man's brain bears to his body, compared to the same proportion in the gorilla or orang, is closely connected with his higher mental powers. . . . On the other hand, no one supposes that the intellect of any two animals or of any two men can be accurately gauged by the cubic contents of their skulls. (Darwin, 1871, p. 37)

Ignoring Darwin, many have tried to tie individual intelligence to gross brain size. If the functional unit of the brain is the brain cell and if larger human brains have more brain cells, does it not follow that brain size and intelligence are related? It depends.

The evolutionary approach that we have been using to explain how the human brain enlarged is based on comparisons *between* species. Special care attends the extension of evolutionary principles to physical comparisons *within* species, especially biological comparisons within or among groups of modern humans. We now illustrate the difficulty of within-species comparisons by considering the complexity of correlating human brain size with intelligence (Deary, 2000).

Large differences appear among the brains of individuals, but the reasons for those differences are numerous and complex. Larger people are likely to have larger brains than smaller people. Men have somewhat larger brains than women, but men are proportionately physically larger. Nevertheless, girls mature more quickly than boys, so in adolescence the brain- and body-size differences may disappear. As people age, they generally lose brain cells, and their brains become smaller.

Neurological diseases associated with aging accelerate the age-related decrease in brain size. Brain injury before or around birth often results in a dramatic reduction in brain size, even in regions distant from the damage. Stress associated with physical or behavioral deprivation in infancy also leads to decreased brain size (Herringa et al., 2013). Neurological disorders associated with a mother's abuse of alcohol or other drugs are associated with conditions such as *fetal alcohol spectrum disorder* (FASD), in which the child's brain size can be greatly reduced. *Autism spectrum disorder* (ASD), a largely genetic condition affecting development, produces a variety of brain abnormalities, including increases or decreases in brain size in different individuals. Both disorders are detailed in Section 24.3.

Brain size changes over an individual's life span. Just as good nutrition early in life can promote larger body size, brain size also will increase. A culturally enriched environment is associated with growth of existing brain cells and thus increased brain size. One way that the brain stores new skills and memories is to add cells and to form new connections among brain cells. These plastic adaptations in turn contribute to increased brain size.

In response to the argument that brain size is related to intelligence, Stephen Jay Gould, in his 1981 book, *The Mismeasure of Man*, reviewed much of the early

(A)

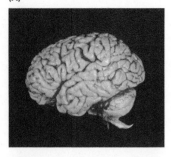

(B)

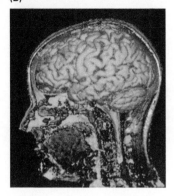

▲ For comparison, photo of a human brain (A) and a virtual brain produced by functional MRI (B). (Part A, Science Source; part B, Collection CNRI/Phototake.)

research and critiqued it on two counts. First, measuring the size of a person's brain is difficult. Even use of modern brain-imaging methods yields no agreement about whether volume or weight is a better measure, and measures of cell-packing density and counts of cell number are yet to be done.

More important, Gould contended that we must consider what is meant by "intelligence." When we compare the behavior of different species, we are comparing their **species-typical behaviors**—behaviors characteristic of all members of a single species. For example, lamprey eels do not have limbs and cannot walk, whereas salamanders do have limbs and can walk, and the difference in brain size between the two species can be correlated with this trait. When we compare behavior *within* a species, however, we are usually comparing how well one individual performs a certain task in relation to others—how well one salamander walks relative to how well another salamander walks, for example.

A century ago, Charles Spearman (1863–1945) performed the first formal analysis of various tests used to rate intelligence, or IQ score. He found a positive correlation among tests and suggested that a single common factor explained them. Spearman named it *g* for general intelligence factor, but it turns out that *g* also is variable. Many factors unrelated to inherent ability—among them opportunity, interest level, training, motivation, and health—influence individual performance on a task.

For example, when IQ tests that were given to young adults of one generation are given to young adults of the next generation, scores increase by as much as 25 points, a phenomenon called the *Flynn effect* (Flynn, 2012). Taken at face value—though it should not be—the increase suggests that human *g* has risen to such a degree in two generations that most young adults fall in the superior category relative to their grandparents. Obviously, the score change has not been accompanied by a similar increase in brain size. It is more likely that education and other life experiences explain the Flynn effect.

People vary enormously in their individual abilities. One may have superior verbal skills but mediocre spatial abilities; another may be adept at solving spatial puzzles but struggle with written work; still another may excel at mathematical reasoning and be average in everything else. Which of these people should we consider the most intelligent? Should certain skills carry greater weight?

Howard Gardner and colleagues (1997) propose the existence of a number of different intelligences (verbal, musical, mathematical, social, and so on). Each type of intelligence is dependent upon the function of a different brain region. Hampshire and colleagues (2012), who presented participants in their study with a battery of typical intelligence assessment tests, support Gardner's idea. As participants took the tests, their brain activity was recorded by brain imaging. The study identified three separate abilities—reasoning, short-term memory, and verbal ability—each associated with a different brain network. The experimenters argue that this finding provides little support for Spearman's *g*. They further suggest that were a wider array of assessments used, additional intelligence networks would be found.

Given the difficulties in measuring brain size and in defining intelligence, it is not surprising that scant research appears in the contemporary literature. If you are wondering whether having a larger brain might mean you could study a little less, consider this: the brains of people who virtually everyone agrees are very intelligent have been found to vary in size from the low end to the high end of the range for our species. The brilliant physicist Albert Einstein had a brain of average size.

The Acquisition of Culture

In evolutionary terms, the modern human brain developed rapidly. Many behavioral changes differentiate us from our primate ancestors, and these adaptations took place more rapidly still, long after the modern brain had evolved. The most remarkable thing that our brains have allowed us to develop is **culture**—the complex learned behaviors passed from generation to generation through teaching and experience.

Cultural growth and adaptation render many contemporary human behaviors distinctly different from those of *Homo sapiens* living 100,000 years ago. Only 30,000 years ago, modern humans created the first artistic relics: elaborate paintings on cave walls and carved ivory and stone figurines. Agriculture appeared still more recently, about 15,000 years ago, and reading and writing were developed only about 7000 years ago.

Most forms of mathematics and many of our skills in using mechanical and digital devices have still more-recent origins. Early *H. sapiens* brains certainly did not evolve to select smartphone apps or imagine traveling to distant planets. Apparently, the things that the human brain did evolve to do contained the elements necessary for adapting to more-sophisticated skills.

Alex Mesoudi and his colleagues (2006) suggest that cultural elements, ideas, behaviors, or styles that spread from person to person—called **memes** (after genes, the elements of physical evolution)—can also be studied within an evolutionary framework. They propose, for example, that individual differences in brain structure may favor the development of certain memes. Once developed, memes would in turn exert selective pressure on further brain development. For example, chance variations in individuals' brain structure may have favored tool use in some individuals. Tool use then proved so beneficial that toolmaking itself exerted selective pressure on a population to favor individuals more skilled in tool fabrication.

Similar arguments can be made with respect to other memes, from language to music, from mathematics to art. Mesoudi's reasoning supports the ongoing expansion of neuropsychology into seemingly disparate disciplines, including linguistics, the arts, and economics. Studying the human brain, far from examining a body organ's structure, means investigating how it acquires culture and fosters adaptation as the world changes and as the brain changes the world.

2.2 Comparative Research in Neuropsychology

Studying nonhuman animals contributes to neuropsychology in countless ways. Similarities in physiology, anatomy, and behavior among humans, monkeys, rats, and other animals demonstrate that studying them all contributes to understanding human brain–behavior relations. And other animals' behavior–brain

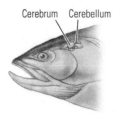

Fish

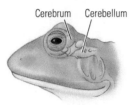

Frog

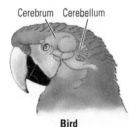

Bird

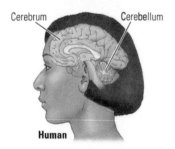

Human

▲ The brains of fishes, frogs, birds, and people have many structures in common, illustrating a single basic brain plan across species having central nervous systems.

relations are interesting in themselves, as bird watchers, pet owners, and animal husbandry confirm.

Three primary lines of research drive neuropsychological investigations with animals: (1) understanding basic brain mechanisms, (2) designing animal models of human neurological disorders, and (3) describing evolutionary and genetic influences on brain development. We consider each line separately.

Understanding Brain Mechanisms

Neuropsychologists design cross-species comparisons to understand the basic mechanisms of brain function—for example, vision. The eye takes vastly different forms in different species. Fruit flies and mammals have eyes that, on the surface, seem to have little in common, and their physical differences were first taken as evidence that the eye evolved a number of times. But studies of the genes responsible for encoding information about how the eye will develop show that the same genes are implicated in all species. Case in point: a gene called *Pax* is responsible for some aspects of eye development in all sighted animals (Nilsson, 2013).

Similarly, *homeobox* genes dictate body segmentation in both fruit flies and humans (Heffer et al., 2013). Thus, genes first discovered in fruit flies govern the human central nervous system's segmentation into spinal cord, brainstem, and forebrain. Variations in eye and nervous system structure in different animal species emerge from slight alterations in genes and in the way the products of those genes interact with the products of other genes. Section 2.3 expands on gene alterations and interactions.

Designing Animal Models of Disorders

The second goal of comparative research is to design animal models of human neurological disorders. Research animals substitute for humans because similar principles presumably underlie the emergence and treatment of a disorder in humans and nonhumans alike. Ideally, researchers want to reproduce the disorder in animals, manipulate multiple variables to understand its cause, and ultimately formulate a treatment.

For example, **Parkinson's disease**, a disorder of the motor system, may affect as many as 1% of humans. Symptoms include tremors, muscular rigidity, and changes in emotion and memory, as detailed in Section 27.6. The causes of Parkinson's disease are many, but the cause for most cases is unknown. Although there are many treatments, there is no cure. Thus, neuropsychologists and other scientists have three goals in relation to Parkinson's disease: prevent it, slow its progression once it has developed, and treat symptoms as the disease progresses.

Parkinson models that have been developed in the mouse, rat, and monkey are aiding in achieving these objectives. Investigations into drug treatment, replacement or grafting of new brain tissue, and rehabilitation all are performed using these animal models before they are applied to humans (Moore et al., 2013).

Scientists have produced animal models of many brain disorders. Animals model the changed social behavior that characterizes schizophrenia, the changed emotional behavior that characterizes depression, and the memory changes that characterize Alzheimer's disease, to name but a few.

Describing Evolutionary Adaptations

Studying the human brain's evolutionary development, its phylogeny, is as important to understanding what humans are as the study of infants is to understanding what adults are. Comparative research on how the mammalian brain and behavior evolved rests on the ancestral lineage of currently living species that most closely resemble those ancestors (Campbell and Hodos, 1970). In the primate lineage, for example, living mammalian species are similar enough to ancestral species to stand in for them (Masterton and Skeen, 1972). Investigators document evolutionary behavior and brain changes leading to the hominid brain. Correspondences between the following four gross cortical-lobe structural developments and new behaviors are charted in **Figure 2.7**:

1. *Occipital cortex.* The presence of a primary visual cortex with a striped appearance (*striate cortex*) confers on the tree shrew an ability to see branches, heights, and the insects it craves. This ability is not important to, and striate cortex is not present in, ground-dwelling animals such as the hedgehog. It is from the tree shrew's ancestors that we inherit our visual abilities and large visual cortex.

2. *Temporal cortex.* The large temporal lobe in the bush baby is related to this animal's ability to select for itself a highly varied diet of insects, fruits, leaves, and more, and, correspondingly, for memory ability. It is from the ancestors of the bush baby that we inherit our equally varied diet and excellent memory.

3. *Frontal lobes.* The large frontal lobes of the rhesus monkey are related to its complex group social life. It is from the rhesus monkey's ancestors that we inherit our large frontal lobes and complex social interactions.

4. *Parietal lobes.* The large parietal lobe that humans share with other apes is a correlate of our ability to perform the skilled movements required in toolmaking. It is from our ape ancestors that we developed our toolmaking ability.

Brain changes in the human lineage can be further investigated with analyses of the genetic bases of primates' neural and behavioral evolution. For example, genetic analysis of this sequence of primates is being used to investigate the neural basis for the origins of language and other behaviors (Geschwind and Konopka, 2012).

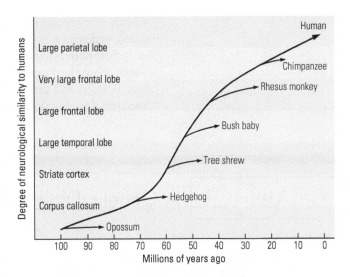

Figure 2.7 ▲

Phylogenetic Lineage
Neuropsychologists regard the evolutionary development of such living mammalian species as hedgehogs, tree shrews, bush babies, monkeys, and apes as closely approximating human ancestors. Phylogenetic relationships thus indicate brain changes that occurred at the branches in this evolutionary sequence. (Adapted with permission from Masterton and Skeen, 1972, © 1972 by the American Psychological Association.)

◎ 2.3 Genes, Environment, and Behavior

Your **genotype** (genetic makeup) influences your physical and behavioral traits, which combine to form your phenotype. Genetic analysis conducted by the Human Genome Project has catalogued the human genome—about 20,000

genes in our species—and today individuals' genomes are routinely documented, as described in the Snapshot. James Watson, the codiscoverer of DNA, was the first person to have his genome catalogued. Researchers have succeeded in sequencing the long-extinct Neanderthal genome as well. The genomes of James Watson and the Neanderthal are surprisingly similar, as might be expected for close hominid relatives.

SNAPSHOT | A Genetic Diagnosis

Fraternal twins Alexis and Noah Beery seemingly acquired brainstem damage perinatally (at or near birth). Typically, such children, who are diagnosed with cerebral palsy, do not get worse with age, but the twins' condition continued to deteriorate. They had poor muscle tone and could barely walk or sit. Noah drooled and vomited; Alexis suffered from tremors.

Their mother, Retta Beery, found a 1991 news report that described a child first diagnosed with cerebral palsy who was then found to have a rare condition, dopa-responsive **dystonia** (abnormal muscle tone). The condition stems from a deficiency in a neurochemical, dopamine, produced by a relatively small cluster of cells in the midbrain (see Section 5.7). When the twins received a daily dose of L-dopa, a chemical that brain cells convert into dopamine, they improved remarkably. "We knew that we were witnessing a miracle," Retta recalled.

A few years later, in 2005, Alexis began to experience new symptoms marked by difficulty breathing. At the time, the twins' father, Joe, worked for Life Technologies, a biotech company that makes equipment used for sequencing

DNA, the molecule that codes our genetic makeup. Joe arranged for the twins' blood samples to be sent to the Baylor College of Medicine's sequencing center.

The twins' genome was sequenced and compared to that of their parents and close relatives. The analysis showed that the twins had an abnormality in a gene for an enzyme that enhances the production not only of dopamine but another chemical made by brainstem cells, serotonin (Bainbridge, 2011).

When the twins' doctors added the chemical that is converted to serotonin to the L-dopa, both twins improved. Alexis competed in junior high school track, and Noah in volleyball at the Junior Olympics. Theirs is the first diagnosis established through genome sequencing that has led to a treatment success, a scientific miracle indeed.

The Human Genome Project, a 13-year, multicountry effort directed toward identifying all human genes and the nucleotide base pairs that comprise each gene, has launched new fields of scientific research and applications, including genome sequencing for the Beery twins. Continuing technological improvements are reducing the time and cost of describing individual genomes and providing routine diagnostic tests for human brain diseases (Alföldi and Lindblad-Toh, 2013).

Alföldi, J., and K. Lindblad-Toh. Comparative genomics as a tool to understand evolution and disease. *Genome Research* 23:1063–1068, 2013.

Bainbridge, M. N., W. Wiszniewski, D. R. Murdock, J. Friedman, C. Gonzaga-Jauregui, I. Newsham, J. G. Reid, J. K. Fink, M. B. Morgan, M. C. Gingras, D. M. Muzny, L. D. Hoang, S. Yousaf, J. R. Lupski, and R. A. Gibbs. Whole-genome sequencing for optimized patient management. *Science and Translation Medicine* 3:87re3, June 15, 2011.

Noah, Retta, Joe, and Alexis Beery at Baylor College standing beside the Solid Sequencer that decoded the twins' genomes. (Courtesy of Retta Beery.)

Studying the influences that genes have on our individual phenotypic traits is the objective of Mendelian genetics, named for Gregor Mendel, whose research led to the concept of the gene (see Section 1.2). But Mendelian genetics cannot explain everything about our phenotypes. Whether a gene is expressed and the extent to which it is expressed can be influenced by the environment. For example, good nutrition and good schooling in early life result in lifelong health benefits, and neglect early in life can impair brain development and lifelong health (Twardosz, 2012). Studying how the environment influences gene expression is the objective of epigenetics. In this section we describe how these two codes, genetic and epigenetic, influence our phenotypes.

Mendelian Genetics and the Genetic Code

The nucleus of each human somatic cell contains 23 pairs of chromosomes, or 46 in all. One member of each chromosome pair comes from the mother and the other comes from the father. The chromosome pairs are numbered 1 to 23, roughly according to size, with chromosome 1 being the largest (**Figure 2.8**).

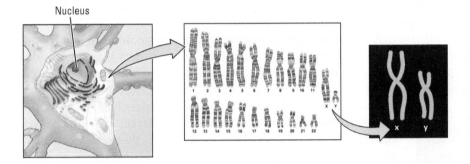

Figure 2.8 ◄

Human Chromosomes The nucleus of a human cell contains 23 chromosomes derived from the father and 23 from the mother. Sexual characteristics are determined by the twenty-third pair, the X and Y sex chromosomes, as contributed by the mother and father. (James Cavallini/Science Source.)

Chromosome pairs 1 through 22, called *autosomes*, contain the genes that contribute to physical appearance and behaviors. The twenty-third pair comprises the *sex chromosomes* that contribute to our physical and behavioral sexual characteristics. The two mammalian sex chromosomes, called X and Y because of their appearance, are shown in Figure 2.8. Female mammals have two X chromosomes; males have an X and a Y.

Because all but your sex chromosomes are matched pairs, each cell contains two copies of every gene, one inherited from your mother, the other from your father. The term "matched" here does not necessarily mean identical, because all gene pairs contain two **alleles**, or alternative forms of a gene. The nucleotide sequences in a pair of alleles may be either identical or different. If they are identical, the two alleles are **homozygous** (*homo* means "the same"). If they are different, the two alleles are **heterozygous** (*hetero* means "different").

The nucleotide sequence that is most common in a population is called the **wild-type** allele, whereas a less frequently occurring alteration that yields a different version of the allele is called a **mutation**. While mutant genes can be beneficial, more often they determine genetic disorders.

Dominant and Recessive Alleles

If both alleles in a gene pair are homozygous, the two encode the same protein, but if the two are heterozygous, they encode two different proteins. Three possible outcomes attend the heterozygous condition when these proteins express a physical or behavioral trait: (1) only the allele from the mother may be expressed; (2) only the allele from the father may be expressed; or (3) both alleles may be expressed simultaneously.

A member of a gene pair that is routinely expressed as a trait is called a *dominant* allele; a routinely unexpressed allele is *recessive*. Alleles can vary considerably in dominance. In complete dominance, only the allele's own trait is expressed in the phenotype. In incomplete dominance, expression of the allele's own trait is only partial. In *codominance*, both of the alleles' traits are expressed completely.

Each gene makes an independent contribution to the offspring's inheritance, even though that contribution may not always be visible in the offspring's phenotype. When paired with a dominant allele, a recessive allele often is not expressed. Still, it can be passed on to future generations and influence their phenotypes when not masked by the influence of a dominant trait.

Genetic Mutations

The mechanism for reproducing genes and passing them on to offspring is fallible. Errors can arise in the nucleotide sequence when reproductive cells make gene copies. The altered alleles are mutations.

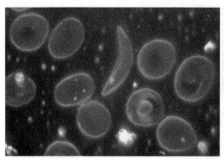

▲ In this micrograph, a sickle cell is surrounded by normal blood cells. (Al Lamme/Phototake.)

A mutation may be as minute as a change in a single nucleotide base. Because the average gene has more than 1200 nucleotide bases, an enormous number of mutations can potentially occur on a single gene. For example, the *BRCA1* (breast cancer) gene, found on chromosome 17, is a caretaker gene that contributes to preventing breast cancer, but more than 1000 different mutations have already been found on it. Thus, in principle, there are more than 1000 different ways to inherit a predisposition to breast cancer from just this gene.

A change in a nucleotide or the addition of a nucleotide in a gene sequence can be either beneficial or disruptive. The mutation that causes sickle-cell anemia is both. The mutated blood cells have an abnormal sickle shape that offers some protection against malaria, but the cells also have poor oxygen-carrying capacity, thus weakening the person who possesses them.

Other genetic mutations are more purely beneficial, and still others are seemingly neutral to the functioning of the organism that carries them. Most mutations, however, have a negative effect. If not lethal, they produce in their carriers debilitating physical and behavioral abnormalities. Each of us carries a surprisingly large number of genetic mutations, some of which may occur during cell division. Neuroscientists know the severe consequences of about 2000 genetic abnormalities that affect the nervous system. For example, an error in a gene could produce a neuron that appears to function normally but does not, or it could produce a neuron that is atypical in both its structure and function.

Applying Mendel's Principles

Gregor Mendel introduced the concept of dominant and recessive alleles in the nineteenth century, when he studied pea plants. Scientists studying Mendelian genetics are gaining insight into how genes, neurons, and behaviors are linked.

Such knowledge may help reduce negative effects of genetic abnormalities—perhaps even eliminate them someday—and contribute to our understanding of regular brain function.

Allele Disorders That Affect the Brain

Among the disorders caused by mutant genes that illustrate Mendel's principles of dominant and recessive alleles is **Tay-Sachs disease**, named for scientists Warren Tay and Bernard Sachs, who first described it. Tay-Sachs is an inherited birth defect caused by the loss of genes that encode the enzyme HexA (hexosaminidase A), necessary for breaking down a class of lipids (fats) in the brain.

Symptoms usually appear a few months after birth and rarely at later ages. The baby begins to suffer seizures, blindness, and degenerating motor and mental abilities. Inevitably, the child dies within a few years. Tay-Sachs mutations appear with high frequency among certain ethnic groups, including Jews of European origin and French Canadians, but the mutation differs in differing populations.

The dysfunctional Tay-Sachs HexA enzyme is caused by a recessive allele of the *HexA* gene on chromosome 15. Distinctive inheritance patterns result from recessive alleles, because two copies (one from the mother and one from the father) are needed for the disorder to develop. A baby can inherit Tay-Sachs disease only when both parents carry the recessive allele. Because both parents have survived to adulthood, both must also possess a corresponding dominant, normal HexA allele for that particular gene pair. The egg and sperm cells produced by this man and woman will therefore contain a copy of one or the other allele. Which is passed on is determined completely by chance.

This situation gives rise in any child of two Tay-Sachs carriers to three different potential gene combinations, as diagrammed in **Figure 2.9**A. If the child

Figure 2.9 ▼

Inheritance Patterns
(A) Recessive condition. A parent with one mutant allele will not show symptoms of the disease but will be a carrier. If both parents carry a mutant allele, each of their offspring stands a 1 in 4 chance of developing the disease. (B) Dominant condition. A person with a single allele will develop the disease. If this person mates with a normal partner, offspring have a 50-50 chance of developing the disease. If both parents are carriers, both will develop the disease, and offspring have a 75% chance of developing it.

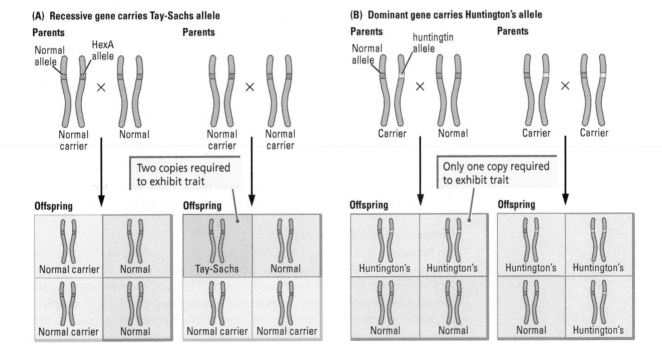

(A) Recessive gene carries Tay-Sachs allele

Parents — Normal allele, HexA allele — Normal carrier × Normal

Parents — Normal carrier × Normal carrier

Two copies required to exhibit trait

Offspring: Normal carrier | Normal / Normal carrier | Normal

Offspring: Tay-Sachs | Normal / Normal carrier | Normal carrier

(B) Dominant gene carries Huntington's allele

Parents — Normal allele, huntingtin allele — Carrier × Normal

Parents — Carrier × Carrier

Only one copy required to exhibit trait

Offspring: Huntington's | Huntington's / Normal | Normal

Offspring: Huntington's | Huntington's / Normal | Huntington's has two normal alleles, he or she will be spared the disorder and cannot pass on the disease. If the child has one normal and one Tay-Sachs allele, he or she, like the parents, will be a carrier of the disorder. If the child has two Tay-Sachs alleles, he or she will develop the disease.

In such a recessive condition, the chance of a child of two carriers being normal is 25%, the chance of being a carrier is 50%, and the chance of having Tay-Sachs disease is 25%. If one parent is a Tay-Sachs carrier and the other is not, then any of their children has a 50-50 chance of being either normal or a carrier. Such a couple has no chance of conceiving a baby with Tay-Sachs disease.

The Tay-Sachs allele operates independently of the dominant allele. As a result, it still produces the defective HexA enzyme, and therefore the person who carries it has a higher-than-normal lipid accumulation in the brain. Because this person also has a normal allele that produces a functional enzyme, the abnormal lipid accumulation is not enough to cause Tay-Sachs disease.

A blood test can detect whether people carry the recessive Tay-Sachs allele, allowing them to make informed decisions about conceiving children. If they avoid having children with another Tay-Sachs carrier, none of their children will have the disorder, although some will probably be carriers. Where genetic counseling has been effective, the disease has been eliminated.

The dominant allele that a carrier of Tay-Sachs possesses produces enough functional enzyme to enable the brain to operate satisfactorily. That would not be the case if the normal allele were recessive, however, as happens with another genetic disorder, **Huntington's disease**. Here, the buildup of an abnormal version of a protein known as *huntingtin* kills brain cells, including cortical cells.

Symptoms can begin anytime from infancy to old age but most often start in midlife. They include abnormal involuntary movements, memory loss, and eventually a complete deterioration of behavior, followed by death. The abnormal *huntingtin* allele is dominant, the recessive allele normal, and so only one defective allele is needed to cause the disorder (Bordelon, 2013).

Figure 2.9B illustrates the inheritance patterns associated with a dominant allele on chromosome 4 that produces Huntington's disease. If one parent carries the defective allele, offspring have a 50% chance of inheriting the disorder. If both parents have the defective allele, the chance of inheritance increases to 75%. Because the abnormal *huntingtin* allele usually is not expressed until midlife, after the people who possess it have already had children, it can be passed from generation to generation even though it is lethal.

As with the allele causing Tay-Sachs disease, a genetic test can determine whether a person possesses the allele that causes Huntington's disease. If a person is found to have it, he or she can elect not to procreate. A decision not to have children in this case will reduce the incidence of the abnormal *huntingtin* allele in the human gene pool. Section 27.6 offers more detail on Huntington's disease.

Chromosome Abnormalities

Single defective alleles are not the only cause of genetic disorders. Some nervous-system disorders are caused by aberrations in a part of a chromosome's DNA or even in an entire chromosome. Such DNA *copy number changes* are also present in different regions of individual human brains. In a small sample of autopsied brains, numerous different copy number errors were found in neurons in the same individuals (McConnell et al., 2013). Some neurons had more than one error. Likely such DNA copy number errors influence the activity of affected neurons and thus have behavioral consequences, both good and bad, of interest to neuropsychologists.

One condition due to a change in chromosome number is **Down syndrome**, usually the result of an extra copy of chromosome 21. One parent (usually the mother) passes on two chromosomes 21 to the child. Combining these two with one chromosome 21 from the other parent yields three chromosomes 21, an abnormal number called a *trisomy*. Although chromosome 21 is the smallest human chromosome, its trisomy affects the expression of genes in many other chromosomes and severely alters a person's phenotype.

People with Down syndrome have characteristic facial features and short stature. They also endure heart defects, susceptibility to respiratory infections, and learning disabilities. They are prone to developing leukemia and Alzheimer's disease. Although people with Down syndrome usually have a much shorter-than-typical life span, some live to middle age or beyond. Improved education for children with Down syndrome, which affects approximately 1 in 700 children, enables them to compensate greatly for the brain changes that cause their learning difficulties.

Genetic Engineering

Geneticists have invented several methods for influencing the traits that genes express, an approach collectively known as *genetic engineering*. In its simplest forms, genetic engineering entails manipulating a genome, removing a gene from a genome, modifying a gene, or adding a gene to the genome via techniques including selective breeding, cloning, and transgenics.

Selective Breeding

Beginning with the domestication of wolves into dogs about 30,000 years ago, many animal species have been domesticated by selectively breeding males and females that display particular traits. Selective breeding of dogs, for example, has produced breeds that can run fast, haul heavy loads, retrieve prey, dig for burrowing animals, climb rocky cliffs in search of sea birds, herd sheep and cattle, or sit on an owner's lap and cuddle. As described by Larson and colleagues (2012), insights into relations among genes, behavior, and disease can be usefully examined in dogs because, as the result of selective breeding, dogs display the most diverse traits of all animal species.

Maintaining spontaneous mutations is one objective of selective breeding. Using this method, researchers create whole populations of animals possessing some unusual trait that originally arose as an unexpected mutation in only one or a few individual animals. In selectively bred laboratory colonies of mice, for example, numerous spontaneous mutations have been discovered and maintained in successive mouse strains.

Some strains of mice move abnormally: they reel, stagger, and jump. Some have immune system diseases; others have sensory deficits and are blind or cannot hear. Some mice are smart, some mice are not, some have big brains, some small, and many display distinctive behavioral traits. Many similar genetic variations can also be found in humans. As a result, investigators can systematically study the neural and genetic bases of the altered behavior in the mice to aid in developing treatments for human disorders.

Figure 2.10 ▲

A Clone and Her Mom
Copycat (top) and Rainbow (bottom), the cat that donated the cell nucleus for cloning. Although the cats' genomes are identical, their phenotypes, including fur color, differ. Even clones are subject to phenotypic plasticity: they retain the capacity to develop into more than one phenotype. (Photographs used with permission of Texas A&M College of Veterinary Medicine and Biochemical Sciences.)

Cloning

More direct approaches to manipulating the expression of genetic traits include altering early embryonic development. One such method is *cloning*—producing an offspring genetically identical to another animal.

To clone an animal, scientists begin with a cell nucleus containing DNA, usually from a living animal, place it in an egg cell from which the nucleus has been removed, and, after stimulating the egg to start dividing, implant the new embryo in the uterus of a female. Because each individual animal that develops from these cells is genetically identical to the donor of the nucleus, clones can be used to preserve valuable traits, to study the relative influences of heredity and environment, or to produce new tissue or organs for transplant to the donor. Dolly, a female sheep, was the first mammal cloned, in 1996, by a team of researchers in Scotland.

Cloning has matured from an experimental manipulation to a commercial enterprise. The first cat to be cloned was called Copycat (**Figure 2.10**). The first rare species cloned was an Asian gaur, an animal related to the cow. One group of investigators anticipates cloning the mastodon, an extinct elephant species, using cells from carcasses found frozen in the Arctic tundra. Another group anticipates cloning the extinct passenger pigeon from the cells of the preserved body of Martha, the last passenger pigeon to die.

Transgenic Techniques

Transgenic technology enables scientists to introduce genes into an embryo or remove genes from it. For example, introducing a new gene can enable goats to produce medicines in their milk. Those medicines can be extracted from the milk and used to treat human diseases (Kues and Niemann, 2011).

When an embryo of one species receives cells from a different species, the resulting *chimeric animal's* cells have genes from both parent species, and its behaviors are a product of those gene combinations. Chimeric animals may display an interesting mix of behaviors of the parent species. For example, chickens that have received Japanese quail cells in early embryogenesis display some aspects of quail crowing behavior rather than chicken crowing behavior, thus providing evidence for the genetic basis of some bird vocalization (Balaban, 2005). The chimeric preparation provides an investigative tool for studying the neural basis of crowing because quail neurons can be distinguished from chicken neurons when examined under a microscope.

In *knock-in technology*, a single gene or many genes from one species added to the genome of another species are passed along and expressed in subsequent generations of **transgenic animals**. One application is studying and treating human genetic disorders. For instance, researchers have introduced the human gene that causes Huntington's disease into lines of mice and monkeys (Gill and Rego, 2009). The animals express the abnormal *huntingtin* allele, display symptoms similar to the disorder in humans, and are being used to study potential therapies.

Knockout technology inactivates a gene so that, for example, a line of mice fails to express it (Tarantino and Eisener-Dorman, 2012). Those "knockout mice" can then be examined both to determine whether the targeted gene is responsible for a human disorder and to examine possible therapies. It is potentially possible to knock out genes related to certain kinds of memory, such as emotional memory, social memory, or spatial memory. Such technology would prove useful in investigating the neural basis of memory.

Phenotypic Plasticity and the Epigenetic Code

Your genotype is not sufficient to explain your phenotype. We all know that if we expose ourselves to the sun, our skin becomes darker; if we exercise, our muscles become larger; if we study, we learn. Your phenotype also changes depending on your diet and as you age. The extent of your phenotypic variation, given a constant genotype, can be dramatic. This **phenotypic plasticity** is due in part to the genome's capacity to express a large number of phenotypes and in part to epigenetics, the influence of environment in selecting one or another of those phenotypes.

Phenotypic plasticity begins with cell division in the developing embryo. The genes that are expressed in a cell are influenced by factors within the cell and outside it, in the cell's environment. Once a fertilized egg begins to divide, each new cell finds itself in a different environment from that of its parent cell. The cell's environment, that is, the cells that surround it, will determine which genes are expressed and so what kind of tissue it becomes, including what kind of nervous system cell it becomes. Later, the external environment and the individual's activity in that environment will influence the structure and function of his or her cells.

The concordance rate between identical twins for a vast array of diseases—including schizophrenia, Alzheimer's disease, multiple sclerosis, asthma, diabetes, and prostate cancer—are between 30% and 60%. For cleft palate and breast cancer, the concordance rate is about 10%. These less-than-perfect concordance rates point to contributing factors other than Mendelian genetic principles (Miyake et al., 2013).

Applying the Epigenetic Code

Epigenetics describes how the genetic code produces different types of cells, explains how the genome codes for different phenotypes, and describes how cell functions go astray to produce diseases ranging from cancer to brain dysfunction. Thus, epigenetics is viewed as a second code; the first code is the genome.

Within each cell, certain genes are expressed (turned on) by a signal, and those genes then produce a particular cell type. A formerly dormant gene becomes activated, resulting in the cell making a specific protein. Certain proteins produce skin cells, whereas other proteins produce neurons.

The specific signals for gene expression are largely unknown, but these signals are probably chemical, and they form the basis of epigenetics. A common epigenetic mechanism that suppresses gene expression during development is **gene methylation** or *DNA methylation*, a process in which a methyl group (CH3) attaches to the DNA nucleotide base pair sequence (**Figure 2.11**). The level of gene methylation in different phenotypes reflects

Figure 2.11 ▾

Gene Methylation

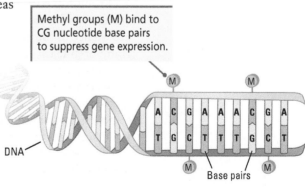

Methyl groups (M) bind to CG nucleotide base pairs to suppress gene expression.

DNA

Base pairs

either an increase or decrease in overall gene expression. Gene expression can be regulated by other epigenetic mechanisms, such as those described in Section 4.1.

To sum up, epigenetic mechanisms can influence protein production, either by blocking a gene so that it cannot be expressed or by unlocking a gene so that it can be expressed. This is where environmental influences come into play. The chemical environment of a brain cell is different from that of a skin cell; therefore, different genes in these cells are activated, producing different proteins and different cell types. The different chemical environments needed to trigger this cellular differentiation could be caused by the activity of other neighboring cells or by chemicals, such as hormones, that are transported in the bloodstream. Some experiential events can also be passed from one generation to the next, as the following study illustrates.

A Case of Inheriting Experience

The idea that traits are passed from parent to child through genes is a cornerstone of Mendelian genetics. Mendel's theory also predicts that individual life experience cannot be inherited. Lars Olov Bygren and colleagues (Kaati et al., 2007), however, found that individuals' nutritional experiences *can* affect their offspring's health.

The investigators focused on Norrbotten, a sparsely populated northern Swedish region. In the nineteenth century, Norrbotten was virtually isolated from the outside world. If the harvest was bad, people starved. According to historical records, the years 1800, 1812, 1821, 1836, and 1856 saw total crop failure. The years 1801, 1822, 1828, 1844, and 1863 brought good harvests and abundance.

Bygren and colleagues identified at random individuals who had been subjected to famine or to plenty in the years just before they entered puberty. Then the researchers examined the health records and longevity of these people's children and grandchildren. The findings seem to defy logic. Descendants of the plenty group experienced higher rates of cardiovascular disease and diabetes and had a life expectancy reduced by more than 7 years compared to the famine group! Notably, these effects were found only in male offspring of males and female offspring of females.

Bygren and colleagues propose that diet during a **critical period**, a developmental window during which some event has a long-lasting influence on the individual, can modify the genetic expression of sex chromosomes—the Y chromosome in males and the X chromosome in females. Further, this change can be passed on to subsequent generations. The timing of dietary experience to the prepubertal period, just before the onset of sexual maturity, is important: this is the time at which gene expression on the sex chromosomes begins.

Bygren and coworkers' seminal findings are supported by many other studies that together make a strong argument for epigenetics and for the idea that some epigenetic influences can be passed on for at least a few generations. Evidence that epigenetic influences play a demonstrable role in determining gene expression is disclosing how our experiences shape our brains to influence whom we become.

SUMMARY

2.1 Human Origins and the Origins of Larger Brains

Hominids diverged from an ancestral ape lineage at least 5 million years ago. In the past 2 million years, a major expansion of the hominid brain and body took place. One early hominid ancestor was probably *Australopithecus*, from whom more humanlike species, among them *Homo habilis* and *Homo erectus*, evolved. Modern humans, *Homo sapiens*, appeared between 200,000 and 100,000 years ago.

Environmental challenges and opportunities that favored adaptability and complex social patterns, changes in physiology, and neoteny all likely stimulated brain evolution in human species. The human brain's structure is quite similar to that of other animals, even relatively simple animals such as rats, but the human brain is large because it has more neurons.

People vary widely in body size and in brain size and have different kinds of intelligence, making simple comparisons of brain size and general intelligence impossible. In studying modern humans, recognizing the great extent to which our behavior is culturally learned rather than inherent in our nervous systems is paramount.

2.2 Comparative Research in Neuropsychology

Three primary lines of research drive comparative investigations with animals: (1) understanding the basic biological mechanisms of the brain, (2) designing animal models of human neurological disorders, and (3) describing the evolutionary development (phylogeny) of the brain.

2.3 Genes, Environment, and Behavior

From each parent, we inherit one of each chromosome in our 23 chromosome pairs. Because all but the sex chromosomes are matched pairs, a cell contains two alleles of every gene. The alleles a person might inherit from a parent depend on that parent's genotype. Sometimes two paired alleles are homozygous (the same); sometimes they are heterozygous (different).

An allele may be dominant and expressed as a trait; recessive and not expressed; or codominant, in which case both it and the other paired allele are expressed in the individual organism's phenotype. One allele is designated the wild type—the most common one in a population—whereas the other alleles are mutations. Genes can undergo mutations that alter their codes by one or more changes in the nucleotide sequence. Most mutations are harmful and may produce abnormalities in nervous-system structure and behavioral function.

Selective breeding is the oldest form of genetic manipulation. Genetic engineering is a newer science in which the genome of an animal is altered. The genetic composition of a cloned animal is identical to that of a parent or sibling, transgenic animals contain new or altered genes, and knockouts have genomes from which a gene has been deleted.

The genome encodes a range of phenotypes, accounting in part for phenotypic plasticity. The phenotype eventually produced is determined by epigenetic influences in the environment. Epigenetic mechanisms can influence gene expression without changing the genetic code.

References

Balaban, E. Brain switching: Studying evolutionary behavioral changes in the context of individual brain development. *International Journal of Developmental Biology* 49:117–124, 2005.

Bordelon, Y. M. Clinical neurogenetics: Huntington disease. *Neurology Clinics* 31:1085–1094, 2013.

Campbell, C. B. G., and W. Hodos. The concept of homology and the evolution of the nervous system. *Brain, Behavior and Evolution* 3:353–367, 1970.

Darwin, C. *The Descent of Man, and Selection in Relation to Sex.* London: J. Murray, 1871.

Deary, I. J. *Looking Down on Human Intelligence: From Psychometrics to the Brain.* Oxford Psychology Series, No. 34. New York: Oxford University Press, 2000.

Dunbar, R. *Grooming, Gossip, and the Evolution of Language.* Cambridge, Mass.: Harvard University Press, 1998.

Falk, D. Brain evolution in *Homo*: The "radiator" theory. *Behavioral and Brain Sciences* 13:344–368, 1990.

Flynn, J. R. *Are We Getting Smarter? Rising IQ in the Twenty-First Century.* Cambridge, UK: Cambridge University Press, 2012.

Fonseca-Azevedo, K., and S. Herculano-Houzel. Metabolic constraint imposes tradeoff between body size and number of brain neurons in human evolution. *Proceedings of the National Academy of Sciences U.S.A.* 109:18571–18576, 2012.

Gallup, G. G., Jr. Chimpanzees: Self-recognition. *Science* 167:86–87, 1970.

Gardner, H. E., M. L. Kornhaber, and W. E. Wake. *Intelligence: Multiple Perspectives.* Fort Worth, Tex., and Toronto: Harcourt Brace College, 1997.

Gardner, R. A., and B. T. Gardner. Teaching sign language to a chimpanzee. *Science* 165:664–672, 1969.

Geschwind, D. H., and G. Konopka. Genes and human brain evolution. *Nature* 486(7404):481–482, June 28, 2012.

Gill, J. M., and A. C. Rego. The R6 lines of transgenic mice: A model for screening new therapies for Huntington's disease. *Brain Research Reviews* 59:410–431, 2009.

Gillespie-Lynch, K., P. M. Greenfield, Y. Feng, S. Savage-Rumbaugh, and H. A. Lyn. A cross-species study of gesture and its role in symbolic development: Implications for the gestural theory of language evolution. *Frontiers in Psychology* 4:160, 2013.

Goodall, J. *The Chimpanzees of Gombe: Patterns of Behavior.* Cambridge, Mass.: Belknap Press of the Harvard University Press, 1986.

Gould, S. J. *The Mismeasure of Man.* New York: Norton, 1981.

Hampshire, A., R. R. Highfield, B. L. Parkin, and A. M. Owen. Fractionating human intelligence. *Neuron* 76:1225–1237, 2012.

Heffer A., J. Xiang, and L. Pick. Variation and constraint in *Hox* gene evolution. *Proceedings of the National Academy of Science U.S.A.* 5:2211–2216, 2013.

Herringa, R. J., R. M. Birn, P. L. Ruttle, C. A. Burghy, D. E. Stodola, R. J. Davidson, and M. J. Essex. Childhood maltreatment is associated with altered fear circuitry and increased internalizing symptoms by late adolescence. *Proceedings of the National Academy of Science U.S.A.* 110(47):19119–19124, November 19, 2013.

Hopkins, W. D., and J. P. Taglialatela. Initiation of joint attention is associated with morphometric variation in the anterior cingulate cortex of chimpanzees (Pan troglodytes). *American Journal of Primatology* 75:441–449, 2012.

Jerison, H. J. *Evolution of the Brain and Intelligence.* New York: Academic Press, 1973.

Johanson, D., and M. Edey. *Lucy: The Beginnings of Humankind.* New York: Warner Books, 1981.

Kaati, G., L. O. Bygren, M. Pembrey, and M. Sjöström. Transgenerational response to nutrition, early life circumstances and longevity. *European Journal of Human Genetics* 15:784–790, 2007.

Kues, W. A., and H. Niemann. Advances in farm animal transgenesis. *Preventative Veterinary Medicine* 102:146–156, 2011.

Larson, G., E. K. Karlsson, A. Perri, M. T. Webster, S. Y. Ho, J. Peters, P. W. Stahl, P. J. Piper, F. Lingaas, M. Fredholm, K. E. Comstock, J. F. Modiano, C. Schelling, A. I. Agoulnik, P. A. Leegwater, K. Dobney, J. D. Vigne, C. Vilà, L. Andersson, and K. Lindblad-Toh. Rethinking dog domestication by integrating genetics, archeology, and biogeography. *Proceedings of the National Academy of Sciences U.S.A.* 109:8878–8883, 2012.

Masterton, B., and L. C. Skeen. Origins of anthropoid intelligence: Prefrontal system and delayed alternation in hedgehog, tree shrew, and bush baby. *Journal of Comparative and Physiological Psychology* 81:423–433, 1972.

McConnell, M. J., M. R. Lindberg, K. J. Brennand, J. C. Piper, T. Voet, C. Cowing-Zitron, S. Shumilina, R. S. Lasken, J. R. Vermeesch, I. M. Hall, and F. H. Gage. Mosaic copy number variation in human neurons. *Science* 342:632–637, 2013.

McKinney, M. L. The juvenilized ape myth—Our "overdeveloped" brain. *Bioscience* 48:109–118, 1998.

Mesoudi, A., A. Whiten, and K. N. Laland. Towards a unified science of cultural evolution. *Behavioural and Brain Sciences* 29:364–366, 2006.

Milton, K. The critical role played by animal source foods in human evolution. *Journal of Nutrition* 133:3893S–3897S, 2003.

Miyake, K., C. Yang, Y. Minakuchi, K. Ohori, M. Soutome, T. Hirasawa, Y. Kazuki, N. Adachi, S. Suzuki, M. Itoh, Y. I. Goto, T. Andoh, H. Kurosawa, M. Oshimura. M. Sasaki, A. Toyoda, and T. Kubota. Comparison of genomic and epigenomic expression in monozygotic twins discordant for Rett syndrome. PLoS ONE, June 21, 2013.

Moore, C. G., M. Schenkman, W. M. Kohrt, A. Delitto, D. A. Hall, and D. Corcos. Study in Parkinson Disease of Exercise (SPARX): Translating high-intensity exercise from animals to humans. *Contemporary Clinical Trials* 36:90–98, 2013.

Nilsson, D. E. Eye evolution and its functional basis. *Vision Neuroscience* 30:5–20, 2013.

Pickering, R., P. H. Dirks, Z. Jinnah, D. J. de Ruiter, S. E. Churchill, A. I. Herries, J. D. Woodhead, J. C. Hellstrom, and L. R. Berger. *Australopithecus sediba* at 1.977 Ma and implications for the origins of the genus *Homo. Science* 333:1421–1423, 2011.

Potts, R., and C. Sloan. *What Does It Mean to Be Human?* Washington, D.C.: National Geographic, 2010.

Stedman, H. H., B. W. Kozyak, A. Nelson, D. M. Thesier, L. T. Su, D. W. Low, C. R. Bridges, J. B. Shrager, N. Minugh-Purvis, and M. A. Mitchell. Myosin gene mutation correlates with anatomical changes in the human lineage. *Nature* 428:415–418, 2004.

Stephan, H., R. Bauchot, and O. J. Andy. Data on the size of the brain and of various parts in insectivores and primates. In C. R. Noback and W. Montagna, eds. *The Primate Brain*, pp. 289–297. New York: Appleton.

Tarantino, L. M., and A. F. Eisener-Dorman. Forward genetic approaches to understanding complex behaviors. *Current Topics in Behavioral Neuroscience,* 12:25–58, 2012.

Twardosz, S. Effects of experience on the brain: The role of neuroscience in early development and education. *Early Education & Development* 23:96–119, 2012.

Zhang, G., Z. Pei, E. V. Ball, M. Mort, H. Kehrer-Sawatzki, and D. N. Cooper. Cross-comparison of the genome sequences from human, chimpanzee, Neanderthal and a Denisovan hominin identifies novel potentially compensated mutations. *Human Genomics* 5:453–484, 2011.

3 Nervous System Organization

Stroke

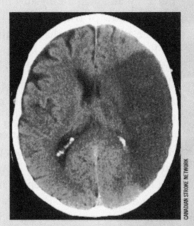

R.S. enjoyed his first job as an usher in a movie theater. After graduating from high school, he became the theater's manager and eventually its owner. He enjoyed the business and loved movies. He had remarkable knowledge of everything cinema and relished discussing its every aspect.

One day while repairing his garage roof, R.S. felt numbness in his left hand, then collapsed and fell to the ground. He had suffered a **stroke**, an interruption of blood flow to the brain that kills brain cells and causes neurological symptoms to appear suddenly. His stroke resulted from **ischemia**, deficient blood flow to the brain due to functional constriction of a blood vessel by a clot.

At a nearby hospital a CT scan showed stroke damage to R.S.'s right frontal cortex. (The dark area at right in the adjoining CT image has been damaged by decreased blood flow.) The U.S. Centers for Disease Control and Prevention estimates stroke to be the third-leading cause of death in the United States and the leading cause of long-term disability.

In the United States, someone suffers a stroke every 40 seconds. Strokes can occur at any age. In developed countries, the rate of stroke is declining with reduced smoking, dietary improvements, and control of blood pressure.

R.S. received no medical treatment for his stroke, and with rehabilitation recovered the ability to walk, although his left leg was stiff. His left arm was rigid and flexed, and he made no attempt to use it.

To his family, R.S. appeared able to resume most of his prestroke activities, but he was apathetic. He no longer enjoyed gardening, took no interest in his business, and no longer talked about movies or watched television. Formerly talkative, R.S. no longer initiated conversation; when he did speak, it was without affect. Ten years after his stroke, despite neuropsychological assessment and repeated attempts at behavioral and physical therapy, R.S. is unchanged.

Unlike the more severe **hemorrhagic stroke**, which results from a burst vessel bleeding into the brain, ischemic stroke can be treated with good results when the drug t-PA is administered within 3 hours. **Tissue plasminogen activator (t-PA)** breaks up clots and allows normal blood flow to return to the affected region.

R.S. was not given the drug within the required 3 hours of his stroke, however, because the attending physician was unsure whether his fall from the garage roof was the result of ischemic stroke or had caused a hemorrhagic stroke resulting from concussion and a burst blood vessel. An anticlotting drug decreases tissue death in ischemic stroke but aggravates cell death in hemorrhagic stroke.

Scientists are developing new treatments for the postacute stroke period, because most patients do not make it to an emergency unit within 3 hours. Scientists are searching for ways to stimulate reparative processes in the brain after ischemic or hemorrhagic stroke, because the poststroke survival period for many patients is long. Neuropsychologists also are interested in developing rehabilitative procedures that help patients cope with and overcome not only motor symptoms but also the apathy that so diminished R.S.'s quality of life.

The complexities that attend the brain and behavior present major challenges to anyone who is trying to explain how one produces the other. The human brain's approximately 85 billion neurons engage in information processing, and its 86 billion glial cells support neuronal functioning (Fonseca-Azevedo and Herculano-Houzel, 2012). Each neuron makes as many as 15,000 connections with other cells.

Neurons in the cortex are organized in layers and in clusters called **nuclei** (from the Latin *nux*, meaning "nut") that have specific functions in mediating behavior. When stained, layers and nuclei reveal distinctive shapes and colors that identify them. Within layers and nuclei, cells that are close together make the most of their connections with one another, but they also make long-distance connections, forming distinctive *fiber pathways* or **tracts** (from Old French, meaning "path").

The human brain has a distinct architecture, as do the brains of each animal species. The features of individual brains also make each one distinctive. Layers and nuclei can differ from one individual to the next and even in each of a single brain's two hemispheres. This anatomical individuation is likely related to the behavioral differences that individuals display.

The brain is also plastic: it can undergo enormous changes during a person's life span. Neurons change their connections with one another. Brains lose and gain neurons and glia. Neuroplasticity mediates changes in development, in learning from experience, and in an individual's ability to compensate for brain damage such as R.S. suffered following his stroke. The brain's common architecture is specified by an individual's genotype, while epigenetic influences, such as those discussed in Section 2.3, mediate the individual's phenotypic plasticity (**Figure 3.1**).

Figure 3.1 ▲

Phenotypic Plasticity These two mice are clones—genetically identical—yet express widely differing phenotypes because their mothers were fed diets with different supplements when pregnant, leading to different body structures, in part as a result of their own eating behaviors. (Randy Jirtle/Duke University Medical Center)

3.1 Neuroanatomy: Finding Your Way Around the Brain

Knowledge about the orderly arrangement of neurons and their connections aids neuropsychologists' efforts to understand brain function. We begin our exploration of nervous system organization by describing the brain's anatomy.

Describing Location in the Brain

The anatomical locations of the brain's layers, nuclei, and pathways are described within three reference frames: with respect to other body parts of the animal, with respect to relative location, and with respect to a viewer's perspective. **Figure 3.2** illustrates the most frequently used sets of orienting terms:

- Figure 3.2A describes brain structures as oriented in the head relative to other body parts. In Latin, *rostrum* is "beak," *caudum* is "tail," *dorsum* is "back," and *ventrum* is "stomach." Accordingly, *rostral, caudal, dorsal*, and *ventral* parts of the brain are located toward those body parts. Occasionally, the terms *superior* and *inferior* are used to refer to structures located dorsally or ventrally.

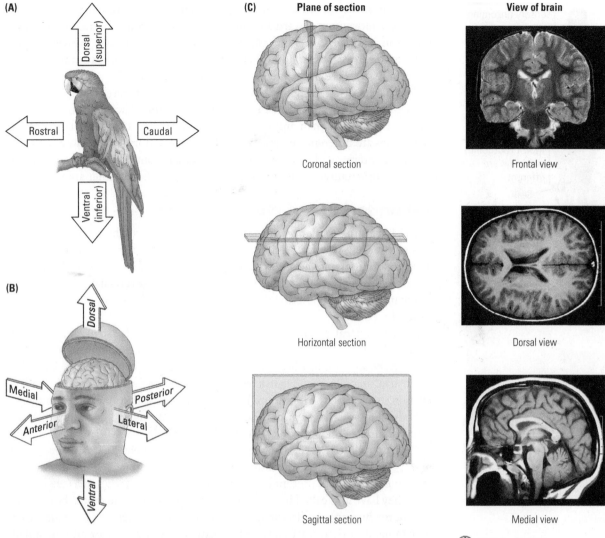

(A) Dorsal (superior) / Rostral / Caudal / Ventral (inferior)

(B) Dorsal / Medial / Anterior / Posterior / Lateral / Ventral

(C) **Plane of section** — Coronal section, Horizontal section, Sagittal section

View of brain — Frontal view, Dorsal view, Medial view

Figure 3.2 ▲

Anatomical Orientation
(A) Terms that describe the brain as oriented in the head relative to other body parts. (B) Terms that describe the human brain from the frame of reference of the face. (C) Sectioning allows viewing the brain's internal structures: a coronal section reveals a frontal view, a horizontal section reveals a dorsal view, and a sagittal section reveals a medial view. (Photographs Dr. D. Armstrong, University of Toronto/Lifeart.)

- Figure 3.2B illustrates how human brain parts are described in relation to one another from the frame of reference of the face. *Anterior* or *frontal* is in front, *posterior* structures are located behind, *lateral* structures are at the side, and *medial* structures are located at the center or between.

- Figure 3.2C illustrates terms that describe the direction of a section through the brain from a viewer's perspective. A *coronal* section is cut in a vertical plane, from the crown of the head down, revealing a *frontal* view of the brain. A *horizontal* section (because the view or cut is along the horizon) produces a *dorsal* view, looking down on the brain from above. A *sagittal* section is cut lengthways, front to back, and reveals a *medial* view, from the side (imagine the brain oriented as an arrow—in Latin, *sagittal*).

The nervous system, like the body, is symmetrical, with left and right sides. Structures that lie on the same side are **ipsilateral**; if they lie on opposite sides, they are **contralateral** to each other. If one lies in each hemisphere—which virtually all do—the structures are **bilateral**.

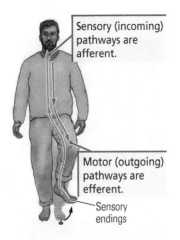

Sensory (incoming) pathways are afferent.

Motor (outgoing) pathways are efferent.

Sensory endings

Structures close to one another are **proximal**; those far from one another are **distal**. Any movement toward a brain structure is **afferent**, whereas movement away from it is **efferent**. Thus, the sensory pathways that carry messages from the body toward the brain and spinal cord are afferent; motor pathways leading to the body from the brain and spinal cord are efferent.

Humans are distinguished in that they stand upright, whereas nonhuman animals typically stand on all fours in a quadruped posture. The spatial orientations of human and nonhuman animal brains are similar, but the spinal-cord spatial orientations are different. As explained in Section 3.4, dorsal and ventral in quadrupeds are anterior and posterior in upright humans, but if humans stand on "all fours," the orientation of the spinal cord is similar to that of other animals.

A Wonderland of Nomenclature

To the beginning student, and perhaps even an expert, the naming of brain parts might seem chaotic. And it is, because neuroscientists have been at it for a long time, and names accumulate as knowledge of brain parts and their functions grows. Consequently, many structures may have several names, often used interchangeably, that describe their appearance, their location, or one or more of their functions.

The **precentral gyrus**, a part of the brain damaged by stroke in R.S. and responsible for his diminished motor ability, has many other names. It is called *gyrus precentralis* in Latin because of its relation to the central gyrus, and "the motor strip" in colloquial English because of its motor functions. It is also called "Jackson's strip," after Hughlings-Jackson, who noted that in epileptic attacks, the body's limbs convulse in an orderly arrangement, suggesting to him that the representation of the body in the brain also is orderly.

Electrophysiologists refer to the precentral gyrus as the *primary motor cortex* or *M1*, to distinguish it from other cortical motor regions. Because they can obtain movements of different body parts after stimulating this area (see Figure 1.12), they have also called it the "somatomotor strip" or "the motor homunculus" (motor human). Additionally, because anatomists such as Gall found that the pyramidal (corticospinal) tract, which extends from the cortex into the spinal cord, comes mainly from this cortical region, they called it "area pyramidalis."

For a lot of brain regions, Greek, Latin, French, and English terminology alternates with slang. Additionally, neuroscientists' imaginations have compared brain structures to body anatomy (mammillary bodies), flora (amygdala, or "almond"), fauna (hippocampus, or "seahorse"), and mythology (Ammon's horn—"the horn of plenty"). Other terms make use of color—substantia nigra ("black substance"), locus coeruleus ("blue area"), and red nucleus—or of consistency, such as substantia gelatinosa ("gelatinous substance").

Some names are puzzling: substantia innominata ("unnamable substance"), zona incerta ("uncertain area"), nucleus ambiguus ("ambiguous nucleus"); others are based entirely on expediency: cell groups A-1 to A-15 or B1 to B9. The longest name for a brain structure is *nucleus reticularis tegmenti pontis Bechterewi*, affectionately known as NRTP because, as you will observe, neuroscientists have a special fondness for abbreviations. We attempt to use consistent and simple terms in this book, but in many cases, because neuroscientists in different fields use different terms in presenting their findings, we must do so as well.

3.2 Overview of Nervous System Structure and Function

From an anatomical standpoint, the central nervous system (CNS) consists of the brain and the spinal cord, both encased in bone. The peripheral nervous system (PNS) encompasses everything else (**Figure 3.3**A). The PNS has two divisions:

- The somatic (body) nervous system (SNS) consists of two sets of inputs and outputs to the CNS. These are the spinal and cranial nerves to and from the sensory organs and the muscles, joints, and skin. The SNS transmits incoming sensory information to the CNS, including vision, hearing, pain, temperature, touch, and the position and movement of body parts, and produces movements in response.

- The autonomic (automatic) nervous system (ANS) controls the functioning of the body's internal organs to "rest and digest" through the **parasympathetic** (calming) **nerves** or to "fight and flee" through the **sympathetic** (arousing) **nerves**.

In the functional organization used in this book, the focus shifts to how the parts of the nervous system work together. In Figure 3.3B, the major divisions of the PNS step up to constitute, along with the CNS, a three-part interactive system.

(A) Anatomical Nervous System Divisions

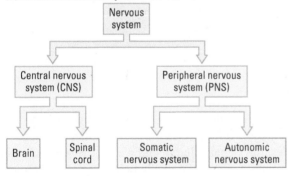

(B) Functional Nervous System Divisions

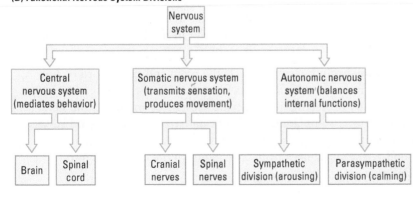

◎ Figure 3.3 ◄

Parsing the Nervous System
(A) Anatomical divisions of the nervous system. (B) A functional organization focusing on how the three parts of the system interact.

Support and Protection

The brain and spinal cord are supported and protected from injury and infection in four ways:

1. The brain is enclosed in a thick bone, the skull, and the spinal cord is encased in a series of interlocking bony vertebrae. Thus, the CNS lies within bony encasements, whereas the SNS and ANS, although connected to the CNS, lie outside them. Lacking bony protection, the PNS divisions are more vulnerable to injury, but they can renew themselves after injury by growing new axons and dendrites. Self-repair is much more limited within the CNS.

2. Within the bony case enclosing the CNS is a triple-layered set of membranes, the **meninges**, shown in **Figure 3.4**. The outer *dura mater* (from the Latin, meaning "hard mother") is a tough double layer of tissue enclosing the brain in a kind of loose sack. The middle *arachnoid membrane* (from the Greek, meaning "resembling a spider's web") is a very thin sheet of delicate tissue that follows the brain's contours. The inner *pia mater* (from the Latin, meaning "soft mother") is a moderately tough tissue that clings to the brain's surface.

Figure 3.4 ▶

Cerebral Security A triple-layered covering, the meninges, encases the brain and spinal cord, which are bathed in cushioning cerebrospinal fluid (CSF).

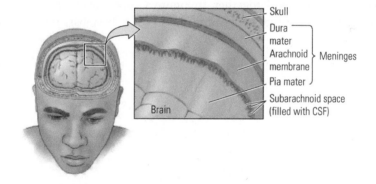

3. The brain and spinal cord are cushioned from shock and sudden pressure changes by the cerebrospinal fluid (CSF), which circulates through the brain's four ventricles, the spinal column, and within the subarachnoid space in the brain's meninges. CSF is continually being made and drained off into the circulatory system through connecting channels among the ventricles. If the outflow in these channels is blocked, as occurs in a congenital condition called **hydrocephalus** (literally, "water brain"), severe intellectual impairments and even death can result from the built-up CSF pressure.

4. The **blood–brain barrier** protects the brain and spinal cord by limiting the movement of chemicals from the rest of the body into the CNS and by protecting it from toxic substances and infection. Glial cells called *astroglia* stimulate the cells of capillaries—minute blood vessels—to form tight junctions with one another, thus preventing many blood-borne substances from crossing from the capillaries into the CNS tissues.

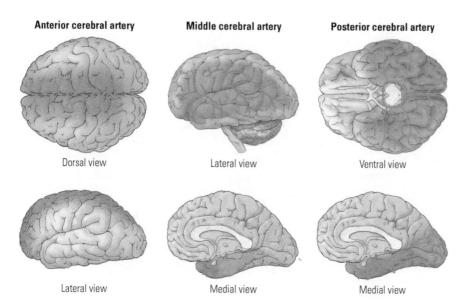

Anterior cerebral artery **Middle cerebral artery** **Posterior cerebral artery**

Dorsal view Lateral view Ventral view

Lateral view Medial view Medial view

Figure 3.5 ◄

Distribution of the Major Cerebral Arteries If you align your hand so that your wrist represents the base of a cerebral artery, your extended digits will spread over the area of cortex corresponding to the area where that artery distributes blood.

Blood Supply

The brain receives its blood supply from two internal carotid arteries and two vertebral arteries that course up each side of the neck. The four arteries connect at the base of the brain, where they enter the skull. They branch off into several smaller arteries that irrigate the brainstem and cerebellum and give rise to three cerebral arteries that irrigate the forebrain. Their distribution zones in the cortex are shown in **Figure 3.5**.

If you place your hand so that the wrist represents the artery trunk at the base of the brain, the extended digits offer an approximate representation of the cortical area irrigated in each zone. Thus, the **anterior cerebral artery** (ACA) irrigates the medial and dorsal parts of the cortex, the **middle cerebral artery** (MCA) irrigates the lateral surface of the cortex, and the **posterior cerebral artery** (PCA) irrigates its ventral and posterior surfaces.

If a blood clot forms in a cerebral artery and causes a stroke, symptoms will vary according to the location of the loss of blood supply. R.S., for example, suffered an MCA ischemic stroke. Note in Figure 3.5 that a large clot in or near the base of an artery will deprive a great deal of the cortex of its blood supply, whereas a smaller clot in the more distal branches of the artery will result in more-restricted damage. Some people have connections between the different arteries, so subsequent to a clot, other arteries can supply blood, thus minimizing a stroke's effects.

The brain's veins, through which spent blood returns to the heart, are classified as external and internal cerebral and cerebellar veins. The venous flow does not follow the course of the major arteries but instead follows its own pattern.

Neurons and Glia

The brain originates in a single, undifferentiated **neural stem cell** (a *germinal cell*). Self-renewing multipotential neural stem cells give rise to the different types of neurons and glia in the nervous system. Neuroscientists, who once thought that

Figure 3.6 ▶

Brain-Cell Origins Brain cells begin as multipotential stem cells that become progenitor cells, the precursors of blasts, which finally develop into specialized neurons and glia. Adult stem cells line the brain's subventricular zone, which surrounds the ventricles, and are located in the spinal cord and the retina of the eye as well.

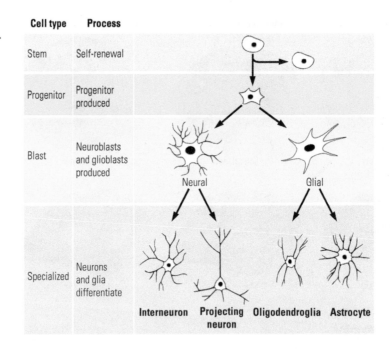

a newborn baby had all the neurons he or she would ever possess, now know that neurons can be lost after birth during typical development. In the adult brain, stem cells that persist can produce new neurons in some brain locations.

A stem cell has extensive capacity for self-renewal. To form a brain initially, a stem cell divides and produces two stem cells, both of which can divide again (**Figure 3.6**). In the adult, one stem cell dies after each division, so the mature brain contains a constant number of dividing stem cells.

In the developing embryo, stem cells give rise to **progenitor cells**, which migrate and act as precursor cells, giving rise to nondividing primitive nervous system cell types called **blasts**. Some, the neuroblasts, differentiate into neurons; others, glioblasts, differentiate into glial cells. These two basic brain-cell types take many forms and constitute the entire adult brain.

Neurons can differ in many ways—in overall size, length and branching of axons, and complexity of dendritic processes as well as in their biochemistry and activity. **Figure 3.7** illustrates some differences in size and shape among the three basic types of neurons from different parts of the nervous system.

Figure 3.7 ▶

Neuron Shapes and Functions (A) Sensory neurons collect information and pass it on to (B) interneurons, whose abundant branches collect information from many sources and link to distinctively large (C) motor neurons, which pass on information to command muscles to move. Note that these cells are not drawn to scale.

(A) Sensory neurons

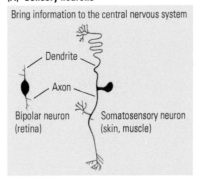

(B) Interneurons

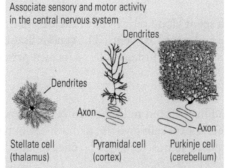

(C) Motor neurons

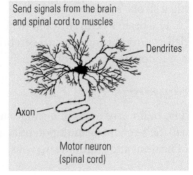

1. *Sensory neurons.* The simplest **sensory receptor**, a cell that transduces sensory information into nervous system activity, is the **bipolar neuron** shown on the left in Figure 3.7A. It consists of a cell body with a dendrite on one side and an axon on the other and is found in the retina of the eye. A **somatosensory neuron** projects from a sensory receptor in the body into the spinal cord. Its dendrite and axon are connected, which speeds information conduction because messages do not have to pass through the cell body (Figure 3.7A, *right*).

2. *Interneurons.* **Interneurons** within the brain and spinal cord link up sensory- and motor-neuron activity in the CNS. The many kinds of interneurons all have multiple dendrites that branch extensively (Figure 3.7B), but like all neurons, a brain or spinal-cord interneuron has only one axon (although it can branch). Interneurons include stellate (star-shaped) cells characterized by many branches, pyramidal cells in the cortex that have a pyramid-shaped cell body, and Purkinje cells of the cerebellum. The pyramidal and Purkinje cells are the output cells of their respective structures.

3. *Motor neurons.* **Motor neurons** located in the brainstem and spinal cord project to facial and body muscles (Figure 3.7C). Together, motor neurons are called "the final common path" because all behavior (movement) produced by the brain is produced through them.

The various types of glial cells have different functions as well. Five types of glia are described in **Table 3.1**. **Ependymal cells** line the brain's ventricles and make CSF. **Astroglia** (star-shaped glia), mentioned earlier in connection with the blood–brain barrier, provide structural support and nutrition to neurons. **Microglia** (tiny glia) fight infection and remove debris. **Oligodendroglia** (few branches) insulate neurons in the CNS, and **Schwann cells** insulate sensory and motor neurons in the PNS. This insulation is called **myelin**.

Gray, White, and Reticular Matter

When a human brain is opened to reveal its internal structures, some parts appear gray, some white, and some mottled. These visually contrasting parts are described as gray matter, white matter, and reticular matter (**Figure 3.8**).

Gray matter acquires its characteristic gray-brown color from the capillaries and neuronal cell bodies that predominate there. Colloquially, the cortex is made up predominantly of layers of neurons, referred to as "our gray matter." **White matter** consists largely of axons that extend from these cell bodies to form connections with neurons in other brain areas. The axons are myelinated (insulated) by

Table 3.1 **Types of glial cells**

Type	Appearance	Features and Function
Ependymal cell		Small, ovoid; secretes cerebrospinal fluid (CSF)
Astrocyte		Star-shaped, symmetrical; nutritive and support function
Microglial cell		Small, mesodermally derived; defensive function
Oligodendroglial cell		Asymmetrical; forms insulating myelin around axons in brain and spinal cord
Schwann cell		Asymmetrical; wraps around peripheral nerves to form insulating myelin

Figure 3.8 ▶

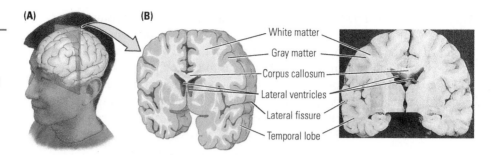

Coronal Section Through the Brain The brain is (A) cut from the top down and (B) frontally viewed at a slight angle. Relatively white regions are composed largely of myelinated nerve fibers; relatively gray-brown areas are composed of cell bodies. The large bundle of fibers joining the two hemi-spheres, visible above the ventricles, is the corpus callosum. Each ventricle is a cavity filled with cerebro-spinal fluid. (Photograph: Arthur Glauberman/Science Source.)

oligodendrocytes and Schwann cells that are composed of the same fatty sub-stance (lipid) that gives milk its white appearance. As a result, areas of the brain that consist of axon pathways appear white.

Reticular matter (from the Latin *rete*, meaning "net") contains a mixture of cell bodies and axons from which it acquires its mottled gray and white, or net-like, appearance. Prominent cell groupings and pathways in the brain can be seen in much more detail when viewed through a microscope after staining (**Figure 3.9**). White and gray matter are sensitive to different stains.

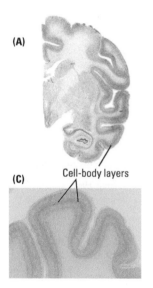

Figure 3.9 ▲

Cortical Layers and Glia Brain sections from a monkey's left hemisphere. (Midline is at left in each image.) Cells stained with a selective cell-body stain [(A) and (C)] for neurons and a selective fiber stain [(B) and (D)] for insulating glial cells (myelin). The staining reveals very different pictures of the brain at a microscopic level [(C) and (D)]. (Courtesy of Bryan Kolb.)

Layers, Nuclei, Nerves, and Tracts

As mentioned in the chapter introduction, large, well-defined groups of cell bodies in the CNS form either layers or nuclei (clusters). Within the PNS, such clusters are called **ganglia**. Tracts (fiber pathways) are large collections of axons projecting toward or away from a nucleus or layer in the CNS.

Tracts carry information from one place to another within the CNS; for example, the corticospinal (pyramidal) tract carries information from the cortex to the spinal cord. The optic tract carries information from the retina of the eye (the retina, strictly speaking, is part of the brain) to other visual centers in the brain. Fibers and fiber pathways that enter and leave the CNS are called **nerves**, the auditory nerve and the vagus nerve, for example, but once they enter the central nervous system, they, too, are called **tracts**.

3.3 Origin and Development of the Central Nervous System

The developing brain, which is less complex than the adult brain, originates as a three-part structure (**Figure 3.10**A). At later stages in development, the front and back components expand greatly and subdivide further, yielding five regions in all (Figure 3.10B). Embryologists describe them in terms of their relative lo-cations (Figure 3.10C).

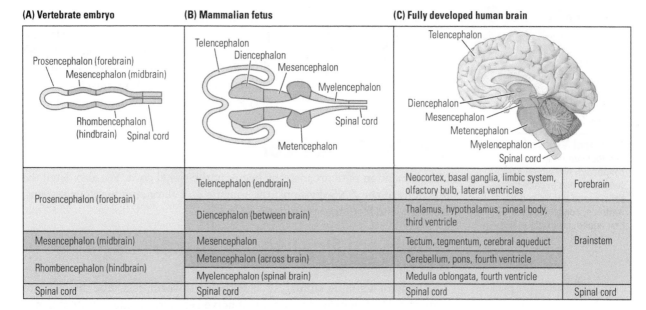

(A) Vertebrate embryo	(B) Mammalian fetus	(C) Fully developed human brain	
Prosencephalon (forebrain)	Telencephalon (endbrain)	Neocortex, basal ganglia, limbic system, olfactory bulb, lateral ventricles	Forebrain
	Diencephalon (between brain)	Thalamus, hypothalamus, pineal body, third ventricle	
Mesencephalon (midbrain)	Mesencephalon	Tectum, tegmentum, cerebral aqueduct	Brainstem
Rhombencephalon (hindbrain)	Metencephalon (across brain)	Cerebellum, pons, fourth ventricle	
	Myelencephalon (spinal brain)	Medulla oblongata, fourth ventricle	
Spinal cord	Spinal cord	Spinal cord	Spinal cord

Figure 3.10 ▲

Steps in Brain Development (A) A three-chambered brain. (B) A five-chambered brain. (C) Medial view through the center of the adult human brain.

The primitive developing brain's three regions are recognizable in Figure 3.10A as a series of enlargements at the end of the embryonic spinal cord. The adult brain of a fish, amphibian, or reptile is roughly equivalent to this three-part brain: the **prosencephalon** ("front brain") is responsible for olfaction, the **mesencephalon** ("middle brain") is the seat of vision and hearing, and the **rhombencephalon** ("hindbrain") controls movement and balance. Here, the spinal cord is considered part of the hindbrain.

In mammals (Figure 3.10B), the anterior prosencephalon develops further to form the cerebral hemispheres (the cortex and related structures), known collectively as the **telencephalon** ("endbrain"). The posterior prosencephalon, referred to as the **diencephalon** ("between brain"), includes the thalamus.

Behind the mesencephalon, the rhombencephalon also develops further, subdividing into the **metencephalon** ("across brain," which includes the enlarged cerebellum) and the **myelencephalon** ("spinal brain"), the lower region of the brainstem.

The human brain is a more complex mammalian brain (Figure 3.10C). As we describe the major structures of the CNS in the sections that follow, we group them according to the three-part scheme of forebrain, brainstem, and spinal cord. Roughly speaking, it is these three subdivisions that constitute the brain's *levels of function* described in Section 1.3. The forebrain is considered the locus of cognitive processes, the brainstem of regulatory functions (drinking, eating, sleeping, etc.), and the spinal cord of more reflexive motor functions. Nevertheless, most behaviors are products not of a single functional level but rather involve all levels of the nervous system.

The brain begins as a tube, and even after it folds and matures, its interior remains "hollow" and is filled with CSF. Four prominent pockets of the hollow region are called **ventricles** ("bladders"), numbered first through fourth. The "lateral ventricles" (first and second) form C-shaped lakes underlying the cerebral cortex, whereas the third and fourth ventricles extend into the brainstem and spinal cord (**Figure 3.11**). The **cerebral aqueduct** connects the third

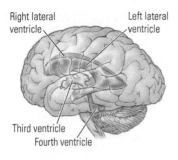

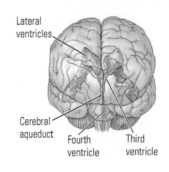

and fourth ventricles. As noted earlier, CSF is produced by ependymal glial cells located adjacent to the ventricles (see Table 3.1). CSF flows from the lateral ventricles out through the fourth ventricle to drain into the circulatory system at the base of the brainstem.

Figure 3.11 ▲

Cerebral Ventricles
The four ventricles are interconnected: two lateral cerebral ventricles, one in each hemisphere, and a third and fourth ventricle, connected by the cerebral aqueduct, in the brainstem.

3.4 The Spinal Cord

Our description of neuroanatomy begins at the spinal cord. We also detail the functions of the PNS divisions, the somatic and autonomic nervous systems, which radiate from the spinal cord.

Spinal-Cord Structure and Spinal Nerve Anatomy

The body of a simple animal, such as the earthworm, is a tube divided into segments. Within its body is a tube of nerve cells also divided into segments. Each nerve-cell segment receives nerve fibers from afferent sensory receptors in the adjacent body part and sends efferent fibers to control that body part's muscles. Thus, each body and nerve-cell segment is a functional unit in the earthworm, although fibers interconnect the segments and coordinate their activity. This basic plan also holds for the human body.

Let us take a look at our "tube of nerves." The spinal cord lies inside the bony spinal column, a series of vertebrae categorized into five anatomical regions from top to tail: cervical (C), thoracic (T), lumbar (L), sacral (S), and coccygeal, as diagrammed in **Figure 3.12**A, where the 30 corresponding spinal-cord segments are labeled within each region.

Figure 3.12B shows this segmental organization within the human body. Each body segment forms a ring, or **dermatome** (skin cut), that encircles the spinal column. Mammalian limbs evolved perpendicular to the spinal cord to accommodate their four-legged stance, but humans' upright posture, on two legs, distorts the dermatomes in the arms and legs, as shown by the pattern in Figure 3.12B.

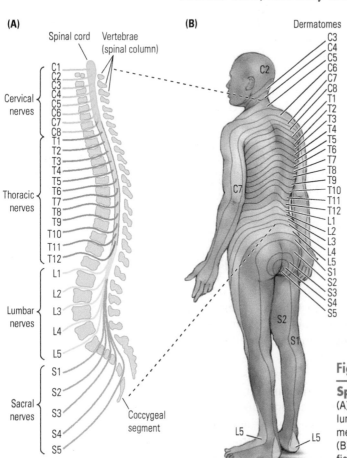

Figure 3.12 ◄

Spinal-Cord Segments and Dermatomes
(A) The five spinal column regions (cervical, C; thoracic, T; lumbar, L; sacral, S; and coccygeal, C vertebrae), shown in medial view along with corresponding spinal-cord segments. (B) Each spinal segment corresponds to a dermatome identified by the segment number, for example, C5 or L2.

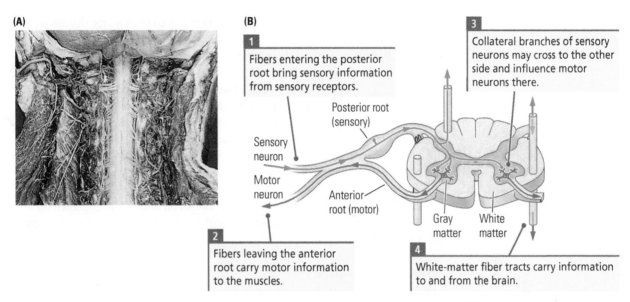

(A)

(B)

1 Fibers entering the posterior root bring sensory information from sensory receptors.

3 Collateral branches of sensory neurons may cross to the other side and influence motor neurons there.

Posterior root (sensory)

Sensory neuron

Motor neuron

Anterior root (motor)

Gray matter

White matter

2 Fibers leaving the anterior root carry motor information to the muscles.

4 White-matter fiber tracts carry information to and from the brain.

🌐 Figure 3.13 ▲

Spinal Nerve Connections
(A) Posterior view with the spinal cord exposed. (B) Cross section of the spinal cord, anterior view, illustrates a sensory neuron in the posterior root and a motor neuron in the anterior root. Collateral branches of sensory fibers may cross to the cord's far side to influence motor neurons on that side and may extend to adjacent spinal segments to influence adjacent body parts. Inner regions of the spinal cord consist of neuronal cell bodies (gray matter); outer regions consist of tracts (white matter) traveling to and from the brain. (Part A from VideoSurgery/Getty Images.)

One result is that as many as six segments (C4 through T2) can be represented on the arm. If you imagine the person in the drawing standing on all fours, you can see how this pattern originated.

Note in Figure 3.12 that each spinal segment connects SNS spinal nerve fibers to the same-numbered dermatome, including the organs and musculature that lie within it. In the main, cervical segments control the forelimbs—in humans, the arms; thoracic segments control the trunk; and lumbar segments control the hind limbs—our legs.

The photo of an exposed spinal cord in **Figure 3.13**A shows that the outer cord consists of white matter tracts. The interior of the cord, shown in cross section in Figure 3.13B, consists of gray matter: it is composed largely of neural cell bodies and has the shape of a butterfly. The cross section reveals the cord's anterior–posterior (dorsal–ventral in quadrupeds) anatomy. In general, the anterior portion of each spinal segment is motor, the posterior sensory.

Afferent fibers enter the posterior spinal cord to bring information in from the body's sensory receptors. These spinal nerve fibers converge as they enter, forming a strand of fibers referred to as a **posterior root**. Efferent fibers exit the anterior spinal cord to carry information from the spinal cord out to the muscles, forming a similar strand of spinal nerve fibers, an **anterior root**.

Spinal-Cord Function and the Spinal Nerves

François Magendie (1783–1855), a French experimental physiologist, reported in a three-page paper in 1822 that he had succeeded in cutting the dorsal roots of one group of puppies and the ventral roots of another group (the youth of the dogs allowed the different surgeries; in adult dogs, the roots are fused). He found that cutting the dorsal roots caused loss of sensation and cutting the ventral roots caused loss of movement.

Eleven years earlier, in 1811, Charles Bell (1774–1842), a Scot, had suggested the opposite functions for each root, basing his conclusions on anatomical information and the results from somewhat inconclusive experiments on rabbits.

When Magendie's paper appeared, Bell hotly disputed priority for the discovery, with some success. Today, the principle that the dorsal or posterior roots in the spinal cord are sensory and the ventral or anterior roots are motor is called the **Bell–Magendie law**.

Magendie's experiment has been called the most important ever conducted on the nervous system. It enabled neurologists for the first time to distinguish sensory from motor impairments and to draw general conclusions about the location of neural damage to spinal-cord segments on the basis of the symptoms displayed by patients. Further major advances toward understanding spinal-cord function came from the work of Charles Sherrington and his students, who showed that the spinal cord retains many functions even after it has been separated from the brain. Sherrington's work had an important influence on improving the treatment of people with spinal-cord injuries, and he was awarded the 1932 Nobel Prize.

Spinal-Cord Injury

Persons whose spinal cords are cut below the cervical segments no longer have control over their legs and are termed **paraplegic**. If the cut is higher, extending into the cervical segments, they are unable to use their arms as well, and are termed **quadriplegic**. A growing understanding of spinal-cord function has led to such tremendous improvements in treatment that spinal-cord patients can lead long and active lives.

In 1987 Canadian paraplegic Rick Hansen, the "man in motion," propelled his wheelchair around the world to campaign for increased awareness of the potential of people with disabilities, removal of barriers, and funding research and treatment for spinal-cord injuries. The late actor Christopher Reeve, famed for his cinematic role as Superman in 1978, became quadriplegic after an equestrian accident, yet continued to make movies and to campaign for medical treatment and research for spinal-cord injuries. They formed, respectively, the Rick Hansen Foundation and Institute in Canada and the Christopher and Dana Reeve Foundation in the United States, both dedicated to treatment of spinal-cord injury.

A main effect of spinal-cord injury is to sever connections between the cord and the brain. Damaged spinal tract fibers do regrow after injury in some vertebrates, such as fish, and in the early developmental stages of other animals such as birds, but they do not regrow in adult mammals. Therefore, research on spinal-cord injury has three main objectives:

1. Following spinal-cord injury, damage in the cord takes hours to days to develop. Arresting the degenerative processes can make an important contribution to sparing function.

2. Inducing fibers to regrow across the damaged section of the spinal cord can restore function. Approaches to establishing regrowth involve removing scar tissue, inducing fibers to regrow by pharmacological treatments, and implanting glial cells in damaged regions to stimulate axon regrowth.

3. Developing aids to movement such as brain–computer interfaces (BCI) and similar marriages of directed neural activity and technology can bypass injury and aid in restoring movement, as detailed in the opening Portrait in Chapter 9.

Spinal Reflexes and Sensory Integration

The spinal cord's neural circuits produce **reflexes**, specific movements elicited by specific forms of sensory stimulation. Each spinal segment contributes to these simple behaviors in the body parts related to that segment. Connections between the segments organize more-complex movements that require the cooperation of many spinal segments. For example, when one leg is withdrawn in response to a painful stimulus, the other leg must simultaneously extend to support the body's weight. In quadrupeds, stepping involves coordinating all four limbs, involving the thoracic and lumber spinal segments working together. Both humans and animals with spinal-cord sections can step if the body is supported. Thus, the spinal cord contains all the connections required for making most of the movements that an animal can make.

Different sensory fibers mediate different reflexes—stepping, postural support, and bladder control are examples. Among the many kinds of sensory receptors in the body are receptors for pain, temperature, touch and pressure, and the sensations of muscle and joint movement. The size of the spinal nerve fiber coming from each kind of receptor is distinctive: generally, pain and temperature fibers are smaller, and those for touch and muscle sense are larger (see Section 8.2).

Stimulation of pain and temperature receptors in a limb produces **flexion** reflexes, which bring the limb inward, toward the body and away from injury. If the stimulus is mild, only the distal part of the limb flexes in response, but with successively stronger stimuli, the size of the movement increases until the whole limb is drawn back. By contrast, stimulation of fine touch and muscle receptors in a limb usually produces **extension** reflexes, which extend the limb outward, away from the body. The extensor reflex maintains contact between the touched part of the limb and the stimulus. For example, the foot or hand touching a surface will maintain contact with the surface and through this reflex will support the body's weight.

Cranial Nerve Connections

Twelve pairs of **cranial nerves** convey sensory and motor signals to and from the head. One set controls the left side of the head; the other set controls the right side. The linkages provided by the cranial nerves between the brain and various parts of the head and neck as well as various internal organs are charted in **Table 3.2** and illustrated in **Figure 3.14**.

Knowledge of the cranial nerves' organization and functions is important for diagnosing brain injury. Cranial nerves can have afferent functions, as for sensory inputs to the brain from the eyes, ears, mouth, and nose, or they can have efferent functions, as for motor control of the facial muscles, tongue, and eyes. Similar to the spinal cord's organization, cranial nerves with sensory functions interface with the posterior part of the brainstem and those with motor function interface with the anterior part. Some cranial nerves have both sensory and motor functions. The spinal accessory and vagus nerves make connections with many internal body organs, including the heart, gut, and glands, via the autonomic nervous system.

Table 3.2 **The cranial nerves**

Number	Name	Function*	Neuropsychological Examination Method	Symptoms Typical of Dysfunction
1	Olfactory	Smell (s)	Various odors applied to each nostril	Loss of sense of smell (anosmia)
2	Optic	Vision (s)	Visual acuity, map field of vision	Loss of vision (anopsia)
3	Oculomotor	Eye movement (m)	Reaction to light, lateral movements of eyes, eyelid movement (ptosis), deviation of eye outward	Double vision (diplopia), large pupil, uneven dilation of pupils, drooping eyelid
4	Trochlear	Eye movement (m)	Upward and downward eye movements	Double vision, defect of downward gaze
5	Trigeminal	Masticatory movements (s, m)	Light touch by cotton baton, pain by pinprick, thermal by hot and cold tubes, corneal reflex by touching cornea, jaw reflex by tapping chin, jaw movements	Decreased sensitivity or numbness of face, brief attacks of severe pain (trigeminal neuralgia), weakness and wasting of facial muscles, asymmetrical chewing
6	Abducens	Eye movement (m)	Lateral movements	Double vision, inward deviation of the eye
7	Facial	Facial movement (s, m)	Facial movements, facial expression, testing for taste	Facial paralysis, loss of taste over anterior two-thirds of tongue
8	Auditory vestibular	Hearing (s)	Audiogram for testing hearing, stimulating by rotating patient or by irrigating the ear with hot or cold water (caloric test)	Deafness, sensation of noise in ear (tinnitus), disequilibrium, feeling of disorientation in space
9	Glossopharyngeal	Tongue and pharynx (s, m)	Testing for sweet, salt, bitter, and sour tastes on tongue; touching walls of pharynx for pharyngeal or gag reflex	Partial dry mouth, loss of taste (ageusia) over posterior third of tongue, anesthesia and paralysis of upper pharynx
10	Vagus	Heart, blood vessels, viscera, movement of larynx and pharynx (s, m)	Observing palate in phonation, touching palate for palatal reflex	Hoarseness, lower pharyngeal anesthesia and paralysis, indefinite visceral disturbance
11	Spinal accessory	Neck muscles and viscera (m)	Movement, strength, and bulk of neck and shoulder muscles	Wasting of neck with weakened rotation, inability to shrug
12	Hypoglossal	Tongue muscles (m)	Tongue movements, tremor, wasting or wrinkling of tongue	Wasting of tongue with deviation to side of lesion on protrusion

*Letters "s" and "m" refer to sensory and motor function, respectively, of the nerve.

Figure 3.14 ▶

Cranial Nerves Each of the 12 pairs of cranial nerves has a different function, detailed in Table 3.2. Some cranial nerves are sensory, others are motor, and still others are both. A common mnemonic device for learning the order of the cranial nerves is, "On old Olympus's towering top, a Finn and German view some hops." The first letter of each word is, in order, the first letter of the name of each nerve.

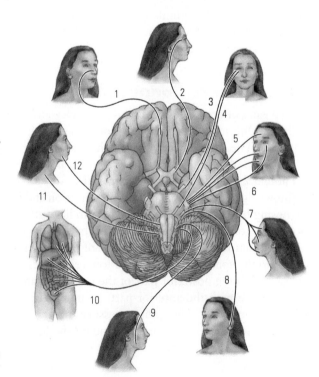

Autonomic Nervous System Connections

The ANS regulates internal organs and glands. Without our conscious awareness, it stays on the job to keep the heart beating, the liver releasing glucose, the pupils of the eyes adjusting to light, and so much more. Autonomic functions kept Terri Schiavo alive after extensive brain damage (see Chapter 1 Snapshot).

The two ANS divisions—sympathetic and parasympathetic—work in opposition. The sympathetic system arouses the body for action, for example by stimulating the heart to beat faster and inhibiting digestion when we exert ourselves during exercise or times of stress, the "fight-or-flight" response. The parasympathetic system calms the body down, for example by slowing the heartbeat and stimulating digestion to allow us to "rest and digest" after exertion and during quiet times. As is illustrated on the left in **Figure 3.15**, spinal nerves do not

Figure 3.15 ▼

Autonomic Nervous System The pathways of the two ANS divisions exert opposing effects on the organs they innervate. All autonomic fibers connect at junctions en route from the CNS to their target organs. (Left) Arousing sympathetic fibers connect to a chain of ganglia near the spinal cord. (Right) Calming parasympathetic fibers connect to individual parasympathetic ganglia near the target organs (center).

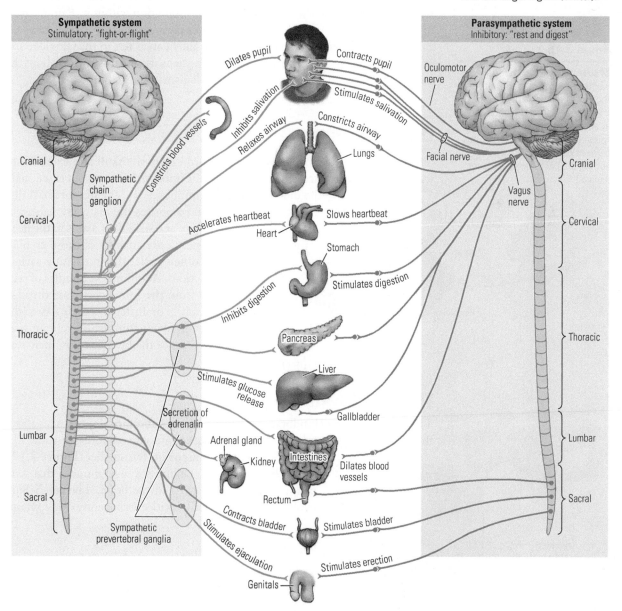

directly control the target organs. Rather, the spinal cord is connected to a chain of autonomic control centers, collections of neural cells called *sympathetic ganglia*, that function somewhat like a primitive brain to control the internal organs.

One part of the parasympathetic system connects directly to the spinal cord—the sacral region as diagrammed at center and on the right in Figure 3.15. However, the greater part of the parasympathetic system derives from three cranial nerves: the vagus nerve calms most of the internal organs, the facial nerve controls salivation, and the oculomotor nerve controls pupil dilation and eye movements. In contrast with the arousing sympathetic system, which forms a chain of ganglia running parallel to the spinal cord, the calming parasympathetic system connects with parasympathetic ganglia near the target organs, as shown at center and on the right in Figure 3.15.

The internal organs, although arranged segmentally in relation to the spinal cord, do not have their own sensory representation within it. Pain in these organs is perceived as coming from the outer parts of the dermatome and so is called **referred pain**. For example, pain in the heart is felt in the shoulder and arm, and kidney pain is felt in the back. Physicians use what is known about the location of referred pains to diagnose problems within the body.

3.5 The Brainstem

The brainstem begins where the spinal cord enters the skull and extends upward into the lower areas of the forebrain. **Figure 3.16** shows its three main regions: the diencephalon, the midbrain, and the hindbrain. A distinctive part of the brainstem comprises the many cranial-nerve nuclei that converge at its core and send their axons to the head muscles. The brainstem core consists of those cranial-nerve nuclei and other nuclei that mediate a variety of regulatory functions. Additionally, bundles of sensory nerve fibers from the spinal cord pass through posterior regions of the brainstem on their way to the forebrain, and motor fibers from the forebrain pass through anterior regions of the brainstem on their way to the spinal cord.

The Hindbrain

The most distinctive hindbrain structure is the **cerebellum**. It protrudes above the brainstem core, and its surface is gathered into narrow folds, or **folia**, like the gyri and sulci of the cortex, but smaller (**Figure 3.17**). At the base of the cerebellum are several nuclei that send connections to other parts of the brain. The cerebellum evolved in size in parallel with the neocortex. It contains

Figure 3.16 ▼

Brainstem Structures Medial view of the brain (left) shows the relation of the brainstem to the cerebral hemispheres. In accord with the plan of the spinal cord, brainstem structures perform both sensory (posterior regions) and motor (anterior regions) functions.

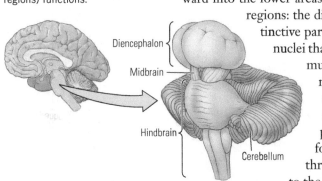

Diencephalon
Midbrain
Hindbrain
Cerebellum

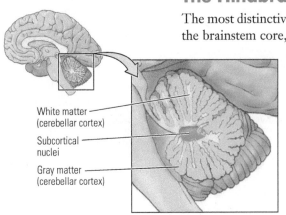

White matter (cerebellar cortex)
Subcortical nuclei
Gray matter (cerebellar cortex)

Figure 3.17 ◄

The Cerebellum Necessary for fine, coordinated movements, the cerebellum, like the cerebrum, has an extensively folded cortex containing gray matter and white matter and subcortical nuclei, detailed in the sagittal section.

about four times more neurons than the cerebral cortex, but they are much more densely packed, rendering its size much smaller.

The cerebellum plays a role in motor coordination and motor learning and may participate in coordinating other mental processes. Damage to it results in equilibrium problems, postural defects, and impairments of skilled motor activity. The parts that receive most of their impulses from the vestibular system (sensory receptors for balance and movement located in the middle ear) help maintain bodily equilibrium. Cerebellar parts receiving impulses mainly from sensory receptors in the body's trunk and limbs control postural reflexes and coordinate functionally related muscle groups.

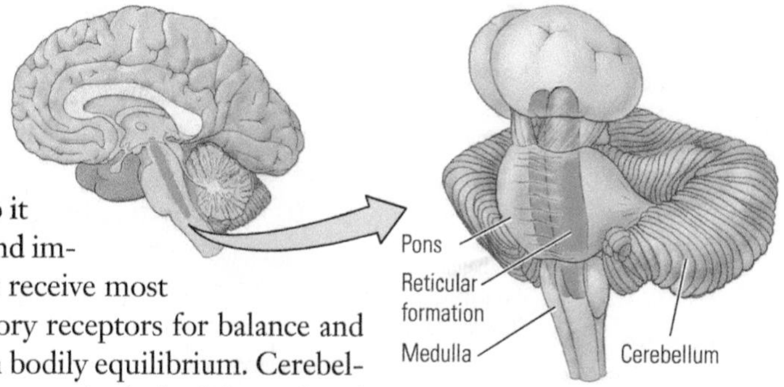

Within the hindbrain's core mixture of nuclei and fibers lies a network, the **reticular formation**, diagrammed in **Figure 3.18**. In 1949, Giuseppe Moruzzi and Horace Magoun stimulated this area electrically in anesthetized cats. The stimulation produced a waking pattern of electrical activity in the cats' cortices. The investigators concluded that the reticular formation's function is to control sleeping and waking—that is, to maintain "general arousal," or "consciousness." As a result, the reticular formation came to be known as the *reticular activating system*. Damage to this area can result in permanent unconsciousness.

Nuclei within the upper (pons) and the lower (medulla) brainstem contain substructures that control vital body movements. Nuclei within the pons (*pons* means "bridge" in Latin) bridge inputs from the cerebellum to the rest of the brain. At the tip of the spinal cord, the medulla's nuclei regulate such vital functions as breathing and the functioning of the cardiovascular system. Damage to this brain region stops breathing and heart function and so can result in death.

The Midbrain

The midbrain, diagrammed in **Figure 3.19**A, has two main subdivisions: a posterior sensory component, the **tectum** ("roof"), the roof of the third ventricle, and, located anteriorly, a motor structure, the **tegmentum**, the "floor" of the third ventricle. The tectum receives a massive amount of sensory information from the eyes and ears. Its two sets of bilaterally symmetrical nuclei, the **superior colliculi** ("upper hills"), receive projections from the retina of the eye. The **inferior colliculi** ("lower hills") receive projections from the ear. Behaviors mediated by the colliculi include locating objects in surrounding space and orienting to those objects, be they visual or auditory.

The nuclei that comprise the tegmentum are related to motor functions (Figure 3.19B). The *red nucleus* controls limb movements, and the **substantia nigra** (black substance) connects to the forebrain, a connection important for rewarding behaviors such as approaching desired objects. The **periacqueductal gray matter** (PAG), made up of cell bodies that surround the cerebral aqueduct, contains circuits for controlling species-typical behaviors (for example, sexual behavior) and for modulating pain responses.

Figure 3.18 ▲

Hindbrain Structures
The principal hindbrain structures integrate both voluntary and involuntary body movement and contribute to sleep–wake cycles.

Figure 3.19 ▲

Midbrain (A) Structures in the midbrain mediate a range of visual- and auditory-related behaviors and are critical in producing orienting movements, species-specific behaviors, and the perception of pain. (B) The tegmentum in cross section, revealing various motor-related nuclei.

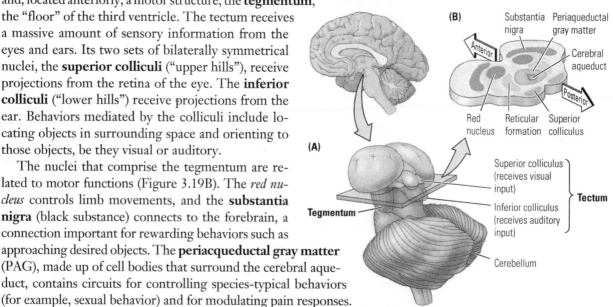

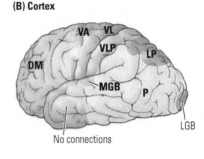

(A) Thalamus

Mammillary bodies
Cingulate gyrus
Basal ganglia
Cerebellum
Basal ganglia
Substantia nigra

Amygdala
Caudate nucleus
Frontal cortex

Areas 17 and 18
Superior colliculus

Auditory

A
DM
VA
VL
VLP
LP
P
LGB
MGB

Somatosensory Visual

(B) Cortex

VA VL
VLP
DM
LP
MGB
P

LGB

No connections

Figure 3.20 ▲

Thalamic Projections
(A) Black arrows indicate the sources of input and output from major thalamic nuclei: anterior nucleus, A; dorsomedial nucleus, DM; ventral anterior nucleus, VA; ventrolateral nucleus, VL; lateral posterior nucleus, LP; ventro-lateral posterior nucleus, VLP; pulvinar, P; lateral geniculate body, LGB; and medial geniculate body, MGB. (B) The cortical areas to which the major thalamic nuclei diagrammed in part (A) project.

The Diencephalon

At the junction of the midbrain and forebrain, the diencephalon (see Figure 3.16) includes three thalamic structures: hypothalamus ("lower room"); epi-thalamus ("upper room"); and thalamus ("inner room" or "chamber").

Although only about 0.3 percent of the brain's weight, the 22 small nuclei and fiber systems that pass through the **hypothalamus** take part in nearly all aspects of motivated behavior—feeding, sexual behavior, sleeping, temperature regulation, emotional behavior, and movement. The hypothalamus connects to and interacts with the pituitary gland to control many endocrine functions.

The largest structure in the diencephalon, the **thalamus**, is composed of 20 nuclei, each projecting to a specific area of the cerebral cortex, as shown in **Figure 3.20**. Almost all the information the cortex receives is first relayed through the thalamus. It serves as a "hub," interconnecting many brain regions:

1. One group of thalamic nuclei relays information from sensory systems to their appropriate targets. For example, the *lateral geniculate body* (LGB) receives visual projections; the *medial geniculate body* (MGB) receives auditory projections; and the *ventrolateral posterior nuclei* (VLP) receive touch, pres-sure, pain, and temperature projections from the body. In turn, these areas project to the visual, auditory, and somatosensory regions of the cortex.

2. Some thalamic nuclei relay information between cortical areas. For example, visual areas of the cortex interconnect with other brain regions through the *pulvinar nucleus* (P).

3. Some thalamic nuclei relay information between the cortex and a number of brainstem regions.

The **epithalamus** is a collection of nuclei at the posterior of the diencephalon. We have met one of its structures, the pineal gland, before. Rather than serv-ing as the seat of the soul, it secretes the hormone melatonin, which influences daily and seasonal body rhythms. Melatonin release during the dark portion of the day–night cycle contributes to the feeling of tiredness associated with our motivation to sleep. Another structure, the habenula, regulates hunger and thirst.

3.6 The Forebrain

Of the three main forebrain structures, two are subcortical: the basal ganglia and the limbic system. Enveloping all is the cerebral cortex. These regions share many connections, forming functional circuits. Nevertheless, each is sufficiently anatomically and functionally distinct to be described separately.

The Basal Ganglia

Lying mainly beneath the anterior regions of the cortex, the **basal ganglia** ("lower knots," referring to "knots below the cortex") are a collection of nuclei that form a circuit with the cortex. The ganglia, shown in **Figure 3.21**, include the *putamen* ("shell"), the *globus pallidus* ("pale globe"), and the *caudate nucleus* ("tailed nucleus").

The caudate nucleus receives projections from all areas of the cortex and sends its own projections through the putamen and globus pallidus to the thalamus and from there to frontal cortical areas. The basal ganglia also have reciprocal connections with the midbrain, especially with the substantia nigra in the midbrain tegmentum (see Figure 3.19B). The basal ganglia are associated with movement and with learning.

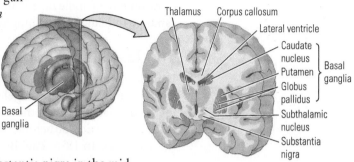

Figure 3.21 ▲

Basal Ganglia This frontal view of the cerebral hemispheres shows the basal ganglia relative to surrounding structures. Two associated brainstem structures instrumental in controlling and coordinating movement, the substantia nigra and subthalamic nucleus, also are illustrated.

The Basal Ganglia and Movement

Much of what is known about the basal ganglia's function comes from studying two general kinds of diseases that occur after they are damaged. These diseases are characterized either by a general loss of movement or by exaggerated movements. As detailed in Section 27.6, they are not disorders of *producing* movements, as in paralysis. Rather, they are disorders of *controlling* movements. The basal ganglia, therefore, must play a role in controlling and coordinating movement patterns, not in activating the muscles. Diseases of excessive movement and loss of movement illustrate its motor functions:

Excessive Movement In *Huntington's disease*, a genetic disorder introduced in Section 2.3, basal ganglia cells die progressively, and associated with this cell death, many involuntary body movements occur almost continuously. These abnormal movements have a "dancelike" quality and collectively were once referred to as *chorea*, which means "dance" in Latin.

The most frequent symptoms in *Tourette's syndrome* are involuntary motor tics, especially of the face and head, and complex movements such as hitting, lunging, or jumping. Tourette's is also characterized by involuntary vocalizations, including curse words and animal sounds. Both diseases are associated with loss of neurons within the basal ganglia.

Loss of Movement *Parkinson's disease* is characterized by many symptoms, among which difficulty in initiating movement and muscular rigidity are predominant. A patient may have trouble getting up from a chair, will walk with a shuffling gait, and have difficulty in reaching for an object. A patient may also display rhythmic tremors of the hands and legs when otherwise resting. Parkinson's disease is associated with loss of connections into and out of the basal ganglia, especially connections from the substantia nigra of the midbrain.

The Basal Ganglia and Learning

The second function of the basal ganglia is supporting associative learning, also referred to as stimulus–response or habit learning, which involves learning relationships between stimuli and their consequences. For example, a bird learns, after a number of experiences, that brightly colored butterflies taste bitter. Its basal ganglia are critical in learning the association between taste and color and in refraining from eating the insects. Similarly, many of our actions are responses to sensory cues—for example, flicking a light switch to turn on a light or turning the handle on a door to open it. People with basal ganglia disorders can have difficulty performing such stimulus–response actions.

The Limbic System

In the course of brain evolution in amphibians and reptiles, a number of three-layered cortical structures developed to sheathe the brainstem periphery. With the subsequent growth of the six-layered **neocortex** ("new bark") in mammals, these older cortical structures became sandwiched between the brainstem and the neocortex. In 1878, Paul Broca named them the *limbic lobe* (in Latin, *limbus* is "edge" or "border"). Their evolutionary origin led some anatomists to refer to them as the *reptilian brain*, a term still in common parlance.

Today, this disparate set of forebrain structures is seen as a functional unit. The **limbic system** plays a role in self-regulatory behaviors including emotion, personal memories, spatial behavior, and social behavior. Among its principal structures, diagrammed in **Figure 3.22**A, are the **amygdala** ("almond"), nuclei in the base of the temporal lobe that participate in emotion, and the **hippocampus** ("seahorse"), a structure lying in the anterior medial region of the temporal lobe that participates in personal memory ("what I did and when I did it"), and spatial navigation. The **cingulate** ("girdle") **cortex**, a three-layered strip of limbic cortex that lies just above the corpus callosum along the medial walls of the cerebral hemispheres, is involved in sexual behavior, among other social interactions.

The limbic lobe has an interesting history in relation to its supposed functions. It receives projections from the olfactory bulbs. On this evidence, early anatomists hypothesized that the limbic structures processed olfactory information, and so the structures became known as the *rhinencephalon*, or "smell-brain." Subsequent experiments have yet to demonstrate precisely what olfactory function the limbic lobe serves, but it is not required simply for identifying odors.

James Papez (1937; MacLean, 1949) suggested that emotion, which at the time had no known anatomic substrate, is a product of the limbic lobe, which had no certain function. Papez proposed that the emotional brain consists of a circuit in which information flows from the mammillary bodies in the

Figure 3.22 ▶

Limbic System (A) The principal limbic structures play roles in emotional and sexual behaviors, motivation, memory, and spatial navigation. (B) Model of the limbic circuit proposed by Papez: the hypothalamic mammillary bodies connect to the hippocampus through the cingulate cortex, and the hippocampus connects to the hypothalamus through the fornix.

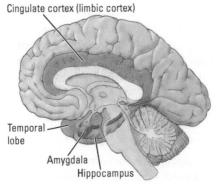

(A) Limbic system, right hemisphere medial view

Cingulate cortex (limbic cortex)

Temporal lobe

Amygdala

Hippocampus

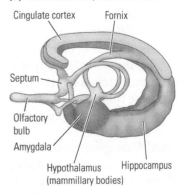

(B) The limbic lobe, dissected out

Cingulate cortex

Fornix

Septum

Olfactory bulb

Amygdala

Hypothalamus (mammillary bodies)

Hippocampus

hypothalamus to the anterior thalamic nucleus to the cingulate cortex to the hippocampus and back to the mammillary bodies (Figure 3.22B).

Input could enter this circuit from other structures to be elaborated as emotion. For example, an idea ("It is dangerous to walk in the dark") from the neocortex could enter the circuit to be elaborated as a fear ("I feel frightened in the dark") and ultimately influence the hypothalamus to release hormones that activate a fight-or-flight arousal response. The hippocampus contains many receptors for the stress hormone corticosterone, which is being investigated in relation to such conditions as posttraumatic stress disorder (see Section 6.5). Other work on the hippocampus associates it with personal memory and spatial behavior, topics elaborated on in Chapters 18 and 21, respectively.

The Neocortex

Anatomists use the term *cortex* to refer to any outer layer of cells. In neuroscience, the terms *cortex* and *neocortex* (new cortex) are often used interchangeably to refer to the outer part of the forebrain, and so, by convention in this book, *cortex* refers to *neocortex* unless otherwise indicated, for example as the older limbic (cingulate) cortex.

The human neocortex can be as large as 2500 square centimeters in area, but its thickness is only 1.5 to 3.0 millimeters. It consists of six layers of cells (gray matter) and is heavily wrinkled. This wrinkling is nature's solution to the problem of confining the huge neocortical surface area within a skull that is still small enough to pass through the birth canal. Just as a sheet of paper that has been crumpled fits into a smaller box than it could when flat, folding in the neocortex permits the brain to fit comfortably within the relatively fixed volume of the skull.

To review the main cortical features introduced in Section 1.1, **Figure 3.23** shows the two nearly symmetrical cerebral hemispheres, left and right, separated

◎ Figure 3.23 ▼

Views of the Human Brain Top, bottom, side, and midline views of the cerebral hemispheres show the locations of the cortical lobes, cerebellum, central sulcus, and longitudinal and lateral fissures. Note that the olfactory bulbs project to the ventral frontal lobe. (Photographs courtesy of Yakovlev Collection National Museum of Health and Medicine, Silver Spring, MD.)

Dorsal view

Central sulcus
Frontal lobe
Parietal lobe
Longitudinal fissure
Occipital lobe

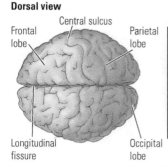

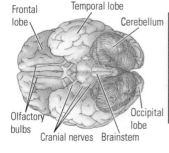
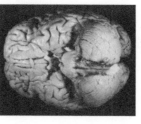

Lateral view

Central sulcus
Frontal lobe
Parietal lobe
Lateral fissure
Temporal lobe
Occipital lobe

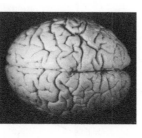
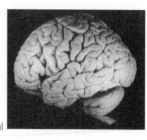

Ventral view

Frontal lobe
Temporal lobe
Cerebellum
Olfactory bulbs
Cranial nerves
Brainstem
Occipital lobe

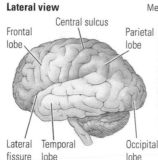
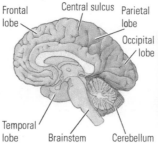

Medial view

Frontal lobe
Central sulcus
Parietal lobe
Occipital lobe
Temporal lobe
Brainstem
Cerebellum

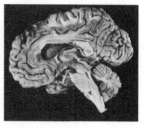

by the longitudinal fissure and each subdivided into four lobes: frontal, parietal, temporal, and occipital. The frontal lobes are bounded posteriorly by the **central sulcus**, inferiorly by the lateral fissure, and medially by the cingulate sulcus—the limbic cortex described in Figure 3.22A.

The anterior boundary of the parietal lobes is the central sulcus, and their inferior boundary is the lateral fissure. The temporal lobes are bounded dorsally by the lateral fissure. On the lateral surface of the brain, no definite boundaries separate the occipital lobes from the parietal and temporal lobes.

Fissures, Sulci, and Gyri

The most conspicuous surface feature of the neocortex is its crinkled tissue, consisting of clefts and ridges. A cleft is called a *fissure* if it extends deeply enough into the brain to indent the ventricles, as do the longitudinal and lateral fissures; it is called a *sulcus* (plural, sulci) if it is shallower. A ridge is called a *gyrus* (plural, gyri).

Figure 3.24 shows the location of important fissures, sulci, and gyri. Their locations and shapes vary somewhat on the two hemispheres of a person's brain, and the location, size, and shape of gyri and sulci vary substantially in the brains of different persons. Adjacent gyri differ in the way that cells are organized within them, and the shift from one kind of arrangement to another is usually in the sulcus.

The major gyri on the outer surface of the neocortex are shown in Figure 3.24A, and those on the medial surface are shown in Figure 3.24B. Note that the cingulate gyrus, part of the limbic system located just above the corpus callosum, spans the inner surface of all four neocortical lobes. Figure 3.24C illustrates the main sulci and fissures on the lateral surface of the cortex, and Figure 3.24D locates some of the main sulci and fissures on the medial surface.

Figure 3.24 ▼

Major Gyri and Sulci
Lateral (A) and medial (B) views of the cortical gyri; lateral (C) and medial (D) views of the cortical sulci.

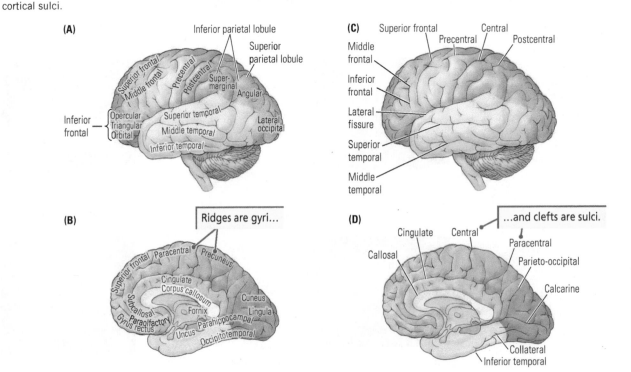

Cortical Organization in Relation to Inputs, Outputs, and Function

Locations of inputs and outputs to the cortex can be represented by maps. A **projection map** (**Figure 3.25**) shows locations on the cortex that process various types of sensory information and those that produce movement.

Because of these specialized regions, each cortical lobe is associated with a specific sense or with movement: vision in the occipital, audition in the temporal, body senses in the parietal, and motor functions in the frontal. This arrangement makes the posterior cortex (parietal, temporal, and occipital lobes) largely sensory and the anterior cortex (frontal lobe) largely motor. A simple theory of cortical function has information flowing from sensory regions to adjacent association regions and then to motor regions for expression in a series of steps.

Primary Areas

Primary areas receive projections from the major sensory systems or send motor projections to the muscles. Note that the lateral view of the brain presented in Figure 3.25 does not represent their entire extent, because these primary areas also extend down into the cortical gyri and fissures. Much of the auditory zone, for example, is located within the lateral fissure. The motor cortex sends projections to brainstem and spinal-cord motor systems. Nevertheless, the primary projection areas of the neocortex are small relative to its total size.

Secondary Areas

Secondary areas adjacent to primary areas and interconnected with them are involved in elaborating information received from primary areas or, in the case of the primary motor area, sending commands to it. In vision, for example, secondary areas are involved in visual aspects that include color, movement, and form.

Tertiary Areas

The majority of cortical areas that lie between the various secondary areas may receive projections from them or send projections to them. These patches of cortex, referred to as **tertiary areas**, or **association cortex**, encompass all cortex not specialized for sensory or motor function. Rather, the association areas mediate complex activities such as language, planning, memory, and attention.

Cortical Function

The organization depicted in the Figure 3.25 projection map allows for generalizing how the cortex functions. Sensory information enters the primary areas and then is passed to the secondary areas, each of which has sensory-related functions (e.g., color, form, motion for vision, and music, words, or other sounds

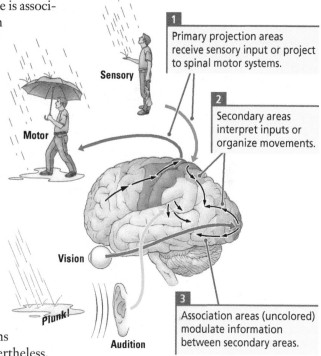

1 Primary projection areas receive sensory input or project to spinal motor systems.

2 Secondary areas interpret inputs or organize movements.

3 Association areas (uncolored) modulate information between secondary areas.

Figure 3.25 ▲

Projection Map Primary areas receive input from the sensory systems or project to spinal motor systems. Secondary areas interpret sensory input or organize movement. Black arrows indicate information flows from primary to secondary sensory areas and from secondary motor areas to primary motor areas. Information also flows from secondary to higher-order association, or tertiary, areas and among association areas of the four cortical lobes.

for audition). The tertiary area in the posterior neocortex receives projections from the secondary areas and forms more complex associations, including ideas or concepts through which we represent the world. This information is then passed on to frontal tertiary areas, where it can be formulated into plans of action that may then be performed by the frontal cortex secondary and primary areas, respectively.

As described in more detail in Section 10.2, many parallel pathways interconnect the primary, secondary, and tertiary regions of the neocortex. Each pathway mediates relatively specific functions. These connections are *reentrant*; that is, each region sends projections back to regions from which they receive connections.

Cellular Organization in the Cortex

Neurons in the neocortex are arranged in six layers (designated by the Roman numerals in **Figure 3.26**). Regional differences among the six layers include the shapes, sizes, and connections of cells. The layers' functions relate to information input and output.

- Inner cortical layers V and VI send axons to other brain areas. Both layers and the pyramidal neurons that compose them are particularly large and distinctive in the motor cortex, which sends projections to the spinal cord. (Large size is typical of cells that send information over long distances.)

- Axons in layer IV receive input from sensory systems and other cortical areas. This layer features large numbers of stellate neurons, small, densely packed cells in the primary areas of vision, somatosensation, audition, and taste–olfaction that receive large projections from their respective sensory organs. Cortical areas rich in layer IV neurons are also called *granular cortex*, referring to their grainy appearance.

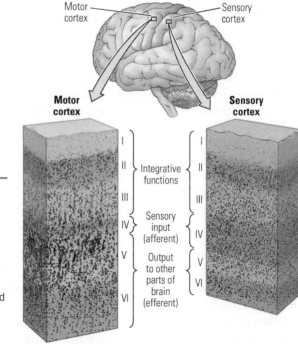

⊙ Figure 3.26 ▶

Layering in the Neocortex As this comparison of cortical layers in the sensory and motor cortices shows, afferent layer IV is relatively thick in the sensory cortex and relatively thin in the motor cortex, whereas efferent layers V and VI are relatively thick in the motor cortex and thin in the sensory cortex.

- Outer layers I, II, and III receive input mainly from layer IV and are well-developed in the secondary and tertiary areas of the cortex to perform their integrative functions.

The regional density of cells in different regions of the cortex led to the creation of **cytoarchitectonic maps** (cell maps) that parcel the cortex into many subregions. An early map, developed by Korbinian Brodmann (1909) and still in wide use, is shown in lateral and medial views in **Figure 3.27**A. To perform his analysis, Brodmann divided the brain at the central sulcus and then examined the front and back halves separately, numbering new conformations of cells as he found them but without following a methodical path over the surface. Thus, the numbers of **Brodmann's map** have no special meaning. He simply named areas 1 and 2 in the posterior section and then switched to the anterior section and named areas 3 and 4 and then switched back again and then looked somewhere else.

Nevertheless, Brodmann's regions correspond quite closely to regions discovered later with the use of noncytoarchitectonic techniques, including electrical stimulation, tract tracing, and analysis of brain injury. Figure 3.27B summarizes some of the relations between areas on Brodmann's map and areas identified according to their known functions. For example, area 17 corresponds to the primary visual projection area, whereas areas 18 and 19 correspond to the secondary visual projection areas. Area 4 is the primary motor cortex. Broca's area, related to the articulation of words (discussed in Section 1.3), is area 44, a region of tertiary cortex. Similar relations exist for other areas and functions.

Newer, more powerful analytical techniques, such as those described in the Snapshot, show that many Brodmann areas can be further subdivided, and new maps, although adhering to Brodmann's outline, further subdivide many of his areas and label them using newer nomenclature. The resulting areas have names consisting of a mixture of numbers, letters, and names—our wonderland of nomenclature. In one such designation the primary areas are

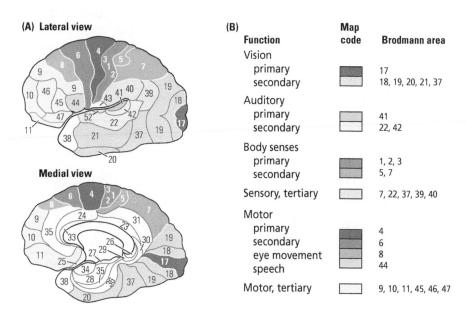

(A) Lateral view

Medial view

(B)

Function	Map code	Brodmann area
Vision		
primary		17
secondary		18, 19, 20, 21, 37
Auditory		
primary		41
secondary		22, 42
Body senses		
primary		1, 2, 3
secondary		5, 7
Sensory, tertiary		7, 22, 37, 39, 40
Motor		
primary		4
secondary		6
eye movement		8
speech		44
Motor, tertiary		9, 10, 11, 45, 46, 47

Ⓔ **Figure 3.27** ◄

Mapping the Cortex
(A) Cortical areas mapped by Brodmann. (Among the numbers missing from original sources of this drawing are areas 12 through 16 and 48 through 51.) (B) Table coordinates known functional areas with Brodmann's cytoarchitectonic areas.

labeled V1, A1, S1, and M1 for vision, audition, somatosensory, and motor. Secondary areas receive higher numbers, for example V2, V3, V4, and so forth for visual secondary areas. Competing numbering systems are described in Part III, where each chapter discusses specific functions of the cortex and its lobes.

Cortical Connections

Given the cortex's regional functional specialization, the connections between and among its regions go a long way toward explaining how higher-level functions are produced. A simple glance at **Figure 3.28** reveals that four types of axon projections interconnect neocortical regions:

1. Long connections between one lobe and another (Figure 3.28A)

2. Relatively short connections between one part of a lobe and another (Figure 3.28B)

3. Interhemispheric connections (commissures) between one hemisphere and the other (Figure 3.28C)

4. Connections through the thalamus

Most interhemispheric connections link **homotopic** points in the two hemispheres—that is, points that correspond to each other in the brain's mirror-image structure. The linkage is especially strong for regions that represent the midline of the body. Thus, the commissures act as a zipper, linking together the representations of the world formed in each hemisphere. The two main interhemispheric commissures—the corpus callosum and anterior commissure—are shown in Figure 3.28C.

The National Institutes of Health launched the Human Connectome Project to map brain pathways. Using brain-imaging techniques to identify nerve fibers selectively, the project uses three-dimensional imaging to visualize the overall organizational "connectome" of the cortex. The idea behind the project is that definitively identifying the brain's pathways, and variations of those pathways in individuals, will lead to understanding the overall function of the cortex (Catani et al., 2013). One of the project's findings is that, if the brain's

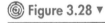

Figure 3.28 ▼

Connections Between Various Cortical Regions

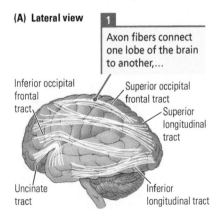

(A) Lateral view

1 Axon fibers connect one lobe of the brain to another,...

Inferior occipital frontal tract

Superior occipital frontal tract

Superior longitudinal tract

Uncinate tract

Inferior longitudinal tract

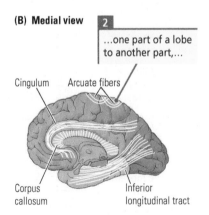

(B) Medial view

2 ...one part of a lobe to another part,...

Cingulum

Arcuate fibers

Corpus callosum

Inferior longitudinal tract

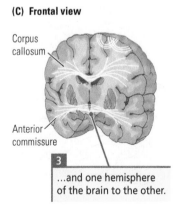

(C) Frontal view

Corpus callosum

Anterior commissure

3 ...and one hemisphere of the brain to the other.

SNAPSHOT | Brainbow and Clarity

Were it not for the discovery of anatomical techniques, the fine structure of the brain would be unknown. New techniques are revealing ever more detailed brain features. Jean Livet and his colleagues at Harvard University (2007) developed a transgenic technique (a form of genetic engineering discussed in Section 2.3) that labels many different neurons by highlighting them with distinct colors. The technique, called "Brainbow," is a play on the word *rainbow*.

In the same way a television monitor produces the full range of colors that the human eye can see by mixing only red, green, and blue, the Brainbow scientists introduced genes that produce cyan (blue), green, yellow, and red fluorescent proteins into the neurons of mice. The red gene is obtained from coral, and the blue and green genes are obtained from jellyfish. (The 2008 Nobel Prize in Chemistry was awarded to Roger Tsien, Osamu Shimomura, and Martin Chalfie for their discovery of fluorescent proteins in coral and jellyfish.)

Owing to chance factors, the extent to which each introduced gene is activated varies from neuron to neuron, with the result that neurons fluoresce in 100 or more different hues. When viewed through a fluorescent microscope sensitive to these wavelengths, individual brain cells and their connections can be visualized because they have slightly different hues, as illustrated in the accompanying micrographs.

There is a problem, however. Tracing the dendrites and axons of a neuron requires the brain to be sliced into thin sections and the neuron reconstructed from successive sections, a difficult and time-consuming task. Kwanghun Chung and colleagues (2013) have found a solution.

Using a chemical method they call "CLARITY," they harden the tissue of the whole brain by binding its proteins in a microscopic scaffold. Then they remove lipid (fat) from the tissue, which renders the brain transparent but leaves the neurons and their connections in place. With use of a fluorescent microscope, any neural element or chemical treated with a fluorescent stain or the Brainbow technique can now be visualized in the whole brain. Thus, neurons highlighted using Brainbow can be visualized in their entirety with their connections revealed as they sit in place within the transparent brain.

CLARITY can visualize any chemical or neuron and can be applied to any brain, including human brains, even those that have been preserved in formalin for many years. Thus, even the brains of deceased patients who suffered from brain disease and whose brains subsequently were stored in brain banks can now be examined to determine the causes of their disease symptoms.

Chung, K., J. Wallace, S. Y. Kim, S. Kalyanasundaram, A. S. Andalman, T. J. Davidson, J. J. Mirzabekov, K. A. Zalocusky, J. Mattis, A. K. Denisin, S. Pak, H. Bernstein, C. Ramakrishnan, L. Grosenick, V. Gradinaru, and K. Deisseroth. Structural and molecular interrogation of intact biological systems. *Nature* 497:332–337, 2013.

Livet, J., T. A. Weissman, H. Kang, R.W. Draft, J. Lu, R. A. Bennis, J. R. Sanes, and J. W. Lichtman. Transgenic strategies for combinatorial expression of fluorescent proteins in the nervous system. *Nature* 450:56–62, 2007.

Cell bodies

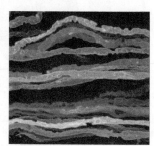

Axons

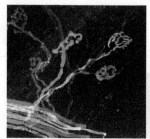

Terminal buttons

Neuronal structures as imaged by Brainbow. (Livet, Draft, Sanes, and Lichtman, Harvard University.)

convolutions are unfolded, they can then be visualized as being connected on a three-dimensional grid—by analogy, like the electrical wiring that connects offices in an office tower.

3.7 The Crossed Brain

A striking feature of the brain's organization is that each nearly symmetrical hemisphere responds mainly to sensory stimulation coming from the contralateral side of the body or sensory world and controls the musculature on that side of the body. The visual system is illustrative.

For animals with eyes located on the side of the head, such as the rat diagrammed on the left in **Figure 3.29**, about 95 percent of the optic fibers from one eye project to the opposite hemisphere. For humans, as diagrammed on the right in the figure, with eyes located at the front of the head, only about 50 percent of the optic fibers from each eye project to the opposite hemisphere. Thus, irrespective of the placement of the eyes, cortical pathways are arranged to ensure that each hemisphere gets visual information from the opposite visual field.

In a similar arrangement, about 90 percent of the motor and somatosensory system fibers cross over in the human spinal cord. Projections from the auditory system go to both hemispheres, but auditory excitation from each ear sends a stronger signal to the contralateral hemisphere (see Figure 11.12). This anatomy results in numerous crossings, or **decussations**, of sensory and motor

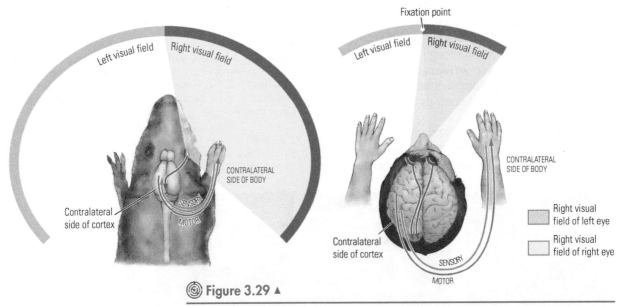

⊚ Figure 3.29 ▲

Crossed Neural Circuits Somatosensory input to the rat (red pathway at left) and human (right) brains is completely crossed: information coming from the right paw or hand, for example, goes to the left hemisphere, and left-hemisphere motor cortex output, traced in blue, projects to the right paw or hand. The rat's eyes are laterally positioned, so virtually all visual input from each eye—traced here (in purple) for the right visual field—travels to the opposite hemisphere. A human's eyes are positioned frontally. As a result, visual-field input is split in two: input from the right side of the world as seen by both eyes (traced in purple) goes to the left hemisphere; input from the left side of the world as seen by both eyes goes to the right hemisphere.

fibers along the midline of the nervous system. Functionally, this crossed organization means that damage to a hemisphere produces symptoms related to perception and movement on the opposite side of the body. Recall from the opening Portrait that R.S.'s stroke to the right cerebral hemisphere impaired movement in his left leg and arm.

SUMMARY

3.1 Neuroanatomy: Finding Your Way Around the Brain

The brain's anatomy is organized but complex, and the names of its many structures provide a wonderland of nomenclature that reflects the rich history behind efforts to describe the brain and determine the functions of its parts.

3.2 Overview of Nervous System Structure and Function

The brain is protected by the skull and by the cushioning meninges. A blood–brain barrier excludes many substances from entry into the CNS as well. The brain's blood supply flows from the internal carotid arteries and the vertebral arteries to distribute blood to specific brain regions through the anterior, middle, and posterior cerebral arteries.

The brain is composed of neurons and glial cells, each present in many forms. The brain is organized into layers, nuclei, and tracts, with layers and nuclei appearing gray and tracts appearing white on visual inspection. Visualizing brain anatomy in greater detail requires that tissue be stained or colored by other techniques to highlight differences in the biochemical structures of different groups of nuclei and tracts.

3.3 Origin and Development of the Central Nervous System

The developing CNS first consists of three divisions surrounding a canal filled with cerebrospinal fluid. In adult mammals, the increased size and complexity of the first and third divisions produce a brain consisting of five separate divisions.

3.4 The Spinal Cord

The spinal cord communicates with the body through posterior (dorsal) roots, which are sensory, and anterior (ventral) roots, which are motor. The spinal cord is also divided into segments, each representing a dermatome, or body segment.

The cranial and spinal nerves of the somatic nervous system carry afferent sensory input to the CNS and transmit efferent motor output from the brain to the body. The autonomic nervous system acts via ganglia either to activate (sympathetic nerves) or to inhibit (parasympathetic nerves) the body's internal organs.

3.5 The Brainstem

The brainstem consists of the diencephalon, the midbrain, and the hindbrain. Hindbrain structures include the cerebellum. The hindbrain core contains the nuclei that give rise to the cranial nerves. The midbrain contains the superior and inferior colliculi (for vision and hearing) in its tectum (roof) and many nuclei for motor function in its tegmentum (floor). The diencephalon consists of three thalamic structures: the epithalamus, including the pineal gland for biorhythms; the thalamus, which relays sensory information to the cortex; and the hypothalamus, which contains many nuclei for regulatory functions such as internal temperature, eating and drinking, and sexual activity.

3.6 The Forebrain

The three functional regions of the forebrain are the basal ganglia, associated with motor coordination; the limbic system, associated with emotion, motivation, and memory; and the neocortex, associated with sensory, motor, and cognitive functions.

The neocortex, or cortex, is a large, thin sheet of neurons organized into six layers and crinkled to form gyri and sulci. The six layers vary in thickness in different cortical regions, thus comprising many subregions.

Individual cortical lobes are associated with general functions: vision in the occipital, audition in the temporal, somatosensation in the parietal, and movement in the frontal. Cortical lobes can be further subdivided into primary, secondary, and tertiary regions, each performing more-complex sensory–motor and associative functions.

The cortex does not function in isolation from its subcortical structures but receives sensory information through the thalamus and works through the basal ganglia to produce movement and through the limbic system to organize emotion and memory.

3.7 The Crossed Brain

In the main, each cortical hemisphere responds to sensory stimulation on the side opposite that hemisphere and produces movements on the opposite side of the body. Visual pathways, for example, ensure that input from each eye travels to the opposite hemisphere.

References

Brodmann, K. *Vergleichende Lokalisationlehr der Grosshirn-rinde in ihren Prinzipien dargestellt auf Grund des Zellenbaues.* Leipzig: J. A. Barth, 1909.

Catani, M., M. Thiebaut de Schotten, D. Slater, and F. Dell'acqua. Connectomic approaches before the connectome. *NeuroImage* 80:2–13, 2013.

Fonseca-Azevedo, K., and S. Houzel. Metabolic constraint imposes tradeoff between body size and number of brain neurons in human evolution. *Proceedings of the National Academy of Sciences U. S. A.* 109:18571–18576, 2012.

MacLean, P. D. Psychosomatic disease and the "visceral brain": Recent developments bearing on the Papez theory of emotion. *Psychosomatic Medicine* 11:338–353, 1949.

Moruzzi, G., and W. H. Magoun. Brain stem reticular formation and activation of the EEG. *Electroencephalography and Clinical Neurophysiology* 1:455–473, 1949.

Papez, J. W. A proposed mechanism of emotion. *Archives of Neurology and Psychiatry* 38:724–744, 1937.

4 The Structure and Electrical Activity of Neurons

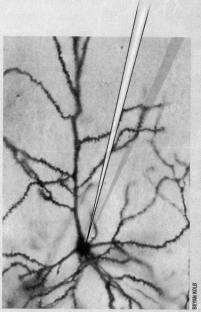

BRYAN KOLB

The subject lay in bed facing a laptop computer on which images of famous people, ordinary people, buildings, or strings of letters from words were briefly displayed. The subject, who suffers from *epilepsy*, a condition characterized by recurrent seizures linked to abnormal electrical discharges, had volunteered for the experiment. (For more about epilepsy, see Sections 7.1 and 26.4.)

Noninvasive recordings from the surface of the skull had failed to pinpoint the location of the epileptic discharges, and so ultrathin wires had been inserted into the subject's temporal lobes to achieve that end by recording the electrical activity of neurons through the wire's uninsulated tip. Once the source is established, surgeons can remove the abnormal brain tissue that produced the epileptic discharges.

In addition to revealing the source of the epileptic discharges, each wire can record the activity of nearby neurons. This *single-cell-recording* technique enables the subjects to participate in an experiment at the University of California at Los Angeles (UCLA). The experiment would reveal how single neurons code information and so contribute to conscious behavior.

One electrode in the subject reveals that a nearby cell produces electrical discharges when the subject sees pictures of the actress Halle Berry. This cell responds to pictures of Halle Berry in different postures; dressed as Catwoman, a movie role she once played; to a drawing of Halle Berry; and to letter strings of her name. The cell does not respond when pictures of other actresses or people are displayed, and it does not respond to pictures of Catwoman played by other actresses.

Quian Quiroga and his coworkers at UCLA (2005) identified other neurons, in the patient described here and in other patients who participated in the study, that respond to pictures of individual persons or of well-known buildings. Such "Halle Berry" neurons confirm that neuronal activity represents our perceptions and actions.

Neurons are the functional units of the nervous system. Scientists believe that many thousands of neurons acting in concert are actually required to form a representation of Halle Berry, but the remarkable response of each neuron contributes to understanding how neurons allow us to create our representations of reality. To discover how single neurons code information, this chapter describes their physical features, the techniques used to study their electrical activity, and how neurons receive information and send messages throughout the nervous system to produce behavior.

4.1 The Neuron's Structure

Neurons share characteristics with other cells in the body, but they also are special. By generating electrical impulses and sending messages to other cells, neurons function as information units: their activity is meaningful with respect to behavior. Neurons also are plastic: they have the capacity to change, allowing them to serve as memory units. Memory, the subject of Chapter 18, is the ability to recall or recognize previous experience, which enables us to make relatively permanent changes in our behavior.

Overview of a Neuron

Figure 4.1 displays the neuron's major external and internal features. Its dendrites feature small protrusions called **dendritic spines** that greatly increase the cell's surface area (Figure 4.1A). A neuron may have from 1 to 20 or more dendrites, each of which may have one or many branches. Each neuron has but a single axon that may branch into **axon collaterals**, which usually emerge from it at right angles. The axon collaterals may divide into a number of smaller branches called **teleodendria** ("end branches") before contacting the dendrites of another neuron.

At the end of each teleodendrion is a knob called an *end foot*, or **terminal button**. The terminal button sits very close to a dendritic spine on another neuron, although it does not touch that spine (Figure 4.1B). This "almost connection" between the surface of the axon's end foot and the corresponding surface of the neighboring dendritic spine plus the space between the two is the **synapse**.

The cell body, or soma, fuels the cell and houses in its nucleus the chromosomes that carry genetic instructions (Figure 4.1C). Extending from the soma, a distinctive enlargement called the **axon hillock** ("little hill") forms the beginning of the neuron's axon.

Information flow through a neuron from dendritic tree to terminal button is illustrated in **Figure 4.2**. Information flows from the dendrites to the cell body to the axon hillock and through the axon to its teleodendria and their terminal buttons. At each terminal button, information is conveyed to the next neuron. Some synapses are **inhibitory**: they decrease the neuron's ability to pass information along to other neurons. Other synapses are **excitatory**: they increase the neuron's ability to pass information along to other neurons.

Information travels through a neuron on a flow of electrical current that begins on the dendrites and travels along the axon to the terminals. In the axon,

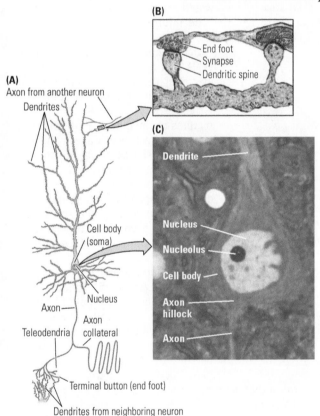

Figure 4.1 ▲

Major Parts of a Neuron (A) A typical neuron's basic structures. (B) An electron micrograph captures the synapse formed where the terminal button of one neuron meets a dendritic spine of another neuron. (C) High-power light microscopic view inside the cell body. (Bryan Kolb)

the summated flow consists of discrete electrical impulses. As each impulse reaches the terminal buttons, they release a chemical message. The message, a **neurotransmitter**, carries the signal across the synapse to influence the target cell's electrical activity—to excite it or inhibit it—and pass the information along.

The balance of this chapter describes the neuron's internal function, how it gains or loses electrical charge, and how these changes in charge enable it to transmit information. Chapter 5 explains how neurotransmitters operate.

The Neuron as a Factory

Neurons, like all living cells, are like miniature factories, and their product is *proteins*, complex organic compounds that form the principal components of all cells. Each gene in a cell's DNA contains plans for making one protein, but retooling along the cellular assembly line enables the cell to make many more proteins than there are genes. **Figure 4.3** diagrams many parts of a neuron that cooperate to make and ship the proteins it uses to regulate its own activity or exports to regulate the activity of other neurons. As we describe them, you will see that the factory analogy is apt indeed.

In our cellular factory, outer walls separate the neuron from the outside world and discourage unwanted intruders. The outer *cell membrane* separates it from its surroundings and allows it to regulate the materials that enter and leave its domain. The cell membrane envelops the cell body, the dendrites and their spines, and the axon and its terminals, forming a boundary around a continuous intracellular compartment.

Unassisted, very few substances can enter or leave a cell because the membrane presents an almost impenetrable barrier. Embedded membrane proteins serve as the factory's gates, allowing some substances to leave or enter and denying the rest passage. Within the cell shown in Figure 4.3, other membranes divide its interior into compartments. This setup allows the cell to concentrate chemicals where they are needed and otherwise keep them out of the way.

Prominent among the cell's internal membranes is the *nuclear membrane*. It surrounds the **nucleus**, which, like the factory's executive offices, houses the blueprints—genes and chromosomes—where the cell's proteins are stored and copied. When needed, genetic instructions or messages are sent to the factory floor, the **endoplasmic reticulum** (ER), an extension of the nuclear membrane where the cell's protein products are assembled.

The finished proteins are packed in a membrane and addressed in the **Golgi bodies** that pass them along to the cell's transportation network. This network is a system of **tubules** that carries the packaged proteins to their final destinations (much like a factory's conveyor belts and forklifts). Other tubules, **microfilaments**, form the cell's structural framework.

Two other vital components of the cellular factory are **mitochondria**, the cell's power plants, which supply it energy, and **lysosomes**, saclike vesicles that

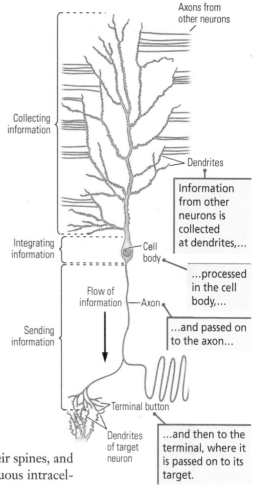

Axons from other neurons

Collecting information

Dendrites

Information from other neurons is collected at dendrites,...

Integrating information

Cell body

...processed in the cell body,...

Flow of information

Axon

...and passed on to the axon...

Sending information

Terminal button

Dendrites of target neuron

...and then to the terminal, where it is passed on to its target.

⊚ **Figure 4.2** ▲

Information Flow in a Neuron

Figure 4.3 ►

A Neuron's Internal Structure
This view inside a typical cell reveals its organelles and other internal components.

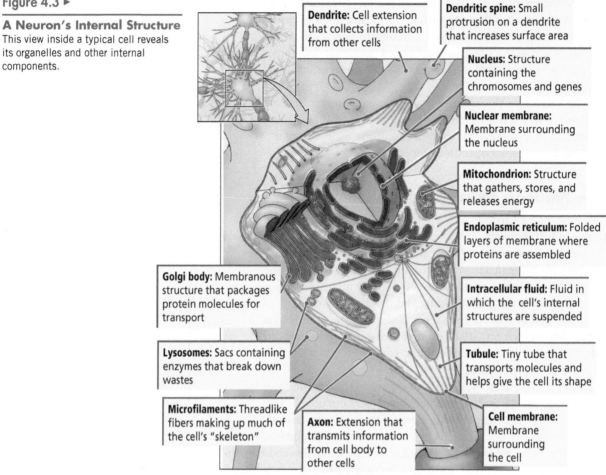

Dendrite: Cell extension that collects information from other cells

Dendritic spine: Small protrusion on a dendrite that increases surface area

Nucleus: Structure containing the chromosomes and genes

Nuclear membrane: Membrane surrounding the nucleus

Mitochondrion: Structure that gathers, stores, and releases energy

Endoplasmic reticulum: Folded layers of membrane where proteins are assembled

Golgi body: Membranous structure that packages protein molecules for transport

Intracellular fluid: Fluid in which the cell's internal structures are suspended

Lysosomes: Sacs containing enzymes that break down wastes

Tubule: Tiny tube that transports molecules and helps give the cell its shape

Microfilaments: Threadlike fibers making up much of the cell's "skeleton"

Axon: Extension that transmits information from cell body to other cells

Cell membrane: Membrane surrounding the cell

not only transport incoming supplies but also move and store wastes. (More lysosomes are found in old cells than in young ones. Cells apparently have trouble disposing of their garbage just as we do.)

With this overview of the cell's internal structure in mind, let us look at some of its components in more detail, beginning with the cell membrane.

The Cell Membrane: Barrier and Gatekeeper

Neurons and glia are tightly packed together in the brain but, like all cells, are separated and cushioned by **extracellular fluid**, water containing dissolved substances. Fluid is found inside a cell as well. This **intracellular fluid**, or *cytoplasm*, also is made up of water and dissolved substances. Separated by the cell membrane, the concentrations of salts and other substances in the two fluids are different.

One substance within the cell's fluids are *salts*, molecules that separate into two parts when dissolved in water. One part carries a positive charge, the other a negative charge, and collectively they are called **ions**. In water, common table salt—sodium chloride (NaCl)—dissolves into sodium ions (Na^+) and chloride ions (Cl^-). These ions form part of the extracellular and intracellular fluids. Other, more complex ions are also present, as are protein molecules, which are hundreds of times larger than the salt ions. Their sizes and charges influence how they cross the cell membrane, and the differences help explain the neuron's information-conducting ability.

Membrane Structure

The cell membrane encases a cell, allowing it to function as an independent unit. The membrane's special double-layer structure makes this possible by regulating the movement of substances into and out of the cell (**Figure 4.4**A). For example, if too much water enters a cell, it can burst; if too much water leaves, the cell can shrivel. The cell membrane helps ensure that neither happens. The membrane also regulates the concentrations of salts and other chemicals on either side, because precise concentrations of chemicals within a cell are essential to its normal functioning.

A molecule called a **phospholipid**, shown in detail in Figure 4.4B, forms the membrane bilayer. Its name comes from its molecular structure, which features a "head" that contains the element phosphorus (P) and two "tails" that are lipid (fat) molecules. The head is polar: it has a slight positive charge in one location and a slight negative charge in another. The tails consist of tightly bound hydrogen and carbon atoms, making them electrically neutral. Figure 4.4C shows the phospholipid's molecular structure.

A glance back at Figure 4.4A shows how the phospholipid molecules align to form a *phospholipid bilayer*, the double-layered cell membrane. The different electrical polarities of the head and tails are the underlying reason that it can form membranes. The head, being polar, is hydrophilic (from the Greek *hydro*, meaning "water," and *philic* meaning "love"—literally, "water loving"): it is attracted to water molecules because they, too, are polar. The nonpolar tails have no such attraction for water: they are hydrophobic, or "water hating" (from the Greek *phobos*, meaning "fear").

Quite literally, then, the head of a phospholipid molecule loves water and the tails hate it. The molecules form a bilayer arranged so that the heads of one

Figure 4.4 ▼

Basic Cell Membrane Structure (A) The cell membrane bilayer, with the tails of each layer facing inward. (B) Conventional symbol for the phospholipid molecule, distinguishing its head and tail regions. (C) Space-filling model of a phospholipid molecule detailing the head's hydrophilic polar regions and the hydrophobic tails, composed of nonpolar fatty acids that do not attract water molecules.

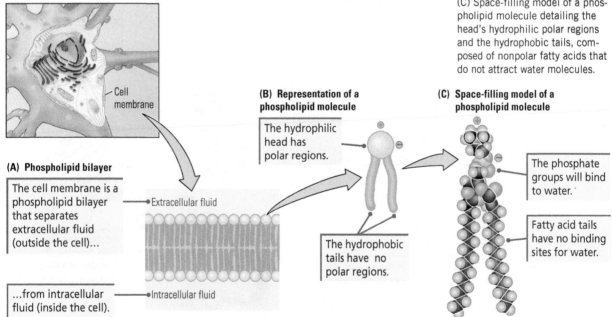

(A) **Phospholipid bilayer**

The cell membrane is a phospholipid bilayer that separates extracellular fluid (outside the cell)...

...from intracellular fluid (inside the cell).

Cell membrane

Extracellular fluid

Intracellular fluid

(B) **Representation of a phospholipid molecule**

The hydrophilic head has polar regions.

The hydrophobic tails have no polar regions.

(C) **Space-filling model of a phospholipid molecule**

The phosphate groups will bind to water.

Fatty acid tails have no binding sites for water.

layer are in contact with the intracellular fluid, and the heads of the other layer are in contact with the extracellular fluid. The tails of both layers nestle inside the bilayer, hidden from water.

How the Cell Membrane Functions

The cell membrane is pliant yet impermeable to a wide variety of substances. It is impenetrable to intracellular and extracellular water because polar water molecules cannot pass through the hydrophobic tails within the bilayer. Phospholipid heads repel the charges carried by other polar molecules in the extracellular and intracellular fluid and so prevent them from crossing the membrane. Thus, only nonpolar molecules, such as oxygen (O_2), carbon dioxide (CO_2), and the sugar glucose, can pass freely through a phospholipid bilayer.

The polar phospholipid-molecule heads allow the cell membrane to regulate salt concentrations within the cell too. Ordinarily, the tightly packed polar surface of the phospholipid membrane prevents ions from passing through it, either by repelling them, binding to them, or blocking their passage if they are large. The cell membrane forms the neuron's secure walls. The cell membrane, however, has embedded protein molecules that act as gates to provide influx and efflux to substances such as large ions and to facilitate delivery of supplies, disposal of wastes, and shipment of products.

The Nucleus: Blueprints for Proteins

In our factory analogy, the nucleus is the cell's executive office, where the blueprints for making proteins—that is, the genes—are stored, copied, and sent to the factory floor. As defined in Section 2.3, *genes*, segments of DNA that encode the synthesis of particular proteins, are contained within the *chromosomes*, the double-helix molecular structures that hold an organism's entire DNA sequence. Chromosomes are like books of blueprints, each containing thousands of genes. Each gene holds the code for making one protein. A chromosome's location in the cell nucleus, its appearance, and the structure of its DNA are shown in **Figure 4.5**.

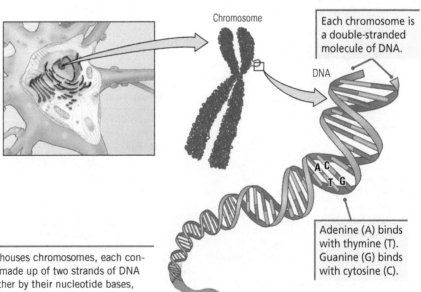

Chromosome

Each chromosome is a double-stranded molecule of DNA.

DNA

A
C
T
G

Adenine (A) binds with thymine (T). Guanine (G) binds with cytosine (C).

Figure 4.5 ▶

A Chromosome The cell nucleus houses chromosomes, each containing many genes. A chromosome is made up of two strands of DNA twisted in a helix and bound to each other by their nucleotide bases, adenine (A), thymine (T), guanine (G), and cytosine (C).

Chromosomes are constantly changing shape and moving in relation to one another. By changing shape, chromosomes unwind to expose different genes so that the genes can be *expressed*, beginning the process of protein formation. Less than 2% of DNA material codes for such functional genes. The rest play a role in regulating gene expression and code for nonfunctional genes as well as for various forms of RNA (described in the next section) that regulate gene expression as part of the epigenetic code.

Each of the two coiled strands of a DNA molecule shown in Figure 4.5 consists of a variable sequence of four *nucleotide bases*, the constituent molecules of the genetic code: *adenine* (A), *thymine* (T), *guanine* (G), and *cytosine* (C). Adenine on one strand always pairs with thymine on the other, whereas guanine on one strand always pairs with cytosine on the other. The attraction that the bases in each pair have for each other binds the two strands of the DNA helix together.

Within the chromosomes, sequences of hundreds to thousands of nucleotide bases spell out the genetic code that scientists represent by their letters—for example ATGCCG. Much as a sequence of letters spells out a word, the sequence of bases codes the order in which **amino acids**, the constituent molecules of proteins, should be assembled to construct a certain protein.

Protein Synthesis: Transcription and Translation

To initiate protein synthesis, the appropriate gene segment of the DNA double helix first unwinds. The exposed sequence of nucleotide bases on one DNA strand then serves as a template to attract free-floating molecules called *nucleotides*. The nucleotides thus attached form a complementary strand of *ribonucleic acid* (RNA), the single-stranded nucleic acid molecule required for protein synthesis. This *transcription* process is shown in steps 1 and 2 of **Figure 4.6**. (To transcribe means "to copy.")

The RNA produced through transcription is much like a single strand of DNA except that the base *uracil* (U), which, like thymine, is attracted to adenine, takes the place of thymine. The transcribed strand of RNA is called *messenger RNA* (mRNA) because it carries the genetic code out of the nucleus to the endoplasmic reticulum, where proteins are manufactured.

Steps 3 and 4 in Figure 4.6 show that the ER consists of membranous sheets folded to form numerous channels. A distinguishing feature of the ER is that it may be studded with *ribosomes*, protein structures that act as catalysts in protein building. When an mRNA molecule reaches the ER, it passes through a ribosome, where its genetic code is read.

In this *translation* process, a particular sequence of nucleotide bases in the mRNA is transformed into a particular amino acid sequence. (To translate

Figure 4.6 ▼

Protein Synthesis The flow of information in a cell is from DNA to mRNA to protein (peptide chain of amino acids).

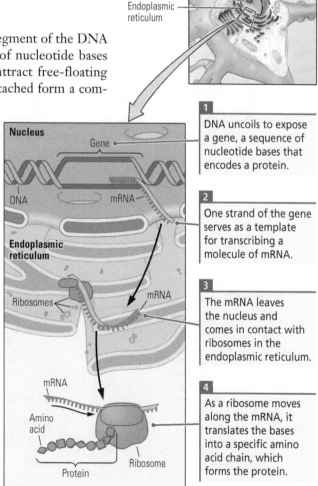

1

DNA uncoils to expose a gene, a sequence of nucleotide bases that encodes a protein.

2

One strand of the gene serves as a template for transcribing a molecule of mRNA.

3

The mRNA leaves the nucleus and comes in contact with ribosomes in the endoplasmic reticulum.

4

As a ribosome moves along the mRNA, it translates the bases into a specific amino acid chain, which forms the protein.

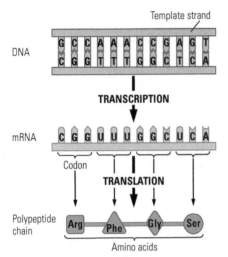

Template strand

DNA

G C C A A A C C G A G T
C G G T T T G G C T C A

TRANSCRIPTION

mRNA

C G G U U U G G C U C A

Codon

TRANSLATION

Polypeptide
chain

Arg Phe Gly Ser

Amino acids

Ⓒ **Figure 4.7** ▲

**Transcription and
Translation** In protein synthesis (see Figure 4.6), a strand
of DNA is transcribed into
mRNA, and mRNA is translated
into a polypeptide chain. Each
sequence of three bases in the
mRNA strand (a codon) encodes
one amino acid. Directed by the
codons, the amino acids link
together to form a polypeptide
chain. The amino acids illustrated
are tryptophan (Trp), phenylalanine (Phe), glycine (Gly), and
serine (Ser).

means to convert one language into another, in contrast to transcription, in which the language remains the same.) *Transfer RNA* (tRNA)
assists in translation.

As shown in **Figure 4.7**, each group of three consecutive nucleotide bases along an mRNA molecule encodes one particular amino
acid. These sequences of three bases are called *codons*. For example, the
codon cytosine, guanine, guanine (CGG) encodes the amino acid ar-
ginine (Arg), whereas the codon uracil, uracil, uracil (UUU) encodes
the amino acid phenylalanine (Phe). As an amino acid is placed in the
chain, it connects to the previously placed amino acid with a peptide
bond, and the chain is thus referred to as a *polypeptide* (meaning "many
peptides") *chain*.

Each nucleotide codon encodes 1 of the 20 different amino acids
found in protein molecules. Just as a remarkable number of words can
be made from the 26 letters of the English alphabet, a remarkable number of peptide chains can be made from the 20 kinds of amino acids that form
proteins. These amino acids can form 400 (20 × 20) different dipeptides (two-
peptide combinations), 8000 (20 × 20 × 20) tripeptides (three-peptide combinations), and an almost endless number of polypeptides.

Applying Epigenetic Mechanisms

A single genome can code for many phenotypes. Epigenetic mechanisms, including *gene (DNA) methylation*, introduced in Section 2.3, create this phenotypic plasticity without altering the base-pair nucleotide sequence of the genes
or changing the genetic code (**Figure 4.8**A). Rather, epigenetic mechanisms
influence protein production in many ways, including unwinding a chromosome so that a gene can be exposed for expression, regulating the initiation and
expression of gene transcription, and regulating gene translation.

Chromosomes are wrapped around supporting molecules of a protein called
a histone. Histone wrapping allows the many yards of a chromosome to be packaged in a small space, as yards of thread are wrapped around a spool. For any
gene to be transcribed into messenger RNA, its DNA must be unspooled from

Ⓒ **Figure 4.8** ▶

**Three Epigenetic
Mechanisms** (A) Methyl (CH₃)
groups (orange circles) may bind
to nucleotide base pairs to block
gene transcription. (B) A methyl
group or other molecules bind to
histone tails, either blocking them
from opening (orange circles) or
allowing them to open for transcription (green squares). (C) The
mRNA message to produce
the protein that a gene codes
may be enabled or, as shown,
blocked by noncoding RNA,
which prevents translation.

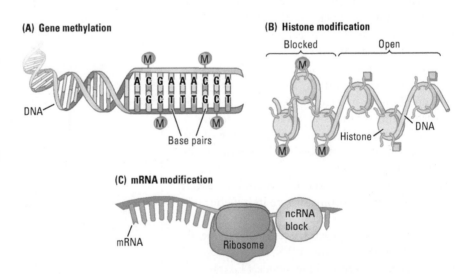

(A) Gene methylation

M   M

A C G A A A C G A
T G C T T T G C T

DNA

M   M

Base pairs

(B) Histone modification

Blocked   Open

M

DNA

Histone

M   M

(C) mRNA modification

ncRNA
block

mRNA   Ribosome

the histones. In *histone methylation* DNA may be unspooled or be stopped from unspooling. In Figure 4.8B, a methyl group (CH₃) binds to the histone tails to block DNA from unspooling. If the methyl group is removed, the chromosome can be unspooled and the DNA exposed. Once unspooled, a gene can be expressed if it receives instructions to begin transcription.

Finally, in *mRNA modification* the mRNA message to produce the protein that a gene codes may be enabled or blocked. In Figure 4.8C, noncoding RNA (ncRNA) binds to mRNA, blocking translation. The cell's environment can influence one or more of these processes and thus regulate gene expression (Charney, 2012). It is through such epigenetic mechanisms that our unique experiences change our brains and enable us to adapt.

Proteins: The Cell's Products

A polypeptide chain and a protein are related, but they are not the same. The relation is analogous to that between a length of ribbon and a bow of a particular size and shape that can be made from that ribbon. **Figure 4.9** shows how proteins are formed when polypeptide chains assume a particular functional shape.

Long polypeptide chains (Figure 4.9A) have a tendency to curl into helices or to form pleated sheets (Figure 4.9B), and these secondary structures, in turn, have a tendency to fold together to form more-complex shapes. The folded-up polypeptide chains constitute a protein (Figure 4.9C). When two or more polypeptide chains combine, the result also is a protein (Figure 4.9D). Many proteins are globular (roundish), and others are fibrous (threadlike), but within these broad categories, countless variations are possible.

Humans have at least 20,000 genes that can therefore make at least that many genetically specified polypeptide chains or proteins. In principle, the nature of the genetic code is quite simple:

$$DNA \rightarrow mRNA \rightarrow protein$$

The epigenetic code, however, can influence each step. DNA can be expressed or blocked, mRNA can be edited—cut into pieces, for example—and each piece can be translated into a different protein. A protein once formed can be edited to a smaller size or be combined with another protein to form a different protein. Thus, the genetic and epigenetic codes in concert result in remarkable protein diversity.

Golgi Bodies and Microtubules: Protein Packaging and Shipment

As many as 10,000 different protein molecules, all manufactured in the cell, may coexist within any one neuron. Some proteins are destined for incorporation into the cellular structure, becoming part of the cell membrane, the nucleus, the ER, and so forth. Other proteins remain in the intracellular fluid, where they act as enzymes, facilitating many of the cell's chemical reactions. Still other proteins are excreted from the cell as hormones or neurotransmitters.

Figure 4.10 illustrates the sequence of steps in which proteins are packaged and shipped to their destinations. The cell contains a set of components, the Golgi bodies, that operate much like a packaging service, dedicated to wrapping,

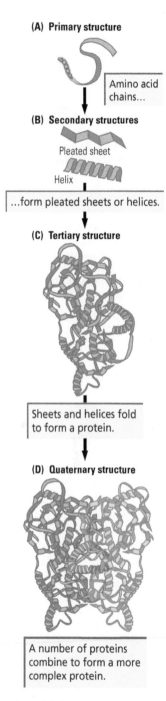

(A) Primary structure

Amino acid chains...

(B) Secondary structures

Pleated sheet

Helix

...form pleated sheets or helices.

(C) Tertiary structure

Sheets and helices fold to form a protein.

(D) Quaternary structure

A number of proteins combine to form a more complex protein.

Figure 4.9 ▲

Four Levels of Protein Structure Whether a polypeptide chain (A) forms a pleated sheet or a helix (B), its ultimate three-dimensional shape (C and D) is determined by the amino acid sequence in the primary structure.

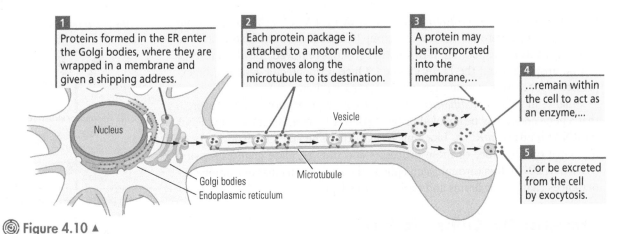

1. Proteins formed in the ER enter the Golgi bodies, where they are wrapped in a membrane and given a shipping address.

2. Each protein package is attached to a motor molecule and moves along the microtubule to its destination.

3. A protein may be incorporated into the membrane,...

4. ...remain within the cell to act as an enzyme,...

5. ...or be excreted from the cell by exocytosis.

Nucleus

Vesicle

Golgi bodies
Endoplasmic reticulum

Microtubule

⊚ Figure 4.10 ▲

Protein Transport Exporting a protein entails packaging, transport, and its function at the destination.

labeling, and shipping. Golgi bodies wrap newly formed protein molecules coming from the ER with membranes and label them to indicate where in the cell they are to go. The packaged proteins are then loaded onto motor molecules to be "walked" along the tubules radiating throughout the cell until they reach their destinations.

If a protein is destined to remain within the cell, it is unloaded into the intracellular fluid. If it is to be incorporated into the cell membrane, it is carried to the membrane and inserts itself there, shedding its covering membrane, as shown in Figure 4.10. Recall that protein molecules are too large to diffuse through the cell membrane. Proteins destined to be excreted, a process called **exocytosis**, remain within their membranes (*vesicles*), which fuse with the cell membrane, allowing the protein to be expelled into the extracellular fluid, perhaps as a neurotransmitter carrying a message to another neuron.

Crossing the Cell Membrane: Channels, Gates, and Pumps

Proteins embedded in the cell membrane serve many functions. One is transporting substances across the membrane. **Figure 4.11** illustrates three categories of such membrane proteins—channels, gates, and pumps. In each case, the protein's function is an emergent property of its shape or its ability to change shape.

1. **Channels**. Some membrane proteins are shaped to form channels, holes through which substances can pass. Different proteins with different-sized channels allow different substances to enter or leave the cell. Figure 4.11A illustrates a protein shaped to form a channel large enough for potassium ions (K^+), but not other ions, to traverse. Other protein molecules serve as channels for other ions and substances.

2. **Gates**. Some protein molecules have the ability to change shape. Figure 4.11B illustrates a **gated channel** that opens and closes to allow Na^+ ions to enter at some times but not at others. Some gates work by changing shape when another chemical binds to them. In these cases, the embedded protein molecule acts as a lock. When a key of the appropriate size and shape is inserted into it and turned, the locking device changes shape and activates the gate. Other gates change shape in response to environmental conditions, such as electrical charge or temperature.

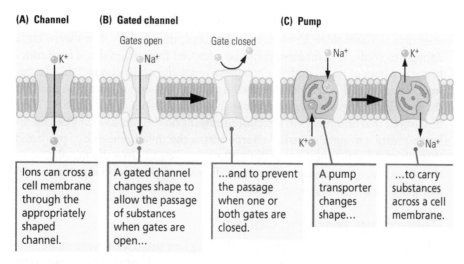

(A) **Channel**

K⁺

Ions can cross a cell membrane through the appropriately shaped channel.

(B) **Gated channel**

Gates open
Na⁺

Gate closed

A gated channel changes shape to allow the passage of substances when gates are open...

...and to prevent the passage when one or both gates are closed.

(C) **Pump**

Na⁺   K⁺

K⁺   Na⁺

A pump transporter changes shape...

...to carry substances across a cell membrane.

Figure 4.11 ◄

Transmembrane Proteins
Channels, gates, and pumps are different proteins embedded in the cell membrane.

3. **Pumps**. Another shape-changing membrane protein acts as a **pump**, or **transporter protein**, a molecule that actively transports substances across the cell membrane. The transporter shown in Figure 4.11C requires energy to change shape and pump Na^+ ions in one direction and K^+ ions in the other. Pumps transport many other substances across the cell membrane as well.

Channels, gates, and pumps contribute to a neuron's ability to convey information, a process whose underlying electrical mechanism is described in Sections 4.2 and 4.3.

4.2 The Neuron's Electrical Activity

The neurons of most animals, including humans, are tiny, on the order of 1 to 20 **micrometers** (μm) in diameter (1 μm = one-millionth of a meter or one-thousandth of a millimeter). The neuron's small size—too small for the eye to see—made it difficult to study at first. Pioneering work with much larger neurons led to the technology that now makes it possible to record from single neurons in the human brain, as described in the opening Portrait.

When British zoologist J. Z. Young (1962) dissected the North Atlantic squid *Loligo*, he noticed its truly giant axons, as much as a millimeter (1000 μm) in diameter. These axons lead to the squid's body wall, or mantle, which contracts to propel the squid through the water. *Loligo*, portrayed in **Figure 4.12**, is not giant. It is only about a foot long. But these particular axons are giants, as axons go. Each is formed by the fusion of many smaller axons into a single large one. Because larger axons send messages faster than smaller axons, these giant axons allow the squid to jet-propel away from predators.

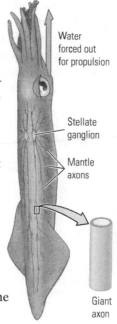

Water forced out for propulsion

Stellate ganglion

Mantle axons

Giant axon

Figure 4.12 ◄

Laboratory Specimen
Loligo's giant axons project from the stellate ganglion to the mantle and form by the fusion of many smaller axons. Their size allows them to convey messages with extreme rapidity, instructing the mantle to contract and propel the squid through the water.

In 1936, Young suggested to Alan Hodgkin and Andrew Huxley, two neuro-scientists at Cambridge University in England, that *Loligo*'s axons were large enough to study. A giant axon could be removed from a squid and kept functional in a bath of liquid designed to approximate the squid's body fluids. In this way, Hodgkin and Huxley determined how neurons send information and laid the foundation for what we now know about neurons' electrical activity. They discovered that differences in ion concentrations on the two sides of a cell membrane create a minute electrical charge across the membrane. They predicted that channels in the membrane must allow the ions to cross the membrane so that the charge can change. They also discovered that the charge can travel along the surface of the membrane.

Recording from an Axon

Hodgkin and Huxley's experiments with the giant squid axon were made possible by the invention of the **oscilloscope**, an instrument that turns electrical fluctuations into visible signals. You may be familiar with one form of oscilloscope, an old, boxy analog television set that uses glass vacuum tubes. The oscilloscope can also be used as a sensitive voltmeter to measure the very small, rapid changes in electrical currents that come from an axon.

Today, oscilloscopes are computerized, but they act on the same principles. **Figure 4.13**A illustrates a digital oscilloscope, which sends a beam of electrons to a screen that glows when struck by the electrons to form a visible trace. In Figure 4.13B, the oscilloscope is connected to a squid axon. Recordings from the axon are made with microelectrodes connected to the oscilloscope. The microelectrodes are insulated wires with minute uninsulated tips. (Such microelectrodes were inserted into to the subject's temporal lobes in the single-cell recording described in the chapter-opening Portrait.) Here, placing the tip of one microelectrode on a squid axon provides an extracellular measure of the electrical current from a very small part of the axon. A second microelectrode with its tip placed inside or elsewhere on the axon is used as a reference.

As shown in Figure 4.13C, a change in charge across the membrane is graphed to represent the neuron's electrical charge in the vicinity of the electrodes. The y axis of the graph indicates the change in charge across the membrane, measured in volts. The x axis of the graph shows time. The sizes of these

Figure 4.13 ▼

Oscilloscope Recording
(A) Basic wave shapes displayed on a digital oscilloscope, which visualizes and measures electrical signals changing in real time. (B) Recording and reference electrodes from the oscilloscope attached to the squid axon. (C) The graph of a trace produced by an oscilloscope, where *S* stands for stimulation. Before and after stimulation, the voltage across the axon membrane shown in part B is represented as −70 mV. (Part A Vanderbilt University/XOS.)

(A) Digital oscilloscope

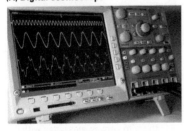

(B) Squid axon

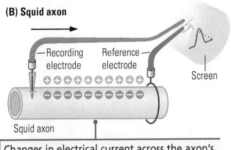

Recording electrode   Reference electrode

Screen

Squid axon

Changes in electrical current across the axon's membrane deflect the electron beam.

(C) Recording electrical charge

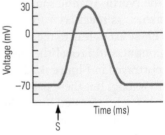

Voltage (mV)

30

0

−70

Time (ms)

S

electrical charges are small, measured in **millivolts** (mV; 1 mV = one-thousandth of a volt), and the changes are rapid, measured in **milliseconds** (ms; 1 ms = one-thousandth of a second).

How the Movement of Ions Creates Electrical Charges

Using the giant squid axon, an oscilloscope, and microelectrodes, Hodgkin and Huxley described a neuron's electrical charge as due to three factors that influence ion movement into and out of cells: (1) concentration gradient, (2) voltage gradient, and (3) membrane structure.

Concentration Gradient

All molecules have an intrinsic kinetic energy: they move constantly. Because of this thermal motion (heat), molecules spontaneously spread out from where they are more concentrated to where they are less concentrated. This spreading out is called **diffusion**.

Requiring no work, diffusion results from the random motion of molecules as they jostle and bounce about, gradually dispersing throughout the solution. Ink poured into water diffuses from its initial point of contact to every part of the liquid. Salts placed in water dissolve into ions surrounded by water molecules. Carried by the random motion of the water molecules, the ions diffuse throughout the solution until every part of it has very nearly the same concentration. When diffusion is complete, the system is in equilibrium, with each component—ions and water molecules—distributed evenly.

When the substance is not evenly dispersed, the term **concentration gradient** describes relative differences in amounts at different locations in a container. As illustrated in **Figure 4.14**A, ink placed in water will start out concentrated at the site of first contact, but even in the absence of mechanical stirring, the ink will quickly spread away from that site.

The ink spontaneously diffuses down a gradient from a high concentration into places of low concentration until it is diffused, distributed equally throughout the water. The process is similar when a salt solution is poured into water.

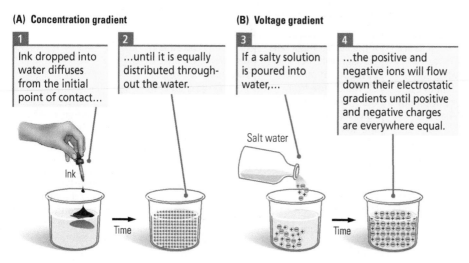

(A) Concentration gradient

1	2
Ink dropped into water diffuses from the initial point of contact...	...until it is equally distributed throughout the water.

(B) Voltage gradient

3	4
If a salty solution is poured into water,...	...the positive and negative ions will flow down their electrostatic gradients until positive and negative charges are everywhere equal.

Ink

Time

Salt water

Time

Figure 4.14 ◄

Moving to Equilibrium

The dissolved salt's concentration is initially high in the location where it enters the water, but the ions soon diffuse until their concentrations are uniform throughout.

Voltage Gradient

When salts dissolve in water, the resulting ions carry an electrical charge. Thus, we can describe their diffusion patterns not only by a concentration gradient but also by a **voltage gradient**—the difference in charge between two regions that allows a flow of current if the two regions are connected. The voltage gradient allows for measuring the relative concentrations of positive and negative electrical charges.

In Figure 4.14B, Na^+ and Cl^- ions move down a voltage gradient from a highly charged area to an area of lower charge just as they move down a concentration gradient from an area of high density to an area of lower density. When the salt is dissolved in water, it diffuses. Diffusion can be described as either movement down a concentration gradient, as shown in Figure 4.14A, or by movement down a voltage gradient, as shown in Figure 4.14B.

Modeling the Cell Membrane

An imaginary experiment illustrates how the third factor, cell membrane structure, influences ion movement. **Figure 4.15**A shows a container of water divided in half by a partition representing the cell membrane. If we place a few grains of NaCl in the left half of the container, the salt dissolves. Sodium and chloride ions diffuse down their concentration and voltage gradients until the water in the left compartment is in equilibrium.

At this point, within the salty side of the container, there are no longer concentration or voltage gradients for either Na^+ or Cl^- ions, because the water everywhere in that side is equally salty. There are no concentration or voltage gradients for these ions within the other side of the container either, because the solid membrane prevents the ions from entering that side. But notice the concentration and voltage gradients for both Na^+ and Cl^- ions *across* the membrane—that is, from the salty side to the freshwater side.

Figure 4.15 ▼

Modeling the Cell Membrane

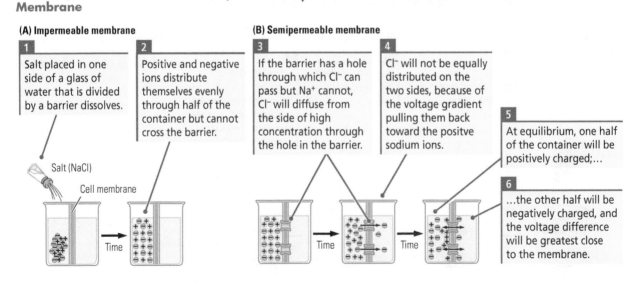

(A) Impermeable membrane

1 Salt placed in one side of a glass of water that is divided by a barrier dissolves.

2 Positive and negative ions distribute themselves evenly through half of the container but cannot cross the barrier.

Salt (NaCl)

Cell membrane

Time

(B) Semipermeable membrane

3 If the barrier has a hole through which Cl^- can pass but Na^+ cannot, Cl^- will diffuse from the side of high concentration through the hole in the barrier.

4 Cl^- will not be equally distributed on the two sides, because of the voltage gradient pulling them back toward the positve sodium ions.

5 At equilibrium, one half of the container will be positively charged;...

6 ...the other half will be negatively charged, and the voltage difference will be greatest close to the membrane.

Time

Time

Recall from Figure 4.11 that protein molecules embedded in the cell membrane act as pores to allow certain kinds of ions to pass through. In our imaginary experiment, we will place a chloride channel in the partitioning membrane and envision how that channel will affect the activity of the dissolved particles.

Chloride ions will now diffuse across the membrane, as shown at the left in Figure 4.15B. The ions will move down their concentration gradient from the side of the container where they are abundant to the side of the container from which they were formerly excluded, as shown in the middle of Figure 4.15B. The sodium ions, in contrast, are still unable to cross the membrane. (Although Cl^- ions are larger than Na^+ ions, Na^+ ions have a greater tendency to hold on to water molecules; as a result, the Na^+ ions are bulkier and unable to enter the chloride channels.)

If the only factor influencing the movement of Cl^- ions were the chloride concentration gradient, the efflux (outward flow) of Cl^- ions from the salty to the freshwater side of the container would continue until Cl^- ions were in equilibrium on both sides. This equilibrium is not achieved because the Cl^- ions carry a negative charge and are attracted back toward the positively charged Na^+ ions (opposite charges attract). Consequently, the concentration of Cl^- ions remains higher in the left half of the container than in the right half, as illustrated on the right in Figure 4.15B.

The efflux of Cl^- ions from the left side of the container to the right side, down the chloride *concentration* gradient, is counteracted by the influx (inward flow) of Cl^- ions down the chloride *voltage* gradient. At some point, an equilibrium is reached in which the concentration gradient of Cl^- ions is balanced by the voltage gradient of their negative charge. At that point,

$$\text{Concentration gradient} = \text{voltage gradient}$$

At this equilibrium, different ratios of positive and negative ions exist on each side of the membrane, so a voltage gradient exists across the membrane. The left side of the container is positively charged because some Cl^- ions have migrated to the other side, leaving a preponderance of positive (Na^+) charges behind them. The right side of the container is negatively charged because some Cl^- ions have entered that chamber, where no ions (of any charge) were before. The charge is highest on the membrane surface, where positive and negative ions accumulate in an attempt to balance each other.

The results obtained in this imaginary experiment are similar to what happens in a real cell. Keep them in mind as we describe and explain how ion channels, gates, and pumps participate in five aspects of the cell membrane's electrical activity: (1) the resting potential, (2) graded potentials, (3) the action potential, (4) the nerve impulse, and (5) saltatory conduction.

The Resting Potential

A neuron at rest maintains an unequal ion distribution that leaves a neuron's intracellular fluid negatively charged relative to the fluid outside the cell. In **Figure 4.16**, when one microelectrode tip is placed on the outer surface of an axon's membrane and another on the membrane's inner surface, the difference in charge, due to the unequal distribution of ions, is about 70 mV.

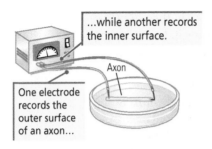

...while another records the inner surface.

One electrode records the outer surface of an axon...

Axon

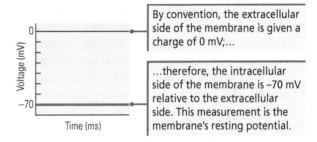

By convention, the extracellular side of the membrane is given a charge of 0 mV;...

...therefore, the intracellular side of the membrane is –70 mV relative to the extracellular side. This measurement is the membrane's resting potential.

Figure 4.16 ▲

Resting Potential The electrical charge recorded across a resting cell membrane produces a store of potential energy.

Although the charge on the outside of the membrane is actually positive, scientists follow the convention of assigning it a charge of 0 mV. The summed charges of the unequally distributed ions give the inside of the membrane a charge of −70 mV relative to the outside. This charge is the membrane's **resting potential**. The resting potential is not identical on every axon. It can vary from −40 mV to −90 mV on axons of different animal species.

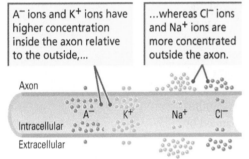

A^- ions and K^+ ions have higher concentration inside the axon relative to the outside,...

...whereas Cl^- ions and Na^+ ions are more concentrated outside the axon.

Axon

Intracellular

Extracellular

Figure 4.17 ▲

Ion Distribution Across a Resting Membrane The number of ions distributed across the resting cell membrane is unequal. Protein ions are represented by A^-.

The Ionic Basis of the Resting Potential

Four kinds of charged particles interact to produce the resting potential: sodium ions (Na^+), chloride ions (Cl^-), potassium ions (K^+), and large protein anions (A^-). As **Figure 4.17** shows, these charged particles are distributed unequally across the axon's membrane, with more protein anions and K^+ ions in the intracellular fluid and more Cl^- and Na^+ ions in the extracellular fluid.

The resting potential represents a store of energy that can change. You might use the idea of potential in the same way when you think about the financial potential of the money that you have in the bank. Just as you have the potential to spend the money at some future time, the cell membrane resting potential stores energy that can be used at a later time. The resting potential can increase or decrease, as you might deposit or withdraw from your bank account, thus increasing or decreasing your potential to spend.

Maintaining the Resting Potential

Embedded in the cell membrane shown in **Figure 4.18** are protein molecules that serve as channels, gates, and pumps to regulate a neuron's resting potential. Protein anions manufactured inside cells remain there because no membrane channels are large enough to enable them to leave the cell. Their charge contributes to the negative charge on the inside of the cell membrane. The negative charge of protein anions alone is sufficient to produce a transmembrane voltage gradient. Because most cells in the body manufacture these large, negatively charged protein molecules, most cells have a charge across their membranes.

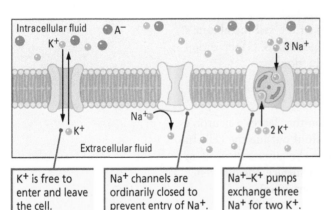

Intracellular fluid

A^-

K^+

$3 Na^+$

Na^+

K^+

$2 K^+$

Extracellular fluid

K^+ is free to enter and leave the cell.

Na^+ channels are ordinarily closed to prevent entry of Na^+.

Na^+–K^+ pumps exchange three Na^+ for two K^+.

Figure 4.18 ◄

Maintaining the Resting Potential Channel gates and pumps in the cell membrane contribute to the transmembrane charge.

To balance the negative charge of the large protein anions in the intracellular fluid, cells accumulate K^+ ions. Potassium ions enter the cell through open potassium channels in the cell membrane, to the extent that about 20 times as much K^+ resides inside the cell as outside it (Figure 4.18, left). If there are 20 times as many positively charged K^+ ions inside the cell as outside it, why should the inside of the membrane still have a negative charge? Shouldn't all those K^+ ions in the intracellular fluid give the inside of the cell a positive charge instead?

No, because not quite enough K^+ ions are able to enter the cell to balance the negative charge of the protein anions. There is a limit on the number of K^+ ions that accumulate inside the cell because, when the intracellular potassium concentration becomes higher than the extracellular concentration, K^+ ions start moving out of the cell, down the K concentration gradient. The inequality in concentration gradient of only a few K^+ ions is sufficient to maintain a relative negative charge on the inside of the membrane.

If Na^+ ions were free to move across the membrane, they could diffuse into the cell and reduce the transmembrane charge. In fact, a cell membrane does have sodium channels, but they are ordinarily closed, blocking the entry of most Na^+ ions (Figure 4.18, center). Still, given enough time, sufficient Na^+ could leak into the cell to reduce its membrane potential to zero. What prevents this?

The high concentration of Na^+ ions outside relative to inside the cell membrane is maintained by the action of a **sodium–potassium pump** (Na^+–K^+ pump), a protein molecule embedded in the membrane that shunts Na^+ ions out of the cell and K^+ ions into it. A neuron membrane's many thousands of Na^+–K^+ pumps work continuously, each one exchanging three intracellular Na^+ ions for two K^+ ions with each pumping action (Figure 4.18, right). The K^+ ions are free to leave the cell through open potassium channels, but closed sodium channels prevent reentry of the Na^+. Consequently, at equilibrium, there are about 10 times as many Na^+ ions on the outside of the axon membrane as there are on the inside.

Chloride ions ordinarily contribute little to the membrane's resting potential. They move in and out of the cell through open chloride channels in the membrane, just as the K^+ ions move through open potassium channels. At equilibrium, the chloride concentration gradient equals the chloride voltage gradient at approximately the membrane's resting potential.

Summarizing the Resting Potential

As summarized in **Figure 4.19**, the unequal distribution of **anions** (negatively charged ions) and **cations** (positively charged ions) leaves a neuron's intracellular fluid negatively charged at about -70mV relative to the fluid outside the cell. Three aspects of the semipermeable cell membrane contribute to this resting potential:

1. Large, negatively charged protein molecules remain inside the cell.

2. Gates keep out Na^+ ions, and channels allow K^+ and Cl^- ions to pass more freely.

3. Na^+–K^+ pumps extrude Na^+ from the intracellular fluid.

Figure 4.19 ▼

Resting Transmembrane Charge

Unequal distribution of different ions causes the inside of the axon to be relatively negatively charged.

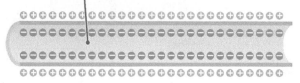

Graded Potentials

The resting potential provides an energy store that the cell can expend if the membrane's barrier to ion movement is suddenly removed. This energy store can also be restored by the flow of ions. If the barrier to the flow of ions is changed, the voltage across the membrane will change. Slight decreases or increases in an axon's membrane voltage are **graded potentials**, highly localized and restricted to the vicinity on the axon where they are produced. A decrease in the voltage on the membrane is termed **depolarization**, and an increase is termed **hyperpolarization**.

For a graded potential to arise, an axon must receive some stimulation that changes the ion flow. Stimulating the axon electrically through a microelectrode is one way to increase or decrease the membrane voltage (to polarize it) and produce a graded potential. Such changes are brief, lasting little more than the duration of the applied current. Just as a small wave produced in the middle of a large, smooth pond disappears before traveling much distance, graded potentials produced on a membrane decay before traveling very far.

If negative current is applied to the membrane, the membrane potential becomes more negative by a few millivolts, increasing its polarity. As illustrated in **Figure 4.20**A at left, it may hyperpolarize from the resting potential of -70 mV to a new, slightly higher potential of, say, -73 mV. For the membrane to become hyperpolarized, the inside must become more negative, which can be accomplished with an efflux of K^+ ions or an influx of Cl^- ions through their respective ion channels as shown in Figure 4.20A, right.

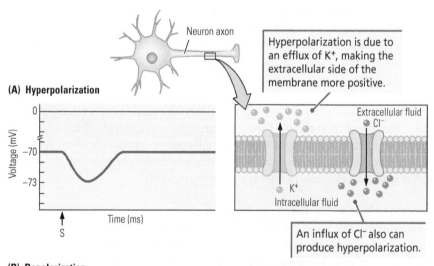

(A) **Hyperpolarization**

Hyperpolarization is due to an efflux of K^+, making the extracellular side of the membrane more positive.

An influx of Cl^- also can produce hyperpolarization.

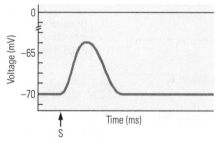

Figure 4.20 ▶

Graded Potentials
(A) Stimulation (S) that increases relative membrane voltage produces a hyperpolarizing graded potential. (B) Stimulation that decreases relative membrane voltage produces a depolarizing graded potential.

(B) **Depolarization**

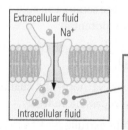

Depolarization is due to an influx of Na^+ through Na^+ channels.

Conversely, if the current applied to the membrane is positive, the membrane potential depolarizes by a few millivolts, decreasing its polarity. As illustrated in Figure 4.20B, left, it may change from a resting potential of −70 mV to a new, slightly lower potential of, say, −65 mV. For the membrane to become depolarized, the inside must become less negative, which can be accomplished by an influx of Na⁺ ions through gated sodium channels as shown in Figure 4.20B, right.

The Action Potential

Electrical stimulation of the cell membrane at resting potential produces localized graded potentials. An **action potential**, by contrast, is a brief but extremely large reversal in the polarity of the axon's membrane, lasting about 1 ms (**Figure 4.21**A).

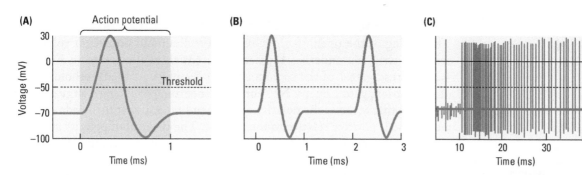

An action potential is triggered when the cell membrane is depolarized to about −50 mV. At this **threshold potential**, the membrane charge undergoes a remarkable change with no further stimulation. The relative membrane voltage suddenly depolarizes until the charge on the inside of the membrane is as great as +30 mV—a total voltage change of 130 mV. Then, almost as quickly, the membrane potential reverses again, becoming slightly hyperpolarized—a reversal of more than 130 mV. After the reversal, the membrane gradually returns to its resting potential at −70 mV.

Figure 4.21B illustrates that each action potential is a discrete event. Figure 4.21C shows that within a time span of about 30 ms a neuron can produce many action potentials. As neurons are the functional units of the nervous system, action potentials are its information units.

The Role of Voltage-Sensitive Ion Channels

Figure 4.22 illustrates the cellular mechanisms that underlie the movement of Na⁺ and K⁺ ions to produce an action potential. A class of gated sodium and potassium channels called **voltage-sensitive channels** are sensitive to the membrane's voltage. These channels are closed at the axon membrane's resting potential, so ions cannot pass through.

When the axon membrane reaches the threshold voltage of about −50 mV, however, the voltage-sensitive channels open to let ions pass. The structure and sensitivity of sodium and potassium channels are different. Voltage-sensitive sodium channels have two gates; one is ordinarily closed and the other open. At the threshold voltage, the closed gate opens and is quickly followed

Figure 4.21 ▲

Measuring Action Potentials (A) Phases of a single action potential. The time scale on the horizontal axis is compressed to chart (B) each action potential as a discrete event and (C) the ability of a membrane to produce many action potentials in a short time.

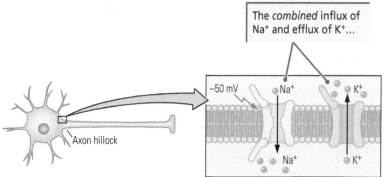

The *combined* influx of Na⁺ and efflux of K⁺...

...results in an action potential that consists of the *summed* voltage changes due to Na⁺ and K⁺.

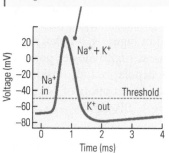

Figure 4.22 ▲

Triggering Voltage-Sensitive Gates to Produce an Action Potential

by the open gate closing. Thus, the duration of ion flow through the sodium channel is brief. The potassium channels, which have one gate, are slower to open and stay open longer.

Phases of the Action Potential and Refractory Periods

The timing of the opening and closing of sodium and potassium voltage-sensitive channels underlies the action potential, as illustrated in **Figure 4.23**. At rest, gate 1 of the sodium channel is closed. At the threshold level of stimulation, gate 1 opens. Na⁺ enters the neuron, producing a large depolarization that reverses the polarity of the membrane so that the inside of the membrane is positive relative to the outside. The reversal of polarity stimulates gate 2 of the sodium channel, which is also voltage sensitive, to close, ending depolarization.

The potassium channels open somewhat more slowly than the sodium channels, and the efflux of K⁺ repolarizes the neuron. K⁺ leaves because the entering Na⁺ replaces the positive charge that potassium maintains on the inside of the cell. As potassium leaves the cell, the membrane depolarizes past its resting potential to the point that the membrane is hyperpolarized before the potassium channels finally close.

Figure 4.23 ▼

Phases of an Action Potential Initiated by changes in voltage-sensitive sodium and potassium channels, an action potential begins with a depolarization. (Gate 1 of the sodium channel opens and then gate 2 closes.) The more slowly-opening potassium channel contributes to repolarization and hyperpolarization until the resting membrane potential is restored.

The dynamic changes in the gates of sodium and potassium channels underlie an important feature of the action potential, its refractory period. If the axon membrane is stimulated during the depolarizing or repolarizing phase of the action potential, it does not respond with a new action potential because the sodium gates are insensitive. The axon in this phase is described as **absolutely refractory**. If, on the other hand, the axon membrane is stimulated during the hyperpolarization phase, a new action potential can be induced, but only if the intensity of stimulation is higher than that which initiated the first action potential. During this phase, the membrane is described as **relatively refractory**. The refractory periods limit the frequency with which action potentials can occur. Thus, the neuron must return to its resting potential before another action potential can occur, making action potentials discrete events.

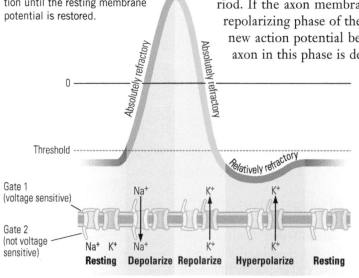

The phases of an action potential are somewhat analogous to the action of a lever-activated toilet. Pushing the lever slightly produces a slight flow of water, which stops when the lever is released. This response is analogous to a graded potential. A harder press of the lever brings the toilet to threshold and initiates flushing, a response that is out of all proportion to the pressure on the lever. This response is analogous to the action potential. During the flush, the toilet is absolutely refractory, meaning that another flush cannot be induced at that time. As the bowl is refilling, the toilet is relatively refractory, meaning that reflushing is possible but harder to bring about. Only after the cycle is completed and the toilet is once again "resting" can the usual flush be produced again.

Poisoning the Action Potential

Direct evidence that voltage-sensitive K^+ and Na^+ channels underlie the action potential comes from experiments that show how each can be blocked selectively, as shown in **Figure 4.24**. A chemical called *tetraethylammonium* (TEA) blocks potassium channels and so blocks potassium efflux but leaves sodium channels intact, as indicated by continued sodium influx at threshold (Figure 4.24, top). The participation of sodium channels in depolarization is indicated by the fact that the chemical *tetrodotoxin* blocks sodium channels (Figure 4.24, bottom) and so prevents sodium influx but does not affect potassium channels, as indicated by spared potassium efflux at threshold.

▼ Pufferfish (The Photo Library— Sidney/Science Source.)

Pufferfish, considered a delicacy in certain countries, especially Japan, secrete tetrodotoxin, so skill is required to prepare this fish for dinner. The fish is lethal to the guests of careless cooks because tetrodotoxin impedes the electrical activity of neurons.

These "poison" experiments highlight ways in which neurons are influenced by environmental chemicals, a theme that we will take up in Chapter 6, as we describe how drugs affect behavior.

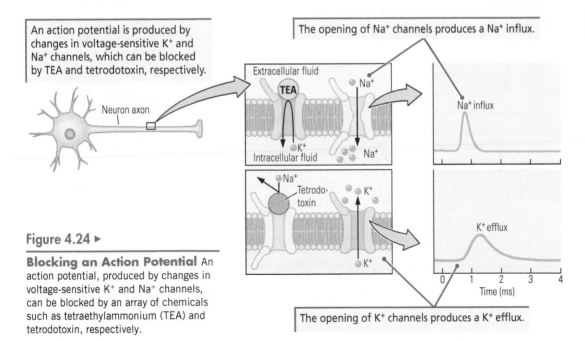

Figure 4.24 ▶

Blocking an Action Potential An action potential, produced by changes in voltage-sensitive K^+ and Na^+ channels, can be blocked by an array of chemicals such as tetraethylammonium (TEA) and tetrodotoxin, respectively.

◎ 4.3 Sending a Message Along an Axon

The action potential does not in itself explain how a neuron sends messages. Sending a message along an axon requires the voltage change that the action potential triggers to move along the axon. We now describe how a voltage change travels along an axon and so carries information for long distances. We also describe why the signal does not decay as it travels and why it nearly always goes in only one direction.

The Nerve Impulse

Suppose you place two recording electrodes at a distance from each other on an axon's membrane and then electrically stimulate an area adjacent to one electrode with a current sufficient to bring the membrane to threshold (**Figure 4.25**). That electrode immediately records an action potential, and shortly afterward so does the second electrode. Somehow the action potential has moved along the axon to induce a **nerve impulse**. Here is how it works.

The total voltage change during an action potential is 100 mV, large enough to bring adjacent parts of the membrane to a threshold of −50 mV. When the adjacent axon membrane reaches −50 mV, the voltage-sensitive channels at that location pop open to produce an action potential there as well. This action potential, in turn, induces a change in the membrane voltage still farther along the axon, and on and on, right down the axon's length.

Figure 4.25 illustrates how each action potential propagates another action potential on the adjacent axon membrane. The word *propagate* means to give birth, which is exactly what happens. Each successive action potential gives birth to another down the length of the axon.

A second consequence of an action potential's refractory period explains why a nerve impulse nearly always travels away from its point of origin. Because the axon membrane is refractory for a brief period during and after an action potential, when an action potential is propagated on an adjacent portion of the membrane, the electrical potential cannot reverse. This ensures that each discrete neural impulse travels in one direction.

To summarize the action of a nerve impulse, another analogy may help. Think of the voltage-sensitive ion channels along an axon as a row of dominoes set on end. When the first domino falls, it knocks over its neighbor, and so on down the line. The wave cannot return to its starting position until the dominoes are set up again. There is also no decrement in the size of the propagated event: the last domino falls exactly the same distance and just as heavily as the first one did.

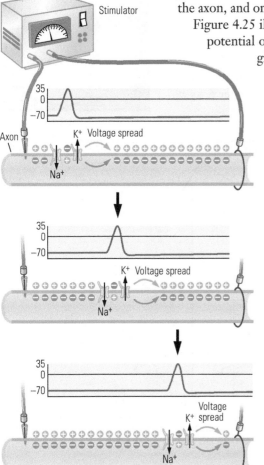

Figure 4.25 ◄

Propagating an Action Potential Voltage sufficient to open sodium channels and potassium channels (top) spreads to adjacent sites of the membrane, inducing voltage-sensitive gates to open there (middle) and spreading the voltage change farther along (bottom). Because the gates are briefly inactivated after closing, the impulse cannot travel back in the direction from which it has come. Here, the voltage changes are shown on one side of the axon membrane only.

Saltatory Conduction and Myelin Sheaths

Large axons convey nerve impulses quickly; smaller axons convey impulses slowly. Because the squid's axons are so large—as much as a millimeter wide—they can propagate nerve impulses very quickly. The largest mammalian axons are only about 30 μm wide, so the speed with which they convey information should not be especially fast. Yet mammalian axons conduct responses with impressive speed. How do they manage to do this with such thin axons?

The mammalian nervous system uses glial cells to enhance impulse speed. Schwann cells in the peripheral nervous system and oligodendroglia in the central nervous system wrap around each axon, forming an insulating *myelin sheath* (**Figure 4.26**). Action potentials cannot be produced where myelin surrounds an axon. The insulating myelin creates a barrier to the flow of electrical current, and the axonal regions that lie under myelin have few voltage-sensitive channels to enable action potentials.

But the axons are not totally encased in myelin. The uninsulated regions between the myelinated segments, called **nodes of Ranvier**, are richly endowed with voltage-sensitive ion channels. Larger mammalian axons tend to be more heavily myelinated than smaller axons, and on larger axons, the nodes are farther apart. Nevertheless, these tiny gaps in the myelin sheath are sufficiently close that an action potential at one node can induce voltage-sensitive gates to open at an adjacent node. In this way, an action potential jumps from node to node, as shown in **Figure 4.27**. This flow of energy is called **saltatory conduction** (from the Latin verb *saltare*, meaning "to leap").

Jumping from node to node greatly increases the speed with which an action potential can travel along an axon. On the largest myelinated mammalian axons, the nerve impulse can travel at a rate as high as 120 meters per second compared with only about 30 meters per second on smaller, less-myelinated axons.

Figure 4.26 ▼

Myelination An axon is insulated by (A) oligodendroglia in the CNS and (B) Schwann cells in the PNS. Each glial cell is separated by a gap, or node of Ranvier.

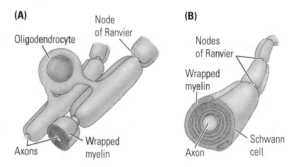

Figure 4.27 ▼

Saltatory Conduction Myelinated stretches of axon are interrupted by nodes of Ranvier, rich in voltage-sensitive channels. In saltatory conduction, the action potential jumps from node to node, carrying the action potential rapidly along.

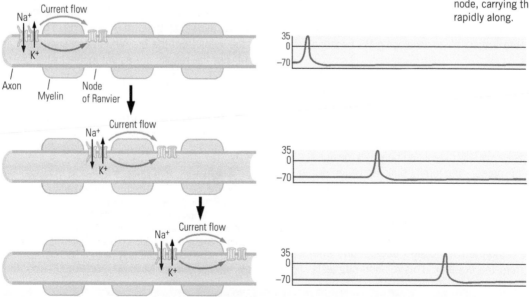

As an analogy, think of how a wave made by spectators consecutively rising to their feet travels around a sports stadium. As one person rises, her immediate neighbor begins to rise also, producing the wave effect. This wave resembles conduction along an uninsulated axon. Now think of how much faster the wave would complete its circuit around the field if only spectators in the corners rose to produce it. This wave effect is analogous to a nerve impulse that travels by jumping from one node of Ranvier to another. Humans and other mammals owe their quick reaction capabilities in part to saltatory conduction in their nervous systems. When myelin breaks down, nerve impulses are disrupted, as detailed in the accompanying Snapshot.

SNAPSHOT | Diagnosing MS

The degenerative nervous-system disorder **multiple sclerosis** (MS) attacks the protective myelin covering of axons, causing inflammation and often destroying the myelin in patches, as shown in the illustration. Eventually, a hard scar, or *plaque*, may form in the affected areas, which is why the disease is called *sclerosis* (from the Greek word meaning "hardness"). When plaque forms, the usual flow of nerve impulses along axons is distorted.

Multiple sclerosis is unpredictable and often disabling. Its cause remains unknown, but researchers believe that it is an autoimmune disease; that is, in MS, the body's immune system malfunctions and starts attacking myelin (Cappellano et al., 2013). Some evidence points to a common virus or bacteria as the disease trigger, and certain people may be more susceptible to developing MS because of genetic factors.

Remissions and relapses are striking features of MS. To counter its unpredictability, magnetic resonance imaging (MRI) is an important diagnostic tool. Imaged by MRI, discrete multiple sclerosis lesions appear around the lateral ventricles and in the white matter of the brain.

Multiple sclerosis is usually diagnosed between the ages of 15 and 40, in the career- and family-building years, but can make its first appearance in young children and in older adults. Prevalence rates range from 1 MS case per 500 people to 1 in 1000. MS is more than twice as likely to develop in women than in men and is seen most commonly in people of northern European background and those living far from the equator. This relation suggests that a lack of vitamin D, obtained from sunlight, may be a contributing factor, and patients frequently use vitamin D_3 and vitamin B_{12} supplements.

Symptoms of MS not only are unpredictable but also vary greatly from person to person and may include vision disturbances such as double or blurred vision. Extreme fatigue, loss of balance, problems with coordination, muscle stiffness, speech problems, bladder and bowel problems, short-term memory problems, and even partial or complete paralysis are common. Among a number of types of MS, symptoms are intermittent in the most common form and progressive in a less common form.

It has been suggested that blood flow from the brain is reduced in MS, allowing a buildup of toxic iron in the brain. Widening the veins from the brain has been suggested as a treatment, but the results are as yet inconclusive (Zamboni et al., 2012).

Normal myelinated nerve fiber

Exposed fiber

Damaged myelin

Nerve affected by MS

Cappellano, G., M. Carecchio, T. Fleetwood, L. Magistrelli, R. Cantello, U. Dianzani, and C. Comi. Immunity and inflammation in neurodegenerative diseases. *American Journal of Neurodegenerative Disease* 2(2):89–107, 2013.

Zamboni, P., A. Bertolotto, P. Boldrini, P. Cenni, R. D'Alessandro, R. D'Amico, M. Del Sette, R. Galeotti, S. Galimberti, A. Liberati, L. Massacesi, D. Papini, F. Salvi, S. Simi, A. Stella, L. Tesio, M. G. Valsecchi, and G. Filippini; Chair of the Steering Committee. Efficacy and safety of venous angioplasty of the extracranial veins for multiple sclerosis. Brave dreams study (brain venous drainage exploited against multiple sclerosis): Study protocol for a randomized controlled trial. Clinicaltrials.gov NCT01371760, 2012.

◎ 4.4 How Neurons Integrate Information

A neuron's extensive dendritic tree is covered with spines, and through the spines it receives thousands of connections from other neurons. Nerve impulses traveling to each of these synapses from other neurons bombard the receiving neuron with all manner of inputs. In addition, a neuron's cell body can receive connections from many other neurons.

How does the neuron integrate this enormous array of inputs into a nerve impulse? In the 1960s, John C. Eccles (1965) and his students performed experiments that helped answer this question, earning Eccles the Nobel Prize in Physiology or Medicine in 1963. Rather than recording from the giant axon of a squid, Eccles recorded from the cell body of large motor neurons in the vertebrate spinal cord. He did so by refining the stimulating and recording techniques developed by Hodgkin and Huxley for studying squid axons.

A spinal-cord motor neuron's extensive dendritic tree has as many as 20 main branches that subdivide numerous times and are covered with dendritic spines. Motor neurons receive input from multiple sources, including the skin, joints, muscles, and brain. To study neuronal integration, Eccles inserted a microelectrode into the spinal cord of a vertebrate animal until the tip was in or right beside a motor neuron cell body. He then placed stimulating electrodes on the axons of sensory nerve fibers (the posterior root) entering the spinal cord (see Figure 3.13B). By teasing apart the fibers of the incoming sensory nerves, he was able to stimulate one fiber at a time.

Excitatory and Inhibitory Postsynaptic Potentials

Figure 4.28 diagrams the experimental setup Eccles used. As shown on the left, stimulating some incoming sensory fibers produced a depolarizing graded potential (reduced the charge toward threshold) on the membrane of the motor neuron to which these fibers were connected. Eccles called these graded potentials **excitatory postsynaptic potentials** (EPSPs). EPSPs increase the probability that an action potential will result. As shown on the right, when Eccles stimulated other incoming sensory fibers, he produced a hyperpolarizing graded potential (increased the charge away from threshold) on the receiving motor-neuron membrane. Eccles called these graded potentials **inhibitory postsynaptic potentials** (IPSPs). IPSPs decrease the probability that an action potential will result.

EPSPs and IPSPs last only a few milliseconds before they decay and the neuron's resting potential is restored. EPSPs are associated with the opening of sodium channels, which allows an influx of Na^+ ions. IPSPs are associated with the opening of potassium channels, which allows an efflux of K^+ ions (or with the opening of chloride channels, which allows an influx of Cl^- ions).

Figure 4.28 ▼

Eccles's Experiment
To demonstrate how input onto neurons influences their excitability, Eccles recorded from the cell body of a motor neuron while stimulating either an excitatory (left) or an inhibitory (right) pathway. Stimulating (S) the excitatory pathway produces a membrane depolarization, or excitatory postsynaptic potential (EPSP). Stimulating the inhibitory pathway produces a membrane hyperpolarization, or inhibitory postsynaptic potential (IPSP).

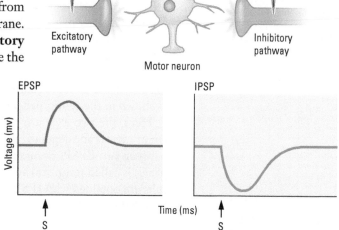

Voltage-Sensitive Channels and the Action Potential

Although the size of a graded potential is proportional to the intensity of stimulation, an action potential is not produced on the motor neuron's cell-body membrane even when an EPSP is strongly excitatory. The cell-body membranes of most neurons do not contain voltage-sensitive channels, but the axon hillock is rich in them (**Figure 4.29**).

To produce an action potential, the summated graded potentials—the IPSPs and EPSPs—on the cell-body membrane must depolarize the membrane at the axon hillock to its threshold voltage. (The actual threshold voltage varies with the type of neuron.) If the threshold voltage is obtained only briefly, just one action potential may occur. If the threshold level is maintained longer, however, action potentials will follow one another in rapid succession, as quickly as the gates on the voltage-sensitive channels can reset. Each action potential is then repeatedly propagated to produce a series of nerve impulses that travel the length of the axon.

Neurons often have extensive dendritic trees, but dendrites and dendritic branches do not have many voltage-sensitive channels and ordinarily do not produce action potentials. And distant branches of dendrites may have less influence in producing action potentials initiated at the axon hillock than do the more proximal dendritic branches, because EPSPs are largely local voltage changes. Consequently, inputs close to the axon hillock are usually more dynamic in their influence than those occurring some distance away, although those distant inputs can have a modulating effect. As in all democracies, some inputs have more say than others (Debanne et al., 2013).

Summation of Inputs

As Eccles's experiment demonstrates, a neuron receives both EPSPs and IPSPs (see Figure 4.28). How do these incoming graded potentials interact? What happens if two EPSPs occur in succession? Does it matter if the time between them is increased or decreased? What happens when an EPSP and an IPSP arrive together?

Temporal Summation

If one excitatory pulse of stimulation is delivered and followed some time later by a second excitatory pulse, one EPSP is recorded, and after a delay, a second EPSP is recorded, as shown at the top in **Figure 4.30A**. These two widely spaced EPSPs do not interact. If the delay between them is shortened so that the two occur in rapid succession, however, a single larger EPSP is produced, as shown in the center panel of Figure 4.30A.

Here, the two excitatory pulses are summed (added together to produce a larger membrane depolarization than either would induce alone). This relation between two EPSPs occurring close together or even at the same time (bottom panel) is called **temporal summation**. Figure 4.30B reveals that equivalent results are obtained with IPSPs. Therefore, temporal summation is a property of both EPSPs and IPSPs.

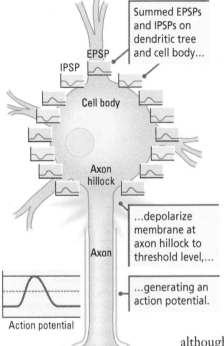

Figure 4.29 ▲

Triggering an Action Potential If the summated graded potentials—the EPSPs and IPSPs—on the dendritic tree and cell body of a neuron charge the membrane to threshold level at the axon hillock, an action potential travels down the axon membrane.

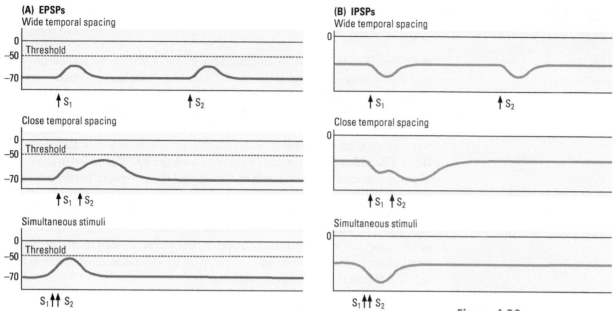

(A) EPSPs

Wide temporal spacing

Threshold

↑ S₁ ↑ S₂

Close temporal spacing

Threshold

↑S₁ ↑S₂

Simultaneous stimuli

Threshold

S₁↑↑ S₂

(B) IPSPs

Wide temporal spacing

↑ S₁ ↑ S₂

Close temporal spacing

↑S₁ ↑S₂

Simultaneous stimuli

S₁↑↑ S₂

Figure 4.30 ▲

Temporal Summation
(A) Two depolarizing pulses of stimulation (S₁ and S₂) separated in time produce two EPSPs similar in size. Pulses close together in time partly sum. Simultaneous EPSPs sum as one large EPSP. (B) Two hyperpolarizing pulses (S₁ and S₂) widely separated in time produce two IPSPs similar in size. Pulses in temporal proximity partly sum. Simultaneous IPSPs sum as one large IPSP.

Spatial Summation

What happens when inputs to the cell-body membrane are located close together or far apart? By using two recording electrodes (R_1 and R_2) we can see the effects of spatial relations on the summation of inputs.

If two EPSPs are recorded at the same time but on widely separated parts of the membrane (**Figure 4.31**A) they do not influence one another. If two EPSPs occurring close together in time are also located close together, however, they sum to form a larger EPSP (Figure 4.31B). This **spatial summation** indicates that two separate inputs occurring very close to one another on the cell membrane and in time will sum. Similarly, two IPSPs produced at the same time sum if they occur at approximately the same place on the cell-body membrane but not if they are widely separated.

The Role of Ions in Summation

Summation is a property of both EPSPs and IPSPs in any combination. These interactions make sense when you consider that the influx and efflux of ions are being summed. The influx of sodium ions accompanying one EPSP is added to

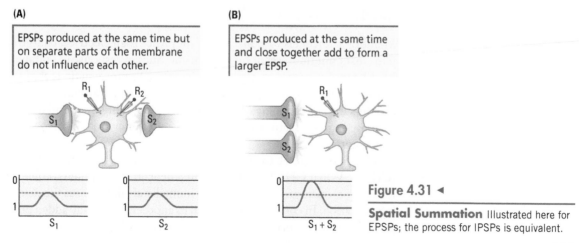

(A)

EPSPs produced at the same time but on separate parts of the membrane do not influence each other.

R_1 R_2

S_1 S_2

S_1 S_2

(B)

EPSPs produced at the same time and close together add to form a larger EPSP.

R_1

S_1

S_2

$S_1 + S_2$

Figure 4.31 ◄

Spatial Summation Illustrated here for EPSPs; the process for IPSPs is equivalent.

111

the influx of sodium ions accompanying a second EPSP if the two occur close together in time and space. If the two influxes of sodium ions are remote in time or in space or in both, no summation is possible.

The same is true regarding effluxes of potassium ions. When they occur close together in time and space, they sum; when they are far apart in either or both ways, there is no summation. The patterns are identical for an EPSP and an IPSP. The influx of sodium ions associated with the EPSP is added to the efflux of potassium ions associated with the IPSP, and the difference between them is summed as long as they are spatially and temporally close together.

A neuron with thousands of inputs responds no differently from one with only a few. It sums all inputs that are close together in time and space. Because of this temporal and spatial summation, a neuron can be said to analyze its inputs before deciding what to do. The ultimate decision is made at the axon hillock, the region that initiates the action potential.

The Versatile Neuron

Dendrites collect information in the form of graded potentials (EPSPs and IPSPs), and the axon hillock initiates discrete action potentials that are delivered to other target cells via the axon. Exceptions to this picture of how a neuron works do exist. For example, some cells in the hippocampus can produce additional action potentials, called *depolarizing potentials*, when the cell would ordinarily be refractory.

A typical neuron does not initiate action potentials on its dendrites because the dendritic membrane does not contain voltage-sensitive channels. In some neurons, however, voltage-sensitive channels on dendrites do enable action potentials. The reverse movement of an action potential from the axon hillock into the dendritic field of a neuron is called **back propagation**. Back propagation signals the dendritic field that the neuron is sending an action potential over its axon, and it may play a role in plastic changes in the neuron that underlie learning. For example, back propagation may make the dendritic field refractory to inputs, set the dendritic field to an electrically neutral baseline, or reinforce signals coming in to certain dendrites (Legenstein and Maass, 2011).

◎ 4.5 Stimulating and Recording with Optogenetics

Membrane channels responsive to light rather than electrical charge and proteins that emit fluorescent light of various hues in response to voltage changes have been discovered in algae and bacteria. A transgenetic technique called **optogenetics** (from the Greek *opto* for "visible") transfers genes for these proteins into the genome of other animals, including mice and monkeys, and then uses light to stimulate the cells and/or a camera to record the cell's light-emitting responses.

The first channel to be used for optogenetics was channelrhodopsin-2 (CHR2). When CHR2 is expressed in a neuron and exposed to blue light, the ion channel opens to Na^+ and K^+ and immediately depolarizes the neuron, causing excitation. In contrast, stimulation of another genetically added protein, the pump halorhodopsin (NpHR), with green-yellow light activates it to pump Cl^-

into the cell, hyperpolarizing the neuron and causing inhibition. If fiber-optic light can be delivered to selective regions of the brain, neurons expressing these proteins will respond immediately: with excitation to a blue light and inhibition to a yellow light. The behavior normally controlled by those neurons will accordingly also be excited or inhibited.

An advantage of optogenetics is that when light-related channels are introduced into select neurons or select populations of neurons, the discrete behaviors produced by those neurons can be elicited, recorded, and studied. Optogenetic methods are in wide use in animal models for investigating neurological diseases, such as Parkinson's disease and Alzheimer's disease, and for investigating neural systems, such as those underlying motivation, emotion, and learning.

Optogenetic techniques will not be applied to studying the human brain any time soon. A thick skull and large brain are obstacles to focal light stimulation and filming. Introducing new genes into the human genome also carries potential risks. Nevertheless, optogenetics provides an elegant confirmation of how neurons function and convey information. The emerging field of **synthetic biology**, the redesign of biological systems, includes coupling light-sensitive proteins to many cellular activities, including protein formation and transport and the mechanisms through which proteins are incorporated into the cell membrane (Bacchus et al., 2013). Using such methods, it is possible to control and film many aspects of the neuronal processes that underlie our behavior.

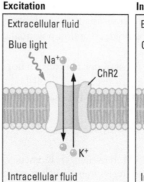
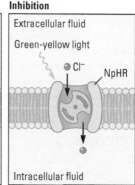

▲ **Lighting Up Neurons**
Specific wavelengths activate light-sensitive proteins expressed in neurons.

SUMMARY

This chapter describes the various parts of a neuron and illustrates how understanding the parts leads to an overall understanding of neuronal function.

4.1 The Neuron's Structure

Cells are "factories" that make protein molecules. Chromosomes in the nucleus contain genes; each gene carries the code for one protein's polypeptide chain. DNA is transcribed into mRNA that carries the code for the polypeptide to a ribosome that translates it into a series of amino acids that form a protein. Epigenetic mechanisms can enable or block gene expression.

The resulting proteins are packaged and shipped by Golgi bodies to microtubules to travel to various destinations within the cell. Some proteins are embedded in the neuron's membrane, forming channels, gates, and pumps that regulate ion flow across the cell membrane. Others leave the cell via exocytosis.

4.2 The Neuron's Electrical Activity

Neurons carry an electrical charge, the resting potential, across their membranes. The charge is produced by unequal concentrations of ions across the membrane, an inequality maintained

and regulated by the membrane's ion channels, gates, and pumps. If the gates on the membrane open briefly, ion efflux or influx can occur, changing the membrane's charge—a graded potential. If a graded potential is sufficient to change the membrane's charge to the threshold, voltage-sensitive sodium and potassium channels open, and an action potential commences.

All neurons communicate by inducing action potentials in other neurons. Thus, understanding their electrical activity leads to an understanding of disorders such as epilepsy and of how consciousness is produced. The channels that underlie ionic flow across the cell membrane are sensitive to various toxins, which explains certain kinds of poisoning; can be altered by genetic mutations, which explains some inherited disorders; and can be influenced by behavior, which explains some kinds of learning.

4.3 Sending a Message Along an Axon

The voltage change induced on the axon membrane by an action potential is sufficiently large to open adjacent voltage-sensitive channels, thus propagating the action potential along the membrane as a nerve impulse. Action potentials can be propagated only at the nodes between glial cells on myelinated axons. This saltatory conduction is especially rapid.

4.4 How Neurons Integrate Information

The summated inputs to neurons from other cells can produce both excitatory postsynaptic potentials and inhibitory postsynaptic potentials. To integrate incoming information, EPSPs and IPSPs are summed both temporally and spatially. If the resulting sum moves the membrane voltage at the axon hillock to threshold, an action potential courses down the axon.

Neurons are versatile. Most of our neurons do not initiate action potentials on dendrites because the cell-body membrane does not contain voltage-sensitive channels. But some voltage-sensitive channels on dendrites do enable action potentials. Back propagation, the reverse movement of an action potential from the axon hillock into the dendritic field of a neuron, may play a role in plastic changes that underlie learning.

4.5 Stimulating and Recording with Optogenetics

Introducing genes that code for channels, pumps, and other cell components that are responsive to light confirms the way in which neurons transmit information and provides a methodology for describing and controlling neuron function.

References

Bacchus, W., D. Aubel, and M. Fussenegger. Biomedically relevant circuit-design strategies in mammalian synthetic biology. *Molecular Systems Biology* 9:691, 2013.

Charney, E. Behavior genetics and postgenomics. *Behavioral Brain Sciences* 35:331–358, 2012.

Debanne, D., A. Bialowas, and S. Rama. What are the mechanisms for analogue and digital signalling in the brain? *Nature Reviews Neuroscience* 14:63–69, 2013.

Eccles, J. The synapse. *Scientific American* 212:56–66, January 1965.

Hodgkin, A. L., and A. F. Huxley. Action potentials recorded from inside nerve fiber. *Nature* 144:710–711, 1939.

Quiroga, R. Q., L. Reddy, G. Dreiman, C. Koch, and I. Fried. Invariant visual representation by single neurons in the human brain. *Nature* 3687:1102–1107, 2005.

Young, J. Z. *The Life of Vertebrates*. New York: Oxford University Press, 1962.

5 Communication Between Neurons

 PORTRAIT Otto Loewi's Dream Breakthrough

Otto Loewi's experiment came to him in a dream. Loewi (1965) enjoyed storytelling, and he recounted that after falling asleep while reading a short novel, he awoke suddenly and completely, with the experiment fully formed. He scribbled the plan on a scrap of paper and went back to sleep. The next morning, he could not decipher what he had written, yet he felt it was important.

All day, Loewi was distracted, looking occasionally at his notes but wholly mystified about their meaning. That night he again awoke in the middle of the night, vividly recalling the ideas in his previous night's dream. This time he remembered them the next morning and immediately set up and successfully performed the experiment.

Loewi's 1921 experiment consisted of electrically stimulating a frog's vagus nerve, which leads from the brain to the heart, while the heart was immersed in a fluid-filled container. Meanwhile, he channeled the fluid in the container to a second container. As illustrated in part A of the accompanying drawing, the second container held a second frog heart that Loewi did not stimulate electrically.

Loewi recorded the beating rates of both hearts. Electrical stimulation decreased the rate of the first heart, but more importantly, the fluid transferred from the first to the second container slowed the beating rate of the second heart (part B of the drawing). Clearly, the fluid carried a message about the speed at which to beat.

But where did the message come from? The only way it could have gotten into the fluid was through a chemical released from the vagus nerve. This chemical must have dissolved in the fluid in sufficient quantity to influence the second heart. The experiment therefore demonstrated that the vagus nerve contains a chemical that tells the heart to slow its rate of beating.

In further experiments, Loewi stimulated another cranial nerve, the accelerator, and observed that the heart rate sped up. The fluid that bathed the accelerated heart increased the beating rate of a second heart that was not electrically stimulated. Together, these complementary experiments showed that chemicals from the vagus nerve and the accelerator nerve modulate heart rate, one inhibiting heartbeat and the other exciting it.

At the time Loewi performed his experiments, most scientists doubted that the chemical reactions required of the neuron for making a chemical, releasing it, inactivating it, and then removing it could take place quickly enough to carry a message from one electrically activated neuron to the next. Nevertheless, in the 40 years that followed, as Otto Loewi's methods were developed for studying neurons in the brain, they proved that most communication between neurons in the central nervous system is indeed chemical.

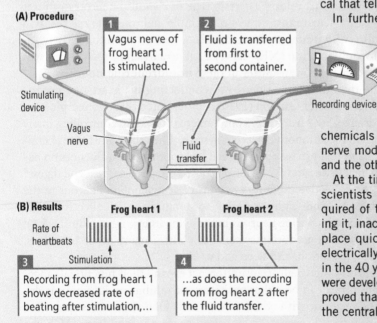

(A) Procedure

1 Vagus nerve of frog heart 1 is stimulated.

2 Fluid is transferred from first to second container.

Stimulating device

Vagus nerve

Fluid transfer

Recording device

(B) Results

Rate of heartbeats

Frog heart 1

Frog heart 2

Stimulation

3 Recording from frog heart 1 shows decreased rate of beating after stimulation,...

4 ...as does the recording from frog heart 2 after the fluid transfer.

We now pursue the story of chemical neurotransmission to the synapse, the site of neurotransmission. Spurred by action potentials, the presynaptic membrane releases chemicals from within the cell to communicate with a target cell. We examine the general function of neural communication first and then consider the general structure of synapses and their variety in the nervous system. You will discover links between groups of neurochemicals and our everyday behavior; links between neurochemicals and neurological disorders; and finally, how drugs, hormones, and toxins can interfere with neurochemicals, replace them or block them, and relieve or cause disorders of brain and behavior.

5.1 Neurotransmitter Discovery

Otto Loewi identified the chemical that communicates a message to inhibit, or slow, a frog's heart rate as **acetylcholine** (ACh) and the chemical that carries an excitatory message to speed up frog heart rate as **epinephrine** (EP), also known as *adrenaline*. In doing so, he discovered a new class of chemicals, the neurotransmitters, which carry messages from one neuron to the next.

Acetylcholine (ACh)

Rather than just two complementary chemicals taking part in these communications, more than 100 may act as neurotransmitters. The confirmed number is about 50. An aside: adrenaline (Latin) and epinephrine (Greek) are the same substance, which is produced by the adrenal glands located atop the kidneys. You may be familiar with the name *adrenaline*, in part because a pharmaceutical company trademarked it. Epinephrine is common parlance in the neuroscience and medical communities and widely known because epinephrine autoinjectors, or "epi pens," are used to treat severe allergic reactions.

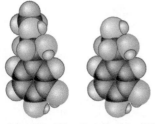

Epinephrine (EP)   Norepinephrine (NE)

▲ ACh inhibits heartbeat; EP and NE excite the heart in frogs and humans, respectively.

Groups of neurons that release a certain type of chemical neurotransmitter are named after that neurotransmitter. For example, neurons that release ACh are called **cholinergic neurons**. In mammals, a neurotransmitter closely related to EP, **norepinephrine** (NE)—also called *noradrenaline* (NA)—replaces EP as the excitatory neurotransmitter in these **noradrenergic neurons**.

At about the time that Otto Loewi was conducting his heart-rate experiments, physiologist Walter Cannon (1920) demonstrated that cholinergic neurons and noradrenergic neurons play complementary roles in controlling many bodily functions in the autonomic nervous system. They thus constitute chemical *activating systems* that produce widespread and coordinated influences on behavior, as explained in Section 5.7. Cannon coined the phrases "rest and digest" to summarize the collective inhibitory actions of acetylcholine neurons in the parasympathetic ANS and "fight or flight" to summarize the collective excitatory actions of norepinephrine neurons in the sympathetic ANS (**Figure 5.1**). The brain also contains activating systems to control many other behaviors, including memory, emotion, and sleep and waking.

The receptors on which neurotransmitters act expand their functional range. Each neurotransmitter can be either excitatory or inhibitory; its action is determined by the receptor with which it interacts. One class of receptors for most neurotransmitters is excitatory and another class is inhibitory. ACh, for example, is inhibitory by means of a receptor on organs of the ANS, including the heart, mediating rest-and-digest behavior, but excitatory on body muscles

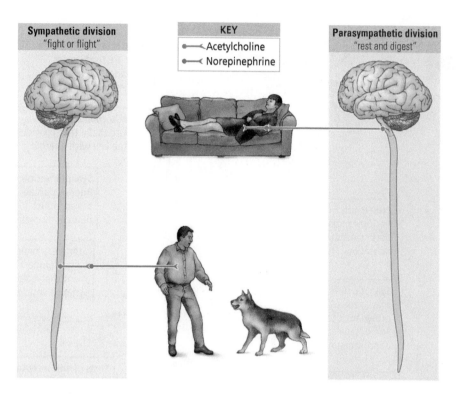

Sympathetic division
"fight or flight"

KEY
— Acetylcholine
— Norepinephrine

Parasympathetic division
"rest and digest"

Figure 5.1 ◄

Controlling Biological Functions in the ANS
(Left) In the sympathetic (arousing) division, cholinergic neurons from the spinal cord activate autonomic noradrenergic neurons that stimulate organs required for fight or flight and suppress those that activate organs used to rest and digest. (Right) In the parasympathetic (calming) division, cholinergic neurons from the spinal cord activate cholinergic neurons in the ANS to inhibit activity in organs used for fight or flight and to excite organs used to rest and digest.

connected to the somatic nervous system. Receptors play other roles too—for example, allowing a neurotransmitter to exert a short-lasting action at one site and a long-lasting action at another.

5.2 The Structure of Synapses

Loewi's discovery about the regulation of heart rate by chemical messengers was the first of two important findings that form the foundation for current understanding of how neurons communicate. The second had to wait nearly 30 years for the invention of the electron microscope, which enabled scientists to see the structure of a synapse. Electron microscopes can project a beam of electrons through a very thin slice of tissue. Their resolution is much higher than that of light microscopes, allowing observation of ultrafine structural details.

Chemical Synapses

The first usable electron micrographs, made in the 1950s, revealed many structures of a typical chemical synapse, as shown in the contemporary micrograph in **Figure 5.2**A. The axon and its terminal are visible in the upper part of this photomicrograph, as is the dendrite in the lower part. The round, granular substances in the terminal (colored blue) are filled with neurotransmitter. The dark band of material just inside the dendrite contains receptors for the neurotransmitter. The terminal and the dendrite do not touch but are separated by a small space.

(A)

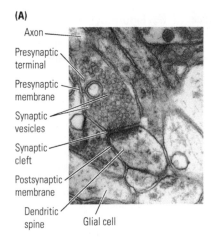

Axon
Presynaptic terminal
Presynaptic membrane
Synaptic vesicles
Synaptic cleft
Postsynaptic membrane
Dendritic spine
Glial cell

Figure 5.2 ▲

Chemical Synapse
(A) Electron photomicrograph of a synapse. Surrounding the centrally located synapse are glial cells, axons, dendrites, and other synapses. (B) Characteristic parts of a synapse. Neurotransmitter, contained in vesicles, is released from storage granules and travels to the presynaptic membrane, where it is expelled into the synaptic cleft by exocytosis. The neurotransmitter then crosses the cleft and binds to receptor proteins on the postsynaptic membrane. (Photomicrograph: Joseph F. Gennaro Jr./Science Source; Colorization: Mary Martin.)

(B)

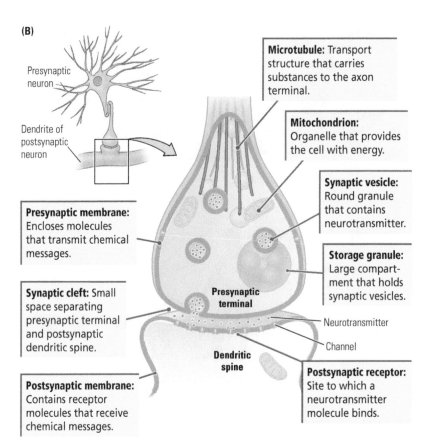

Presynaptic neuron

Dendrite of postsynaptic neuron

Microtubule: Transport structure that carries substances to the axon terminal.

Mitochondrion: Organelle that provides the cell with energy.

Synaptic vesicle: Round granule that contains neurotransmitter.

Storage granule: Large compartment that holds synaptic vesicles.

Presynaptic membrane: Encloses molecules that transmit chemical messages.

Synaptic cleft: Small space separating presynaptic terminal and postsynaptic dendritic spine.

Postsynaptic membrane: Contains receptor molecules that receive chemical messages.

Presynaptic terminal

Neurotransmitter

Channel

Dendritic spine

Postsynaptic receptor: Site to which a neurotransmitter molecule binds.

The three main parts of a synapse, diagrammed in Figure 5.2B, are an axon terminal, the membrane encasing the tip of an adjacent dendritic spine, and the minute space separating the structures—the **synaptic cleft**. On the tip of the dendritic spine is the **postsynaptic membrane**. The patch of dark material within it, shown in Figure 5.2A, consists largely of protein molecules specialized for receiving chemical messages. The dark patches in the **presynaptic membrane**—the membrane of the axon terminal—consist largely of protein molecules, most of them serving as channels and pumps and as receptor sites.

Within the axon terminal are many other specialized structures, including mitochondria (the organelles that supply the cell's energy needs); round granules called **synaptic vesicles**, which contain the chemical neurotransmitter; and tubules that give the terminal button its shape. In some axon terminals, larger **storage granules** hold a number of synaptic vesicles. In the micrograph in Figure 5.2A, you can also see that the synapse (located at center) is closely surrounded by many other structures, including glial cells, other axons and dendritic processes, and other synapses.

Electrical Synapses

Chemical synapses predominate in the mammalian nervous system but are not the only kind of synapse. Some neurons influence each other electrically through a **gap junction**, or *electrical synapse*, where the prejunction and postjunction cell membranes are fused (**Figure 5.3**). Ion channels in one cell membrane connect to ion channels in the adjoining membrane, forming a pore that allows ions to pass directly from one neuron to the next.

This fusion eliminates the brief delay in information flow—about 5 milliseconds per synapse—of chemical transmission. (Compare Figure 5.3 to Figure 5.2B.) For example, the crayfish's gap junctions activate its tail flick, a response that allows it to escape quickly from a predator. Gap junctions in the mammalian brain are found in some regions, where they allow groups of interneurons to synchronize their firing rhythmically. Gap junctions also allow glial cells and neurons to exchange substances.

The possible advantages of chemical synapses center on their plasticity. They are flexible in controlling whether to pass a message from one neuron to the next, they can amplify or diminish a signal sent from one neuron to the next, and they can change with experience to alter their signals and therefore mediate learning. The possible advantages of electrical synapses are speed of impulse transmission and their effect of binding neurons together functionally to enhance their role in teamwork, as might be required for some forms of memory (Bukalo et al., 2013).

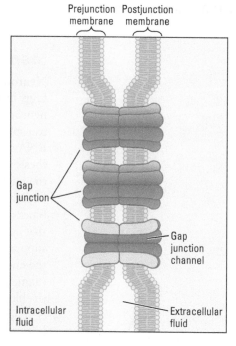

Figure 5.3 ▲

Gap Junction Ion channels span the prejunction and postjunction membranes of an electrical synapse.

5.3 Neurotransmission in Four Steps

Information is transmitted across a chemical synapse in four basic steps illustrated in **Figure 5.4**. Each step requires a different chemical reaction:

1. During *synthesis*, either the transmitter is produced by the cell's DNA and imported into the axon terminal or its building blocks are imported and it is manufactured in the axon terminal.

2. During *release*, the transmitter is transported to the presynaptic membrane and released in response to an action potential.

3. During *receptor action*, the transmitter traverses the synaptic cleft and interacts with receptors on the target cell's membrane.

4. During *inactivation*, the transmitter either is drawn back into the presynaptic axon or breaks down in the synaptic cleft. Otherwise, it would continue to work indefinitely.

Figure 5.4 ►

Synaptic Transmission

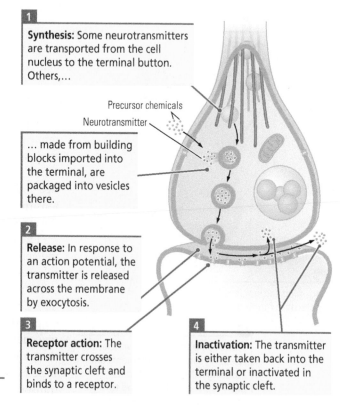

1 Synthesis: Some neurotransmitters are transported from the cell nucleus to the terminal button. Others,...

... made from building blocks imported into the terminal, are packaged into vesicles there.

2 Release: In response to an action potential, the transmitter is released across the membrane by exocytosis.

3 Receptor action: The transmitter crosses the synaptic cleft and binds to a receptor.

4 Inactivation: The transmitter is either taken back into the terminal or inactivated in the synaptic cleft.

Step 1: Transmitter Synthesis and Storage

Neurotransmitters are derived in two basic ways. Some are synthesized as proteins in the cell body according to instructions in the neuron's DNA. These neurotransmitters are then packaged in membranes on the Golgi bodies and transported on microtubules to the axon terminal (see Figure 4.10). Messenger RNA also may be transported to the synapse, where it directs transmitter synthesis within the axon terminal rather than within the ribosomes surrounding the nucleus.

Other neurotransmitters are synthesized in the axon terminal from building blocks derived from food. *Transporter proteins*, molecules in the cell membrane that pump substances across it, absorb these precursor chemicals from the blood supply, as shown in Figure 5.4. Mitochondria in the axon terminal provide the energy for synthesizing neurotransmitters from their precursor chemicals. (Sometimes the transporters absorb entire ready-made neurotransmitters from the blood.)

These two basic modes of synthesis divide most neurotransmitter substances into two large classes: a quicker-acting class derived from nutrient building blocks and a slower-acting class of proteins derived from the cell's DNA. Regardless of their origin, neurotransmitters in the axon terminal are gathered inside membranes that form synaptic vesicles. Depending on the type of neurotransmitter they house, synaptic vesicles are stored in three ways:

1. Some are collected in storage granules.
2. Others are attached to the microfilaments in the terminal button.
3. Still others are attached to the presynaptic membrane, ready to release a neurotransmitter into the synaptic cleft.

When a vesicle is emptied from the presynaptic membrane, others move to take its place so that they, too, stand ready to release their contents.

Step 2: Neurotransmitter Release

Voltage-sensitive calcium channels on the presynaptic membrane play a role in triggering the release of a neurotransmitter from a presynaptic membrane. The surrounding extracellular fluid is rich in calcium ions (Ca^{2+}). As illustrated in **Figure 5.5**, the action potential's arrival opens these voltage-sensitive calcium channels, allowing an influx of calcium into the axon terminal.

The incoming calcium ions bind to other molecules, forming complexes that participate in two chemical reactions: one releases vesicles bound to the presynaptic membrane, and the other releases vesicles bound to filaments in the axon terminal. The vesicles released from the presynaptic membrane empty their contents into the synaptic cleft through *exocytosis*, described in Section 4.1. The membrane surrounding the transmitter substances fuses with the cell membrane. The vesicles that were formerly bound to the filaments are then transported to the membrane to replace the vesicles that were just released there.

Figure 5.5 ▼

Neurotransmitter Release

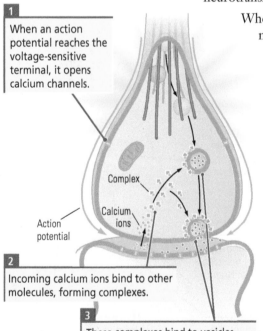

1 When an action potential reaches the voltage-sensitive terminal, it opens calcium channels.

Complex

Action potential

Calcium ions

2 Incoming calcium ions bind to other molecules, forming complexes.

3 These complexes bind to vesicles, releasing some from filaments and inducing others to bind to the presynaptic membrane and to empty their contents by exocytosis.

Step 3: Receptor-Site Activation

A neurotransmitter released from the presynaptic membrane diffuses across the synaptic cleft and binds to specialized protein molecules in the postsynaptic membrane, as shown in Figure 5.5. These transmitter-activated protein molecules are called **receptors** because the sites they occupy on the membrane receive the transmitter substance. The type of neurotransmitter and the kind of receptors on the postsynaptic membrane determine whether the neurotransmitter

- depolarizes the postsynaptic membrane and so has an excitatory action;
- hyperpolarizes the postsynaptic membrane and so has an inhibitory action;
- initiates other chemical reaction sequences that can modulate either the excitatory or the inhibitory effect or influence other functions of the postsynaptic neuron;
- generates new synapses; or
- brings about other changes in the cell.

In addition to acting on the postsynaptic membrane's receptors, a neurotransmitter may interact with **autoreceptors** (self-receptors) on its own presynaptic membrane: it may influence the cell that just released it. Autoreceptors receive messages from their own axon terminal.

How much neurotransmitter is needed to send a message? Bernard Katz (1965) was awarded a Nobel Prize in 1970 for providing an answer. Recording electrical activity from the postsynaptic membranes of muscles, he detected small, spontaneous depolarizations now called *miniature postsynaptic potentials*. The potentials varied in size, but each size appeared to be a multiple of the smallest potential.

Katz concluded that the smallest postsynaptic potential is produced by the release of the contents of just one synaptic vesicle. This amount of neurotransmitter is called a **quantum**. To produce a postsynaptic potential large enough to initiate a postsynaptic action potential requires the simultaneous release of many quanta from the presynaptic cell.

The results of subsequent experiments show that the number of quanta released from the presynaptic membrane in response to a single action potential depends on two factors: (1) the amount of Ca^{2+} that enters the axon terminal in response to the action potential and (2) the number of vesicles docked at the membrane, waiting to be released. Both factors affect the amplitude of a behavioral response produced by synaptic activity and its ability to mediate learning.

Step 4: Neurotransmitter Deactivation

After a neurotransmitter has done its work, it is removed quickly from receptor sites and from the synaptic cleft to make way for other messages sent by the presynaptic neuron. Neurotransmitter deactivation takes place in at least four ways:

1. Diffusion: some of the neurotransmitter simply diffuses away from the synaptic cleft and is no longer available to bind to receptors.
2. Degradation: Enzymes in the synaptic cleft break down the neurotransmitter.

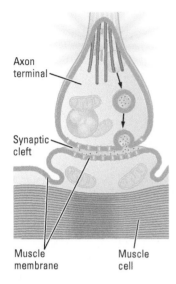

Axon
terminal

Synaptic
cleft

Muscle
membrane

Muscle
cell

Figure 5.6 ▲

Acetylcholine Synapse on a Muscle Cell

3. **Reuptake**: membrane transporter proteins specific to that transmitter may bring the transmitter back into the presynaptic axon terminal for reuse. The by-products of degradation by enzymes also may be taken back into the terminal to be reused in the cell.

4. Some neurotransmitters are taken up by neighboring glial cells. Potentially, the glial cells can also store transmitters for reexport to the axon terminal.

As part of the flexibility of synaptic function, an axon terminal's chemical mechanisms enable it to respond to the frequency of its own use. If the terminal is very active, the amount of neurotransmitter made and stored there increases. For example, all synapses with muscles in the somatic nervous system are cholinergic, using ACh as their neurotransmitter (**Figure 5.6**). Changes in ACh synapse structure and function contribute to getting in shape as a result of intense physical exercise. Exercise that produces a high demand for ACh at nerve–muscle junctions leads to increased ACh being produced in the terminals, thus preparing them to respond to future high demand. In the CNS, similar changes in the synapse contribute to learning, memory, and performance that depend upon the brain keeping in shape.

◎ 5.4 Types of Synapses

So far we have been describing a generic synapse, with features most synapses possess. But the nervous system contains many different kinds of synapses, specialized in regard to location, structure, and function.

Synaptic Variations

Synapses are an extremely versatile chemical delivery system. In one kind, called an **axodendritic synapse** and shown in Figure 5.2, the axon terminal of a neuron meets a dendrite or dendritic spine of another neuron. Another kind of synapse with which you are already familiar is an **axomuscular synapse**, shown in Figure 5.6.

Figure 5.7 shows these and many other types of synapses, including an **axosomatic synapse**, in which an axon terminal ends on a cell body; an **axoaxonic synapse**, in which an axon terminal ends on another axon; and an **axosynaptic synapse**, in which an axon terminal ends at another terminal. Axon terminals that have no specific target but instead secrete their transmitter chemicals nonspecifically into the extracellular fluid are called **axoextracellular synapses**.

In an **axosecretory synapse**, an axon terminal synapses with a tiny blood vessel called a capillary and secretes its transmitter directly into the blood. Synapses need not include axon terminals: dendrites may send messages to other dendrites through **dendrodendritic synapses**. Electrical synapses, shown in Figure 5.3, allow neighboring neurons to synchronize their signals through **somasomatic** (cell body to cell body) connections. Gap junctions also allow glial cells, especially astrocytes, to pass nutrient chemicals to neurons and to receive their waste products.

In summary, a synapse can produce an extremely local effect on neurons or muscles or a very general effect by releasing chemicals diffusely into the brain or into the bloodstream.

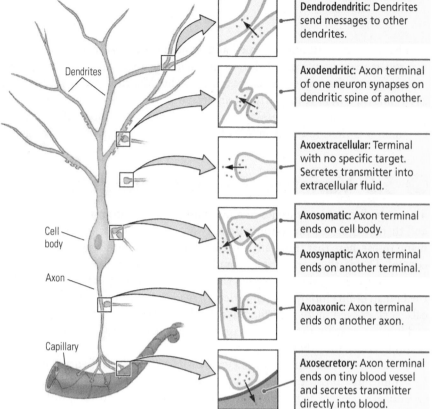

Figure 5.7 ◄

The Versatile Synapse

Dendrodendritic: Dendrites send messages to other dendrites.

Axodendritic: Axon terminal of one neuron synapses on dendritic spine of another.

Axoextracellular: Terminal with no specific target. Secretes transmitter into extracellular fluid.

Axosomatic: Axon terminal ends on cell body.

Axosynaptic: Axon terminal ends on another terminal.

Axoaxonic: Axon terminal ends on another axon.

Axosecretory: Axon terminal ends on tiny blood vessel and secretes transmitter directly into blood.

Excitatory and Inhibitory Messages

Despite their versatility, in the end synapses convey only two types of messages: excitatory or inhibitory. That is to say, a neurotransmitter either increases or decreases the probability that the cell it influences will produce an action potential. In keeping with this dual message system, synapses can be divided into excitatory and inhibitory categories—also known as Type I and Type II synapses, respectively—that differ in location and appearance.

As shown in **Figure 5.8**, Type I excitatory synapses typically are located on the shafts or spines of dendrites; Type II inhibitory synapses are typically located on a cell body. Excitatory synapses have round synaptic vesicles, whereas the vesicles of inhibitory synapses are flattened. Furthermore, the material making up the presynaptic and postsynaptic membranes is denser at an excitatory synapse than it is at an inhibitory synapse, and the excitatory synaptic cleft is wider. Finally, the active zone on an excitatory synapse is larger than that on an inhibitory synapse.

Figure 5.8 ►

Excitatory and Inhibitory Synapses Type I excitatory synapses are found on the spines and dendritic shafts of the neuron, and Type II inhibitory synapses are found on the cell body. Their distinct structural features differ in vesicle shapes, density of material on the presynaptic membrane, cleft size, and size of the postsynaptic active zone.

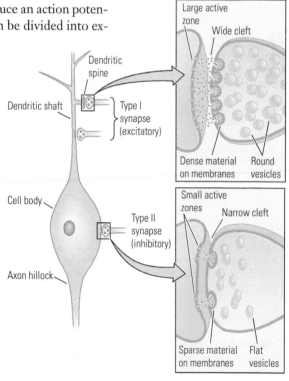

The different locations of Type I and Type II synapses divide a neuron into two zones: an excitatory dendritic tree and an inhibitory cell body. This arrangement suggests that excitation comes in over the dendrites and spreads to the axon hillock, where it may trigger an action potential that travels down the length of the axon. If the message is to be inhibited, the most efficient place to inhibit it is close to the axon hillock, where the action potential originates.

⊚ 5.5 Varieties of Neurotransmitters

The early discoveries of excitatory and inhibitory neurotransmitters by Loewi and their relation to the autonomic nervous system by Cannon suggested to many researchers that the brain must work under much the same type of dual control. That is, there are excitatory and inhibitory brain cells, and NE and ACh are the transmitters through which these neurons work. Today, we know that the human brain employs a wide variety of neurotransmitters, and these chemicals work in even more versatile ways. Each may be excitatory at one location and inhibitory at another, and two or more may team up in a single synapse so that one makes the other more potent.

In this section, we explore how neurotransmitters are identified and how they fit within three broad categories on the basis of their chemical structure. The functional aspects of neurotransmitters interrelate and are intricate, with no simple one-to-one relation between a single neurotransmitter and a single behavior.

Four Criteria for Identifying Neurotransmitters

The experimental criteria used to identify neurotransmitters, shown in **Figure 5.9**, follow from the four-step process of chemical neurotransmission charted in Figure 5.4:

1. The chemical must be *synthesized* in the neuron or otherwise be present in it.

2. When the neuron is active, the chemical must be *released* and produce a *response* in some target cell.

3. The same response (*receptor action*) must be obtained when the chemical is experimentally placed on the target.

4. A mechanism must exist for *deactivating* or removing the chemical from its site of action after its work is done.

By systematically applying these criteria, researchers can determine which of the many thousands of chemical molecules that exist in every neuron are neurotransmitters. They can also synthesize transmitters and use them as drugs, the subject of Chapter 6.

Methodologically, identifying chemical transmitters in the central nervous system is not easy. In the brain and spinal cord, thousands of synapses are packed around every neuron, preventing easy access to a single synapse and its activities. Consequently, for many substances thought to

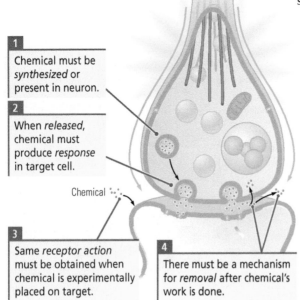

1 Chemical must be *synthesized* or present in neuron.

2 When *released*, chemical must produce *response* in target cell.

Chemical

3 Same *receptor action* must be obtained when chemical is experimentally placed on target.

4 There must be a mechanism for *removal* after chemical's work is done.

Figure 5.9 ▲

Criteria for Identifying a Neurotransmitter

be CNS neurotransmitters, the four criteria needed as proof have been only partly met. A chemical that is suspected of being a neurotransmitter but has not yet met all the criteria for proof is called a *putative* (supposed) *transmitter*.

ACh was the first substance identified as a neurotransmitter in the CNS, a discovery greatly facilitated by a logical argument predicting its presence there even before it was proved experimentally. All motor-neuron axons leaving the spinal cord are cholinergic, and each has an axon collateral within the spinal cord that synapses on a nearby CNS interneuron. The interneuron, in turn, synapses on the motor neuron's cell body. This circular set of connections, termed a **Renshaw loop** after the researcher who first described it, is shown in **Figure 5.10**.

Because the main axon to the muscle releases ACh, investigators suspected that its axon collateral also might release it. Knowing what chemical to look for simplified the task of finding it and then proving that it was in fact also a neurotransmitter in this location. The Renshaw loop acts as a feedback circuit that enables the motor neuron to inhibit itself and not become overexcited in response to excitatory inputs it receives from other parts of the CNS. If the inhibitory neurotransmitter in the Renshaw cell, the amino acid **glycine**, is blocked by the toxin strychnine, motor neurons do become overactive, producing convulsions that interfere with breathing, thus causing death.

Today, the term *neurotransmitter* is used quite broadly. A neurotransmitter may carry a message from one neuron to another by influencing the voltage on the postsynaptic membrane; it may also induce effects such as changing the structure of a synapse. Furthermore, researchers have discovered that neurotransmitters communicate not only in the orthodox fashion, by delivering a message from the presynaptic side of a synapse to the postsynaptic side, but also in some cases, in the opposite direction by *back propagation*, in which the message is sent from the postsynaptic membrane to the presynaptic membrane. Finally, the original idea that each neuron had only one transmitter at all its synapses has been supplanted: different neurotransmitters coexist within the same synapse, and different synapses on the same cell house different neurotransmitters (Sámano et al., 2012).

Three Classes of Neurotransmitters

We can impose some order on the diversity of neurotransmitters by classifying them into three groups on the basis of their chemical composition: (1) small-molecule transmitters, (2) neuropeptide transmitters, and (3) transmitter gases.

Small-Molecule Transmitters

The first neurotransmitters identified are quick-acting **small-molecule transmitters** such as ACh. Typically, they are synthesized from dietary nutrients and packaged for use in axon terminals. When a small-molecule transmitter is

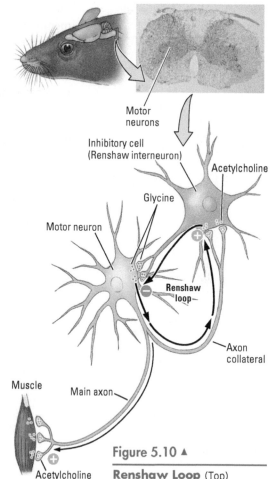

Figure 5.10 ▲

Renshaw Loop (Top) Location of spinal-cord motor neurons that project to the rat's forelimb muscles. (Bottom) In a Renshaw loop, the main motor neuron axon (green) projects to a muscle, and its axon collateral remains in the spinal cord to synapse with an inhibitory Renshaw interneuron (red) that contains the inhibitory transmitter glycine. Both the main motor axon and its collateral terminals contain ACh. When the motor neuron is highly excited (plus signs), it modulates its activity level (minus sign) through the Renshaw loop. (Ian Whishaw.)

released from an axon terminal, it can quickly be replaced at the presynaptic membrane.

Because small-molecule transmitters or their main components are derived from food, diet can influence their levels and activities in the body. This fact is important in the design of drugs that affect the nervous system. Many neuroactive drugs are designed to reach the brain in the same way that small-molecule transmitters or their precursor chemicals do: through ingestion and transport to the brain by the blood. **Table 5.1** lists some of the best-known and most extensively studied small-molecule transmitters, including ACh, the amines, and amino-acid neurotransmitters.

Acetylcholine **Figure 5.11** diagrams how the ACh molecule is synthesized and broken down. ACh is made up of two substances: choline and acetate. Choline is among the breakdown products of fats found in foods such as egg yolk, avocado, salmon, and olive oil; acetate is a compound found in acidic foods, such as vinegar, lemon juice, and apples.

As depicted in Figure 5.11, inside the cell acetyl coenzyme A (acetyl CoA) carries acetate to the synthesis site, and the transmitter is synthesized as a second enzyme, choline acetyltransferase (ChAT), transfers the acetate to choline to form ACh. After ACh has been released into the synaptic cleft and diffuses to receptor sites on the postsynaptic membrane, a third enzyme, acetylcholinesterase (AChE), reverses the process by detaching acetate from choline. These breakdown products can then be taken back into the presynaptic terminal for reuse.

Amines The small-molecule transmitter list includes four amines (chemicals that contain an amine group, NH, in their chemical structure). Some amine transmitters are synthesized by common biochemical pathways and so are related. One such grouping consists of the amines **dopamine** (it plays a role in coordinating movement, in attention and learning, and in behaviors that are reinforcing), NE (NA), and EP (adrenaline). The last two are the excitatory transmitters in the reptilian heart, as we know from Otto Loewi's experiment, and in the mammalian heart, respectively.

Figure 5.12 charts the biochemical sequence that synthesizes these amines in succession. The precursor chemical is tyrosine, an amino acid abundant in food. (Hard cheese and bananas are good sources.) The enzyme tyrosine hydroxylase (enzyme 1 in Figure 5.12) changes tyrosine into

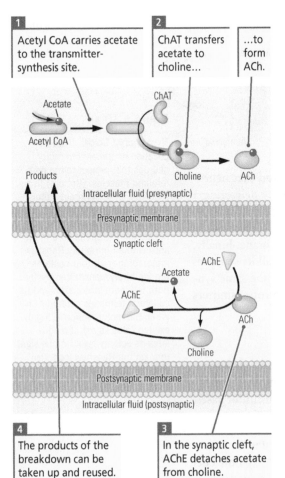

1 Acetyl CoA carries acetate to the transmitter-synthesis site.

2 ChAT transfers acetate to choline... ...to form ACh.

ChAT

Acetate
Acetyl CoA
Products
Choline
ACh
Intracellular fluid (presynaptic)

Presynaptic membrane
Synaptic cleft

AChE
Acetate
AChE
ACh
Choline

Postsynaptic membrane
Intracellular fluid (postsynaptic)

4 The products of the breakdown can be taken up and reused.

3 In the synaptic cleft, AChE detaches acetate from choline.

Figure 5.11 ◄

Chemistry of Acetylcholine Two enzymes—acetyl coenzyme A (acetyl CoA) and choline acetyltransferase (ChAT)—combine the dietary precursors of ACh within the cell, and a third—acetylcholinesterase (AChE)—breaks them down in the synaptic cleft for reuptake.

L-dopa, which is sequentially converted by other enzymes into dopamine, NE, and finally EP.

An interesting aspect of this biochemical sequence is that the amount of the enzyme tyrosine hydroxylase in the body is limited. Consequently, so is the rate at which dopamine, NE, and EP can be synthesized, regardless of how much tyrosine is present or ingested. This **rate-limiting factor** can be bypassed by orally ingesting L-dopa, which is why L-dopa is used in the treatment of Parkinson's disease, a condition brought on by an insufficiency of dopamine.

Serotonin The amine transmitter **serotonin** (5-HT, for 5-hydroxytryptamine) is synthesized differently. Serotonin plays a role in regulating mood and aggression, appetite and arousal, pain perception, and respiration. It is derived from the amino acid tryptophan, which is abundant in turkey, milk, and bananas, among other foods.

Amino Acids Some amino acid transmitters contain carboxyl groups (COOH) in addition to an amine. Two such amino acid transmitters, **glutamate** (Glu) and **gamma-aminobutyric acid** (GABA), are closely related: GABA is formed by a simple modification of Glu in which one carboxyl group is removed (**Figure 5.13**). Glu and GABA are called the workhorses of the nervous system because so many synapses use them.

In the forebrain and cerebellum, Glu is the main excitatory transmitter, and GABA is the main inhibitory transmitter. Type I synapses thus have Glu as a neurotransmitter, and Type II synapses have GABA. So the physical appearance of a synapse provides information about the resident neurotransmitter and its function. Interestingly, Glu is widely distributed in neurons, but it becomes a neurotransmitter only if appropriately packaged in vesicles in the axon terminal. The amino acid transmitter glycine (Gly) is a much more common inhibitory transmitter in the brainstem and spinal cord, where it acts within the Renshaw loop, for example.

Histamine **Histamine** (H) is synthetized from the amino acid histidine. Among its many functions, which include the control of arousal and of waking, histamine can cause the constriction of smooth muscles. When activated in allergic reactions, histamine contributes to asthma, a constriction of the airways. You are probably familiar with antihistamine drugs used to treat allergies.

A few other substances are sometimes classified as small-molecule transmitters. In the future, researchers are likely to find more.

Peptide Transmitters

More than 50 amino acid chains of various lengths form the families of peptide transmitters listed in **Table 5.2**. As explained in Section 4.1, amino acids link together by peptide bonds to form chains, which accounts for the name. Thus, **neuropeptides**, multifunctional chains of amino acids that act as neurotransmitters, are made through the translation of mRNA from instructions in the neuron's DNA (see Figure 4.7).

Although these transmitters are produced in the axon terminal in some neurons, most are assembled on the cell's ribosomes, packaged inside a membrane

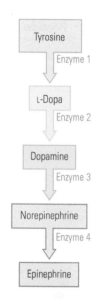

Figure 5.12 ▲

Sequential Synthesis of Three Amines A different enzyme is responsible for successive molecular modification in this biochemical sequence.

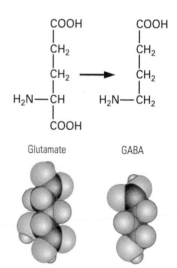

Figure 5.13 ▲

Amino Acid Transmitters (Top) Removing a carboxyl (COOH) group from the bottom of the glutamate molecule produces GABA. (Bottom) Their different shapes allow these amino acid transmitters to bind to different receptors.

Table 5.2 **Peptide neurotransmitters**

Family	Example
Opioids	Enkephaline, dynorphin
Neurohypophyseals	Vasopressin, oxytocin
Secretins	Gastric inhibitory peptide, growth-hormone-releasing peptide
Insulins	Insulin, insulin growth factors
Gastrins	Gastrin, cholecystokinin
Somatostatins	Pancreatic polypeptides
Corticosteroids	Glucocorticoids, mineralocorticoids

Figure 5.14 ▲

Opioid Peptides Parts of some neuropeptide amino acid chains that act on the brain centers for pleasure and pain are similar in structure and also similar to narcotic drugs, such as opium and morphine, that mimic their functions.

by Golgi bodies, and transported on the microtubule highway to the axon terminals. Their synthesis and transport are relatively slow compared to those of small-molecule transmitters. Consequently, neuropeptides form slowly and are not replaced quickly.

Peptides have an enormous range of functions in the nervous system, as might be expected from the large number found there. As described in Section 6.5, they serve as hormones (growth hormone), are active in responses to stress (corticotropin), encourage a mother to bond with her infant (oxytocin), facilitate learning (glucogenlike peptide), and help to regulate eating (cholecystokinin) and drinking (vasopressin) and pleasure and pain (beta-endorphin).

With regard to pleasure and pain, opium—obtained from seeds of the poppy flower—has long been known to produce euphoria and reduce pain. Opium and a group of related synthetic chemicals, such as morphine, appear to mimic the actions of three peptide transmitters: **met-enkephalin**, **leu-enkephalin**, and **beta-endorphin**. (The term *encephalin* derives from the phrase "in the cephalon," meaning "in the brain or head," whereas the term *endorphin* is a shortened form of "endogenous morphine," or morphine made within us.)

All three peptide transmitters contain similar short chains of amino acids that form the biochemically active part of the peptide (**Figure 5.14**). Presumably, opium mimics this part of the chain. The discovery of these naturally occurring opiumlike peptides suggested that one or more of them might have a role in pain management. Opioid peptides, however, are not just pain-specific. These transmitters appear in many locations and provide a variety of functions in the brain, including inducing nausea. Therefore, synthetic opiumlike drugs are still preferred for pain management.

Peptides' amino acid chains are degraded by digestive processes, so unlike the small-molecule transmitters, they are generally not effective if taken orally. If introduced into the blood, their large size may also prevent them from crossing the blood–brain barrier to reach the brain.

Transmitter Gases

The water-soluble gases **nitric oxide** (NO) and **carbon monoxide** (CO) further expand the biochemical strategies that transmitter substances display. As water-soluble gases, they are neither stored in synaptic vesicles nor released from them in the conventional manner; instead, they are synthesized in the cell as needed. Unlike classical neurotransmitters, NO is produced in many regions of a neuron, including the dendrites. On synthesis, each gas diffuses away from the site where it was made, easily crossing the cell membrane and immediately becoming active. Both NO and CO activate metabolic (energy-expending) processes in cells, including those modulating the production of other neurotransmitters.

NO serves as a messenger in many parts of the body. It controls the muscles in intestinal walls, and it dilates blood vessels in brain regions that are in active use, allowing these regions to receive more blood. It also dilates blood vessels in the genital organs and is therefore active in producing penile erections in males. The drug sildenafil citrate (trade name Viagra), the first widely used treatment for male erectile disorder, acts by enhancing the action of NO. NO does not of itself produce sexual arousal.

◉ 5.6 Excitatory and Inhibitory Receptors

When a neurotransmitter is released from the presynaptic membrane, it crosses the synaptic cleft and binds to a receptor on the postsynaptic cell. What happens next depends on the receptor. One class of receptors is excitatory and the other is inhibitory.

Ionotropic Receptors and Excitation

As **Figure 5.15** illustrates, an **ionotropic receptor** has two parts: a binding site for a neurotransmitter and a pore or channel through the membrane. The pore regulates the movement of charged atoms across a cell membrane when a neurotransmitter binds to the binding site. Ionotropic receptors are usually excitatory and increase the likelihood that a neuron will produce an action potential.

When the neurotransmitter attaches to the binding site, the receptor changes its shape, either opening the pore and allowing ions to flow through it or closing the pore and blocking the ion flow. Because the binding of the transmitter to the receptor is quickly followed by the opening or closing of the pore that directly affects the ion flow, ionotropic receptors bring about very rapid changes in membrane voltage.

Structurally, ionotropic receptors are similar to other types of membrane channels, including voltage-sensitive channels. They are composed of a number of membrane-spanning subunits that make up petals forming channel's central pore. Within the pore is a shape-changing segment that causes the pore to open or close, regulating the ion flow through it.

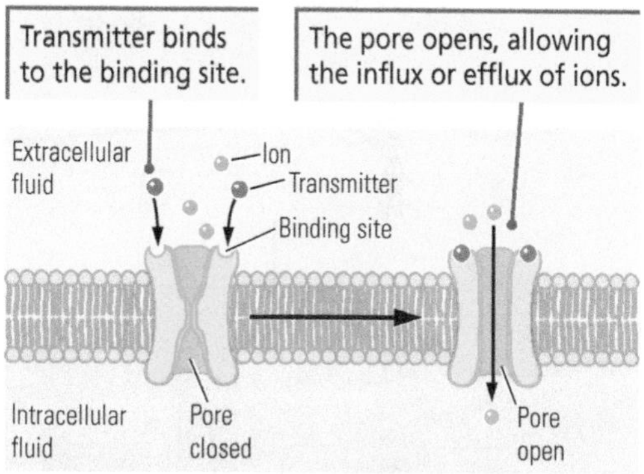

Figure 5.15 ▲

Ionotropic Receptor When activated, these embedded proteins bring about direct, rapid changes in membrane voltage.

Metabotropic Receptors and Inhibition

In contrast to ionotropic receptors, **metabotropic receptors** are usually inhibitory, decreasing the likelihood that a neuron will produce an action potential. A metabotropic receptor's single protein spans the cell membrane but does not possess a pore of its own through which ions can flow. As diagrammed at the top of **Figure 5.16**, the outer part of the receptor has a site for transmitter binding. The receptor's internal part is associated with one of a family of proteins called **guanyl-nucleotide-binding proteins (G proteins** for short) that translates the transmitter's message into biochemical activity within the cell.

A G protein consists of three subunits—alpha, beta, and gamma. The α (alpha) subunit detaches when a neurotransmitter binds to the G protein's associated metabotropic receptor. The detached α subunit then can bind to other proteins within the cell membrane or within its cytoplasm. The α subunit can bind to nearby ion channels, causing them to open or close, and in this way regulate the cell membrane's electrical charge. The α subunit can also bind to other molecules and so induce cascades of metabolic activity that can change the cell's activity or influence gene expression in the cell's nucleus.

Figure 5.16A shows the first effect: opening an ion channel. If the α subunit binds to a nearby ion channel in the membrane, the channel structure changes, modifying the flow of ions through it. If the channel is already open,

(A) Metabotropic receptor coupled to an ion channel

(B) Metabotropic receptor coupled to an enzyme

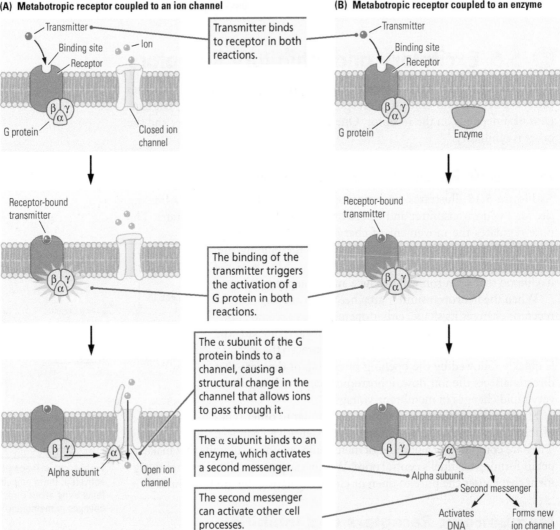

Transmitter binds to receptor in both reactions.

The binding of the transmitter triggers the activation of a G protein in both reactions.

The α subunit of the G protein binds to a channel, causing a structural change in the channel that allows ions to pass through it.

The α subunit binds to an enzyme, which activates a second messenger.

The second messenger can activate other cell processes.

Figure 5.16 ▲

Metabotropic Receptor
When activated, these embedded membrane proteins trigger associated G proteins, thereby exerting indirect effects (A) on nearby ion channels or (B) in the cell's metabolic activity.

the α subunit may close it, or if it is already closed, the α subunit may open it. This change in the channel and the ion flow across the membrane influence the membrane's electrical potential.

The second effect of binding a neurotransmitter to a metabotropic receptor changes the cell's biology. Summarized in Figure 5.16B, the process begins when the detached α subunit binds to an enzyme, which in turn activates another chemical called a **second messenger**. (The neurotransmitter is the first messenger.) A second messenger, as the name implies, carries a message to other structures within the cell. As illustrated at the bottom of Figure 5.16B, the second messenger can

- bind to a membrane channel, causing the channel to change its structure and thus alter ion flow through the membrane.

- initiate a reaction that incorporates protein molecules within the cell into the cell membrane, for example, resulting in the formation of new ion channels.

- influence the cell's DNA to initiate or cease gene expression and thus regulate protein formation.

Excitatory and Inhibitory Receptor Effects

No one neurotransmitter is associated with a single receptor type or a single influence on the postsynaptic cell. At one location, a particular transmitter may bind to an ionotropic receptor and have an excitatory effect on the target cell. At another location, the same transmitter may bind to a metabotropic receptor and have an inhibitory influence.

ACh, for example, has an excitatory effect on skeletal muscles, where it activates an ionotropic receptor. ACh has an inhibitory effect on the heart, where it activates a metabotropic receptor. In addition, each transmitter may bind to several different kinds of ionotropic or metabotropic receptors. Elsewhere in the nervous system, ACh, for example, may activate a wide variety of either receptor type.

◎ 5.7 Neurotransmitter Activating Systems and Behavior

Naming neurons by their chemical neurotransmitters tells us something about the behaviors they influence. Recall, for example, that in the mammalian autonomic nervous system, ACh is associated with the "rest-and-digest" response and noradrenaline with the "fight-or-flight" response.

The idea that specific transmitters, wherever found, form systems with a common function led to the notion that the nervous system could be parsed on the basis of neurotransmitter type. When researchers began to study neurotransmission at the synapse more than a half-century ago, they reasoned that any given neuron would contain only one transmitter at all its axon terminals. Since then, investigators have discovered that different transmitters may coexist in the same terminal or synapse.

Neuropeptides coexist in terminals with small-molecule transmitters, and more than one small-molecule transmitter may be found in a single synapse. In some cases, more than one transmitter may even be packaged within a single vesicle. All these variations result in a bewildering number of neurotransmitter–receptor combinations, which cautions as well against assuming a simple cause-and-effect relation between a neurotransmitter and a behavior.

Nevertheless, neurotransmission can be summarized by concentrating on the dominant transmitter within any given axon terminal. The neuron and its dominant transmitter can then be related to a function or behavior. We now consider some links between neurotransmitters and behavior in the somatic, autonomic, and central divisions of the nervous system.

Neurotransmission in Peripheral Nervous System Divisions

Motor neurons in the somatic nervous system are cholinergic: ACh is their main neurotransmitter. Motor neurons in the brain and spinal cord send their axons to the skeletal muscles, including the muscles of the eyes and face, trunk, limbs, fingers, and toes. As their name implies, SNS motor neurons mediate all our movements. At a skeletal muscle, they are cholinergic, excitatory, and they produce muscular contractions.

Although ACh is the primary neurotransmitter at skeletal muscles, other neurotransmitters found in these cholinergic axon terminals are released onto the muscle along with ACh. One is *calcitonin-gene-related peptide* (CGRP), a neuropeptide that acts through second messengers to increase the force with which a muscle contracts.

The complementary divisions of the autonomic nervous system—sympathetic and parasympathetic—regulate the body's internal environment. Both ANS divisions are controlled by cholinergic neurons that emanate from the CNS at two levels of the spinal cord (see Figure 5.1). The CNS neurons synapse with parasympathetic neurons that contain ACh and with sympathetic neurons that contain NE. Sympathetic noradrenergic neurons prepare the body's organs for fight or flight. Parasympathetic cholinergic neurons prepare the body's organs to rest and digest.

Whether ACh synapses or NE synapses are excitatory or inhibitory on a particular body organ depends on that organ's receptors. During sympathetic arousal, NE turns up heart rate and turns down digestive functions because NE receptors on the heart are excitatory, whereas NE receptors on the gut are inhibitory. Similarly, ACh turns down heart rate and turns up digestive functions because ACh receptors on the heart are inhibitory, whereas those on the gut are excitatory.

The activity of neurotransmitters, excitatory in one location and inhibitory in another, allows the sympathetic and parasympathetic divisions of the ANS to form a complementary regulating system that maintains the body's internal environment under changing circumstances.

Activating Systems of the Central Nervous System

Although many neurotransmitters in the brain and spinal cord likely have specific functions, others appear to have widespread modulatory roles over neural activity in the CNS. These **activating systems**, which form neural pathways that coordinate brain activity through a single neurotransmitter, have been implicated in controlling such functions as motor behavior, arousal, mood, and general brain plasticity.

Each of four small-molecule transmitters—ACh, dopamine, NE, and 5-HT—is among the neurotransmitters featured in the most studied activating systems. The cell bodies of each system's neurons—cholinergic, dopaminergic, noradrenergic, and serotonergic—are located within restricted regions of the brainstem, and their axons are distributed widely throughout the brain and spinal cord. The PET scans in **Figure 5.17** contrast the density of 5-HT neurons and their receptors in a healthy brain with the brain of a person who has Parkinson's disease. These scans reveal that, although the main

Healthy volunteer

Parkinson patient

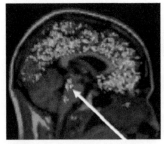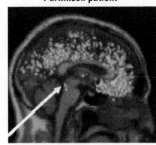

Median raphe

Figure 5.17 ▲

Effects of Parkinson's Disease on the Serotonergic System These PET images capture weak radioactive emissions from an injected tracer compound that binds to serotonin receptors. Autoreceptor density on the cell bodies of the brainstem raphe 5-HT neurons and 5-HT receptors of the terminal buttons in the forebrain are indicated by red for higher density and green for lower density. (Brooks, D.J., Piccini, P. Imaging in Parkinson's disease. The role of monoamines in behavior, *Biological Psychiatry*, 59:908–918, 2006 © Elsevier.)

cause of Parkinson's symptoms is a decrease in dopamine, the disease also affects other neurotransmitters.

You can envision the CNS activating systems as analogous to the power supply to a house. The fuse box is the power source, and from it power lines go to each room, but the electrical devices powered in each room differ. The activating systems are similarly organized in that the cell bodies of their neurons are clustered together in only a few brainstem nuclei, whereas the axons are widely distributed in the forebrain, brainstem, and spinal cord. **Figure 5.18** maps the

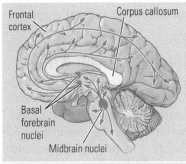

Cholinergic system (ACh)

- Active in maintaining waking electroencephalographic pattern of the cortex.
- Thought to play a role in memory by maintaining neuron excitability.
- Death of cholinergic neurons and decrease in ACh in the neocortex are thought to be related to Alzheimer's disease

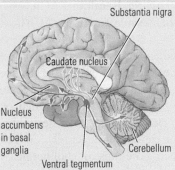

Dopaminergic system (dopamine, or DA)

Nigrostriatal pathways (orange projections)
- Active in maintaining normal motor behavior
- Loss of DA is related to muscle rigidity and dyskinesia in Parkinson's disease

Mesolimbic pathways (purple projections)
- Dopamine release causes feelings of reward and pleasure
- Thought to be the neurotransmitter system most affected by addictive drugs and behavioral addiction
- Increases in DA activity may be related to schizophrenia
- Decreases in DA activity may be related to deficits of attention

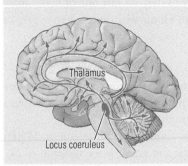

Noradrenergic system (NE)

- Active in maintaining emotional tone
- Decreases in NE activity are thought to be related to depression
- Increases in NE are thought to be related to mania (overexcited behavior)
- Decreased NE activity is associated with hyperactivity and attention-deficit/hyperactivity disorder

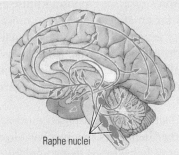

Serotonergic system (5-HT)

- Active in maintaining waking electroencephalographic pattern
- Changes in 5-HT activity are related to obsessive–compulsive disorder, tics, and schizophrenia
- Decreases in 5-HT activity are related to depression
- Abnormalities in brainstem 5-HT neurons are linked to disorders such as sleep apnea and SIDS

Figure 5.18 ◄

Major Activating Systems
Each system's cell bodies are gathered into nuclei (shown as ovals) in the brainstem. The axons project diffusely through the brain and synapse on target structures. Each activating system is associated with one or more behaviors or diseases.

location of each system's nuclei, with arrow shafts tracing the axon pathways and arrow tips indicating axon-terminal locales.

Each activating system is associated with several behaviors and with some disorders, as summarized on the right in Figure 5.18. With the exception of dopamine's clear link to Parkinson's disease, however, most associations between activating systems and brain disorders are far less certain. All these systems are subjects of extensive ongoing research.

The difficulty in making definitive correlations between activating systems and behavior or an activating system and a disorder is that these systems' axons connect to almost every part of the brain. We detail some documented relations between the systems and behavior and disorders here and in many subsequent chapters.

Cholinergic System

The cholinergic system plays a role in normal waking behavior and is thought to function in attention and memory. People with the degenerative **Alzheimer's disease**, which begins with minor forgetfulness, progresses to major memory dysfunction, and later develops into generalized dementia, show a loss of cholinergic neurons at autopsy. One treatment strategy being pursued for Alzheimer's is to develop drugs that stimulate the cholinergic system to enhance alertness, but their beneficial effects are not dramatic. Recall that ACh is synthesized from nutrients in food; thus, the role of diet in maintaining ACh levels also is being investigated.

The brain abnormalities associated with Alzheimer's disease are not limited to cholinergic neurons, however. Autopsies reveal extensive damage to the neocortex and other brain regions, including the loss of neurons and aggregates of abnormal tissue called *plaques*. As a result, what role cholinergic neurons play in the progress of the disorder is not yet clear. Perhaps their destruction causes degeneration in the cortex or perhaps the cause-and-effect relation is the other way around, with cortical degeneration being the cause of cholinergic cell death. Then, too, the loss of cholinergic neurons may be just one of many neural symptoms of Alzheimer's disease, detailed, along with other dementias, in Section 27.7.

Dopaminergic System

As shown in Figure 5.18, two dopaminergic pathways project from the brainstem into other brain regions: the *nigrostriatal* pathway from the substantia nigra and the *mesolimbic* pathway from the ventral tegmentum.

The nigrostriatal DA pathway takes part in coordinating movement. When DA neurons are lost from the substantia nigra, the result is a condition of extreme muscular rigidity, as occurs in Parkinson's disease. Opposing muscles contract at the same time, making it difficult for an affected person to move. Parkinson patients also show rhythmic tremors, especially of the limbs, signaling a release of formerly inhibited movement. Although Parkinson's disease usually arises for no known cause, it can actually be triggered by the ingestion of certain drugs that may act as selective neurotoxins to kill dopamine neurons. (See the Chapter 6 opening Portrait.)

Dopamine in the mesolimbic pathway may be the neurotransmitter most affected in addiction—to food, drugs, and to other behaviors that involve a loss of impulse control. A common feature of addictive behaviors is that stimulating the mesolimbic DA system enhances responses to environmental stimuli, thus making the stimuli attractive and rewarding, as explained in Section 6.4.

Excessive mesolimbic DA activity is proposed to play a role in **schizophrenia**, a behavioral disorder characterized by delusions, hallucinations, disorganized speech, blunted emotion, agitation or immobility, and a host of associated symptoms detailed in Section 27.2. Schizophrenia is one of the most common and debilitating psychiatric disorders, affecting 1 in 100 people.

Noradrenergic System

In the main, behaviors and disorders related to the noradrenergic system concern the emotions. Some symptoms of **major depression**—a mood disorder characterized by prolonged feelings of worthlessness and guilt, disruption of normal eating habits, sleep disturbances, a general slowing of behavior, and frequent thoughts of suicide—may be related to decreases in the activity of noradrenergic neurons. Conversely, some symptoms of **mania** (excessive excitability) may be related to increased activity of these same neurons. Mood disorders are the subject of Section 27.3.

Decreased NE activity also has been associated with both hyperactivity and attention-deficit/hyperactivity disorder (ADHD), elaborated in Section 24.3. Norepinephrine may also facilitate normal brain development and play a role in organizing movements and in learning, by stimulating neuronal plasticity.

Serotonergic System

The serotonergic activating system maintains a waking electroencephalographic (EEG) pattern in the forebrain when we move and thus plays a role in wakefulness, as does the cholinergic system. Like NE, 5-HT plays a role in learning, and some symptoms of depression may be related to decreases in the activity of serotonin neurons. Drugs commonly used to treat depression act on them. Consequently, two forms of depression may exist, one related to norepinephrine and the other to serotonin.

Likewise, some research results suggest that various symptoms of schizophrenia may be related to increased 5-HT activity, which implies different forms of schizophrenia. Increased serotonergic activity is also related to symptoms observed in **obsessive–compulsive disorder** (OCD), a condition in which the affected person compulsively repeats acts (such as hand washing) and has repetitive and often unpleasant thoughts (obsessions). Evidence detailed in the Snapshot on page 136 points to a link between abnormalities in serotonergic nuclei and conditions such as sleep apnea and sudden infant death syndrome (SIDS).

Other Brain Activating Systems

Although the four major activating systems have been implicated in many aspects of behavior and disease, other neurochemical systems also exert general effects on behavior—the histamine, orexin, and opioid systems.

The histamine system's cell bodies in the posterior hypothalamus send projections to the forebrain. Histamine is a small-molecule neurotransmitter and, through a number of receptors, is implicated in controlling sleep and wakefulness. Histamine activity is highest during wakefulness and lowest during sleep, and antihistamine drugs promote sleepiness.

The orexin (also called hypocretin) system, a peptide neurotransmitter system, also has cell bodies in the hypothalamus that project widely to the

SNAPSHOT | Neurochemical Links Between SIDS and Sleep Apnea

Sudden infant death syndrome (SIDS) is the sudden and unexplained death of a seemingly healthy infant under a year old. Typically, a SIDS baby is found dead after having gone to sleep and shows no sign of having suffered.

Although studies have identified risk factors, such as putting infants to bed on their stomach, there remains little understanding of the syndrome's biological causes. SIDS is responsible for roughly 2500 deaths annually in the United States and is the leading cause of death in otherwise healthy infants more than 1 month after birth.

Researchers have examined the brains of babies who died of SIDS and those who died of other causes. Among the SIDS victims, abnormalities appear in the brainstem, including a reduced number of serotonin neurons compared with that in the brainstems of controls (Richerson 2013). Another brainstem nucleus that may be related to these serotonergic neurons is the pre-Bötzinger complex, illustrated at right (Ramirez, 2011). These small, ovoid brainstem neurons control breathing and contain the peptide neurotransmitter substances neurokinin, somatostatin, and mu-opioid.

The same brainstem neuronal systems may also be related to snoring and **sleep apnea**, impairments of breathing during sleep. In sleep apnea, the brain fails to signal the muscles to breathe, so the person has to wake up to do so. Section 26.7 describes the two major types of apneas, a Greek word literally meaning "without breath." People with untreated sleep apnea repeatedly stop breathing during their sleep, sometimes hundreds of times during the night and often for a minute or longer.

Sleep apneas affect more than 12 million Americans, according to the National Institutes of Health. Risk factors include being male, overweight, and older than the age of 40, but sleep apnea can strike anyone at any age, even children. Still, lack of awareness among the public and healthcare professionals leaves the vast majority of those affected undiagnosed and therefore untreated, despite the fact that this serious disorder can have significant consequences.

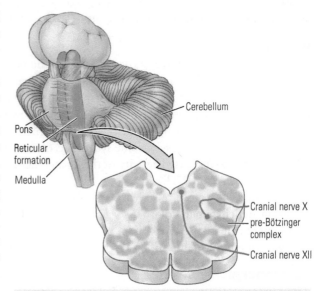

Brainstem nuclei essential for the rhythm of breathing include the pre-Bötzinger complex and cranial nuclei and nerves 10 and 12. The pre-Bötzinger nucleus was named after the label on a wine bottle. (Research from Schwarzacher SW[1], U. Rüb and T. Deller. Neuroanatomcal characteristics of the human pre-Bötzinger complex and its involvement in neurodegenerative brainstem diseases. *Brain* 134 (Pt. 1):24–35, 2011.)

Untreated, sleep apnea can cause high blood pressure and other cardiovascular disease, memory problems, weight gain, impotency, and headaches. Moreover, untreated sleep apnea may be responsible for waking deficiencies ranging from job impairment to accidents such as motor vehicle crashes.

Ramirez, J.-M. The human pre-Bötzinger complex identified. *Brain* 134: 8–10, 2011.

Richerson, G. B. Serotonin: The Anti-SuddenDeathAmine? *Epilepsy Currents* 13(5):241–244, 2013.

forebrain and brainstem. This system is implicated in controlling sleep–waking activity, appetite, and energy expenditure ("orexin" refers to appetite in Greek). Decreased activity in the orexin system can result in an individual uncontrollably collapsing into a dreamlike condition, *narcolepsy*, discussed in Section 26.7.

Opioid systems are anatomically different from activating systems that project from a discrete brain location, because opioid neurons are widespread through the brain and spinal cord. They merit the designation *activating system* in that natural and synthetic opioid drugs, including opium, morphine, and heroin, stimulate opioid neurons and affect behaviors related to emotion, pain, and appetite.

SUMMARY

5.1 Neurotransmitter Discovery

The discovery that neurons communicate with one another by releasing chemicals at their terminals revolutionized neuroscience research. Neurotransmitters released from the presynaptic membrane influence the activity of postsynaptic neurons by binding to receptors on the receiving neuron and changing its electrical activity, either exciting it to make an action potential more likely or inhibiting it to make an action potential less likely. Drugs, hormones, and toxins can mimic neurochemicals or interfere with their activity.

5.2 The Structure of Synapses

A terminal button forms a synapse, which consists of the terminal's presynaptic membrane, a gap, and the postsynaptic membrane. A neurochemical released at the terminal crosses the synaptic gap and activates receptors on the postsynaptic membrane to activate or inhibit the neuron's electrical activity or to change its function in other ways. The existence of 50 neurotransmitter chemicals is confirmed, but more than 100 may be active in the nervous system.

5.3 Neurotransmission in Four Steps

The general steps in transmitter action are (1) neurotransmitter synthesis and storage, (2) release from the axon terminal by exocytosis, (3) action on postsynaptic receptors, and (4) deactivation or reuptake of neurotransmitter substances. Drugs can influence each biochemical event. Thus, understanding how neurotransmitters work can provide insight not only into typical behavior but also into the mechanisms by which many drugs influence behavior.

5.4 Types of Synapses

Neurons can synapse on a cell body, on its axon, on its dendrites, on other synapses, on muscles, and on blood vessels and so mediate a variety of excitatory and inhibitory actions.

Excitation comes in over a neuron's dendrites and spreads to the axon hillock, where it may trigger an action potential that travels down the length of the axon or where the action potential may be inhibited.

5.5 Varieties of Neurotransmitters

The functional aspects of the three main classes of neurotransmitters—small-molecule transmitters, neuropeptides, and transmitter gases—interrelate and are intricate, with no simple one-to-one relation between a single transmitter and a single behavior. Different neurotransmitters can coexist within the same synapse, and different synapses on the same cell can house different neurotransmitters.

5.6 Excitatory and Inhibitory Receptors

An ionotropic receptor has a binding site for a neurotransmitter and a pore that allows ion flow and so mediates excitation—direct and rapid neurotransmitter action. A metabotropic receptor has no pore but, through a second messenger, can influence a variety of metabolic activities in the cell to mediate inhibition—slower neurotransmitter action.

5.7 Neurotransmitter Activating Systems and Behavior

Activating systems of neurons that employ the same principal neurotransmitter influence various general aspects of behavior. Many diseases and other neurological conditions may have their bases in neurotransmitter malfunction in one or another system. For example, the cholinergic, dopaminergic, noradrenergic, and serotonergic activating systems have been associated with brain diseases. Other activating systems include the histamine, orexin, and opioid systems, all of which influence wakefulness. Understanding neurotransmitter function also can facilitate treatments.

References

Brook, D. J., and P. Piccini. Imaging in Parkinson's disease: The role of monoamines in behavior. *Biological Psychiatry* 49:906–918, 2006.

Bukalo, O., E. Campanac, D. A. Hoffman, and R. D. Fields. Synaptic plasticity by antidromic firing during hippocampal network oscillations. *Proceedings of the National Academy of Sciences U. S. A.* 110:5175–5180, 2013.

Cannon, W. B. *Bodily Changes in Pain, Hunger, Fear and Rage.* New York: D. Appleton and Co., 1920.

Iversen, L. L., S. D. Iversen, F. E. Bloom, and R. H. Roth. *Introduction to neuropsychopharmacology.* New York: Oxford University Press, 2009.

Katz, B. On the quantal mechanism of neurotransmitter release. *Nobel Lectures, Physiology or Medicine 1963–1970.* Amsterdam: Elsevier Publishing Company, 1965.

Loewi, O. *The Chemical Transmission of Nerve Action. Nobel Lectures, Physiology or Medicine 1922–1941.* Amsterdam: Elsevier Publishing Company, 1965.

Sámano, C., F. Cifuentes, and M. A. Morales. Neurotransmitter segregation: Functional and plastic implications. *Progress in Neurobiology* 97:277–287, 2012.

6 The Influence of Drugs and Hormones on Behavior

PORTRAIT   The Case of the Frozen Addict

Patient 1: During the first 4 days of July 1982, a 42-year-old man used 4½ grams of a "new synthetic heroin." The substance was injected intravenously three or four times daily and caused a burning sensation at the site of injection. The immediate effects were different from those of heroin, producing an unusual "spacey" high as well as transient visual distortions and hallucinations. Two days after the final injection, he awoke to find that he was "frozen" and could move only in "slow motion." He had to "think through each movement" to carry it out. He was described as stiff, slow, nearly mute, and catatonic during repeated emergency room visits from July 9 to July 11. (Ballard et al., 1985, p. 949)

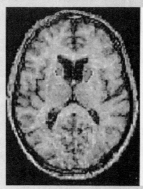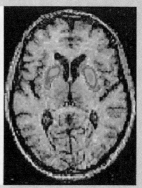

Mendez, et. al. Cell type analysis of functional fetal dopamine cell suspension transplants in the striatum and substantia nigra of patients with Parkinson's disease. *Brain* 2005 Jul;128(Pt 7):1498-510. Epub 2005 May 4.

Thus began a scientific detective story. Patient 1 was one of seven adults hospitalized at about the same time in California. All showed symptoms of severe Parkinson's disease that appeared very suddenly after injecting synthetic heroin sold on the streets in the summer of 1982.

J. William Langston (2008) and colleagues found a contaminant called MPTP (1-methyl-4-phenyl-1, 2, 3, 6-tetrahydropyridine) in the heroin, the result of poor preparation during synthesis. Experimental results in rodents showed that MPTP was not itself responsible for the patients' symptoms but was metabolized into MPP+ (1-methyl-4-phenylpyridinium), a neurotoxin.

The autopsy of one individual who was suspected of having died of MPTP poisoning showed that the victim suffered a selective loss of dopamine (DA) neurons in the substantia nigra. The rest of the brain appeared healthy. Injecting MPTP into monkeys, rats, and mice produced similar symptoms and a similar selective loss of DA neurons in the substantia nigra.

In 1988, Patient 1 received an experimental treatment at University Hospital in Lund, Sweden. DA neurons taken from human fetal brains at autopsy were implanted into his caudate nucleus and putamen (Widner et al., 1992). Patient 1 had no serious postoperative complications and his condition improved after 24 months. He could dress and feed himself, visit the bathroom with help, and make trips outside his home. He responded much better to medication. The MRIs contrast DA levels in the brain of a Parkinson's patient before (left) and 28 months after implantation (right).

This scientific detective story resulted in important discoveries for neuropsychology. The drug MPTP became a new tool for producing animal models of Parkinson's disease. The search for environmental compounds that can mimic MPTP's effects revealed that certain pesticides and herbicides might cause some cases of Parkinson's disease. The finding that grafting neural tissue into the brain of a relatively young person can be beneficial sustains the promise that damaged brains can be restored. Finally, that a drug can quickly and selectively damage the brain raised suspicion that many drugs and related compounds have unsuspected neurotoxic actions.

The study of how drugs affect the nervous system and behavior—**psychopharmacology**—is the subject of this chapter. We begin by looking at ways in which drugs are administered, what routes they take to reach the central nervous system, how they are eliminated from the body, and how they act at the synapse. We next group *psychoactive drugs* based on their major behavioral effects, and then examine individual responses and addiction. Many drug-related principles apply to the action of hormones, the chapter's closing topic.

In considering how drugs produce their effects on the brain, take caution: the sheer number of neurotransmitters, receptors, and possible sites of drug action is astounding. Psychopharmacology research has made important advances, but neuroscientists do not know everything there is to know about any drug.

6.1 Principles of Psychopharmacology

A *drug* is a chemical compound administered to bring about some desired change in the body. Usually drugs are used to diagnose, treat, or prevent illness; to relieve pain and suffering; or to improve an adverse physiological condition. Throughout human history, drugs have also been used as food, for recreation, even as poisons. Today, they are also used as research tools.

Psychoactive drugs are substances that act to alter mood, thought, or behavior, are used to manage neuropsychological illness, and may be abused. Some psychoactive drugs can also act as toxins, producing sickness, brain damage, or death.

Routes of Drug Administration

To be effective, a psychoactive drug has to reach its target in the nervous system. The way in which a drug enters and passes through the body to reach that target is called its *route of administration*. Drugs can be taken orally; inhaled; administered through rectal suppositories; absorbed from patches applied to the skin; or injected into the bloodstream, into a muscle, or even into the brain (**Figure 6.1**).

Taking a drug by mouth is usually convenient and safe, but not all drugs can withstand the acidity of gastric secretions or penetrate digestive-tract walls. To reach the bloodstream, an ingested drug must first be absorbed through the lining of the stomach or small intestine. A liquid drug is absorbed more readily than is a solid. Drugs taken in solid form are not absorbed unless they can be dissolved by the stomach's gastric juices.

Other chemical properties of the drug also affect absorption. A weak acid, such as alcohol, is readily absorbed across the stomach lining. A base, such as a B vitamin, is not as readily absorbed until it reaches the intestines, which have a large surface area to facilitate absorption.

The drug must next enter the bloodstream, where it encounters a different set of barriers. Blood has a high water concentration, so a drug must be *hydrophilic* to mix with it. A *hydrophobic* substance will be blocked from entering the bloodstream. If a drug does make its way into the circulatory system, the blood's 6-liter volume dilutes it.

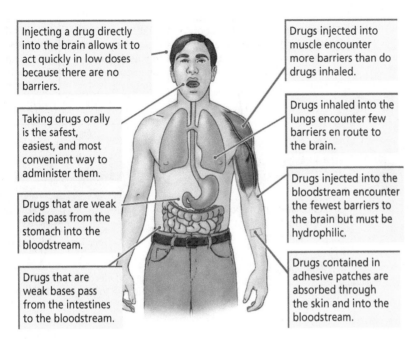

Injecting a drug directly into the brain allows it to act quickly in low doses because there are no barriers.

Taking drugs orally is the safest, easiest, and most convenient way to administer them.

Drugs that are weak acids pass from the stomach into the bloodstream.

Drugs that are weak bases pass from the intestines to the bloodstream.

Drugs injected into muscle encounter more barriers than do drugs inhaled.

Drugs inhaled into the lungs encounter few barriers en route to the brain.

Drugs injected into the bloodstream encounter the fewest barriers to the brain but must be hydrophilic.

Drugs contained in adhesive patches are absorbed through the skin and into the bloodstream.

Ⓢ **Figure 6.1** ◄

Routes of Drug Administration

To reach a neurological target, a drug must also travel from the blood into the extracellular fluid. This part of the journey requires that the drug molecules be small enough to pass through the pores of capillaries, the tiny vessels that carry blood to the body's cells. Even if the drug makes this passage, it encounters other obstacles. The extracellular fluid's volume of roughly 35 liters of water dilutes the drug even further, and if it passes through cell membranes, the drug is at risk of being modified or destroyed by various metabolic processes taking place in the cells.

Routes of Drug Removal

After a drug has been administered, the body soon begins to catabolize (break down) and remove it. Diluted drugs are sequestered in many regions throughout the body, including fat cells. They are also catabolized throughout the body, broken down in the kidneys and liver as well as in the intestine by bile. They are excreted in urine, feces, sweat, breast milk, and exhaled air. Drugs developed for therapeutic purposes are usually designed not only to increase their chances of reaching their targets but also to enhance their survival time in the body, for example, sequestered in fat cells.

The liver is especially active in catabolizing drugs, owing to the presence of a family of catabolizing enzymes called *cytochrome P450*. (Some are also present in the gastrointestinal tract.) Substances that cannot be catabolized or excreted from the body can build up and become poisonous. For instance, the metal mercury is not easily eliminated and can produce severe neurological damage (Eto, 2006).

Drugs that are eliminated from the body can remain problematic. They may be reingested in food and water by many animal species, including humans. Some may then affect fertility, embryonic development, and even the

Figure 6.2 ▶

Blood–Brain Barrier
Capillaries in most of the body allow for the passage of substances across capillary cell membranes, but those in the brain, stimulated by the actions of astrocytes, form the tight junctions of the blood–brain barrier.

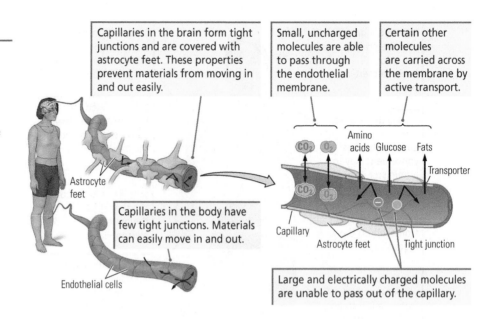

Capillaries in the brain form tight junctions and are covered with astrocyte feet. These properties prevent materials from moving in and out easily.

Small, uncharged molecules are able to pass through the endothelial membrane.

Certain other molecules are carried across the membrane by active transport.

Astrocyte feet

Capillaries in the body have few tight junctions. Materials can easily move in and out.

Endothelial cells

Amino acids Glucose Fats

CO_2 O_2

CO_2 O_2

Transporter

Capillary

Astrocyte feet

Tight junction

Large and electrically charged molecules are unable to pass out of the capillary.

physiology and behavior of adult organisms. This problem can be limited by redesigning waste-management systems to remove drug by-products eliminated by humans as well as by other animals (Radjenović et al., 2009).

Revisiting the Blood–Brain Barrier

Recall from Section 3.2 that the *blood–brain barrier* prevents many substances from entering the brain's rich capillary network. In fact, no neuron is farther than about 50 mm away from a capillary. **Figure 6.2** shows the single layer of thin, flat **endothelial cells** that compose brain capillaries surrounded by the end feet of astrocytes covering about 80 percent of a capillary's outer surface. Astrocytes help maintain the **tight junctions** between the fused membranes of endothelial cells, which allow substances to pass through in only one of two ways:

1. Small molecules such as oxygen and carbon dioxide, which are not ionized and so are fat-soluble, can pass through the capillary wall.

2. Molecules of glucose, amino acids, and other nutrients can be carried across the capillary by **active-transport systems**, specialized protein pumps, such as the sodium–potassium ion pump described in Section 4.2, that convey a particular substance.

The capillary cell walls in the three brain regions shown in **Figure 6.3** lack a blood–brain barrier. The **pituitary gland** of the hypothalamus secretes many hormones into the blood, and other hormones carried to the pituitary gland by the blood trigger their release. The absence of a blood–brain barrier at the **area postrema** of the lower brainstem allows toxic substances in the blood to trigger a vomiting response. The **pineal gland** also lacks a blood–brain barrier and is therefore open to the hormones that modulate the day–night cycles this gland controls.

Figure 6.3 ▼

Barrier-Free Brain Sites

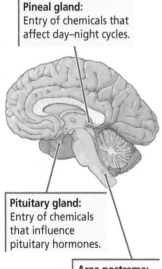

Pineal gland:
Entry of chemicals that affect day–night cycles.

Pituitary gland:
Entry of chemicals that influence pituitary hormones.

Area postrema:
Entry of toxic substances that induce vomiting.

Drug Routes and Dosage

Generally, fewer barriers separate a drug from its target if the drug is inhaled rather than swallowed, and fewer still if it is injected into the blood. The fewest obstacles are encountered if a drug is injected directly into the brain. Given the fearsome obstacles that psychoactive drugs encounter on their journey from mouth to brain, it is clear why inhaling a drug or injecting it into the bloodstream has advantages: these routes of administration bypass the obstacle of the stomach. In fact, with each obstacle eliminated en route to the brain, the drug dosage can be reduced by a factor of 10, and the drug will still have the same effects.

For example, 1 milligram (1000 micrograms, μg) of amphetamine, a psychomotor stimulant, produces a noticeable behavioral change when ingested orally. If inhaled into the lungs or injected into the blood, thereby circumventing the stomach, 100 μg of the drug (1000 $\mu g \div 10$) produces the same results. Similarly, if amphetamine is injected into the cerebrospinal fluid, thereby bypassing both the stomach and the blood, 10 μg is enough to produce an identical outcome, as is 1 μg if dilution in the CSF also is skirted and the drug is injected directly onto target neurons.

This math is well known to sellers and users of illicit drugs. Drugs that can be inhaled or injected intravenously are much cheaper to use because the doses required are a fraction of those needed for drugs taken by mouth, and they reach their brain target quickly.

6.2 Drug Actions in Synapses

Almost all potent psychoactive drugs have been discovered accidentally, either many thousands of years ago or more recently in the case of drugs used to treat neuropsychological illness (**Table 6.1**). Most psychoactive drugs work by influencing the chemical reactions at synapses. Advances in understanding synaptic activity in the brain help explain both the psychoactive effects of drugs and their potential harmful effects. Thus, to understand the psychoactive effects of drugs, we now explore how they modify synaptic activity.

Table 6.1 Drugs used for the treatment of mental illness

Illness	Drug Class	Representative Drug	Common Trade Name	Discoverer
Schizophrenia	Phenothiazines	Chlorpromazine	Largactile, Thorazine	Jean Delay and Pierre Deniker (France), 1952
	Butyrophenone	Haloperidol	Haldol	Paul Janssen (Belgium), 1957
Depression	Monoamine oxidase (MAO) inhibitors	Iproniazid	Marsilid	Nathan S. Kline and J. C. Saunders (United States), 1956
	Tricyclic antidepressants	Imipramine	Tofranil	Roland Kuhn (Switzerland), 1957
	Selective serotonin reuptake inhibitors	Fluoxetine	Prozac	Eli Lilly Company, 1986
Bipolar disorder	Lithium (metallic element)			John Cade (Australia), 1949
Anxiety disorders	Benzodiazepines	Chlordiazepoxide	Valium	Leo Sternbach (Poland), 1940
		Meprobamate	Equanil, Miltown	Frank Berger and William Bradley (Czechoslovakia), 1946

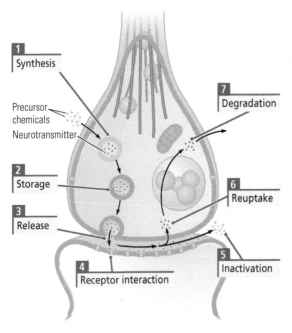

Figure 6.4 ▲

Points of Influence In principle, a drug can modify any of the seven major chemical processes shown in the diagram. Modification(s) can result in reduced or enhanced synaptic transmission, depending on the drug's action as an agonist or antagonist.

Steps in Synaptic Transmission

Figure 6.4 summarizes seven major events that contribute to synaptic neurotransmission. Each is a site of drug action. *Neurotransmitter synthesis* (1) can take place in the cell body, axon, or terminal. The neurotransmitter may then be (2) *stored* in storage granules or in vesicles until it is (3) *released* from the terminal's presynaptic membrane to (4) *act on a receptor* embedded in the postsynaptic membrane. Excess neurotransmitter in the synapse is either (5) *deactivated* or (6) taken back into the presynaptic terminal (*reuptake*) for reuse. The synapse also has mechanisms for (7) *degrading* excess neurotransmitter and removing unneeded by-products.

Each component of neurotransmission entails one or more chemical reactions that drugs can potentially influence. **Agonists** are drugs that increase the effectiveness of neurotransmission; **antagonists** decrease its effectiveness. Agonists and antagonists can work in a variety of ways, but their end results are always the same. To illustrate, consider the neurotransmitter acetylcholine.

Examples of Drug Action: An Acetylcholine Synapse

Figure 6.5 shows how representative drugs and toxins act as agonists or antagonists at the ACh synapse between motor neurons and muscles. Some substances may be new to you, but you have probably heard of others. Two substances named in Figure 6.5 are toxins that influence the release of ACh from the axon terminal:

- **Black widow spider venom** is an agonist because it promotes ACh release to excess. In their insect prey, the excitation caused by excess ACh is sufficient to cause paralysis and death. A black widow spider bite does not contain enough toxin to paralyze a person, though a victim may feel some muscle weakness.

- **Botulinum toxin**, or **botulin**, is a poisonous agent produced by a bacterium that sometimes grows in improperly processed canned foods. Botulin acts as an antagonist because it blocks the release of ACh. The effects of botulin poisoning can last for weeks to months. A severe case can result in paralysis of movement and breathing, leading to death. Botulin also has medical uses. If injected into a muscle, it paralyzes that muscle, blocking unwanted muscular twitches or contractions in conditions such as cerebral palsy. It is also sold under the trade name Botox for use in cosmetic procedures to reduce wrinkles by relaxing muscles, and, because it can also inactivate pain fibers, it is injected into muscles and joints to reduce pain.

Figure 6.5 also includes two drugs that act on ACh receptors:

- **Nicotine**, a chemical in cigarette smoke, acts as an agonist to stimulate cholinergic receptors. The cholinergic receptor at the neuromuscular junction (see Figure 5.6) is called a **nicotinic receptor** because of this action. Nicotine's structure is enough like that of ACh to fit into the ACh receptors' binding sites.

- **Curare**, a poison extracted from the seeds of a South American plant, acts as an antagonist at cholinergic receptors, blocking them and preventing ACh from acting. Curare acts quickly and is cleared from the body in minutes. Large doses, however, arrest movement and breathing long enough to result in death.

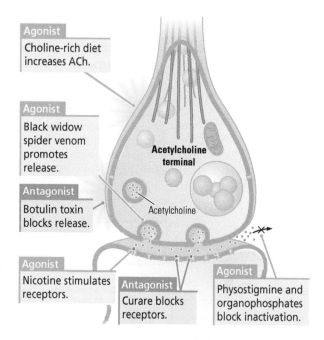

Early European explorers encountered Indians along the Amazon River who killed small animals by shooting them with arrows coated with curare. The hunters themselves were not poisoned when eating the animals because curare cannot pass from the gut into the body. Many curarelike drugs have been synthesized. Some are used to paralyze large animals briefly for identification tagging or examination. Skeletal muscles are more sensitive to curarelike drugs than respiratory muscles are, so an appropriate dose will paralyze an animal but still allow it to breathe.

Figure 6.5 ▲

ACh Agonists and Antagonists Drugs and nutrients can affect ACh transmission by altering its release, its binding to the postsynaptic receptor, and its breakdown or inactivation.

The final drug action shown in Figure 6.5 is that of **physostigmine**, which inhibits acetylcholinesterase (AChE), the enzyme that breaks down ACh. Physostigmine therefore acts as an agonist to increase the amount of ACh available in the synapse. Physostigmine, obtained from a species of African bean, was used as a poison by African tribes. Large doses can be toxic because, like black widow spider venom, they produce excessive excitation at the neuromuscular synapse and so disrupt movement and breathing.

Small doses of physostigmine, however, are used to treat a condition called **myasthenia gravis** (the name means "muscular weakness"), in which muscle receptors are less than normally responsive to ACh, leading to fatigue. Myasthenia gravis tends to affect women and was viewed as a psychological condition—actually termed *tired housewife's syndrome*—until an understanding of the ACh synapse provided the correct explanation and treatment (see Section 26.8).

Physostigmine's action is short-lived, lasting for only a few minutes to at most half an hour, but another class of compounds, called **organophosphates**, bind irreversibly to AChE and consequently are extremely toxic. Many insecticides and herbicides are organophosphates, and they are also used in chemical warfare. One potent organophosphate agent is the lethal nerve gas sarin. Although banned by the Chemical Weapons Convention of 1993, sarin was used by the governments of Iraq, in 1999, and Syria, in 2013, against their own citizens.

Does a drug or toxin that affects neuromuscular synapses also affect ACh synapses in the brain? That depends on whether the substance can cross the blood–brain barrier. Physostigmine and nicotine can readily pass the barrier; curare cannot.

Tolerance

A dramatic example of **tolerance**—the decline in response to the repeated administration of a drug—was described by H. Isbell and coworkers (1955) for a group of prisoner volunteers. These researchers gave the participants enough alcohol daily in a 13-week period to keep them in a constant state of intoxication (**Figure 6.6**A). Yet they found that the participants did not stay drunk for 3 months straight.

In the first days of the experiment, participants showed rapidly rising levels of blood alcohol and behavioral signs of intoxication after consuming alcohol, as shown in the top graph in Figure 6.6B. Between the twelfth and twentieth days, however, blood-alcohol concentrations and the signs of intoxication fell (middle graph), even though the participants maintained a constant alcohol intake.

These results were the products of three different kinds of tolerance:

1. **Metabolic tolerance** develops from an increase in enzymes needed to break down alcohol in the liver, blood, and brain. As a result, the body metabolizes alcohol more quickly, so blood-alcohol levels are reduced.

2. **Cellular tolerance** develops as neurons adjust their activities to minimize the effects of alcohol in the blood. Cellular tolerance helps explain why the behavioral signs of intoxication may be very low despite a relatively high blood-alcohol level.

3. **Learned tolerance** also contributes to the drop in outward signs of intoxication. As people learn to cope with the daily demands of living while under the influence of alcohol, they may show reduced signs of drunkenness.

With repeated administration, the effects of many psychoactive drugs may progressively diminish, owing to tolerance. A dose of 100 mg of morphine is sufficient to cause profound sedation—even death—in some first-time users, but those who have developed tolerance to the drug have been known to take 4000 mg without adverse effects. Long-time amphetamine users may need to take doses 100 or more times as great as those they took initially to produce the same behavioral effect.

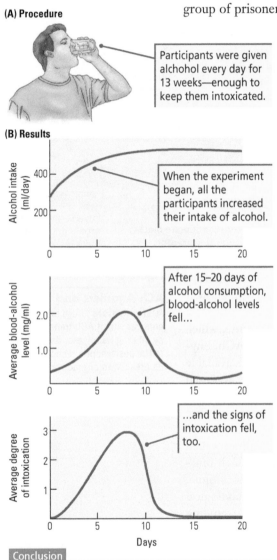

(A) Procedure

Participants were given alchohol every day for 13 weeks—enough to keep them intoxicated.

(B) Results

When the experiment began, all the participants increased their intake of alcohol.

After 15–20 days of alcohol consumption, blood-alcohol levels fell...

...and the signs of intoxication fell, too.

Days

Conclusion

Because of tolerance, much more alcohol was required by the end of the study to obtain the same level of intoxication that was produced at the beginning.

Figure 6.6 ▲

Alcohol Intake, Blood-Alcohol Level, and Behavior Over the first 20 days of steady drinking, the relation between blood-alcohol level and behavioral intoxication changed owing to tolerance. (Data from Isbell et al., 1955.)

Sensitization

Whereas tolerance generally develops with constantly repeated use of a given drug, **sensitization**, increased responsiveness to equal doses of a drug, is much more likely to develop with occasional use. To demonstrate, Terry Robinson and Jill Becker (1986) isolated rats in observation boxes and recorded their reactions to an injection of amphetamine, which stimulates dopamine receptors. Every 3 or 4 days they injected the rats and observed that their motor activity—sniffing, rearing, and walking—was more vigorous with each administration of the same dose of the drug, as graphed in **Figure 6.7**A.

The increased response on successive tests was not due to the animals becoming comfortable with the test situation. Control animals that received no drug did not display a similar escalation. Moreover, the effect of amphetamine was enduring. Even when two injections were separated by months, the animals still showed an increased response to the drug.

Sensitization also develops to drugs with depressive effects. Figure 6.7B shows the changing effects of flupentixol, a dopamine antagonist that blocks

(A) Procedure 1

In the Robinson and Becker study, animals were given periodic injections of the same dose of amphetamine. Then the researchers measured the number of times each rat reared in its cage.

(B) Procedure 2

In the Whishaw study, animals were given different numbers of swims after being injected with flupentixol. Then the researchers measured their speed to escape to a platform in a swimming pool.

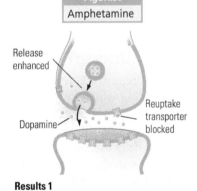

Agonist
Amphetamine

Release enhanced

Dopamine

Reuptake transporter blocked

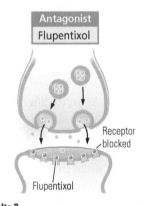

Antagonist
Flupentixol

Receptor blocked

Flupentixol

Results 1

Number of incidents of rearing / Number of injections

Conclusion 1

Sensitization, as indicated by increased rearing, develops with periodic repeated injections.

Results 2

Time to platform (s) / Number of trials

Conclusion 2

Sensitization depends on the occurrence of the behavior; only the number of swims increases the time it takes a rat to reach the platform.

Figure 6.7 ◄

Sensitization from Agonists and Antagonists
(A) Amphetamine stimulates dopamine release and blocks reuptake. Each injection of the same dose of the drug in rats produces a greater effect as measured by an increase in locomotion. (B) The major tranquilizer flupentixol blocks dopamine receptors. After each injection, a swimming trial is slower until the rat can no longer escape from the swimming pool. (Data from Robinson and Becker, 1986, and Whishaw et al., 1989.)

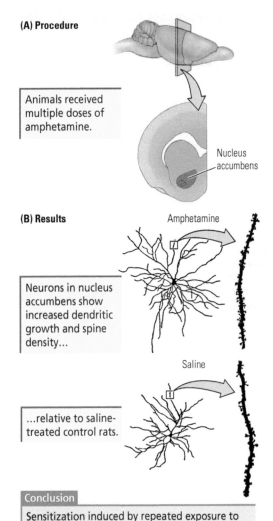

(A) Procedure

Animals received multiple doses of amphetamine.

Nucleus accumbens

(B) Results

Amphetamine

Neurons in nucleus accumbens show increased dendritic growth and spine density...

Saline

...relative to saline-treated control rats.

Conclusion

Sensitization induced by repeated exposure to amphetamine changes the structure of neurons.

Figure 6.8 ▲

Psychoactive Drugs and Plasticity Rats that show sensitization to amphetamine (or to cocaine) undergo increased dendritic growth and increased spine density compared with saline-treated control rats. (Data from Robinson and Kolb, 1997, p. 8495.)

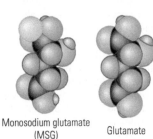

Monosodium glutamate (MSG)

Glutamate

Domoic acid

DA receptors, on the swimming behavior of rats in a study conducted by Ian Whishaw and colleagues (1989). The rats were trained to swim a short distance to a platform in a swimming pool. Once trained, they reached the platform within 1 to 2 seconds of immersion. On the first few swims after the flupentixol injections, the rats swam normally, but in subsequent trials, they began to slow down. After about 12 trials, each separated by a few minutes, the rats simply sank when placed in the water and had to be removed to prevent drowning.

This effect was not simply due to fatigue. If the rats were injected and placed in water only once each day for 12 days, the same pattern of results was obtained. Sensitization to the drug depended on the number of swimming trials, regardless of the time that elapsed between them or the number of times the drug was given. Thus, flupentixol changed dopamine neurons that mediate the behavior only if the rats engaged in the behavior.

Sensitization is long-lasting because it is accompanied by structural changes in the brain that are long-lasting. **Figure 6.8** compares the effects of amphetamine and saline treatments on cells in the nucleus accumbens, a part of the subcortical basal ganglia. Neurons in amphetamine-treated brains have more dendritic branches and an increased number of spines compared with those treated with saline. These plastic changes were not found throughout the brain but were limited to regions that receive a large dopamine projection.

Can Drugs Cause Brain Damage?

As exemplified in the opening Portrait, drugs of abuse can cause brain damage in humans, but determining which drugs do so is difficult. It is hard to sort out other life experiences from drug-taking experiences, to determine genetic susceptibility to drugs, and to identify subtle changes, even when they are associated with repeated drug use. Many natural substances can act as neurotoxins; **Table 6.2** lists some of them. These substances cause brain damage by acting in myriad ways, including poisoning metabolic pathways, blocking synaptic action, and altering development.

In the late 1960s, many reports circulated linking monosodium glutamate, MSG, a salty-tasting, flavor-enhancing food additive, to headaches in some people. In the process of investigating this effect, scientists placed MSG on cultured neurons or injected it into the brains of experimental animals and found it produced neuron death. These findings raised the question of whether large doses of the neurotransmitter glutamate, which MSG resembles structurally, might also be toxic to neurons in some circumstances. It turned out that it is.

Glutamate-receptor activation results in an influx of Ca^{2+} into the cell. Excessive Ca^{2+} may, through second messengers, activate a "suicide gene" in a cell's DNA leading to **apoptosis**, cell death that is genetically programmed. The discovery of this mechanism led to the understanding that a drug might be toxic not only because of its general effect on cell function but also as an epigenetic agent that activates gene processes related to apoptosis.

Many glutamatelike chemicals, including domoic acid, a causal agent in shellfish poisoning; kainic acid, a toxin in seaweed; and ibotenic acid, which is found in some poisonous mushrooms, kill neurons by a similar action. Some psychoactive drugs, such as phencyclidine and ketamine (both once used as anesthetic agents) also act as glutamate agonists, leaving open the possibility that at high doses they, too, can cause neuronal death.

Determining whether recreational drug use causes brain damage is difficult. Chronic alcohol use, for instance, can be associated with damage to the thalamus and limbic system, producing severe memory disorders. Alcohol itself does not cause this damage; rather, it stems from complications related to alcohol abuse, including thiamine (vitamin B_1) deficiencies due to poor diet. Thiamine plays a vital role in maintaining cell-membrane structure.

Nevertheless, some drugs of abuse do produce harmful effects on the body (Milroy and Parai, 2011). The strongest evidence that a recreational drug can cause brain damage and cognitive impairments comes from the study of the synthetic amphetaminelike drug MDMA (also called hallucinogenic amphetamine, *ecstasy*, and in pure powder form, *Molly*) (Büttner, 2011). It is often taken by people to enhance party experiences, for example at a rave, an all-night party featuring lights and music. Findings from animal studies show that doses of MDMA approximating those taken by human users result in the degeneration of very fine serotonergic nerve terminals. In monkeys, the terminal loss may be permanent, as shown in **Figure 6.9**.

Memory impairments and damage revealed by brain imaging have been reported in MDMA users and may be a result of similar neuronal damage (Cowan et al., 2008). MDMA may also contain a contaminant, paramethoxymethamphetamine (PMMA). This toxic amphetamine is also called *Dr. Death* because the difference between a dose that causes behavioral effects and a dose that causes death is minuscule (Vevelstad et al., 2012). Contamination by unknown compounds can occur in any drug purchased on the street.

The psychoactive properties of cocaine are similar to those of amphetamine, and it also has deleterious side effects. Cocaine use is related to the blockage of cerebral blood flow and other changes in blood circulation. Brain-imaging studies also suggest that cocaine use can be toxic to neurons because a number of brain regions are reduced in size in cocaine users (Barrós-Loscertales et al., 2011).

Table 6.2 Some neurotoxins, their sources and actions

Substance	Origin	Action
Alcohol	Fermentation	Alters brain development
Apamin	Bees and wasps	Blocks Ca^{2+} channels
Botulinum toxin	*Clostridium botulinum* bacteria	Blocks ACh release
Caffeine	Coffee bean	Blocks adenosine receptors and Ca^{2+} channels
Colchicine	Crocus plant	Blocks microtubules
Curare	Berry of *Strychnos* vine	Blocks ACh receptors
Domoic acid	Seaweed, shell fish	Mimics glutamate
Ibotenic acid	*Amanita muscaria* and *Amanita pantherina* mushrooms	Similar to domoic acid
Magnesium	Metallic element	Blocks Ca^{2+} channels
Mercury	Metallic element	Blocks many brain enzymes
Rabies virus	Animal bite	Blocks ACh receptors
Reserpine	*Rauwulfia* shrubs	Destroys storage granules
Spider venom	Black widow spider	Stimulates ACh release
Strychnine	Plants of genus *Strychnos*	Blocks glycine
Tetrodotoxin	Pufferfish	Blocks Na^+ ions

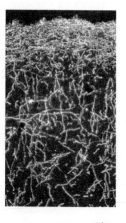 

Figure 6.9 ▲

Drug Damage Treatment with MDMA changes the density of serotonin axons in the neocortex of a squirrel monkey: (left) normal monkey; (right) monkey 18 months after MDMA treatment. (From U.D. McCann, K.A. Lowe, and G.A. Ricaurte, From Long Lasting Effects of Recreational Drugs of Abuse on the Central Nervous System, *The Neuroscientist* 3:401, 1997.)

Some cases of chronic marijuana use have been associated with psychotic attacks. The marijuana plant contains at least 400 chemicals, 60 or more of which are structurally related to its active ingredient, tetrahydrocannabinol. Determining whether a psychotic attack is related to THC or to some other ingredient contained in marijuana or to aggravation of an existing condition is almost impossible (DeLisi, 2008).

6.3 Grouping Psychoactive Drugs

Systematically classifying psychoactive drugs is difficult because most drugs influence many behaviors. Further, drugs with similar chemical structures can have different effects, and drugs with different structures can have similar effects.

The groupings of psychoactive drugs in **Table 6.3** are based on their most-pronounced behavioral or psychoactive effects (Julien et al., 2011). Each of the five groups may contain from a few to many thousands of different chemicals in its subcategories. Most psychoactive drugs have at least three names: a chemical name, a generic name, and a brand name—and some have many street names. The chemical name describes a drug's chemical structure; the generic name is nonproprietary; the capitalized brand name is proprietary to the pharmaceutical company that sells it; growers, sellers, and users all create street names.

Group I: Antianxiety Agents and Sedative Hypnotics

At low doses, antianxiety drugs and sedative hypnotics reduce anxiety; at medium doses, they sedate; and, at high doses, they anesthetize or induce coma. At very high doses, they can kill (**Figure 6.10**). Antianxiety drugs are safer at high doses than sedative hypnotics are.

Table 6.3 **Grouping psychoactive drugs**

Group I Antianxiety agents and sedative hypnotics

Benzodiazepines: diazepam (Valium); Xanax, Klonopin

Barbiturates (anesthetic agents); alcohol

Other anesthetics: gamma-hydroxyburerate (GHB), ketamine (Special K), phencyclidine (PCP, angel dust)

Group II Antipsychotic agents

First generation: phenothiazines: chlorpromazine (Thorazine); butyrophenones: haloperidol (Haldol)

Second generation: clozapine (Clozaril), aripiprazole (Abilify, Aripiprex)

Group III Antidepressants and mood stabilizers

Antidepressants
MAO inhibitors
Tricyclic antidepressants: imipramine (Tofranil)
SSRIs (atypical antidepressants): fluoxetine (Prozac); sertraline (Zoloft); paroxetine (Paxil, Seroxat).

Mood stabilizers
Lithium, sodium valproate, carbamazepine (Tegretol)

Group IV Opioid analgesics

Morphine, codeine, heroin

Endomorphins, enkephalins, dynorphins

Group V Psychotropics

Behavioral stimulants: amphetamine, cocaine

Psychedelic and hallucinogenic stimulants

ACh psychedelics: atropine, nicotine

Anandamide psychedelics: tetrahydrocannabinol (THC)

Glutamate psychedelics: phencyclidine (PCP, angel dust), ketamine (Special K)

Norepinephrine psychedelics: mescaline

Serotonin psychedelics: lysergic acid diethylamide (LSD), psilocybin, MDMA (ecstasy)

General stimulants: caffeine

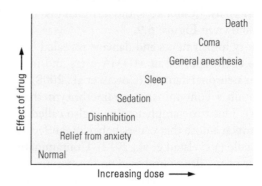

Figure 6.10 ▲

Behavioral Continuum of Sedation
Increasing doses of sedative-hypnotic and antianxiety drugs affect behavior: low doses reduce anxiety and very high doses result in death.

The best-known **antianxiety agents**, also known as minor tranquilizers, are the benzodiazepines such as diazepam. The benzodiazepines are marketed in the widely prescribed drugs Valium, Xanax, and Klonopin. Benzodiazepines are often used by people who are having trouble coping with a major life stress. They are given to aid sleep and also used as presurgical relaxation agents.

The sedative hypnotics include alcohol and barbiturates. Alcohol is well known because it is so widely consumed. **Barbiturates** are sometimes still prescribed as a sleeping medication but are used mainly to induce anesthesia before surgery. Both alcohol and barbiturates induce sleep, anesthesia, and coma at doses only slightly higher than those that sedate.

A characteristic feature of sedative hypnotics is that the user who takes repeated doses develops tolerance: a larger dose is then required to maintain the drug's initial effect. **Cross-tolerance** results when the tolerance developed for one drug is carried over to a different member of the drug group. Cross-tolerance suggests that antianxiety and sedative-hypnotic drugs act on the nervous system in similar ways. One target common to both drug types is a receptor for the inhibitory neurotransmitter gamma-aminobutyric acid, or GABA. The $GABA_A$ receptor, illustrated in **Figure 6.11**, contains a chloride ion channel.

Excitation of the receptor by GABA produces an influx of Cl^- ions through its pore. An influx of Cl^- ions increases the concentration of negative charges inside the cell membrane, hyperpolarizing it and making it less likely to propagate an action potential. The inhibitory effect of GABA, therefore, is to decrease a neuron's firing rate. Widespread reduction of neuronal firing in part underlies the behavioral effects of drugs that affect the $GABA_A$ synapse.

The $GABA_A$ receptor illustrated in Figure 6.11 has binding sites for chemicals other than GABA, including, shown in the panel at left, a barbiturate site and, shown in the center panel, a benzodiazepine site. Activation of each site also promotes an influx of Cl^- ions, but in different ways. Activating the barbiturate site increases the binding of GABA, and of benzodiazepines if present, and maximizes the time the pore is open. Activating the benzodiazepine site enhances the natural action of GABA by influencing the frequency that the ion pore opens in response to GABA. Because the actions at these three sites summate, sedative hypnotics—including alcohol—and antianxiety drugs should not

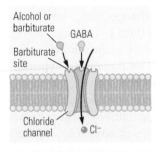

Sedative-hypnotic drugs (alcohol or barbiturates) increase the binding of GABA by maximizing the time the pore is open.

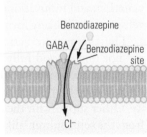

Antianxiety drugs (benzodiazepines) influence the frequency of pore openings.

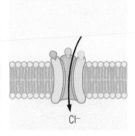

Because of their different actions, these drugs should not be taken together.

⊚ Figure 6.11 ◄

Drug Effects at the $GABA_A$ Receptor Sedative hypnotics act at the barbiturate site (left), and antianxiety agents act at the benzodiazepine site (center). Taken together (right) these two types of drugs can be lethal.

be taken together. Combined doses reportedly contribute to as many deaths as occur annually from automobile accidents in the United States.

The $GABA_A$ receptor also has binding sites that, when active, block the ion pore. Picrotoxin, a compound that blocks the pore, produces overexcitation and epileptic discharges in postsynaptic neurons. Administration of $GABA_A$ agonists can block the action of picrotoxin. Sedative-hypnotic and antianxiety drugs are thus useful in treating epileptic discharges and may act in part through the $GABA_A$ receptor.

Many other psychoactive drugs have sedative-hypnotic and antianxiety actions. They include phencyclidine (PCP, angel dust) and two drugs—gamma-hydroxybutyric acid (GHB) and ketamine (Special K)—that have gained notoriety as date rape drugs. The latter are soluble in alcohol, act quickly, and, like other sedative hypnotics, impair memory for recent events. Because they can be dissolved in a drink, partygoers and clubbers should never accept drinks from anyone, drink from punch bowls, or leave drinks unattended.

Group II: Antipsychotic Agents

The term *psychosis* is applied to behavioral disorders such as schizophrenia, which is characterized by hallucinations (false sensory perceptions) and delusions (false beliefs), among a host of symptoms. The use of antipsychotic drugs has improved the functioning of schizophrenia patients and contributed to reduced numbers housed in institutions over the past half-century. The incidence of schizophrenia is high, about 1 in every 100 people, but antipsychotic drugs are not a cure, and many people with schizophrenia end up living on the streets or incarcerated in jails and prisons.

Antipsychotic agents have been widely used since the mid-1950s, beginning with the development of what are now called first-generation antipsychotics (FGAs), which include a class of drugs called the phenothiazines (e.g., chlorpromazine, Thorazine) and a class called the butyrophenones (e.g., haloperidol, Haldol). FGAs act mainly by blocking the dopamine D_2 receptor. Beginning in the 1980s, newer drugs, such as clozapine (Clozaril) and a number of other compounds, were developed and became the second-generation antipsychotics (SGAs). SGAs weakly block D_2 receptors but also block serotonin $5-HT_2$ receptors. Because antipsychotic drugs produce many side effects including weight gain, agitation, and motivational changes, drugs now in development will likely form a third generation.

The therapeutic actions of antipsychotic agents are not understood fully. The **dopamine hypothesis of schizophrenia** holds that some forms of the disease may be related to excessive dopamine activity. Other support for the dopamine hypothesis comes from the schizophrenialike symptoms of chronic users of amphetamine, a stimulant. As **Figure 6.12** shows, amphetamine is a dopamine agonist. It fosters the release of dopamine from the presynaptic membrane of D_2 synapses and blocks DA reuptake from the synaptic cleft. If amphetamine causes schizophrenialike symptoms by increasing dopamine activity, the argument is

© **Figure 6.12** ▼

Drug Effects at D$_2$ Receptors That the antipsychotic agent chlorpromazine can lessen schizophrenia symptoms, whereas the abuse of amphetamine and cocaine can produce them, suggests that excessive activity at the D_2 receptor is related to schizophrenia.

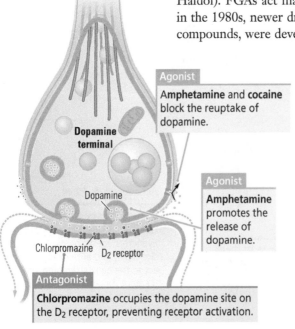

Agonist

Amphetamine and **cocaine** block the reuptake of dopamine.

Agonist

Amphetamine promotes the release of dopamine.

Antagonist

Chlorpromazine occupies the dopamine site on the D$_2$ receptor, preventing receptor activation.

that naturally occurring schizophrenia is related to excessive dopamine action too. Both FGAs and SGAs block the D_2 receptor, which has an immediate effect in reducing motor activity and a longer-term action of alleviating other symptoms in schizophrenia patients.

Other drug models of schizophrenia include the psychotropic stimulant LSD (lysergic acid diethylamide), which produces hallucinations and is a serotonin agonist that acts at the $5\text{-}HT_2$ receptor. Hallucinations are a symptom of schizophrenia, suggesting that excess serotonin action is involved. Two other psychotropic drugs that produce schizophrenialike symptoms, including hallucinations and out-of-body experiences, are phencyclidine and ketamine. As noted previously, formerly used as anesthetics, they also block glutamate receptors, suggesting the involvement of excitatory glutamate synapses in schizophrenia as well (Merritt et al., 2013).

Group III: Antidepressants and Mood Stabilizers

Major depression is a mood disorder characterized by prolonged feelings of worthlessness and guilt, disruption of normal eating habits, sleep disturbances, a general slowing of behavior, and frequent thoughts of suicide. At any given time, about 6 percent of the people experience major depression, and, in the course of a lifetime, 30 percent may experience at least one episode that lasts for months or longer.

Inadequate nutrition, stress from difficult life conditions, acute changes in neuronal function, and damage to brain neurons are among the factors implicated in depression. These factors may be related: nutritional deficiencies may increase vulnerability to stress; stress may change neuronal function, which if unrelieved, may lead to neuron damage.

Among the nutrient deficiencies that may be related to symptoms of depression (Smith et al., 2010) are folic acid and other B vitamins and omega-3 fatty acids, a rich source of vitamin D obtained from fish. Our skin synthesizes vitamin D on exposure to sunlight, but our bodies cannot store it. Vitamin D deficiency is reportedly widespread in people living in northern climates due to inadequate consumption of fish and/or lack of exposure to sunlight in winter months. Although Hoang and colleagues (2011) note an association between vitamin D deficiency and depressive symptoms, little is known about the relationship between long-term deficiencies in nutrients, depression and associated brain changes, and the effectiveness of dietary supplements.

Antidepressant Medications

Several types of drugs have antidepressant effects: **monoamine oxidase (MAO) inhibitors**; **tricyclic antidepressants**, so called because of their three-ringed chemical structure; **second-generation antidepressants**, sometimes called *atypical antidepressants* (see Table 6.3); and the antianxiety agent ketamine. Second-generation antidepressants lack a three-ringed structure, but they share some similarities to the tricyclics in their actions.

Antidepressants are thought to act by improving chemical neurotransmission at serotonin, noradrenaline, histamine, and ACh synapses, and perhaps at dopamine synapses as well. **Figure 6.13** shows the actions of MAO inhibitors and second-generation antidepressants at a serotonin synapse, the synapse on which most research is focused. MAO inhibitors and the tricyclic and

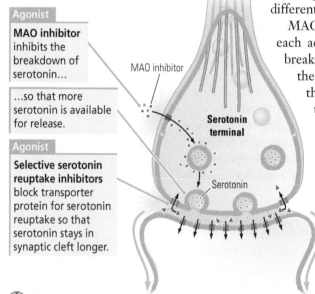

MAO inhibitor inhibits the breakdown of serotonin...

...so that more serotonin is available for release.

Selective serotonin reuptake inhibitors block transporter protein for serotonin reuptake so that serotonin stays in synaptic cleft longer.

Figure 6.13 ▲

Drug Effects at the Serotonin Synapse
Different antidepressant drugs act on 5-HT synapses in different ways to increase the availability of serotonin.

second-generation antidepressants all act as agonists but have different mechanisms for increasing serotonin availability.

MAO inhibitors provide for more serotonin release with each action potential by inhibiting MAO, an enzyme that breaks down serotonin within the axon terminal. In contrast, the tricyclics and second-generation antidepressants block the reuptake transporter that takes serotonin back into the axon terminal. The second-generation antidepressants are thought to be especially selective in blocking serotonin reuptake; consequently, some are also called **selective serotonin reuptake inhibitors** (SSRIs). Because the transporter is blocked, serotonin remains in the synaptic cleft, prolonging its action on postsynaptic receptors.

Although these drugs begin to affect synapses very quickly, their antidepressant actions take weeks to develop. One explanation is that antidepressants, especially SSRIs, stimulate second messengers in neurons to activate the repair of those damaged by stress. Of interest in this respect, one SSRI, fluoxetine (Prozac), increases the production of new neurons in the hippocampus, a limbic structure in the temporal lobes (DeCarolis and Eisch, 2010). As detailed in Section 6.5, the hippocampus is vulnerable to stress-induced damage, and its restoration by fluoxetine is proposed to underlie one of the drug's antidepressant effects (Mateus-Pinherio et al., 2013).

Even so, about 20 percent of patients with depression fail to respond to antidepressant drugs. Recent studies suggest that ketamine can very rapidly alleviate depressive symptoms, a finding that has stimulated the search for similar compounds that do not have ketamine's hallucinogenic properties (Browne and Lucki, 2013).

Of all psychological disorders, major depression is one of the most treatable, and cognitive and intrapersonal therapies are as effective as drug therapies (Comer, 2011). Most people recover from depression within a year of its onset. If the illness is left untreated, however, the incidence of suicide is high.

Mood Stabilizers

Bipolar disorder, once referred to as manic–depressive illness, is characterized by periods of depression alternating with normal periods and periods of intense excitation, or *mania*. According to the National Institute of Mental Health, bipolar disorder can affect as much as 2.6 percent of the adult U.S. population.

The difficulty of treating bipolar disorder with drugs is related to the difficulty of understanding how a disease produces symptoms that appear to be opposites: mania and depression. Consequently, bipolar disorder often is treated with a number of drugs, each directed toward a different symptom. **Mood stabilizers**, which include the salt lithium carbonate, mute the intensity of one pole of the disorder, thus making the other less likely to occur. Lithium does not directly affect mood and so may act by stimulating mechanisms of neuronal repair, such as the production of neuron growth factors.

A variety of drugs effective in treating epilepsy (carbamazepine, valproate) have positive effects, perhaps by muting neuronal excitability during the mania pole. And antipsychotic drugs that block D_2 receptors effectively control the hallucinations and delusions associated with mania. Because all these treatments have side effects, enhancing beneficial effects while minimizing side effects is a major focus of new drug development (Severus et al., 2012).

Group IV: Opioid Analgesics

An *opioid* is any compound that binds to a group of brain receptors that are also sensitive to morphine. The term *narcotic analgesic* was first used to describe these drugs because **opioid analgesics** have both sleep-inducing (narcotic) and pain-relieving (analgesic) properties. Opioids also have two natural sources.

One is opium, an extract from the seeds of the opium poppy, *Papaver somniferum*, shown in **Figure 6.14**. Opium has been used for thousands of years to produce euphoria, analgesia, sleep, and relief from diarrhea and coughing. In 1805, German chemist Friedrich Sertürner synthesized two pure opiates: codeine and morphine. Codeine is often an ingredient in prescription cough medicine and pain relievers: it is converted into morphine by the liver. Morphine, shown at center in Figure 6.14 and named for Morpheus, the Greek god of dreams, is a powerful pain reliever. Despite decades of research, no other drug has been found that exceeds morphine's effectiveness as an analgesic.

The second natural source of opioids is the brain. In the 1970s, several groups of scientists injected radioactive opiates into the brain and identified special receptors to which the opiates bind. At roughly the same time, other groups of investigators identified a number of brain peptides as the neurotransmitters that naturally affect these receptors. The peptides in the body that have opioidlike effects are collectively called **endorphins** (endogenous morphines).

Research has identified three classes of endorphins—*endomorphins, enkephalins* (meaning "in the head"), and *dynorphins*—and three receptors—*mu, kappa,* and *delta*—on which each endorphin is relatively specific. All endorphins and their receptors are found in many brain and spinal-cord regions as well as in other parts of the body, including the digestive system. Morphine most closely mimics the endomorphins and binds most selectively to the mu receptors.

In addition to the natural opioids, many synthetic opioids, such as heroin, affect mu receptors. Heroin is synthesized from morphine but is more fat-soluble and penetrates the blood–brain barrier more quickly, allowing it to produce very rapid but shorter-acting pain relief. Although heroin is a legal drug in some countries, it is illegal in others, including the United States.

Among the synthetic opioids prescribed for clinical use in pain management are hydromorphone, levorphanol, oxymorphone, methadone, meperidine, oxycodone, and fentanyl. All opioids are potently addictive, and abuse of prescription opioids is common. Opioids are also illegally modified, manufactured, and distributed. People who suffer from chronic pain and who use opioids for pain relief also can become addicted; some obtain multiple prescriptions and sell their prescriptions illicitly. Experimental research is being directed toward opioids that affect more than one receptor, activating the mu receptor to lessen pain while blocking the delta receptor to reduce addiction.

Several drugs act as antagonists at opioid receptors. They include *nalorphine* (Lethidrone, Nalline) and *naloxone* (Narcan, Nalone). These drugs are **competitive inhibitors**: they compete with opioids for neuronal receptors.

Figure 6.14 ▲

Potent Poppy Opium is obtained from the seeds of the opium poppy (top). Morphine (center) is extracted from opium, and heroin (bottom) is a powder synthesized from morphine. (Top: Patrick Field/Eye Ubiquitous/Corbis. Center: Science Source. Bottom: Bonnie Kamin/PhotoEdit.)

Because they can enter the brain quickly, they can quickly block the actions of morphine. Many people addicted to opioids carry a competitive inhibitor as a treatment for overdosing. Because they can also be long-acting, competitive inhibitors are used to treat opioid addiction after the addicted person has recovered from withdrawal symptoms.

Researchers have extensively studied whether endorphins that exist in the brain can be used as drugs to relieve pain without producing the addictive effects of morphine. The answer is so far mixed, and the objectives of pain research in producing an analgesic that does not produce addiction may be difficult to realize.

Opioid drugs, such as heroin, are addictive and are abused worldwide. The hypodermic needle was developed in 1853 and used in the American Civil War for the intravenous injection of morphine for pain treatment. This practice reportedly produced 400,000 sufferers of the "soldiers disease" of morphine addiction. Morphine can be administered by many routes, but intravenous injection is preferred because it produces euphoria described as a rush. Morphine does not readily cross the blood–brain barrier, whereas heroin does, and so the latter is even more likely to produce a rush.

If opioids are used repeatedly, they produce tolerance such that, within a few weeks, the effective dose may increase tenfold. Thereafter, many of the desired effects with respect to both pain and addiction are no longer realized. An addicted person cannot simply stop using the drug, however. A severe sickness called withdrawal results if drug use is stopped abruptly.

Because morphine results in both tolerance and sensitization, the morphine user is always flirting with the possibility of an overdose. The unreliability of appropriate information on the purity of street forms of morphine contributes to the risk of overdosing. A lack of sterile needles for injections also leaves the morphine user at risk for many other diseases, including AIDS (acquired immunodeficiency syndrome) and hepatitis.

Opioid ingestion produces a wide range of physiological changes in addition to pain relief, including relaxation and sleep, euphoria, and constipation. Other effects include respiratory depression, decreased blood pressure, pupil constriction, hypothermia, drying of secretions (e.g., dry mouth), reduced sex drive, and flushed, warm skin. Withdrawal is characterized by sicknesslike symptoms that are the physiologically and behaviorally opposite of those produced by the drug. Thus, a major part of the addiction syndrome is the drive to prevent withdrawal symptoms.

Group V: Psychotropics

Psychotropic drugs are stimulants that mainly affect mental activity; motor activity; and arousal, perception, and mood. Behavioral stimulants affect motor activity and mood. Psychedelic and hallucinogenic stimulants affect perception and produce hallucinations. General stimulants mainly affect mood.

Behavioral Stimulants

Behavioral stimulants increase motor behavior as well as elevating a person's mood and alertness. They are used to boost alertness but can be addictive.

Amphetamine is a synthetic compound that was discovered in attempts to synthesize the CNS neurotransmitter epinephrine, which also acts as a hormone to mobilize the body for fight or flight in times of stress. Both amphetamine and

Figure 6.15 ▲

Behavioral Stimulant
Cocaine (left) is obtained from the leaves of the coca plant (center). Crack cocaine (right) is chemically altered to form rocks that vaporize when heated. (Left: Timothy Ross/ The Image Works. Center: Gregory G. Dimijian/Science Source. Right: Tek Image/Science Source.)

cocaine are dopamine agonists that act first by blocking the dopamine reuptake transporter. Interfering with the reuptake mechanism leaves more dopamine available in the synaptic cleft. Amphetamine also stimulates the release of dopamine from presynaptic membranes. Both mechanisms increase the amount of dopamine available in synapses to stimulate dopamine receptors. Amphetamine-based drugs are widely prescribed to treat **attention deficit/hyperactivity disorder** (ADHD) and widely used illicitly as study aids, as reported in the Snapshot.

A form of amphetamine was first used as a treatment for asthma: Benzedrine was sold in inhalers as a nonprescription drug through the 1940s. Soon people discovered that they could open the container and ingest its contents to obtain an energizing effect. Amphetamine was widely used in World War II—and is still used today to help troops and pilots stay alert, increase confidence and aggression, and boost morale—and was used then to improve the productivity of wartime workers. Amphetamine is also used as a weight-loss aid. Many over-the-counter compounds marketed as stimulants or weight-loss aids have amphetaminelike pharmacological actions.

An amphetamine derivative, methamphetamine (also known as meth, speed, crank, smoke, or crystal ice) continues in widespread use. Lifetime prevalence of methamphetamine use in the U.S. population, estimated to be as high as 8 percent (Durell et al., 2008), is related to its ease of manufacture in illicit laboratories and to its potency, thus making it a relatively inexpensive, yet potentially devastating, drug.

Cocaine is a powder extracted from the Peruvian coca shrub, shown in **Figure 6.15**. The indigenous people of Peru have chewed coca leaves through the generations to increase their stamina in the harsh environment and high elevations where they live. Refined cocaine powder can either be sniffed (snorted) or injected. Cocaine users who do not like to inject cocaine intravenously or cannot afford it in powdered form sniff or smoke rocks or crack, a potent, highly concentrated form. Crack is chemically altered so that it vaporizes at low temperatures, and the vapors are inhaled.

Sigmund Freud popularized cocaine in the late 1800s as an antidepressant. It was once a widely used ingredient in soft drinks and wine mixtures promoted as invigorating tonics. It is the origin of the trade name Coca-Cola, because this soft drink once contained cocaine (**Figure 6.16**). The addictive properties of cocaine soon became apparent, however.

Figure 6.16 ▼

Warning Label Cocaine was once an ingredient in a number of invigorating beverages, including Coca-Cola, as this advertisement suggests. (The Granger Collection, NYC. All rights reserved.)

SNAPSHOT | Cognitive Enhancement

A new name for an old game? An article in the preeminent science publication *Nature* floated the idea that certain "cognitive-enhancing" drugs improve school and work performance in otherwise healthy individuals by improving brain function (Greely et al., 2008). The report was instigated in part by reports that up to 20%—and in some schools up to 80%—of high school and university students were using Adderall (mainly dextroamphetamine) and Ritalin (methylphenidate) as a study aid to help meet deadlines and to cram for examinations.

Both drugs are prescribed as a treatment for ADHD, a developmental disorder characterized by core behavioral symptoms of impulsivity, hyperactivity, and/or inattention (see Section 24.3). Methylphenidate and dextroamphetamine are Schedule II drugs, signifying that they carry the potential for abuse and require a prescription when used medically. Their main illicit source is through falsified prescriptions or purchase from someone who has a prescription. Both drugs share the pharmacological properties of cocaine in that they stimulate dopamine release and also block its reuptake (see Section 6.3).

The use of cognitive enhancers is not new. In his classic paper on cocaine, Viennese psychoanalyst Sigmund Freud (1974) stated in 1884, "The main use of coca [cocaine] will undoubtedly remain that which the Indians [of Peru] have made of it for centuries . . . to increase the physical capacity of the body. . . ." Freud later withdrew his endorsement when he realized that cocaine is addictive.

In 1937, an article in the *Journal of the American Medical Association* reported that a form of amphetamine, Benzedrine, improved performance on mental-efficiency tests. This information was quickly disseminated among students, who began to use the drug as an aid to study for examinations. In the 1950s, dextroamphetamine, marketed as Dexedrine, was similarly prescribed for narcolepsy and used illicitly by students as a study aid.

The complex neural effects of amphetamine stimulants center on learning at the synapse by means of habituation and sensitization. With repeated use for nonmedicinal purposes, the drugs can also begin to produce side effects including sleep disruption, loss of appetite, and headaches. Some people develop cardiovascular abnormalities and/or become addicted to amphetamine.

Treating ADHD with prescription drugs is itself controversial, despite their widespread use for this purpose. Aagaard and Hansen (2011) note that assessing the adverse effects of cognitive enhancement medication is hampered because many participants drop out of studies and the duration of such studies is short.

Despite their contention that stimulant drugs can improve school and work performance by improving brain function in otherwise healthy individuals, Greely and coworkers (2008) call for more research into the legal implications related to using cognitive enhancers, their beneficial effects, and the long-term neural consequences of their use.

ROBERT STOLARIK/*THE NEW YORK TIMES*/REDUX

Aagaard, L., and E. H. Hansen. The occurrence of adverse drug reactions reported for attention deficit hyperactivity disorder (ADHD) medications in the pediatric population: A qualitative review of empirical studies. *Neuropsychiatric Disorders and Treatments* 7:729–744, 2011.

Freud, S. *Cocaine Papers* (R. Byck, Ed.). New York: Penguin, 1974.

Greely, H., B. Sahakian, J. Harris, R. C. Kessler, M. Gazzaniga, et al. Towards responsible use of cognitive-enhancing drugs by the healthy. *Nature* 456:702–705, 2008.

Freud also recommended that cocaine could be used as a local anesthetic. Cocaine did prove valuable for this purpose, and many derivatives, such as Novocaine, are used today. These local anesthetic agents reduce a cell's permeability to Na^+ ions and so reduce nerve conduction.

Psychedelic and Hallucinogenic Stimulants

Psychedelic drugs alter sensory perception and cognitive processes and can produce hallucinations. We categorize the major groups of psychedelics by their actions on specific neurotransmitters, here and in Table 6.3 on page 150.

ACh Psychedelics These drugs either block (atropine) or facilitate (nicotine) transmission at ACh synapses.

Anandamide Psychedelics Results from numerous lines of research suggest that this endogenous neurotransmitter plays a role in enhancing forgetting. Anandamide (from the Sanskrit word for "joy" or "bliss") prevents the brain's memory systems from being overwhelmed by all the information to which we are exposed each day. Tetrahydrocannabinol (THC), the active ingredient in marijuana, obtained from the hemp plant *Cannabis sativa*, shown in **Figure 6.17**, acts on endogenous THC receptors for anandamide, the CB1 and CB2 receptors. Thus, THC use may have a detrimental effect on memory or a positive effect on mental overload.

Figure 6.17 ▲

Cannabis sativa The hemp plant is an annual herb that reaches a height between 3 and 15 feet. Hemp grows in a wide range of altitudes, climates, and soils and has myriad practical uses, including the manufacture of rope, cloth, and paper. (Phil Schermeister/Getty Images.)

Evidence points to THC's usefulness as a therapeutic agent for a number of clinical conditions. It relieves nausea and emesis (vomiting) in patients undergoing cancer chemotherapy who are not helped by other treatments, for example, and stimulates the appetite in AIDS patients suffering from anorexia–cachexia (wasting) syndrome. THC has been found helpful for treating chronic pain through mechanisms that appear to be different from those of the opioids. It has also proved useful for treating glaucoma (increased pressure in the eye) and spastic disorders such as multiple sclerosis and disorders associated with spinal-cord injury.

Some studies suggest that THC has neuroprotective properties. It can aid brain healing after traumatic brain injury and slow the progression of diseases associated with brain degeneration, including Alzheimer's disease and Huntington's disease (Sarne et al., 2011). Many reports attest that some ingredients in marijuana reduce epileptic attacks. An oil containing cannabidiol, a compound with few psychoactive effects obtained from a marijuana strain named Charlotte's Web after the first child who used it, is effective in treating childhood epilepsy (Robson, 2014).

For decades, investigations into marijuana's medicinal effects have been made difficult by legal restrictions against THC use. Now that legal restrictions are being reduced in some jurisdictions, widespread use of medicinal THC makes controlled studies difficult to conduct.

Glutamate Psychedelics Phencyclidine (PCP) and ketamine (Special K) can produce hallucinations and out-of-body experiences. Both drugs, formerly used as anesthetics (see Table 6.3, Group I), exert part of their action by blocking glutamate NMDA receptors involved in learning. Other NMDA receptor antagonists include dextromethorphan and nitrous oxide. Although the primary psychoactive effects of phencyclidine last for a few hours, its total elimination rate from the body typically extends for 8 days or longer.

Norepinephrine Psychedelics Mescaline, obtained from the peyote cactus, is legal in the United States for use by Native Americans for religious practices. Mescaline produces pronounced psychic alterations including a sense of spatial boundlessness and visual hallucinations. The effects of a single dose last up to 10 hours.

Serotonin Psychedelics The synthetic drug lysergic acid diethylamide (LSD) and naturally occurring psilocybin (obtained from a certain mushroom) stimulate some serotonin receptors and block the activity of other serotonergic neurons through serotonin autoreceptors. MDMA (ecstasy) is one of several synthetic amphetamine derivatives that affect serotonin neurons.

General Stimulants

General stimulants are drugs that cause an overall increase in cells' metabolic activity. Caffeine, a widely used stimulant, inhibits an enzyme that ordinarily breaks down the second messenger cyclic adenosine monophosphate (cAMP). The resulting increase in cAMP leads to increased glucose production within cells, making more energy available and allowing higher rates of cellular activity.

A cup of coffee contains about 100 milligrams of caffeine, and many common soft drinks contain almost as much—some energy drinks pack as much as 500 milligrams. Excess levels can lead to the jitters. Regular caffeine users who quit may experience headaches, irritability, and other withdrawal symptoms.

6.4 Individual Responses and Influences on Addiction

Any psychoactive drug can act differently on different people at different times. Physical differences—in body weight, sex, age, or genetic background—influence a given drug's effect, as do learned behaviors and cultural and environmental contexts. Anyone potentially can become dependent on or addicted to drugs.

Behavior on Drugs

Ellen, a 19-year-old university freshman, knows the risks of unprotected sexual intercourse. At a homecoming party in her residence hall, Ellen has a great time, drinking and dancing with her friends and meeting new people. She is particularly taken with Brad, a sophomore, and the two of them decide to go back to her room to order a pizza. One thing leads to another, and Ellen and Brad have sexual intercourse without using a condom. The next morning, Ellen is dismayed and surprised by her failure practice safe sex (MacDonald et al., 2000).

What is it about drugs that make people do things they never would do when sober? Risky behavior associated with alcohol use is costly both to individuals and to society. Beyond unprotected sexual activity, people risk drinking and driving, date rape, spousal or child abuse, and other forms of aggression and crime. An early and still widely held explanation of the effects of alcohol is the **disinhibition theory**. It holds that alcohol has a selective depressant effect on the cortex, the brain region that controls judgment, while sparing subcortical structures, those areas responsible for more-primitive instincts, such as desire. Alcohol presumably depresses learned inhibitions based on reasoning and judgment while releasing the "beast" within.

Disinhibition theory excuses alcohol-related behavior with such statements as "She was too drunk to know better" or "The boys had a few too many and got carried away." Does disinhibition explain Ellen's behavior? Not entirely. Ellen had used alcohol in the past and managed to practice safe sex despite the effects of the drug. If alcohol is a disinhibitor, why is it not always so?

Craig MacAndrew and Robert Edgerton (1969) questioned disinhibition theory along just these lines in their book, *Drunken Comportment*. They cite many instances in which behavior under the influence of alcohol changes from one context to another. People who engage in polite social activity at home when consuming alcohol may become unruly and aggressive when drinking in a bar. They cite cultures in which people are disinhibited when sober only to become inhibited after consuming alcohol and cultures in which people are inhibited when sober and become more inhibited when drinking.

MacAndrew and Edgerton suggest that behavior under the effects of alcohol is both learned and specific to culture, group, and setting, and can in part explain Ellen's decision to sleep with Brad. Where alcohol is used to facilitate social interactions, behavior while intoxicated represents a "learned time out" from more-conservative dating rules. But appeals to learning theory have more difficulty explaining Ellen's lapse in judgment regarding safe sex. Ellen had never indulged in unsafe sex before and had never made it a part of her time-out social activities.

Another explanation for alcohol-related lapses in judgment like Ellen's is **alcohol myopia** (nearsightedness), the tendency for people under the influence of alcohol to respond to a restricted set of immediate and prominent cues while ignoring more-remote cues and potential consequences. Once Ellen and Brad arrived at Ellen's room, the sexual cues were more immediate than concerns about long-term safety. Alcohol myopia can explain many lapses in judgment that lead to risky behavior, including aggression, date rape, and reckless driving while intoxicated. After drinking, individuals may have poor insight into their level of intoxication: they may assume that they are less impaired than they actually are (Lac and Berger, 2013).

Addiction and Dependence

B.G. started smoking when she was 13 years old. Now a university lecturer, she has one child and is aware that smoking is not good for her own or her family's health. She has quit smoking many times without success, most recently using a nicotine patch that absorbs the nicotine through the skin, without the smoke.

B.G. has a drug problem. She is one of more than 20 percent of North Americans who smoke. Most begin between the ages of 15 and 35, consuming an average of about 18 cigarettes daily, nearly a pack-a-day habit. Like B.G., most smokers realize that smoking is a health hazard, have experienced unpleasant side effects from it, and have attempted to quit but cannot. B.G. is exceptional only in her white-collar occupation. Today, most smokers are found in blue-collar occupations rather than among professionals.

Substance abuse is a pattern of drug use in which people rely on a drug chronically and excessively, allowing it to occupy a central place in their lives. A more advanced state of abuse is *substance dependence*, popularly known as **addiction**. Addicted people are physically dependent on a drug in addition to abusing it. They have developed tolerance for the drug, and so an addict requires increased doses to obtain the desired effect.

Drug addicts may also experience unpleasant, sometimes dangerous, physical **withdrawal symptoms** if they suddenly stop taking the abused drug. Symptoms can include muscle aches and cramps, anxiety attacks, sweating, nausea, and even, for some drugs, convulsions and death. Symptoms of withdrawal from alcohol or morphine can begin within hours of the last dose and tend to intensify over several days before they subside.

Sex Differences in Addiction

Vast differences among individual responses to drugs are due to differences in age, body size, metabolism, and sensitivity to a particular substance. Larger people, for instance, are generally less sensitive to a drug than smaller people are: their greater volume of body fluids dilutes drugs more. Old people may be twice as sensitive to drugs as young people are. The elderly often have less-effective barriers to drug absorption as well as less-effective processes for metabolizing and eliminating drugs from their bodies. Individuals also respond to drugs in different ways at different times.

Females are about twice as sensitive to drugs as are males, on average, owing in part to their relatively smaller body size but also to hormonal differences. The long-held general assumption that human males are more likely to abuse drugs than are human females led investigators to neglect researching drug use and abuse in human females. The results of more recent research show that females are less likely to become addicted to some drugs than are males, but females are catching up and, for some drugs, are surpassing males in the incidence of addiction (Becker and Hu, 2008).

Although the general pattern of drug use is similar in males and females, females are more likely than males are to abuse nicotine, alcohol, cocaine, amphetamine, opioids, cannabinoids, caffeine, and phencyclidine. Females begin to regularly self-administer licit and illicit drugs of abuse at lower doses than do males, use escalates more rapidly to addiction, and females are at greater risk for relapse after abstinence.

Wanting-and-Liking Theory

To explain drug abuse and addiction, T. E. Robinson and K. C. Berridge (1993) proposed the *incentive-sensitization theory*, also called **wanting-and-liking theory**. Wanting is equivalent to cravings for a drug; liking is the pleasure that drug-taking produces. With repeated drug use, tolerance for liking develops and wanting sensitizes. Liking decreases but wanting increases (**Figure 6.18**).

Opioid brain systems are associated with liking. The first step on the proposed road to drug dependence is the initial experience, when the drug affects a neural system associated with pleasure. At this stage, the user may experience liking the substance—including liking to take it within a social context. With

Figure 6.18 ▼

Wanting-and-Liking Theory Wanting a drug and liking a drug move in opposite directions with repeated drug use. Wanting (craving) is associated with drug cues.

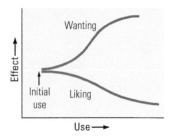

repeated use, liking the drug may decline from its initial level. At this stage the user may begin to increase the dosage to increase liking.

The neural basis of wanting is proposed to be the dopamine system. Many kinds of abused or addictive drugs—including sedative hypnotics, antianxiety agents, opioids, and stimulants—have a common property: they produce **psychomotor activation** by stimulating dopamine systems in some part of their dosage range. This common effect has led to the hypothesis that all abused drugs increase dopamine activity, especially dopamine in the mesolimbic pathways (**Figure 6.19**).

With each use, the drug taker increasingly associates cues related to drug use—be it a hypodermic needle, the room in which the drug is taken, or the people with whom the drug is taken—with the drug-taking experience (Everitt and Heberlein, 2013). The user at this stage makes this association because the drug enhances dopamine-related, classically conditioned cues associated with drug taking. Later encounters with these wanting cues produce enhanced dopamine activity, and this is the neural basis of wanting or craving (Fraioli, 1999).

Ample evidence confirms that abused drugs and the context in which they are taken initially has a pleasurable effect and that habitual users will continue using their drug of choice, even when taking it no longer produces any pleasure. Heroin addicts sometimes report that they are miserable, their lives are in ruins, and the drug is not even pleasurable anymore. But they still want it. What's more, desire for the drug often is greatest just when the addicted person is maximally high, not when he or she is undergoing withdrawal. Finally, cues associated with drug taking—the social situation, sight of the drug, or drug paraphernalia—strongly influence decisions to take, or continue taking, a drug.

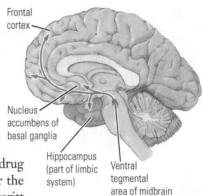

Frontal cortex

Nucleus accumbens of basal ganglia

Hippocampus (part of limbic system)

Ventral tegmental area of midbrain

Figure 6.19 ▲

Mesolimbic Dopamine Pathways and Drug Craving Dopamine cells in the ventral tegmentum project axons to the nucleus accumbens; to the limbic system, including the hippocampus; and to the frontal cortex, suggesting that these areas may play a role in addiction.

Treating Drug Abuse

We can extend wanting-and-liking theory to many life situations. Cues related to sexual activity, food, and even sports can induce a state of wanting, sometimes in the absence of liking. We frequently eat when prompted by the cue of other people eating, even though we may not be hungry and derive little pleasure from eating at that time. The similarities between exaggerating normal behaviors and drug addiction suggest that both depend on the same learning and brain mechanisms. For this reason alone, any addiction is extremely difficult to treat, and legal obstacles, genetic influences, even the drug taken all add extra layers of difficulty.

Legal Obstacles and Social Pressures

Legal proscriptions in relation to drug use are irrational. In the United States, the Harrison Narcotics Act of 1914 made heroin and a variety of other drugs illegal and made the treatment of addicted people by physicians in their private offices illegal. The Drug Addiction Treatment Act of 2000 partly reversed this prohibition, allowing treatment but with many restrictions. In addition, legal consequences attending drug use vary greatly with the drug that is abused and the jurisdiction in which it is used.

From a health standpoint, using tobacco has much greater proven health risks than does using marijuana. The moderate use of alcohol is likely benign.

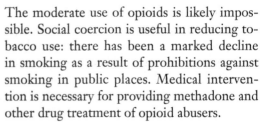

The moderate use of opioids is likely impossible. Social coercion is useful in reducing tobacco use: there has been a marked decline in smoking as a result of prohibitions against smoking in public places. Medical intervention is necessary for providing methadone and other drug treatment of opioid abusers.

Genetic and Epigenetic Influences

Three lines of evidence suggest a genetic contribution to drug use. First, if one twin abuses alcohol, the other twin is more likely to abuse it if those twins are identical (have the same genetic makeup) than if they are fraternal (have only some of their genes in common). Second, people adopted shortly after birth are more

▲ Employees fill prescriptions at a medical marijuana clinic in San Francisco. California is one of many states that have decriminalized the use of medical marijuana. (Jim Wilson/*The New York Times*/Redux)

likely to abuse alcohol if their biological parents were alcoholics, even though they have had almost no contact with those parents. Third, although most animals do not care for alcohol, the selective breeding of mice, rats, and monkeys can produce strains that consume large quantities of it.

Epigenetics offers an alternative to the inheritance explanation of susceptibility to addiction (Robison and Nestler, 2011). Addictive drugs can influence gene regulation relatively directly. By determining which genes are expressed, such drugs can selectively turn off genes related to voluntary control and turn on genes related to behaviors susceptible to addiction. Epigenetic changes in an individual's gene expression are relatively permanent and can be passed along, perhaps through the next few generations, as described in Section 2.3. For these reasons, epigenetics can also account both for the enduring behaviors that support addiction and for the tendency of drug addiction to be inherited.

Successful approaches to drug treatment recognize that addiction is a lifelong problem. Thus, drug addiction must be treated as analogous to the lifelong appropriate diet and exercise required for controlling body weight.

Normal rooster

Capon (rooster with gonads removed)

6.5 Hormones

In 1849, European scientist A. A. Berthold removed the testes of a rooster and found that the rooster no longer crowed. Nor did it engage in sexual or aggressive behavior. Berthold then reimplanted one testis in the rooster's body cavity. The rooster began crowing and displaying normal sexual and aggressive behavior again. The reimplanted testis did not establish any nerve connections, so Berthold concluded that it must release a chemical into the rooster's circulatory system to influence its behavior.

That chemical, we now know, is **testosterone**, the sex hormone secreted by the testes and responsible for the distinguishing characteristics of the male. The effect that Berthold produced by reimplanting the testis can be mimicked by administering testosterone to a castrated rooster, or capon. The hormone is sufficient to make the capon behave like a rooster with testes.

Testosterone's influence on the rooster illustrates some of the ways that this hormone produces male behavior. Testosterone also initiates changes in the size and appearance of the mature male body. In a rooster, for example, testosterone produces the animal's distinctive plumage and crest, and it activates other sex-related organs.

Hierarchical Control of Hormones

Figure 6.20 shows that hormones operate within a hierarchy that begins when the brain responds to sensory experiences and cognitive activity. The hypothalamus produces neurohormones that stimulate the pituitary gland to secrete releasing hormones into the circulatory system. The pituitary hormones, in turn, influence the remaining endocrine glands to release appropriate hormones into the bloodstream. These hormones then act on various targets in the body and send feedback to the brain about the need for more or less hormone release.

Hormones not only affect body organs but also target the brain and neurotransmitter-activating systems there. Almost every neuron in the brain contains receptors on which various hormones can act. In addition to influencing sex organs and physical appearance in a rooster, testosterone may have neurotransmitterlike effects on the brain cells it targets, especially neurons that control crowing, male sexual behavior, and aggression.

Testosterone is transported into these neurons' cell nuclei, where it activates genes. The genes, in turn, trigger the synthesis of proteins needed for cellular processes that produce the rooster's male behaviors. Thus, the rooster develops not only a male body but a male brain as well.

Although many questions remain about how hormones produce complex behavior, the diversity of testosterone's functions clarifies why the body uses hormones as messengers: their targets are so widespread that the best possible way of reaching them all is by traveling in the bloodstream, which goes everywhere in the body.

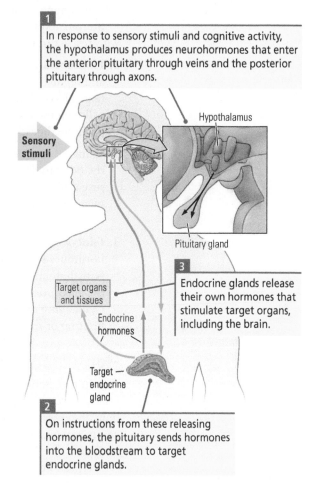

1 In response to sensory stimuli and cognitive activity, the hypothalamus produces neurohormones that enter the anterior pituitary through veins and the posterior pituitary through axons.

Sensory stimuli

Hypothalamus

Pituitary gland

3 Endocrine glands release their own hormones that stimulate target organs, including the brain.

Target organs and tissues

Endocrine hormones

Target endocrine gland

2 On instructions from these releasing hormones, the pituitary sends hormones into the bloodstream to target endocrine glands.

Figure 6.20 ▲

Hormonal Hierarchy

Classes and Functions of Hormones

Hormones can be used as drugs to treat or prevent disease. People take synthetic hormones as replacement therapy if the glands that produce those hormones are removed or malfunction. People also take hormones, especially sex hormones, to counteract the effects of aging and to increase physical strength and endurance and to gain an advantage in sports. In the human body, as many as 100 hormones are classified chemically either as steroids or peptides.

Steroid hormones, such as testosterone and cortisol, are synthesized from cholesterol and are lipid (fat) soluble. Steroids diffuse away from their sites of synthesis in glands, including the gonads, adrenal cortex, and thyroid, easily crossing the cell membrane. They enter target cells in the same way and act on the cells' DNA to increase or decrease protein production.

Peptide hormones, such as insulin, growth hormone, and the endorphins, are made by cellular DNA in the same way as other proteins are made. They influence their target cell's activity by binding to metabotropic receptors on the cell membrane, generating a second messenger that affects the cell's physiology.

Steroid and peptide hormones fall into one of three main functional groups with respect to behavior, and they may function in more than one group:

1. **Homeostatic hormones** maintain a state of internal metabolic balance and regulate physiological systems in an organism. Mineralocorticoids (e.g., aldosterone) control both the concentration of water in blood and cells and the levels of sodium, potassium, and calcium in the body, and they promote digestive functions.

2. **Gonadal (sex) hormones** control reproductive functions. They instruct the body to develop as male (testosterone) or female (estrogen); influence sexual behavior and the conception of children; and, in women, control the menstrual cycle (estrogen and progesterone), the birthing of babies, and the release of breast milk (prolactin, oxytocin).

3. **Glucocorticoids** (e.g., cortisol and corticosterone), a group of steroid hormones secreted in times of stress, are important in protein and carbohydrate metabolism and in controlling sugar levels in the blood and the absorption of sugar by cells. Hormones activated in psychologically challenging events or emergency situations prepare the body to cope by fighting or fleeing.

Homeostatic Hormones

The homeostatic hormones regulate the body's internal environment within relatively constant parameters. An appropriate balance of sugars, proteins, carbohydrates, salts, and water is required in the bloodstream, in the extracellular compartments of muscles, in the brain and other body structures, and in all body cells.

A typical homeostatic function is controlling blood-sugar levels. One group of cells in the pancreas releases insulin, a homeostatic hormone that causes blood sugar to fall by instructing the liver to start storing glucose rather than releasing it and by instructing cells to increase glucose uptake. The resulting decrease in glucose then decreases the stimulation of pancreatic cells so that they stop producing insulin.

Diabetes mellitus is caused by a failure of these pancreatic cells to secrete enough insulin, or any at all. As a result, blood-sugar levels can fall (hypoglycemia) or rise (hyperglycemia). In hyperglycemia, blood-glucose levels rise because insulin does not instruct cells of the body to take up that glucose. Consequently, cell function, including neural function, can fail through glucose starvation, even in the presence of high glucose levels in the blood. Chronic high blood-glucose levels damage the eyes, kidneys, nerves, heart, and blood vessels. Eric Steen and his coworkers (2005) propose that insulin resistance in brain cells may be related to Alzheimer's disease. They raise the possibility that Alzheimer's disease may be a third type of diabetes.

Gonadal Hormones

The gonadal hormones give us our sexual appearance, mold our identity as male or female, and allow us to engage in sex-related behaviors. Sex hormones begin to act on us even before we are born and continue their actions throughout our lives.

The male Y chromosome contains a gene called the sex-determining region, or *SRY*, gene. If cells in the undifferentiated gonads of the early embryo contain an *SRY* gene, they will develop into a testis, and if they do not, they will develop into an ovary. In the male, the testes produce the hormone testosterone, which in turn masculinizes the body, producing the male body, genital organs, and the male brain.

The **organizational hypothesis** proposes that hormone actions in the course of development alter tissue differentiation. Thus, testosterone masculinizes the brain early in life by being taken up in brain cells, where it is converted into estrogen by the enzyme aromatase. Estrogen then acts on estrogen receptors to initiate a chain of events that includes activating certain genes in the cell nucleus. These genes then contribute to the masculinization of brain cells and their interactions with other brain cells.

That estrogen, a hormone usually associated with the female, masculinizes the male brain may seem surprising. Estrogen does not have the same effect on the female brain, because females have a blood enzyme that binds to estrogen and prevents its entry into the brain. Hormones play a somewhat lesser role in producing the female body as well as the female brain, but they control the mental and physical aspects of menstrual cycles, regulate many facets of pregnancy and birth, and stimulate milk production for breast-feeding babies.

Hormones contribute to surprising differences in the brain and in cognitive behavior including, as noted in Section 6.4, playing a role in male–female differences in drug dependence and addiction. The male brain is slightly larger than the female brain after corrections are made for body size, and the right hemisphere is somewhat larger than the left in males. The female brain has a higher rate both of cerebral blood flow and of glucose utilization. Other differences include brain size in different brain regions, including nuclei in the hypothalamus related to sexual function and parts of the corpus callosum that are larger in females, a somewhat larger language region in the female brain, and other cortical gray-matter changes (Koolschijn et al., 2014).

Three lines of evidence, summarized by Elizabeth Hampson and Doreen Kimura (2005), support the conclusion that sex-related cognitive differences result from these brain differences. First, results of spatial and verbal tests given to females and males in many different settings and cultures show that males tend to excel in the spatial tasks tested and females in the verbal tasks. Second, similar tests given to female participants in the course of the menstrual cycle show fluctuations in test scores with various phases of the cycle. During the phase in which the female sex hormones estradiol (metabolized from estrogen) and progesterone are at their lowest levels, women do comparatively better on spatial tasks. During the phase in which levels of these hormones are high, women do comparatively better on verbal tasks. Third, tests comparing premenopausal and postmenopausal women, women in various stages of pregnancy, and females and males with varying levels of circulating hormones all provide some evidence that gonadal hormones affect cognitive function.

Anabolic–Androgenic Steroids

A class of synthetic hormones related to testosterone has both muscle-building (anabolic) and masculinizing (androgenic) effects. These *anabolic–androgenic steroids*, commonly known simply as **anabolic steroids** (and more commonly as roids), were synthesized originally to build body mass and enhance endurance. Russian weightlifters were the first to use them, in 1952, to enhance performance and win international competitions.

Synthetic steroid use rapidly spread to other countries and sports, eventually leading to a ban from use in track and field athletes and then from many other sports competitors as well. Testing policy has led to a cat-and-mouse game in which new anabolic steroids and new ways of taking them and masking them are devised to evade detection.

Today, anabolic steroid use is about equal among athletes and nonathletes. More than 1 million people in the United States have used anabolic steroids not only to enhance athletic performance but also to enhance physique and appearance. Anabolic steroid use in high schools may be as high as 7 percent for males and 3 percent for females.

The use of anabolic steroids carries health risks. Their administration results in the body reducing its manufacture of the male hormone testosterone, which in turn reduces male fertility and spermatogenesis. Muscle bulk is increased, and so is male aggression. Cardiovascular effects include increased risk of heart attacks and stroke. Liver and kidney function may be compromised, and the risk of tumors may increase. Male-pattern baldness may be enhanced, and females may experience clitoral enlargement, acne, increased body hair, and a deepened voice.

Anabolic steroids also have approved clinical uses. Testosterone replacement is a treatment for hypogonadal males. It is also useful for treating muscle loss subsequent to trauma and for recovering muscle mass in malnourished people. In females, anabolic steroids are used to treat endometriosis and fibrocystic breast disease.

⊚ Glucocorticoids and Stress

Stress is a term borrowed from engineering to describe a process in which an agent exerts a force on an object. Applied to humans and other animals, a *stressor* is a stimulus that challenges the body's homeostasis and triggers arousal. Stress responses are not only physiological but also behavioral and include both arousal and attempts to reduce stress. A stress response can outlast a stress-inducing incident and may even occur in the absence of an obvious stressor. Living with constant stress can be debilitating.

The body's response is the same whether the stressor is exciting, sad, or frightening. Robert Sapolsky (2004) argues that, physiologically, a hungry lion and the zebra she is chasing down have exactly the same stress response. It begins when the body is subjected to a stressor and especially when the brain perceives a stressor and responds with arousal. The response consists of two separate sequences, one fast and the other slow.

The left side of **Figure 6.21** shows the fast response. The sympathetic division of the autonomic nervous system is activated to prepare the body and its

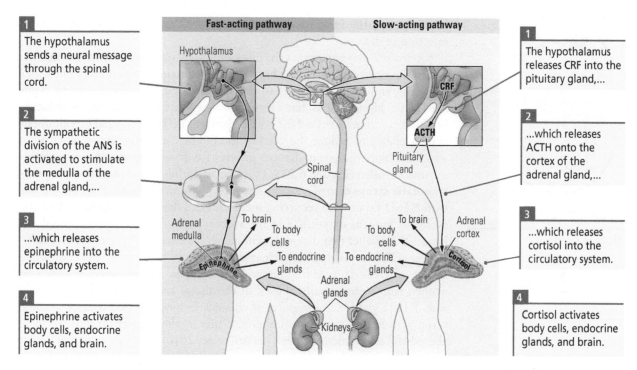

1
The hypothalamus sends a neural message through the spinal cord.

2
The sympathetic division of the ANS is activated to stimulate the medulla of the adrenal gland,...

3
...which releases epinephrine into the circulatory system.

4
Epinephrine activates body cells, endocrine glands, and brain.

1
The hypothalamus releases CRF into the pituitary gland,...

2
...which releases ACTH onto the cortex of the adrenal gland,...

3
...which releases cortisol into the circulatory system.

4
Cortisol activates body cells, endocrine glands, and brain.

Figure 6.21 ▲

Activating a Stress Response Two pathways to the adrenal gland control the body's stress response. The fast-acting pathway primes the body immediately to fight or flee. The slow-acting pathway both mobilizes body resources to confront a stressor and repairs stress-related damage. Abbreviations: CRF, corticotropin-releasing factor; ACTH, adrenocorticotropic hormone.

organs for "fight or flight," and the parasympathetic division for "rest and digest" is turned off. In addition, the sympathetic division stimulates the medulla on the interior of the adrenal gland to release epinephrine. The epinephrine surge (often called the *adrenaline surge* after epinephrine's original name) prepares the body for a sudden burst of activity. Among its many functions, epinephrine stimulates cell metabolism to ready the body's cells for action.

The hormone controlling the slow response is the steroid cortisol, a glucocorticoid released from the outer layer (cortex) of the adrenal gland, as shown on the right side of Figure 6.21. The cortisol pathway is activated slowly, taking minutes to hours. Cortisol has a wide range of functions, including turning off all bodily systems not immediately required to deal with a stressor. For example, cortisol turns off insulin so that the liver starts releasing glucose, temporarily increasing the body's energy supply. It also shuts down reproductive functions and inhibits the production of growth hormone. In this way, the body's energy supplies can be concentrated on dealing with the stress.

◎ Ending a Stress Response

Normally, stress responses are brief. The body mobilizes its resources, deals with the challenge physiologically and behaviorally, then shuts down the stress response. The brain is responsible for turning on the stress reaction and for turning it off. If a stress response is not shut down, the body continues to mobilize energy at the cost of energy storage; proteins are used up, resulting in muscle wasting and fatigue; growth hormone is inhibited, and the body cannot grow; the gastrointestinal system remains shut down, reducing the intake and processing of nutrients to replace used resources; reproductive functions are

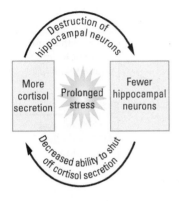

Figure 6.22 ▲

Vicious Circle

inhibited; and the immune system is suppressed, increasing the possibility of infection or disease.

Sapolsky (2005) argues that the hippocampus plays an important role in turning off the stress response. The hippocampus contains a high density of cortisol receptors, and its axons project to the hypothalamus. Cortisol levels are regulated by the hippocampus, but if levels remain elevated because a stress-inducing situation continues, cortisol eventually damages it. The damaged hippocampus is then unable to reduce the cortisol level. Thus, a vicious circle is set up in which the hippocampus undergoes progressive degeneration and cortisol levels are uncontrolled (**Figure 6.22**). This idea underlies one explanation for **posttraumatic stress disorder**: it is a stress response that is not turned off. People with PTSD experience recurring memories and dreams related to a traumatic event for months or years, and the accompanying physiological arousal enhances their belief that danger is imminent (see Chapter 26 opening Portrait).

Research has yet to offer a clear-cut answer as to whether the cumulative effects of stress damage the human hippocampus. For example, research on women who were sexually abused in childhood and subsequently diagnosed with PTSD yields some reports of changes in hippocampal volume as measured with brain-imaging techniques. Other studies report no differences in abused and nonabused women (Landré et al., 2010). Possible explanations for such differing results include the limitations of imaging techniques and individual differences in stress responses.

Humans are long-lived and gather myriad life experiences that complicate simple extrapolations from a single stressful event. Nevertheless, Patrick McGowan and his coworkers (2009) report decreased glucocorticoid-receptor density in the hippocampi of suicide victims who had been sexually abused in childhood compared with that of suicide victims who had not been abused and with that of controls. The decrease in receptors and in glucocorticoid mRNA suggests that childhood abuse induces epigenetic changes in the expression of glucocorticoid genes. The decrease in glucocorticoid receptors presumably renders the hippocampus less able to depress stress responses. The importance of the McGowan study is its suggestion of a mechanism through which stress can influence hippocampal function without necessarily being associated with a decrease in hippocampal volume.

SUMMARY

6.1 Principles of Psychopharmacology
Psychoactive drugs target the central nervous system. The dose required and the route to the brain are successively smaller if the drug is administered orally, to the lungs, into the bloodstream, or directly into the brain. Major barriers to drug action include the stomach lining, dilution by the blood volume, absorption by other body cells, dilution in extracellular fluid, and the blood–brain barrier. The many routes of drug elimination include general metabolism; respiration; and elimination in feces, urine, and sweat.

6.2 Drug Actions in Synapses
Synapses play a central role in determining how drugs produce their effects on behavior. Drugs can influence any biochemical event pertaining to neurotransmission—synthesis of a transmitter; its release from the axon terminal; its interaction at the postsynaptic receptor; and its inactivation, reuptake, or degradation. Any modification of synaptic communication results in increased or decreased transmitter action. In this way, drugs can act as agonists to increase synaptic transmission or as antagonists to decrease it.

Drugs are extremely variable in producing their effects, both with respect to different persons and with respect to the same person on different occasions. A decreased response to a drug with use is called tolerance, whereas an increased response is called sensitization.

6.3 Grouping Psychoactive Drugs

The extraordinary number of psychoactive drugs can be classified according to the behavioral effects they produce. Drugs can act as sedative hypnotics and antianxiety agents, as antipsychotic agents, as antidepressants and mood stabilizers, as opioid analgesics, and as psychotropics. Each group, summarized in Table 6.3 on page 150, contains natural or synthetic drugs or both, and they may produce their actions in different ways.

6.4 Individual Responses and Influences on Addiction

A drug does not have a uniform action on every person. Physical differences—in body weight, sex, age, or genetic background—influence the effects a given drug has on a given person, as do such behaviors as learning and cultural and environmental contexts.

The influence of drugs on behavior varies widely with the situation and as a person learns drug-related behaviors. Alcohol myopia, for example, can influence a person to focus primarily on prominent cues in the environment. These cues may encourage the person to behave in ways that he or she would not normally display.

Females are more sensitive to drugs than males are and may become addicted more quickly to lower doses of drugs than males. The incidence of female abuse of many kinds of drugs currently equals or exceeds male abuse of those drugs.

Initially, drug taking produces pleasure (liking), but with repeated use, the behavior becomes conditioned to associated objects, events, and places. Eventually, those conditioned cues motivate the drug user to seek them out (wanting), which leads to more drug taking. These subjective experiences associated with prominent cues and drug seeking promote craving for the drug. As addiction proceeds, the subjective experience of liking decreases, owing to tolerance, while wanting increases, owing to sensitization.

Drug treatment varies by the drug abused. Whatever the treatment approach, success depends on permanent lifestyle changes. Considering how many people use tobacco, drink alcohol, use recreational drugs, or abuse prescription drugs, finding someone who has not used a drug when it was available is probably a rarity. But some people do seem vulnerable to drug use and addiction because of genetic or epigenetic influences.

6.5 Hormones

Steroid and peptide hormones produced by endocrine glands circulate in the bloodstream to affect a wide variety of targets. Interacting to regulate hormone levels, a hierarchy of sensory stimuli and cognitive activity in the brain stimulates the pituitary gland through the hypothalamus. The pituitary stimulates or inhibits the endocrine glands, which, through other hormones, send feedback to the brain.

Homeostatic hormones regulate the balance of sugars, proteins, carbohydrates, salts, and other substances in the body. Gonadal hormones regulate the physical features and behaviors associated with sex characteristics and behaviors, reproduction, and caring for offspring. Glucocorticoids are steroid hormones that regulate the body's ability to cope with stress—with arousing and challenging situations. Synthetic anabolic steroids that mimic the effects of testosterone and so increase muscle bulk, stamina, and aggression can have deleterious side effects.

Failure to turn stress responses off after a stressor has passed can contribute to susceptibility to PTSD and other psychological and physical diseases. Prolonged stress may activate epigenetic changes that modify the expression of genes regulating hormonal responses to stress, producing brain changes that persist long after the stress-provoking incident has passed.

References

Ballard, P. A., J. W. Tetrud, and J. W. Langston. Permanent human Parkinsonism due to 1-methyl-4-phenyl-1, 2, 3, 6-tetrahydropyridine (MPTP). *Neurology* 35:949–956, 1985.

Barrós-Loscertales, A., H. Garavan, J. C. Bustamante, N. Ventura-Campos, J. J. Llopis, et al. Reduced striatal volume in cocaine-dependent patients. *NeuroImage* 56, 1021–1026, 2011.

Becker, J. B., S. M. Breedlove, D. Crews, and M. M. McCarthy. *Behavioral Endocrinology* (2nd ed.). Cambridge, MA: Bradford, 2002.

Becker, J. B., and M. Hu. Sex differences in drug abuse. *Frontiers in Neuroendocrinology* 29:(1), 36–47, 2008.

Browne, C. A., and I. Lucki. Antidepressant effects of ketamine: Mechanisms underlying fast-acting novel antidepressants. *Frontiers in Pharmacology* 4:161–172, December 27, 2013.

Büttner, A. Review: The neuropathology of drug abuse. *Neuropathology and Applied Neurobiology* 37:118–134, 2011.

Comer, R. J. *Fundamentals of Abnormal Psychology* (7th ed.). New York: Worth Publishers, 2011.

Cowan, R. L., D. M. Roberts, and J. M. Joers. Neuroimaging in human MDMA (Ecstasy) users. *Annals of the New York Academy of Sciences* 1139:291–298, 2008.

DeCarolis, N. A., and A. J. Eisch. Hippocampal neurogenesis as a target for the treatment of mental illness: A critical evaluation. *Neuropharmacology* 58:884–893, 2010.

DeLisi, L. E. The effect of Cannabis on the brain: Can it cause brain anomalies that lead to increased risk for schizophrenia? *Current Opinion in Psychiatry* 21(2):140–150, 2008.

Durell, T. M., L. A. Kroutil, P. Crits-Christoph, N. Barchha, and D. E. Van Brunt. Prevalence of nonmedical methamphetamine use in the United States. *Substance Abuse Treatment, Prevention, and Policy* 3:19, 2008.

Eto, K. Minamata disease: A neuropathological viewpoint. *Seishin Shinkeigaku Zasshi* 108:10–23, 2006.

Everitt, B. J., and U. Heberlein. Addiction. *Current Opinion in Neurobiology* 23:463, 2013.

Fraioli, S., H. S. Crombag, A. Badiani, and T. E. Robinson. Susceptibility to amphetamine-induced locomotor sensitization is modulated by environmental stimuli. *Neuropsychopharmacology* 20:533–541, 1999.

Freud, S. *Cocaine Papers* (R. Byck, Ed.). New York: Penguin, 1974.

Hampson, E., and D. Kimura. Sex differences and hormonal influences on cognitive function in humans. In J. B. Becker, S. M. Breedlove, and D. Crews (Eds.), *Behavioral Endocrinology* (pp. 357–398). Cambridge, MA: MIT Press, 2005.

Hoang, M. T., L. F. Defina, B. L. Willis, D. S. Leonard, M. F. Weiner, and E. S. Brown. Association between low serum 25-hydroxyvitamin D and depression in a large sample of healthy adults: Cooper Center Longitudinal Study. *Mayo Clinic Proceedings* 86:1050–1055, 2011.

Isbell, H., H. F. Fraser, R. E. Wikler, R. E. Belleville, and A. J. Eisenman. An experimental study of the etiology of "rum fits" and delirium tremens. *Quarterly Journal for Studies of Alcohol* 16:1–35, 1955.

Julien, R. M., C. D. Advokat, and J. E. Comaty. *A Primer of Drug Action* (12th ed.). New York: Worth Publishers, 2011.

Koolschijn, P. C., J. S. Peper, and E. A. Crone. The influence of sex steroids on structural brain maturation in adolescence. *PLoS ONE* 9:January 8, 2014.

Langston, W. J. *The Case of the Frozen Addicts.* New York: Pantheon, 2008.

Lac, A., and D. E. Berger. Development and validation of the alcohol myopia scale. *Psychological Assessment* 25:738–747, 2013.

Landré, L., C. Destrieux, M. Baudry, L. Barantin, J. P. Cottier, et al. Preserved subcortical volumes and cortical thickness in women with sexual abuse-related PTSD. *Psychiatry Research* 183:181–186, 2010.

MacAndrew, C., and R. B. Edgerton. *Drunken Comportment: A Social Explanation.* Chicago: Aldine, 1969.

MacDonald, T. K., G. MacDonald, M. P. Zanna, and G. T. Fong. Alcohol, sexual arousal, and intentions to use condoms in young men: Applying alcohol myopia theory to risky sexual behavior. *Health Psychology* 19:290–298, 2000.

Mateus-Pinheiro, A., L. Pinto, J. M. Bessa, M. Morais, N. D. Alves, S. Monteiro, P. Patrício, O. F. Almeida, and N. Sousa. Sustained remission from depressive-like behavior depends on hippocampal neurogenesis. *Translational Psychiatry* 15:3:e210, 2013.

McCann, U. D., K. A. Lowe, and G. A. Ricaurte. Long-lasting effects of recreational drugs of abuse on the central nervous system. *Neurologist* 3:399–411, 1997.

McGowan, P. O., A. Sasaki, A. C. D'Alessio, S. Dymov, B. Labonté, M. Szyf, G. Turecki, and M. J. Meaney. Epigenetic regulation of the glucocorticoid receptor in human brain associates with childhood abuse. *Nature Neurosciences* 12:342–348, 2009.

Merritt, K., P. McGuire, and A. Egerton. Relationship between glutamate dysfunction and symptoms and cognitive function in psychosis. *Frontiers in Psychiatry* 4:151–156, 2013.

Milroy, C. M., and J. L. Parai. The histopathology of drugs of abuse. *Histopathology* 59:579–593, 2011.

Radjenović, J., M. Petrović, and D. Barceló. Fate and distribution of pharmaceuticals in wastewater and sewage sludge of the conventional activated sludge (CAS) and advanced membrane bioreactor (MBR) treatment. *Water Research* 43:831–841, 2009.

Robinson, T. E., and J. B. Becker. Enduring changes in brain and behavior produced by chronic amphetamine administration: A review and evaluation of animal models of amphetamine psychosis. *Brain Research Reviews* 11:157–198, 1986.

Robinson, T. E., and K. C. Berridge. The neural basis of drug craving: An incentive-sensitization theory of addiction. *Brain Research Reviews* 18:247–291, 1993.

Robinson, T. E., and B. Kolb. Persistent structural adaptations in nucleus accumbens and prefrontal cortex neurons produced by prior experience with amphetamine. *Journal of Neuroscience* 17:8491–8498, 1997.

Robison, A. J., and E. J. Nestler. Transcriptional and epigenetic mechanisms of addiction. *Nature Reviews Neuroscience* 12:623–637, 2011.

Robson, P. J. Therapeutic potential of cannabinoid medicines. *Drug Testing and Analysis* 6:24–30, 2014.

Sapolsky, R. M. *Why Zebras Don't Get Ulcers.* 3d ed. New York: Henry Holt and Company, 2004.

Sapolsky, R. M. Stress and plasticity in the limbic system. *Neurochemical Research* 28:1735–1742, 2005.

Sarne, Y., F. Asaf, M. Fishbein, M. Gafni, and O. Keren. The dual neuroprotective-neurotoxic profile of cannabinoid drugs. *British Journal of Pharmacology* 163:1391–1401, 2011.

Severus, E., N. Schaaff, and H. J. Möller, State of the art: Treatment of bipolar disorders. *CNS Neuroscience Therapies* 18:214–218, 2012.

Smith, A. D., S. M. Smith, C. A. de Jager, P. Whitbread, C. Johnston, et al. Homocysteine-lowering by B vitamins slows the rate of accelerated brain atrophy in mild cognitive impairment: A randomized controlled trial. *PLoS ONE* 8:e12244, 2010.

Steen, E., B. M. Terry, E. J. Rivera, J. L. Cannon, T. R. Neely, R. Tavares, X. J. Xu, J. R. Wands, and S. M. de la Monte. Impaired insulin and insulin-like growth factor expression and signaling mechanisms in Alzheimer's disease: Is this type 3 diabetes? *Journal of Alzheimer's Disease* 7:63–80, 2005.

Vevelstad, M., E. L. Oiestad, G. Middelkoop, I. Hasvold, P. Lilleng, et al. The PMMA epidemic in Norway: Comparison of fatal and non-fatal intoxications. *Forensic Science International* 219:151–157, 2012.

Whishaw, I. Q., G. Mittleman, and J. L. Evenden. Training-dependent decay in performance produced by the neuroleptic cis(Z)-Flupentixol on spatial navigation by rats in a swimming pool. *Pharmacology, Biochemistry, and Behavior* 32:211–220, 1989.

Widner, H., J. Tetrud, S. Rehngrona, B. Snow, P. Brundin, B. Gustavii, A. Bjorklund, O. Lindvall, and W. J. Langston. Bilateral fetal mesencephalic grafting in two patients with Parkinsonism induced by 1-methyl-4-phenyl-1, 2, 3, 6 tetrahydropyradine (MPTP). *New England Journal of Medicine* 327:1551, 1992.

7 Imaging the Brain's Activity

 PORTRAIT Angelo Mosso

In the late nineteenth century, Italian physiologist Angelo Mosso (1846–1910) was the first to experiment with the idea that changes in blood flow might provide a way to assess brain function during mental activity (behavior). Mosso knew that the fontanelles—the soft areas on a newborn baby's head where the bones of the skull are not yet fused—pulsate with the rhythm of the heartbeat.

He noticed similar pulsations in two adults who had suffered head injuries that left them with skull defects and observed a sudden increase in the magnitude of those pulsations when the subjects engaged in mental activity. For example, when one subject heard church bells ring and was asked whether the bells signified the time for prayer, the pulsations increased.

While recording the pressure of the pulsations, Mosso simultaneously recorded the patient's blood pressure (part A of the adjoining recordings). Mosso found that when his patient solved mathematical problems, the blood pressure in his brain increased but the pressure in his arm did not (part B). In other words, mental activity was accompanied by a selective increase in brain blood flow.

Mosso's results show that as the brain engages in problem solving, its activity changes. Increased pulsations, for example, suggest increased blood flow, which in turn suggests that the active brain region requires more oxygenated blood to perform ongoing functions. This need for more oxygen in turn suggests that active brain areas signal the circulatory system to increase blood flow to those areas.

Generalizing from this result, if different regions of the brain have different functions, will the energy those regions use reflect that? This idea forms the basis of many recording and imaging techniques developed to determine how the activities of the brain's many regions contribute to ongoing behavior.

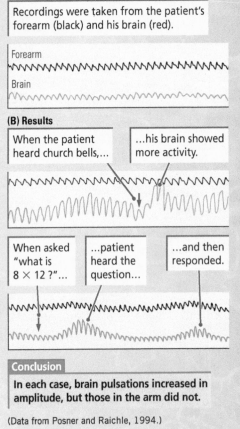

(A) Procedure

Recordings were taken from the patient's forearm (black) and his brain (red).

Forearm

Brain

(B) Results

When the patient heard church bells,...

...his brain showed more activity.

When asked "what is 8 × 12 ?"...

...patient heard the question...

...and then responded.

Conclusion

In each case, brain pulsations increased in amplitude, but those in the arm did not.

(Data from Posner and Raichle, 1994.)

We begin our survey of brain imaging by examining contemporary recording techniques that make use of the brain's electrical activity. Next we examine static techniques that make use of differences in the physical and chemical properties of brain substances. Then we review dynamic techniques that describe the brain's metabolic activity, as in the accompanying PET scan, where brain areas colored red and yellow are more active than those colored green or blue. We end the chapter by comparing uses for selected imaging techniques and surveying their pros and cons.

7.1 Recording the Brain's Electrical Activity

Neurons produce two kinds of electrical activity: graded potentials and action potentials. Researchers have applied the methods they developed for recording the two potentials to experimentation and for clinical applications. Techniques for recording the brain's graded potentials include electroencephalographic (EEG) recording, event-related potential (ERP) recording, and magnetoencephalography (MEG), whereas single-cell recording techniques record action potentials.

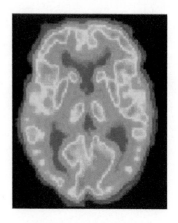

▲ Blood flow in a healthy brain, imaged by PET. (Hank Morgan/ Science Source)

Single-Cell Recording

What is each neuron in the brain doing at any given moment? Single-cell recording techniques address this question. They are refinements of the historic experiments that first detected electrical activity in individual squid axons (see Section 4.2).

In single-cell recording, an electrode is inserted directly into the brain adjacent to a single neuron, recording the neuron's electrical activity on a computer, then correlating the activity with ongoing behavior. Experiments with various animal species can reveal remarkable insights into what single neurons are up to. Although peripheral nervous system cells are accessible for recording, only a few select situations, such as brain surgery, permit researchers such direct access to the central nervous system in a living human brain.

In early studies, only a single recording electrode was used, and a great deal of electronic equipment was required to record from only one cell at a time. Today, miniaturization, computerization, and arrays of hundreds of electrodes allow recording from as many as 2000 individual neurons simultaneously (Nicolelis, 2012).

Action potentials in the brain represent sights, sounds, smells, tastes, pain and temperature sensations, even desire and emotion. A longstanding puzzle in the study of perception is how an action potential in one neuron represents vision, whereas a similar action potential in another similar neuron represents a sound and an action potential in still another neuron records the face of a relative. This puzzle has not been satisfactorily solved, but experiments by Miguel Nicolelis suggest that neurons tune themselves to the sensory input they receive: if they sense light, they see; if they sense touch, they feel.

The Neuronal Code

The many firing patterns of neurons constitute their code. Some discharge at a steady rate; others fire in bursts; still others hardly ever discharge. Some neurons discharge in the morning and evening, in rhythm with the cycle of the day. Others discharge once a year, in sync with some important annual event such as seasonal mating.

More than 100 years ago, theorists speculated that neurons in the visual system might represent our visual world in very much the way a pointillist painter produces a canvas composed of small dots. Bright areas of the visual image might be represented by neurons firing more rapidly, dark areas by reduced or absent firing. The pattern of brightness and darkness across the visual cortex would create a visual image.

The anatomy of the visual system and recordings of single-cell activity at its various levels paint a different picture: a neuronal code that represents visual information. Consider the numbers of neurons at various levels of the visual system, from the receptors in the retina of the eye to the cortical areas that take part in perception. As diagrammed in **Figure 7.1**A and B, a striking decrease in the numbers of neurons occurs at each relay into the visual cortex. Once within the cortical visual association areas, however, the numbers of cells again

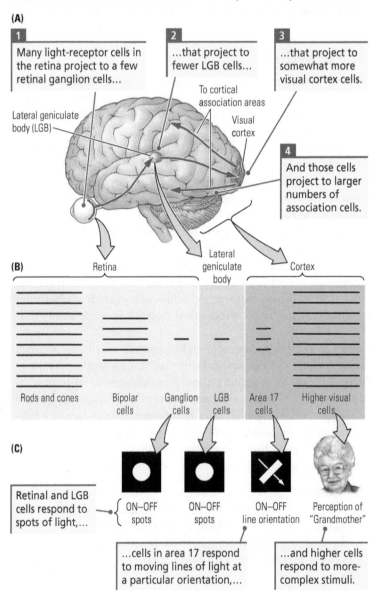

(A)

1 Many light-receptor cells in the retina project to a few retinal ganglion cells...

2 ...that project to fewer LGB cells...

3 ...that project to somewhat more visual cortex cells.

Lateral geniculate body (LGB)

To cortical association areas

Visual cortex

4 And those cells project to larger numbers of association cells.

(B)

Retina

Lateral geniculate body

Cortex

Rods and cones | Bipolar cells | Ganglion cells | LGB cells | Area 17 cells | Higher visual cells

(C)

Retinal and LGB cells respond to spots of light,...

ON–OFF spots

ON–OFF spots

ON–OFF line orientation

Perception of "Grandmother"

...cells in area 17 respond to moving lines of light at a particular orientation,...

...and higher cells respond to more-complex stimuli.

Figure 7.1 ▶

Levels of Processing
(A) Projections from the eye to the visual cortex and from the visual cortex to cortical association areas. (B) Relative numbers of cells at each level of the visual projection in part A, indicated both by the number of lines and by their length. Relatively few neurons carry information from the retina to the visual cortex, but cell numbers increase again in the primary visual cortex and higher association areas. (C) Information coding in the visual pathways.

increase. The changing number of cells argues that visual information must be transmitted as a code, in some ways as a land-based telephone transmission on a single wire conveys all the sounds that a microphone can detect.

Single-cell recording at different levels of the visual relay reveal some of the visual code's features (Figure 7.1C). First, cells along the visual pathway respond only to dots of light, and thereafter cells in the primary visual cortex respond only to bars of light at specific orientations. Cells in higher visual areas respond to more-complex stimuli, including the position and movement of objects and facial features—perhaps a grandmotherly face, perhaps Halle Berry's, as in the Portrait in Chapter 4. Thus, the visual cortex takes information encoded as dots, transfers that information into bars, then transforms bars to more complex representations that tell us what our world "looks" like.

Single-cell recordings made from the human neocortex, usually during neurosurgery, illustrate features of single-cell activity in the human brain. Cortical neurons fire at a relatively low rate of fewer than 3 discharges per minute, which may increase to about 10 discharges per minute when the neurons become more active. Most neurons have a narrow behavioral repertoire, responding to only one kind of sensory event or behavior. Because neuronal activity requires energy, a code expressed in low-level activity is obviously useful.

Neighboring neurons may have very different behavioral repertoires, which suggests that in the brain's association areas, the networks subserving different behaviors interact closely. In Broca's area, where speech is produced, one neuron may be active during word perception, and its neighbor may be active during word production. At the same time, specific stimuli or events may be associated with neuronal activity in a surprisingly large number of areas in both hemispheres.

Inhibition of activity also contributes to the neuronal code. Increased firing by a visual cortex neuron may signal red and decreased firing, green. Well-learned behaviors seem to be encoded by relatively sparse cortical activity, whereas behaviors that are being newly learned are accompanied by much more widespread cortical excitability. These general findings suggest that not only is the type of behavior or stimulus event important for determining whether a neuron changes its firing rate but so are context and experience.

Single-cell recording will always be limited to recordings from relatively small numbers of neurons. Nevertheless, recording from only a few brain cells provides insights into how neurons code behavior and also reveals the contributions of different parts of the brain to behavior. Sampling the contributions of larger groups of neurons requires other techniques.

Electroencephalographic Recording

In the early 1930s, German physiologist Hans Berger developed a technique for recording electrical activity over large regions of the human brain. Berger found that voltage fluctuations, or "brain" waves, could be recorded by placing the leads from a voltmeter on the skull. These recordings are called **electroencephalograms** (*electro* for "electrical," *encephalo* for "brain," and *grams* for "graphs"), or **EEGs**.

In a traditional EEG recording arrangement (**Figure 7.2**), one electrode (a small metal disc called the active electrode) is attached or pasted to the scalp

Figure 7.2 ▼

Polygraph Recording EEG
The first polygraphs used this simple method for noninvasively recording electrical activity in the human brain. (Photograph from Maximilian Stock Ltd./Getty Images; chart from Southern Illinois University/Science Source.)

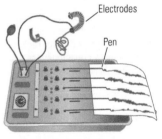

1 Electrodes are attached to the skull, corresponding to specific areas of the brain.

Polygraph pen recorder

2 Polygraph electrodes are connected to magnets, which are connected to pens...

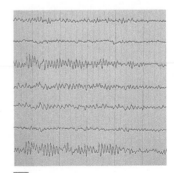

3 ...that produce a paper record of electrical activity in the brain. This record indicates a relaxed person.

to detect the electrical activity in the underlying brain area. A second electrode (the indifferent electrode) is attached elsewhere, on the earlobe perhaps, where no changing electrical activity exists. The two electrodes detect the difference in electrical potentials near the scalp electrode, thus revealing the underlying brain activity.

Electrical fluctuations in the brain are small, usually much less than a millivolt, but when amplified, they can be displayed on a **polygraph** (meaning "many graphs"). In the original polygraph, electrical signals were recorded by pens on long sheets of paper pulled by a motor, allowing the patterns of electrical activity to be traced on the paper. Today, computers, including smartphones, store the patterns and replay the electrical signals on a screen.

▲ EEG waves recorded via computer can match brain-wave activity to specific brain regions and states of consciousness. (AJPhoto/Science Source)

What does the EEG record? Recall that individual neurons produce graded potentials—small depolarizations and hyperpolarizations of membrane voltage (see Figure 4.20). If many neurons undergo graded potential changes at the same time, the signal is large enough to be recorded from as far away as the skull surface. Neocortical neurons are arranged in horizontal layers, and a substantial portion of the EEG signal comes from the large pyramidal neurons of layers V and VI (see Figure 3.26). Thus, the signal recorded by the EEG is the sum of rhythmical graded potentials on many thousands of neurons.

Cell rhythms are produced in a number of ways. Some cells in the thalamus or brainstem act as *pacemakers*, driving the graded potentials of cortical cells. Interneurons within the cortex, connected to many dozens of adjacent cells, also discharge rhythmically, driving those rhythms. Cells also have intrinsic rhythms, and the connections between adjacent neurons can serve to synchronize those patterns. Finally, the cells' rhythms can fluctuate with heart rate or respiration, processes that provide oxygen and glucose to the cells, thus influencing their activity.

No matter how a given signal is produced, the part of the neuron's membrane that produces it is called the signal's **generator**. The many different waves recorded at a single location correspond to the generator's response to changing inputs. That the electrical activity detected through the skull comes from signal generators in the brain has been demonstrated in a number of ways. During surgery, scientists have taken EEG recordings, both from the skull and directly from the underlying brain, and have found that the rhythms from the two locations are similar. The waves in the brain tissue are larger in amplitude (height of wave), however, and larger still the closer they are to the wave-generating cells. In research with animals, microelectrodes placed within neurons demonstrate that these neurons do generate brain waves.

Waves recorded from the skull are **volume conducted** through the brain and through the skull in the manner that waves travel through water. As the electrodes are moved farther from the source, the wave amplitude from a given generator grows smaller. Thus, if a number of electrodes are placed on the skull, amplitude differences can be used to estimate the approximate location of the generator that is producing a given set of waves.

The EEG is a valuable tool for studying states of consciousness, including waking, sleep, and anesthesia; for diagnosing epilepsy and brain damage; and for studying cognitive functions, including neural control of prosthetic devices.

States of Consciousness

Figure 7.3 shows patterns of brain wave activity associated with particular states of consciousness or behavioral states. When a person is aroused, excited, or even just alert, the EEG pattern has a low amplitude (wave height) and a high frequency (number of brain waves per second), as seen in Figure 7.3A. This **beta (β) rhythm** is typical of an EEG taken from anywhere on the skull of an alert participant—not only a human but other animals as well.

In contrast, when a person is calm and resting quietly, especially with eyes closed, rhythmical, larger, slower brain waves emerge (Figure 7.3B). These so-called alpha (α) waves wax and wane in amplitude at a frequency of approximately 11 cycles per second. In humans, the largest alpha rhythms come from the region of the visual cortex at the back of the head. If a relaxed person is disturbed or opens his or her eyes, the alpha rhythm abruptly stops.

Not everyone displays alpha rhythms, and some people display them much more consistently than others. You can buy a small voltmeter for monitoring your own alpha rhythms if you are interested. The voltmeter transforms EEG waves into beeps so that the brain-wave rhythm can be heard. After attaching a lead from one pole of the voltmeter to your skull and attaching the reference wire to your earlobe, you relax with eyes closed and try to make the voltmeter beep in an alpha rhythm. Beeping voltmeters were once promoted as a tool for learning transcendental meditation.

EEG is a sensitive indicator of states other than arousal and relaxation. Figure 7.3C through E illustrates the EEG changes that take place as a person moves from drowsiness to sleep and finally enters deep sleep. As the EEG rhythms become slower in frequency and larger in amplitude, 4- to 7-cycle-per-second theta (θ) waves and finally 1- to 3-cycle-per-second **delta (δ) waves** are produced.

These distinctive brain-wave patterns make the EEG a reliable tool for monitoring waking and other conscious states. Because slower waves also occur during anesthesia, the EEG is useful for estimating the depth of anesthesia. Brain trauma may also result in EEG slowing, making EEG useful for evaluating the severity of head injury. If the brain ceases to function (the condition called brain death), the EEG trace becomes a flat line.

Brain Injury and Epilepsy

The EEG finds useful clinical application in diagnosing brain injury in which electrical signals may be abnormal or absent in damaged tissue. Epilepsy is characterized by changed sensation, mood, or consciousness and/or by convulsions, referred to as seizures (detailed in Section 26.4). The causes of seizure were unknown until EEG experiments demonstrated that different types are associated with different abnormal electrical rhythms in the brain (**Figure 7.4**).

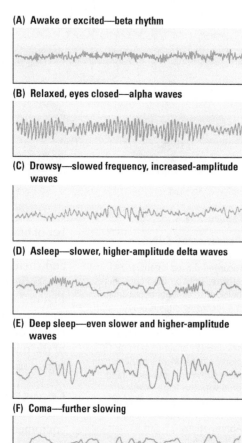

(A) Awake or excited—beta rhythm

(B) Relaxed, eyes closed—alpha waves

(C) Drowsy—slowed frequency, increased-amplitude waves

(D) Asleep—slower, higher-amplitude delta waves

(E) Deep sleep—even slower and higher-amplitude waves

(F) Coma—further slowing

Time (sec)

Figure 7.3 ▲

Characteristic EEG Recordings Brain-wave patterns reflect different states of consciousness in humans. (Data from W. Penfield and H. H. Jasper, *Epilepsy and the Functional Anatomy of the Human Brain.* Boston: Little, Brown, 1954, p. 12.)

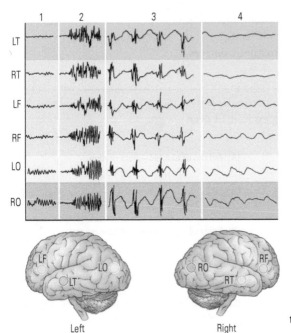

Figure 7.4 ▲

Patterns of Seizure
Examples of EEG patterns recorded during a generalized seizure. Dots on the hemispheres below the readouts approximate the recording sites. Column numbers mark the seizure's stages: (1) typical record before the seizure; (2) onset of seizure; (3) clonic phase, in which the person makes rhythmic movements in time with the large, atypical discharges; and (4) period of coma after the seizure ends. Abbreviations: LT and RT, left and right temporal; LF and RF, left and right frontal; LO and RO, left and right occipital.

In a form of epilepsy called **partial seizure**, abnormal electrical discharges are restricted to only one or a few brain regions. Partial seizure is associated with sensations or emotions (simple partial seizure) or with a brief loss of consciousness (complex partial seizure). By contrast, in **generalized seizures** the abnormal electrical discharges occur in widespread regions of the brain. Generalized seizures are characterized by abnormal body movements and include convulsions (tonic-clonic seizure); falling down without muscle tone (atonic seizure); and loss of consciousness (absence seizure).

EEG recordings can provide information about both the cause of epilepsy and its location. The duration of an epileptic attack correlates closely with the duration of abnormalities in the EEG, large distinctive spikes, slowing of the electrical waves, or brief loss of the EEG signal. This correspondence indicates that epilepsy is associated with abnormal neuronal activity. The EEG likewise can identify the brain region in which the abnormal rhythm is produced: presumably, the focus is the brain region that first generates the abnormal activity. By recording abnormal waves from a number of brain regions, triangulation methods can be used to identify their source.

Alternatively, abnormal EEG waves may originate in a particular location and then recruit adjacent regions, and in that way the abnormality spreads across the brain. Note that the largest abnormal spikes, in the bottom panel of Figure 7.4, appear to come from the right occipital (RO) cortex recording site, suggesting that the abnormality producing the epileptic attack is located in this region of the brain. Computerized techniques are used to make comparisons of the onset times and amplitude of EEG waves and thus to indicate the brain region in which the abnormal waves originate.

Cognitive Function

EEG imaging is also used to study cognitive function. Miniaturization of the equipment allows recordings to be taken from 100 or more sites on the skull. The computer then makes a two-dimensional map of the brain surface, with different colors indicating the relative activity of different brain regions. This technique produces an ongoing "online" representation of the "working" brain.

Coherence theory, which aims to relate the brain's single-cell activity and EEG activity to the information processing required for behavior, proposes that rather than brain activity consisting of a number of conscious "states," a continuum-of-state exists, from high coherence to low coherence (Harris and Thiele, 2011). *High coherence* occurs when the EEG is displaying large, slow waves and the single-cell activity of neurons is highly correlated (**Figure 7.5**A). *Low coherence* occurs when the EEG displays the low-voltage, high-frequency beta pattern and single-cell activity is poorly correlated, with every neuron firing at a different time (Figure 7.5B). In the former state, the brain is idling; in the latter state it is actively processing information.

Coherence theory underlies the idea that measures, even of small differences in EEG activity, can estimate different brain regions' information processing

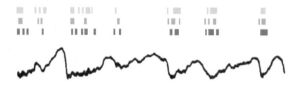

status. Thus, a large number of EEG recording electrodes placed across the skull can map the comparative involvement of different brain regions in ongoing behavior. Coherence theory also underlies the reverse effect—that "brain information" in the form of EEG waves can become a tool to control external devices.

Because EEG signals and the coherence of underlying single-cell activity vary with self-directed behavior, an individual can change his or her brain coherence by "thinking," for example, to learn to control an external device such as a computer or robot via mental activity. Using such *brain–computer interfaces* (BCIs; see Chapter 9 opening Portrait) an individual who is paralyzed can learn to control a computer cursor or command a robot to do chores. Coherence theory also proposes that much more information is contained in single-cell activity than in EEG activity, so single-cell signals will be more effective in controlling BCIs than will EEG waves.

Event-Related Potentials

Event-related potentials are brief changes in an EEG signal in response to a discrete sensory stimulus. ERPs are largely the excitatory and inhibitory graded potentials, the EPSPs and IPSPs that a sensory stimulus triggers on dendrites (see Figure 4.28). An ERP is not easy to detect because the signal is mixed in with many other EEG signals from the brain. One way to detect ERPs is by repeatedly producing the stimulus and then averaging the recorded responses. Averaging cancels out irregular and unrelated electrical activity, leaving only the graded potentials generated by the stimulus event.

To clarify the procedure, imagine throwing a small stone into a lake of choppy water. Although the stone produces a splash, that splash is hard to see among all the lake's ripples and waves. The splash made by the stone is analogous to an ERP caused by a sensory stimulus. If a number of stones of exactly the same size are sequentially thrown, hit exactly the same spot in the water, and produce exactly the same splash, then the splash becomes easier to detect. Using a computer to average out the water's random wave movements would make the regular splashes produced by the stones stand out as clearly as if a single stone had been thrown into a pool of calm water.

Figure 7.6 shows how averaging reveals an ERP in response to a tone. Notice at the top the

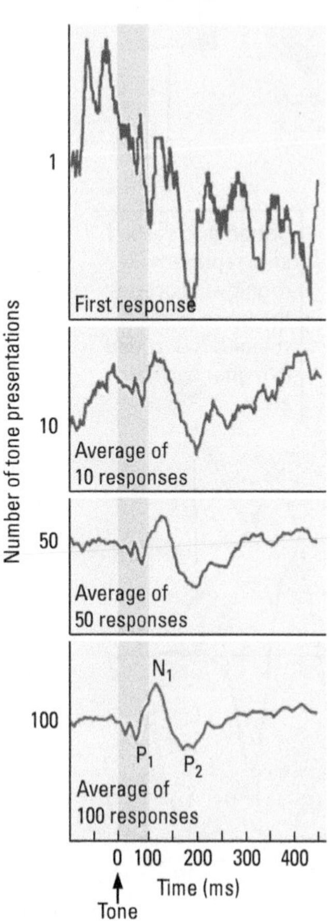

Figure 7.5 ▲

Coherence theory (A) When the EEG displays slow waves (delta pattern), single neurons in a synchronized state discharge rhythmically in phase with the EEG, and the brain is idling. (B) When the EEG displays fast waves (beta pattern), the firing of desynchronized single neurons is uncorrelated, and the brain is actively processing information. (Data from Harris and Thiele, 2011.)

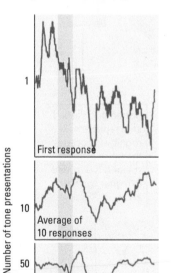

Figure 7.6 ◄

Detecting ERPs In the averaging process for obtaining an auditory ERP, a stimulus tone is presented at time 0 (indicated by the vertical shaded bar), and EEG activity that occurs in response is recorded. After many successive presentations of the tone, the averaged EEG wave sequence develops a more and more distinctive shape until, after 100 presentations, the ERP pattern is sharp and clear. Positive (P) and negative (N) waves that appear at different times after the stimulus repetition are used for analysis.

very irregular EEG made when the tone is first presented. At the bottom, after recordings of more than 100 stimulus presentations are averaged, a distinctive wave pattern—the ERP—appears. An ERP produces a number of negative (N) and positive (P) waves in a period of a few hundred milliseconds after the stimulus.

By convention, the EEG waves depicted as going downward on the ERP graph are called positive, and the waves depicted as going upward are called negative. Positive and negative waves are numbered at the time they are produced. For instance, P_1 in Figure 7.6 is a positive wave produced about 100 ms after the stimulus presentation.

Not all waves in the ERP are unique to a particular stimulus. Some are common to any auditory stimulus the brain perceives. The waves produced at longer latencies, 100 to 300 ms after a stimulus is presented, likely are related to unique properties of the stimulus. For example, the long-latency ERPs produced in response to the spoken words *cat* and *rat* contain distinctive peaks and patterns that allow researchers to differentiate one response from the other.

ERPs have another useful feature. The neural response evoked by a sensory stimulus crosses many synapses between the sensory receptors and the cognitive processing regions in the cortex, where the stimulus information is further processed sequentially in a number of cortical regions. At each neuron in such a pathway, a new ERP is generated. ERP recording can thus map the progress of the response as it makes its way through the nervous system. ERPs can assess both information processing in brain pathways and the health of those pathways themselves.

Figure 7.7 graphs an ERP produced in response to an auditory stimulus. The waves correspond to successive activations of synaptic connections through the auditory pathway from brainstem to cortex. ERP signals identified as I through VI are from brainstem signal generators (neurons in the pathway); those designated N_0 through P_1 are from primary auditory cortex regions (A1); and those designated N_1 through P_3 are from secondary and tertiary (association) regions of the cortex. The dotted lines indicate brain waves associated with thought processes in response to the signal. For example, P_3, produced 300 ms after stimulus presentation, represents decoding the meaning of the sounds.

Figure 7.8 shows a multiple-recording method using 128 electrodes simultaneously to detect ERPs at many sites for cortical mapping. Computerized averaging techniques simplify the masses of recorded neural information into comparisons between electrode sites. At the top of the figure, a participant's ERP is being monitored while he views a picture of a rat that flashes repeatedly in the same place on a computer screen. The P_3 wave recorded on the posterior right side of the participant's head (center diagram) is larger

Figure 7.7 ▼

Brain Mapping with ERP
ERP recorded from the parietal cortex of a participant in response to the presentation of an auditory stimulus. ERP tracks the event's passage through the nervous system. (Data from Neville, 1980.)

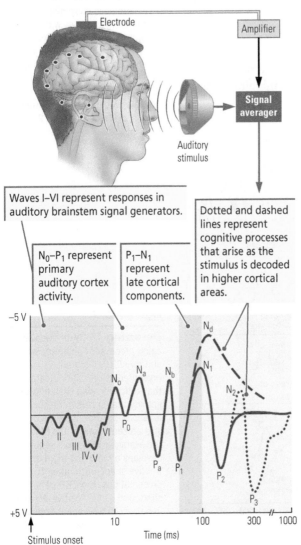

than the same P_3 wave recorded anywhere else, showing that this region is a "hot spot" for processing rats (bottom). Thus, for this particular participant, the right posterior part of the brain is central in decoding the picture of the rat 300 ms after it was presented.

ERPs can reveal when and where in the brain actions are planned and executed. Researchers have identified ERPs called **readiness potentials** produced in the motor cortex later than 300 ms after stimulus presentation. Readiness potentials signal both that the motor cortex is preparing a movement and the part of motor area involved in executing the impending movement.

Magnetoencephalography

When a magnetic field passes across a wire, it induces a current in the wire. When a current flows along a wire, it induces a magnetic field around the wire. This reciprocal relation between electricity and magnetism is also seen in neurons. That is, by generating an electrical field, neural activity also produces a magnetic field. A single neuron produces a micromagnetic field, but the field produced by many neurons can be recorded on the skull surface. Such a **magnetoencephalogram** (MEG) is the magnetic counterpart of the EEG or ERP.

The heart of a MEG probe is a sensing device containing the special superconducting coils needed to detect the brain's very weak magnetic fields. This so-called *SQUID* (superconducting quantum interference device) is immersed in liquid helium to keep it at the low temperature necessary for superconductivity. One or more probes are moved across the surface of the skull, sending signals to the SQUID.

Each probe produces an "isocontour map," a chart with concentric circles (gradients) representing different intensities in the neural magnetic field. Isocontour maps allow investigators to calculate the location of the neurons generating the field in three dimensions. They also convert MEG maps into a graph of electrical events very similar to electrical potentials recorded by EEG instruments.

7.2 Brain Stimulation

Placing an electrode near a neuron and passing an electrical current through it will produce an action potential in that neuron. Neuroscientists discovered long ago that they could learn about the functions of different brain areas by electrically stimulating the tissue. The region's function can be inferred from any resulting behavior. By moving the electrode and repeating the procedure, investigators can construct a functional map of the brain.

The results of the earliest brain stimulation studies indicated that movements are elicited by stimulating the motor cortex, sensations are elicited by stimulating the sensory cortex, and complex cognitive functions such as speech are disrupted by stimulating association areas, such as the cortical speech areas. Electrical stimulation of the brainstem produces many complex behaviors in rats, including mating, aggression, nest building, and food carrying. Many brainstem stimulation sites are positively rewarding: an animal will perform work, such as pressing a bar, to receive the stimulation. Other sites are negatively rewarding: animals will avoid locations at which they had received stimulation.

Electrodes attached to the scalp of a research participant are connected to...

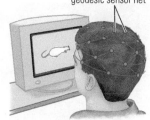

Electrodes in geodesic sensor net

...a computer display of electrical activity, showing a large positive (P_3) wave at the posterior right side of the head.

This electrical activity can be converted to a color representation showing the hot spot for the visual stimulus.

Resting   300 ms after viewing

Figure 7.8 ▲

Using ERPs to Image Brain Activity

Deep Brain Stimulation

Early investigations into electrically stimulating the human brain were directed not only to investigating brain functions but also to controlling brain activity to remediate psychiatric diseases. Elliot Valenstein summarizes this history in his 1975 book, *Brain Control: A Critical Examination of Brain Stimulation and Psychosurgery*. Today, electrodes neurosurgically implanted for **deep brain stimulation** (DBS) is routine (**Figure 7.9**). DBS has application in treating psychiatric, neurological, and psychological conditions (Sankar et al., 2012). DBS stimulation is used to treat depression and obsessive-compulsive disorder when other treatments have failed. DBS can treat epilepsy by coopting activity of neurons involved in abnormal activity and so preventing abnormal discharges.

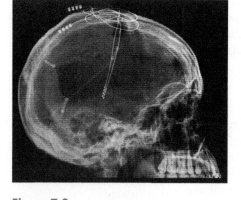

Figure 7.9 ▲

Deep Brain Stimulation
X-ray of a human brain showing electrodes implanted in the thalamus for DBS. (The Cleveland Clinic.)

Parkinsonism is characterized both by tremors and by **akinesia**, absence or poverty of movement (*a*, "not," and *kinesia*, "move"). When DBS electrodes are implanted in the brain in a number of regions of the basal ganglia, including the globus pallidus or subthalamic nucleus, both tremors and akinesia are lessened. Reviews of DBS used for Parkinson's disease document that the treatment improves movement, cognition, and mood as well (Kocabicak et al., 2012).

What limits both experimentation with DBS and its use in treating brain disorders is its invasiveness: the skull must be opened to introduce the electrode. This procedure in itself can damage the brain or introduce infection. Thus, the application of intracranial stimulation techniques is limited to conditions for which other treatment options are limited or nonexistent.

Transcranial Magnetic Stimulation

The relation between magnetism and electricity forms the basis of **transcranial magnetic stimulation** (TMS), a noninvasive method that allows brain stimulation through the skull. A small wire coil in a figure-8 shape is placed adjacent to the skull (**Figure 7.10**A). High-voltage current is passed through the coil in pulses as rapid as 50 times per second. Each electrical pulse produces a rapid increase, then a decrease, in the magnetic field around the coil. The magnetic

Figure 7.10 ▼

Transcranial Magnetic Stimulation (A) In clinical therapy for depression, TMS influences neural activity in a localized brain area. (B) Composite image diagrams how TMS works. (A: Marcello Massimini/University of Milan. B: Composite MRI and PET scan from Tomas Paus, Montreal Neurological Institute.)

(A)

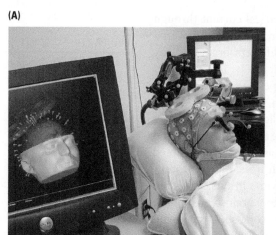

(B)

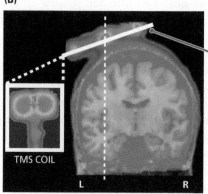

The TMS coil, shown here in a composite MRI and PET-scan photograph, interferes with brain function in the adjacent area.

field penetrates the skull and changes the electrical activity of adjacent neurons (Figure 7.10B).

TMS was originally used by neurosurgeons for stimulating brain tissue, both to monitor its functioning during brain surgery and to identify the tissue's function. From this initial use, it became clear that TMS does not harm brain tissue, even after thousands of pulses of stimulation, and so can be used to stimulate healthy brains through the skull.

To map the brain's functional areas, TMS researchers move the stimulation and note the results, identifying and mapping cortical functions in just the same way as with DBS. TMS is used therapeutically, also like DBS, and for many similar purposes, including treating pain, stroke-induced impairments, movement disorders, and depression (Berlim et al., 2013). Repetitive TMS (rTMS) pulses can inactivate an area of brain tissue for a short time, allowing a TMS researcher to make a temporary virtual lesion in the brain and study its consequences.

7.3 Static Imaging Techniques

Aside from surgery, the first methods for peering into the living brain to see what is "in there" required taking X-rays. The most obvious limitation of X-ray techniques is their output: a static two-dimensional image of what, in contrast, is a dynamic four-dimensional structure. Imaging the third and fourth dimensions had to await the advent of powerful computing techniques.

Imaging by X-Ray

Enhanced X-ray methods continue as important tools for medical diagnosis, especially to the neurologist looking for evidence of a brain tumor, stroke, or abnormality in brain vasculature.

Conventional Radiography

In **conventional radiography**, X-rays pass through the skull onto an X-ray-sensitive film. As they travel through the head, the X-rays are absorbed to different degrees by different tissues: to the greatest degree by dense tissue such as bone, to a lesser degree by neural tissue, and less still by fluids in the blood vessels and ventricles. The developed film reveals a shadowy negative image showing the locations of different kinds of tissue: bone is white, brain is gray, and ventricles black. Radiography is still used for examining the skull for fractures and the brain for gross abnormalities.

Pneumoencephalography

Pneumoencephalography (literally, "air–brain graph") is a method for enhancing conventional X-ray radiography by taking advantage of the fact that X-rays are not absorbed by air. First, a small amount of cerebrospinal fluid is removed from the subarachnoid space in a subject's spinal cord and replaced with air. Then, with the subject sitting upright, X-rays are taken as the air moves up the spinal cord and enters the ventricular system. Because of the air inside them, the ventricles stand out clearly in the resulting image. Although

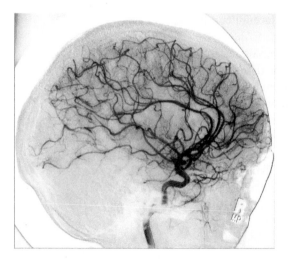

Figure 7.11 ▲

X-Ray Technique Typical carotid angiogram showing the brain's large blood vessels. The face points down toward the right. (Medical Body Scans/Science Source.)

it has diagnostic value—because expanded ventricles can mean loss of brain tissue and because constricted ventricles can indicate the presence of tumors—pneumoencephalography is painful and invasive.

Angiography

Angiography (from the Greek *angeion*, "vessel," and *graph*, "to write") is a method for imaging blood vessels. It is similar to pneumoencephalography except that a substance that absorbs X-rays is injected into the bloodstream (**Figure 7.11**). The presence of this radiopaque material in the blood produces an image of the blood vessels, thus revealing any circulatory abnormalities that might affect blood flow, including dilation, constriction, or abnormalities in blood vessels. Injecting a substance into the bloodstream is dangerous, however, and can be painful. Newer imaging methods thus are supplanting angiography.

Computed Tomography

The modern era of brain imaging began in the early 1970s, when Allan Cormack and Godfrey Hounsfield independently developed an X-ray approach, the **CT scan**, for which they shared the 1979 Nobel Prize. **Computed tomography** (*tomo* means "cut": it images a single section of the brain) involves passing a narrow X-ray beam through the same object at many angles, creating many images. The images are then manipulated using computing and mathematical techniques to create a three-dimensional image (**Figure 7.12**A).

The skull is seen as a white border. The brain's gray matter density does not differ sufficiently from that of white matter for a CT scan to clearly distinguish the two, and so the cortex and its underlying white matter show up as a more or less homogeneous gray. Ventricular fluid is less absorbent, so ventricles and fissures are rendered darker in the CT scan.

Each point on this image represents about a 1-mm-diameter circle of tissue. Called a **voxel**, such an area is a measurement of image resolution, where each pixel represents a voxel. The CT resolution is sufficient for localizing brain tumors and lesions. The lesion revealed in Figure 7.12A appears as a darker area

Figure 7.12 ▼

X-Ray Computed Tomography (A) Horizontal CT scan of a patient who presented with Broca's aphasia. The dark region at the left anterior is the lesion location. (B) Schematic of the horizontal section, with the area of the lesion shaded gray. (C) Lateral view of the left hemisphere with the lesion shaded gray. (Research from Damasio and Damasio, 1989, p. 56 © Elsevier)

(A) CT scan
Lesion

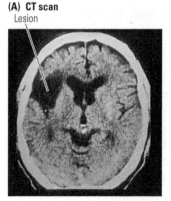

(B) Horizontal section
Anterior

Lesion

Posterior

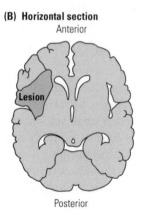

(C) Reconstruction, lateral view
Lesion

Plane of section in parts A and B

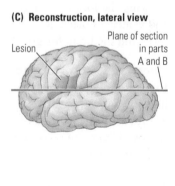

in the CT scan owing to the presence of fewer neurons and more fluid in this region. This patient presented with symptoms of Broca's aphasia, a diagnosis confirmed by the location of the lesion in the left frontal cortex (adjacent to the butterfly-shaped, fluid-filled lateral ventricles), as portrayed in a drawing of the same horizontal section (Figure 7.12B). Figure 7.12C is a lateral drawing of the left hemisphere showing the extent of the lesion, reconstructed from a series of horizontal CT scans.

7.4 Dynamic Brain Imaging

When a brain region is active, the amount of blood, oxygen, and glucose flowing to that region increases. Advances that led from static to dynamic brain imaging allow investigators to measure changes in blood flow and oxygen in the brain and to infer from these measures changes in brain activity. Among the imaging techniques developed around this logic are positron emission tomography, functional MRI, and optical tomography.

Positron Emission Tomography

Researchers use **positron emission tomography** (PET) to study metabolic activity in brain cells engaged in processing brain functions such as language. PET imaging indirectly detects changes in the brain's blood flow (Posner and Raichle, 1994). A PET scanner, shown at left in **Figure 7.13**, consists of a doughnut-shaped array of radiation detectors that encircles a reclining person's head. A small amount of water, labeled with radioactive molecules, is injected into the bloodstream. It poses no danger because the molecules, such as the radioactive isotope oxygen-15 (^{15}O), break down in just a few minutes and are quickly eliminated from the body. A computer reconstructs a color-coded image, as shown at the right of the figure, representing areas of higher and lower blood flow.

Figure 7.13 ▼

PET Scanner and Image
A subject lying in a PET scanner (left). The scanner's design is illustrated in the drawing (center). In the scan (right) the bright red and yellow areas are regions of high blood flow. (PET scanner from Hank Morgan/Science Source; PET scan from Science Source.)

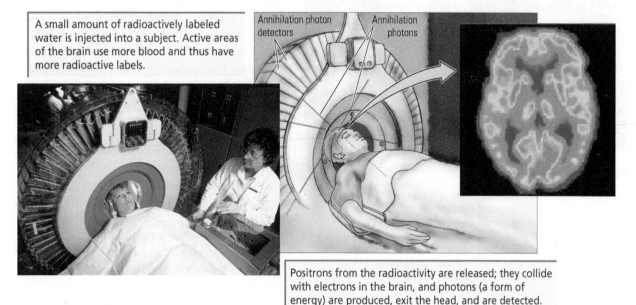

A small amount of radioactively labeled water is injected into a subject. Active areas of the brain use more blood and thus have more radioactive labels.

Annihilation photon detectors   Annihilation photons

Positrons from the radioactivity are released; they collide with electrons in the brain, and photons (a form of energy) are produced, exit the head, and are detected.

(A)

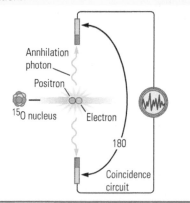

A positron released by an unstable nucleus of ^{15}O meets an electron, and their mass is converted to two annihilation photons traveling in opposite directions.

Annhilation photon

Positron

Annhilation photon

^{15}O nucleus   Electron

180

Coincidence circuit

Opposing radiation detectors record the event when struck simultaneously by annihilation photons.

(B) Annihilation photon detectors

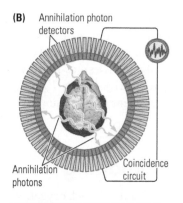

Annihilation photons

Coincidence circuit

Multiple rings of radiation detectors are arranged about the subject's head.

(C)

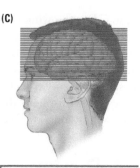

As many as 63 images are recorded simultaneously, in parallel horizontal slices.

Figure 7.14 ▲

The Technique of PET Imaging (Research from Posner and Raichle, 1994, p. 19.)

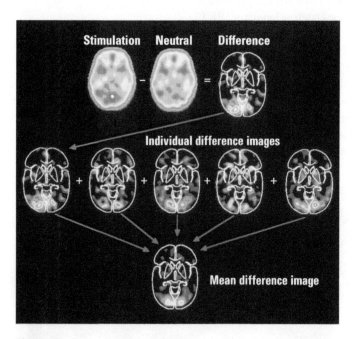

Figure 7.15 ▲

The Procedure of Subtraction In the upper row of scans, the resting condition while looking at a static fixation point (neutral) is subtracted from the experimental condition of looking at a flickering checkerboard (stimulation). The subtraction produces a different scan for each of five experimental participants, shown in the middle row, but all show increased blood flow in the occipital region. The difference scans are averaged to produce the representative image at bottom. (From M. E. Raichle, Malinckrodt Institute of Radiology, Washington University School of Medicine.)

Radioactive molecules such as ^{15}O release positrons (electrons with a positive charge, hence the name of the technique). Positrons are emitted from an unstable atom that is deficient in neutrons and are attracted to the negative charge of electrons in the brain. The subsequent collision of the positively and negatively charged particles leads to their annihilation, which produces energy in the form of two photons (light particles) that leave the area of the annihilation event in exactly opposite directions (**Figure 7.14**A).

In the PET scanner, pairs of radiation detectors, placed opposite each other within a ring encircling the head, detect the photons (Figure 7.14B). The paired detectors record an event only when they are struck by photons simultaneously. Through the use of multiple detectors, PET cameras can image multiple parallel brain slices simultaneously, as shown in Figure 7.14C, to produce an image. The voxel size of each brain-slice image is about 2 mm^3.

PET infers rather than directly measures local neural activity, on the assumption that blood flow increases where neuron activity increases. To do this, PET researchers studying the link between blood flow and mental activity resort to a statistical trick, illustrated in the top row of **Figure 7.15**. They subtract the blood-flow pattern when a participant is in one experimental condition—or in a neutral condition, such as resting—from the pattern imaged when the participant is engaged in a different experimental condition. This subtractive process images the difference in blood flow between the two states. The difference can be averaged across participants (middle row) to yield a representative, average image difference that reveals which brain areas are selectively active during a given experimental condition (bottom).

Generating radioactive materials, which must be prepared in a cyclotron located close to the PET scanner, is very expensive, but the advantages over other imaging methods tend to justify the cost. PET can detect the decay of literally hundreds of radiochemicals to allow for mapping a wide range of brain changes and conditions, including changes in pH, glucose, oxygen, amino acids, neurotransmitters, and proteins. PET can detect relative amounts of a given neurotransmitter; the density of neurotransmitter receptors; and metabolic activities associated with learning, brain poisoning, and degenerative processes possibly related to aging. PET is widely used to study cognitive function, with great success.

Magnetic Resonance Imaging

In **magnetic resonance imaging** (MRI), a large magnet (M) and a specific radiofrequency pulse (R) generate a brain signal that produces an image (I). MRI is used to study both brain anatomy and neural function noninvasively, and because it does not make use of ionizing radiation, it is safe enough to use repeatedly on volunteers and patients, adult and child alike.

The technique is based on the principle that a hydrogen atom's nucleus, which consists of a single proton, behaves like a spinning bar magnet. Each proton has a dipole: one end is a north pole and the other end a south pole. Each spinning proton produces an electrical current. Ordinarily, protons are oriented at random, so a given piece of tissue (all soft tissue contains water, which contains hydrogen) has no net dipole and consequently generates no net electrical current (**Figure 7.16**A).

When hydrogen atoms are placed in a magnetic field, the spinning protons orient themselves with respect to the field's lines of force (Figure 7.16B). In other words, the protons behave like a compass needle that aligns itself north and south with Earth's magnetic field. When aligned, the protons' summed electrical current is large enough to be measured.

Because proton density varies in different brain tissue (cerebrospinal fluid, myelin, neurons), largely in proportion to its water content, the electrical currents produced by the aligned protons are different, higher for some tissues and lower for others. Measures of the electrical current are used to create the MRI image.

Another way to make an MRI image is to perturb the protons when they are aligned and record the changes occurring in the electrical field as the protons realign after the perturbation. A brief radiofrequency pulse is applied to a brain, horizontal to the magnetic field. The pulse forms a second magnetic field that pushes the aligned protons over onto their sides (**Figure 7.17**A). The tipped protons now have two motions: they spin about their own axes and they spin about their

Figure 7.16 ▼

Physics of MRI I (A) Typical random movements of hydrogen protons. (B) Synchronized orientation of protons under the influence of an external vertical magnetic field generates a summed electrical current. Measuring this current is a process used to create an MRI image.

(A)

Each hydrogen atom's proton rotates about its axis, acting as a small magnet with its own north–south dipole. Normally the protons are randomly diffused, so the tissue has no net charge.

(B)

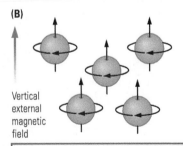

Vertical external magnetic field

When placed in a magnetic field, the protons align in parallel.

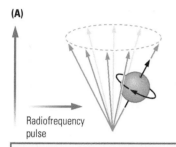

(A)

Radiofrequency pulse

A radiofrequency pulse applied to the tissue pushes the protons to their sides, causing them to wobble about their axes and about their north–south orientation. This motion,...

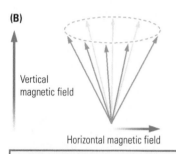

(B)

Vertical magnetic field

Horizontal magnetic field

...called precession, produces measurable vertical and horizontal magnetic fields.

Figure 7.17 ▲

Physics of MRI II (A) Adding a horizontal radiofrequency pulse to the vertical magnetic field perturbs aligned hydrogen protons, tipping them wobbling onto their sides. (B) The precession (wobbling) of protons under these dual influences produces two measurable magnetic fields. Recording changes occurring in the field as protons realign after perturbation is a process used to create MRI images.

longitudinal (north–south) orientation (Figure 7.17B). The protons wobble like a slowly spinning top, a motion called **precession**.

When the horizontal magnetic field is turned off, the synchronously spinning protons begin to relax: they begin to "stand up" again and to fall out of synchrony with one another. Both relaxation processes are measured, using a current detector, by two time constants, T_1 and T_2:

- For T_1, a current detector oriented horizontally to the vertical axis, that is, to the protons' initial alignment, measures how long it takes after the magnetic pulse is turned off for the protons to "right" themselves from their tipped positions and realign with the original magnetic field (**Figure 7.18**A).

- For T_2, a second detector oriented perpendicular to the first measures the rate at which protons lose synchrony about the horizontal axis after the horizontal pulse is turned off (Figure 7.18B).

Protons in differing tissue types have different relaxation rates and corresponding T_1 and T_2 time constants (**Figure 7.19**A). For example, the relaxation rates for cerebrospinal fluid are slower than those for brain tissue. Therefore, at a set time—for example, at the midpoint of relaxation—differences in electrical current related to and indicating the composition of tissue can be measured.

T_1 and T_2 can be translated into brain-image gradients that correspond to its different tissues, with darker gradients indicating low-density tissue and lighter indicating high-density tissue (Figure 7.19B). Either T_1 or T_2 constants are used, though one may be more suitable than the other in a given situation. For example, T_2 imaging is more sensitive than T_1 to differences between damaged tissue and intact tissue and so is useful for detecting lesions.

In the MRI procedure illustrated in **Figure 7.20**, the subject lies prone with his or her head centered within the magnetic coils and must remain as still as possible. (Corrections are made for the slight head and brain movement produced by pulsations of cerebral blood flow.) Density differences in the imaged slice through the head are portrayed as colors, in this case producing a

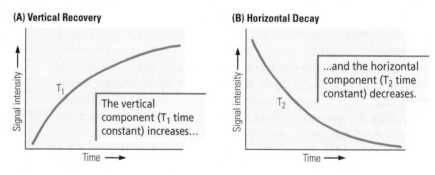

(A) Vertical Recovery

Signal intensity →

T_1

The vertical component (T_1 time constant) increases...

Time →

(B) Horizontal Decay

Signal intensity →

T_2

...and the horizontal component (T_2 time constant) decreases.

Time →

Figure 7.18 ▲

MRI Time Constants When the horizontal radiofrequency pulse is turned off, relaxation in the vertical and horizontal components of the magnetic field provides two time constants. T_1 measures the recovering vertical component of the magnetic field, which increases. T_2 measures the decay of synchronous spinning, the horizontal component of the magnetic field, which decreases.

(A)

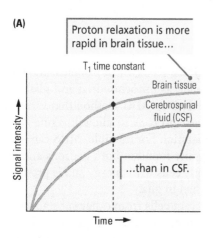

Proton relaxation is more rapid in brain tissue...

T_1 time constant

Brain tissue

Cerebrospinal fluid (CSF)

...than in CSF.

Signal intensity →

Time →

(B) MRI

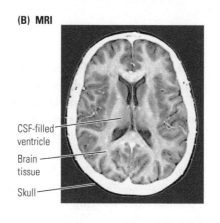

CSF-filled ventricle

Brain tissue

Skull

Figure 7.19 ◄

Translating Relaxation Rates into a Brain Image
(A) Protons have different relaxation rates in different types of tissue. (B) Those differences can be translated into a brain image. (Medical Body Scans/Science Source, Colorization by: Matthew Bologna)

horizontal cross section of the head and of the brain. Although the MRI procedure is safe, the noisy, enclosed magnetic coils produce claustrophobia in some people. People with surgical implants that contain metal should not undergo MRI because of the magnets' strength.

MRI image resolution is derived from the strength of the magnetic field, measured in **teslas**. A 1.5-tesla magnet is referred to as 1.5T magnet; magnets for medical use range from 0.5T to 3.0T. The resolution of a large magnet is 1-cubic-millimeter voxels, twice that of PET. Despite this high image resolution, like PET, each MRI voxel indirectly infers the activity of thousands of neurons.

Magnetic Resonance Spectroscopy

MRI images depict differences in water density in various brain tissues. The hydrogen nuclei in water molecules affected by MRI's magnetic fields constitute 80% of the brain's soft tissue. MRI does not image the remaining 20% of brain

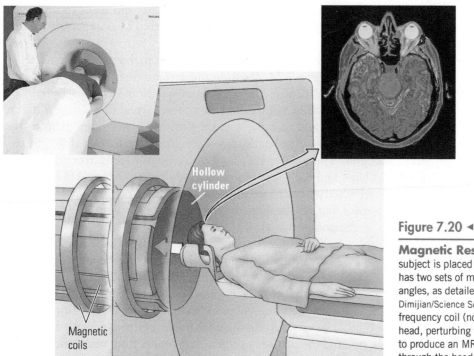

Hollow cylinder

Magnetic coils

Figure 7.20 ◄

Magnetic Resonance Imaging The subject is placed in a long metal cylinder that has two sets of magnetic coils arranged at right angles, as detailed in the drawing. (Gregory G. Dimijian/Science Source.) An additional radio-frequency coil (not shown) surrounds the head, perturbing the static magnetic fields to produce an MRI of a horizontal section through the head, shown in dorsal view at right. (© Bob Schatz)

191

material, including all macromolecules (DNA, RNA, most proteins, and phospholipids); cell membranes; organelles, such as mitochondria; and glial cells. **Magnetic resonance spectroscopy** (MRS) is an MRI method that varies the radiofrequency used for aligning hydrogen protons to allow imaging of the concentrations of that remaining brain material. For example, MRS can image N-acetyl aspartate (NAA), a brain metabolite found in both neurons and glial cells, and creatine, an acid that helps supply cells with energy and is present in much higher concentrations in neurons than in glia.

Thus, MRS imaging can distinguish brain cells from other substances and neurons from glia. MRS can detect brain-cell loss in degenerative diseases such as Alzheimer's, loss of myelin in demyelinating diseases such as multiple sclerosis, and persisting abnormalities in brain metabolism in disorders such as concussion. MRS can also image molecules that participate in transmitting information between neurons. One is choline, the precursor molecule for acetylcholine; another is glutamate, the major excitatory neurotransmitter molecule in the brain. MRS can image many other brain molecules as well, to provide new avenues for investigating brain development, function, and disease.

Diffusion Tensor Imaging

Diffusion tensor imaging (DTI) is an MRI method that detects the directional movements of water molecules to create virtual images of the brain's nerve fiber pathways. (*Diffusion* refers to the movement of water molecules, *tensor* is a linear quality, and *imaging* detects the direction of diffusion.) Water molecules in the ventricles and even in cell bodies move relatively unimpeded in random directions. In nerve fibers, however, their movement is restricted by the tract's orientation and its contents and tends to follow the direction of its longitudinal axis, a property referred to as *anisotropy* (for unequal movement).

DTI tractography is thus used to map the brain's pathways and connectivity, as illustrated in **Figure 7.21**, showing the arcuate fiber pathways that connect Wernicke's and Broca's language areas superimposed on a lateral view of the human brain. The colors shown on these virtual fibers have different orientations and reveal that the arcuate pathway is not homogeneous but consists of a number of subpathways. Each likely mediates a different language function. The images are based on computer reconstructions of bits of actual fibers, and each line represents hundreds of fibers. DTI does not reveal whether fibers are afferent or efferent or the location of synapses, but resolution will improve along with imaging technology (Setsompop et al., 2013).

The Human Connectome Project, a consortium of research centers, is mapping the human brain's connectivity using DTI tractography (Toga et al., 2012). The project's goal is to advance the diagnosis and treatment of conditions such as axon degeneration that might occur in multiple sclerosis, fiber distortion that might occur as a result of tumors, and the damage to fibers that results from traumatic brain injury or stroke. Connectome analysis can also aid in understanding how genes affect brain connections by describing the connectomes

Figure 7.21 ▼

Diffusion Tensor Images of Language Pathways
The pathway connecting Broca's and Wernicke's areas in the brain is revealed by DTI tractography to be composed of subpathways (different colors) representing different aspects of language function. (Research from Marco Catani.)

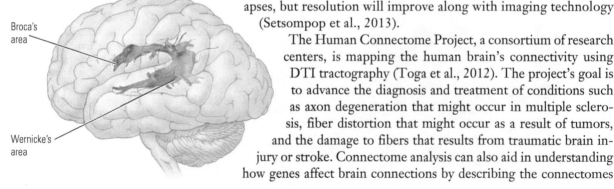

Broca's area

Wernicke's area

of individuals with known genetic diseases, comparing identical twins, and describing sex differences. Finally, connectome analyses can indicate whether epigenetic processes initiated by lifetime experience and learning influence brain connections.

Functional Magnetic Resonance Imaging

As neurons become active, they use more oxygen, resulting in a temporary dip in the amount of oxygen in the blood. At the same time, active neurons signal the blood vessels to dilate to increase blood flow and bring more oxygen to the area. When human brain activity increases, the increase in oxygen produced by increased blood flow actually exceeds the tissue's need for oxygen. As a result, the amount of oxygen in an activated brain area increases (Fox and Raichle, 1986).

An increase in blood oxygen content alters the magnetic properties of the water in the blood. **Functional magnetic resonance imaging** (fMRI) can accurately match these changes in magnetic properties to specific locations in the brain (Ogawa et al., 1990). A measure called the **BOLD contrast**, for blood oxygen level–dependent contrast, provides an index of the brain's relative activity.

Figure 7.22 illustrates the process involved in measuring the BOLD signal. Before neuronal activation, the amount of *deoxyhemoglobin* (hemoglobin without oxygen) and *oxyhemoglobin* (hemoglobin with oxygen) is about equal. (Hemoglobin is a protein in the blood that carries oxygen.) After neuronal activation, the amount of oxyhemoglobin in the blood increases (Figure 7.22, top). The magnetic properties of unoxygenated blood are higher than those of oxygenated blood, and the T_2 signal changes more rapidly in the unoxygenated state than in the oxygenated state (Figure 7.22 middle). Thus, for example, an fMRI measure of a participant viewing a visual stimulus shows the highest blood oxygenation in the visual cortex (Figure 7.22 bottom).

When superimposed on MRI-produced brain images, fMRI changes in activity can be attributed to particular structures. The dense blood-vessel supply to the cerebral cortex allows for a spatial resolution on the order of a 1-cubic-millimeter voxel, about the same resolution as MRI, which affords good spatial resolution of the source of brain activity. Temporal resolution is also quite rapid and follows the fluctuation of oxygenated blood.

Figure 7.23 shows changes in the fMRI signal in the visual cortex of a person who is being periodically stimulated with light. When the light is turned on, the visual cortex (bottom of the brain image) becomes more active than it was during the baseline (no light). In other words, from increases and decreases in the fMRI signal produced by changes in oxygen levels, changes in brain function are inferred.

Which aspects of neuronal function is fMRI measuring? The most metabolically active part of a neuron is presumed to

Figure 7.22 ▼

Blood Oxygen and Brain Activity The different relaxation curves of protons in unoxygenated (blue) and oxygenated (red) blood provide a means for obtaining fMRIs of brain activity. (Research from Kwong et al., 1992, p.5678.)

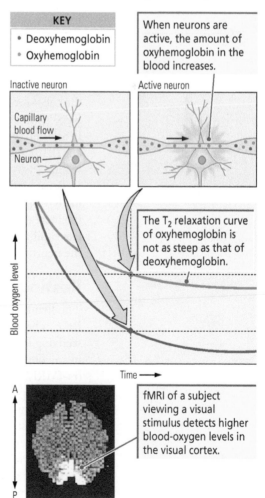

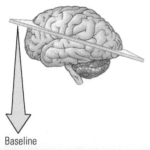

Baseline

Figure 7.23 ▼

Imaging Changes in Brain Activity Functional MRI sequence of a horizontal section at mid-occipital lobe (bottom of each image) in a healthy human brain during visual stimulation. A baseline acquired in darkness (far left) was subtracted from the subsequent images. The participant wore tightly fitting goggles containing light-emitting diodes that were turned on and off as a rapid sequence of scans was obtained in a period of 270 seconds. Note the prominent activity in the visual cortex when the light is on and the rapid cessation of activity when the light is off, all measured in the graph of signal intensity below the images. (Data from Kwong et al., 1992, p. 5676.)

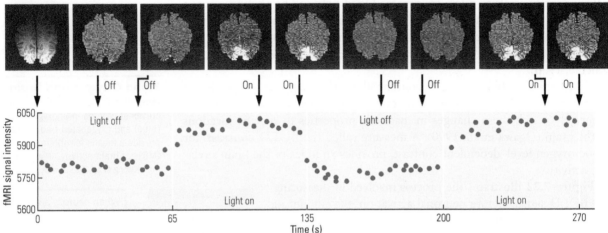

require the most oxygen, so measures of metabolic activity in different parts of the cell—for example, synapses, the cell membrane, or axons—have been made. EPSPs, which ultimately result in cell firing, make the greatest energy demands. IPSPs and the action potential itself have lower energy demands (Murayama et al., 2010). Thus, fMRI is measuring EPSPs and the probability that a neuron will fire, very much the same activity that ERPs measure.

Because glutamate is the major excitatory neurotransmitter in the brain, it is likely responsible in large part for producing both the EPSP on a neuron and the increase in blood flow to the neuron. Glutamate could either directly stimulate capillaries to dilate or activate metabolic pathways that release nitric oxide, the neurotransmitter that causes blood vessels to dilate, to increase blood flow.

Resting-State fMRI

The living brain is always active, even as we rest, sleep, or undergo anesthesia. Researchers have succeeded in inferring brain function and connectivity by studying fMRI signals when participants are in such states, that is, not engaged in any obvious physical or mental activity. This signal, the **resting-state fMRI** (rs-fMRI), is collected when participants are asked to look at a fixed location and to keep their eyes open. The scanner collects brain activity, typically for at least 4-minute-long blocks.

The resting brain is not uniformly active; rather, various brain regions share correlated activity at different times. For example, fields of activity centered on visual regions, auditory regions, movement regions, and so forth, occur. For some regions, such as the basal ganglia, a movement region, functional connectivity, and anatomical connectivity, are highly correlated, but for others, such as those frontal-lobe regions involved in executive function, the correlation is lower. The conclusion is that brain regions that are often used together maintain active relationships even when not in use. This discovery has enabled investigators to map inherent functional relationships in the brain.

In rs-fMRI experiments imaging the electrical activity of neurons across the cortex in mice, neurons in widespread cortical regions likewise become active together. Activity initiated in a primary cortical region, for example the primary visual cortex, then spreads out through secondary and tertiary cortical visual regions. As the wave of activity in visual areas decays, another wave begins in another cortical region, say, in the auditory cortex.

Thus, spontaneous waves of activity circulate from cortical system to cortical system, each lasting on the order of seconds. If a mouse is presented with a sensory stimulus, say a touch on the vibrissae, a wave of activity will immediately begin in the sensory-cortex representation of the vibrissae, then spread over all cortical regions that represent the body senses. These waves of activity form recurring elements, or **motifs**, indicating *functional connectivity* (inherent functional relationships) among cortical systems (Mohajerani et al., 2013).

Finding such functional connectivity motifs in a wide variety of conditions makes rs-fMRI useful for studying the brain's organization. When overall brain function changes, for example as a child's brain is developing or an adult's is aging or a person is learning a new skill, changing motifs in the brain's resting activity may reveal areas where anatomical connectivity changes. Using the same logic, the motifs revealed via rs-fMRI can identify functional brain connections in disease states, such as depression or Alzheimer's disease, and functional connections occurring after brain injury and during recovery (Power et al., 2011).

Optical Tomography

Optical tomography is a noninvasive, dynamic imaging technique that operates on the principle that an object can be reconstructed by gathering light that was transmitted through it. Of course, the object must at least partially transmit light, and soft body tissue, including brain tissue, does and so can be imaged using optical tomography.

In one optical tomography method, functional near-infrared spectroscopy (fNIRS), reflected infrared light infers blood flow because hemoglobin in the blood absorbs light differentially depending upon whether it is unoxygenated or oxygenated. Thus, by measuring the blood's light absorption it is possible to measure the brain's average oxygen consumption, just as fMRI infers brain activity by the increase in oxygenated blood at a brain location. To do so using fNIRS, an array of optical transmitter and receiver pairs is fitted across the scalp, as shown in **Figure 7.24**, and signals are sent over connecting wires or wirelessly. A computer constructs an image of brain function from light intensity differences.

Figure 7.24 ▼

Optical Imaging Apparatus Light injectors (red) and detectors (blue) are distributed in an array across the head. (Hitachi Ltd., Advanced Research Laboratory. Photo by Atsushi Maki.)

The obvious advantage of fNIRS is that it is relatively easy to hook up participants and subjects and record from them throughout life, from infancy to senescence. The disadvantage is that the light does not penetrate the brain very far, so researchers are restricted to measuring cortical activity, as illustrated in the Snapshot. Statistical procedures can average out light absorption by the meninges, skull, and skin overlying the brain, leaving only a measure of brain

---

SNAPSHOT | Tuning in to Language

The search to understand the human brain's organization and operation is driven partly by emerging technologies. Over the past decade, neuroscience researchers have developed dramatic new, noninvasive ways to image the brain's activity in subjects and participants who are awake. The fNIRS technique, illustrated in the accompanying diagram, gathers light transmitted through cortical tissue to image blood-oxygen consumption, or oxygenated hemoglobin, in the brain.

fNIRS allows investigators to measure oxygen consumption in relatively select regions of the cerebral cortex, even

in newborns. In one study (May et al., 2011), newborns (0–3 days old) wore a mesh cap containing the NIRS apparatus, made up of optical fibers, as they listened to the sounds of a familiar or unfamiliar language.

When newborns listened to a familiar language, their brains showed a generalized increase in oxygenated hemoglobin compared to conditions in which they listened to their own language played backward or to an unfamiliar language. Newborn infants can distinguish relationships between sounds, such as "badada" versus "badaga," and whether sound relationships occur at the beginning or at the end of a sequence: "babada" versus "dababa." They can also use prosody (tone of voice) to help discriminate sounds and to aid in learning two languages concurrently. They are at birth prepared to learn language and are actively engaged in doing so (Gervain and Werker, 2013).

The value of NIRS is that it provides a window into the infant brain that would not otherwise be accessible. ERP requires many repetitions of a stimulus to obtain averaging for a meaningful signal, and MRI requires that infants remain still, at best a difficult task. NIRS has limitations in that only cortical activity can be sampled, only a small number of detectors can be fitted onto a cap, and the resolution area is large, on the order of a centimeter. Nevertheless, NIRS is relatively inexpensive, portable, and can be used to ask many basic neuropsychological questions, such as those related to language, as well as to assess other questions related to brain function (Aslin, 2012).

How NIRS Works Light injected through the scalp and skull penetrates the brain to a depth of about 2 cm. A small fraction of the light is reflected and captured by a detector on the scalp surface. Light is reflected from the cortex and also from the tissue above it, as illustrated by the dotted-line curves. The tissue signal then can be subtracted to produce only a brain signal. (Research from L. Spinney, Optical Topography and the Color of Blood, *The Scientist* 19:25–27, 2005.)

Labels on diagram: Light injector, Light detector, Scalp, Skull, Dura mater, Arachnoid layer and cerebrospinal fluid, Cerebral cortex (gray matter), White matter, 2 cm

Aslin, R. N. Questioning the questions that have been asked about the infant brain using NIRS. *Cognitive Neuropsychology* 29:7–33, 2012.

Gervain, J., and J. F. Werker. Prosody cues word order in 7-month-old bilingual infants. *Nature Communications* 4:1490, 2013.

May, L., K. Byers-Heinlein, J. Gervain, and J. Werker. Language and the newborn brain: Does prenatal language experience shape the neonate neural response to speech? *Frontiers in Psychology* 2:222–228, 2011.

oxygenation. Voxel size for the imaged tissue is not high—on the order of centimeters—so resolution is not high. Although up to 100 light emitters and detectors can be fitted around the skull, they are still relatively large, limiting the number of brain locations that can be sampled concurrently.

◎ 7.5 Comparing Brain-Imaging Techniques and Uses

We have considered a wide range of imaging techniques. How do neuropsychology researchers choose among them? The main consideration is the research question being asked.

Some investigators focus on the ways neurons generate electrical activity in relation to behavior or on dynamic changes in brain activity during specific types of cognitive processing. Both approaches are legitimate: the goal is understanding brain–behavior relationships. But investigators must consider practical issues too. Temporal resolution (how quickly the measurement or image is obtained); spatial resolution (how accurate localization is in the brain); and the degree of invasiveness all are pertinent.

Single-cell recording techniques, for example, provide excellent resolution but can be used on humans only in exceptional circumstances. It is impractical to consider MRI-based methods for many studies of children: although the images are highly accurate, the participants must remain absolutely still for long periods. Similarly, studies of brain-injured patients must take into account factors such as the subject's ability to maintain attention for long periods—during neuropsychological testing or imaging studies, for example. And practical problems that attend brain injury, such as motor or language impairment, may limit the methods that researchers can use.

Cost is an ever-present practical consideration. EEG, ERP, and fNIRS are noninvasive and relatively inexpensive (less than $100,000) to set up. MRI-based methods, MEG, and PET are very expensive (more than $2 million) and therefore typically located only in large research centers or hospitals.

Figure 7.25 contrasts the resolution obtained by the CT, PET, and MRI methods with a photograph of a dissected brain. In the photo, gray matter of the cortical surface and white matter of the underlying fibers are easily distinguishable. The photograph's clarity provides a useful frame of reference for evaluating the resolution of other techniques.

X-ray methods provide quick static inexpensive snapshots useful for locating injury to the skull, intracranial bleeding, tumors, and malformations in blood

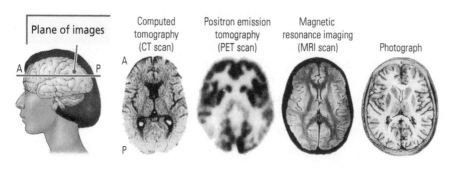

| Plane of images | Computed tomography (CT scan) | Positron emission tomography (PET scan) | Magnetic resonance imaging (MRI scan) | Photograph |

Figure 7.25 ◄

Imaging Contrast The CT, PET, and MRI scans image the same horizontal slice of the brain, viewed dorsally (A, anterior; P, posterior). The fourth image is a photograph of the same brain section removed from a cadaver. (Research from Posner & Raichle, 1994.)

vessels. Thus, CT scans remain the first imaging procedure used to assess possible brain injury or tumors. PET has the advantage of imaging the brain's chemistry and so can identify regions involved in specific behaviors as well as markers of disease states that involve changes in brain chemistry. Obviously, MRI methods produce highly detailed images of brain anatomy, both of cell-rich areas and the fibers that connect them. MRS can detect specific chemical events such as the myelin degeneration that occurs in multiple sclerosis or neuronal degeneration that occurs in Alzheimer's disease.

Imaging Techniques, Pro and Con

The most immediate application of brain imaging is diagnosing brain injury and disease. Once, the only insight into brain disease came at autopsy. The findings clearly were no longer helpful to the patient and were confounded by any number of other lifetime impacts. Today, an immediate diagnosis related to the brain can be made, the course of a disease can be tracked, and the effectiveness of treatment can be assessed.

PET can image an enormous range of chemical events in the brain but is indirect: its measures of chemistry and regional blood flow do not measure neuronal activity. The subtraction process reveals another limitation of PET imaging in that one neutral condition is used as a baseline and subtracted from another condition. The subtraction process provides researchers not with a specific list of what brain areas are taking part in a task but rather with an indication of what areas become relatively more or less active as a task is performed.

Some experiments using PET require a number of subtractions. For example, a state imaged when a participant is resting may be subtracted from a state imaged when the participant is reading a book. This result may be subtracted from a state in which the participant is reading only nouns. Each subtraction provides a more refined view of brain function—but a view that likewise is more artificial.

The strength of fMRI lies in the very detailed information it provides about both regional activity and changes in regional activity in the brain. A drawback is that it takes some time to collect information, and the fMRI procedure takes place in a confined, noisy space difficult for some participants to endure. The confined space and lack of mobility also restrict the types of behavioral experiments that can be performed. A typical solution to the lack of space and mobility is to have participants look at images presented on mirrors and signal their responses with finger movements. Despite these drawbacks, MRI and fMRI provide exceptional information concerning brain structure and function.

Compared with fMRI, fNIRS is inexpensive and portable. The relative ease of recording from participants, especially infants, who cannot remain immobile for fMRI studies, and of recording throughout life, from infancy to senescence, is an obvious advantage of optical tomography techniques such as fNIRS. The disadvantages, so far, are that researchers are restricted to measuring cortical activity and that the spatial resolution is not as good as that of other noninvasive methods. As with more-established imaging methods, however, these disadvantages will continue to be addressed and improved.

Toward Multimodal Brain Atlases

Studies of metabolic and functional processes based on brain imaging have led to the construction of many kinds of brain atlases. Contemporary atlases can locate human brain structures and represent the circuits that these structures form with one another as well as their possible functions (Toga et al., 2006). Early brain maps were derived from one or a few autopsy specimens. Now, brain-imaging methods can sample large populations representing the sexes, individuals of different ages, and people with varying natural and learned abilities. Brain-imaging atlases can represent neural structures and their pathways, neurochemistry, even active genes. Future brain atlases likely will be interactive, providing changing images and views rather than static pages for visualizing function.

Imaging methods improve neuroscientists' ability to test theories. **Figure 7.26**, for example, shows how gray matter thickness changes in a healthy brain from age 5 to age 20. A "bigger-is-better" approach to brain function might lead us to expect that cortical thickness will increase during development as the brain matures. But researchers have found that cortical gray matter in different regions changes in different ways over the course of development.

The frontal cortex, which represents, among other things, executive function, becomes thinner during development. The acquisition of smaller frontal lobes takes a long time and is a correlate of maturity. In other areas of the cortex, such as language areas, gray matter does become thicker. In still other regions, while gray matter overall is thinning, white matter is growing thicker. Thickening and thinning continue into old age, and dynamic representations of brain changes enable investigators to distinguish these lifelong processes (Zhou et al., 2013).

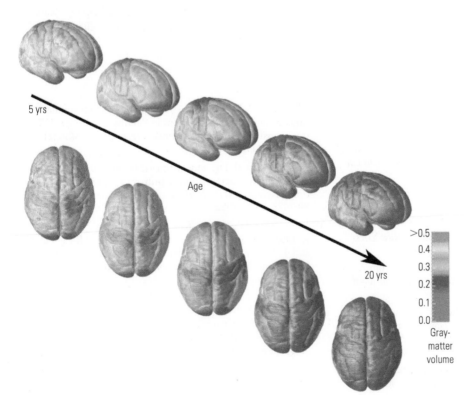

Figure 7.26 ◄

Brain-Imaging Atlas MRI scans of the maturation of gray matter in typical development, showing the length and pattern of maturation. (Image courtesy of Paul Thompson, Kiralee Hayashi, Arthur Toga, UCLA/Nitin Gogtay, Jay Giedd, Judy Rapoport, NIMH.)

SUMMARY

Some brain-imaging methods described in this chapter offer a static image of brain structure; others provide a dynamic image of brain function.

7.1 Recording the Brain's Electrical Activity

From single-cell recordings, we know that neurons employ a code and that cortical neurons organize into functional groups. EEG recordings tell us that when a person is awake and engaged in some behavior, the whole brain is in an active state: the entire neocortex displays the beta-wave pattern (low coherence). Similarly, when a person is resting or sleeping, the entire brain rests or sleeps, as indicated by the slower alpha- and delta-wave patterns (high coherence). ERPs tell us that even though the entire brain is active during waking, certain parts are momentarily much more active than others and the increased activity changes location as information moves from one area of the brain to another.

7.2 Brain Stimulation

Brain stimulation induces changes in the brain's electrical activity. Electrodes can be implanted to stimulate brain tissue directly, as is done for DBS, or for noninvasive signaling through the skull with pulses of transcranial magnetic stimulation.

7.3 Static Imaging Techniques

X-ray imaging methods are sensitive to the density of different parts of the brain, the ventricles, nuclei, and pathways.

Thus, X-rays can be used to assess skull damage, and CT scans can be used to assess brain damage from traumatic brain injury or tumors.

7.4 Dynamic Brain Imaging

Metabolic imaging methods show that any behavior requires collaboration among widespread brain circuits. PET records blood flow and other metabolic changes over time and can reveal the relative activity of brain regions when subtraction procedures are used.

MRI provides exceptionally clear structural images, both of brain nuclei and of fiber pathways, and reveals that different people's brains can be built quite differently. MRS can distinguish gray and white matter to detect degeneration in myelin or neurons.

Records of brain blood flow obtained by using fMRI can be combined with MRI techniques such as diffusion tensor imaging and rs-fMRI to identify the location of changes in the individual brain and to map the brain's functional connectivity.

7.5 Comparing Brain-Imaging Techniques and Uses

Brain-imaging techniques are useful to the neuropsychologist—for diagnosing brain disease, monitoring the brain's physiological and metabolic processes, and testing theories of behavior. Imaging methods are central to many ongoing lines of research into brain function and dysfunction. Subsequent chapters present further examples of their use.

References

Berlim, M. T., F. Van den Eynde, and Z. J. Daskalakis. High-frequency repetitive transcranial magnetic stimulation accelerates and enhances the clinical response to antidepressants in major depression: A meta-analysis of randomized, double-blind, and sham-controlled trials. *Journal of Clinical Psychiatry* 74:122–129, 2013.

Damasio, H., and A. R. Damasio. *Lesion Analysis in Neuropsychology.* New York: Oxford University Press, 1989.

DeArmond, S. J., M. M. Fusco, and M. Dewey. *Structure of the Human Brain: A Photographic Atlas,* 2nd ed. New York: Oxford University Press, 1976.

ffytche, D. H., and M. Catani. Beyond localization: From hodology to function. *Philosophical Transactions of the Royal Society B* 360:767–779, 2005.

Fox, P. T., and M. E. Raichle. Focal physiological uncoupling of cerebral blood flow and oxidative metabolism during somatosensory stimulation in human subjects. *Proceedings of the National Academy of Science U.S.A.* 83:1140–1144, 1986.

Harris, K. D., and A. Thiele. Cortical state and attention. *Nature Reviews Neuroscience* 12(9):509–523, August 10, 2011.

Kocabicak, E., S. K. Tan, and Y. Temel. Deep brain stimulation of the subthalamic nucleus in Parkinson's disease: Why so successful? *Surgery and Neurology International* 3(Suppl 4):S312–S314, 2012.

Kwong, K. K., et al. Dynamic magnetic resonance imaging of human brain activity during primary sensory stimulation. *Proceedings of the National Academy of Sciences U.S.A.* 89:5675–5679, 1992.

Mohajerani, M. H., A. W. Chan, M. Mohsenvand, J. LeDue, R. Liu, D. A. McVea, J. D. Boyd, Y. T. Wang, M. Reimers, and T. H. Murphy. Spontaneous cortical activity alternates between motifs defined by regional axonal projections. *Nature Neuroscience* 16:1426–1435, 2013.

Murayama, Y., F. Biessmann, F. C. Meinecke, K. R. Müller, M. Augath, A. Oeltermann, and N. K. Logothetis. Relationship between neural and hemodynamic signals during spontaneous activity studied with temporal kernel CCA. *Magnetic Resonance Imaging* 28:1095–1103, 2010.

Neville, H. Event-related potentials in neuropsychological studies of language. *Brain and Language* 11:300–318, 1980.

Nicolelis, M. A. Mind in motion. *Scientific American* 307:58–63, 2012.

Ogawa, S. L., L. M. Lee, A. R. Kay, and D. W. Tank. Brain magnetic resonance imaging with contrast dependent on blood oxygenation. *Proceedings of the National Academy of Sciences U.S.A.* 87:9868–9872, 1990.

Posner, M. I., and M. E. Raichle. *Images of Mind*. New York: Scientific American Library, 1994.

Power, J. D., A. L. Cohen, S. M. Nelson, G. S. Wig, K. A. Barnes, J. A. Church, A. C. Vogel, T. O. Laumann, F. M. Miezin, B. L. Schlaggar, and S. E. Petersen. Functional network organization of the human brain. *Neuron* 17:665–678, 2011.

Sankar, T., T. S. Tierney, and C. Hamani. Novel applications of deep brain stimulation. *Surgery and Neurology International* 3(Suppl 1):S26–S33, 2012.

Setsompop, K., R. Kimmlingen, E. Eberlein, T. Witzel, J. Cohen-Adad, J. A. McNab, B. Keil, M. D. Tisdall, P. Hoecht, P. Dietz, S. F. Cauley, V. Tountcheva, V. Matschl, V. H. Lenz, K. Heberlein, A. Potthast, H. Thein, J. Van Horn, A. Toga, F. Schmitt, D. Lehne, B. R. Rosen, V. Wedeen, and L. L. Wald. Pushing the limits of in vivo diffusion MRI for the Human Connectome Project. *NeuroImage* 80:220–233, 2013.

Toga, A.W., K. A. Clark, P. M. Thompson, D. W. Shattuck, and J. D. Van Horn. Mapping the human connectome. *Neurosurgery* 71(1):1–5, July 2012.

Toga, A. W., P. W. Thompson, S. Mori, K. Amunts, and K. Zilles. Towards multimodal atlases of the human brain. *NeuroImaging* 7:952–966, 2006.

Valenstein, E. S. *Brain Control: A Critical Examination of Brain Stimulation and Psychosurgery*. New York: John Wiley and Sons, 1975.

Zhou, D., C. Lebel, A. Evans, and C. Beaulieu. Cortical thickness asymmetry from childhood to older adulthood. *NeuroImage* 83:66–74, 2013.

8 Organization of the Sensory Systems

 Phantoms of the Brain

D.S. injured the nerves in his left arm in a motorcycle accident when he was 19, leaving the limb paralyzed. One year later his arm was amputated above the elbow. When examined 11 years later, D.S. still felt the presence of his missing limb.

The paralysis and pain he experienced prior to amputation had been carried over to a "learned phantom limb" that felt normal in size, was paralyzed, and was excruciatingly painful. Phantom sensations are common. Mobile phone users often report feeling phantom vibrations in response to sounds that resemble the phone's ringtone, for example.

D.S. was treated using the mirror box illusion illustrated here. He simultaneously saw both his intact hand and arm and its reflection at the location where his amputated arm would have been. Double-blind studies demonstrate that when subjects move the intact hand and arm as they look into the mirror box, they experience the illusion that the missing limb is moving. The illusion counteracts unpleasant features of the phantom limb, including cramping and pain.

Vilayanur Ramachandran and colleagues (2009) treated D.S. using the mirror box as he viewed his arm through size-reducing glasses. After many sessions, D.S.'s phantom arm shrank away, leaving only a phantom of his hand and fingers attached to his stump. The pain in his arm was gone but remained in his digits. Shrinking the digits with the size-reducing glasses removed the phantom digits and pain, but only during treatment.

One explanation of phantom-limb sensations is that each part of the body is represented in the brain. In the absence of sensory input from a missing limb, the brain's limb representation can generate both spontaneous and learned sensations, including pain, that are experienced as phantoms. Support for brain representation theory comes from reports that people born missing a limb can experience a phantom limb. Other support comes from case reports of **apotemnophilia**, a disorder in which an individual desires to have a limb amputated. Apparently, abnormalities in the activity of the brain's limb representation are perceived as foreign and unwanted, leading to a desire to have the limb removed.

The many curious findings related to body phantoms demonstrate that the body's neural representation typically is instructed by sensory inputs from the body. Thus, body image is a product of both the brain's representation and the sensory information the body provides to the brain. Moment-to-moment updating of the brain's representation through sensory experience ensures that reality and the inborn body representation are congruent (Makin et al., 2013).

Incongruences between experience and brain representation may not only account for phantom limbs but also explain some conflicts related to sexual identity and to body image and diet linked to the eating disorder anorexia nervosa. This is exaggerated concern with being overweight that leads to inadequate food intake and often excessive exercising; it can lead to severe weight loss and even starvation.

We may believe that we see, hear, touch, smell, and taste real things in a real world. In fact, the only input our brains receive from the "real" world is a series of action potentials passed along the neurons of our various sensory pathways. Although we experience, for example, visual and body sensations as being fundamentally different from one another, the nerve impulses coursing through the neurons in these two sensory systems are nearly identical, as are the neurons themselves.

Neuroscientists understand how nerves turn energy, such as light waves, into nerve impulses. They know the pathways those nerve impulses take to reach the brain. But they do not know how we end up perceiving one set of nerve impulses as what the world looks like and another set as our own motion. At the same time, we realize that our senses can deceive us—that two people can look at the same optical illusion (such as the adjoining photograph of two cheetahs) and see very different images, that a person dreaming does not typically think that the dream images are real, that you often do not think that a picture of you looks like you.

© Gerry Lemmo

In this chapter, we present an overview of how sensory information reaches the cortex, placing special emphasis on three features of sensory organization: (1) many submodalities exist within each sensory system, (2) each submodality is designed for a specific function, and (3) the senses interact.

8.1 General Principles of Sensory-System Function

At first blush, vision, audition, body senses, taste, and olfaction appear to have little in common. But although our perceptions and behaviors in relation to each sense are very different, each sensory system actually is organized according to a similar hierarchical plan. Here we consider the features sensory systems have in common, including receptors and neural relays between receptor and neocortex, sensory coding, and multiple representations within the neocortex.

Sensory Receptors and Neural Relays

Sensory receptors, specialized cells that *transduce*, or convert, energy to neural activity—light photons, for example—have in common properties that provide a rich array of information about our world. All sensory receptors connect to the cortex through a sequence of intervening relay neurons that allow each sensory system to mediate different responses and to interact with other sensory systems.

Sensory Receptors Are Energy Filters
If we put flour into a sieve and shake it, the more finely ground particles will fall through the holes, whereas the coarser particles and lumps will not. Similarly, sensory receptors respond only to a narrow band of energy—analogous

Figure 8.1 ▶

Electromagnetic Spectrum The slice of electromagnetic energy visible to the human eye lies within a narrow range from about 400 nanometers (violet) to 700 nanometers (red). A nanometer (nm) is one-billionth of a meter.

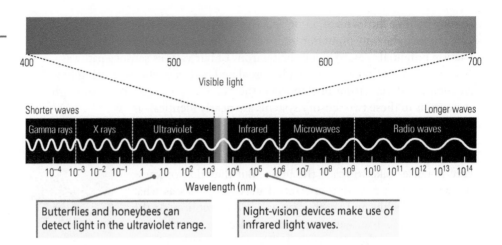

Visible light

Shorter waves   Longer waves

| Gamma rays | X rays | Ultraviolet | Infrared | Microwaves | Radio waves |

Wavelength (nm)

Butterflies and honeybees can detect light in the ultraviolet range.

Night-vision devices make use of infrared light waves.

to particles of certain sizes—within each modality's energy spectrum. Consider the receptors for vision and hearing.

Vision **Figure 8.1** illustrates the tiny slice of the entire electromagnetic spectrum that our visual system can detect. Were our visual receptors somewhat different, we could see in the ultraviolet or infrared parts of the spectrum, as some other animals can.

People who are *color deficient*—often mistakenly said to be *color-blind*—simply lack one or more types of photoreceptors for color vision—the red, blue, and/or green cones. They can see plenty of colors, just not the same colors as people with all three cones can. There are also differences among the visual receptors of individuals who see the typical range of color. Joris Winderickx and his colleagues (1992) reported that about 60 percent of males have one form of the red receptor cone and 40 percent have another form. These groups see red differently. Many females have both forms and hence an enriched color world, not only for reds but also for all of the colors produced by the interactions of other colors with reds.

Audition Compared to such animals as birds and frogs, which hear a relatively narrow range of frequencies, the human hearing range is broad yet far less extensive than that of many other mammals, including whales, dolphins, and dogs. Human auditory receptors respond to sound-wave frequencies between 20 and 20,000 hertz (Hz, cycles per second), but elephants can hear and produce sounds below 20 Hz, and bats can hear and produce sounds as high as 120,000 Hz. Furthermore, humans rapidly lose high-frequency hearing. The frequencies that are most important to us, such as those of speech, fortunately, are in the lower frequencies.

In comparison with the sensory abilities of other animals, those of humans are rather average. Even our pet dogs have "superhuman" powers: they can detect odors that we cannot detect, they can hear the ultrasounds emitted by rodents and bats and the low-range sounds of elephants, and they can see in the dark. We can hold up only our superior color vision. For each species and its individual members, then, sensory systems filter the possible range of sensation to produce an idiosyncratic representation of reality and the behavioral adaptations that characterize the species.

Receptors Transduce Energy

Each sensory system's receptors are specialized to transduce physical or chemical energy into action potentials:

- For vision, light energy is converted to chemical energy in the photoreceptors of the retina, which actually is part of the brain, and this chemical energy is in turn converted to action potentials.

- In the auditory system, air-pressure waves are converted first to mechanical energy, which eventually activates the auditory receptors that produce action potentials.

- In the somatosensory system, mechanical energy activates receptor cells that are sensitive, to say, touch or pressure. Somatosensory receptors in turn generate action potentials. In pain sensation, tissue damage releases chemicals that act like neurotransmitters to activate pain fibers and produce action potentials.

- For taste and olfaction, chemical molecules carried on the air or contained in food fit themselves into receptors of various shapes to activate action potentials.

Thus, each type of sensory receptor transduces the physical or chemical energy it detects to action potentials. **Figure 8.2** illustrates how the displacement of a single hair on the arm results in an action potential that we interpret as touch. The dendrite of a somatosensory neuron is wrapped around the base of the hair. When the hair is displaced in a certain direction, the dendrite is stretched by the displacement.

Na^+ channels in the dendrite's membrane are stretch-sensitive, so they open in response to stretching. If the influx of sodium ions in the "stretch-sensitive" channels is sufficient, the resulting voltage change will depolarize the dendrite to its threshold for an action potential, and the voltage-sensitive K^+ and Na^+ channels will open, resulting in a nerve impulse heading to the brain.

Receptive Fields Locate Sensory Events

Every receptor organ and cell has a **receptive field**, a specific part of the world to which it responds. If you fix your eyes on a point directly in front of you, for example, what you see of the world is the scope of your eyes' receptive field. If you close one eye, the visual world shrinks, and what the open eye sees is that eye's receptive field.

Each photoreceptor points in a slightly different direction and so has a unique receptive field—its "view" of the world. You can appreciate its conceptual utility by considering that the brain uses information from each sensory receptor's receptive field not only to identify that information but also to contrast the information with what a neighboring receptive field is providing.

Receptive fields not only sample sensory information but also help locate sensory events in space and facilitate different actions in space. Because the receptive fields of adjacent sensory receptors may overlap, their relatively different responses to events help us localize sensations. Our lower visual

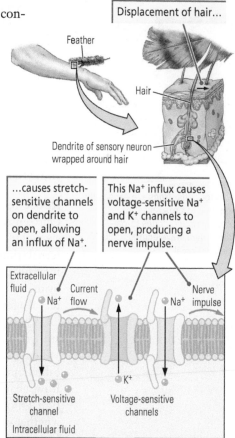

Figure 8.2 ▲

Tactile Stimulation

receptive field facilitates the use of our hands in making skilled actions, whereas our upper visual field facilitates our movements through our more distant surroundings.

Receptors Identify Constancy and Change

Each sensory system answers questions such as, Is something there? And Is it still there? To answer such questions, receptors differ in sensitivity. They may adapt rapidly or slowly to stimulation or react only to a specific type of energy.

Rapidly adapting receptors detect whether something is there. They are easy to activate but stop responding after a very short time. If you touch your arm very lightly with a finger, for example, you will immediately detect the touch, but if you then keep your finger still, the sensation will fade as the receptors adapt. It fades because the rapidly adapting hair receptors on the skin are designed to detect the *movement* of objects on the skin. **Slowly adapting receptors** react to stimulation more slowly. If you push a little harder when you first touch your arm, you will feel the touch much longer because many of the body's pressure-sensitive receptors adapt slowly.

Within the eye, the cup-shaped retina contains thousands of receptor cells, the rods and cones. The rapidly adapting rod-shaped receptors respond to visible light of any wavelength and have lower response thresholds than do the slowly adapting cone-shaped receptors, which are sensitive to color and position. A dog, having mainly black–white vision, is thus very sensitive to moving objects but has more difficulty detecting objects when they are still. With both black–white and color vision, we humans are good at detecting both moving and stationary people and objects.

Receptors Distinguish Self from Other

Our sensory systems are organized to tell us what is happening in the world around us and also what we ourselves are doing. Receptors that respond to external stimuli are **exteroceptive**; receptors that respond to our own activity are **interoceptive**. Objects in the world that we see, that touch us or are touched by us, and that we smell or taste act on exteroceptive receptors: we know an external agent produces them.

When you move, you change the perceived properties of objects in the world and you experience sensations that have little to do with the external world. When you run, visual stimuli appear to stream past, a stimulus configuration called **optic flow**. When you move past a sound source, you hear an **auditory flow**, changes in sound intensity that take place because of your changing location. Optic flow and auditory flow are useful in telling us how fast we are going, whether we are going in a straight line or up or down, and whether we are moving or an object in the world is moving.

Some information about these changes comes to us through our exteroceptive receptors, but we also learn from interoceptive receptors in our muscles and joints and in the vestibular organs of the inner ear. These interoceptive receptors tell us about the position and movement of our bodies. Not only do interoceptive receptors play an important role in helping us distinguish what we ourselves do from what is done to us but they also help us interpret the meaning of external stimuli.

▲ Vision begins in the photoreceptor cells. Rods are especially sensitive to broad-spectrum luminance and cones to particular light wavelengths. (SPL/Science Source)

Try this experiment. Slowly move your hand back and forth before your eyes, and then gradually increase the speed. Your hand will eventually get a little blurry because your eye movements are not quick enough to follow its movement. Now keep your hand still and move your head back and forth. The image of the hand remains clear. When the interoceptive receptors in the inner ear inform your visual system that your head is moving, the visual system responds by compensating for the head movements, and you observe your hand as stationary.

Some psychological conditions appear to be characterized by difficulty in distinguishing between self and other. People who hallucinate perceive events that are being generated internally as coming from outside themselves. They believe that something is there when it is not. In "checking" behavior, those with obsessive–compulsive disorder might return again and again to confirm that they have completed an act such as locking a door. They do not believe that something has been done even when they know they have done it.

Receptor Density Determines Sensitivity

Receptor density is important in determining a sensory system's sensitivity. For example, the tactile receptors on the fingers are numerous compared with those on the arm. This difference explains why the fingers can discriminate touch remarkably well and the arm not so well. You can prove this by moving the tips of two pencils apart to different degrees as you touch different parts of your body. The ability to recognize the presence of two pencil points close together, a measure called **two-point sensitivity**, is highest on the parts of the body having the most touch receptors.

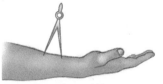

Two-point sensitivity

Our sensory systems use different receptors to enhance sensitivity under different conditions. For example, in the visual system, different sets of photoreceptors respond to light and to color. In the **fovea** (a small area of the retina in which color photoreceptors are concentrated), the receptor cone cells are small and densely packed to make sensitive color discriminations in bright light. In the periphery of the retina, the rod cell receptors for black–white vision are larger and more scattered, but their sensitivity to light (say, a lighted match at a distance of 2 miles on a dark night) is remarkable.

Differences in sensory-receptor density determine the special abilities of many animals, such as excellent olfactory ability in dogs and excellent tactile ability in the digits of raccoons. Variations in receptor density in the human auditory receptor organ may explain such abilities as perfect pitch displayed by some musicians.

Neural Relays Determine the Hierarchy of Motor Responses

All receptors connect to the cortex through a sequence of three or four intervening neurons. Some neural relays in each sensory system are in the spinal cord, others are in the brainstem, and still others are in the neocortex, defining the hierarchy of our motor behavior. For example, the first relay for pain receptors in the spinal cord is related to reflexes that produce withdrawal from a painful stimulus. Even after damage to the spinal cord cuts it off from the brain, a limb will still withdraw from a painful stimulus. Rapidly withdrawing your fingers from a hot stove is thus a reflex produced at the spinal level.

The pain pathway relays in the brainstem, especially in the midbrain **peri-aqueductal gray matter** (PAG) nuclei that surround the cerebral aqueduct (see Figure 3.18), prompt many complex responses to pain stimuli, including behavioral activation and emotional responses. The enduring pain that you feel long after touching a hot stove may be related to neural activity in the PAG.

Pain relays in the neocortex not only localize pain in a body part but also identify the felt pain, its external cause, and possible remedies. The cortex can also adapt to our experience with hot stoves so that we know in advance not to touch one.

The midbrain superior colliculus is a major visual center of the brainstem, and the inferior colliculus is a major auditory center. In animals without visual and auditory areas in the neocortex, these brainstem regions are the main perceptual systems. For animals with cortical visual and auditory areas, these subcortical regions still perform their original functions: locating stimuli in space and guiding movements in relation to them.

Message Modification Takes Place at Neural Relays

The messages sensory systems carry can be modified at neural relays. For example, descending impulses from the cortex can block or amplify pain signals at the level of the brainstem and at the level of the spinal cord. Many of us have had this experience when we are excited, as occurs when we are playing a sport: we may not notice an injury, only to find later that it is severe. This inhibition, or **gating**, of sensory information can be produced by descending signals from the cortex.

Descending messages can also amplify a sensory signal. Later, when we think about the injury, it might feel much more painful because a descending signal from the brain now amplifies the pain signal from the spinal cord. Gating of sensory information occurs in many situations. We have all not "heard" something said to us or failed to "notice" something we have seen. Attention, detailed in Section 22.2, is a form of gating that takes place in the cortex, one that allows us to move efficiently from one action to another.

Central Organization of Sensory Systems

The hierarchical code sent from sensory receptors through neural relays is interpreted in the brain, especially in the neocortex, and eventually translated into perception, memory, and action. The varieties of information produced within each major sensory system determine much of the richness of behavior, and these sensory subsystems, or information channels, are preserved by multiple representations within the neocortex.

Sensory Information Is Coded

Once transduced, all sensory information from all sensory systems is encoded by action potentials that travel along peripheral-system nerves until they enter the brain or spinal cord and then on tracts within the CNS. Every bundle carries the same kind of signal. How do action potentials encode different kinds of sensations (e.g., how vision differs from touch), and how do they encode the features of particular sensations (e.g., how purple differs from blue)?

Parts of these questions seem easy to answer; other parts pose a fundamental challenge to neuroscience. The presence of a stimulus can be encoded by an increase or decrease in a neuron's discharge rate, and the amount of increase or decrease can encode the stimulus intensity. Qualitative visual changes, such as from red to green, can be encoded by activity in different neurons or even by different levels of discharge in the same neuron. For example, more activity by a neuron might signify redder and less activity, greener.

Sensory coding by one neuron is also related to what other neurons are doing. Our ability to perceive colors as constant under a wide range of sensory conditions, for example, is a computation made by the brain. **Color constancy** enables us to see green as green under a wide range of illumination. Thus, the brain is not simply recording sensory stimuli but rather is manipulating sensory input so that it is behaviorally useful.

What is less clear, however, is how we perceive such sensations as touch, sound, and smell as being different from one another. Part of the explanation is that these different sensations are processed in distinct regions of the cortex. Another part is that we learn through experience to distinguish them. A third part is that each sensory system has a preferential link with certain behaviors, constituting a distinct neural wiring that helps keep each system distinct at all organizational levels. For example, pain stimuli produce withdrawal responses, and fine touch and pressure stimuli produce approach responses.

Each Sensory System Is Composed of Subsystems

Within each of our five sensory systems are many subsystems that are surprisingly independent in the behaviors with which they are associated. Neuroscientists have uncovered how many of these subsystems operate but will not know their full extent until all of the subsystems are discovered through further study of the brain. Some well-studied visual subsystems are shown in **Figure 8.3** as separate pathways that connect the retina to the brain's various visual centers.

The pathway from the eye to the suprachiasmatic nucleus (1) of the hypothalamus controls the circadian (daily) rhythms of such behaviors as feeding and sleeping in response to light changes. The pathway to the pretectum (2) in the midbrain controls pupillary responses to light: our pupils constrict in bright light and dilate in dim light. The pathway to the pineal gland (3) controls long-term circadian rhythms through the release of the chemical melatonin in the pineal gland. The pathway to the superior colliculus (4) in the midbrain

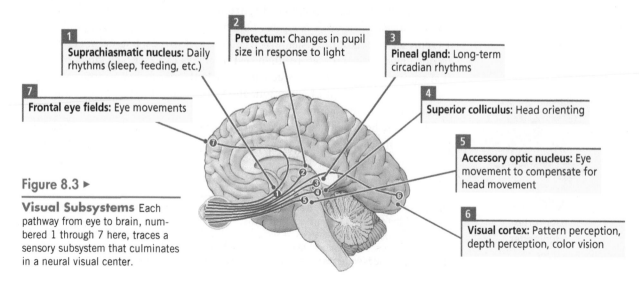

1
Suprachiasmatic nucleus: Daily rhythms (sleep, feeding, etc.)

2
Pretectum: Changes in pupil size in response to light

3
Pineal gland: Long-term circadian rhythms

7
Frontal eye fields: Eye movements

4
Superior colliculus: Head orienting

5
Accessory optic nucleus: Eye movement to compensate for head movement

6
Visual cortex: Pattern perception, depth perception, color vision

Figure 8.3 ▶

Visual Subsystems Each pathway from eye to brain, numbered 1 through 7 here, traces a sensory subsystem that culminates in a neural visual center.

controls head orientation to objects. The pathway to the accessory optic nucleus (5) moves the eyes to compensate for head movements. The pathway to the visual cortex (6) produces pattern perception, depth perception, color vision, and tracking of moving objects. The pathway to the frontal cortex (7) controls voluntary eye movements.

These visual subsystems also have submodalities of their own. In the projection to the visual cortex (6), for example, are pathways for pattern perception, color vision, depth perception, and visual tracking. Each submodality is as independent from another as the systems that encode hearing are independent from those that encode taste. The multiplicity of visual subsystems illustrates that sensory systems have evolved not just to produce sensation but to produce specific behaviors.

Like vision, all sensory modalities contain submodalities that perform distinct and specific roles. One indication that taste, for example, consists of more than one modality is the existence of separate taste pathways. The taste receptors in the front two-thirds of the tongue send information to the brain through the facial nerve (cranial nerve 7), whereas the taste receptors in the posterior third of the tongue send information to the brain through the glossopharyngial nerve (cranial nerve 9). (You can review the locations and functions of the cranial nerves in Figure 3.13 and Table 3.2.)

The human olfactory system has as many as 400 receptor types, each dedicated to detecting a particular odor. In principle, if each smell were linked to a particular behavior, we would have a multitude of olfactory submodalities. One thing that distinguishes animals with excellent olfactory abilities is more receptor types. The mouse, for example, has as many as 1000 kinds of olfactory receptors.

Sensory Systems Have Multiple Neural Representations

Topographic organization is a neural–spatial representation of the body or of areas in the sensory world a sensory organ detects. In most mammals, the neocortex represents the sensory field of each modality—vision, hearing, touch, smell, or taste—not once but many times. How many times a representation occurs is one indication of a species' behavioral complexity.

The squirrel brain depicted in **Figure 8.4**A, for example, has 3 visual areas. Each represents the eye's receptive field topographically. The owl monkey has 14 representations of the visual world (Figure 8.4C). If each visual area responds to one environmental feature, then owl monkeys can "see" 11 kinds of things that squirrels cannot see. Considering that both species live in trees and have color vision, good depth perception, and so on, what those 11 things might be is not immediately obvious.

Monkeys, however, make better use of their fingers, make use of facial expressions, and have a more varied diet than squirrels do, and these differences

(A) Squirrel

(B) Cat

Arrows indicate areas hidden in sulci.

(C) Owl monkey

(D) Rhesus monkey

This drawing represents sulci pulled open to reveal visual areas.

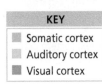

KEY

■ Somatic cortex
■ Auditory cortex
■ Visual cortex

Figure 8.4 ◄

Multiple Sensory Representations Topographic maps of some mammals' brains reveal that the squirrel (A) has 5 somatic areas, 2 or 3 auditory areas, and 2 to 4 visual areas, and the cat (B) has 12 visual areas, 4 somatic areas, and 5 auditory areas. The owl monkey (C) has 14 visual areas, 4 auditory areas, and 5 somatic areas, and the rhesus monkey (D) has 12 visual areas, 4 auditory areas, and 8 somatic areas. (Research from Kaas, 1987.)

might account for some of the monkey's additional visual areas. We humans, in turn, have many more representations than do rhesus monkeys (Figure 8.4D), likely many more than 30, and so we presumably perceive the visual world in ways that rhesus monkeys cannot. (Perhaps some of the additional visual areas are necessary for such cognitive tasks as reading and writing.)

All mammals have at least one primary cortical area for each sensory system. Additional areas are referred to as *secondary areas* because most of the information that reaches them is relayed through the primary area (see Figure 3.27). Each additional representation is probably dedicated to encoding one specific aspect of the sensory modality. Thus, for vision, different areas may take part in the perception of color, of movement, and of form.

8.2 Sensory Receptors and Pathways

We frequently refer to our five senses, but the plethora of sensory receptors and pathways within each system illustrates that many more than five sensory systems are operating. In the sections that follow we limit our discussion to the main sensory receptors and pathways each of the five major senses employs.

Vision

> For I dipped into the future, far as human eye could see,
> Saw the vision of the world, and all the wonder that would be

These lines from Alfred, Lord Tennyson's, poem "Locksley Hall," illustrate that our vision is much richer than the sensory code relayed from the visual receptors in the eye to the visual regions of the brainstem and neocortex. Nevertheless, sensation is this chapter's topic. Subsequent chapters detail the perceptual and neuropsychological aspects of vision that Tennyson evokes.

Photoreceptors

A schematic representation of the eye and its visual-receptor surface, the retina, is presented in **Figure 8.5**. In Figure 8.5A, rays of light enter the eye through the cornea, which bends them slightly, then go through the lens, which bends them to a much greater degree to focus the visual image, upside down and backward, on the receptors at the back of the eye.

The light's having to pass through the layer of retinal cells poses little obstacle to our visual acuity for two reasons. First, the cells are transparent, and the photoreceptors are extremely sensitive: they can be excited by the absorption of a single photon. Second, as detailed in Figure 8.5B, many of the fibers forming the optic nerve bend away from the retina's central part, or fovea, so as not to interfere with the passage of light through the retina. Because of this bending, the fovea as seen in the scanning electron micrograph (SEM) in Figure 8.5C is a depression on the retinal surface.

As noted in Section 8.1, the human retina contains two types of photoreceptive cells. **Rods** are sensitive to dim light. We use them mainly for night vision. **Cones** are better able to transduce bright light and are used for daytime vision. Three types of cones, each type maximally responsive to a different set of wavelengths—red or blue or green—mediate color vision.

Figure 8.5 ▼

Anatomy of the Eye (Part C: SPL/Science Source.)

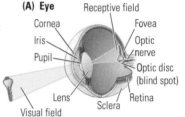

(A) Eye

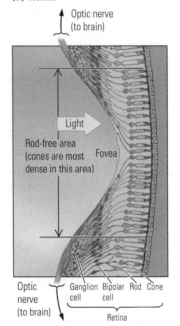

(B) Retina

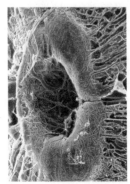

(C) SEM of fovea

The distribution of rods and cones differs across the retina: cones are packed together densely in the foveal region, whereas rods are absent entirely from the fovea and more sparsely distributed over the rest of the retina (Figure 8.5B). Thus, in bright light, acuity is best when looking directly at things; in dim light, acuity is best when looking slightly away.

The photoreceptive cells diagrammed in Figure 8.5B synapse on **bipolar cells** in which they induce graded potentials. Bipolar cells in turn induce action potentials in **retinal ganglion cells** (RGCs). RGC axons collect in a bundle at the optic disc, your blind spot, and leave the eye to form the optic nerve in the brain proper. (Remember that the retina is a part of the brain.) Other retinal cells—including horizontal and amacrine cells—contribute to the retina's processing of visual information.

Visual Pathways

Just before entering the brain, the two optic nerves (one from each eye) meet and form the **optic chiasm** (from the Greek letter X, or chi). At this point, about half the fibers from each eye cross, as illustrated in **Figure 8.6**. So the right half of each eye's visual field is represented in the left hemisphere, and the left half of each eye's visual field is represented in the right hemisphere. Having entered the brain proper, the optic tract, still consisting of RGC axons, diverges to form two main pathways, diagrammed in **Figure 8.7**.

Geniculostriate Pathway The major visual pathway, diagrammed at the top of Figure 8.7 and running from the retina to the lateral geniculate nucleus (LGN) of the thalamus to the primary visual cortex (V1, Brodmann's area 17) is the **geniculostriate pathway**. Its name derives from the knee-shaped appearance of the LGB and the striped appearance of V1. (In Latin, *geniculate* means knee; *stria* are stripes.)

The geniculate pathway takes part in pattern, color, and motion recognition and includes conscious visual functions (Livingston and Hubel, 1988). Symptoms of damage to the geniculostriate system include impairments in pattern, color, and motion perception as well as **visual-form agnosia** (Greek for "not knowing"), the inability to recognize objects (see Section 13.2).

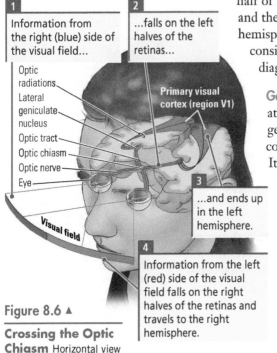

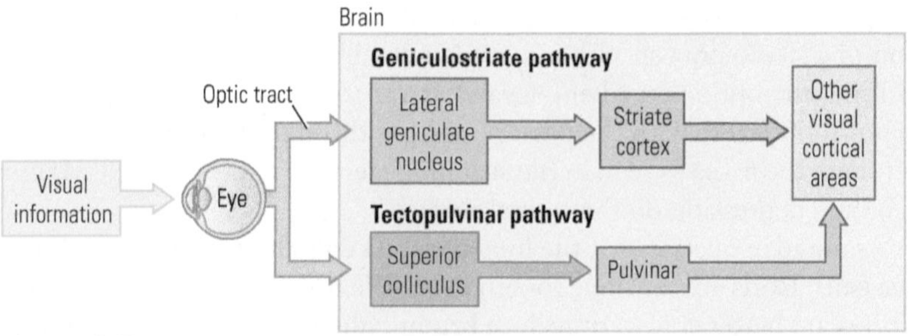

1 Information from the right (blue) side of the visual field...

2 ...falls on the left halves of the retinas...

Optic radiations
Lateral geniculate nucleus
Optic tract
Optic chiasm
Optic nerve
Eye

Primary visual cortex (region V1)

3 ...and ends up in the left hemisphere.

Visual field

4 Information from the left (red) side of the visual field falls on the right halves of the retinas and travels to the right hemisphere.

Figure 8.6 ▲

Crossing the Optic Chiasm Horizontal view of the visual pathways from each eye to region V1 in each occipital hemisphere. In animals such as humans, with eyes at the front of the head, about half of the optic fibers cross at the optic chiasm. In animals such as the rat, with eyes at the sides of the head, as many as 95 percent of the optic fibers cross.

Brain

Geniculostriate pathway

Optic tract

Visual information → Eye → Lateral geniculate nucleus → Striate cortex → Other visual cortical areas

Tectopulvinar pathway

Superior colliculus → Pulvinar

Figure 8.7 ▲

The Major Visual Pathways

The LGN has six well-defined layers: layers 2, 3, and 5 receive fibers from the ipsilateral eye, and layers 1, 4, and 6 receive fibers from the contralateral eye. The topography of the visual field is reproduced in each LGN layer: the central parts represent the central visual field, and the peripheral parts represent the peripheral field.

LGN cells project mainly to layer IV of the primary visual cortex (Brodmann's area 17 or V1), which is very large in primates and appears striped; hence one of its alternative names, striate cortex. The visual field is again topographically represented in V1 as illustrated in **Figure 8.8**—but upside down, inverted, and reversed. The central part of the visual field is represented at the back of the visual cortex, and the periphery is represented toward the front. The upper part of the visual field is represented below the calcarine fissure at the middle of the occipital lobe, and the lower part is represented above the calcarine fissure. Vision for light and for color are separated throughout the geniculostriate pathway and the visual cortices as described in Section 13.1.

Tectopulvinar Pathway The second main visual pathway takes part in detecting and orienting to visual stimulation. As charted at the bottom of Figure 8.7, this **tectopulvinar pathway** relays from the eye to the superior colliculus in the midbrain tectum and reaches the visual areas in the temporal and parietal lobes through relays in the lateral posterior-pulvinar complex of the thalamus.

The pathway to the colliculus constitutes the entire visual system in fish, amphibians, and reptiles and so is capable of sophisticated vision. In mammals, the additional projection from the colliculus to the cortex via the thalamic pulvinar nucleus provides information to the cortex about the absolute (independent of a viewer's visual gaze) spatial location of objects. Among the symptoms of damage to the tectopulvinar system is **visual ataxia** (Greek for "not orienting"), the inability to recognize where objects are located (see Section 14.4).

In summary, two main deficits in visual function stemming from cortical damage, visual agnosia (not knowing what) and visual ataxia (not knowing where), can be linked to the interruption of information from the geniculostriate system and the tectopulvinar system, respectively.

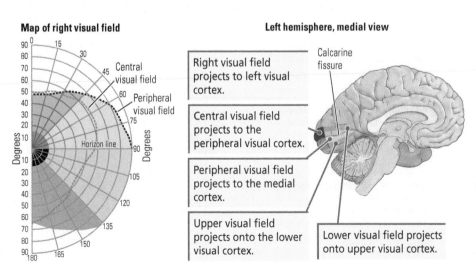

Figure 8.8 ◄

Retinoptic Map Projection of the right visual field map (left) from a medial view of the left hemisphere (right). Note the relation between the visual-field topography and the cortical topography. (Data from Poggio, 1968.)

Hearing

Hearing, or audition, the ability to construct perceptual representations from pressure waves in the air, includes *sound localization*—identifying the source of air-pressure waves—and *echolocalization*—identifying and locating objects by bouncing sound waves off them—as well as the ability to detect the *complexity* of pressure waves. Our nervous systems allow us to interpret this complexity to hear speech and music.

The auditory system itself is complex for two reasons. First, many transformations of pressure waves take place within the ear before action potentials are generated in the auditory nerve. Second, the auditory nerve projects to many targets in the brainstem and cortex. In this section, we describe only its major features.

Auditory Receptors

Changes in air pressure cause sound waves. The frequency, amplitude, and complexity of these changes determine what we hear. We hear the *frequency*, or speed, of pressure changes as changes in pitch; we hear the *amplitude*, or intensity, of pressure changes as loudness; and we hear the complexity of pressure changes as *timbre*, the perceived uniqueness or tonal quality of a sound (**Figure 8.9**). Receptor cells in the inner ear detect these differences in air pressure and convey them to the brain as action potentials. Areas of the cortex in the temporal lobe interpret the action potentials as random noise or as sounds—as language and music, for example.

Structure of the Ear

The human ear's three major anatomical divisions are the outer ear, middle ear, and inner ear (**Figure 8.10**). The outer ear consists of the **pinna**, the external structure which catches waves of air pressure and directs them into the *external ear canal*, which amplifies them somewhat and directs them to the *eardrum* at its inner end. Sound waves striking the eardrum vibrate it at frequencies varying with the waves' frequencies.

On the inner side of the eardrum is the middle ear, an air-filled chamber that contains the three smallest bones in the human body, connected in a series. These three **ossicles**, the *hammer*, *anvil*, and *stirrup*, so-called because of their distinctive shapes, attach the eardrum to the *oval window* of the inner ear.

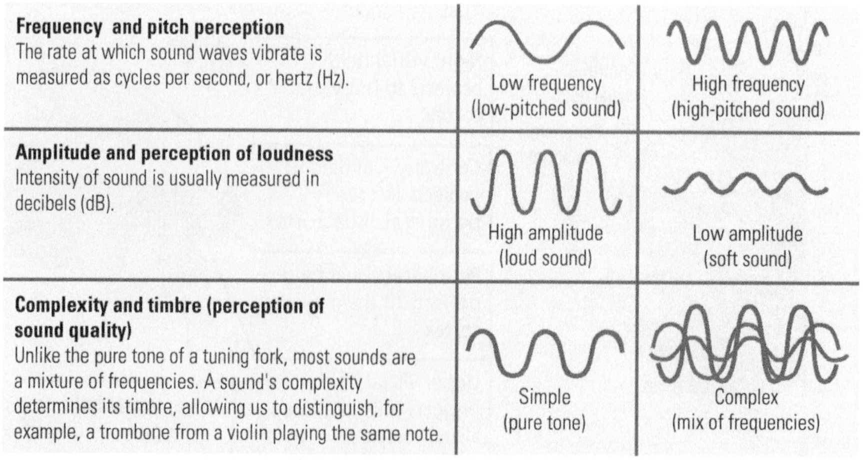

Figure 8.9 ►

Physical Dimensions of Sound Waves The frequency, amplitude, and complexity of sound-wave sensations correspond to the perceptual dimensions of pitch, loudness, and timbre.

Frequency and pitch perception The rate at which sound waves vibrate is measured as cycles per second, or hertz (Hz).	Low frequency (low-pitched sound)	High frequency (high-pitched sound)
Amplitude and perception of loudness Intensity of sound is usually measured in decibels (dB).	High amplitude (loud sound)	Low amplitude (soft sound)
Complexity and timbre (perception of sound quality) Unlike the pure tone of a tuning fork, most sounds are a mixture of frequencies. A sound's complexity determines its timbre, allowing us to distinguish, for example, a trombone from a violin playing the same note.	Simple (pure tone)	Complex (mix of frequencies)

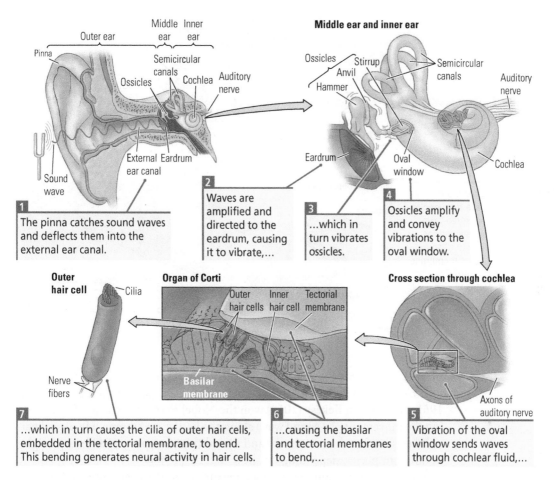

1 The pinna catches sound waves and deflects them into the external ear canal.

2 Waves are amplified and directed to the eardrum, causing it to vibrate,...

3 ...which in turn vibrates ossicles.

4 Ossicles amplify and convey vibrations to the oval window.

7 ...which in turn causes the cilia of outer hair cells, embedded in the tectorial membrane, to bend. This bending generates neural activity in hair cells.

6 ...causing the basilar and tectorial membranes to bend,...

5 Vibration of the oval window sends waves through cochlear fluid,...

Figure 8.10 ▲

Anatomy of the Human Inner Ear

The inner ear consists of the **cochlea**, which contains the auditory sensory receptors called **hair cells**. As detailed in Figure 8.10, the cochlea is rolled up into the shape of a snail shell. It is filled with fluid, and floating in the middle of this fluid is the **basilar membrane**. The hair cells are embedded in a part of the basilar membrane called the *organ of Corti*.

In short, sounds are caught in the outer ear and amplified by the middle ear. In the inner ear they are converted to action potentials on the auditory pathway going to the brain, and we interpret the action potentials as our perception of sound.

Transducing Sound Waves into Neural Impulses

When sound waves strike the eardrum, it vibrates. The vibrations are transferred to the ossicles, producing an action like that of a piston. This back-and-forth action not only conveys the vibrations to the oval window but also amplifies them, much as a drumstick amplifies the movement of the drummer striking a drumhead. In short, pressure waves in the air are amplified and transformed a number of times in the ear: by deflection in the pinna, by oscillation as they travel through the external ear canal, and by the movement of the bones of the middle ear to the cochlea.

The frequency of a sound is transduced by the longitudinal structure of the basilar membrane, which proves to be a sheet of tissue when the cochlea is

(A) Structure of basilar membrane

Basilar membrane

20,000   4,000   1,000   100
Uncoiling of cochlea (Hz)

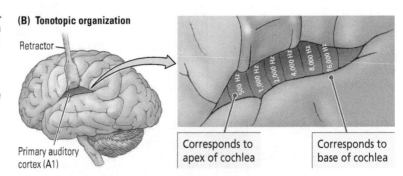

Cochlear base

A narrow, thick base is tuned for high frequencies.

A wide, thin apex is tuned for low frequencies.

Sound waves at medium frequencies cause peak bending of the basilar membrane at this point.

Basilar membrane

Figure 8.11 ▲

Auditory Mapping (A) Unwound cochlea shows the locations of sound-wave frequencies along the basilar membrane, measured from high to low in pitch in cycles per second, or hertz. (B) A tonotopic representation of sound-frequency transfers from the basilar membrane to the primary auditory cortex. A retractor reveals the primary auditory cortex buried within the lateral (Sylvian) fissure.

(B) Tonotopic organization

Retractor

Primary auditory cortex (A1)

500 Hz   1,000 Hz   2,000 Hz   4,000 Hz   8,000 Hz   16,000 Hz

Corresponds to apex of cochlea

Corresponds to base of cochlea

▼ Cochlear implants electronically process incoming sound-wave stimulation directly to the correct tonotopic locations on the basilar membrane via a microphone linked to a small speech-processing computer worn behind the ear. (AP Photo/Gene J. Puskar)

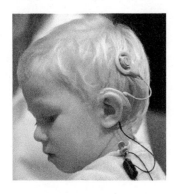

unrolled (**Figure 8.11**A). The basilar membrane is narrow and thick at its base near the round window and thinner and wider at its apex within the cochlea. In 1961, George von Békésy (2014) won the Nobel Prize in Medicine for describing the movement of a sound wave along the basilar membrane. He placed particles of silver on the membrane and filmed them jumping to different heights in different places, depending on the sound frequency.

Higher sound frequencies cause maximum peaks near the cochlear base (that is, near the oval window), and lower sound frequencies cause maximum peaks near the apex (farthest from the oval window). These patterns are roughly analogous to what happens when you shake a rope. If you shake it very quickly, the waves are very small and remain close to the base—the hand holding the rope. But, if you shake the rope slowly, with a broader movement of your arms, the waves reach their peak farther along the rope—toward the apex.

Like the rope, hair cells in the organ of Corti are maximally disturbed at the point at which the wave peaks, producing their maximal neural discharge at that place. A complex signal composed of many frequencies causes several different points along the basilar membrane to vibrate and excites hair cells at all those points.

Single-cell recordings from the primary auditory cortex in the temporal lobes show that different points in the cortex respond maximally to different frequencies, just as occurs in the basilar membrane (Figure 8.11B). This **tonotopic representation**, in which different points on the basilar membrane represent different sound frequencies, also applies to the auditory cortex: there, too, different locations represent different sound frequencies. Thus, projections from hair cells of the organ of Corti form a representation of the basilar membrane in the neocortex.

As in the visual system, each auditory receptor cell has a receptive field, and so does each cell in the higher auditory centers. The receptive field of a hair cell is not a point in space, as it is in the visual system, but rather a particular sound frequency. Thus, in contrast with the retinotopic maps in the visual system, the auditory system is composed of tonotopic (literally, "tone place") maps.

Auditory Pathways

The axons of hair cells leave the cochlea to form the major part of the auditory nerve, the eighth cranial nerve (**Figure 8.12**). This nerve first projects to the level of the medulla in the hindbrain, synapsing either in the dorsal or ventral cochlear nuclei or in the superior olivary nucleus. The axons of neurons in these areas form the lateral lemniscus, which terminates in discrete zones of the inferior colliculus in the midbrain.

The inferior colliculus, the main auditory region in fish, amphibians, and reptiles, plays a role in orienting to sound location. The inferior and superior colliculi are interconnected (see Figure 3.19), and the superior colliculus functions to orient the head toward a sound's direction. The connections between these two areas thus allow conjoint recognition, not only of the direction a sound comes from but also the visual source of the sound.

Two distinct pathways emerge from the colliculus, coursing to the ventral and the dorsal medial geniculate nuclei in the thalamus. The ventral region projects to the core auditory cortex (A1 or Brodmann's area 41), and the dorsal region projects to the secondary auditory regions, thus adhering to the sensory systems' general pattern of having multiple independent ascending pathways to the cortex. As occurs in the visual system pathways, the former auditory pathway identifies the sound and the latter indicates its spatial source.

In contrast with the visual-system pathways, the projections of the auditory system provide both ipsilateral and contralateral inputs to the cortex, so there is bilateral representation of each cochlear nucleus in both hemispheres. As described for the visual system, A1 projects to many other regions of the neocortex, forming multiple tonotopic maps.

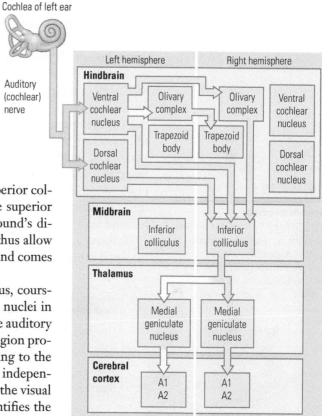

Figure 8.12 ▲

Auditory Pathways
Multiple nuclei process inputs en route to the auditory cortex, charted here for the left ear. Auditory inputs cross to the hemisphere opposite the ear in the hindbrain and midbrain, then recross in the thalamus, so that information from each ear reaches both hemispheres.

Body Senses

Vision and hearing are exteroceptive systems. The somatosensory—literally, "body awareness"—system also has an exteroceptive function: it enables us to feel the world around us. But it is also interoceptive, monitoring internal bodily events and informing the brain about the positions of body segments relative to one another and about the body in space. Three of the four major somatosensory submodalities mediate our perceptions of sensations such as pain, touch, and body awareness. The fourth, composed of a set of interoceptive receptors within the inner ear, mediates balance.

Classifying Somatosensory Receptors

The varied somatosensory receptors in the human body may comprise as many as 20 or more types, but they can all be classified into three groupings based on our sensory perception as illustrated in **Figure 8.13**: nociception, hapsis, and proprioception.

Nociception Nociception (**noxious perception**) is the perception of pain, temperature, and itch. Most nociceptors consist of free nerve endings, as diagrammed at the top of Figure 8.13. When damaged or irritated, these endings secrete chemicals, usually peptides, that stimulate the nerve, producing action potentials that then convey messages about pain, temperature, or itch to the CNS. It is in the CNS, especially the cortex, that pain is perceived, as witnessed in the case of phantom-limb pain described in this chapter's opening Portrait.

People in pain would happily dispense with it. Up to 30 percent of visits to physicians are for pain symptoms, as are 50 percent of emergency room visits. The incidence of people living with pain increases with age, and for many people, pain is a constant companion. But pain is necessary: the occasional person born without pain receptors is subject to body deformities through failure to adjust posture and acute injuries through failure to avoid harmful situations.

As many as eight different kinds of pain fibers exist, judging from the peptides and other chemicals released by these nerves when irritated or damaged.

Figure 8.13 ▼

Somatosensory Receptors Perceptions derived from the body-sense submodalities of nociception, hapsis, and proprioception depend on different receptors located variously in skin, muscles, joints, and tendons.

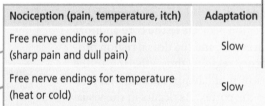

Hair

Nociception (pain, temperature, itch)	Adaptation	Damage or irritation to dendrites or surrounding cells releases chemicals that stimulate dendrites to produce action potentials.
Free nerve endings for pain (sharp pain and dull pain)	Slow	
Free nerve endings for temperature (heat or cold)	Slow	

Hapsis (fine touch and pressure)	Adaptation	Mechanical pressure on the various tissue capsules stimulates dendrites within them to produce action potentials.
Meissner's corpuscle (touch)	Rapid	
Pacinian corpuscle (flutter)	Rapid	
Ruffini corpuscle (vibration)	Rapid	
Merkel's receptor (steady skin indentation)	Slow	
Hair receptors (flutter or steady skin indentation)	Slow	

Proprioception (body awareness)	Adaptation	Movement stretches receptors to stimulate dendrites within them mechanically, producing action potentials.
Muscle spindles (muscle stretch)	Rapid	
Golgi tendon organs (tendon stretch)	Rapid	
Joint receptors (joint movement)	Rapid	

Some chemicals irritate surrounding tissue, stimulating the release of other chemicals to increase blood flow. These reactions contribute to pain, redness, and swelling at the site of an injury.

Many internal organs, including the heart and kidneys and the blood vessels, have pain receptors, but the ganglion neurons carrying information from these receptors lack pathways to the brain. Instead, they synapse with spinal-cord neurons that receive nociceptive information from the body's surface. Consequently, the neurons in the spinal cord that relay pain, temperature, and itch messages to the brain receive two sets of signals: one from the body's surface and the other from the internal organs.

These spinal-cord neurons cannot distinguish between the two sets of signals—nor can we. As a result, pain in body organs is often felt as **referred pain** coming from the body surface. In men, for example, pain in the heart associated with a heart attack may be felt as pain in the left shoulder and upper arm. Pain in the stomach is felt as pain in the midline of the trunk; pain in the kidneys is felt as pain in the lower back. Pain in blood vessels in the head is felt as diffuse pain that we call a headache. (Remember, the brain has no pain receptors.)

Hapsis From the Greek for "touch," **hapsis** is our tactile perception of objects. Haptic receptors enable fine touch, and pressure, allowing us to identify objects we touch and grasp. Haptic receptors, diagrammed at the center of Figure 8.13, occupy both superficial and deep skin layers and are attached to body hairs as well. When touch is lost, not only do we lose the information that it normally provides about the objects we handle or the movements we make, movement is affected as well.

John Rothwell and his coworkers (1982) described a patient, G.O., who was **deafferentated** (lost afferent sensory fibers) by a disease that destroyed touch sensation in his hands. He could not feel when his hand was holding something. G.O. began movements quite normally, but as he proceeded, the movement patterns gradually fell apart. When he tried to carry a suitcase, for example, he would quickly drop it unless he continually looked down to confirm that he was carrying it.

Clearly, G.O.'s lost sense of touch resulted in a motor disability as well. His hands were relatively useless to him in daily life. He was unable to learn to drive a new car. He was also unable to write, to fasten shirt buttons, or to hold a cup.

Proprioception **Proprioception** is the perception of body location and movement. Proprioceptors, diagrammed at the bottom of Figure 8.13, are encapsulated nerve endings sensitive to the stretch of muscles and tendons and to joint movement. We are ordinarily unaware of how proprioception contributes to our movements, but witness what happens when this sense is lost.

Ian Waterman was 19 when he cut his finger while working as a butcher. The resulting inflammation seemed to clear, but Ian began to endure alternating hot and cold spells and was very tired. He was forced to take time off work. About a week later, Ian was taken to the hospital after falling as he tried to get out of bed. He could not move, had no sense of touch or pressure in his hands or feet (although he felt a tingling sensation in both areas), and was having trouble talking.

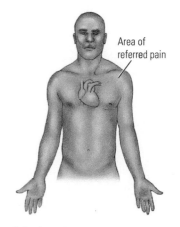

Area of referred pain

▲ During a heart attack, men usually perceive sensations from receptors in the heart as referred pain in the left shoulder and upper arm, while women's symptoms are different and may include back pain, for example.

His physicians had never seen a case like Ian's but finally concluded that he had lost all proprioception. His body was no longer aware of itself, his motor system was helpless, and he was unable to engage in the "melody of movement."

Ian Waterman never recovered from his sensory loss, although with enormous effort he became the first person with this affliction to relearn to walk, to care for himself, and to drive a car. He did so by learning to replace body awareness with vision—by watching his hands as he made them perform and by watching his feet as he made them step. He drove by using vision to estimate his movement speed and direction. But if the lights went out or if his eyes were covered, he lost all ability to control his voluntary movements. Every movement required mental effort that he described as having to perform "a daily marathon" (Cole, 1991).

Somatosensory Pathways

Two major somatosensory pathways diagrammed in **Figure 8.14** extend from the spinal cord to the brain: a posterior spinothalamic tract for hapsis (pressure) and proprioception (body awareness) and an anterior spinothalamic tract for nociception (irritation).

Posterior Spinothalamic Tract The fibers of somatosensory neurons that make up the hapsis and proprioception system are relatively large, heavily myelinated, and for the most part, rapidly adapting. Their cell bodies are located in the

Figure 8.14 ▼

Dual Somatosensory Pathways to the Brain As neurons from the posterior-root ganglia enter the spinal cord, the two somatosensory pathways to the brain diverge.

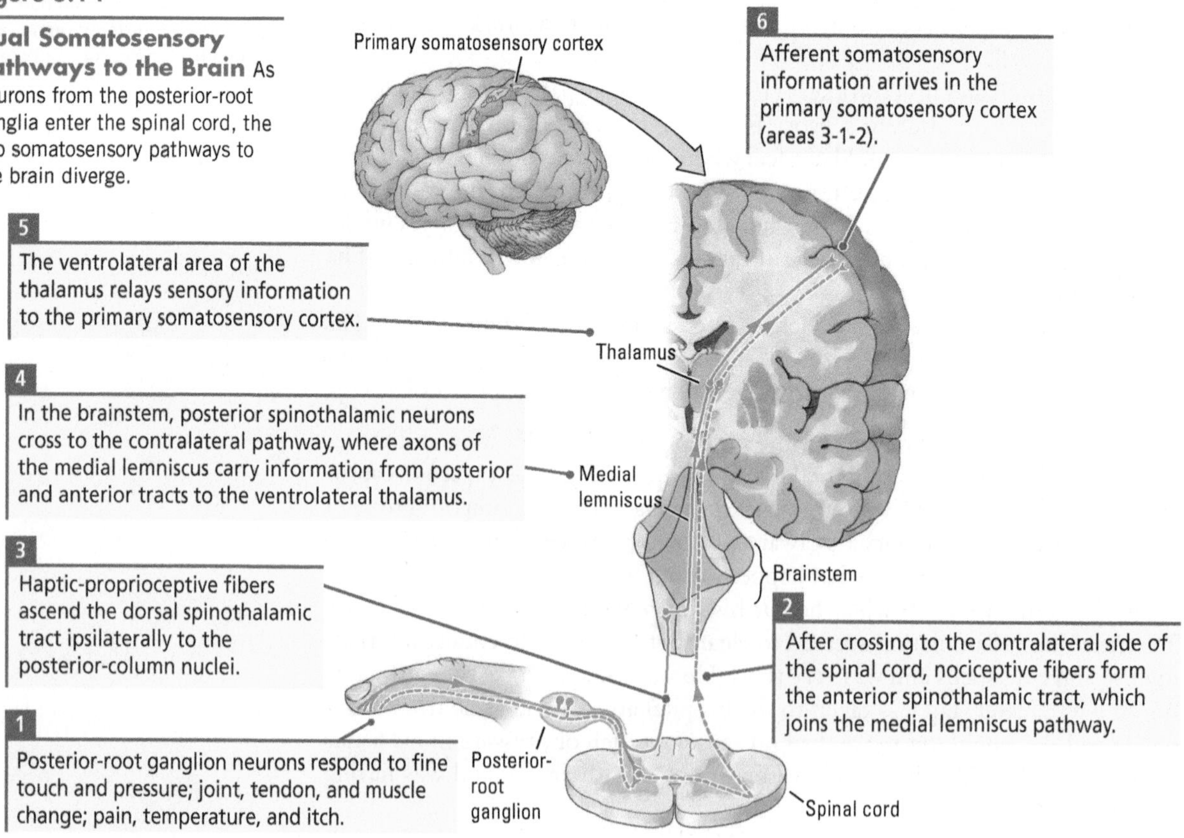

Primary somatosensory cortex

6 Afferent somatosensory information arrives in the primary somatosensory cortex (areas 3-1-2).

5 The ventrolateral area of the thalamus relays sensory information to the primary somatosensory cortex.

Thalamus

4 In the brainstem, posterior spinothalamic neurons cross to the contralateral pathway, where axons of the medial lemniscus carry information from posterior and anterior tracts to the ventrolateral thalamus.

Medial lemniscus

3 Haptic-proprioceptive fibers ascend the dorsal spinothalamic tract ipsilaterally to the posterior-column nuclei.

Brainstem

2 After crossing to the contralateral side of the spinal cord, nociceptive fibers form the anterior spinothalamic tract, which joins the medial lemniscus pathway.

1 Posterior-root ganglion neurons respond to fine touch and pressure; joint, tendon, and muscle change; pain, temperature, and itch.

Posterior-root ganglion

Spinal cord

posterior-root ganglia, their dendrites project to sensory receptors in the body, and their axons project into the spinal cord (detailed in Figure 3.13B).

Recall that the dendrite and axon of each somatosensory neuron are joined into one continuous fiber. In the spinal cord, some branches of these axons make local connections while other branches ascend through the posterior column (the solid red line in Figure 8.14) to synapse in the posterior-column nuclei at the base of the brainstem. The cell bodies in these nuclei send their axons across the spinal cord to form the medial lemniscus, which ascends to synapse in the ventrolateral thalamus. This thalamic nucleus then projects into the primary somatosensory cortex (S1, or Brodmann's area 3-1-2), as well as to area 4, the primary motor cortex.

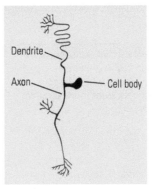

Somatosensory neuron

Anterior Spinothalamic Tract Nociceptive fibers are somewhat smaller, less myelinated, and more slowly adapting than those of the haptic and proprioception pathway. They follow the same course to enter the spinal cord but once there, project to relay neurons in the more central region of the spinal cord, the substantia gelatinosa. The second-relay cells then send their axons across to the other side of the cord, where they form the anterior spinothalamic tract (the dashed red line in Figure 8.14).

These anterior fibers eventually join the posterior hapsis and proprioception fibers in the medial lemniscus. They too terminate primarily in the ventrolateral thalamus as well as in the posterior thalamus, and these messages too are relayed in turn to area 3-1-2 of the cortex. As for vision and hearing, we see two somatosensory pathways, each taking a somewhat different route to the brain and somatosensory cortex. Vision and hearing project mainly to the opposite hemisphere.

A unilateral spinal cord injury that cuts the somatosensory pathways in that half of the spinal cord results in the bilateral symptoms known as Brown-Séquard syndrome, after the two investigators who first described it. As illustrated in **Figure 8.15**, loss of hapsis and proprioception occurs unilaterally on the side of the body where damage occurred, and loss of nociception occurs contralaterally, on the side of the body opposite the injury. Unilateral damage to the points where the pathways come together—that is, to the posterior roots, brainstem, and thalamus—affects hapsis, proprioception, and nociception equally because these parts of the pathways are in proximity.

Unilateral damage to spinal cord causes ... **Cut**

...loss of body awareness and of fine-touch and pressure sensation below the cut on the same side of the body...

...and loss of pain and temperature sensation below the cut on the opposite side of the body.

Figure 8.15 ▲

Effects of Unilateral Spinal Cord Injury

Somatosensory Cortex

In the 1930s, when neurosurgeon Wilder Penfield first stimulated the sensory cortex in conscious epilepsy patients and asked them to report the sensations they felt, he created a topographic map that represents the body surface on the

(A) Penfield's single-homunculus model

Primary somatosensory cortex

Primary somatosensory cortex organized as a single homunculus whose larger areas represent more-sensitive body parts.

(B) Four-homunculi model

Primary somatosensory cortex

Primary somatosensory cortex organized as four separate homunculi. Areas 3a, 3b, and 1 pass information to area 2, which responds to the combined information.

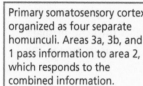

| 3a | 3b | 1 | 2 |

Muscles   Skin (slow)   Skin (fast)   Joints, pressure

Figure 8.16 ▲

Two Models of Somatosensory Homunculi

Figure 8.17 ▶

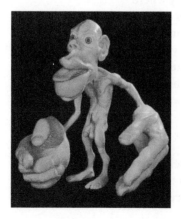

Homunculus The sculpture represents the relative sensitivity of human body parts by size. (Sensory Homunculus (plaster), English School, (20th century)/Natural History Museum, London, UK/The Bridgeman Art Library.)

primary somatosensory cortex, S1 (**Figure 8.16**A). The regions representing feeling in the mouth and eyes are in the ventral part of S1, the regions representing hand and finger sensation are in the middle, and the regions corresponding to feet are in the dorsal area. On this map, called a **homunculus** ("little human") and represented in three dimensions in **Figure 8.17**, the relative sensitivity of body parts are represented by size.

Studies subsequent to Penfield's mainly used monkeys and took advantage of smaller recording electrodes. The results show that the primary somatosensory cortex contains a number of homunculi, one for each of its subregions, 3a, 3b, 1, and 2, as elaborated in the lower part of Figure 8.16B. Each area is dominated by responses to one type of body receptor, although there is overlap. Area 3a represents muscle sense (position and movement of muscles), area 3b represents both slowly and rapidly adapting skin receptors, area 1 represents rapidly adapting skin receptors, and area 2 represents deep pressure and joint sensation. Thus, the body is represented at least four times in S1. A number of other receptor types are represented in each area as well, so it is possible that still more body-representation areas await discovery.

Although Penfield underestimated the number of homunculi, he was correct about the disproportionate sizes of some of its parts relative to others. The density of somatosensory receptors varies greatly from one place to another on the body surface (and varies from species to species), and somatotopic maps manifest this variability. Thus, in the human homunculus, the areas representing the hands and tongue are extremely large, whereas the areas representing the trunk and legs are small.

Like other sensory systems, the somatosensory cortex comprises a primary area and several secondary areas. Thus, S1 (Brodmann's area 3-1-2) sends projections into S2, or Brodmann's areas 5 and 7. Area S1 also sends projections into the adjacent primary motor cortex, M1, or Brodmann's area 4.

The Vestibular System: Motion and Balance

Early in Section 8.1 we asked you to hold your hand in front of you and shake it. Your hand appeared blurry. But when you held your hand still and moved your head back and forth, the hand remained in focus.

In the second observation, interoceptive receptors in the inner-ear **vestibular system** informed your visual system that your head was moving. The visual system responded by compensating for the head movements, and

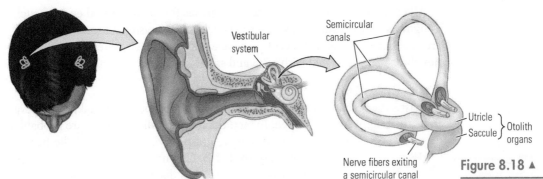

Figure 8.18 ▲

Vestibular System The vestibular organs in each inner ear contain hair cells sensitive to the movement of the head and to gravity.

you observed the hand as stationary. Like other somatosensory submodalities, the vestibular system helps you distinguish between your own behavior and the actions of others.

The inner ear contains the organs that allow you to perceive your own motion and to stand upright without losing your balance. Named for an entrance-way, the vestibular organs contain hair cells that bend when the body moves forward or when the head changes position relative to the body. Shown in **Figure 8.18**, the three *semicircular canals* are oriented in the three planes that correspond to the three dimensions in which we move, so collectively they can represent any head movement. The *otolith organs* detect the head's linear acceleration and respond to changes in head position with respect to gravity. In contrast with the semicircular canals' sensitivity to head movement, the otoliths are sensitive to the head's static position in space.

Fibers from the balance receptors project over the eighth cranial nerve to a number of nuclei in the brainstem. These nuclei interact in the hindbrain to help keep us balanced while we move; they also aid in controlling eye movements at the midbrain level. Ultimately, through its connections in the cerebellum, information from the vestibular system allows us not only to balance but also to record and replay, actively and in the mind's eye, the movements we have made.

Vertigo (from the Latin for "spinning"), a sensation of dizziness when one is not moving, is a dysfunction of the inner ear and can be accompanied by nausea and difficulty maintaining balance while walking. A common way to induce vertigo is to spin, as children do when playing. Vertigo can also occur when a person is looking down from a height, looking up at a tall object, or simply standing up or sitting down. One intoxicating effect of alcohol is vertigo.

Ménière's disease, a disorder of the middle ear resulting in vertigo and loss of balance and named after a French physician, may affect as many as 200 people in 100,000, women more frequently than men, and is most likely to occur in middle age. Symptoms causing dizziness and falling may be caused by impairments in balance receptors in one or both ears and may be brief or last for days or even longer.

The Chemical Senses: Taste and Smell

Unlike carnivores and rodents, primates' gustatory and olfactory systems are considered relatively small in comparison with their well-developed visual systems. Dolphins and whales are mammals whose olfactory system also is small. Nevertheless, taste and smell are sophisticated senses in humans. Their neocortical representations are imaged in the Snapshot.

All of the senses described so far use various forms of physical energy, such as light and air pressure, as stimuli. The stimuli for taste and smell sensations are chemical. Specialized receptors have evolved for each system, for the various chemicals associated with taste and smell.

Taste Receptors

For taste, the receptors are the taste buds, which most people mistakenly believe to be the bumps on the tongue. In fact, the bumps, called *papillae*, are probably there to help the tongue grasp food; the taste buds lie buried around them (**Figure 8.19**). Chemicals in food dissolve in the saliva that coats the tongue and disperse through the saliva to reach the taste receptors. If the tongue is dry, the taste buds receive few chemical signals, and food is difficult to taste. Taste receptors are also found in the gut and elsewhere in the body, where they may play a role in food absorption, metabolism, and appetite.

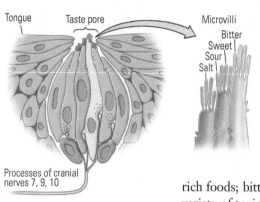

Each of the five main taste-receptor types—sweet, sour, salty, bitter, and umami (savory)—responds to a different chemical component in food. Sweet receptors are sensitive to calorie-rich foods; bitter taste receptors are sensitive to some vegetables and to a wide variety of toxic substances. Salt receptors are related to chemicals necessary for water balance, and sour receptors are sensitive to acidity, especially in fruits. The umami receptor is sensitive to protein and especially sensitive to the food additive monosodium glutamate (MSG).

Figure 8.19 ▲

Anatomy of a Taste Bud

Tastes are related to ingestive behavior as well as to food choice. Animals sensitive to sweet tastes respond with tongue licks and mouth movements designed to take in food when a sweet substance is placed in their mouth. When a bitter substance in placed in their mouth, animals sensitive to bitter tastes make mouth gaping movements and tongue protrusions, as if to expel the substance. Umami-tasting substances induce salivation. The specificity of any given taste receptor is not absolute, however. The perceived taste of any stimulus results from the combined activity of many receptors and perhaps the entire population of taste receptors.

Significant differences in taste preferences exist, both within and between species, as do vast differences in taste among individuals, including humans. Humans and rats like sucrose and saccharin solutions, but dogs reject saccharin, and cats are indifferent to it. Humans have clear individual differences in taste thresholds. Older people generally have higher thresholds, largely because the number of taste buds undergoes a dramatic reduction as we age. Children tolerate spicy foods poorly because their sense of taste is stronger.

As Linda Bartoshuk and colleagues (Rawal et al., 2013) have shown, people termed *supertasters* perceive certain tastes as strong and offensive, whereas others are indifferent to them. Supertasters constitute 25 percent of the population, 50 percent are medium tasters, and 25 percent are nontasters. The groups are distinguished by their sensitivity to the bitter-tasting substance propylthiouracil, to which supertasters are especially sensitive. The advantage of being a supertaster is the avoidance of poisonous substances; the disadvantage is finding many vegetables, brussels sprouts for one, distasteful. Supertasters do eat fewer vegetables than do nontasters.

SNAPSHOT Watching the Brain Make Flavor

After falling from a horse while riding in the mountains of Iran, J.H. required surgery to remove a blood clot from her right frontal cortex. She recovered quickly, but a disability from the accident lingered: she no longer enjoyed food. She had always taken pride in preparing food from many regions of the world. Now hardly a meal went by that did not leave her wishing she could taste what she was eating.

Flavor, a marriage of stimuli from the mouth, nose, and even from vision, plays a role in appreciating foods, including wines (Gonzalo-Diago, 2013). Interactions among tastes affect flavor; for example, bitter taste suppresses the taste of sweet substances. Flavor is also affected by light: sweet tastes sweeter in dim light, hinting at the importance of lighting to the dining experience. Flavor is lost in individuals born without olfactory bulbs, and flavor loss is one of the earliest symptoms of neurological conditions such as Parkinson's disease (Barresi, 2012). Where in the brain does this union of senses take place?

To image the effects of odors and tastes, researchers must first eliminate from the imaging record the effects of air movement through the nostrils and of tongue and mouth movements. The separation of "sniffing" from "smelling" can be accomplished in part by having participants sample air in controlled trials or by anesthetizing the nostrils so that the air movement is not perceived. The usual "sip-and-spit" method employed in laboratory taste tests cannot be used, because mouth movements produce artifacts that interfere with recording the brain image. Special delivery techniques that use droppers or even electrical stimulation of taste buds can partly circumvent the problem.

A review of various imaging studies suggests that the orbitofrontal cortex (OFC), especially in the right hemisphere, plays a special role in perceiving odors and tastes (Zatorre and Jones-Gotman, 2000). The adjoining illustration, for example, combines the results of several independent studies, including studies on odor recognition, odor intensity, and the connection between odor and affect (mood). PET or MRI recorded participants' responses to olfactory stimuli. The locations of brain activity recorded in each study are represented by plus signs.

These summaries of olfactory and taste research suggest that the union of olfaction and taste to produce flavor

(A) Olfactory stimuli **(B) Taste stimuli**

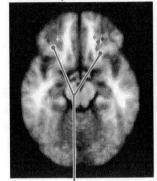 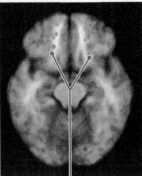

| Left hemisphere | Right hemisphere | Left hemisphere | Right hemisphere |

Neural activity related to flavor is concentrated in the OFC.

Ventral view of horizontal brain sections marks prefrontal cortical locations that respond to (A) olfactory stimuli in six studies and (B) taste stimuli in four studies. (Research from Zatorre and Jones-Gotman, 2000.)

probably takes place in the OFC. Ambience, including the effects of music and light on flavor, also affects this region. In turn, the sensations themselves, singly or in combination, directly influence blood flow in the OFC, further heightening intersensory integration (Frank et al., 2013).

Barresi, M., R. Ciurleo, S. Giacoppo, V. Foti Cuzzola, D. Celi. P. Bramanti, and S. Marino. Evaluation of olfactory dysfunction in neurodegenerative diseases. *Journal of Neurological Sciences* 323: 16–24, 2012.

Gonzalo-Diago, A., M. Dizy, and P. Fernández-Zurbano. Taste and mouthfeel properties of red wines proanthocyanidins and their relation to the chemical composition. *Journal of Agriculture and Food Chemistry* 61:8861–8870, 2013.

Frank, S., K. Linder, L. Fritsche, M. A. Hege, S. Kullmann, A. Krzeminski, A. Fritsche, P. Schieberle, V. Somoza, J. Hinrichs, R. Veit, and H. Preissl. Olive oil aroma extract modulates cerebral blood flow in gustatory brain areas in humans. *American Journal of Clinical Nutrition* 98(5):1320–1366, 2013.

Zatorre, R. J., and M. Jones-Gotman. Functional imaging in the chemical senses. In A. W. Toga and J. C. Mazziota, Eds., *Brain Mapping: The Systems*, pp. 403–424. San Diego: Academic Press, 2000.

The underlying basis for species and individual differences in taste stems from differences in the genes for taste receptors. Two families of metabotropic receptor–producing genes are responsible for sweet, bitter, and umami: at least 3 *TAS1R* (taste family 1 receptor) genes are associated with sweet and as many as 43 *TAS2R* genes are associated with bitter. Genes responsible for sour and salt produce ionotropic receptors. It is likely that taste buds contain many receptor types from the different taste receptor families. For example, it is useful to detect bitter substances that may be poisons, which likely requires many different bitter receptors.

Smell Receptors

The receptor surface for olfaction is the olfactory epithelium located in the nasal cavity and composed of three cell types: receptor hair cells, supporting cells, and an underlying layer of basal cells (**Figure 8.20**). The axons projecting from the olfactory receptors relay onto the ball-like tufted dendrites of glomeruli in the olfactory bulb. From the glomeruli, mitral cells form the olfactory tract (cranial nerve 1). The mitral-cell projection reaches the pyriform cortex and from there reaches the hypothalamus, the amygdala, the entorhinal cortex of the temporal lobe, and the *orbitofrontal cortex* (*OFC*), the area of prefrontal cortex located behind the eye sockets (*the orbits*).

The outer epithelial surface is covered by a layer of mucus in which the receptor cell's cilia are embedded. Odors must pass through the mucus to reach the receptors, which means that changes in its properties (such as occur when we have a cold) may influence how easily we can detect an odor. The area of the olfactory epithelium varies across species. In humans, it is estimated to range from 2 square centimeters to 4 square centimeters; in dogs, the area is about 18 square centimeters; and in cats, about 21 square centimeters. Such differences support the observation that some species are more sensitive to odors than others.

Linda Buck and Richard Axel (1991) received the 2004 Nobel Prize in Medicine for describing the very large family of about 1000 genes in mice (about 400

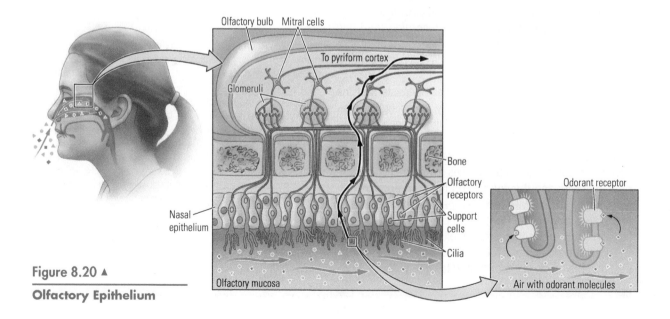

Figure 8.20 ▲

Olfactory Epithelium

in humans) that gives rise to an equivalent number of odorant receptor types. Each type is located on one receptor cell and is sensitive to only a few odors. Receptors of like types project to one of the 2000 glomeruli, and the pattern of activation produced by the glomeruli cells allows humans to distinguish, in principle, 1 trillion odors. It is the summed action of many chemical receptors leading to a particular mosaic of neural activity that the olfactory system identifies as a particular odor.

Taste and Smell Pathways

The chemical senses, like all the others, employ dual pathways to primary and secondary areas in the cortex.

Gustatory Pathways Three cranial nerves carry information from the tongue: the glossopharyngeal nerve (9), the vagus nerve (10), and the chorda tympani branch of the facial nerve (7). All three enter the solitary tract, the main gustatory pathway. At that point, as illustrated in **Figure 8.21**, the pathway divides into two routes. One, shown in red in Figure 8.21, goes to the ventroposterior medial nucleus of the thalamus, which in turn sends out two pathways, one to S1 and the other to a region just rostral to S2 in the insular cortex. The latter region is probably dedicated entirely to taste, because it is not responsive to tactile stimulation.

In contrast, the S1 projection is sensitive to tactile stimuli and is probably responsible for localizing tastes on the tongue. (Those who enjoy wine are familiar with this distinction because wines are described not only by their gustatory qualities but also by the way that they taste on different parts of the tongue.) These areas project in turn to the OFC, in a region near the input of the olfactory cortex, which may be the secondary taste area.

The other route from the solitary tract (shown in blue in Figure 8.21) leads to the pontine taste area, which in turn projects to the lateral hypothalamus and amygdala. Both areas have roles in feeding, although the gustatory input's precise contribution to this behavior is uncertain.

Olfactory Pathways The axons of the olfactory-receptor relays synapse in the olfactory bulb, which is multilayered and may be conceptualized as an analogue to the retina. The major output of the bulb is the lateral olfactory tract, which passes ipsilaterally to the pyriform cortex, the amygdala, and the entorhinal cortex (**Figure 8.22**). The pyriform cortex's primary projection goes to the central part of the dorsomedial nucleus in the thalamus. The dorsomedial nucleus in turn projects to the orbitofrontal cortex, which can be considered the primary olfactory neocortex.

Single-cell recordings from the olfactory pathways suggest two general classes of neurons, some responsive to specific odors and others broadly tuned (Nara et al., 2011). This research also suggests that neurons responsive to specific odors are linked to specific olfactory-related behaviors, but they elicit these behaviors within a context identified by the more broadly tuned neurons.

Accessory Olfactory System

A unique class of odorants is **pheromones**, biochemicals released by one animal that act as chemosignals (chemical signals) to affect the physiology or behavior of another animal. For example, Karen Stern and Martha McClintock (1998)

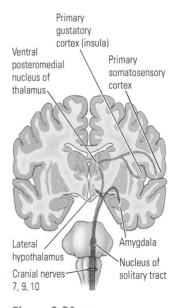

Figure 8.21 ▲

Gustatory Pathways

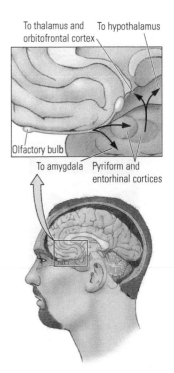

Figure 8.22 ▲

Olfactory Pathways

found that when women reside together, they begin to cycle together and that the synchronization of menstrual cycles is conveyed by odors.

Pheromones appear able to affect more than sex-related behavior. A human chemosignal, androstadienone, has been shown to alter glucose utilization in the neocortex—that is, how the brain uses energy (Jacob et al., 2001). Thus, a chemosignal appears to affect cortical processes even though the signal is not detected consciously.

In many animals, pheromones are unique odors because they are detected by a special olfactory receptor system known as the *vomeronasal organ* made up of a small group of sensory receptors connected by a duct to the nasal passage. The receptor cells in the vomeronasal organ send their axons to the accessory olfactory bulb, which lies adjacent to the main olfactory bulb. The vomeronasal organ connects primarily with the amygdala and hypothalamus and likely plays a role in reproductive and social behavior. Most evidence suggests that humans do not have a vomeronasal organ, so odors that affect human sex-related behaviors must act through conventional olfactory neural pathways.

8.3 Perception

We have reviewed the sensory systems' basic organization, traced their neural pathways from receptors into the cortex, and identified some principles governing their operation and integration. But there is more to **sensation** than registration by the sensory systems of physical or chemical energy from the environment and its transduction into nervous-system activity. Divorced from the richness of interaction with the brain, our description of sensory neuroanatomy and function is incomplete.

Our sensory impressions are affected by the contexts in which they take place, by our emotional states, and by our experiences. All of these factors contribute to **perception**, the subjective experience by the brain of the sensory transduction events outlined in this chapter. Evidence that perception is more than sensation lies in the fact that we transform the same sensory stimulation into totally different perceptions at different times.

We may ignore obvious sensory stimulation yet attend to sensory events that otherwise seem trivial. We can be distracted by a single voice speaking in the background but ignore the babble of many voices. We habituate to sensory events we at first found annoying or be overwhelmed by the absence of sensory stimulation. Still more-dramatic examples of the sensory transformations that comprise perception are illusions, synesthesia, and sensory synergies.

Illusions

An ambiguous image, such as the well-known Rubin's vase shown in **Figure 8.23**A, is a classic illusion. The image may be perceived either as a vase or as two faces. If you fix your eyes on the center of the picture, the two perceptions will alternate, even as the sensory stimulation remains seemingly constant.

The Müller–Lyer illusion in Figure 8.23B demonstrates the influence of context on perception. We perceive the top line as longer than the bottom line, although they are exactly the same length. The contextual cues (the arrowheads) alter the perception of each line's length.

Figure 8.23 ▼

Perceptual Illusions
(A) Edgar Rubin's classic ambiguous or reversible image can be perceived as a vase or as two faces. (B) In the Müller–Lyer illusion, the two lines are equal in length, but owing to the contextual cues provided by the arrowheads, the top line appears longer than the bottom line.

(A) Ambiguous reversible figure

(B) Müller–Lyer illusion

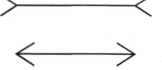

Illusions demonstrate complex perceptual phenomena mediated by the neo-cortex and illustrate that we do not simply respond to sensory information. Our brains transform sensations into information that we find behaviorally useful. Complex visual scenes can contain partly camouflaged objects, and our perceptual systems are designed to search for them. This explains our shifting perception of Ruben's vase. Stimuli similar to the arrowheads in Figure 8.23B occur naturally and help us distinguish an object's distance. When viewed out of context, they present us with the length illusion.

Synesthesia

If you recall shivering on hearing a particular piece of music or the noise of fingernails scratching across a chalkboard, you have felt sound. Such sensory mixing, or **synesthesia** (literally, "feeling together"), is the ability to perceive a stimulus of one sense as the sensation of a different sense. Roughly 4 in 100 people experience synesthesia, which tends to run in families. More than 100 kinds of synesthesia are reported (Chan et al., 2013). Some synesthetes can hear or feel taste; some can see sounds or hear colors; some can taste a rainbow. The most common form of sensory mixing is colored hearing.

Synesthetes are grouped into two general classes. *Projectors* experience sensory mixing as reality. When looking at numbers printed in black text, for example, 7 appears yellow to a projector, whereas 2 looks blue. *Associators* experience sensory mixing in their mind's eye, associating one number with one color and another number with another color but not actually seeing those colors. Projectors and associators can be distinguished by self-reports, and they perform differently on perceptual tests. For example, in the Stroop test (see Figure 16.11) participants read color words, say, RED, printed in a different color, say blue. Projectors take longer than associators to respond, because the color mixes can produce interference.

Zamm and colleagues (2013) used diffusion tensor imaging to measure the extent of fiber connections between the auditory and visual cortices in participants who saw colors when they heard sounds and in participants who did not. Those who displayed synesthesia had more connections than the controls. Rouw and Scholte (2010) examined brain differences in projectors and associators using fMRI and found that projectors show activation associated with sensory mixing in the sensory cortices, whereas associators display sensory activation in association cortices and brain regions associated with memory.

Everyone likely experiences weak forms of synesthesia. Artists—whether writers, musicians, or filmmakers—capitalize on sensory mixing to communicate with their audiences. Synesthesia might serve a similar function by allowing a person to distinguish and classify events rapidly and hold them in memory (Ward, 2013).

Sensory Synergies

Connections between the sensory systems exist at all levels of the nervous system, and their interactions are mediated by these sensory connections. For example, we often rub the area around an injury or shake a limb to reduce the pain sensation. These actions increase the activity in fine touch and pressure pathways and can block information transmission in spinal-cord relays through

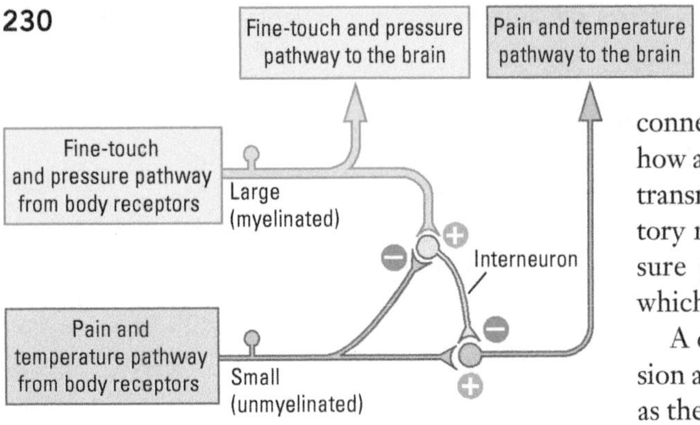

Figure 8.24 ▲

Pain Gate An interneuron in the spinal cord receives excitatory input (plus signs) from the fine-touch and pressure pathway and inhibitory input (minus signs) from the pain and temperature pathway. The relative activity of the interneuron determines whether pain and temperature information is sent to the brain. (Information from R. Melzack, *Puzzle of Pain*, New York: Basic Books, 1973, p. 154.)

connections known as **pain gates**. **Figure 8.24** illustrates how an inhibitory interneuron in the spinal cord can block transmission in the pain pathway. Activating this inhibitory neuron via collaterals from the fine touch and pressure pathway provides the physical substrate through which rubbing an injury or itch can gate sensation.

A dramatic example of sensory interaction between vision and hearing is the visual modification of sound known as the *McGurk effect*. If a recorded speech syllable, such as "ba," is played to a listener who at the same time observes someone whose lips are articulating the syllable "da," the listener hears not the actual sound ba, but the articulated sound da. The viewed lip movements modify the listener's auditory perception. The potency of the McGurk effect highlights the fact that our perception of speech sounds is influenced by vision—here, the facial gestures of a speaker (see Section 19.2).

Interactions between sound and vision extend to music appreciation. Chia-Jung Tsay (2013) asked novice participants to rate musical pieces that had previously been judged by experts in competition. The participants did little better than random when they judged the pieces just by listening or by listening and watching a video of the performance. The participants' judgments were excellent when they viewed only a video of the performance without sound. This dependence on vision did not occur only with novice judges: when experts performed the same task, their ratings were consistent only when they used vision alone. These results suggest that our judgments are generally influenced by vision, even when visual content is not the criterion.

A final example of one sensory system using the neural substrate of another comes from studying blind people who have learned to navigate using echolocation by making brief auditory clicks, shaking keys, or snapping their fingers. When echoed off surrounding objects, the blind echolocators can locate and identify objects. fMRI shows that the auditory cortex is activated by the sounds of the echoes, as is the visual cortex. The echolocators hear the echoes but also employ the visual cortex to "see" the objects (Arnott et al., 2013). Thus, connections from auditory to visual cortex enable the auditory cortex to use the spatial computational systems of the visual cortex. It is likely that we also "see" in our mind's eye, "taste" in our mind's eye the food we see, and "hear" in our mind's eye the objects that we touch.

SUMMARY

Each of the five major sensory systems has different receptors, pathways, and brain targets and comprises many submodalities. That our perceptions are creations of the brain is demonstrated in phantom-limb phenomena, visual illusions, and sensory interaction.

8.1 General Principles of Sensory-System Function

Sensory receptors are energy filters that transduce incoming physical or chemical energy and identify change and constancy in that energy. Neural receptive fields locate sensory events; receptor density determines sensitivity to stimulation. Neural relays between sensory receptors and the brain modify messages and allow the senses to interact. Any sensory information that converges does so in higher cortical areas.

At the same time, the primary brain targets for different modalities and submodalities are discrete. Some sensory systems have both exteroceptive and interoceptive receptors that respond to stimuli outside and within the body, respectively. This division allows us to interpret the stimuli themselves and no doubt helps us to distinguish "self" from "other."

The sensory systems all use a common code, sending information to the brain in the currency of action potentials. We distinguish one sensory modality from another by the source of the stimulation, its target in the brain, and the reflexes and movements made in response to the stimulation. For each sense, mammals represent the world in topographic maps that form multiple neural–spatial representations in the cortex.

8.2 Sensory Receptors and Pathways

The anatomical organization for each sense is similar: each has many receptors, sends information to the cortex through a sequence of three- or four-neuron relays, and diverges into more than one pathway through the brain. Although each sense has a primary cortical target, such as area 17 (V1) for vision, A1 for audition, and S1 for somatosensation, each also targets many other brain regions. For all sensory systems, the primary cortical area projects to a number of secondary areas where sensory information is recoded in more-complex ways.

8.3 Perception

Sensory systems function to allow animals, including humans, to engage in adaptive behavior, so it is not surprising that animals adapted to different environments vary widely in their sensory abilities. Primates and humans in particular have well-developed visual systems. What is perhaps more distinctive about humans is the extent to which we transform sensory information into perceptual information to mediate language, music, and culture. Visual illusions, synesthesia, and sensory synergies all provide evidence that perception is not simply faithful attention to sensation.

References

Arnott, S. R., L. Thaler, J. L. Milne, D. Kish, and M. A. Goodale. Shape-specific activation of occipital cortex in an early blind echolocation expert. *Neuropsychologia* 51:938–949, 2013.

Buck, L., and R. Axel. A novel multigene family may encode odorant receptors: A molecular basis for odor recognition. *Cell* 65:175–187, 1991.

Chan, K. Q., E. M. Tong, D. H. Tan, and A. H. Koh. What do love and jealousy taste like? *Emotion* 13(6):1142–1149, 2013.

Cole, J. *Pride and a Daily Marathon*. London: MIT Press, 1991.

Jacob, S., L. H. Kinnunen, J. Metz, M. Cooper, and M. K. McClintock. Sustained human chemosignal unconsciously alters brain function. *Neuroreport* 12:2391–2394, 2001.

Kaas, J. H. The organization and evolution of neocortex. In S. P. Wise, Ed., *Higher Brain Functions*. New York: Wiley, 1987.

Livingston, M., and D. Hubel. Segregation of form, color, movement and depth: Anatomy, physiology, and perception. *Science* 240:740–749, 1988.

Makin, T. R., J. Scholz, N. Filippini, D. Henderson Slater, I. Tracey, and H. Johansen-Berg. Phantom pain is associated with preserved structure and function in the former hand area. *Nature Communication* 4:1570, 2013.

Nara K., L. R. Saraiva, X. Ye, and L. B. Buck. A large-scale analysis of odor coding in the olfactory epithelium. *Journal of Neuroscience* 31:9179–9191, 2011.

Poggio, G. F. Central neural mechanisms in vision. In V. B. Mountcastle, Ed., *Medical Physiology*. St. Louis: Mosby, 1968.

Ramachandran, V. S., D. Brang, and P. D. McGeoch. Size reduction using Mirror Visual Feedback (MVF) reduces phantom pain. *Neurocase* 99999:1, 2009.

Rawal S., J. E. Hayes, M. R. Wallace, L. M. Bartoshuk, and V. B. Duffy. Do polymorphisms in the TAS1R1 gene contribute to broader differences in human taste intensity? *Chemical Senses* 38(8):719–728, 2013.

Rothwell, J. C., M. M. Taube, B. L. Day, P. K. Obeso, P. K. Thomas, and C. D. Marsden. Manual motor performance in a deafferented man. *Brain* 105:4515–4542, 1982.

Rouw R., and H. S. Scholte. Neural basis of individual differences in synesthetic experiences. *Journal of Neurosciences* 30:6205–6213, 2010.

Stern, K., and M. K. McClintock. Regulation of ovulation by human pheromones. *Nature* 392:177–179, 1998.

Tsay C. J. Sight over sound in the judgment of music performance. *Proceedings of the National Academy of Sciences U. S. A.* 110:14580–14585, 2013.

von Békésy, G. 1961 Nobel Lecture: Concerning the Pleasures of Observing, and the Mechanics of the Inner Ear. *Nobelprize.org*. Nobel Media AB 2013. Web, March 1, 2014.

Ward, J. Synesthesia. *Annual Review of Psychology* 64:49–75, 2013.

Winderickx, J., D. T. Lindsey, E. Sanocki, D. Y. Teller, B. G. Motulsky, and S. S. Deeb. Polymorphism in red photopigment underlies variation in color matching. *Nature* 356:431–433, 1992.

Zamm A., G. Schlaug, D. M. Eagleman, and P. Loui. Pathways to seeing music: Enhanced structural connectivity in colored-music synesthesia. *NeuroImage* 74:359–366, 2013.

9 Organization of the Motor System

PORTRAIT   Mind in Motion

On June 12, 2014, Brazilian Juliano Pinot, 29 and paraplegic, walked onto the soccer pitch and performed the honorary kickoff for the World Cup of Soccer in Brazil. His uniform was an exoskeleton controlled by commands sent from EEG signals in his brain. In turn, feedback from sensors on the soles of his feet enabled his brain to perceive the exoskeleton as part of his body.

The Walk Again Project, led by Miguel Nicolelis (2012), created the demonstration to highlight the success of research in **neuroprosthetics,** a field that develops computer-assisted devices to replace lost biological function. In laboratory experiments, human and primate subjects have learned to use signals from neurons, both EEG waves and single-cell activity, to control neuroprostheses for playing computer games and performing daily functions such as eating. The robotic arms are powered by motors that give them greater strength and dexterity than biological arms, and as portrayed in the adjoining photo, they are lined with sensory receptors that

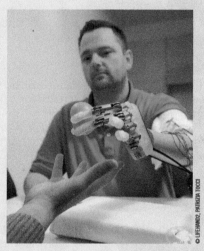

return more sensitive information to the brain than biological hands provide.

Brain–computer interfaces (BCIs) are in wide use now. Cochlear implants consist of only a few electrodes implanted into the auditory nerve, but they restore hearing. Similar implants to the visual system are envisioned to restore sight. The frontier of BCIs is restoring movement. Brain signals sent by a person to an exoskeleton or robot can restore reaching in a lost hand or walking in a lost leg after spinal-cord or brain damage (see Section 14.2). One day, lost bladder and bowel control will similarly be controlled by a subject's thought processes.

This pioneering work on brain–computer interfaces will become part of everyday life. People will use signals sent directly from their brains to turn the lights on or off, command robots, or play computer games. BCIs will in turn remind us to perform tasks, attend meetings, refuse tasty food when we are on a diet, and abstain from drugs and alcohol before we drive.

We can think of the entire nervous system as the motor system, because the nervous system functions to move the body. **Figure 9.1**A shows the stepwise sequence your nervous system performs in directing your hand to pick up a coffee mug. The visual system first inspects the mug to determine what part of it to grasp. The visual cortex relays this information to motor cortex areas that plan and initiate the movement, sending instructions to the part of the spinal cord that controls your arm and hand muscles.

As you grasp the mug's handle, information from sensory receptors in your fingers travels to the spinal cord, and from it messages sent to sensory areas of the cortex interpret touch. The sensory cortex informs the motor cortex that the mug is now being held. Meanwhile, as charted in Figure 9.1B, other central nervous

(A)

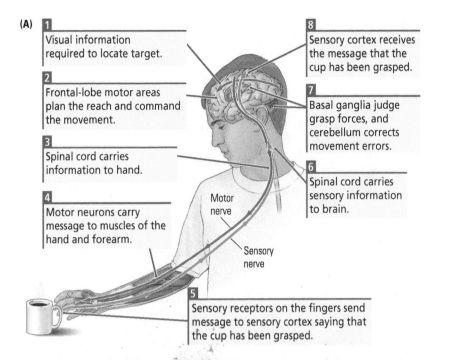

1 Visual information required to locate target.

2 Frontal-lobe motor areas plan the reach and command the movement.

3 Spinal cord carries information to hand.

4 Motor neurons carry message to muscles of the hand and forearm.

Motor nerve

Sensory nerve

5 Sensory receptors on the fingers send message to sensory cortex saying that the cup has been grasped.

8 Sensory cortex receives the message that the cup has been grasped.

7 Basal ganglia judge grasp forces, and cerebellum corrects movement errors.

6 Spinal cord carries sensory information to brain.

(B)

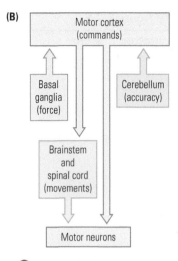

Motor cortex (commands)

Basal ganglia (force)

Cerebellum (accuracy)

Brainstem and spinal cord (movements)

Motor neurons

Figure 9.1 ▲

The Motor System
(A) Movements such as reaching for a cup require the participation of many nervous system components. (B) Major regions of the motor system that participate in all movements.

system regions have been modulating and adjusting the movement. The subcortical basal ganglia help to produce the appropriate amount of force for grasping the handle, and the cerebellum helps to regulate the movement's timing and accuracy.

Functional MRIs of brain activity during tasks such as reaching for an object confirm that widespread brain regions are involved. Indeed, because so many brain areas participate in even the simplest motor tasks, it is difficult, using imaging methods, to map the contributions of specific cortical regions to motor function (Filimon, 2010). Detailing regional contributions to motor control are thus more dependent on single-cell recording and microelectrode brain stimulation techniques (see Sections 7.1 and 7.2).

The term *motor system* is usually reserved for those parts of the nervous system, charted in Figure 9.1B, that take part most directly in producing movement and for the spinal-cord neural circuits that issue commands to muscles through the peripheral nerves. In this chapter, we consider how the brain and spinal cord work together to produce movement and explore how the neocortex, brainstem, basal ganglia, and cerebellum contribute to movement.

9.1 The Neocortex: Initiating Movement

Four neocortical regions produce our skilled movements, as diagrammed in **Figure 9.2**:

1. Lying posterior to the central fissure, the **posterior cortex** specifies movement goals and sends sensory information from vision, touch, and hearing into the frontal regions via multiple routes. The more-direct routes prompt the primary motor cortex to execute relatively automatic movements. Information about movements requiring conscious control takes indirect routes through the temporal and frontal cortex.

◎ Figure 9.2 ▶

Initiating a Motor Sequence

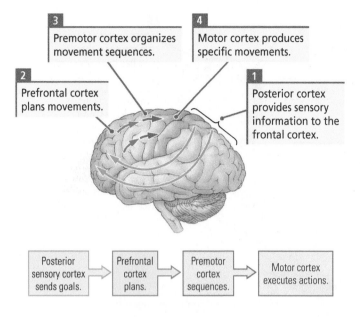

3 Premotor cortex organizes movement sequences.

4 Motor cortex produces specific movements.

2 Prefrontal cortex plans movements.

1 Posterior cortex provides sensory information to the frontal cortex.

Posterior sensory cortex sends goals. → Prefrontal cortex plans. → Premotor cortex sequences. → Motor cortex executes actions.

2. On instructions from the posterior cortex, the **prefrontal cortex** (PFC) generates plans for movements that it passes along to the premotor and motor cortex.

3. The **premotor cortex** immediately anterior to M1 houses a movement repertoire—its lexicon—that, among other things, recognizes others' movements and selects similar or different actions. (The premotor area, corresponding to Brodmann's area 6, includes a ventral region and a dorsal region called the *supplementary motor cortex*.)

4. The lexicon of the **primary motor cortex** (M1, or Brodmann's area 4) consists of more-elementary movements than the premotor lexicon, including hand and mouth movements.

In general then, when a movement goal arises in the posterior cortex, there are two routes for action. If a movement is relatively simple, then the premotor and motor cortex execute the action. If planning is required, the temporal and prefrontal cortices make decisions and then the premotor and motor cortices execute the appropriate movements.

Per E. Roland's (1993) exemplar experiment using cerebral blood flow (which serves as an indicator of neural activity; see the opening Portrait of Chapter 4) illustrates neocortical motor control of simpler versus more complex movements. **Figure 9.3** shows the brain regions that are relatively more active as participants in one such study perform different tasks.

When a participant taps a finger, blood flow increases are limited to the primary somatosensory and motor cortices (Figure 9.3A). When the participant executes a sequence of finger movements, blood flow increases in the premotor cortex as well (Figure 9.3B). And when the participant uses a finger to navigate a drawing of a maze—a task that requires coordinated movements in pursuit of a goal and specific movements corresponding to the shape of the maze—blood flow increases in the prefrontal cortex and regions of the parietal and temporal cortices, too (Figure 9.3C).

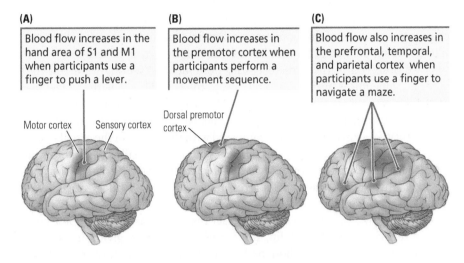

(A) Blood flow increases in the hand area of S1 and M1 when participants use a finger to push a lever.

Motor cortex   Sensory cortex

(B) Blood flow increases in the premotor cortex when participants perform a movement sequence.

Dorsal premotor cortex

(C) Blood flow also increases in the prefrontal, temporal, and parietal cortex when participants use a finger to navigate a maze.

Figure 9.3 ◄

Hierarchical Control of Movement in the Brain
(Research from Roland, 1993, p. 63.)

Mapping the Motor Cortex Using Electrical Stimulation

Body parts specialized for performing skilled movements are widespread among animals. Elephants use their trunks to manipulate objects; dolphins and seals deftly do the same with their noses; and many other animals, including domestic dogs, accomplish the same ends using their mouths. Different bird species have beaks designed for obtaining particular foods, for building nests, and even for making and using tools.

Tails can be handy too. Some marsupials and some New World primates grasp and carry objects with their tails. Horses' lips are dexterous enough to manipulate items as small as a blade of grass. Humans tend to rely primarily on their hands for manipulating objects, but they can do manual tasks with other body parts, such as the mouth or a foot, if they have to. (Some people without arms have become extremely proficient at writing with a foot, for example, and even driving.) What properties of the motor system explain these differences in carrying out skilled movements?

In the 1950s, Wilder Penfield (Penfield and Boldrey, 1958) used brief pulses of electrical stimulation to map the cortices of conscious human patients who were about to undergo neurosurgery. He and his colleagues found that most of the movements induced by their experiments were triggered by stimulation of the precentral gyrus (Brodmann's area 4), the region that, because of its role in movement, is called the primary motor cortex, or M1. Penfield also obtained evidence that movement can be produced by stimulating the dorsal part of the premotor cortex (Brodmann's area 6), and, for this reason, area 6 was designated the supplementary motor cortex.

Just as he had summarized the results of his earlier work on stimulating brain areas involved in sensation by drawing cartoons of representative body parts, Penfield summarized the results of his motor studies using cartoons of body parts to represent the areas of M1 and the premotor cortex where stimulation caused those parts to move. The result was a homunculus ("little human") spread out across the motor cortex, as illustrated for M1 (area 4) in **Figure 9.4**.

▲ Crows are among the animals that, like us humans, make and use tools, often to obtain food as shown here. (Dr. Gavin Hunt/University of Auckland)

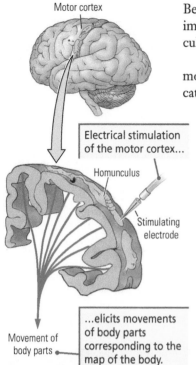

Motor cortex

Electrical stimulation of the motor cortex...

Homunculus

Stimulating electrode

Movement of body parts

...elicits movements of body parts corresponding to the map of the body.

Ⓢ **Figure 9.4** ▲

Penfield's Motor Homunculus Movements are topographically organized in the primary motor cortex. Electrical stimulation of the dorsomedial regions of M1 elicits movements in the lower limbs; stimulation in ventral regions produces movements in the upper body, hands, and face.

Because the body is symmetrical, each hemisphere contains an almost mirror-image representation of this homunculus. Penfield located a secondary homunculus in the supplementary motor cortex (the dorsal portion of area 6).

As we observed in the somatosensory homunculus (see Figure 8.16), the motor homunculus is upside down relative to the actual body, with the feet located dorsally within the central fissure and head located ventrally just above the lateral fissure. The most striking homuncular feature is the disproportionate relative sizes of body parts compared with their sizes in the actual body. The homunculus has very large hands with an especially large thumb. It also has very large lips and a large tongue. In contrast, the trunk, arms, and legs, which constitute most of a real body, occupy much less space, relatively speaking, in the motor cortex.

These size distortions reflect the fact that large parts of the motor cortex regulate hand, finger, lip, and tongue movements, giving us precise, fine motor control over those body parts. Parts of the body over which we have much broader motor control have a much smaller representation in the motor cortex.

Another distinctive feature of the homunculus as sketched according to its representation in the motor cortex is that the arrangement of body parts is somewhat different from that of the real body. For instance, the area of the cortex that produces eye movements is located in front of the area that produces head movement, as is the area that produces lip movement. In addition, the head of the homunculus in Figure 9.4 is oriented with the chin up and the forehead down (rather than the other way around as Penfield originally drew it).

Penfield's homunculus remains a useful concept for understanding the motor cortex's topographic and functional organization, showing at a glance that relatively large brain areas control body parts that make the most complex and finely tuned movements. Penfield's innovation of drawing homuncular maps to represent the body's motor regions influenced other scientists' mapping of other species as homunculi, and similar maps have been produced for species including rodents and a variety of primate species.

Multiple Representations in the Motor Cortex

Penfield's original motor maps were constructed from a few points of electrical stimulation using large electrodes placed on or near the cortical surface and with very brief pulses of electrical stimulation. Refinements of the technique, using microelectrode stimulation and many stimulation sites, eventually revealed many more homunculi than Penfield recognized. There may be as many as 10 homunculi within the motor and premotor cortices, and parts of the homunculi are not arranged as simply as Penfield sketched them.

For example, the loci from which electrical stimulation can elicit a finger movement are not located in a discrete area representing that finger and adjacent to areas representing the other fingers, as Penfield's homunculus suggests. Finger movements can be obtained from many points. Furthermore, many locations from which finger movements are obtained also elicit movements of other body parts. When longer-duration electrical stimulation was used, an explanation for these puzzling results emerged.

Natural Movement Categories

Rather than using brief pulses of electrical stimulation, Michael Graziano (2009) used 0.5-second trains of electrical stimulation in conscious monkeys. He found that stimulation elicits actions that he calls "ethological categories of movement" because these are the movements that the monkey uses in its everyday activities. (*Ethology* is the scientific study of animal behavior under natural conditions.) The drawings in **Figure 9.5** illustrate the end points of several such categories, including defensive postures of the face and body, movement of the hand to the mouth, manipulation and shaping the hand and digits in central body space, outward reach with the hand, and climbing and leaping postures.

Stimulation that causes the hand to move to the mouth, for example, also causes the digits to close with the forefinger positioned against the thumb, the forearm supinated (turned upward), and the wrist flexed such that the grip is aimed at the mouth. Not only is the hand moved precisely to the mouth but the mouth is also opened as if to receive a carried object. The sequence is smooth and coordinated, resembling a spontaneous movement that the monkey might make when reaching for a food item that it brings to its mouth for eating.

The movement categories Graziano observed have the same end irrespective of the location of a monkey's limb or its other ongoing behavior. Electrical stimulation that results in the hand coming to the mouth always recruits that movement, but in a variety of ways depending on the hand's starting point. If

Figure 9.5 ◄

Natural Movement Categories Movement categories evoked by electrical stimulation of the monkey cortex and the motor and premotor regions from which the categories were elicited. (Research from M. S. A. Graziano and T. N. Afalo. Mapping behavioral repertoire onto the cortex. *Neuron* 56:239–251, p. 243, Figure 5, 2007.)

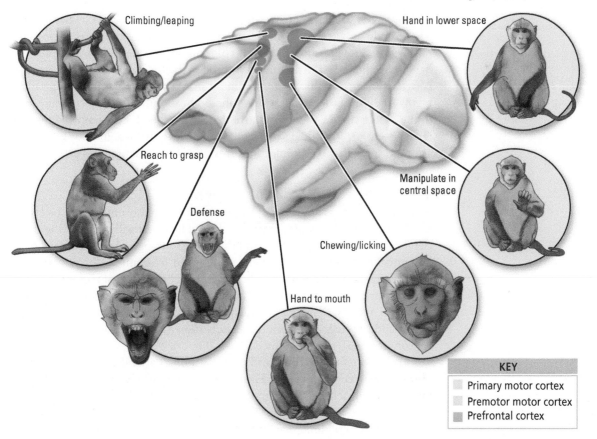

Climbing/leaping

Hand in lower space

Reach to grasp

Manipulate in central space

Defense

Chewing/licking

Hand to mouth

KEY
Primary motor cortex
Premotor motor cortex
Prefrontal cortex

a weight is attached to the monkey's arm, the evoked movement compensates for added load. Nevertheless, movement categories evoked by stimulation lack the flexibility of typical movement: when an obstacle is placed between the hand and the mouth, the hand hits the obstacle. If stimulation continues after the hand has reached the mouth, the hand remains there for the duration of the stimulation.

Figure 9.5 also illustrates the relative cortical locations in the premotor and motor cortex of different movements identified by electrical stimulation in the monkey. Each region represents three types of organization: the body part to be moved, the spatial location to which the movement is directed, and the movement's function. This motor representation shows that many cortical maps of the body exist, but each map represents a different action, the part of space in which an action is to take place, and that action's intended function.

Nevertheless, certain movement types—for example, reaching—cluster together relative to the part of motor cortex from which they are elicited. For example, reaching to different parts of space is elicited from slightly different points in the cortical reaching map. This cortical map also is proposed to be quite flexible, depending on the monkey's past experience, its recent experience, the objects available to reach, and even just-completed actions. At least part of Graziano's conception of cortical control of movement is that arm or body actions function to take the hands to different parts of working space—for example, to spatial locations to grasp objects or to the mouth for eating them.

Among the similarities between Penfield's homunculus and Graziano's maps, whole-body movements of climbing and leaping are located in the dorsal premotor cortex, hand movements of reaching are located more ventrally, and hand movements to the mouth are located in the most ventral part of premotor cortex. Movements that are represented in M1 involve hand-grasping movements to different locations around the body and, in the most ventral portion of the motor cortex, to mouth movements. In general, Graziano's topography is consistent with Penfield's map and with the idea that whole-body movements are represented in the premotor cortex and more discrete movements in the motor cortex.

Visual–Parietal–Motor Connections

The motor cortex is not the only region from which movements can be evoked. Similar functional movements can be elicited by electrically stimulating the parietal cortex (Kaas et al., 2013), and the parietal topography mirrors the motor homunculus. Stepping movements are elicited from more dorsal parietal regions, reaching movements are elicited from medial parietal regions, hand and mouth movements are elicited from more ventral parietal regions. Anatomical studies of the relationships between the topographical regions of the motor cortex and the matching parietal regions show that they have dense anatomical connections.

How do the motor cortex and corresponding parietal cortex topographical regions produce movement? **Figure 9.6** illustrates the answer using reaching for a food item as an example. To perform a reaching movement, visual, somatosensory, and/or auditory information about a target must be sent to the motor cortex. To guide reaching to a target, the visual cortex has to identify both the location of an object and the object it-self—the extrinsic and intrinsic properties of the object, respectively. Based on information about object location, the visual cortex instructs the parietal arm region about the object's location and the hand region about how to shape the digits to grasp the object.

These parietal regions represent the sensory receptors on the body that will be activated when the object is contacted. The reach and grasp regions of the parietal cortex then connect to reach and grasp regions of the motor cortex that will produce the movement over descending pathways to the spinal cord. Thus, the connections from visual cortex to parietal cortex to motor cortex constitute a dual pathway that produces the action of grasping the target (Karl and Whishaw, 2013). In the same way, various combinations of activity in parietal-to-motor cortex pathways underlie the complexity of our movements so that we can catch a basketball as we run and shoot it as we jump, for example.

Each cortical motor region makes a different contribution to movement. The visual cortex identifies the spatial location of the target and its shape. The parietal cortex identifies the body part that will contact the object. The motor cortex in turn represents the elements required to move the arm to the target and shape the digits to grasp it. Nevertheless, the cortex may not actually direct the grasping of an object. While the cortex may be involved in identifying the target, specifying the coordinates required to reach it, and deciding on the precise movement to be used, the movements themselves may be orchestrated in the brainstem or in the spinal cord.

The Movement Lexicon

The results of Graziano's mapping studies lend support to the view that humans have a lexicon, or repertoire, of movement categories in the cortex. Consider the similar ways that different people perform skilled movements. Most people reaching for a small object use a variation of the pincer grip—the thumb and another finger, usually the index finger—to grasp the object (**Figure 9.7**A). By 3 months of age, most healthy babies begin spontaneously to use a pincer grip when making spontaneous hand and finger movements; by 12 months of age they begin to use it to pick up tiny objects such as breadcrumbs; and by 4 years of age they make the movement precisely using visual guidance.

Other evidence in support of the movement lexicon includes, first, that most primate species use this same grip pattern and second, that people who have incurred small lesions of the motor cortex around the thumb region of the homunculus have weakness not only in the thumb but in the other fingers and in the arm as well. The latter finding suggests to Mark

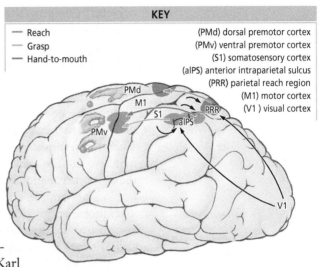

KEY	
— Reach	(PMd) dorsal premotor cortex
— Grasp	(PMv) ventral premotor cortex
— Hand-to-mouth	(S1) somatosensory cortex
	(aIPS) anterior intraparietal sulcus
	(PRR) parietal reach region
	(M1) motor cortex
	(V1) visual cortex

Figure 9.6 ▲

Dual channels for Reaching Reaching for an object employs two movements: directing the hand to the target and shaping the fingers to grasp the target. Two channels mediate a reach and grasp using dual pathways from visual cortex to parietal cortex to premotor and motor cortex. (Research from J. M. Karl and I. Q. Whishaw. Different evolutionary origins for the reach and the grasp: An explanation for dual visuomotor channels in primate parietofrontal cortex. *Frontiers in Neurology* 4:208, December 23, 2013.)

Figure 9.7 ▼

Getting a Grip (Ian Whishaw.)

(A) Pincer grip

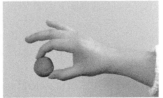

(B) Whole-hand grip

Schieber (1999) that the lesions impair not the hand or individual digit muscles but rather the coordinated action of reaching for and grasping an object. After incurring a lesion in which the pincer grip is lost, a person is likely to substitute a new movement, a whole-hand grip (Figure 9.7B).

Apparently then, the pincer grip and other skilled movements are not entirely learned but are part of the vocabulary in a prewired movement lexicon. They are encoded in the neural connections as basic movement patterns common to the particular species, to be called on and modified as situations demand. The human movement lexicon presumably is more complex than that of the monkey, and the lexicon of primate movements will be different again from those of other mammals such as rodents, carnivores, or pachyderms.

Findings from lesion studies suggest that the premotor cortex and the primary motor cortex share a common movement lexicon and that the repertoire available to the premotor cortex is more complex than that of M1. Brinkman (1984) shows that damage to the premotor cortex does not produce muscle weakness, but it does disrupt more-complex movements. For example, the monkey depicted in **Figure 9.8** is given the task of extracting a peanut wedged in a hole in a table.

Figure 9.8 ►

Premotor Control On a task requiring both hands, a healthy monkey can push a peanut out of a hole with one hand and catch it in the other, but 5 months after the premotor cortex has undergone lesioning, the brain-injured monkey cannot coordinate this movement. (Research from Brinkman, 1984, p. 925.)

If the monkey merely pushes the peanut through the hole with a finger, the peanut will drop to the floor and be lost. The monkey has to catch the peanut by holding one palm beneath the hole while using the other hand to push the peanut out. Five months after the premotor cortex has been ablated, the monkey is unable to make the two complementary movements together. It can push the peanut with a finger and it can extend an open palm, but it cannot coordinate these actions of its two hands. Thus, the premotor cortex plays a greater role in organizing whole-body movements than M1, which controls specific acts.

Note that the lesion made by Brinkman is in the region of the motor cortex identified by Graziano as the climbing region (see Figure 9.5). What is common to climbing and retrieving the peanut is the coordinated use of two hands. Thus, the basic movements elicited in the motor cortex can be extended to other actions through learning by recruiting neural circuitry used for more basic action. For example, a person pitching a baseball (**Figure 9.9**) must coordinate the

Figure 9.9 ►

The Windup Movement patterns used in sports are similar to movements used in everyday activities. Apparently, the nervous system has a set of basic plans for movements.

entire body to deliver the ball to the target. The action requires stepping movements of the leg, constant adjustments of the trunk to maintain balance, and the throwing movement of the arm.

Yet throwing a ball is an elaboration of walking. Both include coordinated movements of diagonal limb couplets: the pitcher has the left arm forward and the right leg back, just as you would if you were stepping forward with your left leg. In an extensive analysis of body reflexes, Tadashi Fukuda (1981) suggested that a large part of learning to move entails learning how to use preorganized movement patterns to achieve both skill and strength. Part of the role of the neocortex in movement must thus be to blend together motor reflexes to form learned skilled actions.

To investigate how motor cortex cells are involved in movement, Edward Evarts (1968) used the simple procedure illustrated in **Figure 9.10**A. He trained a monkey to flex its wrist to move a bar to which differing weights could be attached. An electrode implanted in the wrist region of the motor cortex recorded the activity of neurons there.

The recordings in Figure 9.10B show that these neurons begin to discharge even before the monkey flexes its wrist: they participate in planning the movement as well as initiating it. The neurons continue to discharge during the wrist movement, confirming that they also play a role in executing it. The neurons also discharge at a higher rate when the bar is loaded with a weight, an indication that motor-cortex neurons increase the force of a movement by increasing their firing rate.

Evarts's results also reveal that the motor cortex specifies movement direction. Neurons in the motor-cortex wrist area discharge when the monkey flexes its wrist to bring the hand inward but not when it extends its wrist to move the hand back to its starting position. These neuronal on–off responses, depending on whether the wrist is flexed toward the body or extended away, are a simple way of encoding the direction in which the wrist is moving.

Single-cell recording also shows that movements are not produced simply by the action of a single cell but rather by the coordinated activity of populations of cells. Apostolos Georgopoulos and coworkers (1999) used a method similar to that of Evarts to examine the encoding of movement direction further. They trained monkeys to move a lever in different directions across the surface of a table (**Figure 9.11**A). Recording from single cells in the arm region of the motor cortex, they found that each neuron is maximally active when the monkey moves its arm in a particular direction (Figure 9.11B).

As a monkey's arm moves in directions other than the one to which a particular cell maximally responds, the cell decreases its activity in proportion to the displacement from the "preferred" direction. As illustrated in Figure 9.11B, for

(A) Procedure

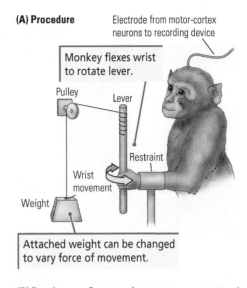

Electrode from motor-cortex neurons to recording device

Monkey flexes wrist to rotate lever.

Pulley

Lever

Restraint

Wrist movement

Weight

Attached weight can be changed to vary force of movement.

(B) Results   Response of motor-cortex neurons to wrist movement

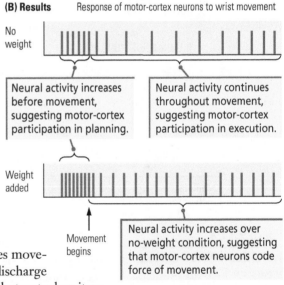

No weight

Neural activity increases before movement, suggesting motor-cortex participation in planning.

Neural activity continues throughout movement, suggesting motor-cortex participation in execution.

Weight added

Movement begins

Neural activity increases over no-weight condition, suggesting that motor-cortex neurons code force of movement.

Figure 9.10 ▲

Corticomotor-Neuron Activity in Planning and Executing Movements (Research from Evarts, 1968, p. 15.)

(A) Procedure

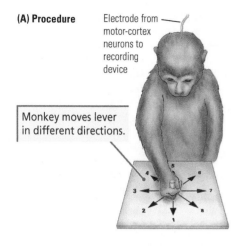

Electrode from motor-cortex neurons to recording device

Monkey moves lever in different directions.

(B) Results   Activity of a single motor-cortex neuron

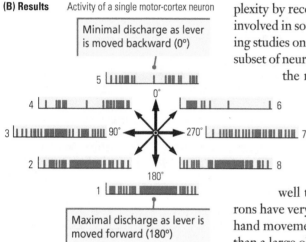

Minimal discharge as lever is moved backward (0°)

Maximal discharge as lever is moved forward (180°)

Figure 9.11 ▲

Individual Motor-Cortex Neurons Tune in to Preferred Directions

(Research from Georgopoulos et al., 1982, p. 1530.)

example, if a neuron discharges maximally as the arm moves directly forward, its discharge is attenuated if the arm moves to one side and ceases altogether if the arm moves backward. Accordingly, the motor cortex calculates both the direction and the distance of movements. In contrast to the view that neurons in the sensorimotor cortex specify direction, a different proposal is that they specify limb position. For example, in reach circuits, neuronal discharge specifies the same posture adopted when the neurons are electrically stimulated (Aflalo and Graziano, 2007).

ⓒ Mirroring Movement

Our movements are anything but robotic. Our actions are learned, situation specific, and often dependent upon our interactions with others. Carlo Umilta and colleagues (2001) provided insights into this complexity by recording the activity of cells in the monkey's motor system involved in social interactions. In the course of their single-cell recording studies on reaching in monkeys, they made a remarkable finding. A subset of neurons in the ventral premotor area discharge not only when the monkey itself makes a movement but also discharge in much the same way when the monkey sees other monkeys make the same movement and even when the monkey sees people make the same movement.

These **mirror system neurons** encode the goal of an action. They do not respond to objects or to isolated hand movements, and they do not respond very well to pictures or videos of movements. Some mirror neurons have very exacting requirements, responding only to a particular hand movement and only if it is used to pick up a small object rather than a large object, for example. Some distinguish whether the object is within reaching distance or lies beyond reach.

Other mirror neurons are more broadly tuned and continue to respond when the grip pattern changes or the size of the target varies. Some will respond when an experimenter picks up a food item by hand or with a pair of pliers. They also respond when the pliers require the experimenter either to close or to open a hand to grasp the object (Cattaneo et al., 2013). Thus, the target of the action is more important to these mirror neurons than are the details of the action required to obtain it. Some mirror neurons can "fill in the blanks" by recognizing a given movement made by a demonstrator, even when the monkey is unable to see part of the movement, as elaborated in the Snapshot on page 244.

Figure 9.12A maps mirror neurons in the monkey's ventral prefrontal cortex that form part of a *core mirror neuron system* including the ventral premotor (F5) and motor cortex and ventral regions of the parietal cortex. Core mirror neurons are more broadly tuned than are other mirror neurons of the premotor cortex and respond to a wide range of actions that might be used in obtaining a goal. Nevertheless, mirror neurons in both regions are transitive in that they respond to actions that obtain goal objects.

Figure 9.12B illustrates the human core mirror neuron system and part of the human *distributed mirror neuron system*. The human core system, like that

(A) Mirror neuron system, rhesus monkey   **(B) Human mirror nueron system**

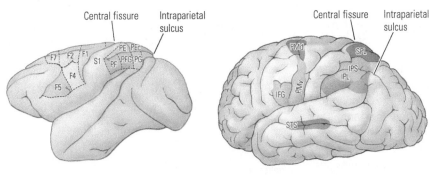

Figure 9.12 ▲

Mirror Neuron Systems (A) In the rhesus monkey, the core mirror neuron system (yellow) comprises the inferior frontal cortex (F5) and inferior parietal cortex (PF and PFG) and is sensitive to transitive movements—those that have a goal. (B) In humans, the core mirror neuron system (yellow) is sensitive to transitive movements and comprises the inferior frontal cortex (IFG, or frontal gyrus); ventral premotor cortex (PMV, or Brodmann's area 6); and inferior parietal cortex (IPL, inferior parietal lobule, and IPS, intraparietal sulcus). The distributed mirror neuron system in humans responds to hand movements (purple) in the dorsal premotor cortex (PMD), and superior parietal lobe (SPL); upper limb movements (blue) in a portion of the superior temporal sulcus (STS); tool use (orange); and intransitive movements in which no object is manipulated (green). (Research from L. Cattaneo and G. Rizzolatti. The Mirror Neuron System. *Archives of Neurology* 66:557–660, 2009.)

of the monkey, responds to transitive actions. The distributed system, however, responds to intransitive actions—movements in which no goal is present. Single-cell recordings identify the brain regions that constitute the monkey's mirror neuron system; in humans EEG and fMRI have identified regions associated with mirror neuron function. In the monkey the core mirror neuron system closely overlaps the parietal–motor circuit involved in manipulating food with the hands and the mouth. In humans the core mirror system includes Broca's area (Brodmann's area 44).

The flexible properties of mirror neurons underlie our ability to imagine movements and, as described in the chapter opening Portrait, allow us to control BCIs. Also included among the mirror neuron system's many suggested functions is the ability to understand the actions of others. The theoretical importance of the mirror neuron system relates to higher cognitive functions. Mirror neuron theory suggests that we understand our own actions and those of others by internally replicating the movements we would use to produce that action. In other words, our cognitive understanding of an action is embodied in the neural systems that produce that action (Bello et al., 2013).

The ability of mirror neurons to participate in self-action as well as in perceiving others' actions suggests that they form the neural substrate for self-awareness, social awareness, and awareness of intention and action in others, and they are likely important for gestural and verbal language. Rizzolatti and coworkers (2014) also suggest that some symptoms of some disorders are related to the mirror neuron system. For example, the absence of **empathy**, the ability to see others' points of view, as occurs in some cases of autism spectrum disorder, may be related to mirror neuron system dysfunction (see Section 24.3). In contrast, Gregory Hickok (2014)

Recording Mirror Neuron Activity

Using a hand, a trunk, or a beak to obtain food and placing it in the mouth to eat is a widespread action among animals. Placing a hand in the mouth is also among the earliest motor actions that develop in human infants. Developing fetuses suck their thumbs, and after birth babies put every object they grasp into their mouths.

In the course of their studies with monkeys, Umilta and colleagues (2001) recorded the activity of an exemplar neuron that discharged when a monkey reached for a food item to place in its mouth for eating. As shown in the accompanying figure, this neuron discharged in much the same way when the monkey observed an experimenter reach for a block (top panel), and it discharged as robustly when the experimenter reached for a target hidden behind a screen (center panel).

It was not the movement of the experimenter's hand per se that excited the neuron, because it did not discharge robustly when the monkey observed the experimenter make a reaching movement in the absence of a target (bottom panel). What turns the mirror neuron on is the act of obtaining the goal, a conclusion supported by many other experiments. Mirror neurons are equally excited when a tool rather than a hand is used and are more excited if the goal is valuable, for example, can be eaten.

Tools extend the hand's function and likely were first used to enhance food acquisition. Many evolutionary theories propose that verbal language may have developed from hand gestures used to signal goal attainment, especially food goals. The close linkage between mirror neurons and goal attainment may explain the flexibility of our skilled movements. If we cannot obtain a goal with a hand reach, we can substitute the mouth, a foot, or a neuroprosthetic BCI.

The discovery of mirror neurons has led to wide-ranging speculation about their role in consciousness and neurological and psychiatric diseases (Thomas, 2012). A conservative view is that mirror neurons function simply to represent the goal of motor action. More speculative views propose that they represent our understanding of actions.

Umilta, M. A., K. Kohler, V. Gallese, L. Fogassi, L. Fadiga, C. Keysers, and G. Rizzolatti. I know what you are doing: A neurophysiological study. *Neuron* 31:155–165, 2001 © Elsevier.

Thomas, B. What's so special about mirror neurons? *Scientific American*, November 2012.

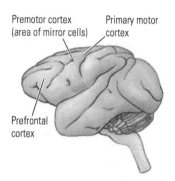

Premotor cortex (area of mirror cells) Primary motor cortex

Prefrontal cortex

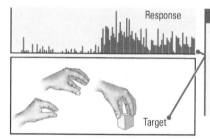

Response

1
A mirror neuron in the monkey's premotor cortex responds when a target is present...

Target

Response

2
...or when it is hidden.

Hidden target

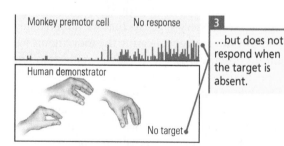

Monkey premotor cell   No response

3
...but does not respond when the target is absent.

Human demonstrator

No target

The mirror neuron would perform in the same way were the monkey to perform the observed movement. (Information from Umilta et al., 2001.)

argues that mirror neurons analyze figure-background relationships. They are not directly related to our understanding of actions, which survives brain injury that damages brain areas rich in mirror neurons.

◎ 9.2 The Brainstem: Motor Control

Beyond the major pathways that carry messages from the cortex to the spinal cord, about 26 pathways to the spinal cord originate in various brainstem locations. These important pathways send information pertaining to posture and balance from the brainstem to the spinal cord, and they control the autonomic nervous system. For all motor functions, the motor neurons are the final common path, but unlike the skilled limb and digit movements organized by the neocortex, those produced by the brainstem tend to be whole-body movements.

The general idea that the brainstem is responsible for many movements performed by animals was most dramatically revealed in a series of studies done by Swiss neuroscientist Walter R. Hess. Hess (1957) developed the technique of implanting and cementing electrodes into the brains of cats and other animals. These electrodes could subsequently be attached to stimulating leads, causing little discomfort to the animal and allowing it to move freely.

When Hess stimulated the brainstem of a freely moving animal, he was able to elicit almost every innate movement that an animal of that species might make. For example, a resting cat could be induced to suddenly leap up with an arched back and erect hair, as though frightened by an approaching dog. The movements would begin abruptly when the stimulating current was turned on and end equally abruptly when the stimulating current was turned off.

These behaviors were performed without vigor when the stimulating current was low but increased in vigor as the stimulating current was increased. Some stimulation sites produced head turning; others produced walking or running; still others produced aggressive or fear movements. The animal's emotional behavior also could be modulated. When shown a stuffed toy, a cat might respond to electrical stimulation of some sites by stalking the toy and to stimulation of other sites with fear and withdrawal.

Other brainstem functions pertain to controlling movements used in eating and drinking and in sexual behavior. The brainstem is also important for posture, for the ability to stand upright and make coordinated movements of the limbs, for swimming and walking, and for movements used in grooming and making nests. Grooming is in fact a particularly complex movement pattern coordinated mainly by the brainstem. When grooming, a rat sits back on its haunches, licks its paws, wipes its nose with its paws, wipes its paws across its face, and finally turns to lick the fur on its body. These movements are always performed in the same order. The next time you dry off after a shower or a swim, attend to the "grooming sequence" that you use. It is very similar to that used by the rat (illustrated in Figure 10.1).

The Basal Ganglia and Movement Force

The basal ganglia, a collection of subcortical nuclei in the forebrain, connect the motor cortex with the midbrain and connect the sensory regions of the neocortex with the motor cortex. As shown in **Figure 9.13**, a prominent structure of

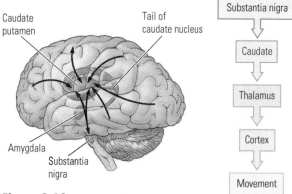

Figure 9.13 ▲

Basal Ganglia Connections The caudate putamen makes reciprocal connections with the forebrain and with the substantia nigra in the midbrain. (Research from Alexander and Crutcher, 1990.)

the basal ganglia is the **caudate putamen**, itself a large cluster of nuclei located beneath the frontal cortex. Part of the caudate extends as a tail (*caudate* means "tailed") into the temporal lobe, ending in the amygdala.

The basal ganglia receive inputs from two main sources: (1) All areas of the neocortex and limbic cortex, including the motor cortex, project to the basal ganglia. (2) The nigrostriatal dopamine pathway extends into the basal ganglia from the substantia nigra, a cluster of darkly pigmented cells in the midbrain (see Figure 5.18). Conversely, as diagrammed in Figure 9.13, the basal ganglia send projections back to both the motor cortex and the substantia nigra.

Two different—in many ways opposite—kinds of movement disorders result from basal ganglia damage, depending on the injury. If cells of the caudate putamen are damaged, unwanted choreiform (writhing and twitching) movements called **dyskinesias** may result. The genetic disorder **Huntington's disease** destroys caudate putamen cells and is characterized by involuntary and exaggerated movements. Such involuntary movements, or **hyperkinetic symptoms**, also related to caudate putamen damage, appear in the unwanted tics and vocalizations peculiar to **Tourette's syndrome**. People with Tourette's syndrome make involuntary movements such as head twists or sudden movements of a hand or arm or will often utter a cry (Friedhoff and Chase, 1982).

In addition to causing *involuntary* hyperkinetic movements, if the cells of the basal ganglia are left intact but its inputs are damaged, the injury results in difficulty *making* movements—that is, in **hypokinetic symptoms**. **Parkinson's disease**, for example, caused by the loss of dopamine cells from the substantia nigra and of their input into the basal ganglia via the nigrostriatal pathway, is characterized by muscular rigidity and difficulty initiating and performing movements. These two opposing sets of symptoms—hyperkinetic and hypokinetic—that occur after basal ganglia damage suggest that one of its major functions is to modulate movement. (Section 27.6 elaborates on both types of motor disorders.)

Steven Keele and Richard Ivry (1991) tried to connect these opposing sets of symptoms by hypothesizing that the basal ganglia's underlying function is to generate the force required for each movement. According to this idea, some types of basal ganglia damage cause errors of too much force and result in excessive movement, whereas other types of damage cause errors of too little force and result in insufficient movement. Keele and Ivry tested their hypothesis by giving healthy participants as well as patients with various basal ganglia disorders a task that tested the ability of both groups to exert appropriate amounts of force.

While looking at a line projected on a television screen, the subjects and controls attempted to produce a second line of the same length by pressing a button with the appropriate amount of force. After several practice trials, both groups were then asked to press the button with appropriate force even when the first line was no longer visible as a guide. Patients with basal ganglia disorders were unable to do this task reliably. The force they exerted was usually too little or too much, resulting in a line too short or too long.

What neural pathways enable the basal ganglia to modulate movement force? Basal ganglia circuits are complex, but Peter Redgrave and coworkers (2011) review evidence that they affect motor cortex activity through two pathways: one inhibitory and the other excitatory. The two pathways converge on an area of the basal ganglia called the internal part of the **globus pallidus** (GPi), as charted in **Figure 9.14**.

The GPi in turn projects to the thalamus (specifically, to the anterior thalamic nucleus), and the thalamus projects to the motor cortex. The GPi acts like a volume control because its output determines whether a movement will be weak or strong. Inputs to the GPi are color-coded in Figure 9.14 to illustrate how they affect movement. If activity in the inhibitory pathway (pink) is high relative to that in the excitatory pathway (green), inhibition predominates in the GPi, and the thalamus is free to excite the cortex, thus amplifying movement. If, on the other hand, activity in the excitatory pathway is high relative to that in the inhibitory pathway, excitation of the GPi will predominate and then inhibit the thalamus, thus reducing input to the cortex and decreasing movement force.

The idea that the GPi acts like a volume control over movement has been instrumental in devising treatments for Parkinson's disease, in which movements become increasingly difficult to perform. Recordings made from cells of the GPi show excessive activity in people with Parkinson's disease, and consistent with the volume-control theory, movements are more difficult to make. If the GPi is surgically destroyed in Parkinson patients or if it is electrically stimulated to interfere with its output, muscular rigidity is reduced, and Parkinson patients are able to make more-normal movements. Thus, the technique of stimulating the GPi or other structures in the basal ganglia circuitry with deep brain stimulation (see Figure 7.9) is one treatment for the rigidity in patients with Parkinson's disease.

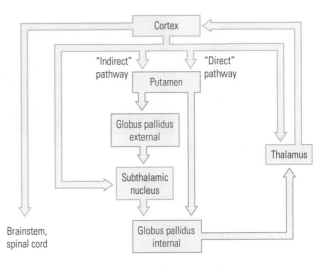

Figure 9.14 ▲

Regulating Movement Force Two pathways in the basal ganglia modulate cortically produced movements. Green pathways are excitatory, red are inhibitory. The indirect pathway excites the GPi, whereas the direct pathway has an inhibitory effect. If activity in the indirect pathway dominates, the thalamus shuts down, and the cortex cannot produce movement. If direct-pathway activity predominates, the thalamus can become overactive, amplifying movement. (Data from Alexander and Crutcher, 1990, p. 269.)

The Cerebellum and Motor Learning

Musicians have a saying: "Miss a day of practice and you're okay, miss two days and you notice, miss three days and the world notices." The enormous amount of practice required to master skilled movements is summarized in **Table 9.1**. The cerebellum seems to be the motor system component that participates in acquiring and maintaining motor skills, from playing a musical instrument to pitching a baseball to texting.

Large and conspicuous, the cerebellum sits atop the brainstem and is clearly visible just behind and beneath the cerebral cortex (**Figure 9.15**). Like the cerebral cortex, it has two hemispheres. A small lobe called the **flocculus** projects from its ventral surface. Despite its small size relative to the neocortex, the cerebellum

Table 9.1 **Repetitions required to master skilled movements**

Activity	Participants	Repetitions
Cigar making	Women	3.0 million cigars
Knitting	Women	1.5 million stitches
Rug making	Women	1.5 million knots
Violin playing	Children	2.5 million notes
Basketball	Professional athletes	1.0 million shots
Baseball pitching	Professional athletes	1.6 million pitches

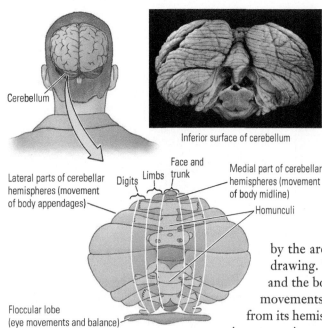

Inferior surface of cerebellum

Cerebellum

Lateral parts of cerebellar hemispheres (movement of body appendages)

Digits   Limbs   Face and trunk

Medial part of cerebellar hemispheres (movement of body midline)

Homunculi

Floccular lobe (eye movements and balance)

Figure 9.15 ▲

Cerebellar Homunculus
The cerebellar hemispheres encode body movements, and the flocculus, visible at the bottom center of the photograph, encodes eye movements and balance. The cerebellum is topographically organized: its more-medial parts represent the midline of the body and its more-lateral parts represent the limbs and digits. (Photograph of cerebellum reproduced from *The Human Brain: Photographic Guide* by H. Williams, N. Gluhbegovic, Wolters Kluwer Health.)

contains about four times more neurons than the neocortex. Evolutionarily, its increased neuron number in large-brained animals, including humans, has been proportional to that of the neocortex.

The cerebellum is divided into several regions, each specializing in a different aspect of motor control. The flocculus receives projections from the vestibular system and so takes part in controlling balance (see Section 8.2). Many of its projections go to the spinal cord and to the motor nuclei that control eye movements.

Different parts of the cerebellar hemispheres subserve different movements, as diagrammed by the areas in Figure 9.15 bordered in white in the bottom drawing. The most medial areas are associated with the face and the body's midline; those more lateral are associated with movements of the limbs, hands, feet, and digits. The pathways from its hemispheres project to cerebellar nuclei in its base, which in turn project to other brain regions, including the motor cortex.

Tumors or damage in midline areas of the cerebellum disrupt balance, eye movements, upright posture, and walking but do not substantially disrupt other movements, such as reaching, grasping, and using the fingers. When lying down, a person with damage to the medial cerebellum may show few symptoms. In contrast, damage to lateral parts of the cerebellum disrupts arm, hand, and finger movements far more than movements of the body's trunk.

Attempts to understand how the cerebellum controls movements center on two major ideas: the cerebellum (1) has a role in movement timing and (2) helps maintain movement accuracy. Keele and Ivry (1991) support the first hypothesis, contending that the cerebellum acts like a clock or pacemaker to ensure that both movements and perceptions are appropriately timed.

In a motor test of timing, subjects with cerebellar damage and control participants are asked to tap a finger in rhythm with a metronome. After many taps, the metronome is turned off, and both groups attempt to go on tapping to the same beat. Those with damage to the cerebellum, especially to the lateral cerebellum, perform poorly.

In a perceptual test of timing, subjects and controls are presented with two pairs of tones. The silent period between the first two tones is always the same length, whereas the silent period between the second two tones changes from trial to trial. Both groups are required to report whether the second silent period is longer or shorter than the first. Those with damage to the cerebellum perform poorly on this task too. The results suggest that the underlying impairment in cerebellar disorders is a loss of timing, both in movement and in perception.

The cerebellum also contributes to maintaining movement accuracy. Tom Thach and coworkers (1992) gathered evidence in support of this hypothesis by having patients and control participants throw darts at a target, as shown in **Figure 9.16**. After a number of throws, both groups donned glasses containing wedge-shaped prisms that displace the apparent location of the target to the left. When a person wearing the glasses throws a dart, it now veers left of the target. All showed this initial distortion in aim; then an important difference appeared.

When control participants see the dart miss the mark, they adjust each successive throw until reasonable accuracy is restored. In contrast, subjects with damage to the cerebellum do not correct for this error. They keep missing the target far to the left time after time.

Next, both groups remove the prism glasses and throw a few more darts. Again, a significant difference emerges. The control participants throw their first darts much too far to the right (corresponding to the previous adjustment that they had learned to make), but soon they adjust until they regain their former accuracy.

In contrast, patients with damage to the cerebellum show no aftereffects from wearing the prisms, seeming to confirm the impression that they had never compensated for the glasses to begin with. This experiment suggests that many movements we make—throwing a dart, hitting a ball with a bat, writing neatly, painting a work of art—depend on moment-to-moment motor learning and adjustments made by the cerebellum.

To better understand how the cerebellum improves motor skills by making required adjustments to movements, imagine throwing a dart yourself. Suppose you aim at the bull's-eye, throw the dart, and find that it misses the board completely. On your next throw, you aim to correct for the original error. Notice that there are actually two versions of each throw: (1) the movement that you intended to make, and (2) the actual movement as recorded by sensory receptors in your arm and shoulder.

If the throw is successful, you need make no correction on your next try. But if you miss, an adjustment is called for. One way to accomplish the adjustment is through the feedback circuit shown in **Figure 9.17**. The cortex sends instructions to the spinal cord to throw a dart at the target. A copy of the same instructions is sent to the cerebellum through the inferior olivary nucleus.

When you first throw the dart, the sensory receptors in your arm and shoulder encode the actual movement and send a message about it through the spinal cord to the cerebellum. The cerebellum now has information about both versions of the movement: what you intended to do and what you actually did. The cerebellum can now calculate the error and tell the cortex how it should correct the movement. When you next throw the dart, you incorporate that correction into your throw.

(A) Procedure

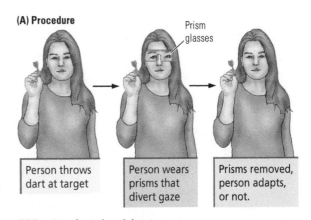

Person throws dart at target

Person wears prisms that divert gaze

Prisms removed, person adapts, or not.

(B) Results—Control participant

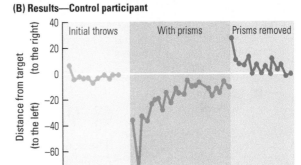

(C) Results—Patient with damage to cerebellum

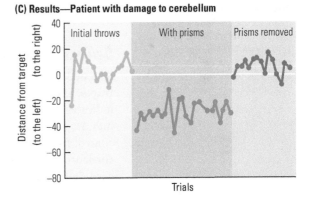

Figure 9.16 ▲

The Cerebellum and Movement Accuracy (A) A person throws darts at a target before, during, and after wearing prisms that divert her gaze to the left. (B) A control participant throws the dart accurately without prisms, adapts when wearing prisms, and shows aftereffects when the prisms are removed. (C) A patient with damage to the cerebellum fails to correct throws while wearing prisms and shows no aftereffect when the prisms are removed. (Research from Thach et al., p. 429.)

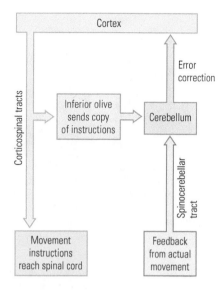

Cortex

Corticospinal tracts

Error correction

Inferior olive sends copy of instructions

Cerebellum

Spinocerebellar tract

Movement instructions reach spinal cord

Feedback from actual movement

Figure 9.17 ▲

Intention, Action, Feedback By comparing the message for the intended movement with the movement that was actually performed, the cerebellum sends an error message to the cortex to improve the accuracy of a subsequent movement.

Many of our cognitive activities require similar practice. When we mispronounce a word or try to pronounce a difficult word that we read, we make a number of attempts until we get it right. When we have a new idea and first try to express it, it may not come out quite right. If we persist, we eventually do get it right. When we draw a picture or write a story, we may have to make many corrections. All these try-and-perfect actions, like dart throwing, likely involve the cerebellum.

In addition to its role in motor learning, the cerebellum participates in coupling movements so the flow of action appears seamless. For example, when we reach for an object, we seamlessly combine two movements, a reach and a grasp (see Figure 9.6). The reach brings the hand to the target, and the grasp positions the fingers on the target. A study of cerebellar subjects reaching for an object shows that although they can perform a reach in isolation and a grasp in isolation, they are impaired in performing the combined movement (Zackowski et al., 2002). Most of our motor actions are like reaching: they require combining a number of simple movements to make a more complex movement.

◉ 9.3 Communicating with the Spinal Cord

The way in which we make movements is represented in the brain's motor cortex, which specializes in skilled movements. The brainstem controls whole-body movements, especially those movements related to species-specific behaviors. The neural circuits for executing these actions are represented in the spinal cord.

Spinal-Cord Pathways

The neocortex sends major projections to the brainstem, as the **corticobulbar tracts**, and to the spinal cord, as the **corticospinal tracts**. (The prefix *cortico-* indicates that these tracts begin in the neocortex, and the terms *bulbar* and *spinal* indicate where the tracts end.) The corticobulbar tracts terminate in nuclei that control facial muscles and thus take part in controlling facial movements. The corticospinal tracts end on interneurons and on motor neurons in the spinal cord that in turn control limb, digit, and body movements.

Axons that form the corticobulbar and corticospinal tracts do not descend only from the primary motor cortex (M1, area 4). Some come from the primary somatosensory cortex (S1, area 3-1-2), others from the premotor cortex (area 6). The part of the corticospinal tract that descends from S1 terminates in posterior-column nuclei of the ascending sensory tracts and modulates sensory signals that are sent to the neocortex (see Figure 8.14). Parts of the tract that originate in M1 and the premotor cortex descend to the interneurons and motor neurons of the brainstem and spinal cord and control movement more directly. Thus, the neocortex both controls movement and modulates sensory information coming in from the body (Leyva-Díaz and López-Bendito, 2013).

The corticobulbar and corticospinal tract axons originate in layer-V pyramidal cells of the neocortex (see Figure 3.26). These motor neurons have especially large cell bodies, in keeping with the fact that they support axons that travel a long way. The corticospinal tract axons descend into the brainstem, sending collaterals to a few brainstem nuclei and eventually emerging on the brainstem's ventral surface, where they form a large bump on each side of that surface. These bumps, known as *pyramids*, give the cortico-spinal tracts their alternative name, the **pyramidal tracts**.

From this location, about 95% of the motor axons descending from the left hemisphere cross over to the right side of the brainstem, whereas a comparable proportion of the axons descending from the right hemisphere cross over to the left side of the brainstem. The remaining axons stay on their original sides. The division produces two cortico-spinal tracts descending on each side of the spinal cord. **Figure 9.18** illustrates the division of motor axons for the tract originating in the left-hemisphere cortex.

The corticospinal-tract fibers that cross to descend into the spinal cord originate mainly in the hand-and-arm and leg-and-foot regions of the cortical homunculi. The fibers that do not cross originate in the trunk regions of the motor homunculi. Therefore, each hemisphere's motor cortex controls the limbs on the opposite side of the body and the trunk on the same side of the body.

Looking at the spinal cord cross section at the bottom of Figure 9.18, you can see the location of the two tracts. Those fibers that cross to the opposite side of the brainstem descend the spinal cord in a lateral location, giving them the name **lateral corticospinal tract**. Those fibers that remain on their original side of the brainstem continue down the spinal cord in an anterior location, giving them the name **anterior corticospinal tract**. The lateral corticospinal tract sends messages to the limbs, whereas the anterior corticospinal tract sends messages to the trunk.

Spinal Motor Neurons

The spinal-cord motor neurons that connect to muscles are referred to as "the final common path" because all movement depends upon them. Interneurons lie just medial to the motor neurons and project onto them. The fibers of the corticospinal tracts make synaptic connections with both the interneurons and the motor neurons, but it is the motor neurons that carry all nervous system commands out to the muscles.

Spinal motor neurons and interneurons are arranged as a homunculus, diagrammed in **Figure 9.19**. Lateral motor neurons project to muscles that control the fingers and hands, intermediate motor neurons project to muscles that control the arms and shoulders, and the most medial motor neurons project to muscles that control the trunk. Axons of the lateral corticospinal tract connect mainly with the lateral motor neurons, whereas axons of the anterior corticospinal tract connect mainly to the medial motor neurons.

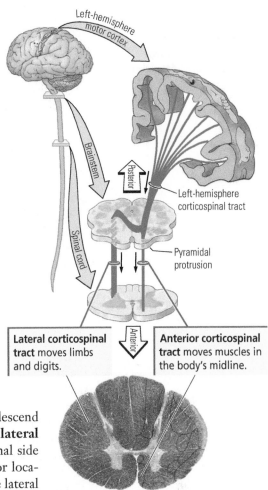

Figure 9.18 ▲

Corticospinal-Tract Pathway Nerve fibers descend from the left-hemisphere motor cortex to the brainstem, producing protrusions called pyramids on the ventral surface of the brainstem where each tract branches into the spinal cord. The lateral corticospinal tract (representing the limbs) crosses the midline, descending into the right side of the spinal cord to move limb and digit muscles on the body's right side. The anterior corticospinal tract (representing the body) remains on the left side. (Photograph of spinal cord reproduced from *The Human Brain: Photographic Guide* by T. H. Williams, N. Gluhbegovic, Wolters Kluwer Health.)

Figure 9.19 ▶

**Relations among
Interneurons, Motor
Neurons, and Muscles**

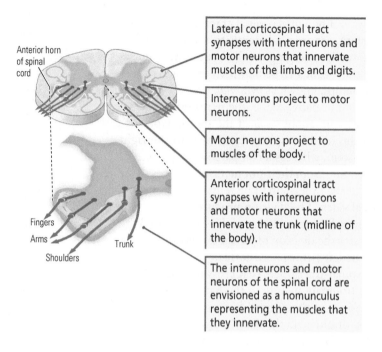

Lateral corticospinal tract synapses with interneurons and motor neurons that innervate muscles of the limbs and digits.

Interneurons project to motor neurons.

Motor neurons project to muscles of the body.

Anterior corticospinal tract synapses with interneurons and motor neurons that innervate the trunk (midline of the body).

The interneurons and motor neurons of the spinal cord are envisioned as a homunculus representing the muscles that they innervate.

Anterior horn of spinal cord

Fingers
Arms
Shoulders
Trunk

Limb muscles are arranged in pairs, as shown in **Figure 9.20**. One member, the **extensor muscle**, moves the limb away from the trunk. The other member, the **flexor muscle**, moves the limb toward the trunk. Connections between spinal cord interneurons and motor neurons cause the muscle pairs to work in concert: when one contracts, the other relaxes. Thus, the spinal cord interneurons and motor neurons relay instructions from the brain and, through their connections, cooperatively organize the movements of many muscles. (Compare the workings of spinal *extension* and *flexion reflexes*, discussed in Section 3.4.)

There is no simple one-to-one relation between an upper motor neuron in the neocortex and a lower motor neuron in the spinal cord. The motor

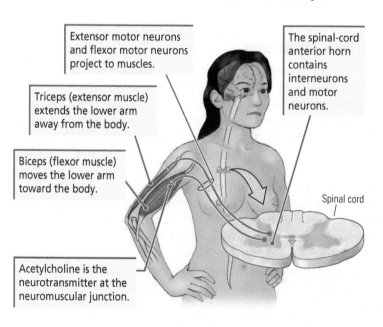

Extensor motor neurons and flexor motor neurons project to muscles.

The spinal-cord anterior horn contains interneurons and motor neurons.

Triceps (extensor muscle) extends the lower arm away from the body.

Biceps (flexor muscle) moves the lower arm toward the body.

Spinal cord

Acetylcholine is the neurotransmitter at the neuromuscular junction.

Figure 9.20 ▶

Muscular Coordination

neurons innervating each muscle are organized in columns that extend through many spinal-cord segments. Upper motor neurons, through their corticospinal connections, synapse with lower motor neurons in these columns and so themselves branch diffusely to many spinal-cord segments. Extensive and distributed corticospinal connections underlie the motor cortex's ability to evoke complex movements.

SUMMARY

Muscle movement in the body is represented in the brain's motor regions. The motor cortex controls skilled movements of the mouth and limbs, the brainstem controls whole-body movements requiring coordination, and the neural circuits for executing all these actions reside in the spinal cord.

9.1 The Neocortex: Initiating Movement

Neocortical circuits from sensory regions to motor regions produce the organized movements of everyday action. Each region produces a specific behavior, for example stepping, reaching, placing an object in the mouth, avoiding threats, and chewing. Similar regions in the motor cortex and parietal cortex are connected. Each receives sensory information concerning vision and touch and connects to the spinal cord, where movement instructions are sent to muscles.

Single-cell recordings in the neocortex suggest that cells in the primary motor cortex specify the movement that is to be made as well as its force and direction. Cells in the premotor cortex are active during more-complex movements in which not only the movement itself but also the movement's target must be considered. One class of premotor cells, mirror neurons, are active when we make a particular goal-oriented movement, when we observe someone else make the same movement, and even when we see only a picture of the movement. Mirror neurons provide a substrate for self-awareness and for social awareness.

9.2 The Brainstem: Motor Control

The basal ganglia's reciprocal connections with the cortex and brainstem contribute to motor control by adjusting the force associated with each movement. Consequently, damage to the basal ganglia can result either in unwanted involuntary movements (too much force being exerted) or in such rigidity that movements are difficult to perform (too little force being exerted). The cerebellum contributes to movement accuracy and control by coordinating movement timing and comparing intended movement with actual movement to calculate any necessary correction, thereby improving movement skill.

9.3 Communicating with the Spinal Cord

The descending corticospinal pathways from the brain into the spinal cord partly cross, so the right and left motor cortices control the limbs on the opposite side of the body and the trunk on the same side of the body. Spinal-cord motor neurons have a homuncular organization, with lateral neurons controlling distal body parts and medial neurons controlling the trunk. Thus, all major parts of the motor system, top to tail, have a topographic organization, with different regions controlling different body parts.

References

Afalo, T.N., and Graziano, M.S.A. Relationship between unconstrained arm movement and single neuron firing in the macaque motor cortex. *Journal of Neuroscience*, 27, 2760–2780, 2007.

Alexander, R. E., and M. D. Crutcher. Functional architecture of basal ganglia circuits: Neural substrates of parallel processing. *Trends in Neuroscience* 13:266–271, 1990.

Bello A., L. Sparaci, S. Stefanini, S. Boria, V. Volterra, and G. Rizzolatti. A developmental study on children's capacity to ascribe goals and intentions to others. *Developmental Psychology* 50(2):504–513, 2013.

Brinkman, C. Supplementary motor area of the monkey's cerebral cortex: Short- and long-term deficits after unilateral ablation and the effects of subsequent callosal section. *Journal of Neuroscience* 4:918–992, 1984.

Cattaneo L., F. Maule, G. Barchiesi, and G. Rizzolatti. The motor system resonates to the distal goal of observed actions: Testing the inverse pliers paradigm in an ecological setting. *Experimental Brain Research* 231:37–49, 2013.

Evarts, E. V. Relation of pyramidal tract activity to force exerted during voluntary movement. *Journal of Neurophysiology* 31:14–27, 1968.

Filimon, F. Human cortical control of hand movements: Parietofrontal networks for reaching, grasping, and pointing. *Neuroscientist* 16:388–407, 2012.

Friedhoff, A. J., and T. N. Chase, Eds. *Advances in Neurology, vol. 35, Gilles de la Tourette Syndrome*. New York: Raven Press, 1982.

Fukuda, T. *Statokinetic Reflexes in Equilibrium and Movement*. Tokyo: University of Tokyo Press, 1981.

Georgopoulos, A. P., J. F. Kalaska, R. Caminiti, and J. T. Massey. On the relations between the direction of two-dimensional arm movements and cell discharge in primate motor cortex. *Journal of Neuroscience* 2:1527–1537, 1982.

Georgopoulos, A. P., G. Pellizzer, A. V. Poliakov, and M. H. Schieber. Neural coding of finger and wrist movements. *Journal of Computational Neuroscience* 6:279–288, 1999.

Graziano, M. *The Intelligent Movement Machine*. New York: Oxford University Press, 2009.

Hess, W. R. *The Functional Organization of the Diencephalon*. London: Grune & Stratton, 1957.

Hickock, G. *The Myth of Mirror Neurons: The Real Neuroscience of Communication and Cognition*. New York: W. W. Norton & Company, 2014.

Kaas, J. H., O. A. Gharbawie, and I. Stepniewska. Cortical networks for ethologically relevant behaviors in primates. *American Journal of Primatology* 75:407–414, 2013.

Karl, J. M., and I. Q. Whishaw. Different evolutionary origins for the reach and the grasp: An explanation for dual visuo-motor channels in primate parietofrontal cortex. *Frontiers in Neurology* 4:208, December 23, 2013.

Keele, S. W., and R. Ivry. Does the cerebellum provide a common computation for diverse tasks? A timing hypothesis. In A. Diamond, Ed., *The Development and Neural Bases of Higher Cognitive Functions. Annals of the New York Academy of Sciences* 608:197–211, 1991.

Leyva-Díaz, E, and G. López-Bendito. In and out from the cortex: Development of major forebrain connections. *Neuroscience* 254:26–44, December 19, 2013.

Nicolelis, M. Mind in motion. *Scientific American* 307:58–63, September 2012.

Penfield, W., and E. Boldrey. Somatic motor and sensory representation in the cerebral cortex as studied by electrical stimulation. *Brain* 60:389–443, 1958.

Redgrave, P., N. Vautrelle, and J. N. Reynolds. Functional properties of the basal ganglia's re-entrant loop architecture: Selection and reinforcement. *Neuroscience* 198:138–151, 2011.

Rizzolatti, G., A. Alberto Semi, and M. Fabbri-Destro. Linking psychoanalysis with neuroscience: The concept of ego. *Neuropsychologia* 55:143-148, 2014.

Roland, P. E. *Brain Activation*. New York: Wiley-Liss, 1993.

Schieber, M. H. Somatotopic gradients in the distributed organization of the human primary motor cortex hand area: Evidence from small infarcts. *Experimental Brain Research* 128:139–148, 1999.

Thach, W. T., H. P. Goodkin, and J. G. Keating. The cerebellum and the adaptive coordination of movement. *Annual Review of Neuroscience* 15:403–442, 1992.

Umilta, M. A., K. Kohler, V. Gallese, L. Fogassi, L. Fadiga, C. Keysers, and G. Rizzolatti. I know what you are doing: A neurophysiological study. *Neuron* 31:155–165, 2001.

Zackowski K. M., W. T. Thach, Jr,, and A. J. Bastian. Cerebellar subjects show impaired coupling of reach and grasp movements. *Experimental Brain Research* 146:511–522, 2002.

10 Principles of Neocortical Function

 PORTRAIT   Hemispherectomy

A.R. was a strictly average boy until the age of 11, when he developed seizures, but only on the right side of his body. In time, persistent right-side weakness emerged along with increasing difficulty in talking, or **dysphasia**, impairment of speech caused by damage to the CNS. Although A.R. was admitted to the hospital many times over the next 6 years, the cause of his seizures and language and motor problems remained undetermined. Initially, he was right-handed but became unable to use that hand and began to write and draw with his left hand.

By age 15, A.R.'s IQ score had dropped by 30 points, and by age 17, his language and emotional problems made psychological testing impossible. At 17, his condition was diagnosed as Rasmussen's encephalitis, a chronic brain infection that slowly leads to a virtual loss of function in one cerebral hemisphere.

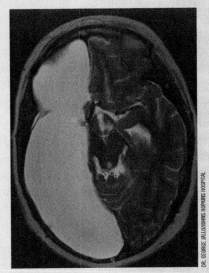

DR. GEORGE JALLO/JOHNS HOPKINS HOSPITAL

Because the only successful treatment is removal of the diseased tissue, most of A.R.'s left cerebral hemisphere was surgically removed, a procedure called **hemispherectomy**. (The adjoining postoperative MRI scan shows a patient's brain in dorsal view after a left hemispherectomy.)

When A.R. was reassessed 10 years later, at age 27, he showed remarkable improvement. His oral language skills appeared to be average. He communicated freely and could both initiate and respond to conversation. He was, however, functionally illiterate, unable to read or write except at a most basic level.

His motor skills also had improved. He could move about on his own, although he still had a significant limp and could only lift his right arm to shoulder level. He could also open and close his hands to grasp objects with his right hand.

People can lose enormous amounts of cerebral tissue and still retain remarkable cognitive and motor abilities. The achievements of hemispherectomy patients such as A.R., even those with severe neuron loss in both hemispheres, prompt the question, What roles do the cerebral hemispheres and subcortical regions play in controlling behavior? To search for answers, in this chapter we focus on the CNS's hierarchical organization from spinal cord to cortex, on the structure of the cortex, and on functional theories of brain organization. We conclude by asking another question: Does the human brain possess unique properties?

10.1 A Hierarchy of Function from Spinal Cord to Cortex

Within the brain's functional hierarchy, higher levels provide an animal with more precision and flexibility in behavior. A.R.'s intelligence test score was 70 (borderline intellectually disabled) after his surgery, much below his childhood IQ score of about 100 (average). Although severely impaired, A.R. nonetheless functioned rather well with so much of his brain gone, for two reasons:

1. **Levels of function.** Subcortical structures can mediate complex behaviors. The relation of the cortex to subcortical structures is analogous to that of a piano player to a piano. The cortex represents the piano player, producing behavior by playing on subcortical keys. This idea dates to Herbert Spencer's mid–nineteenth-century speculation that successive steps in evolution have added new levels of brain and of behavioral complexity. John Hughlings-Jackson adopted Spencer's idea, and it became a central focus of neurological theories in the twentieth and twenty-first centuries (see Section 1.3).

2. **Brain plasticity.** The brain's considerable capacity for change in response to experience, drugs, hormones, or injury is due to its plasticity, as is its ability to compensate for loss of function caused by damage. The brain's resiliency to damage gained popular exposure in 1700, when Joseph Du Verney, in a public demonstration, showed that when a nerve and muscle were dissected away from a frog, the nerve continued to function because it produced muscle contractions when touched.

Indeed, we can trace the focus on functional levels of nervous system organization in part to early findings that the brain has remarkable plasticity. In the 300-odd years since Du Verney's demonstration, it has become clear that both laboratory animals and humans can function surprisingly well with considerable amounts of the brain removed. At the time of his surgery, A.R. had no language ability at all, partly because the dysfunctioning left hemisphere, where language functions are concentrated in most of us, was interfering with the right hemisphere's ability to engage in language functions. Shortly after the left hemisphere was removed, at least some of A.R.'s language functions reemerged, as though the left hemisphere had been suppressing functioning in the right.

We must hasten to point out that the mere fact that people can live fairly normally with large amounts of brain tissue missing does not imply that those brain parts are unnecessary. People can compensate for lost brain tissue just as they can compensate for lost limbs. But this ability does not mean that such people would not be better off with their limbs—or brain—intact.

Throughout the twentieth century, the capacities of animals with extensive regions of the nervous system removed were recorded in many neurologic studies. One study, conducted by Kent Berridge and Ian Whishaw (1992), examined grooming in the rat. Recall from Section 9.2 that rats (like other animals, including ourselves) begin by grooming the head and then work their way down the body. As illustrated in **Figure 10.1**, a rat begins to groom by using its paws, rubbing its nose with symmetrical circular movements.

Figure 10.1 ▼

Grooming Sequences in the Rat

Rats have a fixed grooming sequence, which starts with ellipical strokes to the head,...

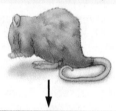

...followed by grooming of each side of the face.

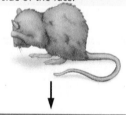

They move to the ears, using bilateral strokes,...

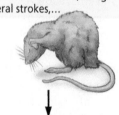

...and then continue moving toward the rear of the body.

Then it sweeps its paws across its face and behind its ears before turning to lick its body. This series of actions can be divided into as many as 50 linked movements.

In examining this movement complex, Berridge and Whishaw found that many levels of the nervous system participate in producing the elements and the syntax (the organization) of grooming behavior: it is produced not by one locus in the brain but rather by many brain areas and levels, from the spinal cord to the cortex. These successive nervous system layers do not simply replicate function; rather, each region adds a different dimension to the behavior.

This hierarchical organization holds not only for grooming but also for virtually every behavior in which we (as well as rats) engage. Understanding the principle of hierarchical organization is critical to understanding how cortical control contributes to behavior. **Figure 10.2** diagrams some functions mediated at different anatomical levels in the nervous system. In the following

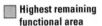

Highest remaining functional area

Behaviors

Spinal (spinal cord)

Reflexes: Responds to appropriate sensory stimulation by stretching, withdrawal, support, scratching, paw shaking, etc.

Low decerebrate (hindbrain)

Postural support: Performs units of movement (e.g., hissing, biting, growling, chewing, lapping, licking) when stimulated; shows exaggerated standing, postural reflexes, and elements of sleepwalking behavior.

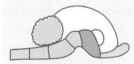

High decerebrate (midbrain)

Spontaneous movement: Responds to simple visual and auditory stimulation; performs automatic behaviors such as grooming; and when stimulated performs subsets of voluntary movements (e.g., standing, walking turning, jumping, climbing).

Diencephalic
(hypothalamus, thalamus)

Affect and motivation: Voluntary movements occur spontaneously and excessively but are aimless; shows well-integrated but poorly directed affective behavior; thermoregulates effectively.

Decorticate (basal ganglia)

Self-maintenance: Links voluntary movements and automatic movements sufficiently well for self-maintenance (eating, drinking) in a simple environment.

Typical (cortex)

Control and intention: Performs sequences of voluntary movements in organized patterns; responds to patterns of sensory stimulation. Contains circuits for forming cognitive maps and for responding to the relationships between objects, events, and things. Adds emotional value.

⊚ **Figure 10.2** ◄

Central Nervous System Hierarchy Anatomical and behavioral levels in the CNS, shown here in an inverted hierarchy from spinal cord to cortex, highlighting the highest remaining functional area at each level.

sections, we note parallel functions that may exist in humans as appropriate. We begin next with the "lowest" CNS level, the spinal cord, then add structures to see how the corresponding behaviors increase in complexity.

The Spinal Cord: Reflexes

Section 3.4 explains the effects of spinal-cord injury, including paraplegia and quadriplegia, and describes how the late actor Christopher Reeve's spinal cord was severed just below the brain in an equestrian accident. Reeve, who portrayed Superman in a series of movies beginning in 1978, survived for nearly

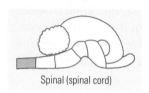

Spinal (spinal cord)

a decade after his injury but was unable to move, or even to breathe without the aid of a respirator. What behaviors could his spinal cord initiate without any descending influence from the brain?

Like Christopher Reeve, an animal whose spinal cord is disconnected from the brain is unable to move voluntarily because the brain cannot communicate with the spinal neurons. Nonetheless, the intact spinal cord can mediate many reflexes, such as limb approach to a tactile stimulus and limb withdrawal from a noxious stimulus (Grillner, 1973).

The spinal cord also contains the neural circuitry to produce stepping responses and walking, provided that body weight is supported. For example, if **spinal** animals are suspended in a hammock and placed such that their limbs are in light contact with a moving treadmill, their legs will begin to make stepping movements automatically, as illustrated in **Figure 10.3**. This behavior tells us that circuitry in the spinal cord, not the brain, produces the stepping movements. The brain's role is control—to make those movements at the right time and place.

Figure 10.3 ▲

Spinal Animal Walking on Treadmill

The Hindbrain: Postural Support

If the hindbrain and spinal cord remain connected after an injury but both are disconnected from the rest of the brain, the subject is called a **low decerebrate**. This type of injury produces a far different syndrome from that produced in an animal with a spinal-cord transection. A spinal animal is alert; a person who has sustained such an injury can still talk, express emotion, and so on. However, a low-decerebrate animal has difficulty maintaining consciousness because many essential inputs to the brain regions above the injury are now disconnected, presumably leaving the forebrain "in the dark."

Sensory input into the hindbrain comes predominantly from the head and is carried over cranial nerves 4 to 12 (see Figure 3.14). Most cranial nerves also have motor nuclei in the hindbrain, whose efferent (outgoing) fibers control muscles in the head and neck. Sensory input to the hindbrain is not limited to the cranial nerves: the spinal somatosensory system has access to hindbrain motor systems, just as the hindbrain has access to spinal motor systems. But sensory input into the hindbrain of the low decerebrate can no longer reach the upper parts of the brain, resulting in a serious disturbance of consciousness.

A classic example reveals the effects of low-decerebrate injury. During extensive studies on cats done early in the twentieth century, researchers such as H. C. Bazett and Wilder Penfield (1922) kept low-decerebrate cats alive for periods of weeks or months. The cats were generally inactive when undisturbed and showed no effective ability to thermoregulate (maintain normal body temperature), but they swallowed food placed on their tongues and so could be fed.

If the animals were stimulated lightly in any of a variety of sensory modalities (such as touch, pain, or sound), they moved from their typical reclining position into a crouch. If the stimulation was stronger, they walked, somewhat unsteadily. These stimuli also elicited such typical affective (emotional) behaviors as biting, hissing, growling, and tail lashing.

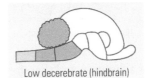

Low decerebrate (hindbrain)

A characteristic behavioral aspect accorded by the hindbrain is a peculiar stiffness called **decerebrate rigidity** due to excessive muscle tone, particularly in the antigravity muscles that hold the body up to maintain posture. These are the body's strongest muscles. When a low-decerebrate animal is placed in an upright position, its limbs extend and its head flexes upward in a posture often referred to as "exaggerated standing."

Against the background of decerebrate rigidity, a variety of postural reflexes can be elicited by changes in head position. If the head of a standing animal is pushed down toward the floor, the front legs flex and the hind legs extend; if the head is pushed upward, the hind legs flex and the front legs extend. The first posture would be used by a typical cat looking under a couch, the second by a typical cat looking upward onto a shelf. Turning the head to the side elicits extension of the limbs on the same side and flexion of the limbs on the opposite side of the body. Usually, this response occurs in a cat that has turned its head to look at some object and is prepared to pursue it.

Typical animals exhibit two types of sleep: *quiet sleep*, characterized by muscle tone and commonly referred to as slow-wave sleep, and *active sleep*, characterized by an absence of muscle tone and commonly referred to as *dream sleep* or *REM sleep* (or rapid eye movement sleep) (**Figure 10.4**). Low-decerebrate animals display both types of sleep at different times. Those left undisturbed gradually lose their rigidity and subside or droop into a prone posture. Any mild stimulus such as a noise or a touch reinstates rigidity. This behavioral change seems analogous to quiet sleep.

Low-decerebrate animals also show a sudden collapse, accompanied by the loss of all body tone, that lasts from 15 seconds to 12 minutes, analogous to active, or REM, sleep. People with an illness called **narcolepsy** similarly collapse uncontrollably into active sleep (see Section 26.9). The results of research with low-decerebrate animals thus demonstrate that the locus of neural centers that produce sleep is in the hindbrain.

The behavioral changes seen in low-decerebrate animals are paralleled in people who enter a persistent vegetative state (PVS) after the type of brainstem damage that essentially separates the lower brainstem from the rest of the brain. R. Barrett and his colleagues (1967) documented numerous cases. Like Terri Schiavo (see the Snapshot on page 14), in a PVS, people may alternate between states of consciousness resembling sleeping and waking, make eye movements to follow moving stimuli, cough, smile, swallow food, and display decerebrate rigidity and postural adjustments when moved. With extraordinary care, PVS patients may live, little changed, for months or years.

Figure 10.4 ▼

Typical Postures of a Cat

Awake

Quiet sleep
(slow-wave sleep)

Active sleep
(REM, or dream, sleep)

The Midbrain: Spontaneous Movement

The next level in the brain organization hierarchy can be seen in an animal with an intact midbrain (mesencephalon) but lacking higher-center function-

High decerebrate (midbrain)

ing. Damage that separates the diencephalon from the midbrain regions containing, in the tectum, the coordinating centers for vision (superior colliculus) and hearing (inferior colliculus) and, in the tegmentum, a number of motor nuclei, produces this condition, called **high decerebration**. Visual and auditory inputs allow the animal to perceive events at a distance, and therefore the high-decerebrate animal can respond to distant objects by moving toward them.

Bard and Macht (1958) report that high-decerebrate cats can walk, stand, resume upright posture when turned on their backs, and even run and climb when stimulated. Bignall and Schramm (1974) found that kittens decerebrated in infancy could orient themselves toward visual and auditory stimuli. The animals could even execute an attack response and pounce on objects at the source of a sound.

In fact, Bignall and Schramm fed the cats by exploiting this behavior: they placed food near the source of the sound. Attacking the sound source, the cats then consumed the food. Although the cats attacked moving objects, they gave no evidence of being able to see, because they bumped into things when they walked.

These experiments demonstrate that all of the subsets of **voluntary movements**—movements that take an animal from one place to another, such as turning, walking, climbing, swimming, and flying—are present at the subcortical level of the midbrain. Animals typically use voluntary movements to satisfy a variety of needs—to find food, water, or a new home territory or to escape a predator, for example. Voluntary movements also are called *appetitive, instrumental, purposive,* or *operant.*

Because they are executed through lower-level postural support and reflex systems, voluntary movements can also be elicited by lower-level sensory input; that is, a pinch or postural displacement can elicit turning, walking, or climbing. Thus, function at the midbrain level is integrated with lower levels by both ascending and descending connections, exactly as the hindbrain and spinal levels are interconnected.

High-decerebrate animals can also effectively perform **automatic movements**, units of stereotyped behavior linked in a sequence. Grooming, chewing food, lapping water, and rejecting food are representative automatic behaviors of the rat. Also variously called *reflexive, consummatory,* or *respondent,* automatic behaviors generally are directed toward completing an act and are not directed specifically toward moving an animal from one place to another.

Grooming provides an excellent example of automatic behavior because it consists of many movements executed sequentially in an organized and stereotyped fashion. Food rejection comprises a similarly complex behavioral series. If high-decerebrate rats are given food when they are not hungry, they perform a series of movements consisting of tongue flicks, chin rubbing, and paw shaking to reject the food. These behaviors are similar to the rejection behaviors of

typical rats—as well as of people, as illustrated in **Figure 10.5**—in response to food they find noxious. If the animals are not sated, they will lap water and chew food brought to their mouths.

Among the accounts of infants born with large parts of the forebrain missing, one child studied by E. Gamper (Jung and Hassler, 1960) nearly a century ago had no brain above the diencephalon and only a few traces of the diencephalon intact. This mesencephalic child was, therefore, anatomically and behaviorally equivalent to a high-decerebrate animal. As shown in **Figure 10.6**, a mesencephalic child shows many behaviors of newborn infants, periodically sleeping and waking, sucking, yawning, stretching, crying, and following visual stimuli with the eyes. However, even though these children can sit up, they show little spontaneous activity and, if left alone, remain mostly in a drowsy state.

Figure 10.5 ▲

Human Reactions to Taste Positive (hedonic) reactions, such as licking the fingers or lips, are elicited by sweet and other palatable tastes. Negative (aversive) reactions, elicited by bitter tastes (such as quinine) and by other unpalatable flavors, include spitting, making a face of distaste, and wiping the mouth with the back of the hand. (Information from K. C. Berridge, Food reward: Brain substrates of wanting and liking. *Neuroscience and Biobehavioral Reviews* 20:6, 1996.)

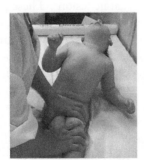
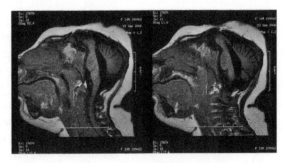

Yvonne Brackbill (1971) studied a similar child and found that in response to moderately loud sounds (60–90 decibels), this infant oriented to stimuli in much the same way as typical infants do. Unlike typical babies, however, this child's responses did not change in magnitude and did not habituate (gradually decrease in intensity) to repeated presentations. Brackbill concluded that the forebrain is not important in producing movements but is important in attenuating and inhibiting them. Babies born with such extensive brain abnormalities usually do not live long, and among those who live for several months—or even for years—the complex behaviors typically seen in infants do not develop.

Figure 10.6 ▲

Mesencephalic Human Child Photos illustrating the rigid postures of a 3-year-old mesencephalic child. MRIs show the absence of the forebrain but the intact lower brainstem and cerebellum. (Carolina Araújo Rodrigues Funayama, Luzia Iara Pfeifer, Ester Silveira Ramos, Patrícia Zambroni Santucci, Israel Gomy, Adolfo Marcondes Amaral Neto Three-year-old child with meroacrania—Neurological signs. *Brain and Development* 33(1):86–89, January 2011 © Elsevier.)

The Diencephalon: Affect and Motivation

A **diencephalic** animal, although lacking the basal ganglia and cerebral hemispheres, has an intact olfactory system, enabling it to smell odors at a distance. The hypothalamus and pituitary also are intact, and their control over hormonal systems and homeostasis no doubt integrates the body's physiology

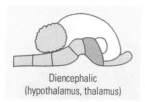

Diencephalic
(hypothalamus, thalamus)

with the brain's activity. Diencephalic animals thermoregulate, for example, but they do not eat or drink well enough to sustain themselves.

The diencephalon adds affective and motivational dimensions to behavior in the sense that it becomes "energized" and sustained. As mentioned earlier, high-decerebrate animals show many component behaviors of rage, but their behaviors are not energetic, well-integrated, or sustained. Walter Cannon and S. W. Britton (1924) studied diencephalic cats and described what they called "quasi-emotional phenomena," or sham rage, such as that usually seen in an infuriated animal. This affective behavior is inappropriately displayed and is thus called sham rage to distinguish it from the directed rage typical of a cat.

Sham rage consists of lashing the tail, arching the trunk, making limb movements, displaying claws, snarling, and biting. A diencephalic animal displays sympathetic nervous system signs of rage, including tail hair erection, sweating of the toe pads, pupil dilation, urination, high blood pressure, high heart rate, and increases in epinephrine and blood sugar. These emotional attacks sometimes last for hours.

Bard removed varying amounts of forebrain and brainstem and found that, for sham rage to occur, at least the posterior part of the hypothalamus must be intact. Clinical reports indicate that similar sham emotional attacks can occur in people who have hypothalamic lesions. These people show unchecked rage or literally die laughing. In addition to sham rage, another pronounced feature of a diencephalic animal's behavior is constant activity. For example, when placed in an open field, it wanders aimlessly.

Sham rage and hyperactivity suggest that the diencephalon energizes an animal's behavior, which may have led some researchers to consider the behaviors affective or motivated. Perhaps a diencephalic animal's hyperactivity should be called *sham motivation* to distinguish it from a typical animal's goal-oriented behavior. In this sense, the diencephalic animal's sham affect and sham motivation are like the exaggerated standing observed in low-decerebrate animals. Under appropriate forebrain control, the behavior can be released for functional purposes, but in the absence of that control, the behavior of a diencephalic animal is excessive and seems inappropriate (see Grill and Norgren, 1978).

The Basal Ganglia: Self-Maintenance

Decortication, removal of the neocortex, leaves the basal ganglia and brainstem intact. Decorticate animals have been studied more closely than any other neu-

Decorticate (basal ganglia)

rologically impaired class because they are able to maintain themselves without special care in laboratory conditions.

The first careful experiments were done by Friedrich Goltz (1960) with decorticate dogs (see Section 1.3), but the most thorough studies have used rats as subjects (e.g., Whishaw, 1989). Within a day after surgery, rats eat and maintain body weight on a wet mash diet and eat dry food and drink water brought in contact with the mouth. With a little training in drinking (holding the water spout to the mouth), they find water and become able to maintain themselves on water and laboratory chow. They have typical sleeping–waking cycles; run, climb, and swim; and even negotiate simple mazes.

They can also sequence series of movements. For example, copulation consists of a number of movements that take place sequentially and last for hours, yet decorticate animals can perform these acts almost normally. As described early in this chapter, grooming also requires the sequential use of about 50 discrete movements, and decorticate rats also perform it normally.

In sum, to a casual observer, a decorticate rat appears indistinguishable from normal animals. In fact, in laboratory exercises in which students are tasked to distinguish between normal and decorticate animals, not only do they find the job difficult, often they fail. A decorticate rat does indeed have a lot of behavioral difficulties, but seeing these problems requires a trained eye. All the elementary movements that animals might make seem to be part of their behavioral repertoire after decortication. They can walk, eat, drink, mate, and raise litters of pups in a seemingly adequate fashion.

What is observed in a decorticate rat, and what is presumably conferred by functions in the basal ganglia, is the ability to link automatic movements to voluntary movements so that the behaviors are biologically adaptive. A major part of this linking probably includes the inhibition or facilitation of voluntary movements. For example, the animal walks until it finds food or water and then inhibits walking to consume the food or water. Thus, the basal ganglia probably provide the circuitry required for the stimulus to inhibit movement so that ingestion can occur.

The Cortex: Intention

What the cortex does also can be ascertained by studying what decorticate animals (with the neocortex alone removed or with the limbic system also removed) do not do. They do not build nests, although they engage in some nest-building behaviors. They do not hoard food, although they might carry food around. They also have difficulty making skilled movements with the tongue and limbs because they are unable to reach for food by protruding the tongue or by reaching with one forelimb.

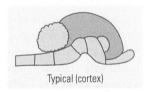

Typical (cortex)

Decorticate animals can perform pattern discriminations in different sensory modalities, but only if these tasks are relatively simple. For example, a decorticate could discriminate two pure tones but would be unable to distinguish complex sounds such as the noises from a lawnmower and an automobile. The results of a series of experiments by David Oakley (1979) show that decorticate animals can perform well in tests of classical conditioning, operant conditioning, approach learning, cue learning, and pattern discrimination. These experiments confirm that the cortex is not essential for learning itself. However, decorticate animals fail at learning, for example, complex pattern discriminations and how to find their way around in a space.

The results of studies of decortication tell us that the cortex does not add much to an animal's behavioral repertoire in the way of new movements. Rather, the cortex appears to extend the usefulness of all behaviors or to make them adaptive in new situations. An animal without a cortex can see and hear and use its limbs for many purposes, but a typical animal with a cortex can make plans and combine movement sequences to generate more-complex behavioral patterns.

🎯 10.2 The Structure of the Cortex

As our summary of the behaviors of animals with only subcortical brain function makes clear, the cortex adds new dimensions to sensory analysis and new levels of movement control. What cortical structures permit these enhancements?

Section 1.4 explains the ideas behind topographic maps that divide up the cortex based on anatomical and functional criteria. Alfred Campbell published the first complete cortical map of the human brain in 1905, based on both cell structure and myelin distribution. Soon after, several alternative versions emerged, the most notable by Korbinian Brodmann, reproduced in **Figure 10.7**.

Based on his studies of myelin development in the cortex, Paul Flechsig (1920) divided cortical regions into (1) an early-myelinating primordial zone including the motor cortex and a region of visual, auditory, and somatosensory cortex; (2) a secondary field bordering the primordial zone that myelinates next; and (3) a late-myelinating (tertiary) zone that he called "association." The three zones are color-coded in Figure 10.7. Flechsig hypothesized psychological functions for his hierarchy: primary zones perform simple sensorimotor functions, whereas the secondary and tertiary zones conduct increasingly complex mental analyses.

Various cortical maps do not correspond exactly, and they use different criteria and nomenclature. As new staining techniques are devised, enabling a truly bewildering variety of subdivisions and redefinitions, estimates of the number of cortical areas in the human brain can range from the approximately 50 areas Brodmann mapped to more than 200! MRI analyses have allowed researchers to create brain atlases with a spatial resolution of about 1 mm. This voxel size allows visualization of gross markers such as sulci, gyri, and subcortical nuclei. It does not allow fine-grained anatomical resolution of cortical regions at a cytoarchitectural level, however. Most recently, MRI has been combined with standard histological analysis to map the human brain objectively in a project known as BigBrain, described in the Snapshot.

Cortical Cells

Nerve cells are easily distinguished in the cortex as **spiny neurons** or **aspiny neurons** by the presence or absence, respectively, of dendritic spines. Much as thorns extend the surface area of rosebush branches, dendritic spines extend the dendrite's surface area. Spiny neurons are excitatory—about 95% of their excitatory synapses are found on the spines—and are likely to have receptors for the excitatory transmitter glutamate or aspartate. (For an extensive series of books on the structure of the cortex, see Peters and Jones, 1984–1999.)

Spiny neurons include **pyramidal cells**—so named for the shape of their substantial cell bodies—whose long axons generally send information from a cortical region to another area of the CNS, for example, within the corticospinal (pyramidal) tracts described in Section 9.3. Spiny **stellate cells** are smaller

Lateral view

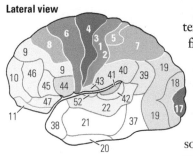

Medial view

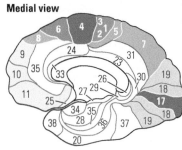

🎯 Figure 10.7 ▲

Brodmann's Map Lateral and medial views highlighted with primary, secondary, and tertiary (association) areas, as described by Paul Flechsig (1920) from his studies of myelin development in the cortex. The primary cortex is brightest (areas 4, 3-1-2, 41, 17), the secondary cortex is medium in tone, and the tertiary is lightest.

SNAPSHOT | Mapping the Human Cortex

BigBrain, a high-resolution three-dimensional atlas compiled by researchers at the Montreal Neurological Institute and Germany's Forschungszentrum Julich, was created by using a large-scale microtome to cut the brain of a 65-year-old female coronally into 7400 20-micrometer sections (see Figure 1.10). The sections were stained for cell bodies (Nissl stain), digitized, and combined by a supercomputer. The freely available BigBrain atlas allows a microscopic view of the entire human brain.

BigBrain will enable testing of new hypotheses about brain connectivity and will redefine traditional neuroanatomy maps such as those created by Brodmann.

Whereas these earlier neuroanatomical analyses were based upon visual inspection of brain sections, the Big-Brain project has used computer analysis to create a **gray level index** (GLI) that calculates brightness differences among the cell bodies and the **neuropil**. Neuropil is any area in the nervous system composed of mostly unmyelinated axons, dendrites, and glial cell processes that forms a synaptically dense region.

As shown in the accompanying illustrations, the shading pattern identified by the GLI differs significantly between areas. These differences allow the computer to identify objective borders between different regions. GLI analysis has allowed even more cortical regions to be identified than was possible with visual inspection alone.

One unexpected outcome of the Big-Brain project is the finding that interbrain variability is much larger than anticipated, leading to the conclusion that neuroscientists cannot present a dogmatic map that represents "the" human brain. The borders of different regions in different people simply are not similar enough, and the total areal differences in a population are at least twofold different. By superimposing the maps of 10 to 20 brains, however, it is possible to create a single probability map that statistically estimates an "average" brain.

(A)

(B)

(C)

(D)

Defining cortical regions objectively. (A) Surface rendering of the three-dimensional reconstructed brain with the frontal pole (anterior part of the frontal lobe) removed. (B) Coronal section 6704 of 7400. (C) The GLI identifies a unique pattern for each cortical area, which allows (D) an objective distinction between cortical regions, in this case Brodmann's areas (BA) 10 and 32. (Amunts et al., 2013, Courtesy Juelich Research Center.)

Amunts, K., C. Lepage, L. Boregeat, H. Mohlberg, T. Dickscheid, M.-E. Rousseau, S. Bludau, P.-L. Bazin, L. B. Lewis, A. M. Oros-Peusquens, N. J. Shah, T. Koppert, K. Zilles, and A. C. Evans. Big-Brain: An ultrahigh-resolution 3D human brain model. *Science* 340:1472–1475, 2013.

star-shaped interneurons whose processes remain within the region of the brain where the cell body is located.

Pyramidal cells are the efferent projection neurons of the cortex, and they constitute the largest population of cortical neurons (70–85 percent). They are found in layers II, III, V, and VI. In general, the largest cells send their axons the farthest. The pyramidal cells of layer V are the largest, projecting from the

Figure 10.8 ▶

Neocortical Cells The most important spiny neuron types, pyramidal cells and stellate cells, are elaborated here along with aspiny stellate and basket cells. The directions of the arrows indicate afferent (up, incoming) or efferent (down, outgoing) neuronal projections. (Research from Szentagothai, 1969.)

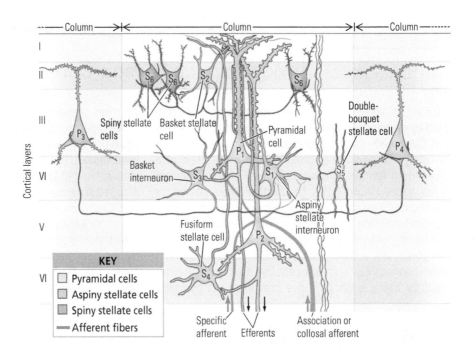

cortex to the brainstem and spinal cord. Those in layers II and III are smaller and project to other cortical regions, as diagrammed in **Figure 10.8**.

Aspiny neurons are interneurons with short axons and no dendritic spines. They are diverse in appearance, with different types named largely on the basis of the configurations of their axons and dendrites. One type of aspiny stellate cell shown in Figure 10.8 is called a *basket cell* because its axon projects horizontally, forming synapses that envelop the postsynaptic cell like a basket. Another, the *double-bouquet* type, has a proliferation of dendrites on either side of the cell body, much as if two bouquets of flowers were aligned stem to stem.

Despite differences in shape, all aspiny neurons are inhibitory and are likely to use gamma-aminobutyric acid (GABA) as a neurotransmitter. Aspiny neurons also use many other transmitters: virtually every classical transmitter and neuropeptide has been co-localized with GABA in aspiny cells. Thus, not only are aspiny cells morphologically diverse, they also show a remarkable chemical diversity.

The BigBrain project has mapped the distribution of excitatory (NMDA) and inhibitory (GABA) receptors, allowing identification of the "receptor fingerprints" for different cortical regions. The receptor maps can then be superimposed on GLI-based maps, yielding an even finer identification of cortical regions. Not surprisingly, the receptor fingerprints highly correlate with GLI profiles described in the Snapshot on page 265.

Cortical Layers, Efferents, and Afferents

Each of the four to six layers of the neocortex has different functions, different afferents, and different efferents. Cells of the middle cortical layers, especially in and around layer IV, constitute an input zone of sensory analysis: they receive projections from other cortical areas and from other areas of the brain. The cells of layers V and VI constitute an output zone, sending axons to other cortical areas or other brain areas.

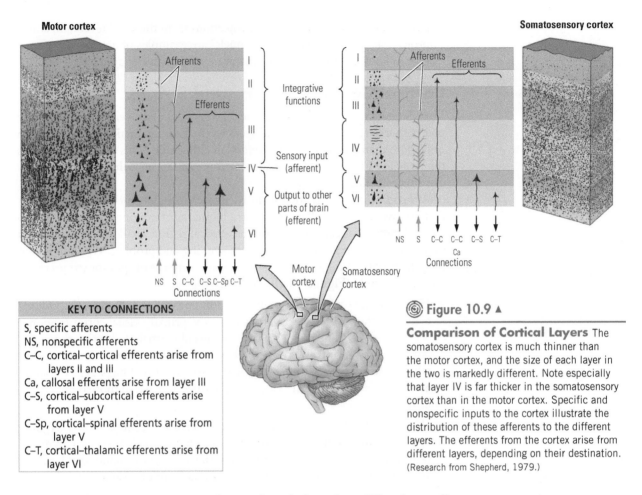

Motor cortex

Somatosensory cortex

KEY TO CONNECTIONS

S, specific afferents
NS, nonspecific afferents
C–C, cortical–cortical efferents arise from
    layers II and III
Ca, callosal efferents arise from layer III
C–S, cortical–subcortical efferents arise
    from layer V
C–Sp, cortical–spinal efferents arise from
    layer V
C–T, cortical–thalamic efferents arise from
    layer VI

Figure 10.9 ▲

Comparison of Cortical Layers The somatosensory cortex is much thinner than the motor cortex, and the size of each layer in the two is markedly different. Note especially that layer IV is far thicker in the somatosensory cortex than in the motor cortex. Specific and nonspecific inputs to the cortex illustrate the distribution of these afferents to the different layers. The efferents from the cortex arise from different layers, depending on their destination. (Research from Shepherd, 1979.)

Thus, the somatosensory cortex has a relatively large layer IV and a small layer V, whereas the motor cortex has a relatively large layer V and a small layer IV. **Figure 10.9** illustrates that the thickness of each layer corresponds to its function and shows that the various cortical layers can be distinguished by the neuronal elements that each contains. The superficial layers (II and III) receive inputs from other cortical areas and can thus integrate information coming to layer IV as well as that from other cortical regions.

Another feature of cortical organization illustrated in Figure 10.9 is that afferents to the cortex are of two general types, specific and nonspecific:

1. **Specific afferents** bring information (e.g., sensory information) to an area of the cortex and terminate in relatively discrete cortical regions, usually in only one or two layers. Specific afferents include projections from the thalamus as well as from the amygdala. Most of these projections terminate in layer IV, although projections from the amygdala and certain thalamic nuclei may terminate in the more superficial layers.

2. **Nonspecific afferents** presumably serve general functions, such as maintaining a level of activity or arousal so that the cortex can process information. They terminate diffusely over large regions of the cortex—in some cases, over all of it. Nonspecific afferents even release their transmitter substances into the extracellular space. Noradrenergic projections

from the brainstem, cholinergic projections from the basal forebrain, and projections from certain thalamic nuclei are examples of nonspecific afferents. (Figure 5.18 diagrams the major neurotransmitter systems.)

Cortical Columns, Spots, and Stripes

Most interactions between the cortical layers take place vertically, within the neurons directly above or below adjacent layers. Less interaction takes place with cells more than a couple of millimeters on either side. This vertical bias forms the basis for a second type of neocortical organization: **columns** or **modules** (see Figure 10.8).

Although these terms are not always interchangeable, the underlying idea is that groups of 150 to 300 neurons form minicircuits ranging from about 0.5 to 2.0 millimeters wide, depending on the cortical region. Evidence for some kind of modular unit comes principally from staining and probing. When the brain is cut horizontally and stained in special ways, patterns of spots or stripes in the cortex are visible (**Figure 10.10**). Some examples:

- If a radioactive amino acid is injected into one eye of a monkey, the radioactivity is transported across synapses to the primary visual cortex (region V1, or area 17). The radioactivity is not evenly distributed across the cortex, however; it travels only to places called *ocular dominance columns*, which connect with the affected eye (Figure 10.10A). The pattern of radioactivity seen in region V1 is a series of stripes, much like those on a zebra's coat.

- When a different technique is used, however, a different pattern emerges. If V1 is stained with cytochrome oxidase, which reveals areas of high metabolic activity by staining mitochondria, the area appears spotted. These spots, known as blobs, have a role in color perception (Figure 10.10B).

- Curiously, if the same stain is applied to area 18, a secondary visual region adjacent to V1, the pattern of staining looks more like stripes (Figure 10.10C) than like spots.

- If the primary somatosensory cortex (area S1) of a rat is stained with succinic dehydrogenase, the cortex shows a pattern of spots known as "barrels" (Figure 10.10D). Each barrel corresponds to a single vibrissa on the rat's face.

Figure 10.10 ▶

Cortical Spots and Stripes
Staining reveals modular patterns. (Research from Purves et al. Iterated patterns of brain circuitry [or how the cortex gets its spots *Trends in Neurosciences* 15(10):362–368, 1992 © Elsevier.)

(A) Ocular dominance columns in area 17

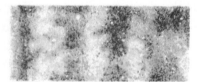

(C) Stripes in area 18

(B) Blobs in area 17

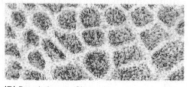

(D) Barrels in area SI

These examples illustrate that many types of cortical modules appear to exist and that the same stain shows a different modular organization in different regions.

A second way to demonstrate the cortex's modular organization is physiological. If a microelectrode is placed in the somatosensory cortex and lowered vertically from layer I to layer VI, for example, all the neurons encountered appear functionally similar. Neurons in each layer are excited, say, by a particular tactile stimulus (e.g., a light touch) in a particular part of the body (e.g., the left thumb).

The cells of layer IV are activated earliest by an afferent input, not surprising considering the direct afferent connections to this layer. Cells of the other layers must have longer latencies: they would have at least one more synapse on an interneuron in layer IV before receiving the sensory input. The pyramidal neurons of layer V are the last to be activated, again as we would expect, because the efferents are there (see Figure 10.8).

The functional similarity of cells across all six layers at any point in the cortex suggests that its simplest functional unit is a vertical column of cells that constitutes a minicircuit. Groups of these columns may be organized in somewhat larger units as well. If an electrode samples the cells of area 17, all of the cells in a column will respond to a line of a given orientation (for example, 45°). If the electrode is moved laterally across the cortex, adjacent columns will respond to successively different orientations (for example, 60°, 90°, and so on) until all orientations covering 360° are sampled. The pattern will then repeat itself. Thus, in the visual cortex, columns are arranged into larger modules.

As interesting as cortical spots, stripes, and columns are, considerable controversy continues over defining a module and what its presence means functionally. One problem is that although modules are apparent in primary sensory regions, they are less apparent in the association or motor areas of the cortex. Another problem is that if we are looking for a common definition of a module's dimensions, then the stripes and spots are a problem because they differ greatly in size.

Furthermore, closely related species often have very different patterns of spots and stripes, an oddity if they are fundamental units of cortical function. Although Old World monkeys have beautiful ocular dominance columns, for example, these columns are not found in New World monkeys, even though the visual abilities of the two groups are similar.

Semir Zeki (1993) suggested that the search for the basic module of cortical organization is like the physicist's search for the basic unit of all matter. The underlying assumption is that the cortical module might be performing the same basic function throughout the cortex. In this view, the evolutionary expansion of the cortex corresponds to an increase in the number of basic units, much as one would add chips to a computer to expand its memory or processing speed. This notion has some appeal, but we are left wondering what the basic function and operation of the cortical module might be.

Dale Purves and his colleagues (1992) offer a provocative answer. Noting that the spots and stripes on the cortex resemble markings on the fur of many animals, they suggest that though these arresting patterns may provide camouflage or broadcast sexual signals, such functions are secondary to the fur's fundamental purpose of maintaining body temperature. By analogy, the researchers propose that some modular patterns in the cortex may well correspond to

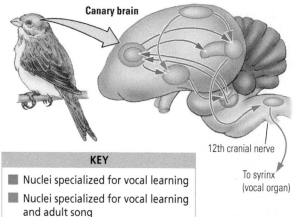

Canary brain

12th cranial nerve

To syrinx
(vocal organ)

KEY

■ Nuclei specialized for vocal learning

■ Nuclei specialized for vocal learning and adult song

Figure 10.11 ▲

Avian Neuroanatomy
Lateral view of the canary brain shows several nuclei that control vocal learning and their connections.

secondary functions of cortical organization. One suggested possibility: cortical modules may be an incidental consequence of synaptic processing in the cortex. As the cortex forms its intrinsic connections to process information, that is, one efficient pattern of connectivity is the vertical module.

The module certainly conforms to an important aspect of cortical connectivity, but it does not *cause* cortical connectivity. There must be an alternative way (or ways) of organizing complex neural activity that does not require a constant module. Consider the bird's brain (**Figure 10.11**).

Birds clearly exhibit complex behavior, and some, such as crows, are extremely intelligent, likely more intelligent than many mammals (such as mice). In spite of their complex behavior, birds lack a cerebral cortex. In their neural organization, different nuclei function rather like cortical layers. Thus we can see that although a cortical organization with columns is a useful arrangement, it is not the only way to organize a brain.

Clearly, a vertical component to cortical organization exists, but the structure and function of a basic module are difficult to define at present. Further, a single way of organizing cortical connectivity across all mammalian species and cortical regions seems unlikely.

Multiple Representations: Mapping Reality

Early ideas about visual, auditory, and somatic function in the cortex held that one or two representations of the external environment are responsible for our basic sensations. When Wilder Penfield and his colleagues stimulated their patients' motor and somatosensory strips at the Montreal Neurological Hospital in the 1950s, they identified two regions of the parietal cortex that appeared to represent localized body parts such as the leg, hand, and face (see Figure 9.4). These *homunculi* were seen as the cortical areas responsible for basic tactile sensations such as touch, pressure, temperature, and itch. Subsequent investigations of nonhuman subjects led to the identification of analogous maps of the visual and auditory worlds. Thus, half a century ago, most neuroscientists believed that the vast majority of the human cortex generally took part in complex mental analyses that we might loosely call **cognition** (knowledge and thought).

Doubt about this simple view of cortical organization arose in the late 1970s and the 1980s, however, as more-refined physiological and anatomical research techniques began to reveal literally dozens of maps in each sensory modality rather than just one or two. For example, between 25 and 32 regions in the monkey cortex have roles in visual functioning, depending on the definition used.

Although the somatosensory and auditory maps are less numerous in the monkey, about 10 to 15 cortical maps in each of these modalities do not duplicate the original maps but rather process different aspects of sensory experience. For example, visual areas are specialized for analyzing basic features such as form, color, and movement. Furthermore, many psychological processes, such as visual object memory and visually guided movements, require visual information.

Sensory Integration in the Cortex

In addition to the demonstration of multiple maps, areas were identified that function in more than one sensory modality (for example, vision and touch). These areas, known as **multimodal cortex**, or **polymodal cortex**, presumably function to combine characteristics of stimuli across different sensory modalities. We can visually identify objects that we have only touched, for example. This implies some common perceptual system linking the visual and somatic systems.

Until recently, neuroscientists believed that several distinct regions of multimodal cortex exist, but it is becoming increasingly clear that multimodal processing is surprisingly pervasive (for a review see Ghazanfar and Schroeder, 2006). **Figure 10.12** summarizes the multisensory areas in the monkey brain and shows that multimodal cortex is found in both primary and secondary cortex. The integration of information from different sensory systems (described as *sensory synergies* in Section 8.3) thus appears to be a basic characteristic of cortical functioning. The convergence of qualitatively different sensory information clearly alters our perception of the world.

Asif Ghazanfar and his colleagues (2005) nicely illustrate this point in a study of neurons in the monkey auditory cortex. When monkeys listened to a recording of another monkey's voice (a coo), the auditory neurons' firing rate increased by about 25% if the voice was accompanied by a visual image of a monkey cooing—but only if the voice and facial movements were in synchrony—the McGurk effect (see Section 8.3). The Ghazanfar study is consistent with our own perception that speech is easier to hear and understand if we can see the speaker's face moving synchronously with the sound.

Multimodal cortex appears to be of two general types, one related to recognizing and processing information and the other to controlling movement related to the information in some manner. This important concept suggests that we have parallel cortical systems: one system functions to understand the world and the other to move us around in the world and allow us to manipulate our world. This distinction is counterintuitive, because our impression is that our sensory and motor worlds are the same. We shall see that they are not.

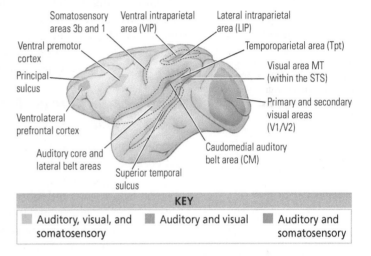

KEY

| ■ Auditory, visual, and somatosensory | ■ Auditory and visual | ■ Auditory and somatosensory |

Figure 10.12 ▲

Multisensory Areas in the Monkey Cortex Colored areas represent regions where anatomical and/or electro-physiological data demonstrate multisensory interactions. Dashed lines represent open sulci. (Research from Ghazanfar and Schroeder, 2006.)

Mapping Reality Through the Cortex

The emerging view is that the cortex is fundamentally an organ of sensory perception and related motor processes. This idea has an interesting implication: animals with more cortex must engage in more sensory processing than do animals with less or no cortex, and must perceive the world differently as well. Harry Jerison (1991) pursued this idea by suggesting that our knowledge of reality is related directly to the structure and number of our cortical maps.

As the number of maps in an animal's brain increases, more of the external world is known to the animal and more behavioral options are available to it.

For instance, animals such as rats and dogs, whose brains lack a cortical region for analyzing color, perceive the world largely in black and white. It must limit their behavioral options, at least with respect to color. Similarly, although it is difficult for us to imagine, dogs are among those species more focused on smell than we are and may know their world through object-specific olfactory images that are as useful to them as our visual images are to us.

Jerison suggested that cortical maps determine reality for a given species and that the more maps a species has, the more complex its internal representation of the external world must be. Thus, if humans have more maps than dogs, then our representation of reality must be more complex than that of a dog. Similarly, if dogs have more maps than mice, then a dog's understanding of the world is more complex than that of a mouse.

This viewpoint implies that the relative intelligence of different mammalian species may be related to the number of maps used by the cortex to represent the world. Dogs would have more olfactory maps than people have and would thus be more intelligent about smells, but the total number of maps in all sensory regions taken together is far greater in humans than in dogs.

Cortical Systems: Frontal Lobe, Paralimbic Cortex, and Subcortical Loops

Connections among cortical areas in a sensory system constitute only a part of all cortical connections. The four other principal connections in the cortical hierarchy are with the frontal lobe, paralimbic cortex, multimodal cortex, and subcortical connections and loops (**Figure 10.13**).

The frontal lobe can be subdivided into (1) primary motor cortex, forming the motor homunculus; (2) premotor cortex lying just in front of the motor cortex; and (3) prefrontal cortex, which occupies the remainder of the frontal lobe (see Figure 9.2). Most sensory regions' proprioceptive fibers connect directly to the primary motor cortex and may project to either the premotor or the prefrontal cortex. Premotor connections participate in ordering movements in time and controlling hand, limb, or eye movements with respect to specific sensory stimuli. Prefrontal projections take part in controlling movements in time and in forming short-term memories of sensory information (detailed in Section 18.5).

The **paralimbic cortex**—phylogenetically older than the neocortex—plays a role in forming long-term memories. It comprises roughly three layers adjacent and directly connected to the limbic structures (**Figure 10.14**). Paralimbic cortex can be seen in two places: (1) on the medial surface of the temporal lobe,

Figure 10.13 ▼

Levels of Cortical Organization The primary sensory cortex projects to interconnected sensory association regions. These regions project to several cortical targets—including the frontal lobe, paralimbic cortex, and multimodal cortex—and to a subcortical target, the basal ganglia. For simplicity, only one of the several levels of association cortex is illustrated here.

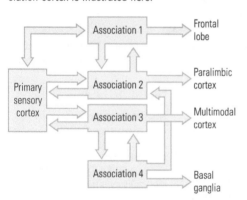

Figure 10.14 ▶

Paralimbic Cortex In these views of the rhesus monkey's cerebral cortex, the rusty color indicates the paralimbic areas in the frontal and temporal lobes and in the cingulate gyrus.

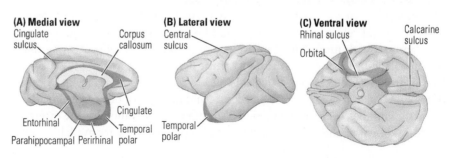

(A) Medial view
Cingulate sulcus
Corpus callosum
Entorhinal
Parahippocampal Perirhinal polar
Cingulate
Temporal

(B) Lateral view
Central sulcus
Temporal polar

(C) Ventral view
Rhinal sulcus
Orbital
Calcarine sulcus

where it is known as *perirhinal cortex, entorhinal cortex*, and *parahippocampal cortex*; and (2) just above the corpus callosum, where it is referred to as *cingulate cortex*.

The neocortex receives all of its sensory input from subcortical structures, either directly from the thalamus or indirectly through midbrain structures such as the tectum. These reciprocal cortical–subcortical connections are feedback loops, or **subcortical loops (Figure 10.15)**. Each level interacts and is integrated with higher and lower levels by ascending and descending connections. Subcortical loops connect the cortex, thalamus, amygdala, and hippocampus; an indirect loop with the striatum connects with the thalamus.

Subcortical loops presumably play some role in amplifying or modulating ongoing cortical activity. Consider, for example, how the amygdala adds affective tone to visual input. A ferocious dog may generate a strong affective response in us as it charges, in part because the amygdala adds affective tone to the visual threat of the dog. Indeed, in the absence of the amygdala, laboratory animals display absolutely no fear of threatening objects. Cats whose amygdala has been removed take leisurely strolls through rooms housing large monkeys, whereas no regular cat would even contemplate doing such a thing.

Cortical Connections, Reentry, and the Binding Problem

We have seen that the cortex has multiple anatomically segregated and functionally specialized areas. How does brain organization translate into our perception of the world as a **gestalt**—a unified and coherent whole? When you look at a person's face, for example, why do shape, color, and size combine into a coherent, unchanging image? This question defines the **binding problem**,

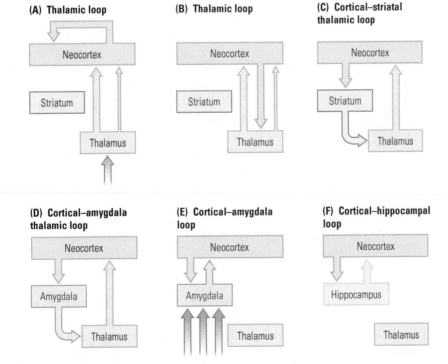

Figure 10.15 ◄

Subcortical Loops Parts (A) and (B) show two thalamic loops. Each feedback loop through the midbrain (parts C–F) presumably functions to modify ongoing cortical activity. Thickness of the arrows represents the relative size of the connections. The arrows into the amygdala in part (E) indicate various subcortical inputs to it.

which is focused on how the brain ties single and varied sensory and motor events together into a unified perception or behavior. How do sensations in specific channels (touch, vision, hearing, smell, and taste) combine into perceptions that translate as a unified experience that we call reality? Three possible solutions to the binding problem present themselves.

One is a high-order cortical center that receives input from all of the different cortical areas and integrates (binds) them into a single perception. Although this hierarchical idea makes sense, unfortunately no such area exists. A second solution is to interconnect all of the different cortical areas so that information is somehow shared. The problem here is that not all cortical areas connect with one another, not even within a single sensory modality. Various researchers have tried to determine the rules of connectivity, but these are beyond the scope of our discussion. (For details, see Felleman and van Essen, 1991; Pandya and Yeterian, 1985; and Zeki, 1993.)

Suffice it to say that only about 40% of the possible *inter*cortical connections within a sensory modality are actually found, which leads us to the third solution: *intra*cortical networks of connections among subsets of cortical regions. This idea has considerable appeal.

First, all cortical areas have internal connections among units with similar properties. These connections link neighboring neurons and synchronize their activity. Second, through a mechanism called **reentry**, any cortical area can influence the area from which it receives input (**Figure 10.16**A). This remarkable interactive aspect of cortical connectivity means that when area A sends information to area B, area B reciprocates and returns a message to area A (Figure 10.16B).

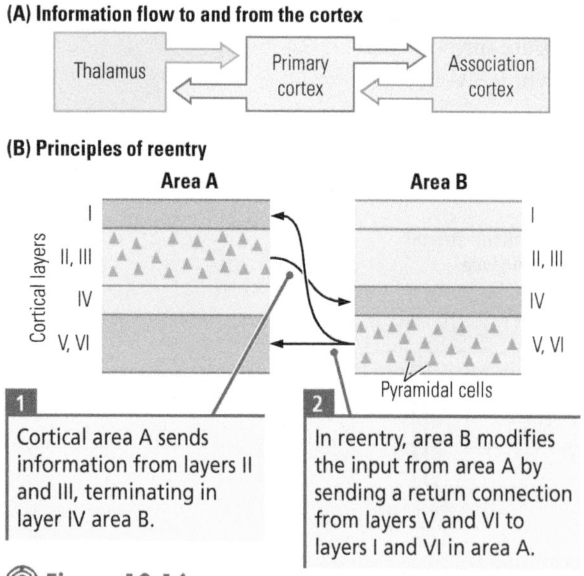

Zeki suggests that an area could actually modify its inputs from another area before it even receives them! An important point detailed in Figure 10.15B is that the connections from areas A and B do not originate from the same layers, suggesting that they play different roles in influencing each other's activity.

How can information flow through intra-areal and interareal connections and interaction through reentry solve the binding problem? Computer modeling suggests that the primary function of the neural connections is to coordinate activity within and between areas to produce a globally coherent pattern, or *integration*, over all areas of the perceptual systems.

Integration requires a way of binding the areas together briefly to form a unified percept. The computer models show that perceptual integration can be almost immediate, on a time scale of 50 to 500 milliseconds. (This concept of cortical organization is likely to be foreign to many readers. We recommend Zeki's readable book for a longer discussion.)

Jerison related the binding problem to his analogy of multiple cortical maps. The evolutionary expansion, in area, of the cortex has implications for a brain with multiple neurosensory channels that are trying to integrate information into a single reality. Because so many different kinds of sensory

(A) Information flow to and from the cortex

Thalamus → Primary cortex → Association cortex

(B) Principles of reentry

Area A   Area B

Cortical layers: I, II, III, IV, V, VI

Pyramidal cells

1 Cortical area A sends information from layers II and III, terminating in layer IV area B.

2 In reentry, area B modifies the input from area A by sending a return connection from layers V and VI to layers I and VI in area A.

Figure 10.16 ▲

Interareal and Intra-areal Connections

(A) Information from the thalamus goes to the primary cortex, which then projects to the association cortex. The reciprocal connections at each level represent feedback loops. (B) A receiving cortical area can modify the inputs that it gets from another area. Reentry holds for all levels of cortical–cortical connectivity.

information reach the cortex, it is necessary somehow to discriminate equivalent features in the external world. It would be useful to the brain to label these equivalencies and organize them.

Suppose that the brain creates labels to designate objects and a coordinate system to locate objects in the external world—that is, in space and time. Suppose also that some sensory information must be both tagged to persist through time (in memory) and categorized to be retrieved (remembered) when needed.

Labels, coordinates, and categories are products of cognition. Viewed in this way, Jerison's analogy of multiple cortical maps provides a basis for thinking about how the information that is arriving at the cortex is integrated into perception and organized as knowledge, thought, and memory. Indeed, injuries to discrete cortical areas alter the way that people perceive the world and the way that they think about it. In Section 13.5 we shall see that one form of sensory deficit, **agnosia** (literally, "not knowing"), renders a partial or complete inability to recognize sensory stimuli. Agnosias are unexplainable as subcortical deficits in elementary sensation or alertness.

◎ 10.3 Functional Organization of the Cortex

To Jerison, knowledge of the world constructed by the brain is the mind. As cortical maps develop, the brain must also develop the mind to organize those maps in a way that produces knowledge of the external world. It is a small jump to the idea that the next step in mental development is language. Language, after all, is a means of representing knowledge.

A Hierarchical Model of Cortical Function

Flechsig was the first to suggest using anatomical criteria to delineate a hierarchy of cortical areas, but Alexander Luria fully developed the idea in the 1960s. Luria (1973) divided the cortex into two functional units:

- The posterior cortex (parietal, occipital, and temporal lobes) is the sensory unit that receives sensations, processes them, and stores them as information (**Figure 10.17**A).

- The anterior cortex (frontal lobe) is the motor unit that formulates intentions, organizes them into programs of action, and executes the programs (Figure 10.17B).

◎ **Figure 10.17 ▼**

Functional Units of the Cortex (A) In traveling from primary to secondary to tertiary zones, sensation is elaborated and integrated into information. (B) Information from the sensory unit travels forward to tertiary motor zones, where it is translated into intention and then into patterns of action in the secondary and primary motor zones. (Research from A.R. Luria. 1973.)

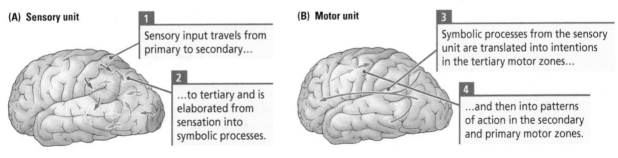

(A) Sensory unit

1 Sensory input travels from primary to secondary...

2 ...to tertiary and is elaborated from sensation into symbolic processes.

(B) Motor unit

3 Symbolic processes from the sensory unit are translated into intentions in the tertiary motor zones...

4 ...and then into patterns of action in the secondary and primary motor zones.

Both of Luria's cortical units are hierarchically structured, with three cortical zones arranged functionally, one above the other. The first zone corresponds to Flechsig's primary cortex; the second to the more slowly developing cortex bordering the primary cortex, labeled *secondary cortex* by Luria; and the third is the most slowly developing cortex, which Luria labeled *tertiary cortex*.

Luria conceived of the cortical units as working in concert along zonal pathways. Sensory input enters the primary sensory zones, is elaborated in the secondary zones, and is integrated in the tertiary zones of the posterior unit. To execute an action, activation is sent from the posterior tertiary sensory zones to the tertiary frontal motor zone for formulation, to the secondary motor zone for elaboration, then to the primary frontal zone for execution.

Consider a simplified example of Luria's model: You are walking along and come upon a soccer game. The actual perception of the movements of players and the ball is in the primary visual area. The secondary visual sensory zone recognizes that those activities constitute a soccer game. In the tertiary zone, the sounds and movements of the game are synthesized into the realization that one team has scored and is ahead and that the game has significance for league standings. By the time the information is integrated in the tertiary sensory zone, it is considerably richer than what we would think of as "sensory." Rather, it has become knowledge.

Information in the tertiary sensory zone activates the paralimbic cortex for memory processing and the amygdala for emotional assessment. These cortical events can then activate, in the tertiary zone of the frontal (motor) cortex, the intention to find a viewing spot and root for your team. The execution of this plan is formulated in the secondary frontal zones. The actual movements required to join the crowd are initiated in the primary motor zone of the frontal cortex.

Using the soccer game example, we can also describe the effects of brain lesions on levels of processing. A lesion in the primary visual zone that produces a blind spot in some part of the visual field might require the spectator to move his or her head backward and forward to see the entire game. A lesion in the secondary visual zone might produce a perceptual deficit, making the person unable to recognize the activity as a soccer game. A lesion in the tertiary sensory zone might make it impossible to abstract the significance of the game—that one team wins.

Damage to the paralimbic cortex leaves no memory of the event, and damage to the amygdala renders the person unresponsive to the event's emotional significance. A lesion in the tertiary motor area might prevent forming the intention to become a soccer player and join a club, buy a uniform, or get to practice on time. A lesion in the secondary motor zone might make it difficult to execute the sequences of movements required in play. A lesion in the primary zone might make it difficult to execute a discrete movement required in the game—for example, kicking the ball.

Evaluating the Hierarchical Model

Luria based his theory on three assumptions:

1. *The brain processes information serially*, one step at a time. Thus, information from sensory receptors goes to the thalamus, then to the primary cortex,

then to the secondary cortex, and finally to the tertiary sensory cortex. Similarly, output goes from tertiary sensory to tertiary motor, then to secondary motor, and finally to primary motor.

2. *Serial processing is hierarchical*: each level adds complexity that is qualitatively different from the processing in the preceding levels. The tertiary cortex could be considered a terminal station insofar as it receives input from the sensorimotor and perceptual areas and performs higher cognitive processes on that input.

3. *Our perceptions of the world are unified and coherent.* Luria's formulation was in accord with the commonsense view that some active process produces each percept, and, naturally, the simplest way to do so is to form it in the tertiary cortex.

The beauty of Luria's theory is that it used the then-known anatomical organization of the cortex to craft a simple explanation for observations that Luria made daily in his clinic and published in 1973. The difficulty is that its basic assumptions have been questioned by newer anatomical and physiological findings. Consider the following problems.

First, a strictly hierarchical processing model requires that all cortical areas be linked serially, but this serial linkage is not the case. We have seen that all cortical areas have reentrant (reciprocal) connections with the regions to which they connect: no simple "feed-forward" system exists. Furthermore, as noted in Section 10.2, only about 40% of the possible connections among different areas in a sensory modality are actually found. Thus no single area receives input from all other areas. This presents a difficulty in actively forming a single percept in one area.

Second, Zeki made an interesting point: because a zone of cortex has connections with many cortical areas, it follows that each cortical zone is probably undertaking more than one operation, which it relays to different cortical areas. Further, the results of the same operation are likely to be of interest to more than one cortical area. This would account for multiple connections.

These principles can be seen in the primary visual cortex, which appears to make calculations related to color, motion, and form. These calculations are relayed to the specific cortical regions for these processes. And the same calculation may be sent to subcortical as well as to cortical regions.

The fact that cortical operations are relayed directly to subcortical areas implies that cortical processing can bypass Luria's motor hierarchy and go directly to subcortical motor structures. Further, the fact that cortical areas can perform multiple calculations that are sent to multiple areas raises a question about what is hierarchical in the processing. Can we assume that areas connected serially are actually undertaking more-complicated operations? An area such as the primary visual cortex, which processes color, form, and movement, might be considered more complex than an area that processes only color.

Finally, Luria assumed that his introspection about perception being a unitary phenomenon was correct. It appears, however, that it is not. We can experience a single percept despite the fact that no single terminal area is producing it. This ability is the essence of the binding problem.

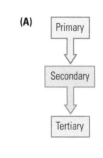

(A)

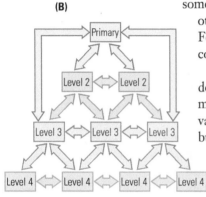

(B)

Figure 10.18 ▲

Two Hierarchical Models
(A) Luria's simple serial hierarchical model of cortical processing.
(B) Felleman and van Essen's distributed hierarchical model features multiple levels of association areas interconnected with one another at each level.

How can we put all of this knowledge together in a meaningful way to see organization in the cortex? Two logical possibilities exist. One is that there is no hierarchical organization but rather some sort of nonordered neural network. As individual organisms gain experiences, this network becomes ordered in some way and therefore produces perceptions, cognitions, and memories. Many neural-network models of brain function propose that this is exactly what happens. However, the results of a wealth of perceptual research suggest that the brain filters and orders sensory information in a species-typical fashion.

The other organizational possibility, suggested by Daniel Felleman and David van Essen (1991), is that cortical areas are hierarchically organized in some well-defined sense, with each area occupying a specific position relative to other areas but with more than one area occupying a given hierarchical level. Felleman and van Essen propose using the pattern of forward and backward connections to determine hierarchical position.

Thus, ascending (or forward) connections terminate in layer IV, whereas descending (or feedback) connections do not enter layer IV but usually terminate in the superficial and deep layers (see Figure 10.16B). Felleman and van Essen also recognize a third type of connection, columnar in its distribution and terminating in all cortical layers. This type of connection is uncommon but provides a basis for placing areas in the same location in the hierarchy.

By analyzing the patterns of connectivity among the visual, auditory, and somatosensory areas, Felleman and van Essen found evidence of what they call a *distributed hierarchical system*. **Figure 10.18** contrasts this model with Luria's model. Notice in Figure 10.18B the several levels of processing and, across the levels, interconnected processing streams that presumably represent different elements of the sensory experience. Note, too, that some connections skip levels and that the number of areas expands as the hierarchy unfolds.

A Contemporary Model of Cortical Function

The Felleman and van Essen model and the process of reentry illustrate that cortical connectivity is not a simple junction of one cortical module with another but rather a dynamic interplay between and among the operations of different regions. Thus, brain areas should be regarded not as independent processors of specific information but instead as areas that act conjointly, forming large-scale neural networks that underlie complex cognitive operations. (See review by Meehan and Bressler, 2012.)

A key principle in understanding cortical networks is the need to identify the anatomical connections that form networks as well as the functional correlations between cortical regions. The Human Connectome Project (www.human connectome.org) is an ambitious venture aimed at charting human brain connectivity using noninvasive neuroimaging in a population of 1200 healthy adults. When complete, the Connectome will provide a comprehensive description of the functional connections between every 1-cubic-millimeter gray matter location and every other 1-cubic-millimeter gray matter location (van Essen and Ugurbil, 2012). Given the human brain's size, the Connectome Project involves at least 100 investigators who expect to be working on it until the year 2020.

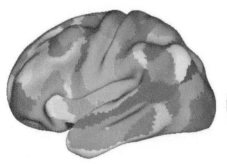
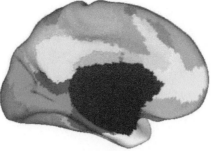

Left hemisphere, lateral view   **Left hemisphere, medial view**

Figure 10.19 ◄

Parcellation of Cerebral Cortical Networks An estimate of 17 cortical networks based upon rs-fMRI data from 1000 participants. Each color represents a network. Some, such as the deep blue auditory areas in the temporal lobe, are localized; others are widely distributed, such as the yellow regions, which reveal prefrontal–posterior parietal connectivity. (Image from Thomas Yeo and Fenna Krienen from Yeo BTT, Krienen FM, Sepulcre J, Sabuncu MR, Lashkari L, Hollinshead M, Roffman JL, Smoller JW, Zöllei L, Polimeni JR, Fischl B, Liu H, Buckner RL. The Organization of the Human Cerebral Cortex Estimated by Intrinsic Functional Connectivity *Journal of Neurophysiology* 106(3):1125–1165, 2011.)

The Connectome Project is based on the observation that a living brain is always active, and researchers have succeeded in inferring brain function and connectivity by studying fMRI signals when participants are resting, that is, not engaged in any specific task. This signal, *resting-state fMRI* (rs-fMRI, introduced in Section 7.4), is collected when participants are asked to look at a fixation cross and to keep their eyes open. The scanner collects brain activity, typically for at least 4-minute-long blocks.

Utilizing rs-fMRI data from 1000 participants, Thomas Yeo and colleagues (2011) parcellated the human cerebral cortex into 17 networks (**Figure 10.19**). The cerebral cortex is made up of primary sensory and motor networks as well as the multiple large-scale networks that form the association cortex. The sensory and motor networks are largely local: adjacent areas tend to show strong functional coupling with one another.

In Figure 10.19, the turquoise and blue-gray regions in the somatosensory and motor cortex and the purple region in visual cortex illustrate these couplings. In contrast, the association networks include areas distributed throughout the prefrontal, parietal, anterior temporal, and midline regions. The distributed yellow regions in the figure show prefrontal–posterior parietal connectivity. Some distributed networks, shown in light red, include temporal, posterior parietal, and prefrontal regions. As the Connectome Project progresses, these networks likely will be broken into much smaller units and similar maps will be generated for other species, such as mice.

◎ 10.4 Do Human Brains Possess Unique Properties?

Scholars who have looked for unique mental abilities in humans form a long tradition. Four allegedly unique abilities are grammatical language; phonological imagery—the ability to use language to make mental images; **theory of mind**, or social cognition—the capacity to understand another's mental state and to take it into account; and certain forms of intelligence, such as intuition. Although the nature and even the presence of such supposedly unmatched capacities remain debatable, we can ask whether the human brain has unique properties.

As discussed in Section 2.1, the human brain is relatively larger than those of other species, but all mammalian species have a common plan of cortical

Figure 10.20 ▶

Locations of von Economo Neurons
(A) The frontal insula at the border of the temporal lobe, the dorsolateral prefrontal cortex, and (B) the anterior cingulate cortex are among the areas that contain von Economo neurons. They bear the name of anatomist Constantin von Economo, who first described them in the 1920s. (Research from Allman et al., 2005 and Cauda et al., 2014.)

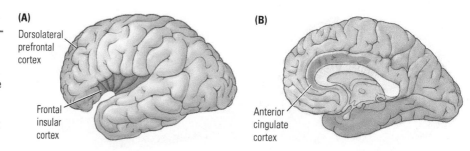

(A)
Dorsolateral prefrontal cortex

Frontal insular cortex

(B)
Anterior cingulate cortex

organization that evolution has modified to suit specific ecological niches (see review by Krubitzer and Kaas, 2005). Three characteristics of the human brain may be special, however.

First, humans have a higher density of cortical neurons than other mammals. The increased neuronal density means that the human brain actually has more neurons than animals with much larger brains, such as whales and elephants. As a result, the human brain possesses a relatively high processing capacity. But it comes at a metabolic cost. Suzana Herculano-Houzel (2012) suggests that our early ancestors solved the metabolic problem by cooking food: cooked food yields more energy than raw food.

The second special characteristic is a class of cortical neurons found only in humans; other great apes; and possibly in macaques, cetaceans, and elephants, but far most abundantly in humans (Cauda et al., 2014). These *von Economo neurons* are large bipolar neurons located in the dorsolateral prefrontal cortex and in deep layers of the insula, shown in **Figure 10.20**A, and in a lateral cortical region of the anterior cingulate cortex (Figure 10.20B).

Figure 10.21 ▶

Mapping Human Cortical Surface Expansion The color scale indicates how many times larger the human surface area is relative to corresponding areas in the macaque monkey. (A) Tertiary regions in the human frontal, temporal, and parietal cortex show the greatest evolutionary expansion. (B) Frontal, temporal, and parietal regions expand postnatally in humans nearly twice as much as other regions. (Jason Hill, et. al. Similar patterns of cortical expansion during human development and evolution, *PNAS*, 107(29):13135–13140, July 20, 2010.)

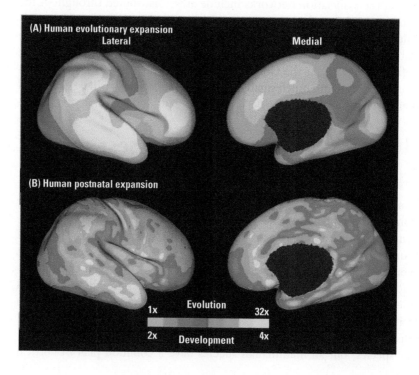

(A) Human evolutionary expansion
Lateral   Medial

(B) Human postnatal expansion

1x Evolution 32x
2x Development 4x

Von Economo neurons develop late in human ontogeny and only reach adult levels by about 4 years of age, possibly through the differentiation of some pre-existing cell type or even through neurogenesis. John Allman and his colleagues (2005) propose that von Economo neurons are associated with the emergence of theory of mind. Even more provocatively, Allman speculates that these cells fail to develop normally in people with *autism spectrum disorder* (ASD), leading to the faulty social intuition characteristic of the disorder (see Section 24.3). Thus, although human and nonhuman primate brains contain mirror neurons (see Section 9.1) that also have been related to ASD, humans have a disproportionate number of von Economo neurons. The broader distribution in humans and other great apes correlates with greater social cognitive abilities and self-awareness (see Section 20.6).

A final difference in the human brain has been the disproportionate expansion of human frontal, temporal, and parietal association areas relative to those of other primates (**Figure 10.21**A). Curiously, as shown in Figure 10.21B, these regions show the greatest postnatal growth as well, perhaps because they are not employed early in life and as a result are influenced more by postnatal experience than regions more mature at birth.

In sum, although humans do not evince any obvious, gross difference in brain organization from that of other mammals, the intrinsic organization of the human neocortex, including the presence of specialized von Economo neurons, may allow the emergence of mental capacities that are qualitatively different from those found in other mammals.

SUMMARY

Human neocortical function is of primary interest to neuropsychologists—the hierarchical levels of function in the CNS and the structure, functional organization, and connectivity of the cortex.

10.1 A Hierarchy of Function from Spinal Cord to Cortex

The functional levels in the CNS begin in the spinal cord and end in the neocortex, as demonstrated by study of animals that have undergone surgical removals of successively more brain tissue. See Figure 10.2 on page 257.

10.2 The Structure of the Cortex

The neocortex comprises two basic types of neurons—spiny and aspiny—organized into about six layers considered sensory, motor, and associational. Their vertical organization in columns, or modules, is revealed in the spots and stripes visible in specific histological preparations and in neuroimaging.

Multiple representations of sensory and motor functions exist in the cortex, and an evolutionary change in mammals has been an increase in their number. A characteristic of cortical connectivity is reentry: each cortical area is reciprocally connected with many other regions in a given sensory modality—but not all.

The cortex processes information about the world in multiple representations that are not formally connected, yet we perceive the world as a unified whole. This conundrum is the binding problem.

10.3 Functional Organization of the Cortex

Cortical activity is influenced by feedback loops not only from other cortical regions but also from subcortical forebrain regions such as the amygdala and hippocampus. Thus the cortex is functionally organized as a distributed hierarchical network. The Human Connectome Project is detailing this network's connectivity.

10.4 Do Human Brains Possess Unique Properties?

Although all mammals' general brain organization is remarkably similar, the frontal, temporal, and parietal association areas in the human brain have expanded disproportionately relative to those of other primates, and unique forms of human cognition seem to exist. One unique cell type, von Economo neurons, may hold the clue to the neural basis of these qualitatively different cognitions, such as social intuition in humans.

References

Allman, J. M., K. K. Watson, N. A. Tetreault, and A. Y. Hakeem. Intuition and autism: A possible role for von Economo neurons. *Trends in Cognitive Science* 9:367–373, 2005.

Bard, P., and M. B. Macht. The behavior of chronically decerebrate cats. In G. E. W. Wolstenholm and C. M. O'Connor, Eds., *Ciba Foundation Symposium on Neurological Basis of Behavior*. London: Churchill, 1958.

Barrett, R., H. H. Merritt, and A. Wolf. Depression of consciousness as a result of cerebral lesions. *Research Publications of the Association for Research in Nervous and Mental Disease* 45:241–276, 1967.

Bazett, H. C., and W. G. Penfield. A study of the Sherrington decerebrate animal in the chronic as well as the acute condition. *Brain* 45:185–265, 1922.

Berridge, K. C., and I. Q. Whishaw. Cortex, striatum, and cerebellum: Control of serial order in a grooming sequence. *Experimental Brain Research* 90:275–290, 1992.

Bignall, K. E., and L. Schramm. Behavior of chronically decerebrate kittens. *Experimental Neurology* 42:519–531, 1974.

Brackbill, Y. The role of the cortex in orienting: Orienting reflex in an anencephalic human infant. *Developmental Psychology* 5:195–201, 1971.

Cannon, W. B., and S. W. Britton. Pseudoaffective medulliadrenal secretion. *American Journal of Physiology* 72:283–294, 1924.

Cauda, F., G. C. Geminiani, and A. Vercelli. Evolutionary appearance of von Economo's neurons in the mammalian cerebral cortex. *Frontiers in Human Neuroscience* doi:10.3389, 2014.

Felleman, D. J., and D. C. van Essen. Distributed hierarchical processing in the primate cerebral cortex. *Cerebral Cortex* 1:1–47, 1991.

Flechsig, P. *Anatomie des menschlichen Gehirns und Rückenmarks*. Leipzig: Georg Thieme, 1920.

Ghazanfar, A. A., J. X. Maier, K. L. Hoffman, and N. K. Logothetis. Multisensory integration of dynamic faces and voices in rhesus monkey auditory cortex. *Journal of Neuroscience* 25:5004–5012, 2005.

Ghazanfar, A. A., and C. E. Schroeder. Is neocortex essentially multisensory? *Trends in Cognitive Science* 10:278–285, 2006.

Goltz, F. On the functions of the hemispheres. In G. von Bonin, Ed., *The Cerebral Cortex*. Springfield, Ill.: Charles C Thomas, 1960.

Grill, H. J., and R. Norgren. Neurological tests and behavioral deficits in chronic thalamic and chronic decerebrate rats. *Brain Research* 143:299–312, 1978.

Grillner, S. Locomotion in the spinal cat. In R. B. Stein, Ed., *Control of Posture and Locomotion*. New York: Plenum, 1973.

Herculano-Houzel, S. The remarkable, yet not extraordinary, human brain as a scaled-up primate brain and its associated cost. *Proceedings of the National Academy of Sciences U.S.A.* 109 Suppl 1:10661–10668, 2012.

Jerison, H. J. *Brain Size and the Evolution of Mind*. New York: American Museum of Natural History, 1991.

Jung, R., and R. Hassler. The extrapyramidal system. In J. Field, H. W. Magoun, and V. E. Hall, Eds., *Handbook of Physiology*, vol. 2, pp. 863–927. Washington, D.C.: American Physiological Society, 1960.

Krubitzer, L., and J. Kaas. The evolution of the neocortex in mammals: How is phenotypic diversity generated? *Current Opinion in Neurobiology* 15:444–453, 2005.

Luria, A. R. *The Working Brain*. Harmondsworth, UK: Penguin, 1973.

Meehan, T. P., and Bressler, S. L. Neurocognitive networks: Findings, models, and theory. *Neuroscience and Biobehavioral Reviews* 36, 2232–2247, 2012.

Oakley, D. A. Cerebral cortex and adaptive behavior. In D. A. Oakley and H. C. Plotkin, Eds., *Brain, Evolution and Behavior*. London: Methuen, 1979.

Pandya, D. N., and E. H. Yeterian. Architecture and connections of cortical association areas. In A. Peters and E. G. Jones, Eds., *Cerebral Cortex*, vol. 4. New York: Plenum Press, 1985.

Peters, A., and E. G. Jones. *Cerebral Cortex*, vols. 1–14. New York: Plenum, 1984–1999.

Purves, D., D. R. Riddle, and A.-S. LaMantia. Iterated patterns of brain circuitry (or how the brain gets its spots). *Trends in Neuroscience* 15:362–368, 1992.

Shepherd, G. M. *The Synaptic Organization of the Brain*, 2nd ed. New York: Oxford University Press, 1979.

Szentagothai, J. Architecture of the cerebral cortex. In H. H. Jasper, A. A. Ward, and A. Pope, Eds., *Basic Mechanisms of the Epilepsies*. Boston: Little, Brown, 1969.

Van Essen, D. C., and Ugurbil, K. The future of the human connectome. *NeuroImage* 62:1299–1310, 2012.

Whishaw, I. Q. The decorticate rat. In B. Kolb and R. Tees, Eds., *The Neocortex of the Rat*. Cambridge, MA: MIT Press, 1989.

Yeo, B. T., F. M. Fienen, J. Sepulcre, M. R. Sabuncu, D. Lashkari et al. The organization of the human cerebral cortex estimated by intrinsic functional connectivity. *Journal of Neurophysiology* 106:1125–1165.

Zeki, S. *A Vision of the Brain*. London: Blackwell Scientific, 1993.

11 Cerebral Asymmetry

| PORTRAIT | Words and Music |

M.S., a 25-year-old mother of two, had a lifetime history of epilepsy. Her seizures were well controlled by medication until after her second child was born. From that time on, she endured about one uncontrolled seizure a month on average. Neurological examination revealed a long-standing cyst in her left temporal lobe as the source of her seizures. M.S. agreed to neurosurgery to remove the cyst and the surrounding abnormal brain tissue.

Initially M.S.'s postoperative course was uneventful, and her seizures appeared to be cured. Unexpectedly, she developed an infection that proved resistant to antibiotics. Within a few days, M.S. suffered extensive damage to her left hemisphere. The illness left her unable either to produce or to understand language, a condition known as *global aphasia*. For weeks, the only words she could say were "I love

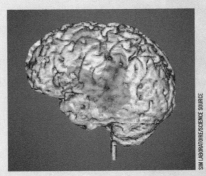

SIM LABORATORIES/SCIENCE SOURCE

you," and she said them to everyone she knew well.

The three-dimensional brain imaged here, constructed on the basis of fMRI and MEG scans, highlights the major left-hemisphere language areas and shows the brain's activity as a person repeats words. Broca's area (frontal operculum), working with the motor cortex, produces the movements needed for speaking. Wernicke's area (planum temporale) regulates language comprehension.

Although M.S. could not use or understand words, talk, or read, her ability to enjoy music was unimpaired. She could use words to sing and could tell immediately if the words in songs were wrong. She sang versions of songs that she had known before her surgery, but learning the words to new songs proved very difficult, Even so, M.S. could learn new tunes and hum along.

The single most curious feature of human brain organization is *cerebral asymmetry*: the left and right cerebral hemispheres have partly separate functions. Cerebral asymmetry is especially apparent in M.S.'s loss of language skills but maintenance of musical skills.

To set the stage for exploring cerebral asymmetry in humans, we address basic anatomical principles first. Next we examine neurological and behavioral research and compare findings between people with damaged brains and those whose brains are intact. In the concluding sections, we compare experimental results to brain scans, contrast sets of theories about cerebral asymmetry, and evaluate the quest to measure behavior. Then in Chapter 12, we examine the biological and environmental factors that produce variations in cerebral asymmetry.

11.1 Anatomical Asymmetries in the Human Brain

In Chapter 10 we focused on how an anatomical and functional hierarchy in the cortex leads to unity of experience and the idea of a mind. **Laterality**, the idea that the two cerebral hemispheres have separate functions, leads to the notion that two different minds control our behavior.

After more than 100 years of studying cerebral asymmetry, neuropsychologists now know that the hemispheres do perform separate functions. Typically, the left hemisphere plays a special role in producing and understanding language and in controlling movement on the right side of the body. The right hemisphere specializes in perceiving and synthesizing nonverbal information, including music and facial expression, and controls movement on the left side of the body.

Four fascinating variables complicate research on laterality:

1. **Laterality is relative, not absolute.** Both hemispheres participate in nearly every behavior; thus, although the left hemisphere is especially important for producing language, the right hemisphere also has some language capabilities.

2. **Cerebral *site* is at least as important in understanding brain function as cerebral *side*.** The frontal lobes are asymmetrical, but their functions are more similar to each other than they are to those of the posterior cortex on the same side. In the absence of neurological data, it is often difficult to localize lesions in neurological patients to one hemisphere even though the site of damage (frontal, say, rather than temporal or parietal) may be immediately obvious. Perhaps it is best to think of many cortical functions as localized and of hemispheric side as being but one feature of the localization.

3. **Environmental and genetic factors affect laterality.** The cerebral organization of some left-handers and females appears less asymmetrical than that of right-handers and males. (We elaborate on these factors in Chapter 12.)

4. **A range of animals exhibit laterality.** Functionally, asymmetry was once believed to be a characteristic related to language and unique to the human brain. Now we know that certain songbirds, rats, cats, monkeys, and apes also have functionally and anatomically asymmetrical brains.

Cerebral Asymmetry

According to John Hughlings-Jackson, Pierre Gratiolet (1815–1865) first observed in the 1860s that the cortical convolutions (gyri and sulci) on the left hemisphere mature more rapidly than those on the right. Anatomical asymmetry was described again later in the nineteenth century by many researchers, but these observations were largely ignored until the 1960s, when Norman Geschwind and Walter Levitsky (1968) described a significant anatomical asymmetry in the temporal lobes.

The **planum temporale** (Wernicke's area) lies just posterior to the primary auditory cortex (Heschl's gyrus) within the Sylvian (lateral) fissure (**Figure 11.1,**

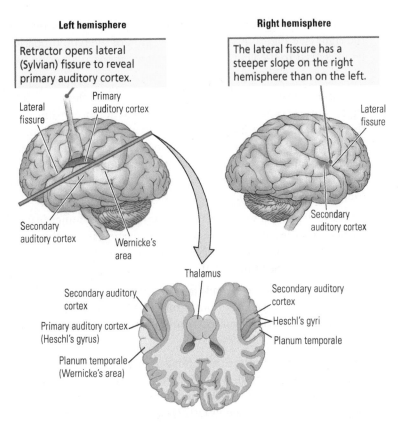

Figure 11.1 ◄

Anatomical Asymmetry
(Top) Viewed laterally, the slope of the lateral (Sylvian) fissure differs in the two hemispheres. (Bottom) The extent of the auditory areas and planum temporale are visible in this ventral view along the lateral fissures. The planum temporale is often larger in the left hemisphere than in the right, whereas two Heschl's gyri appear in the right hemisphere but only one in the left.

top). On average, in 65 of the 100 brains Geschwind and Levitsky studied, the planum temporale in the left hemisphere was nearly 1 cm longer than that in the right hemisphere. Their finding has been replicated by numerous investigators, with the percentage of persons having a larger planum temporale in the left hemisphere varying from 65 percent to 90 percent in different samples. In contrast, the neighboring primary auditory cortex (Heschl's gyrus) is larger in the right hemisphere, where two Heschl's gyri usually reside, compared with only one in the left hemisphere (Figure 11.1, bottom).

MRI scans of living brains confirm eight major anatomical differences between the two hemispheres:

1. The right hemisphere is slightly larger and heavier than the left, but the left contains more gray matter (neurons) relative to white matter (connections).

2. The marked structural asymmetry of the left and right temporal lobes may provide an anatomical basis for their observed specialization in language and in music functions, respectively. (See Geschwind and Levitsky, 1968.)

3. The anatomical asymmetry in the temporal lobes' cortex correlates with an asymmetry in the thalamus, shown in Figure 11.1, bottom drawing. This asymmetry complements an apparent functional asymmetry in the thalamus: the left thalamus is dominant for language functions. (See Eidelberg and Galaburda, 1982.)

4. The slope of the lateral fissure is gentler on the left hemisphere than on the right (see Figure 11.1, top). The region of the temporoparietal cortex lying ventral to the lateral fissure therefore appears larger on the right. (See Toga and Thompson, 2003.)

5. The *frontal operculum* (Broca's area) is organized differently on the left and right. The area visible on the brain surface is about one-third larger on the right than on the left, whereas the area of cortex buried in the region's sulci (ridges) is greater on the left than on the right. This anatomical asymmetry probably corresponds to the lateralization of these regions, the left side affecting grammar production and the right side possibly influencing tone of voice (prosody).

6. The distribution of various neurotransmitters is asymmetrical in both the cortical and the subcortical regions. The particular asymmetries in the distribution of ACh, GABA, NE, and DA depend on the structure under consideration. (See Glick et al., 1982.)

7. The right hemisphere extends farther anteriorly than does the left, the left hemisphere extends farther posteriorly than does the right, and the occipital horns of the lateral ventricles are five times as likely to be longer on the right as on the left.

8. Analysis of cortical surface area imaged in 69 brains that were combined into a single population-averaged brain reveals an unexpectedly broad pattern of asymmetries not visible in individual brains (**Figure 11.2**). David van Essen and his colleagues (2012) calculated the surface areas of multiple regions in each averaged hemisphere and found that, although the overall neocortical surface area was the same in both hemispheres, an overall pattern of asymmetry exists throughout the hemispheres. The largest asymmetries favor the left hemisphere in the Sylvian and medial temporal regions and the right hemisphere in the posterior parietal and dorsolateral prefrontal areas (Figure 11.2A), but an overall pattern of asymmetry was evident across the hemispheres (Figure 11.2B).

Figure 11.2 ▶

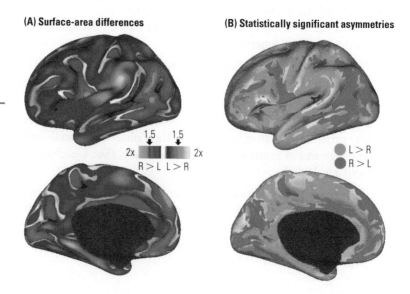

Surface Asymmetry Map (A) Differences in surface area of specific regions in the two hemispheres, averaged across 69 subjects. (B) The statistically significant asymmetries of the averaged hemispheres are illustrated by the color differences shown in the keys. For example, in part A, green, purple, and blue show difference effect sizes for the right hemisphere, which has more surface area than the left (R > L). (van Essen, D. C.; et al. Parcellations and Hemispheric Asymmetries of Human Cerebral Cortex Analyzed on Surface-Based Atlases. *Cerebral Cortex*, 22:10:2241–2262, 2012.)

In spite of the broad population-wide pattern of asymmetries, as a rule of thumb the largest anatomical asymmetries center on the temporoparietal language areas. Moreover, these asymmetries are present before birth, a finding that lends support to the proposition that language is innate in humans. It is thus tempting to speculate that asymmetries evolved to subserve language.

In fact, the brains of australopithecines (see Figures 2.3 and 2.4) shared many anatomical asymmetries with modern humans, but these hominids had no vocal apparatus that allowed language as we conceive of it. In addition, some asymmetries, such as a heavier and larger right hemisphere and a longer lateral fissure, can also be seen in many nonhuman primate species (see Section 12.4). **Table 11.1** reviews the range of reported anatomical asymmetries between the cerebral hemispheres in humans.

With all the emphasis on finding anatomical asymmetries associated with language, we hasten to point out, however, that the two hemispheres have the same surface area and that many regions of the right hemisphere are larger. It is not clear what has driven the right hemisphere advantages listed in Table 11.1. If the left hemisphere has asymmetries

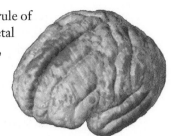

0.05
0.01
0.005
0.001
0.0005
0.0001
0.00002
P value

▲ MRI averaged from brain images of 20 participants shows areas of significant anatomical asymmetry. The greatest appears in the language zones, the least in the anterior temporal lobe and the dorsomedial frontal lobe. (Reprinted by permission from Macmillan Publishers Ltd: Dr. Arthur Toga, Laboratory of Neuro Imaging at UCLA, from Mapping brain asymmetry. *Nature Reviews Neuroscience* 4:37–48, 2003.)

Table 11.1 **Summary of studies demonstrating anatomical asymmetry**

Measure	Basic Reference
Asymmetries Favoring the Left Hemisphere	
Greater specific gravity	von Bonin, 1962
Longer lateral (Sylvian) fissure	Eberstaller, 1884; LeMay and Culebras, 1972
Larger insula	Kodama, 1934
Doubling of cingulate gyrus	Eberstaller, 1884
Higher proportion of gray matter	von Bonin, 1962; Gur et al., 1980
Thicker cortex	Luders et al., 2006
Larger planum temporale	Geschwind and Levitsky, 1968; Galaburda et al., 1978; Teszner et al., 1972; Witelson and Pallie, 1973; Wada et al., 1975; Rubens et al., 1976; Kopp et al., 1977
Larger lateral posterior nucleus	Eidelberg and Galaburda, 1982
Larger inferior parietal lobule	Lemay and Culebras, 1972
Larger area Tpt in auditory cortex	Galaburda and Sanides, 1980
Wider occipital lobe	LeMay, 1977
Longer occipital horn of lateral ventricles	McRae et al., 1968; Strauss and Fitz, 1980
Larger total area of frontal operculum	Falzi et al., 1982
Larger medial temporal lobe	Good et al., 2001
Asymmetries Favoring the Right Hemisphere	
Heavier	Broca, 1865; Crichton-Browne, 1880
Longer internal skull size	Hoadley and Pearson, 1929
Doubling of Heschl's gyrus	von Economo and Horn, 1930; Chi et al., 1977
Larger medial geniculate nucleus	Eidelberg and Galaburda, 1982
Larger area of convexity of frontal operculum	Wada et al., 1975
Wider frontal lobe	LeMay, 1977

related to language, then the right hemisphere must be specialized for some other function(s). After all, given that the two hemispheres are so similar, it is not as though language areas evolved on the left and nothing happened on the right.

Neuronal Asymmetry

Demonstrating gross morphological asymmetries in the human brain is a natural starting point in comparing the two hemispheres structurally. But remember that neurons carry out the brain's activities. Do neuronal structures differ on the brain's two sides?

Identifying structural differences among neurons in any two brain areas is a formidable task, in view of the sheer number of neurons. Nonetheless, Arnold Scheibel and his colleagues (1985) compared the dendritic fields of pyramidal cells in Broca's area, the left frontal operculum (LOP), with those in the facial area of the motor cortex in the left precentral cortex (LPC) and with homologous regions in the right hemisphere.

Their results show that neurons in each region have distinct patterns of dendritic branching, as diagrammed in **Figure 11.3**. The degree or pattern of branching is important, because each branch is a potential location for enhancing or suppressing graded potentials in the dendritic tree (see Section 4.4). More branch points allow the cell more degrees of freedom with respect to its function. Note the abundant branches in neurons in Broca's area (LOP), far more than in the other areas.

Figure 11.3 ▶

Neuronal Asymmetry
Differences in dendritic morphology in neurons in the left and right frontal operculum (LOP, ROP) and in the left and right precentral cortex (LPC, RPC).
(Information from Scheibel et al., 1985.)

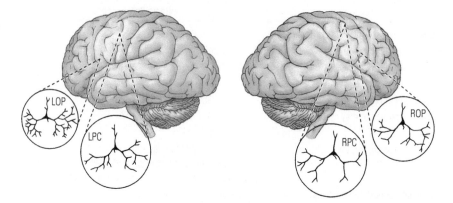

We must approach Scheibel's data on neural asymmetry with caution because the sample size was small ($n = 6$). However, five of the six brains were similar to the pattern shown in Figure 11.3. These five brains came from right-handers; the atypical brain came from a left-handed person.

Genetic Asymmetry

The Human Genome Project, completed in 2003, allows investigators to address the genetic regulation of cerebral asymmetry. Tao Sun and colleagues (2006) compared gene expression levels in the perisylvian regions of the left and right hemispheres of the fetal brain. They found genes that are expressed differently in the two hemispheres, and it is reasonable to predict that epigenetic changes may differentially influence the two hemispheres (e.g., Hrvoj-Mihic et al., 2013).

The mechanism whereby differential gene expression affects anatomical and functional asymmetry remains unknown, although the researchers suggest that some genes may regulate the production of growth factors that would, in turn, facilitate development of specific regions in one hemisphere or the other. A provocative idea is that the asymmetrical expression of genes may account for functional properties such as handedness, which to date has no clear-cut basis. (We return to this idea in Section 12.1.)

11.2 Asymmetries in Neurological Patients

Cerebral asymmetry was first established by studying patients with neurological disease, such as epilepsy, that is lateralized to one hemisphere. Improved neurosurgical treatment for such disorders has provided researchers with a large source of subsequently healthy people who are usually very willing to participate in neuropsychological studies. Current knowledge about both the lateralization and the localization of cortical functions, as reflected in this section, owes a great debt to these patients. Here we consider evidence that demonstrates functional lateralization, emphasizing studies of patients with lateralized lesions and those undergoing surgical disconnection of the hemispheres, brain stimulation prior to neurosurgery, and those in whom one hemisphere was anesthetized.

Patients with Lateralized Lesions

The oldest research on hemispheric specialization infers function from behavioral deficits that arise as a result of strokes or surgery. Such circumscribed, unilateral lesions in the left hemisphere of right-handed patients can produce aphasias that do not develop from lesions in the right hemisphere. The study of patients such as M.S. in the opening Portrait demonstrates that the functions of the two hemispheres are lateralized, or *dissociated*.

To conclude that the cortical area has a special or lateralized function, however, it is also necessary to show that lesions in other brain areas do not produce a similar deficit. In the strongest experimental method for demonstrating lateralization of function, called **double dissociation** by Hans-Leukas Teuber (1955), two neocortical areas are functionally dissociated by two behavioral tests. Performance on each test is affected by a lesion in one zone but not in the other.

Left-hemisphere lesions in right-handed patients consistently produce deficits in language functions (speech, writing, and reading) that are not produced by right-hemisphere lesions. Thus, the two hemispheres' functions are dissociated. However, performing spatial tasks, singing, playing musical instruments, and discriminating tonal patterns are disrupted more by right-hemisphere than by left-hemisphere lesions. Because right-hemisphere lesions disturb tasks not disrupted by left-hemisphere lesions and vice versa, the two hemispheres are doubly dissociated.

A similar logic is used to localize functions within a hemisphere. Behavioral tests that are especially sensitive to damage to a specific locus but not to others

Table 11.2 **Hypothetical double-dissociation behavioral test**

Neocortical Lesion Site	Reading	Writing
102	Impaired	Normal
107	Normal	Impaired

can be used. As illustrated in **Table 11.2**, two hypothetical cortical regions, 102 and 107, are doubly dissociated on tests of reading and writing: damage to area 102 disturbs reading, whereas damage to area 107 impairs writing. In principle, this logic can be extended to dissociate the functions of additional areas concurrently by triple dissociation, quadruple dissociation, and so on.

To illustrate the nature of lateralized functions in neurological cases, we contrast two patients. Neither was aphasic at the time of assessment. The first patient, P.G., a 31-year-old man, had developed seizures in the 6 years preceding his neurosurgery. When he was admitted to the hospital, his seizures were poorly controlled by medication, and subsequent neurological investigations revealed a large tumor in the anterior part of the left temporal lobe.

Preoperative psychological tests showed P.G. to be of superior intelligence, with the only significant deficits being on tests of verbal memory. Two weeks after surgery, psychological testing showed a general decrease in intelligence ratings and a further decrease in the verbal memory scores. Performance on other tests, including tests of recall of complex drawings, was at normal.

The second patient, S.K., had a tumor removed from the right temporal lobe. In contrast with P.G.'s test results, preoperative testing of S.K. showed a low score on recall of complex drawings. Two weeks after surgery, repeat testing showed a marked decrease in performance IQ rating and a decline in the nonverbal memory score, both for simple and for complex designs.

The comparison of these two patients' test results in **Figure 11.4** provides a clear example of double dissociation: subsequent to removal of the left temporal lobe, P.G. was impaired only on verbal tests, whereas subsequent to removal of the right temporal lobe, S.K. was impaired only on nonverbal tests. Furthermore, both patients performed at normal on many tests, providing evidence for localization, as well as for lateralization, of function.

⊚ Figure 11.4 ▼

Double Dissociation

Comparison of psychological test results for (A) patient P.G. after a left temporal lobectomy and (B) patient S.K. after a right temporal lobectomy. The respective regions removed, shown in pink, are as estimated by the surgeon at the time of operation. (Information from Taylor, 1969.)

(A)

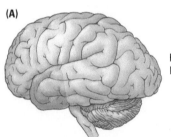

Left temporal lobectomy

Test	Preoperative	Postoperative
Full scale IQ	123	109
Verbal IQ	122	103
Performance IQ	121	114
Memory quotient	96[a]	73[a]
Verbal recall	7.0[a]	2.0[a]
Nonverbal recall	10.5	10.5
Card sorting	6 categories	6 categories
Drawings: Copy	34/36	34/36
Recall	22.5/36	23.5/36

[a] Significantly low score

(B)

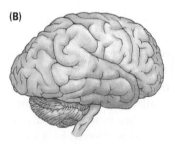

Right temporal lobectomy

Test	Preoperative	Postoperative
Full scale IQ	114	103
Verbal IQ	115	115
Performance IQ	110	89[a]
Memory quotient	121	101
Verbal recall	16.0	12
Nonverbal recall	7.5	5.5[a]
Card sorting	3 categories	3 categories
Drawings: Copy	31/36	28/36[a]
Recall	11/36[a]	13/36[a]

[a] Significantly low score

Commissurotomy Patients

Epileptic seizures may begin in a restricted region of one hemisphere and spread through the fibers of the corpus callosum (the commissure) to the homologous location in the opposite hemisphere. To prevent the spread of a seizure when medication has failed to impose control, **commissurotomy**, the surgical procedure of disconnecting the two hemispheres by cutting the 200 million nerve fibers of the corpus callosum, was performed first in the early 1940s by William Van Wagnen, an American neurosurgeon. The procedure's therapeutic outcome initially appeared too variable, and commisurotomy was abandoned until the 1960s, when research with monkeys and cats by Ron Myers and by Roger Sperry led neurologists to reconsider it (see Section 17.5).

At the time, two California surgeons, Joseph Bogen and Philip Vogel, performed complete sections of the corpus callosum and of the smaller anterior commissure in a new series of about two dozen patients with intractable epilepsy. The procedure was medically beneficial, leaving some patients virtually seizure-free afterward, with minimal effects on their everyday behavior. More extensive psychological testing by Sperry and his colleagues soon demonstrated, however, a unique behavioral syndrome that became a source of new insights into the nature of cerebral asymmetry.

Figure 11.5 illustrates the effect of commissurotomy on typical brain function. After sectioning, the two hemispheres are independent: each receives sensory input from all sensory systems, and each can control the body's muscles, but the two hemispheres can no longer communicate. Because functions in these separate cortexes, or **split brains**, are thus isolated, sensory information

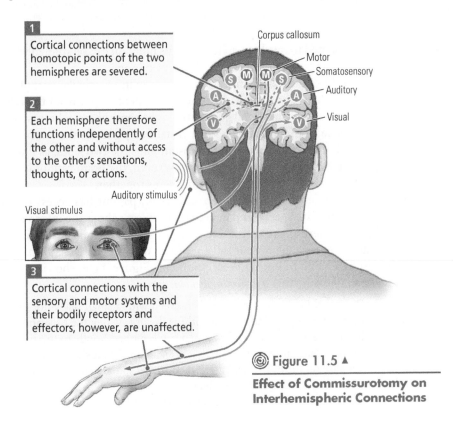

1 Cortical connections between homotopic points of the two hemispheres are severed.

2 Each hemisphere therefore functions independently of the other and without access to the other's sensations, thoughts, or actions.

3 Cortical connections with the sensory and motor systems and their bodily receptors and effectors, however, are unaffected.

Corpus callosum
Motor
Somatosensory
Auditory
Visual

Auditory stimulus

Visual stimulus

Ⓒ Figure 11.5 ▲

Effect of Commissurotomy on Interhemispheric Connections

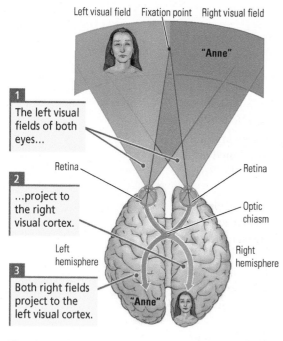

Figure 11.6 ▲

The Visual Fields Both visual fields—not both eyes—are represented in each hemisphere. The entire field left of the fixation point (red region) is represented in the right visual cortex, and the entire field right of the fixation point (blue region) in the left visual cortex.

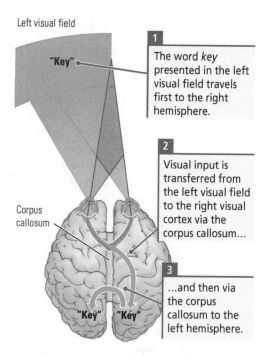

Figure 11.7 ▲

Connecting Both Sides of the Visual World The word *key* presented in the left visual field travels first to the right hemisphere, then through the corpus callosum to the left hemisphere. Commissurotomy prevents the transfer.

can be presented to one hemisphere, and its function can be studied without the other hemisphere having access to the information.

Figure 11.6 illustrates how information seen in a particular part of the visual world by both eyes is sent to only one hemisphere. Input from the left side of the world (the left visual field) goes to the right hemisphere, whereas input from the right side of the world (the right visual field) goes to the left hemisphere. A connection through the corpus callosum joins the two sides, as illustrated in **Figure 11.7**. With the corpus callosum severed, the brain cannot join the different views of the left and right hemispheres together.

When the left hemisphere of a split-brain patient has access to information, it can initiate speech and hence communicate about the information. The right hemisphere apparently has reasonably good recognition abilities but cannot initiate speech, because it lacks access to the speech mechanisms of the left hemisphere. The following description and **Figure 11.8**, showing a different example, illustrate this *split-brain phenomenon*:

> Patient N.G. . . . sits in front of a screen with a small black dot in the center. She is asked to look directly at the dot. When the experimenter is sure she is doing so, a picture of a cup is flashed briefly to the right of the dot. N.G. reports that she has seen a cup. Again she is asked to fix her gaze on the dot. This time, a picture of a spoon is flashed to the left of the dot. She is asked what she saw. She replies, "No, nothing." She is then asked to reach under the screen with her left hand and to select, by

Procedure

The split-brain subject fixates on the dot in the center of the screen while an image is projected to the left or right visual field. He is asked to identify what he sees.

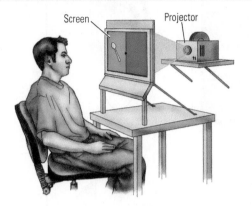

Screen   Projector

🅒 **Figure 11.8 ▲**

Split-Brain Phenomenon Basic testing arrangement used to lateralize visual and tactile information and allow tactile responses. (Information modified from S. P. Springer and G. Deutsch, *Left Brain, Right Brain: Perspectives from Cognitive Neuroscience*, 5th ed. New York: W. H. Freeman and Company, 1998, p. 37.)

Results

| If the spoon is presented to the right visual field, the subject verbally answers, "Spoon." | If the spoon is presented to the left visual field, the subject verbally answers, "I see nothing." |

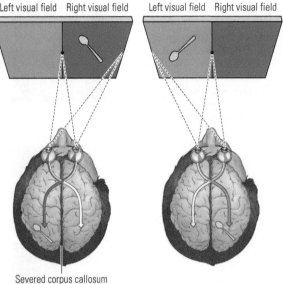

Left visual field   Right visual field   Left visual field   Right visual field

Severed corpus callosum

Conclusion

When the left hemisphere, which can speak, sees the spoon in the right visual field, the subject responds correctly. When the right hemisphere, which cannot speak, sees the spoon in the left visual field, the subject does not respond.

touch only, from among several items the one object that is the same as she has just seen. Her left hand manipulates each object and then holds up the spoon. When asked what she is holding, she says "pencil." (Springer and Deutsch, 1998, p. 36)

Patient N.G.'s behavior clearly demonstrates the different capacities of the two hemispheres when they are not interacting. The speaking left hemisphere could respond to the picture of the cup. The picture of the spoon was presented to the nonspeaking right hemisphere, and with the speaking left hemisphere disconnected from it, N.G. failed to identify the picture. The abilities of the right hemisphere were demonstrated when the left hand, controlled by the right hemisphere, picked out the spoon. But when asked what the still-out-of-sight left hand was holding, the left hemisphere did not know and incorrectly guessed "pencil."

The right hemisphere's special capacities for facial recognition also can be demonstrated in the split-brain patient. Jere Levy and colleagues (1972) devised the chimeric-figures test, which consists of pictures of faces and other patterns that have been split down the center and recombined in improbable ways. When the recombined faces shown in **Figure 11.9** were presented selectively to each hemisphere, split-brain patients appeared unaware of the gross discordance between the pictures' two sides. When asked to pick out the picture they had seen, they chose the face seen in the left visual field—by the right hemisphere—demonstrating that the right hemisphere has a special role in recognizing faces.

In summary, the results of careful and sometimes ingenious studies of commissurotomy patients provide clear evidence of the two cerebral hemispheres'

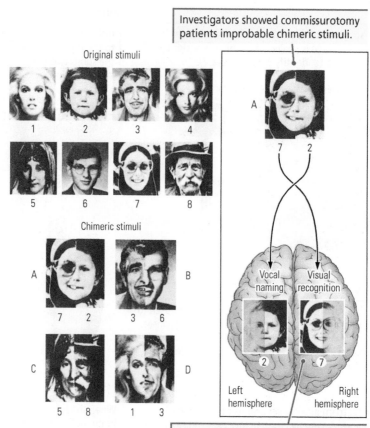

◉ Figure 11.9 ▶

Facial Recognition (Left) To produce chimeric stimuli, Levy and coworkers used photographs 1 through 8 to create composite pictures A through D. (Right) When asked to choose the face they had seen from the array of original pictures 1 through 8, split-brain patients chose the face that had been presented to their left visual field. (Levy, J., C. Trevarthen, and R. W. Sperry. Perception of bilateral chimeric figures following hemispheric deconnexion. *Brain* 95, pp. 61–78. Reprinted with the permission of Oxford University Press, Oxford.)

Original stimuli

Chimeric stimuli

Investigators showed commissurotomy patients improbable chimeric stimuli.

Vocal naming

Visual recognition

Left hemisphere

Right hemisphere

Asked to choose the face that they had seen from the array of original pictures, the patients chose the face that was presented to their left visual field.

complementary specialization. As interesting as these split-brain patients are, they represent only a tiny population, and their two hemispheres are by no means typical. Most had focal lesions, which caused the initial seizure disorder, and some may have had brain damage early in life, leading to a significant reorganization of cerebral function. Thus, generalizations and inferences must be made cautiously from these fascinating patients. We return to them in Chapter 17.

Brain Stimulation

In the early 1930s, Wilder Penfield and his associates at the Montreal Neurological Institute pioneered the use of neurosurgery for epilepsy in patients whose seizures were poorly controlled by drug therapy. The logic of this procedure is to remove the cortical region where the abnormal neural discharge originates. This therapeutic surgery is elective and so can be planned.

Considerable care is taken to ensure that cortical areas critical for controlling speech and movement are not damaged. To identify speech and movement areas and to localize the extent of the epileptogenic tissue, the surgeon stimulates the exposed cortex and records the conscious patient's responses, as

(A) Localizing an epileptogenic focus in the brain

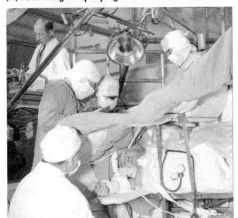

(B) Identifying critical cortical areas

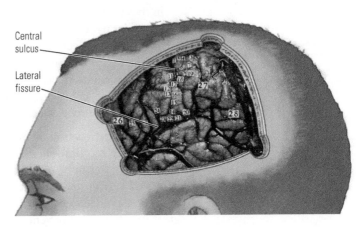

Central sulcus

Lateral fissure

Figure 11.10 ▲

Identifying the Brain's Speech and Movement Areas (A) The patient is fully conscious, lying on his right side with his brain's left hemisphere exposed, and kept comfortable with local anesthesia. In the background, the neurologist studies the electroencephalographic recording from the patient's cortex. The EEG will help to identify the source of seizures. (B) A drawing of the entire skull overlies a photograph of the patient's exposed brain at surgery. The numbered tags identify the points that the surgeon stimulated. The application of a stimulating electrode at points 26, 27, and 28, for example, interfered with speech. (Part A, Courtesy Penfield Archive, Montreal Neurological Institute, McGill University.)

illustrated in **Figure 11.10**. Careful study of hundreds of patients in Montreal by Penfield and his students and more recently by George Ojemann (1983) and his colleagues at the University of Washington provides clear evidence of cerebral asymmetry. Stimulation of the left hemisphere can block the ability to speak, whereas stimulation of the right hemisphere seldom does so.

Applying an electrical current to the cortex of a conscious patient has four general effects—three excitatory and one inhibitory:

1. **The brain has symmetrical as well as asymmetrical functions.** Stimulating the primary motor, somatosensory, visual, and auditory areas and pathways can produce, respectively, localized movements, localized *dysthesias* (numbness or tingling in the skin), light flashes, or buzzing sensations. These effects are typically evoked with about the same frequency by stimulating either hemisphere.

2. **The right hemisphere has perceptual functions not shared by the left hemisphere.** Stimulation can produce what Penfield called "interpretive" and "experiential" responses. That is, patients report specific "memories" in response to specific stimulation. These uncommon but often highly reliable phenomena include alterations in the patient's interpretation of the surroundings—déjà vu, fear, and dreaming states among them—and reproductions of visual or auditory aspects of specific earlier experiences. The phenomena usually arise from tissue showing epileptogenic discharge, but their occurrence reveals an asymmetry: stimulation of the right temporal lobe produces these phenomena more frequently than does stimulation of the left temporal lobe.

3. **Stimulating the left frontal or temporal region may accelerate speech production.** Ojemann suggested that this acceleration may result from a type of "alerting response" and may occur in other cognitive processes, especially memory, although this possibility is difficult to demonstrate unequivocally.

4. **Stimulation blocks function.** This sole inhibitory effect is apparent only when current is applied to left hemisphere temporofrontal areas while a patient is actively engaged in complex functions such as language and

memory. Only when current is applied while a patient is actively engaged in these behaviors is the inhibition apparent. Stimulating the same site in a quiet patient has no discernible effect. Speech disruption is a well-documented effect of left-hemisphere stimulation. Right-hemisphere stimulation, as Ojemann and his colleagues report, disrupts judgments of line orientation, facial expressions, and short-term memory for faces. These effects come almost exclusively from the right temporoparietal cortex, a result consistent with its presumed role in visuospatial behavior.

In summary, cortical stimulation has proved to be a useful tool in demonstrating both localization and lateralization of function. The effect of disrupting stimulation can be ultralocalized, often changing as the site of stimulation is moved even a few millimeters, and it is often very reliable for individual patients. An equally intriguing aspect of data from cortical stimulation is the great variation from patient to patient in the exact location and extent of sites with particular effects on behavior. One can speculate that this variation forms a basis for individual differences in skills because people presumably have different amounts of cortex assigned to particular functions.

Carotid Sodium Amobarbital Injection

Language is usually located in the left hemisphere, but in a small percentage of people, most of them left-handed, the right hemisphere houses language. In the event of elective surgery, preventing inadvertent damage to the speech zones requires that the surgeon be certain of their location. To achieve certainty in doubtful cases, Jun Wada and Theodore Rasmussen (1960) pioneered the technique of injecting sodium amobarbital into the carotid artery to produce a brief period of anesthesia of the ipsilateral hemisphere, as shown in **Figure 11.11**. Today, surgeons normally make injections through a catheter inserted into the femoral artery.

The Wada test results in unequivocal localization of speech, because injection into the speech hemisphere arrests speech for up to several minutes; as speech returns, it is characterized by aphasic errors. Injection into the nonspeech hemisphere may produce no speech arrest or only brief arrest. The advantage of this procedure is that each hemisphere can be studied separately in the functional absence of the anesthetized one. Because the anesthesia lasts several minutes, a variety of functions, including memory and movement, can be studied to determine the capabilities of one hemisphere while the other is anesthetized.

In a typical Wada test, a patient is given a "dry run" to become familiar with the behavioral tests that will be conducted during and after the drug injection. This dry run establishes a baseline performance level against which to compare postinjection performance. The patient is then given a series of simple tasks entailing immediate and delayed memory for both verbal (sentences

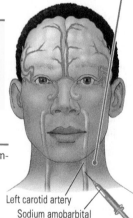

Injecting the left carotid artery briefly anesthetizes the left hemisphere. The person cannot speak, move the right arm, or see on the right visual field. The right hemisphere is awake but for most people is nondominant for speech, so the patient can neither speak nor later report on the experience.

Injection into the right side produces sensory and motor symptoms on the left but no speech disturbance, unless the patient's right hemisphere is dominant for speech.

Figure 11.11 ▲

The Wada Test To avoid damaging speech zones in patients about to undergo brain surgery, surgeons inject sodium amobarbital into the carotid artery. The drug anesthetizes the hemisphere on the side where it is injected (here, the left hemisphere), allowing the surgeon to determine whether that hemisphere is dominant for speech.

Left carotid artery
Sodium amobarbital

or words) and nonverbal (photographs of faces or objects) material, for the same purpose.

Moments before the drug is injected, the supine patient raises both arms and wiggles the fingers and toes. The patient is asked to start counting from 1, and, without warning, the neurosurgeon injects the drug through the catheter for 2 to 3 seconds. Within seconds, dramatic changes in behavior are apparent.

The contralateral arm falls to the bed with flaccid paralysis, and a firm pinch of the skin of the affected limbs elicits no response whatever. If the injected hemisphere is nondominant for speech, the patient may continue to count and carry out the verbal tasks while the temporary hemiparesis is present. Often the patient appears confused and is silent for as long as 20 to 30 seconds but can typically resume speech with urging. When the injected hemisphere is dominant for speech, the patient typically stops talking and remains completely aphasic until recovery from the hemiparesis is well along, usually in 4 to 10 minutes.

Speech is tested by asking the patient to name several common objects presented in quick succession, to count and recite the days of the week forward and backward, and to perform simple object naming and spelling. In addition to aphasia and paresis, patients with anesthesia of either hemisphere are totally nonresponsive to visual stimulation in the contralateral visual field. For example, there is no reflexive blinking or orientation toward suddenly looming objects.

The sodium amobarbital test, like direct brain stimulation, has proved invaluable in determining which hemisphere controls speech. In a series of studies, Brenda Milner and her colleagues (e.g., Rasmussen & Milner, 1977) demonstrated that about 98 percent of right-handers and 70 percent of left-handers show speech disturbance after sodium amobarbital injection into the left hemisphere but not after injection into the right hemisphere. Curiously, roughly 2 percent of the speech functions of right-handers are lateralized to the right cerebral hemisphere, which is roughly the proportion of right-handed people who show aphasia from right-hemisphere lesions.

This finding reminds us that speech is found, albeit rarely, in the right hemisphere of right-handed people. The results for left-handed patients support the view that the pattern of speech representation is less predictable in left-handed and ambidextrous subjects than in right-handers but that the majority of left-handers do have speech represented in the left hemisphere.

Whereas none of the right-handers studied by Milner showed evidence of bilateral speech organization, 15 percent of the non-right-handers displayed some significant speech disturbance subsequent to sodium amobarbital injection on either side. These patients' language functions probably were not symmetrically duplicated in the two hemispheres. Injection of one hemisphere tended to disrupt naming (for example, naming the days of the week), whereas injection of the other hemisphere disrupted serial ordering (for example, ordering the days of the week).

Hence, although people may have bilateral speech representation, it is probably asymmetrical and need not imply that the person has "two left hemispheres." Further study of these patients would probably reveal that visuospatial functions are bilaterally and asymmetrically represented as well, although it is mere conjecture on our part.

11.3 Behavioral Asymmetries in the Intact Brain

Studies of neurological patients demonstrate clear differences between the effects of lesions in the two hemispheres, particularly in language control. The reasons for these differences are not so clear, however, because many problems arise from making inferences about typical brain functioning from clinical results of dysfunctioning brains.

The fact that a specific behavioral symptom is associated with damage to a particular brain area does not necessarily mean that the region once controlled the disrupted function. For example, the fact that a left-hemisphere stroke in the "language areas" disrupts language function in 98 percent of right-handers does not mean that the left hemisphere's function is language. Rather, it means that the left hemisphere executes instructions required for typical language functions.

What are these functions? One experimental approach is to study the typical brain noninvasively and to make inferences about its component functions from the behavior produced by each component. The most common behavioral approach is the laterality experiment, which takes advantage of the sensory and motor systems' anatomical organization to "trick" the brain into revealing its mode of operation. Laterality studies, then, are designed to determine which side of the brain controls various functions. Laterality studies have problems of their own, however, as we shall see.

Asymmetry in the Visual System

The visual system's organization provides an opportunity to present each hemisphere selectively with specific visual information. As shown in Figure 11.6, stimuli in the right visual field travel to the left visual cortex, whereas stimuli in the left visual field project to the right visual cortex. Using a special instrument called a *tachistoscope*, visual information can be presented to each visual field independently.

Participants fixate on a center point marked by a dot or cross (see Figure 11.8). An image is then flashed in one visual field for about 50 milliseconds—briefly enough to allow the image to be processed before the eyes can shift from the fixation point. By comparing the accuracy with which information from the two visual fields is processed, investigators can infer which hemisphere is best suited to processing different types of information.

The simple conclusion to be drawn from the results of more than 50 years of tachistoscopic studies is that information presented to only one visual field is processed most efficiently by the hemisphere specialized to receive it. Words presented to the verbal left hemisphere, therefore, are processed more efficiently than are words presented to the nonverbal right hemisphere. Similarly, a left-visual-field advantage is found for faces and other visuospatial stimuli thought to be processed by the right hemisphere. These results with control participants are consistent with those demonstrated anatomically with neurological patients and reinforce evidence favoring a fundamental difference in the two hemispheres' perceptual processes.

Asymmetry in the Auditory System

The auditory system is not as completely crossed as the visual, because both hemispheres receive projections from each ear (review Figure 8.12). The crossed auditory connections are more numerous, however, and more rapidly conducting than are the ipsilateral projections.

In the early 1960s, Doreen Kimura studied neurological patients while they performed **dichotic-listening tasks**, such as the one illustrated in **Figure 11.12**. In a different task, Kimura presented pairs of spoken digits (say, "2" and "6") simultaneously through headphones, but one digit only was heard in each ear. The subjects heard three pairs of digits, then were asked to recall as many of the six digits as possible, in any order. Kimura noticed that subjects recalled more digits that had been presented to the right ear than to the left.

(A) Monaural presentation

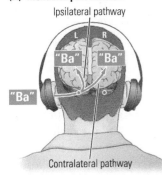 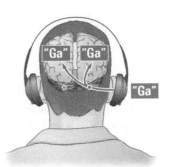

(B) Dichotic presentation

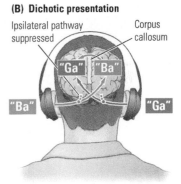

⊚ Figure 11.12 ▲

Kimura's Dichotic Listening Model

(A) Information played to either ear reaches both hemispheres by both ipsilateral and contra- lateral pathways. (B) In dichotic presentation, the contralateral pathways have preferred access to the hemisphere, possibly because the ipsilateral pathways are sup- pressed. Thus, the syllable "ba" presented to the left ear can gain access to the left hemisphere only through the corpus cal- losum. If the callosum is cut, the patient can only report hearing "ga." (Information modified from S. P. Springer and G. Deutsch, *Left Brain, Right Brain: Perspectives from Cognitive Neuroscience*, 5th ed. New York: W. H. Freeman and Company, 1998, p. 99.)

This result led Kimura to propose that when different stimuli are presented simultaneously to each ear, the pathway from the right ear to the speaking hemisphere has preferred access, and the ipsilateral pathway from the left ear is relatively suppressed. Thus, during a dichotic task the stimulus to the left ear must first travel to the right hemisphere then across the cerebral commissures to the left hemisphere. This longer route puts the left ear at a disadvantage, and words played to the right ear are recalled more accurately.

Having found a right-ear advantage for perceiving dichotically presented speech stimuli, the next step was to search for tasks that gave a left-ear superi- ority. In 1964, Kimura reported just such an effect in the perception of melo- dies. Two excerpts of instrumental chamber music were played simultaneously through headphones, one to each ear. After each pair, four excerpts (including the two that had been played dichotically) were presented binaurally (to both ears). The participant's task was to identify the two that had been heard previ- ously. Amazingly, Kimura found a left-ear advantage on this task.

Not all participants show the expected ear advantages in dichotic studies; the effects are not large when they are found (seldom exceeding a twofold difference in accuracy in the two ears); and dichotic results are apparently affected by various contextual and practice effects. Nonetheless, the Kimura studies are seminal in laterality research because her behavioral methods complement results from the neurological literature (**Table 11.3**). As a result, her research opened up an entire field of experimentation to anyone with imagination and a stereo audio device.

Table 11.3 **Ear advantages for various dichotic signals**

Neuropsychological Test	Basic Reference	Neuropsychological Test	Basic Reference
Tests Showing a Right-Ear Advantage		**Tests Showing a Left-Ear Advantage**	
Digits	Kimura, 1961	Melodies	Kimura, 1964
Words	Kimura, 1967	Musical chords	Gelfand et al., 1980
Nonsense syllables	Kimura, 1967	Environmental sounds	Curry, 1967
Formant transitions	Lauter, 1982	Emotional sounds and hummed melodies	King and Kimura, 1972
Backward speech	Kimura and Folb, 1968		
Morse code	Papcun et al., 1974	Tones processed independently of linguistic content	Zurif, 1974
Difficult rhythms	Natale, 1977		
Tone used in linguistic decisions	Zurif, 1974	Complex pitch perception	Sidtis, 1982
Tonal sequences with frequency transitions	Halperin et al., 1973	**Tests Showing No Ear Advantage**	
		Vowels	Blumstein et al., 1977
Ordering temporal information	Divenyi and Efron, 1979	Isolated fricatives	Darwin, 1974
Movement-related tonal signals	Sussman, 1979	Rhythms	Gordon, 1970
		Nonmelodic hums	Van Lancker and Fromkin, 1973

Data source: Noffsinger (1985).

More importantly, Kimura's experiments provide a noninvasive technique for identifying the hemisphere dominant for language—a question of special clinical importance, particularly in left-handed patients. And the dichotic test has other clinical uses. It turns out that patients with left-temporal-lobe damage perform dismally on this task. Patients with damage to the corpus callosum exhibit an almost complete inhibition of words presented to the left ear, even though they can recall words presented to this ear if there is no competing stimulus to the right ear.

Kimura's experiments imply that the left hemisphere is specialized for processing language-related sounds, whereas the right hemisphere processes music-related sounds. There is, however, another interpretation: the asymmetry could be related to the temporal or spectral structure of the sounds—their rhythm and frequency—rather than to language and music per se.

Consider, for example, the finding by George Papcun and colleagues (1974), which showed that Morse-code operators have a right-ear superiority in perceiving the code, even though the sounds are distinguished only by their temporal structures. The results of this study might be taken as evidence that the left hemisphere is specialized not so much for language as for "something else." One possibility is analyzing signals with a complex temporal microstructure. We return to this idea in Section 11.5.

Asymmetry in the Somatosensory System

Experiments on laterality in somatosensation are not as numerous as those on vision and audition. The primary somatosensory system, illustrated in **Figure 11.13**, is almost completely crossed, which allows an easy behavioral comparison of the two sides by testing right and left limbs separately. By blindfolding participants and requiring them to perform various tasks separately with

Figure 11.13 ▼

Primary Sensorimotor Cortex

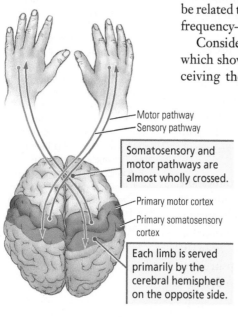

Motor pathway
Sensory pathway

Somatosensory and motor pathways are almost wholly crossed.

Primary motor cortex

Primary somatosensory cortex

Each limb is served primarily by the cerebral hemisphere on the opposite side.

each hand, for example, investigators can identify differences in each hand's efficiency—differences that can be taken to imply functional asymmetry in cerebral organization.

One line of somatosensory research compares the performance of the left and right hands in recognizing shapes, angles, and patterns. The left hand of right-handed participants is superior at nearly all tasks of this type. Both blind and sighted participants read Braille more rapidly with the left hand (Rudel et al., 1974). Some blind children read fluently with the left hand but are totally unable to read with the right. Because Braille patterns are spatial configurations of dots, this observation is congruent with the proposed right-hemisphere role in processing spatial information, a role not shared by the left hemisphere.

A second type of somatosensory test employs an analog of the dichotic-listening procedure, the **dichaptic test**. Participants feel objects, then look at an array of objects and select those that they previously touched. Using this task, Candace Gibson and Philip Bryden (1983) presented children with cutouts of irregular shapes or letters made of sandpaper, which were moved slowly across the fingertips. Their children showed a right-hand advantage for identifying letters and a left-hand advantage for identifying other shapes.

Asymmetry in the Motor System

Neuroscientists have long known that left-hemisphere lesions can produce **apraxia**—severe deficits in making or copying voluntary movement sequences. The logic of studying asymmetry in intact sensory systems reasonably extends to looking for asymmetries in motor control. A difficulty immediately confronts researchers, however: because an asymmetry exists in processing sensory input, studying motor asymmetries is potentially confounded by the fact that the two sides do not start off equal.

For example, if we found that the right hand reacts to verbal stimuli faster than the left hand, we could not conclude that this difference is due to motor asymmetry itself. It could be entirely due to perceptual asymmetry. To overcome such potential pitfalls, two types of experiments have been devised to assess motor asymmetries: (1) direct observation and (2) interference tasks.

Direct Observation

If asymmetry in movement control is inherent, it might be observable as people engage in behaviors that do not require a manual response. For example, perhaps the right hand is more active while performing verbal tasks, whereas the left hand is more active when performing nonverbal tasks, such as listening to music.

To examine this possibility, Kimura and Humphrys (1981) videotaped participants talking or humming. They found that right-handed people tend to gesture with their right hands when talking but are equally likely to scratch themselves, rub their noses, or touch their bodies with either hand. Kimura interpreted the observed gesturing with the limb contralateral to the speaking hemisphere as indicating a relation between speech and certain manual activities.

Differences in gesturing, which favor the right hand in right-handed participants, could simply be due to a difference in preferred hand rather than to functional asymmetry in motor control. Thus, another series of observational studies compared hand-movement asymmetries during analogous verbal and nonverbal tasks.

The procedure consisted of videotaping right-handed participants as they assembled blocks in three tests. The first, a "neutral task," required participants to combine white blocks to form a five-by-five matrix. The second test, a "verbal task," required participants to combine blocks with letters on them in a series of crossword-puzzle tasks. In the third test, a "nonverbal task," participants assembled jigsaw puzzles with the same size blocks as those used in the two preceding tests.

Analysis of the movements showed that in the neutral task, participants manipulated blocks with the right hand while supporting them with the left. Other movements seldom occurred. In the verbal test, most task-directed movements showed a right-hand preference. But in the nonverbal test, task-directed movements showed a leftward shift from the neutral condition, with the right-handed participants now making far more movements with the left hand. These results suggest that the two hemispheres may have complementary roles in movement control—an asymmetry moderated by a native hand preference.

A second directly observed motor asymmetry was reported in performing complex mouth movements. Marilyn Wolf and Melvyn Goodale (1987) performed single-frame analyses of videotaped mouth movements produced when people make verbal or nonverbal sounds. **Figure 11.14** illustrates their principal finding: the right side of the mouth opens more widely and more quickly than the left side for both verbal and nonverbal tasks. These observations support the idea that the left hemisphere has a special role in selecting, programming, and producing verbal and nonverbal oral movements.

Is there an analogous role for the right hemisphere? Indeed there is. Considerable evidence shows that the left side of the face displays emotions more strongly than the right side, and Wylie and Goodale (1988) showed that the onset of facial expressions occurs sooner on the left side of the face. Thus, it is not movement control itself that is asymmetrical but rather its function: movement for a particular purpose.

Interference Tasks

A variety of interference tasks (in common parlance, *multitasking*) examine a well-known phenomenon manifested by most people: performing two complex tasks at the same time is difficult. Perhaps the most interesting interference study known to us is an unpublished experiment by Robert Hicks and Marcel Kinsbourne. They persuaded several unemployed musicians to come to their laboratory daily to play the piano.

The task was to learn a different piece of music with each hand, then play the two pieces simultaneously. When the musicians had mastered this very difficult task, the experimenters asked them to speak or to hum while playing. Speaking disrupted playing with the right hand, and humming disrupted playing with the left hand.

Interference studies provide a useful way to study the roles of the two hemispheres in controlling movement, but much more work is needed before researchers can identify the hemispheres' complementary roles (see reviews by Murphy and Peters, 1994, and by Caroselli et al., 1997). Identifying which types of movements each hemisphere is especially good at controlling will be

(A) Start of speaking "ma"

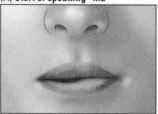

(B) 67 ms later

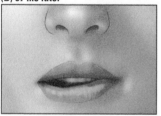

Figure 11.14 ▲

Motor Asymmetry
Successive video frames illustrate that the right side of the mouth opens more quickly and more widely during the production of the syllable "ma" in the sequence "mabopi." (Wolf, M. E., and M. A. Goodale. Oral asymmetries during verbal and non-verbal movements of the mouth. *Neuropsychologia* 25(2):375-395, 1987.)

necessary because these movements will probably be resilient to interference effects. Furthermore, studies should be conducted on the hemispheres' capacities to produce simultaneous finger-versus-limb movements. Perhaps finger movements are more sensitive to interference effects when performed by the right hemisphere than by the left hemisphere.

Studies of interference effects are intriguing because they may offer fresh insight into the cortical organization of the motor systems, but interference effects are poorly understood and appear capricious. In addition, as we become proficient at motor tasks, we are less prone to interference effects. Consider the difficulty of talking while learning to play tennis, an interference paradigm of little challenge to tennis professionals.

◎ What Do Laterality Studies Tell Us about Brain Function?

Laterality studies provide the behavioral complement to anatomical studies of neurological patients, and much current theorizing about the nature of cerebral asymmetry is based on laterality research. However, noninvasive laterality studies are indirect measures, far less precise than direct anatomical measures of brain function. Consider the following problems.

Correlation

Behavioral measures of laterality do not correlate perfectly with invasive measures of cerebral asymmetry. For example, the results of dichotic-listening studies show a right-ear bias for words in about 80 percent of right-handed participants, but sodium amobarbital testing and brain stimulation show language represented in the left hemisphere in more than 98 percent of right-handers. What causes this discrepancy? One possibility is that the behavioral test is measuring several things, only one of which is relative cerebral dominance.

Yet a curious paradox exists: the behavioral tests may correlate with anatomical asymmetries more closely than data from the invasive tests do. From anatomical studies we know that only about 75 percent to 80 percent of brains show a left-side advantage in the posterior lateral area of right-handers, yet 98 percent of these brains show language in the left hemisphere in a sodium amobarbital test.

Esther Strauss and colleagues (1983) propose that the results of laterality studies may provide correlations between anatomy and behavior. One way to test this proposal would be to perform a battery of laterality tests with participants for whom MRIs also are available. Yet the question remains, Why do the results of both the amobarbital test and the brain-stimulation studies show a larger percentage of people with left-hemisphere speech?

Finally, laterality measures do not correlate very highly with one another. We might expect tachistoscopic and dichotic measures in the same participants to be highly concordant, but they are not. Perhaps these tests are not really measuring the same things.

Expectations, Bias, and Skepticism

The behavioral strategies that participants adopt in laterality tasks can alter performance significantly. If participants are instructed to pay particular attention to words entering the left ear in dichotic tasks, they can do so, abolishing the right-ear effect. Participants can also enter tests with preconceived biases that may affect test performance. Finally, laterality effects may simply be a result of experience rather than biological factors. Investigators' suspicions about laterality effects are reinforced by the observation that repeated testing of the same participants does not always produce the same results.

Skepticism regarding the usefulness of laterality research reaches its peak in an insightful and provocative book by Robert Efron (1990). His thesis is that the apparent right–left difference in laterality studies can be explained entirely by the way in which the brain "scans" sensory input. Imagine the following experiment.

Six numbers are presented for 100 milliseconds, in a line going from left to right. Three appear in each visual field such that 1, 2, and 3 fall in the left visual field and 4, 5, and 6 fall in the right visual field. When participants are asked to repeat the numbers that they saw in sequence, they tend to respond: 4, 5, 6, 1, 2, 3. The participants appear to be scanning, from left to right, the contents of the right visual field followed by the contents of the left visual field.

The apparent scanning has nothing to do with actually moving the eyes to read the numbers, because the numbers are present for only 100 milliseconds. That is not enough time for one eye movement. Thus, the sequencing scan is taking place after the presentation of stimuli has ended. We might expect that the longer it takes to scan, the poorer the performance will be at the end of the scan because the information has been decaying.

Subsequent experiments confirm this expectation. Efron's numerous scanning experiments led him to conclude that the brain has a tendency to scan information serially. If so, then the brain must necessarily examine some stimuli before others. If the tendency is to examine stimuli in one visual half-field earlier than those in the other half-field, the result will be a left–right performance asymmetry that entails no hemispheric differences in processing capacity.

There is still a bias in what is scanned first, but that is a different question. Efron does not argue that the two hemispheres are functionally and anatomically identical. He does argue that evidence of laterality does not constitute an explanation and that we should be skeptical when we read descriptions of hemispheric "specialization," asking, What, indeed, is actually lateralized?

11.4 Neuroimaging and Asymmetry

The neuroimaging studies described in Sections 7.1 and 7.4 allow researchers to map cerebral activity in participants as it happens. Localization rather than lateralization of functions is the primary interest in most imaging studies. Because both hemispheres are scanned, however, left–right differences in cerebral activation can be assessed during a wide range of behavioral measures. Virtually all imaging measures, including PET, fMRI, ERP, and MEG, reveal the expected asymmetry in cerebral activation in tasks similar to those used in laterality studies.

As expected, for example, asymmetrical cerebral activity appears when participants either listen to conversation or engage in it (**Figure 11.15**). Thus, when

(A) Left hemisphere, speaking

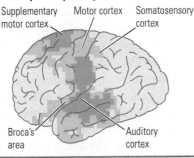

Supplementary motor cortex   Motor cortex   Somatosensory cortex

Broca's area   Auditory cortex

1 Speaking activates the mouth, tongue, and larynx representations in the motor and somatosensory cortices, the supplementary motor area, the auditory cortex, and the left-hemisphere language zones.

(B) Right hemisphere, speaking

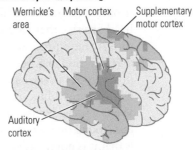

Wernicke's area   Motor cortex   Supplementary motor cortex

Auditory cortex

2 During speech, the mouth area and auditory cortex in the right hemisphere are active but less active than in the left hemisphere.

(C) Left hemisphere, listening

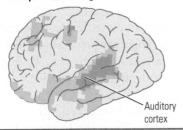

Auditory cortex

3 Sensation changes the blood-flow pattern in the cortex, localizing areas that mediate perception. Here the participants listened to spoken words, resulting in increased activity localized to the auditory cortex.

Figure 11.15 ◄

Relating Brain Function to Regional Blood Flow Images averaged from nine participants show differences in left- and right-hemisphere activity as the blood flow pattern varies with the behavioral task. Light shading indicates the average blood flow level; dark shading indicates higher-than-average blood flow; the absence of shading indicates lower-than-average blood flow. Note: the position of the lateral (Sylvian) and central fissures is approximate; the actual position could be determined only by opening the skull or comparing the blood flow with a structural MRI. The squared-off shapes are an artifact of the recording-and-averaging procedure and thus do not accurately indicate the shapes of brain areas. (Data from Lassen et al., 1978.)

a participant is listening to speech, both hemispheres show regional changes in cerebral activity, especially within the auditory cortex, but the left hemisphere also shows increased activity in Broca's and Wernicke's areas. When speaking, participants also show activity in the motor areas that represent the face and mouth, as well as activity in the supplementary motor cortex (the dorsal premotor area described in Section 9.1).

Curiously, repetition of "automatic" speech, such as naming the days of the week over and over again, fails to increase activity in Broca's area. The idea that this area takes part in producing movement coupled with the results of the sodium amobarbital or stimulation studies discussed earlier would not predict this result. In contrast with the increased activity on the left side during speech perception, right-side activity in the temporal lobe increases when participants hear music.

The mere demonstration of asymmetry will not be the principal advantage of future imaging studies. That advantage will appear in examples in which predicted asymmetries are *not* found, such as the absence of activity in Broca's area during automatic speech.

Performing cognitive tasks during fMRI changes cerebral blood-flow distribution (*perfusion*), which results in alterations of blood-flow velocities in the basal arteries that feed the brain. Changes in arterial blood flow can be measured using a procedure known as *functional transcranial Doppler ultrasonography* (fTCD). Stefan Knecht and colleagues (2000) showed that changes in blood-flow velocity in the basal arteries can be used to identify the language-dominant hemisphere. These researchers tested each patient with both fTCD and the Wada procedure to determine the speaking hemisphere. In every case, both tests found the same hemisphere dominant for speech. The advantage of fTCD is that it is noninvasive and thus may be preferable to the Wada procedure (see Figure 11.11). The question at this point is how the blood flow of people with bilateral speech representation would change with fTCD.

11.5 Theoretical Arguments: What Is Lateralized?

It is tempting to conclude that the functional asymmetries described thus far indicate a fundamental difference in the basic cognitive processes of the left and right cerebral hemispheres. Before considering this conclusion, we first summarize the data, because any theoretical statements are best considered in light of available information.

Table 11.4 summarizes the major data on cerebral lateralization and illustrates the range of functions lateralized principally in the left or right hemisphere. An enormous number of proposals have been made on what is lateralized in the brain. (See Allen, 1983, for a readable summary.) At the broadest level, these theories fall into two groups: specialization theories propose unique functions for each hemisphere, and interaction theories propose cooperation between the hemispheres.

Specialization Models

The extreme unilateral specialization model states that only one hemisphere facilitates a given psychological process—that the left hemisphere alone performs language functions, for example, as has been argued since Broca's time. Eric Lenneberg offers perhaps the most thorough modern version of the left-for-language theory, modified from the theory Hugo Liepmann (1863–1925) proposed a century ago. Liepmann proposed that the left hemisphere is specialized for some form of motor control, which would account for both aphasia and apraxia as the major symptoms of left-hemisphere damage.

Kimura extended this idea, proposing that although the left hemisphere mediates verbal function, it is specialized not for verbal function itself

Table 11.4 **Summary of data on cerebral lateralization**

Function*	Left Hemisphere	Right Hemisphere
Visual system	Letters, words	Complex geometric patterns
		Faces
Auditory system	Language-related sound	Nonlanguage environmental sounds
		Music
Somatosensory	?	Tactile recognition of complex system patterns
		Braille
Movement	Complex voluntary movement	Movements in spatial patterns
Memory	Verbal memory	Nonverbal memory
Language	Speech	Prosody
	Reading	
	Writing	
	Arithmetic	
Spatial processes		Geometry
		Sense of direction
		Mental rotation of shapes

*Functions predominantly mediated by one hemisphere in right-handed people.

but rather for certain motor functions, both verbal and nonverbal. Kimura's argument is based on two premises:

1. Left-hemisphere lesions disturb voluntary movement—an impairment correlated with speech disturbance.

2. Verbal communication among humans evolved from a primarily gestural stage, though with vocal concomitants, to one that is primarily vocal but retains the capacity for gestural communication. Because neurological control of speech and language thus evolved out of a manual system of motor control, the left hemisphere is specialized not for language itself but rather for motor control.

Natalie Uomini and Georg Meyer (2013) used fTCD to compare brain activation during complex stone-tool making (the technique of Acheulean knapping used to make hand axes) and language (word generation) in the same participants. The two tasks caused common cerebral blood flow patterns, supporting the idea that language coevolved with certain types of motor control, as discussed in Section 11.1. Uomini and Meyer suggest that the coevolution of language and Acheulean stone-tool making may explain archeological evidence that shows a rapid and wide spreading of Acheulean tools, possibly due to improved teaching, facilitated by language.

Several researchers (for example, Efron, 1990) suggest that it is not motor control itself that is located in the left hemisphere but rather the capacity for fine resolution of stimuli in time. In other words, because speech analysis and production require fine discrimination over very short intervals, the left hemisphere might be specialized for temporal sequencing. Elaborations of this idea stress the left hemisphere's capacity to make fine discriminations in time, whether or not the stimuli are verbal. (See, for example, Sergent, 1983.) Recall the study described in Section 11.3 of Morse-code operators who displayed a left-hemisphere advantage even though the code is not verbal; it is, rather, a temporal sequence.

Robert Zatorre and his colleagues (2002) expanded Efron's timing idea by emphasizing that speech and musical sounds exploit different acoustical cues: speech is highly dependent on rapidly changing broadband sounds, whereas tonal patterns in music tend to be slower, although small and precise changes in frequency are important. Zatorre proposed that the auditory cortices in both hemispheres are therefore specialized such that temporal resolution is better in the left and spectral resolution is better in the right auditory areas. Zatorre made the point that, because an acoustical system cannot simultaneously analyze both temporal and spectral aspects of sound, the cortical asymmetries related to acoustical processing may have evolved as a solution for optimizing the processing of acoustical stimuli.

Rather than specifying differential processing of specified psychological processes, other specialization models focus on the idea that the two hemispheres might process information in distinctly different ways. The first clear proposal of this sort was made by Josephine Semmes in 1968. On the basis of results from her studies of World War II veterans with penetrating brain injuries, Semmes concluded that the left hemisphere functions as a collection of focal regions, whereas the right hemisphere functions more diffusely.

Her logic was as follows. She had noticed that small lesions in the left hemisphere produced a wide variety of specific deficits (for example, impaired spelling and reading), the precise deficit depending on the locus of the lesion. Similar-sized lesions within the right hemisphere were often without obvious effect. In contrast, large lesions of either hemisphere produced a large number of deficits.

To account for these differences, Semmes argued that a person with a small lesion in the right hemisphere exhibits no deficits because specific functions there are diffusely represented, not localized in discrete regions. A large lesion of the right hemisphere produces many more deficits than would be predicted from the total of smaller lesions because an entire functional field is removed. A large lesion of the left hemisphere produces many deficits simply because many small focal regions have been destroyed; that is, in the left hemisphere, the total is equal to the sum of the parts.

Semmes proposed that this differential hemispheric organization is advantageous for efficient control of their respective functions. The right hemisphere's diffuse organization is advantageous for spatial abilities because spatial analysis requires that different sensations (visual, auditory, tactile) be integrated into a single percept. In the left hemisphere, by contrast, language functions remain discrete individual units.

More recently, differential hemispheric organization has also been shown using noninvasive imaging to study functional connectivity (the connectome; see 10.3) in each hemisphere (e.g., Doron et al., 2012). Stephen Gotts and colleagues (2013), for example, used rs-fMRI to identify the corticocortical interactions between selected left hemisphere regions involved in language and fine motor coordination and right hemisphere regions involved in visuospatial and attentional processing. The left hemisphere showed a strong bias in interacting with itself, whereas the right hemisphere interacted in a more integrated manner with both hemispheres. These results are generally consistent with Semme's ideas based upon her patient studies.

From these basic ideas about the two hemispheres' distinct functions has arisen the idea that each represents a distinct mode of cognitive processing (see Springer and Deutch, 1998). The left hemisphere operates in a more logical, analytical, computerlike fashion, analyzing stimuli input sequentially and abstracting the relevant details, to which it attaches verbal labels. The right hemisphere is primarily a synthesizer, more concerned with the overall stimulus configuration, and organizes and processes information as gestalts, or wholes.

Hemispheric specialization models have stimulated interest among philosophers and the general public. However, it is important to remember that they are based entirely on inference and have jumped a long way from the data, such as those summarized in Table 11.4.

Interaction Models

All interaction models share the idea that both hemispheres have the capacity to perform all functions but do not. The specific reasons have spawned debates, experiments, and models. Three versions of the interaction model:

1. **The two hemispheres function simultaneously but work on different aspects of processing.** This direct analog of the multiple-channel idea of sensory processing (see Section 10.2) takes it one step further, proposing that the two hemispheres represent a class of sensory channel. Although simultaneous processing is generally appealing as a model, this hypothesis

"Integration"

"Segregation"

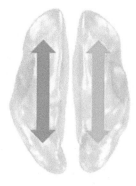

▲ Gotts, Stephen, Joon Jo, Hang, Wallace, Gregory L., Saad, Ziad S., Cox, Robert W., Martin, Alex et al. Two distinct forms of functional lateralization in the human brain. *PNAS*, 10,36 (2013) E3435–E3444.

has yet to offer a satisfactory explanation for the binding problem: how information is combined into a single percept or behavior.

2. **Although the two hemispheres have the capacity to perform a given function, they inhibit or suppress each other's activity.** (See Kinsbourne, 1971, for example, and Moscovitch, 1979.) An entire group of interaction models proposes that the left hemisphere inhibits language processing in the right hemisphere and the right hemisphere inhibits music processing in the left hemisphere. Developmentally, this inhibition model has appeal, because functions such as language appear able to develop in the "wrong" hemisphere if the normally dominant hemisphere is damaged, as illustrated in the Snapshot on page 310. Thus, if the language zones are damaged in infancy, language can develop in the right hemisphere. A difficulty with these models is that none has clearly specified the physiological mechanisms of hemispheric inhibition.

3. **Either the two hemispheres receive information preferentially and thus perform different analyses simultaneously or some mechanism enables each hemisphere to pay attention to specific types of information, thus leading to different hemispheric analyses.** (See, for example, Moscovitch, 1979.) Such interaction models based on information processing are complex, detailed, and based heavily on theories from cognitive psychology. An interesting proposal of the simultaneous-processing models is analogous to networked, or distributed, processing by computer: if one hemisphere is busy, it ought to be able to allocate functions to the other hemisphere. A problem with attention-based information-processing models is that they are necessarily vague on what physiological mechanisms might be responsible for selective attention.

In summary, the question What is lateralized? has no simple or generally accepted answer. There is no shortage of theory. What is needed is more information about the nature of asymmetry and its origins, both developmentally and phylogenetically.

Preferred Cognitive Mode

From the preceding theoretical arguments, we can speculate that individual differences in behavior typically result, at least in part, from individual differences in how the cerebral hemispheres are organized and how functions are lateralized. **Preferred cognitive mode** refers to the use of one type of thought process in preference to another. At one extreme, people who are logical, analytical, and verbal are assumed to rely more on their left hemisphere to solve problems in everyday life, whereas people who are visual, intuitive, and tend to look at the big picture are assumed to rely more on their right hemispheres.

Consider an example, albeit tongue-in-cheek. Two professors, Alpha and Beta, are both excellent scholars, but they work and think in totally different ways.

Alpha is meticulous and leaves no detail to chance: when learning new material, he masters every detail and has total command of the topic. Alpha is verbal and easily wins debates with his quick thinking and elegant arguments. His writing is clear and concise, with flawless grammar and spelling. Alpha, a nationally

SNAPSHOT | Imaging the Brain's Plasticity

The opening Portrait of Chapter 10 explains that hemispherectomy is sometimes performed to treat children with severe seizures. These disorders can arise from progressive viral infections, such as Rasmussen's encephalitis, or as congenital or acquired dysfunction of one cerebral hemisphere. Although such children may have severe behavioral challenges after the surgery, they often compensate remarkably, communicating freely and in some cases showing considerable motor control over the limbs opposite the excised hemisphere.

Using both fMRI and SEPs, Holloway and colleagues (2000) investigated the sensorimotor functions of 17 hemispherectomy patients. Ten showed SEPs in the intact hemisphere when the nerves of the limb opposite the excised hemisphere were stimulated.

Similarly, as illustrated in the adjoining micrographs, fMRI shows that for at least some patients, passive movement of the same limb produces activation in a region of somatosensory cortex that normally responds to the opposite hand. The Holloway team concluded that the responses to the hand ipsilateral to the healthy hemisphere must occur because direct ipsilateral pathways run from that hemisphere to the affected limb.

Curiously, the novel ipsilateral responses were found not only in hemispherectomy patients with congenital disease but also in those with acquired disease, suggesting that although age at injury may be important, other factors must be influencing the cerebral reorganization. The injury-induced reorganization is characteristic of the

Damage to right hemisphere

| Passive movement of the right hand is seen in the left sensorimotor cortex. | Passive movement of the left (hemiplegic) hand shows an abnormal ipsilateral pathway. |

Victoria Holloway, David G. Gadian, Faraneh Vargha-Khadem, David A. Porter, Stewart G. Boyd and Alan Connelly The reorganization of sensorimotor function in children after hemispherectomy. *Brain* Volume 123, Number 12, 1 (December 2000): pp. 2432–2444(13).

brain's plasticity. We return to plasticity in the context of brain development in Section 23.2.

Holloway, V., D. G. Gadian, F. Vargha-Khadem, D. A. Porter, S. G. Boyd, and A. Connelly. The reorganization of sensorimotor function in children after hemispherectomy. *Brain* 123:2432–2444, 2000.

ranked tennis player, is athletic but, curiously, is only mediocre at other sports. With prolonged practice though, he masters them. Alpha's office is neat and tidy, with every item carefully placed in its correct location. On his desk is the project on which he is currently working and nothing else.

Beta appears messy and disorganized compared with Alpha and has poor recall for details. He grasps the heart of an idea quickly, however, and can tie diverse concepts together into a meaningful picture. Communicating his thinking poses a challenge for Beta, however, because he has difficulty expressing his ideas in words. Like Alpha, Beta is athletic, but Beta acquires the general motor skills of new sports rapidly, although he has never been able to become a top participant in any particular event. In contrast with Alpha, who works on only one project at a time, Beta works on several projects concurrently, leading to piles of papers and books in his work space, in contrast to Alpha's meticulous desk.

In both the cognitive and motor skills of Alpha and Beta is a basic difference assumed to correspond to a fundamental difference either in brain organization or in the "dominance" of one hemisphere over the other. Alpha and Beta represent extreme "left-hemisphere" and "right-hemisphere" people, respectively. The fundamental difference between them is their preferred cognitive mode. Alpha is analytical, logical, verbal, and meticulous, whereas Beta is a synthesizer more concerned with organizing concepts and visualizing meaningful wholes.

As intriguing as the Alpha–Beta analysis might be, it is pure speculation, without empirical basis. Factors other than brain organization probably contribute to preferred cognitive mode. For example, the results of a study by William Webster and Ann Thurber (1978) demonstrate that **cognitive set**, the tendency to approach a problem with a particular bias in thought, can affect some tests of lateralization.

They repeated the dichaptic test described in Section 11.3 but added another variable. One group (the gestalt bias) was encouraged to learn the shapes by imagining their overall appearance. A second group (the analytical bias) was encouraged to identify distinctive features of each shape and list them to themselves.

This manipulation of cognitive set demonstrably influenced the degree of left-hand superiority because the gestalt group had a significantly larger performance difference between the hands than did the analytical group. Although the basis for this effect is uncertain, it implies that strategies used by participants can significantly influence tests of lateralization. Thus, differences in preferred cognitive mode can be reasonably assumed to be due to biases in socialization or environmental factors in addition to neuronal, genetic, or constitutional biases. Nevertheless, the idea that individual differences in behavior result in part from individual differences in brain organization is provocative and worthy of serious study.

Measuring Behavior in Neuropsychology

At this point, a brief consideration of the problem of measuring behavior is appropriate. You might think that, of all the procedures used in neuropsychology, the measurement of things or events may be the easiest to perform and replicate. It is not true.

Many measurements of one process lead to inferences about some other processes. For example, if in a study that employs dichotic listening, more words are recalled from the right ear than from the left, the inference is that speech is lateralized to the left hemisphere. The assumptions underlying this inference are simple, yet so many variables affect the result that Phil Bryden (1982) wrote an entire book on the problem.

If a more objective measure of something such as brain size were used, would the results be clearer? This outcome seems unlikely. So many different ways exist to measure objects that almost any result can be obtained. Consider the following example.

Probably everyone has had the feeling that his or her feet are not exactly the same size. Often the difference manifests itself as greater discomfort in one

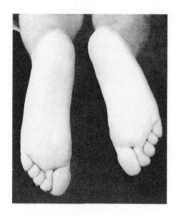

Figure 11.16 ▲

Growth and the Brain
Destruction of the left fronto-parietal region at birth produced this growth asymmetry in the right foot. Such cases demonstrate that growth affecting limb size has a cortical component, quite aside from the effect of disuse on the limb. (Penfield, W., and H. Jasper. *Epilepsy and the Functional Anatomy of the Human Brain*, Boston: Little, Brown, 1954.)

foot when breaking in a new pair of shoes; we have never heard anyone suggest that the shoes might be different sizes. Foot size may be related to differences in brain organization. For example, people in medicine have long known that damage to one hemisphere at an early age leads to smaller limbs on the contralateral side of the body (**Figure 11.16**).

To make inferences about cerebral organization, Jere and Jerome Levy (1978, 1981) attempted to measure differences in foot size among typical people. They measured foot size in 150 persons and found that significantly more right-handed females had larger left than right feet, whereas significantly more right-handed males had larger right than left feet. Just the opposite result was obtained for left-handed females and males.

To report their findings, the Levys measured foot size, converted that measure into shoe size, and then converted differences into a seven-point rating scale. Many studies attempted to repeat the Levys' work. Nicholas Mascie-Taylor and his coworkers (1981) measured foot size by using a "standard anthropometric technique" (described elsewhere as heel to longest toe with the participant seated and the toenails cut). They found that the left foot was longer than the right in both sexes, confirming the results of seven earlier studies. None found handedness effects.

Michael Peters and his coworkers (1981) measured the actual foot length from the heel to the longest toe in 365 seated participants. They found no significant differences between the left and the right foot for any sex or handedness group, and they claimed partial support for their results from three other studies. Another study, in which the outlines of 105 participants' feet were traced on a large sheet of paper, found no differences in foot size with regard to sex or handedness (Yanowitz et al., 1981).

The final score on this series of studies is as follows: one study for sex and handedness effects, eight studies for a left-foot effect, and two studies for no differences, with the results of three additional studies partly supporting no differences. This story—like all good stories—has a sequel, and we refer the interested reader to Peters's (1988) review.

Measuring foot size might seem easy. This series of studies shows that it is not. The results obtained depend on the measuring device, the points across which length is measured, whether participants are seated or standing, the time of day, and perhaps even shoe type worn before measurement. In many of the studies, the importance of these variables was not recognized; in others, the procedure was not described in sufficient detail to permit exact replication. The most objective measure, photography, was not used in any study. A photographic record of the feet would permit a reevaluation of the results at any time by investigators interested in the question of appropriate measurement.

We can derive three lessons from this example, but none of them is that it is impossible to make measurements. The first lesson: if measuring something such as feet is difficult, then inferring something about the brain from such measurements should be done with caution. The second is that nothing is wrong with making multiple measurements. If they correlate, then each is measuring the same thing; if they do not, then either multiple factors are at work or some of the measures are not reliable. The third is that, if a measurement is to be made, it should be the most meaningful one that can be made.

SUMMARY

11.1 Anatomical Asymmetries in the Human Brain

A striking feature of human brain organization is that its two hemispheres are anatomically and functionally asymmetrical. The observed asymmetries can be assumed to represent functional hemispheric specializations. Thus, the increased size of the language areas in certain auditory regions of the temporal lobe presumably corresponds to the special role this tissue plays in processing acoustical stimuli related to language. But given that the total area of the auditory cortex is similar in the two hemispheres, the right hemisphere tissue must be specialized for analyzing some other sound characteristic, most likely the characteristic related to music.

11.2 Asymmetries in Neurological Patients

Analyses of patients undergoing specialized neurological and surgical procedures provide an opportunity to study functional aspects of the hemispheres' anatomical asymmetries. These studies confirm the left hemisphere's special role in language and motor functions and the right hemisphere's complementary role in musical and spatial functions.

11.3 Behavioral Asymmetries in the Intact Brain

The intact brain does not usually reveal its asymmetrical processing in everyday life, but it can be tricked into revealing its processing biases. The simplest way is to strain processing capacity by presenting multiple stimuli simultaneously, as in dichotic listening; or briefly, as in tachistoscopic presentation; or by interference—asking the brain to perform two conflicting tasks simultaneously.

11.4 Neuroimaging and Asymmetry

Asymmetry in the intact brain can also be demonstrated with imaging procedures that measure brain activity as it happens—that is, "online"—using such measures as glucose or oxygen utilization, electrical activity, or blood flow.

11.5 Theoretical Arguments: What Is Lateralized?

Specialization theories propose unique functions for each hemisphere, although agreement on what those underlying unique functions might be has proved elusive. Likely candidates are related to differences in processing sensory inputs and differences in the role of movement control. Interaction theories propose cooperation between the hemispheres: both have the capacity for all functions, but for some reason, they are relatively specialized.

The jury is still out as to why the brain is lateralized. Although it is tempting to conclude that the left hemisphere's function is language, the appropriate conclusion is that the left hemisphere takes part in processes that are necessary for certain aspects of "language." Similarly, the right hemisphere appears to take part in processing required for visuospatial functions. Indeed, at present, we can safely conclude only that we do not know what processes the two hemispheres are specialized to perform.

References

Allen, M. Models of hemispheric specialization. *Psychological Bulletin* 93:73–104, 1983.

Blumstein, S., V. Tartter, D. Michel, B. Hirsch, and E. Leiter. The role of distinctive features in the dichotic perception of words. *Brain and Language* 4:508–520, 1977.

Broca, P. Sur la faculté du langage articulé. *Bulletins et Memoires de la Société D'Anthropologie de Paris* 6:377–393, 1865.

Bryden, M. P. *Laterality: Functional Asymmetry in the Intact Brain.* New York: Academic Press, 1982.

Caroselli, J. S., M. Hiscock, and T. Roebuck. Asymmetric interference between concurrent tasks: An evaluation of competing explanatory models. *Neuropsychologia* 35:457–469, 1997.

Chi, J. G., E. C. Dooling, and F. H. Gilles. Left–right asymmetries of the temporal speech areas of the human fetus. *Archives of Neurology* 34:346–348, 1977.

Crichton-Browne, J. On the weight of the brain: Its component parts in the insane. *Brain* 2:42–67, 1880.

Curry, F. A comparison of left-handed subjects on verbal and nonverbal dichotic listening tasks. *Cortex* 3:343–352, 1967.

Darwin, C. Ear differences and hemispheric specialization. In F. O. Schmitt and F. G. Worden, Eds., *The Neurosciences: Third Study Program.* Cambridge, Mass: MIT Press, 1974.

Divenyi, P., and R. Efron. Spectral versus temporal features in dichotic listening. *Brain and Language* 7:375–386, 1979.

Doron, K.W., D. S. Bassett, and M. S. Gazzaniga. Dynamic network structure of interhemispheric coordination. *Proceedings of the National Academy of Sciences U.S.A.* 109:18661–18668, 2012.

Eberstaller, O. Zur Oberflächenanatomie der Grosshirnhemispharen. *Wiener Medizinische Blätter* 7:479–482, 542–582, 644–646, 1884.

Efron, R. *The Decline and Fall of Hemispheric Specialization.* Hillsdale, N.J.: Erlbaum, 1990.

Eidelberg, D., and A. M. Galaburda. Symmetry and asymmetry in the human posterior thalamus. *Archives of Neurology* 39:325–332, 1982.

Falzi, G., P. Perrone, and L. A. Vignolo. Right-left asymmetry in anterior speech region. *Archives of Neurology* 39:239–240, 1982.

Galaburda, A. M., M. LeMay, T. L. Kemper, and N. Geschwind. Right–left asymmetries in the brain. *Science* 199: 852–856, 1978.

Galaburda, A. M., and F. Sanides. Cytoarchitectonic organization of the human auditory cortex. *Journal of Comparative Neurology* 190:597–610, 1980.

Gelfand, S., S. Hoffmand, S. Waltzman, and N. Piper. Dichotic CV recognition at various interaural temporal onset asynchronies: Effect of age. *Journal of the Acoustical Society of America* 68:1258–1261, 1980.

Geschwind, N., and W. Levitsky. Left–right asymmetries in temporal speech region. *Science* 161:186–187, 1968.

Gibson, C., and M. P. Bryden. Dichaptic recognition of shapes and letters in children. *Canadian Journal of Psychology* 37:132–143, 1983.

Glick, S. D., D. A. Ross, and L. B. Hough. Lateral asymmetry of neurotransmitters in human brain. *Brain Research* 234:53–63, 1982.

Good, C. D., I. Johnsrude, J. Ashburner, R. N. Henson, K. J. Friston, and R. S. Frackowiak. Cerebral asymmetry and the effects of sex and handedness on brain structure: A voxel-based morphometric analysis of 465 normal adult brains. *NeuroImage* 14:685–700, 2001.

Gordon, H. Hemispheric asymmetries in the perception of musical chords. *Cortex* 6:387–398, 1970.

Gotts, S. J., H. J. Jo, G. L. Wallace, Z. S. Saad, R. W. Cox, and A. Martin. Two distinct forms of functional lateralization in the human brain. *Proceedings of the National Academy of Sciences U.S.A.* 110: E3435–3444, 2013.

Gur, R. C., I. K. Packer, J. P. Hungerbuhler, M. Reivich, W. D. Obrist, W. S. Amarnek, and H. Sackheim. Differences in distribution of gray and white matter in human cerebral hemispheres. *Science* 207:1226–1228, 1980.

Halperin, Y., I. Nachson, and A. Carmon. Shift of ear superiority in dichotic listening to temporally patterned nonverbal stimuli. *Journal of the Acoutistical Society of America* 53:46–50, 1973.

Hoadley, M. D., and K. Pearson. Measurement of internal diameter of skull in relation to "pre-eminence" of left hemisphere. *Biometrika* 21:94–123, 1929.

Hrvoj-Mihic, B., T. Bienvenu, L. Stefanacci, A. R. Muotri, and K. Semendeferi. Evolution, development, and plasticity of the human brain: From molecules to bones. *Frontiers in Human Neuroscience* 10:3389, 2013.

Kimura, D. Some effects of temporal-lobe damage on auditory perception. *Canadian Journal of Psychology* 15:156–165, 1961.

Kimura, D. Left–right differences in the perception of melodies. *Quarterly Journal of Experimental Psychology* 16:355–358, 1964.

Kimura, D. Functional asymmetry of the brain in dichotic listening. *Cortex* 3:163–178, 1967.

Kimura D., and S. Folb. Neural processing of background sounds. *Science* 161:395–396, 1968.

Kimura, D., and C. A. Humphrys. A comparison of left- and right-arm movements during speaking. *Neuropsychologia* 19: 807–812, 1981.

King, F., and D. Kimura. Left-ear superiority in dichotic perception of vocal, non-verbal sounds. *Canadian Journal of Psychology* 26:111–116, 1972.

Kinsbourne, M. Eye and head turning indicates cerebral lateralization. *Science* 176:539–541, 1971.

Knecht, S., M. Deppe, B. Dräger, L. Bobe, H. Lohmann, E. Ringelstein, and H. Henningsen. Language lateralization in healthy right-handers. *Brain* 123:74–81, 2000.

Kodama, L. Beitrage zur Anatomie des Zentralnervensystems der Japaner: VIII. Insula Reil ii. *Folia Anatomica Japonica* 12:423–444, 1934.

Kopp, N., F. Michel, H. Carrier, A. Biron, and P. Duvillard. Hemispheric asymmetries of the human brain. *Journal of Neurological Sciences* 34:349–363, 1977.

Lassen, N. A., D. H. Ingvar, and E. Skinhøj. Brain function and blood flow. *Scientific American* 239:62–71, 1978.

Lauter, J. Dichotic identification of complex sounds: Absolute and relative ear advantages. *Journal of the Acoustical Society of America* 71:701–707, 1982.

LeMay, M. Asymmetries of the skull and handedness. *Journal of the Neurological Sciences* 32:243–253, 1977.

LeMay, M., and A. Culebras. Human brain-morphologic differences in the hemispheres demonstrable by carotid arteriography. *New England Journal of Medicine* 287:168–170, 1972.

Levy, J., and J. M. Levy. Human lateralization from head to foot: Sex-related factors. *Science* 200:1291–1292, 1978.

Levy, J., and J. M. Levy. Foot-length asymmetry, sex, and handedness. *Science* 212:1418–1419, 1981.

Levy, J., C. Trevarthen, and R. W. Sperry. Perception of bilateral chimeric figures following hemispheric deconnection. *Brain* 95:61–78, 1972.

Luders, E., K. L. Narr, P. M. Thompson, D. E. Rex, L. Jancke, and A. W. Toga. Hemispheric asymmetries in cortical thickness. *Cerebral Cortex* 16:1232–1238, 2006.

Mascie-Taylor, C. G. N., A. M. MacLarnon, P. M. Lanigan, and I. C. McManus. Foot-length asymmetry, sex, and handedness. *Science* 212:1416–1417, 1981.

McRae, D. L., C. L. Branch, and B. Milner. The occipital horns and cerebral dominance. *Neurology* 18:95–98, 1968.

Moscovitch, M. Information processing and the cerebral hemispheres. In M. Gazzaniga, Ed., *Handbook of Behavioral Neurobiology*, vol. 2. New York: Plenum, 1979.

Murphy, K., and M. Peters. Right-handers and left-handers show differences and important similarities in task integration when performing manual and vocal tasks concurrently. *Neuropsychologia* 32:663–674, 1994.

Natale, M. Perception of nonlinguistic auditory rhythms by the speech hemisphere. *Brain and Language* 4:32–44, 1977.

Noffsinger, D. Dichotic-listening techniques in the study of hemispheric asymmetries. In D. F. Benson and E. Zaidel, Eds., *The Dual Brain*. New York: Guilford Press, 1985.

Ojemann, G. A. Brain organization for language from the perspective of electrical stimulation mapping. *Behavioral and Brain Sciences* 6:189–230, 1983.

Papcun, G., S. Krashen, D. Terbeek, R. Remington, and R. Harshman. Is the left hemisphere organized for speech, language and/or something else? *Journal of the Acoustical Society of America* 55:319–327, 1974.

Penfield, W., and H. Jasper. *Epilepsy and the Functional Anatomy of the Human Brain*. Boston: Little, Brown, 1954.

Peters, M. Footedness: Asymmetries in foot preference and skill and neuropsychological assessment of foot movement. *Psychological Bulletin* 103:179–192, 1988.

Peters, M. B., B. Petrie, and D. Oddie. Foot-length asymmetry, sex, and handedness. *Science* 212:1417–1418, 1981.

Rasmussen, T., and B. Milner. The role of early left-brain injury in determining lateralization of cerebral speech functions. *Annals of the New York Academy of Sciences* 299:355–369, 1977.

Rubens, A. M., M. W. Mahowald, and J. T. Hutton. Asymmetry of the lateral (Sylvian) fissures in man. *Neurology* 26:620–624, 1976.

Rudel, R. G., M. B. Denckla, and E. Spalten. The functional asymmetry of Braille letter learning in normal sighted children. *Neurology* 24:733–738, 1974.

Scheibel, A. B., I. Fried, L. Paul, A. Forsythe, U. Tomiyasu, A. Wechsler, A. Kao, and J. Slotnick. Differentiating characteristics of the human speech cortex: A quantitative Golgi study. In D. F. Benson and E. Zaidel, Eds., *The Dual Brain*. New York: Guilford Press, 1985.

Semmes, J. Hemispheric specialization: A possible clue to mechanism. *Neuropsychologia* 6:11–26, 1968.

Sergent, J. Role of the input in visual hemispheric asymmetries. *Psychological Bulletin* 93:481–512, 1983.

Sidtis, J. Predicting brain organization from dichotic listening performance: Cortical and subcortical functional asymmetries contribute to perceptual asymmetries. *Brain and Language* 17:287–300, 1982.

Springer, S. P., and G. Deutsch. *Left Brain, Right Brain: Perspectives from Cognitive Neuroscience*, 5th ed. New York: W. H. Freeman and Company, 1998.

Strauss, E., and C. Fitz. Occipital horn asymmetry in children. *Annals of Neurology* 18:437–439, 1980.

Strauss, E., B. Kosaka, and J. Wada. The neurological basis of lateralized cerebral function: A review. *Human Neurobiology* 2:115–127, 1983.

Sun, T., R. V. Collura, M. Ruvolo, and C. A. Walsh. Genomic and evolutionary analyses of asymmetrically expressed genes in human fetal left and right cerebral cortex. *Cerebral Cortex* 16:118–125, 2006.

Sussman, H. M. Evidence for left hemisphere superiority in processing movement-related tonal signals. *Journal of Speech and Hearing Research* 22:224–235, 1979.

Taylor, L. B. Localisation of cerebral lesions by psychological testing. *Clinical Neurology* 16:269–287, 1969.

Teszner, D., A. Tzavaras, and H. Hécaen. L'asymetrie droite-gauche du planum temporale: A-propos de l'étude de 100 cerveaux. *Revue Neurologique* 126:444–452, 1972.

Teuber, H.-L. Physiological psychology. *Annual Review of Psychology* 6:267–296, 1955.

Toga, A. W., and P. M. Thompson. Mapping brain asymmetry. *Nature Reviews Neuroscience* 4: 37–48, 2003.

Uomini, N. T., and G. F. Meyer. Shared brain lateralization patterns in language and acheulean stone tool production: A functional transcranial Doppler ultrasound study. *PLoS One* 8:e72693, 2013.

Van Essen, D. C., M. F. Glasser, D. L. Dierker, J. Harwell, and T. Coalson. Parcellations and hemispheric asymmetries in human cerebral cortex analyzed on surface-based atlases. *Cerebral Cortex* 22:2241–2262, 2012.

Van Lancker, D., and V. Fromkin. Hemispheric specialization for pitch and "tone": Evidence from Thai. *Journal of Phonetics* 1:101–109, 1973.

von Bonin, B. Anatomical asymmetries of the cerebral hemispheres. In V. B. Mountcastle, Ed., *Interhemispheric Relations and Cerebral Dominance*. Baltimore: Johns Hopkins University Press, 1962.

von Economo, C. V., and L. Horn. Über Windungsrelief, Masse and Rindenarchitektonik der Supratemporalfläche, ihre individuellen und ihre Seitenunterschiede. *Zeitschrift für Neurologie und Psychiatrie* 130:678–757, 1930.

Wada, J., and T. Rasmussen. Intracarotid injection of sodium amytal for the lateralization of cerebral speech dominance. *Journal of Neurosurgery* 17:266–282, 1960.

Wada, J. A., R. Clarke, and A. Hamm. Cerebral hemispheric asymmetry in humans: Cortical speech zones in 100 adult and 100 infant brains. *Archives of Neurology* 32:239–246, 1975.

Webster, W. G., and A. D. Thurber. Problem solving strategies and manifest brain asymmetry. *Cortex* 14:474–484, 1978.

Witelson, S. F., and W. Pallie. Left hemisphere specialization for language in the newborn: Neuroanatomical evidence of asymmetry. *Brain* 96:641–646, 1973.

Wolf, M. E., and M. A. Goodale. Oral asymmetries during verbal and non-verbal movements of the mouth. *Neuropsychologia* 25:375–396, 1987.

Wylie, D. R., and M. A. Goodale. Left-sided oral asymmetries in spontaneous but not posed smiles. *Neuropsychologia* 26: 823–832, 1988.

Yanowitz, J. S., P. Satz, and K. M. Heilman. Foot-length asymmetry, sex, and handedness. *Science* 212:1418, 1981.

Zatorre, R. J., P. Belin, and V. B. Penhume. Structure and function of auditory cortex: Music and speech. *Trends in Cognitive Sciences* 6:37–46, 2002.

Zurif, E. Auditory lateralization: Prosodic and syntactic factors. *Brain and Language* 1:391–401, 1974.

12 Variations in Cerebral Asymmetry

Individual Responses to Injury

No two brains are alike; indeed, no two hemispheres are even grossly alike, as clearly illustrated in the accompanying photograph, looking down on the brain from above. Anatomically, brains—and hemispheres—differ in size, gyral patterns, gray- and white-matter distribution, cyto-architectonics, vascular patterns, and neurochemistry, among other things. Do variations in anatomical asymmetry correlate with functional asymmetries in the brain?

Consider A.B. and L.P., two middle-aged college graduates who had similar brain injuries but responded very differently. Given their similar injuries and education (both had been psychology majors in college and presumably above average in intelligence before their injuries), we would expect their symptoms to

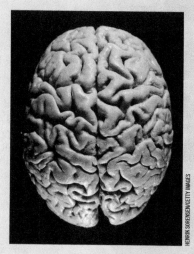

be similar. Instead, they appeared to be opposite.

After an injury to the posterior part of the left temporal lobe, A.B. had verbal difficulties—in reading, speaking, and remembering words. L.P., whose injury was similar, had no language difficulties. But L.P. had trouble recognizing faces and drawing pictures, symptoms that A.B. did not exhibit.

Two significant differences between these people help explain their differing symptoms: A.B. was a right-handed man and L.P. a left-handed woman. These two factors—sex and handedness—influence hemispheric organization and ultimately the effects of cerebral injury. In this case, language in L.P. resided in the right hemisphere, which explains why she had no language impairments.

Handedness and sex are easily identified factors influencing cerebral asymmetry, but they are not the only factors that lead to individual differences in brain organization and behavior. This chapter examines a range of biological and environmental factors that may produce such individual variations. In examining the relations on individual patterns of asymmetry between brain organization and hand preference, sex differences, and genes and environment in the sections that follow, we consider the data before considering theories about differences in patterns of cerebral organization.

12.1 Handedness and Functional Asymmetry

Nearly everyone prefers one hand to the other for writing or throwing a ball. Most people prefer the right hand. Historically, left-handedness has been viewed at best as odd. But it is not rare. An estimated 10 percent of the human population worldwide is left-handed. This proportion is the number of people who write with the left hand. When other criteria are used to determine left-handedness, estimates range from 10 percent to 30 percent of the population.

Marion Annett (1972) constructed a useful distribution of handedness (**Table 12.1**) by asking more than 2000 adults to indicate the hand that they use to perform each of 12 tasks. The evidence of left-handedness on Annett's tasks varies from a low of about 6 percent for cutting with scissors to a high of about 17 percent for dealing cards. Handedness is not absolute. At the extremes, some people are nearly totally left- or right-handed, whereas others are ambidextrous—they use either hand with equal facility.

Anatomical Studies

Hand preference correlates with differential patterns of right–left asymmetry in cerebral blood flow, the parietal operculum, frontal cortex, and occipital region, as summarized in **Table 12.2**. Thus, in comparison with right-handers, a higher proportion of left-handers show no asymmetry or, like L.P. in the opening Portrait, a reversal of left and right anatomical asymmetries.

Are variations in anatomical organization related in any meaningful way to handedness? To answer this question, Graham Ratcliffe (1980) and his colleagues correlated the asymmetry in the course (angle) of the Sylvian (lateral) fissure as revealed by carotid angiogram with the results of carotid sodium amobarbital speech testing (see Figure 11.11). They found that left- and right-handers with speech in the left hemisphere had a mean right–left difference of 27° in the angle formed by the vessels leaving the posterior end of the Sylvian fissure. In left- and right-handers with speech in the right hemisphere or with bilateral speech, the mean difference shrank to 0°.

Thus, the anatomical asymmetry in the population studied by Ratcliffe is related to speech representation and not necessarily to handedness. The location of speech proved a better predictor of individual variation in cerebral organization than did handedness.

Handedness may appear closely related to anatomical anomalies because left-handers display more variation in speech lateralization. A series of studies by P. Yakovlev and Pasko Rakic (1966) are germane. In studying more than 300 brains of right-handers, they found that in 80 percent the pyramidal tract descending to the right hand contains more fibers than does the same tract going to the left hand. Apparently, more fibers descend to the right hand both from the contralateral left hemisphere and from the ipsilateral right hemisphere than descend to the left hand. In addition, the contralateral tract from the left hemisphere crosses at a higher level in the medulla than does the contralateral tract from the right hemisphere.

Table 12.1 **Summary of handedness in performing various tasks**

Task	Left (percent)	Either (percent)	Right (percent)
Dealing cards	17.02	3.32	79.66
Unscrewing jar	6.50	17.49	66.01
Shoveling	13.53	11.89	74.58
Sweeping	13.49	16.89	69.62
Threading needle	13.10	9.74	77.16
Writing	10.60	0.34	89.06
Striking match	9.95	8.74	81.31
Throwing ball	9.44	1.29	89.47
Hammering	9.22	2.54	88.24
Using toothbrush	9.18	8.49	82.33
Using racket	8.10	2.59	89.31
Using scissors	6.20	6.81	86.99

Note: Percentages are based on 2321 respondents.

Data source: Annett, M. A classification of hand preference by association analysis. *British Journal of Psychology* 61:303–321, 1970.

Table 12.2 **Variations in anatomical asymmetry related to handedness**

| Measure | Handedness | ANATOMICAL DIFFERENCES | | |
		Left Larger, percent	Right Larger, percent	No Difference, percent
Blood volume	Right	25	62	13
	Left	64	28	8
Parietal operculum	Right	67	8	25
	Left	22	7	71
Frontal width	Right	19	61	20
	Left	27	40	33
Occipital width	Right	66	9	25
	Left	38	27	35
Occipital horns	Right	60	10	30
	Left	38	31	31

Data sources: Hochberg and LeMay (1975), LeMay (1977), and Carmon et al. (1972).

To date, data are available only for 11 left-handers, but the pattern is remarkably similar to that of right-handers: 9 of the 11 had the typical right-side bias.

A difficulty in accounting for variations in anatomical asymmetries is that some left- and right-handers show a marked dissociation between morphological (structural) and functional asymmetry. Thus, carotid sodium amobarbital testing may show speech to reside in the left hemisphere, but the enlarged temporoparietal speech zone is inferred from other neurological studies to be in the right hemisphere. And a large percentage of the cases of right-handedness summarized in Table 12.2 do not show the expected asymmetries but have reversed asymmetries or no differences at all. These cases pose a significant interpretation problem, and they suggest that other variables, still unknown, also may account for individual differences in both left- and right-handers.

Another place to look for anatomical differences related to handedness is in MRI studies of left- and right-handed participants. Although many investigators have looked in MRI scans for handedness effects, they find little evidence of gross anatomical differences. An exception is the depth of the central fissure. Katrin Amunts and colleagues (2000) found that male right-handers have a significantly deeper fissure on the left than on the right but found no difference in left-handers. How this difference might relate to handedness remains unknown, but given that the central fissure separates motor from somatosensory cortical control of hand movements, it is a promising lead.

Another place to look for handedness-related differences is the interhemispheric connections. Sandra Witelson (1989) studied the hand preference of terminally ill subjects on a variety of unimanual tasks. During postmortem studies of their brains, paying particular attention to the size of the corpus callosum, she found that the cross-sectional area was 11 percent greater in left-handed and ambidextrous people than in right-handed people.

Whether the larger callosum of non–right-handers contains a greater total number of nerve fibers, thicker axons, or more myelin remains to be determined. If the larger callosum results from the number of fibers, the difference will consist of some 25 million fibers. Confirmation of Witelson's result by others will imply greater interaction between the hemispheres of left-handers and will suggest that the pattern of cerebral organization may be fundamentally different in left- and right-handers.

Functional Cerebral Organization in Left-Handers

Although the generalization that cognitive functions are more bilaterally organized in left-handers than in right-handers is widespread in the neurological literature, little evidence exists for it. Using the sodium amobarbital procedure, Charles Branch and colleagues (1964) found that, in left-handers, language is represented in the left hemisphere in 70 percent, in the right hemisphere in 15 percent, and bilaterally in 15 percent.

Similarly, Doreen Kimura (1983) reported the incidence of aphasia and apraxia in a consecutive series of 520 patients selected for unilateral brain damage only. The frequency of left-handedness in her population was within the expected range, and these patients did not have a higher incidence of either aphasia or apraxia than right-handers did. In fact, the incidence of aphasia in left-handed patients was approximately 70 percent of the incidence in right-handers, exactly what would be predicted from the sodium amobarbital studies. Thus, although a small proportion of left-handers have bilateral or right-hemisphere speech, the majority do not.

Henri Hécaen and Jean Sauguet (1971) suggested that left-handers can be subdivided into two genetic populations differing in cerebral organization: familial left-handers, who have a family history of left-handedness, and nonfamilial left-handers, who have no such family history. According to Hécaen and Sauguet, the performance of nonfamilial left-handed patients with unilateral lesions on neuropsychological tests resembles that of right-handed patients. In contrast, familial left-handers perform much differently, suggesting to Hécaen and Sauguet that they have a different pattern of cerebral organization.

In summary, we find little evidence that speech or nonspeech functions in the 70 percent of left-handers with speech represented in the left hemisphere differs from right-handers' cerebral organization of these functions. One caveat: a larger incidence of left-handedness is observed among mentally disabled children and among children with various neurological disorders than is found in the general population.

This finding is not surprising: if the dominant hemisphere is injured at an early age, handedness and dominance can move to the control of what would typically be the nondominant hemisphere. Because there are so many more right-handed children, probability alone dictates that more right-handed children with left-hemisphere damage would switch to right-hemisphere dominance than would switch in the reverse direction. That such switching can take place, however, cannot be used as grounds for predicting cognitive deficits or differences in cerebral organization in the general population of left-handers.

An additional question concerns the cerebral hemisphere organization in left-handers who have right-hemisphere speech. Is there simply a straight reversal of functions from one hemisphere to the other? Unfortunately, little is known about cerebral organization in people who have right-hemisphere speech and otherwise typical asymmetries.

◎ Theories of Hand Preference

The many theories put forward to account for hand preference can be categorized broadly according to their environmental, anatomical, hormonal, or genetic emphasis. Each category shelters widely varied points of view.

Environmental Theories

Environmental theories of handedness stress either its utility, reinforcement for hand use, or a cerebral deficit caused by accident. One utility hypothesis states that it is adaptive for a mother to hold an infant in her left hand to be soothed by the rhythm of her heart, thus leaving her right hand to attend to other activities. Of course, we do not know if right-handedness preceded the behavior and is thus responsible for it rather than being caused by it.

An environmental theory based on reinforcement suggests that handedness is established by a bias in the environment. A child's world is right-handed in many ways that reinforce using that hand. Historically, children in many countries, including the United States, were forced to write with their right hand.

The problem is that in recent decades, children in the United States have been allowed their choice of hand in learning to write, and the incidence of left-handed writing has risen to only 10 percent, which is the norm in most societies that have been studied.

A final category of environmental theory postulates a genetically determined bias toward being right-handed. Left-handedness thus develops through a cerebral deficit caused by accident during development. This idea emerges from correlating statistics on the incidence of left-handedness and neurological disorders in twins. About 18 percent of twins are left-handed, close to twice the occurrence in the population at large. Twins also show a high incidence of neurological disorders that are suspected to result overwhelmingly from intrauterine crowding during fetal development and stress during delivery.

The conclusion that stressful gestation and birth result in an elevated incidence of brain damage is logical. Is left-handedness a form of brain damage? Paul Bakan and his colleagues (1973) extend this logic to nontwins. They argue for a high probability of stressful births among left-handers, which increases the risk of brain damage to an infant and so maintains the statistical incidence of left-handedness. Although the environmental accident theory is intriguing, there is no compelling support for it. For more on genetic relationship and brain structure, see the Snapshot.

Anatomical Theories

Among the several anatomical theories of handedness, two explain hand preference on the basis of anatomical asymmetry.

The first theory attributes right-handedness to enhanced maturation and ultimately greater development of the left hemisphere. Generalizing from this assumption, the theory predicts that nonfamilial left-handers will show an asymmetry mirroring that of right-handers, whereas familial left-handers will show no anatomical asymmetry. These predictions are difficult to assess because no studies have specifically considered anatomical asymmetry with respect to handedness or to familial history and handedness. A major problem with this theory is that it simply pushes the question one step backward, asking not, "Why handedness?" but instead, "Why anatomical asymmetry?"

The second anatomical theory of handedness addresses this question in part. Many animals have a left-sided developmental advantage that is not genetically encoded. For example, there is a left-side bias for the location of the heart, the size of the ovaries in birds, the control of birdsong, the size of the left temporal cortex in humans, the size of the left side of the skull in the great apes, and so on. This predominance of left-favoring asymmetries puts the more celebrated left-hemisphere speech dominance in the more general structural perspective of all anatomical asymmetries.

Hormonal Theories

Norman Geschwind and Albert Galaburda (1987) proposed that early in life, brain plasticity can modify cerebral asymmetry significantly, leading to anomalous patterns of hemispheric organization. Central to their theory is the action of the sex-linked male hormone testosterone in altering cerebral organization during the course of development. Testosterone does affect cerebral organization, as detailed in Section 12.2, so the suggestion that differences in

SNAPSHOT Genetic Influences on Brain Structure

One way to investigate the relative contributions of genes and experience to cerebral organization is to analyze MRIs from typical brains and to vary the genetic relationships among the participants. Thompson and colleagues (2001) varied genetic relatedness by comparing the MRIs of pairs of unrelated people, dizygotic twins, and monozygotic twins. They took advantage of advances in MRI technology that allow detailed mapping of gray-matter distribution across the cerebral hemispheres.

The results are striking, as you can see in the adjoining illustration. The quantity of gray matter, especially in frontal, sensorimotor, and posterior language cortices, ranged from dissimilar in unrelated people to almost identical in monozygotic twins. Because monozygotic twins are genetically identical, we can presume that any differences must be attributable to environmental effects. Curiously, there

was an asymmetry in the degree of similarity: the left-hemisphere language zones were significantly more similar than in the right hemisphere in the monozygotic twins.

The high similarities among monozygotic twins likely account for their highly similar cognitive abilities. Additionally, given that various diseases, such as schizophrenia and some dementias, affect the integrity of the cortex, the high correlation between the brain structures of identical twins could account for the strong genetic component of these diseases.

Thompson, P. M., T. D. Cannon, K. L. Narr, T. van Erp, V. P. Poutanen, M. Huttunen, J. Lonnqvist, C. G. Standertskjold-Nordenstam, J. Kaprio, M. Khaledy, R. Dail, C. I. Zoumalan, and A. W. Toga. Genetic influences on brain structure. *Nature Neuroscience* 4:1253–1258, 2001.

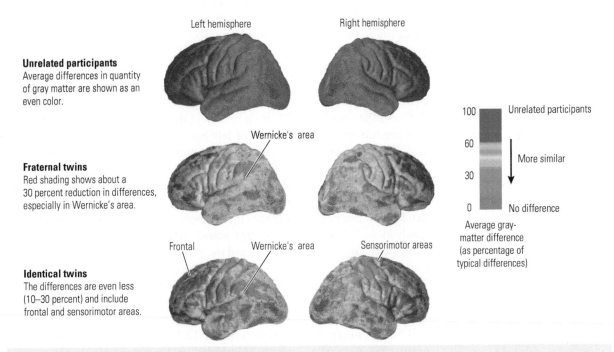

Average differences in quantity of gray matter in each cortical region for identical and fraternal twins compared to average differences between pairs of randomly selected, unrelated persons. (Reprinted by permission from Macmillan Publishers Ltd:

Thompson P. M., Cannon T. D., Narr K. L., van Erp T., Poutanen V. P., Huttunen M., Lonnqvist J., Standertskjold-Nordenstam C. G., Kaprio J., Khaledy M., Dail R., Zoumalan C. I., Toga A. W. "Genetic influences on brain structure," *Nature Neuroscience* 4[12]:1253–1258, 2001.

testosterone level might influence cerebral asymmetry is reasonable, particularly if the testosterone receptors were asymmetrically distributed.

Geschwind and Galaburda suggested that testosterone's effect is largely inhibitory, meaning that higher-than-normal testosterone levels will slow development, possibly acting directly on the brain or indirectly through an action on genes. Central to the Geschwind–Galaburda theory is the idea that testosterone's inhibitory action takes place largely in the left hemisphere, thus allowing the right hemisphere to grow more rapidly, which leads to altered cerebral organization and, in some people, to left-handedness. A further feature of the theory is that testosterone also affects the immune system, leading to more diseases related to a malfunctioning immune system. (A parallel theory of the relation between the immune system and male afflictions had been proposed by Gualtieri and Hicks, 1985.)

The Geschwind–Galaburda theory is elaborate and has generated considerable research. Unfortunately, the bulk of available evidence does not support the model. (For a thorough review, see Bryden et al., 1994.) For example, in one study, Gina Grimshaw and her colleagues (1993) studied handedness in children whose mothers had undergone amniocentesis, thus enabling assessment of fetal levels of testosterone. Increased testosterone levels did not result in increased left-handedness. Nonetheless, the data in the literature do show that left-handers are at greater risk for allergies and asthma, whereas autoimmune disorders such as arthritis are more prevalent in right-handers. These differences still have not been explained.

Genetic Theories

Most genetic models for handedness postulate a dominant gene or genes for right-handedness and a recessive gene or genes for left-handedness (see Hardyck and Petrinovich, 1977, for a review of these models). But the model that best predicts the actual number of left-handers in the population, by Annett (e.g., 2000), rejects this idea in favor of a dominant gene (rs^+) responsible for left-hemisphere speech development.

Annett hypothesized further that the processes necessary for left-hemisphere speech also confer an advantage on motor control in the right hand. The recessive form of the gene (rs^+) results in no systematic bias either for speech or for handedness. If both alleles occurred equally often statistically, then 50 percent of the population would be (rs^{+-}) and the rest would be equally divided, 25 percent (rs^{++}) and 25 percent (rs^{--}). People in the rs^{+-} and rs^{++} groups, constituting 75 percent of the population, would show a left-for-speech and right-handedness shift. The remaining 25 percent, people in the rs^{--} group, would show no bias: half would, by chance, be left-handed.

Thus, Annett's model predicts about 12.5 percent left-handers, which is pretty close to what we see in the population. Unfortunately, her theory neither predicts the number of left-handers with right-hemisphere speech nor attempts to differentiate between familial and nonfamilial left-handers. Similar problems are found with other genetic models.

Clearly, we do not know why handedness develops, and we may never know. Based on the variety of theories just presented, however, no single cause seems likely. Undoubtedly, some genetic basis exists for the development of left-handedness in some people, but how it relates to cerebral organization remains a mystery. Of little doubt, however, is that the asymmetrical representation of language and spatial functions, rather than handedness, is the major factor in cerebral asymmetry.

12.2 Sex Differences in Cerebral Organization

Men and women behave differently: sex is an obvious source of individual variation in human behavior. Substantial anecdotal and experimental evidence reveals cognitive differences between men and women, and several researchers have attempted to relate them to biological differences in brain organization. If one neurological principle can be abstracted to distinguish the sexes, it is that, on average, women tend to be more fluent than men in using language, and men tend to perform better than women in spatial analysis. But sex, like handedness, is not absolute. All men and women exhibit both male and female traits to greater and lesser degrees.

Sex Differences in Children's Behavior

Melissa Hines (2010) argues that the biggest sex difference in behavior can be seen in children's play. Children spend much of their time playing, and play is believed to have a critical role in brain development (e.g., Pellis & Pellis, 2009). Girls and boys differ in their toy, playmate, and activity preferences. Boys tend to prefer toy vehicles and girls tend to prefer dolls.

Children generally prefer playmates of their own sex, and boys spend much more time in rough-and-tumble play than girls do. The sex difference in toy preference is especially interesting and has generally been assumed to result from socialization. Indeed, children tend to choose toys that have been labeled as being "girl" or "boy" toys or those that younger children have seen older children playing with. One surprising finding, however, is that toy preferences, as well as other sex-typed aspects of play, are also influenced by prenatal testosterone.

Beginning at about 7 weeks of gestation, the testes begin to produce testosterone, leading to a vast difference in testosterone concentrations in males and females prenatally. Studies of androgen receptors in the brains of laboratory animals have shown that prenatal exposure to testosterone produces sex differences in brain structure and function (see a review by McCarthy et al., 2009). The relationship between childhood play and prenatal testosterone can be measured in two ways.

The first is to look at play behavior in girls who have been exposed to unusually high levels of testosterone in utero. For example, the children of mothers prescribed androgenic progestins show increased male-typical behavior, whereas those exposed to antiandrogenic progestins show the opposite effects (see reviews by Hines, 2010, 2011).

A second type of study relates fetal testosterone levels in amniotic fluid in normally developing fetuses to male-typical scores on measures of sex-typical play in boys and girls. For example, Bonnie Auyeung and her colleagues (2009) found a significant correlation between fetal testosterone and sexually dimorphic play in both girls and boys. Given that the parents did not know their

Figure 12.1 ▶

Figure 12.1 ▶

Sex Differences in Toy Choice When female and male vervet monkeys have access to children's sex-typed toys, the female (left) inspects a doll much as a human girl would, whereas the male (right) moves the car along much as a human boy would do. (Alexander, G. M., & Hines, M. (2002). Sex differences in response to children's toys in non–human primates (*Cercopithecus aethiops sabaeus*). *Evolution and Human Behavior* 23, 6:467–479. © Elsevier.)

ⓢ **Figure 12.2 ▼**

Tasks Illustrating Sex Differences in Behavior On average, women perform tests of calculation, verbal memory, object memory, fine motor skills, and perception better than men do. Men, on average, perform tests of mathematical reasoning, geometric form perception, mental rotation, target-directed motor skills, and visual imaging better than women do.

children's testosterone levels, it is unlikely that socialization accounts for the sex difference.

Although the Auyeung study did not measure toy preference, studies of monkeys have shown a sex difference in toy preference similar to those seen in human children. For example, as **Figure 12.1** suggests, male vervet monkeys spend more time with such male-typical toys as a car, whereas females prefer such female-typical toys as a doll (Alexander & Hines, 2002). It is not obvious what it is about trucks and cars that attracts males, but it may simply be that males prefer toys that can be moved in space, and those with wheels are especially movable.

Sex Differences in Adult Behavior

In her book *Sex and Cognition*, Kimura (1999) examines five classes of cognitive behaviors and finds compelling sex differences in all—namely, as illustrated in **Figure 12.2**, motor skills, spatial analysis, mathematical aptitude, perception,

Tasks favoring women			Tasks favoring men		
Mathematical calculation	65 73	$13 \times 4 - 21 + 34$ $2(13 + 17) + 18 - \dfrac{20}{4}$	Tests of mathematical reasoning	1650	If only 40% of seedlings will survive, how many must be planted to obtain 660 trees?
Recall of a story, a paragraph, or unrelated words	Story…	Run, flower, casserole, water, explosion, pencil, horse, newspaper, book, pliers, bath, dancer…	Mentally finding a geometric form in a complex picture		
Remembering displaced objects			Mentally rotating a solid object		
Precision, fine motor coordination			Target-directed motor skills		
Rapidly matching items in perceptual tests			Visualizing where holes punched in a folded paper will fall		

and verbal abilities. **Table 12.3** summarizes her major conclusions and shows that the verbal–spatial dichotomy just noted is a gross oversimplification. We briefly consider each class of behavior next.

Motor Skills

An obvious difference in motor skills is that on average men are superior at throwing objects, such as balls or darts, at targets and at catching objects thrown toward them. We could conclude that the average difference is related to practice, but this conclusion is unlikely because such differences are present in children as young as 3 years of age. Furthermore, chimpanzees show a similar sexual dimorphism, although their motor control is far less accurate than that of humans.

In contrast, women have superior fine motor control and surpass men in executing sequential and intricate hand movements. This difference is also unlikely to be related to experience, because young girls are superior to young boys at each of these skills.

Spatial Analysis

Men are superior at spatial analysis tasks requiring mental rotation of objects, such as those illustrated in Figure 12.2, and they are superior at spatial navigation tasks. But the general belief that men are superior to women at spatial analysis holds only for some types of spatial behaviors, as shown in a task illustrated in **Figure 12.3**.

Participants are given a tabletop map on which they must learn a designated route. Although this is not a real-world test of spatial navigation, the findings are consistent with those of studies showing that men have better overall map knowledge than women. On average, men learn such tasks faster and with fewer errors than women do.

Male superiority in spatial-navigation tasks contrasts with female superiority in tests of spatial memory. As illustrated in Figure 12.2, women are better than men at identifying which objects have been moved or displaced. In the map test (Figure 12.3), women have better recall for landmarks along the route. Thus, the spatial information itself is not the critical factor in this sex difference; rather, the critical factor is the required behavior: how the spatial information is to be used.

Mathematical Aptitude

Mathematical ability is perhaps the oldest-established sex difference and undoubtedly the most controversial. On average, men get better scores on tests of mathematical reasoning, whereas women do better on tests of computation (see Figure 12.2).

Camille Benbow and Julian Stanley (1980) conducted perhaps the most provocative studies on mathematical aptitude. In a talent search for mathematically

Table 12.3 **Summary of sex differences in cognitive behavior**

Behavior	Sex Difference	Basic Reference
Motor Skills		
Target throwing and catching	M > F	Hall and Kimura, 1995
Fine motor skills	F > M	Nicholson and Kimura, 1996
Spatial Analysis		
Mental rotation	M > F	Collins and Kimura, 1997
Spatial navigation	M > F	Astur et al., 1998
Geographical knowledge	M > F	Beatty and Troster, 1987
Spatial memory	F > M	McBurney et al., 1997
Mathematical Aptitude		
Computation	F > M	Hyde et al., 1990
Mathematical reasoning	M > F	Benbow, 1988
Perception		
Sensitivity to sensory stimuli	F > M	Velle, 1987
Perceptual speed	F > M	Majeres, 1983
Sensitivity to facial and body expression	F > M	Hall, 1984
Visual recognition memory	F > M	McGivern et al., 1998
Verbal Abilities		
Fluency	F > M	Hyde and Linn, 1988
Verbal memory	F > M	McGuinness et al., 1990

Tabletop Map for Route Learning Men learn routes in fewer trials than women do, but women recall more landmarks along the way. (Courtesy of Bryan Kolb.)

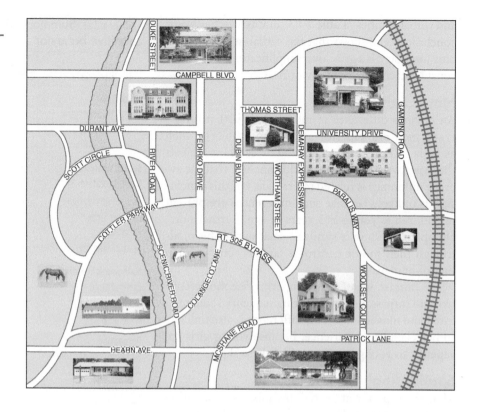

gifted seventh-grade students, they found a 13:1 ratio of high-achieving boys to girls both in the United States and worldwide across different cultures, although the absolute scores varied with educational system (Benbow, 1988). By 2000, the ratio in adolescents had dropped to 4:1 and has been stable since then (Benbow et al., 2000).

More recently, a study by Gijsbert Stoet and David Geary (2013) analyzed the mathematics and reading performance of nearly 1.5 million 15-year-olds in 75 countries. Across nations, boys scored higher than girls in mathematics but lower in reading. The sex difference in reading was three times larger than in mathematics.

Perception

Perception refers to recognizing and interpreting the sensory information we take in from the external world. There would appear to be no a priori reason to expect a sex difference, but the evidence suggests that women are more sensitive to all forms of sensory stimulation except vision. That is not to say that no difference exists in the perception of some types of visual material, however, because women are more sensitive than men to facial expressions and body postures.

Not only do women have lower thresholds for stimulus detection, they also detect sensory stimuli faster than men (see Figure 12.2). Males may have one perceptual advantage, however, in that their drawings of mechanical objects such as bicycles are superior to those of females (**Figure 12.4**A). This particular advantage yields no general advantage in drawing, as illustrated in Figure 12.4B.

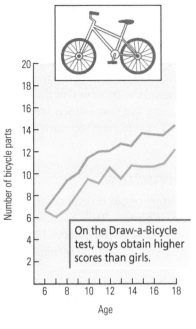

(A) Draw-a-Bicycle

Number of bicycle parts

On the Draw-a-Bicycle test, boys obtain higher scores than girls.

Age

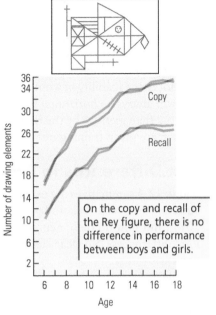

(B) Rey Complex Figure

Number of drawing elements

Copy

Recall

On the copy and recall of the Rey figure, there is no difference in performance between boys and girls.

Age

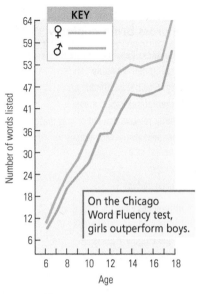

(C) Chicago Word Fluency

KEY
♀
♂

Number of words listed

On the Chicago Word Fluency test, girls outperform boys.

Age

⊚ Figure 12.4 ▲

Performance on Three Neuropsychological Tests by Boys and Girls at Different Ages (Whishaw and Kolb, unpublished.)

Verbal Ability

Women are superior to men on tests of verbal fluency, on average, and they have superior verbal memory (see Figure 12.2). The sex difference in verbal ability has long been known, in part because girls begin talking before boys and appear to be more fluent throughout life. For example, the Chicago Word Fluency test asks participants to write as many words beginning with "s" as possible in 5 minutes and as many four-letter words beginning with "c" as possible in 4 minutes. As Figure 12.4C illustrates, girls performed better—at some ages by as many as 10 words—in a broad study that we did with children.

Effect Size

Although statistically significant sex differences in behavior have been recorded, we can reasonably ask just how significant those differences are. One way to quantify how well statistical significance measures behavioral differences over a range of contexts is to calculate **effect size**, the difference between the mean of an experimental group and a control group as a proportion of a standard deviation in performance. Effect sizes around 0.5 show considerable overlap between the performance of populations of females and males on all the tests. Most effect sizes for the tasks summarized in Table 12.3 are about 0.5, the one exception being target throwing, which is large—on the order of 1.1–2.0.

Genes or Experience?

Sex-related differences, it often is argued, are related to life experience, but Kimura argues compellingly that this relation is unlikely for the cognitive behaviors summarized in Table 12.3. In particular, most if not all of these differences are found in both children and adults and are largely unaffected by training. Training effects certainly exist for most tests but tend to be of similar magnitude in both sexes.

Furthermore, some sex differences seem unrelated to life experience. Consider the test illustrated in **Figure 12.5**. The task is to draw the water line in a series of half-filled, tilted glass jars. Women consistently

⊚ Figure 12.5 ▼

A Water-Level Task The water line must be drawn on each jar.

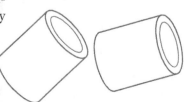

Table 12.4 **Sex differences in gross brain anatomy**

Differences Favoring Female Brains
Larger language areas
Larger medial paralimbic areas
Larger lateral frontal areas
Greater relative amount of gray matter
More densely packed neurons in temporal lobe
More gyri
Thicker cortex

Differences Favoring Male Brains
Larger medial frontal areas
Larger cingulate areas
Larger amygdala and hypothalamus
Larger overall white matter volume
Larger cerebral ventricles
Larger right planum parietale
More neurons overall
Larger brain

Note: For reviews and extensive reference lists, see Cahill, 2009; Hines, 2010; Sacher et al., 2013.

underperform on this task relative to men, a difference seen in both young and old participants and in university students, whether science or non-science majors (Thomas et al., 1973). The difference in performance is due not to the inability of women to understand the concept that the water line will always be horizontal but rather to the fact that women are more affected than men are by the tilt of the jar. The difference remains even if women are given training on the test.

Sex Differences in Brain Structure

Table 12.4 summarizes the extensive literature on sex differences in brain structure (see also reviews by Cahill, 2009; Hines, 2010; Sacher et al., 2013). But how do these neural differences relate to the observed behavioral differences? No clear answer has emerged. One study is suggestive, however.

Eileen Luders and her colleagues (2005) used MRI scans to identify regions of the gray matter that have a high signal intensity—a measure that they call *gray-matter concentration*. Whereas males have more-uniform gray-matter concentration, females have a patchwork of concentration differences, as shown in **Figure 12.6**. Although the investigators do not relate this sex difference to cognitive differences, the conclusion that it must relate is not a stretch. For example, the increased concentration in the peri-Sylvian regions representing the finger areas (see the middle scan) could be related to women's advantage in fine motor skills.

Influence of Sex Hormones

Sex differences in brain structure have been related to differences in the distribution of estrogen and androgen receptors during development. Jill Goldstein and her colleagues (2005) also used MRI scans to compare the brains of men and women, but they concentrated on differences in relative surface area. By correcting for the difference in overall brain size (male brains are larger), Goldstein's team found sexually dimorphic regions in the prefrontal cortex, paralimbic cortex, and the posterior parietal cortex (**Figure 12.7**). Again, it is not a stretch to suggest that these regional differences are related to the sex-related

Figure 12.6 ▶

Sex Differences in Gray-Matter Concentration
Compared to men, women have increased gray-matter concentration in the cortical regions shown in color on these composite MRIs. Not all gray-shaded regions are statistically different in males and females. (Dr. Arthur Toga, Laboratory of Neuro Imaging at UCLA. from "Mapping cortical gray matter in the young adult brain: Effects of gender." *NeuroImage* 26, 2, (2005): pp. 493–501. © Elsevier.)

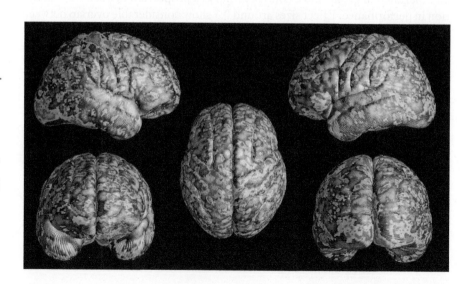

behavioral differences that have been described. But do sex differences exist in anatomical or functional cerebral asymmetries?

Anatomical Asymmetries

Sex differences in overall brain size and in the relative sizes of brain regions does not speak directly to the question, Do sex differences occur in the degree of cerebral asymmetry?

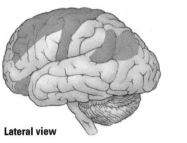

Lateral view

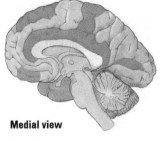

Medial view

Although women's cerebral hemispheres are reportedly more symmetrical than men's, this conclusion is based largely on nonsignificant trends or impressions. However, several reliable sex differences in anatomical asymmetry do exist:

1. Asymmetry (left larger than right) in the planum temporale (Wernicke's area) is seen more often in men than in women. In fact, an MRI study by Jennifer Kulynych and her colleagues (1994) found a large asymmetry in males (left 38 percent larger) but no asymmetry in females. A. Dorion and colleagues (2000) found a similar result but noted in addition that the absolute magnitude of cerebral asymmetry was negatively correlated with the size of the corpus callosum in males but not females. This suggests a sex-dependent decrease in hemispheric connectivity with increasing hemispheric asymmetry.

2. Sandra Witelson and Debra Kigar (1992) quantified the slope of the Sylvian (lateral) fissure with reference to various cortical landmarks, which led to a separate measure of its horizontal and vertical components (**Figure 12.8**A).

   They found that, although the horizontal component is longer in the left hemisphere of both sexes, men had a larger horizontal component in the left hemisphere than did women. There was no difference in the right hemisphere. Thus, male brains have a larger asymmetry in the Sylvian fissure than do female brains. Taken together, the results of the studies of the planum temporale and the Sylvian fissure reinforce evidence for a sex difference in the organization of language-related functions.

3. The asymmetry in the planum parietale, which favors the right hemisphere, is about twice as large in men as in women (Jancke et al., 1994).

4. Numerous studies have found that women have more interhemispheric connections, in both the corpus callosum and the anterior commissure, than do men. The callosal studies have proved controversial, but the consensus appears to be that the posterior part of the callosum (the splenium) is significantly larger in women than in men (Figure 12.8B and **Table 12.5**—but see Luders et al., 2013). The sex difference found in the anterior commissure, a structure that connects the temporal lobes, appears to be less controversial (see Section 17.2). Laura Allen and Roger Gorski (1991) found that women have a larger anterior commissure than do men, even without correcting for brain size. This result is likely due to a difference in the number of neural fibers in the two sexes, which presumably affects how the two hemispheres interact.

⊚ Figure 12.7 ▲

Sex Differences in Brain Volume Relative to Cerebral Size Women's brain volume (purple) in prefrontal and medial paralimbic regions is significantly higher than men's. Men have larger relative volumes (pink) in the medial and orbital frontal cortex and the angular gyrus. Purple areas correspond to regions that have high levels of estrogen receptors during development, pink to regions high in androgen receptors during development. (Data from Goldstein et al., 2001.)

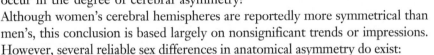

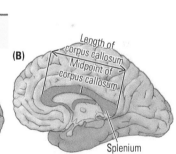

Figure 12.8 ▲

Measuring the Brain
(A) Lateral view of the left hemisphere illustrating the measuring points on the Sylvian (lateral) fissure. (B) The human corpus callosum shown in midsagittal section, indicating the subdivisions typically measured: the entire length and cross-sectional area; the anterior and posterior halves; and the splenium.

Table 12.5 Summary of brain measures in four groups classified by handedness and sex

Group	Number in Group	Age (years)	Brain Weight (g)	Callosal Area (mm²)
Males				
RH	7	48	1442	672
MH	5	49	1511	801[a]
Females				
RH	20	51	1269	655
MH	10	49	1237	697[a]

Note: RH, consistently right-handed; MH, left-handed or ambidextrous.
[a]Differs significantly from other same-sex group.
Data source: Simplified from Witelson (1985).

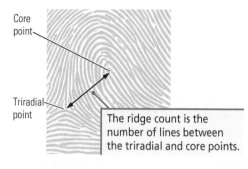

Core point

Triradial point

The ridge count is the number of lines between the triradial and core points.

Figure 12.9 ▲

Fingerprint Pattern

5. The ridges in our fingerprints, established early in fetal life, are asymmetrical: the fingers on the right hand have more ridges than do fingers on the left hand (**Figure 12.9**). Given that this pattern is visible in utero, it could not be influenced by such environmental factors as differences in limb use. Kimura (1999) found that most people have the asymmetry, but women are far more likely to show an atypical pattern, much as seen for brain asymmetries. The critical part of the Kimura studies (and later studies by others) is that the pattern of ridges is correlated with performance on certain cognitive tests.

Kimura also followed up on the studies of others, looking at asymmetries in sexually dimorphic body parts—namely, the size of the testes in men and of the breasts in women. She found that, whereas the right testicle tends to be larger than the left, breasts tend to be larger on the left than on the right. Importantly, the sex difference in gonad size is found in fetuses.

Once again, we must ask what such a finding might mean. At this time, the meaning is not obvious, but one conclusion is inescapable. If an asymmetry in gonad or breast size is sexually dimorphic, then there is every reason to expect sex differences in other body regions, especially in those, such as the brain, that are influenced by gonadal hormones.

The Homosexual Brain

Although few studies consider brain asymmetry and sexual orientation, there is evidence that parts of the hypothalamus of homosexual men differ from those of both heterosexual males and females, who also differ from one another in this regard (see reviews by Gooren, 2006, and by Swaab, 2004). Investigators have looked at the performance of heterosexual and homosexual males and females on tests that reveal sexual dimorphism in heterosexuals. The general finding is that sexual orientation is related to performance. For example, Qazi Rahman and colleagues (2003) found that homosexual men outperform all groups on verbal fluency, a test in which heterosexual women outperform heterosexual men, whereas homosexual women had the lowest scores.

Similarly, an examination of throwing ability (Hall and Kimura, 1995) showed that heterosexual men outperform heterosexual women, whereas homosexual men threw less accurately and homosexual women tend to throw more accurately than their heterosexual counterparts. Differences in sports history

Table 12.6 **Sex differences in imaging studies**

Measure	Result	Representative Reference
EEG	Males more asymmetrical	Corsi-Cabrera et al., 1997
MEG	Males more asymmetrical	Reite et al., 1995
Blood flow	Females > males	Gur et al., 1982
	Females > males in frontal-lobe tests	Esposito et al., 1996
PET	Males > females in anterior blood flow	Haverkort et al., 1999
	Females > males in posterior blood flow	
fMRI	More left-hemisphere activity in language-related tasks in males	Pugh et al., 1996 (but see Frost et al., 1999)
rs-fMRI	Females > males in left-hemisphere connectivity	Tian et al., 2011
	Males > females in right-hemisphere connectivity	

or hand strength did not account for these effects. Although such studies are intriguing, relating them to differences in brain organization is difficult. Perhaps the simplest way to relate sexual orientation to brain and behavior will be the use of noninvasive imaging, although to our knowledge, it has not yet been done.

Sex Differences Revealed in Functional Imaging Studies

The results of virtually all types of functional neuroimaging studies show sex-related differences, as summarized in **Table 12.6** (see review by Sacher et al., 2013). In general, EEG, MEG, and fMRI studies show more-asymmetrical activity in men than in women, particularly in language-related activities. Measures of blood flow, including those obtained using PET, show that women have more rapid overall blood exchange than do men, possibly owing to the difference in neuronal density or the distribution of gray matter and white matter.

Resting-state fMRI studies have shown extensive sex differences in neural connectivity. A review by Julia Sacher and her colleagues (2013) concludes that men show greater connectivity within the right hemisphere, whereas women show greater connectivity in the left hemisphere. It is tempting to relate these connectivity differences to the established sex differences in spatial and verbal abilities, respectively.

A large study by Madhura Ingalhalikar and colleagues (2013) used diffusion tensor imaging to model the connectome in a sample of 949 youths aged 8 to 22 (428 males and 521 females). Their key finding, mapped in **Figure 12.10**, is that females have greater interhemisphere connectivity, whereas males have greater intrahemisphere

(A) Male brain

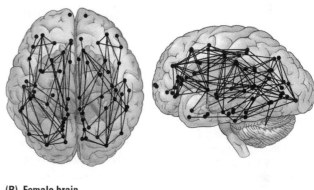

(B) Female brain

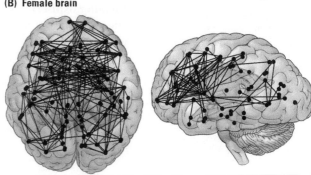

Figure 12.10 ▲

Sex Differences in the Connectome DTI analysis of brain networks, shown in these dorsal and lateral views, shows greater intrahemispheric connections in males (A) and greater interhemispheric connections in females (B). (Ingalhalikar, M., A. Smith, D. Parker, T. D. Satterthwaite, M. A. Elliot, K. Ruparel, H. Hakonarson, R. E. Gur, R. C. Gur, and R. Verma. "Sex differences in the structural connectome of the human brain." *Proceedings of the National Academy of Sciences* U.S.A. 111: 823-828, 2013, Fig. 2.)

connectivity. (Section 11.5 compares theories about male–female connectivity patterns.) The difference was present at a young age and progressed in size into adolescence and adulthood.

These results are consistent with postmortem neuroanatomical results that show greater callosal interhemispheric connectivity in females. Ingalhalikar and colleagues suggest that the DTI results reveal that female brains are designed to facilitate communication between analytical and intuitive processing, leading to superior performance on verbal, attentional, and social cognition tests. Male brains, in contrast, are structured to enhance connectivity between perception and coordinated action, leading to faster and more accurate performance on motor and spatial tasks.

In addition to imaging studies showing differences in hemispheric asymmetry, an even greater number of studies show more generalized differences in a wide range of behavioral tasks but do not necessarily show differences in asymmetry (Gur et al., 2012; Sacher et al., 2013). The main takeaway from all these results: not only do differences exist in the anatomical organization of the male and female brain but differences also exist in these brains' functional activity, a conclusion that is hardly surprising.

Research with Neurological Patients

If female and male brains differ in anatomical organization and connectivity as well as in metabolic activity, as the results of blood-flow, fMRI, and DTI studies indicate, then the effects of injury also might differ between the sexes. Two types of lesion-related differences are possible:

1. **Degree of asymmetry in the lesion effects.** Such a difference might exist if the two hemispheres were more similar functionally in one sex than in the other sex. Indeed, the greater asymmetry in men, as observed in EEG, MEG, and fMRI studies, suggests that men might show more asymmetrical effects of unilateral lesions than women.

2. **Intrahemispheric organization.** Frontal-lobe injury might have greater effects in one sex than in the other, a difference that would be consistent with greater relative volume of much of the frontal lobes of women and the differences in intrahemispheric connectivity.

In fact, there is evidence of both effects.

One way to assess the asymmetry of left- or right-hemisphere lesions is to look at their effects on general tests of verbal and nonverbal abilities. A way of measuring this difference is to examine the pattern of results in the effects of lateralized lesions on the performance and verbal achievement subscales of the Wechsler Adult Intelligence Scale (WAIS; see Section 28.2 for details on this IQ test). By using various statistical procedures with these data, James Inglis and Stuart Lawson (1982) showed that although left- and right-hemisphere lesions in men affect the verbal and performance subscales differently, left-hemisphere lesions in women depressed both IQ scores equally, and right-hemisphere lesions in women failed to depress either IQ score (**Figure 12.11**).

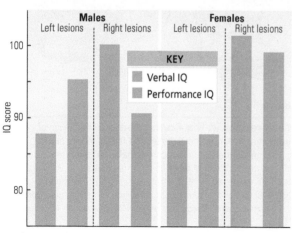

Figure 12.11 ▼

Effects of Injury A clear sex difference emerges in this summary of Inglis and Lawson's (1982) tabulation of studies reporting verbal and performance IQ scores in neurological patients. Males with left-hemisphere lesions exhibited a depression in verbal IQ, whereas males with right-hemisphere lesions exhibited a complementary deficit in performance IQ. In contrast, females with right-hemisphere lesions showed no significant depression on either IQ scale, whereas left-hemisphere lesions depressed both IQ scores equally.

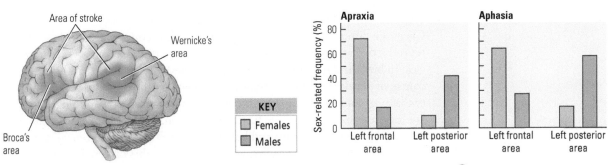

@ Figure 12.12 ▲

Patterns of Injury Evidence for intrahemispheric differences in male–female cortical organization. Apraxia is associated with frontal damage to the left hemisphere in women but with posterior damage in men. Aphasia develops most often with damage to the front of the brain in women but to the rear of the brain in men. (Data from Kimura, 1999.)

Thus, Inglis and Lawson found an equivalent effect of left-hemisphere lesions on verbal IQ score in both sexes, but men with right-hemisphere lesions were more disrupted than women were on the performance IQ test. This finding could imply that right-hemisphere organization differs in men and women. On the other hand, women could be more likely than men to use verbal strategies (that is, a verbal preferred cognitive mode) to solve the tests in the WAIS.

Work by Kimura (1999) shows that the pattern of cerebral organization within each hemisphere also differs between the sexes. Men and women are almost equally likely to be aphasic subsequent to left-hemisphere lesions. But men are likely to be aphasic and apraxic after damage to the left posterior cortex, whereas women are far more likely to experience speech disorders and apraxia after anterior lesions (**Figure 12.12**).

Kimura also obtained data from a small sample of patients that suggest an analogous sex-related difference subsequent to right-hemisphere lesions. Anterior, but not posterior, lesions in women impaired their performance of the block-design and object-assembly subtests of the WAIS, whereas men were equally affected on these tests by either anterior or posterior lesions.

Finally, Esther Strauss and her colleagues (1992) obtained a surprising result. They gave sodium amobarbital to 94 epileptic patients who were being considered for elective surgery after brain damage in infancy. Such left-hemisphere injury is known to lead to a language shift to the right hemisphere, so Strauss expected this shift to take place in patients with left-hemisphere injury.

The unexpected result was a sex difference in the likelihood of cerebral reorganization subsequent to left-hemisphere injury after 1 year of age: girls were unlikely to show reorganization, whereas boys appeared likely to shift language, perhaps as late as puberty. This unexpected result suggests that the male brain may be more plastic after cortical injury, a conclusion that has important implications if it proves reliable.

Taken together, the data from neurological patients support the idea that unilateral cortical lesions have different effects on male and female brains. The precise nature of the differences is still being debated, however.

@ Explanations for Sex Differences

We have considered sex differences in cerebral organization as inferred from studies of behavior, anatomy, imaging, and neurological patients. Five explanations commonly are advanced to account for sex differences: (1) hormonal effects on cerebral function, (2) genetic sex linkage, (3) maturation rate, (4) environment, and (5) preferred cognitive mode.

Hormonal Effects

Clear sex differences are apparent in the neural control of a wide variety of reproductive and nonreproductive behavioral patterns in most vertebrate species. In birds and mammals, the presence of testosterone at critical times in the course of development has unequivocal effects on the organization of both hypothalamic and forebrain structures, and the observed morphological effects are believed to be responsible for the behavioral dimorphism. The influence of gonadal hormones on brain and behavioral development is often referred to as an *inductive*, or *organizing*, *effect*, and in the brain, this organizing effect is said to lead to *sexual differentiation*.

The actions of gonadal hormones (largely androgens) in the course of development are permanent, but the mechanisms of action are still not well understood. Androgens (typically "male" hormones) appear to be converted to estradiol (normally "female" hormones) in the brain, and the binding of this estradiol to receptors leads to masculinization of the brain. Estradiol receptors have been found in the cortices of developing rodents and nonhuman primates, but they are not found in the adults. Regions of the human brain that have clear sex-related differences in adulthood are the same ones that have a high density of estrogen receptors during development (see Figure 12.7).

The principal organizing action of sex hormones is assumed to take place in development, but significant functional effects of hormones might extend into adulthood. One way to test this hypothesis would be to see whether a relation exists between behavior and the level of hormones observed at different times in adults of each sex.

Data collection relating hormone levels to cognitive functions has been made much easier in recent years by the advent of testing hormone levels in saliva. For example, women's performance on certain tasks changes throughout the menstrual cycle as estrogen levels rise and fall (Hampson and Kimura, 1992). High estrogen levels are associated with depressed spatial ability as well as enhanced articulatory and motor capability.

The effect of estrogen fluctuations during the menstrual cycle may be direct or indirect. Estrogen affects catecholamine (e.g., epinephrine and dopamine) levels, and catecholamine levels fluctuate in the estrous cycle in rats. In view of the importance of catecholamines in movement and other behaviors, estrogen could obviously alter behavior through its stimulation of dopamine receptors in particular. Dopamine receptors are located in the prefrontal cortex and medial temporal region, so the possibility that estrogen alters functioning in these regions is reasonable.

Jill Goldstein and her colleagues (2005) investigated this possibility, using fMRI to assess cerebral activity in women at low and high estrogen levels in the menstrual cycle when both groups were shown high-arousal (negative valence) pictures versus neutral pictures. Greater blood oxygenation was found in a variety of cerebral regions including the amygdala, hippocampus, and frontal lobe at the low-estrogen time point versus the high-estrogen point with arousing stimuli. These results are important for understanding fluctuating rates of anxiety and mood as well as cognitive function in women.

Estrogen also directly affects neuronal structure. Catherine Woolley and her colleagues (1990) showed that, in the female rat's estrous cycle, large changes occur in the number of dendritic spines on hippocampal neurons (**Figure 12.13**).

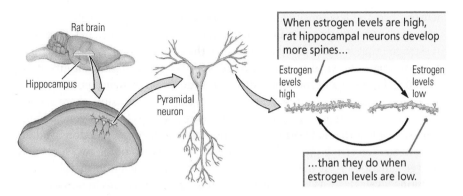

Rat brain

Hippocampus

Pyramidal neuron

When estrogen levels are high, rat hippocampal neurons develop more spines...

Estrogen levels high

Estrogen levels low

...than they do when estrogen levels are low.

Figure 12.13 ◄

Estrogen Effects Dendrites of hippocampal pyramidal neurons at high and low levels of estrogen in the rat's (4-day) estrous cycle reveal far fewer dendritic spines during the low period. (Data from Woolley et al., 1990.)

Thus the number of synapses in the female rat's hippocampus waxes and wanes in 4-day cycles. There is little reason to doubt that similar changes are also taking place in the human brain, albeit on a slower cycle.

In support of the idea that testosterone affects cognition in men, men's levels of testosterone fluctuate both seasonally and daily. Testosterone levels in men are higher in the fall than in the spring, and they are higher in the morning than in the evening. Kimura (1999) showed that men's spatial scores fluctuate with testosterone levels: men with lower testosterone levels have the highest scores. So there appears to be an optimal level of testosterone, and increasing the level is actually detrimental to cognitive performance.

Thus, men perform better on spatial tests in the spring and in the evening. Furthermore, men with lower average levels of testosterone do better both on spatial tests and on mathematical reasoning tests than do those with higher average levels. A reasonable question is whether a relation exists between testosterone level and spatial ability in women. It does. Women with higher levels do better, again suggesting that some optimal hormone level benefits at least some cognitive activities.

Finally, we might ask whether administering testosterone to men with very low levels might improve spatial or other abilities. Bioavailable testosterone levels decline with age in both men and women, and many studies now show that testosterone can enhance spatial cognition and verbal memory in older men (see Janowksy, 2006, for a readable review). Prostate cancer is nearly always androgen responsive, and so men are often given a drug to block testosterone production if they are at high risk for prostate-cancer progression. The results of several studies have now shown that testosterone blockade adversely affects verbal memory and attention but not nonverbal memory. These cognitive effects can be reversed by estradiol, which is a metabolite of testosterone.

The results from studies of men lead to questions about the role of hormone replacement therapy in menopausal women. The data have been controversial, but one consistent finding is that estrogen treatment in postmenopausal women improves verbal fluency and verbal and spatial memory.

Barbara Sherwin (2012) formulated the critical period hypothesis, which holds that estrogen has maximal beneficial effects on cognition in women when it is initiated near the time of natural or surgical menopause. She argues that beginning the hormone treatment 20 years after menopause is too late and without benefit. One explanation is that although estrogen is neuroprotective, neurons become less sensitive to the hormone after a prolonged absence. Another explanation is that so many neurons have died or atrophied in the absence of estrogen that it is not possible to reverse the effect of aging.

In summary, gonadal hormones unquestionably have significant effects on brain development and function. Although little direct evidence points to how these effects might relate to sex differences in cognitive function, there is good reason to suppose that at least some sex differences are related to gonadal hormones. The fact that sex hormones are important to cerebral function in adults leads to an interesting possibility: the cognitive functions of the two sexes may diverge functionally at puberty and begin to converge again in middle age as hormone levels drop. We are unaware of any direct test of this hypothesis.

Genetic Sex Linkage

The major factor proposed in determining variation in spatial ability is genetic. A recessive gene on the X (female) chromosome is postulated to be responsible. A human typically has 46 chromosomes arranged in 23 pairs, one set from the father and one from the mother. The twenty-third pair is composed of the sex chromosomes; if both sex chromosomes are X, the child is female (XX), but if one sex chromosome is X and the other is Y, the child is male (XY).

If a gene for a particular trait, such as spatial analysis, is recessive, the trait will not be expressed in a girl unless the recessive gene is present on both X chromosomes. However, the recessive gene need be present on only one chromosome if the child is a boy. Thus, if a mother carries the gene on both X chromosomes, all of her sons will have the trait, but her daughters will possess it only if their father also carries the recessive gene on his X chromosome. This hypothesis has generated a lot of interest and research, but a thorough review by David Boles (1980) concludes that it has yet to be proved.

Maturation Rate

The results of developmental studies indicate that a fundamental difference in male and female cerebral maturation may help to account for the sex differences observed in adulthood. As has long been known, girls typically begin to speak sooner than boys, develop larger vocabularies in childhood, and use more-complex linguistic constructions than boys do. Furthermore, the speech of young girls may be better enunciated than boys' speech, and girls are generally better readers.

Although developmental studies of laterality in children yield conflicting results, findings from dichotic and tachistoscopic studies often indicate an earlier evolution of cerebral asymmetry in girls than in boys. Because girls typically attain physical maturity at an earlier age than do boys, it is reasonable to propose that the male brain matures more slowly than the female brain and that maturation rate is a critical determinant of brain asymmetry. That is, the more slowly a child matures, the greater the observed cerebral asymmetry.

A study by Deborah Waber (1976) demonstrates just this finding: regardless of sex, early-maturing adolescents perform better on tests of verbal abilities than on tests of spatial ones, whereas late-maturing adolescents do the opposite. Waber's findings imply that maturation rate may affect the organization of cortical function. Because, on average, girls mature faster than boys, superior spatial abilities in boys may relate directly to their relatively slow development.

Environment

Probably the most influential psychological view of sex-related differences is that environmental factors shape the behaviors. For example, boys are expected to exhibit greater independence than girls and thus to engage in activities such as exploring and manipulating the environment—activities that improve spatial skills.

Although it is impossible to rule out social environment as an explanation of sex differences in brain and behavior, experiential effects appear to be relatively smaller than biological effects. It is true that the size of some sex-related cognitive differences (e.g., mathematics scores) have declined in the past 30 years, but the differences persist. Recall that *prenatal* levels of testosterone are related to the expression of male-typical play and that other primate species show a preference for human male-typical toys (see Figure 12.1). In fact, prenatal exposure to testosterone is clearly related to sex differences in cognitive and motor differences, as well as to levels of aggression (Hines, 2010).

One additional consideration here is whether sex hormones alter the way the brain responds to experience. Janice Juraska (1986) found that exposure to gonadal hormones perinatally (near birth) determines the later ability of environmental stimulation to alter the synaptic organization of the cerebrum of rats. Furthermore, she showed that environmentally induced changes in the hippocampus and neocortex are affected differently by gonadal hormones. For instance, the female hippocampus is far more plastic in new environments than the male hippocampus, and this plasticity depends on estrogen.

This type of hormonally mediated selective effect of experience on the brain is important. It provides a route through which experiential factors, including social factors, could influence the male and female brain differently, leading to sex-related variations in brain and behavior.

Preferred Cognitive Mode

As discussed in Section 11.5, the difference in strategies used by men and women to solve problems may be at least partly responsible for the observed sex differences in behavior. Genetic, maturational, and environmental factors may predispose men and women to prefer different modes of cognitive analysis. Women may solve problems primarily by using a verbal mode, for example. Because this cognitive mode is less efficient in solving spatial problems, on average, women exhibit an apparent deficit. By the same logic, on average, women should do better than men at primarily verbal tasks. This proposition has yet to be thoroughly investigated.

Conclusions

At least five significant behavioral differences are sex related: verbal ability, visuospatial analysis, mathematical ability, perception, and motor skills (reviewed in Section 12.1). Although the precise causes of sex-related differences are unknown, biology likely plays a part. Consider the following data.

Richard Harshman and his associates (1983), in a very ambitious study of the interaction of sex and handedness in cognitive abilities, found a significant interaction between sex and handedness: sex-related differences in verbal and visuospatial behavior vary as a function of handedness. (Recall that Witelson found that callosal size also varies by sex and handedness.) It is difficult to imagine how biological or environmental factors alone could account for this result. Thus, the idea that neurological factors that may be modulated by the environment partly account for sex-related differences has plausibility.

12.3 Environmental Effects on Asymmetry

Environmental effects on brain growth in laboratory animals are significant. Therefore, the hypothesis that different environments affect the human brain differently and produce variations in cerebral asymmetry is reasonable. Two broad environmental variables are especially good candidates: culture, especially language, and a range of environmental deficits.

Language and Culture

Most studies of cultural differences center on language. Asian languages such as Japanese and Chinese might promote more right-hemisphere participation than European languages, because the Asian languages appear to have more prosody (or song) and reading pictorial Chinese characters requires more spatial processing. Those who speak two or more languages may develop a different pattern of language organization from those who speak only one.

The results of laterality studies lend some support to the idea that Asian and Native American languages may be represented more bilaterally in the brain than, for example, Spanish. However, as we have seen, laterality studies can be influenced by many factors, such as cognitive strategy and task requirements. Thus, caution is warranted in inferring cultural differences in brain organization from the results of these studies. (Good discussions of the difficulties can be found in Uyehara and Cooper, 1980, as well as in Obler et al., 1982.)

The results of studies of neurological patients provide no evidence for culturally or linguistically based differences in cerebral organization. A good example is a study by Richard Rapport and his coworkers (1983). They evaluated the language functions of seven Chinese–English polyglots whose mother tongues were Malay, Cantonese, or Hokkien. Their methods included the use of carotid sodium amobarbital injection, cortical stimulation, and clinical examination. They found that all of these patients were left-hemisphere dominant for both the Chinese and the English languages; there was no consistent evidence of increased participation by the right hemisphere for oral language functions.

All oral language is probably located in the left hemisphere of bilingual people, but the possibility that their left-hemisphere language zones are larger or slightly different in microorganization from those who speak only a single language cannot be ruled out. Experience is known to alter somatosensory organization, so an analogous effect of experience on the language zones is a reasonable expectation. However, the major effects of language and environment on the brain are likely to be on the development of particular styles of problem solving (that is, preferred cognitive mode), which heavily depend on culture rather than on changes in cerebral asymmetry.

Exposure to multiple languages could be expected to change the typical pattern of brain organization, but again, this change does not appear to take place.

The results of PET studies by Denise Klein and her colleagues (1999) show, for example, that no difference appears in the cerebral activation for various language tasks performed in English and French or in English and Chinese by bilingual participants. In particular, no activation of the right hemisphere was recorded for any task in either language. In a follow-up study by the same group (Klein et al., 2006) the authors showed that in participants who learned their second language after age 5, within the left hemisphere, activation of the second language was more extensive.

The Japanese writing system provides an unusual opportunity for studying cerebral organization because, unlike Indo-European writing, it consists of two types of symbols: phonograms (*kana*) and ideograms (*kanji*). Phonograms are analogous to English letters; each phonogram represents a spoken sound. In contrast, an ideogram represents a unit of meaning, which may correspond to a word or words.

In reading, the brain may process these two types of characters differently; furthermore, the right hemisphere might process *kanji*, whereas the left hemisphere processes *kana*. There is little support for either idea. For example, in a large series of patients, Morihiro Sugishita and his colleagues (1992) found no clear relation between deficits in reading either type of script and locus of left-hemisphere injury. In fact, most of their cases were impaired equally in both forms of reading Japanese.

Some imaging evidence supports the idea that alphabetic language (for example, English) and *kanji* might be processed differently, however. Yun Dong and colleagues (2005) showed that reading pictorial Chinese produces right-hemisphere activation not seen in reading English. The investigators used a phonological task, in which the participants were to determine whether two pictorial words sound similar, and a semantic task, in which they were to determine whether two pictorial words have related meanings. The phonological task activated large regions of the left hemisphere as would be expected (**Figure 12.14**A), whereas the semantic task also activated the right inferior frontal cortex, a result not seen in semantic matching in English (Figure 12.14B).

An interesting question raised by the Dong findings is whether learning pictographic languages alters how the brain processes other types of information. For example, given the visuospatial nature of Chinese pictographs, we could imagine that visuospatial processing might develop differently as children learn the language. There are studies suggesting that native Chinese male participants do not show the male advantage in spatial rotation-type tasks observed in native English-speaking males. The early pictographic language learning may lead to the development of cognitive biases that are more like the typical Western female strategies in visuospatial tasks.

Finally, an intriguing study by Patricia Kuhl and colleagues (2013) asked whether learning a second language early in life might alter the development of cerebral connections. It appears to. Adults who were bilingual (English–Spanish)

Figure 12.14 ▼

Unique Chinese Language Activation (A) In the phonological matching task, subjects had to decide whether Chinese words sounded similar, which activated Broca's area in the left hemisphere. (B) The semantic matching task, requiring subjects to determine whether the words' meanings were related, activated Broca's area and the inferior frontal cortex on the right. Pictographic language appears to require activation of the spatial processing networks in the right hemisphere, which is not normally seen in semantic tasks using alphabetical languages. (Dong, Y., K. Nakamura, T. Okada, T. Hanakawa, H. Fukuyama, J. C. Mazziotta, and H. Shibasaki "Neural mechanisms underlying the processing of Chinese words: An fMRI study." *Neuroscience Research* 52, 2, (2005): pp. 139–145. © Elsevier.)

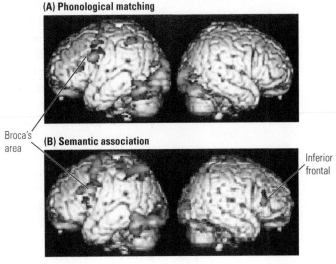

(A) Phonological matching

Broca's area

(B) Semantic association

Inferior frontal

had more diffuse cerebral connectivity than English monolinguals. The researchers propose that bilingual language experience alters connectivity, which in turn is related to increased cognitive flexibility.

Sensory or Environmental Deficits

Both education and congenital deafness are alleged to alter hemispheric specialization. As noted in the preceding section, early pictographic language learning may influence cognitive skills, but the evidence that schooling changes cerebral organization is scanty and inconclusive. Unfortunately, most evidence regarding sensory deficits and asymmetry is based largely on the results of laterality studies, which are difficult to interpret. Furthermore, illiterate aphasics do not appear to differ in hemispheric specialization from those who are educated. But some evidence does indicate that congenital deafness may alter cerebral processing.

Brain Organization in Nonhearing People

As it does to hearing people, left-hemisphere damage produces aphasia in people who converse using American Sign Language (ASL or Ameslan), possibly because of the praxic requirements. But evidence hints that the congenitally deaf may have atypical patterns of cerebral organization.

First, several laboratories report independently that congenitally deaf persons fail to show the usual right-visual-field superiority in linguistic processing tasks. This failure could be interpreted as evidence that, if experience with auditory language is absent, lateralization of some aspect or aspects of nonauditory language function is abolished. Or these data could result from strategy differences (preferred cognitive mode again) due to the absence of auditory experience.

Second, Helen Neville (1977) reported that during the perception of line drawings, visual evoked potentials are significantly larger on the right in children with normal hearing and significantly larger on the left in deaf children who use Ameslan to communicate. Curiously, no asymmetry at all appears in deaf children who cannot sign but merely use pantomime to communicate. From the signers' left-hemisphere effect for line drawings, Neville inferred that the deaf signers acquire their visual signing symbols much as hearing children acquire auditory verbal symbols: with the left hemisphere.

Thus, visuospatial functions may develop in the left hemisphere of people who sign, producing an unexpected left-hemisphere effect. The lack of asymmetry in nonsigners could mean that the absence of language experience somehow abolishes certain aspects of cerebral asymmetry or, alternatively, that the expression of cerebral asymmetry depends on language experience. If the nonsigners learn Ameslan before puberty, they might develop an asymmetrical evoked-potential pattern similar to that of their contemporaries who already sign.

Although congenital deafness may be suspected to affect the development of certain aspects of cerebral lateralization, the results of studies of brain-injured patients show little difference between hearing and nonhearing subjects. Gregory Hickok and his coworkers (2001) studied 34 congenitally deaf patients who had unilateral brain injuries. Left-hemisphere patients performed poorly on all measures of language use, whereas right-hemisphere patients performed poorly on visuospatial tasks—exactly what would be expected in hearing people. Exposure to spoken language was not necessary for hemispheric specialization.

Environmental Deprivation

Evidence pointing to early environment as a factor in asymmetry is based on a study of Genie, an adolescent girl who endured nearly 12 years of extreme social and experiential deprivation and malnutrition in the 1960s (Curtiss, 1978). She was discovered at the age of 13½, after having spent most of her life isolated in a small, closed room. During this time, she was punished for making any noise. After her rescue, Genie's cognitive development was rapid, but her language lagged behind other abilities.

Results of her dichotic listening tests proved provocative for a right-handed person: although both ears showed normal hearing, Genie showed a strong left-ear (hence, right-hemisphere) effect for both verbal and nonverbal (environmental) sounds. In fact, the right ear was nearly totally suppressed, a phenomenon characteristic of people with severe left-hemisphere injury. Genie's right hemisphere appeared to be processing both verbal and nonverbal acoustical stimuli, as would be the case in people who had a left hemispherectomy in childhood (see the opening Portrait in Chapter 10).

At least three explanations for Genie's abnormal lateralization are plausible. First, disuse of the left hemisphere may simply have resulted in degeneration, which seems unlikely. Second, in the absence of appropriate auditory stimulation, the left hemisphere may have lost the ability to process linguistic stimuli. This explanation is possible because, without early exposure to foreign languages, adults have difficulty learning many phoneme discriminations, even though they were able to make these discriminations as infants (see Werker and Tees, 1992). Third, either Genie's left hemisphere was being inhibited by the right or by some other structure or it was performing other functions.

Not all deprivation experiences are as severe as Genie's. This raises the question of how other early experiences might affect brain development. Abandoned Romanian children, for example, were warehoused by the communist regime during the 1970s and 1980s in dreadful state-run orphanages. The children had little environmental stimulation, and, in many cases, a single caregiver looked after as many as 25 children.

After the fall of the communist government, many children about 2 years of age were adopted into homes in the United Kingdom, the United States, Canada, and Australia. Extensive study of these children shows that, even after placement in excellent conditions, the effect of early experience on their brain development is long lasting. At 12 years of age, their average brain size was reduced by as much as 20 percent below normal, there is widespread reduction in cortical thickness, and they have significant cognitive and other behavioral problems (see, e.g., McLaughlin et al., 2013). Little is known about the nature of cerebral asymmetry in these children, but preliminary reports on EEG asymmetries in 24-month-old children suggest that it is not typical of more normally reared children (McLaughlin et al., 2011).

Although not a direct measure of environmental deprivation, socioeconomic status (SES) is a variable that combines income, education, and occupation and is correlated with many social health outcomes. David Boles (2011) reanalyzed laterality studies from the 1970s and 1980s and found reduced laterality in lower SES groups. He suggests that growing up in a low SES environment may either delay brain maturation or reduce functional specialization or both. This finding is provocative and deserves further study.

Epigenetics

We noted in Section 11.1 that differences in gene expression (epigenetics) are likely related to the development of morphological asymmetries in the brain. Early experiences, including prenatal experiences, can produce large changes in gene expression in the cerebral cortex, so it is reasonable to suggest that sensory or environmental deficits could modify gene expression related to the development of cerebral asymmetries.

The powerful effect of experience on epigenetics can be seen in an analysis of monozygotic twins. At birth, monozygotic twins have a genotype in common, but, as they age, they are often observed as not being identical. Mario Fraga (2005) and his colleagues examined gene expression in 3-year-old versus 50-year-old identical twins and found a marked shift in gene expression with aging. The difference was greater in twins who had lived apart and had different lifestyles, including diet and exercise.

Although the Fraga team's study does not speak directly to brain asymmetry, it does show us that genotype, including genes regulating brain function, can be affected by experience. Given that cerebral asymmetry is ultimately controlled by gene expression during development, we can therefore see that alterations in gene expression throughout the lifetime can influence cerebral function. This epigenetic mechanism could provide a powerful means for culture, sex, or abnormal experiences to influence cerebral activity.

Ontogeny of Asymmetry

Anatomical studies generally show that adultlike cerebral asymmetries are present before birth, a result that supports an innate predisposition for cerebral asymmetry in humans. Findings in an MRI study in which Elizabeth Sowell and colleagues (2002) examined asymmetries in the sulcal patterns in a large sample of children, adolescents, and young adults confirm this general impression. Their findings also show that the extent of asymmetries in the sulcal patterns increases even past adolescence and well into adulthood.

Thus, a basic template for cortical development appears to lay down an asymmetrical organization prenatally, and the pattern progresses after birth. Presumably, the environment, especially injury, can influence this pattern. The results of ERP studies by Dennis and Victoria Molfese (1988) confirm a functional asymmetry in which the left hemisphere shows a greater response to speech stimuli as early as 1 week of age. There is apparently little change in this difference during development.

Recall from Section 11.5 the polar theoretical positions that postulate the ontogeny (development in the individual) of cerebral specialization. Unilateral specialization culminates in a left-for-language hypothesis: the left hemisphere is genetically organized to develop language skills; the right hemisphere is dumb. At the opposite pole of cerebral interaction, the parallel-development hypothesis posits that both hemispheres, by virtue of their construction, play special roles, one destined to specialize in language and the other in nonlanguage functions.

Research points to a parallel-development theory that initially permits some flexibility or equipotentiality to explain the bulk of the available data most usefully. The cognitive functions of each hemisphere can be conceived as hierarchical. Simple, lower-level functions are represented at the base of the hierarchy, corresponding to functions in the primary somatosensory, motor, language, or

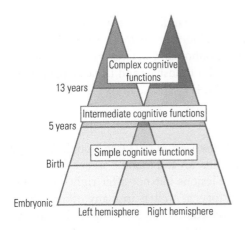

The hemispheres are more highly specialized in older people,...

...whereas there is considerable overlap at birth.

If brain damage occurs early in life, each hemisphere can adopt functions of the other.

Figure 12.15 ◄

Development of Cognitive Function in the Left and Right Hemispheres At birth, the hemispheres' functions overlap considerably, but by adulthood, their functions do not overlap at all. The hemispheres are not themselves becoming more lateralized with respect to a given function; rather, they are developing more highly specialized functions.

visuospatial areas. More-complex, higher-level functions ascend the hierarchy, with the most complex at the top being the most lateralized.

At birth, the two hemispheres overlap functionally because each is processing low-level behaviors. By age 5, newly developing, higher-order cognitive processes have very little overlap, and each hemisphere thus becomes increasingly specialized. By puberty, each hemisphere has developed its own unique functions (**Figure 12.15**). Note that the cerebral hemispheres are not becoming more lateralized during development but rather that developing cognitive functions are built on the lower functions, which are innately located in one hemisphere or the other.

All models of cerebral development must address the question of how functions become restricted to one hemisphere rather than becoming bilateral. The interactive parallel-development hypothesis answers that question. In a series of papers, Morris Moscovitch (1977) emphasizes the possibility that one hemisphere actively inhibits the other, thus preventing the contralateral hemisphere from developing similar functions. This active inhibition presumably develops at about age 5, as the corpus callosum becomes functional.

Moscovitch proposes that this inhibitory process not only prevents the subsequent development of language processes in the right hemisphere but also inhibits the expression of the language processes already in the right hemisphere. Support for this idea comes from the observation that the right hemispheres of commissurotomy patients appear to have greater language abilities than expected from the study of control participants, presumably because the right hemisphere is no longer subjected to inhibition by the left. Furthermore, people born with no corpus callosum demonstrate little or no functional asymmetry as inferred from dichotic listening, suggesting that the absence of interhemispheric connection results in attenuated hemispheric asymmetry (see Netley, 1977). This phenomenon follows directly from the Moscovitch proposal in support of parallel hemispheric development.

12.4 Asymmetry in Nonhuman Animals

Asymmetry is hardly unique to humans. Elements of communicative vocalizations in frogs and salamanders are lateralized to the left side of the brain, for example. Thus, understanding the origins and evolution of lateral asymmetries in the nonhuman brain is germane to understanding the nature of asymmetry in the human brain. Here we present a brief look at the most stimulating and robust data so far gathered on birds and nonhuman primates. For a complete discussion, we recommend the book by John Bradshaw and Lesley Rogers (1993) and a more recent review by Rogers (2014).

Asymmetry in Birds

Fernando Nottebohm made a startling discovery in 1971 (see Nottebohm, 1980). He severed the hypoglossal nerve in canaries and found a severe disruption in the birds' song after left-hemisphere lesions but not after right-hemisphere ones. Subsequent work in his laboratory, as well as in many others, showed anatomical differences in the structures controlling birdsong in the two avian hemispheres and identified many song-related regions as sexually dimorphic. (Brain structures in the two sexes develop differently.)

Curiously, although a left-hemisphere dominance for song has been shown in many species of songbirds (and even in chickens), it is not characteristic of all songbirds. Apparently, the zebra finch has little anatomical or functional asymmetry, even though it sings. The lateralization may not be for singing itself but for some other still-unrecognized feature of bird vocalizations.

Nottebohm's discovery led to interest in the possibility of asymmetry in birds' visual systems because the optic nerves of most birds cross over almost completely at the optic chiasm. Thus, each hemisphere receives nearly all input from a single eye. The beauty of this arrangement is that lateralization of visual function can be investigated by testing birds monocularly. Furthermore, birds have no corpus callosum, and although other small commissures connect the hemispheres, there is less interhemispheric transfer in birds than in mammals.

Lateralization has now been shown for a range of visually guided functions in birds. According to Bradshaw and Rogers, the right-eye system is specialized for categorizing objects, such as food-versus-nonfood items, whereas the left-eye system is specialized for responding to the unique properties of each stimulus (color, size, shape, and so forth), including topographic information. Thus, the left hemisphere of birds appears to be specialized for categorizing objects and the right for processing topographic information.

Asymmetry in Nonhuman Primates

It has become increasingly clear over time that chimpanzees show humanlike asymmetries in both Broca's area and the planum temporale. Such asymmetries are intriguing because they imply that the neuroanatomical substrates for human language were present at least 5 million years ago and vastly predate the emergence of human language.

Rhesus monkeys also have a region that can be called Broca's area. This region controls orofacial actions, and it has connections to parietal and temporal cortex that are similar to a pathway in humans that subserves certain aspects of language processing (Frey, Mackey, and Petrides, 2014). Imaging studies in monkeys show remarkably similar patterns of activation for species-specific vocalizations (e.g., Wilson & Petkov, 2012). Curiously, both human and monkey

Figure 12.16 ▲

Gestural Language
Baboons use the right hand to make communicative gestures. Here a female baboon sends a threat signal to another baboon by rubbing her right hand on the ground rapidly. (© Adrien Meguerditchian.)

studies show more bilateral activity for processing communication sounds than might be expected from studies of human speech areas (see Section 11.1).

Jared Taglialatela and colleagues (2006) looked at the relation between the asymmetry in gestural movements and neuroanatomical asymmetries. Their analysis reveals that chimpanzees that reliably use the right hand for manual gestures have larger left inferior frontal gyri than animals that do not use the right limb as reliably. These results are intriguing, in part because we are unaware of any systematic studies looking at differences in inferior frontal anatomy in human left- versus right-handers.

The results of studies of hand preference in nonhuman primates are controversial, in part because most studies have concentrated on forelimb reaching movements. Peter MacNeilage and his colleagues (1987, 1988) have argued that primates evolved a preference for reaching with one limb (the left) while supporting the body with the other (the right). As the prehensile hand developed and primates began to adopt a more upright posture, the need for a hand used primarily for postural support diminished, and because this hand was free, it became specialized for manipulating objects. They later proposed that the hand specializations were accompanied by hemispheric specializations: a right-hemisphere (left-hand) perceptuomotor specialization for unimanual predation (grasping fast-moving insects or small animals) and a left-hemisphere specialization for whole-body movements, which has led to a strong preference for using the right hand for communicative actions, as illustrated in **Figure 12.16**.

SUMMARY

Considerable variation exists in the individual pattern of left–right hemisphere asymmetry. Neuropsychologists study these anatomical and functional variations—the ontogeny of asymmetry—to separate processes that are lateralized. These studies can offer insight into the nature of cerebral asymmetry in our species (phylogeny).

Systematic relations exist between typical variations in cerebral organization and individual differences in cognitive abilities. Each of us has unique behavioral capacities as well as shortcomings related to cerebral organization. Some asymmetric variation is biologically based, although environmental variables, including epigenetic variables, certainly modify cerebral organization.

12.1 Handedness and Functional Asymmetry
No adequate explanation yet exists for why people are either right- or left-handed. Presumably a neuroanatomical basis must exist, but the only consistent finding is a deeper left

central fissure in right-handers. Some genetic component is likely because left-handedness tends to run in families, but we still must account for nonfamilial left-handedness.

Handedness and language lateralization are clearly related in right-handers, but the left-hemisphere locus of language in most left-handers casts some doubt on that relation. Rather, the major factor in cerebral asymmetry is the asymmetrical representation of language and spatial functions.

12.2 Sex Differences in Cerebral Organization

The most likely explanation for sex differences is that gonadal hormones alter brain organization prenatally and continue to influence brain activity in adulthood. The cerebral cortex in the female brain fundamentally differs in organization from that of the male brain. This altered organization and activity interact with experience to enhance or diminish sex-related differences.

12.3 Environmental Effects on Asymmetry

The nature of experience- and environment-dependent variations in brain organization is not yet understood. Pathological experience in infancy and early childhood appears to affect brain development severely, but less is known about more subtle differences such as those experienced in different cultures. Epigenetics provides one route by which environment can influence cerebral function.

12.4 Asymmetry in Nonhuman Animals

Studies of nonhuman species show that lateral asymmetry is not unique to humans and imply that asymmetry in the human brain far predates the development of human language. A correspondence may exist between the emergence of gestural movements made primarily with the right hand in both apes and monkeys and the emergence of gestural language and asymmetry with a later emergence of human oral language. But cerebral asymmetry is also found in birds, mammals, and even in amphibians, so the general phenomenon is not simply a reflection of gestural language evolution.

References

Alexander, G. M., and M. Hines. Sex differences in response to children's toys in nonhuman primates (*Cercopithecus aethiops sabaeus*). *Evolution and Human Behavior* 23, 6:467–479, 2002.

Allen, L. S., and R. A. Gorski. Sexual orientation and the size of the anterior commissure in the human brain. *Journal of Comparative Neurology* 312:97–104, 1991.

Amunts, K., L. Jancke, H. Mohlberg, H. Steinmetz, and K. Zilles. Interhemispheric asymmetry of the human motor cortex related to handedness and gender. *Neuropsychologia* 38:304–312, 2000.

Annett, M. A classification of hand preference by association analysis. *British Journal of Psychology* 61:303–321, 1970.

Annett, M. The distribution of manual asymmetry. *British Journal of Psychology* 63:343–358, 1972.

Annett, M. Predicting combinations of left and right asymmetries. *Cortex* 36:485–505, 2000.

Astur, R. S., M. L. Ortiz, and R. J. Sutherland. A characterization of performance by men and women in a virtual Morris water task: A large and reliable sex difference. *Behavioural Brain Research* 93:185–190, 1998.

Auyeung, B., S. Baron-Cohen, E. Ashwin, R. Knickmeyer, K. Taylor, G. Hackett, and M. Hines. Fetal testosterone predicts sexually differentiated childhood behavior in girls and boys. *Psychological Science* 20:144–148, 2009.

Bakan, P., G. Dibb, and P. Reed. Handedness and birth stress. *Neuropsychologia* 11:363–366, 1973.

Beatty, W. W., and A. I. Troster. Gender differences in geographic knowledge. *Sex Roles* 16:202–229, 1987.

Benbow, C. P. Sex differences in mathematical reasoning ability in intellectually talented preadolescents: Their nature, effects, and possible causes. *Behavioral and Brain Sciences* 11:169–232, 1988.

Benbow, C. P., D. Lubinski, D. L. Shea, and H. Eftekhari-Sannjani. Sex differences in mathematical reasoning ability at age 13: Their status 20 years later. *Psychological Science* 11:474–480, 2000.

Benbow, C. P., and J. C. Stanley. Sex differences in mathematical ability: Fact or artifact? *Science* 210:1262–1264, 1980.

Boles, D. B. X-linkage of spatial ability: A critical review. *Child Development* 51:625–635, 1980.

Boles, D. B. Socioeconomic status, a forgotten variable in lateralization development. *Brain and Cognition*, 76:52–57, 2011.

Bradshaw, J., and L. Rogers. *The Evolution of Lateral Asymmetries, Language, Tool Use, and Intellect*. New York: Academic Press, 1993.

Branch, C., B. Milner, and T. Rasmussen. Intracarotid sodium amytal for the lateralization of cerebral speech dominance: Observations in 123 patients. *Journal of Neurosurgery* 21:399–405, 1964.

Bryden, M. P., I. C. McManus, and M. B. Bulman-Fleming. Evaluating the empirical support for the Geschwind–Behan–Galaburda model of cerebral lateralization. *Brain and Cognition* 26:103–167, 1994.

Cahill L. Sex differences in human brain structure and function: Relevance to learning and memory. In D. W. Pfaff, et al., Eds., *Hormones, Brain and Behavior*, 2nd ed. New York: Academic Press, 2009.

Carmon, A., Y. Harishanu, E. Lowinger, and S. Lavy. Asymmetries in hemispheric blood volume and cerebral dominance. *Behavioral Biology* 7:853–859, 1972.

Collins, D. W., and D. Kimura. A large sex difference on a two-dimensional mental rotation task. *Behavioral Neuroscience* 111:845–849, 1997.

Corsi-Cabrera, M., C. Arce, J. Ramos, and M. A. Guevara. Effect of spatial ability and sex on inter- and intrahemispheric correlation of EEG activity. *Neurophysiology* 102:5–11, 1997.

Curtiss, S. *Genie: A Psycholinguistic Study of a Modern-Day "Wild Child."* New York: Academic Press, 1978.

Dong, Y., K. Nakamura, T. Okada, T. Hanakawa, H. Fukuyama, J. C. Mazziotta, and H. Shibasaki. Neural mechanisms underlying the processing of Chinese words: An fMRI study. *Neuroscience Research* 52:139–145, 2005.

Dorion, A. A., M. Chantome, D. Hasboun, A. Zouaoui, C. Marsalult, C. Capron, and M. Duyme. Hemispheric asymmetry and corpus callosum morphometry: A magnetic resonance imaging study. *Neuroscience Research*, 36: 9–13, 2000.

Esposito G., J. D. van Horn, D. R. Weinberger, and K. F. Berman. Gender differences in cerebral blood flow as a function of cognitive state with PET. *Journal of Nuclear Medicine* 37:559–564, 1996.

Fraga, M. F., E. Ballestar, M. F. Paz, S. Ropero, F. Setien, M. L. Ballestar, D. Heine-Suner, J. C. Cigudosa, M. Urioste, J. Benitez, M. Boix-Chornet, A. Sanchez-Aguilera, C. Lin, E. Carlsson, P. Poulsen, A. Vaag, Z. Stephan, T. K. Spector, U.-Z. Wu, C. Ross, and M. Esteller. Epigenetic differences arise during the lifetime of monozygotic twins. *Proceedings of the National Academy of Sciences U.S.A.* 102:10604–10609, 2005.

Frey, S., S. Mackey, and M. Petrides. Cortico-cortical connections of areas 44 and 45B in the macaque monkey. *Brain and Language* 131:36–55, 2014.

Frost, J. A., J. R. Binder, J. A. Springer, T. A. Hammeke, P. S. F. Bellgowan, S. M. Rao, and R. W. Cox. Language processing is strongly left lateralized in both sexes: Evidence from functional MRI. *Brain* 122:199–208, 1999.

Geschwind, N., and A. M. Galaburda. *Cerebral Lateralization: Biological Mechanisms, Associations, and Pathology.* Cambridge, MA: MIT Press, 1987.

Goldstein, J. M., L. J. Seidman, N. J. Horton, N. Makris, D. N. Kennedy, V. S. Caviness, Jr., S. V. Faraone, and M. T. Tsuang. Normal sexual dimorphism of the adult human brain assessed by in vivo magnetic resonance imaging. *Cerebral Cortex* 11:490–497, 2001.

Goldstein, J. M., M. Jerram, R. Poldrack, T. Ahern, D. M. Kennedy, L. J. Seidman, and N. Makris. Hormonal cycle modulates arousal circuitry in women using functional magnetic resonance imaging. *Journal of Neuroscience* 25A:9390–9316, 2005.

Gooren, L. The biology of human psychosexual differentiation. *Hormones and Behavior* 50:589–601, 2006.

Grimshaw, G. M., M. P. Bryden, and J. K. Finegan. Relations between prenatal testosterone and cerebral lateralization at age 10. *Journal of Clinical and Experimental Neuropsychology* 15:39–40, 1993.

Gualtieri, T., and R. E. Hicks. An immunoreactive theory of selective male affliction. *Behavioral and Brain Sciences* 8:427–477, 1985.

Gur, R. C., R. E. Gur, W. D. Obrist, J. P. Hungerbuhler, D. Younkin, A. D. Rosen, B. E. Skolnick, and M. Reivich. Sex and handedness differences in cerebral blood flow during test and cognitive activity. *Science* 217:659–660, 1982.

Gur, R. C., J. Richard, M. E. Calkins, R. Chiavacci, J. A. Hansen, W. B. Bilker, J. Loughead, J. J. Connolly, H. Qiu, F. D. Mentch, P. M. Abou-Sleiman, H. Hakonarson, and R. E. Gur. Age group and sex differences in performance on a computerized neurocognitive battery in children age 8–21. *Neuropsychology* 26:251–265.

Hall, J. *Nonverbal Sex Differences*. Baltimore: Johns Hopkins University Press, 1984.

Hall, J. A. Y., and D. Kimura. Sexual orientation and performance on sexually dimorphic motor tasks. *Archives of Sexual Behavior* 24:395–407, 1995.

Hampson, E., and D. Kimura. Sex differences and hormonal influences on cognitive function in humans. In J. B. Becker, S. M. Breedlove, and D. Crews, Eds., *Behavioral Endocrinology*. Cambridge, Mass.: MIT Press, 1992.

Hardyck, C., and L. F. Petrinovich. Left-handedness. *Psychological Bulletin* 84:384–404, 1977.

Harshman, R. A., E. Hampson, and S. A. Berenbaum. Individual differences in cognitive abilities and brain organization: I. Sex and handedness—Differences in ability. *Canadian Journal of Psychology* 37:144–192, 1983.

Haverkort, M., L. Stowe, B. Wijers, and A. Paans. Familial handedness and sex in language comprehension. *NeuroImage* 9:12–18, 1999.

Hécaen, H., and J. Sauguet. Cerebral dominance in left-handed subjects. *Cortex* 7:19–48, 1971.

Hickok, G., U. Bellugi, and E. S. Klima. Sign language in the brain. *Scientific American* 284(6):58–65, 2001.

Hines, M. Sex-related variation in human behavior and brain. *Trends in Cognitive Science* 14:448–456, 2010.

Hines, M. Gender development and the human brain. *Annual Review of Neuroscience* 34:69–88, 2011.

Hochberg, F. H., and M. LeMay. Arteriographic correlates of handedness. *Neurology* 25:218–222, 1975.

Hyde, J. S., E. Fennema, and S. J. Lamon. Gender differences in mathematics performance: A meta-analysis. *Psychological Bulletin* 107:139–155, 1990.

Hyde, J. S., and M. C. Linn. Gender differences in verbal ability: A meta-analysis. *Psychological Bulletin* 104:53–69, 1988.

Ingalhalikar, M., A. Smith, D. Parker, T. D. Satterthwaite, M. A. Elliott, K. Ruparel, H. Hakonarson, R. E. Gur, R. C. Gur, and R. Verma. Sex differences in the structural connectome of the human brain. *Proceedings of the National Academy of Sciences U.S.A.* 111:823–828, 2013.

Inglis, J., and J. S. Lawson. A meta-analysis of sex differences in the effects of unilateral brain damage on intelligence test results. *Canadian Journal of Psychology* 36:670–683, 1982.

Inglis, J., M. Rickman, J. S. Lawson, A. W. MacLean, and T. N. Monga. Sex differences in the cognitive effects of unilateral brain damage. *Cortex* 18:257–276, 1982.

Jancke, L., G. Schlaug, Y. Huang, and H. Steinmetz. Asymmetry of the planum parietale. *Neuroreport* 5:1161–1163, 1994.

Janowsky, J. S. Thinking with your gonads. *Trends in Cognitive Sciences* 10:77–82, 2006.

Juraska, J. Sex differences in developmental plasticity of behavior and the brain. In W. T. Greenough and J. M. Juraska, Eds., *Developmental Neuropsychology*. New York: Academic Press, 1986.

Kimura, D. Sex differences in cerebral organization for speech and praxic functions. *Canadian Journal of Psychology* 37:9–35, 1983.

Kimura, D. *Sex and Cognition*. Cambridge, Mass.: MIT Press, 1999.

Klein, D., B. Milner, R. J. Zatorre, V. Zhao, and J. Nikelski. Cerebral organization in bilinguals: A PET study of Chinese–English verb generation. *Neuroreport* 10:2841–2846, 1999.

Klein, D., K. E. Watkins, R. J. Zatorre, and B. Milner. Word and nonword repetition in bilingual subjects: A PET study. *Human Brain Mapping* 27:153–161.

Kuhl, P. K., T. L. Richards, J. Stevenson, D. D. Can, L. Wroblewski, M. S. Fish, and J. Mizrahi. White-matter microstructure differs in adult bilingual and monolingual brains. *Journal of the Acoustical Society of America* 134:4249.

Kulynych, J. J., K. Vladar, D. W. Jones, and D. R. Weinberger. Gender differences in the normal lateralization of the supratemporal cortex: MRI surface-rendering morphometry of Heschl's gyrus and the planum temporale. *Cerebral Cortex* 4:107–118, 1994.

LeMay, M. Asymmetries of the skull and handedness: Phrenology revisited. *Journal of Neurological Science* 32:243–253, 1977.

Luders, E., K. L. Narr, P. M. Thompson, R. P. Woods, D. E. Rex, L. Jancke, H. Steinmatz, and A. W. Toga. Mapping cortical gray matter in the young adult brain: Effects of gender. *NeuroImage* 26:493–501, 2005.

Luders, E., A. W. Toga, and P. M. Thompson. Why size matters: Differences in brain volume account for apparent sex differences in callosal anatomy: The sexual dimorphism of the corpus callosum. *NeuroImage* 84:820–824, 2013.

MacNeilage, P. F., M. G. Studdert-Kennedy, and B. Lindblom. Primate handedness reconsidered. *Behavioral and Brain Sciences* 10:247–303, 1987.

MacNeilage, P. F., M. G. Studdert-Kennedy, and B. Lindblom. Primate handedness: A foot in the door. *Behavioral and Brain Sciences* 11:737–746, 1988.

Majeres, R. L. Sex differences in symbol–digit substitution and speeded matching. *Intelligence* 7:313–327, 1983.

McBurney, D. H., S. J. C. Gaulin, T. Devineni, and C. Adams. Superior spatial memory of women: Stronger evidence for the gathering hypothesis. *Evolution and Human Behavior* 19:73–87, 1997.

McCarthy, M. M., et al. Sexual differentiation of the brain: Mode, mechanisms, and meaning. In D. W. Pfaff et al., Eds., *Hormones, Brain and Behavior*, 2nd. ed. New York: Academic Press, 2009.

McGivern, R. F., K. L. Mutter, J. Anderson, G. Wideman, M. Bodnar, and P. J. Huston. Gender differences in incidental learning and visual recognition memory: Support for a sex difference in unconscious environmental awareness. *Personality and Individual Differences* 25:223–232, 1998.

McGuinness, D., A. Olson, and J. Chapman. Sex differences in incidental recall for words and pictures. *Learning and Individual Differences* 2:263–285, 1990.

McLaughlin, K. A., N. A. Fox, C. H. Zeanah, and C. A. Nelson. Adverse rearing environments and neural development in children: The development of frontal electroencephalogram asymmetry. *Biological Psychiatry* 70:1008–1015, 2011.

McLaughlin, K. A., M. A. Sheridan, W. Winter, N. A. Fox, C. H. Zeanah, and C. A. Nelson. Widespread reductions in cortical thickness following severe early-life deprivation: A neurodevelopmental pathway to attention-deficit/hyperactivity disorder. *Biological Psychiatry* in press.

Molfese, D. L., and V. J. Molfese. Right-hemisphere responses from preschool children to temporal cues to speech and nonspeech materials: Electrophysiological correlates. *Brain and Language* 33:245–259, 1988.

Moscovitch, M. The development of lateralization of language functions and its relation to cognitive and linguistic development: A review and some theoretical speculations. In S. J. Segalowitz and F. A. Gruber, Eds., *Language Development and Neurological Theory*. New York: Academic Press, 1977.

Netley, C. Dichotic listening of callosal agenesis and Turner's syndrome patients. In S. J. Segalowitz and F. A. Gruber, Eds., *Language Development and Neurological Theory*. New York: Academic Press, 1977.

Neville, H. Electroencephalographic testing of cerebral specialization in normal and congenitally deaf children: A preliminary report. In S. J. Segalowitz and F. A. Gruber, Eds., *Language Development and Neurological Theory*. New York: Academic Press, 1977.

Nicholson, K. G., and D. Kimura. Sex differences for speech and manual skill. *Perceptual and Motor Skills* 82:3–13, 1996.

Nottebohm, F. Brain pathways for vocal learning in birds: A review of the first 10 years. *Progress in Psychobiology and Physiological Psychology* 9:85–124, 1980.

Obler, L. K., R. J. Zatoree, L. Galloway, Jr., and J. Vaid. Cerebral lateralization in bilinguals: Methodological issues. *Brain and Language* 15:40–54, 1982.

Pellis, S., and V. Pellis. *The Playful Brain: Venturing to the Limits of Neuroscience*. London: Oneworld Publications, 2009.

Pugh, K. R., B. A. Shaywitz, S. E. Shaywitz, R. T. Constable, P. Skudlarski, R. K. Fulbright, R. A. Bronen, J. M. Fletcher, D. P. Shankweiler, L. Katz, J. M. Fletcher, and J. C. Gore. Cerebral organization of component process in reading. *Brain* 119:1221–1238, 1996.

Rahman, Q., S. Abrahams, and G. D. Wilson. Sexual-orientation-related differences in verbal fluency. *Neuropsychology* 17:240–246, 2003.

Rapport, R. L., C. T. Tan, and H. A. Whitaker. Language function and dysfunction among Chinese- and

English-speaking polyglots: Cortical stimulation, Wada testing, and clinical studies. *Brain and Language* 18:342–366, 1983.

Ratcliffe, G., C. Dila, L. Taylor, and B. Milner. The morphological asymmetry of the hemispheres and cerebral dominance for speech: A possible relationship. *Brain and Language* 11:87–98, 1980.

Reite, M., J. Sheeder, P. Teale, D. Richardson, M. Adams, and J. Simon. MEG based brain laterality: Sex differences in normal adults. *Neuropsychologia* 33:1607–1616, 1995.

Rogers, L. Asymmetry of brain and behavior in animals: Its development, function, and human relevance. *Genesis* 52(6):555–571, 2014.

Sacher, J., J. Neumann, H. Okon-Singer, S. Gotowiec, and A. Villringer. Sexual dimorphism in the human brain: Evidence from neuroimaging. *Magnetic Resonance Imaging* 31:366–375, 2013.

Sherwin, B. B. Estrogen and cognitive functioning in women: Lessons we have learned. *Behavioral Neuroscience* 126:123–127.

Sowell, E. R., P. M. Thompson, D. Rex, D. Kornsand, K. D. Tessner, T. L. Jernigan, and A. W. Toga. Mapping sulcal pattern asymmetry and local cortical surface gray matter distribution in vivo: Maturation in perisylvian cortices. *Cerebral Cortex* 12:17–26, 2002.

Strauss, E., J. Wada, and M. Hunter. Sex-related differences in the cognitive consequences of early left-hemisphere lesions. *Journal of Clinical and Experimental Neuropsychology* 14:738–748, 1992.

Stoet, G., and D. C. Geary. Sex differences in mathematics and reading achievement are inversely related: Within- and across nation assessment of 10 years of PISA data. *PLoS ONE* 8:e57988, 2013.

Sugishita, M., K. Otomo, S. Kabe, and K. Yunoki. A critical appraisal of neuropsychological correlates of Japanese ideogram (kanji) and phonogram (kana) reading. *Brain* 115:1563–1585, 1992.

Swaab, D. F. Sexual differentiation of the human brain: Relevance for gender identity, transsexualism and sexual orientation. *Gynecology and Endocrinology* 19:301–312, 2004.

Taglialatela, J. P., C. Cantalupo, and W. D. Hopkins. Gesture handedness predicts asymmetry in the chimpanzee inferior frontal gyrus. *Neuroreport* 17:923–927, 2006.

Tian, L., J. Wang, C. Yan, and Y. He. Hemisphere- and gender-related differences in small-world brain networks: A resting-state functional MRI study. *NeuroImage*, 54:191–202, 2011.

Thomas, H., W. Jamison, and D. D. Hummel. Observation is insufficient for discovering that the surface of still water is invariantly horizontal. *Science* 191:173–174, 1973.

Uyehara, J. M., and W. C. Cooper, Jr. Hemispheric differences for verbal and nonverbal stimuli in Japanese- and English-speaking subjects assessed by Tsunoda's method. *Brain and Language* 10:405–417, 1980.

Velle, W. Sex differences in sensory functions. *Perspectives in Biology and Medicine* 30:490–522, 1987.

Waber, D. P. Sex differences in cognition: A function of maturation rate. *Science* 192:572–573, 1976.

Werker, J. F., and R. C. Tees. The organization and reorganization of human speech perception. *Annual Review of Neuroscience* 15:377–402, 1992.

Wilson, B., and C. Petkov. Communication and the primate brain: Insights from neuroimaging studies in humans, chimpanzees and macaques. *Human Biology* 832:175–189, 2012.

Witelson, S. F. The brain connection: The corpus callosum is larger in left-handers. *Science* 229:665–668, 1985.

Witelson, S. F. Hand and sex differences in the isthmus and genu of the human corpus callosum: A postmortem morphological study. *Brain* 112:799–835, 1989.

Witelson, S. F., and D. L. Kigar. Sylvian fissure morphology and asymmetry in men and women: Bilateral differences in relation to handedness in men. *Journal of Comparative Neurology* 323:326–340, 1992.

Woolley, C. S., E. Gould, M. Frankfurt, and B. S. McEwen. Naturally occurring fluctuation in dendritic spine density on adult hippocampal pyramidal neurons. *Journal of Neuroscience* 10:4035–4039, 1990.

Yakovlev, P. I., and P. Rakic. Patterns of decussation of bulbar pyramids and distribution of pyramidal tracts on two sides of the spinal cord. *Transactions of the American Neurological Association* 91:366–367, 1966.

13

The Occipital Lobes

PORTRAIT   An Injured Soldier's Visual World

P.M., a colonel in the British army who fought in North Africa during World War II, was struck by a bullet that went through the back of his brain. Miraculously, P.M. survived, but his vision was severely affected. He completely lost the sight in the right visual field, and only the central part of his left visual field survived. He reported that he could see "normally" in a region of the left visual world that was about the diameter of your fist held at arm's length directly in front of your face.

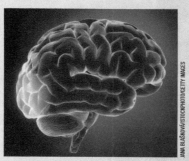

P.M.'s symptoms reveal a topographic map of the visual world in the occipital cortex (see adjoining illustration) and the possibility of seeing through only a small part of it. But what did P.M. experience in the rest of his visual world? Shortly after his injury, he reported that the lost world appeared black, as though the lights were out. Occasionally, however, he was aware that the lost regions were different, "almost gray," although he could never express specifically what exactly was different other than the grayness.

P.M. also experienced a phenomenon that many patients with extensive visual field defects experience: if asked to guess whether a spot of light had blinked in his blind field, he could "guess" at above-chance levels. He was not consciously aware that the light had appeared and was bemused that he could guess, sometimes quite accurately, about the presence or absence of the light.

In spite of his residual central vision, P.M. had two particular—and, for him, aggravating—problems: he found reading very difficult and had difficulty recognizing faces. Curiously, however, P.M. recognized other objects more easily, even though he could not see any more of them than he could of the faces.

Our brains are organized around vision. Our perceptions are predominantly visual, our movements are guided by visual information, our social and sexual behavior is highly visual, our entertainment is largely visual, and our nights are enriched by visual dreams.

In this chapter, we first consider the anatomical organization of the occipital lobes, then examine the visual system's extent within the brain. Next we examine disorders of the visual pathways and of the visual system. Lastly, we shall see why humans' ability to visualize presents neuropsychologists a unique opportunity to study cerebral functioning.

13.1 Occipital Lobe Anatomy

Lying beneath the occipital bone at the back of the skull, the occipital lobes form the posterior pole of the cerebral hemispheres. On each hemisphere's medial surface, the occipital lobe is distinguished from the parietal lobe by the parietal-occipital sulcus, as illustrated in **Figure 13.1**.

No clear landmarks separate the occipital cortex from the temporal or parietal cortex on the lateral hemispheric surface, however, because the occipital tissue merges with the other regions. The lack of clear landmarks makes precisely defining the extent of the occipital areas difficult and has led to massive confusion about their exact boundaries—especially on the brain's ventral surface, where the occipital cortex extends forward to merge with medial and ventral temporal cortices.

Nevertheless, within the visual cortex are three clear landmarks identified in Figure 13.1. Most prominent is the calcarine sulcus, which contains much of the primary visual cortex (V1). The calcarine sulcus divides the upper and lower halves of the visual world. On the ventral surface of each hemisphere are two gyri (lingual and fusiform). The lingual gyrus includes part of visual cortical regions V2 and VP, whereas V4 is in the fusiform gyrus.

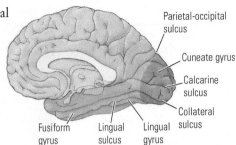

⊚ Figure 13.1 ▲

Medial View Illustrating Major Occipital-Lobe Landmarks

Subdivisions of the Occipital Cortex

A century ago, Brodmann first divided the monkey cortex into three visual regions (areas 17, 18, and 19, shown for the human brain in Figure 10.7). Later studies using imaging and physiological and newer anatomical techniques have produced much finer subdivisions. Although the map is still not complete, the consensus is that the monkey occipital cortex contains multiple visual areas, as illustrated in **Figure 13.2**. Note, too, that many visual areas occupy the adjacent parietal and temporal cortices.

Figure 13.2A shows the locations of these areas on the lateral surface of the monkey brain, and Figure 13.2B shows their locations on a two-dimensional flat map that includes both the lateral areas and those located on the medial surface of the hemisphere. The precise locations of the human homologues are still not settled, but **Figure 13.3** presents flat maps of both monkey and human brains constructed by Dwight Kravitz and his colleagues (2013).

A difficulty in comparing the monkey and human maps is methodological: the monkey maps are based on anatomy and connections, whereas the human maps are now heavily based on noninvasive techniques such as fMRI. Nevertheless, a strong correspondence between monkeys and humans in the early visual areas (V1–V4) is apparent in Figure 13.3, and the additional regions beyond V4 on the human map suggest that humans have more visual processing capacity than monkeys.

A remarkable feature of area V1 is its complex laminar organization—probably the most

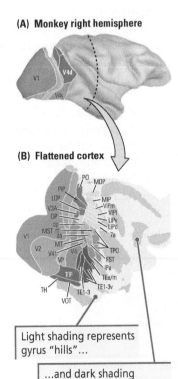

(A) Monkey right hemisphere

(B) Flattened cortex

Light shading represents gyrus "hills"...

...and dark shading represents sulcus "valleys."

Figure 13.2 ◄

Topography of the Macaque Monkey's Visual Cortex (A) The sulci are opened slightly in this nearly normal rendition of the right hemisphere's lateral surface. (B) A flattened cortical surface showing both right lateral and medial regions. Darker areas around the sulci represent regions that are normally curved up (gyri) or down (sulci). (Data from Tootell et al., 2003.)

Figure 13.3 ►

Topography of the Primate Visual Cortex
(A) Flat-map representation of the known retinotopic maps in the macaque, made by inflating the cortical surface to bring the depths of sulci to the surface and cutting along the calcarine sulcus to flatten the map. The various cortical representations of the fovea are marked by an asterisk (*). Arrow tips at lower left indicate direction: D, dorsal; A, anterior. (B) As in (A) but for humans. Note the high correspondence between monkey and human in the early visual areas (V1–V4) and the additional areas anterior to V4 in the human. (Kolster H, et al. The retinotopic organization of the human middle temporal area MT/V5 and its cortical neighbors. *J Neurosci.* 2010; 30:9801–9820, Fig. 16 (A).)

(A) Monkey

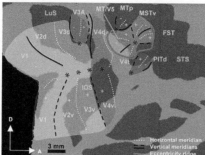

(B) Human

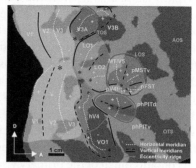

distinct of all cortical areas—illustrated in **Figure 13.4**A. Typically, the neocortex is comprised of six layers, but it is possible to see many more in area V1. This in part because cortical layer IV alone features four distinct layers and appears as a thick stripe, which gives the visual cortex its nickname: **striate cortex**.

Although V1 appears anatomically homogenous, it can be shown actually to be heterogeneous by staining it for cytochrome oxidase, an enzyme crucial in making energy available to cells. Cytochrome-rich areas, the blobs, are separated by interblob regions of little cytochrome activity (see Figure 10.10B). Cells in the blobs take part in color perception; the interblobs have a role in form and motion perception.

The discovery that area V1 is functionally heterogeneous—that a given cortical area may have more than one distinct function—was unexpected. Area V2 also appears heterogeneous when stained with cytochrome oxidase, but instead of blobs, stripes are revealed (see Figure 10.10C). The "thin stripe" takes part in color perception. "Thick stripes" and "pale stripes" have roles in form and motion perception, respectively. Thus, we see that the functional heterogeneity observed in area V1—representing color, form, and motion—is preserved in area V2, albeit organized in a different way, as diagrammed in Figure 13.4B.

The distribution of color function across much of the occipital cortex and beyond (in areas V1, V2, V4) is important because throughout the twentieth century, perception of form or movement was believed to be color-blind. But in fact, color vision is integral to analyzing the position, depth, motion, and structure of objects (see a review by Tanaka et al., 2001).

Although the relative amount of color processing certainly varies across occipital regions, with the major function of area V4 being color processing,

Figure 13.4 ▼

Visual Cortex (A) V1 is highly laminated, as revealed in a cell-body stain (left) or a myelin stain (right) in these sections from a monkey brain. (B) Drawing of a flattened section through the monkey's visual cortex illustrates the blobs in V1 and the stripes in V2.

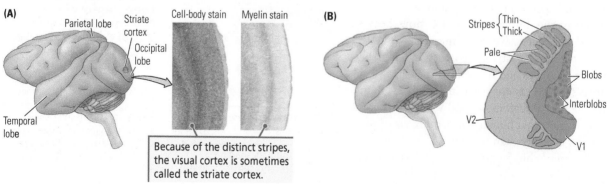

color-related information processing does more than simply allow us to tell red from green. Color also enriches our capacity to detect motion, depth, and position. This point is key. In the absence of significant color analysis, dogs and cats not only see an essentially black-and-white world but also have reduced visual capacities more generally, compared to humans.

But primates' color system is optimized for differentiating edible fruits from a background of leaves and may also be critical for identifying poisonous snakes (Sumner and Mollon, 2000). This ability to differentiate color bestows an important advantage when selecting edible fruits (or spotting dangerous snakes) within a complex scene and is especially important when either is partly occluded by leaves. Color vision provides important information for object recognition. A partly occluded yellow banana is quickly seen, whereas a gray banana would be difficult to detect in a scene viewed in black and white.

Connections of the Visual Cortex

By the late 1960s, the consensus held that the visual cortex is hierarchically organized, with visual information proceeding from area V1 to V2 to V3. Each was thought to elaborate on processing in the preceding area. Today, this strictly hierarchical view is considered too simple and has been replaced by the notion of a distributed hierarchical process with multiple parallel and interconnecting pathways at each level, much as charted in Figure 10.18B.

The wiring diagram of the visual pathways is complex, but it is possible to extract a few simple principles:

- V1 (striate cortex) is the first processing level in the hierarchy, receiving the largest input from the lateral geniculate nucleus of the thalamus and projecting to all other occipital regions.
- V2, the second processing level, also projects to all other occipital regions.
- After V2, three distinct parallel pathways emerge en route to the parietal cortex, the multimodal **superior temporal sulcus** (STS), and inferior temporal cortex for further processing (**Figure 13.5**).

We shall see in more detail next that two pathways emerge: the **dorsal stream** (parietal pathway) participates in the visual guidance of movement, and the **ventral stream**, including both the inferior temporal pathway and the STS pathway, is concerned with object perception (including color and faces) and perceiving certain types of movements.

13.2 A Theory of Occipital-Lobe Function

Areas V1 and V2 are functionally heterogeneous: both segregate processing for color, form, and motion. This heterogeneity contrasts with the functions of the areas that follow in the hierarchy. In a sense, areas V1 and V2 appear to serve as in-boxes into which different types of information are assembled before being sent on to more specialized visual areas.

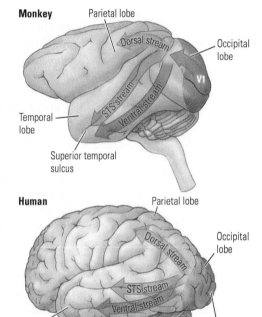

Ⓒ **Figure 13.5** ▲

Visual Streaming In monkey and human brains, the occipito-parietal (dorsal) stream takes part in vision for action, flowing from area V1 to the posterior parietal visual areas. The occipitotemporal (ventral) stream takes part in object recognition and flows from area V1 to the temporal visual areas. Information to and from the dorsal and ventral streams converges in the STS stream, which flows from area V1 into the superior temporal sulcus.

From areas V1 and V2 flow three parallel pathways that convey different attributes of vision. The information derived from the blob areas of V1 goes to area V4, considered a color area. Cells in area V4 are not solely responsive to color, however; some cells respond to both form and color.

Other information from area V1 also goes to area V2 and then to area V5 (also known as middle temporal, or area MT), which is specialized to detect motion. Finally, an input from areas V1 and V2 to area V3 concerns **dynamic form**—the shape of objects in motion. Thus, we see that vision processing begins in the primary occipital cortex (V1), which has multiple functions, then continues in more specialized cortical zones.

Not surprisingly, selective lesions up the hierarchy in areas V3, V4, and V5 produce specific deficits. People who suffer damage to area V4 are able to see only in shades of gray. Curiously, these patients not only fail to perceive colors but also fail to recall colors perceived before their injuries, or even to imagine colors. In a real sense, the loss of area V4 results in the loss of color cognition—the ability to think about color.

Similarly, a lesion in area V5 erases the ability to perceive objects in motion. Objects at rest are perceived, but when the objects begin to move, they vanish. In principle, a lesion in area V3 will affect form perception, but because area V4 also processes form, a rather large lesion of both V3 and V4 would be required to eliminate form perception.

An important constraint on the functions of areas V3, V4, and V5 is that all receive major input from area V1. People with lesions in V1, such as Colonel P.M. in this chapter's opening Portrait, act as though they are blind, but visual input can still get through to higher levels—partly through small projections of the lateral geniculate nucleus to area V2 and partly through projections from the colliculus to the thalamus (the pulvinar) to the cortex. People with V1 lesions seem unaware of visual input and can be shown to retain some aspects of vision only by special testing (see Case D.B. in Section 13.4). Thus, when asked what they see, patients with V1 damage often reply that they see nothing. Nonetheless, they can act on visual information, indicating that they do indeed "see."

Area V1 thus appears primary for vision in yet another sense: V1 must function for the brain to make sense of what the more specialized visual areas are processing. We must note, however, reports of people with significant V1 damage who retain some awareness of visual information, such as motion. John Barbur and his colleagues (1993) suggest that the integrity of area V3 may allow this conscious awareness, but this suggestion remains a hypothesis.

Visual Functions Beyond the Occipital Lobe

Neuroscientists have known for a century that the occipital lobes house vision, but only in the past few decades have they begun to understand the extent of visual processing beyond the occipital lobes. In fact, it is now clear that more cortex is devoted to vision than to any other function in the primate brain.

Visual processing in humans does not culminate in secondary areas such as V3, V4, and V5 but continues within multiple visual regions in the parietal, temporal, and frontal lobes (elaborated in Figures 14.3 and Figure 15.5). Functions have not been assigned to all of these additional visual regions, but evidence is accumulating that different regions have quite specific functions. **Table 13.1** summarizes the putative functions of regions in both the ventral and dorsal streams. For example, in the ventral stream, several regions appear to be tuned selectively to identify body parts such as hands (EBA, extrastriate body area; and FBA, fusiform body area), faces (FFA, fusiform face area), or moving bodies (STSp). Another region, PPA, (parahippocampal place area) has a totally different function—namely, analyzing information about the appearance and layout of scenes.

Although it is tempting to regard each ventral-stream region as an independent visual processor, all are clearly responsive in some degree to all categories of stimuli. The differences among the regions are a matter of *degree*, not the mere *presence*, of activity. An fMRI study by Timothy Andrews and his colleagues (2002) illustrates this. They showed participants the perceptually ambiguous Rubin's vase–face illusion (see Figure 8.23A). The FFA responded more strongly when participants reported seeing the faces than the vase, even though exactly the same physical stimulus gave rise to the two percepts. Such changes were not seen in adjacent visual areas such as the PPA.

Table 13.1 also identifies several dorsal-stream regions specialized for moving the eyes (LIP) or for object-directed grasping (AIP, PRR). Not all neurons in these regions control movements directly. Some appear to be "purely visual" and are presumed to take part in converting visual information into the necessary coordinates for action.

One conclusion we can make is that vision is not unitary but is composed of many highly specific forms of processing. These forms can be organized into five general categories: vision for action, action for vision, visual recognition, visual space, and visual attention.

Vision for Action

This category is visual processing required to direct specific movements. For example, when reaching for a particular object, such as a cup, the fingers form a specific pattern that enables a person to grasp the cup. This movement is obviously guided by vision, because people do not need to shape their hands consciously as they reach.

In addition to guiding grasping, various visual areas guide all kinds of specific movements, including those of the eyes, head, and whole body. A single system could not easily guide all movements: the requirements are too different. Reaching to pick up a jelly bean requires a far different kind of motor control from that required to duck a snowball, but both are visually guided.

Finally, vision for action must be sensitive to the target's movement. Catching a moving ball requires specific information about its location, trajectory, speed, and shape. Vision for action is a function of the parietal visual areas in the dorsal stream.

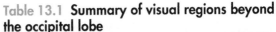

Table 13.1 **Summary of visual regions beyond the occipital lobe**

	Region	Proposed Function
Ventral Stream Regions		
LO	Lateral occipital	Object analysis
FFA	Fusiform face area	Face analysis
EBA	Extrastriate body area	Body analysis
FBA	Fusiform body area	Body analysis
STS	Superior temporal sulcus	Analysis of biological motion
STSp	Superior temporal sulcus (posterior)	Moving-body analysis
PPA	Parahippocampal place area	Analysis of landmarks
Dorsal Stream Regions		
LIP	Lateral intraparietal sulcus	Voluntary eye movement
AIP	Anterior intraparietal sulcus	Object-directed grasping
VIP	Ventral intraparietal sulcus	Visuomotor guidance
PRR	Parietal reach region	Visually guided reach
cIPS	Intraparietal sulcus	Object-directed action

▲ You may consciously decide to reach for an object such as a mug, but your hand forms the appropriate posture automatically, without your conscious awareness.

(A) Control participant

A control's eye movements concentrate on facial features in a photograph and are directed more to the right side of the person's face.

(B) Control participant

Sphere   Bust

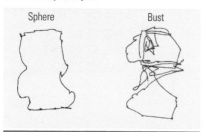

A control's eye movements concentrate on the shapes of the objects examined...

(C) Agnosic subject

Sphere   Bust

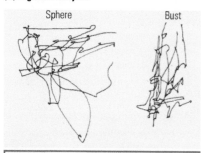

...but those of an agnosic subject are random.

◎ Figure 13.6 ▲

Action for Vision (©1973 A.R. Luria, *The Working Brain: An Introduction to Neuropsychology.* Reprinted with permission of the Perseus Books Group.)

Action for Vision

In a more "top-down" process, the viewer actively searches for only part of the target object and attends to it selectively. When we look at a visual stimulus, we do not simply stare at it; rather, we scan the stimulus with numerous eye movements. These movements are not random but tend to focus on important or distinct features of the stimulus.

When we scan a face, we make multiple eye movements directed toward the eyes and mouth. Curiously, we also direct more eye scans to the left visual field (the right side of the person's face) than to the right visual field (**Figure 13.6**A). This scanning bias may be important in the way that we process faces because it is not found when scanning other stimuli (Figure 13.6B). People with deficits in action for vision are likely to have significant deficits in visual perception (Figure 13.6C), although such deficits have not been studied systematically.

An interesting aspect of action for vision is the eye movements we often make when we visualize information. For example, when people are asked to rotate objects mentally to answer simple questions about the objects' appearance, they usually make many eye movements, especially to the left. When people are acting in the dark—say, searching for objects on a counter—they also make many eye movements. Curiously, if the eyes are closed, these movements stop. Indeed, it appears easier to do many tasks in the dark with closed eyes. Because we act by touch in the dark, the visual system may interfere until the eyes are closed.

Visual Recognition

We enjoy the ability both to recognize objects and to respond to visual information. For example, we can both recognize specific faces and discriminate and interpret different expressions in those faces. Similarly, we can recognize letters or symbols and assign meaning to them.

We can recognize different foods, tools, or body parts, but it is not reasonable to expect that we have different visual regions for each category or object. We do have at least some specialized areas in the temporal regions, however, for biologically significant information, such as faces and hands, as well as regions for objects and places.

Visual Space

Visual information that comes from specific locations in space allows us to direct our movements to objects in that space and to assign meaning to those objects. But spatial location is not unitary. Objects have location both relative to an individual (**egocentric space**) and relative to one another (**allocentric space**).

Egocentric visual space is central to controlling your actions toward objects. It therefore seems likely that visual space is coded in neural systems related to vision for action. In contrast, the allocentric properties of objects are necessary for you to construct a memory of spatial location. A key feature of allocentric spatial coding is its dependence on the identity of particular features of the world. Thus, it is likely to be associated with the regions of visual recognition.

In summary, different aspects of spatial processing probably occur in both the parietal and the temporal visual regions, and respective functions are integrated in areas that interact and exchange information.

Visual Attention

We cannot possibly process all available visual information. This page has shape, color, texture, location, and so on, but its only really important characteristic is its words and images. When you read the page, then, you select specific aspects of visual input and attend to them selectively.

In fact, neurons in the cortex have various attentional mechanisms. Neurons may respond selectively to stimuli in particular places or at particular times or if a particular movement is to be executed, for example. Independent mechanisms of attention are probably required both for guiding movements (in the parietal lobe) and for recognizing objects (in the temporal lobe). We elaborate on attention in Chapter 22.

Visual Pathways Beyond the Occipital Lobe

Vision evolved first for motion, not for recognition. Simple organisms can detect light and move to or from it. For example, the single-cell organism *Euglena* alters its swimming pattern as a function of ambient light levels in different parts of the pond in which it lives. Because sunlight helps manufacture food in this aquatic environment, it is an advantage for *Euglena* to move toward the light.

Notice that *Euglena* need neither "perceive" the light nor make an internal map of the outside world. Rather, only a link of some type between the amount of ambient light and locomotion is necessary. For *Euglena*, vision acts to guide movement—the most primitive form of vision for action.

Even though our vision is far more complicated than that of *Euglena*, much of human vision can be understood without reference to object recognition. Consider, for example, a professional baseball player who swings at a fastball before it is possible for him to perceive what the object actually is. Visual guidance of his movement is independent of his recognition of a baseball.

Nonetheless, as primitive animals interact with their environment, they are adapted to learn more about it. Distinct visual systems thus evolved to recognize objects in the environment. The system of knowing what an object is includes the visual information flow from area V1 to the temporal lobe in the ventral stream. The system controlling visually guided movements includes the flow of information from area V1 to the parietal lobe in the dorsal stream. Although Figure 13.5 suggests a fairly simple flow-through of information along the dorsal and ventral streams, we shall see in Section 15.1 that an interaction with subcortical regions occurs at each step along the ventral stream.

The distinction between the ventral and dorsal streams can be seen clearly in a series of patients studied by David Milner and Melvyn Goodale (2006). They first described D.F., a patient with a selective lesion to the lateral occipital, area LO, illustrated in **Figure 13.7**. D.F.

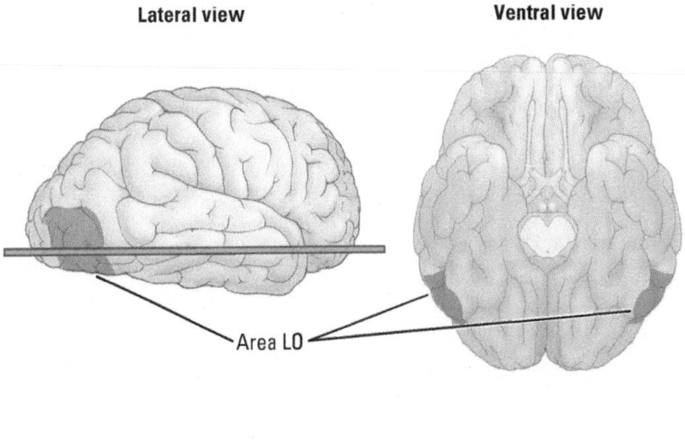

Figure 13.7 ▼

Extent of D.F.'s Lesion
(Left) The right-hemisphere occipital area in red shows that D.F.'s lesion envelops the lateral occipital (area LO). (Right) The ventral view reveals bilateral lesions in LO. (Information from Milner and Goodale, 2006.)

Lateral view   Ventral view

Area LO

was blind but nevertheless shaped her hand appropriately when asked to reach for objects. Her dorsal stream was intact, as revealed by the fact that she could "unconsciously" see location, size, and shape. By contrast, Milner and Goodale note that patients with dorsal-stream damage consciously report seeing objects but cannot reach accurately or shape the hand appropriately when reaching.

Milner and Goodale propose that the dorsal stream be thought of as a set of systems for online visual control of action. Their argument is based on three main lines of evidence:

1. **Visual neurons in posterior parietal regions are unique in that they are active only when the brain acts on visual information.** Their predominant characteristic is that these neurons are active during a combination of visual stimulation and associated behavior. Cells may be active only when a monkey reaches out to a particular object, for example. Looking at an object in the absence of movement does not activate the neurons.

2. **Visual posterior parietal neurons therefore act as an interface between analysis of the visual world and motor action taken on it.** The demands of action have important implications for what type of information must be sent to the parietal cortex—information such as object shape, movement, and location. Each of these visual features likely is coded separately, and at least three distinct pathways within the dorsal stream run from area V1 to the parietal cortex. As illustrated on the right in **Figure 13.8**, one pathway goes from area V1 directly to area V5 to the parietal cortex, a second goes from area V1 to area V3a and then to parietal regions, and a third goes from area V1 to area V2 to the parietal cortex. These three pathways must certainly be functionally dissociable.

3. **Most visual impairments associated with lesions to the parietal cortex can be characterized as visuomotor or visuospatial.** (We return to this point in Section 14.1.)

The Milner–Goodale model is an important theoretical advance in understanding how our visual brain is organized. As detailed in Figure 13.8, the two distinct visual streams have evolved to use visual information in two fundamentally different ways: the dorsal stream for guiding movements and the ventral stream for identifying objects. This model likely can be applied to the organization of the auditory and somatosensory systems as well: both also function to guide movements and identify stimuli. An important point here is that we are conscious of only a small amount of what the brain actually does; even with effort, we cannot gain awareness of much of our sensory processing.

One wrinkle can be added to the Milner–Goodale model: the third stream of visual processing originates from structures associated with both the parietal and the temporal pathways and flows to a region buried in the superior temporal sulcus (see Figure 13.5). The STS is part of the multimodal cortex characterized by **polysensory neurons**—neurons responsive to both visual and auditory or both visual and somatosensory input (see Section 10.2).

The interaction of parietal and temporal streams in the STS stream is probably due to interaction between the dorsal and the

⊚ **Figure 13.8** ▼

Summary of the Visual Processing Hierarchy As shown on the left, the ventral stream takes part in object recognition to allow us to identify objects such as mugs and pens. The dorsal stream takes part in visual action to guide our movements, such as the hand postures for grasping a mug or pen, as illustrated on the right. The dorsal and ventral streams exchange information through polysensory neurons in the STS stream, as shown by the double-headed central arrows. (Research from Goodale, 1993.)

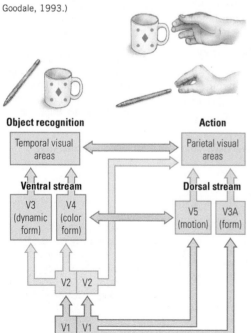

ventral—the "action" and "recognition"—streams. Milner and Goodale suspect that this "third stream" is largely an elaboration of the ventral stream and that the STS stream provides a perceptual representation of biological motion, that is, of the actions of others, as well as visuospatial relations among elements in a scene. (See Rizzolatti and Matelli, 2003, for a different interpretation.)

Imaging Studies of Dorsal and Ventral Streams

Neuroscientists identify brain regions associated with specific visual pathways by measuring regional blood flow as people perform visual tasks. Leslie Ungerleider and James Haxby (1994) reviewed such PET studies, as summarized in **Figure 13.9**.

In studies by Haxby and his colleagues (1999), participants were given two tasks. In the first, participants indicated which of two faces was identical with a sample face. In the second, they were asked to identify which of two stimuli had a dot or square in the same location as in a sample. The results showed activation of the temporal regions for the facial stimuli and activation of the posterior parietal region for the location task (Figure 13.9A). Note also that activation of frontal areas for the spatial task supports the idea that the frontal lobe plays a role in certain aspects of visual processing (see the Snapshot in Section 16.2).

One difficulty in interpreting the spatial-task PET images is that participants have to move their eyes, which activates regions in the dorsal stream, so whether the spatial or the movement components activate the parietal region is not clear. The important point is that different regions take part in the two tasks.

A similar dissociation was identified among the processes that detect motion, color, and shape (Figure 13.9B). Motion detection activates regions in the vicinity of area V5, whereas shape detection activates regions along the STS and the ventral temporal lobe. Color perception is associated with activation of the lingual gyrus (see Figure 13.1), the location of area V4.

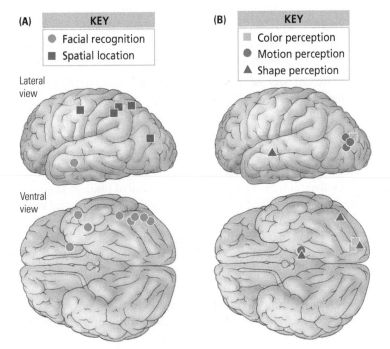

(A)

KEY
● Facial recognition
■ Spatial location

Lateral view

Ventral view

(B)

KEY
■ Color perception
● Motion perception
▲ Shape perception

◎ Figure 13.9 ◄

Imaging Visual Pathways
Summary of results of PET studies illustrates selective activation of (A) cortical regions by tasks of facial recognition (circles) and spatial location (squares), and (B) activation of areas associated with color perception (squares), motion (circles), and shape (triangles). (Data source: Ungerleider and Haxby, 1994.)

In summary, studies of regional blood flow show results consistent with the general notion of two separate visual streams, one to the parietal lobe and the other to the temporal lobe. Separate visual functions clearly reside in different temporal-occipital regions.

Top-Down Predictions in Vision

One characteristic of sensory perception is the speed with which we interpret incoming information. Moshe Bar and his colleagues (see reviews by Kveraga et al., 2007; Panichello et al., 2012) argue that, far from being a passive receiver, the brain continuously employs memories of past experiences, both to interpret moment-to-moment sensory information and to predict the immediate future. For example, a baseball player can anticipate a particular type of pitch to predict the ball's trajectory by combining expectations about the pitch (top-down processing) with online (bottom-up) perception of the ball's rotation and speed—all in less than 500 milliseconds. This ability is not innate but requires years of training.

But where do the top-down predictions arise? Bar proposes that the extensive connections between the prefrontal cortex and both the occipital and temporal lobes make the prefrontal cortex the likely information provider for enhancing visual processing speed.

◎ 13.3 Disorders of Visual Pathways

Before we can consider deficits associated with damage to the visual pathways, we must revisit two key elements in the way the brain organizes the visual fields:

1. The left half of each retina sends its projections to the right side of the brain, whereas the right half of each retina sends its projections to the left side of the brain (**Figure 13.10** at top). Thus, the representation of each side of the visual world seen by each eye is sent to the same place in area V1, and damage to V1 affects vision in both eyes. Conversely, if a visual disturbance is restricted to just one eye, then the damage must be outside the brain, either in the retina or in the optic nerve.

2. Different parts of the visual field are topographically represented in different parts of area V1 (Figure 13.10, bottom). Thus, injury to a specific region of V1 produces a loss of vision in a specific part of the visual world.

Now let us consider what happens when damage is done to different places in the visual pathways, as keyed on Figure 13.10, where standard vision (1) is diagrammed for comparison.

Destruction of the retina or optic nerve of one eye produces (2) *monocular blindness*—loss of sight in that eye. A lesion of the medial region of the optic chiasm severs the crossing fibers, producing (3) **bitemporal hemianopia**—loss of vision of both temporal fields. This deficit can arise, for example, when a tumor develops in the pituitary gland, which sits medially, next to the chiasm. As the tumor grows, it can put pressure on the medial part of the chiasm and produce the loss or disturbance of lateral vision.

A lesion of the lateral chiasm results in a loss of vision of one nasal field, or *nasal hemianopia* (4). Complete cuts of the optic tract, lateral geniculate

◎ **Figure 13.10 ▼**

Effects of Injury Visual defects subsequent to damage at different levels of the visual system, keyed by number. In the visual field key, purple regions denote areas where vision is spared. Black regions denote blind areas in the visual field. (Information from Curtis, 1972.)

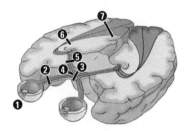

Patient's actual visual field

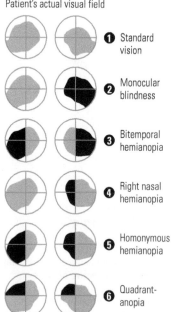

❶ Standard vision

❷ Monocular blindness

❸ Bitemporal hemianopia

❹ Right nasal hemianopia

❺ Homonymous hemianopia

❻ Quadrant-anopia

❼ Macular sparing

body, or area V1 result in (5) **homonymous hemianopia**—blindness of one entire visual field, also illustrated in **Figure 13.11**A. Note also in field 5 of Figure 13.10 that because the disturbance affects information coming from both eyes, we know that the visual defect is present in both eyes.

Indeed, the effects of such injuries enable investigators to determine whether a lesion is in the eye or optic tract versus the optic nerve or brain. The former injuries produce visual disturbance in one eye, whereas the latter injuries produce visual disturbance in the visual field and thus in both eyes. Should this lesion be partial, as is often the case, only a part (quadrant) of the visual field is destroyed (field 6 in Figure 13.10).

Lesions of the occipital lobe often spare the central, or *macular*, region of the visual field. The reason is uncertain. The most reasonable explanation is either (1) that the macular region receives a double vascular supply from both the middle and the posterior cerebral arteries, making it more resilient to large hemispheric lesions, or (2) that the foveal region of the retina projects to both hemispheres, so even if one occipital lobe is destroyed, the other receives projections from the fovea. The first explanation is more likely.

Macular sparing of the central visual field (field 7 in Figure 13.10) helps to differentiate lesions of the optic tract or thalamus from cortical lesions because macular sparing occurs only after unilateral lesions (usually large) to the visual cortex. Macular sparing does not always occur, however, and many people with visual-cortex lesions have a complete loss of vision in one-quarter (**quadrantanopia**) or one-half (*hemianopia*) of the fovea (see Figure 13.11A and B). A curious aspect of both hemianopia and quadrantanopia is that the border between the impaired visual area and the adjacent, intact visual field or quadrant is sharp, much as if a pair of scissors were used to cut away part of the visual field (see Figure 13.10). This sharp demarcation of intact and impaired visual regions is due to the anatomical segregation between left and right and upper and lower visual fields.

Small occipital lobe lesions often produce **scotomas**, small blind spots in the visual field (Figure 13.11C). People are often totally unaware of scotomas because of *nystagmus* (constant tiny involuntary eye movements) and "spontaneous filling in" by the visual system. Because the eyes are usually in constant motion, the scotoma moves about the visual field, allowing the brain to perceive all of the information in the field. If the eyes are held still, the visual system

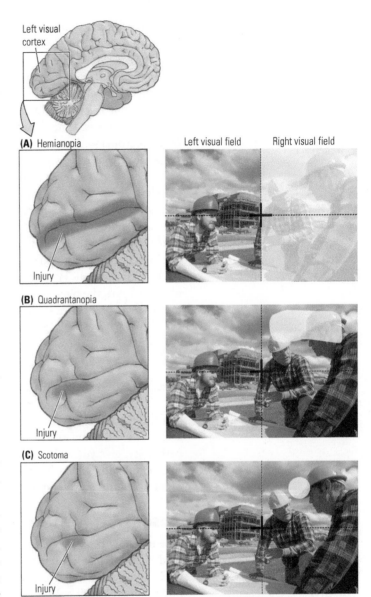

Figure 13.11 ▲

Consequences of Lesions in Area V1 Shaded areas indicate regions of visual loss. (A) A complete lesion of area V1 in the left hemisphere results in hemianopia affecting the right visual field. (B) A large lesion of the lower lip of the calcarine fissure produces a quadrantanopia that affects most of the upper-right visual quadrant. (C) A smaller lesion of the lower lip of the calcarine fissure results in a smaller injury, a scotoma. (Glowimages/Getty Images.)

actually completes objects, faces, and so on, resulting in a regular percept of the stimulus.

The visual system may cover up the scotoma so successfully that its presence can be demonstrated to patients only by "tricking" their visual systems. Such tricking can be achieved by placing objects entirely within the scotoma region of the patient's visual field and, without allowing the patient to shift gaze, asking what the object is. If no object is reported, the examiner moves the object out of the scotoma so that it suddenly "appears" in the intact region of the patient's visual field, thus demonstrating the existence of the blind region.

You can demonstrate a similar phenomenon in your own "blind spot," the region in each eye where axons forming the optic nerve leave the eye and there are no photoreceptors (see Figure 8.5A). Stand beside a table, close or cover one eye, stare at a spot on the table, and move a pencil along the table laterally, from directly below your nose to between 20 and 30 cm toward the periphery. Part of the pencil will vanish when you reach the blind spot. You can move the pencil through the blind spot slowly, and it will suddenly reappear on the other side. Notice that, like a scotoma, the blind spot is not noticeable, even when you look around with just one eye. Our brains typically "fill in" missing bits of the visual world.

13.4 Disorders of Cortical Function

Research into selective disturbances of human visual functions is limited mainly to case studies—recall Colonel P.M., whom you met in the opening Portrait—and these nonsurgical lesions seldom respect the boundaries of specific visual areas. The following case histories, each with distinctly different symptoms and pathology, give you an idea of specific symptoms of injury to the visual cortex. We begin with damage to area V1 and proceed along the hierarchy to higher-order areas and more-complicated visual disturbances.

Case B.K.: V1 Damage and a Scotoma

One morning B.K. awoke to discover that he was hemianopic in the left visual field. Given a history of classic migraine in which the aura was nearly always in the left field, he likely had a migraine stroke. (For a thorough discussion of migraine, see Section 26.6.) Within a few hours, the left lower field began to return, but the left upper quadrant was slow to show any change.

The MRI in **Figure 13.12**A shows a clear **infarct** (dead tissue) in the right occipital area. The size of a visual-field defect is routinely measured with *perimetry*,

Figure 13.12 ▼

Scan of B.K.'s Brain and His Visual-Field Maps
(A) B.K.'s MRI shows the infarct (dark area) in the right occipital area. (B) Map of B.K.'s visual fields 6 months after the stroke. Subnormal vision persists in the upper-left quadrant. (Keith Humphrey/Bryan Kolb.)

(A) MRI scan of B.K.'s brain

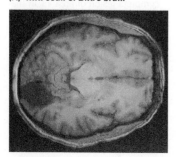

(B) B.K.'s left and right visual fields

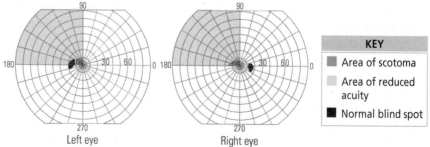

Left eye

Right eye

KEY

■ Area of scotoma

■ Area of reduced acuity

■ Normal blind spot

a standardized method in which the subject fixates on a black dot in the center of a large, white hemisphere. A small light is moved around the field, and the task is to indicate when the light is visible. The brightness and size of the light can be varied to manipulate the difficulty of the task. Performance is mapped by indicating the area of "blindness" on a schematic of the visual fields (Figure 13.12B).

The nature of B.K.'s visual defects can be illustrated best in the context of their poststroke evolution. For the first 2 to 3 days, his visual field appeared dark, much as though a piece of smoked glass were blocking his view of the world beyond. On the fourth day, this darkness had disappeared and was replaced by "visual noise" (a *scintillating scotoma*) throughout much of the field, especially in the area of the scotoma.

A curious phenomenon was first observed during perimetry testing 4 days after the stroke. If the stimulus light was moved into the blind field, B.K. did not perceive it until it moved into another quadrant. Curiously, however, B.K. immediately became aware (in hindsight) that the light had been present in the blind field and could accurately state where it entered. In other words, B.K. perceived location without being able to perceive content. Recall that Colonel P.M also experienced this phenomenon, known as **blindsight**.

In the ensuing 4 to 6 months, the area of blindness decreased somewhat, and acuity in the periphery improved significantly for B.K. Nonetheless, roughly 30 years later, form vision remains poor in the left upper quadrant, outside the scotoma. The scintillating scotoma is still present, showing little change from the first few days after the stroke.

The visual phenomena observed by B.K. indicate that area V1 (and perhaps area V2) probably has an area of total cell death (the dense scotoma). The poor form vision in the rest of the quadrant may be due to a loss of some but not all neurons in area V1, possibly only those that are especially sensitive to a period of reduced blood flow, or **ischemia**. The poor form vision might also be attributed to the fact that other visual areas, especially area V2, remain intact.

B.K.'s symptoms show that other occipital areas are functional, because he perceives color and motion even without form perception in the scotoma. Thus, B.K. can accurately perceive the color or motion of objects that he cannot identify. Those who are myopic (nearsighted) experience a similar phenomenon: the colors of objects or lights can be perceived, but the form is unrecognizable. B.K.'s stroke thus confirms the presence of at least four independent visual functions: form (which is absent), as well as color, movement, and location (which are spared).

The loss of one-quarter of the fovea leads B.K. to make a variety of visual errors. Immediately after the stroke, he was able to read only with great difficulty. When we look at a word, the fixation point is at the center of the word, so for B.K., half of the word is absent. Indeed, he had difficulty finding the edge of the page because it was in the blind field. Normal reading returned as B.K. learned to direct his gaze slightly to the left and upward (probably about 2° in each direction), which allowed words to fall into the normal area of the visual field.

This "recovery" took about 6 weeks. Returning to playing squash and tennis was equally challenging, because when a ball entered the scotoma, it was lost to B.K. Similarly, facial recognition was slower than it had been before the stroke because the information in the left visual field appears to be particularly important for recognizing faces.

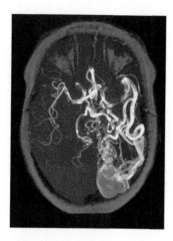

Figure 13.13 ▲

Angioma This MRI looks down on the brain surface of an 18-year-old woman with an angioma. The abnormal cerebral blood vessels (in white) form a balloonlike structure (the blue area at lower right) that caused an infarct around it in the right occipital cortex. (Simon Fraser/Royal Victoria Infirmary, Newcastle upon Tyne/Science Source.)

Case D.B.: V1 Damage and Blindsight

Among the most extensively studied people with visual disturbance from an occipital lesion (see Lawrence Weiskrantz's detailed monograph, 1986) is D.B., whose right calcarine fissure was removed surgically to excise an **angioma**, a collection of abnormal blood vessels that results in abnormal blood flow, imaged for a similar case in **Figure 13.13**. D.B. therefore has a hemianopia based on standard perimetry but nevertheless has surprising visual capacities.

When questioned about his vision in the left field, D.B. usually reports that he sees nothing, as did P.M. and B.K. Occasionally, D.B. indicates that he had a "feeling" that a stimulus was approaching or was "smooth" or "jagged." But according to Weiskrantz, D.B. always stresses that he saw nothing, that typically he is guessing, and that he is at a loss for words to describe any conscious perception.

In contrast, when D.B. was asked to point to locations in the impaired field in which spots of light were turned on briefly, he was surprisingly accurate. His blindsight contrasts with his subjective impression that he saw nothing at all. Furthermore, he appears able to discriminate the orientation of lines that he could not report "seeing." Thus, he can discriminate a 10° difference in orientation (the width of your fist held at arm's length) between two successively presented gratings in his impaired field.

Finally, D.B. can detect some forms of movement. When a vigorously moving stimulus was used, he reported "seeing" something. In this instance, he did not report actually seeing a visual stimulus but rather spoke of complex patterns of lines and grids. These patterns may have been something like B.K.'s moving lines. In summary, D.B. has *cortical blindness*, or blindsight, in which he reports no conscious awareness of "seeing" but still is able to report on the movement and location of objects that he cannot recognize.

Case G.Y. and Related Cases: V1 Damage and Conscious Vision

Weiskrantz's study of D.B. led to intense interest among philosophers and visual neuroscientists, especially related to unconscious vision (see review by Cowey, 2010). This interest led to descriptions of many similar cases, especially G.Y. (Zeki and Ffytche, 1998). Like D.B., G.Y. experienced blindsight, but if a moving stimulus passes through the blind field, G.Y. (and others) are aware that something has happened in the blind field.

Studies of G.Y. using fMRI reveal that when he is aware of a moving stimulus projected to his blind field, activity occurs in V5 and the prefrontal cortex in the hemisphere ipsilateral to the V1 lesion (e.g., Persaud et al., 2011; Ffytche & Zeki, 2011). This suggests that the blind field experience in blindsight reflects severely degraded vision. Perhaps V1 is not necessary for rudimentary visual awareness. The prefrontal activity is presumably related to the brain's attempt to understand the experience, as discussed in Section 13.3.

Case J.I.: V4 Damage and Loss of Color Vision

Oliver Sacks and Robert Wasserman (1987) report the touching story of J.I., an artist who suddenly became color-blind. In 1986, J.I. sustained a concussion in a car accident. His principal symptoms after the injury were an inability to distinguish any colors whatsoever, but his visual acuity had actually improved.

"Within days . . . my vision was that of an eagle—I can see a worm wiggling a block away. The sharpness of focus is incredible."

The effect of losing his color vision, however, was far greater than one might have expected. J.I. could barely stand the pain of living in a world that appeared in shades of gray. He found the changed appearance of people unbearable, because their flesh was an abhorrent gray ("rat colored") to him. He found foods disgusting in their grayish, dead appearance, and he had to close his eyes to eat. He could not even imagine colors any longer. The mental image of a tomato looked as black as its actual appearance was to him. Even his dreams, which had once been vividly colored, were now black and gray.

Detailed visual testing by Sacks and Wasserman, and later by Zeki (1993), revealed that J.I. was color-blind by the usual definitions, but this color blindness was attributed to specific damage to the occipital cortex. His acuity did appear to have improved, however, especially at twilight and at night. Two years after his injury, J.I.'s despair had declined, and he appeared no longer to be able to remember color well.

This failure to remember color is curious, because people who become blind through injury to the eyes or optic nerves do not lose their imagery or memory of color. There is little doubt from J.I.'s case that imagery and memory rely on the operation of at least some cortical structures necessary for the original perception.

Case P.B.: Conscious Color Perception in a Blind Patient

Zeki and his colleagues (1999) describe a man who was electrocuted, resulting in cardiac and respiratory arrest. P.B. was resuscitated but had brain ischemia that produced a large area of posterior cortical damage. He was left virtually blind, although he can detect the presence or absence of light. The interesting visual feature is that P.B.'s capacity to identify and name colors remains intact, as does his ability to name the typical color of imagined objects. Color perception clearly does not require object perception.

P.B.'s vision is in many ways opposite that of J.I.; the results of fMRI studies show that P.B. has activation in areas V1 and V2 in response to colored stimuli. As we reflect on his visual capacity, it is hard to imagine a world that is filled with color but no form, almost like an out-of-focus kaleidoscope that changes as we gaze around the world.

Case L.M.: V5 (MT) Damage and the Perception of Movement

Josef Zihl and his colleagues (1983) report the case of a 43-year-old woman whose bilateral posterior injury resulted from a vascular abnormality. Her primary chronic complaint was a loss of movement vision. She had difficulty pouring tea into a cup, for example, because the fluid appeared to be frozen. And she could not stop pouring, because she could not see the fluid level in the cup rise.

L.M. found being in a room with other people disturbing because she could not see them moving: they suddenly appeared "here or there," but she did not see them move in between. The results of other tests of visual function appeared essentially standard. She could discriminate colors, recognize objects, and read and write.

Her condition is especially intriguing because we would not believe intuitively that such a syndrome is likely. The loss of color or form vision fits with our everyday experience that people can be color-blind or myopic; loss of the ability to see objects moving is counterintuitive indeed. Case L.M. is important because she shows that the brain must analyze the movement of form separately from the form itself.

More recently, Thomas Schenk and his colleagues (2005) also studied L.M. and showed that she not only is unable to perceive movement but also is unable to intercept moving objects by using her hand. Schenk's group mimicked the findings in L.M. by delivering transcranial magnetic stimulation (TMS) to V5. TMS interfered not only with motion perception but also with interception. The inescapable conclusion is that V5 must play a role in both visual streams, much like V1, but it is a role in motion processing.

Case D.F.: Occipital Damage and Visual Agnosia

Visual agnosia is the term coined by Sigmund Freud for an inability to combine individual visual impressions into complete patterns—thus, the inability to recognize objects or their pictorial representations or the inability to draw or copy them. Goodale and Milner and their colleagues (1991) have extensively studied a visual agnosic who suffered carbon monoxide poisoning at age 35, resulting in bilateral damage to the LO region (see Figure 13.7) and unilaterally in the tissue at the junction of the left parietal and occipital cortex.

D.F., whom we met in Section 13.2 in considering Milner and Goodale's distinction between the dorsal and the ventral streams, has essentially normal color vision and can see well enough to get about in the world. Her principal deficit is *visual form agnosia*, a severe inability to recognize line drawings of objects. Thus, although D.F. can recognize many actual objects, she is unable to recognize drawings of them. Furthermore, as illustrated in **Figure 13.14**, although she can draw objects from memory, she has difficulty in drawing objects from life and even more difficulty copying line drawings. D.F. appears to have a serious defect in form perception.

Recall that the remarkable thing about D.F. is her nearly intact ability to guide hand and finger movements toward objects that she cannot recognize. For example, although D.F. had a gross deficit in judging lines as horizontal or vertical, she could reach out and "post" a handheld card into a slot rotated to different orientations, as illustrated in **Figure 13.15**. Indeed, analysis of videos of D.F.'s reaching reveal that, like

Figure 13.14 ▼

Samples of D.F.'s Drawings D.F.'s drawings from memory (A) are superior to her copies (B) of the model line drawings (C). (Servos, P., M. A. Goodale, and G. K. Humphrey. The drawing of objects by a visual form agnostic: Contribution of surface properties and memorial representations. *Neuropsychologia* 31: 251–259, 1993. Figure 2.)

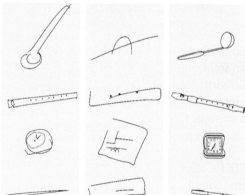

(A) Drawn from memory   **(B) Drawn from the models**   **(C) Line-drawing models**

Figure 13.15 ►

Testing Visuomotor Guidance (A) Apparatus used to test sensitivity to orientation in patient D.F. The task is to "post" the card into the slot as shown. (B) Plots of the card's orientation in a perceptual matching task and in the visuomotor posting task. For illustration, the correct orientation has been rotated to vertical. D.F. was unable to match the orientation of the card to that of the slot unless she made a movement to post it. (Gazzaniga, Michael, ed., *The New Cognitive Neurosciences, second edition*, Figure 26.4, p. 371, © 1999 Massachusetts Institute of Technology, by permission of The MIT Press.)

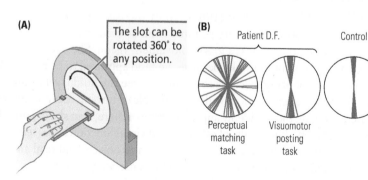

control participants, she began to orient the card correctly even as her hand was being raised from the start position. In other words, D.F. could use visual form information to guide movements to objects (the dorsal stream), but she could not use visual information to recognize those same objects (the ventral stream).

Case V.K.: Parietal Damage and Visuomotor Guidance

Damage to the posterior parietal lobe produces **optic ataxia**, a deficit in visually guided hand movements, such as reaching, that cannot be ascribed to motor, somatosensory, or visual field or acuity deficits. V.K. is a woman with bilateral hemorrhages in the occipitoparietal regions, as described by Lorna Jakobson and her colleagues (1991). Although V.K. initially appeared virtually blind, her symptoms dissipated in a month, and she was left with disordered control of her gaze, impaired visual attention, and optic ataxia. (Collectively, these symptoms are known as *Balint's syndrome*, discussed in Section 14.4.)

V.K. had good form and color vision and could recognize and name objects; however, her ability to reach for objects was grossly impaired. Thus, in contrast to D.F., who was able to reach and orient her hand posture toward different objects that she could not perceive, V.K. was unable to coordinate reaching and grasping for objects that she could perceive.

This difficulty was not merely being unable to direct movements in space, because V. K. could point to objects. What she could not do was to form the appropriate hand postures needed to grasp objects of different shapes, as illustrated in **Figure 13.16**. Taken together, cases D.F. and V.K. suggest that the mechanisms underlying conscious perception of object form are dissociable from the mechanisms controlling visually guided movements to the same objects.

Cases D. and T.: Higher-Level Visual Processes

Two cases described by Ruth Campbell and her colleagues (1986) illustrate an intriguing dissociation of visual functions. D. has a right occipitotemporal lesion associated with a left upper quadrantanopia that extends into the lower quadrant. As would be expected from B.K.'s case, D. had some initial difficulties in reading, but her language abilities were intact. Curiously, she was completely unable to recognize people by their faces and had difficulty identifying handwriting, including her own.

Recall from the opening Portrait that P.M. also had difficulty recognizing faces. His view on the difficulty was that, although he could see the different bits of the face quite clearly, he had trouble putting them all together because, unless a person was a long way off, the entire face did not appear in his visual field all at once.

Figure 13.16 ▼

Grasp Patterns

Representative "grasping axes" for three shapes illustrate the brain's different visual systems for object recognition and movement guidance. At left, patient D.F. with visual form agnosia (ventral-stream deficit); at center, control participant S.H. with no brain damage; and at right, V.K., a patient with bilateral occipitoparietal damage resulting in optic ataxia (dorsal-stream deficit). D.F. does not recognize the object but perceives enough information about shape to control her grasp as she picks it up. In contrast, V.K. recognizes objects but cannot control her movements in relation to them. (Information from Milner and Goodale, 2006.)

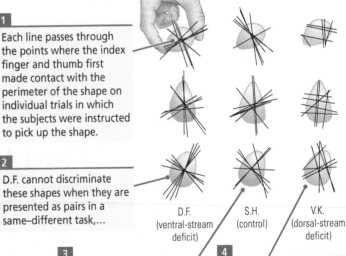

1 — Each line passes through the points where the index finger and thumb first made contact with the perimeter of the shape on individual trials in which the subjects were instructed to pick up the shape.

2 — D.F. cannot discriminate these shapes when they are presented as pairs in a same–different task,...

D.F. (ventral-stream deficit) S.H. (control) V.K. (dorsal-stream deficit)

3 — ...but she and S.H. both place finger and thumb on appropriately opposed points on either side of the shapes.

4 — V.K., whose object recognition is unimpaired, chooses unstable grasp points that often do not pass through the center of mass of the object.

You can imagine what it would be like to try to recognize people by looking at snapshots of different parts of their faces.

The facial-recognition deficit, **prosopagnosia**, is particularly interesting because many prosopagnosics cannot recognize even their own face in a mirror. Although D. could not recognize faces, she could make use of information in faces. For example, when given various tests of lip reading, her scores were completely normal. Furthermore, she could imitate the facial movements and expressions of another person.

In contrast to case D.'s right-side injury, case T. had a left occipitotemporal lesion with a right hemianopia. She had great difficulty reading (**alexia**) and was unable to name colors, even though she could discriminate them. In contrast to D., T. had no difficulty recognizing familiar faces but was impaired in lip reading.

Taken together, cases D. and T. indicate that identifying faces and extracting speech information from faces call on different cortical systems. In addition, the fact that D. has a lesion on the right and a deficit in face identification and that T. has a lesion on the left and a deficit in lip reading suggests an asymmetry in some aspects of occipital-lobe functions. Exactly what visual processes are impaired in the two cases and what the necessary lesions for deficits in facial recognition and lip reading might be remain to be shown.

Conclusions from the Case Studies

The behavior and pathology of the foregoing cases lead to several conclusions:

- Clearly distinct syndromes of visual disturbance exist.

- Some symptoms evince a fundamental dissociation between vision for guiding movements (the dorsal stream) and visual recognition (the ventral stream).

- The dissociability of the symptoms in the various patients implies that our introspective view of a unified visual experience is false. The fact that objects can be seen when they are still but not when they are moving is particularly disturbing: it seems to defy the commonsense view that an object is the same whether it is moving or still. Clearly, the brain does not treat objects in the same way in the two conditions.

◎ 13.5 Visual Agnosia

One difficulty in describing the symptomatology and pathology of agnosia is the bewildering variety of patients and symptoms described in the neurological literature. Another, as Martha Farah (1990) has pointed out, is that lack of agreement on a taxonomy of agnosia makes classifying different patterns of symptoms very difficult. Here we separate visual agnosias into object agnosias and other agnosias.

Object Agnosias

The traditional classification of visual object agnosias distinguishes two broad forms: *apperceptive agnosia* and *associative agnosia*.

Apperceptive Agnosia

Any failure of object recognition in which basic visual functions (acuity, color, motion) are preserved is **apperceptive agnosia**. This category has been applied to an extremely heterogeneous set of patients, but the fundamental deficit is an inability to develop a percept of the structure of an object or objects. In the simplest case, patients are unable to recognize, copy, or match simple shapes, much as in D.F.'s case.

Many patients have another unusual symptom, too, often referred to as **simultagnosia**: patients can perceive the basic shape of an object, but they are unable to perceive more than one object at a time. Thus, if two objects are presented together, only one is perceived. Such patients often act as though they were blind, possibly because they are simply overwhelmed by the task at hand. Imagine trying to see the world one object at a time.

Apperceptive agnosia does not result from a restricted lesion but usually follows gross bilateral damage to the lateral parts of the occipital lobes, including regions sending outputs to the ventral stream. Such injuries are probably most commonly associated with carbon monoxide poisoning, which appears to produce neuronal death in "watershed" regions—that is, regions lying in the border areas between territories of different arterial systems in the brain (diagrammed in Figure 3.5).

Associative Agnosia

The inability to recognize an object despite its apparent perception is **associative agnosia**. Thus, the associative agnosic can copy a drawing rather accurately, indicating a coherent percept, but cannot identify it. Associative agnosia is therefore conceived as being at a "higher" cognitive level of processing that is associated with stored information about objects—that is, with memory.

In effect, failure of object recognition is a memory defect that affects not only past knowledge about the object but also the acquisition of new knowledge. Associative agnosias are more likely with damage to regions in the ventral stream that are farther up the processing hierarchy, such as the anterior temporal lobe.

Other Visual Agnosias

A critical point in understanding the nature of visual agnosia is that the most commonly affected region is the tissue at the occipitotemporal border, which is part of the ventral visual pathway. Visual agnosias do not appear to result from damage to the dorsal stream. Note, however, that agnosias are at least partly dissociable, which means that different streams of visual information processing, such as the STS stream, must flow within the ventral pathway. We now briefly consider three other visual agnosias.

Prosopagnosia

Patients with facial agnosia (recall D. and P.M. in Section 13.4) cannot recognize any previously known faces, including their own as seen in a mirror or photograph. They can recognize people by face information, however, such as a birthmark, mustache, or characteristic hairdo.

Prosopagnosics may not accept the fact that they cannot recognize their own faces, probably because they know who must be in the mirror and thus see themselves. We saw one young woman who was convinced of the severity of her problem only when she was presented with her identical twin sister. When asked who her twin was, she indicated that she had never seen the woman before. Imagine her amazement to discover that the person was her twin.

According to Antonio Damasio and his colleagues (1982), most facial agnosics can tell human from nonhuman faces and can recognize facial expressions. All postmortem studies on facial agnosics have found bilateral damage, and the results of imaging studies in living patients confirm the bilateral nature of the injury in most patients, with the damage centered in the region below the calcarine fissure at the temporal junction. These results imply that facial recognition is probably a bilateral process, but asymmetrical.

Alexia

An inability to read has often been regarded as a symptom complementary to facial-recognition deficits. Alexia is most likely to result from damage to the left fusiform and lingual areas (see Figure 13.1). Either hemisphere can read letters, but only the left hemisphere appears able to combine the letters to form words. Alexia can be conceived as a form of object agnosia, in which there is a perceptual inability to construct wholes from parts, or as a form of associative agnosia in which word memory (the lexical store) is either damaged or inaccessible.

Visuospatial Agnosia

Among this variety of disorders of spatial perception and orientation, one disruptive form is **topographic disorientation**—the inability to find one's way around familiar environments such as one's neighborhood. People with this deficit seem unable to recognize landmarks that would indicate the appropriate direction to travel (see Section 21.1). Most people with topographic disorientation have other visual deficits, especially defects in facial recognition. Thus, it is not surprising to find that the critical area for this disorder lies in the right medial occipitotemporal region, including the fusiform and lingual gyri. Topographic disorientation can be a symptom of such dementias as Alzheimer's disease, discussed in Section 27.8.

13.6 Visual Imagery

Our ability to conjure up mental images of creatures, places, or things that cannot be perceived is central to human thought. Visualization is crucial in problem-solving tasks such as mental arithmetic, map reading, and mechanical reasoning. How crucial can be seen in a patient such as D.F., who was unable to copy drawings or recognize actual objects but who could nonetheless produce drawings of the same objects from memory (see Figure 13.14).

Marlene Behrmann and her colleagues (1992) described another such patient, C.K. The curious thing about C.K. is that although he cannot recognize objects, he can imagine them and draw them in considerable detail from memory. This ability implies some dissociation between the neural system for object perception and that for generating images. We can conclude that neural structures mediating perception and visualization are unlikely to be completely independent, but a deficit in object perception clearly cannot stem simply from a loss of mental representations—that is, memory—of objects.

In the past two decades, cognitive neuroscientists have conducted a flurry of imaging studies designed to identify neural events underlying the generation of a mental image. The results of imaging studies such as the one described in the Snapshot lead to the conclusion that imagery results from a top-down activation of a subset of the brain's visual areas. In other words, at least some cortical areas are used both for perception and for visualization.

SNAPSHOT Generating Mental Images

Conscious manipulation of mental representations is central to many creative human abilities. What is the neural basis for such visual imagery? Alexander Schlegel and colleagues (2013) addressed this question using fMRI while participants either held (maintained) or manipulated a mental image of an abstract figure that had been shown to them. The figure was shown for 2 seconds, and after a 1-second delay the participants had 5 seconds to perform a specified operation in which they either maintained or manipulated the mental image.

The results, illustrated below, found 11 bilateral cortical and subcortical regions of interest (ROIs) showing differential activity levels in the manipulation and maintenance conditions. The cortical regions outside the occipital lobe and ventral stream included two regions of the parietal lobe, the posterior parietal cortex and precuneus lobule, and three

regions of the frontal lobe, the frontal eye fields (participants were moving their eyes with the mental manipulation), dorsolateral prefrontal cortex, and medial prefrontal cortex.

Both the parietal and prefrontal regions appear to be part of a network involved in working memory and attention. The investigators propose that these regions form a core network that mediates conscious operations on mental representations. The precuneus region is relatively larger in humans than in other mammals and is hypothesized to be a hub in several cortical networks related to conscious processing.

Schlegel, A., P. J. Kohler, S. V. Fogelson, P. Alexander, D. Konuthula, and P. U. Tse. Network structure and dynamics of the mental workspace. *Proceedings of the National Academy of Sciences U.S.A.* 110:16277–16282, 2013.

(A) Right hemisphere, lateral view

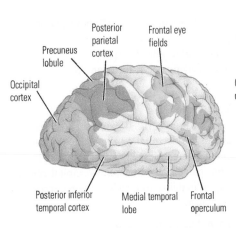

(B) Dorsal view

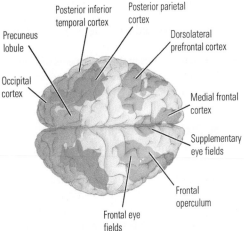

Connectivity in the Mental Workspace ROIs show cortical areas of differential activity as participants either manipulated or maintained mental images. (Research from Schlegel et al., 2013, Figure 2.)

But where is the top-down activity originating? Alumit Ishai (2010) has shown that imagery for faces or objects is modulated by bilateral prefrontal activity and left-hemisphere posterior parietal cortex activity. Curiously, the pattern of activity in prefrontal cortex varied with the image content (faces versus objects), whereas parietal cortex was not content-specific. The top-down prefrontal activity is likely related to the prefrontal activity observed in object perception (see Section 13.2).

Mental rotation of objects is a special category of imagery. Using fMRI, Wilson and Farah (2006) found that object recognition and mental rotation produce distinct patterns of brain activity, independent of stimulus rotation. Object recognition resulted in greater overall activity within right-hemisphere ventral stream visual areas, and mental rotation resulted in greater overall activity within right-hemisphere dorsal stream visual areas.

The dorsal stream involvement in mental rotation makes sense. We can imagine that before a brain can visualize rotating an object, it first has to have actually rotated it manually. It is a small step to presume that visualizing an object rotating requires the activation of at least part of the motor cortex—the regions needed to actually do it.

SUMMARY

Vision is the occipital lobe's function, but visual functions extend beyond the occipital lobe. We consider parietal, temporal, and frontal visual functions, respectively, in Chapters 14, 15, and 16.

13.1 Occipital Lobe Anatomy

Separate anatomical regions within the occipital lobe take part in perceiving form, movement, and color. Occipital structures merely initiate visual processing, because multiple visual systems can be divided into at least three major routes, one going ventrally into the temporal lobe, another going dorsally into the parietal lobe, and a middle route going to the superior temporal sulcus.

The ventral stream participates in various aspects of stimulus recognition. The dorsal stream is for guiding movement in space. The middle STS stream is a part of the ventral stream, which processes biological motion.

13.2 A Theory of Occipital-Lobe Function

Representation of spatial information relies on recognizing cues within the environment. That makes visuospatial recognition dependent on processing in the ventral stream. An important aspect of the dorsal–ventral distinction in visual processing is that neither route is a single system. Rather, clearly dissociable subsystems take part in various functions. Finally, some occipital regions, especially those adjoining the temporal cortex, may be functionally asymmetrical. In particular, there appears to be some specialization for word recognition on the left and for facial recognition and mental rotation on the right.

13.3 Disorders of Visual Pathways

Visual dysfunction can result from injury anywhere in the pathways from the retina to the cortex. Damage to the retina or the axons of the retinal ganglion cells forming the optic nerve produce deficits specific to one eye. Once the optic nerves enter the brain and the information from the two eyes merges, disorders of vision affect information from both eyes and are related to a visual field rather than to an eye.

13.4 Disorders of Cortical Function

Damage to the occipital cortex can produce deficits ranging from blindness in all or part of a visual field to specific deficits in perceiving color, form, and movement.

13.5 Visual Agnosia

Visual agnosia is a loss of knowledge about visual information. Although visual agnosias may result from damage to either the occipital or the temporal lobe, they have different characteristics. The most common form of visual agnosia from damage to the lateral occipital region is object agnosia, an inability to develop a percept about the structure of an object.

13.6 Visual Imagery

Humans are capable of conjuring up mental images—of visualizing what is not physically present. There is a partial dissociation between structures taking part in imagining versus perceiving visual information. Mental rotation is a special case that also involves the dorsal stream.

References

Andrews, T. J., D. Schluppeck, D. Homfray, P. Matthews, and C. Blakemore. Activity in the fusiform gyrus predicts conscious perception of Rubin's vase–face illusion. *NeuroImage* 17:890–901, 2002.

Barbur, J. L., J. D. G. Watson, R. S. J. Frackowiak, and S. Zeki. Conscious visual perception without V1. *Brain* 116:1293–1302, 1993.

Behrmann, M., G. Winocur, and M. Moscovitch. Dissociation between mental imagery and object recognition in a brain-damaged patient. *Nature* 359:636–637, 1992.

Campbell, R., T. Landis, and M. Regard. Face recognition and lip reading: A neurological dissociation. *Brain* 109:509–521, 1986.

Cowey, A. The blindsight saga. *Experimental Brain Research* 200:3–24, 2010.

Curtis, B. Visual system. In B. A. Curtis, S. Jacobson, and E. M. Marcus, Eds., *An Introduction to the Neurosciences*. Philadelphia and Toronto: Saunders, 1972.

Damasio, A. R., H. Damasio, and G. W. Van Hoesen. Prosopagnosia: Anatomical basis and behavioral mechanisms. *Neurology* 32:331–341, 1982.

Farah, M. J. *Visual Agnosia*. Cambridge, Mass.: MIT Press, 1990.

Farah, M. J. The neural basis of mental imagery. In M. S. Gazzaniga, Ed., *The New Cognitive Neurosciences*, 2nd ed. Cambridge, Mass.: MIT Press, 2000, pp. 965–974.

Ffytche, D. H., and S. Zeki. The primary visual cortex, and feedback to it, are not necessary for conscious vision. *Brain* 134:247–257, 2011.

Goodale, M. A. Visual pathways supporting perception and action in the primate cerebral cortex. *Current Opinion in Neurobiology* 3:578–585, 1993.

Goodale, M. A. Perception and action in the human visual system. In M. Gazzaniga, Ed., *The New Cognitive Neurosciences*. Cambridge, Mass.: MIT Press, 2000.

Goodale, M. A., D. A. Milner, L. S. Jakobson, and J. D. P. Carey. A neurological dissociation between perceiving objects and grasping them. *Nature* 349:154–156, 1991.

Haxby, J. V., L. G. Ungerleider, V. P. Clark, J. L. Schouten, E. A. Hoffman, and A. Martin. The effect of face inversion on activity in human neural systems for face and object perception. *Neuron* 22:189–199, 1999.

Ishai, A. Seeing faces and objects with the "mind's eye." *Archives Italiennes de Biologie* 148:1–9, 2010.

Jakobson, L. S., Y. M. Archibald, D. P. Carey, and M. A. Goodale. A kinematic analysis of reaching and grasping movements in a patient recovering from optic ataxia. *Neuropsychologia* 29:803–809, 1991.

Kravitz, D. J., K. S. Saleem, C. I. Baker, L. G. Ungerleider, and M. Mishkin. The ventral visual pathway: An expanded neural framework for the processing of object quality. *Trends in Cognitive Sciences* 17:26–49, 2013.

Kveraga, K., A. S. Ghuman, and M. Bar. Top-down predictions in the cognitive brain. *Brain and Cognition* 65:145–168, 2007.

Milner, A. D., and M. A. Goodale. *The Visual Brain in Action*, 2nd ed. Oxford: Oxford University Press, 2006.

Panichello, M. F., O. S. Cheung, and M. Bar. Predictive feedback and conscious visual experience. *Frontiers in Psychology*, doi: 10.3389, 2012.

Persaud, N., M. Davidson, B. Maniscalco, D. Mobbs, R. E. Passingham, A. Cowey, and H. Lau. Awareness-related activity in prefrontal and parietal cortices in blindsight reflects more than superior visual performance. *NeuroImage* 58:605–611, 2011.

Rizzolatti, G., and M. Matelli. Two different streams form the dorsal visual system: Anatomy and function. *Experimental Brain Research* 153:146–157, 2003.

Sacks, O., and R. Wasserman. The case of the colorblind painter. *New York Review of Books* 34:25–33, 1987.

Schenk, T., A. Ellison, N. J. Rice, and A. D. Milner. The role of V5/MT+ in the control of catching movements: An rTMS study. *Neuropsychologia* 43:189–198, 2005.

Servos, P., M. A. Goodale, and G. K. Humphrey. The drawing of objects by a visual form agnosic: Contribution of surface properties and memorial representations. *Neuropsychologia* 31: 251–259, 1993.

Sumner, P., and J. D. Mollon. Catarrhine photopigments are optimized for detecting targets against a foliage background. *Journal of Experimental Biology* 203:1963–1986, 2000.

Tanaka, J., D. Weiskopf, and P. Williams. The role of color in high-level vision. *Trends in Cognitive Sciences* 5:211–215, 2001.

Tootell, R. B. H., D. Tsao, and W. Vanduffel. Neuroimaging weighs in: Humans meet macaques in "primate" visual cortex. *Journal of Neuroscience* 23:3981–3989, 2003.

Ungerleider, L. G., and J. V. Haxby. "What" and "where" in the human brain. *Current Opinion in Neurobiology* 4:15–165, 1994.

Weiskrantz, L. *Blindsight: A Case History and Implications*. Oxford: Oxford University Press, 1986.

Wilson, K. D., and M. J. Farah. Distinct patterns of viewpoint-dependent BOLD activity during common-object recognition and mental rotation. *Perception* 35:1351–1366, 2006.

Zeki, S. *A Vision of the Brain*. Oxford: Blackwell, 1993.

Zeki, S., S. Aglioti, D. McKeefry, and G. Berlucchi. The neurological basis of conscious color perception in a blind patient. *Proceedings of the National Academy of Sciences U.S.A.* 96:14124–14129, 1999.

Zeki, S., and D. H. Ffytche. The Riddoch syndrome: Insights into the neurobiology of conscious vision. *Brain* 121:25–45, 1998.

Zihl, J., D. von Cramon, and N. Mai. Selective disturbance of movement vision after bilateral brain damage. *Brain* 106:313–340, 1983.

14

The Parietal Lobes

PORTRAIT Varieties of Spatial Information

When H.P., a 28-year-old accountant, was planning his wedding with his fiancée, she noticed that he was making addition errors as he calculated the budget for their reception. At first they joked about it, especially given his occupation, but during the following weeks H.P.'s problem with numbers grew serious. In fact, he was no longer able to perform simple subtraction, such as 30 minus 19, in which the solution requires "borrowing" 10 when subtracting 9 from 0.

H.P. simply put it down to working too hard, but soon he began to have trouble reaching for objects. He was constantly knocking over his water glass because his reach was clumsy and misdirected. Simple manipulations, such as playing with the Rubik's Cube puzzle pictured here, would have become difficult if not impossible for H.P. He began confusing left and right, and reading became difficult. Some words appeared backward or upside down to him: he could not make sense of them.

Finally, H.P. visited a neurologist for testing. It was obvious that something was seriously wrong. That something was a fast-growing tumor in his left parietal lobe. Unfortunately, the tumor was extremely virulent, and within a couple of months, H.P. had died.

The parietal cortex processes and integrates somatosensory and visual information, especially with regard to controlling movement. In this chapter, we first describe parietal-lobe anatomy and then present a theoretical model of parietal-lobe organization. Next we consider the major somatosensory symptoms of parietal injury, survey the most commonly observed disorders of the posterior parietal region, and conclude with a survey of behavioral tests that reliably predict brain injury.

14.1 Parietal Lobe Anatomy

H.P.'s symptoms, described in the opening Portrait, are typical of left parietal injury and illustrative of a curious pattern of symptoms that have challenged neuropsychologists. These symptoms are difficult to model in animals because common laboratory animals such as rats and cats have very modest parietal "lobes." Monkeys with parietal damage show many symptoms similar to those seen in human patients, but symptoms related to language or cognition are difficult to study in monkeys. The fact that humans' parietal lobes have evolved to a much larger size than those of monkeys implies that humans may show some symptoms not seen in monkeys.

Subdivisions of the Parietal Cortex

The parietal region of the cerebral cortex lies between the frontal and occipital lobes, underlying the parietal bone at the roof of the skull. As mapped in **Figure 14.1**A, this area is roughly demarcated anteriorly by the central fissure, ventrally by the lateral (Sylvian) fissure, dorsally by the cingulate gyrus, and posteriorly by the parieto-occipital sulcus. The principal regions of the parietal lobe, mapped in Figure 14.1A and B, include the postcentral gyrus (Brodmann's areas 3-1-2), superior parietal lobule (areas 5 and 7), parietal operculum (area 43), supramarginal gyrus (area 40), and angular gyrus (area 39).

Together, the supramarginal gyrus and angular gyrus are often referred to as the *inferior parietal lobe*. The parietal lobe can be divided into two functional zones: an anterior zone including areas 3-1-2 and 43 and a posterior zone that includes the remaining areas. The anterior zone is the somatosensory cortex; the posterior zone is called the **posterior parietal cortex**.

Over the course of human evolution, the parietal lobes have undergone a major expansion, largely in the inferior region. This size increase makes comparisons of various areas in the human brain with those in the monkey brain confusing, especially because while Brodmann identified areas 39 and 40 in the human brain, he failed to identify them in the monkey. Whether monkeys actually have regions homologous to these areas is debatable. One solution is to consult another anatomist, Constantin von Economo (introduced in Section 10.4).

On von Economo's maps, in which parietal areas are called PA (parietal area A), PB, and so forth, are three posterior parietal areas (PE, PF, PG) that von Economo described in both humans and monkeys (Figure 14.1C). If we use this system, area PF is equivalent to Brodmann's areas 43 and 40 plus part of area 7 and PE to area 5 and the remainder of area 7 (see Figure 14.1B). Similarly, area PG is roughly equivalent to Brodmann's areas 39 and 40. These PG areas are primarily visual and include areas AIP, LIP, cIPS, and PRR (see Table 13.1 and Section 15.1).

An area significantly expanded in the human brain appears to consist of the polymodal parts of area PG and adjoining polymodal cortex in the superior temporal sulcus (STS). Polymodal cells receive inputs from more than one sensory modality. Those in PG respond to both somatosensory and visual inputs, whereas those in the STS (the third visual pathway discussed in Chapter 13) respond to various combinations of auditory, visual, and somatosensory inputs.

The increased size of area PG and the STS is especially interesting, because this region is anatomically asymmetrical in the human brain (see Figure 11.1). The asymmetry may be due to a much larger area PG (and possibly STS) on the right than on the left. If PG has a visual function and is larger in humans, especially in the right hemisphere, then we might expect unique visual symptoms after right parietal lesions. This indeed is the case. Note, however, that PG is also larger on the left in the human than in the monkey. This leads us to expect unique deficits in humans after left-hemisphere lesions. This outcome, too, is the case.

Specific parietal regions take part in the dorsal stream of visual processing, in particular the intraparietal sulcus (cIPS) and the parietal reach regions (PRR) illustrated in the monkey and human in **Figure 14.2**. The monkey regions in Figure 14.2A were mapped by using single-neuron recording techniques, whereas the human regions in Figure 14.2B have been defined by fMRI.

(A) Major parietal lobe gyri and sulci

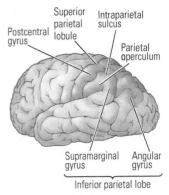

(B) Brodmann's cytoarchitectonic regions

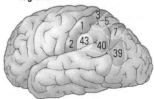

(C) von Economo's cytoarchitectonic regions

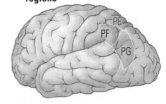

Figure 14.1 ▲

Gross Anatomy of the Parietal Lobe

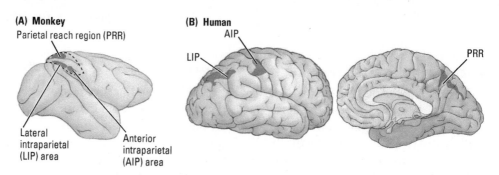

(A) Monkey
Parietal reach region (PRR)

Lateral intraparietal (LIP) area

Anterior intraparietal (AIP) area

(B) Human
AIP

LIP

PRR

Figure 14.2 ▲

Parietal Areas of the Dorsal Stream Homologous regions in the monkey (A) and human (B) that contribute to saccadic eye movement (area LIP), visual control of grasping (area AIP), and visually guided grasping (area PRR). (Part A: Research from Cohen and Andersen, 2002. Part B: Research from Milner and Goodale, 2006.)

The regions in the intraparietal sulcus contribute to controlling saccadic eye movements (area LIP) and visual control of object-directed grasping (AIP). The PRR has a role in visually guided grasping movements. (A **saccade** is a series of involuntary, abrupt, and rapid small movements or jerks made by both eyes simultaneously in changing the point of fixation.)

Connections of the Parietal Cortex

The anterior parietal cortex makes rather straightforward connections. Projections from the primary somatosensory cortex (area 3-1-2 in Figure 14.1B) extend to secondary somatosensory area PE (area 5), which has a tactile recognition function, as well as to motor areas including the primary motor cortex (area 4) and the supplementary motor and premotor regions (area 6) in the frontal lobes. The motor connections must be important for providing sensory information about limb position in movement control (see Section 9.1).

Although more than 100 inputs and outputs have been described for areas 5 and 7 in the monkey (PE, PF, and PG), a few basic principles summarize the connections diagrammed in **Figure 14.3**A and B:

1. Area PE (Brodmann's area 5 plus part of area 7) is basically somatosensory, receiving most of its connections from the primary somatosensory cortex (areas 3-1-2). PE's cortical outputs are to the primary motor cortex (area 4) and to the supplementary motor (SMA) and premotor (6 and 8) regions, as well as to PF. Area PE therefore plays some role in guiding movement by providing information about limb position.

◎ Figure 14.3 ▼

Connections of the Monkey's Parietal Lobe
(A) Major corticocortical projections of the parietal lobe. (B) Posterior parietal and dorsolateral prefrontal projections to cingulate, orbitofrontal, and temporal regions. (C) Subdivisions of the dorsal stream that form the parieto–premotor, parieto–prefrontal, and parieto–medial temporal pathways. (Part C Information modified with permission from Macmillan Publishers, Ltd. Kravitz & Mishkin, A new neural framework for visuospatial processing. *Nature Reviews Neuroscience* 12(4):217–230, March 18, 2011.)

(A) Lateral view

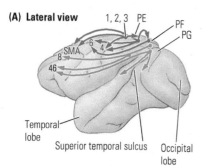

1, 2, 3 PE PF PG SMA 6 4 8 46

Temporal lobe

Superior temporal sulcus

Occipital lobe

(B) Medial view

Parietal lobe Superior temporal sulcus

Dorsolateral prefrontal Occipital lobe

Orbitofrontal cortex

Temporal lobe

Cingulate gyrus

(C) Dorsal visuospatial pathways

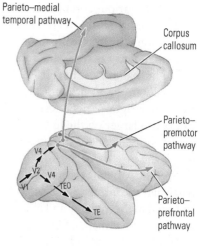

Parieto–medial temporal pathway

Corpus callosum

Parieto–premotor pathway

V4 V2 V4 TEO V1 TE

Parieto–prefrontal pathway

2. Area PF (part of area 7) has heavy input from the primary somatosensory cortex (areas 3-1-2) through area PE. PF also receives inputs from the motor and premotor cortex and a small visual input through area PG. PF's efferent connections are similar to those of area PE, and these connections presumably elaborate similar information for the motor systems.

3. Area PG (part of area 7 and visual areas) receives more-complex connections including visual, somesthetic (skin sensations), proprioceptive (internal stimuli), auditory, vestibular (balance), oculomotor (eye movement), and cingulate (motivational?). MacDonald Critchley (1953) first described area PG as the "parieto-temporo-occipital crossroads," which is apparent from the connectivity. Its function likely corresponds to this intermodal mixing. Area PG is part of the dorsal stream that controls spatially guided behavior with respect to visual and tactile information.

4. The close relation between the posterior parietal connections and the prefrontal cortex (especially area 46) are apparent in the connections between the posterior parietal cortex (PG and PF) and the dorsolateral prefrontal region. Additionally, the prefrontal and the posterior parietal regions project to the same areas of the paralimbic cortex and the temporal cortex as well as to the hippocampus and various subcortical regions. These connections emphasize a close functional relation between the prefrontal and parietal cortices. This relation probably has an important role in controlling spatially guided behavior.

Anatomy of the Dorsal Stream

As originally conceived by Ungerleider and Mishkin (1982), the dorsal stream from the occipital cortex to the posterior parietal regions was conceived of as a "where" pathway. Based upon their studies of patients D.F. and others, Milner and Goodale (1993) hypothesized the dorsal stream as a "how" pathway (see Section 13.2). Since then, our knowledge of the dorsal stream's organization and function has increased vastly, leading Dwight Kravitz and colleagues (2011) to a construct new framework for it.

Kravitz and his colleagues identify three functional pathways leaving the posterior parietal region and traveling to the premotor, prefrontal, and medial temporal regions (Figure 14.3C). The parieto–premotor pathway is proposed as the principal "how" pathway. The parieto–prefrontal pathway is proposed to have visuospatial functions, especially related to visuospatial working memory (see Section 16.1). The parieto–medial temporal pathway, which flows directly to the hippocampus and parahippocampal regions as well as indirectly via the posterior cingulate and retrosplenial cortex, is proposed to have a role in spatial navigation. Thus, the posterior parietal cortex would contribute to the dorsal stream by participating in nonconscious visuospatial behavior, that is, reaching for and grasping objects (illustrated in Figure 13.16).

Kravitz and coworkers emphasize these three pathways within the dorsal stream, but others may well be found. The researchers note connections with V5 and the superior temporal sulcus, regions involved in motion and form processing, as likely candidates. We must caution against seeing these pathways as entirely divergent. The goal of all dorsal stream pathways is to guide visuospatial behavior through motor output, so the parieto–prefrontal and parieto–mediotemporal pathways must eventually influence motor output, though more indirectly than does the parieto–premotor pathway.

14.2 A Theory of Parietal-Lobe Function

If we consider the anterior (somatosensory) and posterior (spatial) parietal zones functionally distinct, we can identify two independent parietal-lobe contributions. The anterior zone processes somatic sensations and perceptions. The posterior zone specializes primarily in integrating sensory input from the somatic and visual regions and to a lesser extent from other sensory regions, mostly for controlling movements—reaching and grasping as well as whole-body movements in space. Remember too, from Section 13.6, that the posterior parietal cortex also plays a significant role in mental imagery, especially related to both object rotation and navigation through space. We are concerned here mostly with posterior parietal zone functions; the anterior zone's somatosensory functions were discussed in Section 8.2.

Imagine having dinner with a friend in a restaurant. You are confronted with cutlery, dishes with food and some without, a basket of bread, a water glass and perhaps a glass of wine or cup of coffee, a napkin, and your companion. Seemingly without effort, you select various utensils and foods as you eat, drink, and chat with your friend.

To do all these things, your brain is faced with several complex tasks. For example, you must reach and correctly grasp a glass or cup, a fork, or a piece of bread. Each movement is directed toward a different place and requires a different hand posture or limb movement or both. You must direct your eyes and head toward various places in space, and you must coordinate your limb and head movements to get food and drink to your mouth.

Furthermore, you must attend to certain objects and ignore others. (You do not take your companion's fork or wine, for example.) You also must attend to the conversation with your friend and ignore other conversations around you. When you eat from your plate, you must choose which utensil you want to use. It would prove both difficult and inappropriate to try to eat your peas using a knife.

Finally, you must also make movements in the correct order. For example, you must cut your food before moving it to your mouth. Similarly, to butter a bit of bread you must pick up a knife, get some butter, spread the butter on the bread, and then eat the buttered bread.

As we think about how the brain manages these tasks, an internal representation of the location of different objects around us seems obvious—a sort of map in the brain of where things are. Furthermore, we assume that the map must be common to all of our senses, because we can move without apparent effort from visual to auditory to tactile information. More than seven decades of clinical observations of patients with parietal injury demonstrate that the parietal lobe plays a central role in creating this brain map. But what precisely *is* the map?

We take for granted that the world around us is as we perceive it and thus that the brain employs a unified spatial map. That is, real space must be mapped topographically in the brain because that is how it appears to us. (Recall the *binding problem* discussed in Section 10.2.)

Unfortunately, scant evidence supports the existence of such a map in the brain. More likely is a series of neural representations of space that vary in two ways. First, different representations serve different behavioral needs. Second, spatial representations vary, from simple ones applicable to controlling simple movements to abstract ones that may represent information such as topographic knowledge. Next we consider each aspect of brain maps in turn.

Behavioral Uses of Spatial Information

David Milner and Melvin Goodale (2006) emphasize that we need spatial information about the location of objects in the world, both to direct actions at those objects and to assign meaning and significance to them. In this sense, spatial information is simply another property of visual information, much like form, motion, and color. Just as form is coded in more than one way in visual processing, so too is spatial information. The critical factor for both form and space lies in how the information is to be used.

Recall the two basic types of form recognition, one for recognizing objects and the other for guiding movements to objects. We can think of spatial information in the same way.

Object Recognition

The spatial information needed to determine relations between objects, independent of what the individual's behavior might be, is very different from the spatial information needed to guide eye, head, or limb movements to objects. In the latter case, visuomotor control must be viewer-centered; that is, the object's location and its local orientation and motion must be determined relative to the viewer. Furthermore, because the eyes, head, limbs, and body are constantly moving, computations about orientation, motion, and location must take place every time we wish to undertake an action. Details of an object's characteristics, such as color, are irrelevant to visuomotor guidance of viewer-centered movements; that is, a detailed visual representation is not needed to guide hand action.

It appears that the brain operates on a "need-to-know" basis. Having too much information may be counterproductive for any given system. In contrast with the viewer-centered system, the object-centered system must be concerned with such properties as the object's size, shape, color, and relative location so that the objects are recognized when they are encountered in different visual contexts or from different vantage points. In this case, the details of the objects themselves (color, shape) are important. Knowing where the red cup is relative to the green one requires identifying each cup.

The temporal lobe codes objects' relational properties. Part of this coding probably occurs in the polymodal region of the superior temporal sulcus and another part in the hippocampal formation. We return to this role of the temporal cortex in Section 15.2.

Movement Guidance

To accommodate the many differing viewer-centered movements (eyes, head, limbs, body, separately and in combinations) requires separate control systems. Eye control is based on the optical axis of the eye, for example, whereas limb control is probably based on the positions of the shoulders and hips. These are vastly different types of movements.

We have considered many visual areas in the posterior parietal region and multiple projections from the posterior parietal regions to the frontal lobe motor structures for the eyes (frontal eye fields, area 8) and limbs (premotor and supplementary motor). Connections to the prefrontal region (area 46) have a role in short-term memory for the location of events in space (see Figure 14.3).

Results of single-cell studies in the posterior parietal lobes of monkeys confirm the posterior parietal's role in visuomotor guidance. The activity of these neurons depends on the concurrent behavior of an animal with respect to visual stimulation. In fact, most neurons in the posterior parietal region are active both during sensory input and during movement. For example, some cells show only weak responses to stationary visual stimuli, but if the animal makes an active eye or arm movement toward the stimulus or even if it just shifts its attention to the object, the discharge of these cells is strongly enhanced.

Some cells are active when a monkey manipulates an object: they respond to its structural features, such as size and orientation. That is, these neurons are sensitive to the features that determine the hand's posture during object manipulation. Other cells move the eye to allow the fine vision of the fovea to examine objects.

John Stein (1992) emphasized that the responses of posterior parietal neurons have two important characteristics in common. First, they receive combinations of sensory, motivational, and related motor inputs. Second, their discharge is enhanced when an animal attends to a target or moves toward it. These neurons are therefore well suited to transforming requisite sensory information into commands for directing attention and guiding motor output. We can predict, therefore, that posterior parietal lesions impair movement guidance (much as in H.P.'s case presented at the chapter's opening) and, perhaps, detection of sensory events.

Sensorimotor Transformation

When we move toward objects, we must integrate movements of various body parts (eyes, body, limbs) with sensory feedback of what movements are actually being made (the *efference copy*) and the plans to make the movements. As we move, the locations of our body parts change, and perceptions of our body must constantly be updated so that we can make future movements smoothly. These neural calculations are called **sensorimotor transformation**. Cells in the posterior parietal cortex produce both the movement-related and the sensory-related signals to make them.

What about the movement-planning aspect of sensorimotor transformation? Although less is known about the role of the parietal cortex in planning, Richard Andersen and his colleagues (Andersen, Burdick et al., 2004) showed that area PRR is active when a participant is preparing and executing a limb movement (see Figure 14.2). Importantly, PRR is coding not the limb variables required to make the movement but rather the desired goal of the movement. Thus, the goal of grasping a cup, for example, is coded rather than the details of the movements toward the cup.

Andersen's group (Andersen, Meeker et al., 2004) devised novel experiments with monkeys: they decoded from parietal neural activity the animals' intentions to reach to position a cursor on a screen. As illustrated in **Figure 14.4**A, monkeys first were trained to make a series of reaches to touch different locations on a computer screen. Their cell activity was analyzed to determine which activity was associated with movement to each location. The monkeys then were

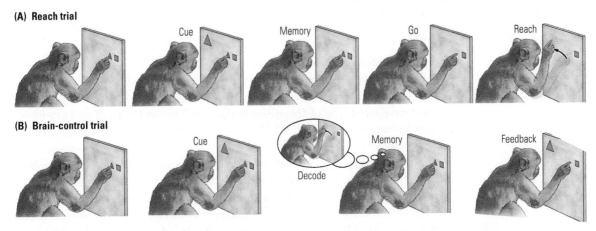

(A) Reach trial

Cue Memory Go Reach

(B) Brain-control trial

Cue Decode Memory Feedback

instructed with a briefly flashed cue to plan to execute a reach to another location but without making a movement.

Their cellular activity was compared with activity associated with actual movements to the requested target. If it was the same as in an actual movement, the monkeys were rewarded with a drop of juice in the mouth and visual feedback showing the correct location (Figure 14.4B). The authors had to use this approach because they could not simply say to the monkeys, "Think about reaching to the target." They had to devise a way for the monkeys to demonstrate that they were thinking about reaching to target.

This type of study is foundational to developing neuroprosthetic devices that enable paralyzed people and amputees to use mental activity to move prosthetics and even to feel what they touch (see Chapter 9 opening Portrait). For example, an array of electrodes can be implanted over the PRR and the recorded activity used to move the mechanical devices. The implications of such advances could go well beyond limb movements. Implants over speech areas might allow a verbal readout of thoughts, thus bypassing cumbersome letter boards and spelling programs. Similarly, one could ask patients questions and have them move a cursor mentally to identify the correct answers, thus gaining access to a wide variety of their thoughts and even emotions.

Miguel Nicolelis and his colleagues (2012) have pioneered neuroprosthetic applications over the past decade. They have designed brain–computer interfaces that allow typical monkeys, and more recently humans with arm paralysis, to move robotic arms to make fine, controlled movements (see Ifft et al., 2013). A key to their success has been technological developments enabling use of multiple recording channels that confer redundancy of control and hence reliability. This led to an ambitious demonstration project in which paraplegics are trained to control the movements of a software body avatar through thought alone. Participants learn to make increasingly complex movements with the goal of walking on a changing terrain or even kicking a ball, aided by an exoskeleton, as described in Chapter 9's opening Portrait.

Perhaps even more remarkably, Nicolelis and his colleagues (Pais-Vierira et al., 2013) have demonstrated that behaviorally meaningful information can be transferred between the brains of two rats. In these experiments an "encoder" rat performed a tactile discrimination task while samples of neural activity were recorded from the parietal cortex. This activity was transmitted through microstimulation electrodes in another rat that learned to make behavioral selections solely via the information provided the encoder rat's brain. Clearly, transforming sensorimotor activity into action using a brain-to-brain interface for real-time sharing is in its infancy and poised to grow.

Figure 14.4 ▲

Moving with the Mind
(A) Monkeys are trained to touch a small central green cue and to look at a red fixation point. A large green cue flashes, and the monkeys are rewarded if they reach to the target after a 1500-millisecond memory period. (B) Monkeys are rewarded if their brain activity indicates that they are preparing to move to the correct target location. (Research from Andersen, Burdick, et al., Cognitive neural prosthetics. *Trends in Cognitive Sciences* 8:486–493, 2004, Figure 1(a). Elsevier.)

Spatial Navigation

When we travel the world, we can take the correct route subconsciously, making the correct turns at choice points until we reach our destination. To do so, we must have some type of "cognitive spatial map" in our brains as well as a mental list of what we do at each spatial location. The internal list is sometimes referred to as *route knowledge.*

Route knowledge is unlikely to be located in a single place in the brain. Findings from both lesion and neuroimaging studies in humans suggest the participation of the medial parietal region (MPR), which includes the parietal region ventral to the PRR as well as the adjacent posterior cingulate cortex, part of the parieto–mediotemporal pathway in the dorsal stream (see Figure 14.3C). Neurons in the dorsal visual stream could be expected to participate in route knowledge, insofar as we must make specific visually guided movements at specific locations in our journey. To explore this idea, Nobuya Sato and colleagues (2006) trained monkeys to perform a navigation task in a virtual environment.

Three-quarters of the cells in the MPR showed responses associated with a specific movement at a specific location. The same movement in a different location did not activate the cells. Thus, like the cells in PRR, which control the planning of limb movements to locations, the cells in MPR control only body movements to specific locations. When the researchers inactivated the MPR pharmacologically, the monkeys became lost and failed to navigate correctly. Thus, the monkeys acted like human patients with medial parietal lesions who often become lost. We return to this condition in Section 21.1.

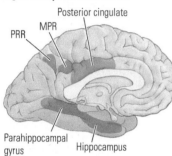

Right hemisphere medial view

Posterior cingulate

PRR MPR

Parahippocampal gyrus

Hippocampus

The Complexity of Spatial Information

The first aspect of our theory of parietal-lobe function considers the uses of spatial information for recognizing objects and guiding movement. The second aspect of spatial representation is complexity. Limb- or eye-movement control is concrete and relatively simple, but other types of viewer-centered representations are complex. For example, the concept of "left" and "right" is viewer-centered but need not require movement. Patients with posterior parietal lesions are impaired at distinguishing left from right, as was H.P, whom we met in the chapter's opening.

Other spatial relations are even more complex. For example, you can visualize objects and manipulate these mental images spatially, as described in the Snapshot. The ability to manipulate objects mentally is likely an extension of the ability to manipulate objects with the hands. Thus, mental manipulation is really just an elaboration of the neural control of actual manipulation, much as visual imagery, discussed in the Snapshot in Chapter 13, is a neural elaboration of actual visual input. Patients with posterior parietal lesions are impaired at mental manipulations.

Other Parietal-Lobe Functions

Three parietal-lobe symptoms do not fit obviously into the simple view of a visuomotor control center: difficulties with arithmetic, aspects of language, and movement sequences. Recall from the opening Portrait that H.P. encountered all three deficits.

In the 1970s, Alexander Luria proposed that mathematics and arithmetic have a quasi-spatial nature analogous to mentally manipulating concrete shapes but entailing the manipulation of abstract symbols, for example to calculate a

SNAPSHOT | Spatial Cognition and White-Matter Organization

The ability to imagine objects in different views is fundamental to spatial cognition. Everyday activities, such as constructional tasks—say, putting a bookshelf together—require an ability to manipulate pieces both mentally and physically. Studies of lesion patients and noninvasive imaging reveal that the posterior parietal cortex carries out mental transformations such as object rotation.

Humans' capacities to perform mental object transformations vary substantially, however, and a significant sex difference favors males in such tasks, at least under some testing conditions (see Section 12.2). Differences in cognitive strategy appear to be important in the sex difference, or the variation could result from differences in the ability to maintain an object's representation in memory as it is manipulated.

The variation could also be related to differences in the underlying neuroanatomy. Thomas Wolbers and his colleagues (2006) hypothesized that the anatomical difference could reside within white-matter organization and correspond to connectivity within the posterior parietal region.

To determine what role white-matter differences play in mental rotation, the researchers gave male participants the difficult mental rotation task illustrated in Figure A. As expected, they found considerable variability among participants, despite controlling for spatial short-term memory ability. They used MRI to characterize white-matter organization in participants' posterior parietal cortex. As shown in Figure B, they recorded a tight relation between mental spatial rotation proficiency and white-matter organization near the anterior part of the intraparietal sulcus.

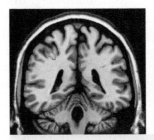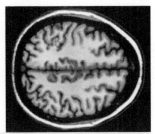

Figure B ▲

Brain Organization and Mental Rotation Scores The part of the intraparietal sulcus shaded yellow and outlined in red in these frontal and dorsal scans correlated strongly with mental rotation scores. (Wolbers, T., E. D. Schoell, and Büchel C. The predictive value of white matter organization in posterior parietal cortex for spatial visualization ability. *NeuroImage* 32:1450–1455, 2006 © Elsevier.)

This indirect anatomical measure of brain organization includes a variety of factors such as myelinization, axon diameter and density, and fiber crossing. Nonetheless, the results support the general idea that details of neuroanatomical organization are related to individual differences in cognitive abilities.

Whether such differences are purely genetic or are influenced by experience remains to be determined. Similarly, because the investigators studied only males, we do not yet know if sex differences in mental rotation are related to sex differences in white-matter organization in the posterior parietal cortex or to other factors, such as experience or preferred cognitive mode, as suggested by Feng and colleagues (2007).

Scheperjans and colleagues (2008) reported that although no sex-related difference appears in the volume of posterior parietal cortex areas, interperson variability in the size of different regions was significantly larger in males. How this variability may contribute to performance differences between men and women in visuospatial manipulations remains an open question.

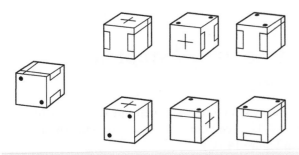

Figure A ▲

Mental Rotation Task The male participants had to determine whether the reference cube on the left might be identical to any of the six cubes on the right. The middle cube in the lower row fits the bill. (T. Wolbers, E. D. Schoell, and C. Büchel. The predictive value of white matter organization in posterior parietal cortex for spatial visualization ability. *NeuroImage* 32:1450–1455, 2006 © Elsevier.)

Feng, J., I. Spence, and J. Pratt. Playing an action video game reduces gender differences in spatial cognition. *Psychological Science* 18:850–855, 2007.

Scheperjans, F., S. B. Eickhoff, L. Homke, H. Mohlberg, K. Hermann, K. Amunts, and K. Zilles. Probabilistic maps, morphometry, and variability of cytoarchitectonic areas in the human superior parietal cortex. *Cerebral Cortex* 18:2141–2157, 2008.

Wolbers, T., E. D. Schoell, and C. Büchel. The predictive value of white matter organization in posterior parietal cortex for spatial visualization ability. *NeuroImage* 32:1450–1455, 2006.

correct solution. Consider subtracting 25 from 52. The "2" and "5" occupy different positions and have different meanings in the two numbers. There must be a "borrowing" from the 10s column in 52 in order to subtract, and so on.

From this perspective, parietal-lobe patients such as H.P. experience **acalculia**, an inability to perform mathematical operations, in this case arithmetic operations, because of the task's spatial nature. Indeed, parietal-lobe patients given simple problems such as 6 minus 4 usually solve them because the spatial demands are few. Even somewhat more difficult problems, such as 984 minus 23, give patients little problem. When more-complex manipulations, such as borrowing, must be made, however, as in 983 minus 24, the patients' abilities break down. Thus, arithmetic operations may depend on the polysensory tissue at the left **temporoparietal junction**, a region where the temporal and parietal lobes meet at the end of the Sylvian fissure.

Language has many demands similar to those of arithmetic. The words *tap* and *pat* have the same letters, but the spatial organization is different. Similarly, the phrases "my son's wife" and "my wife's son" have the same words but very different meanings. These observations have led Luria and others to suggest that language can be seen as quasi-spatial. Patients such as H.P. may understand individual elements clearly, but they cannot understand the whole when the syntax becomes important. This ability, too, may depend on the polysensory region at the temporoparietal junction.

The deficit in organizing individual behavioral elements can be seen in movement as well as in language and arithmetic. People with parietal-lobe injuries have difficulty copying movement sequences, a problem we turn to next.

In summary, the posterior parietal lobe controls visuomotor movement guidance in egocentric (viewer-centered) space. Movement control is most obvious in reaching and eye movements needed to grasp or manipulate objects. The eye movements are important because they allow the visual system to attend to particular sensory cues in the environment. The polymodal region of the posterior parietal cortex is also important in various aspects of mental space, ranging from arithmetic and reading to mental rotation and manipulation of visual images to sequencing movements.

14.3 Somatosensory Symptoms of Parietal Lesions

We now consider somatosensory symptoms associated with damage to the postcentral gyrus—that is, areas 3-1-2 (see Figure 14.1A and B)—and the adjacent cortex (areas PE and PF in Figure 14.1C).

Somatosensory Thresholds

Damage to the postcentral gyrus is typically associated with marked changes in somatosensory thresholds. The most thorough studies of these changes were conducted by Josephine Semmes and her colleagues (1960, 1963) on World War II veterans with missile wounds to the brain and by Suzanne Corkin and her coworkers (1970) on patients who had undergone focal cortical surgery to relieve epilepsy.

Both research groups found that lesions of the postcentral gyrus produce abnormally high sensory thresholds, impaired position sense, and deficits in **stereognosis** (tactile perception, from the Greek *stereo*, meaning "solid"). For example, in the Corkin study, patients performed poorly at detecting a light touch to the skin (pressure sensitivity), determining whether they were touched by one or two sharp points (two-point sensitivity described in Section 8.1), and localizing points of touch on the skin on the side of the body contralateral to the lesion. If blindfolded, these patients also had difficulty reporting whether the fingers of the contralateral hand were passively moved.

Lesions of the postcentral gyrus may also produce a symptom that Luria called **afferent paresis**, loss of kinesthetic feedback that results from lesions to the postcentral gyrus (areas 3-1-2). Finger movements are clumsy because the person has lost the necessary feedback about their exact positions.

Somatoperceptual Disorders

Having typical somatosensory thresholds does not preclude somatosensory abnormalities of other types. First, there is **astereognosis**, the inability to recognize the nature of an object by touch. Tests of tactile perception of objects' qualities, illustrated in **Figure 14.5**, can demonstrate astereognosis. Objects are placed on the palms of blindfolded subjects, or the subjects are told to handle shapes. The task is to match the original shape or object to one of several alternatives solely on the basis of tactile information.

A second somatoperceptual disorder, **simultaneous extinction**, can be demonstrated only by a special testing procedure. The logic of this test is that ordinarily a person confronts an environment in which many sensory stimuli impinge simultaneously, yet the person can distinguish and perceive each individual sensory impression. Thus, a task that presents stimuli one at a time to a person is an unnatural situation that may underestimate sensory disturbances or miss them altogether.

To offer more-complicated and more realistic sensory stimulation, tests for simultaneous extinction present two tactile stimuli simultaneously to the same or different body parts. The objective is to uncover those situations in which both stimuli would be reported if applied singly but only one would be reported if both were applied together, as illustrated in **Figure 14.6**. Failure to report one stimulus is usually called **extinction** and is most commonly associated with damage to the secondary somatic cortex (areas PE and PF), especially in the right parietal lobe.

Numb Touch

Section 13.4 presents evidence of blindsight: visually impaired patients can identify the location of a visual stimulus even though they deny "seeing" it. Jacques Paillard and his colleagues (1983) reported the case of a woman who appears to

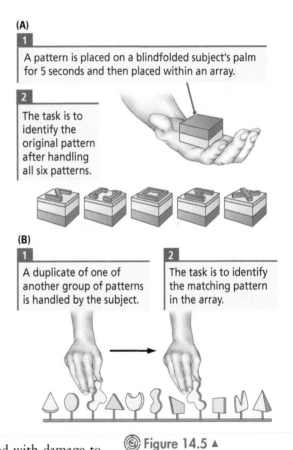

(A)

1 A pattern is placed on a blindfolded subject's palm for 5 seconds and then placed within an array.

2 The task is to identify the original pattern after handling all six patterns.

(B)

1 A duplicate of one of another group of patterns is handled by the subject.

2 The task is to identify the matching pattern in the array.

Figure 14.5 ▲

Tests for Tactile Perception of Objects
Somatosensory abnormalities such as astereognosis can be identified by such neuropsychological tests. (Research from Teuber, 1978.)

When shown two identical objects

Patient sees only the object in his right visual field.

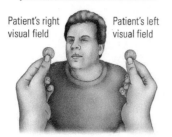

Patient's right visual field

Patient's left visual field

When shown two different objects

Patient sees the object in both visual fields.

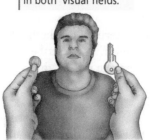

When shown two kinds of an object

Patient sees only the object in his right visual field.

Figure 14.6 ▲

Testing for Extinction in a Stroke Patient The patient responds differently, depending on whether objects in the left and right visual fields are similar or different.

have a tactile analogue of blindsight, which has been referred to both as *blind touch* and *numb touch*. This woman had a large lesion of areas PE, PF, and some of PG, resulting in complete anesthesia on the right side of the body so severe that she was likely to cut or burn herself without being aware of it. Nevertheless, she could point with her left hand to locations on her right hand where she had been touched even though she failed to report feeling the touch.

Although reported in but a single case, the numb touch phenomenon is clearly reminiscent of blindsight. A tactile analog of blindsight is important because it suggests the existence of two tactile systems—one specialized for detection and the other for localization. Such specialization may be a general feature of sensory-system organization.

Somatosensory Agnosias

Astereognosis is one of two major somatosensory agnosias. The other is **asomatognosia**, loss of knowledge or sense of one's own body and bodily condition. Although astereognosis is essentially a disorder of tactile perception, we include it here because it is often described clinically simply as an agnosia.

Asomatognosia is among the most curious agnosias, an almost unbelievable syndrome—until you actually observe it. Varieties of asomatognosia include **anosognosia**, unawareness or denial of illness; **anosodiaphoria**, indifference to illness; **autopagnosia**, inability to localize and name body parts; and **asymbolia for pain**, absence of typical reactions to pain, such as reflexive withdrawal from a painful stimulus.

Asomatognosias may affect one or both sides of the body, although most commonly the left side, as a result of right-hemisphere lesions. An exception comprises the autopagnosias, which usually result from lesions of the left parietal cortex. The most common autopagnosia is **finger agnosia**, a condition in which a person is unable either to point to the various fingers of either hand or to show them to an examiner.

A curious relation exists between finger agnosia and dyscalculia (difficulty in performing arithmetic operations). When children learn arithmetic, they typically use their fingers to count. We might predict that children who are unable to use their fingers to count, such as those with finger agnosia, would have difficulty learning arithmetic. In fact, children with the congenital condition *spina bifida*, which leads to an incompletely formed spinal cord, have finger agnosia and typically are terrible at arithmetic.

◎ 14.4 Symptoms of Posterior Parietal Damage

The clinical literature describes a bewildering array of symptoms of posterior parietal injury. We restrict our consideration here to those most commonly observed.

Bálint's Syndrome

In 1909, Rezsö Bálint described a patient whose bilateral parietal lesion was associated with rather peculiar visual symptoms. The patient had full visual fields and could recognize, use, and name objects, pictures, and colors normally. Nevertheless, he had three unusual symptoms:

1. **He could move his eyes but could not fixate on specific visual stimuli**. Although he spontaneously looked straight ahead, when an array of stimuli was placed in front of him, he directed his gaze 35° to 40° to the right and perceived only what was lying in that direction.

2. **Simultagnosia**. When his attention was directed toward an object, he did not notice other stimuli. With urging, he could identify other stimuli placed before him, but he quickly relapsed into his former neglect. Bálint concluded that the patient's field of attention was limited to one object at a time, a disorder that made reading very difficult because each letter was perceived separately (see Section 13.5).

3. **Optic ataxia**. Bálint used this term to describe the patient's severe deficit in reaching under visual guidance (see also Case V.K. in Section 13.4). The patient could still make accurate movements directed toward the body, presumably by using tactile or proprioceptive information, but could not make visually guided movements.

Although Bálint's syndrome is rare, optic ataxia is a common symptom of posterior parietal lesions that can develop after unilateral as well as bilateral lesions. Consider the following patient described by Antonio Damasio and Arthur Benton:

> She consistently misreached for targets located in the nearby space, such as pencils, cigarettes, matches, ashtrays and cutlery. Usually she underreached by 2 to 5 inches, and then explored, by tact [touch], the surface path leading to the target. This exploration, performed in one or two groping attempts, was often successful and led straight to the object. Occasionally, however, the hand would again misreach, this time on the side of the target and beyond it. Another quick tactually guided correction would then place the hand in contact with the object. . . . In striking contrast to the above difficulties was the performance of movements which did not require visual guidance, such as buttoning and unbuttoning of garments, bringing a cigarette to the mouth, or pointing to some part of her body. These movements were smooth, quick and on target. (Damasio and Benton, 1979, p. 171)

The deficits in eye gaze and visually guided reaching are most likely to result from lesions in the superior parietal region (area PE). Optic ataxia does not accompany lesions in the inferior parietal region, suggesting a clear functional dissociation of the two posterior parietal regions.

Contralateral Neglect and Other Symptoms of Right Parietal Lesions

McDonald Critchley remarked in his 1953 textbook on the parietal lobes that the symptoms of parietal lesions differ widely—one patient showing only a few mildly abnormal signs but another showing an intricate clinical picture with elaborate symptoms. What causes this diversity is still not known. We must keep this uncertainty in mind as we consider the symptoms of right parietal lesions, because the range and severity of symptoms vary widely among individual patients.

Contralateral Neglect

A perceptual disorder subsequent to right parietal lesions was described by John Hughlings-Jackson in 1874. The effect of such lesions was clearly defined 70 years later by Alan Paterson and Oliver Zangwill (1944). A classic paper by John McFie and Oliver Zangwill, published in 1960, reviewed much of the previous work and described several symptoms of right parietal lesions, illustrated in the following patient.

Mr. P., a 67-year-old man, had suffered a right parietal stroke. At the time of our first seeing him (24 hours after admission), he had no visual-field defect or paresis. He did, however, have a variety of other symptoms:

- Mr. P. neglected the left side of his body and of the world. When asked to lift up his arms, he failed to lift his left arm but could do so if one took his arm and asked him to lift it. When asked to draw a clock face, he crowded all the numbers onto the right side of the clock. When asked to read compound words such as *ice cream* and *football*, he read *cream* and *ball*. When he dressed, he did not attempt to put on the left side of his clothing (a form of dressing apraxia) and when he shaved, he shaved only the right side of his face. He ignored tactile sensation on the left side of his body. Finally, he appeared unaware that anything was wrong with him and was uncertain what all the fuss was about (anosagnosia). Collectively, these symptoms constitute **contralateral neglect**.

- Mr. P. was impaired at combining blocks to form designs (constructional apraxia) and was generally impaired at drawing freehand with either hand, at copying drawings, and at cutting out paper figures. When drawing, he often added extra strokes in an effort to make the pictures correct, but the drawings generally lacked accurate spatial relations. In fact, patients showing neglect commonly fail to complete the left side of the drawing, as illustrated in **Figure 14.7**.

- Mr. P. had a topographic disability, being unable to draw maps of well-known regions from memory. He attempted to draw a map of his neighborhood, but it was badly distorted with respect to directions, spatial arrangement of landmarks, and distances. Despite all these disturbances, Mr. P. knew where he was and what day it was, and he could recognize his family's faces. He also had good language functions: he could talk, read, and write normally.

Contralateral neglect as observed in Mr. P. is among the most fascinating symptoms of brain dysfunction. Neglect occurs in visual, auditory, and

Figure 14.7 ▼

Drawings Copied by a Patient with Contralateral Neglect

(Reprinted by permission from Macmillan Publishers Ltd: NATURE, Rossetti, Y., G. Rode, L. Pisella, A. Farne, L. Li, D. Boisson, and M.-T. Perenin. Prism adaptation to a rightward optical deviation rehabilitates left hemispatial neglect. *Nature* 395:166–169, © 1998.)

Model

Patient's copy

somesthetic stimulation on the side of the body or space, or both body and space, opposite the lesion. Neglect may be accompanied by denial of the deficit.

Recovery passes through two stages. **Allesthesia** is characterized by a person's beginning to respond to stimuli on the neglected side as if the stimuli were on the unlesioned side. The person responds and orients to visual, tactile, or auditory stimuli on the left side of the body as if they were on the right.

The second stage of recovery, noted earlier, is simultaneous extinction (see Figure 14.6). The person responds to stimuli on the hitherto neglected side unless both sides are stimulated simultaneously, in which case he or she notices only the stimulation on the side ipsilateral to the lesion.

Neglect presents obstacles to understanding. Where is the lesion that produces this effect? **Figure 14.8**A is a composite drawing of the region damaged, as inferred from brain scans, in 13 patients with neglect as described by Kenneth Heilman and colleagues (1993). A review by Argye Hillis (2006) concludes that damage to both the right intraparietal sulcus (roughly dividing PE and PF) and the right angular gyrus are necessary for contralateral neglect. Furthermore, Neil Muggleton and his colleagues (2006) used transcranial magnetic stimulation (TMS) over these regions to induce neglect in intact persons.

Note, however, that contralateral neglect is occasionally observed subsequent to lesions to the frontal lobe and cingulate cortex as well as to subcortical structures including the superior colliculus and lateral hypothalamus. What is not clear is whether the same phenomenon results from lesions in these various locations.

Why does neglect arise? Two main theories argue that neglect is caused by either (1) defective sensation or perception or (2) defective attention or orientation. The strongest argument favoring the defective sensation or perception theory is that a lesion to the parietal lobes, which receive input from all of the sensory regions, can disturb the integration of sensation into perception. Derek Denny-Brown and Robert Chambers (1958) termed this function *morphosynthesis* and its disruption *amorphosynthesis*.

An elaboration of the defective sensation or perception theory proposes that neglect follows a right parietal lesion because integration of the stimuli's spatial properties becomes disturbed. As a result, although stimuli are perceived, their location is uncertain to the nervous system, and they are consequently ignored. Neglect is thought to be unilateral because, in the absence of right-hemisphere function, the left hemisphere is assumed to be capable of some rudimentary spatial synthesis that prevents neglect of the right side of the world. This rudimentary spatial ability cannot compensate, however, for the many other behavioral deficits resulting from right parietal lesions.

Critchley and later others suggested the second theory, that neglect results from defective attention or orientation—an inability to attend to input that has in fact been registered. Heilman and Watson elaborated on this suggestion. They proposed that neglect is manifested by a defect in orienting to stimuli: the defect results from the disruption of a system whose function is to arouse the person when new sensory stimulation is present.

Object Recognition

Elizabeth Warrington and her colleagues (Warrington and Rabin, 1970; Warrington and Taylor, 1973) described another common symptom of right-parietal lesions: although able to recognize objects shown in familiar views,

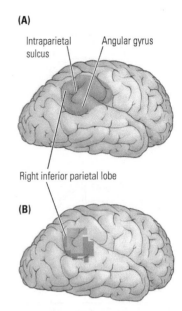

(A)

Intraparietal sulcus   Angular gyrus

Right inferior parietal lobe

(B)

Figure 14.8 ▲

The Locus of Right Parietal Symptoms
(A) Composite map of the imaged region damaged in 13 patients with contralateral neglect as described by Heilman and Watson. The area of greatest overlap is the right inferior parietal lobule. (B) Composite outline of the region of overlap among lesions producing deficits in Warrington and Taylor's recognition test for objects seen in unfamiliar views (Figure 14.9). The area of maximal overlap is lightly shaded. Note the locational similarity in parts A and B.

(A)

(B)

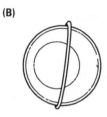

◉ **Figure 14.9** ▲

Objects in Strange Views
Drawing of a bucket in (A) familiar and (B) unfamiliar views. Patients with right parietal lesions have difficulty recognizing objects in unfamiliar views.

patients having these lesions are badly impaired at recognizing objects shown in unfamiliar views (**Figure 14.9**). Warrington concluded that the deficit is not in forming a gestalt, or concept—in this case, of "bucket"—but rather in perceptual classification—the mechanism for categorizing information as being part of the idea of "bucket."

Such misallocation can be seen as a type of a spatial matching in which the common view of an object must be rotated spatially to match the novel view. Warrington and Taylor (1973) suggested that the focus for this deficit is roughly the right inferior parietal lobule, the same region proposed as the locus of contralateral neglect (see Figure 14.8B).

The Gerstmann Syndrome and Other Left Parietal Symptoms

In 1924, Josef Gerstmann described a patient with an unusual disorder subsequent to a left parietal stroke: finger agnosia, an asomatognosia described in Section 14.2 (see Gerstmann, 1957). Gerstmann's patient was unable to name or recognize the fingers on either hand. This symptom aroused considerable interest, and in the ensuing years, three other symptoms were reported to accompany finger agnosia: right–left confusion, **agraphia** (inability to write), and acalculia. These four symptoms collectively became known as the Gerstmann syndrome.

Gerstmann and others argued that these symptoms accompany a circumscribed lesion in the left parietal lobe, roughly corresponding to the angular gyrus (area PG). If these four symptoms arose as a group, the patient was said to demonstrate the Gerstmann syndrome, and the lesions could be localized in the angular gyrus. The Gerstmann syndrome is a doubtful diagnostic tool in routine investigations, but all of the symptoms can be associated with left parietal lesions. Various other symptoms of left parietal lesions are illustrated in the following case history.

On August 24, 1975, S.S., an 11-year-old boy, suddenly had a seizure characterized by twitching on the right side of the body, particularly the arm and face. He was given anticonvulsant medication and remained free of symptoms until September 16, when he began to write upside down and backward. S.S. was immediately referred to a neurologist, who diagnosed a left parietal malignant astrocytoma. Careful neuropsychological assessment revealed a number of symptoms characteristic of left parietal lesions:

- **Disturbed language function.** S.S. was unable to write even his name (agraphia), had serious difficulties reading (dyslexia), and spoke slowly and deliberately, making many errors in grammar (dysphasia).

- **Apraxia.** S.S. was unable to combine blocks to form designs and had difficulty learning a sequence of novel limb movements (see the next subsection).

- **Dyscalculia.** He could not perform mental arithmetic and was unable to solve even simple additions and subtractions.

- **Recall.** He had an especially low digit span, being able to master the immediate recall of only three digits, whether presented orally or visually.

- **Right–left discrimination.** He was totally unable to distinguish left from right, responding at random on all tests of this ability.

- **Right hemianopia.** Probably because his tumor had damaged the geniculostriate connections, as S.S.'s tumor progressed, movement of the right side of his body became disturbed as the tumor placed pressure on the frontal lobe.

At the end of October 1975, S.S. died; neither surgery nor drug therapy could stop the tumor's growth. The symptoms S.S. exhibited resemble those of other patients whom we have seen with left parietal lesions, including H.P., whose story begins this chapter. Curiously, S.S. did not have finger agnosia, one of the Gerstmann symptoms, illustrating the point that even very large lesions do not produce the same effects in every patient.

Apraxia and the Parietal Lobe

Apraxia is a movement disorder in which the loss of skilled movement is not caused by weakness, inability to move, abnormal muscle tone or posture, intellectual deterioration, poor comprehension, or other disorders of movement such as tremor. Among the many apraxias we focus on two: *ideomotor apraxia* and *constructional apraxia*.

In **ideomotor apraxia**, patients are unable to copy movements or to make gestures, for example, to wave hello. Patients with left posterior parietal lesions often present ideomotor apraxia. Doreen Kimura (1977) showed that the deficits in such patients can be quantified by asking them to copy a series of arm movements such as those illustrated in **Figure 14.10**A. Patients with left parietal lesions are grossly impaired at this task, whereas people with right parietal lesions perform it normally.

In **constructional apraxia**, a visuomotor disorder, spatial organization is disturbed. Patients with constructional apraxia cannot assemble a puzzle, build a

(A) Serial arm-movement copying test

(B) Serial facial-movement copying test

Ⓒ Figure 14.10 ◄

Testing for Apraxia
Subjects are asked to copy each movement in a series as accurately as they can. (A) Sample items from a serial arm-movement copying test used to assess ideomotor apraxia. (B) Sample items from a serial facial-movement copying test used to assess constructional apraxia.

tree house, draw a picture, or copy a series of facial movements (Figure 14.10B). Constructional apraxia can develop after injury to either parietal lobe, although debate over whether the symptoms are the same after left- and right-side lesions is considerable (see the review by Benton and Sivan, 1993). Nonetheless, constructional apraxia often accompanies posterior parietal lesions.

You can view both ideomotor and constructional apraxia as movement disturbances resulting from a disruption of the parietofrontal connections that control movement. Vernon Mountcastle proposed that the posterior parietal cortex receives afferent signals not only of tactile and visual representations of the world but also of the body's position and movement (Mountcastle et al., 1975). He proposed that the posterior parietal cortex uses this information to function as "a command apparatus for operation of the limbs, hands, and eyes within immediate extrapersonal space."

Thus, the parietal lobe not only integrates sensory and spatial information to allow accurate movements in space but also functions to direct or guide movements in the immediate vicinity of the body. Ideomotor and constructional apraxia both exemplify dysfunction in this guidance system.

Drawing

Although drawing deficits can arise subsequent to lesions in either hemisphere, those deficits are generally believed to be greater after damage to the right hemisphere than after damage to the left, and right parietal damage is believed to have the greatest influence on drawing ability. This conclusion is consistent with the general idea that the right hemisphere plays a dominant role in spatial abilities, but it may not be correct.

Rather, disturbances in drawing appear to differ depending on whether the lesion is in the right or left hemisphere. For example, Kimura and Faust (1987) asked a large sample of patients to draw a house and a man. Apraxic or aphasic left-hemisphere patients performed poorly, producing fewer recognizable drawings and fewer lines than did right-hemisphere patients. In contrast, right-hemisphere patients tended to omit details from the left side of their drawings and to rotate the drawings on the page.

In sum, drawing is a complex behavior that may require verbal as well as nonverbal (for example, spatial) processes. If asked to draw a bicycle, many people will make a mental checklist of items to include (fenders, spokes, chain, and so on). In the absence of language, we would expect such people to draw less-complete bicycles. Further, if patients are apraxic, there likely is a deficit in making the movements required to draw. Similarly, the parts of a bicycle have a particular spatial organization. If spatial organization is poor, the drawing is likely to be distorted.

Spatial Attention

As we move about the world, a vast array of sensory information confronts us. The nervous system cannot possibly treat it all equally. Rather, the brain must select what information to process. Consider, for example, the sensory overload to which we are subjected when we stop to chat with an old friend in a department store. Several other people may pass nearby, items for purchase will certainly be on display all around, competing sounds (others talking, music, checkout scanners), novel odors, and myriad other stimuli all compete for attention.

Nonetheless, we can orient to a small sample of incoming information and ignore most of the other input. In fact, we may focus to the exclusion of other potentially more important information. Cognitive psychologists refer to this orienting of the sensory systems as *selective attention*: we attend only to particular stimuli.

Michael Posner (Posner et al., 1987) proposed that one function of the parietal cortex is to allow attention to shift from one stimulus to another, a process he calls **disengagement**. Consider our example of dining with a friend in Section 14.2. As we eat, we shift from peas to bread to wine. We are disengaging each time we shift from one food to another.

An aspect of disengagement is that we must reset our visuomotor guidance systems to form the appropriate movements for the next target. We can extend this idea to mental manipulation of objects and spatial information too: we must reset the system for the next operation. We return to the phenomenon of selective attention in Section 22.2.

Disorders of Spatial Cognition

Spatial cognition refers to a broad category of abilities that require using or manipulating spatial properties of stimuli, including the ability to manipulate images of objects and maps mentally. The mental-rotation task illustrated in Figure 12.1 provides a good example. Another is the ability to follow an upside-down map.

There is little doubt that posterior lesions, most likely including the PG region and the polymodal cortex of the superior temporal sulcus, produce deficits in mental-rotation and map-reading tasks. Although it is widely assumed in the neuropsychological literature that the right hemisphere is "spatial" and that deficits in spatial cognition should thus result from right posterior lesions, the clinical evidence is far from convincing. Indeed, there is little doubt that both left- and right-hemisphere lesions produce deficits in spatial-cognition tasks.

The general view, however, is that left- and right-hemisphere lesions have different effects on spatial cognitions. For example, Michael Corballis (1990) suggested that mental rotation requires two different mental operations: (1) imaging the stimulus and (2) manipulating the image. Freda Newcombe and Graham Ratcliff (1990) suggested that the left-hemisphere deficit may result from an inability to generate an appropriate mental image. Visual-imaging deficits result from left occipital lesions, as discussed in Section 13.6. In contrast, the right-hemisphere deficit may result from an inability to perform operations on this mental image.

Deficits in using topographic information are more likely associated with damage to the right hemisphere than to the left. Such disorders include loss of memory of familiar surroundings, inability to locate items such as countries or cities on a map, and inability to find one's way in one's environment. Not surprisingly, such deficits are likely to be associated with other visual deficits (such as contralateral neglect or visual agnosia), but specific disorders of topographic orientation have been described for some patients.

Emillio de Renzi (de Renzi and Faglioni, 1978) concluded that injury to the right posterior hemisphere is a prerequisite for such disorders. Newcombe and

Ratcliff noted that such disorders are often associated with injury to the right posterior cerebral artery and thus likely to include the right occipitotemporal and right hippocampal region. When the parietal cortex is affected, it is most likely to be the inferior part, probably including area PG and the STS.

Left and Right Parietal Lobes Compared

In their classic paper, McFie and Zangwill compared the symptoms of patients with left or right parietal lesions. Although they found some overlapping symptoms, the asymmetry is clear in **Table 14.1**. In addition, as noted earlier, ideomotor apraxia is more likely to be associated with left parietal lesions.

A puzzling feature of the McFie and Zangwill study summarized in Table 14.1 is that lesions to the two hemispheres produce some overlapping symptoms, despite the clear asymmetry. The results of neuropsychological studies tend to emphasize the asymmetry of lesion effects, but the overlapping symptoms are important theoretically. Indeed, as noted earlier, both constructional apraxia and disorders of spatial cognition are poorly lateralized. Many theories of hemispheric asymmetry, discussed in Section 11.5, do not predict such ambiguity in symptom localization and tend to assume far greater dissociation of lesion effects than is actually observed.

One explanation for the overlapping symptoms relates to preferred cognitive mode, a concept introduced in Section 11.5, in which we note that many problems can be solved by using either a verbal cognitive mode or a spatial, nonverbal cognitive mode. Genetic, maturational, and environmental factors may predispose people to use different cognitive modes. For example, you might solve a complex spatial problem, such as reading an upside-down map, either directly, by "spatial cognition" (the directions to travel are intuited spatially), or indirectly, by "verbal cognition" (the spatial information is encoded into words and the problem is solved by being talked through step by step).

People who are highly verbal prefer the verbal mode even when it is less efficient; we expect lesions of the left parietal lobe in these people to disturb functions that ordinarily are disrupted preferentially by right parietal lesions. Little direct evidence favors this explanation of functional overlap, but this provocative idea accounts in part for individual differences as well as for the apparent functional overlap revealed by the results of lesion studies.

14.5 Major Symptoms and Their Assessment

Table 14.2 summarizes the major symptoms of parietal-lobe lesions. Damage to the anterior parietal cortex, including area PE, produces deficits in various somatosensory functions. Damage to the posterior parietal regions produces most other disorders.

Table 14.1 **Effects of left- and right-parietal lesions compared**

	PERCENTAGE OF SUBJECTS WITH DEFICIT*	
	Left (%)	Right (%)
Unilateral neglect	13	67
Dressing disability	13	67
Cube counting	0	86
Paper cutting	0	90
Topographical loss	13	50
Right–left discrimination	63	0
Weigl's Sorting Test	83	6

*Note the small but significant overlap in symptoms of left and right lesions.
Source: Based on data presented by McFie and Zangwill, 1960.

Table 14.2 **Summary of major symptoms of parietal-lobe damage**

Symptom	Most probable lesion site	Basic reference
Disorders of tactile function	Areas 1, 2, 3	Semmes et al., 1960; Corkin et al., 1970
Tactile agnosia	Area PE	Hécaen and Albert, 1978; Brown, 1972
Defects in eye movement	Areas PE, PF	Tyler, 1968
Misreaching	Area PE	Damasio and Benton, 1979
Manipulation of objects	Areas PF, PG	Pause et al., 1989
Apraxia	Areas PF, PG, left	Heilman and Gonzalez Rothi, 1993; Kimura, 1980
Constructional apraxia	Area PG	Benton, 1990
Acalculia	Areas PG, STS	Levin et al., 1993
Impaired cross-modal matching	Areas PG, STS	Butters and Brody, 1968
Contralateral neglect	Area PG right	Heilman et al., 1993
Impaired object recognition	Area PG right	Warrington and Taylor, 1973
Disorders of body image	Area PE?	Benton and Sivan, 1993
Right–left confusion	Areas PF, PG	Semmes et al., 1960
Disorders of spatial ability	Areas PE, PG	Newcombe and Ratcliff, 1990
Disorders of drawing	Area PG	Warrington et al., 1966; Kimura and Faust, 1987

Table 14.2 also lists the regions most likely associated with the deficits, but few studies clearly demonstrate anatomical dissociations of such deficits, in large part because natural lesions rarely respect anatomical boundaries or affect only the neocortex. Additionally, in contrast with the frontal and temporal lobes, which are often implicated in epilepsy and thus may be removed surgically, the parietal lobe is rarely epileptogenic. Surgical removal is rare, as is the opportunity for follow-up research.

Clinical Neuropsychological Assessment

We have seen that restricted lesions of the parietal cortex produce a wide variety of behavioral changes. Behavioral tests used to evaluate brain damage in neurologically verified cases could logically be employed to predict the locus and extent of damage or dysfunction in new cases. (See Section 28.2 for more detail on the rationale behind neuropsychological assessment.)

This section briefly describes the standardized behavioral tests that have proved sensitive and valid predictors of brain injury. Although these tests, summarized in **Table 14.3**, do not assess all symptoms of parietal injury, they do evaluate a broad range of its functions. It would be highly unusual for a person to perform at normal on all these tests yet show other symptoms of parietal-lobe damage. In addition to these tests, Howard Goodglass and Edith Kaplan (1972) described a good series of tests in their "parietal lobe battery."

Somatosensory Threshold

Recall that subsequent to lesions of the postcentral gyrus, the somatosensory threshold increases on the contralateral side of the body. The two-point discrimination test requires a blindfolded subject to report whether he or she felt one or two points touch the skin (usually on the face or palm of the hand). The distance between the points is at first very large (say, 3 centimeters) and

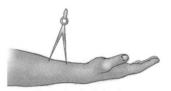

Two-point discrimination

Table 14.3 **Standardized clinical neuropsychological tests for parietal-lobe damage**

Function*	Test	Basic reference
Somatosensory threshold	Two-point discrimination	Corkin et al., 1970
Tactile form recognition	Seguin–Goddard Form Board (tactile patterns)	Teuber and Weinstein, 1954 Benton et al., 1983
Contralateral neglect	Line bisection	Schenkenberg et al., 1980
Visual perception	Gollin incomplete figures Mooney closure	Warrington and Rabin, 1970 Milner, 1980
Spatial relations	Right–left differentiation	Benton et al., 1983
Language		
Speech comprehension	Token	de Renzi and Faglioni, 1978
Reading comprehension	Token	de Renzi and Faglioni, 1978
Apraxia	Kimura Box	Kimura, 1977

*See Table 14.2 for symptoms and probable lesion site(s) associated with some parietal functions.

Note: These standardized tests have been validated on large samples of patients with known localized brain damage.

is gradually reduced until the subject can no longer perceive two points. In extreme cases, the process is reversed: the distance must be increased to find when the subject first perceives two points.

Tactile Form Recognition

In the Seguin–Goddard Form Board Test, a blindfolded subject manipulates 10 blocks of different shapes (star, triangle, and so forth) and attempts to place them in similarly shaped holes on a form board. When this phase of the test is completed, the form board and blocks are removed and the subject is asked to draw the board from memory.

The precise locus of the lesion producing deficits on the Form Board Test is controversial, and no claims have been proved. Nevertheless, research results on tactile performance in monkeys with parietal lesions indicate that blindfolded tactile recognition is probably sensitive to lesions of areas PE and PF, whereas in humans, the drawing part—a test of both memory and cross-modal matching—is probably sensitive to lesions in area PG.

Contralateral Neglect

A variety of tests for contralateral neglect have been devised. We favor the line-bisection test by Thomas Schenkenberg and his colleagues (1980) because it is particularly sensitive: the subject is asked to mark the middle of each of a set of 20 lines. Each line is a different length and located at a different position on the page—some left of center, some in the middle, and some right of center. Patients showing contralateral neglect typically fail to mark the lines on the left side of the page.

Visual Perception

Both the Mooney closure faces test (see Figure 15.16D) and the Gollin incomplete figures test easily assess visual perceptual capacity. Each test presents a series of incomplete representations of faces or objects, and the subject must combine the elements to form a gestalt and identify the picture. These tests are especially sensitive to damage at the right temporoparietal junction, presumably in regions contributing to the ventral visual stream (see Section 15.3).

Spatial Relations

In the right–left differentiation test, a series of drawings of hands, feet, ears, and so on is presented in different orientations (upside down, rear view, and so forth), and the subject's task is to indicate whether the drawing is of the left or the right body part. In a verbal variant of this test, subjects are read a series of commands that are to be carried out (for example, "Touch your right ear with your left hand"). Both tests are very sensitive to left-parietal-lobe damage, but caution is advised: subjects with left-frontal-lobe damage also are often impaired at these tasks.

Language

The Token Test is an easily administered test of language comprehension. Twenty tokens—four shapes (large and small circles, large and small squares) in each of five colors (white, black, yellow, green, red)—are placed in front of a subject. The test begins with simple tasks (for example, touching the white circle) and becomes progressively more difficult (for example, touching the large yellow circle and the large green square).

A token test of reading comprehension can also be given by having the subject read the instructions out loud and then carry them out. We have not considered language a function of the parietal lobe, but the posterior speech zone borders on area PG. Thus, injuries affecting PG often include speech-related temporal cortex, and aphasia is observed.

Apraxia

Unfortunately, no standardized tests analogous to the Token Test for language exist for apraxia. The Kimura Box Test (**Figure 14.11**) is probably the best option. Subjects are required to make consecutive movements, first pushing a button with the index finger, then pulling a handle with four fingers, and lastly pressing a bar with the thumb. Apraxics perform very poorly on this test. Many appear unable to perform this simple series of movements even with extensive practice.

Figure 14.11 ▼

Kimura Box Test Subjects are required to learn a three-step movement series. Apraxic subjects are impaired at this task, and they may be unable to learn it at all. (Research from Kimura, 1977.)

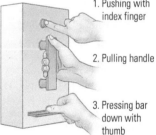

Movement series
1. Pushing with index finger
2. Pulling handle
3. Pressing bar down with thumb

SUMMARY

14.1 Parietal Lobe Anatomy

The parietal lobe can be divided into two broad functional zones. The anterior parietal lobe (somatosensory cortex) primarily participates in somatosensory functions. The posterior parietal cortex can be conceived of as the origin of three distinct pathways in the dorsal visual stream. The parieto–premotor pathway is proposed to be the principal "how" pathway; the parieto–prefrontal pathway to have visuospatial functions; and the parieto–medial temporal pathway to participate in spatial navigation.

14.2 A Theory of Parietal-Lobe Function

Considering the hand as the organ of the parietal lobe, the parietal lobe's primary function is guiding limb movements to place the hand in specific spatial locations. The superior parietal region has expanded in humans to include dorsal-stream areas controlling not only actual movements to manipulate objects but also their mental manipulation and the visuospatial functions related to spatial working memory and spatial navigation. The inferior parietal region has also expanded to support processes related to spatial cognition and such "quasi-spatial" processes as those used in arithmetic and reading. In addition, the inferior parietal cortex is part of a parieto–prefrontal network for spatial attention.

14.3 Somatosensory Symptoms of Parietal Lesions

Damage to anterior somatosensory parietal regions produces deficits in tactile functions ranging from simple somato-sensation to recognizing objects by touch.

14.4 Symptoms of Posterior Parietal Damage

Posterior parietal-lobe injury interferes with the visual guidance of hand and limb movements. Thus, left parietal injury may result in limb apraxias, whereas for right parietal injury, constructional apraxias may result. Left parietal injury also produces a range of cognitive symptoms including deficits in arithmetic calculations and in writing; right parietal injury produces a complementary range of symptoms including contralateral neglect and deficits in spatial cognition.

14.5 Major Symptoms and Their Assessment

Neuropsychologists analyze parietal-lobe functions with tests sensitive to discrete parietal-lobe injuries. Assessments include tests of tactile (anterior parietal) functioning, visual guidance of movement (parieto–premotor pathway), and cognitive (posterior parietal) functions such as spatial orientation, including both copying of complex geometric figures and mental rotation.

References

Andersen, R. A., J. W. Burdick, S. Musallam, B. Pesaran, and J. G. Cham. Cognitive neural prosthetics. *Trends in Cognitive Sciences* 8:486–493, 2004.

Andersen, R. A., D. Meeker, B. Pesaran, B. Breznen, C. Buneo, and H. Scherberger. Sensorimotor transformations in the posterior parietal cortex. In M. S. Gazzaniga, Ed., *The Cognitive Neurosciences III*, pp. 463–474. Cambridge, Mass.: MIT Press, 2004.

Bálint, R. Seelenlähmung des "Schauens," optische Ataxie, räumliche Störung der Aufmerksamkeit. *Monatsschrift für Psychiatrie und Neurologie* 25:51–81, 1909.

Benton, A. L. Constructional apraxia. In F. Boller and J. Grafman, Eds., *Handbook of Neuropsychology*, vol. 2. Amsterdam: Elsevier, 1990.

Benton, A. L., K. de S. Hamsher, N. R. Varney, and O. Spreen. *Contributions to Neuropsychological Assessment.* New York: Oxford University Press, 1983.

Benton, A. L., and A. B. Sivan. Disturbances of body schema. In K. M. Heilman and E. Valenstein, Eds., *Clinical Neuropsychology*, 3rd ed. New York: Oxford University Press, 1993.

Butters, N., and B. A. Brody. The role of the left parietal lobe in the mediation of intra- and cross-modal associations. *Cortex* 4:328–343, 1968.

Cohen, Y. E., and R. A. Andersen. A common reference frame for movement plans in the posterior parietal cortex. *Nature Reviews Neuroscience* 3:553–562, 2002.

Corballis, M. C. Mental rotation: Anatomy of a paradigm. In M. Potegal, Ed., *Spatial Abilities: Development and Physiological Foundations.* New York: Academic Press, 1990.

Corkin, S., B. Milner, and T. Rasmussen. Somatosensory thresholds. *Archives of Neurology* 23:41–58, 1970.

Critchley, M. *The Parietal Lobes.* London: Arnold, 1953.

Damasio, A. R., and A. L. Benton. Impairment of hand movements under visual guidance. *Neurology* 29:170–178, 1979.

Denny-Brown, D., and R. A. Chambers. The parietal lobe and behavior. *Research Publications, Association for Research in Nervous and Mental Disease* 36:35–117, 1958.

de Renzi, E., and P. Faglioni. Normative data and screening power of a shortened version of the Token Test. *Cortex* 14:41–49, 1978.

Gerstmann, J. Some notes on the Gerstmann syndrome. *Neurology* 7:866–869, 1957.

Goodglass, H., and E. Kaplan. *The Assessment of Aphasia.* Philadelphia: Lea & Febiger, 1972.

Hécaen, H., and M. L. Albert. *Human Neuropsychology.* New York: Wiley, 1978.

Heilman, K. M., and L. J. Gonzalez Rothi. Apraxia. In K. M. Heilman and E. Valenstein, Eds., *Clinical Neuropsychology*, 3rd ed. New York: Oxford University Press, 1993.

Heilman, K. M., R. T. Watson, and E. Valenstein. Neglect and related disorders. In K. M. Heilman and E. Valenstein, Eds., *Clinical Neuropsychology*, 3rd ed. New York: Oxford University Press, 1993.

Hillis, A. E. Neurobiology of unilateral spatial neglect. *The Neuroscientist* 12:153–163, 2006.

Ifft, P. J., S. Shokur, Z. Li, M. A. Lebedev, and M. A. Nicolelis. A brain-machine interface enables bimanual arm movements in monkeys. *Science Translational Medicine* 5:210ra154. doi: 10.1126, 2013.

Kimura, D. Acquisition of a motor skill after left hemisphere damage. *Brain* 100:527–542, 1977.

Kimura, D. Neuromotor mechanisms in the evolution of human communication. In H. D. Steklis and M. J. Raleigh, Eds., *Neurobiology of Social Communication in Primates: An Evolutionary Perspective.* New York: Academic Press, 1980.

Kimura, D., and R. Faust. Spontaneous drawing in an unselected sample of patients with unilateral cerebral damage. In D. Ottoson, Ed., *Duality and Unity of the Brain.* Wenner-Gren Center International Symposium Series, vol. 47. New York: Macmillan, 1987.

Kravitz, D. J., K. S. Saleem, C. I. Baker, and M. Mishkin. A new neural framework for visuospatial processing. *Nature Reviews Neuroscience* 12:217–230, 2011.

Levin, H. S., F. C. Goldstein, and P. A. Spiers. Acalculia. In K. M. Heilman and E. Valenstein, Eds., *Clinical*

Neuropsychology, 3rd ed. New York: Oxford University Press, 1993.

McFie, J., and O. L. Zangwill. Visual-constructive disabilities associated with lesions of the left cerebral hemisphere. *Brain* 83:243–260, 1960.

Milner, B. Complementary functional specializations of the human cerebral hemispheres. In R. Levy-Montalcini, Ed., *Neurons, Transmitters, and Behavior*. Vatican City: Pontificiae Academiae Scientiarum Scripta Varia, 1980.

Milner, D.A., and M. A. Goodale. Visual pathways to perception and action. *Progress in Brain Research* 95:317–337, 1993.

Milner, D.A., and M. A. Goodale. *The Visual Brain in Action*. Oxford: Oxford University Press, 2006.

Mountcastle, V. B., J. C. Lynch, A. Georgopoulos, H. Sakata, and C. Acuna. Posterior parietal association cortex of the monkey: Command functions for operation within extrapersonal space. *Journal of Neurophysiology* 38:871–908, 1975.

Muggleton, N. G., P. Postma, K. Moutsopoulou, I. Nimmo-Smith, A. Marcel, and V. Walsh. TMS over right posterior parietal cortex induces neglect in a scent-based frame of reference. *Neuropsychologia* 44:1222–1229, 2006.

Newcombe, F., and G. Ratcliff. Disorders of visuospatial analysis. In F. Boller and J. Grafman, Eds., *Handbook of Neuropsychology*, vol. 2. Amsterdam: Elsevier, 1990.

Nicolelis, M. A. Mind in motion. *Scientific American* 307(3):58–63, 2012.

Paillard, J., F. Michel, and G. Stelmach. Localization without content: A tactile analogue of "blindsight." *Archives of Neurology* 40:548–551, 1983.

Pais-Vieira, M., M. Lebedev, C. Kunicki, J. Wang, and M. A. Nicolelis. A brain-to-brain interface for real-time sharing of sensorimotor information. *Science Reports* 3:1319 doi:10.1038, 2013.

Paterson, A., and O. L. Zangwill. Disorders of space perception association with lesions of the right cerebral hemisphere. *Brain* 67:331–358, 1944.

Pause, M., E. Kunesch, F. Binkofski, and H.-J. Freund. Sensorimotor disturbances in patients with lesions of the parietal cortex. *Brain* 112:1599–1625, 1989.

Posner, M. I., A. W. Inhoff, F. J. Friedrich, and A. Cohen. Isolating attentional systems: A cognitive-anatomical analysis. *Psychobiology* 15:107–121, 1987.

Sato, N., H. Sakata, Y. L. Tanaka, and M. Taira. Navigation-associated medial parietal neurons in monkeys. *Proceedings of the National Academy of Sciences U.S.A.* 103:17001–17006, 2006.

Schenkenberg, T., D. C. Bradford, and E. T. Ajax. Line bisection and unilateral visual neglect in patients with neurologic impairment. *Neurology* 30:509–517, 1980.

Semmes, J., S. Weinstein, L. Ghent, and H.-L. Teuber. *Somatosensory Changes after Penetrating Brain Wounds in Man*. Cambridge, Mass.: Harvard University Press, 1960.

Semmes, J., S. Weinstein, L. Ghent, and H.-L. Teuber. Correlates of impaired orientation in personal and extra-personal space. *Brain* 86:747–772, 1963.

Stein, J. F. The representation of egocentric space in the posterior parietal cortex. *Behavioral and Brain Sciences* 15:691–700, 1992.

Teuber, H.-L. The brain and human behavior. In R. Held, W. Leibowitz, and H.-L. Teuber, Eds., *Handbook of Sensory Physiology*, vol. 7, *Perception*. Berlin: Springer, 1978.

Teuber, H.-L., and S. Weinstein. Performance on a formboard task after penetrating brain injury. *Journal of Psychology* 38:177–190, 1954.

Tyler, H. R. Abnormalities of perception with defective eye movements (Bálints syndrome). *Cortex* 4:154–171, 1968.

Ungerleider, L. G., and M. Mishkin. Two cortical visual systems. In D. J. Ingle, M. A. Goodale, and R. J. W. Mansfield, Eds., *Analysis of Visual Behavior*, pp. 549–586. Cambridge, Mass.: MIT Press, 1982.

Warrington, E. K., M. James, and M. Kinsbourne. Drawing disability in relation to laterality of cerebral lesion. *Brain* 89:53–82, 1966.

Warrington, E. K., and P. Rabin. Perceptual matching in patients with cerebral lesions. *Neuropsychologia* 8:475–487, 1970.

Warrington, E. K., and A. M. Taylor. The contribution of the right parietal lobe to object recognition. *Cortex* 9:152–164, 1973.

15

The Temporal Lobes

When he was 40 years old, H.H., a successful corporate lawyer with a wife and two school-age children, was finding his job increasingly stressful. His wife was taken off guard when H.H. suddenly announced that he was quitting his law firm.

H.H. complained of being so stressed that he simply could not remember the cases on which he was working and felt that he could not continue as a lawyer. He had no plan for how he would support his family but, curiously, seemed unconcerned.

A couple weeks later, H.H. shaved his hair off, donned a flowing robe, and left his family to join a fringe religious group. His wife of 15 years was stunned by this sudden change in behavior: up to this point, H.H. had been an atheist.

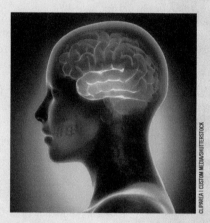

CLIPAREA1 CUSTOM MEDIA/SHUTTERSTOCK

H.H.'s wife was notified 2 weeks later that he had collapsed with a seizure while handing out flowers and peace pamphlets in a large U.S. airport. He was taken to a hospital in a confused state. Neurological examination revealed a left-temporal-lobe tumor. Fortunately, the tumor was operable and was removed.

H.H. was aphasic after his surgery, but this condition cleared in a matter of weeks. He was left with enduring word-finding difficulties, problematic only when he was tired. He continued to complain of verbal-memory problems, however.

H.H.'s wife said that his personality remained transformed, largely because he remained religious. Eventually, H.H. successfully returned to his law firm, although with a reduced caseload compared with that of his pretumor days.

H.H. exhibited symptoms typical of temporal-lobe disorder, including radical changes in affect (emotion) and personality, memory disturbance, and at least a transient disturbance of language. In this chapter, we survey the anatomy of the temporal lobe (highlighted on the brain image above), present a theoretical model of its function, describe the basic symptoms that signal temporal-lobe damage, and briefly describe clinical tests of temporal-lobe function.

15.1 Temporal-Lobe Anatomy

The temporal lobes comprise all of the tissue that lies below the lateral (Sylvian) fissure and anterior to the occipital cortex (**Figure 15.1**). Subcortical temporal-lobe structures include the limbic cortex, the amygdala, and the hippocampal formation (**Figure 15.2**). Connections to and from the temporal lobe extend throughout the brain.

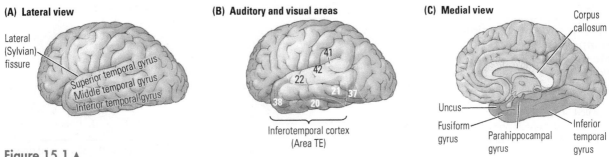

(A) Lateral view

Lateral (Sylvian) fissure

Superior temporal gyrus
Middle temporal gyrus
Inferior temporal gyrus

(B) Auditory and visual areas

41
42
22
21 37
38 20

Inferotemporal cortex
(Area TE)

(C) Medial view

Corpus callosum

Uncus
Fusiform gyrus
Parahippocampal gyrus
Inferior temporal gyrus

Figure 15.1 ▲

Gross Anatomy of the Temporal Lobe (A) Three major temporal-lobe gyri are visible on its lateral surface. (B) Brodmann's areas on the lateral surface, where auditory areas are shown in yellow and visual areas in purple. Areas 20, 21, 37, and 38, the inferotemporal cortex, are often referred to by von Economo's designation, TE. (C) The temporal-lobe gyri visible in a medial view. The parahippocampal gyrus includes areas TF and TH (see Figure 15.3D). The uncus is the anterior extension of the hippocampal formation.

Subdivisions of the Temporal Cortex

Brodmann identified 10 temporal areas, but more-recent studies have identified many more areas in the monkey brain (**Figure 15.3**). Likely, more areas exist in the human brain as well. We can divide the human temporal regions on the lateral surface into those that are auditory (Brodmann's areas 41, 42, and 22 in Figure 15.1B) and those that form the ventral visual stream on the lateral temporal lobe (areas 20, 21, 37, and 38 in Figure 15.1B). The visual regions are often referred to as **inferotemporal cortex** or by von Economo's designation, TE, which was later elaborated by von Bonin and Bailey (Figure 15.3B).

The temporal sulci enfold a lot of cortex, as you can see in the frontal views at the bottom of Figure 15.2. In particular, the lateral (Sylvian) fissure contains tissue forming the **insula**, which includes the gustatory cortex as well as the auditory association cortex.

The superior temporal sulcus (STS) separates the superior and middle temporal gyri and houses a significant amount of neocortex as well. Figure 15.3C diagrams its many subregions of multimodal, or polymodal, cortex, which receive input, from auditory, visual, and somatic regions, from the other two polymodal regions (frontal and parietal), and from the paralimbic cortex (compare Figure 10.12).

The medial temporal region (limbic cortex) includes the amygdala and adjacent cortex (uncus), the hippocampus and surrounding cortex (subiculum, entorhinal cortex, perirhinal cortex), and the fusiform gyrus (see Figure 15.2). The entorhinal cortex is Brodmann's area 28, and the perirhinal cortex comprises Brodmann's areas 35 and 36.

Cortical areas TH and TF, at the posterior end of the temporal lobe in Figure 15.3D, are often referred to as

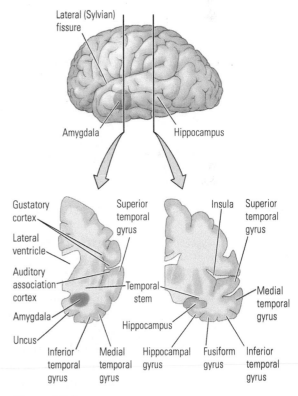

Lateral (Sylvian) fissure

Amygdala
Hippocampus

Gustatory cortex
Lateral ventricle
Auditory association cortex
Amygdala
Uncus

Superior temporal gyrus

Temporal stem

Hippocampus

Inferior temporal gyrus
Medial temporal gyrus
Hippocampal gyrus

Insula
Superior temporal gyrus

Medial temporal gyrus

Fusiform gyrus
Inferior temporal gyrus

Figure 15.2 ▲

Internal Structure of the Temporal Lobe (Top) Lateral view of the left hemisphere illustrating the relative positions of the amygdala and hippocampus buried deep within the temporal lobe. The vertical black lines indicate the approximate location of the coronal sections in the bottom illustration. (Bottom) Frontal views through the left hemisphere map the temporal lobe's cortical and subcortical regions.

Figure 15.3 ▶

Cytoarchitectonic Regions of the Temporal Cortex of the Rhesus Monkey (A) Brodmann's areas. (B) Von Bonin and Bailey's areas. (C) and (D) Lateral and ventral views of Seltzer and Pandya's parcellation showing the multimodal areas in the STS. The subareas revealed in part C are normally not visible from the surface. In D, cortical areas designated TH and TF by von Economo are often referred to as the parahippocampal cortex.

(A) Brodmann's areas

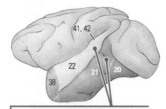

Auditory areas are yellow and visual areas are purple.

(B) Von Bonin and Bailey's areas

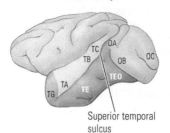

Superior temporal sulcus

(C) Lateral view

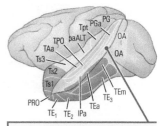

Banks of the STS spread open to show its many subareas.

(D) Ventral view

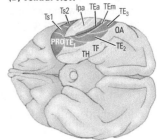

the parahippocampal cortex. The fusiform gyrus and inferior temporal gyrus are functionally part of the lateral temporal cortex (see Figures 15.1C and 15.2).

The cortical region lying along the boundary of the temporal and parietal lobes is often called the **temporal–parietal junction** (TPJ). This abstract label refers roughly to the region at the end of the Sylvian fissure, including the ventral regions of the angular and supramarginal gyri (the inferior parietal lobe shown in Figure 14.1A) and adjacent temporal cortex. The TPJ is consistently shown to be active in neuroimaging studies investigating attention, memory, language, and social processing. Thus, the TPJ is proposed as central to decision making in a social context (see Chapter 22; for a review see Carter and Huettel, 2013).

Connections of the Temporal Cortex

The temporal lobes are rich in internal connections—afferent projections from the sensory systems and efferent projections to the parietal and frontal association regions, limbic system, and basal ganglia. The neocortex of the left and right temporal lobes is connected by the corpus callosum, whereas the medial temporal cortex and amygdala are connected by the anterior commissure.

Results of studies on the monkey's temporocortical connections reveal five distinct types of cortical–cortical connections, illustrated in **Figure 15.4**. Here we list the functions that each projection pathway presumably subserves:

1. **A hierarchical sensory pathway subserves stimulus recognition.**
   The hierarchical progression of connections emanates from the primary and secondary auditory and visual areas, ending in the temporal pole (Figure 15.4A). The visual projections form the ventral stream of visual processing, whereas the auditory projections form a parallel ventral stream of auditory processing.

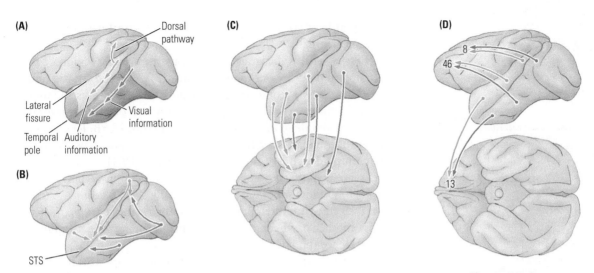

Figure 15.4 ▲

Major Intracortical Connections of the Monkey's Temporal Lobe
(A) Auditory and visual information progress ventrally from the primary regions toward the temporal pole en route to the medial temporal regions. Auditory information also forms a dorsal pathway to the posterior parietal cortex. (B) Auditory, visual, and somatic outputs go to the multimodal regions of the STS. (C) Auditory and visual information goes to the medial temporal region, including the amygdala and the hippocampal formation. (D) Auditory and visual information goes to three prefrontal regions, areas 8 and 46 on the dorsolateral surface and area 13 in the orbital region.

2. **A dorsal auditory pathway is concerned with directing movements with respect to auditory information.** Projecting from the auditory areas to the posterior parietal cortex (Figure 15.4A), this pathway is analogous to part of the dorsal visual pathway, which likely plays a role in detecting the spatial location of auditory inputs.

3. **A polymodal pathway probably underlies stimulus categorization.** This series of parallel projections from the visual and auditory association areas converges in the polymodal regions of the superior temporal sulcus (Figure 15.4B).

4. **A medial temporal projection crucial to long-term memory.** The projection from the auditory and visual association areas into the medial temporal, or limbic, regions goes first to the perirhinal cortex, then to the entorhinal cortex, and finally into the hippocampal formation or the amygdala or both (Figure 15.4C). The hippocampal projection forms the **perforant pathway** that, when disrupted, results in major dysfunction of hippocampal activity.

5. **A frontal-lobe projection necessary for various aspects of movement control, short-term memory, and affect.** This series of parallel projections reaches from the temporal association areas to the frontal lobe (Figure 15.4D).

These five projection pathways play unique roles in the temporal-lobe functions we describe in Section 15.2.

Anatomy of the Ventral Stream

Ungerleider and Mishkin (1982) originally portrayed the ventral stream as a hierarchical pathway traveling from the occipital cortex to the temporal pole. Much more is now known about that pathway, leading Ungerleider, Mishkin, and their colleagues (Kravitz et al., 2013) to propose a modified anatomical and functional network. In their formulation, shown for a macaque brain in

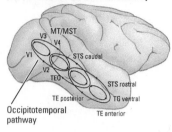

(A) Ventral stream intrinsic connectivity

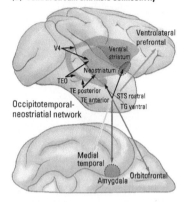

(B) Ventral stream extrinsic connectivity

Figure 15.5 ▲

The Ventral Stream Expanded (A) Far from a single hierarchical pathway moving along the temporal lobe, the intrinsic connectivity of the ventral stream occipitotemporal pathway comprises a series of overlapping, recurrent networks of differing sizes, represented by ovals in the diagram: medial temporal (MT) and medial superior temporal (MST) areas. (B) A schematic of the extrinsic connectivity of the ventral stream occipitotemporal–neostriatial network shows that all temporal visual regions project to the neostriatum. In addition, at least six distinct pathways emanate from the anterior region of area TE. (Information from Kravitz et al., 2013, Figure 2.)

Figure 15.5, at least six distinct cortical and subcortical pathways comprise the ventral stream.

In the first, a set of subcortical projections from every region of the occipitotemporal pathway outlined in Figure 15.5A extends to the **neostriatum** (or *striatum*), comprising the caudate nucleus plus putamen of the basal ganglia. These projections form the occipitotemporal–neostriatal network diagrammed at the top of Figure 15.5B. Kravitz and colleagues propose that this network functions to support types of habit and skill learning dependent on vision (see Section 18.3).

In the second pathway, amygdala-bound projections from inferotemporal regions allow processing of emotionally salient stimuli. A third pathway travels from inferotemporal cortex to the *ventral striatum* (nucleus accumbens, another basal ganglia component) to support the assignment of stimulus valence (potency).

The three remaining pathways illustrated in Figure 15.5B project from inferotemporal cortex to other cortical regions. The medial temporal, orbitofrontal, and ventrolateral prefrontal pathways are involved, respectively, in long-term memory, object–reward associations, and object working memory.

15.2 A Theory of Temporal-Lobe Function

The multifunctional temporal lobe houses the primary auditory cortex, secondary auditory and visual cortex, limbic cortex, and the amygdala and hippocampus. The hippocampus works in concert with cortical object recognition and memory to play a special role in organizing memories of objects in space. The amygdala adds affective tone to sensory input and memories. On the basis of the cortical anatomy, we can identify three basic sensory functions of the temporal cortex:

1. Processing auditory input

2. Visual object recognition

3. Long-term storage of sensory input—that is, memory

Temporal-lobe functions are best understood by considering how the brain analyzes sensory stimuli as they enter the nervous system. Imagine you are hiking in the woods. On your journey, you notice many different birds, and you decide to keep a mental list of the species you encounter so that you can tell your sister, an avid birder.

As you walk along, you suddenly stop and back up—you have encountered a rattlesnake in the middle of the path. You decide to change routes and look for birds elsewhere! What temporal-lobe functions take part in your experience?

Sensory Processes

To search for different birds, you need to be aware of the specific colors, shapes, and sizes of birds that you encounter. This process of object recognition is the function of the ventral visual pathway in the temporal lobe.

You also need to categorize the birds quickly, because they often fly away. You do so by using information that varies in perspective from sighting to sighting (for example, seeing a side view versus a rear view). Developing object categories is crucial to both perception and memory and depends on the inferortemporal cortex, area TE (see Figure 15.1B).

Categorization may require your directed attention because certain characteristics of stimuli likely play a more important role in classification than do others. For example, classifying two different yellow birds requires directing attention away from color and focusing on the birds' shapes, sizes, and other characteristics. Damage to the temporal cortex leads to deficits in identifying and categorizing stimuli. There is no difficulty in locating the stimulus or recognizing that it is present, however, because these activities are functions of the posterior parietal and primary sensory areas, respectively (see Section 14.2).

As you walk along, you may also hear birdsong, and you need to match songs with visual input. This process of matching visual and auditory information is called **cross-modal matching**. It likely depends on the cortex of the superior temporal sulcus.

As you see more and more birds, you must form memories that you can access later. Furthermore, as you see different birds, you must access their names from your memory. These long-term memory processes depend on the entire ventral visual stream as well as the paralimbic cortex of the medial temporal region.

Affective Responses

When you encounter the snake, you first hear its rattle, which alerts you, and you stop. As you scan the ground, you see and identify the rattlesnake, and your heart rate and blood pressure rise. Your affective response is a function of the amygdala. Associating sensory input and emotion is crucial for learning because stimuli become associated with their positive, negative, or neutral consequences, and behavior is modified accordingly.

In the absence of this affective system, all stimuli would be treated equivalently. Consider the consequences of failing to associate the rattlesnake, which is poisonous, with the consequences of being bitten. Or consider being unable to associate good feelings (such as love) with a specific person. Laboratory animals with amygdala lesions become very placid and do not react emotionally to threatening stimuli. For example, monkeys that were formerly terrified of snakes become indifferent to them and may even reach to pick them up.

Spatial Navigation

When you change routes to avoid the snake, you use the hippocampus, which contains cells that code places in space. Together, these cells allow you to navigate in space and to remember where you are.

As we consider these general functions of the temporal lobes—sensory, affective, and navigational—we see that losing them has devastating consequences for behavior: an inability to perceive or remember events, including language, and a loss of affect. But a person lacking these temporal-lobe functions would be able to use the dorsal visual system to make visually guided movements and, under many circumstances, would appear rather typical.

The Superior Temporal Sulcus and Biological Motion

Animals engage in an additional temporal-lobe function we did not consider in the hiking example: *biological motion*, movements that have particular relevance to a species. For example, our eyes, faces, mouths, hands, and bodies make movements that can have social meanings. We shall see that the superior temporal sulcus analyzes biological motion.

The STS receives multimodal inputs that play a role in categorizing stimuli. A major category is social perception, which includes analyzing actual or implied body movements that provide socially relevant information. This information plays an important role in **social cognition**, a theory of mind that allows us to develop hypotheses about other people's intentions. For example, the direction of a person's gaze provides us considerable information about what that person is—or is not—attending to.

Truett Allison and colleagues (2000) proposed that cells in the STS play a key role in social cognition. For example, cells in the monkey's STS respond to various forms of biological motion, including the direction of eye gaze, head movement, mouth movement, facial expression, and hand movement. For social animals such as primates, knowledge about biological motion is critical for inferring the intentions of others. As illustrated in **Figure 15.6**, imaging studies show activation along the STS as people perceive various forms of biological motion.

An important correlate of mouth movements is vocalization, so we might predict that regions of the STS are also implicated in perceiving species-typical sounds. In monkeys, cells in the superior temporal gyrus, which is adjacent to the STS and sends connections to it, show a preference for "monkey calls," and imaging studies in humans show that the superior temporal gyrus is activated both by human vocalizations and by melodic sequences.

We could predict activation in some part of the STS in response to the combination of visual stimuli (mouth movements) and talking or singing. Presumably, talking and singing can be perceived as complex forms of biological motion. We could predict that, if people have temporal-lobe injuries that lead to impairments in analyzing biological motion, there is likely a correlated deficit in social awareness. Indeed, there is.

Studies by David Perrett and his colleagues (see review by Barraclough and Perrett, 2011) illustrate the nature of processing in the STS. They showed that neurons in the superior temporal sulcus may be responsive to particular faces seen head-on, faces viewed in profile, posture of the head, or even to particular facial expressions. Furthermore, auditory sounds that match the facial expression modulate the activity of about 25 percent of these "face cells." Perrett and colleagues (1990) also showed that some STS cells are maximally sensitive to primate bodies moving in a particular direction, another characteristic biological motion (**Figure 15.7**). This finding is remarkable because the basic configuration of the stimulus is identical as the body moves in different directions; only the direction changes.

Visual Processing in the Temporal Lobe

Recall that discrete visual regions beyond those in the occipital lobe, including specialized facial and object-recognition zones, process information within the ventral stream (see Table 13.1). A Herculean study by Uri Hasson and his

(A) Left hemisphere

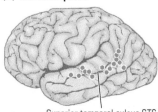

Superior temporal sulcus STS

(B) Right hemisphere

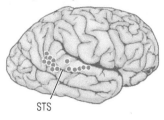

STS

Figure 15.6 ▲

Perceiving Biological Motion Summary of activation (indicated by dots) of the STS region in the left (A) and right (B) hemispheres imaged during the perception of biological motion. (Information from Allison, Puce, and McCarthy, 2000.)

colleagues (2004) demonstrates the role of these regions in natural vision. These investigators allowed participants to freely view a 30-minute segment from the feature film *The Good, the Bad, and the Ugly*, while monitoring cortical activity using fMRI. The investigators reasoned that such rich, complex visual stimulation would be far more similar to ecological vision than are the highly constrained visual stimuli typically used in the laboratory.

Another goal of the free-viewing study was to determine how similar brain activity was in different people by correlating the activity of five individuals watching the same film segment. To do so, the investigators normalized all five brains using a standard coordinate system and then smoothed the data, using sophisticated statistical procedures to allow analysis. They made three principal findings.

First, as shown in **Figure 15.8**A, extensive activity throughout the entire temporal lobe was highly correlated across participants. Thus, the brains of different individuals tended to act in unison during the free viewing, both in the auditory and visual regions of the temporal lobe and in the STS and cingulate regions. This surprising activity coherence implies that a large expanse of the human cortex is stereotypically responsive to naturalistic audiovisual stimuli.

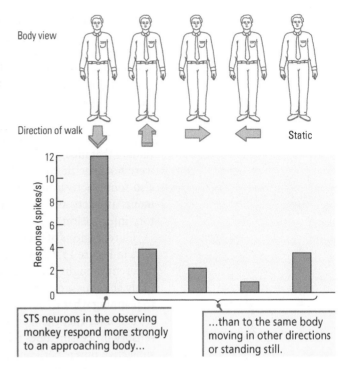

Body view

Direction of walk

Static

STS neurons in the observing monkey respond more strongly to an approaching body...

...than to the same body moving in other directions or standing still.

Figure 15.7 ▲

Neuronal Sensitivity to Body-Movement Direction (Top) Schematic front view of an approaching body. (Bottom) The histogram illustrates a far greater response in STS neurons to a body that approaches the observing monkey than to the same view of the body moving away, to the right and to the left, or stationary. (Data from Perrett et al., 1990.)

(A)

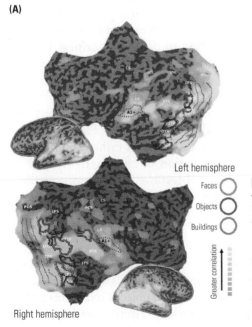

Left hemisphere

Faces
Objects
Buildings

Greater correlation

Right hemisphere

(B)

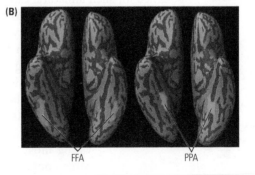

FFA   PPA

Figure 15.8 ◄

Brain Activity During Natural Vision (A) Correlation in brain activity among five participants watching a segment of the movie *The Good, the Bad, and the Ugly*. The ventral stream is coincidentally active in all participants, but there is little coherence in the rest of the brain. (B) Regional selectivity of activity for specific visual stimuli. The fusiform face area (FFA) is active for faces, and the parahippocampal place area (PPA) is active for scenes. (Information modified with permission from Hasson, U., Y. Nir, I. Levy, G. Fuhrmann, and R. Malach. "Intersubject synchronization of cortical activity during natural vision." *Science* 303, 5664 (2004): pp.1634–1640.)

Second, although a general activation of the temporal cortex occurred during the film clip, selective activations were related to the film's precise moment-to-moment content. Figure 15.7B reveals that, when the participants viewed close-ups of faces, they showed high activity in the fusiform face area (FFA) (see Grill-Spector et al., 2004), but when they viewed broad scenes, they showed enhanced activity in the nearby parahippocampal place area (PPA). Later, when Hassan and his colleagues showed participants static views of faces or places, they found increased fMRI signals in precisely the same regions, a finding that nicely validates their free-viewing results. The selective activations were not specific to visual processing, however, inasmuch as the investigators also found activations of the postcentral hand region related to hand movements and activations of the auditory cortex related to specific types of auditory information.

Third, regions of the parietal and frontal lobes showed no intersubject coherence in Figure 15.7A. As participants viewed the film, they may have had widely different thought patterns beyond the sensory processing. Such thoughts were likely about past experiences related to the film content or perhaps even related to planning what to have for supper once the experiment was over. In addition, we can infer that the fact that the film clip produced remarkable coherence in sensory processing does not imply coherence among the different participants' subjective film experiences.

Selective activation of areas FFA and PPA (Figure 15.7B) related to categories of visual stimulation that include widely different exemplars of the specific categories leads us to wonder how specialized cortical regions treat such dissimilar objects equivalently. Not only are different views of the same object linked together as being equivalent but different objects also appear to be linked together as being part of the same category. The automatic categorization of sensory information must be at least partly learned because we categorize manufactured objects such as cars or furniture. It is unlikely that the brain is innately designed for such unnatural categorizations. So how are they learned?

One way to address this question is to look for changes in neural activity as participants learn categories. Kenji Tanaka (1996) began by attempting to determine critical features for activating neurons in the monkey inferotemporal cortex. He and his colleagues presented many three-dimensional animal and plant representations to find the effective stimuli for given cells. Then they tried to determine necessary and sufficient properties of these cells. Tanaka found that activating most cells in area TE requires rather complex features containing a combination of characteristics such as orientation, size, color, and texture. Furthermore, as illustrated in **Figure 15.9**, he found that cells with similar, although slightly different, selectivity tend to cluster vertically in columns.

These cells are not identical in their stimulus selectivity, so an object is likely represented not by the activity of a single cell but rather by the activity of many cells within a columnar module. Tanaka speculated that an object's representation by multiple cells in a module in which selectivity varies from cell

Figure 15.9 ▼

Columnar Organization in Area TE Cells with slightly different selectivities cluster in elongated vertical columns perpendicular to the cortical surface.

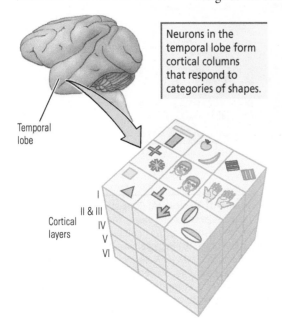

Neurons in the temporal lobe form cortical columns that respond to categories of shapes.

Temporal lobe

Cortical layers

I
II & III
IV
V
VI

to cell and effective stimuli largely overlap can provide the brain a way to minimize the effect of small changes in input images and lead to the categorization of similar objects.

Tanaka and others have described two other remarkable features of inferotemporal neurons in monkeys. First, experience alters the stimulus specificity of these neurons. In a period of 1 year, monkeys were trained to discriminate 28 complex shapes. The stimulus preferences of inferotemporal neurons were then determined from a larger set of animal and plant models. Among the trained monkeys, 39% of the inferotemporal neurons gave a maximum response to some of the stimuli used in training. This percentage compared with only 9% of the neurons in naïve monkeys.

This result confirms that the temporal lobe's role in visual processing is not determined genetically but is subject to experience, even in adults. We can speculate that this experience-dependent characteristic allows the visual system to adapt to different demands in a changing visual environment. This feature is important for human visual recognition abilities that face differing demands depending on the type of environment they are confronting, such as forests, open plains, or urban areas. In addition, experience-dependent visual neurons ensure that we can identify visual stimuli that never have been encountered over the evolution of the human brain.

The second interesting feature of inferotemporal neurons is that they not only may process visual input but also may provide a mechanism for internally representing images of objects. Joaquin Fuster and John Jervey (1982) first demonstrated that, if monkeys are shown specific objects that are to be remembered, neurons in the monkey cortex continue to discharge during the "memory" period (see Figure 18.17). These selective neuronal discharges may provide the basis of working memory for the stimuli. Furthermore, these discharges may provide the basis for visual imagery, discussed in Section 13.6. That is, the discharge of groups of neurons selective for characteristics of particular objects may provide mental images of those objects in their absence.

Are Faces Special?

Most of us probably spend more time looking at faces than at any other single stimulus. Infants prefer to look at faces almost from birth, and adults are excellent at identifying familiar faces despite wide variations in expression and viewing angles, even when the faces are disguised with beards, spectacles, or hats. Faces also convey a wealth of social information, and we humans are unique among primates in spending a good deal of time looking directly at the faces of other members of our species.

The importance of faces as visual stimuli has led to the idea that a special pathway exists in the visual system for analyzing them (see Farah, 1998, for a review). Several lines of evidence support this view. In the first place, results of studies with monkeys show neurons in the temporal lobe specifically tuned to different faces, with some cells attuned to facial identity and others to facial expression. In the second place, inverting a photograph of any object that has a usual right side up makes it harder to recognize, but the effect on faces is disproportionate (see a review by Valentine, 1988).

Similarly, we are particularly sensitive to the configuration of upright faces. The classic "Thatcher illusion" shown in **Figure 15.10** illustrates this effect.

Figure 15.10 ▶

The Thatcher Illusion Look at the face of the late British Prime Minister Margaret Thatcher as presented (upside down) and then invert the page and look again. The inverted face offers a compelling illusion of normalcy, but in the upright view, the reconfigured face appears hideous. Lady Thatcher was the original subject of the illusion that now bears her name. (Thompson P, 1980, "Margaret Thatcher: a new illusion" *Perception* 9(4) 483–484, 1980. Pion Ltd, London.www.perceptionweb.com)

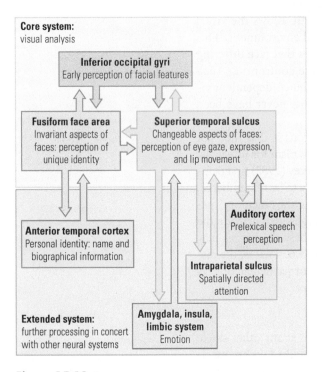

Figure 15.11 ▲

A Model of the Distributed Human Neural System for Face Perception The model is divided into a core system (top), consisting of occipital and temporal regions, and an extended system (bottom), including regions that are part of neural systems for other cognitive and affective functions. (Information from Haxby, Hoffman, and Gobbini, 2000.)

The importance of an upright orientation to facial perception is also seen in imaging studies. For example, James Haxby and his colleagues (1999) showed that the same cortical regions process inverted faces and other visual stimuli, whereas upright faces are processed in a separate face-perception system. This face-perception system is surprisingly extensive and includes regions in the occipital lobe as well as several different temporal lobe regions.

Figure 15.11 summarizes a model by Haxby and colleagues (2000) in which different aspects of facial perception (such as facial expression versus identity) are analyzed in core visual areas in the occipitotemporal part of the ventral stream. Other regions form an "extended system" that includes analysis of other facial characteristics, such as emotion and lip reading. The key point is that facial analysis is unlike other visual stimuli.

Finally, a clear asymmetry exists between the temporal lobes in the analysis of faces. Right temporal lesions have a greater effect on facial processing than do similar left temporal lesions. Even in control participants, researchers can see an asymmetry in face perception.

We presented subjects and controls with photographs of faces, as illustrated in **Figure 15.12**. Photographs B and C are composites of the right or the left sides, respectively, of the original face shown in photograph A. Asked to identify which composite most resembled the original face, controls consistently matched the left side of photograph A to its composite in photograph C. They did so whether the photographs were presented upright or inverted. Furthermore, patients with either right temporal or right parietal removals consistently failed to match either side of the face in either the upright or the inverted presentation.

The results of this split-faces test not only show a temporal-lobe asymmetry in facial processing but also speak to the nature of our perceptions of our own faces. Self-perception provides a unique example of visual perception because your image of your face comes largely from looking in a mirror, where the image is reversed, whereas others have a direct view of your face. Inspecting the images in Figure 15.12 illustrates the implications of this difference.

(A) Original face

(B) Composite of right sides

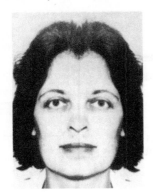

(C) Composite of left sides

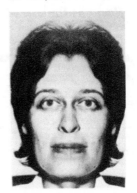

◎ Figure 15.12 ◄

The Split-Faces Test
Participants who were asked which of the two pictures, B or C, more closely resembles picture A chose picture C significantly more often than picture B. Picture C corresponds to the part of picture A falling in the left visual field. Patients with right temporal or parietal removals failed to match either side of the face consistently. (Research from Kolb, B., B. Milner, and L. Taylor, 1983.)

Photograph A is the image that other people see of this woman and, because there is a left-visual-field bias in our perception, most right-handers choose photograph C as the picture most resembling the original. Consider the choice of the woman herself, however. Her common view of her face (in the mirror) is the reverse of ours; hence she is more likely to choose (and in fact did choose) composite photograph B as most resembling her own face.

An intriguing consequence of our biased self-facial image is our opinion of personal photographs. Many people complain about not being photogenic: their photographs are never taken at the correct angle, their hair wasn't just right, and so on. The problem may be rather different: we are accustomed to seeing a mirror image of ourselves. When we view a photograph, we are biased to look at the side of the face that we do not normally perceive selectively in the mirror. Indeed, we appear not to see ourselves as others see us. The more asymmetrical the face, the less flattering the person sees his or her image to be.

Auditory Processing in the Temporal Lobe

As discussed in Section 8.2, sound waves reaching the ear stimulate a cascade of mechanical and neural events—in the cochlea, brainstem, and eventually the auditory cortex—that result in a percept of sound. Like the visual cortex, the auditory cortex has multiple regions, each having a tonotopic map. The precise functions of these maps are poorly understood, but the ultimate goal is to perceive sound-making objects, locate sound, and make movements in relation to sounds.

Many cells in the auditory cortex respond to specific frequencies, often referred to as sound pitches, or to multiples of those frequencies. Two most interesting sound types for humans are language and music.

Speech Perception

Speech differs from other auditory input in three fundamental ways:

1. Speech sounds come largely from three restricted frequency ranges known as *formants*. **Figure 15.13**A illustrates sound spectrograms of different two-formant syllables. Dark bars indicate the frequency bands in more detail in Figure 15.13B, which shows that the syllables differ both in the onset frequency of the second (higher) formant and in the onset time of the consonant. Vowel sounds occupy a constant frequency band, but consonants show rapid changes in frequency.

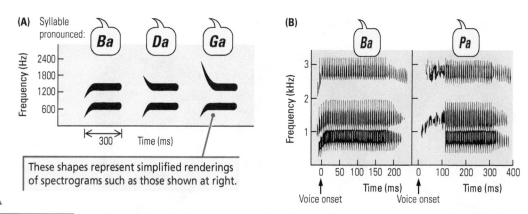

These shapes represent simplified renderings of spectrograms such as those shown at right.

Figure 15.13 ▲

Speech Sounds (A) Schematic spectrograms of three different syllables, each made up of two formants (speech sounds). (B) Spectrograms of syllables differing in voice onset time. (Data from Springer, 1979.)

2. The same speech sounds vary from one context in which they are heard to another, yet all are perceived as being the same. Thus, the sound spectrogram of the letter *d* in English is different in the words *deep, deck,* and *duke,* yet a listener perceives them all as *d.* The auditory system must have a mechanism for categorizing varying sounds as equivalent, and this mechanism must be affected by experience, because a major obstacle to learning foreign languages in adulthood is the difficulty of learning equivalent sound categories. Thus, a word's spectrogram depends on context—the words that precede and follow it. (There may be a parallel mechanism for musical categorization.)

3. Speech sounds change very rapidly in relation to one another, and the sequence of the sounds is critical to understanding. According to Alvin Liberman (1982), we can perceive speech at rates of as many as 30 segments per second, although typical speech is from about 8 to 10 segments per second. Speech perception at the higher rates is truly amazing because it far exceeds the auditory system's ability to transmit all of the speech as separate pieces of auditory information. Nonspeech noise, for example, is perceived as a buzz at a rate of only about 5 segments/per second.

Clearly, the human brain must recognize and analyze language sounds in a special way, much as the bat's echolocation system is specialized in the bat brain. Likely, that special mechanism for speech perception is in the left temporal lobe. This function may not be unique to humans because results of studies in both monkeys and rats show specific deficits in perceiving species-typical vocalizations after left temporal lesions.

Music Perception

Music is fundamentally different from language, which relies on individual auditory elements, whereas music relies on relations between auditory elements. Consider that a tune is defined not by the pitches of its constituent tones but rather by the arrangement of the pitches' duration and the intervals between them. Musical sounds may differ from one another in three aspects: loudness, timbre, and pitch (see Figure 8.9).

- **Loudness,** although related to the intensity of a sound as measured in decibels, refers to the subjective magnitude of an auditory sensation judged by a given person as "very loud," "soft," "very soft," and so forth.

- **Timbre** refers to the distinctive character of a sound, the quality that distinguishes it from all other sounds of similar pitch and loudness. For example, we can distinguish the sound of a violin from that of a trombone even though they may play the same note at the same loudness.

- **Pitch** refers to the position of a sound in a musical scale, as judged by the listener. Pitch is clearly related to frequency, the vibration rate of a sound wave. In regard to speech, pitch contributes to "tone" of voice, known as **prosody**.

Frequency and Pitch Consider the note middle C, described as a pattern of those sound frequencies depicted in **Figure 15.14**. The amplitude of acoustical energy is conveyed by the darkness of the tracing in the spectrogram. The lowest component of this note is the *fundamental frequency* of the sound pattern—264 Hz, or middle C. Frequencies above the fundamental frequency are known as *overtones* or *partials*. Overtones are generally simple multiples of the fundamental (for example, 2 × 264, or 528 Hz; 4 × 264, or 1056 Hz), as shown in Figure 15.14. Overtones that are multiples of the fundamental are known as *harmonics*.

If the fundamental frequency is removed from a note by means of electronic filters, the overtones are sufficient to determine the pitch of the fundamental frequency—a phenomenon known as *periodicity pitch*.

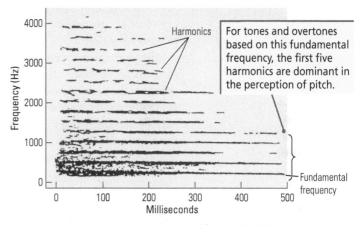

Figure 15.14 ▲

Spectrographic Display of the Steady-State Part of Middle C (264 Hz) Played on a Piano Bands of acoustical energy are present at the fundamental frequency as well as at its integer multiples (harmonics). (Data source: Ritsma, 1967.)

The ability to determine pitch from the overtones alone is probably due to the fact that the difference between the frequencies of the various harmonics is equal to the fundamental frequency (for example, 792 Hz − 528 Hz = 264 Hz = the fundamental). The auditory system can determine this difference, and we perceive the fundamental frequency.

An important aspect of pitch perception is that, although we can generate (and perceive) the fundamental frequency, we still perceive the complex tones of the harmonics, or *spectral pitch*. When individuals hear complex sounds and are asked to judge the direction of shifts in pitch, some will base their judgments on the fundamental and others on spectral pitch. This difference is not related to musical training but rather to a basic difference in temporal-lobe organization.

The primary auditory cortex of the right temporal lobe appears to make this periodicity–pitch discrimination. For example, Robert Zatorre (2001) found that patients with right temporal lobectomies that include the primary auditory cortex (area 41 or **Heschl's gyrus**; see Figure 15.1B) are impaired at making pitch discriminations when the fundamental is absent but make such discriminations normally when the fundamental is present. These patients are also impaired at identifying the direction of a pitch change (see Tramo et al., 2002).

Rhythm Timing is a critical component of music, and two types of time relations are fundamental to the rhythm of musical sequences: segmentation of sequences of pitches into groups based on the duration of the sounds and identification of temporal regularity, or beat, also called *meter*. These two components can be dissociated by having participants tap a rhythm versus keeping time with the beat (such as in spontaneous foot tapping with the strong beat).

Isabelle Peretz and Robert Zatorre (2005) concluded that studies of patients with temporal-lobe injuries as well as neuroimaging studies support the conclusion that the left temporal lobe plays a major role in temporal grouping for rhythm, whereas the right temporal lobe plays a complementary role in meter. But they also noted that a motor component of rhythm is broadly distributed to include the supplementary motor cortex, premotor cortex, cerebellum, and basal ganglia.

Music Memory Music is more than perceiving pitch, rhythm, timbre, and loudness. Peretz and Zatorre reviewed the many other features of music and the brain, including music memory, emotion, performance (both singing and playing), music reading, and the effect of musical training. The contribution of memory to music processing is crucial because music unfolds over time, allowing us to perceive a tune.

Although injury to either temporal lobe impairs learning melodies, retention of melodies is more affected by right temporal injury. Although both hemispheres take part in producing music, the right temporal lobe appears to play a generally greater role in producing melody and the left temporal lobe appears to play a generally greater role in rhythm. Zatorre and Belin (2001) suggested that the right temporal lobe has a special function in extracting pitch from sound, whether the sound is speech or music.

Music and Brain Morphology We learned from Kenji Tanaka's studies of visual learning that cells in the temporal lobe alter their perceptual functions with experience. The same appears true of musical experience. Peretz and Zatorre reviewed noninvasive imaging studies and concluded not only that the brains of professional musicians have more-pronounced responses to musical information than do those of nonmusicians but also that musicians' brains are morphologically different in the area of Heschl's gyrus. Peter Schneider and his colleagues (2005) used MRI to estimate the volume of gray and white matter in Heschl's gyrus and found much larger volumes in both temporal lobes in the musicians (**Figure 15.15**).

The gray-matter differences are positively correlated with musical aptitude: the greater the aptitude, the larger the gray-matter volume. These researchers also found that fundamental-pitch listeners exhibit a pronounced leftward asymmetry of gray-matter volume in Heschl's gyrus, whereas spectral-pitch listeners have a rightward asymmetry, independent of musical training (see Figure 15.15B). The Schneider results imply that innate differences in brain morphology are related to the way in which pitch is processed and that some innate differences are related to musical ability.

Practice and experience with music seem likely to be related to anatomical differences in the temporal cortex as well, but this relation will be difficult to demonstrate without brain measurements before and after intense musical training. Musical training, however, not only is a powerful instrument for inducing brain plasticity in musicians but also may play an important therapeutic role in combating the effects of brain injury and aging (see Section 25.6 and the review by Herholz and Zatorre, 2012).

We have emphasized the role of the temporal lobes in music, but like language, which is distributed in the frontal lobe as well, music perception and performance include the inferior frontal cortex in both hemispheres. Vanessa

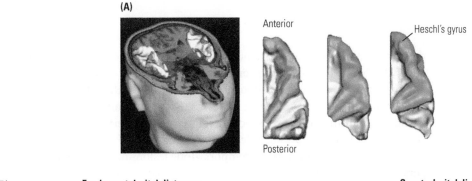

(A)

Anterior

Posterior

Heschl's gyrus

(B)

Fundamental-pitch listeners
Musicians

L

Nonmusicians

Spectral-pitch listeners
Musicians

R

A

Nonmusicians

Sluming and her colleagues (2002) have shown that professional orchestral musicians have significantly more gray matter in Broca's area on the left. This frontal-lobe effect may be related to similarities in aspects of expressive output in both language and music.

Gabriel Donnay and colleagues (2014) explored the role of music in interpersonal communication by measuring activation in the language zones when professional jazz musicians interact to improvise. Such improvisation is akin to a musical conversation: jazz musicians introduce novel melodic material, respond to each other's ideas, and elaborate or modify as they play.

The participants played a keyboard in the fMRI scanner, improvising with another musician in the control room. The results revealed that improvised musical communication—but not a memorized musical piece—activated the left hemisphere cortical regions classically associated with language (Broca's and Wernicke's areas) as well as their right-hemisphere homologues. These data suggest that at least parts of the language networks are not specific for spoken language but rather have some general role in auditory communication broadly defined. Other language regions in the inferior parietal cortex (angular gyrus, supramarginal gyrus) related to semantic processing (knowledge about things) showed reduced activation, suggesting a fundamental difference between the ways music and language convey meaning.

Asymmetry of Temporal-Lobe Function

A comparison of the behavioral effects of left and right temporal lobectomy reveals that specific memory defects vary according to which side has the lesion. Damage to the left temporal lobe is associated with deficits in verbal memory; damage to the right temporal lobe is associated with deficits in nonverbal memory (for example, for faces). Similarly, left temporal lesions are associated with

Figure 15.15 ▲

Music and Brain Morphology (A) At left, a three-dimensional cross section through the head showing the primary auditory cortex (AC) in each hemisphere, with the location of auditory evoked potentials shown at red and blue markers. At right, reconstructed dorsal views of the right AC surface showing the difference in morphology among three people. Heschl's gyrus is shown in red. (B) Examples from individual brains of musicians (top row) and nonmusicians (bottom row) showing the difference in morphology between people who hear fundamental frequency and those who hear spectral pitch. Heschl's gyrus is bigger on the left in the former group and on the right in the latter group and larger overall in the musicians. (Reprinted by permission from Macmillan Publishers Ltd: P. Schneider, V. Sluming, N. Roberts, M. Scherg, R. Goebel, H. J. Specht, H.G. Dosch, S. Bleeck, C. Stippich, and A. Rupp. "Structural and functional asymmetry of lateral Heschl's gyrus reflects pitch perception preference." *Nature Neuroscience* Vol. 8, Issue 9, (2005): pp. 1241–1247.)

deficits in processing speech sounds, whereas right temporal lesions are associated with deficits in processing certain aspects of music.

Little is known, however, about the relative roles of the left and right temporal lobes in social and affective behavior. Right- but not left-temporal-lobe lesions lead to impairments in recognizing faces and facial expressions, so the two sides likely play different roles in social cognition. In fact, clinical experience dictates that left- and right-temporal-lobe lesions have different effects on personality (see Section 20.5).

Although the left and right temporal lobes are relatively specialized in their functions, do not be overly impressed by the apparent asymmetry. Substantial functional overlap is revealed in the relatively minor effects of unilateral temporal lobectomy, a striking result considering that such a large zone of the cerebral hemispheres is removed. Recall, for example, the striking recovery of function by H.H., whom we met in the chapter-opening Portrait.

It is incorrect to assume, however, that removal of both temporal lobes merely doubles the symptoms of damage seen in unilateral temporal lobectomy. Bilateral temporal-lobe removal produces dramatic effects on both memory and affect that are orders of magnitude greater than those observed subsequent to unilateral lesions, as described in Chapter 18.

◉ 15.3 Symptoms of Temporal-Lobe Lesions

Nine principal symptoms are associated with disease of the temporal lobes: (1) disturbance of auditory sensation and perception, (2) disorders of music perception, (3) disorders of visual perception, (4) disturbance in the selection of visual and auditory input, (5) impaired organization and categorization of sensory input, (6) inability to use contextual information, (7) impaired long-term memory, (8) altered personality and affective behavior, and (9) altered sexual behavior. **Table 15.1** summarizes the major symptoms of temporal-lobe damage, lists the most probable lesion sites, and cites basic references. The sections that follow sample the range of temporal-lobe disorders and their clinical assessment.

Table 15.1 **Summary of major symptoms of temporal-lobe damage** ◉

Symptoms	Most Probable Lesion Site	Basic Reference
Disturbance of auditory sensation	Areas 41, 42, 22	Vignolo, 1969; Hécaen and Albert, 1978
Disturbance of visual- and auditory-input selection	Areas TE, STS	Sparks et al., 1970; Dorff et al., 1965
Disorders of visual perception	Areas TE, STS, amygdala	Milner, 1968; Meier and French, 1968
Disorders of auditory perception	Areas 41, 42, 22	Samson and Zatorre, 1988; Swisher and Hirsch, 1972
Disorders of music perception	Superior temporal gyrus	Zatorre et al., 2002
Impaired organization and categorization of material	Areas TE, STS	Wilkins and Moscovitch, 1978; Read, 1981
Poor contextual use	Area TE	Milner, 1958
Disturbance of language comprehension	Area 22 left	Hécaen and Albert, 1978
Poor long-term memory	Areas TE, TF, TH, 28	Milner, 1970
Changes in personality and affect	Area TE, plus amygdala	Blumer and Benson, 1975; Pincus and Tucker, 1974
Changes in sexual activity	Amygdala, plus?	Blumer and Walker, 1975

Disorders of Auditory and Speech Perception

Damage to the primary visual or somatic cortex leads to a loss of conscious sensation, so it is reasonable to predict that bilateral damage to the auditory cortex will produce *cortical deafness*, an absence of neural activity in the auditory regions. Neither clinical nor animal laboratory study results support this prediction. As the Snapshot on page 418 illustrates, auditory hallucinations, which result from spontaneous activity in the auditory regions, are essentially the opposite of cortical deafness.

Auditory hallucination is the perception of sounds (hearing voices) that are not actually present. The auditory cortex plays a role in discriminating two forms of auditory processing—namely, rapidly presented stimuli and complex patterns of stimuli. Language is fast and must be analyzed quickly, whereas music generally contains relatively slower changes in frequency, but the ear must be sensitive to the small differences in frequency important in music.

Impaired auditory processing reveals the difficulty that temporal-lobe patients have in discriminating speech sounds. Although related to the common complaint among patients with left-temporal damage that people are talking too quickly, the problem is not so much the quickness of the speech; rather, it is the patient's inability to discriminate sounds presented quickly. Unimpaired people trying to learn a new language commonly encounter this difficulty.

The problem lies not only in discriminating the speech sounds but also in judging their temporal order. If a control participant is presented with two sounds, a separation of only 50 milliseconds to 60 milliseconds is sufficient to identify which sound was presented first. Patients with temporal-lobe lesions may require as much as 500 ms between two sounds, a tenfold increase, to perform at the same level. Both audioperceptual impairments—discriminating speech sounds and judging the temporal order of sounds—appear more severe after left-temporal-lobe lesions than after right-temporal-lobe lesions, a result suggesting that these auditory skills are especially important in discriminating speech sounds.

The fact that left-temporal-lobe lesions alter speech sound perception ought not be surprising: since the time of Wernicke, lesions of the left temporal association cortex (primarily area 22) have been known to produce aphasia (see Section 1.3). The classical view of **Wernicke's aphasia** associates it with disturbed word recognition, the extreme form being "word deafness," an inability to recognize words as such despite intact hearing of pure tones.

Disorders of Music Perception

As noted earlier, patients with right temporal lesions that include the primary auditory cortex are impaired at making pitch discriminations. Catherine Liegeois-Chauval and her colleagues (1998) pointed out that distinct musical processes may depend on specific cortical sites in the superior temporal gyrus (see Figure 15.1A). In their study of patients with temporal lobectomies, these investigators found that rhythm discrimination was most affected by damage to the right posterior superior temporal gyrus, whereas meter discrimination (for example, distinguishing between a waltz and a march) was more affected by anterior damage to either temporal lobe.

Although it is tempting to compartmentalize music and language on opposite sides of the brain, in fact, only certain characteristics of

▼ The alignment of the holes in this piece of bear femur found in a cave in northern Slovenia suggests that Neanderthals made a flute from it and made music with the flute at least 43,000 years ago. Like modern humans, Neanderthals probably had complementary hemispheric specialization for language and music. (Archive of the Institute of Archaeology ZRC SAZU, photo: Marko Zaplatil.)

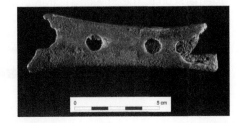

SNAPSHOT | Imaging Auditory Hallucinations

Auditory hallucinations are the most common symptom of schizophrenia, reported by about 65% of people diagnosed with the disease. Auditory hallucinations are not simply sounds: a patient hears fully formed verbal passages that appear to be coming from an external source. The patient's thoughts are usually hostile or paranoid, as in the following example:

> Days later while in the Metropolis again, I was once more startled by those same pursuers, who had threatened me several days before. It was night-time. As before, I could catch part of their talk, but, in the theatre crowds, I could see them nowhere. I heard one of them a woman, say: "You can't get away from us; we'll lay for you and get you after a while!" To add to the mystery, one of these "pursuers" repeated my thoughts aloud verbatim. I tried to elude those pursuers as before, but this time I tried to escape from them by means of subway trains, darting up and down subway exits and entrances, jumping on and off trains, until after midnight. But, at every station where I got off a train, I heard the voices of these pursuers as close as ever. (L. Percy King, from a letter written in the 1940s protesting the writer's imprisonment in a mental hospital and published in Frith [1999], p. 414)

Dierks and colleagues (1999) described an experiment with paranoid schizophrenia patients whose hallucinations could be monitored within one fMRI session. In this study, the verbal hallucinations activated the primary auditory cortex, Broca's area, and the speech zone in the posterior temporal cortex in the left hemisphere, as diagrammed in the adjacent illustration and revealed in the fMRI image. The hippocampus and amygdala also showed some activation.

These results suggest that verbal hallucinations originate in the patients' own inner language systems. The researchers proposed that activation in the auditory cortex leads to the perception that the voices are coming from an external source. The amygdala activity presumably results from the anxiety generated by hearing voices, especially hostile voices, whereas the hippocampal activity may result from the retrieval of auditory memories.

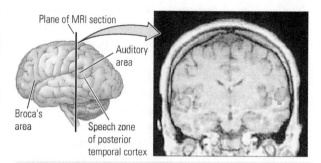

Functional MRI shows activation of primary auditory cortex as a subject with schizophrenia experiences auditory hallucinations. (Dierks, T., D. E. J. Kinden, M. Jandl, E. Formisano, R. Goebel, H. Lanfermann, and W. Singer. "Activation of Heschl's gyrus during auditory hallucinations." *Neuron* 22, 3 (1999): pp. 615–621, 1999. © Elsevier)

In contrast to auditory hallucinations, Oertel and colleagues (2007) report that visual hallucinations do not activate primary visual cortex but rather activate higher visual areas corresponding to the hallucination content (faces, bodies, scenes) and also the hippocampus. The investigators suggest that the hippocampal activation is related to retrieval of visual images from memory and the temporal cortex activity is related to the vividness of the perceptual experience.

The difference between activity in primary sensory regions related to auditory and visual hallucinations likely reflects a fundamental difference in the nature of sensory processing in these regions. Primary visual cortex does not combine basic elements (such as line orientations) into meaningful images, whereas primary auditory cortex does represent meaningful sounds such as syllables.

Dierks, T., D. E. J. Kinden, M. Jandl, E. Formisano, R. Goebel, H. Lanfermann, and W. Singer. Activation of Heschl's gyrus during auditory hallucinations. *Neuron* 22:615–621, 1999.

Frith, C. How hallucinations make themselves heard. *Neuron* 22:414–415, 1999.

Oertel, V., A. Rotarska-Jagiela, V. G. van de Ven, C. Haaenschel, K. Maurer, and D. E. J. Linden. Visual hallucinations in schizophrenia investigated with functional magnetic resonance imaging. *Psychiatry Research: Neuroimaging* 156:269–273, 2007.

musical and language input are analyzed selectively by the two hemispheres. Zatorre (2007) emphasized the key difference: the left hemisphere is concerned more with speed and the right with distinguishing frequency differences, a process called *spectral sensitivity*. He also notes that auditory processing can be influenced by other factors, such as memory and mental imagery. Thus there is an interaction between top-down processes and spectral sensitivity.

That the brain appears to have neural networks dedicated to processing language and music leads to the conclusion that both language and music have biological roots. Although this conclusion seems obvious for language, it is less obvious for music, which has often been perceived as a cultural artifact. But considerable evidence suggests that humans are born with a predisposition for processing music.

Infants show learning preferences for musical scales and are biased toward perceiving the regularities (such as harmonics) on which music is built. Peretz (2001) argued that one of the strongest bits of evidence favoring a biological basis of music is **amusia**: about 4% of people have a condition known as *congenital amusia*. They are tone deaf.

Apparently, amusic people have an abnormality in their neural networks for music, and no amount of training makes much difference. In fact, we have a colleague whose parents were both music teachers, and to their chagrin, she is amusic. She likes to note that she knows that the national anthem is being played because people stand up!

Disorders of Visual Perception

Typically, persons with temporal lobectomies do not have large visual field defects, but they do have deficits in visual perception, a result consistent with the role of the inferotemporal cortex in the ventral stream (Figure 15.5B). Such perceptual deficits were first demonstrated by Milner (1968), who found her patients with right temporal lobectomies impaired in interpreting cartoon drawings in the McGill Picture-Anomalies Test.

For example, one item illustrating a monkey in a cage features an oil painting on the cage wall—an obvious oddity or anomaly. Although patients with right temporal lesions can describe the contents of the cartoon accurately, they are impaired at recognizing the anomalous aspects of this picture and others. Similarly, on instruments such as the Mooney Closure Test or tests requiring the discrimination of complex patterns (**Figure 15.16**), patients with right-temporal-lobe damage perform very poorly. The Mooney figures are all based upon faces, and the performance deficit by right temporal lobe patients likely reflects their general impairment in facial perception and recognition—their performance on the split-faces test, for example (see Figure 15.12).

Furthermore, these patients do not appear able to perceive subtle social signals such as discreet but obvious glances at one's watch, a gesture often intended as a cue to break off

Figure 15.16 ▼

Tests for Visual Disorders
(A) Meier and French's test: the subject must identify the drawing that is different. (B) In this sample from the Gottschaldt Hidden-Figures Test, the task is detecting and tracing the sample (upper drawing) in each of the figures below it. (C) In the Rey Complex-Figure Test, the subject is asked to copy the drawing as exactly as possible. (D) Sample of the Mooney Closure Test, in which the task is to identify the face within the ambiguous shadows. (A: M. J. Meier & L. A. French. (1965) Lateralized deficits in complex visual discrimination and bilateral transfer of reminiscence following unilateral temporal lobectomy, *Neuropsychologia Volume 3, Issue 3, August 1965, Pages 261–272*, Elsevier Limited. B: Kurt Gottschaldt, Über den Einfluß der Erfahrung auf die Wahrnehmung von Figuren 1926, *Psychologische Forschung*, Copyright © 1926, Verlag von Julius Springer. C: Research from Rey, 1941. D: Mooney, C. M., Age in the development of closure ability in children. *Canadian Journal of Psychology/Revue canadienne de psychologie*, Vol 11(4), Dec 1957, 219–226. doi: 10.1037/h0083717)

(A)

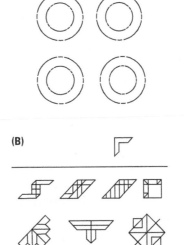

(C)

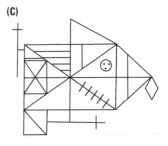

(B)

(D)

a conversation. Presumably, patients fail to perceive the visual signal's significance. Facial signals are a form of biological motion; its analysis is a function of the temporal lobe (see Section 15.2).

Disturbance of Visual- and Auditory-Input Selection

We must select from the wealth of information in our environment. Generally this selectivity is not conscious because the nervous system automatically scans input and selectively perceives the environment. (Conscious control can be exerted, of course, as when you search for an ATM to make a withdrawal.)

Selectivity in auditory perception is best illustrated by the problem of listening to two conversations simultaneously. Because it is impossible to process the two competing inputs concurrently, the auditory system adopts one of two strategies: either one conversation is ignored or attention shifts back and forth from one conversation to the other. In either case, there is a selection of input.

Selective perception in the visual system operates similarly. For example, it is not possible to watch all floor events at a gymnastics meet simultaneously. Either we focus our attention entirely on one event or shift it from event to event.

Let us now consider the person with temporal-lobe damage. Selection of both auditory and visual input is impaired but ordinarily demonstrated only by special testing procedures. Selective attention to auditory input can be tested by dichotic listening (see Figure 11.12). Recall that when subjects are presented with two words simultaneously, one in each ear, control participants report more of the words presented to the right ear; if tonal sequences are presented dichotically, there will be a left-ear advantage.

This right-ear advantage is maintained in patients with temporal-lobe lesions, but left-temporal-lobe lesions result in an overall drop in the number of words recalled. One explanation for this effect is that the nervous system has difficulty focusing selectively on the input into one ear and attempts to process all the input concurrently; as a result, performance drops significantly. H.H. from the opening Portrait had a very difficult time with the dichotic listening test, reporting only a few words even after a prolonged recovery period.

Analogous findings are reported for visual input. If two different visual stimuli are presented simultaneously, one to each visual field, damage to the left temporal lobe impairs recall of content of the right visual field, but damage to the right temporal lobe impairs recall of content in both visual fields. Again, the nervous system may now be unable to focus sufficiently on distinctive features of the stimuli to allow efficient perception and storage of the input. It is noteworthy that right temporal lesions produce bilateral deficits, whereas left temporal lesions produce unilateral ones. This difference implies that the right temporal lobe may have a greater role than the left in selective attention to visual input (see Section 22.2).

Impaired Organization and Categorization

Asked to learn a list of words such as "dog, car, bus, apple, rat, lemon, cat, truck, orange," most of us will organize the words into three categories—animals, vehicles, and fruit. If the list is later recalled, the items are likely to be recalled by category, and recall of the categories is likely to be used as an aid in recalling the items.

The ability to organize material is especially important for language and memory. For example, categorizing makes it possible to comprehend complex, extended sentences, including both the meaning of individual clauses and the information inferred from them. Organization of sensory input appears to be a function of the temporal lobes. Patients with left temporal lobectomies are impaired in their ability to categorize even single words or pictures of familiar objects.

Thus, patients have difficulty placing words or pictures into discrete categories, even when asked to do so, and they also have difficulty in using categories that most of us use automatically. For example, when these patients are given a category name (such as *animal*) and are asked to recall exemplars of the category (such as dog, cat, rat), they have difficulty, even though they are fluent in other types of tests. Given that these patients have difficulty in simple types of categorization tasks studied in the laboratory, you can imagine that their difficulty in spontaneous organization may represent a significant cognitive deficit, especially in memory for complex material.

Neurolinguists propose that another type of categorization may be undertaken in the left temporal lobe. *Semantic categories* are hierarchies of meaning in which a single word might belong to several categories simultaneously. For example, a duck belongs to the categories animal, bird, and waterfowl. Each category is a refinement of the preceding one. Patients with left posterior temporal lesions may show dysphasic symptoms in which they can recognize the broader categorization but have difficulty with the more specific ones.

Inability to Use Contextual Information

The meaning of identical stimuli can vary, depending on context. The word *fall*, for example, can refer to a season or to a tumble, depending on the context. Similarly, context may be a major cue for facial recognition. Most of us have encountered someone completely out of context (for example, while in Paris you encounter a clerk from your neighborhood store at home) and have been unable to recall who the person is until information about the context is provided.

Social situations offer a more complex example of extracting meaning from context. The interpretation of events, and indeed our role in events, depends on the social context. Thus, stimuli may be interpreted in one way when we are with our parents and in a different way when we are with our peers. A simple example of using contextual information can be found in the McGill Picture-Anomalies Test described in the earlier section on disorders of visual perception. The only clue to the correct choice in the McGill anomalies is the context.

Memory Impairment

Interest in the temporal lobes' function in memory was stimulated in the early 1950s by the discovery that bilateral removal of the medial temporal lobes, including the hippocampus and amygdala, results in amnesia for all events after the surgery (**anterograde amnesia**). It is now clear that both the medial temporal regions and the temporal neocortex are important for memory functions (see Section 18.1).

Damage to the inferotemporal cortex specifically interferes with conscious recall of information, the extent of the memory disturbance increasing in direct proportion to the amount of temporal-lobe damage. Lesions of the left temporal lobe result in impaired recall of verbal material, such as short stories and word lists, whether presented visually or aurally; lesions of the right temporal lobe result in impaired recall of nonverbal material, such as geometric drawings, faces, and tunes. Two case histories demonstrate the roles of the left and right temporal lobes in memory.

Mr. B., age 38, was suffering from an astrocytoma in the left temporal lobe. Before onset, he had been a successful executive at an oil company and was noted for his efficiency. As his tumor developed, he became forgetful, and at the time of hospital admission, his efficiency had dropped drastically: he had begun to forget appointments and other important events. Forgetfulness had become such a problem that he had begun to write notes to himself to cover his memory problem, but he often mislaid the notes, leading to even greater embarrassment.

On formal tests of memory, Mr. B. had special difficulty in recalling short stories read to him a few minutes earlier. In one test, he was read the following story from the Wechsler Memory Scale and was asked to repeat it as exactly as possible: "Anna Thompson of South Boston, employed as a scrub woman in an office building, was held up on State Street the night before and robbed of $15. She had four little children, the rent was due and they had not eaten for two days. The officers, touched by the woman's story, made up a purse for her."

Mr. B. recalled: "A woman was robbed and went to the police station where they made her a new purse. She had some children too." This performance is very poor for a person of Mr. B.'s intelligence and education. On the other hand, his immediate recall of digits was good; he could repeat strings of seven digits accurately. Similarly, his recall of geometric designs was within normal limits, illustrating the asymmetry of memory functions, because his right temporal lobe was intact.

Ms. C.'s syndrome complements Mr. B.'s. She was a bright, 22-year-old college student who had an indolent tumor of the right temporal lobe. When we first saw her, after surgery, she complained of memory loss. She performed within normal limits on formal tests of verbal memory, such as the story of Anna Thompson, but was seriously impaired on formal tests of visual memory, especially geometric drawings. For example, in one test, she was shown geometric designs for 10 seconds and then asked to draw them from memory. Ten minutes later, she was asked to draw them again. She had difficulty with immediate recall (**Figure 15.17**) and, after 10 minutes, was unable to recall any of the drawings.

Altered Affect and Personality

Although temporal-lobe disorder has been associated with disturbance of affect in humans for over a century, knowledge about the details of this role is still surprisingly fragmentary. Wilder Penfield and others reported that stimulation of the anterior and medial temporal cortex produces feelings of fear (see Section 11.2), an effect also occasionally obtained from stimulating the amygdala. Recall, too, from the chapter-opening Portrait that H.H.'s wife reported that H.H.'s personality was different after his tumor and surgery from what it had been before.

Temporal-lobe epilepsy has traditionally been associated with personality characteristics that overemphasize trivia and the petty details of daily life.

Figure 15.17 ▼

Impaired Recall The right column shows the sketch Ms. C. drew immediately after viewing each figure in the left column for 10 seconds. Note that her impairment worsens with the more complex figures. Ms. C. was unable to recall even the simplest figure 10 minutes after viewing it. (Bryan Kolb)

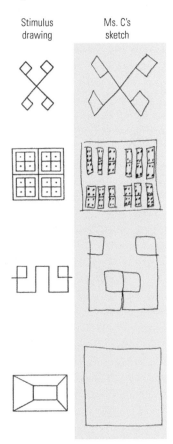

Stimulus drawing   Ms. C's sketch

Symptomatic behaviors include pedantic speech, egocentricity, perseveration in discussions of personal problems (sometimes referred to as stickiness, because one is stuck talking to the person), paranoia, preoccupation with religion, and proneness to aggressive outbursts (Pincus and Tucker, 1974). This constellation of behaviors produces what is described as *temporal-lobe personality*, although very few people's behavior combines all these traits (see Section 20.5).

Similar personality traits arise after temporal lobectomy. A relative asymmetry appears in the symptoms, with right temporal lobectomy more likely associated with these personality traits than left temporal lobectomy. This observation has not been quantified, however, and warrants further study.

Changes in Sexual Behavior

A classic symptom of bilateral temporal-lobe damage that includes the amygdala is a release of sexual behavior. This symptom is not observed after unilateral injury. We return to the effects of amygdala damage on sexual and social behavior in Section 20.3.

◎ 15.4 Clinical Neuropsychological Assessment of Temporal-Lobe Damage

Many standardized assessment tools have proved sensitive and valid predictors of temporal-lobe injury (**Table 15.2**). Like the clinical neuropsychological tests of parietal-lobe function described in Section 14.5, these tests do not assess all possible temporal-lobe symptoms, but it would be highly unusual for a person to perform normally on all of them if there were damage to either temporal lobe.

- Dichotic listening and the Visual Object and Space Perception Battery can assess auditory- and visual-processing capacity, respectively.

- The Wechsler Memory Scale-IV is the best test of general verbal-memory ability. The several subtests often are used separately because the overall memory quotient is affected by nonspecific attentional disorders. For example, two subtests—paired associates and logical stories—are often used as a purer measure of verbal-memory capacity. The paired-associates subtest requires a subject to learn a series of word pairs (for example, north–south, cabbage–pen) such that, when one word is read (north, cabbage), its paired-associate word (south, pen) can be recalled. An example of the logical memory test was presented in Section 15.3 in reference to Mr. B.'s verbal-memory defect.

Table 15.2 **Standardized clinical neuropsychological tests for temporal-lobe damage**   ◎

Function	Test	Basic Reference
Auditory processing capacity	Dichotic words and melodies	Sparks et al., 1970
Visual processing capacity	Visual Object and Space Perception Battery	Lezak et al., 2004
Verbal memory	Revised Wechsler Memory Scale-IV	Hoelzle et al., 2011
Nonverbal memory	Rey Complex Figure	Taylor, 1969
Language	Token	de Renzi and Faglioni, 1978

- The Rey Complex-Figure Test has proven to be one of the best for evaluating nonverbal memory function of the right temporal lobe (see Figure 15.16C). A printed copy of a complex geometric pattern is placed before the subject with the instructions, "Copy the drawing as accurately as you can." Then 45 minutes later, the subject is asked to reproduce as much of the figure as he or she can remember. The scoring criteria provide an objective measure of nonverbal memory, but the test has a drawback: depressed or poorly motivated subjects may perform poorly, not because of right-temporal-lobe damage but because they refuse to try to recall the figure. All tests of nonverbal memory are subject to this complication, and there is no easy solution.

- We recommend the Token Test as the test of choice for language comprehension. However, a deficit in language comprehension could result from a lesion in any of the language zones of the left hemisphere, that is, in the parietal, temporal, or frontal lobes. No current neuropsychological assessment tool can localize the area of damage within the left hemisphere.

SUMMARY

15.1 Temporal-Lobe Anatomy

The temporal lobe consists of four functional zones: (1) one for auditory processes (superior temporal gyrus), (2) one for visual processes (inferotemporal cortex), (3) one for emotion (amygdala), and (4) one for spatial navigation and spatial and object memory (hippocampus and associated cortex).

15.2 A Theory of Temporal-Lobe Function

The temporal lobe adds two features to both auditory and visual information—namely, tone (affect) and categorization. Both are important for understanding sensory input as well as for using it in biologically relevant ways, such as in biological motion. An extensive face-perception system includes regions in the occipital lobe as well as several temporal lobe regions.

Whereas the parietal lobe processes spatial location with respect to movement, the temporal lobe uses spatial location both as a feature of object recognition and for developing memories for object location. Temporal lobe processing of auditory information is specialized for two characteristics: speed and frequency. Language processing requires analysis of rapidly changing sounds, but because people speak at different pitches ranging from high and squeaky to deep and

resonant, our capacity to understand language sounds can tolerate differences in frequencies. Music, by contrast, is relatively slower than language, but differences in frequency are critical to music perception.

15.3 Symptoms of Temporal-Lobe Lesions

The left temporal lobe is more concerned with speed, the right with complex frequency patterns. Damage to temporal lobe auditory regions produces deficits in recognizing language (primarily left) and music (primarily right), as well as in localizing sounds.

Damage to the temporal lobe visual regions disrupts the recognition of complex visual stimuli, such as faces. Damage to medial temporal regions produces deficits in affect, personality, spatial navigation, and object memory.

15.4 Clinical Neuropsychological Assessment of Temporal-Lobe Damage

Neuropsychologists utilize tests that are sensitive to discrete temporal-lobe injuries, including auditory processing (dichotic listening), visual processing (object recognition), memory (both verbal and nonverbal), and language.

References

Allison, T., A. Puce, and G. McCarthy. Social perception from visual cues: Role of the STS region. *Trends in Cognitive Sciences* 4:267–278, 2000.

Barraclough, N. E., and D. I. Perrett. From single cells to social perception. *Philosophical Transactions of the Royal Society B* 366:1739–1752, 2011.

Belin, P., R. J. Zatorre, P. Lafaille, P. Ahad, and B. Pike. Voice-selective areas in human auditory cortex. *Nature* 403:309–312, 2000.

Blumer, D., and D. F. Benson. Personality changes with frontal and temporal lesions. In D. F. Benson and F. Blumer, Eds., *Psychiatric Aspects of Neurologic Disease*. New York: Grune & Stratton, 1975.

Blumer, D., and D. E. Walker. The neural basis of sexual behavior. In D. F. Benson and D. Blumer, Eds., *Psychiatric Aspects of Neurologic Disease*. New York: Grune & Stratton, 1975.

Carter, R. M., and S. A. Huettel. A nexus model of the temporal-parietal junction. *Trends in Cognitive Sciences* 17:328–336, 2013.

de Renzi, E., and P. Faglioni. Normative data and screening power of a shortened version of the token test. *Cortex* 14:41–49, 1978.

Dierks, T., D. E. J. Kinden, M. Jandl, E. Formisano, R. Goebel, H. Lanfermann, and W. Singer. Activation of Heschl's gyrus during auditory hallucinations. *Neuron* 22:615–621, 1999.

Donnay, G. F., S. K. Rankin, M. Lopez-Gonzalez, P. Jira-dej-vong, and C. J. Limb. Neural substrates of interactive musical improvisation: An fMRI study of "Trading Fours" in jazz. *PLoS ONE* 9:e88665, 2014.

Dorff, J. E., A. F. Mirsky, and M. Mishkin. Effects of unilateral temporal lobe removals on tachistoscopic recognition in the left and right visual fields. *Neuropsychologia* 3:39–51, 1965.

Farah, M. J. What is "special" about face perception? *Psychological Review* 105:482–498, 1998.

Fuster, J. M., and J. P. Jervey. Neuronal firing in the infero-temporal cortex of the monkey in a visual memory task. *Journal of Neuroscience* 2:361–375, 1982.

Grill-Spector, K., N. Knouf, and N. Kanwisher. The fusiform face area subserves face perception, not generic within-category identification. *Nature Neuroscience* 7: 555–562, 2004.

Hasson, U., Y. Nir, I. Levy, G. Fuhrmann, and R. Malach. Intersubject synchronization of cortical activity during natural vision. *Science* 303:1634–1640, 2004.

Haxby, J. V., E. A. Hoffman, and M. I. Gobbini. The distributed human neural system for face perception. *Trends in Cognitive Sciences* 4:223–333, 2000.

Haxby, J. V., L. G. Ungerleider, V. P. Clark, J. L. Schouten, E. A., Hoffman, and A. Martin. The effect of face inversion on activity in human neural systems for face and object perception. *Neuron* 22:189–199, 1999.

Hécaen, H., and M. L. Albert. *Human Neuropsychology*. New York: Wiley, 1978.

Herholz, S. C., and R. J. Zatorre. Musical training as a framework for brain plasticity, behavior, function, and structure. *Neuron* 76: 486–502, 2012.

Hoelzle, J. B., N. W. Nelson, and C. A. Smith. Comparison of Wechsler Memory Scale—Fourth Edition (WMS-IV) and Third Edition (WMS-III) dimensional structures: Improved ability to evaluate auditory and visual constructs. *Journal of Clinical and Experimental Neuropsychology* 33: 283–291, 2011.

Kolb, B., B. Milner, and L. Taylor. Perception of faces by patients with localized cortical excisions. *Canadian Journal of Psychology* 37:8–18, 1983.

Kravitz, D. J., K. S., Saleem, C. I. Baker, L. G. Ungerleider, and M. Mishkin. The ventral visual pathway: An expanded neural framework for the processing of object quality. *Trends in Cognitive Sciences* 17:26–49, 2013.

Lezak, M. D., D. B. Howieson, D. W. Loring, H. J. Hannay, and J. S. Fischer. *Neuropsychological Assessment*, 4th ed. Oxford: Oxford University Press, 2004.

Liberman, A. On finding that speech is special. *American Psychologist* 37:148–167, 1982.

Liegeois-Chauvel, C., I. Peretz, M. Babai, V. Laguitton, and P. Chauvel. Contribution of different cortical areas in the temporal lobes to music processing. *Brain* 121:1853–1867, 1998.

Meier, M. S., and L. A. French. Lateralized deficits in complex visual discrimination and bilateral transfer of reminiscence following unilateral temporal lobectomy. *Neuropsychologia* 3:261–272, 1968.

Milner, B. Psychological defects produced by temporal lobe excision. *Research Publications of the Association for Research in Nervous and Mental Disease* 38:244–257, 1958.

Milner, B. Visual recognition and recall after right temporal lobe excision in man. *Neuropsychologia* 6:191–209, 1968.

Milner, B. Memory and the medial temporal regions of the brain. In K. H. Pribram and D. E. Broadbent, Eds., *Biological Basis of Memory*. New York: Academic Press, 1970.

Peretz, I. Brain specialization for music: New evidence from congenital amusia. *Annals of the New York Academy of Sciences* 930:153–165, 2001.

Peretz, I., and R. J. Zatorre. Brain organization for music processing. *Annual Review of Psychology* 56:89–114, 2005.

Perrett, D. I., M. H. Harries, P. J. Benson, A. J. Chitty, and A. J. Mistlin. Retrieval of structure from rigid and biological motion: An analysis of the visual responses of neurones in the macaque temporal cortex. In A. Blake and T. Troscianko, Eds., *AI and the Eye*. New York: Wiley, 1990.

Pincus, J. H., and G. J. Tucker. *Behavioral Neurology*. New York: Oxford University Press, 1974.

Read, D. E. Solving deductive-reasoning problems after unilateral temporal lobectomy. *Brain and Language* 12:116–127, 1981.

Ritsma, R. Frequencies dominant in the perception of pitch of complex sounds. *Journal of the Acoustical Society of America* 42:191–198, 1967.

Samson, S., and R. J. Zatorre. Discrimination of melodic and harmonic stimuli after unilateral cerebral excisions. *Brain and Cognition* 7:348–360, 1988.

Schneider, P., V. Sluming, N. Roberts, M. Scherg, R. Goebel, H. J. Specht, H. G. Dosch, S. Bleeck, C. Stippich, and A. Rupp. Structural and functional asymmetry of lateral Heschl's gyrus reflects pitch perception preference. *Nature Neuroscience* 8:1241–1247, 2005.

Sluming, V., T. Barrick, M. Howard, E. Cezayirli, A. Mayes, and N. Roberts. Voxel-based morphometry reveals increased gray matter density in Broca's area in male symphony orchestra musicians. *NeuroImage* 17:1613–1622, 2002.

Sparks, R., H. Goodglass, and B. Nickel. Ipsilateral versus contralateral extinction in dichotic listening from hemispheric lesions. *Cortex* 6:249–260, 1970.

Springer, S. P. Speech perception and the biology of language. In M. S. Gazzaniga, Ed., *Handbook of Behavioral Neurology: Neuropsychology*. New York: Plenum, 1979.

Swisher, L., and I. J. Hirsch. Brain damage and the ordering of two temporally successive stimuli. *Neuropsychologia* 10:137–152, 1972.

Tanaka, K. Inferotemporal cortex and object vision. *Annual Review of Neuroscience* 19:109–139, 1996.

Tanaka, K. Neuronal mechanisms of object recognition. *Science* 262:685–688, 1993.

Taylor, L. B. Localization of cerebral lesions by psychological testing. *Clinical Neurosurgery* 16:269–287, 1969.

Tramo, M. J., G. D. Shah, and L. D. Braida. Functional role of auditory cortex in frequency processing and pitch perception. *Journal of Neurophysiology* 87:122–139, 2002.

Ungerleider, L.G., and M. Mishkin. Two cortical visual systems. In D. J. Ingle, M. Goodale, and R. J. W. Mansfield, Eds., *Analysis of Visual Behavior*, pp. 549–586. Cambridge, Mass: MIT Press, 1982.

Valentine, T. Upside-down faces: A review of the effect of inversion upon face recognition. *British Journal of Psychology* 79:4571–4591, 1988.

Vignolo, L. A. Auditory agnosia: A review and report of recent evidence. In A. L. Benton, Ed., *Contributions to Clinical Neuropsychology*. Chicago: Aldine, 1969.

Wilkins, A., and M. Moscovitch. Selective impairment of semantic memory after temporal lobectomy. *Neuropsychologia* 16:73–79, 1978.

Zatorre, R. J. Neural specializations for tonal processing. *Annals of the New York Academy of Sciences* 930:193–210, 2001.

Zatorre, R. J. There's more to auditory cortex than meets the ear. *Hearing Research* 229: 24–30, 2007.

Zatorre, R. J., and P. Belin. Spectral and temporal processing in human auditory cortex. *Cerebral Cortex* 11:946–953, 2001.

Zatorre, R. J., P. Belin, and V. Penhume. Structure and function of the auditory cortex: Music and speech. *Trends in Cognitive Sciences* 6:37–46, 2002.

16

The Frontal Lobes

PORTRAIT Losing Frontal-Lobe Functions

E.L., a botany professor at an up-state New York college, was known for his organizational skills. He had developed a large herbarium at the college and truly enjoyed having students work with him on research projects.

Late in the spring semester when he was 60 years old, E.L. began having headaches and felt as if he had the flu, but after a few days of bed rest, he was not getting any better. He eventually visited his physician, who determined that E.L. had an infection in the left frontal lobe. The source was difficult to identify.

Meanwhile, E.L. began to develop cognitive symptoms that his wife found very worrisome. He seemed disorganized, showed little emotion, and although a chapter of his unpublished book was due and he was never late for deadlines, he said that he just could not think of anything to write.

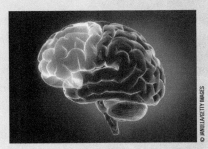

When he arrived for his neuro-psychological assessment, the most striking thing about E.L. was his flat affect and virtual absence of facial expression—symptoms typical of left-frontal-lobe patients. This lack of affect was not associated with a lack of effort on the tests, however, because the assessment ranked his intelligence and general memory scores in the superior range. He did, nevertheless, register significant impairments on tests sensitive to frontal-lobe functions.

Talking with E.L. and his wife of more than 30 years made clear that he was having difficulty not only with his academic work but also in his social interactions with colleagues, friends, and family. He found it difficult to interact even with close friends, and his wife was concerned that her husband was "not the man I married."

All neural roads eventually lead to the frontal lobes. As E.L.'s case makes apparent, when some roads lead nowhere, people can have major problems generating appropriate behavior. In this chapter we consider the frontal lobes' anatomical organization, including information flow to and from them, then consider a general theory of frontal-lobe function, various symptoms associated with frontal injury, and diseases that affect the frontal lobes.

16.1 Frontal-Lobe Anatomy

Children are notorious for their faux pas because they do not recognize that the rules of behavior change with the social and environmental circumstances. Indeed, controlling our behavior in response to the social or environmental situation we are in requires considerable skill. We all have stories about goofing up and behaving inappropriately. Fortunately, most of us do not err often, because our frontal lobes control our behavior with respect to time and place. Yet the frontal lobe can perform such functions only if provided with all relevant and available sensory and mnemonic (that is, memory) information.

Subdivisions of the Frontal Cortex

In the human brain, the frontal lobes, imaged on the previous page in the Portrait, include all the tissue anterior to the central sulcus. This vast area, constituting 30 percent to 35 percent of the neocortex, comprises a multitude of functionally distinct regions that we group into four general categories: primary motor, premotor, prefrontal, and anterior cingulate.

Primary Motor Cortex

The primary motor cortex (M1), designated area 4 in the human brain (**Figure 16.1**) and in the monkey brain (**Figure 16.2**), specifies elementary movements, such as those of the mouth and limbs. M1 also controls movement force and direction. Its cells project to subcortical motor structures such as the basal ganglia and the red nucleus as well as to the spinal cord.

Premotor Cortex

Immediately anterior to the motor cortex in Figures 16.1 and 16.2, the premotor cortex (PM) comprises areas 6, 8, and 44 (Broca's area). PM includes a dorsal region called the *supplementary motor cortex* and, lying below it, three major premotor sectors: the dorsal (PMd) and ventral (PMv) premotor cortex and the inferior frontal gyrus (Broca's area). PMd is active for choosing movements from its movement lexicon. PMv contains *mirror neurons* that recognize

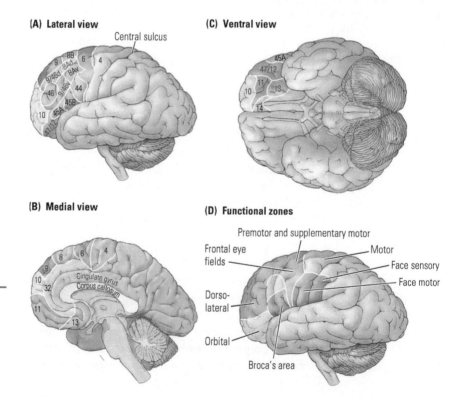

(A) Lateral view

Central sulcus

(C) Ventral view

(B) Medial view

Cingulate gyrus
Corpus callosum

(D) Functional zones

Premotor and supplementary motor

Frontal eye fields

Motor

Face sensory

Face motor

Dorso-lateral

Orbital

Broca's area

Figure 16.1 ▶

Mapping the Human Frontal Lobe (A–C) Petrides and Pandya's (1999) cytoarchitectonic maps of the frontal lobe, redrawn. (D) Approximate boundaries of frontal-lobe functional zones.

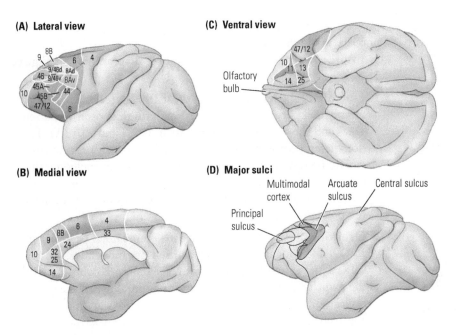

Figure 16.2 ◄

Frontal Areas of the Monkey (A–C) Petrides and Pandya's (1999) cytoarchitectonic maps of the frontal lobe of the rhesus monkey, redrawn. (D) The two major sulci in the monkey frontal lobe are the principal sulcus and the arcuate sulcus, which contains multimodal neurons.

Figure 16.3 ▼

Corticocortical Connections of the Rhesus Monkey Refer to the frontal-lobe areas diagrammed in Figure 16.2. (A) Connections to the dorsolateral surface include projections from posterior parietal as well as temporal regions that contribute to the dorsal and ventral streams. (B) Connections to the inferior frontal region are from the temporal lobe. Connections from the gustatory and olfactory cortices are shown in Figure 16.5.

others' movements and select similar or different actions, as does Broca's area (see Figure 9.12B).

Premotor areas can influence movement directly, through corticospinal projections, or indirectly, through projections to M1. The frontal eye fields (areas 8 and 8A) both receive visual input from posterior parietal region PG and the midbrain superior colliculus, regions that control eye movements and also send projections to these regions (**Figure 16.3**A). PMd and PMv also receive projections from parietal regions PE and PF. All premotor areas receive projections from the dorsolateral prefrontal cortex, implicating this area in controlling limb and eye movements.

Prefrontal Cortex

The peculiarly named prefrontal cortex (PFC), comprising the area anterior to the motor, premotor, and cingulate cortex, derives from Jersey Rose and Clinton Woolsey (1948). They observed that a region in the frontal lobes of all the mammalian species they examined receives projections from the dorsomedial nucleus of the thalamus. They saw this projection as parallel to the projections of the lateral and medial geniculate thalamic nuclei to the visual and the auditory cortex, respectively, and concluded that the dorsomedial projection could define a similar region in different mammalian species.

The prefrontal regions receive significant input from the mesolimbic dopamine cells in the tegmentum. This modulatory input plays an important role in regulating how prefrontal neurons react to stimuli, including stressful stimuli, and probably contributes to our emotional states. Abnormalities in this

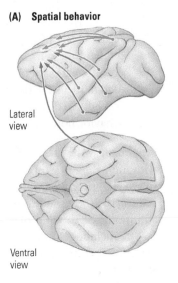

(A) Spatial behavior

Lateral view

Ventral view

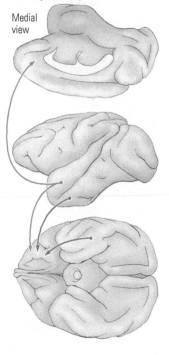

(B) Object recognition

Medial view

(A) Lateral view

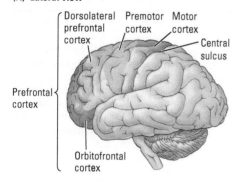

(B) Ventral view

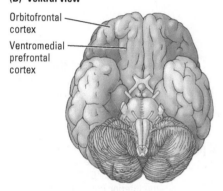

(C) Medial view

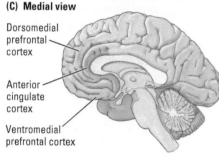

Figure 16.4 ▲

Frontal Regions in the Human Brain Gross subdivisions of the frontal lobe illustrating (A) motor, premotor, and prefrontal lateral, (B) ventral, and (C) medial regions and the anterior cingulate cortex.

projection, discussed in Section 16.6, play central roles in schizophrenia and in drug addiction.

In primates, the PFC's three regions, diagrammed in **Figure 16.4**, are:

1. **Dorsolateral prefrontal cortex** (DLPFC), areas 9 and 46, mainly makes reciprocal connections with the posterior parietal areas and the superior temporal sulcus (see Figure 16.3A). The dorsolateral cortex has extensive connections with regions to which the posterior parietal cortex also projects, including the cingulate cortex, basal ganglia, and superior colliculus. The key to understanding the DLPFC's functions lies in its relation to the posterior parietal cortex (detailed in Figure 14.3).

2. **Orbitofrontal cortex** (OFC), areas 47 and lateral portions of 11, 12, and 13, gains input from all sensory modalities. The OFC's main afferents project from the temporal lobe, including the auditory regions of the superior temporal gyrus, the visual regions of the inferotemporal cortex (area TE), and the STS, and from the subcortical amygdala (see Figure 16.3B). Orbital connections from S2 (somatosensory area 43), gustatory cortex in the insula, and olfactory regions of the pyriform cortex are illustrated in **Figure 16.5**. The OFC projects subcortically to the amygdala and hypothalamus, providing a route for influencing the autonomic nervous system controls changes in blood pressure, respiration, and so on. These physiological changes are important in emotional responses.

3. **Ventromedial prefrontal cortex** (VMPFC), Brodmann areas 10, 14, and 25, the medial parts of areas 11, 12, and 13, and the anterior part of 32, receives cortical connections from the DLPFC, posterior cingulate cortex, and medial temporal cortex. Like the OFC, the VMPFC, shown in Figure 16.4B and C, connects subcortically with the amygdala and with the hypothalamus and also with the periaqueductal gray (PAG) in the brainstem.

The VMPFC is thus linked with structures capable of emotional behavior bodywide.

Anterior Cingulate Cortex

Although the anterior cingulate cortex (ACC) was originally conceived as a relatively primitive limbic cortex, the presence of von Economo neurons (see Figure 10.20) has led to the idea that it is a recent evolutionary development and should be thought of as specialized neocortex. The ACC, shown in Figure 16.4C, includes Brodmann's area 24 and part of 32, and it makes extensive bidirectional connections with motor, premotor, and prefrontal cortex as well as with the insula.

The Connectome and the Frontal Cortex

Continuing research into charting human brain connectivity and the connectome (Sections 10.3 and 17.3) reveals that frontal lobe regions are central to many cortical networks. The most-studied network, called the brain's **default**

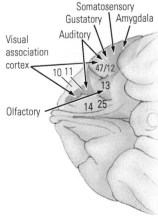

Figure 16.5 ▲

Inputs to the Orbito-frontal Cortex This schematic of the ventral surface of the monkey OFC includes inputs from all major sensory regions as well as from the amygdala. (Data source: Rolls, 1998.)

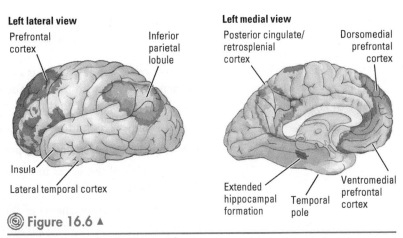

Left lateral view Prefrontal cortex, Inferior parietal lobule, Insula, Lateral temporal cortex

Left medial view Posterior cingulate/retrosplenial cortex, Dorsomedial prefrontal cortex, Extended hippocampal formation, Temporal pole, Ventromedial prefrontal cortex

◉ Figure 16.6 ▲

The Brain's Default Network Brain regions that are more active when participants are resting, that is, in a passive condition, contrasted to brain activity during a wide range of simple active task conditions. Lighter color indicates greater activity. (Research from R. L. Buckner. The brain's default network: Origins and implications for the study of psychosis. *Dialogues in Clinical Neuroscience* 15:352, 2013, Figure 1.)

network (**Figure 16.6**), links a set of far-flung brain regions active in participants who are resting rather than engaging in specific cognitive tasks (Buckner, 2013). Randy Buckner emphasizes, however, that *default network* is a misnomer, because this network is also active during such directed tasks as thinking about one's past (autobiographical memory), thinking about the future, or when the mind is "wandering."

A related **salience network** is seen in correlated activity among the anterior cingulate cortex, supplementary motor cortex, and anterior insular cortex. Valerie Bonnelle and her colleagues (2012) suggest that the salience network is most active when a behavioral change is needed and that it operates to modulate other networks' activities. For example, if the salience network is not functioning properly, the default network shows excessive activity, leading to lapses in attention.

The prefrontal cortex is also a major participant in many cortical networks involved in emotional behaviors (e.g., Roy et al., 2012). The ventromedial prefrontal region plays an especially active role in these networks, and mood disorders result from abnormal activity in these systems (Price and Drevets, 2012).

The frontal lobes' extensive connections with other cortical regions thus can modulate functions of the more posterior cortex. Recall, for example, the role of the prefrontal cortex in visual perception (Sections 13.2, 13.4, and 13.6) and mental imagery (Section 15.3).

16.2 A Theory of Frontal-Lobe Function

Imagine this scenario: On the spur of the moment, you invite friends for dinner. Because you have nothing to serve, you must go shopping after you leave work at 5:00 P.M. Before leaving, you prepare a list of items to buy.

You are working under a time constraint because you must return home before your guests arrive and you need time to prepare. Because the items that you need are not all at the same store, you must plan an efficient travel route.

You also must not be distracted by stores selling items (such as shoes) that you do not need or by extended chats with store clerks or friends whom you might encounter.

The task you have set yourself is a bit rushed, but for most people it offers little challenge. People with frontal-lobe injury, however, cannot manage it. The fundamental requirements of the task that challenge frontal-lobe patients are:

- Planning and selecting from many options
- Ignoring extraneous stimuli and persisting in the task at hand
- Keeping track of the stores to which they have gone and the items that they have already purchased

The behavioral requirements of this task can be described as the temporal (time) organization of behavior, and this sort of sequential organization is the general function of the frontal lobe. Thus, the frontal lobe contains control systems that implement behavioral strategies in response to both internal and external cues. In recent years, it has become fashionable to refer to these temporal systems as *executive functions*, but we do not want to read too much into this label. The premotor and prefrontal regions contribute in different ways to this control function, and so we consider them separately.

Functions of the Premotor Cortex

Whereas the motor cortex executes individual movements, the premotor cortex selects from its lexicon the movements to be executed (see Figure 9.2). Consider a resting dog's behavior. It may get up and respond to its owner's call or it may get up for no apparent reason and wander about the yard.

The dog makes the former movements in response to a specific environmental cue, whereas the latter behavior is a response to an internal event. Richard Passingham (1993) suggested that the premotor region functions primarily to select behaviors in response to external cues, and the supplementary motor region makes a greater internal contribution when no such cues are available.

Just as we choose limb movements, we must select eye movements, which is the function of the frontal eye fields. Like limb movements, eye movements can be made to specific targets that are visible, or they can be made on the basis of internal cues. Thus, we can make eye movements to look at specific objects or we can gaze around, seemingly without purpose. Passingham suggested that area 8 is specialized for stimulus-directed movements, whereas area 8A is responsible for internally driven movements.

The premotor cortex's role in response selection was first shown in controls by Per Roland and his colleagues (1980). They compared cerebral blood flow in participants making either a repetitive movement of one finger or a complex sequence of 16 movements of the fingers of one hand. The blood-flow increase in the supplementary motor cortices in both hemispheres was larger in the sequence task than in the repetitive task. There was, however, no increase in blood flow in the premotor region.

Roland concluded that the supplementary motor region plays a special role in selecting and directing motor sequences. An important aspect of Roland's experiment is that there was no external cue for the movements. That is, production of the movement sequence was self-paced, or internally driven. The results of subsequent studies by others have shown that the premotor cortex is activated when movement sequences are paced externally by a cue.

Not only are motor acts paced by cues, they also can become associated with cues. For example, to drive safely, we must learn that red means stop and green means go. When participants are trained on such arbitrary associations in an fMRI paradigm, functional activity in the premotor cortex increases (see, for example, Amiez et al., 2006).

Functions of the Prefrontal Cortex

The motor cortex is responsible for making movements. The premotor cortex selects movements. The prefrontal cortex controls cognitive processes that select appropriate movements at the correct time and place. This selection may be controlled by internalized information or by external cues, or it may be made in response to context or self-knowledge. We now consider these four aspects of movement selection separately.

Internal Cues

Part of developing internalized information entails developing "rules" that can be used to guide thoughts and actions. The internalized record of what has just taken place is independent of existing sensory information and can be called *temporal memory*, *working memory*, or *short-term memory*. We use **temporal memory** here to refer to a neural record of recent events and their order. These events may be related to things or to movements and thus derive their information from the object-recognition (ventral) or motor (dorsal) streams of sensory processing.

Recall that both the dorsal and the ventral streams project to the prefrontal cortex, although to different areas (see Figure 16.3), which suggests temporal memory for both motor and object information, although the memory will be localized in different places in the prefrontal cortex. The dorsolateral areas are especially engaged in selecting behavior based on temporal memory.

External Cues

People whose temporal memory is defective become dependent on environmental cues to determine their behavior. That is, behavior is not under the control of internalized knowledge but is controlled directly by external cues. One effect is that people with frontal-lobe injuries have difficulty inhibiting behavior directed to external stimuli.

In our dinner-party example, frontal-lobe patients would enter a shoe store or chat with friends as they responded to environmental cues that they encountered. We have probably all experienced occasions when the temporal organization of our behavior failed and we were controlled by external cues rather than internalized information. How many times have you started to do something, been distracted by a question or event, and then been unable to recall what you were going to do? (Sadly, this phenomenon increases with age, which is not reassuring about the state of one's prefrontal cortex.)

One type of environmental cue is feedback about the rewarding properties of stimuli. For example, if you imagine that a certain stimulus, such as a photograph of your grandmother, is always associated with a reward, such as wonderful food, then you learn the association between the visual stimulus (the photo of grandma) and the reinforcement (food). Learning such associations is central to much that we do as we learn about the world, and the orbitofrontal cortex is central to learning by association.

Context Cues

We humans live complex lives. We live in social groups with multiple, simultaneous roles as children, parents, friends, siblings, lovers, workers, and more. Each role is governed by rules of behavior that we are expected to follow: Our behavior around our grandparents is certainly different from our behavior with our high-school friends. Similarly, our behavior varies with the environment: we are quiet in a movie theater or in a library, but we may be noisy at a football game or picnic.

Behavior, then, is context dependent. Hence, behavior that is appropriate at one moment may not be appropriate if the context changes subtly. Jane Goodall's (1986) graphic descriptions of the different behavioral patterns exhibited by chimpanzees illustrate this point beautifully.

The makeup of the social group at any given time dictates the behavior of each chimpanzee. Given the presence and position of certain animals, a particular chimp may be bold and relaxed, whereas with a different group of animals, the chimp is quiet and nervous. An error in evaluating the context can have grievous consequences.

It may be no accident that the frontal lobe has grown so large in highly social primates. We can easily see the importance of social context when we reflect on our behavior with our grandparents versus that with our closest friends. Our tone of voice, use of slang or off-color words, and the content of conversations are vastly different in the two contexts.

Choosing behaviors in context requires detailed sensory information, which is conveyed to the inferior frontal cortex from the temporal lobe. Context also means affective context, and this contribution comes from the amygdala. People with orbitofrontal lesions, which are common in closed-head injury, or traumatic brain injury (TBI), have difficulty with context, especially in social situations, and are notorious for making social gaffes. We consider TBI in detail in Section 26.3.

Autonoetic Awareness

Not only is our behavior under the control of ongoing sensory input, temporal memory, and context but it also is affected by a lifetime of experiences and goals. Endel Tulving (2002) called this autobiographic knowledge **autonoetic awareness** (self-knowledge or awareness of one's self). Tulving's idea is that autonoetic awareness allows one to bind together the awareness of oneself as a continuous entity through time.

Impairment in autonoetic awareness results in a deficit of behavioral self-regulation. Thus our behavior is under the influence of our personal past experiences and life goals for the future, such that we interpret the world in our daily life within our own frames of reference. Patients with medial or ventral frontal injury often lose this self-knowledge and struggle in their daily lives.

Brian Levine and his colleagues (1998) described M.L., a salesman whose orbitofrontal injury resulted from TBI. M.L. noted that maintaining close relations with his wife of 10 years was very difficult: "I have a hard time relating to my wife. I don't know why I married this person. . . . I told myself I must have been happy, and they said I was." This symptom would surely disrupt daily living, but it is not easy to capture via a neuropsychological test, in part because such symptoms are so individual. Section 18.2 expands on autonoetic awareness and memory.

Asymmetry of Frontal-Lobe Function

In keeping with the general complementary organization of the left and right hemispheres, as a rule the left frontal lobe has a preferential role in language-related movements, including speech, whereas the right frontal lobe plays a greater role in nonverbal movements such as facial expressions. Like the asymmetry of the parietal and temporal lobes, asymmetry of frontal-lobe function is relative rather than absolute: results from studies of patients with frontal lesions indicate that both frontal lobes play a role in nearly all behavior. Thus, the laterality of function disturbed by frontal-lobe lesions is far less striking than that observed for lesions in the more-posterior lobes.

Nonetheless, as with the temporal lobe, there is reason to believe that some effects of bifrontal lesions cannot be duplicated by lesions of either hemisphere alone. **Table 16.1** summarizes a study comparing the behavioral effects of unilateral and bilateral frontal lesions. People with bifrontal lesions, for example, are severely impaired in reporting the time of day and in decoding proverbs, effects seldom seen subsequent to unilateral frontal lesions.

Tulving and his colleagues (1994) proposed that the left and right frontal lobes may play different roles in memory processing: the left prefrontal cortex is proposed to have a greater role in encoding information into memory; the right prefrontal cortex is more engaged than the left in memory retrieval. One challenge for Tulving's theory is squaring such a finding with our notions of what cerebral asymmetry represents. Reza Habib and colleagues (2003) speculate that human ancestors possessed fewer mental functions than modern humans and that those functions were bilateral. As more sophisticated mental capacities evolved, the demand for cortical space grew, leading to hemispheric specialization for certain cognitive processes.

Table 16.1 **Relative frequency of defective performance on neuropsychological tests**

Test	PERCENT OF GROUP SHOWING A DEFICIT		
	Left Hemisphere Lesion	Right Hemisphere Lesion	Bilateral Lesion
Verbal fluency	70	38	71
Verbal learning	30	13	86
Block construction	10	50	43
Design copying	10	38	43
Time orientation	0	0	57
Proverbs	20	25	71

Reprinted from *Neuropsychologia*, Vol. 6, Benton, A.L, Differential effects of frontal lobe disease, pg. 53-60, © 1968, with permission from Elsevier.

Heterogeneity of Frontal-Lobe Function

Tim Shallice and Paul Burgess (1991) noted that correlations among performances on tasks sensitive to frontal-lobe injury are relatively low. Among the many explanations offered for low intertest correlations, one is that the tests require different cognitive operations for successful solution. These different functions require different bits of the frontal lobe and related neural networks, and given that the exact site of injury will vary among patients, their performance on the different tests is impaired to different degrees.

As we consider next the symptoms of frontal-lobe injury, then, we must remember that (1) any individual patient is unlikely to show all the symptoms, and (2) the severity of symptoms will vary with lesion location. Few imaging studies have addressed this heterogeneity, and the trend has favored evidence supportive of homogeneity of function. The Snapshot shows, however, that at least in the OFC, evidence of discrete localization of functions exists.

SNAPSHOT | Heterogeneity of Function in the Orbitofrontal Cortex

The large orbitofrontal region includes at least five subregions—namely, Brodmann's areas 10 through 14, diagrammed at right. Different regions have different patterns of connectivity. Area 13, for example, has extensive connections with the amygdala and hypothalamus, whereas area 11 has connections with the ventral visual stream taking part in recognition memory.

OFC function is a challenge to laboratory study because its location makes discrete lesions difficult to produce. Furthermore, although the orbitofrontal cortex is often affected in TBI, these injuries are not focal but tend to be diffuse across the orbital region.

Stephen Frey and Michael Petrides examined functional heterogeneity in the orbital region in two parallel PET studies (Frey and Petrides, 2000; Frey et al., 2000). In one, participants heard either the sounds of violent car crashes, which the investigators suspected would be perceived as unpleasant, or familiar abstract sounds generated from an electronic keyboard. In the other study, participants were presented with novel, abstract visual designs that they had to either commit to memory or just view. Abstract designs were used to prevent participants from verbalizing the images and thus provoking semantic associations.

As shown in the diagram, area 13 showed increased activation in response to the unpleasant auditory stimuli, whereas area 11 showed increased activation when subjects had to learn new visual information. These results show a clear functional dissociation: area 13 (richly connected to the amygdala and hypothalamus) processes unpleasant auditory information; area 11 (medial temporal

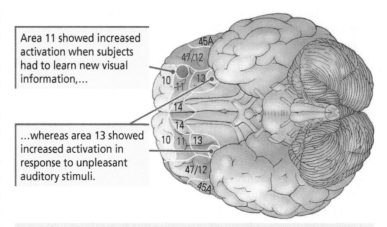

Area 11 showed increased activation when subjects had to learn new visual information,...

...whereas area 13 showed increased activation in response to unpleasant auditory stimuli.

Activation of orbitofrontal areas by sensory stimulation. (Research from Frey and Petrides, 2000, and Frey et al., 2000.)

cortical connections) processes the encoding of new visual information.

We can think of area 13 as a region that can alert an organism to attend to stimuli that have affective qualities. We might predict that people with damage to area 13 would be less responsive to threatening stimuli, and they are. It would be interesting to determine whether orbital areas 11 and 13 both would be implicated if unpleasant stimuli were to be encoded.

Frey, S., P. Kostopoulous, and M. Petrides. Orbitofrontal involvement in the processing of unpleasant auditory information. *European Journal of Neuroscience* 12:3709–3712, 2000.

Frey, S., and M. Petrides. Orbitofrontal cortex: A key prefrontal region for encoding information. *Proceedings of the National Academy of Sciences U.S.A* 97:8723–8727, 2000.

16.3 Symptoms of Frontal-Lobe Lesions

Effects of lesions to the frontal cortex are of primary concern in this section. In an effort to organize the symptoms conceptually, we group them into five major categories (**Table 16.2**). We do not mean to imply that the brain respects these categories but rather that the categories provide a conceptual framework within which to consider the symptoms.

Disturbances of Motor Function

Frontal lesions can impair a person's ability to make a wide variety of movements, to order movement sequences, and even to speak.

Fine Movements, Speed, and Strength

Damage to the primary motor cortex (area 4) is typically associated with a chronic loss of the ability to make fine, independent finger movements, presumably owing to a loss of direct corticospinal projections onto motor neurons

Table 16.2 **Summary of major symptoms of frontal-lobe damage**

Most Probable Symptom	Lesion Site	Basic Reference
Disturbances of Motor Function		
Loss of fine movements	Area 4	Kuypers, 1981
Loss of strength	Areas 4 and 6; dorsolateral	Leonard et al., 1988
Poor movement programming	Premotor; dorsolateral	Roland et al., 1980; Kolb and Milner, 1981
Poor voluntary eye gaze	Frontal eye fields	Guitton et al., 1982
Poor corollary discharge	Premotor; dorsolateral	Teuber, 1964
Broca's aphasia	Area 44	Brown, 1972
Loss of Divergent Thinking		
Reduced spontaneity	Orbital	Jones-Gotman and Milner, 1977
Poor strategy formation	Dorsolateral?	Shallice, 1988
Poor frequency estimate	Dorsolateral	Smith and Milner, 1984
Environmental Control of Behavior		
Poor response inhibition	Prefrontal	Milner, 1964
Impaired associative learning	Dorsolateral	Petrides, 1997
Risk taking and rule breaking	Prefrontal	Miller, 1985
Gambling	Orbital	Bechara et al., 2000
Self-regulatory disorder	Orbital	Levine et al., 1998
Poor Temporal Memory		
Poor working memory	Dorsolateral	Petrides, 2000
Poor delayed response	Dorsolateral	Freedman and Oscar-Berman, 1986
Other Symptoms		
Impaired social behavior	Orbital; dorsolateral	Blumer and Benson, 1975
Altered sexual behavior	Orbital	Walker and Blumer, 1975
Impaired olfactory discrimination	Orbital	Jones-Gotman and Zatorre, 1993
Disorders associated with damage to the facial area	Face	Taylor, 1979

(see Section 9.3). In addition, there is a loss of speed and strength in both hand and limb movements in the contralateral limbs. The loss of strength is not merely a symptom of damage to area 4, because lesions restricted to the prefrontal cortex also lead to reduced hand strength.

Movement Programming

In a classic 1950 paper, Karl Lashley (1960) asked how movements are put together in a particular order. How is it, he asked, that a violinist can play an arpeggio so quickly and flawlessly? Clearly, each note is not "thought of" separately. And how is it that, in a game of tennis, a player can move much too fast to have considered each movement by itself?

Lashley presumed that this function of serially ordering complex chains of behavior in relation to varying stimuli must somehow reside in the neocortex. Although he believed it to be a function of the entire neocortex, it appears more likely to be a frontal-lobe function. Removal of the supplementary motor cortex results in a transient disruption of nearly all voluntary movements (including speech, if removal is on the left). Recovery is rapid, however, and the only permanent disability appears to be in the performance of rapidly alternating movements with the hands or fingers.

The likely reason that relatively minor symptoms result from rather large supplementary motor lesions is that both the left and right premotor cortices participate in movement programming. Both left and right premotor areas show an increase in blood flow during unimanual tasks in humans; in monkeys, cells in both the left and right premotor areas show increased activity regardless of which hand is moving. Each supplementary motor cortex projects bilaterally to the basal ganglia as well.

Further evidence favoring a role for the frontal cortex in movement programming comes from the results of a study in which patients with localized unilateral frontal lobectomies (most did not include the premotor cortex) were asked to copy a series of arm or facial movements (Kolb and Milner, 1981; see Figure 14.10). Although the patients showed mild impairment in copying the arm movements, it was small compared with the performance of patients with left-parietal-lobe lesions. In contrast, patients with both left- and right-frontal-lobe damage were dismal at copying a series of facial movements.

Analysis of the facial-movement task showed that the groups with frontal-lobe lesions made more errors of sequence than did controls or other groups of patients. In other words, patients with frontal-lobe lesions had difficulty ordering the various components of the sequence into a chain of movements. They recalled components correctly but in the wrong order. To be sure, these patients made other sorts of errors as well, especially errors of memory in which items were not recalled. Reproducing movement sequences requires temporal memory, and our impression is that the largest deficits come from dorsolateral lesions.

The observation that frontal injury severely disrupts copying facial but not arm movements implies that the frontal lobe may play a special role in controlling the face, perhaps even including the tongue. Recall from E.L.'s case in the chapter-opening Portrait that patients with frontal-lobe damage exhibit little spontaneous facial expression—a result that accords with a possible special frontal-lobe role in facial control.

Voluntary Gaze

In a number of studies using widely different procedures, frontal-lobe lesions produced alterations in voluntary eye gaze. For example, Hans-Leukas Teuber (1964) presented patients with a screen arrayed with 48 patterns that could be distinguished by shape or color or both (**Figure 16.7**). At a warning signal, a duplicate of 1 of the 48 patterns appeared in a box at the center of the array, and the subject's task was to identify the matching pattern by pointing to it. Patients with frontal-lobe lesions were impaired at finding the duplicate pattern.

Alexander Luria (1973) recorded eye movements as people examined a picture of a complex scene. The eye-movement patterns of the patients with large frontal-lobe lesions were quite different from those of controls or those of patients with more-posterior lesions. For example, if a control were asked about the ages of the people in a picture, his or her eyes fixed on the heads; if asked how they were dressed, the eyes fixed on the clothing. Patients with large frontal-lobe lesions tended to glance over the picture more or less at random, and changing the question about the picture failed to alter the direction or pattern of their eye movements.

Visual search in Luria's task requires internalized knowledge to direct the eyes. Few studies (e.g., Guitton et al., 1982), have tried to localize the voluntary gaze deficits within the frontal lobe, but they seem likely to stem from interrupted activity in the frontal eye fields (see Figure 16.1A, B, and D).

Corollary Discharge

If you push on your eyeball, the world appears to move. If you move your eyes, the world remains stable. Why? Teuber (1964) proposed that for a voluntary movement to take place, a neural signal must produce both the movement and a signal that the movement is going to take place. If the eyes are moved mechanically, as when you press on them, there is no such signal, and the world moves. However, when you move your eyes, you generate a neural signal that movement will happen, and the world stays still. This signal has been termed **corollary discharge**, or **reafference**.

Teuber (1972) argued that a movement command through the motor system effects the movement, and a signal (corollary discharge) from the frontal lobe to the parietal and temporal association cortex presets the sensory system to anticipate the motor act. Thus, a person's sensory system can interpret changes in the external world in light of information about his or her voluntary movement.

When you are running, for example, the external world remains stable even though your sense organs are in motion, because the corollary discharge from the frontal lobe to the parietotemporal cortex signals that the movements are taking place. A frontal-lobe lesion therefore not only can disturb movement production but also can interfere with the message to the rest of the brain that a movement is taking place. By this indirect means, perception of the world by the posterior association cortex is altered.

Evidence that the frontal lobe participates in corollary discharge comes from the results of studies of frontal eye field cells. Emilio Bizzi and Peter Schiller (1970), among others, found that some cells in the frontal eye fields fire simultaneously with eye movements. These cells cannot be causing the eyes to move:

Ⓒ Figure 16.7 ▲

Visual Search Task In Teuber's experiment, the subject must locate and point to a duplicate of the pattern shape or color or both inside the central box.
(Teuber, H. L. The riddle of frontal lobe function in man © McGraw-Hill Education.)

to do so, they would have to fire before the eye movements (just as to accelerate an automobile, you must first depress the gas pedal). Rather, these frontal eye field cells must be monitoring the ongoing movement—a process suspiciously similar to what we would expect from a region controlling corollary discharge.

Speech

Speech entails movement selection. Passingham (1993) suggested that words are responses generated in the context of both internal and external stimuli. If the frontal lobe has a mechanism for selecting responses, then it must select words too. The frontal lobe contains two speech zones: Broca's area (area 44), which we can regard as an extension of the lateral premotor area, and the supplementary speech area, which may be an extension of the supplementary motor area (area 6). See Figure 16.1A and D.

Viewed in this way, Broca's area is critical to retrieving a word on the basis of an object, word, letter, or meaning. Like the premotor area's role in other behaviors, Broca's area selects words on the basis of cues. In contrast, consistent with the general function of the supplementary motor area, the supplementary speech area is required to retrieve words without external cues.

People with strokes in Broca's area are impaired in using verbs and producing appropriate grammar, a symptom known as **agrammatism**. People with strokes that include the supplementary speech area and extend into the adjacent left medial frontal region are often mute. The ability to speak usually returns after a few weeks in people with unilateral lesions but not in those with bilateral lesions. This outcome again supports the supplementary motor areas' bilateral participation in movement selection.

Loss of Divergent Thinking

One clear difference between the effects of parietal- and temporal-lobe lesions and the effects of frontal-lobe lesions is performance on standard intelligence tests. Posterior lesions produce reliable, and often dramatic, decreases in IQ scores, but frontal lesions do not. The puzzle then, is why patients with frontal-lobe damage appear to do such "stupid" things.

Joy Paul Guilford (1967) noted that traditional intelligence tests appear to measure what can be called **convergent thinking**—that there is just one correct answer to each question. Definitions of words, questions of fact, arithmetic problems, puzzles, and block designs all require single correct answers that are easily scored. Another type of intelligence test that emphasizes the number and variety of responses to a single question rather than a single correct answer, can measure **divergent thinking**. An example is asking for a list of the possible uses for a coat hanger. Frontal-lobe injury interferes with the intelligence required by divergent thinking rather than the convergent type measured by standard IQ tests. We explore several lines of evidence that support Guilford's idea in Section 16.4.

Behavioral Spontaneity

Patients with frontal-lobe lesions exhibit a loss of spontaneous speech. Various investigators have quantified this loss by using tests such as the Thurstone Word-Fluency Test (also called the Chicago Word-Fluency Test). Patients are asked to first write or say as many words starting with a given letter as they can think of in 5 min and then say as many four-letter words starting with a given letter in 4 min.

Patients with frontal-lobe lesions have a low word output on this test. For example, when asked to generate as many words as he could think of beginning with a specific letter, E.L., introduced in the opening Portrait, sat for about 2 min before asking if he could use the Latin names of plants. He was assured that he could do so but after another couple of minutes, he remarked, "I can't think of any!" He abandoned the plant names but even with an additional 5 min, he could think of only six words.

Although the principal locus of this defect appears to be in the left orbitofrontal region, lesions in the right orbitofrontal region also may produce a marked reduction in verbal fluency. Again, we see less asymmetry in the frontal lobes. The following case exemplifies low spontaneous verbal fluency resulting from a lesion of the right frontal lobe.

Mrs. P., a 63-year-old woman with a college degree, was suffering from a large astrocytoma of the right frontal lobe. Her performance on a word-fluency test, reproduced in **Figure 16.8**A, illustrates four features of frontal-lobe damage:

(A) Mrs. P's lists

(B) Control's lists

Note the low output, shaky script, and in the four-letter C list, rule breaking.

⊚ Figure 16.8 ▲

Word Fluency Subjects (A) and control participants (B) were given 5 min to write as many English words as possible starting with the letter *s* and 4 min to write as many four-letter words as possible starting with the letter *c*.

1. **Low output.** Mrs. P.'s only 8 words beginning with the letter *s* and 6 words beginning with the letter *c*. (Control participants of similar age and education produce a total of about 60 words in the same time period, as shown in Figure 16.8B.)

2. **Rule breaking.** This is a common characteristic of patients. We told Mrs. P. several times that the words starting with *c* could contain only four letters. She replied. "Yes, yes, I know, I keep using more each time." Even though she understood the instructions, she could not organize her behavior to follow them.

3. **Shaky script.** Her writing was rather jerky, much like that seen in a child learning to write, implying that her tumor had invaded the motor or premotor cortex.

4. **Perseveration.** Mrs. P. insisted on talking throughout the test—complaining that she simply could not think of any more words—and kept looking around the room for objects starting with the required letter.

Marilyn Jones-Gotman and Brenda Milner (1993) devised an ingenious experiment that broadens this deficit via a nonverbal analog. The researchers asked patients to draw as many different designs as they could in 5 min. The drawings were supposed to be not representational but spontaneous—much like the doodles students are prone to draw in the margins of their textbooks. The patients were then asked to draw as many different designs as they could, but this time using only four lines (a circle was counted as a single line).

The results reveal a beautiful analog to the verbal-fluency results: lesions in the right frontal lobe produced a large decrease in the number of different drawings produced. As you can see in **Figure 16.9**, controls drew about

(A) Control

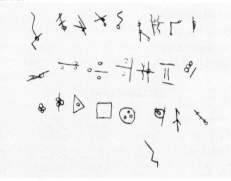

(B) Frontal lobe patient showing perseveration

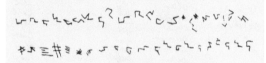

(C) Frontal lobe patient showing lack of spontaneity

Ⓒ Figure 16.9 ▲

Design Fluency In an analog to the word-fluency test, a participant (A) and two subjects (B) and (C) were allowed 5 min to draw as many nonrepresentational doodles as they could. (Jones-Gotman, M., and B. Milner. Design fluency: The invention of nonsense drawings after focal cortical lesions. *Neuropsychologia* 15:653–674, 1977. © Elsevier.)

35 drawings, left-frontal-lobe patients about 24 drawings, and right-frontal-lobe patients about 15 drawings. This deficit appears related to an impoverished output, high perseveration, and, in some cases, representational drawings (the drawing of nameable things). As with verbal fluency, lesions in the orbital cortex or central facial area in the frontal lobe appear to produce larger deficits than do the more-dorsal lesions.

Frontal-lobe patients likely show reduced spontaneity not only in speech or doodling but also in their general behavior. For example, Bryan Kolb and Laughlin Taylor (1981) recorded the spontaneous behavior of frontal-lobe patients as they were taking a battery of neuropsychological tests. Patients with frontal-lobe removals displayed fewer spontaneous facial movements and expressions than did controls or patients with more-posterior lesions. In addition, the number of words spoken by the patients in a neuropsychological interview differed dramatically: patients with left frontal removals rarely spoke, whereas patients with right frontal lesions talked excessively.

Although the range of behaviors studied to date is small, frontal-lobe patients display a general loss of spontaneous behavior. They characteristically appear lethargic or lazy, often having difficulty getting out of bed in the morning, getting dressed, or initiating other daily activities such as going to work. One patient offers a particularly dramatic example. He was a prominent lawyer who had a midline meningioma in the frontal lobe. The tumor was removed surgically, but he was left with bilateral damage to the superior aspect of both frontal lobes.

His IQ score was still superior (over 140), and his memory for legal matters was unimpaired, in part because much of this skill is related to intact convergent thinking processes. Nonetheless, he was unable to function in his profession because he could not get up in the morning to go to work, preferring to stay in bed and watch television. When his wife forced him to get up and go to work, he was disruptive at the office because he could not concentrate on any law-related work: he was distracted by anything else going on in the office. Curiously, he remained an excellent resource for his colleagues; however, they found his behavior intolerable and consequently preferred to consult him by teleconference.

Strategy Formation

Patients with frontal-lobe lesions are especially impaired at developing novel cognitive plans or strategies for solving problems. For example, when Tim Shallice and Margaret Evans (1978) asked subjects questions that require reasoning based on general knowledge and for which no immediate strategy is obvious, they found that frontal-lobe patients performed poorly and often gave bizarre responses.

In a later study, Shallice and Burgess (1991) gave patients a task very much like our dinner-party problem presented in Section 16.2. They gave subjects a list of six errands (for example, "Buy a loaf of brown bread") and an instruction to be at a particular place 15 min after starting. They were also to get answers to four questions (for instance, What is the price of a pound of tomatoes?). They were not to enter shops except to buy something and were to complete the tasks as quickly as possible without rushing.

The frontal-lobe patients found this simple task very difficult. They were inefficient, they broke rules (for example, entered unnecessary shops), and two of the three patients failed at least four tasks. Yet when quizzed, all the patients understood the task and had attempted to comply.

Shallice and Burgess argued that although the frontal lobe may have a general role in planning behavior, it has a critical role in coping with novel situations. They suggested that in contrast to routine situations, coping with a novel one— by which they mean a novel set of external and internal states—entails activating a wide variety of processes to solve the problem. The solution of a familiar task, by contrast, can rely on well-practiced strategies that are more easily accessed.

Environmental Control of Behavior

Perhaps frontal-lobe patients' most commonly observed trait is difficulty in using environmental cues (feedback) to regulate or change their behavior. This difficulty manifests itself in myriad ways.

Response Inhibition

Patients with frontal-lobe lesions consistently perseverate on responses in a variety of test situations, particularly those with changing demands. The best example is observed in the Wisconsin Card-Sorting Test, a standard clinical test of frontal-lobe injury. A subject is presented with four stimulus cards bearing designs that differ in color, form, and number of elements, as represented in **Figure 16.10**. The subject's task is to sort the cards into piles in front of one or another of the stimulus cards. The only help given the subject is to be told whether the choice is correct or incorrect.

The test works on the following principle: the correct solution is, first, color; when the subject has figured out this solution, without warning the correct solution then becomes form. The subject must now inhibit classifying the cards on the basis of color and shift to form. When the subject has succeeded at selecting by form, the correct solution again changes unexpectedly, this time to the number of elements. It will later become color again, and so on.

Shifting response strategies is particularly difficult for people with frontal lesions. They may continue responding to the original stimulus (color) for as many as 100 cards until testing is terminated. Throughout this period, they may comment that they know that color is no longer correct. They nevertheless continue to sort on the basis of color. One person stated (correctly): "Form is probably the correct solution now so this [sorting to color] will be wrong, and this will be wrong, and wrong again."

Perseveration is common on any task that requires a frontal-lobe patient to shift response strategies, thus demonstrating that the frontal lobe is necessary for behavioral flexibility. It is important to note that on card-sorting tasks, subjects must not be given any hint that they are to expect a change in the correct solution, because many frontal-lobe patients improve dramatically when given this warning. The cue apparently lends them enough flexibility to solve the problem.

From the results of Milner's (1964) work, the principal locus of this card-sorting effect appears to be roughly around Brodmann's area 9 in the left hemisphere dorsolateral prefrontal cortex (see Figure 16.1A and D). Lesions elsewhere

Figure 16.10 ▲

Wisconsin Card-Sorting Test The subject is given a deck of cards containing multiple copies of those represented here and presented with a row of four cards selected from among them. The task is to place each card from the deck in front of the appropriate card in the row, sorting by one of three possible categories: color, number of elements, or shape. Subjects are not told the correct sorting category but only whether their responses are correct or incorrect. When a subject selects the correct category 10 consecutive times, the correct solution changes unexpectedly.

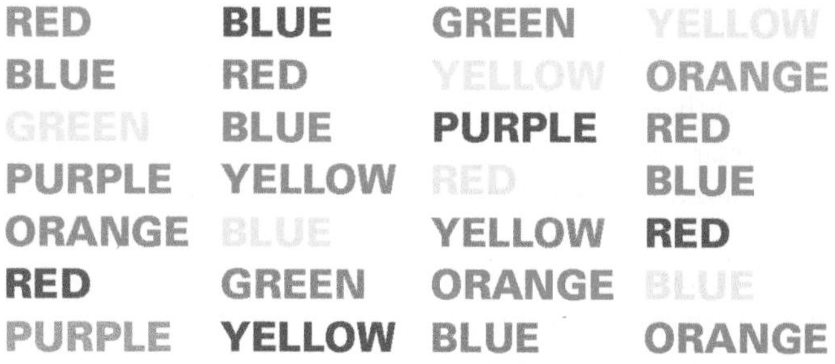

RED   **BLUE**   GREEN   YELLOW

BLUE   RED   YELLOW   ORANGE

GREEN   BLUE   **PURPLE**   RED

PURPLE   YELLOW   RED   BLUE

ORANGE   BLUE   YELLOW   **RED**

RED   GREEN   ORANGE   BLUE

PURPLE   **YELLOW**   BLUE   ORANGE

Figure 16.11 ▲

Stroop Test The task is to name the color of the ink in which each color name is printed as quickly as possible. When the ink color and the color name are the same, the task is simple. When they differ, the tendency is to read the word rather than name the ink color.

in the left frontal lobe, and often in the right frontal lobe, also will produce a deficit, although attenuated, on this task.

The Stroop Test (**Figure 16.11**) further demonstrates loss of response inhibition subsequent to frontal-lobe damage. Subjects are presented with a list of color names. Each name is printed in colored ink but never in the color denoted by the word (for example, the word *yellow* is printed in blue, green, or red ink). The subject's task is to name the color each word is printed in as quickly as possible.

Correct response requires inhibiting reading the color name—difficult even for many controls. Patients with left frontal lesions are unable to inhibit reading the words and thus are impaired in this task (e.g., Perret, 1974).

Risk Taking and Rule Breaking

Frontal-lobe patients are distinguished from other neurological patients in their common failure to comply with instructions. Milner found it especially common on tests of stylus–maze learning in which a buzzer indicates that the patient has made an error and is to stop and start again at the beginning of the maze. Subjects with frontal-lobe lesions tend to disregard the signal, continuing on the incorrect path and making more errors. This behavior is reminiscent of the inability to modify their responses in the card-sorting task.

Lori Miller (1985) gave subjects a task to guess words on the basis of partial information. With each additional clue, a subject was assigned a successively lower point value for a correct answer, but points could be collected only if the answer was correct. An incorrect answer forfeited all the points for an item. Frontal-lobe patients took more risks (and made more mistakes) than did other patients, and the risk taking was greatest in frontal-lobe patients who also had temporal-lobe damage.

Antoine Bechera and colleagues (2000) designed a gambling task to explore the role of the OFC in risk taking. Subjects gradually learn how to play a unique card game. They are presented with four decks of cards and asked to turn over the first card in any deck. Some cards are associated with a payoff ($50 or $100); others result in a $50 or $100 penalty. Each subject is given $2000 in play money, and the goal is to make as much money in the game as possible.

The trick is that the reward and penalty contingencies of each deck differ. For example, one deck may have high payoffs but also high penalties; another may have lower payoffs but also low penalties. The game is set so that playing two of the four decks results in a net loss, whereas playing the other two yields a net gain.

The results from the Bechera studies are clear: controls and patients without frontal damage sample from all the decks for a while but quickly learn which have the best payoff. In contrast, patients with orbitofrontal injuries do not learn this strategy and play predominantly from the bad decks, thus losing all their money.

An important aspect of the task is that no one is allowed to keep a running tally of how they are doing; rather they must "sense" which decks are risky and which are profitable. This ability is clearly a function of the prefrontal cortex, and its loss makes it difficult for orbitofrontal patients to make wise decisions, especially in social or personal matters—that is, situations in which an exact calculation of future outcomes is not possible.

The brain-injury data are consistent with a finding by Ming Hsu and colleagues (2005), who looked at brain activation (fMRI) in subjects engaged in a gambling task in which risk was ambiguous. For example, subjects were asked to bet on whether a card was red or blue without any knowledge of the probability that a card was red or blue. Brain activity was compared to a condition in which they knew that the probability was 50:50.

Patients with orbitofrontal lesions did not find the ambiguous task aversive, but controls found it much more aversive than the known-risk task. The subjective difference was demonstrated by higher activation in the controls' OFC and amygdala during the ambiguous-risk task (**Figure 16.12**). Taken together, the imaging and lesion studies suggest that the OFC is part of a neural decision-making circuit that evaluates degrees of uncertainty in the world.

Self-Regulation

In Section 16.2 we described patient M.L. as typical of people with ventral frontal injuries, who have deficits in regulating their behavior in unstructured situations, in part because of a loss of autonoetic awareness. M.L. had been a salesman, and he knew what his job had been and that he had traveled a great deal. When pressed, however, he was unable to provide a single personal anecdote about this job.

For example, when asked if he traveled to conferences, M.L. said that, yes, he traveled to conferences often; it was a major part of his job. Yet he could not name a single experience he had had at a conference. His autobiographic knowledge was lost.

You can imagine what this impairment would be like if you think about high school. We are all aware of having gone to high school and can describe what high school was like. Presumably, so could patients like M.L. The difference, however, is that we can describe personal events that happened in high school, whereas M.L. would not be able to do so. We can immediately see why M.L. had difficulty relating to his wife: he simply could not recall instances that would explain why they were married. Loss of autobiographic knowledge clearly makes it difficult to put ongoing life events in context and leads to difficulties in regulating behavioral flexibility.

Associative Learning

Patients with large frontal-lobe lesions, it is often claimed, are unable to regulate their behavior in response to external stimuli—that is, to learn from experience. Alexander Luria and Evgenia Homskaya (1964) described patients with massive frontal-lobe tumors who could not be trained to respond consistently with the right hand to a red light and with the left hand to a green light, even though the patients could indicate which hand was which and could repeat the instructions.

In an extensive series of studies, Michael Petrides (1997) examined the ability of both human patients and monkeys with frontal lesions to make arbitrary stimulus–response associations. In one study, Petrides asked frontal-lobe patients to learn arbitrary associations between colors and hand postures, as

Amygdala

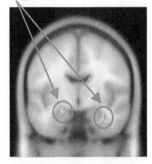

Orbitofrontal cortex

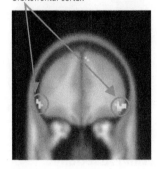

Figure 16.12 ▲

Ambiguity and Brain Activation Controls' amygdala and orbitofrontal cortex show enhanced activity when the probability of risk in a gambling task is ambiguous. (M. Hsu, M. Bhatt, R. Adolphs, D. Tranel, C. F. Camerer. Neural Systems Responding to Degrees of Uncertainty in Human Decision-Making. *Science* 310: 1680–1683, 2005.)

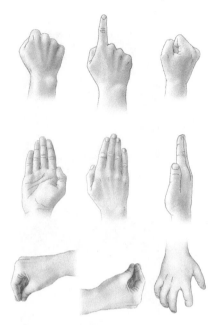

Ⓢ Figure 16.13 ▲

Testing Associative Learning The nine hand postures that constitute responses in the Petrides experiments. In this study, subjects had to learn to associate each hand posture with one of nine colors and to perform the movement in response to the presentation of the appropriate color.

illustrated in **Figure 16.13**. For example, patients were presented with nine colored stimuli, and their task was to learn which posture was associated with which colored stimulus.

Damage to either the left or right hemisphere results in poor performance on this task. Again, the behavioral impairments in frontal-lobe patients could not be attributed to a memory deficit because temporal-lobe patients who performed poorly on other tests of memory performed at normal on these tasks. Rather, the problem is in learning to select, from a set of competing responses, the ones appropriate to the various stimuli.

Poor Temporal Memory

Temporal memory deficits, both in laboratory animals and in human patients, have fascinated researchers for decades.

Studying Temporal Memory in Monkeys

Perhaps the most important experimental discovery for understanding the frontal lobe's functions is Carlyle Jacobsen's (1936) finding that chimpanzees with frontal-lobe lesions are impaired in a **delayed-response test**. In this task, an animal observes a reward being placed under a plaque or in a well. The chimp's view is blocked for a few seconds, and then it is allowed to retrieve the reward.

Animals with prefrontal lesions perform at chance, even with extended practice. Although the behavioral impairment is unlikely to be due to a single deficit, the impairment is difficult to interpret without recourse to some memory difficulty. Four additional experiments are especially germane here.

In the first, Passingham (1985) presented monkeys a task in which the animals were required to open each of 25 doors to obtain a food reward. Food was placed behind each door only once per day, so the animals had to learn not to return to locations where the reward had been obtained already. Passingham found that lesions in area 46 produced marked impairments in this task (see Figure 16.2A). Thus, whereas control monkeys developed a door-opening strategy that led to few repetitions, the lesioned animals were inefficient, often returning to previously accessed doors (**Figure 16.14**A).

In the second experiment, monkeys were trained to fixate on a central spot of light while target lights flashed in different parts of the visual field (Funahashi et al., 1986). The monkeys had to wait for the fixation spot to disappear before moving their eyes to the spot where the target light had been flashed. The researchers found that unilateral lesions in the principal sulcus (part of area 46) impaired the monkeys' ability to remember the location of the target in a restricted region of the contralateral visual field, as illustrated in Figure 6.14B. They interpreted this result as showing that the principal sulcus contains a mechanism for guiding spatial responses on the basis of stored information.

In the third experiment, Mortimer Mishkin and Frederick Manning (1978) trained monkeys in a task known as delayed nonmatching to sample. In this test, a monkey is confronted with an unfamiliar object, which it displaces to find a reward. After a delay, the animal sees the same object paired with a new one. The monkey must recognize the object it saw earlier and move the new one instead to get a reward (Figure 6.14C). Monkeys with lesions of areas 10 and 32 are impaired in this task (see Figure 16.2B). Mishkin and Manning interpreted

Lesion site

Experimental task

(A) Passingham study

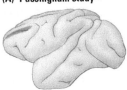

Control   Frontal

Food boxes

1 | The task is to retrieve a food reward from each of 25 food boxes. The control animal seldom returns to a previously visited location, whereas the monkey with a sulcus principalis lesion makes numerous errors.

(B) Funahashi et al. study

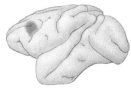

2 | The task is to fixate at the central point, and then after a 3-second delay move the eye to locate the place where a target light had flashed. Correct performance percentage is indicated by the relative positions of the lines along axes drawn through the central fixation point. The monkey performed poorly in one region of the visual field contralateral to the lesion.

(C) Mishkin and Manning study

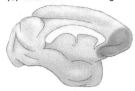

3 | The monkey is shown an object, which is displaced, and a food reward is obtained. The monkey is then presented with two objects after a short delay; the task is to obtain a reward, which is under the novel object. Monkeys with medial lesions are impaired at this task, which is nonspatial.

Figure 16.14 ▲

Testing for Temporal Memory Schematic representations at left show the sites of frontal-lobe lesions in monkeys that correspond to the results of the three experiments illustrated at right. Each result reveals a temporal memory deficit.

the result as showing that this frontal area participates in short-term storage of object information.

In the fourth experiment, a study by Petrides (1991), monkeys were given two tasks. In the first, the animals were presented with three objects and allowed to choose one for reward. The animals were then given an option between the chosen object and one of the two others, with the correct choice being the object that was not previously selected. In the second task, the animals were again presented with three objects and allowed one choice. On this task, however, they were then presented with the previously selected object and two novel objects.

In the first task, a monkey must recall what it did with the objects. In the second task, the monkey must recall only which object was seen before. Monkeys with dorsolateral lesions performed at chance on the first task but performed as well as controls on the second. This result suggests that the DLPFC plays a role in monitoring self-generated responses.

Taken together, these five experiments point to an unequivocal role for the frontal cortex in short-term-memory processes and to the fact that different prefrontal regions control the storage of different types of information. In view of the anatomical connections, area 46 likely takes part in providing an internal

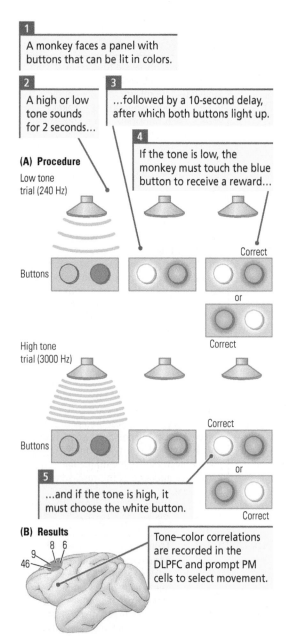

1
A monkey faces a panel with buttons that can be lit in colors.

2
A high or low tone sounds for 2 seconds...

3
...followed by a 10-second delay, after which both buttons light up.

4
If the tone is low, the monkey must touch the blue button to receive a reward...

(A) Procedure

Low tone trial (240 Hz)

Buttons

Correct

or

Correct

High tone trial (3000 Hz)

Buttons

Correct

or

Correct

5
...and if the tone is high, it must choose the white button.

(B) Results

9
46

8 6

Tone–color correlations are recorded in the DLPFC and prompt PM cells to select movement.

Figure 16.15 ▲

Dorsolateral Prefrontal Cells Code Sensory Associations

representation of spatial information, and the dorsomedial regions likely play a similar role with object information.

The results of electrophysiological studies lend further support for the role of area 46, as an experiment by Joaquin Fuster and colleagues (2000) illustrates. Monkeys were trained to associate each of two tones with one of two colors, as illustrated in **Figure 16.15**A. The trick was that a monkey heard the tone and then had to remember that particular tone for 10 s before responding to obtain a reward.

A large contingent of dorsolateral prefrontal cells (in areas 9 and 46) responded selectively to one tone or the other and later—apparently in concert with premotor cells (in areas 6 and 8)—to its associated color (Figure 16.15B). The DLPFC cells appear to integrate sound and color across time. Curiously, in trials on which the animals made errors, the DLPFC cells failed to respond, indicating no temporal correlation of sound and color.

Studying Temporal Memory in Humans

Studies of temporal memory have taken a slightly different slant with human subjects. On the basis of earlier work by others, Brenda Milner, Phil Corsi, and Gabriel Leonard (1991) designed an ingenious memory test for the order in which things have happened, often called **recency memory**. Subjects are shown a long series of cards, each bearing two stimulus items, either words or pictures. On some cards, a question mark appears between the items, and the subjects' task is to indicate which of the two they saw more recently. Successful performance requires the subjects to recall the order of stimulus presentation.

On most test trials, both items have appeared previously, but on some trials, one item is new. In this case, the task becomes one of simple recognition memory. Patients with frontal-lobe lesions perform at normal on the recognition trials but are impaired in judging the relative recency of two previously seen items. Further, the frontal lobes show a relative asymmetry in this regard: the right frontal lobe appears to be more important for nonverbal, or pictorial, recency memory; the left frontal lobe appears to be more important for verbal recency.

In contrast, patients with temporal-lobe lesions are impaired in the recognition test but not in the recency test. This latter finding is curious: it seems analogous to blindsight in that people who fail to recognize items can identify which was observed most recently. Might this suggest a memory location system separate from a memory recognition system?

Petrides and Milner (1982) designed an experiment conceptually similar to Passingham's self-ordering task for monkeys. Subjects were presented with stacks of cards on which were displayed an array of 12 stimuli, including words or drawings in parallel versions of the task. The stimuli in the array remained constant, but the position of each stimulus varied randomly from card to card.

The subjects' task appeared rather simple: go through the stack and point to only one item on each card, taking care not to point to the same item twice. Thus, the subjects themselves initiated the plan to follow and determined the order of responding. Although the task appears easy to us, for frontal-lobe patients it is not: left-frontal-lobe lesions were associated with impaired performance of both verbal and nonverbal versions of the task, whereas right-frontal-lobe lesions were associated with poor performance only on the nonverbal test.

Petrides and Milner suggested that, in contrast with the recency tests, the self-ordered tasks require subjects to organize and carry out a sequence of responses. From the moment subjects begin to respond, they must constantly compare the responses they have made with those that remain to be carried out. Hence, the self-ordered task demands an accurate memory as well as an organized strategy (see also Petrides, 1991).

When questioned afterward about their approach to the task, patients with frontal lesions were less likely than other subjects to report that they had used a particular strategy. When they had, the strategy often appeared both ill-defined and inconsistently used. The deficit is unlikely to be one of simple memory because temporal-lobe patients, who would be expected to have memory defects, performed this task at normal proficiency.

Impaired Social and Sexual Behavior

Social and sexual behaviors require flexible responses that are highly dependent on contextual cues. Frontal-lobe lesions interfere with both. An obvious and striking effect of frontal-lobe damage in humans is a marked change in social behavior and personality.

The most publicized example of personality change subsequent to frontal-lobe lesions is that of Phineas Gage, first reported by John Harlow in 1868. Gage was a dynamite worker who survived an explosion that blasted an iron tamping bar through the front of his head. The bar, shown as part of the reconstruction in **Figure 16.16**, was about 1 m long and 3 cm wide at its widest point.

After the accident, Gage's behavior changed completely. He had been of average intelligence and was "energetic and persistent in executing all of his plans of operation" according to Harlow, who described Gage's personality after the injury as follows:

> The equilibrium or balance, so to speak, between his intellectual faculties and animal propensities seems to have been destroyed. He is fitful, irreverent, indulging at times in the grossest profanity, manifesting but little deference to his fellows, impatient of restraint or advice when it conflicts with his desires, at times pertinaciously obstinate, yet capricious and vacillating, devising many plans of operation, which are no sooner arranged than they are abandoned in turn for others appearing more feasible. A child in his intellectual capacity and manifestations, he has the animal passions of a strong man. (Blumer and Benson, 1975, p. 153)

Gage's injury affected primarily the left frontal lobe from the orbital region upward into the precentral region. Gage's skull has been examined carefully, but the first person with extensive frontal damage to undergo close scrutiny at autopsy was a furrier who fell 30 m from a window. He suffered a compound

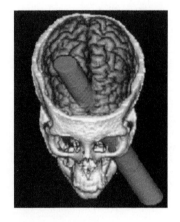

Figure 16.16 ▲

Frontal Injury Reconstruction No autopsy was performed when Phineas Gage died in 1861, but his skull was later recovered. Skull measurements were combined with imaging techniques to reconstruct the accident and determine the probable location of the lesioning. The image makes it obvious that Gage's frontal cortex in both hemispheres was damaged. (Patrick Landmann/Science Source.)

fracture of the frontal bones and severe injury to the right frontal lobe. Remarkably, he was never unconscious and was confused only briefly.

Before the fall, the furrier had been good natured and sociable; afterward he became nasty and cantankerous. Autopsy, about a year after the accident, revealed deep scarring of the orbital part of both frontal lobes, but more extensive on the right.

Pseudodepression and Pseudopsychopathy

From 1900 until about 1950, many excellent psychiatric studies of the effect of brain lesions on personality (especially Kleist's, cited in Zangwill, 1966) found consistently that damage to the orbitofrontal regions is associated with more-dramatic changes in personality than are dorsolateral lesions, although the latter also have significant effects. Clinical descriptions of frontal-lobe lesions' effects on personality abound, and while few systematic studies have been conducted, at least two types of personality change have been clinically observed in such patients.

Dietrich Blumer and Frank Benson (1975) have termed them **pseudodepression** and **pseudopsychopathy**. Patients classified as pseudodepressed exhibit such symptoms as outward apathy and indifference, loss of initiative, reduced sexual interest, little overt emotion, and little or no verbal output. Patients classified as pseudopsychopathic exhibit immature behavior, lack of tact and restraint, coarse language, promiscuous sexual behavior, increased motor activity, and a general lack of social graces. The following two case histories illustrate these personality types.

Pseudodepression

Prior to the accident, the patient had been garrulous, enjoyed people, had many friends and talked freely. He was active in community affairs, including Little League, church activities, men's clubs, and so forth. It was stated by one acquaintance that the patient had a true charisma, "whenever he entered a room, . . . everything became more animated, happy and friendly."

Following the head injury, he was quiet and remote. He would speak when spoken to and made sensible replies but would then lapse into silence. He made no friends on the ward, spent most of his time sitting alone smoking. He was frequently incontinent of urine, occasionally of stool. He remained unconcerned about either and was frequently found soaking wet, calmly sitting and smoking. If asked, he would matter-of-factly state that he had not been able to get to the bathroom in time but that this didn't bother him. . . . He could discuss many subjects intelligently, but was never known to initiate either a conversation or a request. . . . He was totally unconcerned about his wife and children. Formerly a warm and loving father, he did not seem to care about his family. Eventually, the family ceased visiting because of his indifference and unconcern. (Blumer and Benson, 1975, pp. 156–157)

Pseudopsychopathy

A 32-year-old white male was admitted for behavioral evaluation. History revealed that he had sustained a gunshot wound in Vietnam 5 years previously. A high-velocity missile had entered the left temple and emerged through the right orbit. Infection necessitated surgical removal of most of the orbital surface of the right frontal lobe. . . .

Prior to injury he had been quiet, intelligent, proper, and compulsive. He was a West Point graduate and spent the ensuing years as a military officer attaining the rank of captain. Both as a cadet and later as an officer, he was known to be quiet, strict, and rigid. He was considered a good commander, trusted by his men, but never shared camaraderie with his troops or with his peers.

Subsequent to injury, he was outspoken, facetious, brash, and disrespectful. There was no evidence of self-pity, although he frequently made rather morbid jokes about his condition (for example, "dummy's head"). On admission to the hospital, he had just failed at an extremely simple job. (Blumer and Benson, 1975, pp. 155)

Blumer and Benson assert that all elements of pseudodepression and pseudopsychopathy are observable only after bilateral frontal-lobe damage. Nevertheless, some elements of these two rather different syndromes can be observed in most, if not all, persons with unilateral frontal-lobe lesions. Pseudodepression appears most likely to follow lesions of the left frontal lobe, whereas pseudopsychopathic behavior seems likely to follow lesions of the right frontal lobe.

Deficits in Social and Sexual Behavior

Historically, changes in sexual behavior are among the most difficult symptoms of frontal-lobe damage to document properly, largely because of social taboos against investigating people's sexual lives. To date, there are no such empirical studies, but anecdotal evidence suggests that frontal lesions do alter libido and related behavior. Orbitofrontal lesions may introduce abnormal sexual behavior (such as public masturbation) by reducing inhibitions, although the frequency of sexual behavior is not affected. Conversely, dorsolateral lesions appear to reduce interest in sexual behavior, although patients are still capable of the necessary motor acts and can perform sexually if led through the activity "step by step."

The results of several studies show that frontal-lobe lesions in monkeys significantly alter social behavior. In one interesting study (Butter and Snyder, 1972), the dominant (alpha) male was removed from each of several groups of monkeys, and the frontal lobes were removed from half of the alpha monkeys. When the animals were later returned to their groups, they all resumed the position of dominant male, but within a couple of days, all the monkeys without frontal lobes were deposed and fell to the bottom of the group hierarchy.

Analogous studies of wild monkeys show similar results: those with frontal-lobe lesions fall to the bottom of the group hierarchy and eventually die, because they are helpless alone. Exactly how the social behavior of these animals changed is unknown, but the changes are likely as dramatic as those in the social behavior of humans with similar deficits.

Monkeys' social interactions are complex and include significant context-dependent behavior. A monkey's behavior will change in accord with the configuration of the proximal social group, and monkeys may lose this ability after frontal-lobe lesions. There are likely to be additional components of this behavioral change, however, that relate to interpreting species-typical sensory cues, whether they be odors, facial expressions, or sounds.

The deficit in perception of facial expression by human frontal-lobe patients may be related to the loss of cells that code for facial expression. Certain cells in the superior temporal sulcus are especially responsive to facial expression (see Section 15.2), and Edmund Rolls (1998) and his colleagues showed that a population of cells in the orbitofrontal cortex also codes for faces. Some of these face-selective neurons are responsive to facial expression or movement.

It is thus not surprising that patients with orbitofrontal lesions might have difficulty understanding facial expressions. We could speculate that there are also likely to be cells in the prefrontal cortex that are responsive to tone of voice, a verbal analog of facial expression.

Does a Spatial Deficit Exist?

Recall that key to understanding the functions of the dorsolateral prefrontal cortex is its relation to the posterior parietal cortex, which plays a central role in visuomotor guidance of movements in space. Region PG and the superior temporal sulcus play some role in more-complex spatial behavior such as mental rotation (see Section 14.2). These parietotemporal regions provide a major input into the dorsolateral region (see Figure 16.3A), implying some role for this frontal area in spatially guided behavior.

The precise role has been difficult to determine. Clearly, dorsolateral lesions impair short-term memory for the location of events, and this deficit presumably could interfere with selecting behaviors with respect to places in space. Indeed, the delayed-response deficit and the deficit in Passingham's and Goldman-Rakic's tasks (see Figure 16.14A and B) have spatial components.

The DLPFC's role in "spatial thinking" is evident in a blood-flow study by Per Roland and Lars Friberg (1985). They asked participants to imagine walking along a familiar route and taking first a left turn, then a right, and so on, alternating turns along the path. A major increase in blood flow in the dorsolateral region suggests a role for the DLPFC in selecting spatially guided behaviors.

Taken together, results of the blood-flow and lesion studies suggest that the frontal lobe participates in selecting among different visual locations. This may be related to some aspect of attention, an idea to which we return in Section 22.2. Note, however, that little evidence favors a role for the prefrontal cortex in parietal-lobe functions such as topographic orientation or in the ability to mentally manipulate or organize spatial information (see Section 14.1).

Clinical Neuropsychological Assessment of Frontal-Lobe Damage

Considering the number and variety of symptoms associated with frontal-lobe damage, surprisingly few standardized neuropsychological tests are useful for assessing frontal-lobe function. Furthermore, some symptoms of frontal-lobe injury, such as the loss of behavioral self-regulation, are not easily assessed by neuropsychological testing.

Two test batteries have been designed to measure executive functions— EXIT-25 and the Frontal Assessment Battery. Both appear to do so (Dubois et al., 2000; Moorhouse et al., 2009). One difficulty is that although the terms *executive functions* and *frontal functions* are often used interchangeably, they are not synonymous, and patients with focal lesions restricted to the frontal lobe are not impaired on such batteries (e.g., Chapados and Petrides, 2013).

Nonetheless, a number of excellent clinical tests are summarized in **Table 16.3**. As with the parietal- and temporal-lobe tests discussed in Sections 14.5

Table 16.3 **Standardized clinical neuropsychological tests for frontal-lobe damage**

Function	Test	Basic Reference
Response inhibition	Wisconsin Card Sorting	Milner, 1964
	Stroop	Perret, 1974
Verbal fluency	Thurstone Word Fluency	Milner, 1964
		Ramier and Hecaen, 1970
Nonverbal fluency	Design Fluency	Jones-Gotman and Milner, 1977
Motor	Hand dynamometry	Taylor, 1979
	Finger tapping	Reitan and Davison, 1974
	Sequencing	Kolb and Milner, 1981
Language comprehension	Token	de Renzi and Faglioni, 1978
	Spelling	Taylor, 1979
	Phonetic discrimination	Taylor, 1979
Working (temporal) memory	Self-ordering	Owen et al., 1990
Planning	Tower of London	Owen et al., 1995

and 15.4, it would be highly unusual for a person to perform at normal on all these tests if either frontal lobe were damaged.

The Wisconsin Card-Sorting Test (see Figure 16.10) is the best available for assessing dorsolateral prefrontal cortex function. As described earlier, a subject is told to sort the cards into piles in front of one or another of the stimulus cards bearing designs that differ in color, form, and number of elements. The correct solution shifts without the subject's knowledge when he or she has figured out each solution.

The Thurstone Word-Fluency Test illustrated in Figure 16.8 requires subjects to say or write as many words beginning with a given letter as possible in 5 min and then as many four-letter words beginning with a given letter in 4 min. Although subjects with lesions anywhere in the prefrontal cortex are apt to perform this test poorly, patients with left hemisphere dorsomedial lesions above the anterior cingulate region perform the worst. Patients with extensive orbital lesions perform only slightly better, but those with restricted orbital lesions are not impaired.

The Gotman–Milner Design-Fluency Test (see Figure 16.9) also is very useful, although difficult to score. Subjects are asked to draw as many unnameable, abstract drawings as they can in 5 min. Frontal-lobe patients will draw few items, nameable objects, or the same figure repeatedly. The design-fluency task appears most sensitive to right frontal injury.

Two tests, the Tower of Hanoi and the Tower of London, have proved sensitive to frontal injury, although the Tower of London appears a purer test of planning functions. In both tests, a person is presented with several pegs and discs of varying size. The discs must be moved from the presented location to another configuration and location according to different rules. For example, only one disc can be moved at a time, and a large disc may never be placed on a smaller one. Damage to either the left or the right prefrontal cortex produces impairments on these tasks.

The self-ordering task designed by Petrides and Milner and discussed earlier in this section is a good test of temporal memory (see Ross et al., 2007). Patients

454 PART III CORTICAL FUNCTIONS

are presented with a stack of cards. An array of 12 verbal or nonverbal stimuli is displayed in different locations on each card. The task is to point to a new stimulus on each card, taking care not to point to an object twice. Damage to either frontal lobe impairs performance on the verbal task, but the nonverbal task is impaired only by right frontal lesions.

Tests of motor function include tests of strength (hand dynamometry), finger-tapping speed, and movement sequencing. Strength and finger-tapping speed are significantly reduced contralaterally to a lesion in the vicinity of the precentral or postcentral gyri. Motor sequencing can be assessed by using Kolb and Milner's facial-sequence test, although it requires considerable practice to administer and videotaped records should be used for scoring. Simpler tests of movement programming such as the Kimura Box Test (see Figure 14.11) are not suitable because frontal-lobe patients are unlikely to perform very poorly unless the lesion extends into the basal ganglia.

As in preceding chapters, we recommend the Token Test for quick screening for aphasia, to be followed if necessary by more-extensive aphasia testing (see Section 19.6). Although damage to Broca's area is widely believed to result in deficits only in language production and not in comprehension, this notion is not strictly true. Left frontal lesions in the vicinity of Broca's area produce deficits in comprehension as well as in production.

Spelling is seriously impaired by facial-area lesions and can be assessed by any standardized spelling test. Phonetic differentiation (a test described by Stitt and Huntington, 1969, and used for neurological patients by Taylor) is another means of assessing facial-area function. A series of nonsense words, such as *agma*, is presented. The subject's task is to identify the first consonant sound. This test proves difficult even for controls, but subjects with facial-area damage, especially in the left hemisphere, perform most poorly. However, frontal-lobe lesions outside the facial area also may significantly impair performance on this test.

In the absence of language deficits, localizing frontal-lobe damage in either the left or the right hemisphere with neuropsychological tests may prove difficult, presumably because the two frontal lobes' functions overlap significantly. Clinical evaluation of personality as pseudodepressed or pseudopsychopathic (presented earlier in this section) may prove useful in localizing dysfunction to the left or the right hemisphere, respectively, but caution is advised. Unfortunately, no standardized quantitative measures of these symptoms are available.

16.4 Intelligence and the Frontal Lobes

The large evolutionary expansion of the frontal lobe, and especially of the prefrontal cortex, suggests that increased human intelligence relative to that of other primates is related to frontal lobe size. But until recently, the consensus held that intelligence does not reside in the frontal lobes (e.g., Hebb, 1945) because large frontal injuries, including frontal lobotomies, have little effect on intelligence as measured by standard intelligence tests. Yet for more than a century psychologists have searched for other measures of intelligence (e.g., Carroll, 2003; Cattell, 1971; Gardner, 1983; Spearman, 1927), so perhaps intelligence and the frontal lobe can be related to measurements other than IQ score.

Nearly a century ago, Charles Spearman (1927) proposed that some general factor (the *g* factor) contributes to all cognitive activity. Although his idea has been widely criticized, in fact a near-universal positive correlation among cognitive tests suggests that indeed, something like *g* does exist. The best single tests of *g* usually involve problem-solving tasks, which engage **fluid intelligence**, the ability to see abstract relationships and draw logical inferences. Fluid intelligence can be contrasted with **crystallized intelligence**, the ability to retain and use knowledge acquired through prior learning and experience, which is closely related to Wechsler IQ score, as described in the Section 16.3 discussion of convergent thinking.

Brain imaging studies link tests of fluid intelligence to a characteristic pattern of activity, both in dorsolateral and medial prefrontal cortex and in posterior parietal cortex. Jung and Haier (2007) reviewed 37 structural and functional imaging studies and identified a distributed set of brain regions related to fluid intelligence (**Figure 16.17**). Key structures include posterior parietal and prefrontal regions, which the researchers propose are related to processes of integration and abstraction (posterior parietal) and problem solving, evaluation, and hypothesis testing (prefrontal) (see reviews by Colom et al., 2010; Deary et al., 2010). Notably, the activations summarized in Figure 16.17 are asymmetrical, with little overlap between the hemispheres.

One obvious prediction of Jung and Haier's theory is that damage to these regions should significantly impair performance on tests of fluid intelligence. Alexandra Woolgar and colleagues (2010) confirmed this idea in a large study. Damage to frontal or parietal regions, they found, is predictive of fluid intelligence loss, whereas damage beyond these regions is not predictive.

Richard Passingham and Steven Wise (2012) propose that new prefrontal and posterior parietal areas emerged during the evolution of anthropoid apes, eventually leading to disproportionately large prefrontal and parietal regions in the modern human brain. They expanded their hypothesis, suggesting that the resulting prefrontal–parietal networks laid the groundwork for expanding fluid intelligence (general problem solving) in humans (Genovesio, Wise, and Passingham, 2014). Genovesio and coworkers argue that as our ancestors' brains enlarged, greater metabolic demands placed a premium on identifying productive foraging locations that might differ in food quality, volume, and danger in getting to the food. According to this hypothesis, foraging strategies that supported reduced risk-taking and hominid survival also selected for the superior problem-solving capacities that evolved in humans and thus increased our intelligence. The risk-taking behavior frontal lobe patients display illustrates what happens when the newly evolved frontal system dysfunctions.

⊚ Figure 16.17 ▲

Proposed Loci of Fluid Intelligence Brodmann areas (pink and green) proposed to correlate with intelligence. The arcuate fasiculus (yellow) is a likely tract for connecting these brain regions. Green areas show predominantly left-hemisphere correlations, and pink areas show predominantly right-hemisphere correlations. (I.J. Deary, L. Penke, and W. Johnson. The neuroscience of human intelligence differences. *Nature Reviews Neuroscience* 11, March 2010, Fig. 2 p. 208. Figure is modified, with permission, from Jung, R. E. & Haier, R. J. The Parieto-Frontal Integration Theory (P-FIT) of intelligence: converging neuroimaging evidence. *Behav. Brain Sci.* 30,135–154; discussion 154–187, 2007 © 2007 Cambridge University Press.)

16.5 Imaging Frontal-Lobe Function

In general, imaging study results such as those listed in **Table 16.4** show specific activation for prefrontal functions that were identified historically in lesion studies. Thus, for example, many results show dorsolateral prefrontal participation in tasks tapping verbal and nonverbal working temporal memory.

Table 16.4 **Some functional imaging studies of frontal-lobe function**

Presumed Function	Locus of Activation	Basic Reference
Self-ordering	Dorsolateral	Petrides, 2000
Conditioned learning	Dorsolateral	Petrides, 2000
Spatial working memory	Dorsolateral; ventrolateral	Owen et al., 1996
Visuomotor skill learning	Dorsolateral	Doyon et al., 1996
Verbal memory retrieval	Dorsolateral	Buckner et al., 1995
		Tulving et al., 1994
	Orbitofrontal	Petrides et al., 1995
Reversal learning	Orbital and dorsolateral	Hampshire et al., 2012
Encoding visual information	Orbitofrontal	Frey and Petrides, 2000
Evaluation of faces	Ventromedial and orbital	Mende-Siedlecki et al., 2013
Encoding unpleasant auditory information	Orbitofrontal	Frey et al., 2000
Facial expression or recognition or both	Inferior prefrontal	Iidaka et al., 2001
Autobiographic memory	Medial; ventrolateral	Svoboda et al., 2006

A review of frontal-lobe activation patterns associated with a broad range of different cognitive demands—including aspects of perception, response selection, executive functions, working memory, long-term memory, and problem solving—yielded an especially intriguing finding (Duncan and Owen, 2000). Given such a diverse set of presumed cognitive functions, one can reasonably imagine that different frontal lobe regions are active as cognitive tasks that require different cognitive functions are performed. Yet a striking regularity in activation emerged in the research: for most cognitive demands, imaging reveals a similar recruitment of the dorsolateral, ventromedial, and anterior cingulate regions, as summarized in **Figure 16.18**.

The reviewers conclude that although regional specialization exists within the frontal lobes, an integrated frontal-lobe network is consistently recruited

Figure 16.18 ▶

Regular Activation Patterns Prefrontal activation produced by widely different cognitive demands is mapped on lateral and medial views of each hemisphere. Despite the diversity of demands, frontal activations show apparent clustering: most points register within dorsolateral, ventromedial, and anterior cingulate regions.

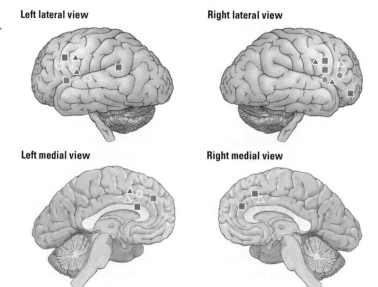

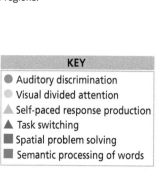

KEY
● Auditory discrimination
○ Visual divided attention
△ Self-paced response production
▲ Task switching
■ Spatial problem solving
■ Semantic processing of words

for solving a diverse set of cognitive problems. How these three regions work in concert to produce behavior is not immediately obvious, but the overlap of activation in controlling such diverse cognitive processes makes the frontal lobe's centrality obvious. Recall, too, the role of the prefrontal cortex in the brain's default network, of the anterior cingulate cortex in the salience network (Section 16.1), and of the prefrontal–parietal network in intelligence (Section 16.4).

⊚ 16.6 Disorders Affecting the Frontal Lobe

Many people with psychiatric or neurological disorders present symptoms characteristic of frontal-lobe injury. Disturbance of frontal function likely contributes significantly to the behavioral symptoms of each disease. In addition, chronic stress alters prefrontal neurons in ways that affect some memory and behavioral functions.

In schizophrenia, an abnormality in the mesolimbic dopamine projection that terminates largely in the frontal lobes, a decrease in blood flow to the frontal lobes and possible frontal-lobe atrophy are believed to contribute. Schizophrenia patients perform poorly on all tests of frontal-lobe function and exhibit abnormalities in eye-movement control, but they perform at normal on tests of parietal-lobe function.

Parkinson's disease results from a loss of dopamine cells in the midbrain substantia nigra and thus from the nigrostriatal pathway. Although the cells' primary projection is to the caudate nucleus, they influence the prefrontal cortex indirectly through the caudate's projection to the dorsomedial nucleus of the thalamus. Parkinson patients are characterized by a lack of facial expression similar to that seen in frontal-lobe patients and are impaired in the Wisconsin Card-Sorting Test and at delayed-response tasks.

Korsakoff's syndrome is a metabolic disorder of the central nervous system often associated with chronic alcoholism, as detailed in Section 18.6. Korsakoff patients have alcohol-induced damage to the dorsomedial thalamus and may have a deficiency in catecholamines in the frontal cortex. They perform poorly on the Wisconsin Card-Sorting Test as well as on tests of spatial memory, such as delayed response.

An inability to control drug-seeking behavior despite aversive consequences characterizes drug addiction (see Section 6.4). Drug addicts typically show impulsive or compulsive behavior or perseveration, all symptoms of frontal-lobe dysfunction. Results of studies with addicts in decision-making tasks, such as the gambling tasks described in Section 16.3, show impairments reminiscent of orbitofrontal patients, and imaging studies show impairments in orbitofrontal blood flow during acute withdrawal and even after long periods of abstinence (for reviews, see Gom et al., 2005, and Schoenbaum et al., 2006).

Addictive drugs change the structure of neurons in both the orbitofrontal and the medial prefrontal regions in rats (for a review, see Robinson and Kolb, 2004). Drug addiction is likely related to abnormalities in prefrontal structure and function that are associated with the maladaptive decision-making characteristic of addictive behavior.

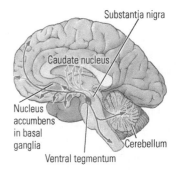

▲ **Dopaminergic Activating System** The nigrostriatal DA pathway (orange projections) takes part in coordinating movement. The mesolimbic DA pathway (purple projections) is greatly affected by addictive drugs. Abnormalities in this pathway may be related to schizophrenia.

▶ Chronic stress experienced by male rats reduces dendritic length (and thus synaptic space) in the medial prefrontal cortex (left) but increases dendritic length in the orbitofrontal cortex (right). (Research from McEwen, B. S., and J. H. Morrison, The brain on stress: Vulnerability and plasticity of the prefrontal cortex over the life course. *Neuron* 79:16–29, 2013, Figure 2, p. 19 © Elsevier.)

Chronic stress

Medial prefrontal cortex

Orbitofrontal cortex

Prolonged stress is correlated with functionally significant changes in the structure of neurons in the PFC that affect temporal memory and goal-directed behaviors (see review by McEwan and Morrison, 2013). Laboratory animal studies have shown that chronic stress in male rats reduces synaptic space in neurons in the medial PFC but increases synaptic space in the orbitofrontal cortex. In contrast, similar stress in female rats produces the opposite effect in medial PFC regions (Garrett and Wellman, 2009). In young adult rats these changes are at least partially reversible with periods of reduced stress, but aged animals show no such recovery. We can speculate that age-related decline in cognitive abilities could partly reflect the chronic effects of stress throughout a lifetime.

SUMMARY

We can conceive of the frontal lobe as the end point for visuomotor and object-recognition functions that originate in the occipital lobe. The frontal lobe's function is to select behaviors with respect to context and internalized knowledge.

16.1 Frontal-Lobe Anatomy

The frontal lobe's four distinct functional zones are primary motor cortex, premotor cortex, prefrontal cortex, and anterior cingulate cortex. The motor cortex specifies elementary movements, whereas the premotor cortex chooses more complex movements from a stored movement lexicon. The prefrontal cortex, through its participation in several extended, integrated networks including the default network and networks involved in socioemotional behaviors, controls cognitive processes that select appropriate movements at the correct time and place. The anterior cingulate cortex forms part of an extended salience network that operates to modulate other cerebral networks.

16.2 A Theory of Frontal-Lobe Function

The premotor cortex can be divided into two functional regions: (1) the lateral area responsible for selecting behaviors in response to environmental cues and (2) the supplementary area responsible for selecting behaviors on the basis of internalized knowledge. The prefrontal cortex can be divided into three general zones: (1) a dorsolateral zone, responsible for selecting behavior with respect to temporal memory; (2) the orbitofrontal cortex, responsible for decision making related to emotion and reward; and, (3) the ventromedial prefrontal region, responsible for selecting behavior with respect to context. Context may be current or based on previous knowledge, including self-knowledge.

16.3 Symptoms of Frontal-Lobe Lesions

The range of symptoms that result from frontal-lobe lesions can be grouped conceptually into several categories: (1) disturbances of motor functions; (2) loss of divergent thinking; (3) impaired response inhibition and inflexible behavior; (4) poor temporal memory; and (5) impaired social and sexual behavior imaging. Left and right frontal lesions have complementary effects in that left frontal lesions are more likely to affect language- or movement-related behaviors, and right frontal lesions are more likely to alter nonlanguage functions, such as emotion.

16.4 Intelligence and the Frontal Lobes

The prefrontal cortex is expanded in hominoids, leading to more complex problem-solving skills in modern humans and expanded participation of the prefrontal cortex in intelligence. Prefrontal activity is proposed to underlie problem solving, evaluation, and hypothesis testing. Although frontal lobe lesions do not affect standard IQ scores, activity in a parieto prefrontal network is associated with measures of problem solving, often referred to as fluid intelligence.

16.5 Imaging Frontal-Lobe Function

Results of imaging studies show frontal participation in tasks with widely different cognitive demands, including attentional tasks, sensory discrimination tasks, motor tasks, spatial problem solving, and the semantic processing of words.

16.6 Disorders Affecting the Frontal Lobe

Frontal lobe dysfunction is implicated in many behavioral disorders, including particularly schizophrenia, Parkinson's disease, Korsakoff's syndrome, and drug addiction. Frontal dysfunction can also result from chronic stress.

References

Amiez, C., P. Kostopoulos, A. S. Champod, and M. Petrides. Local morphology predicts functional organization of the dorsal premotor region in the human brain. *Journal of Neuroscience* 26:2724–2731, 2006.

Bechara, A., D. Tranel, and H. Damasio. Characterization of the decision-making deficit of patients with ventromedial prefrontal cortex lesions. *Brain* 123:2189–2202, 2000.

Benton, A. L. Differential effects of frontal lobe disease. *Neuropsychologia* 6:53–60, 1968.

Bizzi, E., and P. H. Schiller. Single unit activity in the frontal eye fields of unanesthetized monkeys during head and eye movement. *Experimental Brain Research* 10:151–158, 1970.

Blumer, D., and D. F. Benson. Personality changes with frontal and temporal lobe lesions. In D. F. Benson and D. Blumer, Eds., *Psychiatric Aspects of Neurologic Disease*. New York: Grune & Stratton, 1975.

Bonnelle, V., T. E. Ham, R. Leech, K. M. Kinnunen, M. A. Mehta, R. J. Greenwood, and D. J. Sharp. Salience network integrity predicts default mode network function after traumatic brain injury. *Proceedings of the National Academy of Sciences U.S.A.* 109: 4690–4695, 2012.

Brown, J. W. *Aphasia, Apraxia, and Agnosia: Clinical and Theoretical Aspects*. Springfield, Ill.: Charles C Thomas, 1972.

Buckner, R. The brain's default network: Origins and implications for the study of psychosis. *Dialogues in Clinical Neuroscience* 15:351–358, 2013.

Buckner, R. L., M. E. Raichle, and S. E. Petersen. Dissociation of human prefrontal cortical areas across different speech production tasks and gender groups. *Journal of Neurophysiology* 74:2163–2173, 1995.

Butter, C. M., and D. R. Snyder. Alterations in aversive and aggressive behaviors following orbital frontal lesions in rhesus monkeys. *Acta Neurobiologiae Experimentalis* 32:525–565, 1972.

Carroll, J. B. The higher-stratum structure of cognitive abilities: Current evidence supports g and about 10 broad factors. In H. Nyborg, Ed., *The Scientific Study of General Intelligence: Tribute to Arthur R. Jensen*, pp. 5–21. Amsterdam: Pergamon, 2003.

Cattell R. B. *Abilities: Their Structure, Growth and Action*. Boston: Houghton-Mifflin, 1971.

Chapados, C., and M. Petrides. Impairment only on the fluency subtest of the frontal assessment battery after prefrontal lesions. *Brain* 136(Pt 10):2966–2978, 2013.

Colom, R., S. Karama, R. E. Jung, and R. J. Haier. Human intelligence and brain networks. *Dialogues in Clinical Neuroscience* 12:489–501, 2010.

Deary, I. J., L. Penke, and W. Johnson. The neuroscience of human intelligence differences. *Nature Reviews Neuroscience* 11:201–211, March 2010.

de Renzi, E., and P. Faglioni. Normative data and screening power of a shortened version of the Token Test. *Cortex* 14:41–49, 1978.

Doyon J., R. Laforce, G. Bouchard, D. Gaudreau, J. Roy, M. Poirier, P. J. Bedard, F.

Doyon, J., A. M. Owen, M. Petrides, V. Sziklas, and A. C. Evans. Functional anatomy of visuomotor skill learning in human subjects examined with positron emission tomography. *European Journal of Neuroscience* 8:637–648, 1996.

Dubois, B., A. Slachevsky, I. Litvan, and B. Pillon. The FAB: A frontal assessment battery at bedside. *Neurology* 55:1621–1626, 2000.

Duncan, J., and A. M. Owen. Common origins of the human frontal lobe recruited by diverse cognitive demands. *Trends in Neuroscience* 23:475–483, 2000.

Freedman, M., and M. Oscar-Berman. Bilateral frontal lobe disease and selective delayed response deficits in humans. *Behavioral Neuroscience* 100:337–342, 1986.

Frey, S., P. Kostopoulous, and M. Petrides. Orbitofrontal involvement in the processing of unpleasant auditory information. *European Journal of Neuroscience* 12:3709–3712, 2000.

Frey, S., and M. Petrides. Orbitofrontal cortex: A key prefrontal region for encoding information. *Proceedings of the National Academy of Sciences U.S.A.* 97:8723–8727, 2000.

Funahashi, S., C. J. Bruce, and P. S. Goldman-Rakic. Perimetry of spatial memory representation in primate prefrontal cortex. *Society for Neuroscience Abstracts* 12:554, 1986.

Fuster, J. M., M. Bodner, and J. K. Kroger. Cross-modal and cross-temporal association in neurons of frontal cortex. *Nature* 405:347–351, 2000.

Gardner, H. *Frames of the Mind*. New York: Basic Books, 1983.

Garrett, J. E., and C. L. Wellman. Chronic stress effects on dendritic morphology in medial prefrontal cortex: Sex differences and estrogen dependence. *Neuroscience* 162:195–207, 2009.

Genovesio, A., S. P. Wise, and R. E. Passingham. Prefrontal-parietal function: From foraging to foresight. *Trends in Cognitive Sciences* 18:72–81, 2014.

Gom, G., B. Sabbe, W. Hulstijn, and W. van den Brink. Substance use disorders and the orbitofrontal cortex. *British Journal of Psychiatry* 187:209–220, 2005.

Goodall, J. *The Chimpanzees of Gombe*. Cambridge, Mass.: Harvard University Press, 1986.

Guilford, J. P. *The Nature of Human Intelligence*. New York: McGraw-Hill, 1967.

Guitton, D., H. A. Buchtel, and R. M. Douglas. Disturbances of voluntary saccadic eye-movement mechanisms following discrete unilateral frontal-lobe removals. In G. Lennerstrand, D. S. Lee, and E. L. Keller, Eds., *Functional Basis of Ocular Motility Disorders*. Oxford: Pergamon, 1982.

Habib, L., Nyberg, L., and Tulving, E. Hemispheric asymmetries of memory: The HERA model revisited, 3. *Trends in Cognitive Sciences* 7: 241–245, 2003.

Hampshire, A., A. M. Chaudhry, A. M. Owen, and A. C. Roberts. Dissociable roles for lateral orbitofrontal cortex and lateral prefrontal cortex during preference driven reversal learning. *NeuroImage* 59:4102–4112, 2012.

Hebb, D. O. Man's frontal lobes: A critical review. *Archives of Neurology and Psychiatry* 54:10–24, 1945.

Hsu, M., M. Bhatt, R. Adolphs, D. Tranel, and C. F. Camerer. Neural systems responding to degrees of uncertainty in human decision-making. *Science* 310:1680–1684, 2005.

Iidaka, T., M. Omori, T. Murata, H. Kosaka, Y. Yonekura, T. Okada, and N. Sadato. Neural interaction of the amygdala with the prefrontal and temporal cortices in the processing of facial expressions as revealed by fMRI. *Journal of Cognitive Neuroscience* 15:1035–1047, 2001.

Jacobsen, C. F. Studies of cerebral function in primates. *Comparative Psychology Monographs* 13:1–68, 1936.

Jones-Gotman, M., and B. Milner. Design fluency: The invention of nonsense drawings after focal cortical lesions. *Neuropsychologia* 15:653–674, 1977.

Jones-Gotman, M., and R. J. Zatorre. Odor recognition memory in humans: Role of right temporal and orbitofrontal regions. *Brain and Cognition* 22:182–198, 1993.

Jung, R. E., and R. J. Haier. The parieto-frontal integration theory (P-FIT) of intelligence: Converging neuroimaging evidence. *Behavioral and Brain Sciences* 30:135–187, 2007.

Kolb, B., and B. Milner. Performance of complex arm and facial movements after focal brain lesions. *Neuropsychologia* 19:505–514, 1981.

Kolb, B., and L. Taylor. Affective behavior in patients with localized cortical excisions: An analysis of lesion site and side. *Science* 214:89–91, 1981.

Kuypers, H. G. J. M. Anatomy of the descending pathways. In V. B. Brooks, Ed., *Handbook of Physiology; The Nervous System, vol. 2, The Motor Systems*. Baltimore: Williams & Wilkins, 1981.

Lashley, K. S. The problem of serial order in behavior. In F. A. Beach, D. O. Hebb, C. T. Morgan, and H. W. Nissen, Eds., *The Neuropsychology of Lashley*. New York: McGraw-Hill, 1960.

Leonard, G., L. Jones, and B. Milner. Residual impairment in handgrip strength after unilateral frontal-lobe lesions. *Neuropsychologia* 26:555–564, 1988.

Levine, B., S. E. Black, R. Cabeza, M. Sinden, A. R. Mcintosh, J. P. Toth, E. Tulving, and D. T. Stuss. Episodic memory and the self in a case of isolated retrograde amnesia. *Brain* 121:1951–1973, 1998.

Luria, A. R. *The Working Brain*. New York: Penguin, 1973.

Luria, A. R., and E. D. Homskaya. Disturbance in the regulative role of speech with frontal lobe lesions. In J. M. Warren and K. Akert, Eds., *The Frontal Granular Cortex and Behavior*. New York: McGraw-Hill, 1964.

McEwen, B. S., and J. H. Morrison. The brain on stress: Vulnerability and plasticity of the prefrontal cortex over the life course. *Neuron* 79:16–29, 2013.

Mende-Siedlecki, P., C. P. Said, and A. Todorov. The social evaluation of faces: A meta-analysis of functional neuroimaging studies. *Social and Cognitive Affective Neuroscience* 8:285–299, 2013.

Miller, L. Cognitive risk taking after frontal or temporal lobectomy I: The synthesis of fragmented visual information. *Neuropsychologia* 23:359–369, 1985.

Milner, B. Some effects of frontal lobectomy in man. In J. M. Warren and K. Akert, Eds., *The Frontal Granular Cortex and Behavior*. New York: McGraw-Hill, 1964.

Milner, B., P. Corsi, and G. Leonard. Frontal cortex contribution to recency judgements. *Neuropsychologia* 29:601–618, 1991.

Mishkin, M., and F. J. Manning. Non-spatial memory after selective prefrontal lesions in monkeys. *Brain Research* 143:313–323, 1978.

Moorhouse P., M. Gorman, and K. Rockwood. Comparison of EXIT-25 and the Frontal Assessment Battery for evaluation of executive dysfunction in patients attending a memory clinic. *Dementia, Geriatric and Cognitive Disorders* 27:424–428, 2009.

Owen, A. M., J. J. Downes, B. J. Sahakian, C. E. Polkey, and T. W. Robbins. Planning and spatial working memory following frontal lobe lesions in man. *Neuropsychologia* 28:1021–1034, 1990.

Owen, A. M., B. Milner, M. Petrides, and A. C. Evans. Memory for object features versus memory for object location: A positron-emission tomography study of encoding and retrieval processes. *Proceedings of the National Academy of Sciences U.S.A.* 93:9212–9217, 1996.

Owen, A. M., B. J. Sahakian, J. R. Hodges, R. A. Summers, C. E. Polkey, and T. W. Robbins. Dopamine-dependent fronto-striatal planning deficits in early Parkinson's disease. *Neuropsychology* 9:126–140, 1995.

Passingham, R. E. Memory of monkeys (*Macaca mulatta*) with lesions in prefrontal cortex. *Behavioral Neuroscience* 99:3–21, 1985.

Passingham, R. E. *The Frontal Lobes and Voluntary Action*. Oxford: Oxford University Press, 1993.

Passingham, R. E., and S. P. Wise. *The Neurobiology of the Prefrontal Cortex: Anatomy, Evolution, and the Origin of Insight*. New York: Oxford University Press, 2012.

Perret, E. The left frontal lobe of man and the suppression of habitual responses in verbal categorical behavior. *Neuropsychologia* 12:323–330, 1974.

Petrides, M. Functional specialization within the dorsolateral frontal cortex for serial order memory. *Proceedings of the Royal Society, London B* 246:299–306, 1991.

Petrides, M. Visuo-motor conditional associative learning after frontal and temporal lesions in the human brain. *Neuropsychologia* 35:989–997, 1997.

Petrides, M. Mapping prefrontal cortical systems for the control of cognition. In A. W. Toga and J. C. Mazziotta, Eds., *Brain Mapping: The Systems*, pp. 159–176. San Diego: Academic Press, 2000.

Petrides, M., B. Alivisatos, and A. C. Evans. Functional activation of the human ventrolateral frontal cortex during mnemonic retrieval of verbal information. *Proceedings of the National Academy of Sciences U.S.A.* 92:5803–5807, 1995.

Petrides, M., and B. Milner. Deficit on subject ordered tasks after frontal- and temporal-lobe lesions in man. *Neuropsychologia* 20:249–262, 1982.

Petrides, M., and D. N. Pandya. Dorsolateral prefrontal cortex: Comparative cytoarachitectonic analysis in the human and the macaque brain and corticocortical connection patterns. *European Journal of Neuroscience* 11:1011–1136, 1999.

Price, J. L., and W. C. Drevets. Neural circuits underling the pathophysiology of mood disorders. *Trends in Cognitive Sciences* 16:61–71, 2012.

Ramier, A. M., and H. Hecaen. Rôle respectif des atteintes frontales et de la latéralisation lésionnelle dans les déficits de la "fluence verbale." *Revue de Neurologie* 123:17–22, 1970.

Reitan, R. M., and L. A. Davison. *Clinical Neuropsychology: Current Status and Application.* New York: Wiley, 1974.

Robinson, T. E., and B. Kolb. Structural plasticity associated with drugs of abuse. *Neuropharmacology* 47(Suppl 1):33–46, 2004.

Roland, P. E., and L. Friberg. Localization of cortical areas activated by thinking. *Journal of Neurophysiology* 3:1219–1243, 1985.

Roland, P. E., B. Larsen, N. A. Lassen, and E. Skinhoj. Supplementary motor area and other cortical areas in organization of voluntary movements in man. *Journal of Neurophysiology* 43:118–136, 1980.

Rolls, E. T. The orbitofrontal cortex. In A. C. Roberts, T. W. Robbins, and L. Weizkrantz, Eds., *The Prefrontal Cortex: Executive and Cognitive Functions*, pp. 67–86. Oxford: Oxford University Press, 1998.

Rose, J. E., and C. N. Woolsey. The orbitofrontal cortex and its connections with the mediodorsal nucleus in rabbit, sheep and cat. *Research Publications of the Association of Nervous and Mental Disease* 27:210–232, 1948.

Ross, T. P., E. Hanouskova, K. Giarla, E. Calhoun, and M. Tucker. The reliability and validity of the self-ordered pointing task. *Archives of Clinical Neuropsychology* 22:449–458, 2007.

Roy, M., D. Shohamy, and T. D. Wager. Ventromedial prefrontal-subcortical systems and the generation of affective meaning. *Trends in Cognitive Sciences* 16:147–156, 2012.

Schoenbaum G., M. R. Roesch, and T. A. Stalnaker. Orbitofrontal cortex, decision-making and drug addiction. *Trends in Neuroscience* 29:116–124, 2006.

Shallice, T. *From Neuropsychology to Mental Structure.* Cambridge, U.K.: Cambridge University Press, 1988.

Shallice, T., and P. Burgess. Deficits in strategy application following frontal lobe damage in man. *Brain* 114:727–741, 1991.

Shallice, T., and M. E. Evans. The involvement of the frontal lobes in cognitive estimation. *Cortex* 14:294–303, 1978.

Smith, M. L., and B. Milner. Differential effects of frontal-lobe lesions on cognitive estimation and spatial memory. *Neuropsychologia* 22:697–705, 1984.

Spearman C. *The Abilities of Man.* New York: Macmillan, 1927.

Stitt, C., and D. Huntington. Some relationships among articulation, auditory abilities, and certain other variables. *Journal of Speech and Learning Research* 12:576–593, 1969.

Svoboda, E., M. C. McKinnon, and B. Levine. The functional neuroanatomy of autobiographical memory: A meta-analysis. *Neuropsychologia* 44:2189–2208, 2006.

Taylor, L. Psychological assessment of neurosurgical patients. In T. Rasmussen and R. Marino, Eds., *Functional Neurosurgery.* New York: Raven, 1979.

Teuber, H. L. The riddle of frontal lobe function in man. In J. M. Warren and K. Akert, Eds., *The Frontal Granular Cortex and Behavior.* New York: McGraw-Hill, 1964.

Teuber, H. L. Unity and diversity of frontal lobe function. *Acta Neurobiologiae Experimentalis* 32:615–656, 1972.

Tulving, E. Episodic memory: From mind to brain. *Annual Review of Psychology* 53:1–25, 2002.

Tulving E., S. Kapur, F. I. Craik, M. Moscovitch, and S. Houle. Hemispheric encoding/retrieval asymmetry in episodic memory: Positron emission tomography findings. *Proceedings of the National Academy of Sciences U.S.A.* 91:2016–2020, 1994.

Walker, E. A., and D. Blumer. The localization of sex in the brain. In K. J. Zulch, O. Creutzfeldt, and G. C. Galbraith, Eds., *Cerebral Localization.* Berlin and New York: Springer-Verlag, 1975.

Woolgar, A., A. Parr, R. Cusack, R. Thompson, I. Nimmo-Smith, T. Torralva, M. Roca, N. Antoun, F. Manes, and J. Duncan. Fluid intelligence loss linked to restricted regions of damage within frontal and parietal cortex. *Proceedings of the National Academy of Sciences U.S.A.* 107:14899–14902, 2010.

Zangwill, O. L. Psychological deficits associated with frontal lobe lesions. *International Journal of Neurology* 5:395–402, 1966.

17

Cortical Networks and Disconnection Syndromes

At Cross Purposes

D.M., the director of a large psychiatric hospital, began to complain of headaches and memory problems. A neurological examination found a cyst in the third ventricle (see Figure 3.11).

The only available treatment was to drain the cyst and relieve the pressure that was causing D.M.'s symptoms. The surgical procedure was simple and required that the neurosurgeon insert a cannula from the top of the brain through the corpus callosum and a bit of brainstem.

The cyst was drained successfully. D.M. showed good recovery: his headaches disappeared, his memory improved, and he returned to work. A year later, some residual memory difficulties persisted, but D.M. considered himself a lucky man. One new symptom bothered D.M. Throughout his life, he had found assembling large-project jigsaw puzzles relaxing, but he was now having difficulty and was finding the whole experience frustrating.

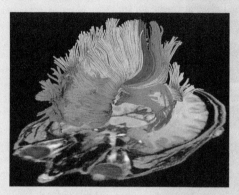

Hofer, Frahm: Topography of the human corpus callosum revisited—Comprehensive fiber tractography using diffusion tensor magnetic resonance imaging. *NeuroImage*, 32(3):989–994, 2006 © Elsevier.

His neurologist discovered that for certain types of tasks, such as puzzles, D.M.'s two hands were not working together. For example, the left hand would pick up one piece and the right hand another, and without realizing it, D.M. would try to put both pieces into the same place, one with each hand. No wonder he was frustrated!

His surgeon had cut a part of the corpus callosum, severing the connections linking the hands in the two hemispheres. D.M.'s right hand literally did not know what his left hand was doing. The diffusion tensor image (DTI) shown here represents the nerve fiber bundles projecting from the corpus callosum into both hemispheres of a male subject. Projections into the prefrontal cortex are green, premotor and supplementary motor areas light blue, M1 dark blue, S1 red, parietal lobes orange, occipital lobes yellow, and temporal lobes purple.

In preceding chapters, we have considered the connections among different cortical regions, most obviously the dorsal and ventral pathways of visual processing and the connectome. But we have not yet considered what happens when cortical pathways are disturbed. This chapter describes the effects of cutting cerebral connections, beginning with a summary of cortical connectivity and the anatomy of cerebral connections.

Next, we consider the structure of brain networks identified by advances in connectome research and revisit Roger Sperry's research on split-brain patients as a model of disconnection syndromes. We then reconsider Norman Geschwind's reinterpretation of three classic symptoms of cortical damage (aphasia, apraxia, and agnosia) as disconnection syndromes.

17.1 Disconnecting Cognitive Functions

To understand D.M.'s symptoms as described in the chapter-opening Portrait, let us look back on the effects that cortical injuries have on behavior. In Chapters 13 through 16, we associate particular behavioral deficits with different brain lesions and from these deficits try to infer the missing region's function. We also consider the results of imaging studies showing localized activity as different behavioral tasks are performed. Two inescapable conclusions emerge from these discussions:

1. **The anatomically defined cortical lobes each engage in a wide range of cognitive activities.** Thus, for example, the temporal lobe appears to play a significant role not only in vision and audition but also in more-complex cognitive functions such as memory, language, and emotion.

2. **Although the cortical lobes engage in different cognitive activities, they overlap remarkably in function.** For example, multimodal frontal lobe cells respond to visual, auditory, somatosensory, olfactory, and taste inputs and participate in such functions as memory, language, and emotion. Clearly, if we presume that the anatomical regions differ in function, then the simplest explanation for how these regions function together is that they participate in neural networks that integrate their varied contributions to virtually every neural function we can describe.

By its very nature, a network implies connections. (Review the connectome in Section 10.3.) The cutting of cerebral connections is called **disconnection**, and the ensuing behavioral effects are called **disconnection syndromes**. We thus can see that D.M.'s disconnection syndrome was an accidental result of his surgical procedure to drain the third ventricle cyst.

The behavioral changes that result from disconnecting cerebral regions can be odd, and they differ from behavioral changes we might expect if either area were damaged but remained connected. **Figure 17.1** illustrates two different forms of disconnection that John Downer (1961) performed on a monkey. In

Figure 17.1 ▼

Downer's Experiment (A) Anatomy of the intact monkey brain. (B) With the commissures severed, the amygdala on the left removed, and an occluder covering the right eye, the monkey displays no species-typical responses to visual stimuli and is described as "tame." (C) With the left eye occluded, the same monkey displays species-typical behavior in response to visual stimuli and is classified as "wild."

(A) Intact monkey

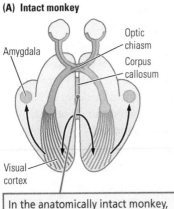

Amygdala

Optic chiasm

Corpus callosum

Visual cortex

In the anatomically intact monkey, the hemispheres are connected by commissures, including the optic chiasm and the corpus callosum.

(B) "Tame" monkey

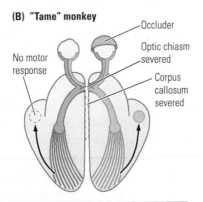

Occluder

Optic chiasm severed

No motor response

Corpus callosum severed

With the commissures disconnected, the right eye covered, and the left amygdala removed, visual information is unavailable to the motor system.

(C) "Wild" monkey

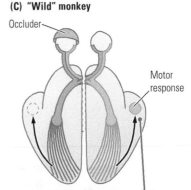

Occluder

Motor response

With the commissures disconnected, the right amygdala intact, and the left eye covered, the circuit in the right hemisphere for activating species-typical behavior is intact.

Downer's study, all commissures connecting the two halves of the brain were cut, and the amygdala on the left side was removed.

Downer then covered one of the animal's eyes with an occluder and presented objects to the other eye. If the objects were presented to the eye ipsilateral to the hemisphere with the ablated amygdala, the animal appeared "tame," even if the objects were typically frightening to monkeys (see Figure 17.1B). If the objects were presented to the eye ipsilateral to the intact amygdala, the animal made its usual species-typical responses to threats and appeared "wild" (see Figure 17.1C). Downer's results can be explained as follows.

For an animal to display species-typical responses to a visual stimulus, information must project from the eye to the visual cortex, through the temporal lobes to the amygdala, and from the amygdala to the brainstem and frontal cortex. These connections activate, respectively, autonomic responses, movements, and facial expressions. When the commissures are disconnected, visual information from one eye can project only to the ipsilateral hemisphere.

If that hemisphere contains an intact amygdala, the circuit for activating species-typical behavior is complete, and behavior will be typical. If the amygdala in the hemisphere is not intact, visual information will be disconnected from motor systems and cannot elicit species-typical behavior. Had the commissures not been cut, the experiment would not have worked, because information from one hemisphere could have crossed to the other, and each eye would thus have had access to the intact amygdala, as diagrammed in Figure 17.1A.

17.2 Anatomy of Cerebral Connections

Three major types of neural fiber pathways connect the neocortex—association, projection, and commissural fibers:

- Association pathways are distinguished as either (1) long fiber bundles that connect distant neocortical areas or (2) short, subcortical, U-shaped fibers that connect adjacent neocortical areas (review Figure 3.27).

- Projection pathways include ascending fibers from lower brain centers to the neocortex, such as projections from the thalamus, and descending fibers from the neocortex to the brainstem and spinal cord.

- Commissural pathways connect the two hemispheres and include principally the corpus callosum, anterior commissure, and hippocampal commissures. The corpus callosum (from the Latin *callus*, meaning "hard body") provides the major connection of neocortical areas. In humans, it is made up of 200 million to 800 million fibers. About half are unmyelinated and quite small. Most, but not all, areas of the two hemispheres are connected.

Figure 17.2 illustrates the patterns of commissural connections between the hemispheres in a rhesus monkey. Most of the primary visual cortex (area V1) is devoid of interhemispheric connections except for that part representing the midline of the visual world, the *visual meridian*. In functional terms, V1 represents the visual world topographically, and there is no need for one half of the representation to be connected to the other.

The motor and sensory areas for distal parts of the limbs (mainly hands and feet) also lack commissural connections. Because their essential function is to work independently of one another, it could be argued that connections are not necessary.

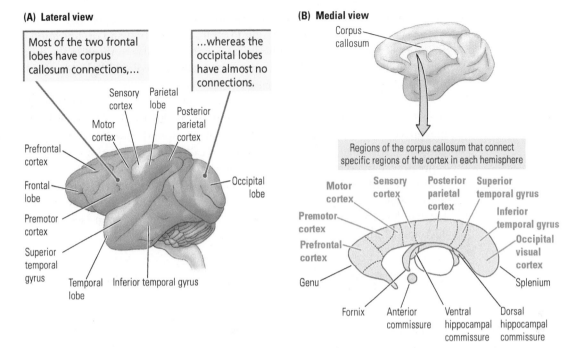

(A) Lateral view

Most of the two frontal lobes have corpus callosum connections,...

...whereas the occipital lobes have almost no connections.

Sensory cortex
Parietal lobe
Posterior parietal cortex
Motor cortex
Prefrontal cortex
Frontal lobe
Premotor cortex
Superior temporal gyrus
Temporal lobe
Inferior temporal gyrus
Occipital lobe

(B) Medial view

Corpus callosum

Regions of the corpus callosum that connect specific regions of the cortex in each hemisphere

Motor cortex
Sensory cortex
Posterior parietal cortex
Superior temporal gyrus
Premotor cortex
Inferior temporal gyrus
Prefrontal cortex
Occipital visual cortex
Genu
Splenium
Fornix
Anterior commissure
Ventral hippocampal commissure
Dorsal hippocampal commissure

🅰 **Figure 17.2** ▲

Patterns of Commissural Connections (A) Areas shaded red show regions in the rhesus monkey cortex that receive projections from the contralateral hemisphere through the corpus callosum. (B) Regions of the corpus callosum showing zones, labeled in red, through which a radioactive label was transported after injections into specific locations in the monkey's cortex. (Research from Pandya and Seltzer, 1986.)

Among the areas that do receive interhemispheric connections, the density of projections is not homogeneous (Figure 17.2A). Cortical areas that represent the body's midline—such as the central meridian of the visual fields, auditory fields, and trunk of the body on the somatosensory and motor cortex—have the densest connections.

The functional utility of this arrangement is that body movements or actions in central space require interhemispheric cooperation. A prominent working hypothesis concerning callosal function is the *zipper hypothesis*: the corpus callosum knits together representations of the body's midpoints and central space that are divided by the longitudinal fissure.

Callosal connections appear to fall into three general classes:

1. Most callosal projections are topographic: they connect to **homotopic areas**—identical points in the two cerebral hemispheres that are related to the body's midline—presumably to knit the two areas together functionally.

2. Projection zones within a hemisphere also maintain close relations with homotopic zones in the contralateral hemisphere. For example, area V1 is connected to area V2, not only within a hemisphere but also across hemispheres. Area V1 in one hemisphere also sends connections to area V2 in the opposite hemisphere.

3. A group of projections has a diffuse terminal distribution, possibly to alert appropriate zones in one hemisphere that the other is active.

The location of fiber projections within the corpus callosum is precise. Figure 17.2B illustrates the pattern in the rhesus monkey. The anterior part of the corpus callosum, called the genu ("knee"), contains the fibers projecting from the prefrontal cortex. Fibers through the body of the corpus callosum, proceeding from front to back, project from the premotor, motor, somatosensory, and posterior parietal cortices. Fibers in the posterior callosum, or splenium, project from the superior temporal, inferior temporal, and visual cortices. In the image shown in the chapter-opening Portrait, the location and organization of fiber projections in the human brain are generally similar to those in the monkey brain, except that the human motor connections (colored light blue in the opening DTI) appear to be more extensive.

The anterior commissure, shown as a circle in Figure 17.2B, is much smaller than the corpus callosum and connects parts of the anterior temporal lobe, amygdala, and the paralimbic cortex of the temporal lobe surrounding the amygdala. In humans born without a corpus callosum, the anterior commissure is greatly enlarged to connect far greater regions of the neocortex.

A variety of individual differences in callosal size and patterns exist. For example, Sandra Witelson (1986) reported that the corpus callosum is larger in left-handers than in right-handers and in women than in men (see Sections 12.1 and 12.2).

⊚ 17.3 Cortical Networks and Hubs

Connectome studies (1) demonstrate that large-scale neural networks underlie complex cognitive operations and (2) seek to unravel neural network architecture and how networks relate to cerebral functions. Brain networks can be extracted using imaging data from DTI tractography (**Figure 17.3**A, at left) and mathematically described as comprising sets of *nodes* (neuronal elements) and

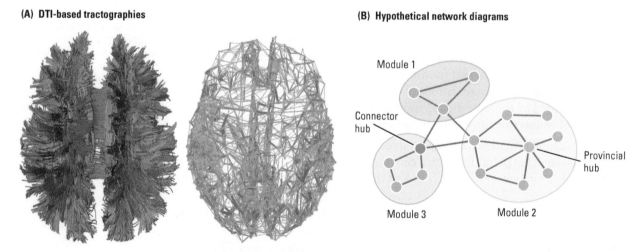

(A) DTI-based tractographies

(B) Hypothetical network diagrams

Module 1

Connector hub

Provincial hub

Module 3

Module 2

Figure 17.3 ▲

From Imaging to Cortical Networks (A) Nerve fibers, imaged at left, run along medial–lateral (red), anterior–posterior (green), and dorsal–ventral (blue) pathways. Imaged at right, a network diagram of cortical nodes (red) and edges (blue). Edge width indicates each connection's strength. (B) Nodes (neuronal elements shown in module 1 as solid circles) connect with other, related nodes clustered into modules that maintain numerous mutual connections but few connections to other modules. Provincial hubs (module 2) are nodes that connect primarily to similar nodes in the same module. Connector hubs (module 3) are nodes that link to connector hubs in other modules (Part A: Patric Hagmann / Lausanne University Hospital (CHUV), Switzerland. From Sporns, Olaf. Structure and function of complex brain networks. *Dialogues in Clinical Neuroscience*, 15:247–262, 2013, Figure 4, p. 252. Part B: M. P. van den Heuvel and O. Sporns. Network hubs in the human brain, *Trends in Cognitive Sciences* 17: 683–696, 2013, Figure 1, p. 685. © Elsevier) *edges* (their interconnections), as imaged in Figure 17.3A, at right).

Nodes interconnect with related nodes and cluster into functional modules, as diagrammed in Figure 17.3B. Individual modules maintain mutual nodal connections but form few connections, called *hubs*, to other modules. *Provincial hubs* are nodes that connect primarily to similar nodes in the same module. *Connector hubs* are nodes that connect with connector hubs in other modules. Mathematical analyses have identified a specific and especially densely connected set of hub regions that require disproportionately high metabolic activity and are believed to factor in efficient communication and functional integration across the brain (for a review, see van den Heuvel and Sporns, 2013).

Figure 17.4 summarizes the findings on the connectivity of cortical hubs in the human brain, including those in the precuneus (a region of the medial parietal lobe lying just in front of the occipital lobe), anterior and posterior cingulate cortex, insular cortex, superior prefrontal cortex, temporal cortex, and lateral parietal cortex. Each hub participates in several dynamic brain networks, as defined by fMRI and MEG recordings, including the *default* and *salience networks* described and illustrated in Section 16.1.

Individual differences in the coupling of cortical hubs have been related to intelligence (Section 16.4) and the "social brain" (Section 20.6). Cortical hubs emerge relatively early in brain development but continue to increase their functional interactions into adolescence. Although studies on the effects of experience on brain network and hub development are few, it is likely that epigenetic effects modify networks, leading to individual differences in a wide range of cognitive skills.

One study, on the effects of early musical training on brain connectivity, provides a compelling example of epigenetic influences on experience. Steele and colleagues (2013) used DTI to compare white matter organization in early- and late-trained musicians. In early-trained musicians (beginning before age 7) the size of the posterior corpus callosum connecting the left and right somatosensory regions increased (**Figure 17.5**). Although this study does not specifically examine connections between the major cortical hubs

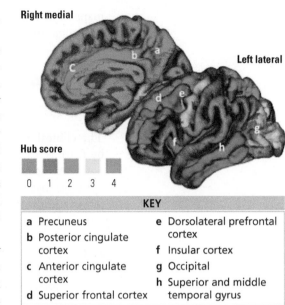

Right medial

Left lateral

Hub score

0 1 2 3 4

KEY	
a Precuneus	**e** Dorsolateral prefrontal cortex
b Posterior cingulate cortex	**f** Insular cortex
c Anterior cingulate cortex	**g** Occipital
d Superior frontal cortex	**h** Superior and middle temporal gyrus

Figure 17.4 ▲

Cortical Hubs The most-connected hubs in the cerebral cortex, mapped here and ranked by degree of connectivity, illustrated by the hub score color. Areas colored red have the highest connectivity. (M.P. van den Heuvel and O. Sporns Network hubs in the human brain, *Trends in Cognitive Sciences* 17: 683–696, 2013, Figure 2B, p. 686. © Elsevier)

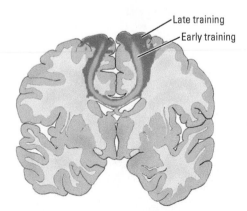

Late training
Early training

Figure 17.5 ◄

Musical Training and the Corpus Callosum Comparative effects of early and late musical training on callosal connectivity in the somatosensory regions in the two hemispheres. Colors on this posterior view represent the degree of difference in density of connections in the two groups. Dark blue depicts an increase in density from 1% to 10% in the late-trained group. Light blue depicts greater than 10% denser connections in the early-trained brains. (Research from Steele, et al., 2013, Figure 2.)

mapped in Figure 17.4, it illustrates that early experience can significantly influence cortical connectivity.

17.4 Behavioral Effects of Disconnection

The clinical effects of callosal disconnection were first seriously considered by Carl Wernicke in 1874 and became a prominent part of early neurology. Wernicke predicted the existence of an aphasic syndrome, **conduction aphasia**, that would result from severing fiber connections between the anterior and the posterior speech zones. In this condition, speech sounds and movements are retained, but speech is impaired because it cannot be conducted from one region to the other. In 1892, Joseph Dejerine was the first to demonstrate a distinctive behavioral deficit resulting from pathology of the corpus callosum.

In a series of papers published around 1900, Hugo Liepmann most clearly demonstrated the importance of severed connections as an underlying factor in the effects of cerebral damage. Having carefully analyzed the behavior of a particular patient, Liepmann predicted a series of neocortical disconnections that could account for the behavior. In 1906, after the patient died, Liepmann published the postmortem findings, which supported his hypothesis.

Liepmann wrote extensively on the principle of disconnection, particularly about the idea that some apraxias might result from disconnection. He reasoned that, if a patient was given a verbal command to use the left hand in a particular way, only the verbal left hemisphere would understand the command. To move the left hand, a signal would then have to travel from the left hemisphere through the corpus callosum to the right hemispheric region that controls movements of the left hand, as illustrated in **Figure 17.6**A.

Interrupting the part of the corpus callosum that carries the command from the left hemisphere to the right would disconnect the right hemisphere's motor region from the command. Thus, although the subject would

Figure 17.6 ▶

Liepmann's Theory of Apraxia (A) Typical response to a verbal command to move the left hand is processed through the left-hemisphere posterior speech zone (areas 22, 39, 40) to the motor cortex, then through the corpus callosum to the right-hemisphere motor cortex (area 4), which controls left hand movement. (B) In the apraxic condition, the verbal command cannot inform the right-hemisphere motor cortex to move the left hand. The jagged line through the callosal area indicates sectioning. A lesion disconnecting the posterior speech zone from the left-hemisphere motor cortex (not shown) would result in bilateral apraxia, as Liepmann proposed, because the verbal command cannot gain access to either left or right motor cortex.

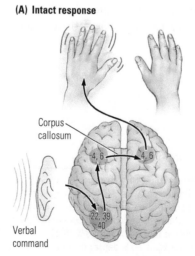

(A) Intact response

Corpus callosum

Verbal command

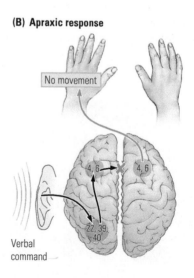

(B) Apraxic response

No movement

Verbal command

comprehend the command, the left hand would be unable to obey it (Figure 17.6B). This apraxia would occur in the absence of the weakness or incoordination of the left hand that would develop in the presence of a lesion of the right-hemisphere motor cortex, which controls the actual movement of the left hand.

Liepmann's deduction, although brilliant, was ignored for a number of reasons. For one, it was published in German and so was not widely read by English-speaking neurologists. Additionally, except in the extremely unusual case of a patient with a natural lesion of only the corpus callosum, any observed behavioral deficits should be attributed to damage of gray matter itself without reference to connections. Finally, the results of numerous animal studies consistently implied that no significant behavioral effects followed the cutting of the corpus callosum. Not until the late 1950s and 1960s did it become clear that the animal-study results were attributable largely to crude behavioral testing.

In the early 1950s, an important series of papers by Ronald Myers and by Roger Sperry (e.g., Myers, 1956: Glickstein and Sperry, 1960) revived interest in the effects of disconnecting neocortical regions. They examined the behavioral effects of severing the corpus callosum of the cat. Their work confirmed others' earlier observations that the experimental animals were virtually indistinguishable from their intact counterparts and indeed appeared intact under most testing and training conditions.

However, unlike those earlier, crude study results, Myers and Sperry's results revealed that under special training procedures, the animals could be shown to have severe deficits. If sensory information was allowed separate access to each hemisphere, each hemisphere could be shown to have its own independent perceptual, learning, and memory processes. The corpus callosum does indeed serve an important function, a conclusion confirmed in subsequent studies by Sperry and his colleagues on the effects of surgical disconnection of the cerebral hemispheres of humans for the treatment of intractable epilepsy.

The success of the Myers and Sperry experiments stimulated interest in other connections within the brain. Geschwind (1965) began to reassess the clinical effects of naturally occurring neocortical lesions as possibly indicating disconnection of various regions of the cerebral hemispheres (see review by Catoni and ffytche, 2005). In parallel work, Mishkin (1979) began to construct animal models of human disconnection syndromes by disconnecting related neocortical regions from one another. These researchers have demonstrated the critical interdependence of these normally connected regions.

In fact, the anatomical organization of the neocortex allows for fairly easy disconnection:

- The primary sensory areas have no direct connections among one another and so can be disconnected quite easily.

- Even in higher-order sensory zones, few if any direct connections exist among sensory systems, and so they can be disconnected easily.

- Because the hemispheres are in large part symmetrical and are connected by only a few projection systems, they are easy to separate and, as noted earlier, are sometimes found separated congenitally.

⊚ 17.5 Hemispheric Disconnection

Results of studies on surgical disconnection of the hemispheres indicate that many symptoms—aphasia, alexia, agnosia, agraphia, **acopia** (inability to copy a geometric design), and apraxia among them—can be demonstrated in the absence of any direct damage to particular cytoarchitectonic or functional neocortical regions. Symptoms can also be present on one side of the body and not the other.

The hemispheres may become completely separated under three conditions. First, in humans, the interhemispheric fibers are sometimes cut as a therapy for epilepsy. Second, people are born with congenitally reduced or absent interhemispheric connections, or **callosal agenesis**. Third, in animals, disconnections are performed to trace functional systems, to model human symptoms, and to answer basic questions about interhemispheric development.

Commissurotomy

As detailed in Section 11.2, **commissurotomy**, the surgical severing of the cerebral commissures, is an elective treatment for intractable epilepsy in cases in which medication proves ineffective. Seizures may begin in a restricted region of one hemisphere (most often in the temporal lobe), then spread through the fibers of the corpus callosum or anterior commissure to the homologous location in the opposite hemisphere. As a result of commissurotomy, each hemisphere retains fibers that allow it to see only the opposite side of the visual world. Likewise, each hemisphere predominantly receives information from the opposite side of the body and controls movements on the opposite side of the body.

The surgery also isolates speech in persons with lateralized speech. Consequently, the dominant hemisphere (usually the left) is able to speak, and the nondominant hemisphere is not. About a year or so is required for recovery from the surgical trauma. Within 2 years, the typical commissurotomy patient is able to return to school or work. A standard medical examination would not reveal anything unusual in these split-brain patients' behavior, and their scores on standardized tests are at normal. The patients' everyday behavior appears similar to that of typical "unified" people.

Specific tests, such as those Sperry and his coworkers obtained with their split-brain patients (e.g., Sperry, 1974), can show differences between the functioning of split-brain patients and that of people with intact cerebral connections. In the split brain, each hemisphere can be shown to have its own sensations, percepts, thoughts, and memories that are not accessible to the other hemisphere. The usual testing procedures include presenting stimuli only to one hemisphere then testing each hemisphere for what transpired. For example, a split-brain patient who is asked to touch an out-of-view object with one hand and then find a similar object with the other hand is unable to match the objects (see Figure 11.8).

Odors presented to one nostril cannot be identified by the other, objects seen in one visual field cannot be recognized in the other, and so on. Although the hemispheres function independently, they both do so at a high level, even in language skills. The nondominant hemisphere, although unable to speak, can understand instructions, read written words, match pictures to words, and match written to spoken words. Nondominant language ability is best for nouns and poorest for verbs.

The nondominant hemisphere performs in a superior fashion on a variety of spatial tasks, including copying designs, reading facial expressions, and fitting forms into molds. The nondominant hemisphere also has a concept of self and can recognize and identify social relations and pictures of the person in a social relation as well as pictures of family members, acquaintances, pets and belongings, and historical and social figures. Each hemisphere also has a general awareness of body states such as hunger and fatigue.

Callosal Agenesis and Early Transections

Agenesis of the corpus callosum is a surprisingly common cerebral malformation in humans, with an incidence in the general population of about 5 per 1000 and 2 to 3 per 100 in children with developmental disabilities (Bedeschi et al., 2006). Although several different chromosomal abnormalities are found in many, but not all, patients, the cause of callosal agenesis is not known.

In contrast to the results obtained with adult commissurotomy patients, persons born without a corpus callosum can perform interhemispheric comparisons of visual and tactile information. The interpretation of these results is that the patients have enhanced conduction in the remaining commissures (for example, for vision) and that they develop enhanced abilities to use their few uncrossed projections (for example, for tactile information).

These patients do have significant neuropsychological deficits, however, although most patient samples are small, so there is considerable variability in findings. Nonetheless, Vanessa Siffredi and her colleagues (2013) performed a meta-review of neuropsychological articles and found several consistent effects. A large effect on general intelligence is evident in a significantly reduced Wechsler IQ score, averaging 15 points below the population average. The majority of patients also have impaired expressive and receptive language deficits, impairments in visual and spatial reasoning, and a range of memory deficits including short-term verbal and visual memory and long-term verbal memory.

Most patients also have impaired motor skills and difficulties in information processing speed, as illustrated in a study by Maryse Lassonde (1986). She presented paired stimuli to six patients with callosal agenesis, asking them if the pairs were the same or different. Letters, numbers, colors, or forms were used. Either the pairs were presented one above the other in one visual field (intrahemispheric task) or one stimulus was presented in one visual field and the other stimulus in the other visual field (interhemispheric task).

The acallosal group was equally accurate in identifying same–different pairs under both conditions. Their reactions, however, were very slow for both forms of presentation. Lassonde suggested that the callosum participates in hemispheric activation as well as in information transfer. Thus, the acallosal group

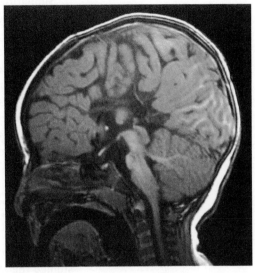

▲ Complete agenesis of the corpus callosum. MRI reveals that the cingulate gyrus, and thus the anterior cingulate cortex, also is absent. (From V. Siffredi, V. Andersen, R. J. Leventer, and M. M. Spencer-Smith. Neuropsychological profile of agenesis of the corpus callosum: A systematic review. *Developmental Neuropsychology* 38:36–57, 2013, Figure 1, p. 37.)

has alternative ways of obtaining the interhemispheric transfer of information but not of activation.

A particularly interesting question concerns the development of language laterality and other hemispheric asymmetries in regard to agenesis patients (Jeeves, 1986). One explanation of why language is lateralized to one hemisphere is that it gets a start there, and then that hemisphere actively inhibits its development in the other. In people with callosal agenesis, the opportunity for such an inhibitory process to work is much reduced, yet the lateralization of language and other functions in most of these people is similar to that in the general population. They also tend to be right-handed, as is the general population. Thus, the corpus callosum and other commissures are not necessary for the development of asymmetries.

Similarities exist in the effects of callosal agenesis and the effects of transections made early in life. Lassonde and coworkers (1986) compared the performance of five children, aged 6 to 16 years, on interhemispheric transfer of tactile information and motor learning. The younger children were less affected by callosal transection than the older children.

The researchers suggested that the younger children come to rely on ipsilateral pathways to obtain information and execute movements. That older children are more impaired suggests that, if transections are done early, ipsilateral pathways may make new connections, become functionally validated, or simply become more sensitive.

⊚ 17.6 Disconnecting Sensorimotor Systems

Roger Sperry (1974), Michael Gazzaniga (1970), and others have extensively studied the effects of hemispheric disconnection on behaviors related to both sensory and motor systems. Their findings are summarized here, followed by a consideration of partial disconnection effects.

Olfaction

Of all the senses, only the olfactory system connections are not crossed. Input from the left nostril goes straight back to the left hemisphere, and input from the right nostril goes directly to the right hemisphere. Fibers traveling through the anterior commissure join the olfactory regions in each hemisphere, just as fibers traveling through the corpus callosum join the motor cortex of each hemisphere (see Figure 17.2).

A patient whose anterior commissure is severed cannot name odors presented to the right nostril because the speaking left hemisphere is disconnected from the information. The right hemisphere has the information but no control of speech. The olfactory function is still intact, however, because the patient can use the left hand to pick out an object, such as an orange, that corresponds to the odor smelled.

In this case, no connection with speech is necessary because the right hemisphere both contains the olfactory information and controls the left hand. If requested to use the right hand, the patient would be unable to pick out the object, because the left hemisphere, which controls the right hand, is disconnected from the sensory information. Thus, the patient appears intact using one hand (**Figure 17.7**A) and **anosmic** (lacking the sense of smell) with the other (Figure 17.7B).

Vision

The visual system is crossed, so information flashed to one visual field travels selectively to the contralateral hemisphere. Recall that by using this fact, researchers have demonstrated left- and right-visual-field superiority for different types of input. For example, verbal material (such as words) is perceived more accurately when presented to the right visual field, presumably because the input travels to the left, speaking, hemisphere. On the other hand, visuo-spatial input (such as a map) produces a left-visual-field superiority, because the right hemisphere appears to be superior to the left in analyzing spatial information.

Note, however, that the visual-field superiority observed in controls is relative. That is, words presented to the left visual field, and hence right hemisphere, are sometimes perceived, although not as accurately or consistently as when presented to the right visual field. The relative effects occur because either hemisphere potentially has access to input to the opposite hemisphere through the corpus cal-losum, which connects the visual areas.

A commissurotomy patient no longer has such access: the connection is severed. Given that speech is usually housed in the left hemisphere of right-handed persons, visual information presented to the left visual field will be disconnected from verbal associations because the input goes to the right, nonlinguistic, hemisphere. Similarly, complex visual material presented to the right visual field will be inadequately processed, because it will not have access to the right hemisphere's visuospatial abilities. Thus, if material is appropriately presented, aphasia, agnosia, alexia, and acopia can be demonstrated, as follows, in a patient who ordinarily exhibits none of these symptoms.

If verbal material is presented to the left visual field, a commissurotomy patient will be unable to read it or to answer questions about it verbally because the input is disconnected from the left-hemisphere speech zones. Presenting the same verbal material to the right visual field presents no difficulties because the visual input projects to the verbal left hemisphere.

Similarly, if an object is presented to the left visual field, the patient will be unable to name it and thus will appear agnosic and aphasic. If presented to the right visual field, this same object will be correctly named, because the left visual cortex perceives the object and has access to the speech zones. Thus, the split-brain patient is aphasic, alexic, and agnosic if verbal material or an object requiring a verbal response is presented visually only to the right hemisphere, but this person appears intact if material is presented to the left hemisphere.

A further deficit can be seen if the patient is asked to copy a complex visual figure. Because the right hemisphere controls the left hand, we might predict that the left hand will be able to copy the figure but the right hand, deprived

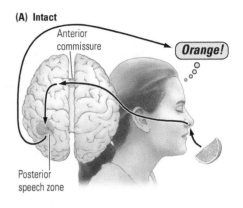

(A) Intact

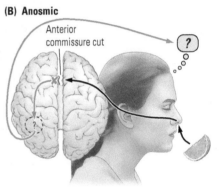

(B) Anosmic

Figure 17.7 ▲

Anosmia (A) In the intact condition, olfactory input to the right nostril travels directly back into the right hemisphere and crosses the anterior commissure, thus gaining access to the left (speech) hemisphere. (B) Anosmia results from sectioning the anterior commissure. (The jagged line indicates the lesion.) With the pathway severed, the information is blocked, and the left hemisphere has no way of knowing what odor the right hemisphere perceived.

of the expertise of the right hemisphere, will be severely impaired. This result is indeed the case: the left hand draws the figure well, whereas the right hand cannot and is thus acopic.

Somatosensory Functions

Like the visual system, the somatosensory system is completely crossed. Sensations of touch in the left hand travel to the right hemisphere, and those in the right hand travel to the left hemisphere. An object placed in the left hand can be named because the tactile information projects to the right hemisphere, crosses to the left, and subsequently has access to the speech zones.

Similarly, if a person is blindfolded and the right hand is molded to form a particular shape, the left hand is able to copy the shape. The tactile information goes from the right hand to the left hemisphere, then across the corpus callosum to the right hemisphere, and the left hand forms the same shape.

If, however, the two hemispheres are disconnected, the somatosensory functions of the left and right parts of the body become independent. For example, if some object is placed in the left hand of a blindfolded callosal patient who is then asked to choose the presented object from an array of objects, the left hand can pick out the object, but the right hand cannot. If an object is placed in a blindfolded patient's right hand, the patient can name it but cannot do so if the object is placed in the left hand because the sensory input is disconnected from the left (speech) hemisphere.

Disconnection effects can also be demonstrated without using objects. If the callosal patient is blindfolded and one hand is shaped in a particular way, for example, the opposite hand is unable to mimic the posture. One hand has no way of "knowing" what the other hand is doing in the absence of input coming from the opposite hemisphere through the corpus callosum. If the patient is not blindfolded, however, he or she can find out what the opposite hand is doing simply by looking at it.

Audition

The auditory system is more complex than the other sensory systems because it has both crossed and uncrossed connections. Although the left hemisphere appears to receive most of its input from the right ear, it also receives input from the left ear. Therefore, words played into the left ear can travel directly to the left hemisphere or can go to the right hemisphere and then to the left hemisphere through the corpus callosum.

In controls, dichotic-listening tasks clearly show that the contralateral input is preferred: words presented to the right ear are selectively perceived over words presented to the left ear. Remember, however, that this difference is relative, because some words presented to the left ear also are reported (see Figure 11.12).

This bilateral anatomical arrangement appears to reduce the effects of disconnection; nevertheless, one effect has been demonstrated. In the dichotic-listening task, input from the left ear is totally suppressed: the patient reports only those words played to the right ear. That is, digits or words played to the right ear are reported, but no input to the left ear is reported. This effect is surprising because words played to the left ear, even under these conditions, would be expected to attain some direct access to the left hemisphere. This direct access does not appear to exist when the hemispheres are disconnected.

Movement

Because the motor system is largely crossed, we might predict that hemispheric disconnection will induce motor difficulties. Here, we consider responses to verbal commands and tasks requiring the two hands to cooperate.

On any task in which the left hand must either respond to a verbal command or write in response to verbal material, a form of apraxia and agraphia could be expected because the left hand would not receive instructions from the left hemisphere. That is, the left hand would be unable to obey the command (apraxia) or to write (agraphia). These disabilities would not be seen in the right hand because it has access to the speech hemisphere.

Similarly, if a patient is asked to use the right hand to copy a geometric design, it might be impaired (acopia) because it is disconnected from the right hemisphere, which ordinarily has a preferred role in rendering. These symptoms of disconnection are in fact observed in commissurotomy patients, although the deficit's severity declines significantly with the passage of time after surgery, possibly because the left hemisphere's ipsilateral control of movement is being used.

A second situation that might produce severe motor deficits in commissurotomy patients is one in which the two arms must be used cooperatively. Ordinarily, one hand is informed of what the other is doing through the corpus callosum. Bruno Preilowski (1975) and later Dahlia Zaidel and Roger Sperry (1977) examined the effect of disconnecting this type of bimanual cooperative movement.

Patients were severely impaired at alternating tapping movements of the index fingers. Likewise, in a task similar to using an Etch A Sketch, one requiring tracing a line inclined at an angle, callosal patients did very poorly. This task requires the use of two cranks, one operated by each hand; one crank moves the tracing pen vertically, and the other moves it horizontally.

A high degree of manual cooperation is required to trace a diagonal line smoothly. Disconnecting the hemispheres severely retards this cooperation because the left and right motor systems cannot gain information about what the opposite side is doing, except indirectly by a patient's watching them. Recall from the chapter-opening Portrait D.M.'s frustration with assembling his jigsaw puzzles.

Dramatic illustrations of conflict between hands abound. In one case, a patient repeatedly picked up a newspaper with his right hand and laid it down with his left hand. He performed this sequence several times until finally the left hand threw the newspaper on the floor. Another patient was described by a physiotherapist: "He was buttoning his shirt with his right hand and the left hand was coming along just behind it undoing the buttons just as quickly as he could fasten them."

As in the praxic impairments described earlier, however, instances of intermanual conflict are generally confined to the first postoperative months and again seem related to the patient's age and the extent of extracallosal damage. A note of interest is that the same patients, while inhibiting these episodes of intermanual conflict, could use their left hands in a purposeful and cooperative manner when "not thinking of what they were doing" (Preilowski, 1975, p. 119). For example, they could pour coffee from a pot held in the right hand into a cup held by its handle with the left hand. The aforementioned peculiarities in motor functions were observed only in complete-split-brain patients, not in patients with partial disconnections.

Effects of Partial Disconnection

Would a partial section of the corpus callosum have effects as severe as those of a complete disconnection? Surgeons have experimented with partial hemispheric disconnection, hoping to attain the same clinical relief from seizures but with fewer neuropsychological side effects.

Partial disconnection, in which the posterior part of the corpus callosum is left intact, appears to combine markedly milder effects than those of complete commissurotomy with the same therapeutic benefits. For example, Sperry and his colleagues (e.g., Gazzaniga, 2005; Sperry, 1974) found that patients with partial disconnection are significantly better at motor tasks such as those needed to use the Etch A Sketch.

Results of research on monkeys with partial commissurotomies suggest that the posterior part of the corpus callosum (splenium) subserves visual transfer (as does the anterior commissure), whereas the region just in front of the splenium affects somatosensory transfer (see Figure 17.2B). The functions of the more anterior parts of the corpus callosum are largely unknown, but the transfer of motor information is presumed to be one such function. The effect of transecting the anterior versus the posterior part of the callosum is illustrated nicely in the Snapshot.

SNAPSHOT | An fMRI Study of Disconnection

Various imaging studies reveal that if one hand is subjected to tactile stimulation, areas S1 and S2 in both the contralateral and the ipsilateral hemispheres become activated. To relieve drug-resistant epilepsy, M.C., age 41, underwent a partial callosotomy that severed the anterior corpus callosum. Because his seizures were unaffected by the surgery, M.C. later had the posterior callosum severed as well.

M.C. was placed in an MRI scanner a week before the second surgery, and his fMRI was recorded in response to the brushing of his palm and fingers of the right or left hand with a sponge at the rate of about 1 Hz (part A of the adjoining illustration). He was retested in the same manner 6 months after the second surgery. Part B shows that, whereas M.C. retained bilateral activation in response to tactile stimulation of either hand after the first surgery, he showed activation only in the contralateral hemisphere after the second surgery.

This result is due to the absence of callosal transfer of the tactile information after the posterior callosum was severed. This loss of activation was correlated with a functional loss as well: before the second surgery, M.C. was able to name objects placed in either hand, whereas after the second surgery, he could no longer name objects placed in his left hand.

(A) Before second surgery

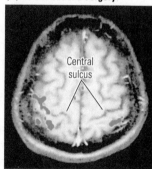

Central sulcus

(B) After second surgery

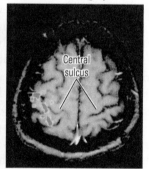

Central sulcus

Activation in response to tactile stimulation. (A) Before the second disconnection surgery, M.C. showed bilateral activation of somatosensory cortex, whereas after it (B), he showed only unilateral activation. The second surgery prevented the transfer of information from one hemisphere to the other. (Fabri et al., 2001, p. 1071.)

Fabri, M., G. Polonara, M. Del Pesce, A. Quatrinni, U. Salvolini, and T. Manzoni. Posterior corpus callosum and interhemispheric transfer of somatosensory information: An fMRI and neuropsychological study of a partially callosotomized patient. *Journal of Cognitive Neuroscience* 13:1071–1079, 2001.

◎ 17.7 Lesion Effects Reinterpreted As Disconnection Syndromes

In 1965, Geschwind wrote a theoretically significant paper titled "Disconnexion Syndromes in Animals and Man" that tied together a vast amount of literature and anticipated many of the effects of callosal surgery. Geschwind's thesis is that certain types of behavioral deficits result from disconnections between the hemispheres, within a hemisphere, or both. That is, symptoms such as aphasia and agnosia can be thought of as resulting from the *disconnection* of cortical regions rather than necessarily from *damage* to cortical regions.

The value of this paper is not its review of the data but rather its reintroduction of the concept first proposed by Dejerine and Liepmann nearly 70 years earlier: disconnection of neocortical regions can cause a variety of neurological symptoms. To demonstrate the utility of the model, we consider only the three classic symptoms of left hemisphere damage (apraxia, agnosia, and alexia) and one of right hemisphere damage (contralateral neglect).

Apraxia

As noted in earlier sections, if a lesion of the corpus callosum disconnects the left hand from the left hemisphere, that hand is unable to respond to verbal commands and is considered apraxic. Suppose, however, that the right hand is unable to respond to verbal commands. Geschwind speculated that this deficit results from a lesion in the left hemisphere that disconnects its motor cortex (which controls the right hand) from the speech zone (see Figure 17.6B). Thus, the right hand cannot respond to verbal commands and is considered apraxic.

Although Geschwind's model can explain bilateral apraxia in some patients, we must emphasize that disconnection is not its only cause. Because the posterior cortex has direct access to the subcortical neural mechanisms of arm and body movements (see Section 9.2), parietal input need not go through the motor cortex except to control finger movements. Further, as noted in earlier sections, patients with sections of the corpus callosum are initially apraxic but show substantial recovery despite a disconnection of the motor cortex of the left and right hemispheres.

Agnosia and Alexia

Geschwind theorized that agnosia and alexia can result from a disconnection of the posterior speech area from the visual association cortex. Both symptoms can be produced by a lesion that disconnects the visual association region on the left from the speech zone or by a lesion that disconnects the right visual association cortex from the speech zone by damaging the corpus callosum, as illustrated in **Figure 17.8**. Thus, a patient who has such a lesion, although able to talk, is unable to identify words or objects because the visual information is disconnected from the posterior speech zone in the left hemisphere.

Figure 17.8 ▼

Geschwind's Model of Disconnection Agnosia and alexia can result from disconnection of the visual cortex from the posterior speech zone. (A) Typically, visual input from both hemispheres travels to the posterior speech zone and association cortex, where it is processed to allow speech describing the written word or the object. (B) In the absence of this connection, processing of visual input is no longer possible, and agnosia and alexia result. The jagged lines indicate the lesion of the pathway through the posterior region of the corpus callosum.

(A) Intact

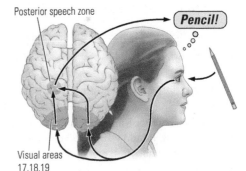

Posterior speech zone

Pencil!

Visual areas 17,18,19

(B) Agnosic and alexic

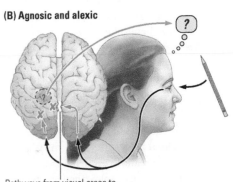

?

Pathways from visual areas to posterior speech zone cut

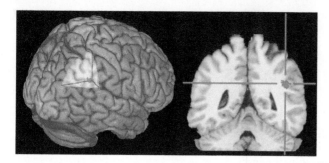

Figure 17.9 ▲

Anatomy of Contralateral Neglect The subregion of lesion overlap most associated with neglect in patients with right-hemisphere stroke (left) lies within the white matter just subcortical to the anteroventral part of the angular gyrus (right). (Mort, D. J., P. Malhotra, S. K. Mannan, C. Rorden, A. Pambakian, C. Kennard, and M. Husain. The anatomy of visual neglect. *Brain* 126(9):1986–1977, Fig. 3, 2003.)

Contralateral Neglect

Geschwind did not discuss contralateral neglect, but disconnection also can partly account for this syndrome. Damage to the right parietotemporal junction is most commonly associated with neglect (described in Section 14.4). MRI analysis confirms this location in a large group of patients and shows that white-matter damage is most closely associated with neglect, as illustrated in **Figure 17.9**. Patients with gray-matter excisions in the parietal lobe do not show contralateral neglect.

Hubs and Connectivity in Brain Dysfunction

Abnormal connectivity and hub-region function have been proposed as at least a partial explanation for a range of neurological and psychiatric brain disorders discussed in Chapters 26 and 27 (e.g., van den Heuvel and Sporns, 2013). Analyses of schizophrenic brains have shown reduced frontal-hub connectivity in patients as well as in their offspring. Developmental studies have found abnormalities in cases of autism spectrum disorder, with greater connectivity in some hubs and lesser in others (Shi et al., 2013). Neurodegenerative conditions such as frontotemporal dementia and Alzheimer's disease also show abnormalities in frontal and parietal hub connections.

Hub disconnection may be especially relevant to symptoms that result from traumatic brain injury. Patients who have had a head trauma often exhibit severe chronic impairments unrelated to the amount of gray-matter injury. Often, disruption of connectivity in cortical hub regions of people undergoing the effects of TBI involves impaired levels of consciousness or awareness.

SUMMARY

17.1 Disconnecting Cognitive Functions

Historically enigmatic, now well understood, the functions of the corpus callosum and associated forebrain commissures are, in general, to allow the two hemispheres to engage in complementary functions and to do so in concert.

17.2 Anatomy of Cerebral Connections

There is more to connectivity than interhemispheric connections. Intrahemispheric connections, including long fiber bundles that connect distant cortical areas and short fibers that connect adjacent areas, allow each hemisphere to work as a coordinated unit. The major interhemispheric connection is the corpus callosum, which joins most neocortical regions. The anterior commissure connects the medial temporal regions, especially the amygdalae.

17.3 Cortical Networks and Hubs

Brain networks can be extracted from imaging data generated by DTI tractography, then mathematically described and converted into diagrams as comprising nodes, hubs,

modules, and their interconnections. Connector hubs participate in dynamic networks underlying efficient communication and functional integration across the cerebral cortex. Individual differences in the coupling of cortical hubs have been related to individual differences in cognitive abilities.

17.4 Behavioral Effects of Disconnection

Disconnection of either inter- or intrahemispheric connections can produce a variety of neurological syndromes including apraxia, aphasia, agnosia, and acopia. Such classic symptoms thus may result either from damage to specific cortical regions or from damage to the connections between the cortical regions.

17.5 Hemispheric Disconnection

The cerebral hemispheres are sometimes surgically disconnected for the relief of intractable seizures. Split-brain patients (both total and partial disconnections) and those with callosal agenesis show a variety of symptoms that demonstrate functional asymmetries between the hemispheres.

17.6 Disconnecting Sensorimotor Systems

Researchers have taken advantage of disconnection syndromes to study functions in discrete cortical regions. This approach has proved especially useful in studies examining the sensory systems' hierarchical organization.

17.7 Lesion Effects Reinterpreted As Disconnection Syndromes

Many neurological symptoms can be interpreted as resulting from disconnection of cortical regions or of hubs within a hemisphere. For example, neurological symptoms such as apraxia, agnosia, alexia, and contralateral neglect all can be associated with the disconnection of specific cortical regions within the left or right hemisphere. Abnormal connectivity and/or hub-region function constitute another type of disconnection syndrome and partially explain a range of neurological and psychiatric brain disorders.

References

Bedeschi, M. F., M. C. Bonaglia, R. Grasso, A. Pellegri, R. R. Garghentino, M. A. Battaglia, A. M. Panarisi, M. Di Rocco, U. Balottin, N. Bresolin, M. T. Bassi, and R. Borgatti. Agenesis of the corpus callosum: Clinical and genetic study in 63 young patients. *Pediatric Neurology* 34:186–193, 2006.

Catani M., and D. H. ffytche. The rises and falls of disconnection syndromes. *Brain* 128: 2224–2239, 2005.

Downer, J. L. Changes in visual gnostic functions and emotional behavior following unilateral temporal pole damage in the "split-brain" monkey. *Nature* 191:50–51, 1961.

Gazzaniga, M. S. *The Bisected Brain*. New York: Appleton-Century-Crofts, 1970.

Gazzaniga, M. S. Forty-five years of split-brain research and still going strong. *Nature Reviews Neuroscience* 6:653–659, 2005.

Geschwind, N. Disconnexion syndromes in animals and man. *Brain* 88:237–294, 585–644, 1965.

Glickstein, M., and R. W. Sperry. Intermanual somesthetic transfer in split-brain rhesus monkeys. *Journal of Comparative and Physiological Psychology* 53:322–327, 1960.

Jeeves, M. A. Callosal agenesis: Neuronal and developmental adaptions. In F. Lepore, M. Ptito, and H. H. Jasper, Eds., *Two Hemispheres—One Brain*. New York: Liss, 1986.

Lassonde, M. The facilitatory influence of the corpus callosum on intrahemispheric processing. In F. Lepore, M. Ptito, and H. H. Jasper, Eds., *Two Hemispheres—One Brain*. New York: Liss, 1986.

Lassonde, M., H. Sauerwein, G. Geoffroy, and M. Decarie. Effects of early and late transection of the corpus callosum in children. *Brain* 109:953–967, 1986.

Mishkin, M. Analogous neural models for tactile and visual learning. *Neuropsychologia* 17:139–152, 1979.

Mort, D. J., P. Malhotra, S. K. Mannan, C. Rorden, A. Pambakian, C. Kennard, and M. Husain. The anatomy of visual neglect. *Brain* 126:1986–1997, 2003.

Myers, R. E. Functions of the corpus callosum in interocular transfer. *Brain* 57:358–363, 1956.

Pandya, D. N., and B. Seltzer. The topography of commissural fibers. In F. Lepore, M. Ptito, and H. H. Jasper, Eds., *Two Hemispheres—One Brain*. New York: Liss, 1986.

Preilowski, B. Bilateral motor interaction: Perceptual-motor performance of partial and complete "split-brain" patients. In K. J. Zulch, O. Creutzfeldt, and G. C. Galbraith, Eds., *Cerebral Localization*. Berlin and New York: Springer, 1975.

Shi, F., L. Wang, Z. Peng, C. Y. Wee, and D. Shen. Altered modular organization of structural cortical networks in children with autism. *PLoS ONE* 8:e63131, 2013.

Siffredi, V., V. Andersen, R. J. Leventer, and M. M. Spencer-Smith. Neuropsychological profile of agenesis of the corpus callosum: A systematic review. *Developmental Neuropsychology* 38:36–57, 2013.

Sperry, R. W. Lateral specialization in the surgically separated hemispheres. In F. O. Schmitt and F. G. Worden, Eds., *Neurosciences: Third Study Program*. Cambridge, Mass.: MIT Press, 1974.

Sporns, O. Structure and function of complex brain networks. *Dialogues in Clinical Neuroscience* 15:247–262, 2013.

Steele, C. J., J. A. Bailey, R. J. Zatorre, and V. B. Penhune. Early musical training and white-matter plasticity in the corpus callosum: Evidence for a sensitive period. *Journal of Neuroscience* 33:1282–1290, 2013.

van den Heuvel, M. P., and O. Sporns. Network hubs in the human brain. *Trends in Cognitive Sciences* 17:683–696, 2013.

Witelson, S. F. Wires of the mind: Anatomical variation in the corpus callosum in relation to hemispheric specialization and integration. In F. Lepore, M. Ptito, and H. H. Jasper, Eds., *Two Hemispheres—One Brain*. New York: Liss, 1986.

Zaidel, D., and R. W. Sperry. Some long term motor effects of cerebral commissurotomy in man. *Neuropsychologia* 15:193–204, 1977.

18

Learning and Memory

In 1953, when Henry Gustav Molaison, better known as Patient H.M., was 27 years old, he underwent elective surgery to relieve intractable epilepsy. When William Scoville operated on H.M., he inadvertently opened one of the most widely studied cases of memory impairment in neuropsychological history (Scoville and Milner, 1957). H.M.'s disorder was documented in more than 100 scientific publications during his lifetime.

H.M. experienced generalized epileptic seizures that had grown progressively worse in frequency and severity despite very high doses of medication. Scoville performed a bilateral medial-temporal-lobe resection in an attempt to stop the attacks. Afterward, H.M's seizures lessened, but he experienced severe amnesia that persisted until his death on December 2, 2008 (Annese et al., 2014). A postmortem photo of H.M.'s brain, in ventral view, clearly shows areas of scarring from the operation in both hemispheres (white outlines), including a mark visible on the parahippocampal gyrus of the right hemisphere (black arrow) produced by oxidation of one of the surgical clips Scoville inserted.

H.M.'s IQ was above average (118 on the Wechsler Adult Intelligence Scale), and he performed at normal

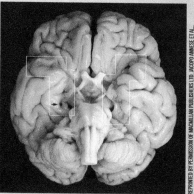

REPRINTED BY PERMISSION OF MACMILLAN PUBLISHERS LTD: JACOPO ANNESE ET AL., POSTMORTEM EXAMINATION OF PATIENT H.M.'S BRAIN BASED ON HISTOLOGICAL SECTIONING AND DIGITAL 3D RECONSTRUCTION, *NATURE COMMUNICATIONS* JAN 28, 2014; 5: 3122. FIGURE 1

on perceptual tests. H.M.'s memory of events that took place before the surgery was good, as was his capacity to recall remote events such as incidents from his school days or jobs that he held in his late teens or early twenties. For events that occurred after his surgery, H.M.'s memory was extremely limited: he was unable to describe the work he was doing after 6 months of employment, find his way to the house he had moved into after surgery, or even remember that he had just eaten a meal.

Given what was known about memory before H.M.'s experience, the discovery that **amnesia**, partial or total memory loss, can result from a localized brain lesion was a surprise. Perhaps even more surprising was that H.M. was unimpaired in learning some things, including motor skills; remembering faces; and retaining short-term memories, such as remembering a telephone number or a name for a short period of time (Milner et al., 1968).

The case of H.M. reveals two novel things about memory. First, many kinds of memory exist, each mediated by different neural systems, and second, selective brain damage can result in the loss of memory abilities.

The study of H.M.'s amnesia and of other patients with brain damage reveals that our multiple memory systems, charted in **Figure 18.1**, constitute largely independent neural processes. *Long-term memories* are of three general types—explicit, implicit, and emotional—each supported by different brain pathways. *Short-term memory* calls on a separate set of neural pathways. In this chapter we describe these different memory systems, their neural substrates, and the insights that knowledge about the many kinds of memory brings to our understanding of our own memories. We begin by surveying the effects of amnesia on learning and remembering.

⊚ 18.1 Learning, Memory, and Amnesia

In his classic book, *Remembering*, Fredric Bartlett emphasized that remembering cannot be regarded as the mere revival of previous experience; rather, remembering is an active process of reconstruction. "So long as the details which can be built up are such that they would give a 'reasonable' setting," Bartlett stated, "most of us are fairly content, and are apt to think that what we build we have literally retained" (Bartlett, 1932, p. 176).

Daniel Schacter and Donna Addis (2007), who use the term *gist* to describe the objective of reconstructing a memory, make the point that the gist serves the adaptive purpose of allowing us to anticipate and respond to situations in the future in ways that benefit from our past experiences. Thus, memory does not just allow us to recreate the past, it is prospective in allowing us to imagine or anticipate the future and so respond adaptively "next time." Because the gist is adaptive, details are often unimportant. As such, the shortcut nature of the gist renders it prone to errors of commission as well as of omission. Schacter describes such errors as the seven sins of memory.

An adaptive "sin" that experimental control participants commit far more often than amnesic subjects illustrates the sacrifice in accuracy that gist formation incurs. Participants are given a study list of words (*tired, bed, awake, rest, dream, night, blanket, dose, slumber, snore, pillow, peace, yawn,* and *drowsy*). A presented lure word (for example, *sleep*) is related to the words on the study list. On a subsequent old–new recognition test containing studied words (for example, tired and dream), new words unrelated to the study list (for example, butter) as well as new lure words related to the study-list items, such as *mattress*, are presented.

Controls frequently claim that they have previously studied the lure words. Amnesic patients with damage to the hippocampus and related structures in the medial temporal lobe show significantly reduced false recognition of nonstudied words that are related, either semantically or perceptually, to previously studied words. Apparently, controls form and retain a well-organized semantic or perceptual gist of a list of related study items. This gist causes them to respond to lure words but also allows them to reject unrelated words, whereas amnesic subjects may form a better list memory but retain only a weak or degraded gist.

The notion that we have multiple memory systems allows for other errors caused by favoring one kind of memory over others. For example, witnesses at an accident can usually give the gist of what they observed. They can note the temporal and spatial sequence of the action, identify the participants, and note the autobiographical framework of how they became an observer.

Yet when quizzed on the details, the fallibility of memory becomes apparent. Each observer may recall details not remembered by others. In addition, recollection can be distorted. Observers can be *primed* (sensitized) by other witness's stories and by photographs or videos of the occasion to remark, "Oh yes, I remember that also," even when the stories, photographs, or videos are distorted.

A simple example of the relation between such perceptual bias and memory reconstruction is illustrative. If people are asked to draw an upright glass half

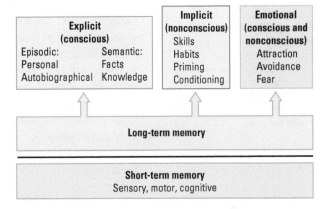

Figure 18.1 ▲

Multiple Memory Systems The broadest classification of memory distinguishes transient *short-term memory* for recent sensory, motor, or cognitive information from relatively permanent *long-term memory.* Conscious, long-term memories may be *explicit*—events and facts that you can spontaneously recall—and either *episodic*, for personal experiences (your first day at school), or *semantic*, for facts (England is in Europe). *Implicit*, nonconscious memories (say, riding a bicycle) consist of learned skills, conditioned responses, and events recalled on prompting. *Emotional memory* for the affective properties of stimuli or events (your first kiss) is vivid and has characteristics of implicit and explicit memory.

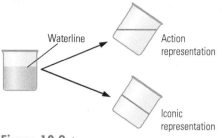

Waterline
Action representation
Iconic representation

Figure 18.2 ▲

Perception Affects Memory Those who encode a glass of water as an action image will render the waterline horizontally, whereas those who encode it as an icon will render the waterline at a slant, rotating it with the glass.

full of water as a tilted glass, some represent the glass with the water level in a horizontal position while others represent it with the waterline tilted (**Figure 18.2**). The former suggests encoding a spatial or action representation of the image, whereas the latter suggests encoding the representation as an icon. In Section 12.2 we report a sex difference in the representation of this image, with females more likely to report the icon and males the action. Both are accurate, but obviously quite different, perceptions.

As a student, you may have problems with different kinds of memory when studying for and taking examinations. A rule of thumb is that you remember things in the way that you learned them. If you learn the gist, you will not do well when asked for details. If you just read over material or underline important passages or both, you will not do well when asked to recount the material in detail.

You can prevent the unpleasant experience of "I knew the information but had a mental block when I had to produce it" by performing the same operations during the study phase that will be required of you during the test phase. Effective studying consists of practicing for an exam as it will be administered. These sessions usually require top-down rather than bottom-up processing if examiners are interested in more than the gist, and they usually are.

Varieties of Amnesia

The first evidence that the temporal lobes might play a role in human memory preceded H.M. by 50 years, when Vladimir Bekhterev (1900) autopsied the brain of a patient who had shown a severe memory impairment. He discovered a bilateral softening in the medial temporal cortex. The bilateral surgical excision made in H.M.'s brain, illustrated in **Figure 18.3**, shows just how small a region of damage to the medial temporal lobes can produce severe amnesia.

Other patients with bilateral temporal cortex damage, whom Brenda Milner (1970) and her coworkers had described in the 1950s, confirmed not only the temporal lobe's role in memory but also the special contributions made by different structures within the temporal lobes to different kinds of memory.

Area of lesion

(A)

Entorhinal cortex   Amygdala

(B)

Collateral   Entorhinal   Hippocampus
sulcus   cortex

(C)

Hippocampus

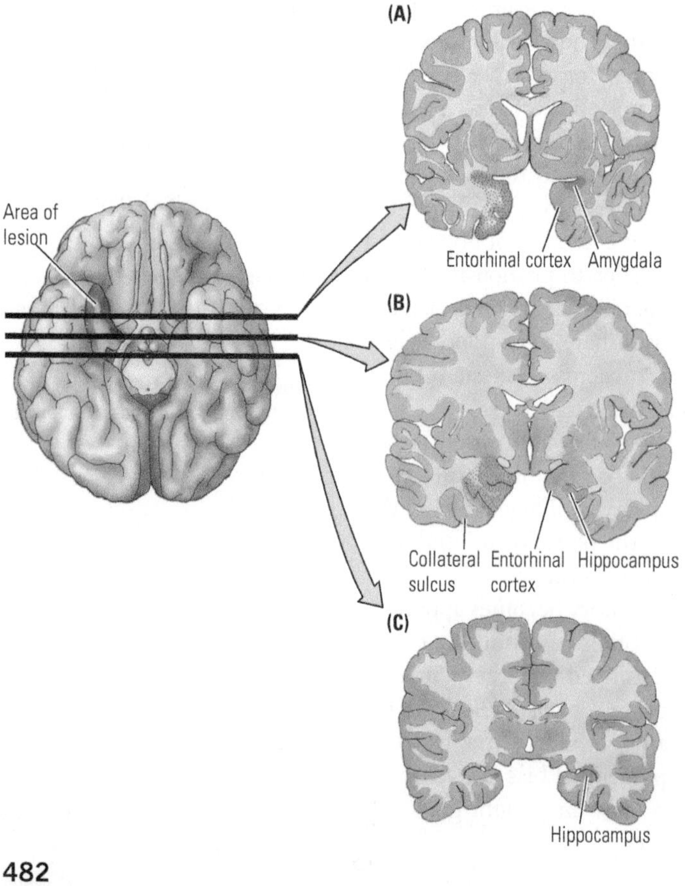

Figure 18.3 ◄

Extent of H.M.'s Surgery (Left) H.M.'s brain viewed ventrally, with the area of only the right-hemisphere lesion shown, in purple. (Right) In sections A, B, and C, which are based on MRI scans made in 1997, the left hemisphere (right sides of the diagrams) is intact to show the relative locations of affected medial temporal structures. Because the lesion, shaded purple on the left in each diagram, ran along the walls of both medial temporal lobes, the extent of damage in H.M.'s brain can be seen in the right hemisphere in several cross sections. (Research from Corkin et al., 1997.)

Recall from Section 15.3, for example, that damage to the inferotemporal cortex (area TE) specifically interferes with conscious recall of information, the extent of the memory disturbance increasing in direct proportion to the amount of temporal-lobe damage. Other causes of amnesia, and presumably other ways of disrupting or damaging the medial temporal lobe and its pathways, also offer insight into the neural bases of learning and memory.

Childhood Amnesia

We have all experienced amnesia to some degree. The most dramatic example of forgetting common to us all is **childhood (infantile) amnesia**, an inability to remember events from infancy or early childhood. The early years of life are generally regarded as critical in our development. We acquire many skills, including language, and much knowledge in those years but for the most part do not remember the experiences through which we acquired them. One reason for this failure to remember is that memory systems mature at different rates. Personal memories of our early years may be lost because the system central to storing adult episodic memory is not yet mature.

Another reason that childhood memories may be lost is that the brain plays an active role in deleting them, perhaps to make room for new memories. Katherine Akers and colleagues (2014) find that childhood amnesia also occurs in some nonhuman animals. During the period for which amnesia occurs in experimental mice, for example, many new neurons are being added to the hippocampus. In precocial species, including the guinea pig, hippocampal neurogenesis is largely complete before birth, and they do not display infantile amnesia. The investigators suggest that as new hippocampal neurons form new connections, they participate in forming new memories, but in doing so they disrupt neural circuits that support memories already acquired. More-permanent memories are formed only after the acquisition of new neurons by the hippocampus slows.

Amnesias Rare and Common

Adults also forget, as witnessed by occasional reports of people who turn up far from home with no knowledge of their former lives but with skills and language intact. Referred to as a **fugue state**, memory loss of personal history is sudden and usually transient. *Fugue* means "flight," and one interpretation is that the person has in effect fled a former life to form a new one. Perhaps the basis of the fugue state is the temporary suppression of medial-temporal-lobe memory systems.

Damage to restricted brain areas can cause amnesia that takes very curious forms. Clinical reports describe people who become amnesic for the meaning of nouns but not verbs, and vice versa, or amnesic for recognizing animals but are not *prosopagnosic* (amnesic for human faces). Simona Siri and colleagues (2003) describe a patient with herpes simplex encephalitis who was severely amnesic for fruits and vegetables but less so for animals and birds, suggesting a partial dichotomy in memory between plant and animal categories.

We all experience little everyday amnesias: we forget people's names or faces or where we put our keys. This kind of forgetting can increase with advancing age, in so-called senior moments. Its onset is typically characterized by amnesias for the names of people we do not often meet and for items we encounter in news media and in conversation. For some people, memory disorders of aging can become incapacitating, as happens in *Alzheimer's disease*, characterized

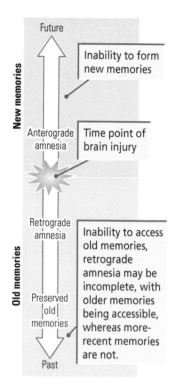

Figure 18.4 ▲

Varieties of Amnesia
Among the possible consequences of brain injury on old and new memories, retrograde amnesia may be incomplete, with older memories being better preserved than newer memories.

by the extensive loss of past memories and accompanied by neuronal loss that begins in the medial temporal lobe and then extends to other brain areas (see Section 27.7).

Anterograde and Retrograde Amnesia

H.M.'s memory, like that of other amnesic patients, consists of two parts. H.M. was unable to acquire new memories, a condition called **anterograde amnesia**, but he lost only some memories that must have been accessible to him before his surgery, a form of memory loss called **retrograde amnesia** (**Figure 18.4**).

The term *anterograde* refers to the future with respect to the time at which a person incurred damage to his or her brain. Because so many aspects of his ability to learn and remember appeared to be affected, H.M.'s severe anterograde amnesia is referred to as *global anterograde amnesia*. He was impaired in spatial and topographic learning and in learning about the events that took place around him, including the death of his loved ones. He showed sparse learning of new words and remembered only a few events or people who had made news after his injury. As H.M. himself said, "Every day is alone in itself, whatever enjoyment I've had, and whatever sorrow I've had."

The term *retrograde* signifies that memory loss extends back in time relative to the time of brain injury, as shown in Figure 18.4. H.M.'s retrograde amnesia was not as complete as his anterograde amnesia; he remembered many things he had learned before his surgery. He knew who he was; he could read, write, and speak; and he retained most of the skills he acquired before his surgery. Typically, memory is much better for events that took place earlier in life than for more-recent events. H.M. knew the way to the house where he lived before his surgery, for example.

For other patients, the extent of anterograde and retrograde amnesia can be quite variable (Smith et al., 2013). Both anterograde and retrograde amnesia occur in other clinical conditions, such as Alzheimer's disease. As the condition progresses, retrograde amnesia becomes more and more severe until almost all memory is affected.

Time-Dependent Retrograde Amnesia

Traumatic brain injury (TBI) commonly produces **time-dependent retrograde amnesia**, with the injury's severity determining how far back in time the amnesia extends. For example, after a head trauma, a transient loss of consciousness followed by a short period of confusion and retrograde amnesia is typical. The retrograde extent of the amnesia (the period of personal history it covers, extending from the present to the more-distant past) generally shrinks with the passage of time, often leaving a residual amnesia of only a few seconds to a minute for events immediately preceding the injury.

The duration of such posttraumatic amnesias can vary, however, as described in the opening Portrait of L.D. in Chapter 1. In a classic study, in one group of patients with severe head injuries, 10 percent had duration of less than 1 week, 30 percent had duration of 2 to 3 weeks, and the remaining 60 percent had duration of more than 3 weeks (Whitty and Zangwill, 1966). Sometimes isolated events, such as the visit of a relative or some unusual occurrence, are retained as islands of memory during this amnesic period.

Three Theories of Amnesia

The peculiar uncoupling of anterograde and retrograde amnesia presents a puzzle. What makes the memory systems underlying these two forms of amnesia partially independent? Three differing theoretical views each use the same evidence, from case and group studies of patients who have sustained medial-temporal-lobe damage and from extensive testing of learning and memory in animals.

System Consolidation Theory

As articulated by Larry Squire and Peter Bayley (2007), **system consolidation theory** states that the hippocampus *consolidates* new memories, a process that makes them permanent. When consolidation is complete, the memories are stored elsewhere in the brain. That is, memories are held in the hippocampus for a time, then gradually consolidated in a new location, the neocortex.

Consolidation theory explains why older memories tend to survive cases of hippocampal damage—they have been transferred elsewhere for storage— whereas more-recent memories are likely to be lost—they still reside in the hippocampus. If damage is limited to the hippocampus, retrograde amnesia may extend back for only a few years because only recently acquired memories remain there. As more of the temporal lobe, a region where longer-term memories are stored, is affected, retrograde amnesia can extend back for one to two decades or longer, depending on lesion size.

Multiple-Trace Theory

Lynn Nadel and Morris Moscovitch (1997) propose that **multiple-trace theory** accounts for individual differences in amnesias:

- **In any learning event memories of many types are encoded in parallel in different brain locations.** For example, autobiographic memory depends on the hippocampus and frontal lobes; factual semantic memory depends on temporal-lobe structures; and general semantic memory, on the remaining cortical areas.

- **Memories change throughout a person's life as they are recalled, reevaluated, and restored.** Autobiographic events, for example, through being recalled and discussed, can also be stored as factual memory and perhaps even as general memory (Cabeza and Moscovitch, 2013). Thus, the very process through which memories change as they are reused places them in different brain locations. This transformation results in memory that is recoded with use and thus changed from one type to another.

- **Different kinds of memory, being stored in different locations, are differentially susceptible to brain injury.** Because of this memory organization, after brain injury usually only some aspects of memory will be affected, and more important, older memories will be more resistant to disruption than newer memories.

Reconsolidation Theory

As described by Natalie Tronson and Jane Taylor (2007), **reconsolidation theory** proposes that memories will rarely consist of a single trace or neural substrate. We frequently recall memories, think about them, and discuss them with others. In storytelling or gossiping, a memory is not only recalled but also shared and elaborated on by others.

Each time a memory is used, it is reconsolidated: the memory reenters a labile phase and is then restored as a new memory (Schwabe et al., 2014). Each use of memory is associated with a new phase of storage, resulting in many different traces for the same event. Reconsolidation complicates the study of amnesia because spontaneous recall and even investigating a subject's memory will change the memory that is the object of investigation. Case in point: a witness's memory for an accident consists of multiple traces, one for each time the accident is recalled. And the difficulty in studying childhood amnesia lies in separating memories that an individual recalls for the first time from those he or she has recalled numerous times and those that have been contributed to by reminders from others, such as a parent (Wang and Peterson, 2014).

These three theories suggest that memory storage or memory type or frequency of use contributes to the extent of amnesia. Because of the complexity of memory storage, we can expect wide individual differences in the degree to which people display anterograde and retrograde amnesia after a traumatic event. In the sections that follow, we describe the three categories of long-term memory—explicit, implicit, and emotional—in detail, and then turn to the characteristics of short-term memory.

◎ 18.2 Long-Term Explicit Memory

Explicit memory for events and facts is conscious and intentional and consists of personal experiences, or *episodic memories* (what you did last night) and fact-based *semantic memories* ($2 \times 2 = 4$, for students who memorized the times table). Both types of explicit memory depend on conceptually driven top-down processing, in which a person reorganizes the data to store it. Later recall of information is thus greatly influenced by the way in which the information was originally processed.

Episodic Memory

Episodic (autobiographic) memory, a person's recall of singular events, is uniquely different from other neurocognitive memory systems in that it is memory of life experiences centered on the person himself or herself—a life history. The following excerpts illustrate a simple test for the presence of autobiographic memory. In reading through it, note the neuropsychologist's persistence in trying to determine whether the subject, G.O., can recall a single personal event or experience. Had he not been so persistent, G.O.'s impairment in episodic memory might well have been missed.

> *Do you have a memory of when you had to speak in public?*
>
> Well yes, I'm a call centre trainer with Modern Phone Systems; so I did a lot of speaking because I did a lot, a lot of training all across Canada. I also went to parts of the States.
>
> *Do you remember one time that you were speaking? Can you tell us about one incident?*

Oh yes! Well I trained thousands and thousands of clients on a wide variety of topics including customer service, inbound and outbound telemarketing. Handling difficult customers.

. . .

So what we're looking for is one incident or one time that you gave a training session or any other speeches that you want to tell us about. A specific incident.

Oh well I customized a lot of material for many, many companies. And I also did lots of training at the home office.

OK, so what we're asking is do you remember one time that you gave a talk?

Oh! yes I do.

One specific time not over a series of times, one time, can you tell us about that?

Oh sure yes, it was at the home office and yes, many many people were there.

. . .

I'm getting the impression that you have a really good memory for all the training that you've done but you don't seem to be able to come up with a specific talk that maybe stands out in your mind for any reason? Would you agree with that?

Oh yes well I always trained customer service.

So there was no talk that maybe something went wrong or something strange happened?

No, No I was a very good trainer. (Levine, 2000)

Autonoetic Awareness of Time

One function of autobiographical memory is providing us with a sense of continuity. Endel Tulving (2002) terms this *autonoetic awareness*, or self-knowledge, which allows us to bind together the awareness of our self as a continuous entity through time. Autonoetic awareness further allows us to travel in subjective time, either into the past or into the future. Patients with hippocampal and frontal cortical injury often lose self-knowledge and have real difficulty in daily living resulting from a deficit of behavioral self-regulation and the ability to profit from past experience in making future decisions (see Section 16.2). Tulving proposes that "time travel" is a memory ability that characterizes humans but not nonhuman animals and depends on maturation and so will not be found in babies and young children.

Tulving's patient Kent Cochrane, usually referred to as patient K.C., illustrates the effects of losing autobiographic memory. At age 30, as a result of a motorcycle accident, K.C. had a serious TBI with extensive lesions in multiple cortical and subcortical brain regions, including the medial temporal lobes, and consequent severe amnesia. Nevertheless, most of K.C.'s cognitive capabilities were intact and indistinguishable from those of typical, healthy adults.

His intelligence and language were at normal; he had no problems with reading or writing; his ability to concentrate and to maintain focused attention were standard; his thought processes were clear; he could play the organ, chess, and various card games; his ability to visualize things mentally was intact; and his performance on short-term-memory tasks was at normal. K.C. knew many objective facts concerning his own life, such as his date of birth, the address of his home for the first 9 years of his life, the names of some of the schools that he attended, the make and color of the car that he once owned, and the fact that his parents had owned and still owned a summer cottage.

He knew the location of the cottage and could easily find it on a map. He knew the distance from his home to the cottage and how long it took to drive there in weekend traffic. He also knew that he had spent a lot of time there. His knowledge of mathematics, history, geography, and other school subjects, as well as his general knowledge of the world, was not greatly different from that of others at his educational level.

Along with all these typical abilities, however, K.C. had dense amnesia for personal experiences. He could not recollect any autobiographic events, whether one-time happenings or repeating occurrences. This inability to remember any episodes or situations in which he was present covered his whole life from birth, although he did retain immediate experiences for a minute or two. In short, he could not "time travel," either to the past or future. He could not say what he would be doing later in the day, the next day, or at any time in the rest of his life. In short, he could not imagine his future any more than he could remember his past.

Because the damage to K.C.'s brain was diffuse, it is difficult to say which constellation of injuries accounted for his asymmetrical retrograde amnesia, in which episodic memory is lost but semantic memory is spared. Brian Levine and his coworkers (1998) described similar symptoms for M.L., whose lesion was more localized.

Densely amnesic for episodic experiences predating his injury, M.L. showed damage to the right ventral prefrontal cortex and underlying white matter, including the **uncinate fasciculus**, a fiber pathway that connects the temporal lobe and ventral prefrontal cortex (**Figure 18.5**). Because H.M. also displayed a complete loss of autobiographic memory both from before and after his surgery, autobiographic memory must depend on the medial temporal lobe as well as the ventral prefrontal cortex and the connections between them made by the uncinate fasciculus.

Semantic Memory

Knowledge about the world—all nonautobiographical knowledge—is categorized as **semantic memory**. It includes the ability to recognize family, friends, and acquaintances; information learned in school, such as specialized vocabularies and reading, writing, and mathematics; and knowledge of historical events

Figure 18.5 ▼

Brain Regions of Episodic Memory (Left) The ventral frontal and temporal lobes are reciprocally connected by the uncinate fasciculus pathway, shown in blue in the adjacent diffusion tensor image (right). (Diffusion tensor image from Field, A. S. Diffusion tensor imaging of cerebral white matter. *American Journal of Neuroradiology* 25:356–369, 2004, Fig. 7B.)

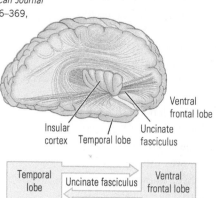

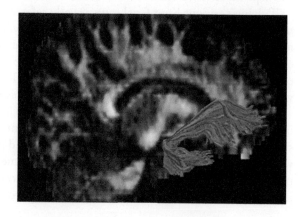

and of historical and literary figures—for example the answer to the question, Who was Charles Darwin?

Tulving's patient K.C. retained his semantic memory. He recalled the information he learned in school, he remembered that his parents had a cabin, and he knew where it was. He also remembered the games he learned before his injury, and he played them well. Similarly, H.M. retained semantic memory from before his surgery, and he acquired some semantic memories after his surgery—he knew that he had had brain surgery, for example. Not only is semantic memory different from episodic memory, it does not depend on the medial-temporal-lobe–ventral-prefrontal-lobe memory system that subserves episodic memory. Rather, semantic memory depends on the temporal- and frontal-lobe regions adjacent to the neural regions that subserve episodic memory.

Neural Substrates of Explicit Memory

Growing evidence indicates that neural systems, each consisting of several structures, support different kinds of memory. On the basis of animal and human studies, including many we have reviewed to this point, Herbert Petri and Mortimer Mishkin (1994) propose a largely temporal–frontal-lobe neural basis for explicit memory. This system comprises much of Mishkin's expanded ventral stream "what" pathway (see Figure 15.5).

Figure 18.6A illustrates the neural structures Petri and Mishkin assign to explicit memory. Most are in the temporal lobe or closely related to it, including the hippocampus, the rhinal cortices adjacent to the hippocampus in the temporal lobe, and the prefrontal cortex. Nuclei in the thalamus also participate, inasmuch as many connections between the prefrontal cortex and the temporal cortex are made through the thalamus. The regions that make up the explicit-memory circuit receive input from the neocortex and from the ascending systems in the brainstem, including the acetylcholine, serotonin, and noradrenaline activating systems (Figure 18.6B).

The following sections describe explicit-memory functions of different brain regions. We begin with medial-temporal-lobe structures—the hippocampus and perirhinal cortex—and move to the temporal and prefrontal cortices and other brain regions to which these structures connect.

Figure 18.6 ▼

Neural Circuit Proposed for Explicit Memory
(A) General anatomical areas of explicit memory. (B) Flow of information, beginning with inputs from the sensory and motor systems that are not considered part of the explicit memory circuit.

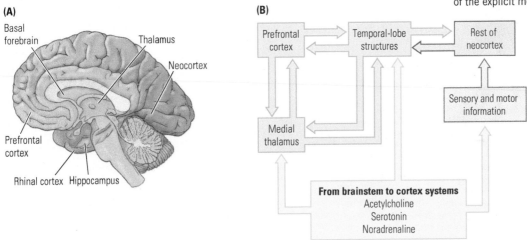

Hippocampal Anatomy

Fifty years ago, neuroanatomist H. Chandler Elliott (1969) described the hippocampus as "quite archaic and vestigial, possibly concerned with primitive feeding reflexes no longer emergent in man." Quite to the contrary, this structure, small in comparison with the rest of the human forebrain, plays a dominant role in discussions of memory today. We describe hippocampal anatomy in some detail, both in reference to its position as a way station between the posterior sensory cortex and the frontal cortex and in reference to its intrinsic complexity. (It was named *hippocampus*—Greek for "seahorse"—in the sixteenth century, either for its resemblance to the half-horse–half-fish that pulled the sea god Poseidon's chariot or for the small, horselike fish itself.)

The hippocampus, a limbic structure that extends in a curve from the lateral neocortex of the medial temporal lobe toward the brain's midline, has a tubelike appearance (**Figure 18.7**A). It consists of two gyri, **Ammon's horn** (the horn of plenty, the mythological goat's horn from which fruits and vegetables flow endlessly), and the **dentate gyrus** (from the Latin *dentatus*, meaning "toothlike," because its main cell layer has a sharp bend like the edge of a tooth).

Each gyrus contains a distinctive type of cell (Figure 18.7B). Ammon's horn contains pyramidal cells, and the dentate gyrus cells are stellate (star-shaped) **granule cells**. The pyramidal cells of Ammon's horn are divided into four groups: CA1, CA2, CA3, and CA4 (CA standing for *cornu Ammonis*, the Latin name for Ammon's horn). For structural and functional reasons, the cells of the two gyri are differentially sensitive to *anoxia* (lack of oxygen) and to many toxins. With mild anoxia, CA1 cells are the most likely to die; with more-severe anoxia, other CA cells and finally the dentate gyrus cells will die.

Figure 18.7 ▼

Hippocampal Formation
(A) Lying medially within the temporal lobe, the hippocampus is connected to temporocortical structures by the perforant path and to the brainstem mammillary bodies and subcortical nucleus accumbens and anterior thalamus by the fimbria-fornix pathway. (B) Cross section through the hippocampus shows the locations of Ammon's horn, with its pyramidal cells (CA1 through CA4), and the dentate gyrus. (C) Neocortical structures project to the hippocampus through the entorhinal cortex, which receives feedback from the subiculum.

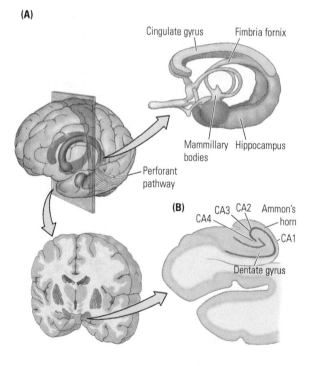

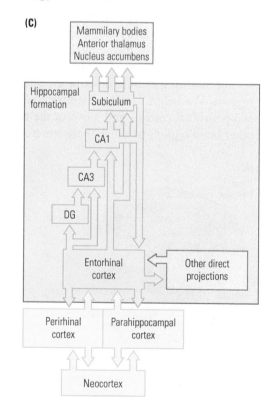

The hippocampus is reciprocally connected to the rest of the brain through two major pathways. The **perforant pathway** (because it perforates the hippocampus) connects the hippocampus to the posterior temporal cortex, as shown in Figure 18.7A. The other pathway, called the **fimbria fornix** ("arch fringe" because it arches along the edge of the hippocampus), connects the hippocampus to the thalamus, prefrontal cortex, basal ganglia, and hypothalamus.

It is through these two pathways that the hippocampus functions as a way station between the posterior neocortex and the frontal cortex, basal ganglia, and brainstem. Within the hippocampus, input from the neocortex goes to the dentate gyrus, which projects to Ammon's horn. Thus, granule cells are the sensory neurons of the hippocampus, and pyramidal neurons are its motor cells. CA1 cells project to another part of the temporal lobe called the subiculum, and the subicular cells project back to the temporal cortex and forward to the thalamus and brainstem (Figure 18.7C).

◎ Case Histories of Hippocampal Function

Although evidence from the amnesic patient H.M. suggested a prominent role in memory for the hippocampus, H.M.'s hippocampal lesion was incomplete and included areas of the temporal lobe as well as the amygdala. Debate continues over what contribution the hippocampus makes to memory. It is a complex structure, and each patient with damage to the hippocampus whose case history we describe here has somewhat different lesions.

Larry Squire and Peter Bayley (2007) describe two patients, R.B. and D.G., whose lesions are limited to the CA1 region of the hippocampus and who have a limited retrograde amnesia covering perhaps 1 or 2 years. They also describe L.M. and W.H., who have more extensive but still incomplete hippocampal damage. Their retrograde amnesia covers 15 to 25 years. Patient E.P., with complete hippocampal damage plus some damage to surrounding structures, has retrograde amnesia covering 40 to 50 years.

These patients' amnesia suggests that the hippocampus itself is important in retaining memory after learning, and adjacent cortices are responsible for memory extending farther back in time. Squire and Bayley's consolidation theory, outlined in Section 18.1, proposes that the earliest memories can be accessed directly in the neocortex and so survive temporal-lobe lesions.

In contrast with the patients Squire and Bayley described, for whom some limit on retrograde amnesia exists, Lisa Cipolottie and her colleagues (2001) report that V.C., a patient whose hippocampus was entirely removed, though surrounding structures were undamaged, has retrograde amnesia that covers his entire life before the lesion was incurred. V.C.'s case suggests that the complete loss of the hippocampus results in complete retrograde and anterograde amnesia for explicit information from all age periods of life.

Cases of Early Hippocampal Damage The symptoms seen in adult cases of hippocampal damage led some researchers to hypothesize that if such damage occurred in infancy, the persons would be described not as amnesic but as severely mentally disabled. That is, they would be unable to speak, being unable to learn new words; unable to socialize, being unable to recognize other people; and unable to develop problem-solving abilities, being unable to remember solutions to problems.

Faraneh Vargha-Khadem and her colleagues (1997) report on three cases in which hippocampal damage was incurred early in life: for one subject, just after birth; for another, at 4 years of age; and for the third, at 9 years of age. None can reliably find his or her way in familiar surroundings, remember where objects and belongings are usually located, or remember where the objects were last placed. None is well oriented as to date and time, and all must frequently be reminded of regularly scheduled appointments and events, such as particular classes or extracurricular activities. None can reliably recount the day's activities or remember telephone conversations or messages, stories, television programs, visitors, holidays, and so on.

According to all three sets of parents, these everyday memory losses are so disabling that none of the affected persons can be left alone, much less lead lives commensurate with their ages or social environments. They are not mentally disabled, however. All have fared well in mainstream educational settings. They are competent in speech and language, have learned to read, and can write and spell. When tested for factual knowledge, they score in the average range. When tested on memory for faces and objects, they also score in the average range, although they are impaired on tasks requiring object–place associations and face–voice associations.

Cases of Damage to Neural Hippocampal Connections Taken together, the evidence suggests that the hippocampus is important for episodic memory, whereas semantic memory is the responsibility of adjacent structures. The complexity in the symptoms displayed by different patients relates to the fact that the lesions are seldom selective and vary widely from patient to patient. Not only is it difficult to establish that a lesion is restricted to the hippocampus but even if it is so restricted, the lesion nevertheless damages projections to and from other brain regions. Disconnecting the hippocampus can produce amnesia similar to that following hippocampal damage. David Gaffan and Elizabeth Gaffan (1991) describe a series of patients who sustained damage to the fimbria-fornix pathway, which connects the hippocampus to the frontal lobes and brainstem while sparing the hippocampus itself (see Figure 18.7A). These patients display retrograde and anterograde amnesia similar to that seen in patients with temporal-lobe damage, although perhaps not as extensive.

Hippocampal Function

What does the evidence we have reviewed tell us about the function of the hippocampus? Even though the specific hippocampal contribution to memory is debatable, studies of hippocampal patients allow us to draw four conclusions: (1) anterograde memory is more severely affected than retrograde memory, (2) episodic memories are more severely affected than semantic memories, (3) autobiographic memory is especially severely affected, and (4) "time travel" is diminished.

The hippocampus may also contribute to our ability to vary memory details when remembering—for example, recalling at one time only that an accident involved a bus and a car while recalling at another time extensive details related to the accident. Jordan Poppenk and colleagues (2013) review the many anatomical differences between the anterior hippocampus (area closer to the frontal

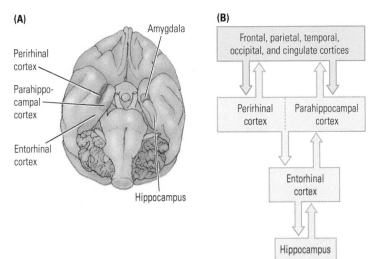

(A)

Amygdala

Perirhinal cortex

Parahippo-campal cortex

Entorhinal cortex

Hippocampus

(B)

Frontal, parietal, temporal, occipital, and cingulate cortices

Perirhinal cortex

Parahippocampal cortex

Entorhinal cortex

Hippocampus

Figure 18.8 ◄

Medial Temporal Structures Participating in Memory (A) Rhesus monkey brain, ventral view, visualizing subcortical medial temporal regions. On the left are the perirhinal cortex, the para-hippocampal cortex, and the entorhinal cortex. On the right, the amygdala and hippocampus are not directly visible because they lie beneath the medial temporal cortical regions illustrated on the left. (B) Input from the sensory areas in the cortex flows to the medial temporocortical, parahippocampal, and perirhinal regions, then to the entorhinal cortex, and finally to the hippocampus, which feeds information back to the medial temporal cortical regions.

lobes) and the posterior hippocampus (area closer to the temporal lobes). They suggest that the anterior hippocampus provides a coarse-grained representation of events, whereas the posterior area provides a fine-grained representation. Presumably, by accessing different memory subpathways through the hippocampus we can access and recount either abbreviated or elaborated versions of our life experiences.

The Temporal Cortex

When Suzanne Corkin and her colleagues (1997) used MRI to reexamine the extent of H.M.'s temporal-lobe removal, they found that the resection had removed portions of temporal cortex adjacent to the hippocampus (see Figure 18.3). Temporal-lobe areas bordering the rhinal fissure (called *rhinal cortex*) include the perirhinal cortex and the **entorhinal cortex**, which provides a major route for neocortical input to the hippocampal formation (**Figure 18.8**).

These regions, which project to the hippocampus, are often damaged in patients with medial-temporal-lobe lesions. Therefore, conventional surgeries and many forms of brain injury that affect the hippocampus may also damage the rhinal cortex or the pathways from it to the hippocampus. Discriminating between deficits that stem from rhinal cortex damage and deficits that result from disconnection or damage to the hippocampus is difficult.

Elizabeth Murray (2000) has used neurotoxic lesion techniques selectively to damage cells and spare fibers of either the hippocampus or the rhinal cortex in monkeys, then examine the specific contributions of each structure to amnesia. In Murray's studies, monkeys reach through the bars of their cages to displace objects under which a reward may be located (**Figure 18.9**A). To find the reward, the animals must use their abilities to (1) recognize objects or (2) recognize a given object in a given context.

A *matching-to-sample task* tests object recognition. A monkey sees a sample object that it displaces to retrieve a food reward hidden underneath. After a brief interval, the monkey is allowed to choose between the sample and a different object and is rewarded for choosing the familiar object. In an alternative *non-matching-to-sample* version, the monkey must choose the novel object

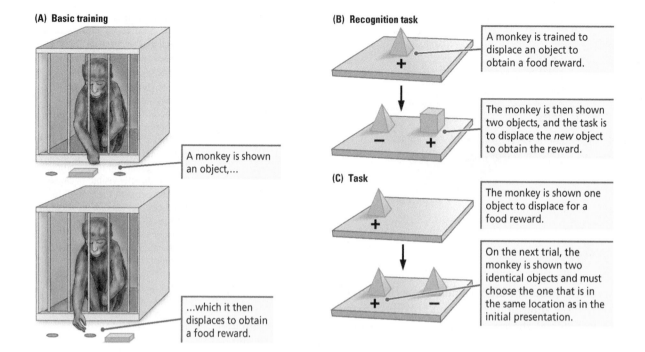

(A) Basic training

A monkey is shown an object,...

...which it then displaces to obtain a food reward.

(B) Recognition task

A monkey is trained to displace an object to obtain a food reward.

The monkey is then shown two objects, and the task is to displace the *new* object to obtain the reward.

(C) Task

The monkey is shown one object to displace for a food reward.

On the next trial, the monkey is shown two identical objects and must choose the one that is in the same location as in the initial presentation.

Figure 18.9 ▲

Two Memory Tasks for Monkeys

(Figure 18.9B). Delays can be introduced between the sample and the matching–nonmatching parts of both tests.

A contextual version of the task requires a monkey to choose an object by using cues based on the object's spatial location. The task may require choosing an object that remains in the same place, as shown in Figure 18.9C, or an object that appears in the same location in a visually presented scene in a picture.

In these studies of memory for objects and contexts, animals with selective hippocampal removal displayed no impairments on the object-recognition tests but were impaired when the test included context. In contrast, animals with rhinal lesions displayed severe anterograde and retrograde impairments on the object-recognition tests. The conclusion: object recognition (factual, or semantic, knowledge) depends on the rhinal cortices, whereas contextual knowledge (autobiographic, or episodic, knowledge) depends on the hippocampus.

Alex Clarke and Lorraine Tyler (2014) support this conclusion. They used fMRI to image participants' brains as they named a wide range of objects—animal, mineral, or vegetable, just like the guessing game. Activation in the ventral stream, from visual to perirhinal cortex, reflected object categories. General categories activated areas closer to primary visual cortex, and specific objects activated perirhinal cortex. If the object in the guessing game is to name a specific item, for example, the racehorse that won the 1973 Triple Crown, the category guessing (animal) would begin toward the visual cortex, and the identification of the winner, Secretariat, would occur in rhinal cortex. Personal knowledge—that you saw the races or have watched them on YouTube or got the right answer in this guessing game—is a function of the hippocampus.

Hemispheric Specialization for Explicit Memory

A variety of investigations reveal that asymmetries in explicit memory exist in all neocortical lobes.

Temporal Cortex

Because one treatment for epilepsy is removal of the affected temporal lobe, including both neocortical and limbic systems, many patients have undergone such surgery and have subsequently undergone neuropsychological study. The results of these studies suggest significant differences in the memory impairments stemming from damage to the left and right hemispheres. They also show that the temporal neocortex contributes significantly to these functional impairments.

After right-temporal-lobe removal, patients are impaired on face-recognition, spatial-position, and maze-learning tests (**Figure 18.10**). Impairments in memory for spatial position are illustrated by performance on the Corsi block-tapping test, illustrated in **Figure 18.11**A, in which a subject learns to tap out a sequence on a block board. Just as there is a memory span for digits (about seven), a similar memory span codes for locations in space. In the Corsi (1972) test, patients and controls are tested on sequences of block locations that contain one item more than the number their memory span can accommodate. One sequence, however, is repeated every third trial. Controls learn the repeated sequence in several trials, although they still have trouble with the novel

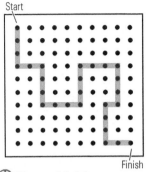

ⓒ Figure 18.10 ▲

Visually Guided Stylus Maze The black circles represent metal bolt heads on a wooden base. The task is to discover and remember the correct route by trial and error, indicated here by the orange line. Deficits on this task are correlated with the amount of hippocampus damage in the right hemisphere.

(A) Corsi block-tapping test

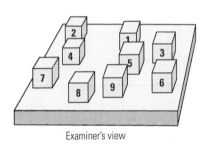

Examiner's view

(B) Hebb recurring-digits test

```
1  4  3  9  2  8  6  7  5
3  6  4  5  7  2  1  9  8
5  9  1  3  4  8  6  2  7  (R)
8  5  2  1  6  9  3  7  4
7  1  4  8  3  2  5  9  6
5  9  1  3  4  8  6  2  7  (R)
2  9  3  5  6  1  8  7  4
8  4  6  9  5  3  7  1  2
5  9  1  3  4  8  6  2  7  (R)
```

(C) Learning-acquisition curve

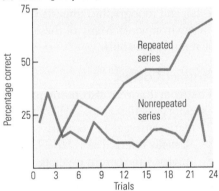

(D) Performance

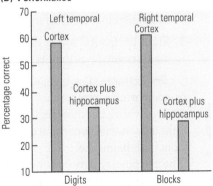

ⓒ Figure 18.11 ◄

Assessing Temporal-Lobe Role in Memory (A) The Corsi block-tapping test requires a person to copy a sequence the examiner taps out. The blocks' numbers are visible on the examiner's side of the board only, and one numerical sequence repeats. (B) In the Hebb recurring-digits test, people are given multiple series of nine numbers, two digits longer than the usual digit-span memory. One series repeats (R) every third trial. (C) Performance on repeated series improves as the number of trials increases, but the nonrepeating series shows no improvement. (D) Patients with left-hemisphere medial temporal lesions are impaired on the Hebb recurring-digits test; subjects with right-hemisphere medial-temporal-lobe damage are impaired on the Corsi block-tapping test. (Research from Corsi, 1972.)

sequences. Subjects with damage to the right temporal lobe either do not learn the repeated sequence or learn it very slowly.

Left-temporal-lobe lesions result in functional impairments in recalling word lists, consonant trigrams, and nonspatial associations. Lesions may also cause impairments on the Hebb recurring-digits test illustrated in Figure 18.11B. This test is similar to the block-tapping test in that subjects are given lists of digits to repeat that exceed their digit spans. Among the lists is one digit sequence that repeats. Patients with left-temporal-lobe lesions do not display the typical learning-acquisition curve, illustrated in Figure 18.11C, but instead fail to learn the repeated digit sequence.

Brenda Milner (1965) doubly dissociated the effects on several memory tasks from damage to each hemisphere's temporal cortex. She concluded that lesions of the right temporal lobe result in impaired memory of nonverbal material. Lesions of the left temporal lobe, on the other hand, have little effect on the nonverbal tests but produce deficits on verbal tests such as the recall of previously presented stories and word pairs, as well as the recognition of words or numbers and recurring nonsense syllables. The results of these studies, graphed in Figure 18.11D, indicate that not only the medial temporal lobe but also the adjacent temporal neocortex are associated with severe memory deficits.

Parietal and Occipital Cortex

Cortical injuries in the parietal, posterior temporal, and occipital cortices sometimes produce specific long-term memory difficulties. Examples include color amnesia, prosopagnosia, object anomia (inability to recall the names of objects), and topographic amnesia (inability to recall the location of an object in the environment). Many of these deficits appear to develop in the presence of bilateral lesions only.

Frontal Cortex

The frontal cortex also participates in memory, including autobiographical memory, as described earlier. An interesting pattern of hemispheric asymmetry emerges in comparisons between memory encoding and retrieval. Usually referred to as *HERA*, for hemispheric encoding and retrieval asymmetry, this pattern predicts:

1. Left prefrontal cortex differentially more engaged in encoding semantic information than in retrieving it.

2. Left prefrontal cortex differentially more engaged in encoding episodic information than in retrieving it.

3. Right prefrontal cortex differentially more engaged in episodic memory retrieval than is the left prefrontal cortex.

For example, Tulving and coworkers (1994) showed that the left orbitofrontal cortex is preferentially active during memory encoding of words or series of words, but these regions do not retrieve this information. Rather, the right dorsolateral prefrontal cortex (DLPFC) and the posterior parietal cortex in both hemispheres are active during memory retrieval (**Figure 18.12**).

The asymmetry between encoding and retrieving may be related to hemispheric asymmetry in the use of language and spatial processes. Most information storage may include language use in some way, whereas retrieval may

Figure 18.12 ▼

Hemispheric Encoding and Retrieval Asymmetry (HERA) Active cortical areas, revealed by PET, during acquisition or recall of verbal information. During acquisition, activation appears in the left ventrolateral prefrontal cortex (areas 10, 46, 45, and 47). During recall of the same material, activation occurs in the right premotor cortex (areas 6 and 8), in prefrontal areas 9 and 10, and in the parietotemporal cortex bilaterally (areas 7 and 40). (Research from Tulving et al., 1994.)

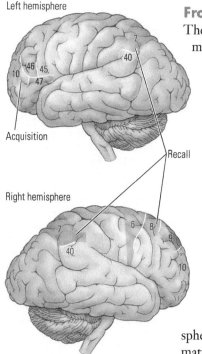

Left hemisphere

Acquisition

Recall

Right hemisphere

additionally tap spatial processes to locate stored information. Thus, Roberto Cabeza and Lars Nyberg (2000), in a review of 275 PET and fMRI studies, note that brain activation during memory encoding and retrieval is likely due to general processes the brain employs to handle information as well as to local processes related to storing and retrieving specific kinds of information.

18.3 Long-Term Implicit Memory

The implicit–explicit memory distinction is especially vivid in H.M., whom you met in the chapter-opening Portrait. H.M. exhibited severe explicit-memory defects on many neuropsychological tests yet was surprisingly competent at some forms of implicit learning. **Implicit memory** of learned skills, conditioned reactions, and short-term events, is nonconscious and unintentional. Using language and performing motor skills, such as riding a bicycle or playing a sport, access implicit memory, which is encoded in much the same way as it is received. Processing is data driven, or bottom-up, and depends simply on sensory or motor information: it does not require manipulation by higher-level cortical processing. Implicit memory depends upon many of the neural structures that constitute the dorsal stream action pathway (see Figure 14.3C).

Milner trained H.M. on a mirror-drawing task that requires drawing a third outline between the double outline of a star while looking only at the reflection of the star and the pencil in a mirror (**Figure 18.13**A). This task is difficult at first even for controls, but they improve with practice. Patients with amnesia can also display a typical learning curve on this task, as did H.M., but like him, may not remember ever performing it (Figure 18.13B). When Suzanne Corkin (1968) trained H.M. on a variety of manual tracking and coordination tasks, his initial performance tended to be inferior to those of controls, but he showed nearly standard improvement from session to session. Yet again, he had no explicit memory of ever performing the tasks.

Sparing of Implicit Memory in Amnesia

Other forms of implicit memory also survive in amnesic patients. One entails the experimental technique of **priming**, in which a stimulus is used to sensitize the nervous system to a later presentation of the same or a similar stimulus. In

 Figure 18.13 ▼

Test of Motor Memory
(A) The mirror-drawing task.
(B) Patient H.M.'s performance over three training sessions.
(Research from Milner, 1965.)

(A)

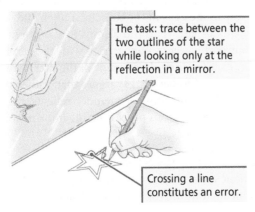

The task: trace between the two outlines of the star while looking only at the reflection in a mirror.

Crossing a line constitutes an error.

(B)

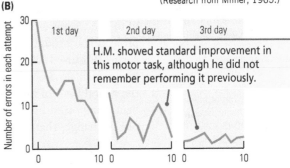

Number of errors in each attempt

1st day   2nd day   3rd day

H.M. showed standard improvement in this motor task, although he did not remember performing it previously.

a typical priming task, a person is first given a list of words to read, then given a list containing only the beginnings of words. The task is to complete each incomplete item with the first word that comes to mind.

If one of the priming words is TAB, the person might complete it as *table, tablet, tabby, tabulation,* or something similar. If one of the words on the first list is *table,* however, a person is more likely to complete TAB as *table* than as any other possibility, showing that he or she remembers the word. The first list primed the person to give a certain response later on. Amnesic subjects perform as well on priming as controls do, indicating that they remember what was on the first study list even as they report no conscious recollection of ever having seen it.

In another priming demonstration, subjects and controls are shown an incomplete sketch and asked what it is. If they fail to identify the sketch, they are shown another slightly more complete sketch. This process continues until they eventually recognize the picture. When controls and amnesic patients are shown the same sketch at a later date, both groups will identify it at an earlier stage than was possible for them the first time. Thus, both groups indicate through their performance that they remember the previous experience of seeing the lion in **Figure 18.14** completed, even though the amnesic subjects cannot consciously recall ever seeing the sketches before.

The independence of implicit from explicit memory can be demonstrated in other ways. If asked to think about the meaning of a word or the word's shape, controls' explicit recall of the word is greatly improved. Yet their scores on word completion, which taps implicit memory, are not affected by this manipulation. This is the **depth-of-processing effect**. On the other hand, if controls are presented with a word in one modality (for example, hearing the word) and are tested for recall in another modality (say, writing the word or identifying by reading), their scores on a word-completion test are greatly reduced, but their explicit recall is little affected, a phenomenon called a **study–test modality shift**.

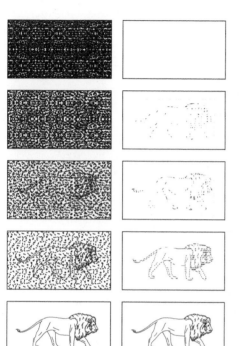

⊚ Figure 18.14 ▲

Gollin Incomplete-Figures Test Subjects and participants are shown a series of drawings in sequence, from least to most clear. Identifying the object from the first sketch is impossible; most people must see several panels to identify it correctly. On a retention test some time later, however, they identify the image sooner than they did on the first test, indicating memory for the image. Amnesic subjects also show improvement after priming, even though they forget taking the test before. (Republished with permission of AMMONS SCIENTIFIC LTD., from Perceptual and motor skills, Gollin, E. S., Developmental studies of visual recognition of incomplete objects, 11:289–298, 1960; permission conveyed through Copyright Clearance Center, Inc.)

Neural Substrates of Implicit Memory

Herbert Petri and Mortimer Mishkin (1994) suggested a brain circuit for implicit memory that includes the entire neocortex and basal ganglia structures (the caudate nucleus and putamen). The basal ganglia receive projections from all regions of the neocortex as well as from dopamine cells in the substantia nigra and send projections through the globus pallidus and ventral thalamus to the premotor cortex (**Figure 18.15**). The motor cortex shares connections with the cerebellum, which also contributes to implicit memory. In a review of the literature on the neural basis of implicit memory, Paul Reber (2013) argues that, rather than being supported by a discrete neural circuit, implicit memory reflects instead plastic changes that take place in the brain regions processing the information.

Motor Cortex Plasticity

In the pursuit rotor task, a person attempts to keep a stylus in a particular location on a rotating turntable about the size of a vinyl record album. The task draws on skills similar to those needed in mirror drawing. When researchers

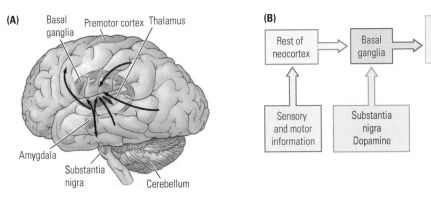

(A) Basal ganglia, Premotor cortex, Thalamus, Amygdala, Substantia nigra, Cerebellum

(B) Rest of neocortex → Basal ganglia → Ventral thalamus → Premotor cortex; Sensory and motor information; Substantia nigra Dopamine

Figure 18.15 ◄

Neural Circuit Proposed for Implicit Memory (A) The general anatomical areas of implicit memory. (B) Information flow through the implicit memory circuit begins with inputs from the sensory and motor systems, which themselves are not considered part of the circuit.

used PET to record regional cerebral blood flow as controls learned to perform this task, they found that performance is associated with increased cerebral blood flow in the motor cortex, basal ganglia, and cerebellum (Grafton et al., 1992). Acquisition of the skill was associated with a subset of these structures, including the primary motor and supplementary motor cortices and the pulvinar nucleus of the thalamus.

A more dramatic demonstration of motor cortex plasticity in implicit learning comes from a study by Alvaro Pascual-Leone and his colleagues (1994), who found that acquiring implicit knowledge requires motor cortex reorganization not required for explicit-memory performance. Participants were required to press one of four numbered buttons, using a correspondingly numbered finger, in response to numbered cues provided on a video monitor. For example, when number 1 appears on the screen, push button 1 with finger 1. The measure of learning was the decrease in reaction time between the cue's appearance and the pushing of the button on successive trials.

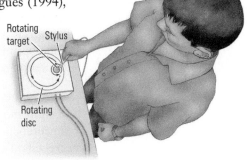

▲ A person who attempts the pursuit rotor task must keep the stylus in contact with a metal disc that is moving in a circular pattern on a turntable, which also is moving in a circular pattern.

Two groups were tested with sequences of 12 cues. For the control group, there was no order to the sequences, but the sequence presented to the other group was repeated so that after they learned the pattern, they could anticipate the cue and so respond very quickly. The implicit-memory component of this task was improvement in reaction time with practice; the explicit-memory component was the participants' recognition of the sequence, which enabled them to generate responses without needing the cues.

Transcranial magnetic stimulation mapped the motor-cortex area representing the limb making the responses; muscle activity in the limb was recorded simultaneously. Researchers thus discovered which cortical areas send commands to the muscles at various times in the course of learning. Here, Pascual-Leone and colleagues found that the cortical area controlling the limb appeared to increase in size as implicit learning took place. When the participants knew the sequence of stimuli and thus had explicit knowledge of the task, however, the motor cortex area active during task performance returned to its baseline dimensions. Thus, acquiring implicit knowledge requires cortical plasticity not required for explicit-memory performance.

The Basal Ganglia

Evidence from other clinical and experimental studies supports a formative role for basal ganglia circuitry in implicit memory. In a study of patients with **Huntington's disease**, a hereditary disorder characterized by *choreas* (ceaseless, involuntary movements) stemming from cellular degeneration in the basal ganglia, patients were impaired in the implicit mirror-drawing task illustrated in Figure 18.13. Patients with temporal-lobe lesions were unimpaired (Martone et al., 1984). Conversely, the patients with Huntington's disease were unimpaired on verbal recognition, an explicit-memory task.

J.K.'s case is illustrative. He was above average in intelligence and worked as a petroleum engineer for 45 years. In his mid-70s, he began to show symptoms of *Parkinson's disease* (in which the projections from the dopaminergic cells of the brainstem to the basal ganglia die), and by about age 78, he started having memory difficulties. Curiously, J.K.'s memory disturbance primarily affected tasks he had done all his life. He once stood at the door of his bedroom, frustrated by his inability to recall how to turn on the lights. He remarked, "I must be crazy. I've done this all my life, and now I can't remember how to do it!" When he was seen trying to turn the radio off with the remote control for the television set, he explained, "I don't recall how to turn off the radio; so I thought I would try this thing!"

J.K. clearly displayed an implicit memory deficit. In studies of patients with Parkinson's disease, Elise Anderson and colleagues (2014) report improvements in implicit memory when Parkinsonian subjects are given L-dopa treatment. This dopamine precursor restores basal ganglia dopamine, with subsequent deterioration of performance when treatment is withheld.

The Cerebellum

Cortical motor regions also receive projections through the thalamus from the cerebellum. Kyu Lee and Richard Thompson (2006) demonstrated the cerebellum's important position relative to the brain circuits taking part in motor learning (see Figure 9.15). They also suggest that the cerebellum plays an important role in a form of nonconscious learning called **classical (Pavlovian) conditioning**, in which a neutral stimulus is paired with a stimulus that evokes behavior.

In the Lee–Thompson model, a puff of air paired with a stimulus, such as a tone, is administered to a rabbit's eyelid. Eventually, whenever the tone is sounded, the conditioned rabbit blinks even though the air puff does not occur. Lesions to pathways from the cerebellum abolish this *conditioned response* but do not stop the rabbit from blinking in response to an actual air puff, the *unconditioned response*. This evidence suggests that the cerebellum mediates learning discrete, adaptive, behavioral responses.

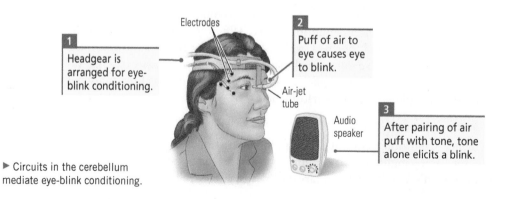

1 Headgear is arranged for eye-blink conditioning.

Electrodes

2 Puff of air to eye causes eye to blink.

Air-jet tube

Audio speaker

3 After pairing of air puff with tone, tone alone elicits a blink.

▶ Circuits in the cerebellum mediate eye-blink conditioning.

◎ 18.4 Long-Term Emotional Memory

Like implicit memory, **emotional memory** for the affective properties of stimuli or events relies on bottom-up processing. But emotional memory, which is arousing, vivid, and available on prompting, likewise has the intentional, top-down element of explicit memory. We use internal cues both in processing emotional events and in initiating their spontaneous recall.

Evoking Negative Emotions

In **fear conditioning**, a noxious stimulus is paired with a neutral stimulus to elicit an emotional response. A rat or other animal is placed in a box that has a grid floor through which a mild but noxious electrical current can pass. (This shock is roughly equivalent to the static-electrical shock we get when we rub our feet on a carpet, then touch a metal object or another person.) When the tone is later presented without the shock, the animal will act afraid. It may become motionless and may urinate in expectation of the shock. A novel stimulus, such as a light, presented in the same environment has little effect on the animal. Thus, the animal tells us that it has learned to associate the tone with the shock.

Although both eye-blink, a nonemotional form of conditioning, and fear conditioning are Pavlovian, different parts of the brain mediate learning in each case. Circuits of the amygdala mediate fear conditioning, and circuits of the cerebellum mediate eye-blink conditioning. Emotional memories contain both implicit (nonconscious) and explicit (conscious) aspects: people can react with fear to specific identifiable stimuli, and they can also fear situations for which they do not seem to have specific memories.

In a common pathology, **panic disorder**, people show marked anxiety but cannot identify a specific cause. Thus, emotional memory can be seen as separate from explicit and implicit memory. Perhaps the difficulty people have in coping with posttraumatic stress is that the emotional memory evoked by stress is dissociated from other stress-related memories.

Neural Substrates of Emotional Memory

Emotional memory has a unique anatomical component—the amygdala (**Figure 18.16**A). The amygdala consists of a number of nuclei, the basolateral complex, the cortical nucleus, the medial nucleus, and the central nucleus. The

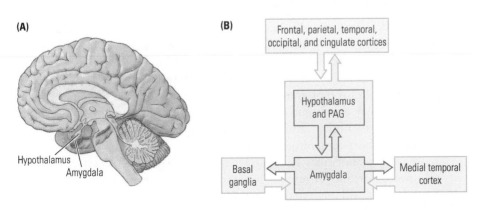

(A)

Hypothalamus
Amygdala

(B)

Frontal, parietal, temporal, occipital, and cingulate cortices

Hypothalamus and PAG

Basal ganglia ⟷ Amygdala ⟷ Medial temporal cortex

Figure 18.16 ◄

Neural Circuit Proposed for Emotional Memory
(A) The key structure in emotional memory is the amygdala. (B) Information flow in emotional memory.

basolateral complex can be further subdivided into the lateral, the basal, and the accessory basal nuclei. The amygdala connects to autonomic systems that control such functions as blood pressure and heart rate and to the hypothalamus, which controls hormonal systems. A number of early neuropsychological studies on monkeys that had received amygdala damage noted their tameness.

Damage to the amygdala abolishes emotional memory but has little effect on implicit or explicit memory. The amygdala has especially close connections with medial temporal cortical structures (Figure 18.16B). It projects to structures taking part in producing autonomic responses—namely, the hypothalamus and brainstem periaqueductal gray matter (PAG). In addition, the amygdala links to the implicit-memory system through its connections with the basal ganglia. Joseph LeDoux (2012) argues that these connections should be regarded as a survival circuit that prompts us to fight or flee, as the situation dictates.

Unique Aspects of Emotional Memory

Emotionally arousing experiences spark vivid memories, a fact confirmed both by animal and human studies and detailed in Chapter 20. Emotionally significant experiences, pleasant and unpleasant, reactivate hormonal and brain systems that act to stamp in these vivid memories by modulating memory circuits in the rest of the brain. Future experiences can reactivate these circuits, for example in circumstances that require a rapid fight-or-flight response.

A study of severely demented patients by Bob Sainsbury and Marjorie Coristine (1986) illustrates the nonconscious aspect of emotional remembering. The patients were believed to have severe cortical abnormalities but intact amygdalar functioning. The researchers first established that their ability to recognize photographs of close relatives was severely impaired.

The patients were then shown four photographs, one of which depicted a relative (either a sibling or a child) who had visited during the preceding 2 weeks. The task was to identify the person whom they liked better than the others. Although the subjects were unaware that they knew anyone in the photographs, they consistently preferred the photographs of their relatives. This result suggests that each patient, although demented, still had an emotional memory that guided his or her preference.

◉ 18.5 Short-Term Memory

In 1890, William James drew a distinction between memories that endure only briefly and longer-term memories. Not until 1958, however, did Donald Broadbent specifically postulate separate short- and long-term memory systems. **Short-term memory**, also called **working memory** or *temporal memory*, is a neural record of recent events and their order. We use the short-term system to hold sensory events, movements, and cognitive information, such as digits, words, names, or other items, for a brief period.

Because short-term information may be related to objects or to movements, short-term memory may be related to the ventral (object-recognition) or dorsal (motor) streams of sensory processing. Both streams project to the prefrontal cortex, although to different places (see Figure 16.3). Thus, short-term memory for motor and for object information is mediated by locations defined by the dorsal and ventral streams, respectively, to two different regions of the frontal cortex.

Short-Term Memory and the Temporal and Parietal Lobes

Elizabeth Warrington and Larry Weiskrantz (1978) describe patient K.F., who had received a left posterior-temporal lesion that resulted in an almost total inability to repeat verbal stimuli such as digits, letters, words, and sentences. In contrast, his long-term recall of paired-associates words or short stories was nearly standard. K.F.'s condition contrasts starkly with that of H.M. and other medial-temporal-lobe subjects, who retain functional short-term memory (Allen et al., 2014).

Warrington and Weiskrantz also found that some patients apparently have defects in short-term recall of visually presented digits or letters but have standard short-term recall for the same stimuli presented aurally. Russian neuropsychologist Alexander Luria (1968) described patients with just the opposite difficulty: specific deficits for aurally presented but not visually presented verbal items. Short-term-memory deficits can also result from damage to the polymodal sensory areas of the posterior parietal and posterior temporal cortex. Warrington and Weiskrantz present several cases of specific short-term-memory deficits in patients with lesions at the junction of the parietal, temporal, and occipital cortices.

Short-Term Memory and the Frontal Lobes

Damage to the frontal cortex is the recognized cause of many short-term memory impairments for tasks in which subjects must temporarily remember the locations of stimuli. The tasks themselves may be rather simple: given this cue, make that response after a delay. But as one trial follows another, both animals and people with frontal-lobe lesions start to mix up previously presented stimuli.

⊚ Neuropsychological Testing for Short-Term Memory Function

L. Prisko (1963) devised a compound stimulus task in which two stimuli in the same sensory modality are presented in succession, separated by a short interval. A subject's task is to report whether the second stimulus is identical with the first. In half the trials, the paired stimuli were the same; in the other half, they were different. Thus, the task required that the subject remember the first stimulus to compare it with the second while suppressing the stimuli that had been presented in previous trials. The Snapshot on page 504 describes another compound-stimulus paradigm.

Similarly, two tasks, one verbal and one nonverbal, were used in another test (Corsi, 1972). Subjects were required to decide which of two stimuli had been seen more recently. In the verbal task, they were asked to read word pairs presented on a series of cards (for example, *cowboy–railroad*). From time to time, a card appeared bearing two words with a question mark between them. Subjects had to indicate which word they had read more recently.

Ladislas von Meduna developed **electroconvulsive therapy** (ECT), the first electrical brain-stimulation treatment, in 1933 because he thought that people with epilepsy could not be schizophrenic and therefore that seizures could cure insanity. At first, the therapeutic seizures were induced with a drug called Metrazol, but in 1937, Ugo Cerletti and Lucio Bini replaced Metrazol with electricity.

ECT does not cure schizophrenia, but a review by Max Fink (2014) finds that it can be effective in treating major depression. A drawback to ECT is that it can temporarily impair memory (Sackheim, 2014). This observation led to using ECT to study memory, but its use for severe depression has grown rare with the advent of noninvasive treatments such as transcranial magnetic stimulation (TMS).

According to *system consolidation theory*, described in Section 18.1, long-term memories are not formed instantaneously but require biochemical and structural changes that take some time. Neuroscientists reasoned that if an animal was given a learning experience, application of ECT at different times afterward could be used to map the duration of changes required for memory formation.

But the results of many experiments using ECT suggest that many memory-forming changes take place after a single experience, each with its own time course for consolidation. Recent experiences are related to transitory, short-term memory storage, whereas longer-term experiences are related to long-term memory formation.

More-refined application of brain stimulation makes use of noninvasive TMS. A magnetic coil is placed over the skull to stimulate the underlying brain area (Section 7.2). TMS can be used either to induce behavior or to disrupt ongoing behavior. Justin Harris and colleagues (2002) presented two vibratory stimuli to participants' fingertips and asked them to state whether the stimuli were the same or different. TMS delivered within 600 ms of the first stimulus disrupted choice accuracy, but TMS after 900 ms did not.

Harris (2006) further demonstrates that the primary sensory cortex is the site for short-term memory of somatosensory stimulation and that a memory can be formed within 900 ms. Thus, short-term memories are encoded at low hierarchical levels of the nervous system.

Jacinta O'Shea and colleagues (2007) used a pop-out paradigm to study the specificity of short-term memory. (If the same stimulus is presented repeatedly in a number of pictures, participants identify its shape and location more quickly.) They found that TMS applied to the frontal eye fields, a premotor cortex site of visual short-term memory, disrupted memory for location but not for form. Thus, different neural locations encode different stimulus features, such as form and location, hence different short-term memories, separately.

Fink, M. What was learned: Studies by the consortium for research in ECT (CORE) 1997–2011. *Acta Psychiatrica Scandinavica* 129(6):417–426, 2014.

Harris, J. A. Psychophysical investigations into cortical encoding of vibrotactile stimuli. *Novartis Foundation Symposium* 270:238–245, 2006.

Harris, J. A., C. Miniussi, I. M. Harris, and M. E. Diamond. Transient storage of a tactile memory trace in primary somatosensory cortex, *Journal of Neuroscience*, 22:8721, 2002.

O'Shea, J., N. G. Muggleton, A. Cowey, and V. Walsh. Human frontal eye fields and spatial priming of pop-out. *Journal of Cognitive Neuroscience* 19:1140–1151, 2007.

Sackeim, H. A. Autobiographical memory and electroconvulsive therapy: Do not throw out the baby. *Journal of ECT* April 21, 2014.

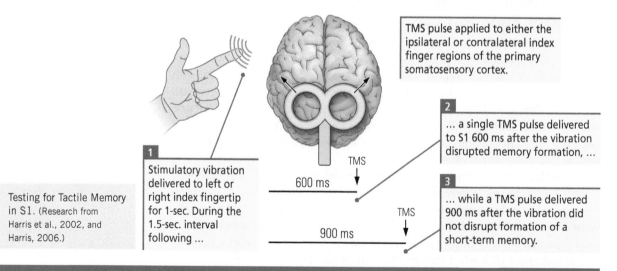

TMS pulse applied to either the ipsilateral or contralateral index finger regions of the primary somatosensory cortex.

1 Stimulatory vibration delivered to left or right index fingertip for 1-sec. During the 1.5-sec. interval following ...

2 ... a single TMS pulse delivered to S1 600 ms after the vibration disrupted memory formation, ...

3 ... while a TMS pulse delivered 900 ms after the vibration did not disrupt formation of a short-term memory.

TMS
600 ms
TMS
900 ms

Testing for Tactile Memory in S1. (Research from Harris et al., 2002, and Harris, 2006.)

Sometimes, both words had been seen before; at other times, only one word had been seen. In the latter case, the task became a simple test of recognition, whereas in the former case, it was a test of *recency memory*. Patients with left temporal removals showed a mild deficit in recognition, in keeping with their verbal memory difficulty; frontal-lobe patients performed at normal. On the recency test, however, both frontal-lobe groups (left and right) were impaired, with the left-side group significantly worse.

The nonverbal task was identical to the verbal task except that the stimuli were photographs of paintings rather than words. Patients with right-temporal-lobe removals showed mild recognition deficits, consistent with their visual-memory deficit, whereas those with right-frontal-lobe lesions performed at normal. On the recency test, the frontal-lobe groups were impaired, but now the right-side group was significantly worse.

Interference Tasks

Morris Moscovitch (1982) devised a task in which patients were read five different lists of 12 words each and instructed to recall as much of each list as they could immediately after presentation. In the first four lists, all words were drawn from the same taxonomic category, such as sports; the words in the fifth list came from a different category, such as professions.

Controls showed a decline from list 1 to list 4 in the number of words recalled correctly; that is, they exhibited **proactive interference**: the earlier lists interfered with learning new information. But they also exhibited an additional phenomenon on list 5: they recalled as many words as they did for list 1, thus demonstrating *release from proactive interference*. Frontal-lobe patients also showed strong proactive interference, as would be expected from the Prisko experiments, but they failed to show release from proactive interference on list 5.

Another memory deficit in patients with frontal-lobe lesions has been demonstrated in a test of movement copying (shown in Figure 14.10). When patients with cortical lesions were asked to copy complex arm and facial movements, in addition to making errors of sequence, frontal-lobe patients made many errors of intrusion and omission (Kolb and Milner, 1981). That is, when asked to copy a series of three discrete facial movements, frontal-lobe patients left one movement out (error of omission) or added a movement seen in a previous sequence (error of intrusion).

Dorsal- and Ventral-Stream Participation in Short-Term Memory

The results of experiments with monkeys confirm that different prefrontal areas take part in different types of short-term memory. Joaquin Fuster (1989) demonstrated that if monkeys are shown objects they must remember for a short period before making a response, neurons in the frontal cortex fire during the delay. This finding suggests that these neurons are active in bridging the stimulus–response gap. Patricia Goldman-Rakic (1992) examined this phenomenon further in two tasks, one testing memory for the location of objects and the other memory for object identity.

For the first task, a monkey was required to fixate on a point in the center of a screen while a light was flashed in some part of its visual field. After a variable delay of a few seconds, the monkey was required to shift its eyes to look at the

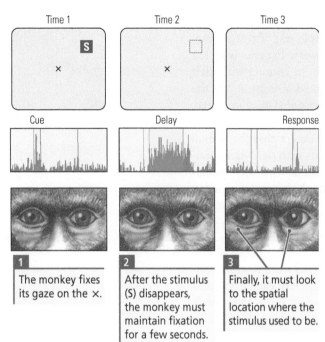

Figure 18.17 ▲

Testing Short-Term Memory Single cells can code spatial location of objects. During the delay in step 2, single cells in area 8 code the location of the second stimulus in memory. (Data from Goldman-Rakic, P.S. Working memory and the mind. *Scientific American* 267(3):111–117, 1992.)

point where the light had been. In the second task, as the monkey fixated on the center of the screen, one of two objects appeared on the screen. The monkey was required to look to the left in response to one stimulus and to the right in response to the other (**Figure 18.17**). Cells that code spatial vision are located in area 8 of the premotor cortex, whereas cells that code object recognition are located in areas 9 and 46 of the DLPFC (**Figure 18.18**A).

Michael Petrides and his coworkers (1993) used PET and MRI to demonstrate similar function–anatomy relations in humans. Their model posits two short-term-memory systems, for spatial and object memory (Figure 18.18B).

A spatial vision test required participants to point to one of eight patterns on each of eight cards in response to a colored bar at the top of the card. That is, in response to a cue, participants had to search for a specific pattern. Performance of this task was accompanied by increased activity in area 8 of the left hemisphere.

In contrast, an object task required participants to point to a different pattern in an array of eight patterns repeated on eight successive cards, which meant that they had to keep track of the patterns they had indicated already. During this task, the researchers found increased regional cerebral blood flow in the mid-dorsolateral prefrontal cortex (areas 9 and 46, mainly on the right).

Taken together, these studies confirm that the dorsal and ventral visual pathways from the parietal cortex and from the temporal lobes project to

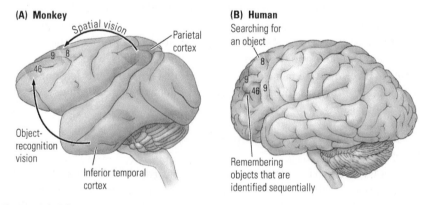

Figure 18.18 ▲

Two Short-Term Memory Systems in the Frontal Cortex (A) Results of single-cell-recording experiments show that premotor area 8, which receives projections from the parietal cortex, participates in short-term memory for object location in space (dorsal stream). DLPFC areas 9 and 46 participate in short-term memory for visual object recognition (ventral stream) and receive information from the inferior temporal cortex. (B) Results of PET-recording experiments show that area 8 searches for an object when a stimulus is presented, and areas 9 and 46 remember objects identified in sequence. (Part A information from Wilson et al., 1993; part B information from Petrides et al., 1993.)

different prefrontal cortical regions and support two kinds of short-term memory. The dorsal stream enables vision for action and the ventral stream, vision for perception.

◎ 18.6 Neurological Diseases and Long-Term Memory

Memory impairments result not only from diffuse brain damage but also from brain diseases such as transient global amnesia, herpes simplex encephalitis infections, Alzheimer's disease, and Korsakoff's syndrome.

Transient Global Amnesia

Concussion, migraine, hypoglycemia, and epilepsy, as well as interrupted blood flow from either a transient ischemic stroke or an embolism, are among the many possible causes of **transient global amnesia**. Described as loss of old memories and inability to form new ones, the condition is acute, with a sudden onset and usually a short course (Fisher and Adams, 1958). Transient global amnesia can be a one-time event, but Hans Markowitsch (1983) suggests, even so, that some memory loss can be permanent. Indeed, significant chronic memory loss is typical in transient global amnesia but usually overlooked because of the dramatic recovery and because careful memory testing after recovery is seldom done.

Herpes Simplex Encephalitis

Antonio Damasio and his coworkers (1991) describe several herpes simplex encephalitis cases in which temporal-lobe damage is accompanied by severe memory impairments. They describe one such patient, Boswell, in considerable detail. Boswell resembles many temporal-lobe-injury patients in having extensive anterograde amnesia while demonstrating typical intelligence and language abilities and performing at normal on implicit-memory tests.

Boswell is different, however, in that his retrograde amnesia is far more severe than that displayed by most temporal-lobe-injury patients: he is entirely unable to retrieve information from any part of his life history. The damage to the medial temporal cortex probably accounts for his anterograde amnesia, whereas additional damage in the lateral temporal cortex, the insula (diagrammed in Figure 18.5), and the ventromedial prefrontal cortex probably contributes to his retrograde amnesia.

Damasio suggests that in Boswell and other herpes simplex encephalitis patients, the insula may be especially implicated in retrograde amnesia. On the basis of study results using PET imaging, Michael and Marcus Raichle (1994) report that the insula is active when participants perform a well-practiced verbal task but inactive when they perform a novel verbal task. This finding seems consistent with Damasio's suggestion that the insula accesses previously acquired memories.

▼ Horizontal brain sections of two patients with selective retrograde amnesia for autobiographic information. (Left) An amnesic patient who contracted herpes simplex encephalitis. The right frontal and temporal lobes are dark, corresponding to a metabolic reduction in the right temporal frontal region (arrow). (Right) A patient with psychogenic amnesia. Again, a significant metabolic reduction is visible in the right temporal frontal area (arrow). (Markowitsch, H. J. Functional Neuroimaging Correlates of Functional Amnesia. *Memory*, Vol. 7, Issue 5-6, Plate 2. (1999): pp. 561–584.Reprinted by permission of Psychology Press Ltd., Hove.)

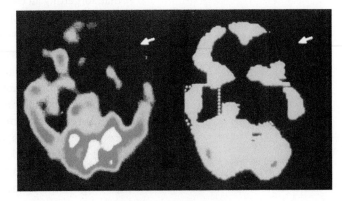

Alzheimer's Disease

Alzheimer's disease exhibits both a progressive loss of cells and the development of cortical abnormalities. It is characterized at first by anterograde amnesia and later by retrograde amnesia as well. Among the first areas of the brain to show histological change is the medial temporal cortex, but as the disease progresses, other cortical areas are affected.

Here, too, the pattern of brain change and the pattern of memory deficit suggest that damage to the medial temporal cortex is related to anterograde amnesia and that damage to other temporal association and frontal cortical areas is related to retrograde amnesia. Alzheimer's-related amnesia is displayed mainly on tests of explicit memory, but eventually, implicit memory also may suffer.

Korsakoff's Syndrome

Long-term alcoholism, especially when accompanied by malnutrition, has long been known to degrade memory. In the late 1800s, Russian physician Sergei Korsakoff called attention to a syndrome that he found to accompany chronic alcoholism, the most obvious symptom being a severe loss of memory. He wrote:

> The disorder of memory manifests itself in an extraordinarily peculiar amnesia, in which the memory of recent events, those that just happened, is chiefly disturbed, whereas the remote past is remembered fairly well. This reveals itself primarily in that the patient constantly asks the same questions and repeats the same stories. At first, during conversation with such a patient, it is difficult to note the presence of psychic disorder; the patient gives the impression of a person in complete possession of his faculties; he reasons about everything perfectly well, draws correct deductions from given premises, makes witty remarks, plays chess or a game of cards, in a word, comports himself as a mentally sound person. Only after a long conversation with the patient, one may note that at times he utterly confuses events and that he remembers absolutely nothing of what goes on around him: he does not remember whether he had his dinner, whether he was out of bed. On occasion the patient forgets what happened to him just an instant ago: you came in, conversed with him, and stepped out for one minute; then you come in again and the patient has absolutely no recollection that you had already been with him. . . . With all this, the remarkable fact is that, forgetting all events, which have just occurred, the patients usually remember quite accurately the past events, which occurred long before the illness. (Oscar-Berman, 1980, p. 410)

Korsakoff's syndrome has been studied intensively since a seminal article, published in 1971 by Helen Sanders and Elizabeth Warrington, because Korsakoff patients are far more readily available than are persons with other forms of global amnesia. Six major symptoms constitute the syndrome: (1) anterograde amnesia; (2) retrograde amnesia; (3) **confabulation**, in which patients glibly produce plausible stories about past events rather than admit memory loss (the stories are plausible because they tend to be based on past experiences; a man once told us, for example, that he had been at the Legion with his pals, which, though untrue, had been his practice in the past); (4) meager content in conversation; (5) lack of insight; and (6) apathy (patients lose interest in things quickly and generally appear indifferent to change).

The symptoms of Korsakoff's syndrome may appear suddenly, within the space of a few days. The cause is a thiamine (vitamin B_1) deficiency resulting from prolonged intake of large quantities of alcohol. The syndrome, which is usually progressive, can be arrested by massive doses of vitamin B_1 but cannot be reversed. Prognosis is poor, with only about 20 percent of patients showing much recovery in a year on a B_1-enriched diet. Many patients demonstrate no recovery even after 10 to 20 years.

The vitamin deficiency kills cells in the medial part of the diencephalon—the "between brain" at the top of the brainstem—including the medial thalamus and the mammillary bodies of the hypothalamus. The frontal lobes of 80 percent of patients show atrophy.

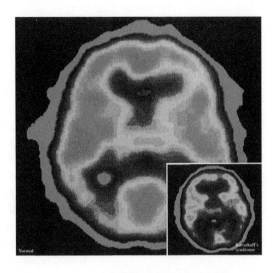

▲ PET scans from a healthy patient (larger image) and a Korsakoff patient (inset) reveal reduced activity in the frontal lobes of the diseased brain. (The frontal lobes lie at the bottom center of each scan.) Red and yellow represent areas of higher metabolic activity; activity is lower in the darker areas. (Dr. Peter R. Martin, from *Alcohol Health & Research World*, Spring 1985, 9, cover.)

Neurotransmitter Activating Systems and Memory

At least three neurotransmitter systems—cholinergic, serotonergic, noradrenergic, mapped in Figure 5.18—ascending from the brainstem to the forebrain are implicated in memory. Other ascending transmitter systems, including the histamine and orexin systems, are less studied but may also contribute to memory.

Loss of cholinergic cells is related to, and may even be responsible for, the amnesia displayed by patients with Alzheimer's disease. Curiously, in animal experiments, selective lesions of an ascending system have not produced amnesia, but conjoint damage to at least two systems has produced memory impairments. Cholinergic cells project from the basal forebrain to the frontal lobes and the temporal lobes and help maintain a waking EEG pattern. Selective damage to these cells is not associated with memory impairment. Serotonergic cells in the midbrain that project to the limbic system and cortex also are active in maintaining a waking EEG. If this cell group only is removed in animals, no serious memory difficulty results.

Profound amnesia can be produced, however, if the serotonergic cells and the cholinergic cells are damaged together. Cornelius Vanderwolf (1988) demonstrated that animals receiving such treatment behave as if the entire neocortex has been removed in that they no longer display any intelligent behavior. Additionally, cortical EEG recordings from such animals show a pattern typical of sleep, even though the animals can be behaviorally active.

Another example of the ascending systems' conjoint activity occurs between the cholinergic and the noradrenergic systems. Pharmacological blocking of either system has little effect on learning, but if both systems are blocked together, experimental rats are extremely impaired on learning tasks (Decker et al., 1990). Because many diseases of aging are associated with the loss of neurons from the ascending projections of the cholinergic, serotonergic, or noradrenergic systems, cell loss in more than one of these systems could be a cause of amnesia even when cortical or limbic structures are intact.

◎ 18.7 Special Memory Abilities

We began our discussion by noting that a primary purpose of explicit memory is to allow us to make good decisions and that our memories thus need not be perfectly detailed. The gist is sufficient. Some people—among them musicians, dancers, and athletes—may display exceptional implicit memory, but in practice every experience leaves an implicit memory trace in everyone. Those who do possess extraordinarily detailed memory display exemplary episodic, or autobiographical, recall.

Some people with **Asperger's syndrome**, a form of autism spectrum disorder in which intellectual function is high, can display excellent memory abilities. Others' special memory abilities are restricted, for example, to superior autobiographical memory. Here we describe, first, a case of special semantic memory ability described by Luria and second, people who display almost complete autobiographical memory.

Savant Syndrome

S. was a newspaper reporter with an extraordinary ability to form explicit memories that he could not forget. The fact that, unlike other reporters, he never took notes at briefings brought him to his employer's attention. When questioned on the matter, S. responded by repeating verbatim the transcript of the briefing they had just attended.

At his employer's urging, S. went to see a psychologist and met Alexander Luria, who began studying S.'s remarkable memory ability, a case study that endured for the following 30 years. Luria (1968) published an account of his investigation, and to this day *The Mind of a Mnemonist* is one of the most readable case studies in the literature of memory.

To sample these abilities, consider **Table 18.1**. S. could look at a table like this for 2 or 3 minutes and then repeat it from memory: by columns, by rows, by diagonals, in reverse, or in sums. Tested unexpectedly 16 or more years later, S. could still reproduce the table, reciting the columns in any order or combination, without error.

For a good part of his life, S. supported himself as an mnemonist—an entertainer who specializes in feats of memory. In the course of his career, he memorized hundreds of such lists or lists of names, letters, nonsense syllables, and so on; after memorizing any of them, he was able to recall it at any later date.

S.'s ability to commit information to memory hinged on three processes. First, he visualized stimuli mentally, recalling them simply by reading from this internal image. Second, he experienced **synesthesia**, or *sensory mixing*, which usually entails perceiving a stimulus of one sense as the sensation of a different sense, as when sound produces a sensation of color (see Section 8.3). But for S., a word invoked multisensory impressions of sound, splashes of color, odor, taste, texture, and even temperature! Finally, S. employed the pegboard technique many mnemonists use: he kept a collection of standard images in his mind and associated them with new material he wanted to remember. This trick and others employed by mnemonists offer insight into how explicit memories are usually formed and how such understanding can

Table 18.1 Type of table S. memorized

6	6	8	0
5	9	3	2
1	6	8	4
7	9	3	5
4	2	3	7
3	8	9	1
1	0	0	2
3	4	2	1
2	7	6	8
1	9	2	6
2	4	6	7
5	5	2	0
x	0	1	x

Note: With only 2 to 3 minutes of study of such a table, S. was able to reproduce it in reverse order, horizontally, or vertically, and to reproduce the diagonals.

improve memory in typical people as well as in people with memory impairments. Here are some examples from S.:

> Even numbers remind me of images. Take the number 1. This is a proud, well-built man; 2 is a high-spirited woman; 3 a gloomy person (shy, I don't know); 6 a man with a swollen foot; 7 a man with a mustache; 8 a very stout woman—a sack within a sack. As for the number 87, what I see is a fat woman and a man twirling his mustache. (Luria, 1968)

Did S. pay a price for his memory abilities? Luria's position clearly is that he did. He characterizes S. as a person with little aim in life, seemingly dull and superficial, and suggests that S. was unable to reason, to categorize, and to see order in things as ordinary people can. He also had little ability to use or understand metaphors (for example, the phrase "to weigh one's words"); he visualized and interpreted them literally and so was puzzled by what they meant. S. often had difficulty understanding simple statements and had even more difficulty understanding the sense of poetry.

Superior Autobiographical Memory

A research group headed by James McGaugh has collected several cases of individuals who display *highly superior autobiographical memory*, or *HSAM* (LePort et al., 2012). They display virtually complete recall for events in their lives, usually beginning around age 10, and can often describe any episode, including the day of the week that it occurred and the date. Their recall can include the weather and social and public events.

They use no memory strategy as aids and are, as a group, otherwise quite ordinary; that is, their performance on formal memory tests is not unusual. Brain imaging of those who display HSAM reveals increased gray matter in the temporal and parietal lobes and increased size of fiber projections between the temporal lobe and the frontal cortex. These brain regions, when damaged, have been associated with impairments in autobiographical memory.

Unlike S., people with HSAM generally cope well with life, although some display obsessive-compulsive behaviors. Some also report that they ruminate on past memories and experience enjoyable memories again and again. One individual with HSAM, known to us, elaborates his conversation by recounting details, including the date, the weather, and coincident activities of family members. This takes some patience on the part of the listener.

SUMMARY

Our multiple memory systems operate independently of one another (review Figure 18.1).

18.1 Learning, Memory, and Amnesia

Research results find differences in the processes of acquiring and storing memory. For example, anterograde amnesia, the inability to form new memories, is often more severe than retrograde amnesia, the inability to retrieve old memories.

The medial temporal and inferior frontal lobes and the circuits within and between them mediate long-term learning and explicit memory, including episodic memory, related to personal experiences, and semantic memory, related to facts. Explicit memories are often lost after medial temporal damage, while long-term implicit memory, such as motor skills, and the ability to form new memories are usually spared. Opposing theories of amnesia argue for memory-system consolidation, multiple-trace memory, or reconsolidated memory.

18.2 Long-Term Explicit Memory

A neural system consisting of the prefrontal cortex, medial temporal lobe, and subcortical temporal-lobe structures, including the hippocampus, rhinal cortex, and connections with the ventral prefrontal cortex, is the likely location of conscious explicit memory. Episodic memory is especially dependent on the hippocampus and ventral prefrontal cortex, where damage can be associated with the loss of all retrograde autobiographic memory and an inability to imagine a personal role in future events.

18.3 Long-Term Implicit Memory

Motor memory, priming, and conditioning constitute implicit memory, a nonconscious neural system consisting of pathways connecting the basal ganglia, motor cortex, and cerebellum. Deficits in learned motor skills and habits are associated with damage to the basal ganglia; and the loss of conditioned responses, with damage to the cerebellum.

18.4 Long-Term Emotional Memory

Neural systems centered in the amygdala of the limbic system, subcortical to the temporal lobes, encode our emotional recollections of affective experiences. These recollections share aspects of explicit and implicit memory.

18.5 Short-Term Memory

Sensory regions of the neocortex mediate short-term (working, temporal, or recency) memory for items held in mind for seconds to minutes. The dorsal stream traversing the parietal and frontal cortex participates in short-term memory for locations, whereas the ventral stream from the sensory regions forward into the inferior temporal–dorsolateral prefrontal cortex mediates short-term memory for objects.

18.6 Neurological Diseases and Long-Term Memory

Memory impairments can result from diffuse brain damage and from brain disease, as occurs in transient global amnesia, herpes simplex encephalitis infections, Alzheimer's disease, and Korsakoff's syndrome. Neurotransmitter activating systems also contribute to neurological diseases that affect memory.

18.7 Special Memory Abilities

People can display extraordinary semantic or autobiographical memory. The very neural circuits that produce memory deficits when damaged may be enhanced in those who possess savant syndrome or superior autobiographic memory. Thus, special abilities may coexist alongside islands of intellectual weakness.

References

Akers, K. G., A. Martinez-Canabal, L. Restivo, A. P. Yiu, A. De Cristofaro, H. L. Hsiang, A. L. Wheeler, A. Guskjolen, Y. Niibori, K. Ohira, B. A. Richards, T. Miyakawa, S. A. Josselyn, and P. W. Frankland. Hippocampal neurogenesis regulates forgetting during adulthood and infancy. *Science* 618:598–602, 2014.

Allen, R. J., F. Vargha-Khadem, and A. D. Baddeley. Item-location binding in working memory: Is it hippocampus-dependent? *Neuropsychologia* 59:74–84, 2014.

Anderson, E. D., F. B. Horak, M. R. Lasarev, and J. G. Nutt. Performance of a motor task learned on levodopa deteriorates when subsequently practiced off. *Movement Disorders* 29:54–60, 2014.

Annese, J., N. M. Schenker-Ahmed, H. Bartsch, P. Maechler, C. Sheh, N. Thomas, J. Kayano, A. Ghatan, N. Bresler, M. P. Frosch, R. Klaming, and S. Corkin. Postmortem examination of patient H.M.'s brain based on histological sectioning and digital 3D reconstruction. *Nature Communications* 5:3122, 2014.

Bartlett, F. C. *Remembering*. Cambridge, U.K.: Cambridge University Press, 1932.

Bekhterev, V. M. Demonstration eines Gehirns mit Zerstörung der vorderen und inneren Theile der Hirnrinde beider Schlafenlappen. *Neurologisches Zentralb* 19:990–991, 1900.

Broadbent, D. E. *Perception and Communication*. London: Pergamon, 1958.

Cabeza, R., and L. Nyberg. Imaging Cognition II: An empirical review of 275 PET and fMRI studies. *Journal of Cognitive Neuroscience* 12:1–47, 2000.

Cabeza, R., and M. Moscovitch. Memory systems, processing modes, and components: Functional neuroimaging evidence. *Perspectives on Psychological Science* 8:49–55, 2013.

Cipolotti, L., T. Shallice, D. Chan, N. Fox, R. Scahill, G. Harrison, J. Stevens, and P. Rudge. Long-term retrograde amnesia: The crucial role of the hippocampus. *Neuropsychologia* 39:151–172, 2001.

Clarke A., and L. K. Tyler. Object-specific semantic coding in human perirhinal cortex. *Journal of Neuroscience* 34:4766–4775, 2014.

Corkin, S. Acquisition of motor skill after bilateral medial temporal-lobe excision. *Neuropsychologia* 6:255–265, 1968.

Corkin, S., D. G. Amaral, R. G. Gonzalez, K. A. Johnson, and B. T. Hyman. H.M.'s medial temporal lobe lesion: Findings from magnetic resonance imaging. *Journal of Neuroscience* 17:3964–3979, 1997.

Corsi, P. M. *Human Memory and the Medial Temporal Region of the Brain*. Ph.D. dissertation. Montreal: McGill University, 1972.

Damasio, A. R., D. Tranel, and H. Damasio. Amnesia caused by herpes simplex encephalitis, infarctions in basal forebrain, Alzheimer's disease and anoxia/ischemia. In L. Squire and G. Gainotti, Eds., *Handbook of Neuropsychology*, vol 3. Amsterdam: Elsevier, 1991.

Decker, M. W., M. T. Gill, and J. L. McGaugh. Concurrent muscarenic and beta-adrenergic blockade in rats impairs place learning in a water maze and retention of inhibitory avoidance. *Brain Research* 513:81–85, 1990.

Elliott, H. C. *Textbook of Neuroanatomy*. Philadelphia: Lippincott, 1969.

Fisher, C. M., and R. D. Adams. Transient global amnesia. *Transactions of the American Neurological Association* 83:143, 1958.

Fuster, J. M. *The Prefrontal Cortex*. New York: Raven, 1989.

Gaffan, D., and E. Gaffan. Amnesia in man following transection of the fornix: A review. *Brain* 114:2611–2618, 1991.

Goldman-Rakic, P. S. Working memory and the mind. *Scientific American* 267(3):111–117, 1992.

Gollin, E. S. Developmental studies of visual recognition of incomplete objects. *Perceptual and Motor Skills* 11:289–298, 1960.

Grafton, S. T., J. C. Mazziotta, S. Presty, K. J. Friston, S. J. Frackowiak, and M. E. Phelps. Functional anatomy of human procedural learning determined with regional cerebral blood flow and PET. *Journal of Neuroscience* 12:2542–2548, 1992.

James, W. *The Principles of Psychology*. New York: Holt, 1890.

Josselyn S. A., and P. W. Frankland. Infantile amnesia: A neurogenic hypothesis. *Learning and Memory* 16:423–433, 2012.

Kolb, B., and B. Milner. Performance of complex arm and facial movements after focal brain lesions. *Neuropsychologia* 19:491–503, 1981.

LeDoux, J. Rethinking the emotional brain. *Neuron* 73:653–676, 2012.

Lee, K. H., and R. F. Thompson. Multiple memory mechanisms in the cerebellum? *Neuron* 51:680–682, 2006.

LePort, A. K., A. T. Mattfeld, H. Dickinson-Anson, J. H. Fallon, C. E. Stark, F. Kruggel, L. Cahill, and J. L. McGaugh. Behavioral and neuroanatomical investigation of Highly Superior Autobiographical Memory (HSAM). *Neurobiology of Learning and Memory* 98:78–92, 2012.

Levine, B. Autonoetic consciousness and self-regulation in patients with brain injury. *International Journal of Psychology* 35:223, 2000.

Levine, B., S. E. Black, R. Cabeza, M. Sinden, A. R. Mcintosh, J. P. Toth, and E. Tulving. Episodic memory and the self in a case of isolated retrograde amnesia. *Brain* 121:1951–1973, 1998.

Luria, A. R. *The mind of a mnemonist*. New York: Basic Books, 1968.

Markowitsch, H. J. Transient global amnesia. *Neuroscience and Biobehavioral Reviews* 7:35–43, 1983.

Martone, M., N. Butlers, M. Payne, J. T. Baker, and D. S. Sax. Dissociations between skill learning and verbal recognition in amnesia and dementia. *Archives of Neurology* 41:965–970, 1984.

Mazzucchi, A., G. Moretti, P. Caffara, and M. Parma. Neuropsychological functions in the follow-up of transient global amnesia. *Brain* 103:161–178, 1980.

Milner, B. Visually-guided maze learning in man: Effects of bilateral hippocampal, bilateral frontal, and unilateral cerebral lesions. *Neuropsychologia* 3:317–338, 1965.

Milner, B. Memory and the medial temporal regions of the brain. In K. H. Pribram and D. E. Broadbent, Eds., *Biology of Memory*. New York: Academic Press, 1970.

Milner, B., S. Corkin, and H.-L. Teuber. Further analysis of the hippocampal amnesic syndrome: 14-year follow up study of H.M. *Neuropsychologia* 6:215–234, 1968.

Moscovitch, M. Multiple dissociations of function in amnesia. In L. S. Cermak, Ed., *Human Memory and Amnesia*. Hillsdale, N.J.: Lawrence Erlbaum, 1982.

Murray, E. Memory for objects in nonhuman primates. In M. S. Gazzaniga, Ed., *The New Cognitive Neurosciences*, 2nd ed., pp. 753–763. London: MIT Press, 2000.

Nadel, L., and M. Moscovitch. Memory consolidation, retrograde amnesia and the hippocampal complex. *Current Opinion in Neurobiology* 7:212–227, 1997.

Oscar-Berman, M. Neuropsychological consequences of long-term chronic alcoholism. *American Scientist* 68:410–419, 1980.

Pascual-Leone, A., J. Grafman, and M. Hallett. Modulation of cortical motor output maps during development of implicit and explicit knowledge. *Science* 263:1287–1289, 1994.

Petri, H. L., and M. Mishkin. Behaviorism, cognitivism, and the neuropsychology of memory. *American Scientist* 82:30–37, 1994.

Petrides, M., B. Alivisatos, A. C. Evans, and E. Meyer. Dissociation of human mid-dorsolateral from posterior dorsolateral frontal cortex in memory processing. *Proceedings of the National Academy of Sciences U.S.A.* 90:873–877, 1993.

Poppenk, J., H. R. Evensmoen, M. Moscovitch, and L. Nadel. Long-axis specialization of the human hippocampus. *Trends in Cognitive Science* 17:230–240, 2013.

Posner, M. I., and M. E. Raichle. *Images of Mind*. New York: Scientific American Library, 1994.

Prisko, L. *Short-Term Memory in Focal Cerebral Damage*. Ph.D. dissertation. Montreal: McGill University, 1963.

Reber, P. J. The neural basis of implicit learning and memory: A review of neuropsychological and neuroimaging research. *Neuropsychologia* 51:2026–2042, 2013.

Sainsbury, R., and M. Coristine. Affective discrimination in moderately to severely demented patients. *Canadian Journal on Aging* 5:99–104, 1986.

Sanders, H. I., and E. K. Warrington. Memory for remote events in amnesic patients. *Brain* 94:661–668, 1971.

Schacter, D. L., and D. L. Addis. The cognitive neuroscience of constructive memory: Remembering the past and imagining the future. *Philosophical Transactions of the Royal Society of London B* 362:773–786, 2007.

Schwabe, L., K. Nader, and J. C. Pruessner. Reconsolidation of human memory: Brain mechanisms and clinical relevance. *Biological Psychiatry* 76:274–280, 2014.

Scoville, W. B., and B. Milner. Loss of recent memory after bilateral hippocampal lesions. *Journal of Neurology, Neurosurgery & Psychiatry* 20:11–21, 1957.

Siri, S., E. A. Kensinger, S. F. Cappa, and S. Corkin. Questioning the living/nonliving dichotomy: Evidence from a patient with an unusual semantic dissociation. *Neuropsychology* 17:630–645, 2003.

Smith, C. N., J. C. Frascino, R. O. Hopkins, and L. R. Squire. The nature of anterograde and retrograde memory impairment after damage to the medial temporal lobe. *Neuropsychologia* 51:2709–2714, 2013.

Squire, L. R., and P. J. Bayley. The neuroscience of remote memory. *Current Opinion in Neurobiology* 17:185–196, 2007.

Tronson, N. C., and J. R. Taylor. Molecular mechanisms of memory reconsolidation. *Nature Reviews Neuroscience* 8:262–275, 2007.

Tulving, E. Episodic memory: From mind to brain. *Annual Review of Psychology* 53:1–25, 2002.

Tulving, E., S. Kapur, F. I. M. Craik, M. Moscovitch, and S. Houle. Hemispheric encoding/retrieval asymmetry in episodic memory: Positron emission tomography finding. *Proceedings of the National Academy of Sciences U.S.A.* 91:2016–2020, 1994.

Vanderwolf, C. H. Cerebral activity and behavior: Control by central cholinergic and serotonergic systems. *International Review of Neurobiology* 30:255–340, 1988.

Vargha-Khadem, F., D. G. Gadian, K. A. Watkins, W. Connelly, W. Van Paesschen, and M. Mishkin. Differential effects of early hippocampal pathology on episodic and semantic memory. *Science* 277:376–380, 1997.

Wang, Q., and C. Peterson. Your earliest memory may be earlier than you think: Prospective studies of children's dating of earliest childhood memories. *Developmental Psychology* 50, 1680–1686, 2014.

Warrington, E. K., and L. Weiskrantz. Further analysis of the prior learning effect in amnesic patients. *Neuropsychologia* 16:169–177, 1978.

Whitty, C. W. M., and O. L. Zangwill. Traumatic amnesia. In C. W. M. Whitty and O. L. Zangwill, Eds., *Amnesia.* London: Butterworth, 1966.

Wilson, F. A. W., S. P. O. Scalaidhe, and P. S. Goldman-Rakic. Dissociation of object and spatial processing domains in primate prefrontal cortex. *Science* 260:1955–1958, 1993.

19 Language

K.H., a Swiss-born architect, was a professor of architecture at a major U.S. university. Although German was his first language and he was fluent in French and Italian, his primary language had become English.

He had been an outstanding student, excelling at writing and meticulous about his spelling and grammar. When his mother complained that he was making spelling and grammatical errors in his letters to her, written in German, he was astonished. He suspected that he was forgetting his German and resolved to prevent that from happening.

A few weeks later, K.H. asked a colleague to review a manuscript he had just completed, written in English. His colleague commented that K.H. must be working too hard because the manuscript was filled with uncharacteristic errors. At about the same time, K.H. noticed that the right side of his face felt "funny." A neurologist found a small tumor at the junction of the motor–face area and Broca's area in the left hemisphere. (The accompanying diffusion tensor image models the ventral and dorsal

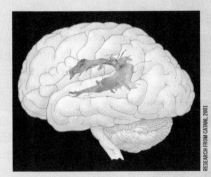

RESEARCH FROM CATANI, 2001

stream language pathways connecting Broca's and Wernicke's areas within the brain.)

The tumor was benign and was removed surgically. In the first few days after the surgery, K.H. was densely aphasic: he could neither talk nor understand oral or written language. Although he had been warned that aphasia was likely and that it would be temporary, he was visibly upset. By the end of the first week, he could understand oral language, but his speech was still unintelligible, and he could not read.

By the end of the second week, K.H. was speaking German fluently but had difficulty with English, although it was certainly understandable. He was still unable to read in any language but believed that he could read German and could be convinced otherwise only when he was informed that the book he was supposedly reading was upside down! His reading and English slowly improved, but even now, years later, K.H. finds spelling in any language difficult, and his reading is slower than would be expected for a person of his intelligence and education.

Using language is a precious ability, yet we tend to take it for granted, as K.H. did before he was stricken. Think about how much your daily life depends on your ability to talk, listen, and read. We even talk to ourselves. As children, we learn language long before we can catch a ball or ride a bicycle, using words to identify and learn about our environment. We use language to inform and persuade and to entertain ourselves with poetry, song, and humor. Indeed, much humor is based on nuances of language and on double entendres. Using language is our most complex skill, and we can approach its study in many ways. One place to start is by considering what language is.

19.1 What Is Language?

The word language derives from *langue*, an Anglo-French word for "tongue," referring to a convention that describes language as the use of sound combinations for communication. But language also includes the idea that this use of sounds is guided by rules that, when translated into other sensory modalities, allow for equivalent communication through gestures, touches, and visual images. Many other animal species have evolved forms of communication, but no other species uses language as humans do. That said, no universal agreement has emerged on what language is, and differences in defining language also lead to differences of opinion about how the brain produces language.

Language Structure

Like most people, you probably think of words as the meaningful units of language. Linguists break language down differently (**Table 19.1**). They view words as consisting of fundamental language sounds, called **phonemes**, that form a word or part of a word. Phonological analysis determines how we link phonemes together.

We combine phonemes to form **morphemes**, the smallest meaningful units of words, such as a base (*do* in un*do*), an affix (*un* in *un*do or *er* in do*er*), or an inflection (*ing* in do*ing* or *s* in girl*s*). Some morphemes are themselves complete words; others must be combined to form words.

A **lexicon** comprises a memory store that contains words and their meanings—hypothetically, all of the words in a given language. Words are strung together in patterns that conform to the language's rules of grammar—its **syntax**. A key aspect of syntax is appropriate choice of verb tense.

The meaning connected to words and sentences is referred to, collectively, as **semantics**. Vocal intonation—the tone of voice, called **prosody**—can modify the literal meaning of words and sentences by varying stress, pitch, and rhythm. **Discourse**, the highest level of language processing, involves stringing together sentences to form a meaningful narrative.

This linguistic discussion emphasizes the acoustical nature of basic language components, but analogs exist in the visual nature of reading, the touch language of Braille, and in the movement language of signing, for example in American Sign Language (ASL, or Ameslan). A morpheme in ASL is the smallest meaningful movement.

Table 19.1 Components of a sound-based language

Phonemes	Individual sound units whose concatenation, in particular order, produces morphemes
Morphemes	Smallest meaningful units of a word, whose combination forms a word
Lexicon	Collection of all words in a given language; each lexical entry includes all information with morphological or syntactical ramifications but does not include conceptual knowledge
Syntax	Grammar—admissible combinations of words in phrases and sentences
Semantics	Meanings that correspond to all lexical items and all possible sentences
Prosody	Vocal intonation—the tone of voice—which can modify the literal meaning of words and sentences
Discourse	Linking sentences to constitute a narrative

The traditional criterion linguists use to recognize language is the presence of words and word components; another characteristic of human language is its use of syllables made up of consonants and vowels. Our mouths are capable of producing consonants and combining them with vowels to produce syllables. Nonhuman species do not produce syllables, primarily because they do not produce consonants.

Producing Sound

The basic anatomy that enables humans to produce sound consists of two sets of parts, one set acting as the sound source and the other as filters, as modeled in **Figure 19.1**A and charted in Figure 19.1B. Air exhaled from the lungs drives oscillations of the **vocal cords** (*vocal folds*), folds of mucous membrane attached to the vocal muscles, located in the **larynx**, or "voice box," the organ of voice. The rate of vocal-fold oscillation (from about 100 Hz in adult men to 500 Hz in small children) determines the pitch (low to high frequency) of the sound produced.

Acoustical energy thus generated then passes through the vocal tract (pharyngeal, oral, and nasal cavities) and finally out through the nostrils and lips. As this energy passes through the vocal tract, its structures group sound waves specific to each vowel sound, called **formants**. Formants modify the emitted sound, allowing specific frequencies to pass unhindered but blocking transmission of others (review Figure 15.13). Filtering plays a crucial role in speech: the length and shape of the vocal tract determine formant characteristics, which are modified rapidly during speech by the movements of the articulators (tongue, lips, soft palate, and so on). Formants emphasize sound frequencies that are meaningful in speech.

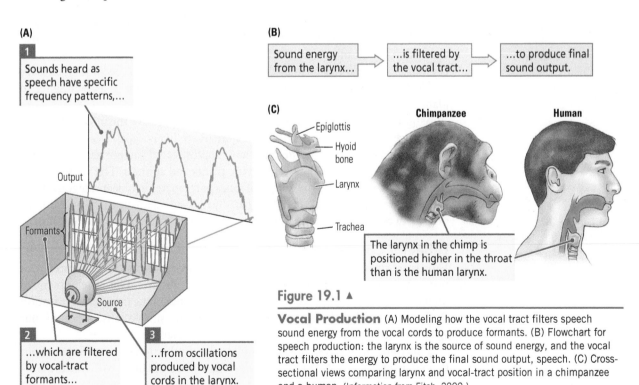

(A)

1 Sounds heard as speech have specific frequency patterns,...

Output

Formants

Source

2 ...which are filtered by vocal-tract formants...

3 ...from oscillations produced by vocal cords in the larynx.

(B)

Sound energy from the larynx... → ...is filtered by the vocal tract... → ...to produce final sound output.

(C)

Epiglottis

Hyoid bone

Larynx

Trachea

Chimpanzee

Human

The larynx in the chimp is positioned higher in the throat than is the human larynx.

Figure 19.1 ▲

Vocal Production (A) Modeling how the vocal tract filters speech sound energy from the vocal cords to produce formants. (B) Flowchart for speech production: the larynx is the source of sound energy, and the vocal tract filters the energy to produce the final sound output, speech. (C) Cross-sectional views comparing larynx and vocal-tract position in a chimpanzee and a human. (Information from Fitch, 2000.)

The vocal apparatus that produces formants marks a major difference between us and other apes. The human oral cavity is longer than in other apes, and the human larynx is situated much lower in the throat, as shown in Figure 19.1C. Starting at about 3 months of age, the human larynx begins a slow descent toward its adult position, reaching it after 3 to 4 years. A second, shorter descent takes place in human males at puberty.

Descent of the human larynx is a key evolutionary and developmental innovation in speech. By allowing the tongue to move both vertically and horizontally within the vocal tract, a lowered larynx enables us to vary the area of the oral and pharyngeal tubes independently, adding to the variety of sounds we can produce easily. Sound energy fuels our primary means of communicating, but language exists in forms other than sound, including gestures, the touch language of Braille, and the visual languages of reading and ASL. Whatever our definition of language, it need not involve sound.

Core Language Skills

Four core skills underlie human language: (1) categorizing, (2) category labeling, (3) sequencing behaviors, and (4) mimicry. One or another of these core skills may be present in other animal species, including other apes, songbirds, even bees. Before we review evidence of core language skills in other animals, we consider their roles in human language. These four abilities are similar to and likely depend upon neural circuits that you have encountered in earlier chapters.

Categorization

Multiple parallel hierarchical neural channels function to process incoming sensory stimulation. As the cortex expands and the number of channels that process parallel sensory information increases, binding (integrating) the information into a single perception of reality becomes more difficult. The brain must determine which of myriad kinds of sensory information reaching the cortex correspond to a given object in the external world. Thus, it becomes necessary to categorize information, for example to tag some qualities as belonging to plants and others as belonging to animals.

Assigning tags to information makes it easier to perceive the information and to retrieve it later when needed. Most animals are likely capable of categorizing objects to some extent, and humans have sophisticated categorization systems, informal as well as formal, for classifying plants and animals. The ventral visual stream coursing through the temporal lobes participates in object categorization, and the dorsal stream may also participate by making relatively automatic distinctions between objects, such as plant versus animal or human versus nonhuman.

Labeling Categories

Words are the ultimate categorizers, but using words as tags to label categories rests on a preexisting perception of what categories are. The development of human language may have entailed selection for novel means of categorization that not only allowed for combining and grouping simple sensory stimuli but also provided a means of organizing events and relations.

This categorizing system can stimulate the production of word forms about that concept (the category); conversely, it can cause the brain to evoke the concepts in words. Thus, a man who was once a painter but is now color-blind can know and use the words (labels) for colors, even though he can no longer perceive or imagine what those labels mean. He has, in a sense, lost his concept of color, but his words can still evoke it. In contrast, certain brain-lesion patients retain their perception of color, and thus the concept, but have lost the language with which to describe it. They experience colors but cannot attach labels to them.

Thus, labeling a category includes not only identifying it, a function of the temporal lobes, but also organizing information within the category—as, for example, within the category label *tools*. This is a function of the motor cortices in the frontal lobes within the dorsal visual stream.

Sequencing Behavior

Human language employs transitional larynx movements to form syllables. Left-hemisphere structures associated with language form part of a system that has a fundamental role in ordering vocal movements such as those used in speech. We can also sequence face, body, and arm movements to produce nonverbal language. Sequencing words to represent meaningful actions likely makes use of the same dorsal-stream frontal cortex circuits that sequence motor action more generally.

Mimicry

Mimicry fosters language development. Athena Vouloumanos and Janet Werker (2007) find that from birth, babies show a preference for listening to speech over other sounds. When they begin to babble, they are capable of making the sounds used in all languages. They also mimic and subsequently prefer the language sounds made by the people in their lives.

By some estimates, in the formative years, children may add as many as 60 new words each day to their vocabularies. Motor system *mirror neurons* respond when we see others make movements and also when we make the same movements (see the Snapshot on page 244). One view related to mimicry is that mirror neurons in the cortical language regions are responsible for our ability to mimic the sounds, words, and actions that comprise language.

19.2 Searching for the Origins of Language

Two theoretical approaches attempt to explain language origins. **Discontinuity theory** proposes that language evolved rapidly and appeared suddenly, occurring in modern humans in the last 200,000 years or so. **Continuity theory** proposes that language evolved gradually: similarities in the genes and behaviors of ancestral hominid species, when uniquely modified in modern humans, produced language. The Snapshot on pages 520–521 describes how one gene that has been related to human language supports the idea from continuity theory that a language gene may exist.

The search for the origins of language is not merely idle curiosity. If we can determine which capacities were precursors of human language and why they were selected, we will have taken a giant step toward understanding how language came to be represented in our brains. It is likely that the continuity and

SNAPSHOT Genetic Basis for an Inherited Speech and Language Disorder

Almost half of the members of three generations of the KE family are affected by a severe disorder of speech and language inherited as an autosomal (non–sex chromosome) dominant trait (Vargha-Khadem et al., 2005). The impairment, displayed by 15 of 37 family members (**Figure A**), is best characterized as a deficit in sequencing articulation patterns, rendering speech sometimes agrammatical and often unintelligible. The orofacial aspect affects the production of sound sequences, which makes the deficit resemble Broca's aphasia.

Affected KE family members scored poorly when tested on repeating nonwords and on verbal and performance IQ tests, including such nonverbal subtests as picture completion and picture arrangement. They were also impaired on most tests of language function. The affected members were impaired on tests of mouth movement (oral praxis), including simple movements of clicking the tongue and movement sequences (such as blowing up the cheeks then licking the lips then smacking the lips).

MRI analysis of the affected family members' brains showed significantly less gray matter than typical in the caudate nuclei (**Figure B**) as well as in sensorimotor cortex, inferotemporal

cortex, cerebellum, and left inferofrontal cortex (Watkins et al., 2002). These brain regions are associated with producing facial movements necessary for language.

Genetic analysis of the KE family identified a mutation that affects the ability of the gene *foxhead P2*, or *FOXP2*, to regulate the transcription of other genes. The mutation is a single nucleotide polymorphism (SNP), or one base change, that renders the protein inactive. *FOXP2* regulates the expression of over 300 genes during development and during learning, mainly by blocking their expression, and the genes regulated by *FOXP2* are different in different brain regions and also other body regions, including the lungs. This has led to a search among these genes for

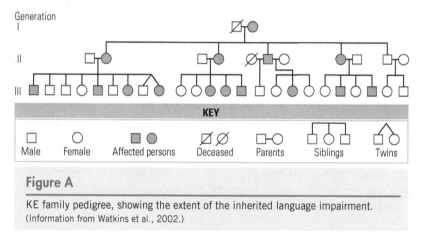

Figure A

KE family pedigree, showing the extent of the inherited language impairment. (Information from Watkins et al., 2002.)

discontinuity theories are both correct: language is what brains do, but the specific form that language takes varies from species to species, and this explains both the origins and the structure of language as humans use it.

Continuity Theory

Continuity theory considers many lines of evidence, including the adaptation of animal vocalization for language (Schoenemann, 2012). Perhaps it is a tribute to the imagination with which speculators approached the question of *which* vocalizations, in 1866, that the Linguistic Society of Paris banned future discussion of vocalization theory. We will not let that ban deter us.

Gordon Hewes (1977) reviews many variants of animal vocalization theory, including the *pooh-pooh* theory (language evolved from noises associated with strong emotion), the *bow-wow* theory (language evolved from noises first those that may be related to language impairments. One gene regulated by *FOXP2* is *CNTNAP2*, has been implicated in specific language-related disorders and in autism spectrum disorder (Nudel and Newbury, 2013).

FOXP2 is highly conserved in that it is similar in many nonhuman animal species, where it also plays a role in the development of many parts of the brain as well as other body organs. The gene is expressed in brain areas that regulate song learning in birds, singing in whales, and ultrasonic vocalizations in mice. *FOXP2* mutations in these species affect sound production.

FOXP2 has undergone two mutations over the course of hominid evolution. Such rapid evolution suggests that these mutations may have altered neuronal circuitry in the brain's motor regions to enable movements that contribute to human speech. Introducing the human gene variant, including the two mutations, into mice produced 34 changes in genes expressed in the mutant mice, alterations in dendritic morphology of brain cells, and alterations in the frequency of ultrasonic vocalizations.

The discovery of the *FOXP2* gene mutation in the KE family has led to the identification of other *FOXP2* mutations in other individuals with language disorders and in some individuals with schizophrenia. However, not all individuals with reading and learning disabilities have abnormalities in this gene.

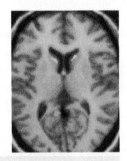

Figure B

Graph (left) records the average volume of the caudate nucleus at various locations along its extent in affected and unaffected family members. MRI (right) locates parts of the caudate nucleus (yellow areas) near the ventricles. (Information and MRI from Watkins, K. E., N. F. Dronkers, and F. Vargha-Khadem. MRI analysis of an inherited speech and language disorder: structural brain abnormalities. *Brain*, Vol. 125, Issue 3, [2002]: pp. 465–478.)

Nudel, R., and D. F. Newbury. *FOXP2. Wiley Interdisciplinary Reviews: Cognitive Science* 4:547–560, 2013.

Vargha-Khadem, F., D. G. Gadian, A. Copp, and M. Mishkin. *FOXP2* and the neuroanatomy of speech and language. *Nature Reviews Neuroscience* 32:131–138, 2005.

Watkins, K. E., N. F. Dronkers, and F. Vargha-Khadem. MRI analysis of an inherited speech and language disorder: structural brain abnormalities. *Brain*, Vol. 125, Issue 3, (2002): pp. 465–478.

made to imitate natural sounds), the *yo-he-ho* theory (language evolved from sounds made to resonate with natural sounds), and the *sing-song* theory (language evolved from noises made while playing or dancing).

Scientific evidence that vocalization contributes to language origins comes from studying chimpanzees. The results of Jane Goodall's studies on the chimpanzees of Gombe in Tanzania indicate that our closest relatives have as many as 32 separate vocalizations. Goodall (1986) noted that the chimps seem to understand these calls much better than humans do, although her field assistants, the people most familiar with the chimps, can distinguish them well enough to claim that the actual number is higher than 32. **Figure 19.2** illustrates the wide range of vocalizations made by free-living chimpanzees.

Jared Taglialatela and his coworkers (2003) recorded vocalizations made by the chimp Kanzi, noting that he made both communicative sounds and sounds when eating. As the Portrait on page 28 reports, these investigators found that

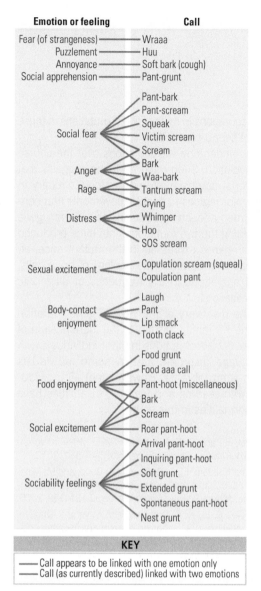

Emotion or feeling	Call
Fear (of strangeness)	Wraaa
Puzzlement	Huu
Annoyance	Soft bark (cough)
Social apprehension	Pant-grunt
Social fear	Pant-bark
	Pant-scream
	Squeak
	Victim scream
	Scream
Anger	Bark
	Waa-bark
Rage	Tantrum scream
	Crying
Distress	Whimper
	Hoo
	SOS scream
Sexual excitement	Copulation scream (squeal)
	Copulation pant
Body-contact enjoyment	Laugh
	Pant
	Lip smack
	Tooth clack
Food enjoyment	Food grunt
	Food aaa call
	Pant-hoot (miscellaneous)
	Bark
	Scream
Social excitement	Roar pant-hoot
	Arrival pant-hoot
	Inquiring pant-hoot
Sociability feelings	Soft grunt
	Extended grunt
	Spontaneous pant-hoot
	Nest grunt

KEY

⎯⎯ Call appears to be linked with one emotion only
⎯⎯ Call (as currently described) linked with two emotions

Figure 19.2 ▲

Precursors of Language
Chimpanzee calls and the emotion or feeling with which they are most closely associated. (Goodall, J. *The Chimpanzees of Gombe.* Cambridge, Mass.: Harvard University Press, 1986. Permission granted by The Jane Goodall Institute.)

Kanzi's food peeps were structurally different in different contexts. Thus, "chimpanzeeish" as a primitive form of communication can be thought of as a stepping-stone to human language and speech.

Varied evidence supports the contribution gestures make to language evolution. Many animals communicate with movement: at the simplest, when one animal moves, others follow. We have all observed the gestures displayed by a dog that wants us to open a door. We understand these gestures and might make similar gestures when asking the dog to go through the door.

We can observe the rudiments of subject-object-verb (SOV) syntax in movements such as reaching for a food item (Schouwastra and de Swart, 2014). The subject is a person, the object is the food, and the verb is the reach. Clearly, our pet dog watching us reach for a food item understands. According to this idea, language begins in the brain regions that produce movement, but the notable adaption in human language is its specialization for communication.

Nonverbal gestures are closely related to speech. David McNeill (2005) reports that hand and body gestures accompany more than 90% of our verbal utterances. Most people gesture with the right hand when they speak: their gestures are produced by the left hemisphere, as is most language. Gestures thus form an integral component of language, suggesting that our language comprises more than speech: the neural basis of language is not simply a property of brain regions controlling the mouth but includes the motor system more generally.

As early as 1878, John Hughlings-Jackson suggested that a natural experiment would support the idea that gestural language is related to vocal language. The loss of certain sign-language abilities by people who had previously depended on sign language (for example, ASL), he reasoned, would provide the appropriate evidence that gestural language and vocal language depend on the same brain structure. Hughlings-Jackson even observed a case that seemed to indicate that a left-hemisphere lesion disrupted sign language, as it would vocal language.

Doreen Kimura (1993) confirmed that lesions disrupting vocal speech also disrupt signing. Of 11 patients with signing disorders subsequent to brain lesions, 9 right-handers had disorders subsequent to a left-hemisphere lesion similar to one that would produce aphasia in a speaking person. One left-handed patient had a signing disorder subsequent to a left-hemisphere lesion, and another left-handed patient had a signing disorder subsequent to a right-hemisphere lesion. These proportions and the location of the lesions are identical with those found for vocal patients who become aphasic (see Section 12.3). Such results support the idea that some language systems that control vocal speech also control signing.

Aaron Newman and his colleagues (2002) used fMRI to study brain areas active in bilingual speakers during speech and during signing. Their results support the idea that verbal language and sign language depend on similar neural structures. The Newman study also compared "native signers," who acquired sign language early in life, with "late signers," who learned sign language later in life. As is illustrated in **Figure 19.3**, both native and late signers show activation in the left-hemisphere frontal and temporal lobes.

You may be familiar with the *cocktail-party effect*. When listening to speech in a noisy environment, we can "hear" what a speaker is saying much better if we can see the speaker's lips. A phenomenon called the *McGurk effect*, after its originator, Harry McGurk (Skipper et al., 2007), offers another demonstration of "seeing" sounds. When viewers observe a speaker say one word or syllable while they hear a recording of a second word or syllable, they "hear" the articulated word or sound that they saw and not the word or sound that they actually heard. Or they hear a similar but different word entirely. For example, if the speaker is mouthing "ga" but the actual sound is "da," the listener hears "ga" or perhaps the related sound "ba." The McGurk phenomenon is robust and compelling.

You may also have read the transcript of a conversation that took place between two or more people. It can seem almost incomprehensible. Had you been present, however, your observation of the speakers' accompanying gestures would have provided clarity. Taken together, studies on vocalization and studies on gestures, including signing, show that communication is more than vocalization and that what makes us humans special is the degree to which we communicate.

Discontinuity Theory

Discontinuity theories emphasize the syntax of human languages and propose that language arose quite suddenly in modern humans (Berwick et al., 2013). One emphasis is recognizing the unique species-specific "computational core" of human language—its sounds, syntax, and semantics.

Another approach of discontinuity theory attempts to trace language origins by comparing similarities in word use. For example, Morris Swadish (1971) developed a list of 100 basic lexical concepts that he expected would be found in every language. These concepts included such words as "I," "two," "woman," "sun," and "green." He then calculated the rate at which these words would have changed as new dialects and languages emerged. His estimates suggest a rate of change of 14% every 1000 years. When he compared the lists of words spoken in different parts of the world today, he estimated that, between 10,000 and 100,000 years ago, everyone spoke the same language.

According to Swadish's logic, language would have had its origins at about the time when everyone spoke the same language, because diversification would have begun almost as soon as language developed. Of course, Swadish's approach may identify the origin of languages used today, but it cannot speak to the possibility that other languages preceded modern language families. Hominid species have been around for millions of years. How can we rule out the possibility that one of them spoke much earlier than 100,000 years ago?

Philip Lieberman (2003) studied the vocal-tract properties that enable modern humans to make the sounds used for language (see Figure 19.1C). Neither

Native signers

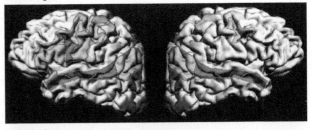

Late signers

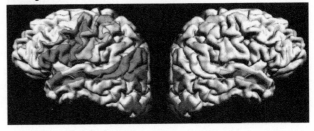

Figure 19.3 ▲

Signing Structures These fMRI images compare responses in native signers (top) and late signers (bottom) to American Sign Language sentences (red) and to meaningless signlike gestures (green). Like spoken or written English, ASL activates extensive regions of the left hemisphere (images at left), as well as activating right-hemisphere superior temporal and inferior parietal regions (images at right). Right-hemisphere activation in native signers includes brain regions not active in later-learning signers. (Reprinted by permission from Macmillan Publishers Ltd: Newman, A. J., D. Bavelier, D. Corina, P. Jezzard, and H. J. Neville. A critical period for right hemisphere recruitment in American Sign Language processing. *Nature Neuroscience* 5(1): 76–80, 2001.)

modern apes nor newborn humans can produce all of the sounds used in human speech. Lieberman concludes that language appeared along with the lowered vocal tract in modern humans, within about the past 200,000 years.

Another argument for recent language development is that the ability to write and the ability to speak have a lot in common. Both require very fine movements and many movement transitions. Therefore, speech and writing could have appeared at about the same time. Alexander Marshack (1971) found that the first symbols attributed to humans date to about 30,000 years ago, adding to the evidence that speech appeared before or at least at about this time.

Peter MacNeilage (1998) argues that the critical feature of language is *articulation*, basically what the mouth does. The mouth is usually opened once for each vocal episode, and the shape of the cavity between the lips and the vocal tract modulates the sound. Articulation is unique to humans and is employed in virtually every utterance of every language (with the exception of a few words consisting of a single vowel).

In human speech, the mouth alternates more or less regularly between a relatively open (for vowels) and a relatively closed (for consonants) configuration. To MacNeilage, the question this observation raises is not how the vocal tract changed but how the brain changed to provide the motor control necessary for the mouth to make syllables. Many of these changes, he reasons, are likely related to the development of fine mouth movements made in eating the foods that comprise modern human diet.

What seems to link these separate lines of evidence, making the discontinuity theory's recency hypothesis plausible, is that modern humans first appeared within the past 200,000 years. The evolution of *Homo sapiens* was quite sudden, their vocal tract was low, they were capable of making deft mouth movements, they created art, and one of their adaptive strategies was vocal language. Nevertheless, mounting evidence indicates that Neanderthals and some of our other hominid cousins were more similar to us than they were different. It would be surprising if they did not have some form of language. Evidence supporting this idea would push the origins of language much further back in time.

Experimental Approaches to Language Origins

Research on language origins considers the many types of communication different animal species employ, including birdsong, the elaborate songs and clicking of dolphins and whales, and the dances of honeybees. Each contains elements of the core skills underlying language. Language-like abilities are present in many different brains, even brains extremely different from our own.

Irene Pepperberg's 30-year study of Alex, an African gray parrot, represents a remarkable contribution to language research. Alex could categorize, label, sequence, and mimic. Pepperberg (2008) could show Alex a tray of four corks and ask, "How many?" Alex would reply, "Four." He correctly applied English labels to numerous colors, shapes, and materials and to various items made of metal, wood, plastic, or paper. He used words to identify, request, and refuse items and to respond to questions about abstract ideas, such as the color, shape, material, relative size, and quantity of more than 100 different objects. Birds do not possess a neocortex, but parrots'

▼ The African gray parrot Alex, shown here with Irene Pepperberg and a sampling of the items he could count, describe, and answer questions about. Alex died in 2007, aged 31. (Wm. Munoz.)

forebrains have cortexlike connection and house an enormous number of neurons, comparable to much larger primate brains. This anatomy likely accounts for Alex's ability to learn forms of "thought," "speech," and "language."

Evidence for Language in Nonhuman Apes

A definitive test of the continuity and discontinuity theories is whether our closest relatives, chimps, as well as other apes, can use language. Chimpanzees share with humans some behaviors and anatomy related to language, including handedness and left-right asymmetry in language areas of the brain (Hopkins, 2013). In the 1940s, Keith and Catherine Hayes (1950) raised Vicki, a chimpanzee, as a human child. They made a heroic effort to get her to produce words, but she produced only four sounds, including a poor rendition of "cup," after 6 years of training.

Beatrice and Allen Gardner (1978) used a version of American Sign Language to train Washoe, a year-old chimp they brought into their home. They aimed to teach Washoe ASL hand signs for various objects or actions (called *exemplars*). These signing gestures, analogous to words in spoken language, consist of specific movements that begin and end in a prescribed manner in relation to the signer's body (**Figure 19.4**).

Washoe was raised in an environment filled with signs. The Gardners molded her hands to form the desired shapes in the presence of exemplars, reinforcing her for correct movements, and they used ASL to communicate with each other in Washoe's presence. She did learn to understand and to use not only nouns but also pronouns and verbs. For example, she could sign statements such as "You go me," meaning "Come with me." Attempts to teach ASL to other species of great apes (gorilla, orangutan) have had similar success.

David Premack (1983) formalized the study of chimpanzee language abilities by teaching his chimpanzee, Sarah, to read and write with variously shaped and colored pieces of plastic, each representing a word. Premack first taught Sarah that different symbols represent different nouns, just as Washoe had been taught in sign language. Sarah learned, for example, that a pink square was the symbol for banana. She was then taught verbs so that she could write and read such combinations as "give apple" or "wash apple."

Premack tested Sarah's comprehension by "writing" messages to her—that is, by hanging up a series of symbols—then observing her response. Much more complicated tutoring followed, in which Sarah mastered the interrogative ("Where is my banana?"), the negative, and finally the conditional (if . . . then). Sarah learned a fairly complicated communication system, analogous in some ways to simple human language.

Duane Rumbaugh launched Project Lana, which called for teaching the chimp Lana to communicate by means of a computer-programmed keyboard (Rumbaugh and Gill, 1977). Computer-based training facilitates collecting the large volume of data the language-training procedures generated. The keyboard was composed of nine stimulus elements and nine main colors that could be combined in nearly 1800 lexigrams

Figure 19.4 ▼

Exemplars from American Sign Language
The Gardners and others taught such symbols to the chimpanzees in their studies. (Information from Gustason et al., 1975.)

Cat: Draw out two whiskers with thumb and index finger

Caterpillar: Pull hand along arm

Fruit: Fingertip and thumbtip on cheek; twist

Orange: Squeeze fist in front of chin

Me: Index finger points to and touches chest

Fond: Cross arms over heart

(A) Design elements

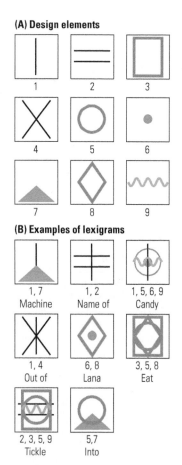

(B) Examples of lexigrams

Figure 19.5 ▲

Lana's Keyboard Yerkish consists of nine basic design elements (A) that are combined to form lexigrams (B). (von Glaserfeld, E. The Yerkish language and its automatic parser. D. M. Rumbaugh, Ed. *Language Learning by a Chimpanzee.* New York: Academic Press, 1977. © Elsevier.)

to form a language now known as Yerkish, shown in **Figure 19.5** (Savage-Rumbaugh et al., 1986).

Lana had simply to type out her messages on the keyboard. She was trained first to press keys for various single incentives. The requirements became increasingly complex, and she was taught to compose statements in the indicative ("Tim move into room"), the interrogative ("Tim move into room?"), the imperative ("Please Tim move into room"), and the negative ("Don't Tim move into room"). Eventually, Lana was composing strings of six lexigrams.

Kanzi spontaneously learned to communicate with Yerkish by watching his mother Matatla's failed training session. Kanzi's knowledge of English words has exceeded his knowledge of Yerkish lexigrams. To facilitate his learning, his keyboard was augmented with a speech synthesizer. When he was 6 years old, Kanzi was tested on his comprehension of multisymbol utterances. He responded correctly to 298 of 310 spoken sentences of two or more utterances. Joel Wallman (1992) concluded that Kanzi's use of lexigrams constitutes the best evidence available to date for the referential application of learned symbols by an ape.

Conclusions from Investigations of Language Origins

In considering the rudimentary abilities of other animal species to acquire some aspects of language, two explanations address its neural basis. The first holds that when the brain reaches a certain level of complexity, it has the ability to perform some core language skills, even in the absence of a massive neocortex with dedicated neural structures. This view is applicable to modern humans' ability to read and write. We acquired these behaviors so recently that it is unlikely the brain specifically evolved to engage in them.

Another view is that all brains have communicative functions, but the ways that communication takes place varies from species to species. Apes, as social animals, clearly have a rudimentary capacity to use sign language. They use gestures spontaneously (Hobaiter et al., 2014), and formal training can foster this skill. Nevertheless, apes also have a much greater predisposition to understand language than to produce it, which derives from observing and responding to the many social behaviors of their compatriots. Anyone watching films of apes' performance in response to human vocal commands cannot help but be impressed by their level of understanding. Taken together, this body of research supports the view of continuity theorists that the basic capacity for languagelike processes was present to be selected for in the common ancestor of humans and apes.

19.3 Localization of Language

Current ideas about where in the brain language processes are located come from several basic lines of inquiry: anatomical studies, studies of brain lesions in human patients, studies of brain stimulation in awake human patients, and brain-imaging studies. As each line of research is exploited, new language-related brain regions are added to its neural circuitry. In a reanalysis of the preserved brains of Broca's first two patients (detailed in Section 1.3), Nina Dronkers and colleagues (2007) found that brain regions lying outside Broca's area, if not responsible for, contributed to, their aphasia. Brain imaging studies, aphasia analyses, and neural modeling concur in showing that a large network in the temporal, parietal, and frontal lobes, including both hemispheres, contributes to language.

Anatomical Areas Associated with Language

The anatomical landmarks researchers use to describe brain regions associated with language vary considerably and undergo constant revision. Some refer to sulci, others to Brodmann's areas, and still others to areas associated with syndromes, such as Broca's area and Wernicke's area. **Figure 19.6** illustrates various approaches to labeling the cortical regions most frequently described as core to language:

- Figure 19.6A includes the inferior frontal gyrus and the superior temporal gyrus, in which Broca's area (green) and Wernicke's area (yellow), respectively, are located. Parts of surrounding gyri, including the ventral parts of the precentral and postcentral gyri, the supramarginal gyrus, the angular gyrus, and the medial temporal gyrus, also lie within the core language regions.

- Figure 19.6B depicts the language areas in accord with Brodmann's mapping. Broca's area includes areas 45 and 44, and Wernicke's area includes area 22. Language regions also include parts of areas 4, 6, 9, 3-1-2, 40, 39, and 21.

- In Figure 19.6C the lateral fissure is retracted, showing the language-related areas found within it, including the insula, a large region of the neocortex lying within the dorsal bank of the lateral fissure; Heschl's gyrus (primary auditory cortex); and parts of the superior temporal gyrus referred to as the anterior and posterior superior temporal planes (aSTP and pSTP). Together, Heschl's gyrus, aSTP, and pSTP constitute the **planum temporale**.

(A) Fissures and gyri

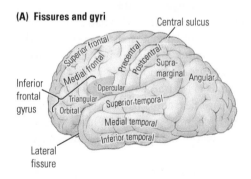

(B) Brodmann's areas

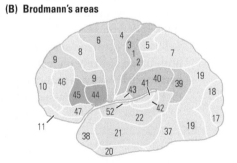

(C) Insula and medial superior temporal gyrus

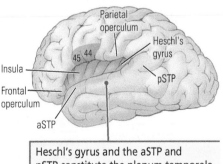

Heschl's gyrus and the aSTP and pSTP constitute the planum temporale.

Figure 19.6 ▲

The Brain's Core Language Regions
Areas associated with language functions are shown (A) in relation to fissures and gyri, (B) in relation to Brodmann's areas, and (C) with the lateral fissure retracted to expose the insula and the medial bank of the superior temporal gyrus.

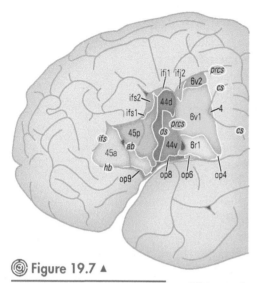

Figure 19.7 ▲

Subdivision of Broca's Area Anatomical map of Broca's area that includes areas 44 and 45 with subdivisions, three subdivisions added to area 6, and a plethora of smaller regions. (Research from Amunts K, Lenzen M, Friederici AD, Schleicher A, Morosan P, Palomero-Gallagher N, Ziles K. Broca's region: novel organizational principles and multiple receptor mapping. *PLoS Biology* 2010 Sep 21; 8[9] e1000489. Figure 9.)

This survey by no means details all language regions in the brain. **Figure 19.7** diagrams an updated anatomical reconceptualization of Broca's area (areas 44 and 45) and some brain regions surrounding Broca's area now suggested to be involved in language. The findings were derived from analyzing various receptor types in these areas' neurons (Amunts et al., 2010):

- Brodmann's areas 44 and 45 each consist of two subdivisions, an anterior and posterior region in area 45 and a dorsal and ventral region in area 44.

- Ventral premotor area 6, related to facial movements and containing mirror neurons, has three subdivisions.

- Surrounding and wedged between these regions and subdivisions in Figure 19.7 are numerous smaller areas. At present, no imaging or behavioral work assigns functions to these small areas.

This modern reconceptualization of the anatomy within and surrounding Broca's area points to a conclusion: many challenges remain before we fully understand the anatomical basis of language.

Still other regions taking part in language include dorsal premotor area 6 (the supplementary motor area), responsible for the rhythmic mouth movements that articulate sounds; parts of the thalamus, dorsolateral parts of the caudate nucleus, and the cerebellum; visual areas (required for reading), sensory pathways, and motor pathways; and pathways connecting all of these various regions. In addition, many right-hemisphere regions participate in language.

Neural Connections Between Language Zones

Broca and Wernicke identified speech areas in patients who had lesions from stroke. Wernicke's early neurological model of language and its revival in the 1960s by Norman Geschwind, as the **Wernicke–Geschwind model**, were both based entirely on lesion data. As diagrammed in **Figure 19.8**, the three-part model proposes that comprehension is (1) extracted from sounds in Wernicke's area and (2) passed over the arcuate fasciculus pathway to (3) Broca's area to be articulated as speech. Other language functions access this comprehension–speech pathway as well.

The Wernicke–Geschwind model has played a formative role in directing language research and organizing research results. A contemporary language model, based on recent anatomical and behavioral studies, is illustrated in **Figure 19.9**. As proposed by Evelina Fedorenko and Sharon Thompson-Schill (2014), the temporal and frontal cortices are connected by pairs of dorsal and ventral

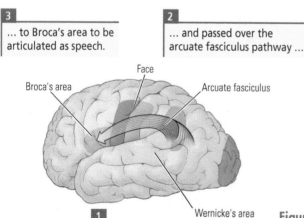

3 ... to Broca's area to be articulated as speech.

2 ... and passed over the arcuate fasciculus pathway ...

1 Comprehension is extracted from sounds in Wernicke's area ...

Figure 19.8 ◄

Wernicke–Geschwind Model The classical anterior and posterior speech zones, connected by the arcuate fasciculus.

language pathways, which are viewed as extensions of the dorsal and ventral visual streams.

The double-headed arrows on both paired pathways in Figure 19.9 indicate that information flows both ways between the temporal and frontal cortex. Information from vision enters into the auditory language pathways via the dorsal and ventral visual streams and contributes to reading. Information from body-sense regions of the parietal cortex also contributes to the dorsal and ventral language pathways and likely contributes to touch language such as Braille. Noteworthy in this new model, the ventral premotor region of area 6 is a target of the dorsal language stream, and Brodmann's area 47, located anterior to area 45, is a target in the ventral language stream.

At the simplest level of analysis, the dorsal language pathways are proposed to transform sound information into motor representation—to convert phonological information into articulation. The ventral language paths are proposed to transform sound information into meaning—to convert phonological information into semantic information (Poeppel et al., 2012). Information flow in the dorsal pathway is bottom-up, as occurs when we are asked to repeat nonsense words or phrases. Thus, the temporal cortex assembles sounds by phonetic structure and passes them along to the frontal cortex for articulation. No meaning is assigned to sounds in this pathway. Information flow in the ventral pathway is proposed to be more top-down, assigning meaning to words and phrases, as occurs when we assign a specific meaning to a word, such as "hammer," that has various meanings.

The dorsal and ventral language pathways are engaged in syntax, with the dorsal pathway categorizing sounds in terms of frequency of association and the ventral pathway extracting meaning from the grammatical organization of words. Both sets of language pathways are also proposed to be involved in short- and long-term memory for the phonetic and semantic components of speech, respectively. Nonverbal speech, including reading and sign language from visual cortex and Braille from parietal cortex, also uses these pathways.

We can speculate that some aphasic patients who can read but not understand the meaning of what they read have damage to the ventral language pathways. Similarly, some patients who cannot articulate words but can understand them might have damage to the dorsal pathways. Patients with damage to both language pathways would not be able to repeat words (mediated by the dorsal pathways) or assign meaning to words (mediated by the ventral pathways).

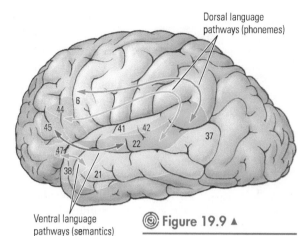

Ⓒ Figure 19.9 ▲

Dual Language Pathways Dorsal language pathways convey phonological information for articulation; ventral pathways, semantic information for meaning. All are involved in syntax and may contribute to short- and long-term memory for language. (Research from Berwick, R. C., A. D. Friederici, N. Chomsky, and J. J. Bolhuis. Evolution, brain, and the nature of language. *Trends in Cognitive Science* 17:89-98, February 2013, Figure 2.)

Speech Zones Mapped by Brain Stimulation and Surgical Lesions

Wilder Penfield and others identified the neocortical language zones, particularly those pertaining to speech, using intracortical stimulation during surgery. Statistical analyses of results from hundreds of patients have contributed to

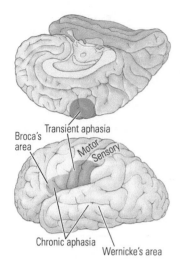

Broca's area   Transient aphasia   Motor   Sensory

Chronic aphasia   Wernicke's area

◎ Figure 19.10 ▲

Speech Interference
Regions where electrical stimulation or surgical lesions have been shown to affect speech. Damage to Broca's and Wernicke's areas produces chronic aphasia; damage to the sensory and motor areas produces transient aphasia; and damage outside these areas does not produce aphasia.

mapping these regions, which include the classical Broca's and Wernicke's areas in the left hemisphere as well as the sensory and motor representations of the face and the supplementary speech area in both hemispheres.

Cortical stimulation produces either positive effects, eliciting vocalization that is not speech but rather a sustained or interrupted vowel cry, such as "Oh," or negative effects, inhibiting the ability to vocalize or to use words properly, including a variety of aphasialike errors diagrammed in **Figure 19.10**:

- *Total speech arrest or an inability to vocalize spontaneously.* This error results from stimulation throughout the shaded zones in Figure 19.10.

- *Hesitation and slurred speech.* Hesitation results from stimulation throughout the zones shaded in Figure 19.10, whereas slurring results primarily from stimulation of the dorsal regions in Broca's area and the ventral facial regions of premotor and motor cortex.

- *Distortion and repetition of words and syllables.* Distortion differs from slurring in that the distorted sound is an unintelligible noise rather than a word. These effects result primarily from stimulating Broca's and Wernicke's areas, although occasionally from stimulating the face area as well.

- *Number confusion while counting.* For example, a patient may jump from "6" to "19" to "4," and so on, resulting from stimulation of Broca's or Wernicke's area.

- *Inability to name objects despite retained ability to speak.* An example is, "That is a . . . I know. That is a. . . ." When the current was removed, the patient was able to name the object correctly. Another example is, "Oh, I know what it is. That is what you put in your shoes." After withdrawal of the stimulating electrodes, the patient immediately said "foot" (Penfield and Roberts, 1959, p. 123). Naming difficulties arise from stimulation throughout the anterior (Broca's) and posterior (Wernicke's) speech zones.

- *Misnaming and perseverating.* Misnaming may occur when the subject uses words related in sound, such as "camel" for "comb," uses synonyms, such as "cutters" for "scissors," or perseverates by repeating the same word. For example, the subject may name a picture of a bird correctly but may also call the next picture—of a table—a bird. Misnaming, like other naming difficulties, occurs during stimulation of both the anterior and the posterior speech zones.

George Ojemann (2003) reported that during stimulation of Broca's area, patients were unable to make voluntary facial movements, and stimulation of these same points may also disrupt phonemic discrimination and gestures, such as hand movements, associated with speech. Most reports agree that the extent of the cortical language zones as marked by electrical stimulation and surgical lesions varies considerably among subjects. It is noteworthy that these classic studies were performed using single nouns, and brain regions involved in speech would likely be larger and perhaps somewhat different were verbs and sentence stimuli also used (Rofes and Miceli, 2014). We can add to this point that brain stimulation would be unlikely to elicit narrative as in storytelling, a behavior that lesion studies suggest is contributed by the right hemisphere.

Speech Zones Mapped by Transcranial Magnetic Stimulation (TMS)

Intracortical microstimulation and lesions have numerous drawbacks as methods for studying the neural basis of language: the procedures are performed during surgery in which a portion of the skull is removed, and the patients often have preexisting brain conditions that may lead to anomalous language organization. In contrast, TMS can be used noninvasively to explore the neural basis of language in healthy people.

TMS can interfere with neural function, producing a virtual lesion lasting from tens of milliseconds to as long as an hour. At appropriate frequencies and intensities, TMS can prime neurons to enhance reaction times for behaviors dependent on the region that is stimulated (Rogic et al., 2014). TMS is relatively easy to use, can be used repeatedly, and when combined with MRI, can allow predetermined brain regions to be examined under controlled experimental conditions. TMS has drawbacks in that the stimulator produces a sound that can cue a participant or subject to the stimulation. In addition, the stimulation must pass through the scalp, skull, and meninges and can cause muscle contractions, discomfort, and pain. Finally, the stimulation does not easily access regions located deep within sulci. Nevertheless, as reviewed by Luigi Cattaneo (2013), mapping language regions with TMS aids in defining cortical contributions of language.

TMS can also be used to evaluate connections between brain regions, such as brain regions used for selecting words and brain regions used for producing sounds. For example, a movement of the lips produced by TMS to the motor cortex might be enhanced if a person thinks of a word such as "hammer," which produces a lip movement when said. Presumably, the part of the brain thinking "hammer," is connected to the part of the brain being stimulated to produce the lip movement.

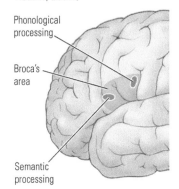

▼ Stimulation of the anterior and posterior extent of Broca's area by TMS inhibits semantic and phonological processing, respectively. (Information from Devlin and Watkins, 2007.)

TMS has been used to map specific brain regions, such as Broca's area (Kim et al., 2014). A number of brain-imaging studies suggest that the anterior region of Broca's area is implicated in semantic processing (processing the meaning of words) and the posterior region of Broca's area is implicated in phonological processing (the production of words). For example, participants were presented word pairs on a computer screen and required to decide whether the words meant the same thing (say, "gift" and "present") or sounded the same (say, "key" and "quay"). Stimulation of the anterior region of Broca's area increased reaction times for the semantic condition but not for the phonological condition, whereas stimulation of the posterior region of Broca's area increased the reaction time for the phonological condition but not for the semantic condition.

Speech Zones Mapped by Brain-Imaging Techniques

Using fMRI to measure brain areas implicated in language, Jeffery Binder and his colleagues (1997) reported that sound-processing areas make up a remarkably large part of the brain. These researchers presented either tones or meaningful words to 30 right-handed participants. Half were male and half were female. Tone stimuli consisted of a number of 500- and 750-Hz pure tones presented in sequence. The participants pressed a button if they heard two 750-Hz tones in a sequence. Word stimuli were spoken English nouns designating animals (for example, "turtle"). Participants pushed a button if an animal was both native to the United States and used by humans. A rest condition consisted of no stimulus presentations.

By subtracting the activation produced by tones from the activation seen during the rest condition, the researchers identified brain regions responsive to tones. By subtracting the activation produced by words from the activation produced by tones, they identified brain regions responsive to words. Binder and coworkers found that words activate widespread brain regions, including areas in the occipital, parietal, temporal, and frontal lobes; the thalamus; and the cerebellum (**Figure 19.11**).

Figure 19.11 ▶

Aural Activation Left-hemisphere brain regions, shaded red, and the cerebellum (not shown), were activated while participants listened to speech, as measured by fMRI. Participants listened to spoken English nouns designating animals and were required to decide, in each case, whether the word indicated an animal native to the United States and used by humans. (Research from Binder et al., 1997.)

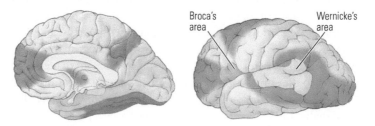

Using PET and a wider range of stimuli, a number of research groups have identified more-specific functions for some of these language areas, summarized in **Figure 19.12**. Steven Petersen's group (1988) used a variety of conditions to identify speech regions. In a word-generation task, they passively presented words (in some cases, pseudo-words or pseudo-sounds) either visually or aurally

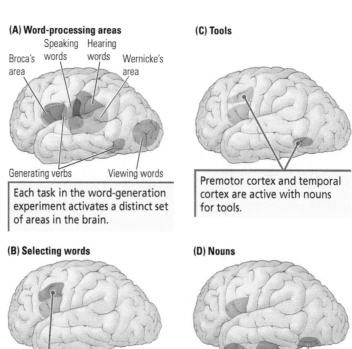

(A) Word-processing areas

Speaking Hearing
words words
Broca's   Wernicke's
area   area

Generating verbs   Viewing words

Each task in the word-generation experiment activates a distinct set of areas in the brain.

(C) Tools

Premotor cortex and temporal cortex are active with nouns for tools.

(B) Selecting words

Premotor cortex is active in a task requiring matching a noun to one of four target words.

(D) Nouns

Persons   Animals   Tools

Locations in area TE are active for nouns of different kinds.

⊚ Figure 19.12 ▶

Brain Areas Activated by Language Tasks Results obtained with the use of PET to monitor blood flow were analyzed by using subtraction methods. (Part A: research from Posner and Raichle, 1994; part B: research from Wagner et al., 2001; part C: research from Martin et al., 1996; part D: research from Damasio et al., 1996.)

to a passive participant. In the next, an output task, the participant was to repeat the word. Finally, in an association task, the participant was to suggest a use for the object named by the target word (for example, if "cake" were presented, the participant might say "eat").

The investigators monitored blood flow using PET and analyzed their data using a subtraction technique. In the sensory (reading or listening) tasks, they identified changes from baseline blood flow by taking the difference between the activities in the two states. In the output task, they subtracted the sensory activity, and in the association task, they subtracted the output activity. (Figure 7.15 explains the subtraction technique.)

The results, summarized in Figure 19.12A, illustrate the involvement of many brain regions in language and reveal some specific contributions of each region:

- No overlap occurred in visual and auditory activation during the passive task, implying that processing word forms in the two modalities is completely independent.

- During the speaking tasks, bilateral activation occurred in the motor and sensory facial areas and the supplementary speech area as well as activation of the right cerebellum.

- Generating verbs activated the frontal lobe, especially the left inferior region, including Broca's area. The verb-generation task also activated the posterior temporal cortex, anterior cingulate cortex, and cerebellum.

Other investigators have identified still other activated areas, depending on task demands. Anthony Wagner and colleagues (2001) presented participants with a single cue word and four target words. The task was to indicate which target word was most closely and globally related to the cue, thus measuring the participant's ability to retrieve meaningful information. An area in the left premotor cortex just dorsal to Broca's area became active during this task (Figure 19.12B).

Alex Martin and his colleagues (1996) asked participants to name tools or animals and subtracted activation produced by the brain response to animals from the response to tools. Naming tools activates a region of premotor cortex also activated by imagined hand movements (Figure 19.12C). Finally, Antonio Damasio and colleagues (1996) reported that naming persons, animals, and tools activates specific locations in area TE, the inferotemporal lobe (Figure 19.12D).

In summary, the results of imaging studies confirm that the classical anterior and posterior speech zones of Broca's and Wernicke's areas are involved in language, and they also implicate other regions. Imaging further suggests that Wernicke's area may deal largely with analyzing auditory input and that Broca's area does not simply represent speech movements but also is involved in syntax and memory. Finally, the results provide evidence that "language" is mapped onto circuits ordinarily also engaged in more-primary functions: visual attributes of words are represented in visual areas, auditory attributes are mapped onto auditory brain regions, motor attributes are mapped onto motor regions, and so on.

◎ Neural Networks for Language

Hundreds of anatomical, brain lesion, and brain imaging studies have demonstrated that language-related functions can be localized to specific brain regions connected by neural pathways. What is less clear is whether these language-related regions are specialized for language or serve other functions as well. In the 1800s, scientists who mapped language using locations and connecting pathways were criticized as "diagram makers." This criticism deterred no one. Nevertheless, even if a region has a primary role in language, it is still appropriate to ask what localization means. The word "hammer," for example, can signify the object or the action and can be a command or a question. Are all these meanings of "hammer" localized in the same brain region, or are they located at different places in the brain? How are the word and its many meanings represented?

Many current language models are based on the idea that language is widely distributed in cortical and other brain structures. Even single words are widely distributed, which is one way they acquire their many meanings. We describe two language-network models that illustrate its distribution in the cortex. Be aware, however, that whereas computer networks are precise, proposed language networks are speculative. First, it is difficult to establish whether single neurons or groups of neurons are the proper network elements, and second, information usually flows one way in computer networks, but brain–network flow is two-way.

Core Language Network

Fedorenko and Thompson-Schill (2014), who outlined the dual language pathways shown in Figure 19.9, propose that, of a number of brain networks, one is a *core language network*. Their version, illustrated in **Figure 19.13**A, consists of five functional modules, each involved in a particular function, such as hearing

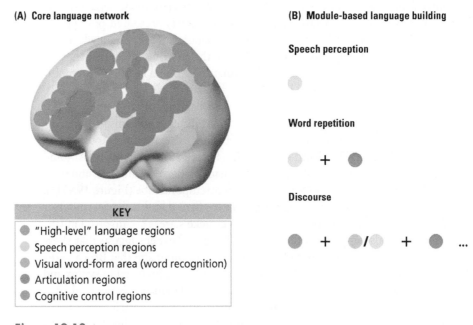

(A) Core language network

(B) Module-based language building

Speech perception

Word repetition

Discourse

KEY
- "High-level" language regions
- Speech perception regions
- Visual word-form area (word recognition)
- Articulation regions
- Cognitive control regions

Figure 19.13 ▲

Neural Language Network (A) The core network consists of five sets of modules (colored regions). (B) Activation of one module is required for speech perception (top), coactivation of two modules is required for word repetition (center), and coactivation of many modules is required for discourse (bottom). (Part A: Fedorenko, E., and Thompson-Schill, S. L. Reworking the language network. *Trends in Cognitive Sciences* Vol. 18(3):120–126, 2014, Figure 2.; part B: research from E. Fedorenko, and S. L. Thompson-Schill, Reworking the language network, *Trends in Cognitive Science*, 18:120–126, 2014, Figure 2.)

(yellow), converting sound to meaning (red) or articulating language (purple). Each module consists of multiple nodes (the circles) that likely serve a common function; that is, a single node could be active in producing phonemes, representing animal words, representing word actions, and so on.

Fedorenko and Thompson-Schill propose that high-level language activity, such as discourse, would involve many functional modules (Figure 19.13B), whereas activity in only a few modules, or even a single module, would generate a language subfunction, such as recognizing that a sound is a word. By interacting with other brain networks, for example an attentional network, language can be focused, as might occur when two people hear only each other at a noisy party.

The advantage of the core language network idea is that it allows one to see at a glance the distribution of language across the left hemisphere and to see that different parts of the network serve different functions. By imagining that a module can act alone or in cooperation with other modules, we can imagine various degrees of language complexity, from distinguishing phonemes to engaging in discourse. We can also make predictions, for example about what happens following damage to one or another module or different combinations of modules.

Nodes and Neural Webs for Language

As noted earlier in this section, the word "hammer" has many meanings. Is the word localized in the brain with its different meanings coded in neighboring neurons, or is it distributed throughout the cortex so that the written word "hammer" appears in a visual pathway and the action word "hammer" is located in the motor cortex, and so forth?

Riitta Salmelin and Jan Kujala (2006) suggest that meaning comes through the connections (*edges* in network jargon; see Section 17.3) between nodes proposed to comprise neural webs. Here again, nodes can be single cells or collections of cells, and a web consists of nodes and their two-way connections. The nodes and their connections can be local or widely distributed across the cortex. The idea is that by combining information from many parts of the brain, individual words can take on many different meanings and can represent language in its many forms—spoken or written, for example.

Figure 19.14 illustrates some representative neural webs for individual words. If a word contains visual content, the web includes visual brain areas; if it contains motor content, the web includes motor areas. Any given web will include nodes within primary and secondary auditory areas as well as within primary and secondary motor regions. The objective of creating neural webs to represent language-related brain regions is not to eventually produce a wiring diagram but rather to illustrate one way that the brain might produce language. We can see from these examples that language, even at the level of single words, is widely distributed across the cortex.

Figure 19.14 ▼

Neural Webs for Language Tasks Nodes are symbolized by circles, and edges (interconnecting axonal pathways) are represented by lines. In this model, different word-related tasks use different neural webs. (Information from Salmelin, R., and J. Kujala. Neural representation of language: Activation versus long-range connectivity. *Trends in Cognitive Sciences* 10:519–525, 2006.)

(A) Word sounds

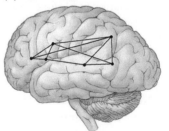

(C) Tool-related word

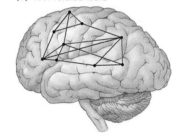

(B) Face-related word

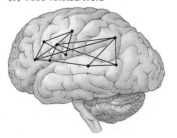

(D) Animal-related word

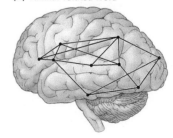

19.4 Language Disorders

In describing how neuropsychologists classify symptoms of language impairment we must first recognize that symptom classification was originally linked to brain regions (Broca's aphasia and Broca's area, for example). Improved anatomical analysis suggests that such precise correlations do not exist. Standard language function depends on the complex interaction of sensory integration and symbolic association, motor skills, learned syntactical patterns, and verbal memory. *Aphasia* may refer to a language disorder apparent in speech, in writing (also called **agraphia**), or in reading (also called **alexia**) produced by injury to brain areas specialized for these functions. Thus, disturbances of language due to severe intellectual impairment, to loss of sensory input (especially vision and hearing), or to paralysis or incoordination of the musculature of the mouth (called **anarthria**) or hand (for writing) are not considered aphasic disturbances. These disorders may accompany aphasia, however, and they complicate its study.

Howard Goodglass and Edith Kaplan (1972) divide language disturbances into 10 basic types that we group into disorders of comprehension and disorders of production in **Table 19.2**. Most were described in Part III chapter discussions of parietal-, temporal-, and frontal-lobe functions. The one exception is **paraphasia**, the production of unintended syllables, words, or phrases during speech. Paraphasia differs from difficulties in articulation in that sounds are correctly articulated, but they are the wrong sounds: people with paraphasia either distort the intended word (for example, "pike" instead of "pipe") or produce a completely unintended word (for example, "my mother" instead of "my wife").

Despite disagreement among experts concerning the number of types of aphasias, certain classification systems are widely used (for example, see Mazzocchi and Vignolo, 1979). The system we present in **Table 19.3**, based on correlations of lesion locations among stroke patients, groups aphasias into three broadly defined categories:

1. **Fluent aphasias:** fluent speech but difficulties either in auditory verbal comprehension or in the repetition of words, phrases, or sentences spoken by others.

2. **Nonfluent aphasias:** difficulties in articulating but relatively good auditory verbal comprehension.

3. **Pure aphasias:** selective impairments in reading, writing, or recognizing words in the absence of other language disorders.

Within each category, Table 19.3 lists subtypes, including Wernicke's aphasia, transcortical aphasia, conduction aphasia, anomic aphasia, and Broca's aphasia.

Fluent Aphasias

Fluent aphasias are impairments related mostly to language input or reception. The impression of a listener who did not speak the language of a fluent aphasic would be that the subject was speaking easily and correctly.

Table 19.2 Summary of symptoms of language disorders

Disorders of Comprehension
Poor auditory comprehension
Poor visual comprehension

Disorders of Production
Poor articulation
Word-finding deficit (anomia)
Unintended words or phrases (paraphasia)
Loss of grammar and syntax
Inability to repeat aurally presented material
Low verbal fluency
Inability to write (agraphia)
Loss of tone in voice (aprosidia)

Information from Goodglass and Kaplan, 1972.

Table 19.3 **Classification of aphasic syndromes**

Syndrome	Type of Speech Production	Type of Language Errors
Fluent Aphasias		
Wernicke (sensory)	Fluent speech without articulatory disorders	Neologism or anomias, or paraphasias, poor comprehension; poor repetition
Transcortical (isolation syndrome)	Fluent speech without articulatory disorders; good repetition	Verbal paraphasias and anomias; poor comprehension
Conduction	Fluent, sometimes halting speech, but without articulatory disorders	Phonemic paraphasias and neologisms; phonemic grouping; poor repetition; fairly good comprehension
Anomic	Fluent speech without articulatory disorders	Anomia and occasional paraphasias
Nonfluent Aphasias		
Broca (expressive), severe	Laborious articulation	Speechlessness with recurring utterances or syndrome of phonetic disintegration; poor repetition
Broca (expressive), mild	Slight but obvious articulatory disorders	Phonemic paraphasias with anomia; agrammatism; dysprosody
Transcortical motor	Marked tendency to reduction and inertia; without articulatory disorders; good repetition	Uncompleted sentences and anomias; naming better than spontaneous speech
Global	Laborious articulation	Speechlessness with recurring utterances; poor comprehension; poor repetition
"Pure" Aphasias		
Alexia without agraphia	Normal	Poor reading
Agraphia	Normal	Poor writing
Word deafness	Normal	Poor comprehension; poor repetition

Reprinted from *Cortex*, Vol. 15, Mazzocchi, R., and L. A. Vignolo., Localization of lesions in aphasia: Clinical–CT scan correlations in stroke patients, pages 627–654, © 1979, with permission from Elsevier.

Wernicke's aphasia, or **sensory aphasia**, is the inability to comprehend words or to arrange sounds into coherent speech even though word production remains intact. Alexander Luria proposed that sensory aphasia has three characteristic deficits—in classifying sounds, producing speech, and writing (Luria and Hutton, 1977).

The first, hearing and making sense of speech sounds, demands the ability to qualify sounds—that is, to recognize the different sounds in the system of phonemes that are the basic speech units in a given language. For example, in the Japanese language, the sounds "l" and "r" are not distinguished; a Japanese-speaking person hearing English cannot distinguish these sounds because the necessary template was never laid down in the brain. Thus, although this distinction is perfectly clear to English-speaking persons, it is not clear to native Japanese. This problem is precisely what a person with Wernicke's aphasia has in his or her own language: the inability to isolate the significant phonemic characteristics and to classify sounds into known phonemic systems. Thus, we see in Wernicke's aphasia a deficit in sound categorization.

The second characteristic of Wernicke's aphasia is a speech defect. The affected person can speak, and may speak a great deal, but he or she confuses phonetic characteristics, producing what is often called **word salad**, intelligible words that appear to be strung together randomly. The third characteristic is a writing impairment. A person who cannot discern phonemic characteristics cannot be expected to write because he or she does not know the graphemes (pictorial or written representations of a phoneme) that combine to form a word.

Transcortical aphasia, sometimes called *isolation syndrome*, is curious in that people can repeat and understand words and name objects but cannot speak spontaneously, or they cannot comprehend words although they can repeat them. Comprehension could be poor because words fail to arouse associations. Production of meaningful speech could be poor because, even though word production is at normal, words are not associated with other cognitive activities in the brain.

Conduction aphasia is paradoxical: people with this disorder can speak easily, name objects, and understand speech, but they cannot repeat words. The simplest explanation for this problem is a disconnection between the "perceptual word image" and the motor systems producing the words.

People with *anomic aphasia* (sometimes called **amnesic aphasia**) comprehend speech, produce meaningful speech, and can repeat speech, but they have great difficulty finding the names of objects. For example, we saw a patient who, when shown a picture of a ship anchor, simply could not think of the name and finally said, "I know what it does. . . . You use it to anchor a ship." Although he had actually used the word as a verb, he was unable to access it as a noun. Difficulties in finding nouns appear to result from damage throughout the temporal cortex (see Figure 19.12D). In contrast, verb-finding deficits are more likely to come from left frontal injuries (see Figure 19.12A).

Although the extent to which the brain differentiates between nouns and verbs may seem surprising, we can see that they have very different functions. Nouns are categorizers. Verbs are action words that form the core of syntactical structure. It makes sense, therefore, to find that they are separated in such a way that nouns are a property of brain areas controlling recognition and classification, and verbs are a property of brain areas controlling movement.

Nonfluent Aphasias

In nonfluent aphasia (Broca's aphasia, or **expressive aphasia**), a person continues to understand speech but has to labor to produce it: the person speaks in short phrases interspersed with pauses, makes sound errors, makes repetitious errors in grammar, and frequently omits function words. Only the key words necessary for communication are used. Nevertheless, the deficit is not one of making sounds but rather of switching from one sound to another.

Nonfluent aphasia can be mild or severe. In one form, *transcortical motor aphasia*, repetition is good, but spontaneous production of speech is labored. In *global aphasias*, speech is labored and comprehension is poor.

Pure Aphasias

The pure aphasias include *alexia*, an inability to read; *agraphia*, an inability to write; and word deafness, in which a person cannot hear or repeat words. These disorders may be quite selective. For example, a person is able to read but not write or is able to write but not read.

◎ 19.5 Localization of Lesions in Aphasia

Beginning students of language are intrigued by the simplicity of the Wernicke–Geschwind model, where Wernicke's area is associated with speech comprehension, Broca's area is associated with speech production, and the fibers connecting them translate meaning into sound (see Figure 19.7). As earlier sections explain, however, the neural organization of language is more complex and requires consideration of the brain's many pathways and anatomical regions related to language.

Four variables to keep in mind summarize why studying the neural basis of language is itself so complex:

1. **Most of the brain takes part in language in one way or another.** It makes sense that a behavior as comprehensive and complex as language would not be the product of some small, circumscribed region of the brain.

2. **Most of the patients who contribute information to studies of language have had strokes, usually of the middle cerebral artery (MCA). Figure 19.15**A illustrates the location of this artery and its tributaries. Because stroke results from arterial blockage or bleeding, all core language areas may be damaged or only smaller regions may be damaged, depending on where stroke occurs. Individual differences in the tributary pattern of the MCA add to the variation seen in stroke symptoms and outcomes. The artery supplies subcortical areas as well, including the basal ganglia, a region that includes the caudate nucleus and is important in language (Figure 19.15B).

3. **Immediately following stroke, symptoms are generally severe but improve considerably as time passes.** Thus, the symptoms cannot be easily ascribed to damage in a particular brain region.

4. **Aphasia syndromes described as nonfluent (Broca's) or fluent (Wernicke's) consist of numerous varied symptoms, each of which may have a different neural basis.**

Cortical Language Components

In studying a series of stroke patients with language disorders, Nina Dronkers and her coworkers (1999) correlate different symptoms of nonfluent and fluent aphasia with specific cortical regions. Their analysis suggests that nonfluent aphasia consists of at least five kinds of symptoms: apraxia of speech (difficulty in producing sequences of speech sounds), impairment in sentence comprehension, recurring utterances, impairment in articulation of sounds, and impairment in working memory for sentences.

Their analysis suggests that the core deficit, apraxia of speech, comes from damage to the insula. Impairments in sentence comprehension seem to be associated with damage to the dorsal bank of the superior temporal gyrus and the middle temporal gyrus; recurring utterances seem to stem from damage to the arcuate fasciculus; and impairments in working memory and articulation seem to be associated with damage to ventral frontal cortex.

Concerning fluent aphasia, Dronkers and her colleagues propose that most of the core difficulties, especially the lack of speech comprehension, come from damage to the medial temporal lobe and underlying white matter. Damage in this area not only destroys local language regions but also cuts off most of the occipital, temporal, and parietal regions from the core language region. The researchers also propose that damage to the temporal cortex contributes to

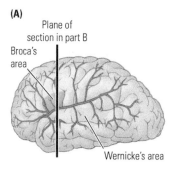

(A)

Plane of section in part B

Broca's area

Wernicke's area

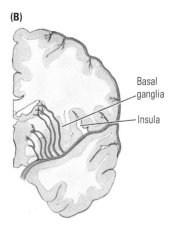

(B)

Basal ganglia

Insula

Figure 19.15 ▲

Middle Cerebral Artery
The amount of damage to the cortex by blockage or bleeding of the middle cerebral artery (red) can vary widely in the neocortex (A) and the basal ganglia (B), depending on the location of the blockage or bleeding.

deficits in holding sentences in memory until they can be repeated. Thus, these patients appear to have impairment in the "iconic" memory for sounds but are not impaired in comprehension.

Subcortical Language Components

At the same time that Broca was describing a cortical center for speech control, Hughlings-Jackson proposed that subcortical structures are critical to language. In 1866 he wrote: "I think it will be found that the nearer the disease is to the basal ganglia, the more likely is the defect of articulation to be the striking thing, and the farther off, the more likely it is to be one of mistakes of words." Yet when Alison Rowan and her colleagues (2007) used MRI and behavioral tests specifically to examine the language abilities of young patients who had had a basal ganglia stroke, they concluded that the language deficits most likely derive from subtle damage to the neocortex.

Other evidence indicates that the thalamus participates in language. Findings by George Ojemann (2003), in which the thalamus was electrically stimulated, indicate that the pulvinar nucleus and the lateral-posterior–lateral-central complex of the left thalamus have a role in language that is not common to other subcortical structures. Stimulation of the left ventrolateral and pulvinar thalamic nuclei produced speech arrest, difficulties in naming, perseveration, and reduced talking speed. Stimulation of the thalamus has also been reported to have a positive effect on memory because it improves later retrieval of words heard during the stimulation. As a result, some researchers propose that the thalamus influences language function by activating or arousing the cortex.

When the thalamus is damaged by electrical current applied for the treatment of abnormal movements, a variety of speech and language disturbances have been found in association with lesions of the left ventrolateral thalamus or the pulvinar nucleus or both. Symptoms include postoperative dysphasia, which is usually transitory; increased verbal-response latency; decreases in voice volume; alterations in speaking rate and slurring or hesitation in speech; and impaired performance on tests of verbal IQ and memory.

Right-Hemisphere Contributions to Language

Although it is well established that the left hemisphere of right-handed people is dominant in language, the right hemisphere also has language abilities. The best evidence comes from studies of split-brain patients in whom the linguistic abilities of the right hemisphere have been studied systematically with the use of various techniques for lateralizing input to one hemisphere (such as shown in Figure 11.8).

The results of these studies show that the right hemisphere has little or no speech but surprisingly good auditory comprehension of language, including both nouns and verbs. There is some reading ability but little writing ability in the right hemisphere. In addition, although the right hemisphere can recognize words (semantic processing), it has little understanding of grammatical rules and sentence structures (syntactical processing).

Complementary evidence of the right hemisphere's role in language comes from studies of people who have had left *hemispherectomies*. If the left hemisphere is lost early in development, the right hemisphere can acquire considerable language abilities (detailed in Ch10's opening Portrait), although people with left hemispherectomies are by no means typical. Left hemispherectomy in adulthood produces severe deficits in speech but leaves surprisingly good auditory comprehension. Reading ability is limited, and writing is usually absent. In general, left hemispherectomy appears to result in language abilities reminiscent of those achieved by the right hemisphere of commissurotomy patients.

The effects of right-hemisphere lesions on language functions provide further indication that the right hemisphere is capable of language comprehension, especially of auditory material, even though it usually does not control speech. For example, aphasia is rare after right-hemisphere lesions, even after right hemispherectomy (some left-handers excepted), but more-subtle linguistic impairments bubble up, including changes in vocabulary selection, in responses to complex statements with unusual syntactical construction, and in comprehending metaphors. In addition, right orbitofrontal lesions reduce verbal fluency and lead to deficits in prosody—both for comprehending tone of voice and for producing emotional vocal tone.

The contrasts in right- and left-hemisphere functioning in language have been summarized as follows. The wife of a patient with Broca's aphasia comments that her husband understands everything said, even though he cannot match spoken words with their pictured representations and cannot follow two-step commands. The wife of a patient with an equivalent right-hemisphere lesion comments that her husband has difficulty following a conversation, makes irrelevant remarks, and generally seems to miss the point of what people are saying, even though he performs quite well on the same tests failed by the patient with a left-hemisphere lesion.

Thus, the right hemisphere has considerable language comprehension, whereas the left-hemisphere's major contribution to language is syntax (**Table 19.4**). Syntax has many components, including producing, timing, and sequencing movements required for speaking as well as understanding the rules of grammar.

Table 19.4 **Language activities of the two hemispheres**

Function	Left Hemisphere	Right Hemisphere
Gestural Language	+	+
Prosodic Language		
Rhythm	+ +	
Inflection	+	+
Timbre	+	+ +
Melody		+ +
Semantic Language		
Word recognition	+	+
Verbal meaning	+ +	+
Concepts	+	+
Visual meaning	+	+ +
Syntactical Language		
Sequencing	+ +	
Relations	+ +	
Grammar	+ +	

Reprinted from *Cortex*, Vol. 22, Benson, D. F., Aphasia and lateralization of language, pages 71–86, © 1986, with permission from Elsevier.

◎ 19.6 Neuropsychological Assessment of Aphasia

Widespread interest in establishing a standardized, systematic procedure for assessing aphasia, both to provide clinical descriptions of patients and to facilitate comparison of patient populations in neuropsychological research, goes back nearly 80 years. Among the numerous tools for assessing aphasia (Lezak et al., 2012), we summarize a few in **Table 19.5**, with basic references.

The first group, aphasia test batteries, contains varied subtests that systematically explore the subject's language capabilities. They typically include tests of (1) auditory and visual comprehension; (2) oral and written expression, including tests of repetition, reading, naming, and fluency; and (3) conversational speech.

Because test batteries have the disadvantages of being lengthy and requiring special training to administer, some brief aphasia screening tests also have been devised, including conversational analysis and some simpler formal tests

Table 19.5 **Summary of major neuropsychological tests of aphasia**

Test	Basic Reference
Aphasia Test Batteries	
Boston Diagnostic Aphasia Test	Goodglass and Kaplan, 1972
Functional communicative profile	Sarno, 1969
Neurosensory center comprehensive examination for aphasia	Spreen and Benton, 1969
Porch Index of Communicative Ability	Porch, 1967
Minnesota Test for Differential Diagnosis of Aphasia	Schuell, 1965
Wepman–Jones Language Modalities Test for Aphasia	Wepman and Jones, 1961
Aphasia Screening Tests	
Conversation analysis	Beeke, Maxim, and Wilkinson, 2007
Halstead–Wepman Aphasia Screening Test	Halstead and Wepman, 1959
Token Test	de Renzi and Vignolo, 1962

listed under the second group in Table 19.5. The Halstead–Wepman Aphasia Screening Test and the Token Test are often used as part of standard neuropsychological test batteries because they are short and easy to administer and score. Screening tests do not take the place of the detailed aphasia test batteries, but they offer efficient means of discovering the presence of a language disorder. If a detailed description of the linguistic deficit is then desired, the more comprehensive aphasia batteries may be given.

Although theoretical models and test batteries may be useful for evaluating and classifying the status of a patient with aphasia, they are no substitute for continued experimental analysis of language disorders. Whereas the test batteries attempt to classify patients into a number of groups, a psychobiological approach concentrates on individual differences and peculiarities and, from these differences, attempts to reconstruct the brain's language-producing processes.

On the practical side, John Marshall (1986) notes that only about 60% of aphasic patients will fit into a classification scheme such as the one presented in Table 19.3 on page 537. Similar inadequacies have been noted in other classification methods. For example, most patients with language impairment show a deficit in naming that can be elicited by having them look at pictures of objects and attempt to identify them.

The naming deficit can vary from subject to subject. One subject might be able to name a violin, another might know only that it is a musical instrument, another that it is a stringed instrument, and still another that it is similar to a cello and not a trumpet. Some subjects have highly selective naming deficits, such as being unable to name buildings or people or colors or objects found inside houses. Studying such differences can offer important insight into the neural organization of language.

Assessing Developmental Language Disorders

Assessment of reading disorders, detailed in Section 24.2, is a specialized branch of language research for several reasons. First, analyzing reading is more objective than analyzing writing and speaking. Second, a large pedagogical science of reading is available. Finally, in addition to the **acquired dyslexias** (impairments in reading subsequent to brain damage), cases of **developmental dyslexia** (failure to learn to read during development) are common and require diagnosis and remediation.

Max Coltheart (2005) argues that model building is the most objective approach to studying reading. A model is much like an algorithm—a set of steps to follow to answer a question. Reading models are used to test reading-disabled people, both as a way of defining the impairment and as a way of testing the model's utility.

The model-building approach views reading as composed of a number of independent skills or subsystems, one or another of which may not be functioning in an impaired reader. The modeling approach thus differs from classical neurological approaches in two ways: (1) the latter define dyslexia according to whether it arises in conjunction with other disorders, such as *dysgraphia* or *dysphasia*, and (2) the primary intent is to correlate the impairment with the locus of brain damage.

Analyzing Acquired Dyslexia

The model-building approach can be traced to an analysis by James Hinshelwood (1917) in which he identified different types of reading disorders: (1) the inability to name letters (letter blindness), (2) the inability to read words (word blindness), and (3) the inability to read sentences (sentence blindness). Hinshelwood's taxonomy and its subsequent elaboration led to the current hypothesis that reading is composed of a number of independent abilities that may each have an independent anatomical basis.

Figure 19.16 charts a series of questions that an examiner might ask to identify the following impairments:

1. **Attentional dyslexia.** When one letter is present, letter naming is standard. When more than one letter is present, letter naming is difficult. Even if a letter is specially colored, underlined, has an arrow pointing to it, and is pointed to by the tester, it may be named incorrectly when it is among other letters. The same phenomenon may occur for words when more than one word is present.

2. **Neglect dyslexia.** Persons displaying this impairment may misread the first half of a word (for example, reading "whether" as "smother") or they may misread the last part of a word (for example, reading "strong" as "stroke").

3. **Letter-by-letter reading.** Affected persons read words only by spelling them out to themselves (aloud or silently). Silent spelling can be detected by the additional time required for reading long words. Frequently, an affected person can write but then has difficulty reading what was written.

4. **Deep dyslexia.** The key symptoms are semantic errors: persons with deep dyslexia read semantically related words in place of the word that they are trying to read (for instance, "tulip" as "crocus" and "merry" as "Christmas"). Nouns are easiest for them to read; followed by adjectives; then verbs (function words), which present the greatest

Figure 19.16 ▼

Analyzing Acquired Dyslexia (Information from Coltheart, 2005.)

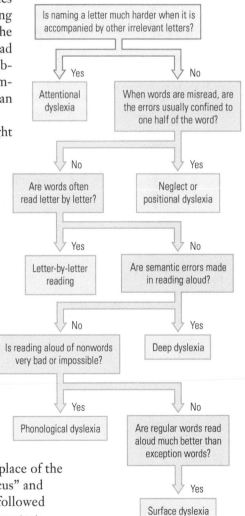

difficulty. Those with deep dyslexia also find it easier to read concrete words than abstract ones and are completely unable to read nonsense words. They are also generally impaired at writing and in short-term verbal memory (*digit span*).

5. **Phonological dyslexia.** The one symptom is an inability to read nonwords aloud; otherwise reading may be nearly flawless.

6. **Surface dyslexia.** The surface dyslexic cannot recognize words directly but can understand them by using letter-to-sound relations, that is, if it is sounded out. This reading procedure works well as long as the words are regular and can be sounded out ("home," "dome"), but not if the words are irregular ("come" will be read as "comb"). *Regular words* have consistent phoneme-grapheme relationships, whereas *irregular words* do not and must be memorized. Spelling is also impaired but is phonetically correct. Surface dyslexia does not develop in languages that are totally phonetic and sounded out as they are written (such as Italian). Surface dyslexia is a common symptom of children who have difficulty in learning to read.

Modeling Speech from Print

Central to the model-building idea of reading is the **dual-route theory**, which proposes that reading written language is accomplished by using two distinct but interactive procedures, the lexical and nonlexical routes. Reading by the lexical route relies on the activation of orthographic (picture) or phonological (sound) representations of a whole word. The lexical route can process all familiar words, both regular and irregular, but it fails with unfamiliar words or nonwords, because it lacks a means for representing them.

In contrast with the whole-word retrieval procedure used by the lexical route, the nonlexical route uses a subword procedure based on sound-spelling rules. The nonlexical route can succeed with nonwords (for example, "klant") and regular words that obey letter-sound rules, but it cannot succeed with irregular words that do not obey these rules (for example, "winding," "choir").

The application of the dual-route theory is that typical readers compute sense and sound in parallel, whereas, in the dyslexic reader, one process or the other may be absent. In deep dyslexia, a subject is unable to process for sound and reads for sense. The subject may misread the word "bird" as "butterfly," both words referring to flying animals. In surface dyslexia, a subject is able to process for sound but not for sense. The subject might pronounce English words correctly and even read fluently but still not realize what he or she is saying. Stephen Rapcsak and his colleagues (2007) propose that the dual-route theory is effective in diagnosing both developmental and acquired dyslexia.

Figure 19.17 charts a model illustrating the dual-route theory. Note the quite separate ways of obtaining speech from print and a still different way of producing letter names. The important features of the dual-route approach are that it does not depend on function–anatomy relations, it can be applied to language disorders other than dyslexia, and it can lead to hypotheses concerning the anatomical organization of language.

Figure 19.17 ▼

Dual-Route Model Speech from print can follow a number of routes and can be independent of comprehension or pronunciation. (Information from Coltheart, 2005.)

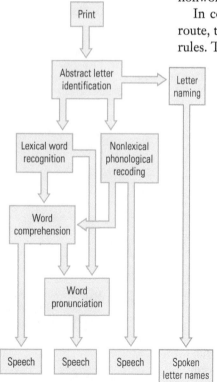

SUMMARY

19.1 What Is Language?

Language allows humans to organize sensory inputs by assigning tags to information. Tagging allows us to categorize objects and ultimately concepts and to speak to ourselves about our past and future. Language also includes the unique motor act of producing syllables as well as the ability to impose grammatical rules. Both dramatically increase the functional capacity of language.

19.2 Searching for the Origins of Language

Continuity theorists propose that language has a long evolutionary history; discontinuity theorists propose that language evolved suddenly in modern humans. The evolution of language represents not the development of a single ability but rather the parallel development of multimodal processes. Investigations of language origins are directed toward understanding the component skills necessary for language and the genes that contribute to languagelike processes in different animal species.

19.3 Localization of Language

Language functions occupy a vast cortical area. Functions such as generating verbs versus nouns or understanding visual versus auditory information are found in precise locations. Language, like other cerebral functions, is organized in a series of parallel hierarchical channels that can be modeled as neural networks. Neural networks propose that language is generated by cortical areas in which phonemes and syntax involve connections between different cortical regions, even at the level of individual words.

19.4 Language Disorders

Traditional classifications of language disorders characterize fluent aphasias, in which speech can be expressed; nonfluent aphasias, in which speaking is impaired; and pure aphasias, which may be highly selective. Various combinations of fluent and nonfluent types are identified, depending on the disorder.

19.5 Localization of Lesions in Aphasia

One contemporary language model proposes paired dorsal and paired ventral language pathways connecting temporal- and frontal-lobe language areas. The dorsal pathways mediate phonology, and the ventral pathways mediate semantics. Both pairs of pathways are involved in short- and long-term memory for language. Subcortical structures and the right hemisphere also contribute to language, revealing its wide distribution through the brain.

19.6 Neuropsychological Assessment of Aphasia

Assessment tools developed to describe language disorders include tests of perceptual disorders, disorders of comprehension, and disorders of speech production. The complexities of language render it difficult to group every disorder with any single assessment tool.

Reading analysis lends itself to a model-building approach. Dual-route theory proposes that reading can be accomplished in two ways: by either (1) a lexical route in which words are recognized as wholes, or (2) a nonlexical approach in which words are recognized by using letter-sound rules. Acquired or developmental dyslexia can include impairments in lexical routes, nonlexical routes, or both.

References

Amunts, K., M. Lenzen, A. D. Friederici, A. Schleicher, P. Morosan, N. Palomero-Gallagher, and K. Zilles. Broca's region: Novel organizational principles and multiple receptor mapping. *PLoS Biology* 8(9):e1000489, September 21, 2010.

Beeke, S., J. Maxim, and R. Wilkinson. Using conversation analysis to assess and treat people with aphasia. *Seminars in Speech Language* 28(2):136–147, 2007.

Benson, D. F. Aphasia and lateralization of language. *Cortex* 22:71–86, 1985.

Berwick, R. C., A. D. Friederici, N. Chomsky, and J. J. Bolhuis. Evolution, brain, and the nature of language. *Trends in Cognitive Science* 17:89–98, 2013.

Binder, J. R., J. A. Frost, T. A. Hammeke, R. W. Cox, S. M. Rao, and T. Prieto. Human brain language areas identified by functional magnetic resonance imaging. *Journal of Neuroscience* 17:353–362, 1997.

Catani, M., R. J. Howard, S. Pajevic, and D. K. Jones. Virtual in vivo interactive dissection of white matter fasciculi in the human brain. *NeuroImage* 17:77–94, 2002.

Cattaneo L. Language. *Handbook of Clinical Neurology* 116:681–691, 1913.

Coltheart, M. Modelling reading: The dual-route approach. In M. J. Snowling and C. Hulme, Eds., *The Science of Reading: A Handbook*, pp. 6–23. Malden, Mass.: Blackwell, 2005.

Damasio, H., T. J. Grabowski, D. Tranel, R. D. Hichwa, and A. R. Damasio. A neural basis for lexical retrieval. *Nature* 380:499–505, 1996.

de Renzi, E., and L. A. Vignolo. The Token Test: A sensitive test to detect disturbances in aphasics. *Brain* 85:665–678, 1962.

Devlin, J. T., and K. E. Watkins. Stimulating language: Insights from TMS. *Brain* 130:610–622, 2007.

Dronkers, N. F., B. B. Redfern, and R. T. Knight. The neural architecture of language disorders. In M. S. Gazzaniga, Ed., *The New Cognitive Neurosciences*, pp. 949–958. Cambridge, Mass.: MIT Press, 1999.

Dronkers N. F., O. Plaisant , M. T. Iba-Zizen, and E. A. Cabanis. Paul Broca's historic cases: High resolution MR imaging of the brains of Leborgne and Lelong. *Brain* 130:1432–1441, 2007.

Fedorenko, E., and S. L. Thompson-Schill. Reworking the language network. *Trends in Cognitive Science* 18:120–126, 2014.

Fitch, W. T. The evolution of speech: A comparative review. *Trends in Cognitive Science* 4:258–267, 2000.

Gardner, R. A., and B. T. Gardner. Comparative psychology and language acquisition. *Annals of the New York Academy of Sciences* 309:37–76, 1978.

Goodall, J. *The Chimpanzees of Gombe*. Cambridge, Mass.: Harvard University Press, 1986.

Goodglass, H., and E. Kaplan. *The Assessment of Aphasia and Related Disorders*. Philadelphia: Lea & Febiger, 1972.

Gustason, G., D. Pfetzing, and E. Zawoklow. *Signing Exact English*. Silver Spring, Md.: Modern Signs Press, 1975.

Halstead, W. C., and J. M. Wepman. The Halstead-Wepman aphasia screening test. *Journal of Speech and Hearing Disorders* 14:9–15, 1959.

Hayes, K. J., and C. Hayes. The intellectual development of a home-raised chimp. *Proceedings of the American Philosophical Society* 95(2):106–109, April 30, 1951.

Hewes, G. W. Language origin theories. In D. M. Rumbaugh, Ed., *Language Learning by a Chimpanzee*. New York: Academic Press, 1977.

Hinshelwood, J. *Congenital Word-Blindness*. London: H. K. Lewis, 1917.

Hobaiter, C., D. A. Leavens, and R. W. Byrne. Deictic gesturing in wild chimpanzees (Pan troglodytes)? Some possible cases. *Journal of Comparative Psychology*128:82–87, 2014.

Hopkins, W. D. Neuroanatomical asymmetries and handedness in chimpanzees (Pan troglodytes): A case for continuity in the evolution of hemispheric specialization. *Annals of the New York Academy of Science* 1288:17–35, 2013.

Kellogg, W., and L. Kellogg. *The Ape and the Child*. New York: McGraw-Hill, 1933.

Kim, W. J., Y. S. Min, E. J. Yang, and N. J. Paik. Neuronavigated vs. conventional repetitive transcranial magnetic stimulation method for virtual lesioning on the Broca's area. *Neuromodulation* 17:16–21, 2014.

Kimura, D. *Neuromotor Mechanisms in Human Communication*. Oxford: Oxford University Press, 1993.

Lezak, M. D., D. B. Howieson, E. D. Bigler, and D. Tranel, *Neuropsychological Assessment*, 5th ed. New York: Oxford University Press, 2012

Lieberman, P. Motor control, speech and the evolution of human language. In M. H. Christianson and J. R. Hurford, Eds., *Language Evolution*, pp. 255–271. Oxford: Oxford University Press, 2003.

Luria, A. R., and J. T. Hutton. A modern assessment of basic forms of aphasia. *Brain and Language* 4:129–151, 1977.

MacNeilage, P. F. The frame/context theory of evolution of speech production. *Behavioral Brain Sciences* 21:499–511, 1998.

Marshack, A. *The Roots of Civilization: The Cognitive Beginnings of Man's First Art, Symbol, and Notation*. New York: McGraw-Hill, 1971.

Marshall, J. C. The description and interpretation of aphasic language disorder. *Neuropsychologia* 24:5–24, 1986.

Martin, A., C. L. Wiggs, L. G. Ungerleider, and J. V. Haxby. Neural correlates of category-specific knowledge. *Nature* 379:649–652, 1996.

Mazzocchi, R., and L. A. Vignolo. Localization of lesions in aphasia: Clinical–CT scan correlations in stroke patients. *Cortex* 15:627–654, 1979.

McNeill, D. *Gesture and Thought*. Chicago: University of Chicago Press, 2005.

Newman, A. J., D. Bavelier, D. Corina, P. Jezzard, and H. J. Neville. A critical period for right hemisphere recruitment in American Sign Language processing. *Nature Neuroscience* 5:76–80, 2002.

Ojemann, G. A. The neurobiology of language and verbal memory: Observations from awake neurosurgery. *International Journal of Psychophysiology* 48:141–146, 2003.

Penfield, W., and L. Roberts. *Speech and Brain Mechanisms*. Princeton, N.J.: Princeton University Press, 1959.

Pepperberg, I. M. *Alex and Me: How a Scientist and a Parrot Discovered a Hidden World of Animal Intelligence—And Formed a Deep Bond in the Process*. New York: Collins, 2008.

Petersen, S. E., P. T. Fox, M. I. Posner, M. Mintun, and M. E. Raichle. Positron emission tomographic studies of the processing of single words. *Journal of Cognitive Neuroscience* 1:153–170, 1988.

Poeppel, D., K. Emmorey, G. Hickok, and L. Pylkkänen. Towards a new neurobiology of language. *Journal of Neuroscience* 32:14125–14131, 2012.

Porch, B. E. *Index of Communicative Ability*. Palo Alto, Calif.: Consulting Psychologists Press, 1967.

Posner, M. I., and M. E. Raichle. *Images of Mind*. New York: Scientific American Library, 1994.

Premack, D. The codes of man and beasts. *Behavioral and Brain Sciences* 6:125–167, 1983.

Rapcsak, S. Z., M. L. Henry, S. L. Teague, S. D. Carnahan, and P. M. Beeson. Do dual-route models accurately predict reading and spelling performance in individuals with acquired alexia and agraphia? *Neuropsychologia* 45:2519–2524, 2007.

Ricklan, M., and I. S. Cooper. Psychometric studies of verbal functions following thalamic lesions in humans. *Brain and Language* 2:45–64, 1975.

Rofes, A., and G. Miceli. Language mapping with verbs and sentences in awake surgery: A review. *Neuropsychological Reviews* 24:185–199, 2014.

Rogić, M., V. Deletis, and I. Fernández-Conejero. Inducing transient language disruptions by mapping of Broca's area with modified patterned repetitive transcranial magnetic stimulation protocol. *Journal of Neurosurgery* 120(5):1033–1041, March 2014.

Rowan, A., F. Vargha-Khadem, F. Calamante, J. D. Tournier, F. J. Kirkham, W. K. Chong, T. Baldeweg, A. Connelly, and D. G. Gadian. Cortical abnormalities and language function in young patients with basal ganglia stroke. *Neuro-Image* 36:431–440, 2007.

Rumbaugh, D. M., and T. V. Gill. Lana's acquisition of language skills. In D. M. Rumbaugh, Ed., *Language Learning by a Chimpanzee*. New York: Academic Press, 1977.

Salmelin, R., and J. Kujala. Neural representation of language: Activation versus long-range connectivity. *Trends in Cognitive Sciences* 10:519–525, 2006.

Sarno, M. T. *The Functional Communication Profile: Manual of Directions*. New York: Institute of Rehabilitation Medicine, New York University Medical Center, 1969.

Savage-Rumbaugh, E. S., K. McDonald, R. A. Sevcik, W. D. Hopkins, and E. Rubert. Spontaneous symbol acquisition and communicative use by pygmy chimpanzees (*Pan paniscus*). *Journal of Experimental Psychology: General* 115:211–235, 1986.

Schoenemann, P. T. Evolution of the brain and language. In M. A. Hofman and D. Falk, Eds., *Progress in Brain Research* 195:443–459, 2012.

Schouwstra, M., and H. de Swart. The semantic origins of word order. *Cognition* 131:431–436, June 2014.

Schuell, H. *Differential Diagnosis of Aphasia with the Minnesota Test*. Minneapolis: University of Minnesota Press, 1965.

Skipper J. I., V. van Wassenhove, H. C. Nusbaum, and S. L. Small. Hearing lips and seeing voices: How cortical areas supporting speech production mediate audiovisual speech perception. *Cerebral Cortex* 17:2387–2399, 2007.

Spreen, O., and A. L. Benton. *Neurosensory Center Comprehensive Examination for Aphasia*. Victoria, Canada: University of Victoria, 1969.

Swadish, M. *The Origin and Diversification of Language*. J. Sherzer, Ed. Chicago: Aldine-Atherton, 1971.

Taglialatela, J. P., S. Savage-Rumbaugh, and L. A. Baker. Vocal production by a language-compentent *Pan paniscus*. *International Journal of Primatology* 24:1–17, 2003.

von Glaserfeld, E. The Yerkish language and its automatic parser. In D. M. Rumbaugh, Ed., *Language Learning by a Chimpanzee*. New York: Academic Press, 1977.

Vouloumanos, A., and J. F. Werker. Listening to language at birth: Evidence for a bias for speech in neonates. *Developmental Science* 10:159–164, 2007.

Wagner, A. D., E. J. Paré-Blagoev, J. Clark, and R. A. Poldrack. Recovering meaning: Left prefrontal cortex guides controlled semantic retrieval. *Neuron* 31:329–338, 2001.

Wallman, J. *Aping Language*. Cambridge, U.K.: Cambridge University Press, 1992.

Wepman, J. M., and L. V. Jones. *Studies in Aphasia: An Approach to Testing*. Chicago: University of Chicago Education-Industry Service, 1961.

20

Emotion and the Social Brain

 PORTRAIT Agenesis of the Frontal Lobe

The year was 1912. After a difficult 22-hour labor, a baby boy was born. J.P. weighed 11.5 pounds but dropped to 5 pounds following postpartum complications. S. S. Ackerly (1964) reports that J.P. appeared to recover from his early trauma and by age 1 was walking and talking and displaying apparently typical intelligence. But he was a problem child. He was hyperactive and showed no emotion but anger, which he expressed in temper tantrums.

As J.P. grew to school age, he began to wander away. Police would find him miles from home, but evidently he never showed any fear of being lost. Even severe whippings did not deter him. School was a real problem. Although he was extremely well mannered most of the time, J.P. unexpectedly engaged in inappropriate behaviors such as exposing himself and masturbating in the classroom.

Growing up, he developed no close friendships and was generally disliked. The community blamed his parents for most of the boy's problems, but nothing they did helped. As an adolescent, J.P. pawned his

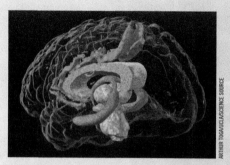

ARTHUR TOGA/UCLA/SCIENCE SOURCE

mother's rings, stole his uncle's car, and drove to Chicago from Kentucky to spend the money. At 19, when his criminal record for theft began to mount, a psychiatrist began to investigate the nature of his behavioral problems, eventually finding that J.P.'s right frontal lobe was missing and his left was only 50 percent of typical size. It was the 1930s, and few treatment options existed.

As an adult, J.P. could not hold down a job for more than a few weeks, largely because of his erratic behavior. One moment, he was charming; the next, he was reacting out of all proportion to some seemingly trivial matter. Even at age 50, J.P.'s behavior had not changed: he remained hyperactive and alone, largely detached from anything that gives meaning to life, such as love or friendship. He had virtually no social feelings at all and evidently was unable to understand what such feelings would be like or to react to emotions in others.

Absent frontal lobes, J.P. had no social skills and showed very little emotion except anger, which took the form of temper tantrums.

Emotion, like memory, entails cognitive processes that may either be conscious or lie outside our awareness. We begin this chapter by exploring the nature of emotion and what neuropsychologists have learned about how the brain produces and processes emotions. We next review theories of emotion developed over the past century and cortical asymmetry in processing emotion. Then we consider how emotion contributes to social behavior and the social brain. We end the chapter by detailing how emotion contributes to our sense of self.

20.1 The Nature of Emotion

J.P.'s behavior, as described in the Portrait, was extreme and certainly uncommon. More typical is the observation that seemingly minor brain injury can change a person's personality. To neuropsychologists, impairments of movement, perception, language, or memory affect not only how a person expresses and reacts to emotion but also how others perceive that person's emotions. Not so evident to observers, however, is a person's subjective feeling of emotion.

Indeed, some view emotion as an inconvenient remnant of our evolutionary past, a nonconscious time when humans literally were driven by such "instincts" as emotion. They believe that humans are fundamentally rational, but emotion is older than thought. People such as J.P., with blunted or lost emotions, may behave in a completely rational manner most of the time, but when making personal and social decisions, they act irrationally.

Antonio Damasio (2000) emphasizes that emotion is a cognitive process that actually contributes to logical thinking. He argues that unconscious and conscious signals emanating from the neural machinery underlying emotion significantly influence the mechanisms of reasoning. Note the contrast between neuropsychologists' use of the word "unconscious" as a synonym for nonconscious brain activity and Freud's use of it as a hidden or repressed component of the mind. Neuropsychologists use "unconscious" as shorthand for nineteenth-century German scientist Hermann von Helmholtz's notion of **unconscious inference**—processes outside awareness and learned by experience whereby observers use knowledge to perceive and make decisions.

What Are Emotions?

Neuropsychologists view **emotion**, the cognitive interpretation of subjective feelings, as an inferred behavioral state called **affect**, a conscious, subjective feeling about a stimulus, independent of where or what it is. Affective behavior is internal and subjective. Most psychological theories rank emotions along two dimensions labeled by such dichotomies as pleasant/unpleasant, arousing/not arousing, or rewards/punishers (**Figure 20.1**). Regardless of the words we use, these positive and negative aspects distinguish emotion from other neuropsychological processes.

Components of Emotion

The experience of emotion has four principal behavioral components, and each can be quantified as well as observed—in principle:

1. **Psychophysiology.** Physiological components include central and autonomic nervous system activity and the resulting changes in neurohormonal and visceral (somatic) activity. Emotion changes heart rate, blood pressure, distribution of blood flow, perspiration, and the digestive system, among others, as well as the release of hormones that may affect the brain or the ANS (detailed in Figure 3.15). Although the topic of debate, at least some emotional states—happiness versus sadness, for example—can likely be differentiated by the associated physiological changes each engenders.

⊚ **Figure 20.1** ▲

Two-dimensional space of emotion Emotions are rated on this grid as ranging from pleasant to unpleasant and varying in arousal (intensity). (Anderson, D. J., and R. Adolphs. A framework for studying emotions across species. *Cell* 157:187–200, 2014. © Elsevier.)

2. **Distinctive motor behavior.** Facial expression, tone of voice, and posture all express emotional states. These motor behaviors are especially important to observing emotions because they convey overt action that can differ from observed verbal behavior. Our perception of a person who says that he is fine but is sobbing uncontrollably is different from our perception of the same person when he is smiling.

3. **Self-reported cognition.** Cognitive processes are inferred from self-reports. Cognition operates in the realm of both *subjective* emotional feelings (feeling love or hate, feeling loved or hated) and *other cognitive processes* (plans, memories, or ideas).

4. **Unconscious behavior.** This component incorporates von Helmholtz's unconscious inference—cognitive processes of which we are not aware that influence behavior. We may make decisions on the basis of "intuition" or a hunch or other apparently unfounded bases. In Section 16.3, for example, we describe a gambling task in which participants gradually changed their behavior to optimize the outcome but seemed unconscious of why they had chosen to play certain decks of cards over others to win the game. (Frontal-lobe patients, by contrast, behaved irrationally: they failed to choose these decks, lost all their play money, and had to "borrow" more to continue the experiment.)

A contemporary theory of emotion must include at least these four principal behavioral components. The theoretical distinction among physiology, movement, self-reports, and unconscious action is significant because researchers detect little correlation among the physical states of emotion when all of them are measured in the same participants. A brief review of a century's research on emotion, next, sets the stage for exploring the anatomy of emotion and discussing contemporary theories in depth later.

20.2 Historical Views

Interest in the biology of emotion dates to Darwin's book, *The Expression of the Emotions in Man and Animals*, published in 1872. Darwin believed that because emotional behavior is determined by evolution, human emotional expression could be understood only in the context of its expression in other animals. Although Darwin's book was a bestseller in its time, its influence was short-lived, and it was temporarily forgotten.

Investigating the Anatomy of Emotion

Psychologists began to speculate about emotions at the turn of the twentieth century, but they had little knowledge about the neural basis of emotional behavior. By the late 1920s, physiologists had begun to examine the relation among autonomic, endocrine, and neurohumoral (neurotransmitter) factors and inferred emotional states, with particular emphasis on measuring indices such as heart rate, blood pressure, and skin temperature.

Philip Bard made one of the first major anatomical discoveries about emotion while working in Walter Cannon's laboratory in the late 1920s. Friedrich Goltz's studies in the 1890s had shown that, reminiscent of J.P.'s behavior, decorticated dogs could show strong "rage" responses to seemingly trivial stimuli: the dogs behaved as though a seriously threatening stimulus confronted them. Working with cats, Bard showed that this response depended on the diencephalon, the "between brain," which includes the thalamus and hypothalamus. He found that if the diencephalon was intact, animals showed strong "emotional" responses, but if the animals were decerebrate (see Figure 10.2), leaving the diencephalon disconnected from the midbrain, they were unemotional.

Results of studies by many investigators, spanning the 1940s through the 1960s, show that stimulating different hypothalamic regions elicits different "affective responses" in cats. Behaviors associated with attacking another cat (piloerection, hissing, baring of teeth) or attacking a prey animal (crouching, whiskers and ears forward, pouncing)—including eating the animal—can result.

The lesion and stimulation studies on the diencephalon led to the idea that the thalamus and hypothalamus contain the neural circuits for the overt expression of emotion and for autonomic responses such as changes in blood pressure, heart rate, and respiration. The cortex was envisioned as inhibiting the thalamus and hypothalamus. Conversely, the thalamus was seen as activating the cortex during autonomic arousal, presumably to help direct the emotion to the appropriate stimulus.

The Emotional Brain

In 1937, James Papez proposed the first major theory in the neurology of emotion. The structure of the "limbic lobe" forms the anatomical basis of emotion, Papez reasoned, and the limbic structures act on the hypothalamus to produce emotional states. Although for Papez, the neocortex played no part in producing emotional behavior, he did believe the cortex to be necessary for transforming events produced by limbic structures into our experience of emotion.

The Papez theory had appeal: it combined behavioral phenomena having no known neurological substrates with anatomical structures having no known function. The idea of an emotional brain gained instant broad approval because Freudian thinking predominated in the 1930s. That an ancient, deep part of the central nervous system controls emotions and instincts in Freud's unconscious, with the neocortex producing consciousness, was a concept with natural appeal for the psychology of the time.

Cortical Connections of Emotion

Two more contributions from the 1930s shed light on the nature of the cortical structures and connections implicated in emotion. In both cases, investigators were studying something other than emotion and made serendipitous findings that fundamentally changed our thinking about the emotional brain.

Klüver–Bucy Syndrome

In 1939, Heinrich Klüver and Paul Bucy announced the rediscovery of an extraordinary behavioral syndrome first noted by Sanger Brown and Edward Schaefer in 1888. *Klüver–Bucy syndrome* subsequently has been observed in people with a variety of neurological diseases. An obvious aspect of this extraordinary set of behaviors is lack of affect. For example, animals displaying

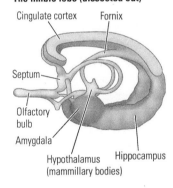

The limbic lobe (dissected out)

Cingulate cortex   Fornix

Septum

Olfactory bulb

Amygdala

Hypothalamus   Hippocampus
(mammillary bodies)

▲ Papez proposed that this group of subcortical limbic structures, acting on the hypothalamus, produces emotions.

Klüver–Bucy syndrome show no fear whatsoever of threatening stimuli such as snakes or "threat" signals from humans or other animals, situations in which healthy animals show strong aversion.

The behavioral syndrome, induced experimentally from bilateral anterior temporal lobectomy in monkeys, includes the following:

- Tameness and a loss of fear
- Indiscriminate dietary behavior: willingness to eat many types of previously rejected foods
- Greatly increased autoerotic, homosexual, and heterosexual activity, with inappropriate object choice (for example, sexual mounting of chairs)
- Hypermetamorphosis, a tendency to attend and react to every visual stimulus
- A tendency to examine all objects by mouth
- Visual agnosia

Klüver–Bucy syndrome can also be observed in humans. Wendy Marlowe and colleagues (1975) reported on a patient with Klüver–Bucy symptoms that resulted from meningoencephalitis (inflammation of the brain and the meninges). This man exhibited a flat affect and engaged in oral exploration of all objects within his grasp, including the plastic wrapper from bread, cleaning pastes, ink, dog food, and feces.

> The patient's sexual behavior was a particular source of concern while in hospital. Although vigorously heterosexual prior to his illness, he was observed in hospital to make advances toward other male patients by stroking their legs and inviting fellatio by gesture; at times he attempted to kiss them. Although on a sexually mixed floor during a portion of his recovery, he never made advances toward women, and, in fact, his apparent reversal of sexual polarity prompted his fiancée to sever their relationship. (Marlowe et al., 1975, p. 56)

The appearance of Klüver–Bucy syndrome in humans and monkeys apparently requires that the amygdala and inferior temporal cortex be removed bilaterally. H.M., the amnesic patient featured throughout Chapter 18, did not exhibit the syndrome, despite bilateral removal of the medial temporal structures. Furthermore, monkeys with bilateral amygdalectomies do not show Klüver–Bucy syndrome unless the temporal cortex also is removed.

Psychosurgery

At about the time of Klüver and Bucy's discovery, Carlyle Jacobsen made a less dramatic, but in many ways even more important, discovery. Jacobsen studied the behavior of chimpanzees in a variety of learning tasks subsequent to frontal-lobe removals. In 1935, he reported his findings on the effects of the lesions at the Second International Neurology Congress in London. He casually noted that one particularly neurotic chimp appeared more relaxed after the surgery, leading a Portuguese neurologist, Egas Moniz, to propose that similar lesions in people might relieve various behavioral problems. Thus was born psychosurgery and the frontal lobotomy.

Unbelievably, frontal lobotomies were performed on humans with no empirical basis. Not until the late 1960s was any systematic research done on the

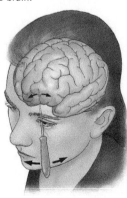

▼ In this psychosurgical procedure, a transorbital leukotomy, the inferior frontal cortex is disconnected from the rest of the brain.

effects of frontal-lobe lesions on the affective behavior of nonhuman animals. Experimental findings by several laboratories clearly confirm the results of frontal lobotomies on humans: frontal-lobe lesions in rats, cats, and monkeys have severe effects on social and affective behavior across the board.

20.3 Candidate Structures in Emotional Behavior

A consistent principle of neural organization is that multiple systems control virtually every behavior. Sensory information enters the cortex through multiple distinctly different sensory channels. When stimuli have been processed, information travels through multiple parallel systems subserving different functions.

Processing Emotional Stimuli

Visual information from the occipital lobe follows a ventral route through the temporal lobe to assist in object recognition, and a dorsal route through the parietal lobe assists in controlling movement. In keeping with this general principle of brain organization, we can speculate that multiple systems, both cortical and subcortical, contribute to the experience of an emotion.

Neural systems must process sensory stimuli as significant to social behavior. Presumably, sensations are species-specific for olfactory (pheromones), tactile (especially to sensitive body zones), visual (facial expressions), and auditory (phonemes, crying, screaming, and so forth) stimuli. Arguably, these socially significant stimuli are processed by the same systems that analyze other sensory inputs, but at least some sensory systems may be separate. Olfaction in cats provides a good example.

In many mammals, a receptor organ (Jacobson's organ) is specialized to analyze species-typical odors. When animals such as cats encounter certain odors (especially urine from other cats), they close their nostrils and appear to stare off into space with an odd look on their faces, a behavior known as *flehmen* (**Figure 20.2**). Actually, the cats are forcing the air through the roof of the mouth and into a special duct connected to the accessory olfactory system that allows the air access to Jacobson's organ. (The accessory olfactory system functions to analyze species-specific odors and has direct connections to the hypothalamus and amygdala.)

Virtually the only odors that produce flehmen in cats come from other cats, including urine and ear wax but not feces. This neural system is thus specialized for species-typical odors. (Curiously, we have found that human urine also is often effective.) The system shows habituation (repeated exposure to the same urine reduces the likelihood of flehmen), and cats appear able to remember the odors of familiar cats. Thus, they do not show flehmen to their own urine or to that of cats with which they live. Urine from novel cats will produce prolonged episodes of flehmen, and urine from familiar but not co-resident cats will produce shorter episodes.

The analysis of faces provides an example of processing emotion in primates. Cells in the superior temporal sulcus of monkeys are specialized for faces, and

Figure 20.2 ▼

Flehmen A cat sniffs a urine-soaked cotton ball (top), begins the gape response of the flehmen (center), and follows with the full gape response (bottom). This behavior is mediated by the accessory olfactory system. (Bryan Kolb.)

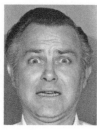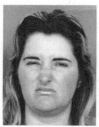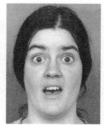

⊚ Figure 20.3 ▲

Universality of Emotion
Paul Ekman and his colleagues showed these photographs to people in societies throughout the world—ranging from hunting-and-gathering tribes to postindustrial enclaves—and found that humans of all cultures, regardless of experience, recognize facial expressions of basic emotions.
(Paul Ekman, Ph.D./ Paul Ekman Group, LLC.)

humans also show activity in the fusiform face area (V4 in the ventral temporal lobe) in response to faces. Paul Ekman and colleagues (Ekman and Friesen, 1984) demonstrated that throughout the world, people universally recognize basic facial expressions—anger, fear, disgust, surprise, happiness, and sadness (**Figure 20.3**). Cultural differences exist in the details of facial expressions, suggesting that expressions of emotion can contain nonverbal accents that identify the expresser's nationality or culture. Temporal-lobe neurons can be tuned by experience (Section 15.2), and faces appear to provide another example of such tuning.

Higher-level brain systems possibly process other aspects of sensory information, including internally generating feelings. In addition to multiple systems that may encode specific species-typical information, a general cortical system may identify affective attributes of external stimuli. An interesting experiment by Michael Gazzaniga and Joseph LeDoux (1978) illustrates such a system. They presented split-brain patients with visual information to one or the other visual field. The task was to describe the stimulus verbally and to rate it on a five-point scale from "dislike very much" to "like very much."

The results are striking. As expected, only the items in the right visual field (and therefore sent to the left, speaking, hemisphere) were described accurately. In contrast, the split-brain patients' five-point rating was identical for stimuli in each visual field. Clearly, the pathways that process the affective significance of stimuli are distinct from the pathways that process their objective properties.

This distinction is reminiscent of the difference between knowing what a stimulus is and knowing where it is, as illustrated by blindsight (see Section 13.4). There may be a third system that processes affect. We have all recognized an odor, sound, or other physical stimulus, even though we cannot identify it in that moment. We may say that we have a "feeling" or "intuition" about the stimulus.

The effect is often true of sounds that may elicit a certain feeling because of the context in which we typically hear them. For example, music associated with being at some place or with some person may elicit emotional feelings when heard in another context, such as an elevator. We may not realize why we are suddenly melancholy or unusually happy. Recall from Section 18.4 that emotional memories are generally unconscious.

Brain Circuits for Emotion

In the early 1930s, when the psychiatrist described in the opening Portrait was beginning to study J.P., the limbic lobe (including the amygdala) and prefrontal cortex were identified as brain regions implicated in emotion. Although the original limbic structures Papez identified in the late 1930s focused on the hippocampus and its connections with the hypothalamus, modern views of the limbic system focus as closely on the amygdala and prefrontal cortex. **Figure 20.4** shows the amygdala lying adjacent to the hippocampus in the temporal lobe, with the prefrontal cortex lying just anterior.

Figure 20.5A diagrams the contemporary notion of the limbic system's extent, and Figure 20.5B schematically illustrates the limbic circuit. The hippocampus, amygdala, and prefrontal cortex all connect with the hypothalamus. The mammillary nucleus of the hypothalamus connects to the anterior thalamus, which in turn connects to the cingulate cortex. Connections from the cingulate cortex complete the circuit by connecting to the hippocampus, amygdala, and prefrontal cortex.

Although the entire circuit is important to emotional behavior, the prefrontal cortex (especially the orbitofrontal and ventromedial regions) and amygdala hold the key to understanding the nature of emotional experience. The orbitofrontal cortex is especially important in emotion because it represents positive and negative rewards and learns which previously neutral stimuli are associated with positive and negative rewards and when these associations change (for an extensive review, see Rolls, 2014).

In a meta-analysis of fMRI studies examining pleasure coding in prefrontal cortex, Berridge and Kringelbach (2013) conclude that pleasure appears most faithfully represented by activity in the OFC, particularly in a mid-anterior subregion (**Figure 20.6**). Evidence suggests activity of this mid-anterior zone tracks changes in subjective pleasantness ratings of chocolate and delicious drinks, such as when pleasure intensity is diminished by switching the taster's state from hunger to satiety, and may also encode pleasures of sexual orgasm, drugs, and music. The medial orbital area also codes subjective pleasure ratings

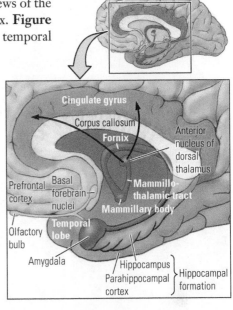

Figure 20.4 ▲

Emotional Circuitry The limbic lobe, which encircles the brainstem, consists of the cingulate gyrus and hippocampal formation, the amygdala, the mammillothalamic tract, and the anterior thalamus.

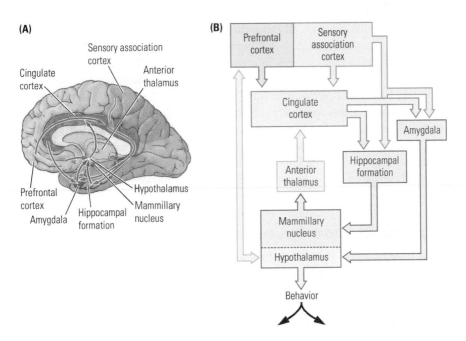

Figure 20.5 ◄

Contemporary View of the Limbic System
(A) A network of structures including the cortex, thalamus, hypothalamus, hippocampal formation, and amygdala forms the basis of emotional experience.
(B) In a schematic representation of the major connections in the limbic circuit, the prefrontal and sensory regions connect with the cingulate cortex, hippocampal formation, and amygdala. The last two structures connect with different regions in the hypothalamus, which in turn connects with the cingulate cortex through the thalamus.

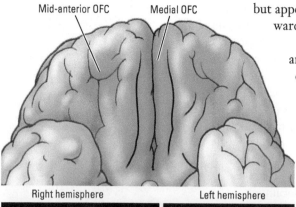

Mid-anterior OFC   Medial OFC

Right hemisphere   Left hemisphere

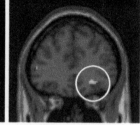

Medial OFC   Mid-anterior OFC

Figure 20.6 ▲

Subjective Pleasure Coded by Orbitofrontal Cortex Pleasant sensations are related to increased activation in OFC. (Top) The mid-anterior region (shaded red) most faithfully represents sensory pleasures, and although the medial OFC (shaded blue) also encodes pleasant sensations, the region apparently is more involved in predicting reward. (Bottom) MRI scans show activation in the medial and mid-anterior OFC regions in response to pleasurable sensations. (Berridge, K. C., and M. L. Kringelbach. Neuroscience of affect: Brain mechanisms of pleasure and displeasure. *Current Opinion in Neurobiology* 23:294–303, 2013. © Elsevier.)

but appears more concerned with monitoring and predicting reward value than with the pleasure of the experience per se.

Named for the Greek word meaning "almond," the amygdala is formed by three principal subdivisions—corticomedial, basolateral, and central areas. Like the prefrontal cortex, the amygdala receives inputs from all sensory systems; to be excited, the cells of the amygdala, like those of the prefrontal cortex, require complex stimuli (such as faces). Many amygdalar cells are multimodal; in fact, some respond to visual, auditory, somatic, gustatory, *and* olfactory stimuli, just as prefrontal cells do. The amygdala can therefore create a complex image of the sensory world, and this image is especially sensitive to stimuli that might be threatening or dangerous.

Bilateral damage to the amygdala renders animals extremely tame and fearless (e.g., Klüver–Bucy syndrome), with a general lack of emotional responsiveness. The amygdala appears to be part of a system that provides rapid and reliable identification of affectively significant stimuli, both pleasant and unpleasant (Pessoa and Adolphs, 2010). The amygdala's hedonic role is also seen in studies showing that neurons in the monkey amygdala may respond mainly to either rewarding or punishing stimuli (Rolls, 2014). This has led to the idea that the amygdala plays a central role in attaching hedonic values to both emotional and other environmental stimuli.

◎ 20.4 Neuropsychological Theories of Emotion

One theme runs through all modern theories of emotion: emotion and cognition are intimately related and likely entail overlapping neural systems. It therefore follows that changes in cognitive abilities will be related to changes in emotion and vice versa. (For a thorough review of theories of emotion, see Scherer, 2000.) Here we outline three current theories that represent the major lines of thinking in cognitive neuroscience regarding emotion: appraisal theories, notably Antonio Damasio's somatic marker hypothesis (1996); Joseph LeDoux's cognitive–emotional interaction theory (2000); and cognitive asymmetry as summarized in Guido Gainotti's lateralization theory (2000). The reader is directed to books and reviews by these authors listed in the end-of-chapter References.

Appraisal Theories of Emotion

This broad class of theories argues that our emotions are extracted from our appraisal of internal and external events, which causes an affective response. The general idea stems from the late nineteenth century, when William James began to argue that an emotion consists of a change in body and brain states in response to the evaluation of a particular event. For example, if you encounter a poisonous snake as you walk along a path, physiological changes—including increases in heart rate, respiration, and sweating—take place. You interpret these physiological changes as fear.

Most versions of appraisal theory are psychological in nature and generally independent of neuropsychological considerations. One exception is Damasio's *somatic marker hypothesis*: when a person is confronted with a stimulus of biological importance, the brain and the body change as a result. Damasio would call the physiological changes in response to the poisonous snake "somatic markers."

On this basis, we could predict that a reduction in the bodily reaction to a stimulus should reduce the intensity of emotions. **Figure 20.7** illustrates that people with spinal-cord injuries do indeed experience reduced emotionality, the loss being proportional to the level of the injury on the spinal cord.

Whereas James was really talking about intense emotions such as fear or anger, Damasio's theory encompasses a much broader range of bodily changes. For example, there may be a change in motor behavior, facial expression, autonomic arousal, or endocrine status as well as neuromodulatory changes in how the brain processes emotional information and other information. Hence, for Damasio, emotions engage those neural structures that represent body states and those structures that somehow link perceptions of external stimuli to body states.

Somatic markers thus are linked to external events and influence cognitive processing. Damasio's theory uniquely specifies that the neural control of emotions includes both the brain structures that represent body states and the activity of neuromodulatory activating systems that link them and can produce global changes in neural processing, including, at the extremes, depression or mania.

A key aspect of Damasio's somatic marker hypothesis is that emotion is fundamental to the individual's survival within a particular environment. The environment for mammals (certainly for humans) encompasses not only physical surroundings but also the social environment. Emotions therefore affect the survival of members of a social group.

This social aspect is of great importance for humans and includes social development, social communication, and even culture. Neuropsychologists have barely addressed these topics, and virtually nothing is known about the neural underpinnings of social emotions such as jealousy, pride, and embarrassment. Given that the frontal lobe has expanded so extensively in human evolution, social emotions probably require some form of frontal-lobe processing, but that they actually do so remains conjecture. Investigators are making strides in this area, however.

Finally, Damasio's theory emphasizes that emotion is not only a fundamental experience for all higher animals but also a necessary one in order for us humans to make rational decisions—especially in situations in which a person faces risk or conflict, as described in the Snapshot on page 558. People with reduced emotions, such as frontal-lobe patients, thus show impairments in personal or social matters, especially when they include possible risk or conflict. The role of our emotions, especially subtle emotional states, is obviously not always conscious, and thus we may be unable to account for why we behave in certain ways.

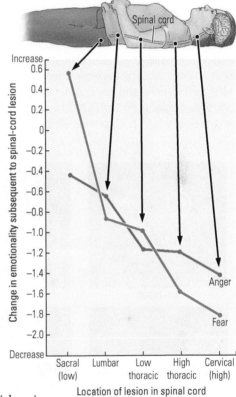

Figure 20.7 ▲

Losing Emotion Spinal injury reduces the experience of emotion. The extent of emotional loss is greatest when the lesion is high on the spinal cord. (Data from J. Beatty. *Principles of Behavioral Neuroscience.* Dubuque, Iowa: Brown & Benchmark, 1995, p. 339.)

SNAPSHOT | Brain Activation in Social Cognition

Human decisions are strongly influenced by emotions. Take regret, for example, an emotion associated with a decision that turns out badly. Typically, regret embodies a feeling that some outcome would have been better had we made a different decision. Regret is a common experience, and people try to anticipate and avoid it by making choices they believe have a higher probability of a positive outcome. Imaging and patient data alike point to the orbitofrontal cortex as key in mediating the experience of regret.

Nathalie Camille and her colleagues (2004) presented control participants and orbitofrontal patients with a gambling task in which both groups were asked to rate their emotional states after making a choice that led either to a $50 or $200 win or to a $50 or $200 loss. When participants learned that the choice led to a $50 win but an alternative choice would have led to a $200 win, they experienced strong negative emotion, whereas learning that the alternative would have led to a $200 loss produced feelings of relief.

After several trials, the participants began making choices that optimized profitable outcomes, even if smaller than they might have been, largely to prevent feeling regret at losing. In contrast, orbitofrontal patients reported no regret and did not adjust their behavior to minimize losses. The absence of regret in the orbitofrontal patients suggests that they failed to grasp the concept of being responsible for one's own decisions—a concept that clearly biased the thinking of controls.

Georgio Coricelli and his colleagues (2007) used fMRI to investigate cerebral activity in controls when they participated in the gambling task. In the early stages, regret at choices was correlated with increased activity in the orbitofrontal and anterior cingulate cortex and the medial temporal regions. As the participants began to make choices that reduced the probability of regret, increased activity in the orbitofrontal cortex and amygdala preceded the choices, suggesting that the same neural system mediates both the experience and the anticipation of regret (see the adjoining figure).

These studies show that the orbitofrontal cortex contributes to optimizing our life choices. They also show that it is possible to begin to understand individual differences in traits such as regret because they may be related to individual differences in orbitofrontal activity.

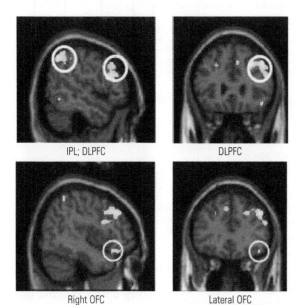

IPL; DLPFC

DLPFC

Right OFC

Lateral OFC

Enhanced activity in dorsolateral prefrontal cortex (DLPFC), parietal cortex (inferior parietal lobule, IPL), and right OFC was observed when control participants experienced regret. (Coricelli, G., R. J. Dolan, and A. Sirigu. Brain, emotion and decision making: the paradigmatic example of regret. *Trends in Cognitive Science* 11(6): 258–265, 2007 © Elsevier.)

Camille, N., G. Coricelli, J. Sallet, P. Pradat-Diehl, J. R. Duhamel, and A. Sirigu. The involvement of the orbitofrontal cortex in the experience of regret. *Science* 302:1167–1170, 2004.

Coricelli, G., R. J. Dolan, and A. Sirigu. Brain, emotion and decision making: The paradigmatic example of regret. *Trends in Cognitive Sciences* 11:258–265, 2007.

Cognitive-Emotional Interactions

This class of theory argues that emotions evolved to enhance animals' survival, and as the brain evolved, cognitive and emotional processes grew more and more interrelated. In contrast with Damasio, Joseph LeDoux (2000) has not tried to account for all emotions but rather has chosen one—namely, fear—as an exemplar of how to study brain–behavior relations in emotion.

In LeDoux's view, all animals inherently detect and respond to danger, and the related neural activities eventually evolve to produce a feeling—in this case, fear. When a mouse detects a cat, fear is obviously related to predation. In most situations prey animals' fear is related either to predation or to danger from others, in this case cats, that may take exception to their presence in a particular place. For humans, however, fear is a much broader emotion that today is only rarely of predation (depending on one's taste in reading, video, or gaming entertainments) but routinely includes stress—situations in which we must "defend" ourselves on short notice.

Modern humans face wide-ranging physical and psychological dangers, from sports injuries to terrorism, as well as more subtle dangers such those posed by chronic stress. An important implication of LeDoux's theory is that our fear system includes both unconscious fear responses, such as the mouse's response to the cat, and conscious awareness of feeling fear. He presumes, however, that the neural system underlying fear is similar in both unconscious and conscious responses and that the neural basis of fear can be studied by using a model system, which is fear conditioning.

Most behavioral studies of fear employ classical conditioning, the pairing of some initially neutral stimulus, such as a tone, with some biologically significant event, such as pain from a shock. Rats (and people) rapidly learn when a neutral stimulus is paired with a negative event (such as a shock). In this case, the auditory information (the tone) passes through the auditory pathways to the thalamus, which in turn sends the information to the cortex and to the amygdala, as charted in **Figure 20.8**.

The key brain structure in developing a conditioned fear is the amygdala, which sends outputs to stimulate hormone release and activate the ANS and thus generates emotion that we interpret in this case as fear. Physiological measures of fear conditioning can measure autonomic functioning (for example, heart rate or respiration), and quantitative measures can measure behavior (for example, standing motionless) after the tone is heard.

Damage to the amygdala interferes with fear conditioning, regardless of how it is measured. People with temporal-lobe damage that includes the amygdala are impaired at fear conditioning, and imaging studies show activation of the amygdala during fear conditioning (see, for example, LaBar and colleagues, 1998). How does the amygdala "know" that a stimulus is dangerous? LeDoux proposes two possibilities. Both implicate neural networks, one genetically evolved and one shaped by learning.

Figure 20.8 ▼

Processing an Emotional Stimulus Information about an emotion-laden stimulus travels from the sensory thalamus to the amygdala and cortex. The cortex feeds back to the amygdala, where several projections initiate stress-hormone release, activate the autonomic nervous system, evoke emotion and suppress pain, and stimulate arousal. The hippocampus provides information related to context. (Information from LeDoux, 2000.)

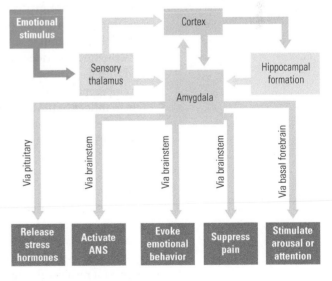

Genetically based neural networks in the amygdala evolve with the animal (for example, fearing the scent or appearance of a predator). Rats born in the laboratory show fear responses to the sound of owls or the scent of predators even though they have never encountered them. Most primates show intense fear of snakes on their first encounter, which suggests that a "snake detector" has evolved to sensitize us to stimuli associated with danger. John Downer's split-brain monkey with one amygdala removed (see Figure 17.1) had no fear of a snake from the side of brain lacking the amygdala but showed intense fear from the intact side.

Similarly, neurons in the amygdalae of primates evolved a sensitivity to negative facial expressions of others. This evolution makes sense because presumably a cue to the presence of a threatening stimulus is the behavior of one's social group toward the stimulus.

Neural networks based in the amygdala likely also learn from experience about dangerous stimuli for which evolution could not prepare us. We may have learned, for instance, that a person wearing a certain type of insignia (such as one characteristic of a violent gang) is typically dangerous, whereas a person wearing another insignia (such as a police badge) is typically not dangerous.

LeDoux proposes that these circuits in the amygdala interact with cortical circuits to influence affective behavior. For example, if the amygdala functions to identify stimuli that signal danger, then the amygdala can act through the brainstem-activating systems to arouse the cortex and essentially to regulate cortical attention (awareness) to specific stimuli.

An important aspect of fear is context: a particular stimulus can be dangerous in one setting but not in another, and this distinction is clearly important to our behavior. A highly poisonous snake is extremely dangerous when suddenly encountered on a pathway but presents no danger behind a glass wall in a zoo. Furthermore, environmental contexts may acquire emotional properties through prior experiences (classical conditioning). If poisonous snakes are repeatedly encountered on a particular path in the woods, then the path itself becomes threatening.

Although the evidence is incomplete regarding exactly how context is associated with fear, the evidence is clear that hippocampal damage interferes with the development of contextual fear associations. How hippocampal activity typically acts to influence the association of context and fear remains to be understood.

How can the amygdala influence our thoughts about emotion-laden stimuli? People have all sorts of fears and worries that can interfere with everyday life, and for some people, these fears become debilitating. People suffer from panic disorders, posttraumatic stress disorder, obsessive–compulsive disorders, anxiety disorders, and phobias. The extreme power of fear-related events to affect cognition suggests that evolution has crafted a powerful mechanism for forming such associations.

It is important in this context to recall that frontal-lobe patients show little anxiety or fear-related behavior. The orbital and medial prefrontal regions have significant reciprocal connections with the amygdala, suggesting that amygdalo-prefrontal circuits play a significant role in the formation of thoughts about fearful stimuli. The prefrontal cortex is possibly somehow modified in people with pathological fears and anxieties, making it difficult for them to extinguish learned fears or to suppress fears of evolutionarily significant events.

Finally, we must point out that cognitive–emotional interactions are not just related to negative stimuli. Neurons in the amygdala of monkeys respond to a range of facial expressions, and electrical stimulation of the amygdala is highly rewarding (for an extensive review, see Rolls, 2014).

Cognitive Asymmetry and Emotion

We have seen in both Damasio's and LeDoux's theories that emotion entails cognitive appraisals. Because significant asymmetries exist in a variety of cognitive functions, it follows that related emotional systems also must be lateralized. This idea can be traced back at least to the 1930s, when clinicians reported detailed observations of patients with large unilateral lesions, noting an apparent asymmetry in the effects of left- and right-hemisphere lesions on emotional behavior. Through the decades in neuropsychology, many versions of asymmetry theories of emotional control have been compiled. The reader is directed to the reviews by Gainotti (2000) and by Tucker and colleagues (2000) for details.

The best-known early descriptions, contemporary with J.P.'s case presented in the chapter-opening Portrait, are those of Kurt Goldstein (1939), who suggested that left-hemisphere lesions produce "catastrophic" reactions characterized by fearfulness and depression, whereas right-hemisphere lesions produce "indifference." The results of the first systematic study of these contrasting behavioral effects, by Gainotti in 1969, showed that catastrophic reactions were found in 62 percent of his left-hemisphere sample compared with only 10 percent of his right-hemisphere cases. In contrast, indifference was common in the right-hemisphere patients, found in 38 percent compared with only 11 percent of the left-hemisphere cases.

Significantly, however, Gainotti reported that catastrophic reactions were associated with aphasia and that indifference reactions were associated with contralateral neglect. A key point to remember in regard to Goldstein's and Gainotti's observations is that if the left hemisphere is damaged extensively, then the behavior that we observe is in large part a function of what the right hemisphere can do. Thus, if we observe a catastrophic reaction after a left-hemisphere injury, one conclusion is that this behavior is coming from the right hemisphere. This conclusion leads directly to the idea that the right hemisphere normally plays a major role in producing strong emotions, especially emotions regarded as negative, such as fear and anger.

Gainotti concludes that the two sides of the brain play complementary roles in emotional behavior, the right hemisphere being more engaged in the automatic components of emotion and the left hemisphere in the overall cognitive control of emotion. The left hemisphere is presumed to have this general control because of language.

This idea is similar to one proposed by Gazzaniga (1994), who suggests that a general control function of the speaking hemisphere characterizes the differences in thinking between humans and other animals. He calls the speaking hemisphere the "interpreter." An experiment using split-brain patients illustrates Gazzaniga's meaning. Each hemisphere is shown the same two pictures, such as a picture of a match followed by a picture of a piece of wood. A series of other pictures is then shown, and the task is to pick out a third picture that has an inferred relation with the other two. In our example, the pertinent third picture might be a bonfire.

The right hemisphere is incapable of making the inference that a match struck and held to a piece of wood could start a bonfire, whereas the left hemisphere can easily arrive at this interpretation. Evidently, the speaking left hemisphere can make logical inferences about sensory events that the non-speaking right hemisphere cannot make. Gainotti applies this general idea to emotion and concludes that the right hemisphere generates emotional feelings, whereas the left hemisphere interprets these feelings, presumably through its language abilities, and produces a conceptual (cognitive) level of emotional processing (affective behavior).

◎ 20.5 Asymmetry in Emotional Processing

Emotional and cognitive behavior overlap in all three principal neuro-psychological theories of emotional behavior. We now turn our attention to studies that focus on the nature of this overlap. Since the 1990s, interest has shifted toward the Damasio and LeDoux theories, which focus on site within the cerebral hemispheres. But in the 1970s and 1980s, there was considerable interest in cerebral asymmetry, the possibility that the two hemispheres play complementary roles in controlling emotional behavior. We briefly consider the asymmetry literature, providing examples of research on producing and interpreting emotional behavior as well as on changes in personality associated with temporal-lobe lesions. These latter changes segue into the social brain.

Producing Emotional Behavior

Mood is inferred largely from affect—facial expression, tone of voice, and frequency of talking—and so it is sensible to measure these behaviors first in analyzing emotional behavior in brain-damaged people. **Table 20.1** summarizes a range of experimental measures of emotional behavior. The general picture

Table 20.1 **Production of emotional behavior in neurological patients**

Behavior	Characteristics	Basic Reference
Clinical behavior of patients with natural lesions	Catastrophic reactions from left-hemisphere lesions; indifference from right-hemisphere lesions	Gainotti, 1969; Goldstein, 1939
Facial expression	Reduced by frontal lesions	Kolb and Milner, 1981
	Reduced by right-hemisphere lesions	Buck and Duffy, 1980; Borod et al., 1986
	Asymmetry altered	Bruyer, 1986
Spontaneous speech	Decreased by left-frontal-lobe lesions; increased by right-frontal-lobe lesions	Kolb and Taylor, 1981
Tone, or prosody, of speech	Right-hemisphere lesions impair mimicry of emotional states	Tucker et al., 1977; Kent and Rosenbek, 1982
Temporal-lobe traits	Temporal-lobe personality	Bear and Fedio, 1977; Waxman and Geshwind, 1974; Fedio and Martin, 1983
Sodium amytal	Catastrophic reactions to left injection; indifference reactions to right injection	Terzian, 1964; Rossi and Rosandini, 1974
	No evidence of asymmetric effects	Rovetta, 1960; Kolb and Milner, 1981

is that left-hemisphere lesions, especially left-frontal-lobe lesions, produce a flattening of mood and in many people an appearance of depression, especially after strokes that produce language difficulties.

Facial expression is among the most obvious cues to emotion in humans, and overall, studies of neurological patients find a reduction in the frequency and intensity of facial expressions in people with anterior lesions relative to those with more-posterior lesions. For example, whether facial expressions are measured in terms of frequency, quantitative scoring of facial-movement elements, or subjective rating by judges, both left- and right-frontal-lobe patients show a reduction in facial expression relative to temporal-lobe groups (**Figure 20.9**A). This result is obtained whether the expressions are spontaneous or posed (e.g., Kolb and Taylor, 2000).

In contrast with the reduction in facial expression from both left- and right-frontal-lobe lesions, the effects of side of the lesion on spontaneous talking in frontal-lobe patients differ. Right-frontal-lobe lesions appear to increase talking markedly, whereas left-frontal-lobe lesions decrease it (Figure 20.9B). Without doubt, friends and relatives of frontal-lobe patients would perceive loss of facial expression and changes in talkativeness as marked changes in personality.

Spoken language carries two types of information: content and prosody. Typically, content is a function of the left hemisphere, and there is reason to suspect that tone of voice is a function of the right. For example, when Don Tucker and his colleagues (1977) asked patients to express particular affective states such as anger, happiness, and sadness as they read emotionally neutral sentences, patients with right-hemisphere lesions produced the sentences with relatively flat affect compared with patients with left-hemisphere lesions. This absence of tone in speech has been termed **aprosodia**, and it can be measured on a wideband spectrogram (see Kent and Rosenbek, 1982).

Abnormalities in tone of voice in right-hemisphere patients led Elliott Ross (1981) to propose a set of aprosodias analogous to aphasias in left-hemisphere

Figure 20.9 ▼

Emotional Expression in Neurological Patients Relative frequency of facial expressions (A) and spontaneous talking (B) during routine neuropsychological testing. (Data sources: Kolb and Milner, 1981, and Kolb and Taylor, 1981.)

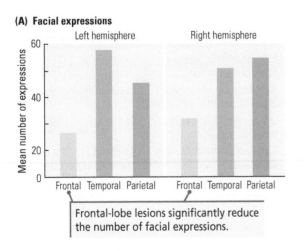

(A) Facial expressions

Frontal-lobe lesions significantly reduce the number of facial expressions.

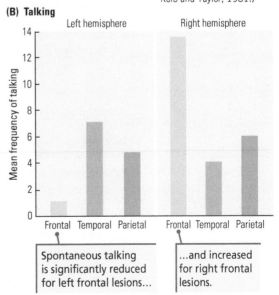

(B) Talking

Spontaneous talking is significantly reduced for left frontal lesions...

...and increased for right frontal lesions.

speech. For example, *motor aprosodia*, an inability to produce affective components of language, is proposed to result from damage to Broca's area in the right hemisphere. *Sensory aprosodia*, a deficit in interpreting the emotional components of language, is presumed to result from damage to the region in the right hemisphere analogous to Wernicke's area.

Ross and Monnot (2008, 2011) used the Aprosodia Battery to assess stroke patients and found that although both left- and right-hemisphere lesions affect prosody, different patterns of deficits follow left- and right-side brain damage. They concluded that affective prosody is a dominant and lateralized function of the right hemisphere. They also found a decline in accuracy of prosody processing in aging, which they took as evidence for a general decline of right-hemisphere cognitive functions in aging.

Interpreting Emotional Behavior

Emotional behavior might appear atypical not only because a person is unable to produce the appropriate behavior (an expression, say), but also because he or she misinterprets the social or emotional signals coming from others. The importance of *interpretation symptoms* in understanding personality change after injury has led to the development of a variety of clinical tests of emotional perception, which are summarized by Joan Borod and her colleagues (2000). As summarized in **Table 20.2**, right-hemisphere lesions produce deficits in a range of measures, especially including comprehending humor, as well as judging mood, both in tone of voice and facial expression.

The ability to be humorous and to comprehend humor is one of humankind's most intriguing behaviors. It certainly contributes to personality and is a basic ingredient in social life. In a study looking at humor in patients with focal injuries in various brain areas, those with right-frontal injuries were the most affected in that they reacted less than other patients, with diminished

Table 20.2 **Interpretation of emotional behavior in neurological patients**

Experiment	Characteristics	Basic Reference
Judgment of mood in others	Right-hemisphere lesions impair comprehension.	Heilman et al., 1993
	Right-temporal-lobe lesions impair perception of intonation.	Tompkins and Mateer, 1985
Judgment of propositional affect	Left-hemisphere lesions impair comprehension.	Kolb and Taylor, 1981
Comprehension of verbal humor	Right-hemisphere lesions alter appreciation.	Gardner et al., 1975; Shammi and Stuss, 1999
Matching emotional expressions	Right-hemisphere lesions impair performance.	DeKosky et al., 1980; Kolb and Taylor, 1981;
	Left-hemisphere lesions impair performance.	Bowers et al., 1987; Young et al., 1993
Judgment of emotional expressions	Bilateral amygdala lesions impair perception of negative expressions.	Adolphs et al., 1999

laughter and smiling, and failed to grasp the punch lines of jokes (Shammi and Stuss, 1999).

We should note here that not only do right-frontal-lobe patients fail to comprehend humor, in our experience, their efforts at humor exhibit a perverse aspect. For example, we had one patient who liked to introduce himself as "Campbell, with a p, like in swimming."

Like humor, facial expression is a kind of social glue that bonds humans together: a lot of information passes between and among us simply through the nuances of facial expression. Patients with lesions of the right temporal or right frontal lobe or both have difficulty recognizing facial expressions. To illustrate: participants were asked to choose the appropriate facial expression for each of a set of cartoons in which one face was blank, as illustrated by social situations 1 and 2 in **Figure 20.10** (Kolb and Taylor, 2000). As summarized in **Figure 20.11**A, both frontal- and temporal-lobe patients were impaired at this test, but curiously, there was no asymmetry: lesions of either hemisphere were equally effective in disrupting performance, regardless of the appropriate emotion (Kolb and Taylor, 2000).

One explanation is that although the right hemisphere may be dominant for processing faces and facial expressions, the left hemisphere may play a role in understanding context. We noted earlier that Gazzaniga's studies of split-brain patients led him to conclude that the left hemisphere acts as an "interpreter" of behavior. This function may also be true of social situations.

Are different facial expressions (frightened or happy, for example) analyzed by different cerebral regions? Recall, for example, that the amygdala is believed to perceive fear selectively, and the results of studies by Ralph Adolphs and his colleagues (1999) show that patients with bilateral amygdala lesions are impaired at recognizing negative expressions (such as fear) but not at recognizing happy faces. In a similar study, Bryan Kolb and Laughlin Taylor (1981) showed that patients with unilateral frontal-lobe lesions were severely impaired at matching negative but not positive faces to the appropriate Ekman face (see Figure 20.3). Patients with right, but not left, temporal or parietal lesions showed a similar pattern of deficits, as illustrated in Figure 20.11B.

Thus, facial expressions appear not to be a single stimulus category; rather, different expressions may be processed separately in the brain. An fMRI study addressed this idea by comparing the cerebral activation for fear and disgust (Phillips et al., 1997). Given that expressions of disgust are typically related to bad-tasting food, the researchers predicted that perceiving expressions of

Figure 20.10 ▼

Testing Social Cognition
Examples of cartoon situations in which patients were asked either to produce the appropriate expression for the blank face or to choose the appropriate expression from several choices. Figure 20.3 shows a representative range of choices. (Research from Kolb and Taylor, 2000.)

Situation 1

Situation 2

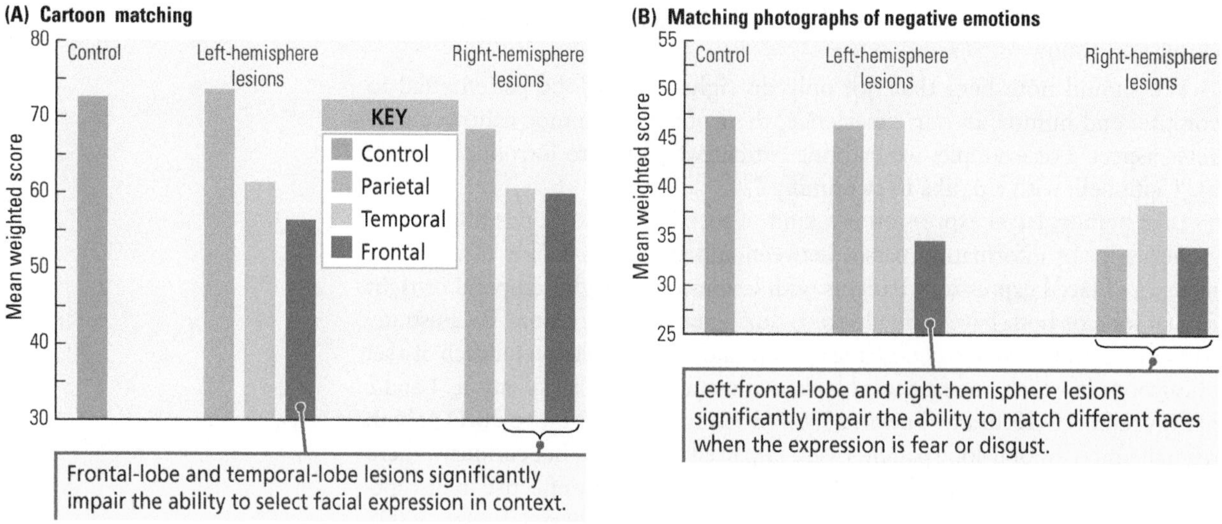

(A) Cartoon matching

Control Left-hemisphere lesions Right-hemisphere lesions

Mean weighted score

KEY
- Control
- Parietal
- Temporal
- Frontal

Frontal-lobe and temporal-lobe lesions significantly impair the ability to select facial expression in context.

(B) Matching photographs of negative emotions

Control Left-hemisphere lesions Right-hemisphere lesions

Mean weighted score

Left-frontal-lobe and right-hemisphere lesions significantly impair the ability to match different faces when the expression is fear or disgust.

Figure 20.11 ▲

Matching Facial Expressions (A) Performance of controls and surgical-excision patients on a test of matching facial expressions to cartoon situations such as those shown in Figure 20.11. (B) Performance of the same groups tested on matching photographs of negative emotions to the appropriate Ekman face (see Figure 20.3). Lesions throughout the right hemisphere disturb this ability. (Data source: Kolb and Taylor, 2000.)

disgust might include the gustatory cortex, located in the insula within the temporal lobe. That is exactly what they found: fearful expressions activate the amygdala, whereas disgust expressions activate the insula.

Temporal-Lobe Personality

The general clinical impression is that temporal-lobe patients exhibit a clear personality change. For example, epilepsy patients and their friends were asked to complete rating scales of behaviors such as "anger," "sadness," or religiosity, and the patients were found to display a distinctive set of traits (Bear and Fedio, 1977), summarized in **Table 20.3**, sometimes referred to as temporal-lobe personality (see also Section 15.3).

The epileptic patients self-reported a distinctive profile of humorless sobriety, dependence, and obsession. Raters differentiated the temporal-lobe patients on the basis of nearly every trait in Table 20.3 but rated them most strongly on the traits described as "viscosity," "hypermoralism," and "anger."

Table 20.3 **Behaviors attributed to temporal-lobe epileptics**

Altered sexual interest	Loss of libido and hyposexualism or hypersexual episodes, exhibitionism, fetishism, transvestism
Anger and aggression	Heightened temper, irritability, and overt hostility: rape and other violent crimes, including murder
Emotionality	Deepened emotion; sustained, intense bipolar disorder and exhilarated mood
Guilt	Self-scrutiny and self-recrimination
Hypermoralism	Scrupulous attention to rules without distinguishing significant from minor infractions
Obsessiveness	Ritualism; orderliness; compulsive attention to detail
Humorlessness, sobriety	Overgeneralized, overbearing concern; humor lacking or idiosyncratic
Hypergraphia	Extensive diary keeping, detailed note taking; writing poetry, autobiography, or novel
Paranoia	Suspicious, overinterpreting motives and events; paranoid schizophrenia diagnosis
Religiosity	Deep religious beliefs; often idiosyncratic multiple conversions or mystical states
Sadness	Discouraged, fearful, self-depreciating; depression diagnosis; suicide attempt
Viscosity	"Stickiness"; tendency to repetition

Source: Data, in part, from Bear and Fedio, 1977.

Furthermore, right- and left-temporal-lobe patients could be distinguished: the right-temporal-lobe patients were described as more obsessional, and the left-temporal-lobe patients as more concerned with "personal destiny."

◉ 20.6 The Social Brain and Social Cognition

Traditionally, studying the social brain was limited to examining the effects of brain injuries on both human patients and laboratory animals. With the increasing sophistication of noninvasive imaging over the past two decades, social and cognitive psychologists now observe brain activation while participants engage in social cognitive tasks, as exemplified in the Snapshot in Section 20.4. The interdisciplinary field of **social neuroscience** seeks to understand how the brain mediates social interactions.

Although advances in imaging technology tempt us to think that major insights into the social brain no longer require lesion studies, Justin Feinstein (2013) makes the compelling case that lesion studies do not always support conclusions drawn from noninvasive imaging. We need to combine both types of analyses. Thus we begin here by reviewing the effects of frontal lesions in monkeys and frontal and temporal lesions in humans before exploring social neural networks, our awareness of "self," and using our cognitive capacity to control emotion.

Frontal Lesions in Monkeys

Spouses or relatives often complain of personality changes in brain-damaged patients, but the parameters of these changes have been poorly specified in humans. Even descriptions of behavioral changes in people such as Phineas Gage (see Figure 16.16) are typically general and subjective and seldom reported objectively. Results of research on animals, particularly nonhuman primates, however, make possible the identification of six behavioral changes associated with emotional processes after frontal lesions.

1. **Reduced social interaction.** Especially after orbitofrontal and anterior cingulate lesions, monkeys become socially withdrawn and even fail to reestablish close relations with family members. The animals sit alone; seldom if ever engage in social grooming or contact with other monkeys; and in a free-ranging natural environment, become solitaries, leaving the troop altogether.

2. **Loss of social dominance.** As reported in Section16.3, after orbitofrontal lesions, monkeys that were formerly dominant in a group fail to maintain their dominance, although the fall from power may take weeks to complete, depending on the aggressiveness of other monkeys in the group.

3. **Inappropriate social interaction.** Monkeys with orbitofrontal lesions fail to exhibit the appropriate gestures of submission to dominant animals and may approach any other animal without hesitation, irrespective of that animal's social dominance. This behavior often results in retaliatory aggression from the dominant, intact animals. Similarly, when approached by dominant animals, monkeys with frontal lesions may simply ignore

them or run away rather than performing typical submissive gestures, such as allowing mounting.

4. **Altered social preference.** When a healthy monkey is released into a large enclosure that has conspecifics behind a glass barrier, it will generally sit against the glass next to an animal sitting on the opposite side. Although healthy animals prefer to sit beside intact monkeys of the opposite sex, monkeys with large frontal lesions prefer to sit with other frontal-lesion monkeys of the same sex, presumably because they are less threatening.

5. **Reduced affect.** Monkeys with frontal lesions largely abandon facial expressions, posturings, and gesturings in social situations. (Lesions of the cingulate or visual association cortex seem to have no effect.) Thus, monkeys with frontal lesions show a drastic drop in the frequency and variability of facial expressions and are described as "poker faced." This is not a simple loss of facial muscle control, because the animals do produce expressions, but not often.

6. **Reduced vocalization.** Lesions of the frontal cortex reduce spontaneous social vocalizations. Indeed, after anterior cingulate lesions, rhesus monkeys effectively make no typical vocalizations at all.

In general then, lesions of the monkey OFC produce marked changes in social behavior. In particular, lesion monkeys become less socially responsive and fail to produce or respond to species-typical stimuli. Damage to the paralimbic cortex produces milder effects, the animals showing reduced social interaction. An important point is that despite the significant changes in the sensory processing abilities of animals with visual association lesions, very few obvious changes in their affective behavior are observed.

The changes in emotional processes in monkeys with frontal lesions are especially intriguing because they suggest that similar changes might be found in humans with frontal-lobe injuries. In particular, because monkeys fail to make appropriate vocal and gestural behaviors and fail to respond typically to those made by conspecifics, we can predict that humans with frontal-lobe injuries or abnormalities, such as those J.P. endured, will show similar changes in social behavior. Furthermore, disorders characterized by significant changes in social interactions, such as schizophrenia, also might result from frontal dysfunction.

Cerebral Lesions in Humans

Frontal and temporal lesions in humans result in deficits in producing facial expressions and social speech, impair the perception of facial expressions and emotions relative to specific social contexts, and change personality (Table 20.3). Lesions to the insula not only increase pain threshold but also impair the ability to recognize pain in someone else. This finding is consistent with imaging studies showing increased activity in the insula during tasks assessing empathy for pain (Gu et al., 2012). Amygdala lesions impair the recognition of fear in others.

A long history of case studies shows that bilateral damage to the ventromedial prefrontal region produces grave impairments of social conduct, decision making, and emotion processing (for a review, see Damasio et al., 2012). Such patients are also described as having poor judgment regarding their personal and occupational affairs and making poor decisions in laboratory tasks designed to measure complex decision making. Most case studies have focused primarily on patients with bilateral lesions, largely because such patients usually have ruptured aneurysms in the anterior cerebral or anterior communicating arteries, which lead to bilateral lesions, or from surgical treatment of midline tumors, which also lead to bilateral injury.

Dan Tranel and his colleagues (2002, 2007) reported on a patient sample with unilateral ventromedial frontal lesions on either the left or right side. They found a profound asymmetry: patients with right-side lesions showed the profound disturbances described earlier, leading the investigators to describe them as meeting the criteria for "acquired sociopathy." (Patients with large right frontal lesions, as reported in Section 16.3, can be described as pseudopsychopathic.) In contrast, the patients with left-side lesions displayed typical social and interpersonal behavior, stable employment, and more-or-less unchanged personalities and decision-making ability. Tranel and coworkers conclude, insofar as social, decision-making, and emotional functions are concerned, that the right-side component of the ventromedial prefrontal system may be critical and the left-side component less important.

Finally, isolated case histories suggest social changes related to lesions in the temporal–parietal junction (TPJ) and anterior cingulate cortex.

Social Neural Networks

To identify brain regions implicated in social behavior, Daniel Kennedy and Ralph Adolphs (2012) reviewed lesion studies of brain-injured patients and fMRI activation in healthy participants. **Figure 20.12**A lists individual cerebral

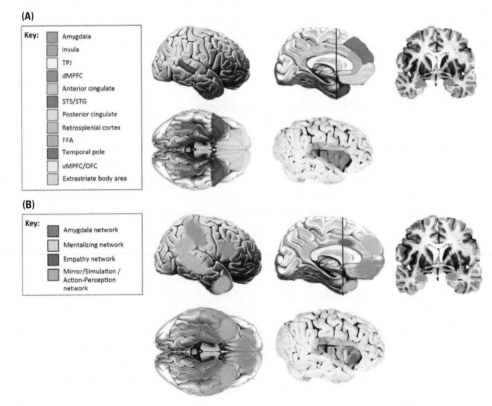

(A)

Key:
- Amygdala
- Insula
- TPJ
- dMPFC
- Anterior cingulate
- STS/STG
- Posterior cingulate
- Retrosplenial cortex
- FFA
- Temporal pole
- vMPFC/OFC
- Extrastriate body area

(B)

Key:
- Amygdala network
- Mentalizing network
- Empathy network
- Mirror/Simulation / Action-Perception network

Figure 20.12 ◄

The Social Brain: From Structures to Networks (A) Structures believed to be involved in social cognition based on studies of brain-injured patients and fMRI activation in healthy participants. TPJ, temporoparietal junction; dMPFC, dorsomedial prefrontal cortex; STS/STG, superior temporal sulcus/gyrus; FFA, fusiform face area; vMPFC/OFC, ventromedial prefrontal cortex/orbitofrontal cortex. (B) Proposed social networks. (Kennedy, D. P., and R. Adolphs. The social brain in psychiatric and neurological disorders. *Trends in Cognitive Sciences* 16:559–572, 2012, Figure 1, page 561. © Elsevier.)

structures implicated in social behavior, and Figure 20.12B demarks four social-related brain networks that tie these regions together:

1. **Amygdala network.** Including the orbitofrontal cortex and temporal cortex as well as the amygdala, this network's functions range from triggering emotional responses to detecting socially relevant stimuli.

2. **Mentalizing network.** This collection of structures related to thinking about the internal states of others includes the superior temporal sulcus and anterior temporal cortex, providing a mechanism for understanding others' actions.

3. **Empathy network.** Structures recruited when individuals empathize with others include the insula and cingulate cortex. The empathy network can attribute intentions to others, something we humans do automatically. Indeed, humans seem compelled to attribute intentions and other psychological motives even to nonhumans and abstract animations. Fulvia Castelli and colleagues (2000) showed participants animations of "interacting" triangles (one triangle mocking another, and so on) versus animations characterized as random. fMRI images showed that the attribution state primed by the triangle animation increased activation in participants' medial prefrontal regions, their basal temporal regions (fusiform gyrus and temporal poles adjacent to the amygdala), and their STS and occipital areas.

4. **Mirror/stimulation/action–perception network.** Activated when observing the actions of others, this network includes the mirror neuron systems of the parietal and premotor cortex (detailed in Figure 9.12B) and is also thought to be involved in developing our concept of self, discussed next.

We have described only the cortical components of these social networks, but most likely they also recruit subcortical regions such as the nucleus accumbens, globus pallidus, hypothalamus, and ventral tegmentum (see review by Berridge and Kringelbach, 2013).

The Self and Social Cognition

We humans are aware not only of the actions and intentions of others but also of our own: we are self-aware. Two distinct neural networks in frontal-lobe structures appear to be critical for generating the "self": (1) a right frontoparietal network that overlaps the mirror/stimulation/action–perception network, and (2) a cortical midline network.

Humans and apes have a unique ability to recognize themselves—the *self-face*—in a mirror. The right hemisphere of a split-brain patient can recognize the self-face, and the physiological reaction to the self-face is greater for the right than the left hemisphere. Both imaging and patient data provide evidence that a right frontoparietal network controls recognition of the self-face.

Lucina Uddin and her colleagues (2007, 2011) showed, for example, that self-face recognition activates right frontal and parietal regions, as illustrated in **Figure 20.13**. The activated regions overlap with regions that contain mirror neurons, and the activated neurons have been proposed to provide a link between self-perception and associated mental states of the self and of understanding others' intentions. Uddin and colleagues proposed that the right frontoparietal mirror-neuron areas act as bridges between self and other, by co-opting a system for recognizing the actions of others to allow for recognition of the actions of self. Self-recognition not only involves faces: in a parallel study with voices, Uddin's group (Kaplan et al., 2008) showed that listening to one's own voice also increases activity in the right inferior frontal gyrus. They conclude that the inferior right frontal region may contribute to a multimodal, abstract self-representation.

Actions of the self are only part of what we would call self-awareness. A more abstract mental self also exists. Matthew Lieberman (2007) proposed that the processes that focus on one's own (or another's) mental states rely on medial frontal regions. In one study, Jason Mitchell and colleagues (2005) asked participants to perform one of two types of semantic judgment: "Does this description refer to a potential psychological state of the target [a person or a dog]?" or "Does this description refer to a physical part of the target?" fMRI shows that activation increased selectively in the medial frontal region in the psychological state condition regardless of whether the target was a person or dog. This medial frontal system, it is proposed, acts to monitor psychological states in others as well as in the self.

Because the frontoparietal mirror neuron network and the medial frontal network seem to be involved in self–other representations, they likely interact to maintain self–other representations across multiple neural domains. The nature of this interaction and the details of how the self develops and changes likely will arouse considerable research interest over the coming decade.

Cognitive Control of Emotion

Humans have amazing emotional range, and we also have the cognitive capacity to control our emotions. For example, we may have expectations about how a stimulus might feel (e.g., a syringe injection of penicillin), and our expectations can alter the actual feeling when we experience the event. Nobukatsu Sawamoto and colleagues (2000) found that nonpainful stimuli are perceived as painful when participants expect pain and that this response is correlated with activation of the cingulate cortex, a region associated with pain perception.

The use of cognitive processes to change an existing emotional response has also been studied using noninvasive imaging. Kevin Ochsner and James Gross (2005) reviewed such studies and concluded that when participants reappraise self-emotions there is concurrent activation of the prefrontal and cingulate cortex. In one study these researchers showed participants aversive photos and instructed them to think about the personal relevance of each image as it appeared.

In one condition the participants were asked to increase both their negative affect and their sense of subjective closeness to pictured events—to imagine themselves or a loved one as the central figure in a photo. In a second condition they were to decrease their negative affect by increasing their sense of objective distance, viewing pictured events from a detached, third-person perspective. The investigators observed that both up- and down-regulating negative emotion recruits prefrontal and anterior cingulate regions.

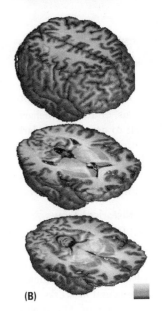

(A)

(B)

Figure 20.13 ▲

The Neural Basis of Self-Recognition Humans are capable of self-recognition in a mirror or photograph. Brain activity during the presentation of self-faces or similar or different face morphs (A) provides a way to investigate selective brain activation for self-face. Self-faces typically activate the right frontoparietal network, as shown in (B). Repetitive transcranial magnetic stimulation (rTMS) of those regions interferes with self-recognition. (From L. Q. Uddin et al. The self and social cognition: the role of cortical midline structures and mirror neurons. *Trends in Cognitive Sciences* 11(4):153–157, 2007. © Elsevier.)

In summary, social neuroscience is radically changing our understanding of how the brain participates in humans' complex social behavior. Historical lesion studies tended to focus on the perception and production of social behavior, but the contemporary perspective is allowing insights into the very nature of how the brain allows humans to think about themselves and about one another.

SUMMARY

20.1 The Nature of Emotion

Emotions, or affective behaviors, are easily recognized but difficult to quantify. Similarly, it is easy to identify brain structures in which injury can disrupt emotional behavior but difficult to determine what roles different structures play in emotional behavior, which entails cognitive processes that may either be conscious or lie outside our awareness.

20.2 Historical Views

Darwin first drew attention to the biology of emotion, but not until the late 1920s did physiologists begin to look for its neural and endocrine correlates. They emphasized the role of thalamic and hypothalamic structures. Papez expanded the putative neural networks to include forebrain structures of the limbic system. The important role of the cerebral cortex in emotion emerged only in the past 40 years.

20.3 Candidate Structures in Emotional Behavior

Multiple neural systems control different aspects of emotional behavior. The key candidate structures include the frontal lobes, primarily the inferior frontal cortex; the amygdala and associated paralimbic cortex; and the hypothalamus. To the extent that changes in behavioral functions such as perception, movement, memory, and language affect our emotional behavior, we can see that the vast cortical regions taking part in cognitive processing also take part in producing emotion.

20.4 Neuropsychological Theories of Emotion

A theme that runs through all major theories of emotion, especially Damasio's somatic marker hypothesis, LeDoux's cognitive–social interaction theory, and Gainotti's asymmetry theory, is that emotion and cognition are intimately related and are likely controlled by overlapping neural systems.

20.5 Asymmetry in Emotional Processing

Studies of changes in emotional behavior after cerebral injury focus largely on changes in producing and perceiving emotions. Overall, lesions of the left and right hemispheres have different effects on emotional behaviors, and damage to the right hemisphere appears to produce larger effects. This asymmetry should not overshadow the importance of cortical site in understanding emotional behavior. Both the frontal lobes and the amygdala play special roles in emotional control, especially on behaviors related to producing and interpreting facial expression. The left amygdala appears to play a special role in generating one particular emotion: fear.

20.6 The Social Brain and Social Cognition

Studies of frontal and other cerebral injuries in monkeys and in humans identify a wide range of social behavioral changes and often, personality changes. Humans display an asymmetry in the effects, with the right-side injuries, especially frontal lobe injuries, producing much larger behavioral changes than left-hemisphere damage.

Social neuroscientists have identified cerebral networks implicated in social behavior, including an amygdala network, mentalizing network, empathy network, and mirror/stimulation/action–perception network. Preliminary work points to a fundamental role for the prefrontal and anterior cingulate regions in processes related to our sense of self and how beliefs and expectations affect emotional processing.

References

Ackerly, S. S. A case of paranatal bilateral frontal lobe defect observed for thirty years. In J. M. Warren and K. Akert, Eds., *The Frontal Granular Cortex and Behavior*, pp. 192–218. New York: McGraw-Hill, 1964.

Adolphs, R., D. Tranel, S. Hamann, A. W. Young, A. J. Calder, E. A. Phelps, A. Anderson, G. P. Lee, and A. R. Damasio. Recognition of emotional expression in nine individuals with bilateral amygdala damage. *Neuropsychologia* 37:1111–1117, 1999.

Anderson, D. J., and R. Adolphs. A framework for studying emotions across species. *Cell* 157:187–200, 2014.

Bear, D. M., and P. Fedio. Quantitative analysis of interictal behavior in temporal lobe epilepsy. *Archives of Neurology* 34:454–467, 1977.

Berridge, K. C., and M. L. Kringelbach. Neuroscience of affect: Brain mechanisms of pleasure and displeasure. *Current Opinion in Neurobiology* 23:294–303, 2013.

Borod, J. C., E. Koff, M. Perlman Lorch, and M. Nicholas. The expression and perception of facial emotion in brain-damaged patients. *Neuropsychologia* 24:169–180, 1986.

Borod, J. C., M. H. Tabert, C. Santschi, and E. H. Strauss. Neuropsychological assessment of emotional processing in brain-damaged patients. In J. C. Borod, Ed., *The Neuropsychology of Emotion*, pp. 80–105. New York: Oxford University Press, 2000.

Bowers, D., H. B. Coslett, R. M. Bauer, L. J. Speedie, and K. M. Heilman. Comprehension of emotional prosody following unilateral hemispheric lesions: Processing defect versus distraction defect. *Neuropsychologia* 25:317–328, 1987.

Brown, S., and E. A. Schaefer. An investigation into the functions of the occipital and temporal lobe of the monkey's brain. *Philosophical Transactions of the Royal Society Series B* 179:303–327, 1888.

Bruyer, R. *The Neuropsychology of Face Perception and Facial Expression*. Hillsdale, N.J.: Lawrence Erlbaum, 1986.

Buck, R., and R. J. Duffy. Nonverbal communication of affect in brain-damaged patients. *Cortex* 16:351–362, 1980.

Castelli, F., F. Happe, U. Frith, and C. Frith. Movement and mind: A functional imaging study of perception and interpretation of complex intentional movement. *NeuroImage* 12:314–325, 2000.

Coricelli, G., R. J. Dolan, and A. Sirigu. Brain, emotion and decision making: The paradigmatic example of regret. *Trends in Cognitive Science* 11:258–265, 2007.

Damasio, A. R. The somatic marker hypothesis and the possible functions of the prefrontal cortex. *Philosophical Transactions of the Royal Society of London B Biological Sciences* 351:1413–1420, 1996.

Damasio, A. R. A second chance for emotion. In R. D. Lane and L. Nadel, Eds., *Cognitive Neuroscience of Emotion*, pp. 12–23. New York: Oxford University Press, 2000.

Damasio, A. R., S. W. Anderson, and D. Tranel. The frontal lobes. In K. Heilman and E. Valenstein, Eds., *Clinical Neuropsychology*, 5th ed., pp. 417–465. New York: Oxford University Press, 2011.

DeKosky, S. T., K. M. Heilman, D. Bowers, and E. Valenstein. Recognition and discrimination of emotional faces and pictures. *Brain and Language* 9:206–214, 1980.

Ekman, P., and W. V. Friesen. *Unmasking the Face*. Palo Alto, Calif.: Consulting Psychology Press, 1984.

Fedio, P., and A. Martin. Ideative–emotive behavioral characteristics of patients following left or right temporal lobectomy. *Epilepsia* 254:S117–S130, 1983.

Feinstein, J. S. Lesion studies of human emotion and feeling. *Current Opinion in Neurobiology* 23:304–309, 2013.

Gainotti, G. Reactions "catastrophiques" et manifestations d'indifference au cours des atteintes cerebrales. *Neuropsychologia* 7:195–204, 1969.

Gainotti, G. Neuropsychological theories of emotion. In J. C. Borod, Ed., *The Neuropsychology of Emotion*, pp. 214–236. New York: Oxford University Press, 2000.

Gardner, H., P. K. Ling, L. Flamm, and J. Silverman. Comprehension and appreciation of humorous material following brain damage. *Brain* 98:399–412, 1975.

Gazzaniga, M. *Nature's Mind*. New York: Basic Books, 1994.

Gazzaniga, M., and J. E. LeDoux. *The Integrated Mind*. New York: Plenum, 1978.

Goldstein, K. *The Organism: A Holistic Approach to Biology, Derived from Pathological Data in Man*. New York: American Books, 1939.

Gu X., Z. Gao, X. Wang, X. Liu, R. T. Knight, P. R. Hof, and J. Fan. Anterior insular cortex is necessary for empathetic pain perception. *Brain* 135:2726–2735, 2012.

Heilman, K. M., D. Bowers, and E. Valenstein. Emotional disorders associated with neurological diseases. In K. M. Heilman and E. Valenstein, Eds., *Clinical Neuropsychology*, 3rd ed. New York: Oxford University Press, 1993.

Kaplan, J. T., L. Aziz-Zadeh, L. Q. Uddin, and M. Iacoboni. The self across the senses: An fMRI study of self-face and self-voice recognition. *SCAN* 3:218–223, 2008.

Kennedy, D. P., and R. Adolphs. The social brain in psychiatric and neurological disorders. *Trends in Cognitive Sciences* 16:559–572, 2012.

Kent, R. D., and J. C. Rosenbek. Prosodic disturbance and neurological lesion. *Brain and Language* 15:259–291, 1982.

Klüver, H., and P. C. Bucy. Preliminary analysis of the temporal lobes in monkeys. *Archives of Neurology and Psychiatry* 42:979–1000, 1939.

Kolb, B., and B. Milner. Observations on spontaneous facial expression after focal cerebral excisions and after intracarotid injection of sodium amytal. *Neuropsychologia* 19:505–514, 1981.

Kolb, B., and L. Taylor. Affective behavior in patients with localized cortical excisions: Role of lesion site and side. *Science* 214:89–91, 1981.

Kolb, B., and L. Taylor. Facial expression, emotion, and hemispheric organization. In R. D. Lane and L. Nadel, Eds., *Cognitive Neuroscience of Emotion*, pp. 62–83. New York: Oxford University Press, 2000.

LaBar, K. S., J. C. Gatenby, J. C. Gore, J. E. LeDoux, and E. A. Phelps. Human amygdala activation during conditioned fear acquisition and extinction: A mixed-trial fMRI study. *Neuron* 20:937–945, 1998.

LeDoux, J. E. Cognitive–emotional interactions. In R. D. Lane and L. Nadel, Eds., *Cognitive Neuroscience of Emotion*, pp. 129–155. New York: Oxford University Press, 2000.

Leiberman, M. D. Social cognitive neuroscience: A review of core processes. *Annual Review of Psychology* 58:259–289, 2007.

Marlowe, W. B., E. L. Mancall, and J. J. Thomas. Complete Klüver–Bucy syndrome in man. *Cortex* 11:53–59, 1975.

Mitchell, J. P., R. B. Mahzarin, and C. N. Macrae. General and specific contributions of the medial prefrontal cortex to knowledge about mental states. *NeuroImage* 28:757–762, 2005.

Ochsner, K. N., and J. J. Gross. The cognitive control of emotion. *Trends in Cognitive Sciences* 9:242–249, 2005.

Papez, J. W. A proposed mechanism of emotion. *Archives of Neurology and Psychiatry* 38:725–744, 1937.

Pessoa, L., and R. Adolphs. Emotion processing and the amygdala: From a 'low road' to 'many roads' of evaluating biological significance. *Nature Reviews Neuroscience* 11:773–783, 2010.

Phillips, M. L., A. W. Young, C. Senior, M. Brammer, C. Andrews, A. J. Calder, E. T. Bullmore, D. I. Perrett, D. Rowland, S. C. R. Williams, J. A. Gray, and A. S. David. A specific neural substrate for perceiving facial expressions of disgust. *Nature* 389:495–498, 1997.

Rolls, E. T. *Emotion and Decision-Making Explained*. Oxford: Oxford University Press, 2014.

Ross, E. D. The aprosodias: Functional–anatomical organization of the affective components of language in the right hemisphere. *Archives of Neurology* 38:561–569, 1981.

Ross, E. D., and M. Monnot. Neurology of affective prosody and its functional–anatomic organization in right hemisphere. *Brain and Language* 104: 51–74, 2008.

Ross, E. D., and M. Monnot. Affective prosody: What do comprehension errors tell us about hemispheric lateralization of emotions, sex and aging effects, and the role of cognitive appraisal? *Neuropsychologica* 49:866–877, 2011.

Rossi, G. F., and G. Rosadini. Experimental analysis of cerebral dominance in man. In C. J. Millikan and F. L. Darley, Eds., *Brain Mechanisms Underlying Speech and Language*, pp.167–174. New York: Grune & Stratton, 1974.

Rovetta, P. Discussion of paper "Amytal intracaroitides per lo studio della dominanza emisferica." *Rivista di Neurologia* 30:460–470, 1960.

Sawamoto, N., M. Honda, T. Okada, T. Hanakawa, M. Kanda, H. Fukuyama, H. Konishi, and H. Shibasaki. Expectation of pain enhances responses to nonpainful somatosensory stimulation in the anterior cingulate cortex and parietal operculum/posterior insula: An event-related functional magnetic resonance imaging study. *Journal of Neuroscience* 20:7438–7445, 2000.

Scherer, C. Psychological theories of emotion. In J. C. Borod, Ed., *The Neuropsychology of Emotion*, pp. 137–162. New York: Oxford University Press, 2000.

Shammi, P., and D. T. Stuss. Humour appreciation: A role of the right frontal lobe. *Brain* 122:657–666, 1999.

Terzian, H. Behavioral and EEG effects of intracarotid sodium amytal injection. *Acta Neurochirurgica* 12:230–239, 1964.

Tompkins, C. A., and C. A. Mateer. Right hemisphere appreciation of intonational and linguistic indications of affect. *Brain and Language* 24:185–203, 1985.

Tranel, D., A. Bechara, and N. L. Denburg. Asymmetric functional roles of right and left ventromedial prefrontal cortices in social conduct, decision making, and emotional processing. *Cortex* 38:589–612, 2002.

Tranel D., J. Hathaway-Nepple, and S. W. Anderson. Impaired behavior on real-world tasks following damage to the ventromedial prefrontal cortex. *Journal of Clinical and Experimental Neuropsychology* 29:319–332, 2007.

Tucker, D. M., D. Derryberry, and P. Lau. Anatomy and physiology of human emotion: Vertical integration of brainstem, limbic, and cortical systems. In J. C. Borod, Ed., *The Neuropsychology of Emotion*, pp. 56–79. New York: Oxford University Press, 2000.

Tucker, D. M., R. T. Watson, and K. M. Heilman. Discrimination and evocation of affectively intoned speech in patients with right parietal disease. *Neurology* 27:947–950, 1977.

Uddin, L. Q., M. Iacoboni, C. Lange, and J. P. Keenan. The self and social cognition: The role of cortical midline structures and mirror neurons. *Trends in Cognitive Sciences* 11:153–157, 2007.

Uddin, L. Q. Brain connectivity and the self: The case of cerebral disconnection. *Consciousness and Cognition* 20:94–98, 2011.

Waxman, S. G., and N. Geschwind. Hypergraphia in temporal lobe epilepsy. *Neurology* 24:629–636, 1974.

Young, A. W., F. Newcombe, E. H. de Haan, M. Small, and D. C. Hay. Face perception after brain injury: Selective impairments affecting identity and expression. *Brain* 116:941–959, 1993.

21

Spatial Behavior

Whenever he left his room in the hospital, he had trouble in finding the way back, because at any chosen point of the route he did not know whether to go right, left, downstairs, or upstairs (on one occasion, he walked from the main floor down to the basement instead of going up to the first floor, where his bed was located). When he eventually arrived in front of his own room, he did not recognize it unless he chanced to see some distinguishing feature. . . .

When taken to sections of the city he knew before his illness and required to lead the way, he tried hard to find familiar landmarks, such as a signboard, the name of a street, the tramcar numbers, etc., but this information, though effectively indicating to him he was near his home, failed to provide clues for choosing the right direction. . . .

Required to provide verbal information concerning routes or places well known before the disease, he performed fairly well as long as he could rely on purely verbal knowledge. Thus, he was able to give the names of the intermediate stations on the railway line he used daily or the location of the main building of the city. Yet, he met with considerable difficulty when the way had to be retraced from spatial memory; for instance, when required to tell how he would walk between two sites chosen at random in the city, he could only say the initial street and then he became confused. . . .

He grossly mislocated cities and states on a map of his country as well as of Europe, a task with which he was familiar, since he had been a post office clerk. (Adolph Meyer's patient, summarized by de Renzi, 1982, p. 213)

The patient described in the Portrait was examined in the early 1900s and is but one of many whose spatial–perceptual impairments add insight into one of our most complex behaviors. Our bodies occupy, move through, and interact with other entities in space and time; our brains mentally rotate and manipulate spatial representations. People, as well as other animate and inanimate objects, occupy space and maintain relations in space with one another and with us.

This chapter begins with an overview of brain control of spatial behavior and then describes spatial impairments that result from brain injury. We continue by outlining how the dorsal and ventral visual streams contribute to spatial abilities and survey various experimental models used to study spatial behavior. After reviewing factors that seem to affect individual performance on spatial tests, we discuss the relationships among spatial memory, episodic memory, imagination, and future thinking.

21.1 Spatial Behavior and Spatial Impairments

Spatial behavior refers to all of the behaviors we and other animals use to guide all or parts of our bodies through space. **Topographic memory**, the ability to move through space from one place to another, derives from the idea that movements take place between or in relation to points or objects that are spatially distinct, such as the points on a map. (*Topography* refers to mapmaking.)

In their book, *The Hippocampus As a Cognitive Map*, John O'Keefe and Lynn Nadel (1978) argue that as we and other animals travel, we create brain representations of the environment in the form of **cognitive maps**. We then use these maps to guide new trips through the same environment. The idea that we use cognitive maps to navigate in space has appeal because maps offer simple representations of vast amounts of information. The map of Napoleon's 1812 military campaign in Russia shown in **Figure 21.1** vividly records the

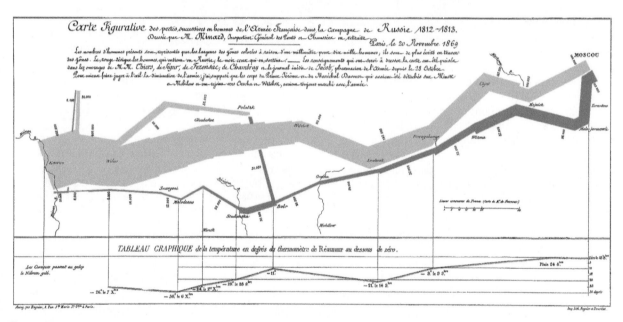

Figure 21.1 ▲

Efficient Data Storage This map, drawn by Charles Joseph Minard, may well be the best statistical graph ever drawn. Minard portrays the losses in Napoleon's army in the Russian campaign of 1812. Beginning at the left on the Polish–Russian border near the Niemen, the thick green band represents the size of French army (422,000 men) as it invaded Russia. The band's width represents the size of the army at each position.

Napoleon reached Moscow, at the right side of the map, with 100,000 men. The path of Napoleon's retreat from Moscow in the bitterly cold winter, depicted by the dark blue band, is tied to temperature and time scales. The remains of the Grande Armée struggled out of Russia with 10,000 men, little more than 2 percent of the soldiers who began the campaign. (E. J. Marey. *La Méthode Graphique*, Paris: Masson, 1885.)

Grande Armée's vast attrition on his disastrous winter trip to Moscow and back to France. To describe the losses in mere words would require substantially more space than the map occupies.

Explaining Spatial Behavior

The challenge to scientists studying spatial behavior is to discover how the brain represents various kinds and properties of space. Space breaks down into subspaces of various kinds (**Figure 21.2**). One is the body's surface—the *body space*—on which such things as clothing or contact with external objects can be localized. A variety of perceptual impairments affect the body schema, causing body disorientation and body neglect (Rousseaux et al., 2014).

Other subspaces include the *grasping space* surrounding the body and the *distal space* that the body moves through. Our grasping space is monitored by the ventral visual field and our traveling space by the dorsal visual field. Fredrico Nemmi and colleagues (2013) recorded fMRIs from participants observing a demonstrator tap a sequence on several blocks (Corsi Block Tapping Task) within grasping space or walk the same sequence on blocks in distal space. They observed differences in the pattern of brain activation, suggesting differences in the way that the brain codes grasping and distal spaces.

Space also has a time dimension of past and future, or *time space*, diagrammed in Figure 21.2. This encompasses Tulving's concept of *autonoetic awareness*, self-knowledge that allows one to bind together the awareness of oneself as a continuous entity through time. In Section 18.2 we point out the special role played by the hippocampus and orbitofrontal cortex in this time travel. Our time space expands from infancy to adulthood as we learn about the past and speculate on the future.

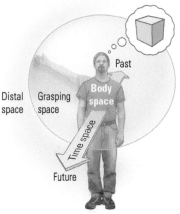

Figure 21.2 ▲

Compartments of the Body Space and Time Space

⊚ Clinical Descriptions of Spatial Impairments

Early accounts of cerebral organization describe spatial processing in humans as a special function of the right hemisphere. John Hughlings Jackson first proposed the theory that the right hemisphere might have some special perceptual function complementary to the left hemisphere's language function. In his 1874 paper titled "On the Nature of the Duality of the Brain," he predicted that a person with damage restricted to the posterior part of the right hemisphere would have a distinctive syndrome:

> The patient would have difficulty in recognizing things; he would have difficulty in relating what had occurred, not from lack of words, but from a prior inability to revive images of persons, objects and places, of which the words are symbols. . . . He could not put before himself ideal images of places one after another; could not re-see where he had been, and could not therefore tell of it in words. (Jackson, 1915, p. 14)

Subsequently, several investigators described cases of spatial–perceptual difficulties, confirming Jackson's prediction that such disorders exist. But most of the patients described appeared to have bilateral damage rather than unilateral right-hemisphere damage. Experiences with brain-injured soldiers in World War I (1914–1918) advanced the understanding of spatial disturbances, but the possibility of a special association between spatial deficits and right-hemisphere damage was largely ignored. The more systematic work of Henri Hécaen and his coworkers (1951, 1980) and Oliver Zangwill (1960) forced a reexamination of the right hemisphere's role in spatial performance. The following descriptions of topographical impairments include the contribution of the right hemisphere.

Topographic Disorientation

Abundant clinical reports describe patients who, following brain injury, have **topographic disorientation**, a gross disability in finding their way about in relation to salient environmental cues, even in environments familiar to them before the onset of their injuries. In 1890, Otfrid Foerster described a 44-year-old postal clerk who developed blindness on the right side of the visual field (a right hemianopia), followed a few days later by blindness on the left side of the visual field (a left hemianopia), a situation that left him with only a small, central area of vision (review Figure 13.10). This patient's most striking disability, however, was impairment in remembering where objects were located and in building up a picture—a cognitive map—of a route.

When blindfolded, he was unable to point toward furniture in his room or to remember the location of a toilet only a few steps away from his room. His amnesia was retrograde, extending back to things he knew before the onset of his disability. He could not describe or draw the spatial arrangement of his office or home or of well-known places in his city. He also could not draw general maps of the world or the city, although he could express some geographic ideas verbally.

Multiple variations in the symptoms of topographic disorientation have been described. Some patients are unable to name buildings or landmarks that were formerly familiar to them. Others retain this ability. Some patients can describe routes and draw maps but become disoriented when they actually visit the locations, because they cannot identify familiar buildings or landmarks. Other patients can navigate routes but cannot describe or draw maps of them. Some patients can navigate in familiar places but become disoriented in new places, and others can eventually learn to navigate in new places by painstakingly memorizing buildings and landmarks and the routes from one to another.

Topographic disorientation can occur because an individual fails to recognize previously familiar individual landmarks, can no longer compute the relationship between landmarks, or is impaired in spatial guidance. Any form of topographic disorientation can occur as an anterograde or a retrograde impairment of spatial memory. People who lose the ability to navigate in environments that were familiar before their injuries have *retrograde spatial amnesia*. People who have *anterograde spatial amnesia* retain the ability to navigate in environments that were familiar before their injuries but cannot navigate in novel environments. Patients may display both conditions, losing all topographic ability. Next we describe some examples of selective deficits in topographic disorientation.

Egocentric Disorientation

Patients described as having **egocentric disorientation** have difficulty perceiving the relative location of objects with respect to the self. They have either unilateral or bilateral injuries in the posterior parietal cortex **(Figure 21.3)**. Although they are able to gesture toward objects as long as their eyes are open, this ability is completely lost when their eyes are closed.

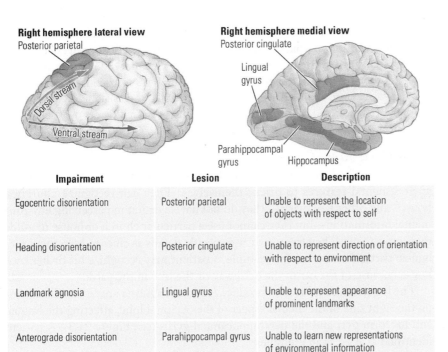

Right hemisphere lateral view
Posterior parietal

Dorsal stream

Ventral stream

Right hemisphere medial view
Posterior cingulate

Lingual gyrus

Parahippocampal gyrus

Hippocampus

Impairment	Lesion	Description
Egocentric disorientation	Posterior parietal	Unable to represent the location of objects with respect to self
Heading disorientation	Posterior cingulate	Unable to represent direction of orientation with respect to environment
Landmark agnosia	Lingual gyrus	Unable to represent appearance of prominent landmarks
Anterograde disorientation	Parahippocampal gyrus	Unable to learn new representations of environmental information
Spatial-mapping or memory deficit	Hippocampus	Anterograde and retrograde amnesia, especially for rich spatial details

(@) **Figure 21.3** ◄

Right-Hemisphere Brain Injuries and Spatial Deficits (Left) Arrows show the dorsal stream and ventral stream in a lateral view of the right hemisphere. (Right) The subcortical structures linked to spatial impairments are shown in a medial view of the right hemisphere. Table relates lesion location to impairment.

Their performance is impaired on a wide range of visuospatial tasks, including mental rotation (the ability to visualize the appearance of three-dimensional objects from different perspectives) and the ability to judge distances between objects. These patients are uniformly impaired in way-finding tasks both in formerly familiar and in novel environments. A case reported by Levine and coworkers (1985) exemplifies the condition.

This patient could not reach accurately for visual objects in central or peripheral visual fields even though he could identify them. He could not tell which of two objects was closer or which was to the left or the right. He could not find his way about and even got lost in his own home. His spatial imagery was also impaired. He could not describe how to get from his house to the corner store, a trip he had frequently made before his injury. His was not a general memory impairment, because he was able to describe the store and the proprietor.

Heading Disorientation

Patients said to have **heading disorientation** are unable to set a course to where they want to go, even though they are able to recognize landmarks, to recognize their own location in relation to landmarks, and to describe where they want to go. In short, they have no "sense of direction." This condition has been associated with injury in the right posterior cingulate cortex (see Figure 21.3). The following description of a patient is representative:

> [A]s he was driving his taxi in the same city [in which he had worked for years], he suddenly lost his understanding of the route to his destination. As he could quickly recognize the buildings and landscapes around

him, he was able to determine his current location. However, he could not determine in which direction he should proceed. He stopped taking passengers and tried to return to the main office, but didn't know the appropriate direction in which to drive. Using the surrounding buildings, scenery, and road signs, he made several mistakes along the way. He remembered, during this time, passing the same places over and over again. (Takahashi et al., 1997, p. 467)

Landmark Agnosia

Patients described as having **landmark agnosia** are unable to use prominent environmental features to orient themselves. They can recognize churches, houses, and other landmarks—they do not have a deficit in perceiving environmental information—but they cannot use a particular church or house to guide their movement. They frequently use specific details as clues to help them recognize particular objects; for example, a patient may recognize his or her own house because of the car in the driveway or the tree in the yard.

The lesion sites reported to produce landmark agnosia are either bilateral or on the right side of the medial aspect of the occipital lobe, affecting the lingual and fusiform gyri and the parahippocampal gyrus (see Figure 21.3). A patient identified as A.H. is an example:

> He complained a lot of his inability to recognize places. "In my mind's eye I know exactly where places are, what they look like. I can visualize R . . . Square without difficulty, and the streets that come into it. . . . I can draw you a plan of the roads from Cardiff to the Rhondda Valley. . . . It's when I'm out that the trouble starts. My reason tells me I must be in a certain place and yet I don't recognize it. It all has to be worked out each time." His topographic memory was good, as could be inferred from his accurate descriptions of paths, roads, the layout of the mine-shafts [the patient was an engineer] and from his excellent performance in drawing maps of places familiar to him before his illness. (Pallis, 1955, p. 219)

Anterograde Disorientation

In **anterograde disorientation**, patients have no problem navigating in formerly familiar environments but experience difficulty in novel environments because of an inability to learn about unfamiliar objects by looking at them. If shown a novel object, they are not likely to be able to select it from an array of objects a short while later. In contrast, they *are* able to recall auditory and tactile information that is novel. Damage in the parahippocampal gyrus of the inferior ventral cortex on the right side is associated with this condition (see Figure 21.3).

Ross (1980) describes a patient who was unable to recognize faces and was also unable to find his way in familiar locations. He had to consult notes and maps in order to get to school. There were differences in his spatial abilities relative to places that were familiar before his injury, in which he was spatially comfortable, and those after his injury, in which he became lost. He had no difficulty reaching for objects.

Spatial Distortion

People can experience a variety of distortions in spatial perception, seeing themselves as too small or too large relative to their spatial world, as did Alice in Wonderland. They can have out-of-body experiences, seeing themselves as occupying a space at a distance from their body or imagine that they have more than one body or see people or objects that are not there. We examined a woman who experienced a spatial distortion in which certain portions of her world ceased to exist for her.

When she was 80 years old, L.A. had a left medial parietal stroke that extended into the cingulate cortex. A former professor of language who presented with only slight **dysarthria** (difficulty in producing speech caused by incoordination of the speech apparatus), her spatial disorientation first became apparent in the hospital. During a walk, she stopped and declared that she could go no farther because that is where the hospital ended. When released from the hospital, she refused to return to her home of 20 years because, she declared, it was in a place that was not there. Even after her daughter found her a new apartment, she would often refuse to talk about her former home: she became upset by the fact that it was in a place that did not exist.

◉ 21.2 Dorsal- and Ventral-Stream Contributions to Spatial Behavior

The dual-stream theory proposed by Leslie Ungerleider and Mortimer Mishkin (1982) and featured prominently throughout this book had its foundation in explaining spatial behavior. From an origin in visual cortex, a pathway, or stream, projects through the temporal lobes and identifies objects, a pathway Ungerleider and Mishkin term the "what" pathway. A second pathway or stream projects through the parietal lobes and guides movement, a pathway they term the "where" pathway. In order for the "where" pathway to guide spatial navigation in relation to objects, the two pathways are proposed to synthesize the "what" and "where" in the frontal lobes. The theory therefore identifies parietal cortex as the formative part of the "where" pathway, temporal cortex as a formative part of the "what" pathway, and frontal cortex synthesis all as playing prominent roles in spatial navigation.

David Kravitz and coworkers (2011) propose a new anatomy that features three dorsal-stream targets. Visual information enters a domain in parietal cortex that then sends projections to premotor cortex, prefrontal cortex, and the medial temporal lobe. As is illustrated in **Figure 21.4**, the three projections organize visually guided action, spatial navigation, and spatial memory, respectively. The following sections outline the contributions that the brain regions comprising these projections make to spatial behavior.

The Dorsal Stream in Parietal Cortex

Not surprisingly, considering that this region forms the common component of the dorsal stream projections, damage to the parietal cortex results in many varied spatial impairments. Researchers now recognize about eight different defects of visual exploration that in most known instances result from bilateral parietal lesions but do not all coincide in every such case (**Table 21.1**). Disorders of visuospatial exploration stemming from such damage were first described by Rezsö Bálint (1909)

Figure 21.4 ▼

Three Dorsal Stream Projections for Visuospatial Processing
The parieto–prefrontal projection to the frontal eye fields (area 8) regulates eye movements to spatial targets. The parieto–premotor projection to cortical area 6 regulates body, head, and arm movements, and the parieto–medial temporal projection participates in route knowledge. (Information from Kravitz & Mishkin. A new neural framework for visuospatial processing. *Nature Reviews Neuroscience* 12(4):217–230, 2011, Figure 1C, p. 230.)

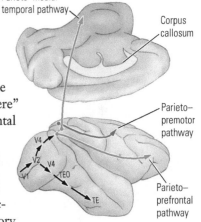

Table 21.1 **Deficits in visuospatial exploration**

Displaced visual attention
Inability to perceive more than one stimulus
Defective visual control of movement (optic ataxia)
Inability to follow a moving target
Defective accommodation and convergence
Inability to maintain fixation
Inability to direct gaze to targets voluntarily (gaze apraxia)
Abnormal visual search

Left hemisphere   Right hemisphere

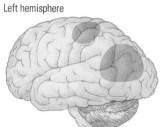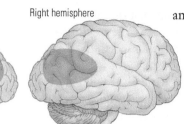

Figure 21.5 ▲

Areas of Softening Bálint Described in His Patient's Brain (Information from de Renzi, 1982.)

and then by Gordon Holmes. The condition is referred to as Bálint's syndrome (detailed in Section 14.4).

Bálint's patient had bilateral damage to the occipital and parietal cortex that included parts of the dorsal temporal lobes. He also had a zone of unilateral damage to the dorsal parietal and motor cortex (**Figure 21.5**). He had come to Bálint's attention after a stroke, and his condition remained unchanged for 6 years.

This man had complete visual fields; was reportedly capable of eye movements; and recognized and named colors, objects, and pictures. When presented with visual stimuli, he directed his gaze 35° to 40° to the right of them and saw only what was in his direct line of sight. Only after prompting would he look to the left and notice that the stimuli were there. After his attention had been directed to an object, he noticed nothing else—a response that was true for objects of all sizes, from a pin to a human figure. The patient would not look over a picture or scene but fastened on the first item that he saw in it.

The impairment resulted in a reading defect because he focused on a single letter, and only with difficulty could he work backward through a word to decode it. The patient was also impaired in reaching. If asked to grasp an object or point to a target, he groped and hit the target only by chance. Misreaching extended to attempting to light a cigar in the middle. The patient was also unable to estimate distance and could not tell which of two objects was the closer.

Gordon Holmes described a group of World War I soldiers who had penetrating missile wounds to the brain (Holmes and Horax, 1919). Their most notable symptoms were various impairments in eye movement. They had difficulty in looking at a stimulus, whether it was presented visually or aurally, in maintaining visual fixation, in following a moving target, in keeping the eyes focused on an approaching object, and in blinking in response to a visual threat.

These patients also failed to comprehend the spatial features of a stimulus that they were looking at and could recognize. That is, they had trouble judging the location of objects in space, estimating distance, discriminating length and size, and evaluating depth and thickness. As a result, they ran into objects when walking and had difficulty in reading and in counting scattered objects. The patients also sometimes failed to notice objects placed before them, and like Bálint's patient, did not notice anything else once their attention had been attracted by a stimulus.

Since these early reports, there have been many accounts of patients with similar problems, although the precise symptoms vary, depending on how an injury was acquired, whether it was bilateral, and where it was located. **Figure 21.6** depicts misjudgment by a patient studied by Truett Allison and his colleagues (1969) who had bilateral posterior cortical lesions resulting in small lower-temporal-quadrant-field defects, accompanied by dramatic deficits in the visual control of reaching and other movements (optic ataxia) and by deficits in eye movements:

Figure 21.6 ▲

A Visuospatial Deficit
A patient with Bálint's syndrome attempts to pour fluid into a glass. (Research from Allison et al., 1969.)

A manifestation of visual disorientation noted by the nursing staff five months after operation was when he attempted to light a cigarette. He took it out of the packet and put it in his mouth, then clumsily took a match out of the matchbox and lit it, afterwards directing the flame towards his lower lip, missing the cigarette. . . . He could not pour fluid from a bottle into a glass but spilled it on the tablecloth. He was unable to shake hands without first groping for the proffered hand. It could be demonstrated that visual memory was intact and did not contribute to his errors. When an object (e.g., a matchbox) was held up either above his head, to the right, or to the left and he was asked to note its position, close his eyes for a moment, and then point in the general direction in which he had seen the object, he did this correctly. Therefore, it appeared that his ability to remember the position of an object in space was not impaired. (Allison et al., 1969, pp. 324–326)

To differentiate the many deficits of such patients investigators have focused on two aspects of visual function: visual localization and depth perception. For example, to demonstrate a disorder of spatial localization independent of a disorder of reaching or pointing, Julia Hannay and her coworkers (1976) projected one or two dots on a screen for 300 milliseconds. Two seconds later, they projected an array of numbers, and the subjects were asked to pick the number (or numbers) located in the same position (or positions) as the dot (or dots).

Patients with right-hemisphere lesions were impaired at this task in comparison with controls and subjects with left-hemisphere lesions. This deficit is not simply a manifestation of neglect, because errors were distributed equally in the left and right visual fields. It is not surprising that a person who is unable to receive a sense impression of the location of points in space would have a hard time directing his or her movements, resulting in an apparent spatial deficit.

In another example, researchers designed an experiment using random dot stereograms to study the cues necessary to perceive depth (Carmon and Bechtoldt, 1969). Looking into eyepieces, patients and controls saw an apparently random array of dots. When viewed with one eye alone, the array had no contour or depth and looked rather like a complex crossword puzzle with black and white boxes. However, when the array was viewed as a stereogram—both eyes open and each looking independently at left-eye and right-eye views of the same image—a striking figure–background contour suddenly appeared (a figure appeared to float in front of a background) because of slight disparities between the images shown to the left and right eye.

Most intact participants and patients with left-hemisphere damage easily perceived the contour, but most patients with right-hemisphere damage did very badly at this test, illustrating a defect in depth perception. The result supports the idea that at least some part of the mechanism for depth perception is more strongly represented in the right hemisphere.

The parietal cortex is closely linked to body senses, and its likely contribution is to provide a spatial coordinate system related to the body—to aid us in locating objects in space relative to ourselves, in egocentric coordinates. In the absence of this system, a patient still sees an object but is not able to direct eye or hand movements toward it accurately because the object cannot be located relative to his or her body.

Various investigators have identified neurons in the monkey posterior parietal cortex that respond to stimuli presented within a monkey's grasping space. These cells—or some of them—project to the motor system to guide the limbs and the body moving voluntarily toward targets in various spatial locations. The parietal cortex also contains neurons that have a role in directing body, hand, and eye movements toward stimuli, providing further evidence that the parietal cortex has a special role in directing movements to targets relative to body coordinates.

The Dorsal Stream in Frontal Cortex

As the recipient of at least two dorsal-stream projections from the parietal cortex, the frontal cortex is also important in spatial discriminations (see Figure 21.4). The most dramatic demonstration comes from experiments by Richard Nakamura and his coworkers (1986). They spared all of the visual areas of the posterior cortex while removing the entire cortex anterior to it in monkeys. The monkeys failed to show any signs of vision, but recordings of single-cell activity in the visual areas revealed that the cells were functioning normally. Thus, removal of the frontal cortex renders animals chronically blind and unable to navigate even though the visual system is functioning.

Findings in a number of studies demonstrate that more-selective impairments follow more-restricted lesions in the visual-to-frontal-cortex pathways. Because the premotor and motor cortices are responsible for organized movements, including locomotion, reaching, bringing the hands to the mouth, and avoidance movements, damage to these regions impairs motor behavior in response to visual stimuli. For example, if the hand area of the motor cortex is disconnected from the visual centers, a monkey can no longer use a hand to locate food and pick it up (Haaxma and Kuypers, 1975).

It is difficult to distinguish impairments in detecting objects from impairments in spatial behavior. Some features of object-detection impairments, however, do suggest that the underlying cause is a spatial impairment relative to body-centered coordinates. Patricia Goldman-Rakic (1987) reported an orienting deficit, using rhesus monkeys with small lesions in the dorsolateral prefrontal lobe along the principal sulcus, which comprises the monkey's frontal eye fields.

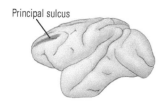

Principal sulcus

Rhesus monkey brain

The monkeys had been trained to fixate on a spot of light in the center of a television monitor. A second dot was flashed briefly in the monkeys' visual fields. The monkeys were reinforced with food for waiting until the fixation spot disappeared before directing their gaze to the new visual target. Monkeys with unilateral lesions failed to direct their gaze to the new target after even very short delays. If there was no delay, however, they performed at normal. Varying the location of the lesion produced selective deficits associated with different parts of the visual field.

There is a parallel to these eye-movement results in experiments that require monkeys to reach toward a target. If a monkey with lesions in the principal sulcus is given a delayed-response task in which the object's location is the relevant variable, impairments are observed after short delays (see Figure 16.14A). Discrimination tasks that do not require memory for spatial location are not impaired by these lesions.

Michael Petrides and Brenda Milner (1982) reported a somewhat analogous deficit in people with frontal-lobe damage. Their patients were presented with a set of pages that each contained an array of the same visual stimuli, but the stimuli were presented in a different order on each page. They were asked to point to one of the stimuli on each page but to do so without pointing to the same page location twice. Thus, the patients had to remember the locations of the selections that they had made previously. The frontal-lobe patients displayed impairments at this task.

The Dorsal and Ventral Streams in Temporal Cortex

An extensive literature implicates the temporal lobes in spatial behavior, but controversy abounds about the precise nature of the deficits caused by damage there and the anatomical regions related to specific deficits. Spatial theories vary from proposing that the temporal lobes have a direct and specific role in spatial navigation to proposing that their role in memory is more generalized and that anterograde spatial deficits arise as part of an anterograde memory impairment.

In fact, both proposals are likely correct. The temporal lobes receive a dorsal stream projection that is involved in spatial navigation. The temporal lobes also receive a ventral-stream projection that mediates object perception (Kravitz et al., 2013). The temporal lobes are thus positioned to combine egocentric (body-wise) spatial guidance with allocentric (external) spatial guidance related to objects. We must point out, however, that both the dorsal- and ventral-stream projections to the temporal lobes are complex, with projections routed through numerous temporal-lobe regions including the cingulate cortex, the parahippocampal gyrus, entorhinal cortex, and various cell fields of the hippocampus. Thus, parceling out the contributions of each subpathway, their many targets, and their combined actions is not straightforward.

The dorsal- and the ventral-stream pathways both converge on the hippocampus (see the Snapshot on page 586). E.P.'s case, reported by Edmond Teng and Larry Squire (1999), illustrates the possible contributions of the temporal lobes, and especially the hippocampus, in spatial memory:

> E.P. was a 76-year-old former laboratory technician who became amnesic in 1992, after an episode of herpes simplex encephalitis. He had extensive bilateral damage to the hippocampus and surrounding areas, including the parahippocampal gyrus. The experimenters identified five individuals who had attended E.P.'s high school and who had since moved away, as had E.P. The subjects were asked to describe how they would navigate from their homes to different locations in the area served by the school, how they would navigate between different locations in the area, and how they would navigate if the most logical routes were blocked off. E.P. scored as well as the control subjects on these tests. In contrast, when E.P. was asked to describe how he would navigate in his present environs, a location to which he had moved after his brain injury, he was unable to provide any responses to any questions. (Teng and Squire, reprinted by permission from Macmillan Publishers Ltd: *NATURE*, © 1999, p. 675.)

In their study of K.C., a patient with a similar hippocampal plus parahippocampal gyrus lesion, Shayna Rosenbaum and her colleagues (2005) report that, although the patient could produce what they called a "schematic cognitive map" of the environment in which he had lived before his injury, his memory of that environment's rich contextual details was impaired (see Figure 21.3). For example, when shown a photograph of the neighborhood in which he had lived before his brain injury, K.C. had difficulty identifying the viewpoint from which

SNAPSHOT | Imaging the Hippocampi of London Taxi Drivers

To examine brain regions associated with topographic memory, Katherine Woollett and Eleanor Maguire (2011, 2012) recruited licensed London taxi drivers as participants. Official London taxi drivers must train for 4 years and pass stringent examinations of spatial knowledge before receiving a license. The fact that these drivers had such an extensive knowledge of London meant that all of them could be tested with the same stimuli: the city's topography.

The taxi drivers were given a number of tasks, two of which required topographic knowledge:

1. Given a starting and destination point in the greater London area, they were asked to describe overtly, while undergoing a PET scan, the shortest legal route between the two points.

2. They were required to recall and describe the appearance of individual world-renowned landmarks that were not in London and that they had never visited.

A control task for the driving-sequence test was the recall of a film plot. As a control for the renowned-building test, the participants were asked to describe individual frames from a film.

PET-scan images were superimposed onto the MRI reconstructions of each driver's brain. The brain areas activated during the spatial test included the occipitotemporal areas, medial parietal cortex, posterior cingulate cortex, parahippocampal gyrus, and right hippocampus (shown in the illustration). The nonspatial tasks did not activate the right hippocampus.

Woollett and Maguire used MRI to image the hippocampus. Increases in gray-matter volume (neurons) were found in the right and left hippocampi; no increases were seen in other parts of the brain. Analysis of hippocampal volume indicated that control participants had larger anterior hippocampal areas and London taxi drivers had larger posterior hippocampal areas. In addition, the measures indicated that the right posterior hippocampus increased in size as a function of years spent as a taxi driver.

To control for the influence of motion and the effects of stress in driving, the taxi drivers were compared with bus drivers. Bus drivers, who follow set routes, did not display hippocampal changes similar to those observed in taxi drivers.

The scientists suggest that the "mental map" of London used by the taxi drivers in delivering their passengers is located in the right posterior hippocampus. Furthermore, they propose that this region of the hippocampus expands to accommodate the map. This finding is confirmed in part by the study of a taxi driver, T.T., who had sustained bilateral hippocampal damage. In a virtual test of navigation, T.T. retained knowledge of the topography of London and its landmarks and could even navigate major routes. When he left the major routes, he became lost, however.

Findings from rodent studies have established that new cells are generated in the subgranular zone of the hippocampus and migrate to join its granular layer. The survival of these new cells conjointly with the use of the mental map may underlie the expansion of the right hippocampus in humans. The expansion comes at a cost, however, indicated both by the relative decrease in size of the anterior hippocampus and by poorer performance on the part of taxi drivers compared with bus drivers on tests of new spatial information.

Woollett, K., and E. A. Maguire. Acquiring "the Knowledge" of London's layout drives structural brain changes. *Current Biology* 21:2109–2114, 2011.

Woollett, K., and E. A. Maguire. Exploring anterograde associative memory in London taxi drivers. *Neuroreport* 23:885–888, October 24, 2012.

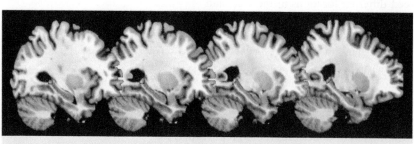

After a 4-year course devoted to learning London's street layout, trainees who qualified as licensed taxi drivers show increased gray-matter volume in the most posterior part of the hippocampus (orange and yellow areas). (From Woollett, K., and E. A. Maguire Acquiring "the Knowledge" of London's layout drives structural brain changes, *Current Biology* 21(24):2109–2114, 2011. © Elsevier.)

the photograph was taken, and he was unable to describe the surrounding environment that was not visible in the photograph. Rosenbaum and colleagues suggest substantial retrograde amnesia for the richer contextual features of space.

In this respect, it is noteworthy that the amnesic patient H.M., profiled throughout Chapter 18, had extensive anterograde amnesia but could solve some simple spatial problems. Véronique Bohbot and Suzanne Corkin (2007) asked control participants and patient H.M. to locate a sensor under a carpet by stepping on it. When a control stepped on the sensor, it activated a tone through a speaker. In order to solve the task, the participants needed to form a memory of the location of the sensor in relation to surrounding room cues.

H.M., whose right parahippocampal gyrus was intact, could learn the location of one sensor but not two. Presumably, the right parahippocampal gyrus is sufficient for learning a single location, but additional temporal-lobe structures, including the hippocampus, are necessary for more complex spatial memory, including the memory of having previously performed and learned the task.

Robert Astur and his coworkers (2002) presented a virtual spatial-navigation problem to participants and to patients with unilateral left- or right-hippocampal damage. The participants used a joystick to move about in a virtual three-dimensional swimming pool, trying to escape from the water by finding a platform hidden just beneath the surface as quickly as possible. The computer gave them both auditory and visual feedback when they had succeeded.

The view on the screen was a 60° first-person field of view, approximately the same visual field seen by the human eye. When participants and patients pushed the joystick to the right, the view on the screen panned to the right, and so on. Each participant or patient was given 20 trials, and each trial might start from any of the four different starting locations around the edge of the virtual pool. Then participants and patients each were given a probe trial in which the escape platform was removed from the pool, and the time that he or she spent searching for the hidden platform at its former location was measured.

Astur and colleagues report that both left- and right-hippocampal groups were severely impaired in solving the spatial-navigation task and in searching for the platform at a location where it had formerly been hidden. Whether the deficit can be ascribed to the hippocampal damage alone is unclear because the overlying cortex and amygdala also were damaged, but the results confirm a role for the right hemisphere and also demonstrate that the left hemisphere is important.

21.3 Experimental Models of Spatial Behavior

Nonhuman animals have evolved a remarkable range of behavior in relation to space. They know migration routes, secure locations, locations of food sources and of places where they have cached food, and locations for mating and raising young. They also know when and how to move between all of these locations. As a result, neuropsychologists have abundant behavioral paradigms available for investigating the richness of nonhuman animal spatial behavior.

We humans are similar to other animals in that we store objects in many places where we intend to find them at a later date. We know the locations of many places, including those at which we play, study, or shop. We also keep track of our present location and our starting location so that we can return if we wish. We also maintain an "online" inventory of the locations of our friends and family. And like other animals, we use a variety of sensory information to guide our spatial behavior.

In keeping with the many applications of spatial skills to problem solving, human and nonhuman animal species have evolved various strategies that together form their spatial behavior. The distinctive nature of many of these spatial abilities suggests that they are mediated by distinctive neural circuits. In this section, we illustrate some of these spatial behaviors, including route following, piloting, food caching, and dead reckoning.

Route Following

Perhaps the simplest spatial behavior is following a trail or moving toward an object or cue, behaviors referred to as *route following*. This form of spatial behavior is also called *cue learning*, implying that a response is being made to a specific cue, or *taxon navigation*, implying movement toward or away from a specific cue. Some animals direct their movements toward the light of the sun, moon, or stars; other animals direct their movements toward the dark—examples of route following in which a light gradient forms the route.

Migrating salmon follow routes in a number of ways. They follow olfactory cues, presumably following the gradient strength of the cue, to swim many hundreds of miles from their feeding grounds in the ocean to return to their spawning grounds in the river in which they hatched. In turn, their offspring use an inherited magnetic compass to return to the feeding grounds in the ocean (Putman et al., 2014).

Route following is an everyday activity for us humans. Following a road or path, moving toward a landmark, or even reaching for an object that we can see are examples of route following. We also use maps to plan the routes to different places and follow instructions from others or from a satellite guidance system that tells us to "turn left at the second traffic light, go two blocks" and you are there. For places we can see, say a library that we intend to enter, route following consists of walking directly toward the target. As described in Section 21.1, if we are unable to identify familiar places, the impairment is referred to as *landmark agnosia*.

Piloting

Piloting is the ability to take a course to a place that is not directly marked by a cue or route. The pilot who guides a ship into a harbor may take a very irregular path by using a variety of landmarks that provide a spatial representation of the harbor and the obstacles to be avoided to enter safely. Piloting is also referred to as *topographic guidance* because it is guided by a rich array of environmental cues, or *cognitive mapping* on the assumption that guidance is provided by neural processes that represent the environment in maplike coordinates. Piloting also is referred to as *place learning*, on the assumption that the goal of our trip is to reach a specific place, or *locale navigation*, which again emphasizes the importance of location.

Figure 21.7 depicts four tasks used for studying route following and piloting abilities in rats. Figure 21.7A shows a typical research room containing a

(A) Morris water task

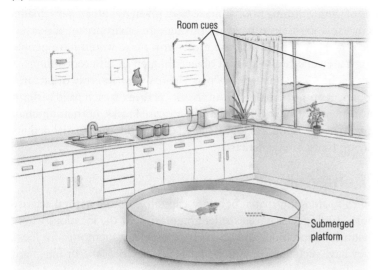

Room cues

Submerged
platform

 **Figure 21.7** ◄

Tasks Used to Study Spatial Behavior in Rodents (A) The swimming-pool task requires an animal to learn the location of a visible or hidden (submerged) platform. The only cue to the hidden platform position is its spatial relation to cues about the room. (B) The radial-arm maze was designed as a test of foraging behavior in animals. A rat must learn either which alleys marked by a local cue contain food or which arms marked by distal cues contain food. Both (C) the T-maze and (D) the Grice box test left–right differentiation as well as the ability of animals to alternate their responses. These various tasks usually are presented in open rooms so that in addition to local cues, animals can use the many surrounding room cues as aids to orientation.

(B) Olton radial-arm maze   **(C) T-maze**   **(D) Grice box**

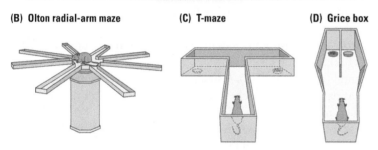

rich array of visual cues such as cupboards, pictures, and windows. In the center of the room is a swimming pool used in the Morris water task (named after its inventor, Richard Morris). In this test of spatial abilities, a rat must escape from the water onto a platform, which can be visible or hidden under the water.

If the platform is visible, it serves as a cue for route navigation: the rat can take a direct route toward it. If the platform is hidden, the rat must learn to use surrounding room cues to pilot to the platform. (Rats are well suited to this task. They are excellent swimmers, but their small size puts them at risk for hypothermia if they stay in the water for long, so they are highly motivated to escape from the pool.)

The mazes illustrated in Figure 21.7B, C, and D are used for other laboratory tests of spatial navigation. In the Olton radial-arm maze (named for its inventor, David Olton) an animal can walk from arm to arm, thus following a route. Marking a specific alley with a distinctive color or cue also makes the task into a route-learning task. An animal can also learn that some arms contain food but others do not. Because the arms appear similar, an animal must learn their locations in relation to the room's topography, and thus the solution to task is one of piloting. In the T-maze and Grice box (named after its inventor, G. Robert Grice), a correct response might consist of learning to go to only one location, a route task, or learning to alternate locations on every trial, a piloting task.

At the end of Section 21.2 we described a human version of the rat swimming pool piloting task: individuals walk through a room until they depress a hidden switch that indicates location by making a sound. Then we described virtual versions of the swimming pool or maze tasks given to human participants by having them use a joystick to navigate through an environment displayed on a computer screen. A corollary of the radial-arm maze would have people navigate through a virtual house to find objects hidden in different rooms. A human analogy of the Grice box task has participants view an array of pictures on a sequence of pages on which they point to one picture on each page without pointing to the same picture twice. In all of these spatial tasks, both nonhuman animals and humans with temporal lobe damage display piloting spatial deficits without displaying route or cue deficits.

Caching Behavior

Some approaches to studying spatial behavior capitalize on the natural activity of a species. Some bird species have excellent memories for the locations where they have previously found food, and others have excellent memories for locations where they have cached food. Among birds that *scatter hoard*, or hide food in different locations, the abilities of two major families, the chickadee and tit family (Paridae) and the jay and nutcracker family (Corvidae), provide rich insights into spatial memory.

Chickadees store insect prey and seeds in scattered sites that typically include furrows in tree bark, conifer needle clusters, moss, and other natural hiding places (Sherry and Hoshooley, 2010). A small number of food items, often only one, are stored at each site, and cache sites are not reused. Sites may be scattered throughout a number of acres. Estimates of the number of items cached by a bird in a year total in the thousands. The items are left for periods ranging from hours to weeks before the bird returns to retrieve them.

The birds use distal spatial cues rather than local landmarks to recall the locations of their caches. Distal spatial cues are objects at some distance from a cache site, and local cues are close to the cache site. To illustrate the difference, if cues in the vicinity of a food item are disturbed, a bird's ability to find the food is not disturbed. Similarly, removing an artificial cue, such as a colored object, from a cache site does not prevent the bird from retrieving the food at that location. If distal cues are removed or displaced, however, the bird's search in a location is disrupted or displaced.

If the caches on one side of an aviary are pilfered, the birds learn to avoid that side of the aviary. If cache sites marked by certain colored tapes are pilfered but cache sites marked by different-colored tapes are not, the birds do not learn to differentiate between the colors, even though independent tests show that the birds can easily tell one color from another. The results of these experiments and many similar ones indicate that birds use distal spatial cues rather than local landmarks to mark the location of their cached food. Members of the crow family not only keep track of the locations of cached food, they also conceal the food from onlookers, and they remember whether food is perishable or durable so that they can time their returns to retrieve the food for eating (Legg and Clayton, 2014).

Results of studies comparing birds that cache food with birds that do not cache food indicate that the hippocampus is considerably larger in the birds that cache (**Figure 21.8**). Hummingbirds remember a remarkable number of previously visited flowers and do not visit those flowers again until some time

Figure 21.8 ▼

Inferring Spatial Memory Graph relating hippocampal volume to forebrain volume in three food-storing (left) and ten non-food-storing (right) families of songbirds. Hippocampi of birds that cache food, such as the black-capped chickadee, are about twice as large as the hippocampi of birds, such as the sparrow, that do not. (Data from D. F. Sherry, L. F. Jacobs, and S. J. C. Gaulin, Spatial memory and adaptive specialization of the hippocampus. *Trends in Neuroscience* 15:298–303, 1992.)

has passed so that nectar is replenished. Hummingbirds have the largest hippocampi relative to body size of all birds studied, suggesting that the hippocampus contributes to their remarkable spatial memory (Ward et al., 2012).

If the hippocampus is damaged in birds that cache food, they continue to cache but are unable to retrieve the food. As summarized by David Sherry and his colleagues (Hall et al., 2014), changes in *neurogenesis*—in the number of cells added to the hippocampus—are related to food-storing behavior. Precursor cells migrate into the hippocampus and differentiate into new neurons during the season in which birds are storing food. Food storing in chickadees reaches its maximum in autumn, continues through the winter, and decreases in spring and summer. Both hippocampal neurogenesis and hippocampal size reach a maximum in autumn and decrease in spring. Food-storing experience also correlates with hippocampal size. If a food-storing marsh tit is prevented from storing food early in development, the relative size of its hippocampus lags behind that of age-matched controls. If neurogenesis is prevented, the food-storing behavior of birds is relatively impaired.

Taken together, the findings in these studies, showing that food-caching birds can remember hundreds of locations at which food is stored, use distal spatial cues to locate food, and require the hippocampus to do so, suggest once again that the hippocampus plays an important role in spatial behavior. Because we humans are cachers as well, it follows that our hippocampal processes function much like those of caching birds.

Dead Reckoning

Dead reckoning—derived from the phrase *deduced reckoning*—is a form of navigation that depends on cues generated by an animal's own movement. It refers to an animal's ability to know how far it has traveled and where it is in relation to a starting point, to monitor its speed and travel time, and to change direction as necessary. Dead reckoning behavior is sometimes referred to as *path integration* to indicate that integrating an outward path provides information about present location and information about how to set a direct course homeward.

Charles Darwin (1893) was the first to suggest that animals could use dead reckoning to navigate. Subsequently, many researchers have confirmed that animals do so, as do humans. When we speak of a person having a "sense of direction" or "sense of distance," most likely we are describing a conscious awareness of spatial location derived from the brain's skill at dead reckoning.

Dead reckoning was an early form of navigation used by sailors; Columbus used it on his journeys between Europe and Central America, for example. Using a compass to monitor direction, a sailor calculated speed by throwing a piece of wood overboard at a certain point on the bow. As the ship moved past the piece of wood, a sailor chanted until the wood had passed a certain point on the stern. The chant was written in such a way that the last word spoken corresponded to a specific speed. If sailors could additionally tell time (for example, by using sun and star sightings), they could locate their position.

In other words, knowing direction, speed, and travel time allowed sailors to record their progress accurately. Using a reverse record of the outbound trip ensured an accurate return journey, and the homeward journey could be direct even though the outward trip was circuitous. Dead reckoning is still used today

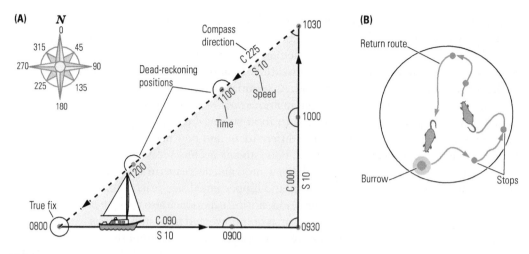

Figure 21.9 ▲

Dead Reckoning by Sailors and by Rats (A) A ship starts from a known location, arrives at a destination, and returns to the starting point without using external cues. The starting point is at 0800 hours, the compass direction (C) is 90°, and the speed (S) is 10 knots. Time, direction, and speed are noted at each directional change, and dead-reckoning location is calculated and recorded each hour. The return trip (dashed line) can be calculated from the plots made on the outbound trip. (B) A rat foraging for food makes a number of turns, stops before finding the food, and on finding the food, returns directly home. The rat does not have a clock, compass, or speedometer and so must have internal processes for dead reckoning.

when fog interferes with the use of visual beacons; all that a sailor needs is a speedometer, watch, and compass (**Figure 21.9**A). The invention of clocks that could keep time at sea greatly facilitated navigation.

Nonhuman animals have no mechanical means for measuring speed, time, and direction when they navigate by dead reckoning but rather derive this information from their own movements, collectively called *self-movement cues*. In principle, sensory cues, including from the proprioceptive and vestibular systems, can provide the necessary information. For example, sensory flow, including *optic flow*, gradients of sound and odors, and even wind resistance provide information about movement speed and direction. Activation of the vestibular system indicates movement speed, turns, and duration, thus providing important cues for dead reckoning.

In addition, an animal may monitor its movements by using the efferent (output) copy of movement commands. That is, when an animal voluntarily decides to travel to a certain location, it can retain the instructions that it sends to its muscles. This efferent copy can be used to infer how far it has traveled and the direction that it has taken.

By using these cues to compute velocity and direction over time, an animal can keep track of its location in relation to a starting point. Then, by reversing these computations, the animal is able to return to that starting point (Figure 21.9B). Such behavior is useful when the starting point is a home to which the animal must return. Dead reckoning is especially useful if an animal is traveling about in the dark, is in a new place where the environmental cues are unfamiliar, or is in a place where the visual cues often change.

The results of a number of experiments suggest that the hippocampal formation also contributes to dead reckoning. In a testing situation in which rats emerge from a hidden burrow to forage on a circular table for large food pellets, when a rat finds a food pellet, it carries the pellet back to its refuge for eating (Whishaw et al., 2001).

The outward trip made by a rat as it is looking for food is circuitous, but the homeward trip is direct. When foraging in the light, a rat is able to use both room cues and self-movement cues for guidance. If the rat is tested in the dark and all olfactory and auditory cues are removed, the rat can return home only if it can access a record of the body movements made on the outward trip to calculate the homeward trip. It must dead-reckon.

Healthy rats are very accurate at returning home in both the light and the dark. If the hippocampal formation is damaged, however, the rats are accurate in the light but not in the dark. The finding that damage to the hippocampus disrupts dead reckoning as well as some forms of spatial mapping indicates that they are related and that the hippocampus participates in both forms of spatial navigation.

The trick in giving similar dead reckoning tasks to humans is the necessity of removing other guidance cues, such as room cues or cues that can be derived from counting steps or counting turns and their directions. Participants are sometimes blindfolded, taken by the hand, and walked on a short route, say a triangle. Then they are asked to repeat the trip from memory. Or the blindfolded participant might be walked along an irregular path, then asked to return to the starting point. People can also be given computer-based tests that require them to remember movements of objects in a featureless environment.

Like rats, humans are good at these tasks, and dead reckoning tests can assess the function of brain regions following brain injury or evaluate brain regions that are active during the tests (Wolbers et al., 2007). Results from both testing paradigms suggest the involvement of temporal lobes and the hippocampus in dead reckoning (Worsley et al., 2001).

Neuropsychological Tests of Spatial Behavior

Tests used for measuring human spatial abilities vary from tests of real-world spatial abilities to virtual tests and computer simulations of spatial tasks. Their sheer number and variability has so far precluded a systematic comparison of the universe of spatial tests.

A noteworthy example of a real-world test is one used in Mary-Lou Smith and Brenda Milner's (1981) studies of patients who had undergone elective surgery to remove the hippocampus as a treatment for epilepsy. These researchers employed 16 small toys spread out over a table as stimulus objects (**Figure 21.10**A). A subject was told that the test's purpose was to measure the ability to estimate prices and that the task consisted of estimating the average price of a real object represented by the toy.

The subject was told to point to a toy, name it, and think of a price. After 10 seconds, the price was asked for and the subject was instructed to move on to another toy, and so on. Then the subject was moved away from the table and asked to recall the objects on it. After this test of object recall, a sheet of brown paper the same size as the original table was placed before the subject, and he or she was asked to place the toys on it in their original arrangement. The two recall tests were then repeated 24 hours later.

Scores were given for recall of the objects' names and for their locations. The location score was the measure of the distances between the objects' original locations and the patient's immediate recollection of where the objects had been, as well as between the

◉ Figure 21.10 ▼

Test of Spatial Memory
(A) In this test of spatial memory for objects, showing a typical arrangement of 16 toys in 16 fixed locations, subjects are required to point to the objects and estimate their individual prices. The objects are then removed, and the subjects are asked to indicate where in the array each object was. (B) Graph of the performances of left-temporal and right-temporal patients and of controls on the recall of absolute location indicates impairment in the right-temporal group. (Task and data source: Smith and Milner, 1981.)

(A) Test of spatial memory

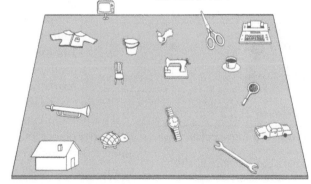

(B) Results

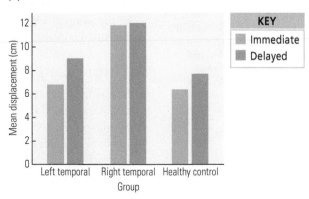

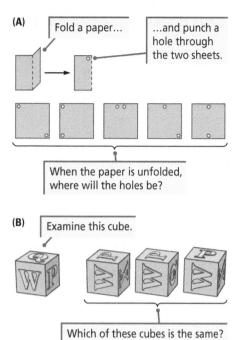

(A) Fold a paper... ...and punch a hole through the two sheets.

When the paper is unfolded, where will the holes be?

(B) Examine this cube.

Which of these cubes is the same?

Figure 21.11 ▲

Measuring Spatial Abilities Sample test items for (A) a visualization test and (B) an orientation test. As you work on the orientation sample, note that no letter appears on more than one face of a given cube. (Information from Halpern, 1986.)

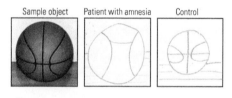

Sample object | Patient with amnesia | Control

Figure 21.12 ▲

Boundary Expansion When asked to draw an object presented within a border (left), subjects with hippocampal damage produce a more accurate rendition of the object relative to the size of the border (center) than do controls (right), who draw the object in a reduced size relative to the border. (Mullally S. L., H. Intraub, and E. A. Maguire. Attenuated Boundary Extension Produces a Paradoxical Memory Advantage in Amnesic Patients. *Current Biology* 22(4):261–268, 2012, Figure 3.)

original locations and the patient's delayed recollection of where the objects had been. On the measure of name recall, patients with right- and with left-hippocampus damage were moderately impaired, with the left-hippocampal patients having lower scores than the right-hippocampal patients.

The results for the spatial component of the experiment, graphed in Figure 21.10B, indicate a selective participation of the right hippocampus in spatial memory. Scores for the left-temporal group were comparable to scores for the control group, but placement errors for the right-temporal group were extremely high on both immediate and delayed recall tests. Many variations of this test have been derived, including computer-based tests in which subjects and controls are required to name and relocate objects on a virtual table.

Visualization tests evaluate the ability to manipulate, rotate, twist, or invert two- or three-dimensional stimulus objects mentally. The underlying ability seems to entail a process of recognition, retention, and recall of a configuration whose parts move and change place, as when an object is manipulated in three-dimensional space or a flat pattern is folded and unfolded (**Figure 21.11**A). *Orientation tests* evaluate comprehension of the arrangement of elements within a visual stimulus pattern and the aptitude to remain unconfused by the changing orientation in which a spatial configuration may be presented (Figure 21.11B).

Sinéad Mullally and her colleagues (2012) describe an interesting test in which amnesic patients, including patients with hippocampal damage, display spatial performance superior to that of control participants. Subjects are presented with a picture within a frame and are asked to draw it (**Figure 21.12**). Amnesic patients produce an accurate drawing of the object relative to the size of the frame, whereas controls draw the object with a reduced size relative to the frame.

The phenomenon of **boundary expansion** (expansion of the space between the object and the frame) displayed by control participants but not by amnesic patients is obtained in other sensory modalities. For example, asked to touch an array of objects within a frame and then to position the objects within the frame in a test, the control participants expand the boundary by reducing the area in which the objects are replaced. The interpretation of the boundary expansion is that amnesic patients produce a literal rendition of the sample, whereas the participants attempt to place the object within an extended context.

Single-Cell Recording and Spatial Behavior

Studying the spatial behavior of small animals has advantages. They are good at solving spatial tasks, and as they do, their single-cell activity can be recorded. Single-cell recordings made from dorsal and ventral stream structures, including parietal cortex, rhinal cortices, and the hippocampus and its input and output pathways have led to discovering a remarkable variety of neurons that seem to be involved in spatial behavior.

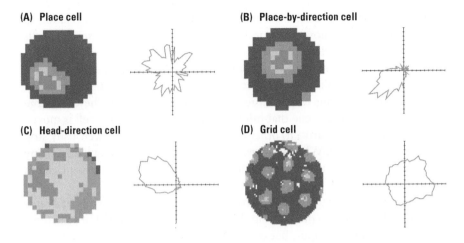

Figure 21.13 ◄

Classes of Spatially Related Cells in the Hippocampal Formation
The X-Y coordinates at the right indicate the directional selectivity of the cell recorded at the left. (A and B) Place cells discharge when a rat is at a spatial location, irrespective of its orientation. (C) Head-direction cells discharge when the rat's head points in a given direction, irrespective of its location. (D) Grid cells discharge at many locations, forming a virtual grid that is invariant in the face of changes in the rat's direction, movement, or speed. (Courtesy of John O'Keefe. Research from Andersen et al., 2007, Fig. 11.21.)

Some cells indicate ongoing locomotion, some signal boundaries such as walls or the edges of tables, while others keep time, tracking movement duration or rest periods. Some even predict upcoming movements (Kraus, 2013). Among these cell types, most experimental investigation has been directed to place cells, head-direction cells, and grid cells (**Figure 21.13**). We describe their properties in the context of theories about route learning, place learning, and dead reckoning (Barry and Burgess, 2014). The Nobel Prize in Physiology or Medicine 2014 was awarded to John O'Keefe, May-Britt Moser, and Edvard I. Moser "for their discoveries of cells that constitute a positioning system in the brain."

Place Cells

Place cells, first described by John O'Keefe and Jonathan Dostrovsky (1971; Best et al., 2001), discharge when an animal enters a specific location in its environment (Figure 21.13A). Within a short time of a rat being placed in a novel environment, hippocampal formation place cells begin to discharge in relation to the animal's location. For some cells, whether the rat walks to a place itself or is carried there by the experimenter does not seem to matter. *Place-by-direction cells* encode not only the rat's location but also the direction and speed of its movement (Figure 21.13B).

If the rat is walking on a straight path, active place cells are more likely to code by direction as well as location. If the lights are turned off after the animals have explored a new environment, place cells maintain their activity relative to the previously visualized cue locations. If a rat is removed temporarily then returned after the environmental cues have been changed, place cells modify their activity to represent the new environment. If the rat is present when a cue is removed, place cells are more likely to maintain their original firing relations.

Moving a few visual cues has little effect on the pattern of activity displayed by place cells, but if all room cues are rotated, the cells will then discharge with respect to the cues' new locations. If a rat is exploring a maze for food, some place cells will discharge when it is in a particular part of the maze. Moreover, these cells may discharge, say, only if the rat is intending to make a left turn but not if it is intending to make a right turn.

Although place cells seem to prefer visual cues, they can also be influenced by olfactory, vestibular, tactile, and auditory cues. For example, place cells in blind animals respond to cues that the animals discover by touch. If one of a number of cups in an apparatus contains water, some place cells will fire in relation to that cup. If the cup is moved, the preferred firing location for those place cells changes with the cup's location.

If an animal is placed in an environment with only one visual cue, then this single cue will determine where place cells discharge. If the single cue is removed, the cells continue to discharge, but the location at which they discharge begins to drift. If a visual cue that influences the firing of a place cell is moved about unpredictably relative to other cues, then the place cells eventually stop responding to that cue. When numerous cells are recorded concurrently, many that are active in one environment will not be active when the rat is placed in another environment.

Place-cell activity is closely linked to an animal's ability to move, so if a rat is restrained, the cells stop discharging. Place cells can be recorded in structures other than the hippocampus, but only hippocampal place cells appear to have the special versatility that allows them to change activity in response to changes in environmental cues. Nevertheless, some hippocampal place cells appear to have invariant properties. Longnian Lin and colleagues (2007) found cells in the hippocampus of mice that are activated only by a nest or bed. They argue that the hippocampus can represent higher-order "concepts" in addition to representing object location.

Head-Direction Cells

Jeffrey Taube (2007) summarized the extensive body of research suggesting the existence of hippocampal formation cells that indicate direction. These **head-direction (HD) cells** discharge whenever a rat points its head in a particular direction (Figure 21.13C). Different cells have different preferred directions. For example, one HD cell might discharge whenever the rat points its head to the west; another will discharge whenever the rat points its head to the south.

The firing of head-direction cells is not related to the position of the animal's trunk and does not significantly depend on whether the rat is still or moving. Furthermore, HD cells do not adapt as time passes but maintain their rate of discharge as long as the rat's head is pointing in the preferred direction.

A head-direction cell is not activated by the presence of a particular object in the environment. Rather, such a cell is responsive to direction itself, similar to a compass needle, which continues to point north when the compass is moved. Nevertheless, surrounding cues influence HD cells. If a rat is taken to a novel environment, its HD cells will quickly develop a preferred orientation there. If the rat is then removed from that environment while the cues are rotated and is subsequently returned, the HD cells' preferences will rotate with the cues. If the cues are rotated while the rat is in the environment, the preferred direction of HD cells is not as greatly influenced.

If the lights are turned off, head-direction cells maintain their tuning for many minutes. When a rat is allowed to explore two environments connected by a tunnel, its HD cells will maintain the same preferred direction in both environments. But if the cues in one environment are rotated while the rat is absent and the rat is then returned to that environment, the HD cells' preferences will again rotate with the cues. When the rat enters the tunnel and crosses to the second, unperturbed environment, the HD cells revert to their former orientation.

Head-direction cells are not limited to orienting the animal in a horizontal plane; they maintain their directional tuning when the animal climbs up or down as well. HD cells continue to discharge when the rat is restrained, unlike place cells, which stop firing in such a situation. Whereas place cells may fire in one environment but not in another and at different rates on different occasions, every HD cell is locked into a network that is constantly active, depending only on head direction.

Grid Cells

First described by Torkel Hafting and his colleagues (2005), **grid cells** fire at regularly spaced nodes that appear to divide an environment into a grid. Each grid cell discharges at regular spatial intervals, as if discharges marked nodes forming the points of equilateral triangles (Figure 21.13D). The nodes represent points throughout the environment in which an animal is placed, forming a grid. The grid is invariant in the face of changes in the animal's direction, movement, or speed.

Different cells at the same location have the same grid spacing and orientation relative to the environment. They differ, however, in node location such that the firing peaks of one grid cell are slightly shifted from those of its neighbor. Cells located in different parts of the medial entorhinal cortex demark grids of different sizes, as if to map the size of the environment. The orientation of the grids demarked by each cell can be oriented to different cues in the environment and can be influenced by the direction that an animal is facing.

Location of Spatial Cells

The brain regions that house place cells, head-direction cells, and grid cells are largely different. **Figure 21.14** shows that place cells are most often recorded in the entorhinal cortex, subiculum, and hippocampus. Head-direction cells are recorded in the lateral mammillary nuclei, anterior thalamus, cingulate cortex, and postsubicular regions of the hippocampus. Grid cells are recorded in the medial entorhinal cortex.

Figure 21.14 ▼

Locating Spatial Cells
Locations in the rat brain (sagittal section) where place cells, head-direction cells, and grid cells have been recorded. Although the relations among the three systems are not well understood, investigators have established that the head-direction system mediates navigation in relation to the animal's own location, the place-cell system mediates navigation by using environmental cues, and the grid-cell system signals the size of a space and the animal's position within it.

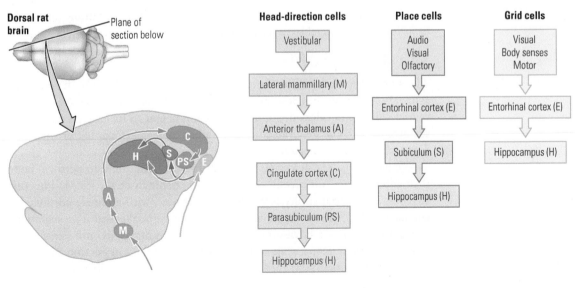

This anatomical organization suggests that interactions among these three temporal lobe regions and their three classes of cells form the substrate of much of our spatial behavior.

- The place system allows an animal to navigate by using the relations between environmental cues (allocentric guidance).
- The head-direction system allows an animal to navigate in relation to its own spatial position (egocentric guidance).
- The grid system provides a spatial framework that indicates the size of a space and the animal's location in that space. Grid cells may provide a frame of reference similar to that provided by the latitude and longitude lines of a map.

Place cells, head-direction cells, and grid cells have been reported in primates, including humans. Edmund Rolls and J. Z. Xiang (2006) report, however, that place cells are far less likely than head-direction cells to be recorded in monkeys, which instead seem to possess many "view cells"—cells that discharge when a monkey looks in particular directions. Therefore, place cells and head-direction cells may possibly be closely linked to eye movements in primates and to body movements in rats.

One way of thinking about the contributions of spatial cells—on the assumption that we humans also have these cell types—is to envision the place-cell system as telling us where things are in the world, the grid system indicating how big our present navigating environment is, and the head-direction and grid systems telling us where we ourselves are. Add in time cells (Howard et al., 2014), and the temporal lobe has all of the ingredients both to create topographic maps and to keep track of personal location with dead reckoning.

⊚ 21.4 Individual Differences in Spatial Abilities

Chapter 12 examines a range of biological and environmental factors that produce individual variations in cerebral asymmetry, including sex and handedness. In this section, we review differences attributed to these variations that appear to influence individual spatial abilities.

Sex-Related Differences

The study of spatial abilities dates to the early part of the twentieth century, in association with studies designed to predict mechanical aptitude. As interest in spatial abilities developed, studies eventually began to include mixed age and sex groups, and the generalization that adult males perform better than adult females gradually emerged.

We have reviewed evidence that adult human males tend to perform better than adult females on certain spatial tests (Harshman et al., 1983). This male advantage in spatial ability is generally contrasted with a female advantage in language skills, fine motor movements, and perceptual speed. Past experience and testing methods, however, influence both advantages in both sexes.

In the tests of virtual water-maze learning described in Section 21.3, Astur and his coworkers (1998) reported one of the largest sex differences favoring human males. Maguire and her colleagues (1999), however, compiled evidence that females are more likely to navigate by using landmarks, whereas males are more likely to use spatial-mapping procedures (see Figure 12.3). This provides one explanation for the Astur results.

Debora Saucier and her colleagues (2007) suggest that sex differences in spatial ability apply not only to the task but also to the part of space in which a task is performed. They suggest that males excel in performing tasks in distant space, whereas the female advantage is most obvious in peripersonal space. The relevance of such laboratory-based tasks to real-world spatial problems is unclear, as Ariane Burke and colleagues (2012) report no sex difference in a real-world test of spatial abilities.

Research results also suggest that females and males differ in their abilities at such skills as chess, mathematics, music, and art, endeavors thought to involve spatial ability. Mathematical aptitude has received the closest scrutiny. Findings in a large number of studies reveal that males outperform females on tests of quantitative ability. In the United States, scores on the Scholastic Aptitude Test and the Johns Hopkins University mathematical talent search indicate that these differences become apparent in adolescence and are more evident at the high end of the performance scale.

Apart from environmental influences, possible explanations for differences between male and female performance are experiential and hormonal. For example, differences may emerge as a result of the action of hormones on neural organization and function. Alternatively, they may be genetically sex-linked and determined by a recessive gene on the X chromosome. The difficulty in obtaining consistent values for sex differences not only relates to testing procedure but also includes previous experiences. Males are much more likely than females to spend a substantial proportion of their time engaged in activities that involve spatial navigation. Where people live in environments that reduce sex-related roles, it is likely that sex differences in cognitive function will accordingly be muted.

Genetic Contributions

The explanation for a genetic basis for male and female differences in spatial ability is evolutionary: they enhance reproductive success. During the formative period in the evolution of modern humans, for example, differentiated roles in food gathering may have been adaptive.

A primary occupation of males was hunting, which requires an ability to find one's way about a large area. Hunting also requires the ability to throw rocks and spears and aim arrows. Males endowed with these spatial skills would be more successful than those who were not, and consequently would be "selected" in the Darwinian sense. Primary roles for females included foraging locally and cooking, behaviors that would draw upon object memory.

At present, however, evidence for the hunter–gatherer sex difference theory is sparse and unsupported by comparative studies on predatory versus nonpredatory nonhuman animals (Clint et al., 2012). And again, within the context of postindustrial societies, the muting of sexually dimorphic roles such as hunting and gathering may also mute the development of cognitive differences.

Mark McGee (1979) suggested that spatial skills are heritable through an X-linked recessive gene. Females have two X chromosomes, and males have one. Thus, traits that are carried by a single gene on the X chromosome are said to be *sex-linked*: if such a gene is recessive, more males than females will be affected. Under this arrangement, according to the usual estimates, 50 percent of males and 25 percent of females will carry the gene and have enhanced spatial abilities. In other words, about one-fourth of females will score above the male median on tests of spatial abilities, a finding obtained in most studies.

The recessive-gene hypothesis has been put to a number of tests and has not emerged unscathed. According to the hypothesis, certain correlations should emerge in the offspring of different families, but these correlations have not been obtained. Another problem concerns the tests used to obtain scores for correlations. Studies using different tests have obtained different correlations, raising the possibility that different kinds of spatial abilities may exist. The results suggest either that alternative inheritance models should be considered or that sex-related differences have other explanations.

Hormonal Influences

Three lines of evidence suggest that hormones influence sex differences in spatial abilities, including findings from (1) developmental studies, (2) studies of persons with chromosomal–hormonal abnormalities, and (3) investigations of the relation between androgenicity and spatial abilities.

Sex differences in spatial performance are found more reliably in adults than in prepubescent children, suggesting that such differences may be partly attributable to hormonal changes during puberty. Prenatal or early postnatal sex-related hormonal influences could account for differences obtained with prepubescent children. Results from studies of patients with **Turner's syndrome**, a disorder found in females born with a single X chromosome rather than the typical XX pair, seem to support this hypothesis (Ross et al., 2006). Turner's patients' intelligence and verbal ability scores are distributed throughout the normal range, but their spatial abilities are impaired, and they display alterations in the neural organization of the parietal cortex. Their scores are extremely low on tests of mental rotation, the Wechsler Adult Intelligence Scale block-design test, the spatial subtest of the Primary Mental Abilities Test, the Road-and-Map Test of Direction Sense, and tests of imaginary movements and direct rotation. These spatial impairments are associated with abnormalities in the parietal cortex.

These results are counterintuitive and at variance with the recessive-gene hypothesis, which would predict that females with a single X chromosome ought to be similar to males, who also have one X chromosome. Females with Turner's syndrome produce no gonadal hormones, which questions the idea that gonadal hormones influence spatial abilities. Current proposals from studies examining this hypothesis are that levels of androgens (masculinizing hormones) or the balance between estrogen and androgens might determine spatial abilities.

There are many possible explanations of how hormones might influence the neural systems responsible for spatial abilities. Early in life, hormones may influence neural connections, neural growth, and cell death, thus sculpting a spatial neural system in which some individuals have enhanced abilities. In favor of this idea, boys who display excess androgen have increased gray matter in cortical structures constituting the dorsal stream (Mueller et al., 2011). On the other hand, hormones might selectively modulate neural function in these systems through still-unknown mechanisms.

Handedness and Spatial Ability

Left-handedness is often proposed to confer a special spatial advantage. Left-handers reportedly are disproportionately represented in engineering and architecture faculties. Leonardo da Vinci and Michelangelo were left-handed. In the realm of sport, left-handedness is common among tennis players and baseball pitchers.

Although left-handedness is a frequently reported advantage in sporting events, it may be largely attributable to the fact that left-handers have vastly more opportunities to practice against right-handers than vice versa (Harris, 2010). Nevertheless, if the right hemisphere disproportionately contributes to spatial behavior and if some left-handers' speech also resides in the right hemisphere, coextensive control of space and of language may accord left-handers cognitive advantages in some endeavors.

21.5 Episodic Memory, Scene Construction, and Theory of Mind

A body of evidence suggests that spatial abilities are special and that they derive from a dedicated neural system. Evidence also suggests that spatial memory deficits and episodic memory deficits occur together. This raises a question: Is spatial memory just a subcategory of episodic memory?

Spatial Activity in Episodic Memory

Stuart Zola-Morgan and his coworkers (1986) favor the idea that the hippocampus has a role in memory and that episodic memory impairment includes an obligatory spatial memory impairment. They describe R.B., a male postal worker who, at 52 years of age, underwent coronary bypass surgery. During the procedure, arterial blood flow to his brain was reduced temporarily, to dire effect. Until his death 5 years later, R.B. exhibited marked anterograde amnesia as well as spatial impairments. A postmortem examination revealed a bilateral loss of all cells in CA1, a restricted part of the hippocampus (see Figure 18.7B).

Even the findings in studies on birds, although seemingly consistent with a special role for the hippocampus in spatial behavior, are amenable to an episodic memory interpretation. Nicola Clayton and her colleagues (2007) report that if birds are given especially tasty or perishable items to store, they are likely to retrieve those items before retrieving other ones. A food-storing bird also considers whether other birds are watching and takes preventative measures to protect cached food if they are. Thus, to be useful, some episodic memories need a spatial tag, once again supporting the idea that spatial memory is a form of episodic memory.

Spatial Memory as Distinct from Episodic Memory

An argument for the idea that spatial memory is distinct from other episodic memory comes from studying people who have no known brain injury and who display selective spatial disabilities. Giuseppi Iaria and Jason Barton (2010) identified a cognitive disorder they call **developmental topographic disorientation** (DTD). It is characterized by an inability to segregate landmarks and derive navigational information from them, navigate through a nonverbal process, or generate cognitive maps. Individuals with DTD are frequently lost or disoriented even in their own homes or in the surrounding neighborhood. They need to be accompanied when walking or driving to work or school, which frequently leaves them at risk for getting lost. One subject was even convinced that north was always the direction that she was facing.

DTD is a lifelong condition frequently displayed by other family members. Given a battery of nonspatial and spatial tests, people with DTD perform at control levels on the nonspatial tests but are impaired on all spatial tests, including left–right orientation, landmark navigation, route following, and place learning. DTD's neural basis is not known, but it likely derives from abnormalities in dorsal stream projections. With respect to the question of whether spatial memory is just another form of episodic memory, this evidence would indicate that it is not.

Spatial and Episodic Memory as Hippocampal Functions

Now we discuss two possible explanations advanced for why episodic and spatial memory deficits co-occur after hippocampal damage.

Dual-Contribution Theory

In the first explanation, the dorsal- and ventral-stream projections that mediate both memory functions course through the hippocampus but remain at least partially independent within the hippocampus and related structures. Thus, dorsal-stream projections to the medial temporal lobe contribute to spatial memory; ventral-stream processes contribute to episodic memory; and damage to the hippocampus impairs both.

Michael Prerau and colleagues (2014) support this *dual-contribution theory* with a single-cell recording study. They trained rats to turn left or right in a T-maze, shown in Figure 21.7C, and recorded from cells in the entorhinal cortex and CA1 in the hippocampus. The entorhinal cortex cells discharged when the rat made turns, whereas the CA1 cells discharged as the rats passed salient visual cues. This result suggests that object memory and spatial memory, although separate, co-occur.

Scene Construction Theory

Eleanor Maguire and Sinéad Mullally (2013) have a different take. They suggest that the hippocampus functions for neither spatial memory nor episodic memory but rather employs both to create more; namely, spatially coherent scenes that involve four elements: spatial navigation, episodic memory, imagining, and future thinking (**Figure 21.15**). Their **scene construction theory**

Figure 21.15 ▼

Elements of Scene Construction Theory The hippocampus employs four elements to construct spatially coherent scenes: spatial navigation, episodic memory, imagining, and future thinking. All four elements are lost together in people with hippocampal damage. (Eleanor A. Maguire, Sinéad L. Mullally, The hippocampus: a manifesto for change. Journal of Experimental Psychology, General 2013 142, 4, 1180-1189, Figure 2.)

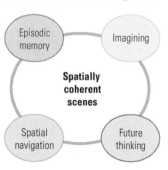

(SCT) is based on numerous lines of evidence, including their finding that all four elements of spatially coherent scenes are lost together in people with hippocampal damage.

Adding to the evidence that Maguire and Mullally present for SCT is that people with intact hippocampi attempt to place objects or events within a larger spatial context to form a scene. (Recall from Figure 21.12 the boundary expansion behavior displayed by control participants, who when drawing an object displayed in a frame, expand the boundary between an object and the frame, whereas amnesic patients do not.) Scene construction theory thus predicts that for information to be biologically useful, it has to be "packaged" as a composite of past experience, present context, and future prospects.

Scene construction theory also argues that most of our spatial imagination, future thinking, and even memory distortion is related to scene construction. Even our daytime and nighttime dreaming is composed of scenes. It follows from SCT that dorsal- and ventral-stream neural pathways, including the hippocampus, are ultimately designed not to store individual spatial and episodic memories but to produce higher-order "memory composites" in the form of spatially coherent scenes.

Theory of Mind

An illustration of the use of scenes in everyday behavior is exemplified in *social cognition*, or theory of mind, the ability to attribute mental states—desires, beliefs, intentions, pretending, knowledge—to ourselves and others and to understand that others experience similar states (see Figure 15.6). Theory of mind can be studied in amnesic patients and controls by giving them a picture, for example of a family having a picnic, and questioning them about the family members' activities—past, present, and future.

Social cognition can also be studied by asking subjects and controls to compare the consequences of a present versus a future decision: Would you accept $50 now or $100 in 2 weeks? Amnesic subjects, including patients with no hippocampus, do demonstrate that they have theory of mind, but it is stereotypical in its features and probably based on the semantic knowledge of what people may typically do, have done, or might do. In contrast, control participants provide richer descriptions and make more complex decisions.

Participants are especially skilled in predicting the theories of mind of relatives and close associates by virtue of their personal familiarity with recent or past episodic events—that is, the context (Rabin et al., 2013). It is not so much scene construction that distinguishes the hippocampus's function; more, it is that the scene's context is personal, immediate, and relevant.

SUMMARY

21.1 Spatial Behavior and Spatial Impairments

Evidence obtained from brain-injured people suggests that the right hemisphere and the temporal lobes, especially the hippocampus, play special roles in spatial behavior. Nevertheless, a variety of spatial behaviors reflecting body space, grasping space, and distal space have different neural controls, as does time space.

Humans display various spatial deficits depending upon lesion location. They may be impaired in mapping space, discriminating object location relative to themselves, approaching objects, or acquiring new spatial information, and they may experience spatial distortions relative to themselves in space or in space relative to themselves.

21.2 Dorsal- and Ventral-Stream Contributions to Spatial Behavior

From its origins in visual cortex, the dorsal stream enters a domain in parietal cortex that sends projections to premotor cortex, the frontal eye fields in dorsolateral prefrontal cortex, and the medial temporal cortex. These projections coordinate spatial behavior relative to the body, eye movement, and environmental location. The ventral stream projection to the medial temporal lobes mediates knowledge about objects. Frontal cortex produces behaviors that coordinate spatial and object memory.

21.3 Experimental Models of Spatial Behavior

Researchers have modeled spatial behavior in human and nonhuman animals. Route following includes moving toward or away from landmarks or cues or following a sensory gradient such as an odor trail. Piloting includes using landmarks or cues to plot routes or locate places in relation to those cues. Caching involves storing and subsequently locating objects.

Dead reckoning entails using self-movement cues to locate a present position and to return to a starting location. These spatial behaviors key into the activity of specialized hippocampal formation neurons, including place and place-by-direction cells, head-direction cells, grid cells, and time cells.

21.4 Individual Differences in Spatial Abilities

Several lines of evidence suggest that sex and handedness influence human spatial abilities. Thus, sex hormones and cortical organization can influence spatial behavior. Tests of spatial abilities are useful in indicating both the site and the side of brain injury in humans.

21.5 Episodic Memory, Scene Construction, and Theory of Mind

Impairments in spatial memory and episodic memory after hippocampal damage present a puzzle: Are they different or a shared function? Scene construction theory proposes that the hippocampus functions to integrate new information, including spatial navigation, episodic memory, imagining, and future thinking, into spatially coherent scenes. All of these elements are important for developing social cognition, a personalized theory of mind.

References

Allison, R. S., L. J. Hurwitz, J. G. White, and T. J. Wilmot. A follow-up study of a patient with Bálint's syndrome. *Neuropsychologia* 7:319–333, 1969.

Astur, R. S., M. L. Ortiz, and R. J. Sutherland. A characterization of performance by men and women in a virtual Morris water task: A large and reliable sex difference. *Behavioural Brain Research* 93:185–190, 1998.

Astur, R. S., L. B. Taylor, A. N. Mamelak, L. Philpott, and R. J. Sutherland. Humans with hippocampus damage display severe spatial memory impairments in a virtual Morris water task. *Behavioural Brain Research* 132:77–84, 2002.

Bálint, R. Seelenlahmung des "Schauens," optische Ataxie, raumlielie Störung der Aufmerksamkeit. *Monatsschrift für Psychiatrie und Neurologie* 25:51–81, 1909.

Barry, C., and N. Burgess. Neural mechanisms of self-location. *Current Biology* 24:330–339, 2014.

Best, P. J., A. M. White, and A. Minai. Spatial processing in the brain: The activity of hippocampal place cells. *Annual Review of Neuroscience* 24:459–486, 2001.

Bohbot, V. D., and S. Corkin. Posterior parahippocampal place learning in H.M. *Hippocampus* 17:863–872, 2007.

Burke, A., A. Kandler, and D. Good. Women who know their place: Sex-based differences in spatial abilities and their evolutionary significance. *Human Nature—An Interdisciplinary Biosocial Perspective* 23:133–148, 2012.

Carmon, A., and H. P. Bechtoldt. Dominance of the right cerebral hemisphere for stereopsis. *Neuropsychologia* 7:29–39, 1969.

Clayton, N. S., J. M. Dally, and N. J. Emery. Social cognition by food-caching corvids: The western scrub-jay as a natural psychologist. *Philosophical Transactions of the Royal Society of London: Biological Sciences* 362:507–522, 2007.

Clint, E. K., E. Sober, and T. J. Garland. Male superiority in spatial navigation: Adaption or side effect? *Quarterly Review of Biology* 87:289–313, 2012.

Corkin, S. Tactually-guided maze-learning in man: Effects of unilateral cortical excisions and bilateral hippocampal lesions. *Neuropsychologia* 3:339–351, 1965.

Corkin, S. The role of different cerebral structures in somaesthetic perception. In E. C. Carterette and M. P. Friedman, Eds. *Handbook of Perception*, vol. 6. New York: Academic Press, 1978.

Darwin, C. On the origin of certain instincts. *Nature* 7:417–418, 1873.

de Renzi, E. *Disorders of Space Exploration and Cognition*. New York: Wiley, 1982.

Goldman-Rakic, P. S. Circuitry of primate prefrontal cortex and regulation of behavior by representational memory. In V. B. Mountcastle, F. Plum, and S. R. Geiger, Eds. *Handbook of Physiology, vol. 5, Higher Functions of the Brain*. Bethesda, Md.: American Physiological Society, 1987.

Haaxma, R., and H. G. Kuypers. Intrahemispheric cortical connexions and visual guidance of hand and finger movements in the rhesus monkey. *Brain* 98:239–260, 1975.

Hafting, T., M. Fyhn, S. Molden, M. B. Moser, and E. I. Moser. Microstructure of a spatial map in the entorhinal cortex. *Nature* 436:801–806, 2005.

Hall, Z. J., S. Delaney, and D. F. Sherry. Inhibition of cell proliferation in black-capped chickadees suggests a role for neurogenesis in spatial learning. *Developmental Neurobiology* 74(10):1002–1010, 2014.

Halpern, D. F. *Sex Differences in Cognitive Abilities*. Hillsdale, N.J.: Lawrence Erlbaum, 1986.

Hannay, H. J., N. R. Varney, and A. L. Benton. Visual localization in patients with unilateral brain disease. *Journal of Neurology, Neurosurgery and Psychiatry* 39:307–313, 1976.

Harris, L. J. In fencing, what gives left-handers the edge? Views from the present and the distant past. *Laterality* 15:15–55, 2010.

Harshman, R. A., E. Hampson, and S. A. Berenbaum. Individual differences in cognitive abilities and brain organization I: Sex and handedness differences in ability. *Canadian Journal of Psychology* 37:144–192, 1983.

Hécaen, H., J. de Ajuriaguerra, and J. Massonet. Les troubles visuoconstructifs par lésions pariéto-occipitales droites: Role des perturbations vestibulaires. *Encephale* 1:122–179, 1951.

Hécaen, H., C. Tzortzis, and P. Rondot. Loss of topographical memory with learning deficits. *Cortex* 16:525–542, 1980.

Holmes, G., and G. Horax. Disturbances of spatial orientation and visual attention, with loss of stereoscopic vision. *Archives of Neurology and Psychiatry* 1:385–407, 1919.

Howard, M. W., C. J. MacDonald, Z. Tiganj, K. H. Shankar, Q. Du, M. E. Hasselmo, and H. Eichenbaum. A unified mathematical framework for coding time, space, and sequences in the hippocampal region. *Journal of Neuroscience* 26: 4692–4707, 2014.

Iaria, G., and J. J. Barton. Developmental Topographical Disorientation: A newly discovered cognitive disorder. *Experimental Brain Research* 206:189–196, 2010.

Jackson, J. H. On the nature of duality of the brain. *Brain* 38:80–103, 1915.

Kraus, B. J., R. J. Robinson, 2nd, J. A. White, H. Eichenbaum, and M. E. Hasselmo. Hippocampal "time cells": Time versus path integration. *Neuron* 78:1090–1101, 2013.

Kravitz, D. J., K. S. Saleem, C. I. Baker , and M. Mishkin. A new neural framework for visuospatial processing. *Nature Reviews Neuroscience* 12:217–230, 2011.

Kravitz, D. J., K. S. Saleem, C. I. Baker, L. G. Ungerleider, and M. Mishkin. The ventral visual pathway: An expanded neural framework for the processing of object quality. *Trends in Cognitive Science* 17:26–49, 2013.

Legg, E. W., and N. S. Clayton. Eurasian jays (*Garrulus glandarius*) conceal caches from onlookers. *Animal Cognition* 17(5):1223–1226, 2014.

Levine, D. N., J. Warach, and M. J. Farah. Two visual systems in mental imagery: Dissociation of "what" and "where" in imagery disorders due to bilateral posterior cerebral lesions. *Neurology* 35:1010–1015, 1985.

Lin, L., G. Chen, H. Kuang, D. Wang, and J. Z. Tsien. Neural encoding of the concept of nest in the mouse brain. *Proceedings of the National Academy of Sciences U.S.A.* 104:6066–6071, 2007.

Maguire, E. A., and S. L. Mullally. The hippocampus: A manifesto for change. *Journal of Experimental Psychology General* 142:1180–1189, 2013.

McGee, M. G. Human spatial abilities: Psychometric studies and environmental, genetic, hormonal, and neurological influences. *Psychological Bulletin* 86:889–918, 1979.

Mueller, S. C., D. P. Merke, E. W. Leschek, S. Fromm, C. Grillon, B. R. Cornwell, C Vanryzin, and M. Ernst. Grey matter volume correlates with virtual water maze task performance in boys with androgen excess. *Neuroscience* 197:225–232, 2011.

Mullally, S. L., H. Intraub, and E. A. Maguire. Attenuated boundary extension produces a paradoxical memory advantage in amnesic patients. *Current Biology* 22:261–268, 2012.

Nakamura, R. K., S. J. Schein, and R. Desimone. Visual responses from cells in striate cortex of monkeys rendered chronically "blind" by lesions of nonvisual cortex. *Experimental Brain Research* 63:185–190, 1986.

Nemmi, F., M. Boccia, L. Piccardi, G. Galati, and C. Guariglia. Segregation of neural circuits involved in spatial learning in reaching and navigational space. *Neuropsychologia* 51:1561–1570, 2013.

O'Keefe, J., and J. Dostrovsky. The hippocampus as a spatial map: Preliminary evidence from unit activity in the freely-moving rat. *Brain Research* 34:171–175, 1971.

O'Keefe, J., and L. Nadel. *The Hippocampus As a Cognitive Map*. New York: Clarendon Press, 1978.

Pallis, C. A. Impaired identification of faces and places with agnosia for colors. *Journal of Neurology, Neurosurgery and Psychiatry* 18:218–224, 1955.

Petrides, M., and B. Milner. Deficits on subject-ordered tasks after frontal- and temporal-lobe lesions in man. *Neuropsychologia* 20:249–292, 1982.

Prerau, M. J., P. A. Lipton, and H. B. Eichenbaum. Characterizing context-dependent differential firing activity in the hippocampus and entorhinal cortex. *Hippocampus* 24:476–492, 2014.

Putman, N. F., M. M. Scanlan, E. J. Billman, J. P. O'Neil, R. B. Couture, T. P. Quinn, K. J. Lohmann, and D. L. Noakes. An inherited magnetic map guides ocean navigation in juvenile Pacific salmon. *Current Biology* 24446–24450, 2014.

Rabin J. S., N. Carson, A. Gilboa, D. T. Stuss, and R. S. Rosenbaum. Imagining other people's experiences in a person with impaired episodic memory: The role of personal familiarity. *Frontiers in Psychology* 3:588, 2012.

Rolls, E. T., and J. Z. Xiang. Spatial view cells in the primate hippocampus and memory recall. *Reviews of Neuroscience* 17:175–200, 2006.

Rosenbaum, R. S., S. Kohler, D. L. Schacter, M. Moscovitch, R. Westmacott, S. E. Black, F. Gao, and E. Tulving. The case of K.C.: Contributions of a memory-impaired person to memory theory. *Neuropsychologia* 43:989–1021, 2005.

Ross, E. D. Sensory-specific and fractional disorders of recent memory in man I: Isolated loss of visual recent memory. *Archives of Neurology* 37:193–200, 1980.

Ross, J., D. Roeltgen, and A. Zinn. Cognition and the sex chromosomes: Studies in Turner syndrome. *Hormone Research* 65:47–56, 2006.

Rousseaux, M., J. Honoré, and A. Saj. Body representations and brain damage. *Neurophysiological Clinics* 44:59–67, 2014.

Saucier, D., A. Lisoway, S. Green, and L. Elias. Female advantage for object location memory in peripersonal but not extrapersonal space. *Journal of the International Neuropsychological Society* 13:683–686, 2007.

Sherry, D. F., and J. S. Hoshooley. (2010). Seasonal hippocampal plasticity in food-storing birds. *Philosophical Transactions of the Royal Society. B: Biological Sciences* 365:933–943.

Smith, M. L., and B. Milner. The role of the right hippocampus in the recall of spatial location. *Neuropsychologia* 19:781–793, 1981.

Takahashi, N., M. Kawamura, J. Shiota, N. Kasahata, and K. Hirayama. Pure topographic disorientation due to a right retrosplenial lesion. *Neurology* 49:464–469, 1997.

Taube, J. S. The head direction signal: Origins and sensory-motor integration. *Annual Review of Neuroscience* 30:181–207, 2007.

Teng, E., and L. R. Squire. Memory for places learned long ago is intact after hippocampal damage. *Science* 400:675–677, 1999.

Ungerleider, L.G., and M. Mishkin. Two cortical visual systems. In D. J. Ingle, M. A. Goodale, and R. J. W. Mansfield, Eds., *Analysis of Visual Behavior*, pp. 549–586. Boston: MIT Press, 1982.

Ward, B. J., L. B. Day, S. R. Wilkening, D. R. Wylie, D. M. Saucier, and A. N. Iwaniuk. Hummingbirds have a greatly enlarged hippocampal formation. *Biological Letters* 8:657–659, 2012.

Whishaw, I. Q., D. J. Hines, and D. G. Wallace. Dead reckoning (path integration) requires the hippocampal formation: Evidence from spontaneous exploration and spatial learning tasks in light (allothetic) and dark (idiothetic) tests. *Behavioural Brain Research* 127:49–70, 2001.

Wolbers, T., J. M. Weiner, H. A. Mallot, and C. Büchel. Differential recruitment of the hippocampus, medial prefrontal cortex, and the human motion complex during path integration in humans. *Journal of Neuroscience* 27:9408–9416, 2007.

Worsley, C. L., M. Recce, H. J. Spiers, J. Marley, C. E. Polkey, and R. G. Morris. Path integration following temporal lobectomy in humans. *Neuropsychologia* 39:452–464, 2001.

Zangwill, O. L. *Cerebral Dominance and Its Relation to Psychological Function*. Edinburgh: Oliver & Boyd, 1960.

Zola-Morgan, S., L. Squire, and D. G. Amaral. Human amnesia and the medial temporal region: Enduring memory impairment following a bilateral lesion limited to field CA1 of the hippocampus. *Journal of Neuroscience* 6:2950–2967, 1986.

22

Attention and Consciousness

PORTRAIT A Curious Case of Neglect

After returning from a trip abroad at age 28, R.P. developed a terrible headache and flulike aches and fever. The flu symptoms disappeared after a few days, but the headache remained for several weeks. During this time, R.P. noticed that she was unusually clumsy and started having difficulty recognizing people's faces.

We first met R.P. 2 years later. Among a variety of visuoperceptual problems, she presented especially severe deficits in facial recognition, a mental neglect of the left side of space, and constructional apraxia.

- The face-recognition deficit was so severe that R.P. was unable to recognize her identical twin sister except by movement and voice.
- The mental neglect was intriguing. Before her illness, R.P. had earned a master's degree in library science, and she was an excellent cook. Having friends over for supper had been a joy of her life. Now entertaining was impossible: she could not remember where in her kitchen, items were kept especially items on her left side. Those who show

DENNIS O'BRIEN

hemispatial neglect, including the dog pictured here that has a right-hemisphere brain tumor, behave as though the left side of the world were not present.

- R.P.'s apraxia was not severe, but she was unable to assemble things. A bookshelf unit that she had bought was still in boxes. R.P. noted, in fact, that she could not even imagine how the unit could be put together.

Imaging studies found abnormally low blood flow in the superior parietal regions in both hemispheres and throughout the right temporal lobe, but the causes of R.P.'s symptoms were never really understood. It seems likely that a viral infection caused her symptoms and the abnormal blood flow.

R.P. had one other persisting symptom: her social cognition was impaired. She had been duped on two occasions by con artists who tricked her into giving them money for bogus projects. She complained that she did not seem to be able to tell when people were untrustworthy.

Attention and consciousness are properties of the nervous system that direct complex actions of body and brain. They are not *epiphenomena*— properties that emerge simply because the brain is complex. At chapter end, we address questions about the neural basis of consciousness and why we are conscious. Along the way, we explore the evidence of how we select our behaviors and delve deeper into the deficits R.P. showed—in attention and visual guidance of movements, in recognizing faces, and in identifying others' intentions.

◎ 22.1 Defining Attention and Consciousness

Donald Hebb (1980) and others have argued that the central question in neuropsychology is the relation between the mind and the brain. The question is easy to ask, yet grasping what it is that we need to explain it is not so easy. How do we select information on which to act? How do we select behaviors?

Worms and other simple animals have a limited sensory capacity and an equally limited behavioral repertoire. Animals such as dogs have a much more sophisticated sensory capacity and a corresponding increase in behavioral options. Primates, including humans, have even further developed sensory capacity and behavioral complexity.

Thus, as sensory and motor capacities increase, so does the problem of selection, both of information and of behavior. Furthermore, as the brain expands, memory increases, providing an internal variable to stimulus interpretation and to response selection. Finally, as the number of sensory channels increases, the need to correlate the different inputs to produce a single "reality" arises. We first encountered this problem in Section 10.2 when we examined the binding problem.

One way to consider these evolutionary changes is to posit that as the brain expands to increase sensorimotor capacity, so does some other process (or processes) that takes part in selecting sensory and motor behaviors. One proposed process for selective awareness and response to stimuli is **attention**, narrowing or focusing awareness selectively to a part of the sensory environment or to a class of stimuli.

The concept of attention implies that we somehow focus a "mental spotlight" on certain sensory inputs, motor programs, memories, or internal representations. This spotlight might be unconscious, in that we are not aware of the process, or it might be conscious, as when we scan our memory for someone's name. The development of language should increase the likelihood of conscious attention, but it is unlikely that all conscious processing is verbal. One can speculate, for example, that Archimedes's "eureka" insight entailed more than just verbal, conscious processing.

The point is, as sensorimotor capacities expand, so do the processes of attention and consciousness. In broad terms, *consciousness* is synonymous at a primary level with awareness and at a secondary level with awareness of awareness. A gradual evolutionary increase in consciousness correlates with the ability to organize sensory and motor capacities. The most-evolved organizer is language. This implies an increased processing capacity for attention.

Earlier in your reading, you encountered conditions such as blindsight and numb touch, both problems of attention and conscious awareness. Patients can describe the location of sensory information for which they have no conscious awareness (see Sections 13.4 and 14.3). Similarly, amnesic patients such as H.M., whose case is profiled throughout Chapter 18, can display implicit memory even when they have no conscious recollection of having been in a room before, let alone having learned a task.

R.P. and others who have right posterior parietotemporal lesions show hemispatial neglect: they behave as though the left side of the world were not present. That this problem is not one of sensory input was illustrated beautifully in experiments—showing that such patients have a cognitive as well as behavioral hemispatial neglect. For example, when asked to imagine a familiar scene from a particular perspective, patients neglected the left side, but when asked to imagine the same scene from a perspective 180° removed, they described the previously neglected regions and this time neglected the previously described regions!

The close relation between consciousness and attention has led to a question: Are these processes distinct, or are they different manifestations of the same brain process? Christof Koch and Naotsugu Tsuchiya (2007) have argued that consciousness and attention are fundamentally different and require two distinct brain processes. For them, the key difference is that attention is primarily a top-down process that selects information from a specific part of the sensory world, such as a point in space or an object, and in doing so, takes time. Consciousness, by contrast, is not so selective: it simply summarizes all information pertinent to the individual and its environment.

Thus, as consciousness gives us the gist of the world, attention focuses on specific features in the world. Keep this distinction in mind as we look more closely at the nature of attention and of consciousness.

◎ 22.2 Attention

Attention has an uneven history. During contrasting periods in psychology, the existence of attentional processes and specific attentional systems either were simply assumed or their existence completely rejected. Behaviorists, for example, held that a full account of behavior is possible in strictly physiological terms, with no reference to cognitive concepts such as attention or even consciousness.

The emergence of cognitive science led to a reevaluation of the behaviorist perspective. Investigators in both cognitive science and neuroscience have returned to the position first espoused by William James in the late 1800s: "Everyone knows what attention is. It is the taking possession by the mind, in clear and vivid form, of one out of what seems several simultaneously possible objects or trains of thought."

Automatic and Conscious Processing Compared

An area of agreement in cognitive psychology is that certain behaviors can be performed with little, if any, focused attention, whereas others are highly sensitive to the allocation of attention. *Automatic processes* are unconscious: direct behavior occurs without intention, involuntarily, without awareness, and without interfering with ongoing activities. Automatic processing may be an innate property of sensory information processing, or extended training may produce it.

Operations that are not automatic have been referred to by various terms—controlled, effortful, attentive, and conscious. Unlike automatic processes, conscious operations require focused attention. Automatic processes are bottom-up and conscious processes top-down. Stopping at a red light is an example of bottom-up processing, whereas actively searching for a street sign at which to make a turn is an example of top-down processing.

Bottom-up processing is data driven: it relies almost exclusively on the stimulus information being presented in the environment. In contrast, top-down processing is conceptually driven, relying on information already in memory. That includes whatever expectation might exist regarding the task at hand. Viewed in this way, we can reasonably presume that automatic and conscious processing require at least some different cortical circuits. One hypothesis is that whatever unique cortical circuits are recruited in attentive processing must include processes of consciousness.

Another way to examine the difference between automatic and conscious processing is to try it yourself. Consider the following experiment. Anne Treisman and her colleagues (1986, 1988) presented participants with boxed arrays of stimuli such as the four shown in **Figure 22.1**. The task in each case is to identify the target that is different from all the others. Try it now.

Did you find some targets easier to find than others? Treisman's participants did as well. Response times differ dramatically depending on the nature of the stimulus. When the task requires identifying a target with an *extra* line, as at the upper left in Figure 22.1, search time is independent of the number of distractors. Apparently, the target visually pops out of the display. But when the task requires the participant to find a target distinguished by the *lack* of a feature present in the other items, as on the upper right, the time taken to find the target varies directly with the number of distractors. Evidently, in this case we must subject the items in the display to a serial search.

The result of Treisman's experiment is not intuitive. After all, each case requires the same discrimination between the same two stimuli. Thus, we can infer:

- Certain aspects of visual processing are automatic. We need not focus attention on any particular aspect of the visual field. Analysis requires only a specific visual feature, such as a vertical line (the pop-outs in Figure 22.1), to locate the target.

- Other aspects of visual processing depend on focused attention to locate the conjunction—the combination of features, such as circles and lines—that leads to the target. **Conjunction search** is a serial process, as if a mental spotlight were scanning from one location to another, searching for particular combinations of sensory information. In the lower panels of Figure 22.1, for example, the conjunction of shading and form identifies the target.

In principle, it should be possible to develop feature processing with practice. Treisman and her colleagues have studied this possibility intensively, but they conclude that although practice can speed up feature processing, it remains dependent on specific automatic neural associations between features as well as on serial-processing pathways. Feature processing appears to be innate to the visual system.

Treisman (1986) has explained her results with a perceptual model of **feature search**, the cognitive strategy for scanning for specific features of stimuli. As illustrated in **Figure 22.2**, a stimulus registered in area V1 is broken down into separate feature maps. This information is then serially processed in parallel pathways (for example, to area V3, V4, or V5). Because no single visual area specifically integrates or conjoins different features of the object, bits of the visual

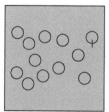
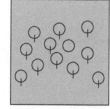
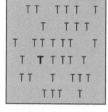
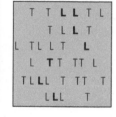

Figure 22.1 ▲

Visual Processing Tasks
(Left) Feature search. Here, the ♀ and the **T** visually "pop out" of the display automatically. (Right) Serial search. You must scan from symbol to symbol to locate the ○ and the **T** in each display. (Bottom) Conjunction search. With focused attention, the combination of line weight and form identifies the target. (Research from Treisman and Gormican, 1988.)

world must be processed serially, presumably using some sort of reentry process (see Figure 10.16B).

The idea is that attention is directed to each location in turn and that features present in the same "fixation" of attention are combined to form a single object. Michael Posner and Marcus Raichle (1993) suggested that in a sense, the attentional process provides the "glue" that cements features into a unitary object. When the features have been assembled, the object can be perceived and held in memory as a unit.

A clear prediction from Treisman's theory is that neurons in the visual areas outside area V1 and probably outside area V2 should respond differentially, depending on whether attention is focused on the corresponding receptive field. In the following section, we consider neurophysiological evidence that these neurons do indeed respond differentially.

A question that arises from the results of feature-detector research is, What constitutes a feature? Treisman presumes that features are the properties the visual system codes cells to detect. Perhaps features are biologically significant stimuli. John Eastwood and his colleagues (2001) presented participants with displays of happy and sad emoji faces similar to those shown in **Figure 22.3**. The task was to identify the odd face, which could be a happy face in a sea of sad ones or vice versa. Before you try this one, turn your book upside down.

Participants were faster at detecting sad faces, upside down or right side up. When Eastwood and coworkers redid the experiment with abstract targets that signified either a happy or a sad state, participants still found the sad-related feature faster.

Given that the features should be equally conspicuous in the happy and sad conditions, it follows, biologically, that something is more important about detecting sad (negative) than happy (positive) stimuli. As mentioned in Section 20.4, certain cells in the amygdala are especially tuned to fear-related stimuli, so negative stimuli (potentially dangerous or threatening features as well as sad ones) appear to be attended to very efficiently and to demand attention more than do targets for more-positive features.

From an evolutionary perspective, favoring the nervous system attentive to stimuli that can influence an animal's survival makes sense. The evolution of biological targets is likely more important to survival than are the simpler targets detected by cells in area V1.

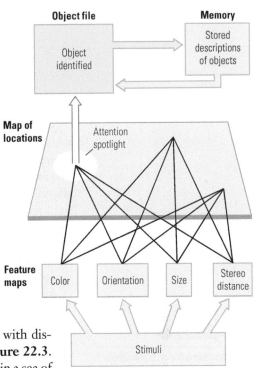

Figure 22.2 ▲

Treisman's Model of Feature Search Beginning at the bottom of the illustration, early vision encodes some simple and useful properties of a scene in a number of feature maps, which may preserve the spatial relations of the visual world but do not themselves make spatial information available to subsequent processing stages. Instead, focused attention selects and integrates the features it maps at particular locations. At later visual stages, the integrated information creates and updates recognition "files" on perceptual objects. In turn, the perceptual file contents are compared with descriptions stored in a recognition network (memory). (Research from Treisman, 1986.)

 **Figure 22.3** ◄

Feature-Search Demonstration Visual displays in which participants must detect happy or sad faces. Participants detect sad faces faster, even if presented upside down. (Research from Eastwood et al., 2001.)

Neurophysiological Evidence of Attention

Any experiment purporting to demonstrate that the focus of attention determines the responses of neurons must meet one important criterion. The *same stimulus* must activate a neuron at one time and not at another. This condition rules out the possibility that the changes in neural activity are somehow related to the actual features of the stimulus target.

Jeffrey Moran and Robert Desimone (1985) trained a monkey to hold a bar while it gazed at a fixation point on a screen. A sample stimulus (for instance, a vertical red bar, as illustrated on the left in **Figure 22.4**) appeared briefly at one location in the receptive field, followed about 500 milliseconds later by two stimuli: one at the same location and another in a separate one. The key point: both targets were in the cell's receptive field, but only one was in the correct location. When the test stimulus was identical with the sample and in the same location, the animal was rewarded if it released the bar immediately. In this way, the same visual stimulus could be presented to different regions of the neurons' receptive fields, but the importance of the information varied with its location.

As the animals performed the task, the researchers recorded cell firing in area V4. Cells in V4 are sensitive to color and form; therefore, different neurons responded to different conjunctions of features. A given cell might respond to one stimulus (for example, a horizontal green bar) but not to another (for example, a vertical red bar). These stimuli were presented either in the correct location or in an incorrect location for predicting reward.

The critical result is the behavior of the neuron in response to the effective target stimulus, illustrated on the right in Figure 22.4. When the effective stimulus was presented in the correct location, the cell was highly active. When the *same stimulus* was presented in an incorrect location, however, the cell was not responsive. When attention is focused on a place in the visual world, neurons appear to respond only to stimuli appropriate to that place.

Figure 22.4 ▼

Demonstrating Selective Attention A monkey performing an attentional task demonstrates that even though a given neuron typically responds to a stimulus in many locations, the neuron can adapt to attend selectively to information in a specific region of its receptive field. (Data source: Moran and Desimone, 1985.)

Experimental procedure

Monkeys were trained to release a bar when a certain stimulus was presented in a certain location. The monkeys learned to ignore stimuli in all other locations.

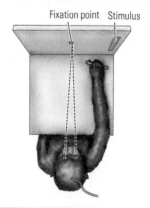

Fixation point   Stimulus

Results

During performance of this task, researchers recorded the firing of neurons in visual area V4, which are sensitive to color and form. Stimuli were presented in either rewarded or unrewarded locations.

Pretraining recordings:

Rewarded location   Unrewarded location

Strong response   Strong response

Before training, neurons responded to stimuli in all locations.

Posttraining recordings:

Rewarded location   Unrewarded location

Strong response   Baseline response

After training, neurons responded only when the visual stimuli were in the rewarded location.

Conclusion

A neuron can learn to respond selectively to information in its receptive field.

Ineffective stimuli remained so regardless of where they appeared in the visual field. Moran and Desimone considered the possibility that visual areas activated earlier (V1) or later (TE) in visual processing also might show attentional effects. Cells in area V1 showed no attentional effects, whereas cells in area TE did. Presumably, features detected in area V1 were too simple to direct attention, whereas those detected in TE could do so.

Moran and Desimone's results are also theoretically important to the general matter of space. The cells showing constraints in spatial attention were in areas V4 and TE, both parts of the ventral object-recognition stream. Thus, neurons in this system are coding spatial location, consistent with David Milner and Melvyn Goodale's (2006) idea that both the dorsal and the ventral streams of visual processing play a role in perceiving space, but their roles are different (as elaborated in Sections 13.2, 14.1, 15.2, and 21.2).

Note that Moran and Desimone's monkey did not actually have to move. If it did, we would predict that cells in the posterior parietal cortex would be sensitive to attentional demands. Vernon Mountcastle and his colleagues (e.g., 1995) report just such results. They found that posterior parietal cells are active when animals reach to obtain an object, such as food, but are not active when the same movements are made for other reasons. Notice that these cells are responding not to the features of the stimuli but rather to the movements needed to get to them. There appear to be two types of visual attention, one related to selecting stimuli and the other to selecting and directing movements.

Divided Attention

Attention can affect neurons in other ways as well. Daniel Kahneman (1973) noted that perceptual systems do not always work at peak efficiency. One explanation is that we can process only so much information at once, and if we are overloaded, a "bottleneck" in processing occurs. Kahneman proposed that the capacity to perform mental activity is limited and must be allocated among concurrent activities.

For Kahneman, one aspect of attention is the amount of effort directed toward a particular task. If a task is routine (such as driving on a road without much traffic), little attentional focus is used, and the driver can carry on a conversation. When the driver is turning across traffic at a busy intersection, however, attention must be focused on the task and the conversation briefly interrupted. Some process must be active to shift and focus attention in response to changing task demands.

In fact, in many jurisdictions, for a driver to use a phone in a moving vehicle is illegal because evidence clearly shows that attention is divided when we perform the two tasks concurrently. You may have noticed that when you attempt a difficult maneuver with a car, such as parking in a tight spot, you turn down your music. We see this problem whenever we multitask—reading and watching television at the same time, for instance. We can pay attention to only one task at any particular instant. If we try to divide our attention among several tasks, performance on each task suffers.

Selective Attention

Hedva Spitzer, working with Moran and Desimone (1988), wondered if cells in area V4 might vary their firing characteristics in accord with the amount of effort needed to solve a particular visual problem. She and her colleagues trained

(A) Preferred range

(B) Easy discrimination

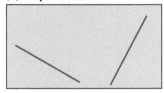

(C) Difficult discrimination

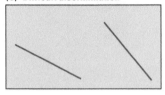

ⓢ **Figure 22.5** ▲

Effort and Attention
(A) Range of line orientations to which a given cell will respond. (B) Easy condition. The left line is within the orientation preference of the cell, but the right line is outside this range. (C) Difficult condition. Both line orientations fall within the cell's preferred range of response. (Information from Spitzer, H., R. Desimone, and J. Moran. Increased attention enhances both behavioral and neuronal performance. *Science* 240:338–340, 1988.)

monkeys, much as Moran and Desimone had in their experiment, except that they varied the difficulty of the task by taking advantage of the fact that cells respond to a range of stimuli (**Figure 22.5**A). Thus, a given V4 cell responds optimally to a given orientation and color. This tuning is not precise, however, and the cell will respond to orientations and colors that approximate the preferred range.

Spitzer and her colleagues reasoned that it should be easy for a cell to discriminate between a stimulus within its preferred orientation or color and a stimulus outside this orientation or color. For example, an easy discrimination would be one in which the test stimulus is orthogonal (oriented at 90°) to the sample (Figure 22.5B). In contrast, a difficult discrimination would be one in which both stimuli are within the range of a cell's preferred orientations—say, if the difference in orientation were only 22.5°, which is within the acceptable range for most cells (Figure 22.5C). They trained animals to make this discrimination, and the animals' performance confirmed that the finer discrimination was more difficult: 93 percent of responses were correct under the easy conditions compared with 73 percent under the difficult conditions.

The change in area V4 cells' response characteristics is intriguing. First, under the difficult condition, the cells increased their firing rate by an average of about 20 percent. Second, the cells' tuning characteristics changed. Whereas the cells tolerated an orientation difference of about 81° under the easy condition, under the difficult condition, the same cells became more selective: the orientation range dwindled to 53°.

The second, more difficult task is explaining both the behavioral and electrophysiological results, which indicate that increasing the effort needed to perform a perceptual task can affect how the visual system processes information. It requires increased attention to the differences between stimuli, as neurons in area V4 manifested in their changing stimulus selectivity.

Cells in the pulvinar, a thalamic nucleus, also respond to visual stimuli in a way that implies selectivity. One hypothesis on how this attentional effect can alter the cell's activity involves a signal from the pulvinar that projects to secondary visual areas in the tectopulvinar system (charted in Figure 8.7). Steven Petersen and coworkers (1987) found that neurons in the pulvinar respond to stimuli more vigorously when the stimuli are targets of behavior than when the same stimuli are not targets of behavior. In the larger view, when a visual stimulus is present but has no meaning for the animal, neuronal firing rate is low. When the same stimulus signifies a reward, the cells become more active.

Because the pulvinar complex projects to the posterior parietal cortex, temporal cortex, and prefrontal cortex, it may participate in directing Treisman's attention "spotlight" to different parts of space. Petersen and colleagues found that disrupting the pulvinar does disrupt spatial attention. The pulvinar receives visual input from the midbrain colliculus, which is known to play a role in orienting to visual information, so a collicular–pulvinar spotlight may be at work.

How is the collicular–pulvinar spotlight turned on? At present, we must be satisfied only with observations. As for attention, that knowledge of task demands can somehow alter the activity of neurons in the visual system seems the essence of a top-down process.

Parallel Processing of Sensory Input

Even when a spotlight has been directed to a part of the sensory world, the brain still has an attentional problem. If a single object falls in the mental spotlight, the visual system can bind together all of its visual elements to form the single object. But if multiple objects, on a cluttered desk, say, capture the attentional spotlight, the visual system has a binding problem insofar as the different objects must be retained as separate items.

Electrophysiological studies in monkeys show that the neurons in area TE appear able to process items from cluttered scenes in parallel. One way in which the brain could do this is by having cells sensitive to complex configurations. A neuron could respond to a square above a circle but not to a circle above a square, for example. But we could not possibly have enough complex neurons to decipher a really cluttered scene. Another solution is to select items serially. In this way, a scene would be processed in very brief cycles that allow us to process items in parallel (for example, see Woodman and Luck, 2003).

Another form of parallel processing is cross-modal. We typically must allocate attention both within and between modalities as we process simultaneous visual, auditory, and somatosensory inputs. A consistently reported sensory interaction is the demonstrated decreases in auditory activation to specific auditory inputs when participants must also attend to a visual stimulus.

Jennifer Johnson and Robert Zatorre (2006) presented participants with geometric shapes and melodies—visual and auditory stimuli—either separately or together. The participants were to perform a task requiring that they attend to the stimuli. fMRI recorded greater brain activation in the secondary auditory cortex when attention was directed to the auditory stimulus and in the visual cortex when attention was directed to the visual stimulus. Thus, selective attention led to increased activation in relevant sensory cortices and decreases in irrelevant regions.

More interesting, however, was the response to dividing attention between the two modalities. Here, fMRI recorded no change in sensory cortical activation relative to a passive baseline condition of exposure to the competing stimuli, and in fact the sensory activation was less than the sum of the activities seen in the unimodal conditions. The major change in activation was actually in the left dorsolateral prefrontal cortex (DLPFC; **Figure 22.6**). The contrasting results of the selective and bimodal conditions suggest that distinct neural processes control the two forms of attentional processing.

When we multitask, by using the phone or talking while driving for instance, we likely must recruit additional prefrontal cortex. If the PFC is already engaged—say, in planning a driving route—attention to one or more of the concurrent tasks will likely be lost. A common observation: when drivers are turning left across traffic they speak more slowly and may completely stop speaking to focus their attention.

Functional Imaging and Attention

One place to start our search for neural correlates of attention in healthy humans is to look at attentional processes in the visual system that parallel those already studied in monkeys. Maurizio Corbetta and his colleagues (1993) designed the experiment illustrated in **Figure 22.7**A. A row of boxes streamed across a screen viewed by participants who fixated on another box located

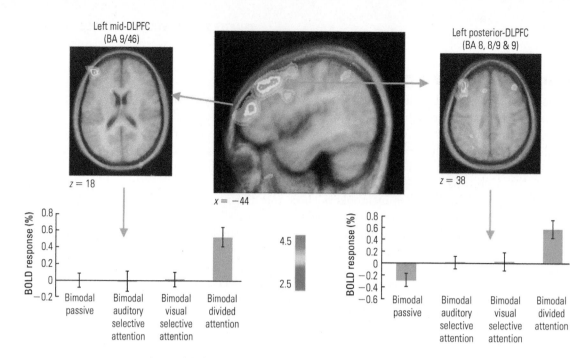

Figure 22.6 ▲

Divided Attention Recruits DLPFC Prefrontal cortices activated during the bimodal divided-attention condition compared with the bimodal passive condition. When participants attend only to auditory or visual stimuli, there is no activation of the frontal lobe. But to attend to both modalities simultaneously requires a recruitment of the DLPFC. Color bar indicates level of significant activity (*t* values) at each voxel. Abbreviations: BA, Brodmann's area; BOLD, blood-oxygenation-level–dependent MRI. (Reprinted from *Neuroimage*, Vol. 31, Johnson, J. A., and R. J. Zatorre, Neural substrates for dividing and focusing attention between simultaneous auditory and visual events, pages 1673–1681, © 2006, with permission from Elsevier.)

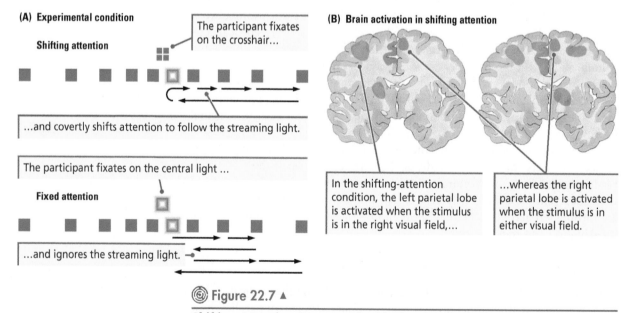

(A) **Experimental condition**

Shifting attention

The participant fixates on the crosshair...

...and covertly shifts attention to follow the streaming light.

The participant fixates on the central light ...

Fixed attention

...and ignores the streaming light.

(B) **Brain activation in shifting attention**

In the shifting-attention condition, the left parietal lobe is activated when the stimulus is in the right visual field,...

...whereas the right parietal lobe is activated when the stimulus is in either visual field.

Figure 22.7 ▲

Shifting Attention Compared with Fixed Attention (A) Experimental setups for the shifting and fixed conditions. (B) A summary of frontal-view PET scans for the shifting-attention task reveals that activation of the parietal cortex increases compared with the fixed-attention task and is more extensive in the right parietal lobe. (Research from Corbetta et al., 1993.)

just above the row. The task required participants to maintain fixation on the upper box and to do one of two things: (1) shift attention as a light moved from box to box across the row or (2) maintain fixation on the central box and ignore the movement of the light. Thus, as in the Moran and Desimone study of monkeys, the stimuli presented were identical, but the attentional requirements differed.

The results are clear. Relative to the fixed-attention task, attending to the moving light increased activation in the posterior parietal cortex (Figure 22.7B). Furthermore, if the moving light was presented to the left visual field, only the right parietal cortex was activated; if the moving light was presented to the right visual field, both left and right parietal cortices were activated. In other words, the right parietal cortex was active when the stimulus was in either the left or the right visual field, but the left parietal cortex was active *only* when the stimulus was in the contralateral (right) visual field.

Two distinct foci of activation appeared in the right parietal lobe as well, one corresponding to the left visual field and the other corresponding to the right visual field. These findings may explain why patients with right posterior parietotemporal lesions show more-pronounced contralateral neglect than do patients with left-hemisphere lesions. In the absence of the left parietal cortex, a representation of the right visual field remains in the right parietal cortex. But, as in the case of R.P. in the chapter opening, in the absence of the right parietal cortex, there is no representation of the left visual field, and the region is neglected.

An intriguing aspect of this study is that no activation was recorded in area V4, such as might be predicted from the results of electrophysiological studies of monkeys. An explanation is that the task did not require integrating different stimulus properties; rather, it simply required a record of where something was. This possibility was confirmed in a parallel study by the same researchers.

In this case, Corbetta and his colleagues (1991) presented participants with a screen with a small white spot in the center (**Figure 22.8**). Each target stimulus (frame 1, for example) was a spatially random distribution of 30 elements, all identical in shape and color and moving horizontally as a coherent sheet to the left or right. The shape, color, speed of movement, or all three might be changed in the second stimulus (frame 2). A stimulus was presented for 400 milliseconds, followed by a second stimulus 200 milliseconds later.

Participants had two tasks: in the "selective attention" task, to report whether the two frames differed for a specific stimulus feature (for example, color); in the "divided attention" task, participants were to indicate a change in *any* feature. The fundamental difference between the two tasks is that the selective task requires adopting a specific mental set for a specific feature, whereas the divided task does not. The researchers posited that the selective task would require more focused attention and the divided task would require more memory. Therefore, they predicted a different pattern of cortical activation in the two tasks.

PET measurements showed that the selective-attention task activated specific visual regions, the region varying with the

◉ Figure 22.8 ▼

Selective-Attention Compared with Divided-Attention Tasks Frames 1 and 2 model stimulus displays. The selective-attention task is to determine if there is a change from frame 1 to frame 2 in a particular feature (color, shape, speed of movement). In the divided-attention task, participants report a change in any of the features. (Research from Corbetta et al., 1991.)

Selective-attention task: Were objects moving at different speeds in the two frames?

Divided-attention task: Was any feature of the two frames different?

Stimulus displays

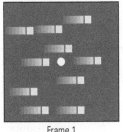

Frame 1

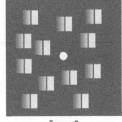

Frame 2

Participants were shown frame 1...

...and, one-fifth second later, frame 2.

feature detected. Thus, attention to color activated a region probably corresponding to area V4, whereas attention to shape activated regions corresponding to areas V3 and TE. The selective task also activated the insula, posterior thalamus (probably pulvinar), superior colliculus, and orbitofrontal cortex.

In contrast, the divided-attention task activated a mutually exclusive set of areas. Thus, although there was no activation of visual areas beyond the activation on passive presentation of the stimuli, the anterior cingulate and DLPFC were active. The important point is that the stimuli were identical in the two conditions, even though the tasks were different. The selective-attention task led to increased activation of visual areas that presumably were recruited to solve it.

Taken together, the results of the Corbetta studies show that different cortical areas are activated in different attentional tasks:

- The parietal cortex is activated for attention to location; the occiptotemporal cortex is activated for attention to features such as color and form.

- The anterior cingulate and prefrontal areas show activation during both visual tasks. Thus, attention appears generally to require activation of both the anterior cingulate and some prefrontal areas in addition to activation of specific sensory areas related to a particular modality, such as vision or touch.

Do these activations outside the visual areas indicate the existence of some general attentional system, or are they specific to visual attention? What about other sensory systems? One way to answer these questions is to examine attentional processes in other sensory systems. For example, the somatosensory system also must select stimuli for processing, so we can reasonably ask whether it has an attentional organization that parallels that of the visual system.

A PET study was undertaken in which participants had to direct their attention to either the roughness or the length of tactile stimuli (Burton et al., 1999). The same stimulus was used, but the feature attended to varied. In control conditions, the participants were stimulated but did not attend to any particular feature. As would be predicted, tactile stimulation activated areas S1 and S2, but during the attentional task, posterior parietal cortex also registered activation. This activation did not overlap foci seen in studies of visual attention. Thus, it appears that distinct regions in the posterior parietal cortex participate in attention to different types of sensory inputs.

ⓒ Networks of Attention

In 1990 Mike Posner and Steve Petersen published a seminal article on networks of attention. Since then, about 5,000 imaging papers on attention and cognitive control have been published, an overwhelming volume of scientific evidence related to brain mechanisms of attention. Fortunately, Petersen and Posner have reviewed this newer evidence and presented a comprehensive integrative theory outlining several discrete networks of attention (Petersen and Posner, 2012).

Three concepts are central to their theory. First, the attention system is anatomically separate from the sensory systems that process incoming information and produce behaviors. Second, attention is not a single process but includes networks of distributed anatomical areas. Third, these diverse areas form three distinct networks, each representing a different set of attentional processes, namely, alerting, orienting, and executive control.

Alerting Network

It has been known for nearly 70 years that the ascending reticular activating system (RAS) in the midbrain functions to maintain alertness (e.g., Moruzzi and Magoun, 1949). A key component of the RAS is the neuromodulating noradrenergic projection from the locus coeruleus (see Figure 5.18) in the brainstem to the forebrain, which acts to prepare regions, especially in prefrontal and posterior parietal cortex, for detecting stimuli rapidly. For example, a warning cue provides no information about what is to follow, but when it appears, an experimental participant's orientation and response to the target automatically speed up.

Drugs that enhance noradrenergic release improve the alerting effect, whereas drugs that block it block the effect. Drugs acting on other neuromodulators, such as acetylcholine, do not influence the alerting system. One of the system's effects is to suppress other cerebral processing, likely by increasing activity in anterior cingulate cortex and related structures.

Orienting Network

The orienting system prioritizes sensory input by selecting a sensory modality (e.g., vision, audition, touch) or a location in space. Imaging studies over the past decade have identified two brain networks, shown in **Figure 22.9**A, related to

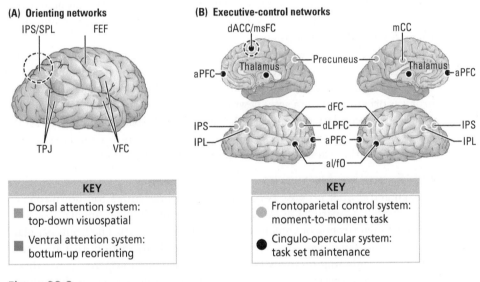

(A) Orienting networks IPS/SPL FEF TPJ VFC

(B) Executive-control networks dACC/msFC Precuneus Thalamus mCC Thalamus aPFC aPFC dFC IPS dLPFC IPS IPL aPFC IPL aI/fO

KEY

- Dorsal attention system: top-down visuospatial
- Ventral attention system: bottom-up reorienting

KEY

- Frontoparietal control system: moment-to-moment task
- Cingulo-opercular system: task set maintenance

Figure 22.9 ▲

Networks of Attention (A) The dorsal orienting network (purple), which includes the frontal eye fields (FEF) and intraparietal sulcus/superior parietal lobe (IPS/SPL), operates in a top-down process to synchronize visuospatial orienting-system activity. The ventral system (blue), which includes the temporoparietal junction (TPJ) and ventral frontal cortex (VFC), synchronizes orienting-system activity with incoming bottom-up sensory input. (B) The frontoparietal executive control system (green) operates moment to moment, while the cingulo–opercular (anterior insular) control system (black) shows sustained activity during task performance. Abbreviations: dACC/msFC, dorsal anterior cingulate cortex; aPFC, anterior prefrontal cortex; dlPFC, dorsolateral prefrontal cortex; dFC, dorsal frontal cortex (prefrontal cortex); aI/fO interor insula/frontal operculum; IPL, inferior parietal lobule; mCC, middle cingulate cortex. (Petersen, S. E., and M. I. Posner. The Attention System of the Human Brain: 20 Years After. *Annual Review of Neuroscience* 35:73–89, 2012, Figure 2.)

orienting to external stimuli. Asking participants to orient to an arrow cue when it appears prompts activity in a dorsal system of the frontal eye fields and the intraparietal sulcus, shown in yellow in Figure 22.9A. For attention to switch elsewhere, the brain must disengage from the first orientation and move to engage another stimulus. This activates a more-ventral network, shown in blue, consisting of regions in the temporoparietal junction (TPJ) and the ventral frontal cortex.

Just as noradrenergic projections from the brainstem modulate the alerting network, the brainstem cholinergic system modulates both orienting networks. This action largely appears to be on the TPJ region. The activity of the noradrenergic and cholinergic systems can be doubly dissociated, insofar as they modulate only the alerting or orienting systems, respectively.

Dorsal Orienting Network The dorsal system is strongly right-lateralized, and so lesions in this region are central to the neglect syndrome described in the chapter-opening Portrait. Thus, although neglect traditionally has been associated with posterior parietal regions, injuries elsewhere, such as the prefrontal cortex, can also induce neglect symptoms. The dorsal orienting network operates in a top-down process to synchronize visuospatial orienting-system activity.

Ventral Orienting Network The pulvinar nucleus in the thalamus influences activity in the ventral orienting network. Pulvinar neurons respond to the same stimuli more vigorously as targets of behavior than when these stimuli are not targets of behavior. That is, when a visual stimulus is present but has no meaning for the animal, the cells have a low firing rate. When the same stimulus signifies a reward, the cells become more active.

Because the pulvinar complex projects to the posterior parietal, temporal, and prefrontal cortices, it may play some role in directing Treisman's attentional "spotlight" to different parts of space. The ventral orienting network synchronizes orienting-system activity with incoming, bottom-up sensory input in primary and secondary regions (e.g., V1 and higher visual areas). One effect is to reduce the influence of other, competing sensory inputs in a winner-take-all competition within various levels of sensory and association systems.

Dual Executive Networks

Petersen and Posner propose two executive networks with a top-down role: a dorsolateral-PFC–parietal network and an anterior cingulate/medial frontal–anterior insular (frontal operculum) network (Figure 22.9B). The frontoparietal network, shown in green, is thought to relate to task instructions that are transient at the beginning of a new task, whereas the cingulo-opercular network, black areas, shows sustained activity across a task. Although activity in regions within each network is highly correlated, the two sets of regions do not correlate strongly with one another.

The Petersen–Posner dual executive network is not universally embraced. Although we are convinced by the evidence for it, some investigators prefer a single, unified executive network theory that includes all these regions (see Posner, 2012, and Power et al., 2011).

Attentional Networks and Self-Control

Humans are capable of voluntarily controlling cognition and emotion. This is a form of attention. For example, if participants are asked to avoid arousal as they process erotic events or to avoid emotion when looking at pictures with a negative tone, they can do so. Such demonstrations of self-control correlate with enhanced activation in the lateral prefrontal and cingulate regions of the attentional networks.

Young children are not as self-controlled as most adults (a trait often called *self-regulation* in developmental psychology). Posner, Rothbart, Sheese, and Voelker (2012) propose that during infancy, children's self-regulation is largely based on their orientation to sensory events, and it is not until the executive attentional systems begin to mature, beginning at about 3 to 4 years of age, that they develop the capacity to control emotions and cognitions (see Section 23.2).

Impaired Attentional Networks

Chronic stress alters the structure and epigenetics of rats' prefrontal cortices and is a well-known risk factor for many neuropsychiatric conditions discussed in Chapter 27, including schizophrenia, depression, and anxiety disorders. All include deficits in the cognitive control of attention. It is thus reasonable to suggest that stress might interfere with the frontoparietal executive attentional networks, leading to impaired performance on attentional tasks. It does.

Liston and her colleagues (2009) compared the performance of healthy adults on a difficult attention-shifting task while scanning their brains using fMRI. Half of the participants were medical students, tested after 4 weeks of psychosocial stress as they prepared for a major academic examination. The other half, who had been matched with the medical students for age, gender, and occupation, were relatively unstressed.

Stress selectively impaired the medical students' performance on the attentional task: fMRI revealed decreased activity in DLPFC, anterior cingulate, premotor, and posterior parietal cortices during the test. When these participants were rescanned on the test a month after the exam, their task performance was no longer impaired, nor was their attentional network activation reduced.

These results highlight the therapeutic potential of stress-reduction interventions for people with chronic stress, whether they are university students or people showing neuropsychiatric symptoms. These results also support the hypothesis that attention is related to activity in the prefrontoparietal networks diagrammed in Figure 22.9B.

Mechanisms of Attention

The Posner and Petersen model does not specify how the executive attentional system might influence neuronal activity in sensory areas. How does the spotlight choose important events from among all of the ongoing sensory information? Although several mechanisms are possible, one is generating increasing interest: the attentional system induces synchrony across a population of neurons that assess some sensory signal.

Figure 22.10 illustrates how a change in synchrony across a population of neurons can be effected by shifting

Figure 22.10 ▼

Inducing Neural Synchrony Ernst Niebur and his colleagues suggest how synchrony may modify the representation of attended stimuli. In the unattended condition, outputs arrive asynchronously on neuron 3 and are unlikely to lead to action potentials. In the attended condition, neural outputs that are in synchrony and thus summate on neuron 3 are more likely to generate excitatory postsynaptic potentials (EPSPs) that lead to action potentials. (Information from Niebur et al., 2002.)

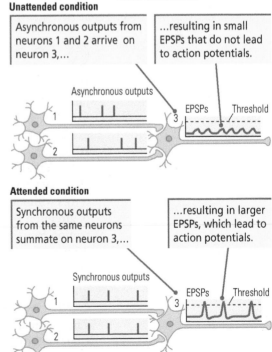

Unattended condition

Asynchronous outputs from neurons 1 and 2 arrive on neuron 3,...

...resulting in small EPSPs that do not lead to action potentials.

Asynchronous outputs

EPSPs   Threshold

Attended condition

Synchronous outputs from the same neurons summate on neuron 3,...

...resulting in larger EPSPs, which lead to action potentials.

Synchronous outputs

EPSPs   Threshold

the temporal positions of action potentials slightly so that two inputs to a given neuron arrive together. When this event happens, the excitatory postsynaptic potentials (EPSPs) are summed and thus more likely to initiate an action potential in the postsynaptic neuron (detailed in Section 4.4).

Ernst Nieber and his colleagues (2002) proposed that this synchrony can be induced by sending simultaneous action potentials to all neurons in a given population. Each neuron that receives the simultaneous input is nudged toward a firing threshold, thus enhancing the synchronous firing of all neurons receiving the input.

Peter Hellyer and his colleagues (2014) asked participants to perform an attention-demanding task during fMRI scanning. They recorded increased activity in the frontoparietal dorsal executive attention network and decreased activity in the brain's default network (mapped in Figure 16.6). These changes were accompanied by increased synchrony in the attention network. Synchrony was sustained during the period of intense concentration on the task, as well as in other specific networks not thought to be part of the attentional network.

The investigators concluded that the processes of attention increase synchrony globally in the brain. They tested this idea using a computerized model of neuron activity and found similar effects, namely, that increasing activity in the attention network increases brain synchrony globally. They were able to increase activity in the default network in their model as well, but that had the opposite effect—a loss of global synchrony.

Although the optimal signal for inducing synchrony is not entirely clear, many researchers believe it to be a signal of about 40 Hz. Many researchers also believe that synchrony may be an important clue to solving the binding problem. We return to the idea of synchrony in cognitive processing in concluding our discussion of consciousness and the binding problem in Section 22.4.

◎ 22.3 Inattention

Each year more than 30,000 people are killed and more than 2 million are injured in automobile accidents in the United States. Most traffic accidents result from human error, and inattention is one of the biggest causes. A commonplace example: one driver seemed not to see another and made a left-hand turn directly into the path of the oncoming vehicle.

Sometimes the cause is obvious (the driver was using a smartphone or other electronic device), but many times there is no obvious cause. On the surface, errors without apparent cause seem incomprehensible. Understanding failures of attention is obviously important, and it complements the study of how attention facilitates perception. Most studies of inattention are based either on demonstrations in cognitive-science laboratories or on observations of sensory neglect in patients. We consider each separately.

Absence of Visual Attention

Three popular tasks for demonstrating what Marvin Chun and René Marois (2002) refer to as the "dark side of attention" are *inattentional blindness*, *change blindness*, and *attentional blink*.

Inattentional Blindness

Here, participants fail to notice an event that occurs as they are performing another task. A simple example of inattentional blindness is a failure to notice a dot flashed on a computer monitor during performance of a visual task. Perhaps the most stunning example of inattentional blindness was exhibited in an experiment by Daniel Simons and Christopher Chabris (1999).

Participants were shown a video in which two teams are passing a basketball back and forth. The task is to count the number of passes made by one team. After about 45 seconds, a person wearing a gorilla suit enters the frame, walks across the display and exits the other side 5 seconds later. Remarkably, on average, more than 70 percent of the participants did not see the gorilla. (You can view shortened versions of the displays at https://www.youtube.com/watch?v=vJG698U2Mvo.)

Participants are often shocked when shown the clip again and asked to look for the gorilla, sometimes even exclaiming, "I missed *that*?" Now, when participants have been alerted to expect unusual events, they readily detect them. In many ways, failure to see the gorilla is like failure to see an oncoming car. If a person is focused on counting passes—or reading street signs, fiddling with the radio, talking or texting on a phone—his or her ability to perceive other, usually obvious, visual events is suppressed.

Change Blindness

Here, a participant fails to detect changes in the presence, identity, or location of objects in scenes. Like inattentional blindness, change blindness is most likely to occur when people do not expect changes. Simons (2000) conducted an experiment in which about 50 percent of real-world observers failed to note that the identity of a person with whom they were conversing had changed when the switch occurred during a brief occlusion, as a worker carried a door between the conversants.

This type of inattentiveness seems as preposterous as failing to see the gorilla, but the experimental results are similar. For example, participants may take seconds to notice that an item is appearing and disappearing from a scene on a video screen. Again, when participants have been told to expect change, they notice it more quickly.

Attentional Blink

Participants display this phenomenon when they fail to detect a second visual target presented within 500 milliseconds of the first one. Attention to the first target prevents awareness of the second one, even if it is extremely conspicuous. Once again, participants have no difficulty detecting the second target if they are told to ignore the first one. Presumably, the visual system is taxed to the limit by requiring participants to process so much information in such a short time.

Understanding Failures of Attention

The three paradigms of inattention are similar in that each shows a failure to attend to stimuli that are quite detectable. The visual system must be filtering the information out, but when? Is it filtered out during an early stage of processing, or is it retained at a nonconscious level?

The latter appears to be correct. Clever imaging experiments have shown, for example, that in change-blindness experiments, the changing stimulus activates ventral-stream regions; in attentional-blink experiments, event related potential

(ERP) evidence reveals that the second stimulus was processed. But why do the unattended stimuli remain outside conscious awareness? One reason would be that the executive attentional network, in conjunction with the posterior parietal orienting system, selectively activates areas in the ventral stream.

This explanation implies not that conscious perception takes place in the frontoparietal network but rather that this network acts to filter information. A prediction from this conclusion, and our next topic, is that people with damage to this network should have deficits in conscious perception.

Sensory Neglect

We first encountered **sensory neglect**, a condition in which a person does not respond to sensory stimulation, in discussing the effects of parietal-cortex lesions. Patients with lesions at the temporoparietal junction (TPJ; see Figure 14.8) behave as if the left side of the surrounding space had ceased to exist. We encountered sensory neglect again in describing its effect on R.P.'s social life in the opening Portrait.

The results of imaging studies, such as those portrayed in Figure 22.7B, show that the right parietal region is engaged when attended stimuli are in the right or left visual fields, whereas the left parietal region is engaged only for stimuli in the right visual field. When the right parietal region is damaged, no backup system exists for the left side of space, and it is excluded from conscious awareness. When neglect patients are presented with two stimuli simultaneously, they show extinction and ignore the stimulus on the left side, as illustrated in the chapter-opening Portrait.

Yves Rossetti and his colleagues (1998) wondered whether it is possible to modify the attentional system to attend to left-side information. In the 1960s, many investigators performed experiments by fitting prisms to the eyes of laboratory animals and humans. (Figure 9.16 illustrates the setup.) Whatever the experimental participant saw was displaced to one side or another. Such manipulations were initially disrupting, but after wearing the prisms for a few hours, the distortions diminished, and healthy participants performed acts, such as reaching for objects, normally.

Rossetti placed prisms that induced a 10° shift of the visual field to the right on two patients with contralateral neglect. In contrast with the earlier experiments, however, the patients wore the prisms only for about 5 minutes each day. In the course of the prism adaptation, the patients made 50 pointing movements to stimuli presented 10° to the left or right of the midline.

The results were stunning. One neglect patient (F.D.) showed an immediate reduction in the field defect, as illustrated in **Figure 22.11**. This improvement was surprisingly long-lived, lasting for at least 2 hours after prism removal, and in patient F.D.'s case, performance was even better after 2 hours. In contrast, M.Y.R., a patient who wore neutral goggles, showed no change.

Of the two likely explanations for the prism effect, one is that the activity in either the healthy left or the remaining right parietal region was recruited to deal with the distorted visual inputs. The other explanation is that a cerebellar or frontal region was recruited. Cerebellar lesions impair the adaptation to prisms, so the activity in the cerebellum is likely important for motor aspects of the adaptation (see Section 9.2). The frontal lobe may have a complementary role related to attention more than to direct motor control.

(A) With prisms (patient F.D.)

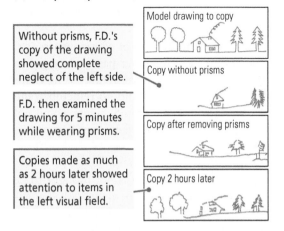

Without prisms, F.D.'s copy of the drawing showed complete neglect of the left side.

F.D. then examined the drawing for 5 minutes while wearing prisms.

Copies made as much as 2 hours later showed attention to items in the left visual field.

(B) Control patient (patient M.Y.R.)

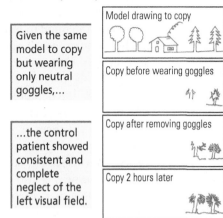

Given the same model to copy but wearing only neutral goggles,...

...the control patient showed consistent and complete neglect of the left visual field.

⊚ Figure 22.11 ▲

The Prism Effect Two patients with contralateral neglect were asked to copy the same drawing. Both displayed complete neglect of the left side. Patient F.D. then wore prisms for 5 minutes. Control patient M.Y.R. wore neutral goggles. In both the immediate postprism test and 2 hours later, F.D.'s drawings (A) show attention to items in the left visual field, whereas M.Y.R.'s drawings (B) show no change. (Reprinted by permission from Macmillan Publishers Ltd: *NATURE*, Rossetti, Y., G. Rode, L. Pisella, A. Farne, L. Li, D. Boisson, and M.-T. Perenin. Prism adaptation to a rightward optical deviation rehabilitates left hemispatial neglect. *Nature* 395:166–169, © 1998.)

Frontal, but not parietal or temporal, lesions in monkeys disrupt prism adaptation (Bossom, 1965). The frontal lobe's role in the Rosetti study may have been mediated by the executive attentional network, which became activated as the patients adapted to the sensory distortion. The frontal lobe's role need not be strictly attentional, however. As noted in Section 16.3, the frontal lobe is central in controlling movements through *corollary discharge*, the signal from the motor system to the sensory system indicating what movement has been produced.

Frontal-lobe involvement in directing attention leads us to wonder whether frontal lesions would also produce a neglect syndrome. Although not as common as neglect in patients who have parietal-lobe injuries, neglect in both humans and laboratory animals with frontal-lobe injuries—especially injuries in area 6, the premotor cortex—has been reported on numerous occasions. The neglect in frontal-lobe patients is quite unlike that seen in parietal-lobe patients, however: it tends to be directed only to the region related to perceiving grasping space, leaving the perception of distant space intact (see Figure 21.2).

Anna Berti and Francesca Frassinetti (2000) described a patient who, after a right frontal stroke, exhibited a selective neglect of peripersonal space. The neglect was apparent in a line-bisection task in which the patient used a light pen to bisect near or distant lines: bisection of the near lines showed neglect, but bisection of the distant lines did not. Curiously, when the patient acted on far lines by using a stick to touch the lines, the impairment appeared in distant space. Using the stick apparently extended personal space to include all of the space between the body and the stimulus. Evidently, the frontal attentional system can influence the way in which we perceive space.

⊚ 22.4 Consciousness

Conscious experience is probably our most familiar mental process, yet its workings remain mysterious. Everyone has a vague idea of what being conscious means, but consciousness is easier to identify than to define. Definitions range from the view that it merely refers to complex thought processes to the more slippery implication that it is the subjective experience of awareness or of "inner self." Nonetheless, there is general agreement that, whatever conscious experience is, it is a process. We define **consciousness** as the level of responsiveness of the mind to impressions made by the senses.

Descartes proposed one of the first modern theories of consciousness (see Section 1.2). He proposed that the abilities to remember past events and to speak were the primary abilities that enable consciousness. In preceding chapters, we have encountered people who have lost the ability to remember and who have lost the ability to speak. Those who knew these patients would not have described them as no longer being conscious. In fact, consciousness is probably not a single process but a collection of many processes, such as those associated with seeing, talking, thinking, emotion, and so on.

Consciousness is also not always the same. A person is not thought to be equally conscious at each age of life; young children and adults with dementia are usually not considered to experience the same type of consciousness as healthy adults do. Indeed, part of the maturation process is becoming fully conscious. And consciousness varies across the span of a day as we pass through various states of sleep and wakefulness.

Most definitions of consciousness exclude simply being responsive to sensory stimulation or simply being able to produce movement. Thus, animals whose behavior is simply reflexive are not conscious. Similarly, the isolated spinal cord, although a repository for many reflexes, is not conscious. Machines that are responsive to sensory events and are capable of complex movements are not conscious. Many normal physiological functions of humans, such as the beating of the heart, are not conscious processes. Similarly, many nervous system processes, including simple sensory processes and motor actions, are not conscious. Consciousness requires processes that differ from all of the aforementioned.

Some people have argued that certain mental processes are much more important for consciousness than others. Language is often argued to be essential because language fundamentally changes the nature of human consciousness. Michael Gazzaniga suggested that language acts as an "interpreter," which he believes led to an important difference between the functions of the cerebral hemispheres (see Section 20.4).

People who are aphasic have not lost conscious awareness, however; nor have people whose right hemisphere is removed. Patient H.M., whom we first met in the Chapter 18 Portrait, had a dense amnesia, yet he was quite conscious and could engage in intelligent conversations. In sum, although language may alter the nature of our conscious experience, any single brain structure seems unlikely to equate with consciousness. Rather, viewing consciousness as a product of all cortical areas, their connections, and their cognitive operations makes more sense.

The simplest explanation for why we are conscious is that consciousness provides adaptive advantage. That is, either our construct of the sensory world or our selection of behavior is enhanced by being conscious. Consider visual consciousness. Francis Crick and Christof Koch (1992) noted that an animal such as a frog acts a bit like a zombie when it responds to visual input. Frogs respond to small, preylike objects by snapping; they respond to large, looming objects by jumping. These responses are controlled by different visual systems and are best thought of as being reflexive rather than conscious. But these visual systems work well for the frog, so why add consciousness?

Crick and Koch suggested that reflexive systems are fine when the number of such systems is few, but as the number grows, a reflexive arrangement becomes inefficient, especially if systems are in conflict. When the amount of information about some event increases, it is better to produce a single complex representation and make it available for a sufficient amount of time to the parts of the brain (such as the frontal lobe) than to choose among many different but possible plans for action.

We still need the ability to respond quickly and, presumably, unconsciously. In the human brain, the ventral stream is conscious, but the dorsal stream, which acts more rapidly, is not. The action of the unconscious "online" dorsal stream can be seen anecdotally in many athletes. To hit a baseball or a tennis ball traveling at more than 90 or even 100 miles per hour requires athletes to swing before they are consciously aware of actually seeing the ball. Conscious awareness of the ball comes just after an athlete hits it.

The results of a series of experiments by Jeannerod's group (1994) show a similar dissociation between behavior and awareness in healthy volunteers making grasping movements. **Figure 22.12** illustrates the results of a representative experiment. Participants were required to move one hand and grasp one of three rods as quickly as possible. The correct target was determined on any given trial by a light.

On some trials, unbeknownst to the participants, the light jumped from one target to another, and they were asked to indicate if such a jump had taken place. As is shown in Figure 22.12, participants were able to make the trajectory correction "online," but to the surprise of many, on some trials they were actually grasping the target before they were aware that it had moved. As with athletes, conscious awareness of the stimulus event occurred after the movement took place. Clearly, no thought was required to make the movement, just as frogs appear to catch flies without thinking about it.

Such movements contrast, however, with conscious movements directed toward a specific object. If we are reaching toward a bowl to grasp a jellybean of a specific color, we must be aware of the difference among red, green, and yellow jellybeans, and we must direct our reach toward the desired color. When we must discriminate and respond differentially to particular stimuli, we need conscious, ventral-stream action. Consciousness allows us to select behaviors that correspond to the nuances of sensory inputs.

The Neural Basis of Consciousness

Consciousness must be a function of numerous interacting neural systems, presumably including sensory areas, memory structures, and perhaps structures underlying other processes such as emotion and executive functions. The problem for a theory of the neural basis of consciousness is to explain how all these systems can be integrated.

We have returned to the binding problem that we first encountered in Section 10.2, in which we recounted that Harry Jerison suggested one solution to the binding problem within the sensory domain: temporal integration. Crick and Koch (1998) went further and proposed that binding is the solution to consciousness.

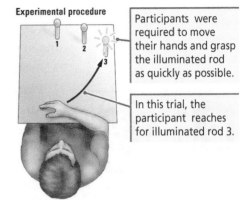

Experimental procedure

Participants were required to move their hands and grasp the illuminated rod as quickly as possible.

In this trial, the participant reaches for illuminated rod 3.

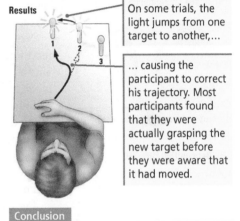

Results

On some trials, the light jumps from one target to another,...

... causing the participant to correct his trajectory. Most participants found that they were actually grasping the new target before they were aware that it had moved.

Conclusion

It is possible to dissociate behavior and conscious awareness.

Figure 22.12 ▲

Dissociating Behavior and Conscious Awareness Black arrows indicate paths that the hand follows to grasp the illuminated rod. On some trials, the light switched unexpectedly from one target to another. The switch elicited a smooth and rapid movement correction. Participants were asked to respond vocally to indicate that they were aware of the target switch. On some trials, the dissociation between motor and vocal responses was such that, to their surprise, participants had already grasped the target some 300 ms before they emitted the vocal response. (Research from Frith et al., 1999.)

Before re-examining these ideas more closely, we need to re-examine the processes believed to be prerequisites of consciousness. Most investigators agree that at least four processes must take part:

1. **Arousal**: waking the brain up via nonspecific neuromodulatory systems

2. **Perception**: detection and binding of sensory features

3. **Attention**: selection of a restricted sample of all available information

4. **Working memory**: short-term storage of ongoing events

Andreas Engel and Wolf Singer (2001) proposed that all four processes either require or modify the operation of an overall binding process and that binding is implemented by the transient and precise synchronization of neural discharges in diffuse neural networks. The general idea is that neurons that represent the same object or event fire their action potentials in a temporal synchrony with a precision of milliseconds.

No such synchronization should take place among cells that are part of different neural networks. The idea of synchrony was proposed earlier as a mechanism of attention (see Figure 22.10). Taken further, without attention to an input, there is no awareness of it (see Taylor, 2002, for more on this point).

What is the synchronizing mechanism? Neuronal groups exhibit a wide range of synchronous oscillations (6–80 Hz) and can shift from a desynchronized state to a rhythmic state in milliseconds. Thus, we can predict that when we become consciously aware of some event, evidence of synchronous activity should appear among widely separated brain regions (contrast coherence theory and consciousness, discussed in Section 7.1).

Figure 22.13 illustrates this process in regard to synchronous activity in the gamma range (roughly 40 Hz) recorded when participants viewed Mooney faces, either right side up or upside down. When viewed upright, faces can be found, but when viewed inverted, finding the face is impossible. A participant's task was to find the face and push one of two buttons to signify its presence or absence.

Figure 22.13 shows a marked difference in neural activity in the two conditions. About 200 milliseconds after the stimulus presentation (Figure 22.13A), synchrony was recorded in the left hemisphere in the upright-face condition, inasmuch as electrodes in all lobes showed synchronous activity (Figure 22.13B) followed by a period of asynchrony in most of both hemispheres (Figure 22.13C). Such desynchronization is postulated as necessary because there is a shift between synchrony in different neural assemblies. Finally, a return of synchrony coincided with the participant's button pressing (Figure 22.13D). Notice in the inverted condition shown at right that there was no synchrony during the analysis of the stimulus, as shown in Figure 22.13A and B, but there was during the motor response shown in Figure 22.13D.

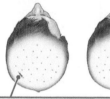

Face perceived   Face not perceived

(A) Image presented (0–180 ms)

Image perception is followed by...

(B) Recognition (180–360 ms)

... synchronous activity over the left hemisphere.

(C) Synchrony scatter (360–540 ms)

Brief asynchrony in both hemispheres...

(D) Motor response (540-720 ms)

...is followed by synchrony when the participant presses the button.

Figure 22.13 ◄

Shadow of a Perception Average scalp distribution of phase synchrony in EEG recorded from electrodes on the scalp marked by dots. The blue lines indicate synchrony, the red lines asynchrony. (A) When participants were shown an upright Mooney face, they were able to perceive a face, whereas when shown the figure inverted, they did not perceive a face. Synchrony is correlated with recognition of the face (B) and the motor response. A period of asynchrony (C) precedes motor activity (D). (Top: Research from Mooney, Craig M., Age in the development of closure ability in children. *Canadian Journal of Psychology/Revue canadienne de psychologie* 11(4):219–226, 1957, doi: 10.1037/h0083717. Parts A–D: Research from Rodriguez et al., 1999.)

A review of the evidence on synchrony and consciousness concludes that phase synchrony acts not only to bind the sensory attributes but also to bind all dimensions of the cognitive act, including associative memory, emotional tone, and motor planning (Thompson and Varella, 2001). However, all studies to date are correlative. No direct evidence shows that changes in synchrony lead to changes in either behavior or consciousness. A search for such evidence is the likely direction of studies on consciousness both in laboratory animals and in humans over the coming decade.

Cerebral Substrates of Consciousness

Little is known about the cerebral regions essential for consciousness. One way to investigate is to identify which brain structures are inactive when we are unconscious and active when we are conscious. **Figure 22.14**A summarizes the cortical regions that are compromised when people are in a coma, in a persistent vegetative state (PVS), asleep, or under general anesthesia. The DLPFC, medial frontal cortex, posterior parietal cortex, and posterior cingulate cortex are inactive in all of these states.

Figure 22.14B illustrates brain activation in a quiet resting state and identifies two distinct neural networks of structures that are either correlated (red to orange) or anticorrelated (blue to green) with parietal cortex. Again, we see evidence of a general frontoparietal network. We return to this network shortly, in considering emotion and consciousness.

A second way to look for cerebral substrates of consciousness is to look for structures that might synchronize activity. Crick and Koch (2005) introduced the novel idea that a little-studied brain region may play a central role in the processes that bind diverse sensory attributes. The **claustrum**, meaning "hidden away," is a thin sheet of gray matter that lies ventral to the general region of the insula in the human brain. Its connectivity is unique in that the claustrum receives input from virtually all cortical regions and projects back to almost all these regions.

Virtually nothing is known about the functions of the claustrum in any mammalian species, in large part because it is almost impossible to damage selectively. Crick and Koch proposed that its unique anatomy is compatible with a global role in integrating information to provide the gist of sensory input on a fast time scale.

Mohamad Koubeissi and his colleagues (2014) stimulated the claustrum of an epileptic patient in the course of using deep brain electrodes to record signals from different brain regions to work out where her seizures originated. One electrode was positioned next to the claustrum, an area that had never been stimulated before. When it was, the patient lost consciousness until the stimulation stopped. Then she awoke.

The stimulation is believed to have disrupted the claustrum's activity, leading to unconsciousness. Just as

Figure 22.14 ▼

Neural Substrates Necessary for Consciousness (A) Data from functional imaging show that a frontoparietal network (areas in black) is compromised in coma, vegetative state, sleep, and under general anesthesia. These regions appear to be necessary for consciousness. Abbreviations: F, prefrontal; MF, medial frontal; P, posterior parietal; Pr, posterior cingulate. (B) In a quiet but awake resting state, two distinct networks of structures are either correlated (color coded red to orange) or anticorrelated (blue to green) with the parietal cortex, indicated by the arrow. (Tsuchiya, N., and R. Adolphs. Emotion and consciousness. *Trends in Cognitive Sciences* Vol. 11, Issue 4, Fig. 3, pg. 161 [2007]: pgs. 158–167 © Elsevier.)

(A)

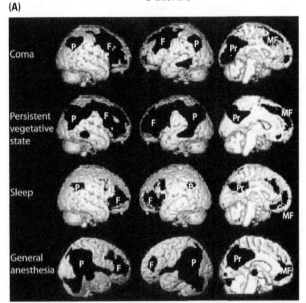

(B)

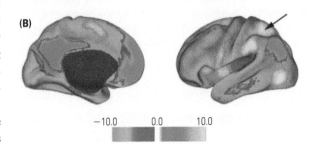

−10.0   0.0   10.0

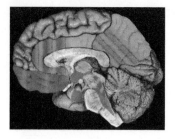

Figure 22.15 ▲

Linking Emotion and Consciousness Note the overlap in brain regions critical to emotional state (blue), emotional feeling (red), and level of consciousness (green). (Tsuchiya, N., and R. Adolphs. Emotion and consciousness. *Trends in Cognitive Sciences* Vol. 11, Issue 4, Fig. 3, pg. 160 [2007]: pgs. 158–167 © Elsevier.)

the ignition switch is critical for starting the car, activity in the claustrum appears to be critical for coordinating activity through diffuse brain systems to produce consciousness. Although we caution that the patient's brain was epileptic and thus not typical, this result nonetheless is provocative.

Emotion and Consciousness

In raising the question of whether a relation exists between emotion and consciousness, Naotsugu Tsuchiya and Ralph Adolphs (2007) began with the observation that considerable overlap appears in the brain regions underlying these quite different experiences and the experience of self, as summarized in **Figure 22.15**. The principal overlap appears in the medial frontal cortex and posterior cingulate cortex, regions that we have identified as central to the concept of self-awareness (see Section 20.6).

SNAPSHOT Stimulating Nonconscious Emotion

Faces convey considerable information about others' moods and intentions, an ability that R.P., described in the opening Portrait, apparently had lost when it came to gauging people's trustworthiness. Yi Jiang and Sheng He (2006) used fMRI to examine hemodynamic (blood flow) changes as measured by blood-oxygenation-level–dependent (BOLD) MRI when participants viewed neutral, fearful, and scrambled faces that were either visible or rendered invisible through intraocular suppression, produced by showing the face image to the nondominant eye and a scrambled face to the dominant eye (part A of the adjoining illustration).

Using this procedure, the face can be completely suppressed from awareness. The fusiform face area (FFA), superior temporal sulcus (STS), and amygdala responded strongly to the visible faces, as would be expected (see Sections 13.2 and 20.3). When the faces were made invisible, however, activity in the FFA was much reduced, and the STS was active only when fearful faces were shown (part B of the illustration). The amygdala still responded strongly to the visible faces but was much more active when the faces showed fear (part C of the illustration).

For the invisible-face condition, activity in the amygdala was correlated with that in the STS but not in the FFA. Thus, even though the participants were not consciously aware of having seen the faces, the STS and amygdala responded strongly to the fearful face and less so or not

(A) Invisible condition

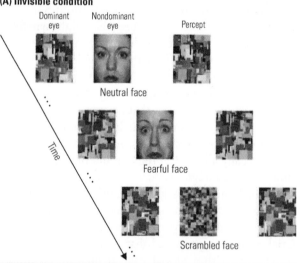

Responding to invisible faces. (A) Faces are rendered invisible to the participants by presentation of scrambled patterns to the dominant eye and the face to the nondominant eye. The dominant eye suppresses face perception. (B and C) BOLD fMRI responses of the fusiform face area (FFA), superior temporal sulcus (STS), and amygdala to the invisible and visible faces. All areas had strong responses to the visible face images, but the STS did not respond to the invisible or neutral faces. (Jiang, Y., and S. He. Cortical responses to invisible faces: Dissociating subsystems for facial-information processing. *Current Biology* 16:(20)2023–2029, Figure 2A. © Elsevier)

Tsuchiya and Adolphs further asked whether consciousness is essential to experience emotion. Although it seems unlikely that we experience emotion when we are not conscious—in a coma or vegetative state—considerable evidence shows that we can have nonconscious emotions. In fear conditioning to subliminal stimuli, for example, a person develops emotional responses without conscious awareness of their triggering stimuli. The pathway for this learning includes the amygdala and related subcortical structures (see Figure 18.16).

Neuroimaging studies, such as the one described in the Snapshot, also show amygdala activation to emotional stimuli of which participants are not consciously aware. Whether emotional processing is necessary for consciousness, however, is less clear. If it is, the implication is that a severe impairment in emotional experience would lead to compromised consciousness, an idea that is novel and currently wide open for future study.

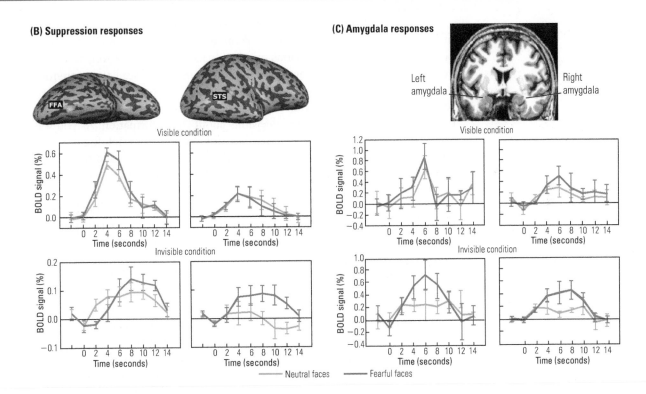

at all to the neutral face. The study thus shows that nonconscious stimuli can evoke emotional states.

How did the suppressed image manage to activate the FFA and STS? Jiang and He hypothesize that the face information may travel through subcortical pathways to eventually reach the STS, FFA, and amygdala. Findings from studies on blindsight patients support the idea that unperceived fearful stimuli can activate fear-related activity in the amygdala.

Jiang, Y., and S. He. Cortical responses to invisible faces: Dissociating subsystems for facial-information processing. *Current Biology* 16:2023–2029, 2006.

Nonconscious Processing

Humans have a rich mental life, and we tend to think that conscious thought controls our behavior. But we have seen many examples that contradict this notion, including blindsight, priming, dorsal stream processing, Jeannerod's experiment presented in Figure 22.12, and more. If conscious thought really controlled people's behavior, accurately reporting and explaining behavior would be simple (see reviews by Masicampo and Baumeister, 2013; Newell and Shanks, 2014).

In a now classic paper entitled "More Than We Could Know," Richard Nisbett and Tracey Wilson (1977) showed that when people are asked to explain their actions, they can provide explanations, but often inaccurately and ignoring many factors that clearly influenced their behavior. Nisbett and Wilson conclude that humans have little introspective access to higher-order cognitive processes. On the basis of his studies of split-brain patients, Michael Gazzaniga (2000) concluded that people explain their behaviors by fabricating stories. Asked to explain their behaviors, his patients were quick to provide plausible, although incorrect, explanations. A rich literature shows that when participants are duped, their explanations for their behavior are clearly false (e.g., Johansson et al., 2005).

The nature of nonconscious thinking has had a long history, since the time of Freud's psychodynamic theories of the early twentieth century. Contemporary views of the nonconscious mind are varied and not yet well studied by neuropsychologists, the exception being the thousands of studies on attention. Nonetheless, it is clear that given the amount of information processed by the sensory systems every second, we could not possibly be processing most of it consciously. Yet we are making decisions about this information. As you walk down the street, for example, you may be thinking about a recent discussion but still navigate successfully around people and objects and manage to maintain your balance over uneven surfaces. (For readable lay summaries of unconscious processing, see Leonard Mlodinow, 2008, 2012.)

The systematic study of conscious versus nonconscious processing has led to the general idea of dual systems of information processing. Automatic processes (system 1) generate rapid, nonconscious responses with little or no "thought." A parallel system (system 2) is conscious—more controlled and based on relevant knowledge (e.g., Evans, 2009; Morewedge and Kahneman, 2010; and see the discussion of automatic and conscious processing in attention in Section 22.1).

Daniel Kahneman expanded this idea in his 2011 book, *Thinking, Fast and Slow*. He proposes that system 1 is fast-thinking, instinctive, emotional, and unconscious. We have little control over this system. In contrast, system 2 is slow-thinking, effortful, deliberate, and logical. This system can perform complicated computations, but it is selective. Fast system 1 does most of our mental work.

Neuroeconomics, a growing interdisciplinary field, is attempting to understand how the brain makes decisions by combining neuroscience, cognitive and social psychology, and behavioral economics and increasingly by emphasizing noninvasive imaging studies (Glimcher and Fehr, 2014). Anticipate an explosion of neuroimaging papers related to neuroeconomics topics in the coming decade, much as we have seen for the study of attention and consciousness in the past decade. Studies of unconscious patients, as shown in Figure 22.14A, provided a basis for this endeavor, including the work of Adrian Owen and his colleagues, discussed in the Snapshot in Section 1.3.

SUMMARY

22.1 Defining Attention and Consciousness

Attention and consciousness are not epiphenomena resulting from the brain's complexities. Rather, both are properties of the nervous system that direct complex actions of the body and the brain. Neuropsychologists have not quantified attention or consciousness. Still, it is possible to hypothesize that they are functions of one or another brain region and to theorize about how brain processes produce both phenomena.

22.2 Attention

Attention focuses the nervous system on aspects of the world and on aspects of the brain itself. Attentional processes can be demonstrated using behavioral, neurophysiological, and imaging techniques. Together these methods have identified several parallel neural networks and systems for conscious attention, including an alerting network that is unconscious and two sets of attention-related networks.

A dorsal system from the frontal eye fields to the intraparietal sulcus, paired with a more ventral system consisting of regions in the temporoparietal junction (TPJ) and the ventral frontal cortex, functions as a bottom-up orienting system that prioritizes sensory input. A dorsolateral prefrontal–parietal system paired with an anterior cingulate/medial frontal–anterior insular (frontal operculum) system

functions as an executive system with a top-down role in maintaining attention.

22.3 Inattention

Impairments in the attentional orienting and executive systems, either by injury or other factors such as chronic stress, interfere with cognitive processing. As demonstrated by the paradigms of inattentional blindness, change blindness, and attentional blink, inattention ("the dark side of attention"), is necessary fallout from focusing attention on specific information.

22.4 Consciousness

Consciousness, a property of complex brains, binds diverse aspects of sensory information into a single perceptual event that we experience as reality. Consciousness is hypothesized to be a property of synchronized brain activity that may implicate the claustrum or cingulate regions. Most mental processing is not conscious, which leads to the general idea that dual systems of information processing employ automatic processes (system 1, fast thinking) to generate rapid, unconscious responses with little or no "thought" and a parallel system (system 2, slow thinking) that employs conscious control based on relevant knowledge.

References

Berti, A., and F. Frassinetti. When far becomes near: Remapping of space by tool use. *Journal of Cognitive Neuroscience* 12:415–420, 2000.

Bossom, J. The effect of brain lesions on adaptation in monkeys. *Psychonomic Science* 2:45–46, 1965.

Burton, H., N. S. Abend, A.-M. K. MacLeod, R. J. Sinclair, A. Z. Snyder, and M. E. Raichle. Tactile attention tasks enhance activation in somatosensory regions of parietal cortex: A positron emission tomography study. *Cerebral Cortex* 9:662–674, 1999.

Chun, M. M., and R. Marois. The dark side of visual attention. *Current Opinion in Neurobiology* 12:184–189, 2002.

Corbetta, M., F. M. Miezin, S. Dobmeyer, G. L. Shulman, and S. E. Petersen. Selective and divided attention during visual discrimination of shape, color, and speed: Functional anatomy by positron emission tomography. *Journal of Neuroscience* 11:2383–2402, 1991.

Corbetta, M., F. M. Miezin, G. L. Shulman, and S. E. Petersen. A PET study of visuospatial attention. *Journal of Neuroscience* 13:1202–1226, 1993.

Crick, F., and C. Koch. The problem of consciousness. *Scientific American* 267:152–159, 1992.

Crick, F., and C. Koch. Consciousness and neuroscience. *Cerebral Cortex* 8:97–107, 1998.

Crick, F., and C. Koch. What is the function of the claustrum? *Philosophical Transactions of the Royal Society: Biological Sciences* 360:1271–1279, 2005.

Eastwood, J. D., D. Smilek, and P. M. Merikle. Differential attentional guidance by unattended faces expressing positive and negative emotion. *Perception and Psychophysics* 63:1004–1013, 2001.

Engel, A. K., and W. Singer. Temporal binding and the neural correlates of sensory awareness. *Trends in Cognitive Sciences* 5:16–25, 2001.

Evans, J. S. B. T. How many dual-process theories do we need? One, two, or many? In J. S. B. T. Evans and K. Frankish, Eds., *Two Minds*, pp. 33–54, Oxford University Press, 2009.

Frith, C., R. Perry, and E. Lumer. The neural correlates of conscious experience. *Trends in Cognitive Sciences* 3:105–114, 1999.

Gazzaniga, M. Cerebral specialization and interhemispheric communication: Does the corpus callosum enable the human condition? *Brain* 123:1293–1326, 2000.

Glimcher, P. W., and E. Fehr. *Neuroeconomics*, 2nd ed. New York: Academic Press.

Hebb, D. O. *Essay on Mind*. Hillsdale, N.J.: Lawrence Earlbaum, 1980.

Hellyer, P. J., M. Shanahan, G. Scott, R. J. Wise, D. J. Sharp, and R. Leech. The control of global brain dynamics: Opposing actions of frontoparietal control and default mode networks on attention. *Journal of Neuroscience* 34: 451–461, 2014.

Jeannerod, M. The representing brain: Neural correlates of motor intention and imagery. *Behavioral and Brain Sciences* 17:187–245, 1994.

Johansson, P., L. Hall, S. Sikstrom, and A. Olsson. Failure to detect mismatches between intention and outcome in a simple decision task. *Science* 310:116–119, 2005.

Johnson, J. A., and R. J. Zatorre. Neural substrates for dividing and focusing attention between simultaneous auditory and visual events. *NeuroImage* 31:1673–1681, 2006.

Kahneman, D. *Attention and Effort.* Englewood Cliffs, N.J.: Prentice-Hall, 1973.

Kahneman, D. *Thinking, Fast and Slow.* New York: Macmillan, 2011.

Koch, C., and N. Tsuchiya. Attention and consciousness: Two distinct brain processes. *Trends in Cognitive Sciences* 11:16–22, 2007.

Koubeissi, M. Z., F. Bartolomei, A. Beltagy, and F. Picard. Electrical stimulation of a small brain area reversibly disrupts consciousness. *Epilepsy and Behavior* 37C:32–35, 2014.

Liston, C., B. S. McEwen, and B. J. Casey. Psychosocial stress reversibly disrupts prefrontal processing and attentional control. *Proceedings of the National Academy of Sciences U.S.A.* 106:912–917, 2009.

Masicampo, E. J., and R. F. Baumeister. Conscious thought does not guide moment-to-moment actions—It serves social and cultural functions. *Frontiers in Psychology* doi: 10.3389, 2013.

Milner, A. D., and M. A. Goodale. *The Visual Brain in Action,* 2nd ed. Oxford: Oxford University Press, 2006.

Mlodinow, L. *The Drunkard's Walk: How Randomness Rules Our Lives.* New York: Pantheon Books, 2008.

Mlodinow, L. *Subliminal: How Your Unconscious Mind Rules Your Behavior.* New York: Pantheon Books, 2012.

Moran, J., and R. Desimone. Selective attention gates visual processing in the extrastriate cortex. *Science* 229:782–784, 1985.

Morewedge, C. K., and D. Kahneman. Associative processes in intuitive judgment. *Trends in Cognitive Sciences* 14:435–440, 2010.

Moruzzi, G., and H. W. Magoun. Brainstem reticular formation and activation of the EEG. *Electroencephalography and Clinical Neurophysiology* 1:455–473, 1949.

Mountcastle, V. B. The parietal system and some higher brain functions. *Cerebral Cortex* 5:377–390, 1995.

Newell, B. R., and D. R. Shanks. Unconscious influences on decision making: A critical review. *Behavioral and Brain Sciences* 378:1–61, 2014.

Niebur, E., S. S. Hsiao, and K. O. Johnson. Synchrony: A neuron mechanism for attentional selection? *Current Opinion in Neurobiology* 12:190–194, 2002.

Nisbett, R. E., and T. D. Wilson. Telling more than we can know: Verbal reports on mental processes. *Psychological Review* 84:231–259, 1977.

Petersen, S. E., and M. I. Posner. The attention system of the human brain: 20 years after. *Annual Review of Neuroscience* 35:73–89, 2012.

Petersen, S. E., D. L. Robinson, and J. D. Morris. Contributions of the pulvinar to visual spatial orientation. *Neuropsychologia* 25:97–106, 1987.

Posner, M. I. *Cognitive Neuroscience of Attention.* New York: Guilford, 2012.

Posner, M. I., and S. E. Petersen. The attention system of the brain. *Annual Review of Neuroscience* 13:25–42, 1990.

Posner, M. I., and M. E. Rachle. *Images of Mind.* New York: Scientific American Library, 1993.

Posner, M. I., M. K. Rothbart, B. E. Sheese, and P. Voelker. Control networks and neuromodulators of early development. *Developmental Psychology,* 48:827–835, 2012.

Power, J. D., A. L. Cohen, S. M. Nelson, G. S. Wig, K. A. Barnes, J. A. Church, A. C. Vogel, T. O. Laumann, F. M. Miezin, B. L. Schlaggar, and S. E. Petersen. Functional network organization in the human brain. *Neuron* 72:665–678.

Rodriguez, E., N. George, J. P. Lachaux, J. Martinerie, B. Renault, and F. J. Varela. Perception's shadow: Long-distance synchronization of human brain activity. *Nature* 397:430–433, 1999.

Rossetti, Y., G. Rode, L. Pisella, A. Farne, L. Li, D. Boisson, and M.-T. Perenin. Prism adaptation to a rightward optical deviation rehabilitates left hemispatial neglect. *Nature* 395:166–169, 1998.

Schall, J. D., and D. P. Hanes. Neural basis of saccade target selection in frontal eye field during visual search. *Nature* 366:467–469, 1993.

Simons, D. J. Attentional capture and inattentional blindness. *Trends in Cognitive Sciences* 4:147–155, 2000.

Simons, D. J., and C. F. Chabris. Gorillas in our midst: Sustained inattentional blindness for dynamic events. *Perception* 28:1059–1074, 1999.

Spitzer, H., R. Desimone, and J. Moran. Increased attention enhances both behavioral and neuronal performance. *Science* 240:338–340, 1988.

Taylor, J. G. Paying attention to consciousness. *Trends in Cognitive Sciences* 6:206–210, 2002.

Thompson, E., and F. J. Varela. Radical embodiment: Neural dynamics and consciousness. *Trends in Cognitive Sciences* 5:418–425, 2001.

Treisman, A. Features and objects in visual processing. *Scientific American* 254(11):114–124, 1986.

Treisman, A., and S. Gormican. Feature analysis in early vision. *Psychological Review* 95:15–30, 1988.

Tsuchiya, N., and R. Adolphs. Emotion and consciousness. *Trends in Cognitive Sciences* 11:158–167, 2007.

Woodman, G. F., and S. J. Luck. Serial deployment of attention during visual search. *Journal of Experimental Psychology: Human Perception and Performance* 29:121–138, 2003.

23 Brain Development and Plasticity

PORTRAIT   Plasticity and Language

Alex had a congenital condition known as Sturge–Weber syndrome affecting his left hemisphere. Faraneh Vargha-Khadem and colleagues (1997) reported that by age 8, Alex had failed to develop speech, and his comprehension of single words and simple commands was equivalent to that of an average 3-year-old.

At 8½ years of age, Alex's left hemisphere was removed to alleviate his poorly controlled seizure condition, allowing discontinuation of anticonvulsant medication by the time he was 9 years old. At that time, Alex unexpectedly began to acquire speech and language. By age 15, he had the expressive and receptive language capacities of a 10-year-old, which is remarkable given that he had no expressive language at all when he was 9.

Although Alex still has severe cognitive difficulties compared with average children his age, he appears to

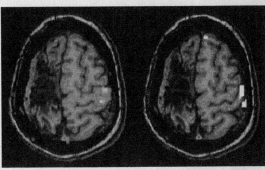

Holloway, V., D. G. Gadian, F. Vargha-Khadem, D. A. Porter, S. G. Boyd, and A. Connelly. The reorganization of sensorimotor function in children after hemispherectomy. *Brain* 123, 12: (2000) pp. 2432–2444, Fig. 2.

have undergone little disadvantage from his protracted period of mutism and limited language comprehension. This outcome contrasts with the widely held view that early childhood is a critical period for acquiring the components of speech and language, including phonology, grammar, prosody, and semantics (detailed in Table 19.1).

Alex's case suggests that it is possible to develop clearly articulated, well-structured, and appropriate language for the first time as late as age 9 and with the right hemisphere alone. His progress provides an unusually good example of brain plasticity during development. The fMRI images shown here record similar sensorimotor plasticity in a child with congenital left-hemisphere damage: the right hemisphere shows activation during movement of the left hand (A) and similar activation during passive movement by the hemiplegic right hand (B).

Why does the brain appear to be flexible in compensating for injury early in life? A parallel question is whether one kind of environment is more likely than others to stimulate plastic changes in the damaged or, indeed, even the healthy brain. To answer such questions, we need first to examine healthy brain development and how it influences behavior.

23.1 Approaches to Studying Brain Development

Behavioral changes resulting from neural function can be examined in three ways. The first approach is to look at nervous system maturation and correlate it with the development of specific behaviors. For example, we can link the

635

development of certain brain structures to the development of, say, grasping or crawling in infants.

As brain structures develop, their functions emerge and are manifested in behaviors that we can observe. Thus, structures that develop quickly exhibit their functions sooner than structures, such as the frontal lobes, that develop more slowly. And, because the human brain continues to develop well past adolescence, it is not surprising that some behavioral abilities do not emerge until that time.

The second approach is the converse of the first: looking at a growing child's behavior, then making inferences about neural maturation. For example, as language emerges in the young child, we expect to find corresponding changes in the neural structures that control language. In fact, we do find such changes.

At birth, children do not speak, and even extensive speech training would not enable them to do so. The neural structures that enable people to speak are not yet mature enough. As language emerges, we can conclude that the speech-related structures in the brain are undergoing the necessary maturation.

The same reasoning can be applied to frontal-lobe development. As frontal-lobe structures mature, beginning in adolescence, we look for related behavioral changes. But we can also do the reverse: because we observe new abilities emerging in the teenage years, we infer that they must be controlled by late-maturing neural structures.

The third approach to studying the relation between brain and behavioral development is to identify and study factors that influence both. From this perspective, the mere emergence of a certain brain structure is not enough: we must also know the experiences that shape how the structure functions and that therefore lead to certain kinds of behaviors being produced. Some experiences that influence brain function are related to the effects of hormones, injuries, and abnormal genes.

Logically, if behavior is influenced by one of these experiences, then structures in the brain that are changed by that experience are responsible for the behavioral outcomes. For example, we might study how an abnormal secretion of a hormone affects both a certain brain structure and a certain behavior. We can then infer that because the observed behavioral abnormality results from the abnormal functioning of the brain structure, that structure must typically play some role in controlling the behavior. In the following sections, we consider some of the findings obtained by using these different approaches to studying brain development and plasticity.

23.2 Development of the Human Brain

At the moment an egg is fertilized by a sperm, a human embryo consists of just a single cell. But this cell soon begins to divide, and by the fourteenth day, the embryo consists of several sheets of cells with a raised area in the middle. It looks something like a fried egg. The raised area is the primitive body. By 3 weeks after conception, it possesses a primitive brain, which is essentially a sheet of cells at one end of the embryo. This sheet of cells rolls up to form a

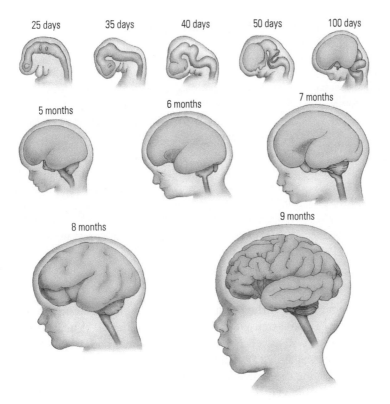

Figure 23.1 ◄

Prenatal Brain Development In these diagrams of embryonic and fetal stages of human brain development, forebrain areas are represented in yellow, the midbrain in teal, the hindbrain in purple, and the spinal cord in red. (Republished with permission of ABC-CLIO, from L. Balter, Ed., *Parenthood in America: An Encyclopedia*, 2000; permission conveyed through Copyright Clearance Center, Inc.)

structure called the **neural tube**, much as a flat sheet of paper can be curled to make a cylinder.

The body and the nervous system change rapidly in the next 3 weeks of development. By 7 weeks (49 days), the embryo begins to resemble a miniature person, and, as **Figure 23.1** shows, by about 100 days after conception, the brain looks distinctly human; however, it does not begin to form gyri and sulci until about 7 months. By the end of the ninth month, the brain has the gross appearance of the adult human organ, even though its cellular structure is different.

The results of research into the development of the child's brain have identified a series of changes that take place in a fixed sequence, as summarized in **Table 23.1**. This program of development has two extraordinary features. First, nervous-system subcomponents form from cells whose destination and function are largely predetermined before they migrate from the ventricular wall where they originate. Second, development is marked by an initial abundance of cells, branches, and connections, with an important part of subsequent maturation consisting of **apoptosis**, cell death that is genetically programmed, or pruning back of the initial surfeit.

Deficits in the genetic program, intrauterine trauma, the influence of toxic agents, or other factors may lead to peculiarities or errors in development that contribute to obvious and severe deformities, such as those listed in **Table 23.2**. Less-pronounced deficits may lead to such problems as learning disabilities or may appear only as subtle changes in behavior.

Table 23.1 Stages of brain development

1. Cell birth (neurogenesis; gliogenesis)
2. Cell migration
3. Cell differentiation
4. Cell maturation (dendrite and axon growth)
5. Synaptogenesis (formation of synapses)
6. Cell death and synaptic pruning
7. Myelogenesis (formation of myelin)

Table 23.2 **Types of abnormal development**

Type	Symptom
Anencephaly	Cerebral hemispheres, diencephalon, and midbrain are absent.
Holoprosencephaly	Cortex forms as a single undifferentiated hemisphere.
Lissencephaly	Brain fails to form sulci and gyri and corresponds to that of a 12-week embryo.
Micropolygyria	Gyri are more numerous, smaller, and more poorly developed than typical.
Macrogyria	Gyri are broader and less numerous than typical.
Microencephaly	Development of the brain is rudimentary and the person has low-grade intelligence.
Porencephaly	Cortex has symmetrical cavities where cortex and white matter should be.
Heterotopia	Displaced islands of gray matter appear in the ventricular walls or white matter, caused by aborted cell migration.
Callosal agenesis	Entire corpus callosum or a part of it is absent.
Cerebellar agenesis	Parts of the cerebellum, basal ganglia, or spinal cord are absent or malformed.

Neuron Generation

The neural tube is the brain's nursery. The multipotential **neural stem cells** lining it have an extensive capacity for self-renewal. When a stem cell divides, it produces two stem cells; one dies and the other lives to divide again. This process repeats again and again throughout a person's lifetime. In an adult, neural stem cells line the ventricles, forming the **subventricular zone**.

If lining the ventricles were all that stem cells did throughout a human life span, they would seem like an odd kind of cell to possess. But stem cells have another function: they give rise to **progenitor (precursor) cells**. These progenitor cells also divide, but they eventually produce nondividing cells known as **neuroblasts** and **glioblasts** that mature, respectively, into specialized neurons and glial cells (review Figure 3.6).

Neural stem cells, then, give rise to all of the many specialized brain and spinal cord cells. Stem cells continue to produce neurons and glia not just into early adulthood but also in an aging brain, at least in the olfactory bulb and hippocampus. The fact that neurogenesis can continue into adulthood and even into senescence is important: it means that when injury or disease causes neurons to die in an adult, perhaps the brain can be induced to replace those neurons. Unfortunately, we do not yet know how to instruct stem cells to carry out this replacement process. Consequently, injury to central nervous system tissue usually is permanent.

A contentious question concerns what the new neurons might be doing in adult brains (see Gould et al., 1999). The production of new neurons continuously throughout the life span suggests that perhaps old neurons are dying. They are. In fact, given the balance of cell generation and death in the olfactory bulb and hippocampus, we might speculate that adding new neurons and consequently their novel contribution to neural circuits could play a role in forming new memories, whereas the death of neurons and subsequent loss of neural circuits could be related to the loss of old memories.

The survival of new neurons in the hippocampus does appear to be related to experience: animals that learn tasks requiring activation of the hippocampus retain more newly formed neurons than do animals trained on tasks that do not require hippocampal circuitry (see Sections 18.2 and 21.3). The question of whether postnatal neurogenesis occurs in the cortex is far from settled, however, and is bound to remain controversial for some time (see Rakic, 2002, for a provocative review). Using isotropic fractionation, a novel method for counting neurons, Priscilla Mortera and Suzana Herculano-Houzel (2012) showed a major increase in the number of neurons in the rat cortex during adolescence followed by a significant drop beginning in early adulthood. The authors have not conducted a comparable study in primates.

Cell Migration and Differentiation

The production of neuroblasts destined to form the cerebral cortex is largely complete by the middle of gestation (4½ months), whereas the cell migration to various regions continues for a number of months, even postnatally, with some regions not completing migration until about 8 months after birth. During the last 4½ months of gestation, the brain is especially delicate and is extremely vulnerable to injury or trauma, including asphyxia.

Apparently, the brain can more easily cope with injury during neuron generation than it can during cell migration and differentiation. One reason may be that after general neurogenesis has stopped, it does not naturally start again. If neurogenesis is still progressing, however, the brain may be able to replace its own injured cells or perhaps allocate existing healthy cells differently.

Cell migration begins shortly after the first neurons are generated, but it continues for weeks after neurogenesis is complete. At the completion of general neurogenesis, cell differentiation begins, in which neuroblasts become specific types of neurons (see Figure 3.6). Cell differentiation is essentially complete at birth, although neuron maturation, which includes the growth of dendrites, axons, and synapses, continues for years and in some parts of the brain may continue into adulthood.

The cortex is organized into various areas that differ from one another in their cellular makeup. How are different areas established in the course of development? Pasko Rakic and his colleagues (2009) argue that the subventricular zone contains a primitive map of the cortex that predisposes cells born in a certain subventricular region to migrate to a certain cortical location. For example, one region of the subventricular zone may produce cells destined to migrate to the visual cortex, whereas another region produces cells destined to migrate to the frontal lobes.

But how do the cells know where these different parts of the cortex are located? The answer is that they travel along "roads" made of **radial glial cells**, each of which has a fiber extending from the subventricular zone to the cortical surface, as illustrated in **Figure 23.2**. The cells from a given region of the subventricular zone need only follow the glial road, and they will end up in the right location.

The advantage of this system is that as the brain grows, the glial fibers stretch, but they still go to the same place. Figure 23.2B shows a cell migrating perpendicularly to the radial glial fibers. Although

Figure 23.2 ▼

Development of Cortical Maps (A) Neuroscientists hypothesize that the map for the cortex is represented in the subventricular zone. (B) Radial glial fibers extend from the subventricular zone to the cortical surface. (C) Neurons migrate along the radial glial fibers, which take them from the protomap in the subventricular zone to the corresponding region in the cortex. (Information from P. Rakic, Neurons in Rhesus Monkey Cerebral Cortex: Systematic Relation Between Time of Origin and Eventual Disposition. *Science* 183:425, 1974.)

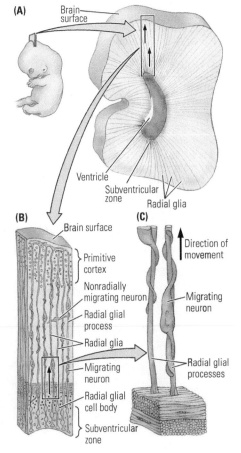

most cortical neurons follow the radial glial fibers, a small number appear to migrate by following some type of chemical signal. We do not yet know why some neurons function in this different way.

A distinctive feature of neuronal migration in the cerebral cortex is that its layers develop from the inside out, much as layers are added to a ball. The neurons of innermost layer V1 migrate to their locations first, followed by those destined for layer V, and so on. In this way, successive waves of neurons pass earlier-arriving neurons to assume progressively more exterior positions in the cortex. The formation of the cortex is a bit like building the ground floor of a house first, then the second floor, and so on, until the roof is reached. The materials needed to build higher floors must pass through lower floors to get to their destinations.

Migration can stop prematurely, leaving a group of cells that belong in an outer layer instead scattered among inner layers of cells. Verne Caviness and Richard Sidman (1973) conducted a major study of disturbed cell migration in the cerebellar cortex of a genetically mutant mouse called the reeler mouse. In this animal, the first cells to be generated lie near the surface and those generated last lie deepest, producing a cortical organization that is inverted compared with that of a healthy mouse. Despite their aberrant position, the cells receive and send out appropriate connections, but the mice exhibit an atypical, reeling movement. Failed or incomplete cell migration in humans also has been described, although the consequences differ from those in the reeler mouse, the most common effect in humans being disorders such as dyslexia or epilepsy.

Neural Maturation

After neurons have migrated to their final destinations and differentiated into specific neuron types, they begin the process of growing dendrites to provide the surface area for synapses with other cells. They also extend their axons to appropriate targets to initiate the formation of other synapses. These processes are part of neural maturation.

Two events take place in the development of a dendrite: (1) dendritic *arborization*, or branching, and (2) the growth of *dendritic spines*. As illustrated in **Figure 23.3**, dendrites begin as simple, individual processes protruding from the cell body. Later, they develop increasingly complex extensions that look much like the branches of trees visible in winter. This event is arborization. The dendritic branches then begin to form spines, on which most dendritic synapses take place.

Although dendritic development begins prenatally in humans, it continues long after birth. In contrast with the development of axons, which grow at the rate of a millimeter (mm) per day, dendritic growth proceeds at a relatively slow rate, measurable in micrometers (μm) per day. The disparity between the developmental rates of axons and dendrites is important, allowing the faster-growing axon to contact its target cell before that cell's dendrites are completely formed and enabling the axon to influence dendritic differentiation.

A major enigma in developmental neurobiology is the mechanism that initiates and guides axonal growth. Axons have specific targets that they must reach if the

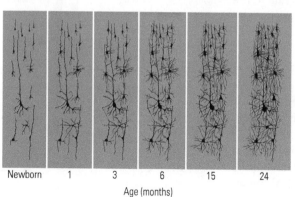

Figure 23.3 ▼

Neural Maturation In postnatal differentiation of the human cerebral cortex around Broca's area, the neurons first display simple dendritic fields. These fields become progressively more complex until a child reaches about 2 years of age, paralleling the behavioral development of language. (From E. Lenneberg, *Biological Foundations of Language*, New York: Wiley, 1967, pp. 160–161.)

Newborn   1   3   6   15   24

Age (months)

neuron is to survive and become functional. Some axons seem to grow by being pulled from their cell body by a structure that is growing away from the region, such as a muscle growing away from the spinal cord early in development. Other axons traverse enormous distances and cope with such obstacles as being moved to another location, having their cell body rotated, or having their target moved. Some axons follow an electrical or chemical gradient or a particular physical substrate. Some send out many branches or shoots, and when one of them reaches an appropriate target, the others follow. Several such mechanisms possibly operate simultaneously or sequentially.

Appropriate neural pathway formation can be disrupted in many ways. An axon may fail to reach its target if its way is blocked, as can happen after scarring from head trauma in the early months of life. The development of axons can also be disrupted by anoxia, the ingestion of toxic materials, malnutrition, or some other disturbance.

Several reports of anomalous fiber systems in mutant strains of mice suggest that abnormalities can also have a genetic basis. Mouse strains have been bred in which the corpus callosum is abnormally sized or is absent and mouse strains in which the fiber pathways in the hippocampal system are abnormal. In a number of albino animal species and possibly also in human albinos, the ipsilateral optic pathway is reduced in size and area of distribution.

Axonal development can also be disrupted if the axonal system's target is damaged, in which case the system may degenerate or may connect with an inappropriate target. Should the latter occur, the behavior supported by the invaded area may be affected too. In a well-documented study of atypical fiber growth, Gerald Schneider (1979) showed that if the optic tectum in a hamster is removed on one side at birth, the fibers that should project to it project instead to the opposite side. This aberrant pathway is functional, but in a curious way.

If a visual stimulus is presented to the eye contralateral to the damaged tectum, the hamster turns in the direction opposite that of the stimulus. The message has traveled from the eye to the tectum that would ordinarily receive input from the opposite side of the world. The irregularities of posture and movement seen in children with certain kinds of **athetosis** (slow, involuntary movement) and **dystonia** (imbalances in muscle tone) may arise because fiber systems meant to support posture and movement have connected to the wrong target.

To some extent, axons appear capable of overcoming obstacles to reach their target. For example, if the spinal cord is partly sectioned, pyramidal-tract axons that should pass through the damaged part of the cord may cross over to the undamaged side of the cord and then complete their journey to the appropriate target by recrossing the cord. Axons may also substitute for other axons. If the pyramidal cells of one hemisphere of the cortex are destroyed early in life, the axons of pyramidal cells from the other hemisphere will occupy the missing cells' targets. A developing brain can adjust its growth in many ways to achieve functional connections if its normal development is hindered.

Synapse Formation and Pruning

The number of synapses in the human cerebral cortex is staggering, on the order of 10^{14}. Our genetic program could not possibly produce this huge number of connections by assigning each synapse a specific location. It is more likely

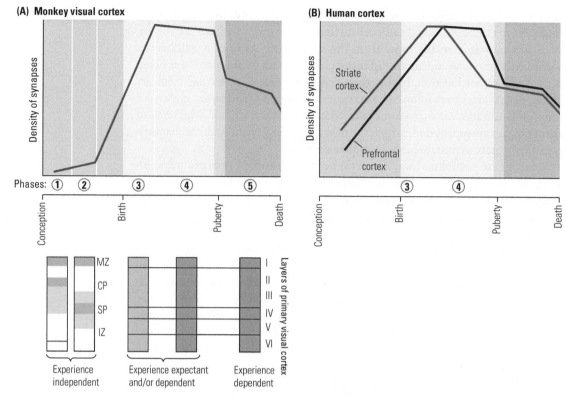

Figure 23.4 ▲

Phases of Synapse Formation and Pruning
(A) Five phases of synaptogenesis between conception and death in the primate visual cortex are identified. The shading in the vertical bars below the graph indicates areas of synapse formation during each phase. (B) Changes in the relative density of synapses in the human visual cortex and prefrontal cortex as a function of age. (Data source: J.-P. Bourgeois, Synaptogenesis in the Neocortex of the Newborn: The Ultimate Frontier for Individuation, in C. A. Nelson and M. Luciana (Eds.), *Handbook of Developmental Cognitive Neuroscience*, Cambridge, MA: MIT Press.)

that only the general outlines of neural connections in the brain are predetermined. The vast array of specific synaptic contacts is then guided into place by a variety of cues and signals.

Five distinct phases of synapse formation in the cerebral cortex of primates are shown in **Figure 23.4**A for the macaque. The first two phases take place in early embryonic life and are characterized by the generation of low-density synapses represented by the areas of shading in the vertical bars below the graph. The synapses formed in phases 1 and 2 differ in their origin, but both groups are thought to be generated independently of experience.

In phase 3, the number of synapses grows rapidly. The rate in the macaque peaks at about 40,000 synapses per second. This phase begins before birth and continues until nearly 2 years of age in humans. Phase 4 is characterized by an initial plateau in synapse number followed by a rapid elimination of synapses that continues through puberty. The rate of loss may be maximal during puberty, although it is not shown in Figure 23.4B.

The reduction in synapses is dramatic; they may fall to 50 percent of the number present at age 2. And just as synapses can be formed very rapidly during development, they may be lost at a rate of as many as 100,000 per second in adolescence. It should not surprise us that teenagers are so moody, considering that their brains are undergoing such rapid organizational changes.

In phases 3 and 4, synapses are formed both by experience-expectant and by experience-dependent mechanisms (Figure 23.4A). *Experience expectant* means that synaptic development depends on the presence of certain sensory experiences for the organization of cortical circuits. For example, in the visual cortex, the synapses depend on exposure to features such as line orientation, color, and movement. The general pattern of these synapses is presumed to be common to all members of a species—provided that the individual members receive the appropriate experience. *Experience dependent* refers to the generation of synapses that are unique to an individual organism because they are produced in response to experiences that are unique and personal. For example, in the visual system, these synapses can correspond to learning specific visual information such as the features of a particular face.

Phase 5 is characterized by a plateau in synapse number through middle age followed by a slow, steady decline in synaptic density with advancing age and a final, rapid drop during senescence before death. All phase 5 synapses are experience dependent.

As graphed in Figure 23.4B, synapse loss is not the same over the entire cortex: synapse loss from primary sensory areas such as V1 precedes synapse loss from prefrontal cortex, for example. In fact, synaptic loss from prefrontal cortex appears to continue at least until age 30 (**Figure 23.5**). The static, even slightly declining number of synapses in adulthood remains perplexing. After all, we continue to learn throughout adulthood, and presumably memory formation requires forming new synapses, so why don't we see an increase in synapse number corresponding to the formation of neural circuits underlying new memories? The only simple conclusion is that experience modifies existing memory circuits, and the generation of new synapses is somehow balanced by the loss of old ones. But we are still left with the problem of how we maintain so many memories for so long.

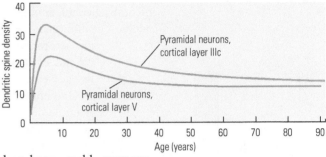

Glial Development

The birth of glial cells (both astrocytes and oligodendrocytes; see Table 3.1) begins after most neurons are formed and continues throughout life. Although axons can function before they are encased by myelin, regular adult function is attained only after myelination is complete. Consequently, myelination is useful as a rough index of cerebral maturation.

In the early 1920s, Paul Flechsig (1920) noticed that myelination of the human cortex begins just after birth and continues until nearly 18 years of age. He also noticed that some cortical regions are myelinated by 3 to 4 years of age, whereas others show virtually no myelination at that time. **Figure 23.6** shows one of Flechsig's brain maps, with areas shaded according to early or late myelination. Flechsig hypothesized that the areas maturing earliest control relatively simple movements or sensory analyses, whereas the late-myelinating areas control the highest mental functions. Investigators currently use MRI analyses to look at myelin development.

◎ The Adolescent Brain

Adolescence is a period generally defined as beginning at the onset of puberty and ending as one takes on adult social roles. Chronologically, its typical span ranges from ages 10 to 17 in girls and 12 to 18 in boys. Although the tendency has been to see brain maturation as linear, it has become clear that the adolescent brain is

Figure 23.5 ▲

Dendritic Spine Growth and Pruning in DLPFC
Spine density on pyramidal neurons in the dorsolateral prefrontal cortex across the life span. Density peaks around age 5, then a decline continues into the thirties before stabilizing at adult levels. (Data source: Petanjek et al., 2011, p. 13283, Figure 2B.)

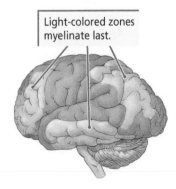

Figure 23.6 ▲

Progress of Myelination in the Human Cortex The fact that the light-colored zones are very late to myelinate led Flechsig to propose that they are qualitatively different in function from those that mature earlier.

qualitatively different from the child or adult brain. The brain in adolescence is characterized both by rapid synaptic pruning and also the growth of connections, especially those related to the prefrontal cortex, and by differences in the volume of gray and white matter and levels of transmitters such as dopamine and GABA (see review by Sturman and Moghaddam, 2011). These changes in the adolescent brain are among the most dramatic and important in the human life span.

Adolescents also behave differently from children or adults. They engage in more risk taking, impulsive choices, and preferences for novelty and reward and in less inhibitory control. Psychoactive drugs also have different effects in adolescence than in adulthood, and the incentive value in using drugs such as nicotine, alcohol, amphetamine, cocaine, and marijuana is greater than among adults. The difference in drug effects is related to overexpression of dopaminergic, serotonergic, and endocannabinoid receptors across both cortical and subcortical regions, followed by a pruning to adult levels in late adolescence.

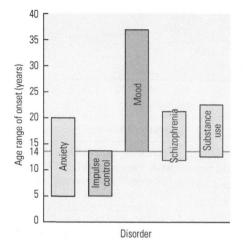

Figure 23.7 ▲

(Data from T. Paus, M. Keshavan, and J. N. Giedd, Why Do So Many Psychiatric Disorders Emerge During Adolescence? *Nature Reviews Neuroscience* 9:947–957, 2008.)

One important aspect of adolescent brain development is that it is a time of high vulnerability to the onset of mental disorders. The peak onset for any mental disorder is estimated to be 14 years (Paus et al., 2008), although there are differences across disorders (**Figure 23.7**). Anxiety disorders, psychosis (including schizophrenia), mood disorders (bipolar disorder, depression), eating disorders, and substance abuse most commonly emerge during adolescence.

Rapid brain change during adolescence is related to pubertal hormones as well as to stressful psychosocial factors—relationships with parents and peers and at school, for example. From an evolutionary perspective the attendant neurobiological and associated behavioral changes in adolescence optimize the brain for the challenges ahead in adulthood. However, the brain's plasticity in adolescence can also make it vulnerable to psychopathology that can endure throughout the individual's life.

23.3 Imaging Studies of Brain Development

MRI and fMRI techniques are revolutionizing the study of human brain development. Early studies of gray-matter volumes showed that, whereas a decline in gray-matter volume beginning at 6 to 7 years of age continues through adolescence, white-matter volumes increase in the same time frame. A study by Nitin Gogtay and colleagues (2004) at the National Institute of Mental Health (NIMH) quantified the changes in gray-matter density at specific cortical points by using serial MRI scans of groups of children, each group followed for an 8-year period.

This study reveals a shifting pattern of gray-matter loss, which is presumably due to neuron and synaptic pruning, beginning in the dorsal parietal and sensorimotor regions and spreading laterally, caudally, and rostrally as shown in **Figure 23.8**. The first regions to mature are primary cortical regions controlling basic sensory and motor functions. Parietal regions controlling spatial and language skills mature at puberty (age 11–13 years). Tertiary cortical areas such as the prefrontal cortex begin to mature last, in late adolescence, and continue into adulthood.

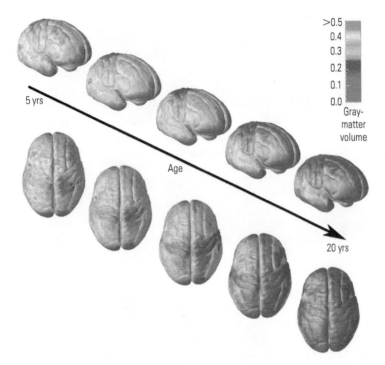

Figure 23.8 ◄

Progressive Changes in Cortical Thickness
Trajectory of cortical gray-matter density in groups of children, each scanned longitudinally every 2 years for 8 years. The reduction in gray-matter density begins in primary areas and spreads to secondary and tertiary regions.
(Paul Thompson, Kiralee Hayashi, and Arthur Toga, UCLA; and Nitin Gogtay, Jay Giedd, Judy Rapoport, NIMH.)

The trajectory of cortical maturation appears to continue until at least age 30. A large-scale study by Elizabeth Sowell and her colleagues (2003) raises the intriguing possibility that cortical sculpting may continue even longer. These investigators collected MRIs from a large sample of healthy people 7 to 87 years of age. Significant decline in gray-matter density continued until age 60, with no decline after that. The question of when maturational changes shift to degenerative changes of aging remains unanswered.

Few studies have considered the cognitive correlates of cortical thinning, but we would predict a negative correlation between cognitive performance and cortical thickness. Another study by Sowell and her colleagues (2004) confirms this prediction by correlating performance on the vocabulary subtest of the Wechsler Intelligence Scales with cortical thickness, as shown in **Figure 23.9**.

$P = .1–.05$
$P = .05–.01$
$P < .01$

Figure 23.9 ◄

Brain–Behavior Correlations for Vocabulary and Cortical Thickness The probability of significant negative correlation, indicated by the color regions, corresponds to brain areas in which greater cortical thinning is negatively correlated with greater vocabulary improvement. (Toga, A. W., P. M. Thompson, and E. R. Sowell. Mapping brain maturation. *Trends in Neuroscience*, 29[3]:148–159, 2006. © Elsevier)

◎ **Figure 23.10** ▶

Neurodevelopmental Disorder–Specific Cortical Patterns Differences in gray-matter density relative to control (arbitrarily set at 0) are color coded in Williams syndrome (WS), attention-deficit/hyperactivity disorder (ADHD), and fetal alcohol spectrum disorder (FASD). Each disorder has a unique pattern of brain development. (Arthur W. Toga, Paul M. Thompson and Elizabeth R. Sowell. Mapping brain maturation. *Trends in Neurosciences* 29(3):155, fig. 7, 2006. © Elsevier)

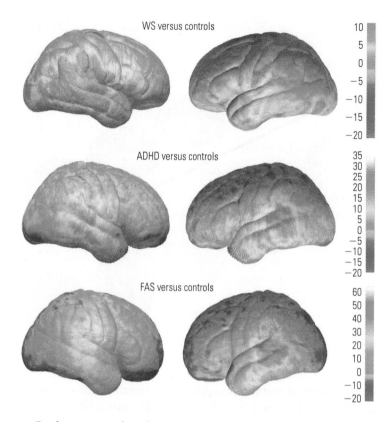

In the course of studying "normal" changes in gray matter, it has also been possible to assess group differences between healthy children and those displaying neurodevelopmental disorders. Such comparisons now routinely find disorder-specific patterns of brain development (Giedd and Rapoport, 2010). The images in **Figure 23.10** show percentage differences in gray-matter density between typically developing controls and children with genetic disorders of brain development (for example, Williams syndrome, a mental-retardation disorder); those with neuropsychiatric and neurodevelopmental disorders (respectively, schizophrenia and attention-deficit/hyperactivity disorder, for example); and those exposed to teratogens such as drugs in the course of development (for example, fetal alcohol spectrum disorder).

Cortical abnormalities in children with neurodevelopmental disorders may not be permanent. Shaw and colleagues (2007) followed about 500 children, either typically developing or with ADHD. They found that reduced volume of prefrontal cortex was not permanent but rather reflected a delay in cortical development by about 2½ years, suggesting that ADHD is characterized by a delay rather than a deviance in cortical development. Note that a delay in reaching peak cortical volume also implies a delay in the synaptic pruning that characterizes adolescence. The delayed cortical development seen in ADHD is a novel hypothesis that will guide both research and treatment for the foreseeable future.

In contrast, imaging of patients with childhood-onset schizophrenia shows a 10 percent decrease in cortical gray volume. Moreover, in adolescence they exhibit a progressive loss of regional gray-matter volume, particularly in frontal and temporal regions. This gray-matter loss correlates with the emergence of more-severe psychiatric symptoms. In sum, although researchers have only begun to use functional imaging in developmental studies, MRI and fMRI promise to transform our understanding of both typical and atypical brain development.

In one study, cortical activity was recorded by fMRI while children and adults performed a task of response inhibition that is presumed to entail the prefrontal cortex (Casey et al., 2001). The area of prefrontal activation was nearly four times as large in the children as in the adults, suggesting that, with age, cortical areas may become more specific in their participation in particular tasks. Another interpretation could be that the task was more difficult for the children, and thus to perform it required more activation in a child's brain than in an adult's brain.

The development of functional near-infrared spectroscopy (fNIRS; see Section 7.4 Snapshot) has made it possible to study behavior-related hemodynamic changes in young children (e.g., Moriguchi and Hiraki, 2013) without having to keep the head and body still, as fMRI requires. fNIRS enables researchers to study the emergence of prefrontal activity related to working memory, inhibitory control of behavior, and cognitive shifting (such as required in the Wisconsin Card-Sorting Task described in Section 16.3). Three-year-old children perform poorly in such tasks, whereas six-year-olds perform much better. fNIRS data reveal that the younger children display generalized increases in blood flow across the frontal lobe, whereas in older children the activity is more localized. These results are consistent with the fMRI findings discussed earlier in this section.

◎ 23.4 Development of Problem-Solving Ability

It seems reasonable to assume that as a particular brain area matures, a person will exhibit behaviors corresponding to the maturation of that brain structure. The strongest advocate of this view has been Eric Lenneberg, who published a seminal book, *Biological Foundations of Language*, in 1967. A principal theme is that children's acquisition of language is tied to the development of critical language areas in the cerebral cortex.

This idea immediately stimulated debate about the merits of correlating brain and behavioral development. Today this relation is widely accepted, although the influence of experience and learning on behavior is still considered critical. Psychologists believe that behaviors cannot emerge until the neural machinery for them has developed; however, when the machinery is in place, related behaviors develop quickly and are shaped significantly by experience. We use the development of problem solving as an example.

The first person to try to identify stages of cognitive development was Swiss psychologist Jean Piaget (e.g., 1971). He realized that children's behavior could be used to make inferences about their understanding of the world. For example, a baby who lifts a cloth to retrieve a hidden toy is showing an understanding that objects continue to exist even when out of sight, a behavior corresponding to the concept of *object permanence*.

An absence of understanding also can be seen in children's behavior, as illustrated by a very young child's difficulty in grasping the principle of *conservation of liquid volume*, which is not displayed until about age 7. In a typical example, a child might watch a colored fluid being poured from a short fat beaker into a tall cylindrical one. Because the second beaker is taller, young children do not understand that the amount of liquid remains constant despite the difference in appearance.

Having studied children's performance on such tasks, Piaget concluded that cognitive development is a continuous process. Children's strategies for exploring the world and their understanding of it are constantly changing. These changes are not simply the result of acquiring specific pieces of knowledge. Rather, at certain points in development fundamental changes take place in the organization of a child's apparatus for learning about the world, and with these changes come new understandings.

Piaget identified four major stages of cognitive development, which are summarized in **Table 23.3**. Stage 1 is the sensorimotor period, from birth to about 18 to 24 months of age. During this period, babies learn to distinguish between themselves and the external world; they come to realize that objects exist even when out of sight; and they gain some understanding of cause-and-effect relations. In stage 2, the preoperational period, roughly from ages 2 to 6 years, children acquire the ability to form mental representations of things in their world and to represent those things in words and drawings. Stage 3 is the period of concrete operations, from about 7 to 11 years of age. Now children are able to manipulate mentally concrete ideas such as volumes of liquid and dimensions of objects. Finally, stage 4 is the period of formal operations, which is usually reached after age 11. Children are now able to reason in the abstract, not just in concrete terms.

If we take Piaget's stages as rough approximations of qualitative changes that take place in children's thinking as they grow older, we can ask what changes in the brain might produce them. One place to look is in the relative rate of brain growth. After birth, the brain does not grow uniformly but instead tends to increase in mass suddenly during irregularly occurring periods commonly called **growth spurts**.

In an analysis of brain-to-body weight ratios, Epstein (1978) found consistent spurts in brain growth from 3 to 10 months (accounting for an increase of 30 percent in brain weight by the age of 1½ years) as well as between ages 2 and 4, 6 and 8, 10 and 12, and 14 and 16+ years. Brain weight increased by about 5 percent to 10 percent in each of these 2-year periods. The brain growth takes place without a concurrent increase in the number of neurons, so it is most likely due to the growth of glial cells and synapses. Although synapses themselves would be unlikely to add much weight to the brain, the growth of synapses is accompanied by increased metabolic demands, which causes neurons to become larger, new blood vessels to form, and new astrocytes to be produced.

Table 23.3 **Piaget's stages of cognitive development**

Typical age range	Description of the stage	Developmental phenomena
Birth to 18–24 months	*Stage 1: Sensorimotor* Experiences the world through senses and actions (looking, touching, mouthing)	Object permanence Stranger anxiety
About 2–6 years	*Stage 2: Preoperational* Represents things with words and images but lacks logical reasoning	Pretend play Egocentrism Language development
About 7–11 years	*Stage 3: Concrete operational* Thinks logically about concrete events; grasps concrete analogies and performs arithmetical operations	Conservation Mathematical transformations
About 12+ years	*Stage 4: Formal operational* Reasons abstractly	Abstract logic Potential for mature moral reasoning

Source: From PSYCHOLOGY 10e, by David G. Myers. Copyright 2013 Worth Publishers. Used with permission of the publisher.

We would expect such an increase in the complexity of the cortex to generate more-complex behaviors, so we might predict significant, perhaps qualitative, changes in cognitive function during each growth spurt. The first four brain growth spurts coincide nicely with the four main stages of cognitive development Piaget described. This correspondence suggests that significant alterations in neural functioning accompany the onset of each Piagetian stage. At the same time, differences in the rate of brain development or perhaps in the rate at which specific groups of neurons mature may account for individual differences in the age at which the various cognitive advances Piaget identified emerge. Although Piaget did not identify a fifth stage of cognitive development in later adolescence, the growth spurt during that time implies that one does occur, and more recent evidence showing major changes in the adolescent brain confirm this.

A difficulty in linking brain growth spurts to cognitive development is that growth spurts are superficial measures of changes taking place in the brain. We need to know what neural events are contributing to brain growth and just where they are taking place. A way to find out is to observe children's attempts to solve specific problems that are diagnostic of damage to discrete brain regions in adults. If children perform a particular task poorly, then whatever brain region is engaged in that task in adults must not yet be mature in children. Similarly, if children can perform one task but not another, the tasks apparently require different brain structures, and these structures must mature at different rates.

William Overman and Jocelyne Bachevalier (2001) used this logic to study the development of forebrain structures participating in learning and memory in young children and monkeys. **Figure 23.11** shows the test situations that they presented to their experimental subjects. The first task was simply to learn to displace an object to obtain a food reward. After the subjects learned this task, they were trained on two

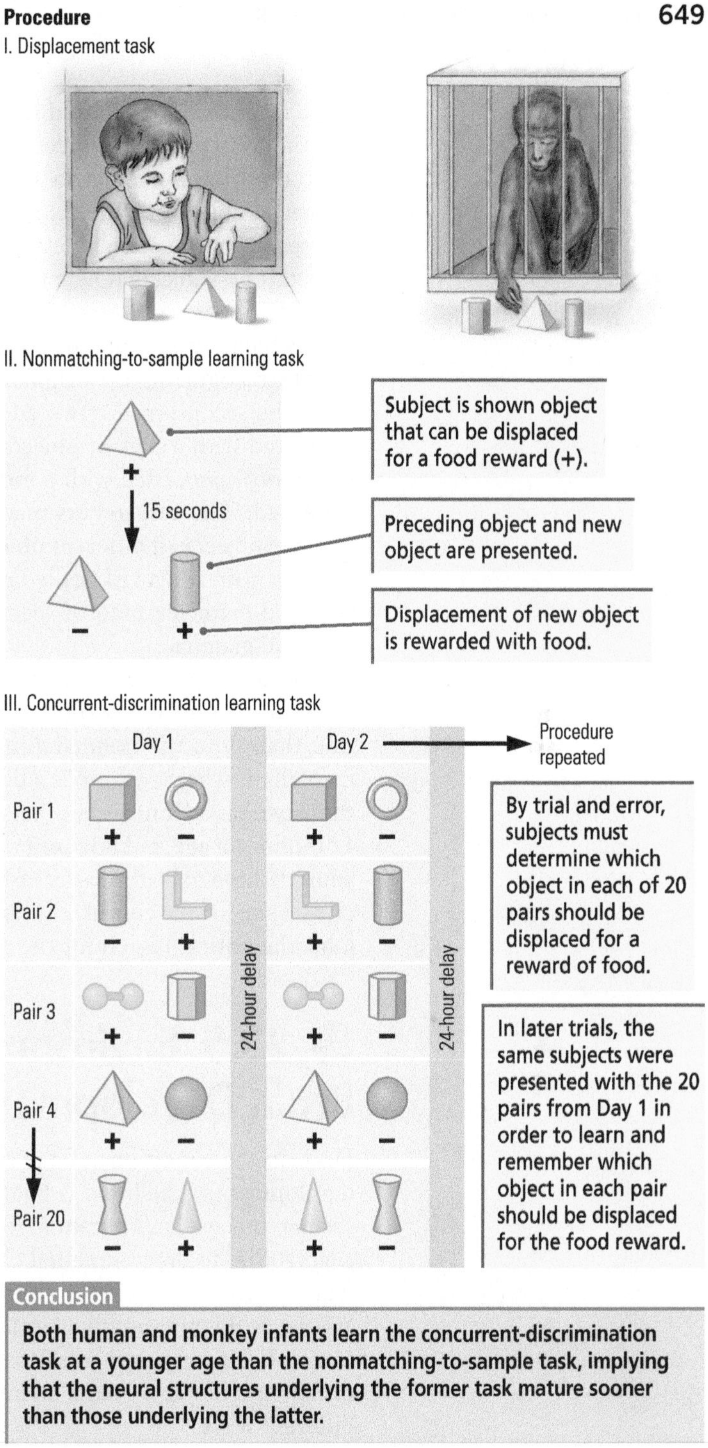

Procedure

I. Displacement task

II. Nonmatching-to-sample learning task

Subject is shown object that can be displaced for a food reward (+).

Preceding object and new object are presented.

Displacement of new object is rewarded with food.

III. Concurrent-discrimination learning task

By trial and error, subjects must determine which object in each of 20 pairs should be displaced for a reward of food.

In later trials, the same subjects were presented with the 20 pairs from Day 1 in order to learn and remember which object in each pair should be displaced for the food reward.

Conclusion

Both human and monkey infants learn the concurrent-discrimination task at a younger age than the nonmatching-to-sample task, implying that the neural structures underlying the former task mature sooner than those underlying the latter.

Figure 23.11 ▲

Demonstrating Cognitive Development This experiment is designed to show the order in which forebrain structures participating in learning and memory mature. In these versions of the Wisconsin General Test Apparatus, the experimental subject's task is to displace an object to reveal a food reward. The nonmatching-to-sample task requires maturation of the temporal lobe, and the concurrent-discrimination task requires maturation of the basal ganglia. (Research from Object Recognition Versus Object Discrimination: Comparison Between Human Infants and Infant Monkeys, by W. H. Overman, J. Bachevalier, M. Turner, and A. Peuster, 1992. *Behavioral Neuroscience*, 106, p. 18.)

more tasks that are believed to measure the functioning of the temporal lobes and the basal ganglia, respectively.

In the first of these two additional tasks, the children and monkeys were shown an object that they could displace to receive a food reward. After a brief (15-second) delay, two objects were presented: the original object and a novel object. The subjects now had to displace the novel object to obtain the food reward. This *nonmatching-to-sample* task is thought to measure object recognition, which is a function of the temporal lobes. The subject can find the food only by recognizing the original object and *not* displacing it.

In the second of the two additional tasks, the children and monkeys were presented with a pair of objects and had to learn that one object in that pair was always associated with a food reward, whereas the other object was never rewarded. The researchers made the task more difficult by sequentially giving the subjects 20 different object pairs. Each day the subjects were given one trial per pair. This task, called *concurrent discrimination*, is thought to measure trial-and-error learning of specific object information, which is a function of the basal ganglia.

Adults easily perform both tasks but describe the concurrent task as the more difficult of the two because it requires remembering far more information than does the nonmatching-to-sample task. The key question developmentally is whether there is a difference in the age at which children can solve these two tasks. It turns out that children can solve the concurrent task by about 12 months of age, but not until about 18 months of age can they solve what most adults believe to be the easier task. These results imply that the basal ganglia, the critical site for the concurrent task, mature more quickly than does the temporal lobe, the critical region for the nonmatching-to-sample task.

23.5 Environmental Effects on Brain Development

How do the conditions of a person's early environment affect nervous system development? The brain is pliable, as suggested by the term **brain plasticity**, the nervous system's potential for physical or chemical change that enhances its adaptability to environmental change and its ability to compensate for injury. These constantly accruing changes in brain structure accompany experience: at least at the microscopic level, neural structure can be molded into different forms. Brains exposed to different environmental experiences—not only external ones but also events taking place within a person's body—are molded in different ways.

Although the precise mechanism driving plastic changes is poorly understood, accumulating evidence points to epigenetic changes inferred from altered gene methylation and gene expression. Importantly, evidence exists that these epigenetic changes can cross to subsequent generations (discussed in Section 2.3). Thus, grandchildren can show epigenetic changes similar to those seen in their grandparents, even though the grandchildren may not have been directly exposed to the same experiences as the grandparents.

Internal events include the effects of hormones, injury, nutrients, microbiota, and gestational stress. Early in life, the developing brain is especially responsive to these internal factors, which in turn alter the way that the brain reacts to external experiences later in life. In this section, we explore a range of environmental influences—both external and internal—on brain development.

Developmental Effects of Aversive Environments

The results of studies regarding the fate of the wave of Romanian orphans adopted into families after the fall of its communist regime in the 1980s provide clear evidence that (1) early experience has profound effects on brain development, and (2) age at adoption is critical. In general, infants adopted before 6 months of age have average IQs, whereas those adopted at 18 months or older have an IQ drop of 15 or more points, smaller brains, as well as a host of serious chronic cognitive and social deficits that do not appear to be easily reversed (e.g., Johnson et al., 2010; Lawler et al., 2014; Rutter, 2004). One bright spot is evidence for increased white-matter volume in institutionalized children who are placed in foster homes, suggesting that some remediation may be possible (Sheridan et al., 2012; see Section 24.4).

In the 1960s, Genie, whom we met in Section 12.3, experienced severe social and experiential deprivation as well as chronic malnutrition after having spent most of her 13 years isolated in a small, closed room. She showed severe retardation in cognitive development, especially language. Although the experiences of the Romanian (and other) orphans and of Genie are extreme, less-severe aversive early experiences can also profoundly alter brain development and health in adulthood. In a study of over 170,000 people, Robert Anda and colleagues (Anda et al., 2006) showed that such aversive childhood experiences (ACEs) as verbal or physical abuse, a family member's addiction, or loss of a parent are predictive of physical and mental health in middle age.

People with two or more ACEs, for example, are 50 times more likely to acquire addictions or attempt suicide. Women with two or more ACEs are five times more likely to have been sexually assaulted by age 50. We hypothesize that early aversive experiences promote these ACE-related susceptibilities by compromising frontal-lobe development. Consider that most victims of sexual assault know their attacker. Abnormal frontal-lobe development would make a person less likely to judge a particular situation as dangerous.

The general tendency is to think of environmental effects as beginning after birth, but growing evidence reveals that prenatal experiences also can influence brain development. For example, in an extensive series of studies in rats, a mother's prenatal tactile experience, stress, or exposure to psychoactive drugs have been shown to change fundamentally the dendritic organization of and later, the behavior of, offspring (see reviews by Kolb et al., 2012; 2013). Tactile stimulation of a pregnant woman improves motor and cognitive outcome; stress has the opposite effect. Furthermore, evidence is emerging that prenatal exposure to therapeutic drugs such as antidepressants (SSRIs, for example) also may interfere with healthy brain development in both rats and human children (see Oberlander et al., 2008, for a human study), as does exposure to nicotine.

The U.S. National Institute on Drug Abuse (NIDA; 2009) estimates that babies are exposed to nicotine in utero in 22 percent of all live births to women under age 25 in the United States. The rate drops to about 10 percent in older pregnant women. Alcohol consumption by pregnant women of all ages is about 10 percent, and the effects of alcohol consumption in the etiology of fetal alcohol effects are well-documented (see Section 24.3). Even low doses of commonly prescribed drugs, including antidepressants and antipsychotics, appear to alter prenatal neuron development in the prefrontal cortex. It manifests after birth in abnormalities in behaviors controlled by the affected regions (see review by Halliwell et al., 2009).

NIDA also estimates that 5.5 percent of expectant mothers, approximately 221,000 pregnant women each year in the United States, use an illicit drug at least once during the course of their pregnancies. And what about caffeine? More than likely most children were exposed to caffeine (from coffee, tea, cola and energy drinks, and chocolate) in utero.

The precise effects of drug intake on brain development are poorly understood, but the overall conclusion from current knowledge is that children with prenatal exposure to a variety of psychoactive drugs have an increased likelihood of later drug use (Malanga and Kosofsky, 2003). Many experts suggest that, although again poorly studied, childhood disorders—learning disabilities and attention-deficit-hyperactivity disorder (ADHD) are examples—may be related to prenatal exposure to drugs such as nicotine or caffeine or both. Malanga and Kosofsky (2003) note poignantly, "society at large does not yet fully appreciate the impact that prenatal drug exposure can have on the lives of its children."

Environmental Influences on Brain Organization

The simplest way of measuring the effects of environment on the nervous system is by documenting differences in brain size. The results of studies of animal brain size reveal that certain cortical areas are as much as 10 percent to 20 percent smaller in domestic animals than in animals of the same species and strain raised in the wild. These differences are apparently related to factors encountered early in life, because animals born in the wild and later domesticated have brains the same size as those of animals raised in the wild. The part of the brain that seems to be most affected by a domestic upbringing is the occipital cortex, which is reduced in size by as much as 35 percent in some animals. This reduction may be related to smaller eye and retina size.

Benefits of Complex Environments

Exposure to a complex rather than impoverished environment increases brain size, most noticeably of the neocortex, with the greatest increase being in the occipital cortex. Related to increased size are increases in density of glial cells, length of dendrites, density of spines (the location of most excitatory synapses), and size of synapses. Curiously, although many have assumed that the young brain will show greater changes in response to experience than an older brain will, young and adult brains may actually respond differently to the same experience.

For example, housing animals in complex environments with changing objects to play with increases the length of pyramidal-cell dendrites in the cortices of both younger and older animals. However, spine density *decreases* in young animals and *increases* in the older animals (**Figure 23.12**). Both younger and older animals show similar functional benefits, performing better than their

Figure 23.12 ▼

Effects of Complex Housing on Rats A comparison of the effects of 3 months of complex housing, beginning at different ages, on (A) dendritic length and (B) spine density. Although all three age groups show similar increases in dendritic length, a qualitative difference in spine density emerges: juveniles show a drop, whereas adults show an increase. (Data source: Kolb et al., 2003.)

(A) Dendritic length

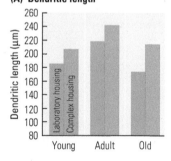

(B) Spine density

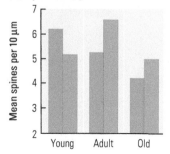

impoverished counterparts on a number of tests of skilled motor behavior as well as on tests of learning and memory.

We can speculate that the qualitative differences in experience-dependent synaptic changes at these different times in life must have some functional implications. One possibility is that an animal whose brain is stimulated during development may more easily change its brain in response to experience later in life. One example is children who are exposed to different languages in development and who then learn additional languages later in life more quickly than do peers whose early experience was unilingual. Another example, shown in studies of laboratory animals, is that one function of play is to render the brain more plastic in adulthood (e.g., Himmler et al., 2013).

The fact that very early experience can alter brain structure and behavior in adulthood leads to the question of whether prenatal experiences—those taking place in phase 1, 2, or early phase 3 synaptogenesis—also might alter brain development. The results of several studies show that newborns can identify the maternal voice that they heard in utero, so it seems possible that prenatal experience *can* influence brain development.

Robbin Gibb and her colleagues manipulated prenatal experience in rats either by placing the pregnant dams in complex environments or by giving them daily tactile stimulation (e.g., Gibb et al., 2014). This experience resulted in larger brains in the offspring, a result that could be due either to increased numbers of neurons or glia or both or to increased numbers of synapses. The larger-brained offspring then showed superior performance on both cognitive and motor tasks, just like animals raised in complex environments postnatally (see review by Kolb et al., 2013).

Gibb's group also manipulated the preconceptual paternal experience by placing males in complex environments for several weeks before mating them with females. The offspring showed that this preconceptual experience accelerated behavioral development and showed increased gene expression in hippocampal and prefrontal cortex (Mychasiuk et al., 2012).

Effects of Diet and Nutrients

Maternal diet during gestation has long been known to alter the offspring's brain development and later behavior, but the mechanisms are only beginning to be examined. In a remarkable study, Paula Dominguez-Salas and her colleagues (2014) showed that maternal diet at conception significantly altered gene methylation in newborns. (Increased gene methylation, for example, means that fewer genes are expressed and thus that body and brain will develop differently in the two groups.) The Dominguez-Salas group studied infants in rural Gambia who had been conceived in either the dry season or the rainy season. Gambians' diets are dramatically different during these two seasons, and so was gene methylation in the infants' blood (**Figure 23.13**).

An even more surprising effect of early experience is emerging from studies of the bacteria in the developing gut, the mother's vaginal tract, and other regions, together referred to as the prenatal *microbiome*. Accumulating evidence points to a correlation between microbiotic composition and the child's brain and behavior. Host-supporting species (probiosis) alter behavior and biochemical parameters in a different direction from that of pathogenic species (dysbiosis; see review by Cryan and Dinan, 2012).

Figure 23.13 ▼

Diet and Gene Expression The diets of women in rural Gambia vary with the season. Babies conceived in the rainy season show a significant increase in gene methylation (fewer genes expressed) compared with babies conceived in the dry season. Boxes map the interquartile range. (Data source: Dominguez-Salaz et al., 2014, Figure 3B.)

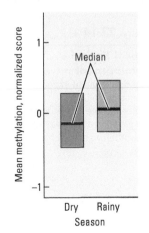

Rochellys Diaz Heitz and her colleagues (2011) manipulated gut bacteria in developing mice and showed related alterations in brain and behavior. The role of the microbiome in understanding brain and behavior has led to the concept of *psychobiotics* as a new class of psychotropic drug (Dinan et al., 2013; see Section 27.9). Given the likelihood of geographical variations in the microbiome, we have a provocative mechanism for differences in brain and behavioral development, possibly related to geographical differences in gut bacteria. One can speculate, given that culture is geographical, that brain differences related to culture could have a partial basis in different microbiomes.

Experience and Neural Connectivity

Disturbances of the optics of the eye early in life (for example, cataracts and astigmatism) cause long-lasting impairments of vision even after the optical defects are corrected. Adults who have had lifelong cataracts removed to allow light to finally reach the retina have difficulty learning the identity of objects by looking at them. These visual impairments, called **amblyopia**—deficits of vision without obvious impairment of the eye—are thought to be caused by changes in the central nervous system. The results of behavioral studies have shown that amblyopia can be produced in animals; the process has been analyzed extensively in studies of cats and monkeys.

Torsten Wiesel and David Hubel (1965) approached the problem by asking how the functional organization of the visual system of kittens might be altered by eliminating the visual input to one eye. The researchers were aware that inputs from each eye go to adjacent alternating *ocular dominance columns* in area V1. (In each column, the alternate eye is dominant, as shown in **Figure 23.14**). This alternating arrangement of inputs from the two eyes presumably plays an important role in merging the images from each eye.

The specific question Wiesel and Hubel asked was whether restricting visual experience to one eye might alter the structure of the ocular dominance columns. They discovered that if one eye is sewn shut for a time in early life, the eye appears to be essentially blind for a period of weeks after opening, although its function does improve somewhat with time. The results of cell-recording studies show that either stimulation in the deprived eye cannot activate cells in the cortex or, in those few cases in which it can, the cells are highly atypical. The results also show that the earlier the deprivation takes place, the shorter the length of deprivation required to produce effects and the more severe the effects.

These results confirm that environmental deprivation can retard development and that early deprivation is the most damaging. Findings from later studies by other researchers have shown that one reason for the deprived eye's atypical functioning is that the connections from that eye have been weakened by the lack of visual experience, as illustrated in Figure 23.14. Apparently, visual experience is necessary to validate (that is, to reinforce) functional connections in the brain. In the absence of activity, the synapses are lost. This principle of

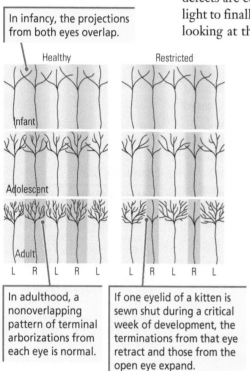

In infancy, the projections from both eyes overlap.

Healthy   Restricted

Infant

Adolescent

Adult

L R L R L   L R L R L

In adulthood, a nonoverlapping pattern of terminal arborizations from each eye is normal.

If one eyelid of a kitten is sewn shut during a critical week of development, the terminations from that eye retract and those from the open eye expand.

Figure 23.14 ▲

Critical Period in Development In the postnatal development of ocular dominance columns in the cat, axons enter the cortex, where they grow large terminal arborizations. Abbreviations: L, left eye; R, right eye.

"use it or lose it" can be applied to the nervous system in general, although the effect of experience is not always as severe as that seen in the example of the deprived eye.

Can the visual system be changed by manipulation less drastic than complete sensory deprivation? Kittens were fitted with lenses that brought a set of horizontal stripes into focus on one retina and a set of vertical stripes into focus on the other (see Hirsch and Spinelli, 1971). After later removal of the lenses, the eye that had seen horizontal stripes during the exposure period responded only to a stimulus oriented close to the horizontal, and the eye that had seen vertical stripes responded only to a stimulus oriented close to the vertical. These findings have been confirmed for kittens raised in an environment of stripes only or spots only or in an environment organized to be devoid of movement. In fact, work by Colin Blakemore and Donald Mitchell (1973) indicates that 1 hour of exposure on day 28 after birth in kittens is sufficient to bias a cortical unit to respond to a particular pattern.

Overall, this work suggests that the visual system is genetically programmed to make standard connections and standard responses, but it can lose much of this capacity if it is not exercised during the early months of life. When part of the system is deprived, some degree of capacity is lost. Moreover, the remaining functional areas inhibit the deprived part of the system, reinforcing the defect—although removal of the inhibition can permit some degree of recovery. Finally, if the environment is so arranged that the visual system is exposed to stimuli of one type, the cells in the system develop a preference for those stimuli.

Plasticity of Representational Zones in the Developing Brain

The tendency for cortical organization to be influenced by experience can be seen not only in the brain subjected to restricted experience but also in the brain subjected to enriched experience. Consider, for example, the effect of practicing some skill, such as playing a musical instrument, for hours a day for many years in childhood. Thomas Elbert and his colleagues (2001) studied bowed-string-instrument players as a model for how experience can alter the organization of the sensorimotor maps of the hand. The second through fifth digits of the left hand are continuously engaged in fingering the strings, whereas the thumb, which grasps the neck of the instrument, is less active. The right hand moves the bow, which also requires much less finger movement.

Neuroimaging showed that representation of the fingers of the left hand not only occupied more space than did the thumb or the fingers of the right hand but also that the amount of change was proportional to the age at which musical training began, as illustrated in **Figure 23.15**. The representational zone of the left-hand fingers was largest in participants who had begun

Figure 23.15 ▼

Effects of Enrichment This graph plots the age at which participants began practicing on stringed instruments against the amount of neural activation that they showed in response to tactile stimulation of the fifth digit of the left hand. (Data source: Elbert et al., 2001.)

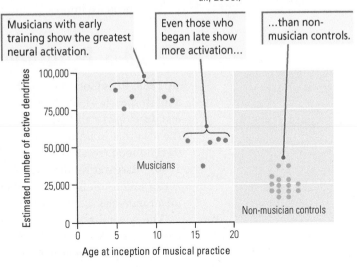

Figure 23.16 ▼

Infant Wearing an ERP Recording Cap The graph illustrates the mismatch negativity signal. One wave (teal) is a standard signal from one sound, and the other (orange) comes from a deviant signal. The MMN is the difference between the waves. If the brain detects that two signals are different, a mismatch will be recorded, but if the brain does not discriminate between the signals, there will be no MMN. (Data from Kuhl, 1999.)

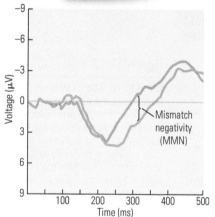

regular practice before age 13—that is, before puberty. Even if training began later in life, the representation of the relevant digits still exceeded the representation seen in participants without musical training. A later study found similar effects on the representation of piano-music frequencies in the auditory cortexes of piano players (the study represented in Figure 15.15).

A characteristic of human speech perception is that adults are skilled at distinguishing speech sounds in their native language but often have difficulties making sound distinctions in other languages. For example, the difficulty that Japanese or Korean speakers have in making the distinction between "r" and "l" in English is well known. Janet Werker and Richard Tees (1983) compared the ability of infants to discriminate speech sounds taken from widely disparate languages, such as English, Hindi (from India), and Salish (a Native American language). Their results showed that young infants can discriminate between the speech sounds of different languages without previous experience, but their ability to do so declines over the first year of life.

In studies by others, event-related potentials (ERPs) have been used to examine this phenomenon, with the use of *mismatch negativity* (MMN). If a repeated speech sound, such as "l, l, l, . . . " is played to an infant and a different sound, such as "r," is embedded in the middle, the ERP will show a negative deflection—a mismatch negativity—if the baby's auditory system detects the difference in sound (**Figure 23.16**). In studies by various groups (see reviews by Elbert et al., 2001, and by Kuhl, 1999), MMNs were detected for language-specific speech sounds in infants at 6 months of age, but 12-month-old infants no longer made many of the distinctions. These results imply that the auditory representation of sounds is altered by each infant's linguistically biased environment.

Knowledge of how experience reorganizes the cortex can be used to treat cognitive deficits in children. For example, some preschool children with no apparent psychiatric or neurological impairment have great difficulty learning language, in which case their condition is referred to as a *specific language impairment*. One theory suggests that such impairments may be caused by an abnormal representation of speech sounds in the auditory system. If so, then specific training ought to produce improvement. It does. (See Chapter 24 for more details.)

◎ 23.6 Brain Injury and Plasticity

By 1868, Jules Cotard—who knew that damage to the left frontal cortex could abolish speech—had observed children with left frontal lesions who nevertheless developed standard adult language functions. This observation originated the idea that brain injury has milder and more short-lived effects if sustained in childhood (recall Alex's case in the chapter-opening Portrait). Then in the 1930s, Margaret Kennard (e.g., 1942) compared the effects of unilateral motor-cortex lesions on infant and adult monkeys and found that impairments in the infant monkeys seemed milder than those in the adults.

The generalization that sparing of function follows infant lesions became known as the *Kennard principle*. For a time, the idea received wide acceptance, but neuroscientists began to realize that earlier may not always be better and can sometimes be worse. Donald Hebb (1949), for example, showed that children who incur prefrontal injuries in infancy or early childhood have very poor outcomes. The ultimate effect of a brain injury depends on the behavior affected, the extent and location of damage, and the precise age at which the injury occurs. With respect to cognitive function in humans, it is clear that speech survives early brain damage, but some elements of syntax and some nonlanguage functions may not survive, and general intellectual ability may decline.

Effects of Age

Age is an important determinant of the effects of early lesions. Three critical age divisions have been identified: before 1 year, between 1 and 5 years, and older than 5 years. Lesions incurred before age 1 tend to produce disproportionately greater impairments than do those incurred later. Lesions incurred between 1 and 5 years of age are followed by some reorganization of brain function, including the rescue of language functions. Lesions incurred later than age 5 permit little or no sparing of function.

For example, in a comparison of the effects of lesions incurred before and after age 1, earlier lesions reduced IQ more than did later lesions (see Riva and Cazzaniga, 1986). An implication of the age-related effects of injury on language development is that the brain's manner of acquiring languages differs at different times in development. Further evidence for this hypothesis is described in the Snapshot on page 658.

Effects of Brain Damage on Language

Language deficits resulting from cerebral injury in young children are usually short-lived, and an injured child usually seems to recover almost fully. This is the case even though language disorders subsequent to right-hemisphere damage are more frequent in children than in adults, the incidence being about 8 percent in children and 2 percent in adults (**Table 23.4**).

Théophile Alajouanine and F. Lhermitte (1965) studied 32 cases of childhood aphasia, finding writing deficits in all and reading deficits in about half of the children, in addition to their speech difficulties. Six months after injury, the researchers observed total recovery of spontaneous language in about one-third of these subjects and noted significant improvement in all of the others. When reexamined 1 year or more after injury, 24 of the 32 children had standard or almost standard language—although 14 still had some degree of dysgraphia—and 22 of the children were eventually able to return to school.

Similarly, Henri Hécaen (1976) followed postinjury recovery from aphasia and related symptoms in 15 children with left-hemisphere

Table 23.4 **Summary of studies of aphasia resulting from unilateral lesions**

Study	Age range of subjects	Number of cases	Percentage with right-hemisphere lesions
Childhood Lesions			
Guttman, 1942	2–14	15	7.00
Alajouanine and Lhermitte, 1965	6–15	32	0.00
McCarthy, 1963	After language acquisition	114	4.00
Basser, 1962*	Before 5	20	35.00
Hécaen, 1976	3½–15	17	11.00
Total	2–15	198	8.00
Adult Lesions			
Russell and Espir, 1961	—	205	3.00
Hécaen, 1976	—	232	0.43
Total	—	437	1.60

*The Basser study, which describes 35 percent of young children with right-hemisphere lesions as having aphasia, is thought to be inaccurate because many of the subjects may have had bilateral lesions.

Source: S. D. Krashen. Lateralization, language learning, and the critical period: Some new evidence, *Language Learning*, 23:63–74, 1973, John Wiley & Sons, Inc., with modifications from Hécaen, 1976.

SNAPSHOT | Distinct Cortical Areas for Second Languages

Children generally find it easier than adults to acquire more than one language and to speak each one with a native accent. In asking whether the age at language acquisition might influence how that language is represented in the brain, Karl Kim and his colleagues (1997) used fMRI to determine the spatial relation between native and second languages in the cortex.

Bilingual participants were instructed to describe in their minds, without speaking aloud, the events that had taken place during a certain period of the preceding day (for example, in the morning). On different scans, they used different languages. Some participants had learned a second language as children, whereas others learned a second language as adults.

As would be expected in a sentence-generation task, both Broca's and Wernicke's areas were activated. Imaging revealed a difference between childhood and adult acquisition of the second language in activating Broca's area but no difference in Wernicke's area.

As shown in the illustration, activation in Broca's area overlapped virtually completely for the childhood-acquisition participants, but an anatomical separation of the two languages appeared in the adulthood-acquisition group. This spatial separation of the two languages in Broca's area suggests that language acquisition may alter the functional organization of Broca's area.

Thus, as human infants learn languages, Broca's area undergoes modification according to the nature of the languages being learned. Once modified, the region appears to resist subsequent modification, which necessitates utilizing adjacent cortical areas for the second language learned as an adult.

Kim, K. H. S., N. R. Relkin, K. Young-Min Lee, and J. Hirsch. Distinct cortical areas associated with native and second languages. *Nature* 388:171–174, 1997.

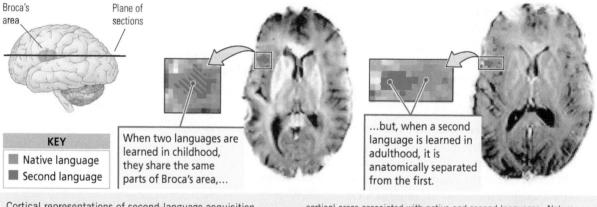

Broca's area
Plane of sections

KEY
■ Native language
■ Second language

When two languages are learned in childhood, they share the same parts of Broca's area,...

...but, when a second language is learned in adulthood, it is anatomically separated from the first.

Cortical representations of second-language acquisition. (Reprinted by permission from Macmillan Publishers Ltd: Kim, K. H. S., N. R. Relkin, K. Young-Min Lee, and J. Hirsch. Distinct cortical areas associated with native and second languages. *Nature* 388(6638):171–174, 1997.)

unilateral lesions, as summarized in **Table 23.5**. Besides speech disorders, nearly all of the children exhibited disorders of writing and calculation. Of these 15 children, 5 showed complete recovery within 6 weeks to 2 years. Most of the remaining children showed considerable improvement; in many cases, the only remaining deficit was a mild difficulty in writing, a finding similar to that of Alajouanine and Lhermitte.

Bryan Woods and Hans-Leukas Teuber (1973) studied about 50 patients with prenatal or early postnatal brain damage to either the left or the right

Table 23.5 **Frequency of different symptoms in 15 cases caused by left-hemisphere lesions in childhood**

Symptom	Number of cases	Percentage	Evolution of symptoms
Mutism	9	60	From 5 days to 30 months
Articulatory disorders	12	80	Persistent in 4 cases
Auditory verbal comprehension disorders	6	40	Persistent in 1 case
Naming disorders	7	46	Persistent in 3 cases
Paraphasia	1	7	Disappearance
Reading disorders	9	60	Persistent in 3 cases
Writing disorders	13	86	Persistent in 7 cases
Facial apraxia	2	—	Transient
Acalculia	11	—	(Not reported)

Source: Reprinted from *Brain and Language*, Vol. 3, Hécaen, H., "Acquired aphasia in children and the ontogenesis of hemispheric functional specialization," pages 114–134, Copyright 1976, with permission from Elsevier.

hemisphere. Using healthy siblings as controls, they came to the following conclusions:

1. Language survives early left-hemisphere injury.

2. Much of this survival seems attributable to appropriation of a potential language zone in the right hemisphere.

3. This shift of language location has a price: specifically, some kinds of visuospatial orientation are impaired.

4. Early lesions of the right hemisphere produce deficits similar to those produced by such lesions in adulthood.

In other words, if a child sustains a left-hemisphere lesion that produces right hemiplegia, language functions are recovered to a remarkably greater degree than after a comparable lesion in an adult, presumably because some or all language abilities move to the right hemisphere. Presumably, language crowds into the right hemisphere at the expense of visuospatial functions. On the other hand, a right-hemisphere lesion, which produces left hemiplegia, does not impair language ability.

A summary of this pattern of results, obtained from verbal and performance IQ scores of the Wechsler Adult Intelligence Scale, is shown in **Figure 23.17**. Left-hemisphere lesions depress both verbal and performance scores. Right-hemisphere lesions depress only performance scores. In a subsequent study, Woods (1980) examined the effects of lesions incurred earlier than age 1. The main finding was that right-hemisphere lesions impaired both verbal and performance IQ scores. Daria Riva and L. Cazzaniga (1986) confirmed these results and noted that lesions incurred before 1 year of age produce more-severe overall impairments than do those incurred after age 1.

Not all aspects of language function are spared after lesions incurred between the ages of 1 and 5. Woods (1987) found that, on a speech-shadowing task, which requires a person to repeat passages of speech as they are

Figure 23.17 ▼

IQ Scores on Subtests of the Wechsler Adult Intelligence Scale The adults tested had a lesion of the left or the right hemisphere in infancy, as determined by the occurrence of hemiparesis. Note that both verbal and performance scores are depressed by left-hemisphere lesions, whereas only performance scores are depressed by right-hemisphere lesions. (Average IQ score is 100.) The results suggest that, if language moves to the right hemisphere, its usual functions are sacrificed to accommodate the shift. The results also suggest that right-hemisphere functions do not shift sufficiently to interfere with language. (Data from Teuber, 1975.)

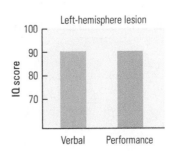

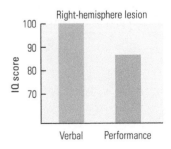

read, adult right- and left-hemisphere lesions produce equal impairments. Virtually identical impairments are observed subsequent to early-childhood lesions, even though speech is significantly spared in the early left-hemisphere lesions.

Reorganization of Language

The evidence that language is spared after early brain damage because its control is transferred to the opposite hemisphere raises three questions. What actual language functions are transferred? What type of brain damage causes the transfer? During what age range can transfer can take place? Ted Rasmussen and Brenda Milner (1975, 1977) addressed the first two questions experimentally, but the third has not yet been answered completely.

Using carotid sodium amobarbital injection and dichotic-listening tests (see Sections 11.2 and 11.3), Rasmussen and Milner localized language in a large number of patients who underwent left-hemisphere injury early in life and returned to the hospital years later because of complications. They found that the patients sorted into three groups, as shown in **Table 23.6**. In the first group, speech was in the left hemisphere; in the second group, it was represented bilaterally; and in the third group, it was in the right hemisphere. The patients who had speech in the left hemisphere were found to have damage that did not invade the anterior speech zone (Broca's area) or the posterior speech zone (Wernicke's area).

Examples of brain damage that did not produce a shift in language lateralization are shown in **Figure 23.18**A. Both exemplar lesions are large, yet the dichotic-listening test showed a right-ear advantage (a sign that a person's speech is localized in the left hemisphere). In the sodium amobarbital tests following left-hemisphere injection, the patients were mute both on naming tasks (for example, identifying objects as an experimenter holds each up and asks, "What is this?") and on repetition tasks (for example, "Name the days of the week in order."). The locations of the anterior and posterior speech zones are shown in green and yellow, respectively, in Figure 23.18A.

Table 23.6 **Changes in hemispheric speech representation after early brain damage**

		PERCENTAGE WITH SPEECH REPRESENTATION		
	Handedness	Left	Bilateral	Right
No early damage	Right	96	0	4
	Left or mixed	70	15	15
Early damage	Right	81	7	12
	Left or mixed	28	19	53

Data source: Rasmussen and Milner, 1975, pp. 248–249.

(A) No shift in language

Early brain damage

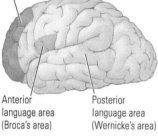

Anterior language area (Broca's area)

Posterior language area (Wernicke's area)

(B) Complete shift of language

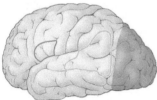

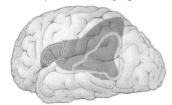

(C) Shift of anterior speech functions

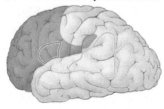

(D) Shift of posterior speech functions

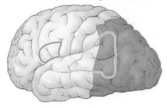

Figure 23.18 ◄

Reorganization of Language Relations between early brain damage and hemisphere changes in language organization: (A) Anterior and posterior lesions (red), after which language remained in the left hemisphere. (B) An anterior–posterior lesion causes all language to move to the right hemisphere. (C) An anterior lesion causes bilateral representation, with the anterior speech zone shifting to the right hemisphere. (D) A posterior lesion also causes bilateral representation, with the posterior speech zone shifting to the right hemisphere. (Research from Rasmussen and Milner, 1977.)

An example of a lesion that produced a complete shift of language to the right hemisphere is illustrated in Figure 23.18B. This patient showed a left-ear advantage on the dichotic-listening test and was mute for naming and repetition after right-hemisphere sodium amobarbital injection. Note that the lesion invaded both the anterior and the posterior speech zones, which was typical for patients who developed right-hemisphere speech after early left-hemisphere lesions.

Examples of the lesions in patients who had bilateral speech are shown in Figure 23.18C and D. The patient whose lesion is shown in Figure 23.18C at age 6 incurred a large left-frontal-lobe lesion that included the anterior language zone. At age 18, the patient was right-handed and had a right-ear advantage for digits and a left-ear advantage for melodies. On the sodium amobarbital tests, a left-hemisphere injection produced a disturbance in series repetition (counting, reciting the days of the week forward or backward, or oral spelling), but naming was less disturbed. A right-hemisphere injection produced a disturbance in both series repetition and naming.

With the assumptions that the right-ear advantage for digits is an indication of left-hemisphere speech and that the absence of series repetition after left-hemisphere sodium amobarbital injection is an indication of intact speech in the left posterior speech zone, we can conclude that the lesion did not cause a complete shift of speech from the posterior left speech zone. Because naming was disturbed after a right-hemisphere injection of sodium amobarbital, the left-hemisphere speech functions of the anterior zone are assumed to have shifted to the right hemisphere.

The patient whose lesion is shown in Figure 23.18D had a large posterior lesion that was incurred at 2½ years of age. Testing at age 16 showed that she was left-handed and had a left-ear advantage for both digits and melodies. Sodium amobarbital tests showed that naming was disturbed by both left- and right-hemisphere injections, whereas she performed series repetition competently after the left but not the right hemisphere was injected. In this case, the large posterior lesion incurred early in life seems to have caused speech functions of the posterior zone to shift to the right, whereas the anterior speech zone still retained some speech function.

The results described so far, particularly those of Rasmussen and Milner (1975, 1977), show that speech has a strong affinity for the left hemisphere and will not abandon it unless an entire center is destroyed; even then, it might shift only partly to the other hemisphere. This affinity is thought to be based on the innate anatomical organization of the left hemisphere. In examining their patients with early left-hemisphere lesions, Rasmussen and Milner also noted that childhood injuries to the left hemisphere after 5 years of age rarely caused a change in speech patterns.

They thus inferred that recovery after about age 6 is due not to transfer to the other hemisphere but to intrahemispheric reorganization, possibly with intact surrounding zones acquiring some control over speech. Further evidence comes from Woods and Teuber's study. Recall from Figure 23.17 that left- but not right-hemisphere lesions cause a decline in both verbal and performance IQ scores, a result that argues against the idea that the right hemisphere has equal potential for language.

Although the evidence supports the left-for-speech hypothesis, there is reason to believe that functional validation is still required; that is, practice with language is necessary to establish left-hemisphere preeminence. Woods (1987; Woods and Teuber, 1973) reported that if left-hemisphere lesions occur before the first birthday, both verbal and performance IQ scores are severely depressed. If left-hemisphere lesions occur after age 1, neither verbal nor performance IQ score is affected. Right-hemisphere lesions at any age lower only performance IQ score. The effects of lesions before age 1 might be due to a disruption of verbal functions that had not yet been sufficiently validated or that perhaps were disrupted by the invasion of performance functions. We must note, however, that this suggestion is speculative, that IQ score is at best an imprecise measure of language, and that a more systematic study of these patients—one using linguistic tests—is called for.

Absence of Language After Bilateral Lesions

Bilateral cortical lesions in children are rare. Nevertheless, a number of reports suggest that, when bilateral lesions do occur, the plasticity required for the acquisition or reacquisition of language subsequent to injury is absent. Faraneh Vargha-Khadem and Gordon Watters (1985) report such a case.

A.C. was born after a healthy pregnancy, but the delivery was difficult and required forceps. The next day, A.C. began to have epileptic seizures. He was given anticonvulsants and after a couple of weeks of treatment was seizure-free. When he began to walk, he had left hemiparesis that affected the left limbs. His language development was much delayed and he did not advance beyond a few two-word utterances. A.C.'s rare attempts to form sentences could not be understood. Although he could follow instructions, suggesting a somewhat preserved capacity for comprehension, he did poorly on the Token Test, which evaluates the ability to follow a number of sequentially presented instructions, and very poorly on most other tests of language ability. At the same time, his performance on the nonverbal parts of IQ tests suggested that he had at least average intelligence.

A CT scan performed at age 6½ indicated that A.C. had a lesion largely restricted to Broca's area in the left hemisphere and another lesion restricted to the middle part of the sensorimotor cortex on the right side. Thus, even though A.C. had a spared Broca's area on the right and spared posterior speech zones on both the left and the right, he failed to acquire language as he might be expected to have done had he received only a unilateral left-hemisphere lesion. The reason that A.C. failed to show sufficient plasticity to develop more-standard language is not known, but this case history strongly suggests that for some reason, plasticity depends on at least one intact hemisphere.

◎ 23.7 Studying Plasticity After Early Brain Injury

The mechanisms mediating recovery of function after brain injury sustained in infancy can be studied experimentally in laboratory animals by systematically varying the age at injury and its location. We first consider the behavioral effects of injury, then look at what the anatomical correlates might be.

Effects of Early Brain Lesions on Behaviors Later in Life

We have already considered the relation between age at injury and functional outcome in human infants. We might expect to see a similar phenomenon in laboratory animals, and as noted in Section 23.6, Kennard showed that motor-cortex lesions in infant monkeys allow better functional outcome than do similar lesions in adulthood. This view was presumed to be correct until the 1970s, when contradictory findings began to emerge from laboratory studies. As in all fields of science, reality has proved much more complex than our descriptions of it, and we now know that many factors influence the general dependability of the Kennard principle. These factors include the brain region injured, precise developmental stage at injury, age at assessment, type of behavior measured, and exposure to gonadal hormones (for a review, see Kolb, 1995).

Since the early 1980s, we (the authors) have removed virtually every region of the rat cortical mantle at varying ages, ranging from embryonic day 18 to adolescence (see Kolb et al., 2013, for a review). Our general finding is that recovery varies with the precise embryological age at which the removal took place (**Table 23.7**). If the cortex is injured bilaterally during neurogenesis, functional recovery is virtually complete.

The brain's ability to compensate for injury incurred at the time of neurogenesis is remarkable. Sam Hicks and Constance D'Amato (1973) demonstrated as long as 40 years ago, when they found that if the developing brain was irradiated at the early stages of cortical neurogenesis (which effectively killed the entire cerebrum), that the brain compensated by regenerating a substantial proportion of the lost cells. In short, the cerebrum was destroyed by the treatment, and the stem cells responded by overproducing new cortical neurons that rebuilt about 50 percent of what was lost.

In contrast, if a rat's cortex is injured in the first few days after birth, which is a time of neural migration and cell differentiation, the effect is functionally devastating: the animal shows much more severe effects of injury than would be expected even if it had been aged at the time of injury. This poor outcome is not a function of lesion size or of damage to particular cortical areas. Rather, something about the cortex during this developmental time makes it especially vulnerable. For example, damage at this time may disturb synaptogenesis or may even alter stem-cell activity. When this phase of development has ended, however, the brain is especially able to compensate for injury.

Rats incurring cortical injuries at 7 to 12 days of age show behavioral capacities in adulthood that exceed those of animals receiving similar lesions at any other time. In fact, on some behavioral tests, these animals show virtually complete recovery. Importantly, far more extensive recovery is seen in the ability to

Table 23.7 Summary of the effects of frontal cortical injury at different ages in the rat

Age at Injury	Behavioral Result	Anatomical Result
E18	Functional recovery	Gross anomalies in structure Brain size close to standard
P1–P5	Dismal functional outcome	Small brain, dendritic atrophy Abnormal connectivity
P7–P12	Functional recovery	Neurogenesis; astrogenesis Increased synapse number
P120	Partial return of function	Dendritic atrophy, then regrowth

Abbreviations: E18, embryonic day 18; P followed by number, postnatal day.
Data source: Kolb and Gibb, 2007.

perform cognitive tasks, such as learning how to solve various spatial-navigation problems, than is seen in the performance of motor-function tests.

These findings are further complicated when we examine the effects of removing an entire hemisphere (*hemispherectomy*, described in the Chapter 10 Portrait) or the cortex of an entire hemisphere (*hemidecortication*), which are sometimes used as a treatment for disorders such as severe epilepsy. The earlier the hemidecortical removal in such cases, the greater the extent of functional recovery.

Thus, rats with hemidecortication on the day of birth have a far better functional outcome than do animals with later hemidecortications. One explanation for this result is that the lesion does not interfere with migration and differentiation in the intact hemisphere—presumably where recovery is being mediated. The connection between unilateral injury and increased likelihood of recovery is reminiscent of the effects of cortical injuries on language in human infants. Recall A.C.'s case, in which his bilateral injury resulted in permanent aphasia.

The only other laboratory species regularly used for studies of early brain injury are cats and rhesus monkeys. In comparing these species with rats, one must take care to remember that rats, cats, and monkeys are not born at the same developmental age. Rats are born in a more immature state than are cats, although both species are helpless at birth, and some time elapses before their eyes are mature enough even to open. Cats at birth are much more immature than monkeys, which are actually more mature than human newborns. **Figure 23.19** compares the approximate relative developmental ages at birth of rats and humans. Jaime Villablanca and colleagues (1993) emphasize the age-at-birth confound and conclude that, like newborn rats, kittens with prenatal injuries are functionally better off than kittens receiving lesions slightly later, during the time of synaptogenesis, as would be predicted from Figure 23.19.

The importance of the site of injury in the developing brain is shown nicely in studies by Jocelyne Bachevalier and Mort Mishkin (1994), who varied the size and location of temporal-lobe injury in infant monkeys. In their first studies, they and their colleagues examined the effects of neonatal visual-system lesions on the performance of the delayed nonmatching-to-sample task illustrated in Figure 23.11. In adult monkeys, lesions of the medial temporal cortex and of more lateral neocortex (area TE) severely impair performance on the task, especially when the intervals between presentations of the objects are increased. The researchers removed these areas in monkeys that were 1 to 2 weeks old, then tested them on the nonmatching task, beginning at 10 months of age. The monkeys with medial temporal lesions were nearly as impaired as monkeys that received lesions as adults, whereas the monkeys that received TE lesions in infancy performed much better than monkeys that received lesions as adults.

These results suggest that functional recovery may be better after some brain injuries than others. In further studies, Bachevalier and colleagues (2001) examined the social behavior of monkeys that received lesions of the medial temporal

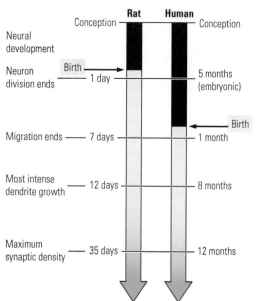

Figure 23.19 ▲

Developmental Age This diagram compares the developmental ages of the rat brain and the human brain at various times after conception. Note that day of birth is unrelated to the stage of neural development.

area as infants. As they develop, these monkeys shun social contact with other monkeys and display stereotypical behavior, excessive self-directed behavior, and a lack of facial expression. In short, these animals appear autistic.

If the temporal-lobe lesions are restricted to the amygdala and entorhinal cortex, the autistic behavior is present but is not as severe. If the lesion is restricted to the parahippocampal gyrus and hippocampus, the autistic behavior emerges only in adulthood. Monkeys that receive damage to TE neonatally are not autistic but are hyperactive. Their behavior is annoying to adult monkeys, who do not like to interact with them.

Effects of Early Brain Lesions on Brain Structure Later in Life

In principle, the brain could show plastic changes that might support recovery after early injury in three ways:

1. **Changes in the organization of the remaining intact circuits in the brain.** The general idea is that the brain could reorganize in some way "to do more with less." It is unlikely that a complexly integrated structure such as the cerebral cortex could undergo a wholesale reorganization of cortical connectivity. Instead, recovery from cortical injury would be most likely to result from a change in the intrinsic organization of local cortical circuits in regions directly or indirectly disrupted by the injury. Although significant reorganization of cortical connectivity in the young brain might be possible, the overwhelming evidence in experimental animals is that such reorganization is rare and just as likely to be associated with abnormal functioning as with recovery.

2. **Generation of new circuitry.** We have already seen that cerebral reorganization can be stimulated by experience in the healthy brain, and it seems reasonable to expect that experience or some other treatment, such as a drug, could influence reparative processes in the remaining brain or could enhance the production of new circuitry. Once again, the induced neuronal changes would most likely take place in the intrinsic organization of the cortex rather than throughout the brain as a whole.

3. **Generation of neurons and glia to replace at least some lost neurons.** As stated earlier, the stem cells that give rise to the brain's neurons and glia remain active in the subventricular zone throughout life. Thus, perhaps neurogenesis could be stimulated after injury, especially in development, and these new neurons could replace those lost to injury or disease (see, for example, Kolb et al., 1998).

Evidence exists that supports all three of these possible explanations for cerebral plasticity after early injury (Kolb et al., 2013).

Factors Influencing Plasticity After Early Cortical Injury

The healthy brain is affected by a wide variety of factors, ranging from general sensory experience to gonadal hormones and **neurotrophic factors**, chemical compounds that support growth and differentiation in developing neurons and

Table 23.8 **Summary of the effects of factors on plasticity after early cortical lesions**

Treatment	Behavioral Result	Anatomical Result
Tactile stimulation	Recovery after P4 frontal, motor, or parietal lesions	Dendritic growth, neurotrophic factors increased, acetylcholine increased
Handling	No effect	Synaptic pruning
Prenatal tactile stimulation of dam	Recovery after P4 frontal lesions	Dendritic growth
Complex rearing from weaning	Recovery after P4 frontal or parietal lesions	Dendritic growth
Nicotine	Recovery after P3 frontal lesions	Acetylcholine increased dendritic change?
Choline supplement	Enhanced recovery after P4 lesions	Increased dendritic growth
Hormone depletion	Blocks recovery after P7 frontal lesions	Blocks dendritic changes
Noradrenaline depletion	Blocks recovery after P7 frontal lesions	Blocks dendritic hypertrophy

Abbreviation: P followed by number, postnatal day.

Data sources: Research from Kolb, Comeau, and Gibb (2008), and Kolb, Halliwell, and Gibb (2010).

may act to keep neurons alive in adulthood. It is reasonable to suppose that all of these factors will also influence the damaged brain. Although virtually all research to date has been done in rats, the evidence is compelling that a wide range of factors can facilitate functional recovery (**Table 23.8**).

Perhaps one of the most potent treatments is tactile stimulation. A series of studies have shown that stroking infant rats with a soft brush for 15 minutes three times a day for 10 days after a perinatal lesion of the frontal, parietal, or motor cortex can stimulate significant functional recovery in adulthood (Kolb and Gibb, 2010). The tactile stimulation promotes synaptogenesis in the remaining cortex, possibly because the treatment increases the production of growth factors in the skin that pass into the blood to stimulate reparative processes in the cortex.

Even more interesting is Gibb and colleagues' (2014) finding that prenatal experiences, including complex housing or tactile stimulation of pregnant dams with a child's hairbrush throughout pregnancy, not only can alter the synaptic organization of the as-yet-unborn progeny's brain in adulthood but also can facilitate recovery from cortical injury incurred in infancy. The mechanism of this behavioral effect is not yet known, although we can speculate that it may be related to the increased production of one or more neurotrophic factors, likely resulting from changes in gene expression.

SUMMARY

23.1 Approaches to Studying Brain Development

Brain development can be studied by correlating it with specific behaviors, by studying cognitive development and making inferences about which brain structures must be maturing, and by studying factors that influence brain and behavioral development. The merging of all three types of evidence has led to our current understanding of brain development and plasticity.

23.2 Development of the Human Brain

The process of brain maturation in humans is long, lasting well beyond adolescence. Neurons, the brain's elementary components, are born, migrate, and as their processes elaborate, establish connections with other neurons. Because the brain contains such a large number of cells and an even larger number of connections, the newborn brain possesses more neurons and connections than it needs, then prunes them back to a stable adult level. The adolescent brain is fundamentally different from both child and adult brains, and this difference correlates with the unique set of behaviors observed in adolescents.

23.3 Imaging Studies of Brain Development

The increased use of MRI techniques across the life span and the introduction of fNIRS have led to a new understanding of brain maturation processes. The human cortex is sculpted by a reduction in cortical thickness beginning before age 4 and continuing until at least 30 years of age. These changes take place first in the brain's primary regions and later in secondary and tertiary regions and are inversely correlated with measures of cognitive development.

23.4 Development of Problem-Solving Ability

Behavioral and cognitive capacities follow parallel sequences of development, from the rudimentary to the complex. Stages of cognitive development identified by Piaget correlate with growth spurts in the brain. Neuropsychological measures of cognitive development correlate with changes in brain structure in the basal ganglia and cerebral cortex. Development does not take place without sensory input, however: experience has major effects on healthy brain development. These

effects can be seen not only in the morphology of the cerebral cortex and patterns of cortical connectivity but also in its representational maps.

23.5 Environmental Effects on Brain Development

Just as "normal" experiences shape brain development, abnormal experiences alter brain structure and behavior. Furthermore, perturbations of the brain in the course of development can significantly alter brain development and result in severe behavioral abnormalities.

23.6 Brain Injury and Plasticity

The brain's sensitivity to experience or injury varies with time because during discrete periods in the course of development, different brain regions are particularly sensitive to different events. Functional recovery after early injury may result from modification of remaining circuits, generation of new (abnormal) circuits, or generation of neurons and glia.

23.7 Studying Plasticity After Early Brain Injury

Various factors can influence recovery from early cortical injury, including experience, hormones, stress, drugs, and neurotrophic factors. These factors stimulate neurogenesis, gliogenesis, and synaptic remodeling.

References

Alajouanine, T., and F. Lhermitte. Acquired aphasia in children. *Brain* 88:653–662, 1965.

Anda, R. F., V. J. Felitti, J. D. Bremner, J. D. Walker, C. Whitfiedd, B. D. Perry, S. R. Dube, and W. H. Giles. The enduring effects of abuse and related adverse experiences in childhood: A convergence of evidence from neurobiology and epidemiology. *European Archives of Psychiatry and Clinical Neuroscience* 256:174–186, 2006.

Bachevalier, J., L. Malkova, and M. Mishkin. Effects of selective neonatal temporal lobe lesions on socioemotional behavior in infant rhesus monkeys (*Macaca mulatta*). *Behavioral Neuroscience* 115:545–559, 2001.

Bachevalier, J., and M. Mishkin. Effects of selective neonatal temporal lobe lesions on visual recognition memory in rhesus monkeys. *Journal of Neuroscience* 14:2128–2139, 1994.

Basser, L. Hemiplegia of early onset and the faculty of speech with special reference to the effects of hemispherectomy. *Brain* 85:427–460, 1962.

Blakemore, C., and D. E. Mitchell. Environmental modification of the visual cortex and the neural basis of learning and memory. *Nature* 241:467–468, 1973.

Bourgeois, J.-P. Synaptogenesis in the neocortex of the newborn: The ultimate frontier for individuation? In C. A. Nelson and M. Luciana, Eds. *Handbook of Developmental Cognitive Neuroscience*. Cambridge, Mass.: MIT Press, 2001.

Casey, B. J., K. M. Thomas, and B. McCandliss. Applications of magnetic resonance imaging to the study of development. In C. A. Nelson and M. Luciana, Eds. *Handbook of*

Developmental Cognitive Neuroscience, pp. 137–147. Cambridge, Mass.: MIT Press.

Caviness, V. S., Jr., and R. L. Sidman. Time of origin of corresponding cell classes in the cerebral cortex of normal and reeler mutant mice: An autoradiographic analysis. *Journal of Comparative Neurology* 148:141–152, 1973.

Cryan, J. F., and T. G. Dinan. Mind-altering microorganisms: The impact of gut microbiota on brain and behaviour. *Nature Reviews Neuroscience* 13:701–712, 2012.

Diaz Heijtz, R., S. Wang, F. Anuar, Y. Qian, B. Bjorkholm, A. Samuelsson, M. Hibberd, H. Forssberg, and S. Pettersson. Normal gut microbiota modulates brain development and behavior. *Proceedings of the National Academy of Sciences U.S.A.* 108:3047–3052, 2011.

Dinan, T. G., C. Stanton, and J. F. Cryan. Psychobiotics: A novel class of psychotropic. *Biological Psychiatry* 74:720–726, 2013.

Dominguez-Salas, P., S. E. Moore, M. S Baker, A. W. Bergen, S. E. Cox, R. A. Dyer, et al. Maternal nutrition at conception modulates DNA methylation of human metastable epialleles. *Nature Communications* doi: 10.1038/ncomms4746, 2014.

Elbert, T., S. Heim, and B. Rockstroh. Neural plasticity and development. In C. A. Nelson and M. Luciana, Eds. *Handbook of Developmental Cognitive Neuroscience*, pp. 191–204. Cambridge, Mass.: MIT Press, 2001.

Epstein, H. T. Growth spurts during brain development: Implications for educational policy and practice. In J. S.

Chard and A. F. Mirsky, Eds. *Education and the Brain*. Chicago: University of Chicago Press, 1978.

Flechsig, P. *Anatomie des menschlichen Gehirns und Ruckenmarks*. Leipzig: Georg Thieme, 1920.

Gibb, R., C. Gonzalez, and B. Kolb. Prenatal enrichment and recovery from perinatal cortical damage: Effects of maternal complex housing. *Frontiers in Behavioral Neuroscience* doi: 10.3389/fnbeh.2014.00223, 2014.

Giedd, J. N., and J. L. Rapoport. Structural MRI of pediatric brain development: What have we learned and where are we going? *Neuron* 67:728–734, 2010.

Gogtay, N., J. N. Giedd, L. Lusk, K. M. Hayashi, D. Greenstein, A. C. Valtuzis, T. F. Nugent III, D. H. Herman, L. S. Clasen, A. W. Toga, J. L. Rapoport, and P. M. Thompson. Dynamic mapping of human cortical development during childhood and adolescence. *Proceedings of the National Academy of Sciences of the U.S.A.* 101:8174–8179, 2004.

Gould E., P. Tanapat, N. B. Hastings, and T. J. Shors. Neurogenesis in adulthood: A possible role in learning. *Trends in Cognitive Science* 3:186–192, 1999.

Guttman, E. Aphasia in children. *Brain* 65:205–219, 1942.

Halliwell, C., W. Comeau, R. Gibb, D. O. Frost, and B. Kolb. Factors influencing frontal cortex development and recovery from early frontal injury. *Developmental Rehabilitation* 12:269–278, 2009.

Hebb, D. O. *The Organization of Behavior*. New York: McGraw-Hill, 1949.

Hécaen, H. Acquired aphasia in children and the ontogenesis of hemispheric functional specialization. *Brain and Language* 3:114–134, 1976.

Hicks, S. P., and C. J. D'Amato. Effects of ionizing radiation on developing brain and behavior. In G. Gottlieb, Ed. *Studies on the Development of Behavior and the Nervous System*, pp. 35–72. New York: Academic Press, 1973.

Himmler, B.T., S. M. Pellis, and B. Kolb. Juvenile play experience primes neurons in the medial prefrontal cortex to be more responsive to later experiences. *Neuroscience Letters* 556:42–45, 2013.

Hirsch, H. V. B., and D. N. Spinelli. Modification of the distribution of receptive field orientation in cats by selective visual exposure during development. *Experimental Brain Research* 13:509–527, 1971.

Holloway, V., D. G. Gadian, F. Vargha-Khadem, D. A. Porter, S. G. Boyd, and A. Connelly. The reorganization of sensorimotor function in children after hemispherectomy. *Brain* 123:2432–2444, 2000.

Johnson, D. E., D. Guthrie, A. T. Smyke, S. F. Koga, N. A. Fox, C. H. Zeanah, and C. A. Nelson. Growth and associations between auxology, caregiving environment, and cognition in socially deprived Romanian children randomized to foster vs ongoing institutionalized care. *Archives of Pediatric Adolescent Medicine* 164:507–516, 2010.

Kennard, M. Cortical reorganization of motor function. *Archives of Neurology* 48:227–240, 1942.

Kolb, B. *Brain Plasticity and Behavior*. Hillsdale, NJ: Lawrence Erlbaum, 1995.

Kolb, B., W. Comeau, and R. Gibb. Early brain injury, plasticity, and behavior. In C. A. Nelson and M. Luciana, Eds. *Handbook of Developmental Cognitive Neuroscience*, 2nd ed. MIT Press: Cambridge, Mass., 2008.

Kolb, B., and R. Gibb. Brain plasticity and recovery from early cortical injury. *Developmental Psychobiology* 49:107–118, 2007.

Kolb, B., and R. Gibb. Tactile stimulation facilitates functional recovery and dendritic change after neonatal medial frontal or posterior parietal lesions in rats. *Behavioural Brain Research* 214:115–120, 2010.

Kolb, B., R. Gibb, and G. Gorny. Experience-dependent changes in dendritic arbor and spine density in neocortex vary with age and sex. *Neurobiology of Learning and Memory* 79:1–10, 2003.

Kolb, B., R. Gibb, G. Gorny, and I. Q. Whishaw. Possible brain regrowth after cortical lesions in rats. *Behavioural Brain Research* 91:127–141, 1998.

Kolb, B., C. Halliwell, and R. Gibb. Factors influencing neocortical development in the normal and injured brain. In M. S. Blumberg, J. H. Freeman, and S. R. Robinson, Eds. *Developmental and Comparative Neuroscience: Epigenetics, Evolution, and Behavior*. New York: Oxford University Press, 2010.

Kolb, B., R. Mychasiuk, A. Muhammad, and R. Gibb. Brain plasticity in the developing brain. *Progress in Brain Research*, 207:35–64, 2013.

Kolb, B., R. Mychasiuk, A. Muhammad, Y. Li, D. O. Frost, and R. Gibb. Experience and the developing prefrontal cortex. *Proceedings of the National Academy of Sciences U.S.A.* 109 Suppl. 2:17186–17193, 2012.

Krashen, S. D. Lateralization, language learning, and the critical period: Some new evidence. *Language Learning* 23:63–74, 1973.

Kuhl, P. K. The role of early experience in early language development: Linguistic experience alters the perception and production of speech. In N. A. Fox, L. A. Leavitt, and J. G. Warhol, Eds. *The Role of Early Experience in Infant Development*, p. 120. New Brunswick, N.J.: Johnson & Johnson Consumer Companies, 1999.

Lawler, J. M., C. E. Hostinar, S. B. Mliner, and M. R. Gunnar. Disinhibited social engagement in postinstitutionalized children: Differentiating normal from atypical behavior. *Developmental Psychopathology* 26:451–464, 2014.

Lenneberg, E. *Biological Foundations of Language*. New York: John Wiley, 1967.

Malanga, C. J., and B. E. Kosofsky. Does drug abuse beget drug abuse? Behavioral analysis of addiction liability in animal models of prenatal drug exposure. *Developmental Brain Research* 147:47–57, 2003.

McCarthy, G. Quoted in Krashen, S. D. Lateralization, language learning, and the critical period: Some new evidence. *Language Learning* 23:63–74, 1973.

Moriguchi, Y., and K. Hiraki. Prefrontal cortex and executive function in young children: A review of NIRS studies. *Frontiers in Human Neuroscience* doi:10.3389, 2013.

Mortera, P., and S. Herculano-Houzel. Age-related neuronal loss in the rat brain starts at the end of adolescence.

Frontiers in Neuroanatomy doi: 10.3389/fnana.2012.00045, 2012.

Mychasiuk, R., S. Zahir, N. Schmold, S. Llnytskyy, O. Kovalchuk, and R. Gibb. Parental enrichment and offspring development: Modifications to brain, behavior and the epigenome. *Behavioural Brain Research* 228:294–298, 2012.

National Institute on Drug Abuse (NIDA, 2009). http://www.drugabuse.gov/publications/topics-in-brief/prenatal-exposure-to-drugs-abuse

Oberlander, T. F., R. J. Bonaguro, S. Misri, M. Papsdorf, C. J. Ross, and E. M. Simpson. Infant serotonin transporter (SLC6A4) promoter genotype is associated with adverse neonatal outcomes after prenatal exposure to serotonin reuptake inhibitor medications. *Molecular Psychiatry* 13:83–88, 2008.

Overman, W. H., and J. Bachevalier. Inferences about functional development of neural systems in children via the application of animal tests of cognition. In C. A. Nelson and M. Luciana, Eds. *Developmental Cognitive Neuroscience*, pp. 109–124. Cambridge, Mass.: MIT Press, 2001.

Overman, W. H., J. Bachevalier, M. Turner, and A. Peuster. Object recognition versus object discrimination: Comparison between human infants and infant monkeys. *Behavioral Neuroscience* 106:15–29, 1992.

Paus, T., M. Keshavan, and J. N. Giedd. Why do so many psychiatric disorders emerge during adolescence? *Nature Reviews Neuroscience* 9:947–957, 2008.

Petanjek, Z., M. Judas, G. Simic, M. R. Rasin, H. B. M. Uylings, et al. Extraordinary neoteny of synaptic spines in the human prefrontal cortex. *Proceedings of the National Academy of Sciences U.S.A.* 108:13281–13286, 2011.

Piaget, J. *Biology and Knowledge*. Chicago: University of Chicago Press, 1971.

Rakic, P. Neurogenesis in adult primate neocortex: An evaluation of the evidence. *Nature Reviews Neuroscience* 3:65–71, 2002.

Rakic, P., A. E. Ayoub, J. J. Breuning, and M. H. Dominguez. Decision by division: Making cortical maps. *Trends in Neuroscience* 32:291–301, 2009.

Rasmussen, T., and B. Milner. Clinical and surgical studies of the cerebral speech areas in man. In K. J. Zulch, O. Creutzfeldt, and G. C. Galbraith, Eds. *Cerebral Localization*. Berlin and New York: Springer, 1975.

Rasmussen, T., and B. Milner. The role of early left-brain injury in determining lateralization of cerebral speech functions. *Annals of the New York Academy of Sciences* 299:355–369, 1977.

Riva, D., and L. Cazzaniga. Late effects of unilateral brain lesions sustained before and after age one. *Neuropsychologia* 24:423–428, 1986.

Russell, R., and M. Espir. *Traumatic Aphasia*. Oxford: Oxford University Press, 1961.

Rutter, M., T. G. O'Connor, and the English and Romanian Adoptees (ERA) Study Team. Are there biological programming effects for psychological development? Findings from a study of Romanian adoptees. *Developmental Psychology* 40:81–94, 2004.

Schneider, G. E. Is it really better to have your brain injury early? A revision of the "Kennard Principle." *Neuropsychologia* 17:557–583, 1979.

Shaw, P., K. Eckstrand, W. Sharp, J. Blumenthal, J. P. Lerch, D. Greenstein, L. Clasen, A. Evans, J. Giedd, and J. L. Rapoport. Attention-deficit/hyperactivity disorder is characterized by a delay in cortical maturation. *Proceedings of the National Academy of Sciences U.S.A.* 104:19649–19654, 2007.

Sheridan, M. A., N. A. Fox, C. H. Zeanah, K. A. McLaughlin, and C. A. Nelson. Variation in neural development as a result of exposure to institutionalization early in childhood. *Proceedings of the National Academy of Sciences U.S.A.* 109:12927–12932, 2012.

Sowell, E. R., B. S. Peterson, P. M. Thompson, S. E. Welcome, A. L. Henkenius, and A. W. Toga. Mapping cortical change across the human life span. *Nature Neuroscience* 6:309–315, 2003.

Sowell, E. R., P. M. Thompson, C. M. Leonard, S. E. Welcome, E. Kan, and A. W. Toga. Longitudinal mapping of cortical thickness and brain growth in normal children. *Journal of Neuroscience* 24:8223–8231, 2004.

Sturman, D. A., and B. Moghaddam. The neurobiology of adolescence: Changes in brain architecture, functional dynamics and behavioral tendencies. *Neuroscience and Biobehavioral Reviews* 35:1704–1712, 2011.

Teuber, H.-L. Recovery of function after brain injury in man. In *Outcomes of Severe Damage to the Nervous System*, Ciba Foundation Symposium 34. Amsterdam: Elsevier-North Holland, 1975.

Toga, A. W., P. M. Thompson, and E. R. Sowell. Mapping brain maturation. *Trends in Neuroscience* 29:148–159, 2006.

Vargha-Khadem, F., L. J. Carr, E. Brett, C. Adams, and M. Mishkin. Onset of speech after left hemispherectomy in a nine-year-old boy. *Brain* 120:159–182, 1997.

Vargha-Khadem, F., and G. V. Watters. Development of speech and language following bilateral frontal lesions. *Brain and Language* 25:167–183, 1985.

Villablanca, J. R., D. A. Hovda, G. F. Jackson, and C. Infante. Neurological and behavioral effects of a unilateral frontal cortical lesion in fetal kittens II: Visual system tests, and proposing a "critical period" for lesion effects. *Behavioral Brain Research* 57:79–92, 1993.

Wiesel, T. N., and D. H. Hubel. Comparison of the effects of unilateral and bilateral eye closure on cortical unit responses in kittens. *Journal of Neurophysiology* 28:1029–1040, 1965.

Werker, J. F., and R. C. Tees. Developmental changes across childhood in the perception of non-native speech sounds. *Canadian Journal of Psychology* 37:278–286, 1983.

Woods, B. T. The restricted effects of right-hemisphere lesions after age one: Wechsler test data. *Neuropsychologia* 18:65–70, 1980.

Woods, B. T. Impaired speech shadowing after early lesions of either hemisphere. *Neuropsychologia* 25:519–525, 1987.

Woods, B. T., and H.-L. Teuber. Early onset of complementary specialization of cerebral hemispheres in man. *Transactions of the American Neurological Association* 98:113–117, 1973.

24 Neurodevelopmental Disorders

 PORTRAIT   Life Without Reading

Ms. P., 19 years old, was working as a nurse's aide and had found her work so enjoyable that she was considering entering a nursing program. Because she had not completed high school and had a generally poor academic record, she came to us for guidance in deciding whether she could handle such a program.

Ms. P. had difficulty with language skills, and her reading skills were so poor that she was unable to pass the written examination for a driver's license. In view of Ms. P.'s interest in furthering her nursing education, we decided to test her reading abilities and to administer a complete neuropsychological battery. The results confirmed that she had difficulty reading. Her overall IQ score was 85 on the Wechsler Adult Intelligence Scale, but there was a 32-point difference between her verbal IQ of 74 and her performance (nonverbal) IQ of 106.

Specific tests of left-hemisphere function confirmed this discrepancy: although her verbal memory, verbal fluency, spelling, reading, and arithmetic scores were extremely low, her spatial skills were good, as were her nonverbal memory and her performance on tests such as the Wisconsin Card-Sorting Test and the

THE KOBAL COLLECTION AT ART RESOURCE, NY

Semmes Body-Placing Test. In short, her language skills were those of a 6-year-old, although she had attended school for 11 years, but her other abilities were typical for a person of her age.

In view of her deficient language skills, we advised Ms. P. that handling a nursing program would be difficult. We also considered it unlikely that she would to be able to develop the necessary language skills, especially because—as we discovered inadvertently—none of her five brothers and sisters could read either.

We explained to Ms. P. that she was by no means intellectually disabled, but that just as some people had poor musical ability, she had poor verbal ability and that it was possible to compensate. (We arranged for an oral administration of the driver's test, which she passed.)

Finally, we explained Ms. P.'s problem to her husband, who held a master's degree. In the short time that they had been married, he had grown frustrated with her inability to balance their checkbook, read recipes, and so forth. They now had an understanding of the problem, which we hoped would help them work out domestic routines to minimize its effect.

The Portrait illustrates one type of **neurodevelopmental disorder**, also called a *learning disability*, generally defined by performance in a specific school subject that falls significantly below average and seems to originate in abnormal brain development. Ms. P.'s difficulty with language skills made school arduous and frustrating and continued to cause her problems as an adult. Countless people with learning disabilities struggle to make adequate adjustments in their lives, and those with severe neurodevelopmental disorders need various degrees of lifelong assistance or care.

In this chapter, we survey neurodevelopmental disorders of learning, attention, social behavior, and general intellectual functioning. We expand on *savantism*, introduced in Section 18.7 and characterized by mental handicaps combined with a talent that may far exceed the abilities of the general population. (You may have seen the movie *Rain Man*, in which real-life savant Kim Peek is portrayed by actor Dustin Hoffman, shown in the Portrait.) We conclude the chapter by surveying research on adult outcomes of neurodevelopmental disorders.

⊚ 24.1 Neurodevelopmental Disorders

At school, most children are required to master a core curriculum. Some are unable to meet any demands of their school system; others learn, but only with difficulty. Among them, some repeat one or more grades, some graduate but fail to master certain subject areas, and some even graduate without mastering basic knowledge in any area. For those who fail to learn, the educational experience leaves emotional and attitudinal scars that may persist throughout life.

By no means are all causes of learning difficulties that children encounter in school neurodevelopmental. A child may be disturbed by an unhappy home life, be enduring abuse, be bored by school, dislike school, dislike a teacher, or have a physical handicap. But the difficulty could also result from brain dysfunction or brain damage. Some school systems are equipped to assess and distinguish the causes of learning problems, but most have no resources for either assessment or remediation. Even when a school is unequipped to deal with learning problems, however, if a child is not learning effectively, the question of whether the cause is brain damage or dysfunction or something else will arise.

Formal definitions of neurodevelopmental disorders encompass a wide variety of school-related problems—in interpersonal skills and intellectual achievement as well as difficulty in school. Because reading is central to success in school, inability to read—**dyslexia** (from the Greek *dys*, for "impaired," and *lexia*, for "word")—is central to the study of neurodevelopmental disorders. The World Health Organization (1992) defines dyslexia as a "disorder manifested by difficulty in learning to read despite conventional instruction, adequate intelligence, and sociocultural opportunity. It is dependent upon fundamental cognitive disabilities which are frequently of constitutional [mental or physical] origin."

This and similar definitions pose difficulties. What is meant by "conventional instruction"? By "adequate intelligence"? To comprehend the difficulty of arriving at satisfactory definitions, knowing some history behind contemporary ideas about dyslexia is helpful.

Historical Background and Evolution of Understanding

Dyslexia emerged within the context of *aphasia*, the loss of language ability resulting from brain injury. James Hinshelwood (1895), a Glasgow eye surgeon, and the following year Pringle Morgan, a general practitioner in the English town of Seaford, proposed independently that prerequisite brain areas were absent or abnormal in students who could not learn to read. It seemed logical to conclude that **developmental dyslexia**, which is acquired before birth or during early postbirth years, is similar in nature to **acquired dyslexia**, which is due to brain damage after the person has learned to read (see Section 19.7). Learning deficits in other spheres, such as mathematics, also would be due to some underlying brain problem.

Samuel T. Orton (1937) proposed that dyslexia is due to delayed function, not anatomical absence. Orton noted that dyslexia was correlated with left-handedness and with tendencies to reverse or invert letters and words when learning to read or write. He termed such dyslexia *strephosymbolia* (from the Greek, meaning "twisted symbols"). Orton thought that the nondominant hemisphere, usually the right, which he postulated reversed images of things, was excessively dominant or not sufficiently controlled. He suggested that, if an instructor was clever or persevering, education could establish "normal" dominance of reading in the left hemisphere, and the problem would be resolved.

When sociologists and educational psychologists became interested in learning disabilities, many supposed that environmental rather than neurological explanations accounted for learning impairments. This stance was perhaps motivated by the hope that environmental causes could be reversed more easily than neurological ones.

The term *learning disability* originated in an address given by Samuel A. Kirk in 1963. Kirk argued for better descriptions of children's school problems, but he excluded children with sensory and mental disorders from the group he labeled learning-disabled. Members of Kirk's audience, influenced both by his address and by his definition, later joined together to form the Association for Children with Learning Disabilities and further popularized the expression he had coined. More recently, the American Psychiatric Association's (2013) *Diagnostic and Statistical Manual of Mental Disorders* (DSM-5) adopted the term *neurodevelopmental disorder*.

To emphasize the overabundance and consequent confusion and inaccuracy engendered by the wide variety of terms long used to label learning disorders, Edward Fry (1968) published a tongue-in-cheek "Do-It-Yourself Terminology Generator" from which about 2000 labels can be constructed. You can try it for yourself in **Table 24.1**. From time to time, terms in wide use may take on pejorative connotations and be dropped in favor of new terms. The DSM-IV formally defined the term *retarded* as certain low scores on IQ tests, for example, but it is absent from the DSM-5.

Today, improved understanding of brain function and methods of behavioral testing, brain imaging, and identifying brain regions implicated in learning difficulties are proposed to result in improved diagnoses of neurodevelopmental disorders related to symptoms and their treatment. Neuroscientists now recognize that, for a host of reasons, a person may display selective impairments in, say, music, mathematics, or spatial navigation alongside otherwise healthy and even exemplary behavioral function in other areas. Neuroscientists also recognize that a variety of factors in early life contribute to brain health and consequently to adequate learning adjustments.

Table 24.1 **"Do-it-yourself terminology generator"**

Directions: Select any word from first column, then add any word from second and third columns. If you do not like the result, try again. It will mean about the same thing.

Secondary	Nervous	Deficit
Minimal	Brain	Dysfunction
Mild	Cerebral	Damage
Minor	Neurological	Disorder
Chronic	Neurologic	Desynchronization
Diffuse	CNS	Handicap
Specific	Language	Disability
Primary	Reading	Retardation
Developmental	Perceptual	Deficiency
Disorganized	Impulsive	Impairment
Organic	Visual-motor	Pathology
Clumsy	Behavior	Syndrome
Functional	Psychoneurologic	Complex

Source: Fry, E. A do-it-yourself terminology generator. *Journal of Reading* 11:428–430, 1968. Copyright © 1968 by the International Reading Association (www.reading.org).

Incidence of Neurodevelopmental Disorders

In the United States, the National Association for Learning Disabilities estimates that 5 percent of the school-age population is learning-disabled. A problem that complicates calculations of prevalence estimates related to neurodevelopmental disorders is that they are emerging conditions. When children enter first grade, few are categorized as learning-disabled, largely because a common method of defining learning disabilities is to estimate how far a person is behind an expected norm: for example, if a person is 2 years behind in academic progress as determined by a standardized test, that person is labeled learning-disabled.

When this criterion is used, fewer than 1 percent of 6-year-olds and 2 percent of 7-year-olds are learning-disabled, until, at age 19, 25 percent meet the criterion. This pattern of emerging incidence develops because the learning-disabled are falling behind at a rate proportional to the degree of their impairments.

Further complicating the process of calculating and utilizing prevalence rates is the variation in scholastic achievement from one school system to another. Achievement tests are often used to determine grade-equivalent performance, but even nondisabled school populations do not all display equivalent performance. Prevalence rates might be obtained by asking teachers to report the number of children in their classes who are receiving special help, but many schools have no resources for special education and cannot provide such information.

Nevertheless, the National Assessment of Educational Progress found, as of 2014 in the United States, that as many as one-third of schoolchildren lacked fundamental reading skills and that reading proficiency was not improving overall. Linking diagnosis to special assistance in the classroom also has an effect on the incidence of neurodevelopmental disorders. For example, when the diagnosis autism spectrum disorder (ASD) was linked to special funding for instruction, the incidence of ASD diagnoses increased.

Types of Neurodevelopmental Disorders

The DSM-5 recognizes many categories of childhood disorders, including the neurodevelopmental disorders summarized in **Table 24.2**. The classification and incidence of neurodevelopmental disorders correspond to the emphasis

Table 24.2 Summary DSM-5 classification of neurodevelopmental disorders

Diagnostic category	Description
Intellectual disability	Impairment that affects adaptive functioning in conceptual (language, etc.); social (interpersonal relations); and practical (self-management) domains
Communication disorder	Impairment in verbal and nonverbal communication
Autism spectrum disorder	Impairment in social interactions; repetitive behavior patterns
Attention-deficit/hyperactivity disorder	Impairments in attention to detail and hyperactivity exemplified by excessive talking, fidgeting, or an inability to remain seated in appropriate situations
Specific learning disorder	Persistent difficulties in reading, writing, arithmetic, or mathematical reasoning skills during formal schooling

Data source: American Psychiatric Association. *Diagnostic and Statistical Manual of Mental Disorders*, 5th ed. Washington, D.C.: American Psychiatric Association, 2013.

Table 24.3 Symptoms associated with neurodevelopmental disorders

1. Hyperactivity
2. Perceptual–motor impairments
3. Emotional lability
4. General coordination deficits
5. Disorders of attention (short attention span, distractibility, perseveration)
6. Impulsivity
7. Disorders of memory and thinking
8. Specific learning disabilities, including especially those of reading (dyslexia), arithmetic, writing, and spelling
9. Disorders of speech and hearing
10. Neurological signs and irregular EEG

placed on communication disorders, on self-control, and on certain academic specialties in most public school systems. **Table 24.3** lists symptoms that can be associated with neurodevelopmental disorders.

Good behavior, reading, arithmetic, and spelling are emphasized, and learning-disability classifications correspond to this focus. Although art, music, and physical education are taught in many schools, referrals for failure in these areas are uncommon. If art, rather than reading, were the core subject in the early school years, cataloging types of disabilities would be different. Nevertheless, disabilities can interfere with acquiring reading, spatial orientation, mathematics, and social skills. We focus next on reading disabilities.

24.2 Learning Disorders That Affect Reading

The study of reading disabilities is central to the analysis of learning disorders, and the complexity of reading illustrates how many different influences can affect performance. Reading requires letter-identification skills, phonological skills (converting letters into sounds by using certain rules), grapheme-association skills (using the visual gestalt of a word to access a previously learned sound), sequencing skills (in which a number of sounds are analyzed and combined in sequence), and short-term-memory skills (to retain pieces of information as they are sequentially extracted from written material).

Acquired information is important, including a **lexicon**, a memory store that contains words and their meanings, knowledge of the ways in which they can be combined, and information about the ideas with which they can be associated. Thus, reading is a multiprocess and multistage behavior (see Section 19.1). As such, one would expect that it could be disrupted in many ways. In the following sections, we describe types of reading, causes of reading disabilities, and the role of neuropsychological evaluation in reading.

Types of Reading

Reading is mastered in either of two ways: (1) phonetically, by decoding the sounds of words, or (2) graphemically, by using the image of the word to access its sound. Phonetic, or **phonological reading**, converts a letter or group of letters into sounds (*phonemes*) that cue the meaning of a word: the sounds achieved by analyzing letter groups lead to a pronunciation, which then accesses the lexicon for the word's meaning and connections. In **graphemic reading** (also called *lexical* or *whole-word reading*) the word is memorized. Many English words are irregular and must be memorized. Graphemic reading is also how Arabic numerals (1, 2, 3) and international symbolic road and direction signs must be read and learned.

Fluent reading thus requires both strategies. After learning to read phonetically and becoming fluent, readers become more dependent on grapheme reading. This progression may explain why fluent readers have difficulty finding typographic errors when they proofread. Rather than reading phonologically, they read graphemically and need to read only part of a word before recognizing its meaning and shifting attention to the next word. If the spelling error is not within the part of the word actually read, it will not be noticed.

Given the differences between these two reading processes, different reading impairments arise at different ages. A child who is incompetent in the phonological procedure has difficulty in the early stages of reading. A child who is competent in the phonological procedure but incompetent in the grapheme procedure will have difficulty later on. A child who is impaired in phonetic reading will be hampered in making the transition to graphemic reading. Moreover, these impairments do not exhaust the classifications of poor readers.

People with poor short-term auditory memory may not make proper sense of written material because they quickly forget words and phrases as they proceed. This type of disability may be particularly obvious at older ages, when reading material becomes more complex. People with poor long-term memory may not understand the sense of words despite good decoding skills, simply because they do not recall information about the words' meanings. This situation is similar to that faced by a person who speaks only English trying to read Italian. She can sound out the words by using general phonetic rules, but not knowing what the words mean, cannot understand what she is reading. In fact, people with dementia often behave in this way. They can read, but they understand nothing.

Further compounding the understanding of the causes of learning disabilities is lack of uniformity in the teaching of reading. The disagreement between advocates of initiating reading instruction with phonological versus graphemic, or "whole word," reading has been referred to as a "war." Carol Connor and coworkers (2014) suggest that more-scientific approaches to reading, such as algorithm-guided individual instruction, can maximize the benefits of both systems. This approach emphasizes building skills via individualized assessment and instruction. The algorithm approach can capitalize on new technologies including e-readers, which allow users to vary print size, font type and size, line length, letter and/or background color, and can provide word pronunciation at a touch.

Causes of Reading Disorders

It would be helpful if reading deficits displayed themselves in a straightforward manner. Unfortunately, they do not. Language plays a high-level role in managing our mental processes and thus is affected by and affects other behaviors. People with dyslexia exhibit a wide range of symptom clusters as well as individual variations including deficits in attention, eye movement, brain development, memory, coordination, spatial abilities, movement sequencing, map reading, and visuospatial processing. Despite the variability and complexity of symptoms associated with reading disabilities, several theories, including the phonological, attention, sensory, and motor theories, posit primary causes.

Phonological Deficiency

Impairments in language and reading may stem from children's difficulties in consciously decomposing words into their constituent speech sounds—an ability called *phonemic awareness*. An early investigation describes the sound-categorization ability of children who have not yet started to read (Bradley and Bryant, 1983). Children were given three or four words and asked to pick out the word that does not have a sound (phoneme) in common with the others. For example, in the series "hill, pig, pin," "hill" is the correct choice; in the series "cot, pot, hat," "hat" is the correct choice, and in the series "pin, bun, gun," "pin" is the correct response.

When the same children were older and had started to learn to read, those initially weak at sound categorization later fell behind in reading and spelling. This outcome argues that the initial insensitivity to rhyme and alliteration causes subsequent reading impairment because if a child who was initially impaired was given special training in rhyme and alliteration, his reading was far less impaired after reading training began. A meta-analysis of brain imaging studies suggests that impairments in phoneme use and recognition are associated with language regions of the left hemisphere (DeWitt and Rauschecker, 2012). According to this view, reading impairments stem from impairments within the brain's language-processing systems.

Attentional Deficiency

Some theorists propose that reading impairments can stem from problems not directly related to language use. Impairments in separating stimuli have been found in all sensory modalities in reading-disabled people, as have impairments in producing movements. Thus, language-impaired persons may require longer intervals between stimuli before they can detect two separate lights or two separate touches, and they may be impaired in producing rapid movements. They may also be impaired in sound-frequency discriminations and in detecting a target sound obscured by background noise.

The attention hypothesis suggests that the central problem could be "sluggish attention shifting": it is attention to and selection of a letter and not the identification of the letter and its associated sound that contributes to dyslexia (Ruffino et al., 2014). The suggestion is that the problem arises in the parietal-lobe association areas that receive input from all sensory systems, then initiate movements, including eye movements during reading. Such an attention deficit leads to an inability to switch attention and affects many sensory domains, and so produces reading impairments.

Sensory Deficiency

Because reading depends on detecting words both visually and aurally, sensory impairments have been examined in association with reading disabilities. People with dyslexia reportedly have no difficulty hearing speech in quiet conditions but do have difficulty hearing in speech-noisy conditions, which suggests that they are impaired in sensory discrimination (Dole et al., 2014).

Paula Tallal and her coworkers (1993; for a review, Tallal, 2013) examined the sensory detection abilities of children with learning disabilities and found them impaired in detecting sound events that take place in rapid succession. If two tones are presented in succession very quickly, for example, impaired children will hear them as one tone. If the interval between the tones is gradually increased, a point will be reached at which they are heard as two tones. For most people, a separation of about 10 to 40 milliseconds is required before two tones are discriminated. For some people with reading disabilities, a much longer separation is needed (**Figure 24.1**).

This finding's relevance to language impairments is that *stop consonants* ("ba," "da," "ga," "pa," and "ta") contain a transition period in which the sounds change very rapidly, usually within 40 milliseconds. When stop consonants are used as stimuli, reading-impaired people have difficulty differentiating one consonant from another, whereas they have no difficulty in detecting vowels. They also have no difficulty in detecting stop consonants if the transition period is lengthened. A detection difficulty in infants is predictive of later language impairment.

Tallal and coworkers suggest that remediation of language-related disorders should focus on training in sound discrimination. For example, they reason that if a child has difficulty in discriminating "da" from "de" when the sounds are presented at a typical rate, then first slowing the presentation down so that the sounds' durations are dragged out makes the discrimination easier.

Tallal's group constructed computer games called Fast ForWord® in which subjects, who are rewarded each time they make a correct discrimination (either between verbal or nonverbal stimuli), gradually work their way from simple to more-complex discrimination problems. They also designed computerized listening exercises that teach phonological discrimination using acoustically modified speech. The computer-based exercises measure each subject's initial performance level, then lead the subject through extensive daily training for several weeks, after which the subject's performance level moves closer to standard. Training in sound-processing rates improves temporal integration on the discrimination tasks (see the Snapshot).

The magnocellular visual theory is similar to the auditory sensory theory, except it postulates that reading deficits originate in the magnocellular part of the visual system, which processes black–white vision and movement. If a child's detection of visual motion is disturbed, he or she may have difficulty reading because the words on the page appear to jump around. The magnocellular theory suggests that if children read through a color filter or with only one eye, their perception of word movement can be reduced and reading can be improved. Using fMRI imaging of V5, the motion processing area in the dorsal stream, Olumide Olulade and colleagues (2013) also conclude that activity in V5 is sluggish in poor readers but argue that poor reading is causative and not the result of impaired magnocellular activity.

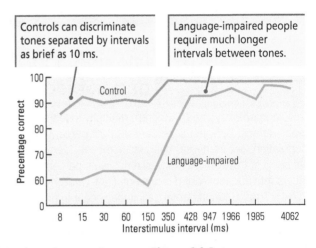

Figure 24.1 ▲

Sound-Detection Ability
Percentage of trials in which controls and language-impaired subjects discriminate two tones separated by different interstimulus intervals. (Data source: Tallal et al., 1993.)

Motor Deficiency

One motor theory of reading disabilities is the cerebellar theory (Mariën et al., 2014). The cerebellum, classically associated with movement, also participates in higher cognitive functions, including timing, coordination, and attention—skills relevant to reading. Although cerebellar damage in adults does not abolish any language skills, if tests sensitive to higher functions were administered, the cerebellar theory proposes that impairments might emerge.

Although no agreement exists with respect to the cerebellum's precise role in language, its dysfunction should be expected to impair language learning. In particular, reading requires rapid sensory processing and attentional shifts,

SNAPSHOT | Imaging Sound Perception in Controls and Subjects with Dyslexia

Developmental dyslexia—inherent difficulty in learning to read—affects between 5 percent and 20 percent of the population, yet its neural basis is unknown. Many studies suggest impairment in translating visual perception of letters into auditory sound representations (Murphy et al., 2014). Thus, a fundamental deficit may occur in processing rapidly changing sensory signals, an ability necessary for language comprehension. This *rapid-processing hypothesis* suggests that subjects given training in discriminating rapidly changing acoustical signals would improve their ability to discriminate among the signals and thus improve their comprehension of auditory language.

Elise Temple and her colleagues (2003) tested a group of adults with a history of developmental dyslexia and a matched group of control participants on discriminating rapid acoustical signals while obtaining fMRI images of their brain activity. The images reveal a specific disruption of neural responses to transient, rapidly changing acoustical stimuli in the adults with developmental dyslexia. The largest activation in the controls was in the left prefrontal region, between the middle and superior frontal gyri in Brodmann's areas 46, 10, and 9.

Analysis of the dyslexic readers revealed no increase in left frontal response to the rapid relative to the slow stimuli. The illustration shows examples of rapid and slowed nonspeech acoustical signals (A) and examples of participants' and dyslexic subjects' fMRI responses to rapid auditory stimuli (B). Note the greater activation of left prefrontal cortex in unimpaired readers.

Dyslexic subjects then underwent a training program designed to improve rapid processing, after which they were re-examined using fMRI. After training, some subjects improved on tests of rapid auditory processing and auditory language comprehension, and their fMRIs showed significantly increased activity in the left prefrontal cortex.

Taken together, these results suggest that a subset of people with dyslexia are impaired in their sensitivity to rapidly changing acoustical stimuli and that fMRI can assist in diagnosing and treating the impairment.

Murphy, C. F. B., L. O. Pagan-Neves, and H. F. Wertzner. Auditory and visual sustained attention in children with speech sound disorder. *PLoS ONE* 9:e93091, 2014.

Temple, E., G. K. Deutsch, R. A. Poldrack, S. L. Miller, P. Tallal, M. M. Merzenich, and J. D. Gabrieli. Neural deficits in children with dyslexia ameliorated by behavioral remediation: Evidence from functional MRI. *Proceedings of the National Academy of Sciences of the U.S.A.* 100:2860–2865, 2003.

(A) Sound signals

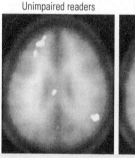

(B) fMRI responses, dorsal view

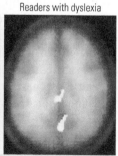

Analyzing sound perception in unimpaired readers and readers with dyslexia. (A) Rapid and slowed nonspeech acoustic signals used as test stimuli and in training. (B) fMRI responses to rapid auditory stimuli in unimpaired controls and subjects with dyslexia. (A): E. Temple. Brain mechanisms in normal and dyslexic readers. *Current Opinion in Neurobiology* Vol. 12, Issue 2:178-183, 2002. © Elsevier. (B): E. Temple et al., *Proceedings of the National Academy of Sciences of the United States of America* 97, 25:13907-13912, 2000. Copyright © 2000 National Academy of Sciences, U.S.A.

and the cerebellar theory proposes that cerebellum dysfunction in these respects should be reflected in reading impairments. Catherine Stoodley and John Stein (2013), in reviewing the evidence supporting a role for the cerebellum in dyslexia, argue instead that abnormalities in language networks include abnormalities in the cerebellum, but the cerebellar abnormalities are not causal for dyslexia.

Multicausal Approaches

Among the remarkable number of causative theories of learning disorders in general and of reading disorders in particular, many are supported by substantial experimentation, tests sensitive to the relevant deficits, and brain imaging and autopsy studies. A parsimonious interpretation of this widely ranging evidence is the likelihood that subpopulations of disabled readers display different deficits. Franck Ramus and his coworkers (2003) attempted to evaluate all of the theories in a single study by giving a small population of 17 disabled readers an extensive series of cognitive, sensory, motor, and reading tests.

The investigators found that their subjects all had language impairments in the use of sounds. A subset of subjects had sensory deficits in both the visual and the auditory domains. A second group had motor deficits, and of these subjects, most also had auditory deficits. A third group had language deficits with neither sensory nor motor symptoms. Ramus and colleagues suggest that the major cause of reading disability lies in language processes stemming from language-related brain areas, but other areas related to attentional, sensory, or motor function may additionally be impaired and contribute to the disability.

In keeping with a multicausal view of reading disorders, Amaia Carrion-Castillo and colleagues (2013) summarize research on nine different regions of nine different chromosomes on which gene mutations are suspected to be involved in dyslexia. Candidate genes in any of these regions, when identified, will likely contain many mutations. Research directed toward identifying genes in these regions and their specific effects on reading are aided by longitudinal studies on individuals at risk for dyslexia. For example, the Dutch Dyslexia Program (van der Leij and Maassen, 2013) follows 300 children at risk for dyslexia. The program facilitates genetic comparisons of children who acquire dyslexia and those who do not and also facilitates correlating specific reading deficits with individual genetic results.

ⓒ Neuropsychological Evaluation

Assessment approaches to dyslexia rest on the assumptions that the neuropsychological test can identify impairments and suggest strategies for remediation. Neuropsychological testing strategy does provide a comprehensive evaluation that is useful for counseling, as Ms. P.'s case in the chapter-opening Portrait demonstrates. Indeed, neuropsychological testing often is favored because it provides evidence both that a neurodevelopmental impairment is causative and that extra instructional resources are required.

Neuropsychological testing assesses performance on a wide range of tasks, providing insight on all areas of brain function (see Section 28.3). Most learning-disabled children are not dyslexic or dyscalculic (unable to do math)

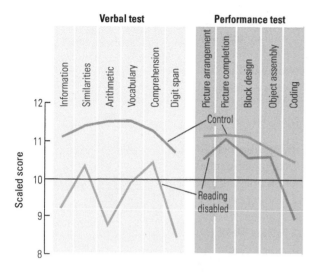

	Reading-disabled	Control
Verbal IQ	98	108
Performance IQ	102	106
Full-scale IQ	100	107
Number of subjects	1521	554

Figure 24.2 ▲

The ACID Profile Intelligence test profiles of developmentally dyslexic subjects and controls. Note the low scores on arithmetic, coding, information, and digit span (ACID) typical of children with reading disabilities. (Data sources: Rugel, 1974, and Whishaw and Kolb, 1984.)

alone but rather have several associated symptoms of which teachers and parents may be unaware. Discovering these associated deficits helps the adults in a learning-disabled child's life to understand the difficulties with which the child is struggling. Neuropsychological tests can also help distinguish between children who have central reading impairments and those whose problems have emotional or social causes.

Many studies focus on the IQ subtest results of learning-disabled children. These analyses attempt to correlate learning impairments with performance on the subtests of the Wechsler Intelligence Scale for Children (WISC). **Figure 24.2** presents a compilation of the results from studies in which, collectively, a total of 1521 reading-disabled children and 554 control children were tested and compared (Rugel, 1974).

The dyslexic group displays low scores on four subtests: *a*rithmetic, *c*oding, *i*nformation, and *d*igit span. This *ACID profile* is typical of many such studies. Dyslexic children characteristically have an overall IQ score that averages about 7 points lower than the same score attained by control children, but their mean IQ score is roughly 100. Children above age 8 show the ACID profile, whereas those younger than 8 may not show a deficit in the information or arithmetic subscales because they have yet to acquire information or arithmetic skills (Whishaw and Kolb, 1984). Although the deficits in digit span and coding are commonly seen with dyslexia, there is no agreement that these deficits are necessarily related to a reading disorder.

Many researchers have commented on the wide differences between verbal IQ score and performance IQ score in persons with dyslexia (recall Ms P.'s results). Some experts believe that two types of dyslexia can be identified on the basis of these scores. Generally speaking, however, the subscores of a child with dyslexia vary greatly (the child will score in the high range on some subtests, in the low range on others, and in the average range on still others). Nevertheless, for an experienced counselor, a pattern displayed by any child may be meaningful.

In a comparison of the performance of a dyslexic group with that of a control group on other sections of a composite test battery, other tests that also discriminate between the two groups depended in part on the person's age. This age dependence is particularly evident in three tests:

- In a test of left–right differentiation (**Figure 24.3**), neither children with dyslexia nor age-matched controls score above chance if they are younger than 8 years old. After age 8, the control children perform well, whereas the children with dyslexia continue to perform at chance.

- Another emerging difference appeared on tests of word fluency (for example, "Give as many words beginning with the letter 'S' as you can"). Dyslexic and control scores are similar in children younger than 8 years but diverge increasingly in older age groups, suggesting that fluency performance in the control group improves with age, whereas the dyslexic group's fluency remains almost static.

- A third pattern was obtained on the Semmes Body-Placing Test (another test of left–right discrimination). Here, significant group differences emerge only in adults, and these differences depend on the fact that adult controls' performance on the tests was virtually perfect. These observations suggest to us that although the tests can be applied with some success to children, they must be interpreted with caution in younger children, and retesting at different ages is worthwhile.

Neuropsychological tests with the objective of investigating learning disabilities must be accompanied by specific tests of functional impairments. In examinations for dyslexia, for example, reading tests should also be given. Many supplementary tests also can provide insights into specific aspects of learning impairments (Asbjornsen et al., 2014).

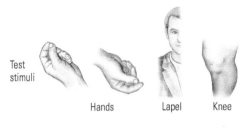

Test stimuli

Hands   Lapel   Knee

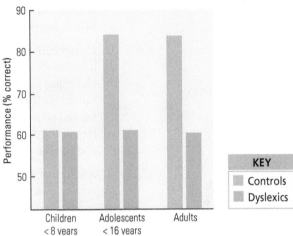

KEY
Controls
Dyslexics

Children < 8 years   Adolescents < 16 years   Adults

Performance (% correct)

⊚ Figure 24.3 ▲

Performance Comparison
Scores of controls and dyslexic subjects on a left–right discrimination test show significant group differences among adolescent and adult groups but not among children younger than age 8. (Data from Whishaw and Kolb, 1984.)

⊚ 24.3 Nonlanguage Neurodevelopmental Disorders

Common among the six nonlanguage neurodevelopmental disorders described in this section—attention-deficit/hyperactivity disorder, cerebral palsy, hydrocephalus, autism spectrum disorders, fragile-X syndrome, and fetal alcohol spectrum disorder—are children's difficulty in comprehending aspects of their environment, pretending and anticipating, interpreting others' facial and emotional gestures, and performing skilled movements. These disabilities can seriously compromise independent living in adulthood.

Attention-Deficit/Hyperactivity Disorder

Attention-deficit/hyperactivity disorder (ADHD), characterized by core behavioral symptoms of impulsivity, hyperactivity, and/or inattention, is distinguished from other types of learning disabilities in that an affected child displays behavioral problems in school. All aspects of school performance are usually disrupted. In addition to hyperactivity, children with ADHD may have specific learning disabilities, which possibly contribute.

The Centers for Disease Control and Prevention reports that about 5 percent of children in the United States are diagnosed with ADHD, and boys are twice as likely as girls to be affected by it. Diagnoses of ADHD have steadily increased, and in some jurisdictions it is applied to as many as 12 percent of school-aged children. ADHD may be diagnosed less often in girls in part because of symptom differences: girls are more likely to display inattention and are less likely to act out, while boys are more likely display hyperactivity and impulsivity.

The DSM-5 lists two main diagnostic criteria, each with several symptoms. A specified number of symptoms that interfere with functioning and development must be present:

1. **Inattention** Six or more symptoms of inattention in children up to age 16, five or more in adolescents 17 and older and adults; symptoms of inattention have been present for at least 6 months and are inappropriate for the developmental level. Symptoms include avoiding tasks and distractibility as well as inability to pay attention to details, hold attention on tasks, listen, follow instructions, organize, and finish work.

2. **Hyperactivity and Impulsivity** Six or more symptoms of hyperactivity–impulsivity in children up to age 16, five or more for adolescents 17 and older and adults; symptoms of hyperactivity–impulsivity have been present for at least 6 months to an extent that is disruptive and inappropriate for the person's developmental level. Symptoms include fidgeting, not remaining seated, running about, talking excessively, and inability to play and to take turns.

Additional diagnostic conditions also must be met. Several inattentive or hyperactive–impulsive symptoms present before age 12 years; several symptoms present in two or more settings (e.g., at home, school, or work; with friends or relatives; in other activities); and clear evidence that the symptoms interfere with or reduce the quality of social, school, or work functioning.

In infancy, hyperactive children exhibit poor and irregular sleep, colic, and feeding problems and do not like being cuddled or held still for long. Later, they are described as learning to run rather than to walk and as being driven to handle and play with everything. By the time they reach kindergarten, they are demanding, inattentive, and do not play well with other children. People outside the home may begin to reject a hyperactive child because of his behavior.

By the time the child enters school, his high activity level, low tolerance for frustration, poor concentration, and poor self-esteem lead to referral for assessment. By adolescence, many of these children are failing in school, and 25 percent to 50 percent have encountered problems with the law. Their behavior remains restless, they withdraw from school, and they fail to develop social relations and maintain steady employment.

Hyperactivity is the most common behavioral disturbance among children. Incidence estimates vary because different definitions and cultural differences in tolerance of hyperactive behavior exist. The American Psychiatric Association suggests a prevalence rate of between 3 percent and 5 percent, with a higher incidence in boys than in girls.

Numerous brain-imaging studies suggest wide-ranging structural and connection irregularities in people diagnosed with ADHD (Rubia et al., 2014). The suggested causes of hyperactivity are also extensive and include brain damage, encephalitis, genetics, food allergies, high lead concentrations, and various home and school environments. This evidence also suggests that circuits in frontal brain regions, especially ventral frontal regions including the basal ganglia, impair self-regulatory behavior and contribute to ADHD. Impaired self-regulation leads not only to disruption in ongoing actions but also to failure to learn from experience (Berger et al., 2013).

Therapy includes counseling for the child and parents and careful structuring of home and school environments. Beginning in the 1960s and continuing to the present, treatment with stimulant drugs has been popular. Brand names include Adderall, Concerta, Dexedrine, and Ritalin, among others. Many nonstimulant drugs, including Strattera and Intuniv, are reportedly effective, and antidepressant drugs are sometimes prescribed for treatment.

The effectiveness of drug treatment as a long-term solution is controversial (Taylor, 2014). In some countries, drug treatments are underprescribed over concerns about illegal use; in other countries drugs are overprescribed in that the number of users exceeds the number of people diagnosed with ADHD. Drugs may control ADHD symptoms because they allow the person to concentrate on the task at hand, and as reported in the Chapter 6 opening Portrait, they are used as *cognitive enhancers* for the same reason. Consequently, prescription drugs are funneled into the underground drug market to be used recreationally and for cognitive enhancement.

Cerebral Palsy

Cerebral palsy was originally defined as a disorder primarily of motor function caused by brain trauma in the course of fetal development or birth. Any simple definition is difficult, however. First, trauma can occur both prenatally and, by some definitions, within the first 5 years postnatally. Second, motor symptoms take many forms, from mild impairments in a single limb to more severe impairments that compromise movement of the entire body. Third, various kinds of accompanying impairments, including cognitive and emotional impairment, epilepsy, and impairment of other body functions, may occur. Fourth, the causes are diverse and include blood clots, infections, and a wide range of traumatic brain injuries.

As a consequence, cerebral palsy cannot accurately be called a disease, a syndrome, or even a condition; it will take a different form in each person, depending on the nature of the brain damage. The term **cerebral palsy** is therefore most useful in an administrative sense, as a category of persons who are disabled in many different ways by disorders due to nonprogressive brain abnormalities. Because brain damage is the underlying cause, cerebral palsy is not curable, but it is often amenable to therapy and training and, more importantly, to environmental modifications that aid the affected individual.

Cerebral palsy was first described in 1853 by London physician William Little, who recognized that motor dysfunction displayed by some babies results from abnormal parturition (delivery), difficult labor, premature birth, or asphyxia. Little also recognized the permanence of the disabilities and their associated intellectual impairments; effects on personality (such as irritability and temper tantrums); and epilepsy. More important, he pointed out that these problems could be severely aggravated by subsequent improper training and education. Subsequent definitions of cerebral palsy have attempted to incorporate many other symptoms that are not strictly motor (Colver et al., 2014).

The incidence of cerebral palsy is estimated at about 3.5 per 1000 births, The greatest influence, prematurity, can increase incidence a hundredfold. The numbers of males and females afflicted are about equal. Estimates of the degree of impairment suggest that about 10 percent require no special services, 65 percent need services on an occasional basis, and about 25 percent need special schooling or custodial care. When cases of cerebral palsy are categorized by motor symptoms, about 50 percent of persons with the disorder are spastic (their limbs resist being moved), about 25 percent are *athetoid* (they make slow involuntary movements), about 10 percent are afflicted with rigidity (muscles around joints are stiff), and about 10 percent are *ataxic* (have difficulty making voluntary movements).

Among cerebral palsy's many causes, **Table 24.4** details the most frequent. Lesions of the corticospinal tracts, basal ganglia, brainstem, and cerebellum are presumed to be responsible for the motor disorders, but establishing clear-cut relations between lesions and clinical findings has proved difficult. Furthermore, because symptoms are not limited to motor function but can include any function controlled by the brain, lesions may include any part of the nervous system.

There are no specific treatments for cerebral palsy, but physical therapy, creating small lesions to the spinal cord, and the injection of Botox to immobilize

Table 24.4 **Potential causes of cerebral palsy**

Hereditary

Static—familial athetosis, familial paraplegia, familial tremor

Progressive—demyelinating diseases of viral or undetermined origin (chromosomal breakages are rare in cerebral palsy, as are disorders of metabolism)

Congenital (acquired in utero)

Infectious rubella, toxoplasmosis, cytomegalic inclusions, herpes simplex, other viral or infectious agents

Maternal anoxia, carbon monoxide poisoning, strangulation, anemia, hypotension associated with spinal anesthesia, placental infarcts, placenta abruptio

Prenatal cerebral hemorrhage, maternal toxemia, direct trauma, maternal bleeding, diathesis

Prenatal anoxia, twisting or kinking of the cord

Miscellaneous toxins, drugs

Perinatal (obstetrical)

Mechanical anoxia—respiratory obstruction, narcotism due to oversedation with drugs, placenta previa or abruptio, hypotension associated with spinal anesthesia, breech delivery with delay of the after-coming head

Trauma—hemorrhage associated with dystocia, disproportions and malpositions of labor, sudden pressure changes, precipitate delivery, caesarean delivery

Complications of birth—"small for date" babies, prematurity, immaturity, dysmaturity, postmaturity, hyperbilirubinemia and isoimmunization factors (kernicterus due to Rh factor, ABO incompatibility), hemolytic disorders, respiratory distress disorders, syphilis, meningitis, and other infections, drug-addiction reactions, hypoglycemic reactions, hypocalcemic reactions

Postnatal–Infancy

Trauma—subdural hematoma, skull fracture, cerebral contusion

Infections—meningitis, encephalitis, brain abscess

Vascular accidents—congenital cerebral aneurism, thrombosis, embolism, hypertensive encephalopathy, sudden pressure changes

Toxins—lead, arsenic, coal-tar derivatives

Anoxia—carbon monoxide poisoning, strangulation, high-altitude and deep-pressure anoxia, hypoglycemia

Neoplastic and late neurodevelopmental defects—tumor, cyst, progressive hydrocephalus

Source: Denhoff, E. Medical aspects. In W. M. Cruickshank, Ed., Cerebral Palsy Syracuse, N.Y.: Syracuse University Press, 1976, p. 35. Reprinted with permission.

muscles have been used to relieve muscle cramps and to promote movement in immobilized limbs. The most important factors that improve the quality of life of affected individuals are environmental changes that improve physical care, enhance educational opportunities, and encourage social well-being.

Hydrocephalus

Characterized by increased volume of the cerebrospinal fluid (CSF), **hydrocephalus** can be caused in two ways. In one, more likely to develop in adults, enlarged ventricles can be a secondary result of shrinkage or atrophy of surrounding brain tissue. In the other, more typical cause of hydrocephalus—especially in infants—obstruction in the flow of CSF results in a buildup of pressure in one or more ventricles, which eventually causes their expansion. Whether a simple overproduction of CSF is ever a cause of hydrocephalus is uncertain.

Figure 24.4 is a drawing made from a cast of the ventricular system in a healthy brain. In a living brain, the ventricles are filled with CSF (Mortazavi, Adeeb, and Grissenauer, 2014). The usual volume in an adult is only about 130 milliliters; about one-third is in the spinal cord's great lumbar cistern. The CSF is made by the choroid plexus in the ventricles, most of it in the lateral ventricles (Mortazavi, Grissenauer, and Adeeb, 2014). From there, it flows through the interventricular foramina (windows) of Monro into the third ventricle, through the cerebral aqueduct, and into the fourth ventricle. It finally escapes through three little holes in the roof of the fourth ventricle. These holes are the two laterally located foramina of Luschka and the medial foramen of Magendie. (The mnemonic is lateral, Luschka; medial, Magendie.) The fluid then enters the subarachnoid space beneath the arachnoid membrane of the meninges and spinal cord. It is absorbed into the veins and carried away by the bloodstream.

Circulation in the ventricles can be blocked at either interventricular foramen, causing increased pressure followed by the expansion of either lateral ventricle. CSF can also be blocked at the level of the cerebral aqueduct (causing hydrocephalus of the first three ventricles) or by closure of the foramina in the roof of the fourth ventricle (producing hydrocephalus of the entire ventricular system). Any sudden obstruction of CSF flow causes a rapid rise in intracranial pressure, ventricular dilation, and finally, coma. A gradual obstruction, such as by a tumor, causes a less-rapid increase in pressure and consequent dilation, and the symptoms may include the gradual appearance of visual disturbances, palsies, dementia, and so on.

Infant hydrocephalus, characterized by a conspicuous enlargement of the head, usually develops during the first few months of life, affecting as many as 27 of 100,000 newborn babies. In about 14 percent of these cases, a malformation impedes CSF circulation; most other cases result from inflammation or trauma, although about 4 percent are due to tumors. As the ventricles distend, they push the cerebral hemispheres into a balloon shape. Because the skull bones of an infant are not yet fused, continued pressure causes the head to expand in all directions. If expansion damages the cortex, intelligence may be impaired and dementia may result. If the cortex is not damaged, intelligence

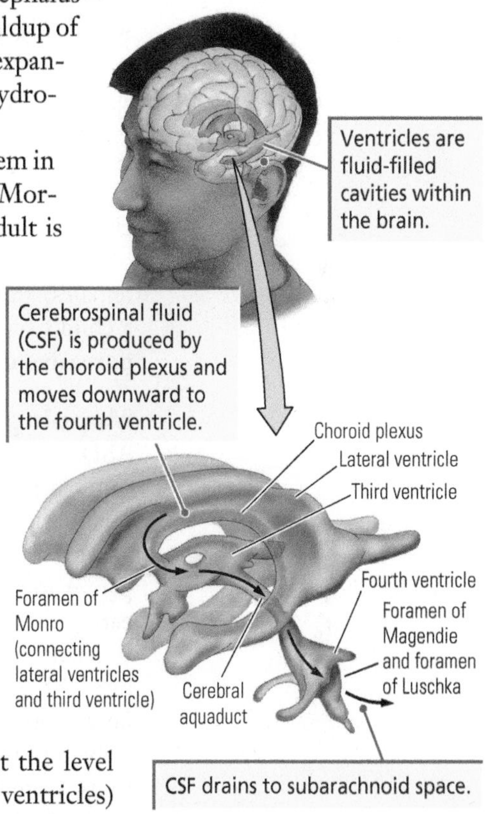

Ventricles are fluid-filled cavities within the brain.

Cerebrospinal fluid (CSF) is produced by the choroid plexus and moves downward to the fourth ventricle.

Choroid plexus
Lateral ventricle
Third ventricle
Fourth ventricle
Foramen of Magendie and foramen of Luschka
Foramen of Monro (connecting lateral ventricles and third ventricle)
Cerebral aqueduct

CSF drains to subarachnoid space.

Figure 24.4 ▲

Cerebral Ventricles (Top) Drawing of a cast of the healthy brain's ventricular system viewed laterally. (Bottom) Arrows indicate the direction of flow of cerebrospinal fluid. A blockage of CSF flow in the narrower parts of the ventricles (for example, the cerebral aqueduct) can cause hydrocephalus.

may be unimpaired even after the cortex has been stretched into a sheet of tissue less than a centimeter thick.

Hydrocephalus can be treated with some success by inserting a valve into one lateral ventricle and a tube that passes into a jugular vein to drain into the cardiac atrium. Untreated, hydrocephalus often causes death or severe mental or motor disabilities.

Autism Spectrum Disorders

The term *autism* was first used by Leo Kanner and Hans Asperger in the 1940s to describe individual children without obvious signs of focal cerebral disease who display such symptoms as severely impaired social interaction, a bizarre and narrow range of interests, language and communication abnormalities, and in some cases, preserved intellect. Some are severely impaired, others can function on their own, and still others have exceptional abilities in some areas, such as music, art, or mathematics.

The disorder is now referred to as **autism spectrum disorder** (ASD) to include children with either mild or severe symptoms. Other rare, very severe disorders included in the autism spectrum are Rett syndrome, which affects mainly females, and childhood disintegrative disorder, which affects mainly males. If a child's symptoms do not meet the specific criteria for ASD, the diagnosis is **pervasive developmental disorder not otherwise specified** (PDD-NOS).

Mapping the Autism Spectrum

ASD is estimated to affect as many as 1 to 3.5 of every 1000 children; is four times as prevalent in boys as in girls; and has no known racial, ethnic, or social boundaries. Its incidence is reported to have increased dramatically in the past 30 years, but Ashley Wazana and her colleagues (2007) calculate that the apparent increase is due to methodological factors such as better reporting and earlier diagnosis.

Many infants on the autism spectrum behave oddly from birth, avoiding physical contact with caregivers by arching their backs or going limp when held. Approximately one-third of children diagnosed with ASD develop typically until between 1 and 3 years of age, when caregivers begin to notice symptoms. Common among them are a failure to interact socially and an insistence on sameness. One possible reason for the latter may be an inability to understand and cope with novel situations. People affected by ASD may exhibit repeated body movements (hand flapping, rocking), unusual facial movements and features, unusual responses to people or unusual attachments to objects, and resistance to any change in routine. In some cases, aggressive or self-injurious behavior or both are seen as well.

A less-severe condition of withdrawal in children is **Asperger's syndrome**. These children, although withdrawn, exhibit early speech and good grammar, but they also exhibit narrow, repetitive play, poor peer relations, and a need for routine and sameness. They may excel in some aspect of behavior, such as reading, calculations, music, or art. **Hyperlexia** describes unusual reading ability in otherwise cognitively impaired persons, such as children with Asperger's syndrome. It is marked by precocious development of reading abilities between the ages of 3 and 5 years. Often these children teach themselves to read. Reading may not be completely fluid because many of those affected have articulatory defects and prosodic irregularities of intonation and rate of speech. Generally, reading comprehension is impaired, and children show emotional withdrawal, occasional *echolalia* (pathological repetition of others' speech), and symptoms of autism.

Those who exhibit Asperger's syndrome can develop exceptional memory abilities, such as an unusual ability to remember words, television shows, names of streets, the weather, birthdays, and so forth. Commonly displayed skills include calendar calculations (some can tell the day of a person's birthday in any year of a 1000-year period); mathematical ability; musical ability, including the ability to play new pieces of music after hearing them once; sculpting; drawing; and peculiar feats of memory, such as recalling what the weather was like on every day of the person's life, retention of the names of all visitors ever received and the dates of their visits, and the date of every burial in a parish in a 35-year time span as well as the names of all the attendees.

Related to Asperger's syndrome is **savant syndrome**, first described by John Langdon Down in 1887 as *idiot savant syndrome*. Affected persons have a narrow range of special abilities, and a common symptomatic triad is retardation, blindness, and musical genius. The oxymoronic *idiot savant* was coined by combining the word *idiot*, at one time an accepted label for a subcategory of intellectual disability, with *savant*, which means "knowledgeable person." The term has endured despite its now-pejorative connotation. Savants are characterized by mental challenges resulting from a developmental disability or mental illness combined with a talent that far exceeds their other abilities (talented savants) or the abilities of the general population (prodigious savants). The syndrome affects males about six times as frequently as females. The special skill can appear quite suddenly and disappear equally quickly.

Anatomical Correlates of ASD

Extensive research shows that brain abnormalities in various types of ASD correlate with the degree of impairment displayed by an autistic person. For example, impairments in *explicit memories* (memories for daily events) might be related to temporal-lobe abnormalities, and impairments in *implicit memory* (learned skills and conditioned responses) might be related to parietal and cerebellar abnormalities. Although retrospective studies show that head size prebirth is normal in autistic children, by age 1, head and brain are larger than normal. This finding suggests that plastic processes related to development, including cell division, cell loss, and synaptic pruning, are atypical. Such changes in developmental processes would lead to widespread brain abnormalities.

More-specific changes in brain structure are hypothesized as well. John Allman and his colleagues (2005) propose that large frontal cortex cells called *von Economo neurons* (see Figure 10.20) fail to develop normally, resulting in abnormal social development in affected persons. Patricia Rodier (2000) suggests that one cause of autism may be an abnormality in the expression of genes central in brainstem development. She found that an area in the caudal part of the pons is small in autistic subjects and that several nuclei in this area, including the facial nucleus, which controls facial musculature, are small or missing (**Figure 24.5**, top). Many autistic children have subtle facial abnormalities that may be due to abnormalities of the facial nerve (Figure 24.5,

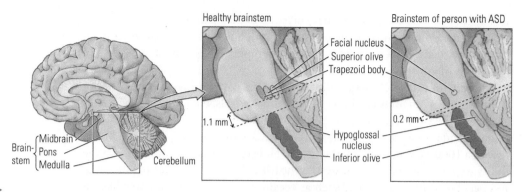

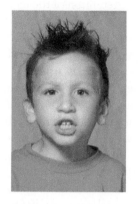

@ Figure 24.5 ▶

Anatomical Correlates of ASD (Top) Changes to the brainstem in ASD include reduced size of the posterior part of the pons. Several nuclei in this region, including the facial nucleus, superior olive, and trapezoid body, are either smaller than typical or missing. (Bottom) A child with ASD may have some characteristic physical anomalies. The corners of the mouth may be unusually low in relation to the upper lip, the tops of the ears may flop over (left), and the ears may be a bit lowered and have an almost square shape (right). (Top: Research from Rodier, © 2000 by Scientific American, Inc., all rights reserved. Bottom: Kallista Images/Getty Images.)

bottom). Perhaps mutation of the *HOSA1* gene, which plays a role in brainstem development, or interference in the expression of this gene, is responsible for some cases of autism.

Evidence that the cerebellum controls conditioned responses suggests that the desire for sameness and avoidance of novelty characteristic of autism also may be related to cerebellar abnormality (Becker and Stoodley, 2013). One feature of conditioned learning is **habituation**, in which a response to a stimulus weakens with repeated presentations. Absent the ability to habituate to ongoing events, a person may find such stimuli especially noxious and so avoid them in favor of maintaining sameness. This theory could explain, for example, why people with autism report that the sound of traffic, to which most people quickly habituate, remains for them frighteningly loud.

In an attempt to define networks in the autistic brain, Feng Shi and colleagues (2013) hypothesized that cortical thickness provides a good index of the brain's modular organization and thus, regions of similar cortical thickness should group together as functional modules. They identified three modules—frontal, parietal, and temporal—in the cortex of preadolescent children. They then estimated the connectivity between and within these modules and found (1) fewer connections between modules in the autistic group, and (2) increased within-module connections in the frontal module. Shi's group proposes that the frontal module in the autistic group both "talks" to itself more and "talks" less with the rest of the brain than in the control group. Although this analysis presents averaged results for a large group of individuals, future analyses of individual cases could well provide insights into the symptoms of individual cases of ASD.

Genetic Contributions to ASD

ASD is proposed to be under strong genetic influence. In some families, autism is highly heritable; in others, heritability is lower. Variable concordance is reported for identical twins, with a low-end estimate of about 0.5, which although high, also points to the contribution of epigenetic factors (Sandin et al., 2014).

A fascinating line of inquiry into the gene contribution to ASD implicates a gene *domain of unknown function*, DUF 1220, located in the long arm of chromosome 1. DUF 1220 is a base sequence, likely forming a gene, which features a large number of copies. DUF 1220 is unstable, and copy number can vary from around 55 to 90, with an average number about 70. In this respect, DUF 1220 is like the CAG base pair repeats related to Huntington's disease (Section 27.7), but rather than three base pairs repeating, an entire gene repeats. A high number of DUF 1220 repeats is correlated with the symptoms of ASD (Davis et al., 2014).

Three lines of evidence tie the copy number of DUF 1220 to brain development. First, copy number is found to increase in the primate lineage along with increases in brain size, with an especially large increase in modern humans. Second, copy number is found to be smaller in humans who display microencephaly and larger in humans who display macroencephaly. Third, investigations of the effects of DUF 1220 on brain development suggest that it is related to brain-cell division such that with higher copy number, more brain cells are produced.

The Davis group suggests that the instability of DUF 1220 has allowed the evolution of a large human brain with the consequent deleterious side effect of autism. In ASD, the increased DUF 1220 copy number causes the production of excess numbers of neurons, which if not eliminated have poorly formed connections. Some unknowns remain in the theory, including why copy number changes occur and why high copy number does not always produce a brain characteristic of ASD. The theory does explain many autistic individuals' large brains, their highly variable symptoms, and ASD's genetic basis.

Other Possible Causes of ASD

Other evidence supports a viral cause for ASD: women have an increased risk of bearing an autistic child after exposure to rubella in the first trimester of pregnancy, for example. Some suspect that industrial toxins and other environmental pollutants can cause autism. The evidence for these causes is uncertain. Concern is voiced as well that mercury used as a preservative in vaccines, and vaccines themselves, can trigger ASD, but no scientific support for this view has emerged. Many well-done, large-scale studies fail to show a link between mercury and autism.

Fragile-X Syndrome

Fragile-X syndrome, a common inherited cause of mental impairment and ASD, affects about 1 in 2000 males and 1 in 4000 females. About 1 in 259 women and 1 in 800 men carry the fragile-X gene and could pass it on to their children. Fragile-X syndrome is characterized by facial abnormalities and by mental disabilities ranging from subtle learning disorders to severe intellectual impairment. It is associated with attention deficits, hyperactivity, anxiety and unstable mood, and behaviors characteristic of ASD. Physical characteristics include a long face, large ears, flat feet, and hyperextensible joints, especially fingers. Boys are typically more severely affected than girls in that most boys with fragile-X syndrome are typically learning-disabled compared with only about one-third of affected girls.

Fragile-X syndrome is caused by an abnormality of the *FMR1* gene located on the long arm of the X chromosome (Bagni and Oostra, 2013). When functional, *FMR1* encodes a protein (*FMRP*) that participates in translating mRNA into protein in neurons, including in their axons and dendritic spines. The protein participates in synapse formation and maturation and is related to the production of receptors for glutamate and GABA. The mutation occurs in a stretch of CGG base pair repeats in the X chromosome DNA. This sequence of repeats is prone to increase in length as it passes from generation to generation.

When the number of CGG repeats exceeds a critical level of about 200, their expanded area encourages *methylation* that extends to blocking the promoter region of the *FMR1* gene, halting production of *FMRP*. Examination of neurons in affected persons at autopsy shows that dendritic spines are poorly formed and more numerous than typical. Thus, the protein encoded by the *FMR1* gene may be required for healthy development and elimination of synapses. MRI scans of children with fragile-X syndrome show cortical thinning; an unusually small caudate nucleus; and an increase in ventricular size, which suggests a general loss of brain cells.

Symptoms in females are generally less severe than those in males because females have two X chromosomes: if one is abnormal, the other is usually able to manufacture the necessary protein. This difference suggests that—in theory at least—if a normal copy of the *FMR1* gene could be inserted into brain cells, neuronal abnormalities could be reduced.

A number of animal models of fragile-X syndrome have been produced, and the knockout *Fmr1* mouse model is the most extensively studied. These mice are prone to epilepsy, learning impairments, and hyperactivity—symptoms that mimic human fragile-X symptoms. Gene replacement therapy has been explored in neurons cultured in a dish and in a mouse that had previously lacked the fragile-X gene.

Because *FMRP* affects both glutamate and GABA receptors, experimental studies and clinical trials have been conducted with drug antagonists of glutamate receptors or agonists of GABA receptors. The former treatment is reportedly beneficial to a subset of patients, while the latter treatment reportedly improves some social deficits in patients. Thus, some hope of treatment success exists for people affected by fragile-X syndrome.

Fetal Alcohol Spectrum Disorder

The term *fetal alcohol syndrome*, coined by Kenneth Jones and David Smith in 1973, describes a pattern of physical malformation and intellectual impairment observed in children born of alcoholic mothers. These disorders are now included under the umbrella of **fetal alcohol spectrum disorder** (FASD).

As illustrated in **Figure 24.6**A, children with FASD may have irregular facial features, including a smooth philtrum (the fissure below the nose), thin upper lip, and short palpebral fissures (the distance across the eyelids). They also have a range of brain irregularities, from small brains with abnormal gyri (Figure 24.6B) to brains of typical size with abnormal clusters of cells and misaligned

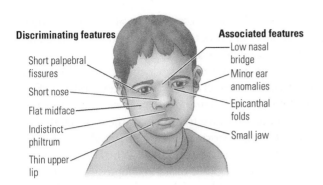

Discriminating features

Short palpebral fissures

Short nose

Flat midface

Indistinct philtrum

Thin upper lip

Associated features

Low nasal bridge

Minor ear anomalies

Epicanthal folds

Small jaw

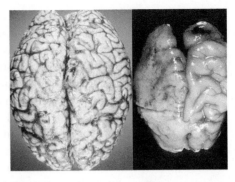

Figure 24.6 ▲

Fetal Alcoholism Spectrum Disorder
(A) Diagram of characteristic facial features that indicate FASD. (B) The convolutions characteristic of a healthy child's brain (left) are grossly underdeveloped in the brain of a child with FASD. (Part A: Research from Streissguth and Connor, 2001. Part B: Courtesy of Sterling K. Clarren, M.D., Professor of Pediatrics, University of British Columbia Faculty of Medicine.)

cells in the cortex. Among their physical characteristics are small stature and a tendency to be thin.

Related to the anatomical anomalies observed in FASD are certain behavioral symptoms. Children commonly display varying degrees of learning disabilities and lowered intelligence scores as well as hyperactivity and other social problems.

The recognition of FASD stimulated widespread interest in the effects of alcohol consumption by pregnant women. Pronounced FASD is found in the offspring of approximately 6 percent of alcoholic mothers. Its incidence in different geographic regions varies widely, depending on the pattern and degree of alcohol abuse in those locations. Ann Streissguth and Paul Connor (2001) suggest that about 1 in 700 to 1 in 100 newborns in the United States have FASD. An especially high incidence in child-care settings and among prison populations suggests that these are at-risk populations (Lange et al., 2013).

Fetal alcohol syndrome is not an all-or-none diagnosis (Pruett et al., 2013). Alcohol-induced abnormalities can range from hardly noticeable physical and psychological effects to full-blown FASD. Severity is related to when, how much, and how frequently alcohol was consumed during a pregnancy as well as to many other individual factors. The worst effects occur if drinking takes place in the first 3 months, which unfortunately may be a time when many women do not know that they are pregnant. Severe FASD is also more likely to be caused by binge drinking, which produces high blood-alcohol levels. Other factors related to a more severe outcome are poor maternal nutrition and use of other drugs, including nicotine.

A major and complex question FASD raises is how much alcohol is too much to consume during pregnancy, because the effects of alcohol on a fetus depend on so many factors. To be completely safe, it is best not to drink at all in the months preceding pregnancy as well as during it. This conclusion is supported by findings that as little as one alcoholic drink per day during pregnancy can lead to decreased intelligence test scores in offspring. This advice extends to males as well as females, both because it is likely that if a male consumes alcohol, his partner does too and because alcohol may produce epigenetic changes in sperm that affect fetal development (Abel, 2004; Stouder et al., 2011).

FASD, in its full-blown and milder forms, teaches important lessons. Alcohol is a widely used drug that poses risks when used inappropriately but when used in moderation, may have health benefits. Even so, women who are pregnant should completely avoid alcohol. Yet women most at risk for bearing FASD babies often are poor and not well educated, with alcohol-consumption problems that predate pregnancy and little access to prenatal care. Often they are unaware of the dangers that alcohol poses to a fetus and do not understand the need to abstain from drinking while they are pregnant.

Among the suggestions related to mechanisms by which alcohol produces its characteristic effects are general effects on cell division and maturation as well as epigenetic effects. An interesting idea relates to possible effects on a potassium channel called Kir2.1 that allows K^+ to move freely across the cell membrane and thus is important for maintaining a normal resting potential across both neuronal and non-neuronal cell membranes (Bates, 2013). When the channel is blocked, downstream effects on cell metabolism result in apoptosis (cell death). Such effects may account for physical and brain abnormalities seen in FASD. Supporting evidence for Kir2.1's role in FASD is that mutations in genes that produce it, and knockouts of these genes in mice, produce physical and behavioral symptoms that resemble FASD. Alcohol does have an inhibitory effect on Kir2.1 channels, suggesting that their dysregulation contributes to development of FASD.

⊚ 24.4 Developmental Influences on Neurodevelopmental Disorders

A century ago, neurodevelopmental disorders were widely accepted as inherited. Since then, it has become clear that many nongenetic factors, including structural damage and toxic effects, hormonal effects, and environmental deprivation, also influence the incidence of neurodevelopmental disorders.

Structural Damage and Toxic Effects

When a childhood learning disorder—dyslexia is an example—resembles a symptom seen in brain-damaged adults, it is only natural to wonder whether structural damage of a similar nature, such as birth trauma, encephalitis, anoxia, or an early-childhood accident, causes the learning disorder. This no doubt is the case for a small minority of affected children, but many neurological symptoms associated with brain damage in adults are not typically observed in children. For example, children with developmental dyslexia do not have *hemianopia* (blindness in half of the visual field) or *scotomas* (blind spots in the visual field), symptoms present in a large percentage of brain-damaged adults with dyslexia. Likewise, the results of EEG and CT-scan studies usually do not support a structural-damage hypothesis: abnormal EEGs similar to those correlated with known brain damage do not correlate consistently with neurodevelopmental disorders.

Subtler changes in brain structure can be produced in many ways. Possible causal factors include poor nutrition, drug use, and exposure to environmental contaminants. Clearly, exposure to environmental toxins such as mercury and some other metals can lead to learning disorders. As is reviewed by Jessica Reyes (2014), it is possible to infer causal relations between environmental toxins and the incidence of learning disabilities and crime. She notes, for example, increases in school performance and decreases in violent crime following the removal of lead from automobile gasoline in the 1970s. Nevertheless, it is generally hard to identify both the presence and the extent of toxins retrospectively and equally difficult to identify a toxin as a causative agent in a neurodevelopmental disorder.

Hormonal Effects: The Geschwind–Galaburda Theory

The higher incidence of neurodevelopmental disorders in males than in females raises the question of whether hormones that differentiate the male brain during development contribute. Norman Geschwind and Albert Galaburda (1985) propose that gonadal hormones may affect brain development and learning. The seed of their hypothesis lies in the observation that the *planum temporale* (Wernicke's area in the auditory cortex, which represents speech in the left hemisphere) is asymmetrical—larger on the left and smaller on the right in most right-handers. This typical anatomical asymmetry is considered the basis of an underlying neural asymmetry that gives rise to the left hemisphere's dominance in language. Because males show greater deviance from this asymmetrical pattern, it is possible that testosterone plays a role.

During embryonic development, the male fetal gonads produce high levels of testosterone, comparable to levels in adult males. The Geschwind–Galaburda theory proposes that the embryonic surge of testosterone delays left-hemisphere development, allowing the right hemisphere both space and time for greater development. Thus, males in general have some comparatively better-developed areas in the right hemisphere that presumably would endow them with excellent spatial skills.

If the testosterone-induced asymmetry produces some particularly large right-hemisphere areas, special abilities, such as precocious mathematical reasoning ability, may result. Alternatively, perhaps testosterone also produces some casualties characterized by brain abnormalities and learning disabilities. The theory proposes that testosterone also affects immune-system development, with a consequent increase in susceptibility to autoimmune disorders (migraines, allergies, asthma, thyroid disorders, and ulcerative colitis among them) and explains their high incidence, both among males in general and among males with exceptional abilities.

The appeal of the Geschwind–Galaburda theory is that it accounts for the general observation that females tend to do better than males at language-related tasks and males tend to do better than females at spatial tasks. It also accounts for the high incidence both of precocity and of learning disabilities among males. The proposed rightward shift in cerebral dominance further suggests an explanation for the high incidence of left-handedness among the precocious and among the learning-disabled.

And because testosterone's effects on the brain will in some ways parallel its effects on the immune system, the theory accounts for the high incidence of autoimmune disease in the precocious and learning-disabled male populations. Additionally, the theory allows for deviations in hormonal functions to produce increased incidences of learning disorders, precociousness, left-handedness, and autoimmune disorders in females. Another appealing aspect: the theory is testable and can be explored using animal models.

The first dissection of the brain of a person with a reading disability was performed on a 12-year-old boy who died of cerebral hemorrhage (Drake, 1968). The boy's intelligence had tested in the normal range, but in school he had been impaired in arithmetic, writing, and reading. The autopsy revealed atypical gyral patterns in the parietal lobes, an atrophied corpus callosum, and neurons that should have migrated to the cortex within the underlying white matter.

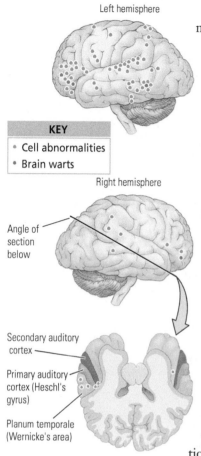

KEY

- Cell abnormalities
- Brain warts

Left hemisphere

Right hemisphere

Angle of section below

Secondary auditory cortex

Primary auditory cortex (Heschl's gyrus)

Planum temporale (Wernicke's area)

Figure 24.7 ▲

Proposed Hormonal Effects Red and blue dots mark locations of cell abnormalities and brain warts, respectively, found at autopsy in the brain of a person diagnosed as being reading-disabled. The horizontal section illustrates the typical asymmetrical hemispheric pattern of the planum temporale. (Research from Galaburda et al., 2006.)

Later, Albert Galaburda's group (2006) examined the brain of a 20-year-old man who had had a reading disability despite average intelligence. Visual inspection showed nothing irregular, but microscopic examination revealed several anomalies. Polymicrogyria (numerous small convolutions) and other architectonic abnormalities were found in left frontal and parietal cortex. The locations of the anomalous brain regions are shown in **Figure 24.7**. Subcortical abnormalities in the medial geniculate and the lateral posterior nuclei of the thalamus were discovered as well. Since the original study, this group has reported similar findings in other cases.

More-recent support for the idea that high levels of gonadal hormones can alter brain development comes from studies that correlate serum hormone levels prenatally with the subsequent diagnosis of ASD (Baron-Cohen et al., 2014). This relationship has led to the suggestions that in some respects, ASD symptoms are related to exaggerated male brain features and that the excessive expression of sex hormones alters the epigenetic profile of the developing brain.

Environmental Deprivation

Environmental deprivation can have long-lasting consequences for physical and intellectual function (see Sections 12.3 and 23.5). Children raised in orphanages with adequate physical care but inadequate social stimulation fail to thrive. They fall below age norms in both physical and intellectual development. In the 1970s, the Communist regime then governing Romania outlawed all forms of birth control and abortion. The consequence of the hundreds of thousands of unwanted pregnancies that resulted were unwanted children who were placed in orphanages where the conditions were appalling.

After the Communist government fell and the outside world moved to intervene, hundreds of these children were placed in adoptive homes throughout the world. Initially malnourished and small in size, they improved spectacularly in their adoptive homes. Their average height and weight became almost normal, and most achieved healthy motor and cognitive development. A significant number were learning-disabled, however, and many had psychosocial problems—difficulty in developing secure attachments with adults and healthy relations with peers. Children who were adopted before 6 months of age had significantly better outcomes than did those adopted at older ages (Miller et al., 2009).

People in postindustrial societies continue to adopt children from developing countries—children who have been subjected to various degrees of deprivation. Even in the most economically advanced countries, many children suffer varying degrees of deprivation and abuse. Accordingly, environmental deprivation continues as a leading cause of learning disorders. Interventions work best within the first 3 years of life (Bulut, 2013), but for many children who suffer deprivation at older ages, intervention is less effective.

The Birthday Effect

A subtle variant on environmental deprivation is called the the **birthday effect**, or influence of birth date on subsequent success at sports or school. The finding comes from studies undertaken by Roger Barnsley and his colleagues (1985) of birthdays of North American hockey players. In senior hockey leagues, the investigators found a negative correlation between birth month and number of players. More than 30 percent of players had birth dates in the first quarter of the year (16 percent in January), whereas fewer than 15 percent had birth dates in the last quarter of the year (5 percent in December). Furthermore, a disproportionate number of superstars had first-quarter birthdays.

This birth discrepancy is not present in beginning hockey leagues but emerges progressively as players advance through the leagues. The explanation appears straightforward. Players enter the most junior league according to age—children must be 8 years old between January 1 and December 31 of the year in which they enter Mite hockey. Equal numbers of children born in each month enter. But children born in January enter hockey almost a year earlier than children born in December, who in effect have had to wait a year. The younger, smaller children are at a developmental disadvantage from the outset. They receive less playing time and reinforcement and are more likely to drop out. In sports not regulated by entrance age, such as high school football, parents use the birthday effect to advantage by delaying the age at which their children start school.

Research on the effects of relative age on educational achievement produce similar results. Lars Lien and his coworkers (2005) find—as parents who understand the birthday effect know—that children entering school at a younger age perform at a significantly lower level than do their older classmates and have more emotional problems. Throughout schooling, socioemotional skills are an important prerequisite for optimal learning (Huang, 2014).

An interesting variation on the birthday effect is documented for children born preterm. Those enrolled in school based on their actual birthday do not perform as well as preterm children who enter school based on their "expected" birthday—the due date projected for full-term birth (Odd, 2013). Thus, maturational age, although not a primary factor in learning disabilities, can worsen performance of learning-disabled children.

◎ 24.5 Adult Outcome of Neurodevelopmental Disorders

The variety of views on outcomes for children with neurodevelopmental disorders range in level of optimism. In the most optimistic outcome study, reported by MacDonald Critchley (1964), 20 dyslexic boys attended a private school and received special instruction using training methods. As adults, two became medical doctors, two college professors, one a lawyer, two research scientists, six owners or managers of businesses, one a school principal, three teachers, one an actor, one a factory foreman, and one a skilled laborer. The popular press periodically reports similar, though perhaps not so absolute, successes at various private schools for learning-disabled children.

Most outcome studies do not report such optimistic conclusions, and the most thorough are frankly pessimistic about academic outcomes. Otfried Spreen (1988) examined the progress of 203 learning-disabled people and healthy, aged-matched peers over a long period with assessments, personal interviews, parental interviews, and other observations. He reports that the learning-disabled group suffered through a miserable and usually short school career, then experienced a miserable social life full of disappointments and failures. They also had a relatively poor chance of obtaining advanced training and skilled employment. They did not, however, have a higher incidence of juvenile delinquency or psychiatric problems than the general population. The disabled group and their parents were largely in agreement concerning factual information, but parents tended to regard learning disabilities as having had more serious effects on the well-being, happiness, and social interaction of their children than were reported by the disabled people themselves.

The affected people's memories of their childhood were less detailed than the control people's. As subjects aged, they developed firmer plans for their future and made better occupational adjustments, but they also gave increasingly negative descriptions of their school experiences. The eventual social adjustments of the females were worse than those of the males. The effects of learning disabilities early in life have negative consequences on physical as well as mental health in adulthood (Haider et al., 2013).

To summarize, careful assessment in evaluating the particular cognitive deficits of each learning-disabled child is invaluable. After problem areas are identified, specialized teaching programs can be devised to circumvent impairments. There may be little point in trying to teach a given child a particular skill that he or she is clearly not capable of learning. Perhaps the educational program for that child should instead be directed toward acquiring skills that can be used to gain employment.

Counseling is an important part of the educational process, both for the learning-disabled child and for the parents. It should focus not only on overcoming negative attitudes toward the educational system but also on understanding the child's unique challenges and on devising strategies for circumventing them if possible. Because learning disabilities experienced early in life have lifelong consequences, counseling and support should be directed accordingly toward adult adaptation. Finally, we cannot overemphasize the influence of personalized attention and practice. Learning takes time and repetition, and even small increments in skill acquisition can have beneficial consequences.

SUMMARY

24.1 Neurodevelopmental Disorders

A variety of disorders that appear in childhood, and persist throughout life, interfere with progress at school, work, and in social situations. The acquisition of reading in school is central, and understandably, disorders that result in reading impairments are an obstacle to satisfactory academic progress.

24.2 Learning Disorders That Affect Reading

Reading is a complex activity that can be disrupted in many ways. Research focuses on causes that include deficits in phonological awareness and in attention shifting as well as impairments in rapid sensory discrimination, in memory, and in fine motor skills.

24.3 Nonlanguage Neurodevelopmental Disorders

Several common disabilities unrelated to language, including ADHD and ASD, cerebral palsy and hydrocephalus, and fragile-X and fetal alcohol syndromes, lead to academic and social difficulties. Many conditions are associated with general, diffuse damage that varies from case to case. Causes include genetically based abnormalities in brain development, brain injury in utero, and deleterious environmental influences, including the use of alcohol during pregnancy.

24.4 Developmental Influences on Neurodevelopmental Disorders

Environmental conditions can influence brain function and developmental success—brain injury; effects of hormones, toxins, and drugs; and environmental deprivation among them. Even subtle influences, such as the age at which a child begins school, can significantly affect school success.

24.5 Adult Outcome of Neurodevelopmental Disorders

Although people with relatively mild neurodevelopmental disabilities do make adequate adjustments in later life, the effects of their disabilities and negative learning experiences are long-lasting. People with severe neurodevelopmental disabilities need lifelong assistance and care.

References

Abel, E. L. Paternal contribution to fetal alcohol syndrome. *Addiction Biology* 9:127–133, 2004.

Allman, J. M., K. K. Watson, N. A. Tetreault, and A. Y. Hakeem. Intuition and autism: A possible role for von Economo neurons. *Trends in Cognitive Sciences* 9:367–373, 2005.

American Psychiatric Association. *Diagnostic and Statistical Manual of Mental Disorders*, 4th ed. Washington, D.C.: American Psychiatric Association, 1994.

American Psychiatric Association. *Diagnostic and Statistical Manual of Mental Disorders*, 5th ed. Washington, D.C.: American Psychiatric Association, 2013.

Asbjornsen, A. E., J. E. Obrzut, and J. D. Oyler. A cross-cultural comparison of verbal learning and memory functions in reading disabled American and Norwegian adolescents. *Scandinavian Journal of Psychology* 55:115–122, 2014.

Bagni, C., and B. A. Oostra. Fragile X syndrome: From protein function to therapy. *American Journal of Medical Genetics* 161:2809–2821, 2013.

Barnsley, R. H., A. H. Thompson, and P. E. Barnsley. Hockey success and birth date: The relative age effect. *Canadian Association of Health, Physical Education, and Recreation* November–December, 23–27, 1985.

Baron-Cohen, S., B. Auyeung, B. Nørgaard-Pedersen, D. M. Hougaard, M. W. Abdallah, L. Melgaard, A. S. Cohen, B. Chakrabarti, L. Ruta, and M. V. Lombardo. Elevated fetal steroidogenic activity in autism. *Molecular Psychiatry* doi:10.1038/mp.2014.48, 2014.

Bates, E. A. A potential molecular target for morphological defects of fetal alcohol syndrome: Kir2.1. *Current Opinion in Genetics & Development* 23:324–329, 2013.

Becker, E. B. E., and C. J. Stoodley. Autism spectrum disorder and the cerebellum. *International Review of Neurobiology* 113:1–34, 2013.

Berger, I., O. Slobodin, M. Aboud, J. Melamed, and H. Cassuto. Maturational delay in ADHD: Evidence from CPT. *Frontiers in Human Neuroscience* 7:691. doi:10.3389/fnhum.2013.00691. eCollection 2013.

Bradley, L., and P. E. Bryant. Categorizing sounds and learning to read: A causal connection. *Nature* 301:419–421, 1983.

Bulut, S. Intelligence development of socio-economically disadvantaged pre-school children. *Annales de Psicologia* 29:855–864, 2013.

Carrion-Castillo, A., B. Franke, and S. E. Fisher. Molecular genetics of dyslexia: An overview. *Dyslexia* 19:214–240, 2013.

Cobrinik, L. Unusual reading ability in severely disturbed children. *Journal of Autism and Childhood Schizophrenia* 4:163–175, 1974.

Colver, A., C. Fairhurst, and P. O. D. Pharoah. Cerebral palsy. *The Lancet* 383: 1240–1249, 2014.

Connor, C. McD., M. Spencer, S. L. Day, S. Giuliani, S. W. Ingebrand, and F. J. Morrison. Capturing the complexity: Content, type, and amount of instruction and quality of the classroom learning environment synergistically predict third graders' vocabulary and reading comprehension outcomes. *Journal of Educational Psychology* 106(3):762–778, August 2014.

Critchley, M. *Developmental Dyslexia*. Springfield, Ill.: Charles C Thomas, 1964.

Cruickshank, W. M., Ed. *Cerebral Palsy*. Syracuse, N.Y.: Syracuse University Press, 1976.

Davis, J. M., V. B. Searles, N. Anderson, J. Keeney, L. Dumas, and J. M. Sikela. DUF1220 dosage is linearly associated with increasing severity of the three primary symptoms of autism. *PLoS Genetics* 10:e1004241, 2014.

DeWitt I., and J. P. Rauschecker. Phoneme and word recognition in the auditory ventral stream. *Proceedings of the National Academy of Sciences U.S.A.* 21:109(8):E505-14, 2012.

Dole, M., F. Meunier, and M. Hoen. Functional correlates of the speech-in-noise perception impairment in dyslexia: An MRI study. *Neuropsychologia* 60:103–114, June 4, 2014.

Drake, W. Clinical and pathological findings in a child with a developmental learning disability. *Journal of Learning Disabilities* 1:468–475, 1968.

Fry, E. A do-it-yourself terminology generator. *Journal of Reading* 11:428–430, 1968.

Galaburda, A. M., J. LoTurco, F. Ramus, R. H. Fitch, and G. D. Rosen. From genes to behavior in developmental dyslexia. *Nature Neuroscience* 9:1213–1217, 2006.

Geschwind, N., and A. M. Galaburda. *Cerebral Lateralization*. Cambridge, Mass.: MIT Press, 1985.

Haider, S. I., Z. Ansari, and L. Vaughan. Health and wellbeing of Victorian adults with intellectual disability compared to the general Victorian population. *Research in Developmental Disabilities* 34:4034–4042, 2013.

Hinshelwood, J. Word blindness and visual memory. *Lancet* 2:1564–1570, 1895.

Huang, F. L. Further understanding factors associated with grade retention: Birthday effects and socioemotional skills. *Journal of Applied Developmental Psychology* 35:79–93, 2014.

Lange, S., K. Shield, and J. Rehm. Prevalence of fetal alcohol spectrum disorders in child care settings: A meta-analysis. *Pediatrics* 132:E980–E995, 2013.

Lien, L., K. Tambs, B. Oppedal, S. Heyerdahl, and E. Bjertness. Is relatively young age within a school year a risk factor for mental health problems and poor school performance? A population-based cross-sectional study of adolescents in Oslo, Norway. *BMC Public Health* 5:102, 2005.

Little, W. J. *Deformities of the Human Frame*. London: Longmans, 1853.

Mariën, P., H. Ackermann, M. Adamaszek, C. H. Barwood, A. Beaton, J. Desmond, E. De Witte, A. J. Fawcett, I. Hertrich, M. Küper, M. Leggio, C. Marvel, M. Molinari, B. E. Murdoch, R. I. Nicolson, J. D. Schmahmann, C. J. Stoodley, M. Thürling, D. Timmann, E. Wouters, and W. Ziegler. Consensus paper: Language and the cerebellum: an ongoing enigma. *Cerebellum* 13(3):386–410, June 2014.

Miller, L., W. Chan, L. Tirella, and E. Perrin. Outcomes of children adopted from Eastern Europe. *International Journal of Behavioral Development* 23(4)289–298, 2009.

Mortazavi, M. M., N. N. Adeeb, and C. J. Griessenauer. The ventricular system of the brain: A comprehensive review of its history, anatomy, histology, embryology, and surgical considerations. *Child's Nervous System* 30:19–35, 2014.

Mortazavi, M. M., C. J. Griessenauer, and N. Adeeb. The choroid plexus: A comprehensive review of its history, anatomy, function, histology, embryology, and surgical considerations. *Child's Nervous System* 40:205–214, 2014.

National Assessment of Educational Progress. *The Nation's Report Card* National Center for Education Statistics, Washington, D.C., 2014.

Odd, D., D. Evans, and A. Emond. Preterm birth, age at school entry and educational performance. *PloS One* 8, e76615, 2013.

Olulade, O. A., E. M. Napoliello, and G. F. Eden. Abnormal visual motion processing is not a cause of dyslexia. *Neuron* 79(1):180–190, July 10, 2013.

Orton, S. T. *Reading, Writing, and Speech Problems in Children*. New York: Norton, 1937.

Pruett, D., E. H. Waterman, and A. B. Caughey. Fetal alcohol exposure: Consequences, diagnosis, and treatment. *Obstetrical and Gynecological Survey* 68:62–69, 2013.

Ramus, F., S. Rosen, S. C. Dakin, B. L. Day, J. M. Castellote, S. White, and U. Frith. Theories of developmental dyslexia: Insights from a multiple case study of dyslexic adults. *Brain* 126:841–865, 2003.

Reyes, J. W. *Childhood Lead and Academic Performance in Massachusetts*, Federal Reserve Bank of Boston Working Paper, 2014.

Rodier, P. M. The early origins of autism. *Scientific American* 282(2):56–63, 2000.

Rubia, K., A. Alegria, and H. Brinson. Imaging the ADHD brain: Disorder-specificity, medication effects and clinical translation. *Expert Review of Neurotherapeutics* 14:519–538, 2014.

Ruffino, M., S. Gori, D. Boccardi, M. Molteni, and A. Facoetti. Spatial and temporal attention in developmental dyslexia. *Frontiers in Human Neuroscience* 22:331.doi: 10.3389/fnhum.2014.00331, 2014.

Rugel, R. P. WISC subtest scores of disabled readers: A review with respect to Bannatyne's categorization. *Journal of Learning Disability* 17:48–55, 1974.

Sandin, S., P. Lichtenstein, and R. Kuja-Halkola. The familial risk of autism. *Journal of the American Medical Association* 17:1770–1777, 2014.

Shi, F., L. Wang, C-W. Wee, and D. S. Shen. Altered modular organization of structural cortical networks in autistic children. *PLoS ONE* 8(5): e63131.doi:10.1371/journal.pone.0063131, 2013.

Spreen, O. *Learning Disabled Children Growing Up*. New York: Oxford University Press, 1988.

Stoodley, C. J., and J. F. Stein. Cerebellar function in developmental dyslexia. *The Cerebellum* 12:267–276, 2013.

Stouder, C., E. Somm, and A. Paoloni-Giacobino. Prenatal exposure to ethanol: A specific effect on the H19 gene in sperm. *Reproductive Toxicology* 31:507–512, 2011.

Streissguth, A. P., and P. D. Connor. Fetal alcohol syndrome and other effects of prenatal alcohol: Developmental cognitive neuroscience implications. In C. A. Nelson and M. Luciana, Eds. *Handbook of Developmental Cognitive Neuroscience*, pp. 505–518. Cambridge, Mass.: MIT Press, 2001.

Tallal, P. Fast ForWord®: The birth of the neurocognitive training revolution. *Progress in Brain Research* 207:175–207, 2013.

Tallal, P., S. Miller, and R. H. Fitch. Neurobiological basis of speech: A case for the preeminence of temporal processing. In P. Tallal, A. M. Galaburda, R. R. Llinas, and C. von Euler, Eds. *Temporal Information Processing in the Nervous System*. New York: New York Academy of Sciences, 1993.

Taylor, E. Uses and misuses of treatments for ADHD. The second Birgit Olsson lecture. *Nordic Journal of Psychiatry*, Volume 68 Issue 4: 236–242, 2014.

van der Leij, A., and B. Maassen. Dutch Dyslexia Programme. *Dyslexia* 19:189–190, 2013.

Wazana, A., M. Bresnahan, and J. Kline. The autism epidemic: Fact or artifact? *Journal of the American Academy of Child Adolescent Psychiatry* 46:721–730, 2007.

Whishaw, I. Q., and B. Kolb. Neuropsychological assessment of children and adults with developmental dyslexia. In R. N. Malatesha and H. A. Whitaker, Eds. *Dyslexia: A Global Issue*. The Hague: Martinus Nijhoff, 1984.

World Health Organization. International Classification of Diseases and related health problems (ICD-10). Geneva, WHO, 1992.

25 Plasticity, Recovery, and Rehabilitation of the Adult Brain

PORTRAIT | Concussion

Early in 2011, 50-year-old former Chicago Bears defensive back Dave Duerson died of a self-inflicted gunshot wound. Duerson had played 11 seasons in the National Football League, was on two Super Bowl–winning teams, and received numerous awards. He left behind a note asking that his brain be studied.

As a pro player he received at least 10 concussions, none serious enough to cause him to leave the game. After retiring from football, Duerson obtained a business degree from Harvard. He pursued a successful business career until he began to experience problems in decision-making and temper control. Eventually, Duerson's business and marriage failed.

After his suicide, neuroscientists at Boston University's Center for the Study of Traumatic Encephalopathy did study his brain as part of a long-term longitudinal study. Duerson's diagnosis, **chronic traumatic encephalopathy (CTE)**, is a progressive degenerative disease found in individuals with a history of multiple concussion and other closed head injuries (detailed in Section 26.3) and characterized by neurofibrillary tangles, plaques, and cerebral atrophy and expanded ventricles due to cell loss.

Concussion, or *mild traumatic brain injury* (MTBI), is common in sports, especially contact sports such as American and Canadian football, hockey, and rugby. During 2012–2013, sports-related concussions in U.S. high school students numbered 294,000, and a study of two Canadian university hockey teams (one men's team, one women's team) during the 2011–2012 season recorded concussion in 11 of 45 players (Helmer et al., 2014). The National Football League estimates that one in three players will have cognitive issues later in life. Concussion also results from falls and from vehicular accidents. The incidence is likely higher than 6 per 1000 individuals.

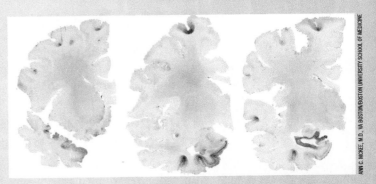

Most concussions go unrecognized. For those that are diagnosed, little apparent pathology appears after relatively short rest periods, the usual treatment. In the Helmer study, MRIs found inflammatory changes in white matter 72 hours after injury. The changes had resolved when the players were rescanned after 2 months. Yet the relationship is well established between concussion and a range of degenerative diseases that occur later in life—dementias including Alzheimer's disease, as well as Parkinson's disease, motor neuron disease, and CTE. This relationship suggests that concussion can initiate a cascade of pathological events that, over years, develop into CTE (Gavett et al., 2010).

To test for cell death postmortem, researchers stain for accumulation of the **tau protein** (dark brown areas in the illustration), a sensitive marker for neuronal degeneration. In three coronal sections through Duerson's anterior right hemisphere, degenerating brain tissue appears in frontal cortex and medial temporal lobe.

The unknowns about CTE are many. What we do know is that many professional athletes, especially football and hockey players, have developed CTE. Clearly, more care needs to be taken, beginning in childhood, to prevent concussion and to ensure that it is treated, even though what constitutes adequate treatment remains uncertain.

Dave Duerson's experience vividly illustrates the difficulty of stimulating functional recovery after brain injury. After a healthy brain has been injured, it will forevermore be coping with damaged circuits. When the damaged brain is also coping with age-related changes, it is not uncommon for symptoms to emerge long after injury. Nonetheless, some restitution of function often is achieved, in part because of the brain's plasticity and in part because brain-injured people learn to compensate. We begin this chapter by considering 10 principles of plasticity in the healthy brain. We then examine how the brain responds to injury, and finally, how various rehabilitation protocols may stimulate change in the damaged brain.

@ 25.1 Principles of Brain Plasticity

Many details remain to be learned about brain plasticity. Here we reflect on what is known by identifying principles that govern plastic changes in the brain and provide a framework for understanding the nature of plasticity.

Principle 1: Plasticity is common to all nervous systems, and the principles are conserved.

Although most current work on brain plasticity is conducted on mammals, many early ideas regarding plasticity came from studying invertebrates and other non-mammals, such as birds. Even the simplest animals, such as the tiny worm *Caenorhabditis elegans*, which has only 302 neurons, can learn to make associations between sensory events, such as smells, and consequences, such as mild shocks. Such changes are remarkably similar across phylogeny. For any animal to learn by association, the nervous system must undergo some change that codes for it.

Principle 2: Plasticity can be analyzed at many levels.

As summarized in **Table 25.1**, neuroscientists investigate brain plasticity at many levels, ranging from behavior, the most complex, to the simplest, molecules.

Behavior

Learning and remembering new information must entail changes in nervous-system cells—changes that would constitute a neural record of the learned information. A comprehensive survey of what studying behavioral change has contributed to the research on nervous system plasticity is beyond the scope of this discussion, but the following example illustrates how such research is conducted.

Humans show a remarkable ability to adapt to a visually rearranged world. Wolfgang Köhler (1964) fitted participants with special glasses made of prisms that inverted the visual field and reversed left and right, so that a participant would see the world upside down and backward. For the first few days of constantly wearing these glasses, a participant's struggle to navigate an upside-down, backward world was confusing and debilitating, but within a few days, the world seemed to right itself. The participant once again was able to dress, eat, walk about, and perform other daily activities with ease. Eventually, a participant could even perform complex activities such as skiing and riding a bicycle. When

▲ *Caenorhabditis elegans*, a small roundworm about 1 mm long that lives in soil, was the first species to have all of its neurons, synapses, and genome described. (Sinclair Stammers/Science Source.)

Table 25.1 Plasticity: Levels of analysis @

1. Behavior
2. Neural imaging
3. Cortical maps (invasive and noninvasive)
4. Physiology (e.g., long-term potentiation, unit recording, stimulation)
5. Synaptic organization
6. Mitotic activity
7. Molecular structure

the glasses were finally removed, the participant again needed time to adjust, because the world again appeared distorted, just as when first fitted with the prisms.

The adaptation of Köhler's subjects to the transformed visual world included several behavioral changes, each associated with changes in certain brain regions (Sugita, 2001). One region is the premotor cortex. If healthy monkeys are fitted with such prisms, they adapt to the change just as the human participants did. But if a monkey's premotor cortex has been inactivated, the animal has great difficulty. Another locus of change is the posterior parietal cortex. Dottie Clower and her colleagues (1996) used PET to locate changes in regional blood flow in participants adapting to prisms and found that when they used their eyes to guide them in reaching for objects, activation in the posterior parietal cortex greatly increased.

The properties of cells in the visual cortex were found to change as healthy monkeys adapted to prisms (Sugita, 2001). Normally, cells in area V1 would respond only to cells in the contralateral visual field, but with adaptation, the cells began to respond to stimuli in the ipsilateral field as well. These changes disappeared soon after the prisms were removed. Parallel changes were also seen in other ventral-stream pathways, such as area V4.

Whatever plastic changes support prism adaptation, they presumably correspond to changes in synaptic organization, although the consistency and dependability of adaptation in both humans and monkeys suggest that the connections necessary for the adaptation are already in place. If so, adaptation would be a matter of enhancing the efficiency of these connections relative to the connections used for seeing the "normal" visual world.

Much remains to be learned about the nature of the plastic changes in the visually adapting brain, but clearly, by studying novel situations in which behavior changes dramatically, researchers can make inferences about the nervous system's plasticity. Understanding such processes not only is of general interest with respect to how the healthy brain functions but also can offer insight into ways of stimulating functional recovery after injury. Recall, for example, that Yves Rossetti used prism adaptation as a way of stimulating recovery from contralateral neglect in stroke patients (see Figure 22.11).

Cortical Maps

As described in Sections 8.1 and 10.1, in each sensory system multiple maps provide topographic representations of the external world. The homunculi that represent the motor and somatosensory cortices exemplify these representations. The motor maps' size and organization can be determined by stimulating the cortex either directly, with microelectrodes, or transcranially, using magnetic stimulation to induce movements or by using functional imaging to map the areas activated when participants are engaged in different behaviors.

The results of studies in rats, monkeys, and humans demonstrate that specific motor training can increase the size of motor map components. Recall from Section 23.3 that violinists' motor maps have a larger representation of the digits of the left hand than do nonmusicians' maps. Randy Nudo and his colleagues (1996, 1997) directly examined motor-map changes in squirrel monkeys that the researchers trained to retrieve food objects from either small or large wells (**Figure 25.1**A). To obtain food from the small wells, the animals had to use a pincer grasp; to obtain food from the large wells, they used gross movements of the whole hand and wrist. When the researchers mapped the motor cortex with

(A)

Difficult task

One group of monkeys was trained to retrieve food from a small well.

Simple task

Another group of monkeys was trained to retrieve food from a large well.

(B)

The motor representation of digit, wrist, and arm was mapped.

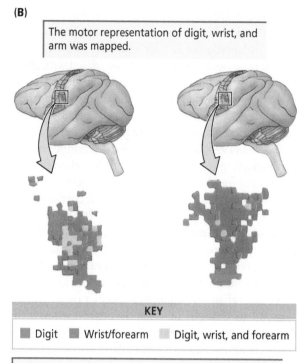

KEY		
■ Digit	■ Wrist/forearm	■ Digit, wrist, and forearm

The digit representation in the brain of the animal with the more difficult task is larger, corresponding to the neuronal changes necessary for the acquired skill.

Figure 25.1 ▲

Effects of Motor Training (A) To test the differential effects of motor-skill acquisition and motor use on the functional organization of the squirrel monkey motor cortex, the training procedures consisted of practice retrieving small food pellets from either a small or a large well. The monkey is able to insert the entire hand into the large well but only one or two fingers into the small well. (B) Maps of brain activity during forelimb movements, produced by microelectrode stimulation of the cortex, show systematic neural changes in the animals trained with the small well (left) but not with the large one (right). (Information from Nudo et al., 1997.)

microelectrodes, they found that the area representing the digits had increased in the animals making pincer movements, whereas no similar change took place in animals making larger movements (Figure 25.1B).

As for motor maps, experience modifies sensory maps. For example, Christo Pantev and his colleagues (1998) used MEG to map a 25 percent increase in the cortical representation for the musical scale in musicians compared with nonmusicians. This enlargement correlated with the age at which the musicians began to practice music. Josef Rauschecker (2001), who notes that early blindness results in an expansion of the auditory-responsive areas in the parietal and occipital lobes—areas that would not have auditory functions in sighted people—actually claims that this finding lends credibility to the generalization that blind people have greater musical abilities than the sighted.

Extensive study of plasticity in somatosensory representations by Michael Merzenich and his colleagues (for a review see Nahum et al., 2013) showed that map organization can be changed by manipulating afferent inputs to the cortex. For example, if the afferent nerve from one or more digits is cut, representation of the remaining digits expands, presumably allowing greater sensitivity in those digits. If two digits are sewn together, a single digit area replaces the two formerly separate digit areas on the map.

Such changes are not always adaptive. *Focal hand dystonia*, the loss of motor control of one or more digits because of increased muscle tone, can result from repetitive, synchronous movements of the digits, such as those made by musicians over a lifetime of playing. In golfers, the condition is called "the yips."

(A)

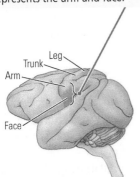

In the control monkey, this area of the somatosensory cortex represents the arm and face.

Leg
Trunk
Arm
Face

This normal pattern is illustrated by a normal face.

(B)

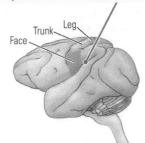

In the denervated monkey, the area of the somatosensory cortex that formerly represented the arm has been taken over by expansion of the face area.

Trunk
Leg
Face

This expansion is illustrated by an elongated face.

Figure 25.2 ▲

Somatosensory Plasticity
The neural face representations, mapped by electrical recordings in a healthy (A) and a denervated (B) monkey, are shown right side up for simplicity. Note in part B that only the lower part of the neural face area has expanded. (Information from Pons et al., 1991, p. 1858.)

Thomas Elbert and colleagues (2001) studied the somatosensory maps of musicians with focal hand dystonia and found smaller-than-normal distances between the digit representations, much as in people with webbed fingers. Presumably, the musical training inadvertently caused the mapped representations of the digits to fuse. A logical extrapolation is that dystonia should be treatable by training affected persons to make independent asynchronous finger movements. Indeed, Victor Candia and his colleagues (1999) confirmed it.

One well-known example of somatosensory plasticity is described repeatedly in the extensive literature concerning studies of people and monkeys with amputations. In a classic study, Tim Pons and his colleagues (1991) mapped the somatosensory representation of monkeys that had been deprived of somatosensory input to one limb by a nerve transection 12 years earlier. The researchers found that the denervated hand and arm area responded to tactile stimulation of the face on the affected side of the body. Most surprising was that the changes in the map were large—covering more than 1 cm—as shown in **Figure 25.2**. The major change was an expansion of the face area to invade the denervated limb area.

Parallel studies conducted with people have yielded similar results (see review by Elbert et al., 2001). But what happens to the original map? Vilayanur Ramachandran and William Hirstein (1998) demonstrated that the original maps remain and can be detected by lightly stimulating the face (**Figure 25.3**). Other studies document similar rearrangements of sensory maps subsequent to amputation of other body parts. Salvatore Aglioti (1999) found that in women who have

(A)

(B)

Figure 25.3 ▶

Mapping an Amputated Hand (A) When an amputee is stroked lightly on the face with a cotton swab, he or she experiences the sensation of the missing hand being lightly touched. (B) Touching different parts of the amputee's face and noting what part of the hand each touch evokes allow for mapping a representation of the hand on the face. As in the typical somatosensory cortex map, the area representing the thumb is disproportionately large. (Information from Ramachandran and Hirstein, 1998, p. 1603.)

Cotton swab

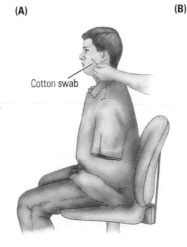

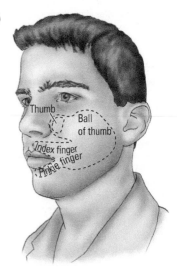

Thumb
Ball of thumb
Index finger
Pinkie finger

(A) Enhanced response
Procedure

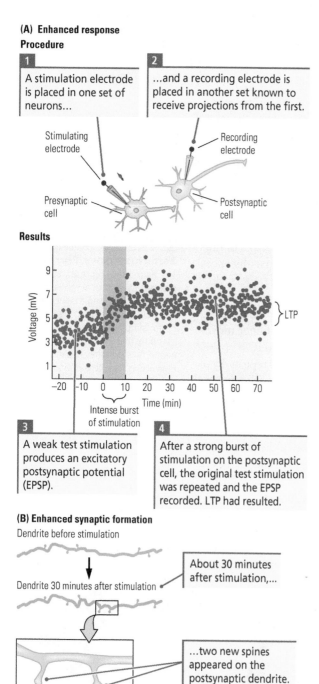

1. A stimulation electrode is placed in one set of neurons...

2. ...and a recording electrode is placed in another set known to receive projections from the first.

Stimulating electrode

Recording electrode

Presynaptic cell

Postsynaptic cell

Results

Intense burst of stimulation

3. A weak test stimulation produces an excitatory postsynaptic potential (EPSP).

4. After a strong burst of stimulation on the postsynaptic cell, the original test stimulation was repeated and the EPSP recorded. LTP had resulted.

(B) Enhanced synaptic formation

Dendrite before stimulation

Dendrite 30 minutes after stimulation

About 30 minutes after stimulation,...

...two new spines appeared on the postsynaptic dendrite.

Figure 25.4 ▲

Demonstrating Long-Term Potentiation (A) Each dot on the graph represents the size of an EPSP in response to a single test stimulus. (B) New dendritic spines can grow in conjunction with LTP. (Data source: Bliss and Lømo, 1973.)

undergone bilateral mastectomies, somatosensory representation of the nipples relocates to the earlobes (see very readable book by Ramachandran and Blakeslee, 1998).

Physiology

The general hypothesis tested in physiological studies of brain plasticity is that electrical stimulation can change the nervous system. Two primary methods are *long-term potentiation* and *kindling*.

High-frequency electrical stimulation applied briefly to the hippocampus resulted in a long-term change in the efficiency of synapses activated by the stimulation (Bliss and Lømo, 1973), a phenomenon called **long-term potentiation** (LTP). Brief pulses of current were delivered to a neuron for a period of a few seconds, and the magnitude of the response was recorded from neurons known to receive projections from the stimulated neuron (**Figure 25.4**A). After a stable baseline of response—the excitatory postsynaptic potential (EPSP)—to the stimulation was established, the stimulation was changed to a high-frequency burst, driving the system very hard. (Think of this burst as a training stimulus.) After a brief rest period, the original test pulse was presented again, and this time the magnitude of the response (that is, the EPSP) was greater than before, demonstrating that LTP had occurred.

Under optimal experimental conditions, this enhanced response can persist indefinitely and can be shown to correlate with changes in dendritic length and spine density in the postsynaptic neuron (see Figure 25.4B). This synaptic change has been adopted by many as a general model of how learning might take place.

Kindling refers to the development of persistent seizure activity after repeated exposure to an initially subconvulsant stimulus. Like LTP, kindling is presumed to activate mechanisms similar to those activated for at least some kinds of learning. It can be demonstrated in most forebrain structures and, like LTP, is associated with a change in synaptic organization and with a variety of molecular-level events, such as the production of *neurotrophic growth factors* (for a review, see Teskey, 2001).

Synaptic Organization

Synaptic organization has been studied by using Golgi-type stains to reveal dendritic arborization and by using electron-microscope technology to inspect synapse number and size. Inasmuch as both these approaches require postmortem tissue, studies of synaptic changes in human brains have necessarily been limited.

In one series of human synapse studies, Bob Jacobs and his colleagues (1993) predicted that predominant life experiences, such as a person's occupation, should alter the structure of dendritic trees. In comparing somatosensory cells in the trunk area, finger area, and supramarginal gyrus, they found wide individual differences (**Figure 25.5**). Especially large differences in trunk and finger neurons were found in people who had achieved a high level of finger dexterity and maintained it for long periods (as would a court reporter, for example). In contrast, no trunk–finger difference was found in the brain of a person whose career as a sales representative had required far less specialized finger use and thus made less-complex demands on the finger neurons.

The results of Golgi-type studies of the brain tissue of laboratory animals support the conclusions seen in humans. Experience-dependent changes are seen in every species of animal tested, from fruit flies and bees to rats, cats, and monkeys (for a review, see Kolb and Whishaw, 1998).

Mitotic Activity

In mammals, both the olfactory bulbs and the hippocampus incorporate new neurons into their existing circuitry throughout life. The olfactory-bulb cells are generated by stem cell mitosis along the wall of the lateral ventricles, in the subventricular zone (see Figure 23.2). The olfactory precursor cells migrate from the anterior part of the subventricular zone along a pathway known as the rostral migratory stream until they reach the olfactory bulb, where they differentiate into neurons. In contrast, the precursor cells in the hippocampus are located between the granule-cell layer and the hilus, as illustrated in **Figure 25.6**.

Debate about whether new neurons are produced in the cerebral cortex of the healthy, noninjured brain has been vigorous, but there is little doubt that new neurons *are* produced in the injured cortex. Their presence has led to the idea that a treatment for cortical injury might be to increase the number of cortical cells produced. Any neurons produced in the intact cerebral cortex, however, are clearly produced in rather small numbers.

Newly generated neurons in the olfactory bulb and hippocampus are assumed to have some function, but the

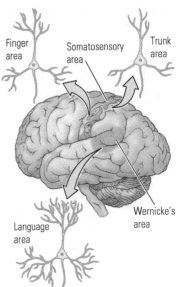

Figure 25.5 ▲

Experience and Neuronal Complexity Cells that represent the body's trunk area perform less-demanding computations than those performed by cells representing the finger region and are therefore less complex in structure. In contrast, cells engaged in higher-level cognitive functions (such as language, in Wernicke's area) perform more-demanding computations than are performed by cells engaged in finger functions and are even more complex in structure.

Figure 25.6 ▶

Neurogenesis in the Hippocampus (A) Section through the hippocampus illustrates the dentate gyrus, where a granule cell is extending its dendrites upward and sending an axon to a pyramidal cell. (B) Displayed over the time course of cell division and maturation, precursor cells differentiate into immature neurons, migrate to the appropriate location, and grow mature connections. (Information from Ormerod, B. K., and L. A. M. Galea. Mechanism and function of adult neurogenesis. In C. A. Shaw and J. C. McEachern, Eds. *Toward a Theory of Neuroplasticity*. Lillington, N.C.: Taylor & Francis, 2001, pp. 85–100.)

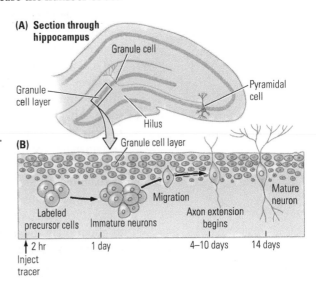

Table 25.2 Effects of various factors on cell proliferation and hippocampal granule-neuron survival

Factor	Effect on Proliferation	Effect on Survival
Adrenal steroids	Down	No change
Aging (rats)	Down	Down?
Adrenalectomy	Up	Up
Dentate gyrus lesions	Up	Up
Running-wheel activity	Up	Unknown
High levels of estradiol	Up	Up
Serotonin agonists (e.g., Prozac)	Unknown	Up
Hippocampal-dependent learning	No change	Up
Season (reduced daylight)	Up	Up
Kindling	Up	No change
Exposure to stress	Down	Down?

Data source: Ormerod and Galea, 2001.

nature of that function is not yet known. Certain possibilities are suggested by the principle that if new neurons are being produced, room must be made for them or the brain cavity will fill up. Therefore, the new neurons are being generated to replace lost ones, or they somehow stimulate the death of old neurons, or the new neurons themselves may be destined to be short-lived.

New neurons likely do replace old ones; however, their survival is not certain and can be affected by many types of experience. **Table 25.2** summarizes some factors that influence neuron generation and neuron survival in the hippocampus. Note especially that when animals engage the hippocampus to solve a neuropsychological problem, survival of new granule cells is enhanced.

We can speculate that cell survival is related to successful acquisition of the task. If so, the implication is that learning could be compromised if cell proliferation or survival or both were compromised. Stress is correlated with decreases in hippocampal-cell proliferation and survival, which comports with evidence that stress reduces mental efficiency and may especially impair some forms of memory.

Perhaps even more interesting is the relation between chronic stress and depression and the finding that antidepressants that stimulate serotonin production (SSRIs such as fluoxetine) also increase neuron generation in the hippocampus. These observations suggest that the therapeutic activity of antidepressants may be related to their ability to stimulate neurogenesis, which in turn may alter mental activity.

Molecular Structure

The studies using cortical maps, Golgi stains, or physiological techniques to show that the brain changes in response to experience are phenomenological: they describe and classify but do not explain. If we wish to know why the brain changes or understand how, we need to look at the mechanisms that actually produce synaptic change. In the final analysis, we must look at how different proteins are produced, which ultimately means looking at the effects of experience on genes.

Genetic screening techniques—for example, *gene-chip arrays*—allow researchers to analyze bits of brain tissue and determine which genes have been affected by a particular experience. In the gene-chip technique, a miniature grid (on a chip about 1 cm in diameter) that can identify as many as 10,000 genes, each in a different location on the grid, is exposed to a homogenate of tissue. If certain genes are present in the tissue, they will react with a substance at one of the locations on the chip.

Such techniques are undoubtedly powerful, providing a lot of information about which genes change, for example, when an animal is housed in a complex rather than a deprived environment. As yet, what the changes actually tell us about brain function is far from clear. For example, rats placed in complex environments for different lengths of time significantly increased the activity of more than 100 genes (of 11,000 genes screened in a study by Rampon et al., 2000) in response to the experience.

Knowing that genes change is only the start. The real question is what the changes mean. Nonetheless, the effort to understand how experience alters genes is an important step in understanding how to enhance (or reduce) plastic changes in the brain, especially changes that take place after injury.

Principle 3: The two general types of plasticity derive from experience.

Two types of plasticity can be distinguished in the healthy brain (Black, Greenough, and Wallace 1997). *Experience-expectant plasticity* occurs largely during development. For different brain systems to develop requires specific types of experience. A good example is the development of ocular dominance columns found in the primary visual cortex, described in Figure 23.14.

Experience-dependent plasticity reflects brain changes necessary to modify neuronal ensembles that are already present. Experience-dependent plasticity can be seen in a variety of situations, as when animals learn to solve problems and topographic maps expand or shrink in response to the experience or in response to abnormal experiences such as psychoactive drugs or injury. Such experiences both increase and decrease synapse numbers, often in the same animals but in different brain regions. The key points for both types of plasticity are that the synaptic changes are all dependent on experiences, and they reflect modifications of a basic phenotype shaped by development.

Principle 4: Similar behavioral changes can correlate with different plastic changes.

It is tempting to conclude that a behavioral change, such as learning to solve a new problem, engenders plastic changes, such as increased synapse number in some brain region, that are similar to those seen for learning other tasks that may involve some other brain region(s). But changes in synapse number reflect changes in neural networks, and therefore synapse number could increase in learning one task but decrease in learning another. In fact, when a person is learning a single task, synapses in one part of the brain could increase while synapses in another brain area decrease. Even in the same localized region, such as a cortical column, synapse numbers can increase in one layer and decrease in another. Synaptic changes simply reflect changes in neuronal ensembles underlying the new behavior.

Evidence of unique plastic changes in different brain regions can also be seen in molecular measures. For example, Richelle Mychasiuk and her colleagues (2013) found completely different changes in gene expression in the prefrontal cortex and hippocampus in response to psychoactive drugs such as amphetamine. The differing changes in gene expression would suggest different mechanisms of synaptic changes in the two regions related to the same experience.

Principle 5: Experience-dependent changes interact.

As we travel through life, we encounter an almost infinite number of experiences that could alter brain organization. Until recently, virtually no experimental studies have attempted to determine how the experiences of a lifetime interact, a property referred to as *metaplasticity*. Terry Robinson and his colleagues have attempted to address this question in a series of studies (see review by Robinson and Kolb, 2004) in which animals received stimulant drugs (amphetamine, cocaine, methylphenidate, or nicotine) before placement in complex environments (e.g., Kolb et al., 2003).

Complex environments typically produce extensive increases in dendritic arborization and spine density, but these increases are completely blocked by the earlier exposure to stimulants. An obvious question is whether complex housing would alter the drug effects. It does. Animals given several months of complex-housing experience before they receive repeated doses of nicotine show a much-reduced response to the drug. Thus, one reason for individual differences in susceptibility to drug addiction may likely be related to predrug experiences.

One common experience of everyday life is stress. It is known to produce striking changes in dendritic morphology and neurogenesis (see a review by McEwen, 2007). It is not surprising then to find that stress interacts with other experience-dependent changes related to drugs, brain injury, complex housing, and so on.

Principle 6: Plasticity is age-dependent.

A universal truism about growing older is that learning new motor tasks becomes more difficult. It is possible to learn to play tennis well at age 40, but no tennis newbie this age is going to win Wimbledon. Thus, the brain's plasticity changes in response to similar experiences across the life span. One reason is that similar experiences trigger different plastic responses at different ages. For example, when the adolescent brain is shedding synapses, we might anticipate that learning a complex skill like tennis would induce a different plastic change than in a middle-aged brain that is no longer rapidly pruning.

Another reason for age-related differences in plasticity is that metaplastic changes depend upon previous experience. Once the brain has been changed by nicotine, for instance, it will likely respond to other experiences differently later in life. We also saw in Section 23.6 that injury at different ages leads to differing plastic changes, and we shall see next that this is true not only during development but in adulthood as well.

Principle 7: Plastic changes are time-dependent.

Synaptic changes may be stable or may change over time. For example, rats placed in complex environments show increased dendritic length in medial prefrontal cortex after 4 days of complex housing, but the increase is transient: it has disappeared after 14 days. In contrast, sensory cortex shows no obvious signs of change after 4 days but exhibits clear and seemingly permanent changes after 14 days (Comeau et al., 2010). These changing patterns of synaptic organization are likely related to changes in gene expression. For example, Rampon and colleagues (2000) found that different sets of genes are expressed either acutely or chronically in response to complex housing.

Principle 8: Plasticity is related to an experience's relevance to the animal.

Some behaviors can be learned in just one trial; others may seem impossible to learn. Food aversions, for example, can be related to a single incidence of illness, a phenomenon called *taste aversion learning*. If we encounter a food with a novel flavor that we pair with illness, we have an immediate and persistent aversion to the taste. This type of learning is obviously relevant to our survival, and the brain is clearly prepared to make the taste–illness association. In contrast, learning the theory of relativity can be painfully slow, reflecting the separation between the material and its relevance to our well-being.

Principle 9: Plasticity is related to the intensity or frequency of experiences.

Some learning can occur in a single trial, but most learning is much slower and requires multiple exposures to experiences. Slower behavioral change likely reflects a slow plastic change as well. It is often said that becoming an expert at something requires 1 million repetitions, although experimental evidence shows that even smaller numbers of repetitions can make a big difference. For example, when rats are given amphetamine daily with differing repetitions (e.g., 0, 2, 8, 20, 40) there is an escalating increase in the size of the plastic changes in prefrontal neurons with added doses (e.g., Kolb et al., 2003). The increase is not linear but rather gets smaller with repeated doses, just as our improvement in learning a new game such as tennis is relatively rapid in the beginning but slows over time.

Principle 10: Plasticity can be maladaptive.

We have emphasized the positive side of plastic changes in the brain. But plastic changes can have a dark side. For example, exposure to mind-altering drugs such as amphetamine, cocaine, nicotine, and morphine produce alterations in dendritic length and spine density, the details of the changes varying with the particular drug (see a review by Robinson and Kolb, 2004).

Some maladaptive behaviors of drug addicts have been proposed to result from drug-related changes in prefrontal morphology. After all, drug addicts have many behavioral symptoms reminiscent of frontal-lobe-injured people. Other examples of plasticity gone awry include the development of pathological pain, pathological response to sickness, epilepsy, and dementia.

Changes in brain maps can also be maladaptive. Focal hand dystonia, the loss of motor control of one or more digits, can result from repetitive synchronous movements of the digits, such as those made by musicians in a lifetime of playing. Thomas Elbert and his colleagues (2001) studied the somatosensory maps of musicians with focal hand dystonia and found that they contained smaller-than-normal distances between the representations of the digits. Presumably, the musical training inadvertently caused the mapped representations of the digits to fuse. A logical extrapolation of this finding is that dystonia should be treatable by training affected persons to make independent asynchronous finger movements. Indeed, Victor Candia and his colleagues (1999) found it to be the case.

◎ 25.2 Can Plasticity Support Functional Recovery After Injury?

Clinical neurologists have long known that some recovery of function is possible after injury to the nervous system, but the nature and mechanisms of the mediating processes remain poorly understood. Significant here is the lack of a generally accepted definition of what constitutes "recovery." The word could mean a complete return of function, a marked improvement in function, or indeed any degree of improvement. Another problem is lack of knowledge concerning what plastic changes might take place in the nervous system after injury. Knowing the nature of these changes will influence how we conceptualize processes related to recovery. Let us explore these problems briefly before considering brain plasticity and behavior after injury.

Compensation Compared with Recovery

We like to call the question of compensation "the problem of the three-legged cat." When cats are struck by automobiles, they commonly suffer severe injury to a back leg. The usual veterinary treatment is to remove the affected leg. Initially, the cats have a great deal of difficulty getting around, leading their owners to wonder, in despair, whether the cats would not be better off dead. Fortunately, cats are resilient: within a few weeks, they seem as agile as before the amputation. This restoration of mobility is often so complete that an observer may not even realize that a leg is missing. The cat has regained lost functions but has not recovered its lost leg. Rather, the cat has compensated for its difficulties and developed new behavioral strategies for locomoting through the world.

Many would argue that that is exactly what happens after brain injury. People do not actually recover lost behaviors or capacities; instead, they develop a new way of functioning to compensate. Consider a case that we have already encountered. In Section 13.4 we encountered B.K., who had a stroke that left him with a left-upper-field defect in which one-quarter of the fovea was devoid of pattern vision.

B.K. was initially unable to read and was seriously impaired at recognizing faces. With the passage of time, he regained both these abilities, but not because his lost visual functions were somehow magically restored. Instead, B.K. learned to direct his vision so that parts of words that once disappeared into the scotoma are now captured in the lower visual fields. Similarly, when looking at a face, he directs his gaze to the person's right eye, a shift that places most of the face in the functioning part of his visual field and allows him to recognize the person. It is important to note that B.K. did not set out consciously to learn these strategies. They developed spontaneously. Thus, although he had "recovered" the ability to read and recognize faces, the original behaviors did not return.

Is all post-brain-injury improvement compensation, or do some improvements actually constitute functional restitution? As stated in Section 23.6, some functional recovery is clearly possible in the infant brain, the best example being the partial return of language functions after left hemispherectomy. But even this "recovery" is not complete; it includes compensation in the sense that the right hemisphere now controls talking, a function that develops at the expense of some other, typical right-hemisphere functions. The extreme view is that actual restitution of function is possible only if the injured brain can be replaced and stimulated to function like the original brain—a tall order that, in the near future, seems an unlikely option for the adult brain.

A goal for those studying rehabilitation, therefore, is finding ways of stimulating plastic responses in the brain to provide for the best possible compensation.

We have seen, for example, that cortical maps can change in response to experience, including amputation. Is it not reasonable, then, to suppose that if the brain itself is injured, there may be a way to encourage its maps to reorganize? However, we might find that plastic changes after cerebral injury could actually make functional outcome worse.

Consider a hypothetical example in which, instead of a limb being amputated, the cortical representation of a limb was damaged by stroke (which could be thought of as "amputation" of the arm representation in the brain). If the arm representation were to reappear in the face area, the person's arm movements might improve, but his or her facial movements could be compromised. If such a change interfered with speech, the problem would not be trivial. Fortunately, deleterious effects of plastic changes are not common.

What Happens When a Brain Is Injured?

Although we may be able to point to a specific immediate cause of brain injury (stroke is such a cause), the damage that is then wrought on the brain is not the result of a single causative event. Rather, a cascade of cellular events following on the initial event can seriously compromise not only the injured part of the brain but other brain regions as well. Consider what happens after a stroke when the blood supply to one of the cerebral arteries is interrupted.

The lack of blood, called *ischemia*, results in a sequence of events that progresses even if blood flow is restored. In the first seconds to minutes, as illustrated in **Figure 25.7**, changes occur in the ionic balance of the affected regions, including changes in pH and properties of the cell membrane. These ionic changes result in a variety of pathological events, such as the release of massive amounts of glutamate and the prolonged opening of calcium channels. The open calcium channels in turn allow toxic levels of calcium to enter the cell, not only producing direct toxic effects but also instigating various second-messenger pathways that can prove harmful to the neurons.

In the ensuing minutes to hours, mRNA is stimulated, altering the production of proteins in the neurons and possibly proving toxic to the cells. Next, brain tissues become inflamed and swollen, threatening cellular integrity far removed from the site of injury. Finally, a form of neural shock—Constantin von Monakow called it **diaschisis**—occurs. As von Monakow (1960) noted, after the brain is injured, not only are local neural tissue and its function lost but areas related to the damaged region also undergo a sudden withdrawal of excitation or inhibition. Such sudden changes in input can lead to temporary loss of function, both in areas adjacent to an injury and in regions that may be quite distant.

Stroke may also be followed by changes in metabolism or in glucose utilization of the injured hemisphere or in both—changes that may persist for days. Like diaschisis, these metabolic changes can severely affect the functioning of otherwise healthy tissue. After a cortical stroke, for example, metabolic rate throughout the rest of the hemisphere has been shown to decrease by about 25 percent.

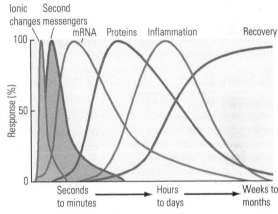

Figure 25.7 ▲

Results of Ischemia The cascade of changes taking place after a stroke. In the first seconds to minutes, ionic changes are followed by changes in second messengers and RNA production. Changes in protein production and inflammation follow, then slowly resolve in hours to days. Recovery follows and takes weeks to months or years.

Treatments for cerebral injury are directed at various targets in the post-injury cascade. For example, *neuroprotectant* drugs can block calcium channels or prevent ionic imbalance, possibly protecting neurons from the cascade of toxic events that follow an ischemic episode. Other drugs can reduce swelling or enhance metabolic activity. The effects of neuroprotectants and anti-inflammatory drugs are quite different from the effect of treatments aimed at stimulating plasticity and functional compensation.

◎ 25.3 Examples of Functional Restitution

The return of function is seldom sudden. An examination of the stages of functional restitution and associated behaviors often reveals a slow reemergence that resembles the sequence of developmental stages in infants. We consider two common examples of functional restoration after cortical stroke: recovery of movement and of language. We then examine some characteristics of functional improvement in two particular populations: soldiers with head injuries and neurosurgical cases. Finally, we look at prospects for patients returning to work and having a "normal" life after cerebral injury.

Recovery from Motor-Cortex Damage

Tom Twitchell (1951) described recovery from *hemiplegia* (paralysis on the side of the body contralateral to the injury) produced by thrombosis, embolism, or stroke of the middle cerebral artery in humans. The hemiplegia appeared immediately after the damage occurred, marked by complete flaccidity of the muscles and loss of all reflexive and voluntary movements. The recovery sequence closely parallels the development of reaching and of the grasp response Twitchell (1965) described in infants.

Recovery took place over a period of days or weeks and followed an orderly sequence: (1) return of reflexes; (2) development of rigidity; (3) grasping facilitated by or occurring as part of other movements; and (4) development of voluntary grasping, which entailed recovery of movement sequentially in the shoulder, elbow, wrist, and hand—first in the flexor musculature and then in the extensor musculature (review Figure 9.20). Voluntary grasping continued to improve until independent finger movements were well developed. Complete recovery of arm use, when it occurred, appeared between 23 and 40 days after the lesion. About 30 percent of patients reached this last stage of recovery; the others showed arrested recovery at one of the preceding stages.

Recovery from Aphasia

Andrew Kertesz (1979) reviewed the prospects of recovery from aphasia, using the case histories of his own patients as examples. **Figure 25.8** graphs the recovery of a typical patient

◎ **Figure 25.8** ▼

Recovery from Aphasia
Initial deficits and recovery in stroke patients with different language disorders and in a post-trauma patient. Each line is a representative patient. (Data source: Kertesz, 1979.)

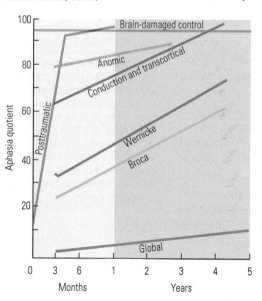

from each of his subgroups. (The "aphasia quotients" used on the graph's *y* axis were derived from the patients' scores on the Western Aphasia Battery, which tests spontaneous speech content, fluency, comprehension, repetition, and so forth.) Kertesz made the following generalizations:

1. Posttrauma (head-injury) patients showed the most rapid and often almost complete recovery, whereas recovery in stroke patients was less pronounced and in some groups, almost absent.

2. Initial deficits were least severe in *anomic* patients (people who are unable to generate the names for common objects) and most severe in global aphasics, with intermediate severity seen in other groups. The actual rate of recovery, given initial impairments, was often quite similar in all groups.

3. When recovery occurred, patients tended to progress to one of the other stages, but recovery usually stopped in those with anomic aphasia.

4. Most recovery took place in the first 3 months (illustrated only for the posttrauma patient in Figure 25.8), with some additional recovery over the next 6 months and less in the 6 months following. Thereafter, there was little or no recovery.

5. Some evidence pointed to younger patients showing better recovery; the effects of intelligence, occupation, and sex in those patients, if present, were slight.

6. The language components most resistant to brain damage were naming, oral imitation, comprehension of nouns, and yes–no responses—functions that may be partly mediated by the right hemisphere.

Recovery from Traumatic Lesions

Hans-Leukas Teuber (1975) described the deficits of wounded war veterans as assessed in tests given 1 week after each had an open head injury and again 20 years later. These patients are excellent candidates for study: they underwent standardized testing after induction into the army, they were young at the time of injury, the immediate aftermath of the injury is documented, and the kind and extent of recovery can be documented through prolonged follow-up examinations by veterans' services. Teuber's results, summarized in **Figure 25.9**,

⊚ Figure 25.9 ◄

Recovery from Brain Trauma Estimated improvement, based on initial examination (no later than 1 week after injury) and follow-up examination (20 years later), for some body regions (extremities, sides of face) for which symptoms were recorded (reflex changes, paralysis, weakness) in the motor system; for noted sensory losses in the somatosensory system; for the visual field (diminution in number of quadrants known to be affected); and for symptoms interpreted as dysphasia. Note the advantage of younger age at the time of wounding. (Data source: Teuber, H.-L. Recovery of function after brain injury in man. In Outcome of Severe Damage to the Nervous System: Ciba Foundation Symposium 34. Amsterdam: Elsevier North-Holland, 1975. Figs. 10 & 11, pp. 176–177.)

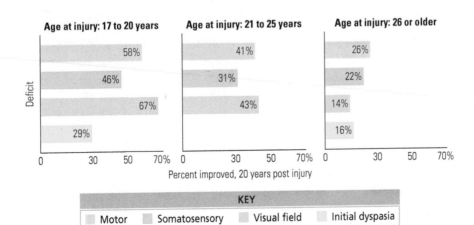

KEY

Motor   Somatosensory   Visual field   Initial dyspasia

reveal, on average, that 42 percent of these veterans showed some recovery from motor defects, 36 percent showed some recovery from somatosensory defects, 43 percent showed some recovery from visual defects, and 24 percent showed some recovery from initial dysphasia.

Two comments about Teuber's analysis are germane. First, more than 50 percent of this patient population showed no recovery at all, and the failure of more than 75 percent to show recovery from dysphasia is not encouraging. The latter percentage is in line with Alexander Luria's (1972) report that 66 percent of his dysphasic patients showed no recovery. Second, the usefulness of Teuber's analysis is limited, because the assessments are not quantitative: there is no estimate of the *degree* of recovery.

Jay Mohr and his coworkers (1980) undertook a study of a larger population, Vietnam War veterans. In general, their results are consistent with Teuber's, in that a great deal of recovery of function is seen subsequent to penetrating brain injury. In fact, Mohr reports more-extensive recovery from aphasia (34 percent) than does Teuber, and reports that recovery continued for years after injury.

More recently, Josef Zihl and Yves von Cramon (1986) reported that practice in locating lights led to an increase in the visual field of partly blind patients, an improvement that would not have taken place without the practice. What effect specific therapy might have had on the patients reported in the veteran studies is unknown.

Recovery from Surgical Lesions

Surgery to remove brain tumors or relieve epilepsy often damages parts of the brain that were intact and functional before the operation. Assessment tests have been administered to patients within days of tumor surgery and as long as 20 years after surgery to evaluate such damage and gauge recovery. Unfortunately, recovery seems to have been so infrequent that the breakdown of data at different test–retest intervals is not reported. **Table 25.3** summarizes results from some studies in which tests were given a few days before surgery, within 20 days after surgery, and 1 to 20 years after surgery. After dorsolateral frontal lesions, no recovery occurred in card sorting; after right temporal lesions, no recovery in recall of the Rey figure (see Figure

Table 25.3 Performance on neuropsychological tests by patients with cortical lesions

Test	Lesion	Preop	Postop	Follow-up	Control	Reference
Card-sorting categories	Frontal	3.3	1.4	1.3	4.6	Milner, 1963
Card-sorting errors	Frontal	54.9	73.2	78.2	37.7	Milner, 1963
Rey-figure copy score	Right temporal	31.2	30.6	29.8	34.9	Taylor, 1969
Rey-figure recall score	Right temporal	15.4	15.3	13.8	24.2	Taylor, 1969
Finger-position sense	Central					
Incidence of deficit (%)						
Ipsilateral		24.0	14.0	6.0	—	Taylor, 1969
Contralateral		36.0	43.0	65.0	—	Taylor, 1969
Arm-movement copying	Left parietal		73.0	75.8	90.2	Kolb and Milner, 1981

15.16C); and after parietal lesions, no recovery in finger-position sense or arm-movement copying.

The finding of no recovery is also reported in some other studies. Marilyn Jones-Gotman and Brenda Milner (1977) tested patient groups on spontaneous drawing tasks within 2 weeks of surgery and 1 or more years later. The subjects were told to draw as many unnameable objects as they could within 5 minutes (see Figure 16.9). Although all patient groups showed some reduction in performance level relative to control groups, patients with right frontal lesions were the most impaired, and there were no differences in performance between patients tested shortly after surgery and those tested more than a year later.

There also seems to be little or no recovery in memory after bilateral medial-temporal-lobe removal. In a 14-year follow-up, Milner and her colleagues (1968) reported that the amnesic patient H.M., profiled in Chapter 18, had a presurgical IQ score of 104, a 2-year-follow-up score of 112, and a 9-year-follow-up of 118. Yet despite this improvement in intelligence test score, H.M.'s anterograde amnesia remained essentially unchanged for the rest of his life.

In some studies of patients with longstanding lesions, a degree of recovery has been noted on some tests. Milner reported in 1975 that patients with left temporal lesions had preoperative memory scores of 12, early postoperative scores of 4.4, and 5- to 20-year-follow-up scores of 8. This improvement is significant. Similarly, Colin Blakemore and Murray Falconer (1967) studied paired-associates learning in 86 temporal-lobectomy patients for as long as 10 years after surgery. They found that the deficit lasted for 2 to 3 years, after which they saw progressive recovery, provided the patients were young.

One explanation for improved memory is illustrated in a study by Marilyn Jones (1974), who demonstrated substantial memory improvement in left-temporal-lobe patients taught to use imagery (for example, they imagine an elephant with a bouquet of flowers in its trunk for the associate word pair "bouquet–elephant"). Hence, recovery could be due to developing alternative memory strategies. Another possibility is that the temporal cortex must have rather special properties that allow rapid memory storage. Those properties probably also make it especially prone to epilepsy. If any temporal cortex remains intact, it possibly retains a special capacity for plasticity uncharacteristic of other brain areas.

Return to Daily Life

A person's capacity to work and earn a living clearly depends on many behavioral abilities and configurations of abilities. Brain damage may affect some more than others, but people can compensate in many ways. For example, when gainful employment is used as a measure of recovery, as was done for veterans injured in the Korean War, the resulting recovery rates are quite high: approximately 80 percent (Dresser et al., 1973). This is the highest rate of any we have found in the literature and strongly suggests that some factor, such as behavioral compensation, is operating.

Such a high recovery rate does not minimize the difficulties of the 20 percent who were not employed. Furthermore, it does not take into consideration the quality of employment. In fact, work may not be a sensitive index of recovery. For example, of 54 patients with closed head injuries, 48 were back at work within 2 years, but many were restricted in their work activity and reported that they had not regained their full working capacity (Oddy and Humphrey, 1980).

Other aspects of the veterans' lives also were restricted because these patients had not fully resumed their leisure activities and social contacts. Interestingly, of all social relations aspects, those with siblings declined most. The researchers emphasized that therapy should be directed not only toward returning to work but also toward pursuing leisure activities and social relations.

One way to examine the chronic effects of brain damage and how those affected cope is to study the self-reports of people who have brain damage. Generally, little attention is given to self-reports, but they can provide valuable insight into questions of recovery. Fredrick Linge, a clinical psychologist, described the changes he underwent after brain damage in an automobile accident.

Linge was in a coma for the first week after the accident and was not expected to recover significantly. Nevertheless, he did succeed in returning to a demanding clinical practice about a year after his accident. Even so, he was changed by the brain damage and had to make lifestyle and work routine adjustments to cope. He describes his adjustments in the following way:

> In learning to live with my brain damage, I have found through trial and error that certain things help greatly and others hinder my coping. In order to learn and retain information best, I try to eliminate as many distractions as possible and concentrate all my mental energy on the task at hand. . . . In the past I enjoyed a rather chaotic life style, but I now find that I want "a place for everything and everything in its place." When remembering is difficult, order and habit make the minutiae of daily living much easier.
>
> I cannot cope with anger as well as I was able to do before my accident. . . . [O]nce I become angry, I find it impossible to "put the brakes on" and I attribute this directly to my brain damage. It is extremely frightening to me to find myself in this state, and I still have not worked out a truly satisfactory solution, except insofar as I try to avoid anger-provoking situations or try to deal with them before they become too provoking.
>
> My one-track mind seems to help me to take each day as it comes without excessive worry and to enjoy the simple things of life in a way that I never did before. As well, I seem to be a more effective therapist, since I stick to the basic issues at hand and have more empathy with others than I did previously. (Linge, 1980, pp. 6–7)

Linge's self-report shows that assessments of recovery cannot be limited to measures such as reemployment or even levels of renewed social contacts. Such measures may fail to indicate the ways in which a person has changed and the coping mechanisms that he or she has learned to employ. Linge was a professional psychologist who lived in a social milieu in which people were willing to help him reestablish himself. Many people do not have such extensive support systems and resources and will have a much more difficult recovery. Linge's comments also demonstrate that the brain-damaged person must change not only the external environment but the internal environment as well.

◎ 25.4 Research on Plasticity in the Injured Brain

Just as plasticity in the healthy brain can be investigated at different levels, so too can plasticity in the injured brain. To date, most work has focused on changes in maps, determined either by functional imaging or by brain stimulation. We consider each method in turn.

Functional Imaging After Cerebral Injury

Functional changes observed after stroke provide an excellent window into cerebral plasticity. If patients can recover from stroke despite having lost significant cortical areas, then we can conclude that some type of change has taken place in the remaining parts of the brain. Functional-imaging techniques, especially PET, fMRI, and TMS, can be used repeatedly in the weeks and months after stroke to document changes in cerebral activation that might correlate with functional improvement. Several reviews of such studies have led us to the following conclusions (see especially reviews by Johansson, 2012, and Rijntjes and Weiller, 2002):

1. **If the primary sensorimotor cortex survives a stroke, some functional improvement is likely with the passage of time.** Even if hemiparesis immediately follows the stroke and the efferent fiber tracts may be damaged, thus causing the hemiparesis, the remaining cortex may yet become activated. Functional improvement is correlated with the appearance of this activation.

2. **Activation of motor areas during limb movements recruits cortical areas along the rim of cortical injury.** In addition, particular movements often activate larger areas of motor cortex. For example, hand or limb movements often activate regions of the face area, possibly because of intact pyramidal-tract fibers leaving the face area (see Figure 25.3).

3. **The motions of stroke patients activate much larger cortical areas, especially parietal and premotor areas, than do similar movements by controls.** These regions of activation are extended for both language and motor functions. The relation between recovery and activation is not always straightforward, however, as shown in the Snapshot on pages 718–719.

4. **Reorganization is not restricted to one hemisphere: similar changes take place bilaterally.** Thus, although performing a unilateral motor task largely activates only the contralateral cortex, the brains of stroke victims show a marked increase in bilateral activation. Increased activation in the contralateral hemisphere is especially notable in patients with language disturbances in which regions opposite the language areas (so-called homologous areas) show activation.

Using Imaging to Study Recovery

Nick Ward and Richard Frackiowiak (2006) used fMRI to study a large group of stroke patients and controls as they performed an isometric hand-grip task. The advantage of using such a task is that all subjects and participants were capable of doing it, although their abilities varied considerably. The experiments aimed to answer two questions:

1. Does the task-related activation pattern differ in controls and stroke patients?

2. Do the degree of task-related brain activation and the outcome correlate?

Based on the existing literature, the obvious expectation was that patients with better recovery would show greater recruitment of those perilesional regions presumed to assist in the recovery. The results were surprisingly different.

The 20 stroke patients all had cortical infarcts, but none extended into M1. Hand-grip activated a motor network of cortical and subcortical regions including motor cortex, premotor cortex, supplementary motor cortex, anterior cingulate cortex, and parietal cortex. About half of the patients showed overactivations of cortex relative to the control group. These novel activations were found not only in the expected motor regions but also in the prefrontal and insular cortex in the lesion hemisphere as well as in M1 and S1 in the contralateral hemisphere.

Curiously, when Ward and Frackowiak correlated fMRI activation and recovery, they found an inverse correlation in several brain regions, as shown in part A of the illustration. Especially apparent is that subjects with a poorer outcome had extensive activation in *both* hemispheres.

One explanation is that the patients with poorer recovery may have had infarcts that made direct access to M1 difficult, requiring the activation of less-efficient parallel pathways. In attempting to reconcile the results with previous studies by others who had found a positive correlation between activation and recovery, Ward and Frackowiak suggested that the measures of recovery might be the critical difference and emphasized the importance of *detailed* outcome measurements.

They then asked how brain activation might be related to recovery longitudinally. They performed repeated fMRIs over time in individual patients and correlated performance with outcome. As expected, a bilateral overactivation appeared in motor regions immediately after stroke, but as time passed, these activations lessened, and other regions began to show activation, as shown in part B of the illustration.

Ward and Frackowiak suggest that different mechanisms may facilitate recovery at different time points after stroke. Early on, any voluntary movement is associated with massive recruitment of motor areas, but with the

5. **Capacity for reorganization declines with increasing size of stroke and increasing age.** The relation to stroke size is likely due to the fact that the presence of incompletely damaged regions, such as Wernicke's area, is a good predictor of functional improvement. Recall that the severity of the initial deficit in aphasia correlates with later outcome (see Figure 25.8). Presumably, the extent of the initial deficit is related to the extent of injury.

6. **Variability among stroke victims is considerable.** Variability is probably related to differences in the degree of prestroke activations and is particularly true of language. People who show the greatest bilateral activation for language functions after stroke are probably those who already had some bilateral activation before the stroke, as with left-handers. Michel Rijntjes and Cornelius Weiller (2002) note that the extent of right-hemisphere activation during language tasks is highly variable and that the activation pattern in people who have exhibited recovery from Wernicke's aphasia is remarkably similar to the maximal areas of right-hemisphere activation seen in healthy brains.

passage of time, new learning of motor control will be related to the precise amount and site of the anatomical damage. This conclusion is supported by Ian Whishaw and his colleagues (e.g., Alaverdashvili et al., 2008), whose work with rat models suggests that recovery after

M1 damage is related to the animals' relearning the lost movements.

Alaverdashvili, M., A. Foroud, D. H. Lim, and I. Q. Whishaw. "Learned baduse" limits recovery of skilled reaching for food after forelimb motor cortex stroke in rats: A new analysis of the effect of gestures on success. *Behavioural Brain Research* 188:281–290, 2008.

Ward, N. S., and R. S. J. Frackowiak. The functional anatomy of cerebral reorganization after focal brain injury. *Journal of Physiology, Paris* 99:425–436, 2006.

(A)

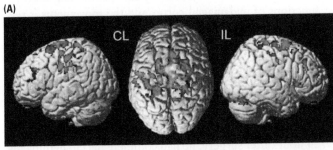

(B)

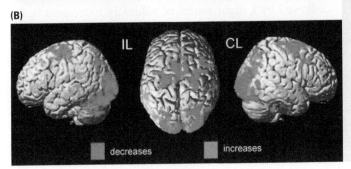

decreases   increases

(A) Brain regions in which a linear inverse correlation is observed between recovery and task-related fMRI brain activation across 20 patients. (Frontal lobes are at the top in the central image. CL, contralesional; IL, ipsilesional.) (B) Results of single-subject longitudinal analysis (over multiple sessions) examining for linear changes in task-related brain activations as a function of recovery. The patient had a left-side pontine infarct resulting in right hemiparesis. The results are rendered onto a canonical brain. Red areas represent recovery-related decreases in task-related activation, and green areas represent the equivalent recovery-related areas. (Ward, N. S., and S. J. Frackowiak. The functional anatomy of cerebral reorganization after focal brain injury. *Journal of Physiology, Paris* 99(4–6):425–436, 2006. © Elsevier.)

In conclusion, functional improvement after stroke corresponds to a change in functional organization of the remaining brain, as shown in functional-imaging studies. However, such studies are usually reported only for patients who show good recovery. Even so, these studies typically provide little detailed information about the treatments the patients might have received.

Physiological Mapping After Cerebral Injury

Randy Nudo and his coworkers (1997) mapped the hand and digit areas of the squirrel monkey motor cortex. When they subsequently removed a part of the digit area, use of the contralateral hand was reduced. When they remapped the motor cortex, the researchers found that the monkeys were unable to produce movements of the lower part of the arm, wrist, and digits, as illustrated in **Figure 25.10**. The hand area had disappeared from the cortical map, and only a representation of the stump of the upper arm remained.

They subjected additional animals to the same procedure, except that after surgery, they provided therapy for the affected limb. The good limb was bound

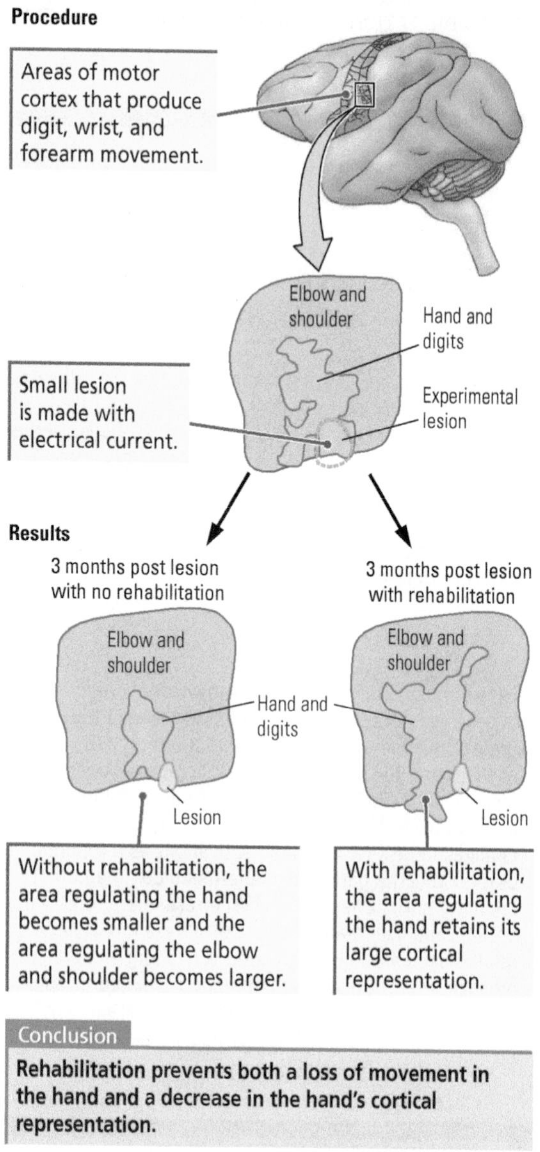

Areas of motor cortex that produce digit, wrist, and forearm movement.

Elbow and shoulder

Hand and digits

Small lesion is made with electrical current.

Experimental lesion

Results

3 months post lesion with no rehabilitation

Elbow and shoulder

Hand and digits

Lesion

Without rehabilitation, the area regulating the hand becomes smaller and the area regulating the elbow and shoulder becomes larger.

3 months post lesion with rehabilitation

Elbow and shoulder

Lesion

With rehabilitation, the area regulating the hand retains its large cortical representation.

Conclusion

Rehabilitation prevents both a loss of movement in the hand and a decrease in the hand's cortical representation.

Figure 25.10 ▲

Use It or Lose It (Information from Nudo et al., 1996.)

so that the monkey was forced to use the affected limb. When the researchers again examined the motor maps of these monkeys, the hand and digit area was present, except for the area that had been removed originally. Nevertheless, the therapy brought about some recovery of use in the digits represented by the missing area. Presumably, the cortical representations of the remaining digits mediated movements made by the digits that had lost their cortical representation.

The importance of therapy is central in the Nudo experiments. Therapy is necessary for maintaining both the functions of undamaged cortex and the movements it represents. Therapy can also promote compensation for affected body parts.

The form of plasticity Nudo and his coworkers described may explain recovery in the following case reported by Paul Bucy and his coworkers (1964). They studied a man whose pyramidal tract was sectioned in the lower brainstem as a treatment for involuntary movements. During the first 24 hours after surgery, he had complete flaccid hemiplegia, followed by a slight return of voluntary movement in his extremities. By the tenth day, he could stand alone and walk with assistance. By the twenty-fourth day, he could walk unaided. Within 7 months, maximum recovery seemed to have been reached, and he could move his feet, hands, fingers, and toes with only slight impairment.

At autopsy 2½ years later, about 17 percent of his pyramidal tract fibers were found to be intact. The recovery of his ability to move his toes and fingers seems attributable to that remaining 17 percent, which did the job formerly done by the entire tract. We venture that if the man had been discouraged from using the afflicted limbs, his recovery would have been lessened.

◎ 25.5 Variables Affecting Recovery

In addition to lesion size, several other variables affect the rate of recovery from brain damage. Yet these variables, including age, sex, handedness, intelligence, and personality, are not fully discussed in many papers: measurements are difficult to make; many patient groups are small, which lessens the validity of any statistics derived from them; or a particular researcher simply may not consider them important. Overall, recovery from brain damage seems likely to be best if the patient is a young, intelligent, optimistic, left-handed female.

Youth is among the easier variables to measure. Teuber and his coworkers (1975) found that on a number of tests, recovery from head injuries by soldiers is greater in the 17-to-20 age group than in those in the 21-to-25 age group, which in turn is greater than in the 26+ age group (see Figure 25.9). Milner (1975) reported that patients older than 40 who have removals near the posterior temporal speech zone in the left hemisphere show less recovery than do younger patients. But note that age does not always appear significant in studies of recovery, as reported by Kertesz (1979).

The fact that age is a contributing factor to the onset of many kinds of brain damage complicates analyses of age effects. Strokes and other brain abnormalities are common in older people, who are more likely in any case to be declining in motor and cognitive function owing to normal aging processes. Thus, recovery may tend to be obscured by aging.

Handedness and sex, both for much the same reason, may influence the outcome of brain damage. Recall from Section 12.2 that several theories argue that female and male brains differ in both anatomy and functional organization, with imaging studies revealing less functional lateralization in the female. Considering the imaging evidence in brain-injured patients discussed earlier, if females have more bilateral functional activation, then they should show more functional recovery. Likewise, familial left-handers appear to be less lateralized in function than right-handers, again providing an advantage for recruiting undamaged regions after brain injury.

Highly intelligent and, usually, well-educated people are generally believed to have better recovery than are those with lower intelligence. There is no clear reason for this difference, although whatever neural properties allow for higher intelligence may also provide an advantage after injury. People of higher intelligence may have more-plastic brains and thus respond better to injury—a possibility that is not easy to prove. Alternatively, people of higher fluid intelligence (Section 16.4) may be able to generate more strategies to compensate for injury than less-intelligent people can.

Although a very intelligent person's ultimate recovery may be excellent in relation to the recovery of others, the actual residual deficit may be the same simply because the very intelligent person typically would function at a higher level. Thus, in our experience, highly intelligent people generally complain more than others about the negative effects of residual deficits on quality of life.

The role of personality in recovery is difficult to evaluate, but optimistic, extroverted, and easygoing people are widely thought to have a better prognosis after brain injury. One reason could be that people who are more optimistic about recovering are more likely to comply with rehabilitation programs. Unfortunately, brain damage may have a negative influence on personality. For example, patients may develop postinjury depression and as a result would be expected to show poor, or at least slow, recovery until the depression is treated. Indeed, stroke patients are now commonly prescribed antidepressants such as SSRIs, which are believed to aid in recovery.

(A) Male brain

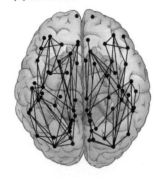

(B) Female brain

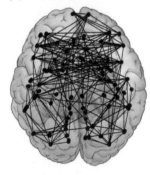

▲ DTI analysis of brain networks, shown in these dorsal views, shows greater intrahemispheric connections in males (A) and greater interhemispheric connections in females (B). (Ingalhalikar, M., A. Smith, D. Parker, T. D. Satterthwaite, M. A. Elliott, K. Ruparel, H. Hakonarson, R. E. Gur, R. C. Gur, and R. Verma. Sex differences in the structural connectome of the human brain. *Proceedings of the National Academy of Sciences U.S.A.* 111: 823–828, 2013, Figure 2.)

⊚ 25.6 Therapeutic Approaches to Recovery After Brain Damage

We conclude by reviewing five major experimental therapeutic approaches to recovery following brain damage:

1. Rehabilitation procedures consist of a variety of experiential, behavioral, and psychological therapies.

2. Pharmacological therapies are intended to promote recovery in the immediate postsurgery period.

3. Brain stimulation increases brain activity.

4. Brain-tissue transplants and stem-cell-induction techniques are being developed in the hope of restoring healthy brain function.

5. Diet provides the building blocks for plastic changes.

Rehabilitation procedures are used widely, with mixed results; drug therapy, stimulation, implantation techniques, and diet are moving past the animal-experimentation stage into preliminary clinical trials.

Rehabilitation

It would seem logical that people with brain injuries should be placed in some sort of rehabilitation program. Surprisingly, however, neuroscientists as yet have little information concerning the value of different kinds of rehabilitation, the optimal timing for initiating a program, or even the optimal duration of rehabilitative therapy. Although both speech and physical therapies are often assumed to be effective, the role of any specific therapy—the kinds of changes that it brings about and how or why they take place—is a matter of debate (see reviews by Teasell et al., 2009, and by Nahum et al., 2013).

Consider, for example, that patients undergoing speech therapy not only receive speech training but also have daily contact with a therapist. Much of this interaction is social and not strictly related to language. The importance of such stimulation cannot be overstated. For example, evidence is growing that patients who are placed in a dedicated stroke unit, rather than treated as outpatients, are likely to have a better outcome. In a dedicated unit, a variety of professional rehabilitation therapists work together and provide patients with social stimulation for much of the waking day.

Results of studies of laboratory animals consistently show that the single most successful treatment strategy for optimizing functional recovery is placing animals in complex, stimulating environments. But far from suggesting that rehabilitation therapies are not useful, these results reinforce that specific types of training can alter motor maps. Consider three more examples: movement therapy, tactile stimulation, and cognitive rehabilitation.

Movement Therapy

Based on the observation that after stroke, many patients have initial hemiparesis; develop strategies to use the unimpaired opposite limb; and in so doing, fail to attempt to use the impaired limb, Edward Taub and his colleagues developed **constraint-induced movement therapy** (Unwatte & Taub, 2013). The goal of this therapy, which is accomplished by placing the unaffected limb in a sling and forcing the patient to perform daily activities with the impaired limb, is to induce patients to use the affected limb for several hours a day for a period of weeks.

Patients are also given various tasks to practice with the affected limb—tasks such as picking up objects or turning the pages of magazines. Constraint-induced therapy is effective in stimulating sometimes-dramatic improvement in using the affected limb. An explanation for the improvement is that the motor training stimulates plastic changes in the brain, leading to an enlargement of the motor representation of the affected arm and hand.

Joachim Leipert and colleagues (2005) measured this increase by using TMS both before and after 12 days of constraint-induced therapy. They found that the training stimulated a dramatic increase in the cortical area representing the paretic hand (a 50 percent increase in map size after 12 days of training and still present 6 months later). The location of the map expansion varied from patient to patient, presumably because the precise area of injury varied from person to person. Parallel studies conducted on monkeys by Nudo's group yielded similar results (see Figure 25.10).

Tactile Stimulation

Tactile stimulation, either as massage or lighter stimulation, has the potential to offer patients significant benefits. Physiotherapists have long used massage in treating brain-injured patients, but few studies have examined its efficacy. However, laboratory studies of both adult and infant cortically injured rats record benefits from tactile stimulation using light touch with a fine brush several times daily for 15 minutes for 2 to 3 weeks after the brain injury (e.g., Gibb et al., 2010; Kolb and Gibb, 2010). The stimulation is correlated with changes in dendritic length or spine density in cortex adjacent to the injuries. The mechanism is proposed to be enhanced release of neurotrophic factors, such as fibroblast growth factor-2 (FGF-2), by the skin. Such factors pass through the blood–brain barrier and stimulate FGF-2 receptors in the brain.

Cognitive Rehabilitation

The most critical problems faced by many brain-injured people are not strictly sensory or motor but rather are more-complex cognitive problems, such as memory disturbances or spatial disorientation. These patients need cognitive rehabilitation, and a logical place to find it is the burgeoning field of cognitive training in aging adults without brain injury. Nori Jacoby and Merav Ahissar (2013) review this literature and conclude that although people improve with training, suggesting significant plasticity in the older brain, the chronic effects are generally mild and with limited generality to novel tasks (but see Merzenich, 2013).

Nonetheless, interest in improving such training programs is intense, as reviewed by Nahum and colleagues (2013) and Van Vleet and DeGutis (2013). Treating patients in hospitals is expensive, triggering a push for outpatient programs, often called "community neurorehabilitation" (see review by Chard, 2006). Even though the long-term benefits remain poorly understood, several cognitive programs are available for brain-injured adults (see Prigatano, 2001; Wilson, 2011).

A broader matter, however, is the difficulty of coping with residual cognitive deficits outside the clinic. For example, a person with spatial disorientation might benefit somewhat from practicing various paper-and-pencil tasks, but in the end, the patient may continue to struggle with the real-world problem of finding his or her way home. Thus, therapy for brain damage often requires creativity and initiative on the part of the therapist trying to develop techniques that are relevant to an individual patient.

We were once asked to recommend a therapy for a depressed motorcycle racer who had suffered extensive brain damage after crashing a hang glider. We half-seriously suggested a tricycle, which his caregivers then had constructed for him. His attitude improved dramatically, and he was soon racing the tricycle around the hospital grounds and taking trips to town. The exercise and attitude change helped him tackle other tasks that furthered his recovery.

Substitution systems may be useful for some patients. For example, visual information can be recorded with a video camera and transformed by computer into a tactile message presented on the skin as a partial substitute for vision. Various machines, especially computers, can be used to perform specific tasks. For patients with memory problems, a system called SenseCam designed by Microsoft for other applications can prove beneficial.

The procedure involves wearing a small camera on a lanyard around the neck. The camera automatically takes a photo at fixed time periods, say, every 20 minutes. At the end of the day, the wearer downloads the photos to a computer and reviews the day. Silva and colleagues (2013) report not only that participants have improved memory for the day's events but that the improvement also generalizes to other neuropsychological tests of memory. As this technology moves into the clinic, it promises significant benefits for people with brain injuries that impair memory.

▲ SenseCam (Source: Microsoft.)

Other Behavioral Therapies

Robotic devices (e.g., Hidler et al., 2009); behavioral shaping; bilateral arm training (Lin et al., 2010); body weight–supported treadmill training (Dobkin et al., 2006; Duncan et al., 2007); task-oriented physical therapy (Jonsdottir et al., 2010); and music therapy (Schneider et al., 2007) have also proven to be effective treatments. The reasons for their effectiveness are unknown, but presumably such techniques lead to synaptic changes that may be identified in mapping studies using noninvasive imaging or *transcortical direct current stimulation* (tDCS). Indeed, a study by Amengual and colleagues (2013) used music-supported therapy followed by TMS and found improved motor functions correlated with plastic changes in the form of increased cortical excitability following the training.

Pharmacological Therapies

Interest in using pharmacological therapies for ameliorating the effects of brain damage is longstanding. The general idea is to use compounds that facilitate plastic changes in the brain. For example, psychoactive drugs such as amphetamine, nicotine, and marijuana stimulate changes in cortical and subcortical circuits in the healthy brain.

The hope is that using such compounds in the injured brain can stimulate synaptic changes that might facilitate functional recovery (see review by Feeney, 1997). Research results suggest that the rate of recovery can be increased if pharmacological treatments and experience are combined shortly after brain damage. The success of such treatments in the laboratory has led to clinical trials using amphetamine with stroke patients—with mixed results. A key factor is lesion size, because stimulants are most effective in cases of restricted injuries. Even so, many clinical trials have focused on patients with larger lesions, but with limited success.

Other types of pharmacotherapies take advantage of compounds that enhance axonal sprouting after cerebral injury. The injured brain, however, spontaneously produces endogenous compounds—one is called Nogo-A—that inhibit axon sprouting and regeneration and synapse formation, (for a review, see Kempf and Schwab, 2013). Administering an antibody to Nogo-A stimulates axon generation and increased synaptogenesis in cortical pyramidal neurons, which is correlated with functional recovery in studies of both rats and monkeys (e.g., Hamadjida et al., 2012). Because Nogo-A is an endogenous molecule found in oligodendrocytes and some neurons, it is reasonable to suspect that its expression might be affected by other therapies, such as constraint-induced therapy, and this appears to be the case (e.g., Zhao et al., 2013).

Electrical Stimulation

One effect of brain injury is reduced activity in perilesional regions. Several strategies pioneered in the early 2000s include increasing blood pressure (Hillis, 2007); low-level electrical stimulation (Teskey et al., 2003); and TMS (Rauschecker et al., 2002). All these techniques would seem to carry the risk of complications, but preliminary clinical trials have proved very promising and without complication.

Vagus nerve stimulation provides a novel form of electrical stimulation. Low-level vagal stimulation releases acetylcholine and norepinephrine. An advantage over direct drug administration is that vagus nerve stimulation can be precisely temporally controlled during, for example, different forms of behavioral therapy (see review by Hays et al., 2013). Vagus nerve stimulation has been shown to be a safe and approved method for managing intractable epilepsy and depression in more than 60,000 patients. Laboratory studies have shown vagal stimulation effective in enhancing memory and in treating stroke in rats, and this success is being translated into clinical trials to treat sensory, motor, and cognitive dysfunction in humans after brain injury.

Brain-Tissue Transplants and Stem-Cell Induction

The idea of transplanting neural tissue in mammals and the techniques for doing so date back more than a century. Yet until recently, the possibility that neural transplantation could have practical application was viewed as remote. In the 1980s, researchers discovered that if fetal tissue containing immature cells was extracted from particular brain regions and then inserted into the appropriate region of a recipient animal, the fetal tissue would grow and integrate into the host brain. Such a procedure would be impractical for repairing damage to a complex circuit such as the neocortex, but perhaps transplantation of specific cell types, such as dopaminergic cells from the brainstem, could benefit patients missing those cells—Parkinson patients, for example (see Chapter 6 opening Portrait).

More than 100 Parkinson patients have now received fetal stem-cell transplants. Improvements have been reported in some cases, but a large study by Curt Freed and his colleagues (2001) is not encouraging. By and large, the relief from symptoms has been minor or only short-lived. Perhaps the transplants do not grow sufficiently in the large human brain, are not adequately incorporated into brain circuitry, or are affected by the same disease process that is causing the original loss of dopamine cells.

Another approach to transplanting fetal tissue is to stimulate stem-cell growth within the host brain by using growth factors. Knowing that the brain is capable of making new neurons even in adulthood, researchers hypothesize that it ought to be possible to potentiate the production of new neurons after injury. If these new neurons can then be induced to migrate to the site of injury and integrate into that part of the brain, they may be able restore some level of functioning there.

Many studies have used a variety of growth factors to stimulate proliferation of neural stem cells after injury (for a review, see Dibajnia and Morshead, 2013). Many growth factors act directly on their respective receptors but may also mediate proliferation of precursor cells, although Dibajnia and Morshead point out that they may have indirect effects too, via modulation of the immune response, protection of neurons in the region around an injury, and the production of blood vessels.

Significant challenges block moving to the clinic with compounds to increase the proliferation of neural *precursor cells*—stem cells that are able to differentiate into neurons, astrocytes, or oligodendrocytes. Many of these compounds are powerful mitogens (chemicals that encourage cell division), leading to potentially harmful effects. Another challenge is the route of delivery of activation factors. Peripheral routes (intravenous, subcutaneous, intraperitoneal) may have widespread systemic effects, and the activation factors may not enter the brain in sufficient strength to produce the required number of neurons. Direct injection into brain tissue or ventricles is invasive and could lead to other complications. Additionally, there is the problem of the much greater distance that proliferating cells would have to migrate in humans compared to rodents. Finally, older brains have fewer neural precursor cells in the subventricular zone, likely making it more difficult to stimulate enough cells to make a difference. Clearly, transition to clinical use is some time away.

Diet

Predicting that vitamin and/or mineral supplements might facilitate recovery from brain injury is reasonable. Dietary choline supplementation in laboratory animals during the perinatal period leads to enhanced spatial memory in various spatial navigation tasks and increases the levels of nerve growth factor in the hippocampus and neocortex. Evidence is growing that vitamin/mineral supplements may improve mood and reduce aggression in adults and adolescents with various disorders and reduce social withdrawal and anger in children with ASD (for reviews, see Rucklidge and Kaplan, 2013, and Popper, 2014). Few studies of such supplements address recovery from brain injury, although several reports have shown enhanced recovery from early brain injuries in lab animals (e.g., Halliwell et al., 2009).

SUMMARY

25.1 Principles of Brain Plasticity

The brain is not a static organ: it changes constantly throughout life. Underlying this brain plasticity, neuroscientists have identified some basic principles. Here are 10:

1. Plasticity is common to all nervous systems, and the principles are conserved.

2. Plasticity can be analyzed at many levels.
3. The two general types of plasticity derive from experience.
4. Similar behavioral change can correlate with different plastic changes.
5. Experience-dependent changes interact.
6. Plasticity is age-dependent.

7. Plastic changes are time-dependent.

8. Plasticity is related to an experience's relevance to the animal.

9. Plasticity is related to the intensity or frequency of experiences.

10. Plasticity can be maladaptive.

25.2 Can Plasticity Support Functional Recovery After Injury?

Brain damage is a major cause of loss of function. A cascade of damaging molecular events unfolds within the first 48 hours after a brain injury followed by an extended period of repair that may last for years. The brain can compensate for injury, but true recovery of function is probably impossible without regenerating lost brain tissues and restoring the original connections. The practical definition of restitution of function must be based on the extent to which a patient regains an acceptable quality of life.

25.3 Examples of Functional Restitution

Functional restitution after brain injury is slow, often revealing a gradual reemergence of functions that resembles the sequence of developmental stages in infants.

25.4 Research on Plasticity in the Injured Brain

Most studies of plasticity in the injured human brain use noninvasive neuroimaging to show altered brain-activation patterns in both sensory and motor maps. Dynamic changes in brain activation appear to occur in the course of recovery, representing different recovery processes at work as time passes.

25.5 Variables Affecting Recovery

Recovery shows considerable variance from person to person. Functional improvement is affected by a variety of factors, including age, handedness, sex, intelligence, personality, and treatment.

25.6 Therapeutic Approaches to Recovery After Brain Damage

Therapy for brain injury currently includes (1) rehabilitation emphasizing the repeated use of affected limbs or cognitive processes, (2) pharmacological treatments designed to stimulate brain plasticity and to reduce inflammation, (3) electrical stimulation intended to increase brain or vagus nerve activity, (4) stem-cell treatments consisting of either the endogenous induction of neurogenesis or transplantation of stem cells to replace neurons lost to disease or injury, and (5) diet.

References

Aglioti, S. "Anomalous" representations and perceptions. In J. Grafman and Y. Christen, Eds. *Neuronal Plasticity: Building a Bridge from the Laboratory to the Clinic*, pp. 79–91. New York: Springer, 1999.

Amengual, J. L., N. Rojo, M. Vecina de las Heras, J. Marco-Pallarés, J. Grau-Sánchez, S. Schneider, L. Vaquero, M. Juncadella, J. Montero, B. Mohammadi, F. Rubio, N. Rueda, E. Duarte, C. Grau, E. Altenmüller, T. F. Münte, and A. Rodríguez-Fornells. Sensorimotor plasticity after music-supported therapy in chronic stroke patients revealed by transcranial magnetic stimulation. *PLoS ONE* 8:e61883. doi:10.1371/journal.pone.0061883, 2013.

Black, J. E., W. T. Greenough, and C. S. Wallace. Experience and brain development. *Child Development* 58:539–559, 1997.

Blakemore, C. B., and M. A. Falconer. Long-term effects of anterior temporal lobectomy on certain cognitive functions. *Journal of Neurology, Neurosurgery, and Psychiatry* 30:364–367, 1967.

Bliss, T. V. P., and T. Lømo. Long-lasting potentiation of synaptic transmission in the dentate area of the anesthetized rabbit following stimulation of the perforant path. *Journal of Physiology* 232:331–356, 1973.

Bucy, P. C., J. E. Keplinger, and E. B. Siqueira. Destruction of the "pyramidal tract" in man. *Journal of Neurosurgery* 21:385–398, 1964.

Candia, V., T. Elbert, E. Altenmuller, H. Rau, T. Schafer, and E. Taub. Constraint-induced movement therapy for focal hand dystonia in musicians. *Lancet* 353:42, 1999.

Chard, S. E. Community neurorehabilitation: A synthesis of current evidence and future research directions. *NeuroRx: Journal for American Society for Experimental NeuroTherapeutics* 3:525–534, 2006.

Clower, D. M., J. M. Hoffman, J. R. Voraw, T. L. Faber, R. P. Woods, and G. E. Alexander. Role of posterior parietal cortex in the recalibration of visually-guided reaching. *Nature* 383:618–621, 1996.

Comeau, W., R. McDonald, and B. Kolb. Learning-induced structural changes in the prefrontal cortex. *Behavioural Brain Research* 214:91–101, 2010.

Dibajnia, P., and C. M. Morshead. Role of neural precursor cells in promoting repair following stroke. *Acta Pharmacologia Sinica* 34:78–90, 2013.

Dobkin, B., D. Apple, H. Barbeau, M. Basso, A. Behrman, D. Deforge, J. Ditunno, G. Dudley, R. Elashoff, L. Fugate, S. Harkema, M. Saulino, and M. Scott. Weight-supported treadmill vs over-ground training for walking after acute incomplete SCI. *Neurology* 66:484–493, 2006.

Dresser, A. C., A. M. Meirowsky, G. H. Weiss, M. L. McNeel, A. G. Simon, and W. F. Caveness. Gainful employment following head injury. *Archives of Neurology* 29:111–116, 1973.

Duncan, P. W., K. J. Sullivan, A. L. Behrman, S. P. Azen, S. S. Wu, S. J. E. Nadeau, et al. Protocol for the Locomotor Experience Applied Poststroke (LEAPS) trial: A randomized controlled trial. *BMC Neurology* 39:1471–2377, 2007.

Elbert, T., S. Heim, and B. Rockstroh. Neural plasticity and development. In C. A. Nelson and M. Luciana, Eds. *Handbook of Developmental Cognitive Neuroscience*, pp. 191–204. Cambridge, Mass.: MIT Press, 2001,

Feeney, D. M. From laboratory to clinic: Noradrenergic enhancement of physical therapy for stroke or trauma patients. *Advances in Neurology* 73:383–394, 1997.

Freed, C. R., P. E. Greene, R. E. Breeze, W. Y. Tsai, W. DuMouchel, R. Kao, S. Dillon, H. Winfield, S. Culver, J. Q. Trojanowski, D. Eidelberg, and S. Fahn. Transplantation of embryonic dopamine neurons for severe Parkinson's disease. *New England Journal of Medicine* 344:710–719, 2001.

Gavett, B. E., R. A. Stern, R. C. Cantu, C. J. Nowinski, and A. C. McKee. Mild traumatic brain injury: A risk factor for neurodegeneration. *Alzheimer's Research Therapy* 25:18 doi:10.1186/alzrt42.

Gibb, R., C. L. R. Gonzalez, W. Wegenast, and B. Kolb. Tactile stimulation facilitates recovery following cortical injury in adult rats. *Behavioural Brain Research* 214:102–107, 2010.

Halliwell, C., W. Comeau, R. Gibb, D. O. Frost, and B. Kolb. Factors influencing frontal cortex development and recovery from early frontal injury. *Developmental Rehabilitation* 12:269–278, 2009.

Hamadjida, A., A. F. Wyss, A. Mir, M. E. Schwab, A. Belhaj-Saif, and E. M. Rouiller. Influence of anti-Nogo-A antibody treatment on the reorganization of callosal connectivity of the premotor cortical areas following unilateral lesion of primary motor cortex (M1) in adult macaque monkeys. *Experimental Brain Research* 223:321–340, 2012.

Hays, S. A., R. L. Rennaker, and M. P. Kigard. Targeting plasticity with vagus nerve stimulation to treat neurological diseases. *Progress in Brain Research* 107:275–300, 2013.

Helmer, K. G., O. Pasternak, E. Fredman, R. I. Preciado, I. K. Koerte, T. Sasaki, M. Mayinger, A. M. Johnson, J. D. Holmes, L. A. Forwell, E. N. Skopelja, M. E. Shenton, and P. S. Echlin. Hockey concussion educational project, Part 1. Susceptibility-weighted imaging study in male and female ice hockey players over a single season. *Journal of Neurosurgery* 120:864–872, 2014.

Hidler, J., D. Nichols, M. Pelliccio, K. Brady, D. D. Campbell, and J. H. Kahn.

Multicenter randomized clinical trial evaluating the effectiveness of the Lokomat in subacute stroke. *Neurorehabilitation Neural Repair* 23:5–13, 2009.

Hillis, A. E. Pharmacological, surgical, and neurovascular interventions to augment acute aphasia recovery. *American Journal of Physical Medicine and Rehabilitation* 86:426–634, 2007.

Jacobs, B., M. Schall, and A. B. Scheibel. A quantitative dendritic analysis of Wernicke's area in humans II: Gender, hemispheric, and environmental factors. *Journal of Comparative Neurology* 327:97–111, 1993.

Jacoby, N., and M. Ahissar. What does it take to show that a cognitive training procedure is useful? A critical evaluation. *Progress in Brain Research* 107:121–140.

Johansson, B. B. Multisensory stimulation in stroke rehabilitation. *Frontiers in Human Neuroscience* doi:10.3389/fnhum.2012.

Jones, M. K. Imagery as a mnemonic aid after left temporal lobectomy: Contrast between material-specific and generalized memory disorders. *Neuropsychologia* 12:21–30, 1974.

Jones-Gotman, M., and B. Milner. Design fluency: The invention of nonsense drawings after focal cortical lesions. *Neuropsychologia* 15:653–674, 1977.

Jonsdottir, J., D. Cattaneo, M. Recalcati, A. Regola, M. Rabuffetti, and M. Ferrarin. Task-oriented biofeedback to improve gait in individuals with chronic stroke: Motor learning approach. *Neurorehabilitation and Neural Repair* 24:478–485, 2010.

Kempf, A., and M. E. Schwab. Nogo-A represses anatomical and synaptic plasticity in the central nervous system. *Physiology* 28:151–163, 2013.

Kertesz, A. *Aphasia and Associated Disorders*. New York: Grune & Stratton, 1979.

Köhler, W. Perceptual organization and learning. *American Journal of Psychology* 7:311–315, 1958.

Kolb, B., and R. Gibb. Tactile stimulation facilitates functional recovery and dendritic change after neonatal medial frontal or posterior parietal lesions in rats. *Behavioural Brain Research* 214:115–120, 2010.

Kolb, B., G. Gorny, Y. Li, A. N. Samaha, and T. E. Robinson. Amphetamine or cocaine limits the ability of later experience to promote structural plasticity in the neocortex and nucleus accumbens. *Proceedings of the National Academy of Sciences U.S.A.* 100:10523–10528, 2003.

Kolb, B., and B. Milner. Performance of complex arm and facial movement after focal brain lesions. *Neuropsychologia* 19:491–504, 1981.

Kolb, B., R. Mychasiuk, A. Muhammad, and R. Gibb. Plasticity in the developing brain. *Progress in Brain Research* 107:35–64, 2013.

Kolb, B., and I. Q. Whishaw. Brain plasticity and behavior. *Annual Review of Psychology* 49:43–64, 1998.

Leipert, J. Transcranial magnetic stimulation in neurorehabilitation. *Acta Neurochirurgica Supplement* 93:71–74, 2005.

Lin, K. C., Y. A. Chen, C. L. Chen, C. Y. Wu, and Y. F. Chang. The effects of bilateral arm training on motor control and functional performance in chronic stroke: A randomized controlled study. *Neurorehabilitation and Neural Repair* 24:42–51, 2010.

Linge, F. What does it feel like to be brain-damaged? *Canada's Mental Health* 28:4–7, 1980.

Luria, A. R. *The Man with a Shattered World*. New York: Basic Books, 1972.

McEwen, B. S. Physiology and neurobiology of stress and adaptation: Central role of the brain. *Physiological Reviews* 87:873–904, 2007.

Merzenich, M. *Soft-wired: How the New Science of Brian Plasticity Can Change Your Life*. San Francisco: Parnassus Publishing, 2013.

Milner, B. Effect of different brain lesions on card sorting. *Archives of Neurology* 9:90–100, 1963.

Milner, B. Psychological aspects of focal epilepsy and its neurosurgical management. *Advances in Neurology* 8:299–321, 1975.

Milner, B., S. Corkin, and H.-L. Teuber. Further analysis of the hippocampal amnesic syndrome: 14-year follow-up study of H.M. *Neuropsychologia* 6:215–234, 1968.

Mohr, J. P., G. H. Weiss, W. F. Caveness, J. D. Dillon, J. P. Kistler, A. M. Meirowsky, and B. L. Rish. Language and motor disorders after penetrating head injury in Viet Nam. *Neurology* 30:1273–1279, 1980.

Mychasiuk, R., A. Muhammad, and B. Kolb. Persistent gene expression changes in NAc, mPFC, and OFC associated with previous nicotine or amphetamine exposure. *Behavioural Brain Research* 256:655–651, 2013.

Nahum, M., H. Lee, and M. M. Merzenich. Principles of neuroplasticity-based rehabilitation. *Progress in Brain Research* 107:141–174, 2013.

Nudo, R. J., E. J. Plautz, and G. W. Millikan. Adaptive plasticity in primate motor cortex as a consequence of behavioral experience and neuronal injury. *Seminars in Neuroscience* 9:13–23, 1997.

Nudo, R. J., B. M. Wise, F. SiFuentes, and G. W. Milliken. Neural substrates for the effects of rehabilitative training on motor recovery after ischemic infarct. *Science* 272:1793, 1996.

Oddy, M., and M. Humphrey. Social recovery during the year following severe head injury. *Journal of Neurology, Neurosurgery, and Psychiatry* 43:798–802, 1980.

Ormerod, B. K., and L. A. M. Galea. Mechanism and function of adult neurogenesis. In C. A. Shaw and J. C. McEachern, Eds. *Toward a Theory of Neuroplasticity*, pp. 85–100. Lillington, N.C.: Taylor & Francis, 2001.

Pantev, C., R. Oostenveld, A. Engelien, B. Ross, L. E. Roberts, and M. Hoke. Increased auditory cortical representation in musicians. *Nature* 392:811–814, 1998.

Pons, T. P., P. E. Garraghty, A. K. Ommaya, J. H. Kaas, E. Taum, and M. Mishkin. Massive cortical reorganization after sensory deafferentation in adult macaques. *Science* 272:1857–1860, 1991.

Popper, C. Single-micronutrient and broad-spectrum micronutrient approaches for treating mood disorders in youth and adults. *Child and Adolescent Psychiatric Clinics of North America* 23:591–672, 2014.

Prigatano, G. P. *Principles of Neuropsychological Rehabilitation.* New York: Oxford University Press, 2001.

Ramachandran, V. S., and S. Blakeslee. *Phantoms in the Brain.* New York: HarperCollins, 1998.

Ramachandran, V. S., and W. Hirstein. The perception of phantom limbs: The D. O. Hebb lecture. *Brain* 121:1603–1630, 1998.

Rampon C., C. H. Jiang, H. Dong, Y. P. Tang, D. J. Lockhart, P. G. Schultz, J. Z. Tsien, and Y. Hu. Effects of environmental enrichment on gene expression in the brain. *Proceedings of the National Academy of Sciences U.S.A.* 97:12880–12884, 2000.

Rauschecker, J. P. Cortical plasticity and music. *Annals of the New York Academy of Sciences* 930:330–336, 2001.

Rauschecker, J. P. Cortical map plasticity in animals and humans. *Progress in Brain Research* 138:73–88, 2002.

Rijntjes, M., and C. Weiller. Recovery of motor and language abilities after stroke: The contribution of functional imaging. *Progress in Neurobiology* 66:109–122, 2002.

Robinson, T. E., and B. Kolb. Structural plasticity associated with drugs of abuse. *Neuropharmacology* 47(Suppl. 1):33–46, 2004.

Rucklidge, J. J., and B. J. Kaplan. Broad-spectrum micronutrient formulas for the treatment of psychiatric symptoms: A systematic review. *Expert Reviews* 13: 49–73, 2013.

Schneider, S., P. E. Schonle, E. Altenmuller, and T. Munte. Using musical instruments to improve motor skill recovery following a stroke. *Journal of Neurology* 254:1339–1346, 2007.

Silva, A. R., S. Pinho, L. M. Macedo, and C. J. Moulin. Benefits of SenseCam: Review on neuropsychological test performance. *American Journal of Preventive Medicine,* 44:402–407, 2013.

Sugita, Y. Global plasticity of adult visual system. In C. A. Shaw and J. C. McEachern, Eds. *Toward a Theory of Neuroplasticity*, pp. 44–50. Philadelphia: Taylor & Francis, 2001.

Taylor, L. Localization of cerebral lesions by psychological testing. *Clinical Neurosurgery* 16:269–287, 1969.

Teasell, R., N. Foley, K. Salter, S. Bhogal, N. Bayona, J. Jutai, and M. Speechley. *Evidence-Based Review of Stroke Rehabilitation*, 12th ed. *Top Stroke Rehabilitation* 16:463–488, 2009.

Teskey, G. C. Using kindling to model the neuroplastic changes associated with learning and memory, neuropsychiatric disorders, and epilepsy. In C. A. Shaw and J. C. McEachern, Eds. *Toward a Theory of Neuroplasticity*, pp. 347–358. Lillington, N.C.: Taylor & Francis, 2001.

Teskey, G. C., C. Flynn, C. D. Goertzen, M. H. Monfils, and N. A. Young. Cortical stimulation improves skilled forelimb use following a focal ischemic infarct in the rat. *Neurological Research* 25:794–800, 2003.

Teuber, H.-L. Recovery of function after brain injury in man. In *Outcome of Severe Damage to the Nervous System: Ciba Foundation Symposium 34.* Amsterdam: Elsevier North-Holland, 1975.

Twitchell, T. E. The automatic grasping response of infants. *Neuropsychologia* 3:247–259, 1965.

Twitchell, T. E. The restoration of motor function following hemiplegia in man. *Brain* 74:443–480, 1951.

Unwatte, G., and E. Taub. Constraint-induced movement therapy: A method for harnessing neuroplasticity to treat motor disorders. *Progress in Brain Research* 107:379–401, 2013.

Van Vleet, T. M., and J. M. DeGutis. The nonspatial side of spatial neglect and related approaches to treatment. *Progress in Brain Research* 107:327–350, 2013.

von Monakow, C. Lokalisation der Hirnfunktionen. *Journal für Psychologie und Neurologie* 17:185–200, 1911. Reprinted in G. von Bonin. *The Cerebral Cortex.* Springfield, Ill.: Charles C Thomas, 1960.

Wilson, B. A. 'Cutting edge' developments in neuropsychological rehabilitation and possible future directions. *Brain Impairment* 12, 33–42, 2011.

Zhao, S., M. Zhao, T. Xiao, J. Jolkkonen, and C. Zhao. Constraint-induced movement therapy overcomes the intrinsic axonal growth-inhibitory signals in stroke rats. *Stroke* 44:1698–7105, 2013.

Zihl, J., and D. von Cramon. Visual field rehabilitation in the cortically blind? *Journal of Neurology, Neurosurgery, and Psychiatry* 49:965–967, 1986.

26 Neurological Disorders

PORTRAIT   Posttraumatic Stress Disorder

Life is filled with stress. Routinely, we cope. But some events are so physically threatening, and often emotionally shattering, that people experience long-term consequences. Flashbacks and nightmares persist long after any physical danger has passed. These symptoms can lead to emotional numbness and a diagnosis of **posttraumatic stress disorder** (PTSD).

Traumatic events that may trigger PTSD include violent assault, natural or human-caused disaster, accident, and war. An estimated one in six veterans of the conflicts in Iraq and Afghanistan, including many not directly exposed to combat, developed symptoms of PTSD, including intrusive, unwanted thoughts; avoiding thoughts related to stressful events; negative cognitions and moods; and altered arousal and reactivity responses. Understanding the neural basis and identifying new PTSD treatments has spurred intense interest. Nevertheless, treatment is often difficult, and most sufferers receive no or little treatment.

As recently as 1980, when PTSD acquired its name, it was labeled a "psychological" problem in individuals who were trying to repress unpleasant experiences. Treatment was psychotherapy. Patients were encouraged to imagine and talk about the stressful experiences they endured. Today, PTSD is widely considered a neurological condition, and more treatment options are available.

In **virtual-reality (VR) exposure therapy**, a controlled virtual-immersion environment combines realistic

COURTESY ALBERT "SKIP" RIZZO, PH.D., USCICT

street scenes, sounds, and odors, allowing people to relive traumatic events (Gonçalves et al., 2012). The Virtual Iraq and Afghanistan Simulation is customized for war veterans to start with benign events—such as children playing— and gradually adds increasingly stressful components, culminating in such traumatic events as a roadside bomb exploding in the virtual space around an armored personnel carrier, illustrated here.

To make Virtual Iraq realistic, the system pumps in smells, stepping up from the scent of bread baking to body odor to the reek of gunpowder and burning rubber. Speakers provide sounds while off-the-shelf subwoofers mounted under the subject's chair re-create movements. VR exposure therapy is now used prior to stress exposure for soldiers, police, firefighters, and other first responders, as a means of preventing PTSD from developing (Rizzo et al., 2011).

Many unknowns related to PTSD remain, including how stress injures the brain, especially the frontal lobes and hippocampus (Wingenfeld and Wolf, 2014); why some people do not experience PTSD following extremely stressful events; and the extent to which PTSD is associated with other health events, including previous stressors, diabetes, and head trauma (Costanzo et al., 2014). That said, assessment and treatment options for most of those who endure PTSD are poor: over half of all war veterans, for example, receive no assessment or treatment.

Our responses to stressful events were once considered mainly psychological, but the medical and psychological communities now recognize that responses characteristic of PTSD can also trigger physical changes in the brain. We begin this chapter by describing the examination a neurologist typically performs on a patient. Then we survey several common neurological disorders and their treatment—from vascular insults and head trauma to epilepsy; from tumors, headaches, and infections to disorders of the spinal cord and sleep disorders.

◎ 26.1 The Neurological Examination

People suspected of sustaining a nervous system disorder are usually examined by a **neurologist**, a physician specializing in the treatment of brain injury or dysfunction. The neurologist takes the patient's history, makes a general assessment of the patient's physical condition, and perhaps recommends additional tests—an electroencephalagram (EEG) or a brain scan, for example, and neuropsychological assessment—as indicated by the history or the initial examination. At the end of this initial assessment, the neurologist compiles a case summary.

The Patient's History

The neurologist's first step is to ask the patient about the problem. Information is collected about the patient's background, with particular attention to any history of disease, accidents, and the occurrence of symptoms such as headache, loss of consciousness, and sleep disturbances. Family background is reviewed as well because many diseases, such as epilepsy, have a high familial incidence.

While the history is being taken, the neurologist observes the patient's behavior, assessing mental status, watching facial features for abnormalities or asymmetries, listening for speech abnormalities, and observing posture. The patient's state of awareness is described with adjectives such as *alert*, *drowsy*, *stuporous*, *confused*, and so forth. Any evidence of delusions and hallucinations is reported. Facial expression and behavior can reveal whether the patient is agitated, anxious, depressed, apathetic, or restless.

The neurologist may test some simple aspects of memory by reciting a series of digits and asking the patient to repeat it. In addition, the neurologist may look to see whether the patient is left- or right-handed and ask about the history of handedness in the family, because handedness can be a clue to which hemisphere controls speech. A number of simple tests for speech may be given, such as asking the meaning of words, having rhymes or words repeated (for example, "la-la," "ta-ta"), having objects named, and having the patient read and write.

The Physical Examination

The neurologist uses many tools in the course of the physical examination to assess the patient's nervous system functioning. Tools range from basic—a blood-pressure cuff—to sophisticated imaging technologies **(Figure 26.1)**. A

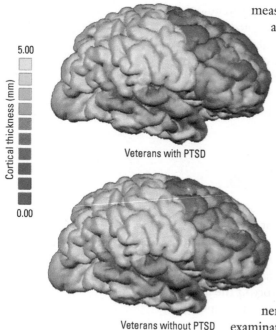

Veterans with PTSD

Veterans without PTSD

Figure 26.1 ▲

Cortical Thickness and PTSD Blue shading reflects reduced cortical thickness in group-averaged brains of veterans with PTSD (top) compared with veterans without PTSD (bottom). (Geuze, E., Westenber, H.G.M., Heinecke, A., de Kloet, C.S., Goebel, R & Vermetten, E. Thinner prefrontal cortex in veterans with posttraumatic stress disorder. *NeuroImage*, Vol. 41, Issue 3:675-681 Figure 2, page 678, 2008 © Elsevier.)

measuring tape records head and body size, the size of skin lesions, and so on; a stethoscope reveals the sounds of the heart and blood vessels. An otoscope allows the neurologist to examine the auditory canal and eardrum; a flashlight elicits pupillary reflexes, and tongue depressors elicit the gag reflex and abdominal and plantar (sole of the foot) reflexes.

A vial of coffee is useful in assessing smell, and vials of salt and sugar can assess taste. A 256-Hz tuning fork tests vibratory sensation and hearing. A cotton wisp will elicit the corneal reflex and test sensitivity to light touch; plastic tubes test temperature sensations; pins test pain sensation; and a rubber-headed hammer elicits muscle stretch reflexes, such as the knee-jerk reflex. Some coins and keys are useful in testing object recognition through touch.

A critical part of the neurological examination is the study of the head. Its general features, such as size and shape, are assessed, and a detailed examination is made of the sensory and motor functioning of its 12 sets of cranial nerves. Cranial-nerve malfunctions discovered in this part of the examination can be important clues to the location and nature of nervous system damage.

The motor system in other parts of the body is examined to assess muscle bulk, tone, and power; to test for the occurrence of involuntary muscle movements, such as shaking and tremors; and to assess the status of reflexes. In addition, coordination is examined by having a patient perform such tasks as walking heel to toe in a straight line, touching the neurologist's finger and his or her own nose repeatedly, making rapid alternating finger movements, tapping the foot as rapidly as possible, and so on. Generally, all of the muscles are tested in head-to-foot order, and the status of each is recorded on a standard chart.

A sensory examination includes investigating sensitivity to painful stimulation, touch, and temperature as well as analyzing vibration sense, joint-position sense, two-point discrimination, tactile localization, object identification, and the ability to identify numbers or letters traced on the skin with a blunt object. Sensory tests allow assessment of individual sensory system functioning and provide information about the location of possible dysfunctions.

Suspected nervous system problems are further investigated with tests of the blood, saliva, and stool, and neural assessment with EEG, CT scans, and MRI. To understand the neural basis of PTSD, for example, and develop treatments for patients, brain imaging has revealed significant reductions, bilaterally, in the volume of the hippocampus and amygdala within the temporal lobes and of the frontal cortex. Reduced cortical thickness is associated with reduced cerebral blood flow and deficits in performance on neuropsychological tests of frontal- and temporal-lobe function.

Predisposing factors that may contribute to PTSD include reduced volume in brain areas such as the hippocampus and amygdala, susceptibility to stress, and a life background characterized by poor social support (van Zuiden et al., 2013). In response to sudden catastrophic events, for example, people frequently display a sequence of adaptive responses. An initial response is shock:

the individual is apathetic and unable to respond. A period of suggestibility follows, in which the individual willingly follows directions.

A final phase is recovery, which often features exaggerated talking during which the events associated with the catastrophe are recounted and repeatedly discussed. Perhaps, if the recovery stage does not occur, there is no stress resolution, and continuing stress contributes to the patient's PTSD symptoms. VR exposure therapy then may substitute for the recovery stage.

26.2 Cerebral Vascular Disorders

Vascular problems can affect healthy central nervous system functioning, because blood-vessel disease or damage can greatly—even totally—reduce the flow of oxygen and glucose to a brain region. If such interference lasts longer than 10 minutes, all cells in the affected region die. Most disease of the cerebral vascular system develops in the arterial system (review Figure 3.5); disease of venous drainage is uncommon in the CNS. Cerebral vascular diseases are among the most common causes of death and chronic disability in the Western world.

Types of Cerebral Vascular Disease

A **cerebral vascular accident (CVA)**, or **stroke**, is the sudden appearance of neurological symptoms as a result of interrupted blood flow. Stroke can result from a wide variety of vascular disorders, but not all vascular disorders produce stroke. The onset of dysfunction can be insidious, spanning months or even years. Stroke often produces an **infarct**, an area of dead or dying tissue resulting from an obstruction of the blood vessels supplying the area. Stroke is the most common cause of death worldwide. As you read this paragraph, someone in the United States will have a CVA.

If the flow through small blood vessels, such as capillaries, is interrupted, the effects are more limited than the often-devastating consequences of damage to large vessels. If a stroke or other cerebral vascular disorder is in one restricted part of a vessel (and other parts of the system are relatively healthy), the prognosis can be rather good because vessels in the surrounding areas can often supply blood to at least some of the deprived area. On the other hand, if a stroke affects a region supplied largely by weak or diseased vessels, the effects can be much more serious because there is no possibility of compensation. In addition, the surrounding weak zones themselves may be at increased risk of stroke.

In the long run, a small vascular lesion in a healthy brain will have a good prognosis for substantial recovery of function. In the event of preexisting vascular lesions, the effects of the new lesions may be extremely variable. The lesions can be cumulative and obliterate a functional zone of brain tissue, producing serious consequences. As with other lesions, the behavioral symptoms subsequent to vascular lesions depend on the location of damage.

Of the numerous vascular disorders that affect the CNS, the most common are *ischemia*, *migraine stroke*, *cerebral hemorrhage*, *angiomas*, and *arteriovenous aneurysms*.

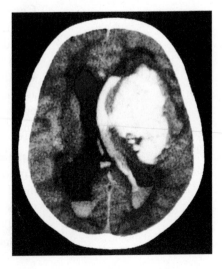

▼ False-color CT scan shows a dorsal view of internal bleeding (yellow/orange) due to a cerebrovascular accident. The front of the brain is at top. The main mass of blood (*hematoma*) is at upper right. To the left, blood abnormally fills a ruptured ventricle. Farther left, a healthy ventricle (black) helps to circulate the brain's cerebrospinal fluid. This stroke resulted in aphasia and hemiplegia. (ZEPHYR/Science Source)

Cerebral Ischemia

Ischemia refers to any of a group of disorders in which the symptoms are caused by vessel blockage preventing a sufficient supply of blood to the brain. In **thrombosis**, for example, some of the blood in a vessel has coagulated to form a plug or clot that has remained at the place of its formation. An **embolism** is a clot or other plug brought through the blood from a larger vessel and forced into a smaller one, where it obstructs circulation. An embolism can be a blood clot, air bubble, oil or fat deposit, or small mass of cells detached from a tumor. Curiously, embolisms most often affect the middle cerebral artery of the brain's left side (see Figure 3.5).

Reduction in blood flow can also result from other factors that narrow the vessel. The most common example of such narrowing is a condition marked by thickening and hardening of the arteries, called **cerebral arteriosclerosis**. When ischemia is temporary, it may be termed **cerebral vascular insufficiency** or **transient ischemia**, indicating the variable nature of the disorder with the passage of time. The onset of transient attacks is often abrupt and in many cases experienced as fleeting sensations of giddiness or impaired consciousness.

Migraine Stroke

While relatively rare compared with other types, **migraine strokes** are believed to account for a significant proportion of strokes in people under 40 years of age, especially women. The immediate cause of these strokes is probably some form of vasospasm—constriction of blood vessels—but the underlying cause of the vasospasm remains a mystery.

Since the late 1800s, physicians have recognized that migraine stroke may lead to infarcts and permanent neurological deficits. The classic migraine stroke is experienced as a transient ischemic attack with a variety of neurological symptoms, including impaired sensory function (especially vision, as detailed, for example, in Case B. K., Section 13.4); numbness of the skin (especially in the arms); difficulties in moving; and aphasia. The precise symptoms depend on the vessels affected, however, and the posterior cerebral artery is most commonly affected.

Cerebral Hemorrhage

Cerebral hemorrhage is a massive bleeding into the substance of the brain. The most frequent cause is high blood pressure, or *hypertension*. Other causes include congenital defects in cerebral arteries, blood disorders such as leukemia, brain trauma, and toxic chemicals. The onset of cerebral hemorrhage is abrupt, and the bleeding may quickly prove fatal. It usually occurs when a person is awake, presumably because the person is more active and thus has higher blood pressure. Prognosis is poor in cerebral hemorrhage, especially if the patient is unconscious for more than 48 hours.

Angiomas and Aneurysms

Angiomas are congenital collections of abnormal vessels that divert the normal flow of blood. These capillary, venous, or **arteriovenous malformations** (AVMs) are masses of enlarged and tortuous cortical vessels that are supplied by one or more large arteries and are drained by one or more large veins, most often in the field of the middle cerebral artery. Because they cause abnormalities in the amount and pattern of blood flow and are inherently weak, angiomas may lead to stroke or to an inadequate distribution of blood in the regions surrounding the vessels. In some cases, they cause arterial blood to flow directly into veins only briefly, or sometimes not at all, after servicing the surrounding brain tissue.

Aneurysms are vascular dilations resulting from localized defects in a vessel's elasticity. They can be visualized as balloonlike expansions of vessels that are usually weak and prone to rupture. Although aneurysms are usually due to congenital defects, they may also develop from hypertension, arteriosclerosis, embolisms, or infections. A characteristic symptom of an aneurysm is severe headache, which may be present for years, because the aneurysm is exerting pressure on the *dura mater*, which is richly endowed with pain receptors.

Treating Cerebral Vascular Disorders

The variety of approaches to treatment of vascular disorders includes drug therapy and surgery. Anticoagulant therapy (for example, tissue-plasminogen activator, or t-PA) to remove or dissolve a clot is useful only in ischemic episodes and if delivered within 3 hours. It is not administered if bleeding is suspected because it aggravates bleeding. Therefore it is important that every effort be made to shorten the time between the occurrence of a stroke and treatment.

Following stroke, neuroprotectant drugs that limit the changes leading to cell death can be administered. These include drugs to block calcium channels, reduce edema, and regulate neural activity. For individuals prone to stroke, a variety of antiplatelet agents—aspirin is one—can reduce the likelihood of blood clotting and so serve as a preventive measure. Once a stroke has occurred, a variety of brain changes occur over a number of days (see Figure 25.7). Treatments to reduce these processes include vasodilators to dilate the vessels, drugs to reduce blood pressure, and salty solutions or steroids to reduce *cerebral edema* (the accumulation of fluid in and around damaged tissue).

Surgical techniques are not always practical. For example, the only certain cure for an aneurysm is total removal, which is usually not feasible. Aneurysms are sometimes painted with various plastic substances to prevent them from rupturing. In regard to cerebral hemorrhage, it may be necessary to perform surgery to relieve the pressure of blood from the ruptured vessel on the rest of the brain.

The most effective approach to vascular disorders is prevention. Organizations, including the American Heart Association and National Institutes of Health, offer advice on prevention, as do primary care and vascular physicians. The development of procedures both to prevent and to treat stroke is an active area of research (Kersten et al., 2014). Age is an unavoidable risk factor, as is the growing incidence of **metabolic syndrome**, a combination of medical disorders, including obesity and insulin abnormalities, which collectively increases the risk of developing cardiovascular disease and diabetes. Accordingly, preventive measures include lifestyle choices, such as healthy diet and weight control, exercise, stress control, moderate consumption of alcohol, and avoidance of smoking and cigarette smoke. Preventive measures also include drug therapy to control blood pressure.

⊚ 26.3 Traumatic Brain Injuries

Traumatic brain injury (TBI) commonly results from automobile and industrial accidents, war injuries, sports injuries, and injuries due to other accidents (see Chapter 1 Portrait). According to the Defense and Veteran's Brain Injury Center, more than 250,000 U.S. soldiers wounded in the Iraq and Afghanistan wars sustained TBI. Back at home, cerebral trauma or injury from a blow to the head is the most common form of brain damage in people under age 40. Estimates of the annual incidence of TBI are increasing as knowledge about brain trauma has improved (Ghobrial et al., 2014). TBI is about eight times as frequent as breast cancer, AIDS, spinal-cord injury, and multiple sclerosis combined.

The two most important factors in the incidence of head injury are age and gender (**Figure 26.2**). Sports account for about 20 percent of TBI, with injuries occurring most commonly in contact sports such as American football, hockey, rugby, and lacrosse (Selassie et al., 2013). Heading a ball in soccer can also cause TBI, but the incidence and severity of such injury await further study. The difficulty in evaluating TBI in sports relates to the underreporting of *concussion* (mild TBI) and the problem of tracking repeated injuries. Children and the elderly are more likely to have head injuries from falls than are others, and males between 15 and 30 years of age are very likely to incur brain injuries, especially from automobile and motorcycle accidents.

⊚ **Figure 26.2 ►**

Traumatic Brain Injury in the United States Based on combined reports of emergency-room visits, hospitalizations, and deaths, this chart graphs the average annual rates of TBI per 100,000 people. (Data source: Centers for Disease Control report *TBI in the United States: Emergency Department Visits, Hospitalizations, and Deaths*, 2004; 2012.)

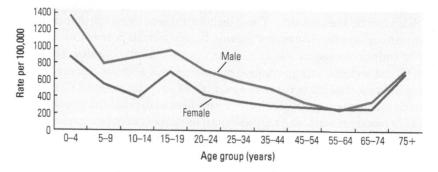

Head injury can affect brain function by damaging the brain directly; by disrupting blood supply; by inducing bleeding, increased intracranial pressure, and swelling, thus opening the brain to infection; and by scarring brain tissue, which can then become a focus for later epileptic seizures. Brain imaging of glucose metabolism indicates long-term depression of brain activity following TBI (**Figure 26.3**), and 90 percent of people who have had concussion report migrainelike headaches as long as a year after the incident.

⊚ **Figure 26.3 ►**

PET imaging shows brain glucose metabolism reduced as a result of concussion (left) to levels nearly as low as those imaged for severe brain trauma (center). Image at right shows glucose metabolism in a healthy brain. (Courtesy UCLA/ Bergsneider.)

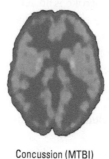 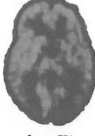 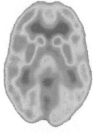 

Concussion (MTBI)   Severe TBI   Healthy   CMRglc mg/100mg/min

TBI can have many other consequences. For example, one study of adolescents admitted to the New York City jail system found that as many as 50 percent reported previous TBI (Kaba et al., 2014). The two main types of brain trauma are open- and closed head injuries.

Open Head Injuries

Open head injuries are TBIs in which the skull is penetrated, as in gunshot or missile wounds, or in which fragments of bone penetrate the brain. In many cases, the injury does not cause the victim to lose consciousness.

Recovery from open head injury can be remarkable, as the case of Gabrielle "Gabby" Giffords illustrates. In January 2011, an assailant shot Giffords, a U.S. Representative from Arizona, in the head. The bullet passed from the front of her skull on the left side through her brain to the rear of the skull and thus passed completely through her left hemisphere. After part of her skull was removed and bone fragments were removed from the brain, she was placed in an induced coma. She subsequently underwent several reconstructive surgeries and received intense rehabilitation that allowed her to relearn to walk, to regain substantial speech, and to learn to write with her left hand. Although she resigned from the House of Representatives, she remains politically active along with her husband, former astronaut Mark Kelly, in support of responsible gun ownership (Giffords et al., 2011).

Open head injuries tend to produce distinctive symptoms that may undergo rapid and spontaneous recovery. The neurological signs may be highly specific, and many of the effects of the injuries closely resemble those of the surgical excision of a small area of cortex. The specificity of neurological symptoms subsequent to open head injuries from a series of wars has given rise to a number of studies of their neuropsychological consequences (Newcombe, 1969; Luria, 1973; Teuber et al., 1960).

▲ (Top) Days before a gunshot to the head left her near death in January 2011, U.S. Representative Gabrielle Giffords (D-AZ) reenacted her swearing-in with House Speaker John Boehner. A year later she resigned her House seat to concentrate on her recovery. (Bottom) By 2013, Giffords, who had regained limited speech, was traveling the country to urge support for background checks on gun purchasers. Mobility on her right side remained limited. (Top: AP/Wide World Photos. Bottom: Al Drago/MCT/Newscom.)

Closed Head Injuries

Closed head injuries result from a blow to the head, which can subject the brain to a variety of mechanical forces, illustrated in **Figure 26.4**:

- Damage at the site of the blow, a bruise (contusion) called a **coup**, is incurred where the brain has been compacted by the bone's pushing inward, even when the skull is not fractured.

- The pressure that produces the coup may push the brain against the opposite side or end of the skull, producing an additional bruise, known as a **contrecoup**.

- Brain movement may cause twisting or shearing of nerve fibers, producing microscopic lesions. These lesions may occur throughout the brain but are most common in the frontal and temporal lobes. In addition, twisting and shearing may damage the brain's major fiber tracts, especially those crossing the midline, such as the corpus callosum and anterior commissure. As a result, connection between the two sides of the brain may be disrupted, leading to a disconnection syndrome (see Section 17.5).

◎ **Figure 26.4** ▶

Results of TBI Brain regions most frequently damaged in closed head injury are indicated by pink and blue shading. A blow can produce a contusion both at the site of impact (coup) and at the opposite side of the brain (contrecoup), owing to compression of the brain against both the front and the back of the skull or to both sides.

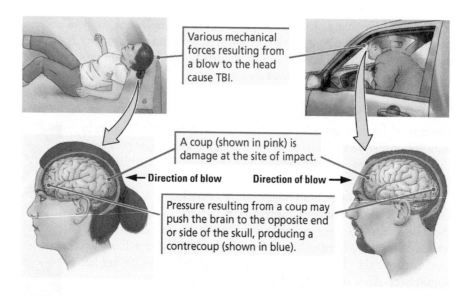

Various mechanical forces resulting from a blow to the head cause TBI.

A coup (shown in pink) is damage at the site of impact.

◄— **Direction of blow**   **Direction of blow** —►

Pressure resulting from a coup may push the brain to the opposite end or side of the skull, producing a contrecoup (shown in blue).

- Bruises and strains caused by the impact may produce cerebral hemorrhage. Because the blood is trapped within the skull, it acts as a growing mass, or **hematoma**, exerting pressure on surrounding structures.

- As with blows to other parts of the body, blows to the brain produce edema (swelling), another source of pressure on brain tissue.

Closed head injuries resulting from traffic accidents are particularly severe because the head is moving when the blow is struck, thereby increasing the impact's velocity and multiplying the number and severity of small lesions throughout the brain. Computed tomographic (CT) scans of accident victims in prolonged **coma** (loss of consciousness) show diffuse brain injury and enlarged ventricles, signs associated with poor outcomes.

Closed head injuries are commonly accompanied by coma. According to Muriel Lezak and coworkers (2012), the duration of unconsciousness can serve as a measure of the severity of damage because it correlates directly with mortality, intellectual impairment, and deficits in social skills. The longer a coma lasts, the greater the possibility of serious impairment and death.

Two kinds of behavioral effects result from closed head injuries: (1) discrete impairment of the specific functions mediated by the cortex at the site of the coup or contrecoup lesion, and (2) more generalized impairments from widespread trauma throughout the brain. Discrete impairment is most commonly associated with damage to the frontal and temporal lobes, the areas most susceptible to closed head injuries. More-general impairment, resulting from minute lesions and lacerations scattered throughout the brain and from tears due to movement of the hemispheres in relation to each other, is characterized by a loss of complex cognitive functions, including reductions in mental speed, concentration, and overall cognitive efficiency.

Patients generally complain of an inability to concentrate or to do things as well as they could before the accident, even if their intelligence rating remains well above average. In our experience, highly skilled people are the most affected by closed head injuries because they are acutely aware of any cognitive loss that prevents them from returning to their former competence level.

Closed head injuries that damage the frontal and temporal lobes also tend to have significant effects on personality and social behavior. Relatively few victims of traffic accidents who have sustained severe head injuries ever resume their studies or return to gainful employment; if they do reenter the workforce, they do so at a level lower than that before their accidents.

Often, the chronic effects of closed head injuries are not accompanied by any obvious neurological signs, and the patients may therefore be referred for neuropsychological evaluation (the subject of Chapter 28). Thorough neuropsychological assessments are especially useful in these cases for uncovering cognitive deficits that are not apparent on cursory examination. **Table 26.1** summarizes the pathological effects of closed head injury.

Once people sustain a head injury, they are more likely to sustain subsequent head injuries, both because behavioral changes post injury may prompt them to become more careless and because they may continue the activity that resulted in the injury. The effects of even mild head injuries can be cumulative. For example, it is well-established that a boxer will sustain a significant level of brain injury even though the periods of unconsciousness experienced by the boxer may have been few and of short duration. Boxers who endure repeated concussion can subsequently suffer *dementia pugilistica* (DP), colloquially "punch-drunk syndrome" or "boxer's dementia" (Foerstl et al., 2010).

Repetitive head injury is likely to occur in many contact sports, but because each incidence may be relatively mild, such effects may be difficult to track. For example, 30 percent of bouts of extreme fighting are stopped owing to a head blow, but the number of blows to the head that cause TBI is not known. Surprisingly, fewer brain injuries may be incurred in extreme fighting than in boxing because fighters can tap out when injured and fights are stopped quickly when one fighter has an advantage.

Another area of concern is the effect of concussion in American football, ice hockey, and other sports in which the risk of suffering multiple concussions over an athletic career is significant (see Chapter 25 Portrait). As many as 10 percent of individuals who have repeatedly had concussion—and an estimated one in three National Football League players—may later display symptoms of dementia and, with age, the accumulation of *tau protein*, a marker for neuronal degeneration, in the frontal and temporal cortices (Tartaglia et al., 2014). Understanding of the relationship between the number of concussions and subsequent *chronic traumatic encephalopathy* (CTE), or even of whether the current treatment of rest from competition following a concussion is an optimal measure, remains poor. Resting from competition, however, does remove the possibility of an immediate repeat occurrence.

Table 26.1 Brain injuries subsequent to closed head trauma

Primary Brain Injuries, Immediate on Impact
Coup and contrecoup contusions
Fiber shearing or stretching
Macroscopic and microscopic lesions
Laceration or depression from skull penetration or fracture

Secondary Injuries
Intracranial hemorrhage and edema
Ischemic or bleed-induced damage
Increased intracranial pressure or distortion
Effects of multiple injuries and hypoxia

Injurious Effects, Delayed
Degeneration of gray and white matter
Hydrocephalus

Behavioral Assessment of Head Injury

Although neuroradiological measures can provide objective indicators of neural status after head injury, behavior is the most important measure of nervous system integrity. In the immediate postinjury period, the two most obvious behavioral symptoms are coma and amnesia. Clinical judgment of the depth of coma was largely subjective and unreliable a generation ago, when the Glasgow Coma Scale (GCS; **Table 26.2**) began to provide an objective indicator of the degree of unconsciousness and of recovery from unconsciousness. Other similar scales and brain imaging can supplement the results, but the GCS remains a useful coma assessment (Knox et al., 2014).

In this scale, three indices of wakefulness are evaluated—eye opening (E), motor response (M), and verbal response (V)—and summed. A score of 8 or less is often used as a criterion for severe closed head injury, with a score ranging from 9 to 12 being a criterion for moderate injury. A shortcoming of the scale as a measure of the severity of brain injury is that as many as 50 percent of brain-injury victims admitted to hospitals have scores ranging from 13 to 15, indicating an absence of coma, and yet, later, such patients may undergo many of the consequences of head injury.

The length of *posttraumatic amnesia* (PTA) is an alternative measure of an injury's severity. Definitions of PTA vary (some include the period of coma; others are restricted to the period of anterograde amnesia), but the best evidence reveals that duration of amnesia is correlated with later memory disturbance. A commonly used PTA scale is as follows: amnesia lasting less than 10 minutes corresponds to very mild injury; amnesia lasting 10 to 60 minutes

Table 26.2 **The Glasgow Coma Scale**

Response	Points	Index of Wakefulness
Eye Opening (E)		
None	1	Not attributable to ocular swelling
To pain	2	Pain stimulus is applied to chest or limbs
To speech	3	Nonspecific response to speech or shout; does not imply that the patient obeys command to open eyes
Spontaneous	4	Eyes are open; does not imply intact awareness
Motor Response (M)		
No response	1	Flaccid
Extension	2	"Decerebrate," adduction, internal rotation of shoulder, and pronation of the forearm
Abnormal flexion	3	"Decorticate," abnormal flexion, adduction of the shoulder
Withdrawal	4	Normal flexor response; withdraws from pain stimulus with abduction of the shoulder
Localizes pain	5	Pain stimulus applied to supraocular region or fingertip causes limb to move to attempt to avoid it
Obeys commands	6	Follows simple commands
Verbal Response (V)		
No response	1	(Self-explanatory)
Incomprehensible	2	Moaning and groaning, but no recognizable words
Inappropriate	3	Intelligible speech (e.g., shouting or swearing), but no sustained or coherent conversation
Confused	4	Patient responds to questions in a conversational manner, but the responses indicate varying degrees of disorientation and confusion
Oriented	5	Normal orientation to time, place, and person

Note: The summed Glasgow Coma Scale is equal to E + M + V (3–15 points).

Source: Research from Teasdale, G., and B. Jennett. The Glasgow Coma Scale. *Lancet* 2:81–84, 1974.

corresponds to mild injury; amnesia lasting 1 to 24 hours corresponds to moderate injury; amnesia lasting 1 to 7 days corresponds to severe injury; amnesia lasting more than 7 days corresponds to very severe injury.

A problem with using amnesia as a measure is that no consistent method is used to measure it. Researchers evaluate amnesia variously, by retrospective questioning, by measures of disorientation, or infrequently, by neuropsychological assessment. Each method yields a different estimate of severity and, hence, of the extent of injury. Besides which, skill in assessment is required and skilled assessors are seldom available.

Recovering from and Preventing Head Injury

Reportedly, recovery from head trauma may continue for 2 to 3 to many years, but the bulk of cognitive recovery takes place in the first 6 to 9 months (Karr, 2014). Recovering memory functions appears to be somewhat slower than recovering general intelligence, and the ultimate level of memory performance is lower than other cognitive functions. People with brainstem damage, as inferred from oculomotor disturbance, have a poorer cognitive outcomes, and this is probably true of people with *initial dysphasias* or *hemiparesis* as well.

One difficulty in assessing the effects of mild TBI on subsequent neuropsychological function is that concussions frequently do not lead to significant changes as detected by neuropsychological tests. Where prominent impairments are detected, the prognosis for significant recovery of cognitive functions is good, but less optimism attends the recovery of social skills or personality, areas that often change significantly following closed head injury. The results of numerous studies support the conclusion that the quality of life—in regard to social interactions, perceived stress levels, and enjoyment of leisure activities—is significantly reduced and that this reduction is chronic (Gregorio et al., 2014).

Head injury is preventable, and the number-one preventive measure is recognizing that concussions have severe immediate and long-term consequences *and* cumulative effects (Solomon and Kuhn, 2014). Concussion from participation in sports can be minimized and even prevented by adopting appropriate rules, emphasizing safe coaching, and developing protective headgear. Workplace concussion is preventable, and workplace education is a priority in major industries but less widely practiced in small businesses and farming. Other major sources of head injury include vehicle accidents and combat. Here too, many avenues for prevention exist.

26.4 Epilepsy

Epilepsy is a brain disorder caused by *seizure*—spontaneous, abnormal discharges of brain neurons as a result of scarring from injury, infections, or tumors. The definition of epilepsy requires the occurrence of at least one epileptic seizure, but the disorder is often characterized by recurrent seizures associated with a disturbance of consciousness and by its neurobiologic, cognitive, psychological, and social consequences.

Recurrent epileptic seizures of various types that register on an EEG are associated with disturbances of consciousness (see Figure 7.5). Epileptic episodes have been called *convulsions*, *seizures*, *fits*, and *attacks*, but none of these terms

Table 26.3 Precipitating factors of seizure in susceptible persons

Drugs
    Alcohol
    Analeptics
    Excessive anticonvulsants
    Phenothiazines
    Tricyclic antidepressants
Emotional stress
Fever
Hormonal changes
    Adrenal steroids
    Adrenocorticotrophic hormone (ACTH)
    Menses
    Puberty
Hyperventilation
Sensory stimuli
    Flashing lights
    Laughing
    Reading, speaking, coughing
    Sounds, for example music or bells
Sleep
Sleep deprivation
Trauma

Source: Information from Pincus, J. H., and G. J. Tucker. *Behavioral Neurology.* New York: Oxford University Press, 2003.

on its own is entirely satisfactory because the character of the episodes can vary greatly. Epileptic seizures are common: 1 person in 20 will experience at least one seizure in his or her lifetime.

Symptomatic seizures can be identified with a specific cause, such as infection, trauma, tumor, vascular malformation, toxic chemicals, very high fever, or other neurological disorder. **Idiopathic seizures** appear to arise spontaneously and in the absence of other CNS diseases. **Table 26.3** summarizes the great variety of circumstances that appear to precipitate seizures. Although their range is striking, a consistent feature is that the brain is most epileptogenic when it is relatively inactive and the patient is still.

Although epilepsy has long been known to run in families, its incidence is lower than a one-gene model would predict. More likely, people with certain genotypes are predisposed to seizure, given certain environmental circumstances. The most remarkable clinical feature of epileptic disorders is the widely varying length of intervals between attacks—from minutes to hours to weeks or even years. In fact, describing a basic set of symptoms to be expected in all or even most people with the disorder is almost impossible. At the same time, three particular symptoms occur in many types of epilepsy:

1. **Onset of an aura**, a subjective sensation, perceptual experience, or motor phenomenon that precedes and marks the onset of an epileptic seizure or migraine.

2. **Loss of consciousness**, ranging from complete collapse in some people to simply staring off into space in others, and often accompanied by amnesia in which the victim forgets the seizure itself and the period of lost consciousness.

3. **Movement**, as seizures commonly have a motor component, although the characteristics vary considerably. Some people shake during an attack; others exhibit automatic movements, such as rubbing the hands or chewing.

Typically, EEG confirms the diagnosis of epilepsy. In some people with epilepsy, however, seizures are difficult to demonstrate in this way except under special circumstances (when challenged by a flashing light, for example, or in an EEG recorded during sleep). Moreover, not all people with an EEG suggestive of epilepsy actually have seizures. Some estimates suggest that one person in five has an abnormal EEG pattern—far more than the number of people thought to have epilepsy.

Classifying Seizures

Several schemes for classifying epilepsy have appeared through the years. Here we discuss four commonly recognized types: *focal seizures*, *generalized seizures*, *akinetic seizures*, and *myoclonic spasms*.

Focal Seizures

John Hughlings-Jackson hypothesized in 1870 that focal seizures probably originate from the point (*focus*) in the neocortex representing the region of the body where the movement is first seen. He was later proved correct. A **focal seizure** begins in one place, then spreads. In a Jacksonian focal seizure, for example, the attack begins with jerking movements in one part of the body (for example, a finger, a toe, or the mouth), then spreads to adjacent parts. If the attack begins with a finger, the jerks might spread to other fingers then to the hand, the arm, and so on, producing the so-called "Jacksonian march."

Complex partial seizure, a type of focal seizure that originates most commonly in the temporal lobe and somewhat less frequently in the frontal lobe, is characterized by three common manifestations: (1) subjective experiences that presage the attack, such as forced, repetitive thoughts, sudden alterations in mood, feelings of déjà vu, or hallucinations; (2) **automatisms**, or *automatic behaviors*; that is, performing nonreflexive acts without conscious volition—repetitive stereotyped movements such as lip smacking or chewing or activities such as undoing buttons; and (3) postural changes, as when the person assumes a catatonic, or frozen, posture.

Generalized Seizures

Generalized seizures are bilaterally symmetrical, without focal onset, and can be characterized by loss of consciousness and by stereotyped motor activity. Generalized seizure typically comprises three stages: (1) a *tonic stage*, in which the body stiffens and breathing stops; (2) a *clonic stage*, in which rhythmic shaking occurs; and (3) postseizure, a postictal depression, during which the patient loses affect and is confused. About 50 percent of generalized seizures are preceded by an aura.

Akinetic Seizures and Myoclonic Spasms

Akinetic seizures are ordinarily seen only in children. Usually, an affected child collapses suddenly and without warning. These seizures are often of very short duration, and the child may get up after only a few seconds. The fall can be dangerous, however, and a common recommendation is to have children wear padded helmets until the seizures can be controlled by medication. **Myoclonic spasms** are massive seizures that basically consist of a sudden flexion or extension of the body and often begin with a cry.

ⓒ Treating Epilepsy

The treatment of choice for epilepsy is an anticonvulsant drug such as diphenylhydantoin (DPH, Dilantin), phenobarbital, or one of several others. Anticonvulsants inhibit the discharge of abnormal neurons by stabilizing the neuronal membrane. If medication fails to alleviate the seizure problem satisfactorily, surgery can be performed to remove the focus of abnormal functioning in patients with focal seizures. *Deep brain stimulation* (DBS, shown in Figure 7.9) has been used experimentally to treat subjects who are not responsive to medication. Whereas treatment may be beneficial following anterior thalamic, hippocampal, and cerebellar stimulation, DBS treatment is invasive and requires further assessment with long-term trials (Sprengers et al., 2014).

26.5 Tumors

A **tumor**, or *neoplasm*, is a mass of new tissue that persists and grows independently of its surrounding structures and has no physiological use. Brain tumors grow from glia or other support cells, not from neurons. The rate at which

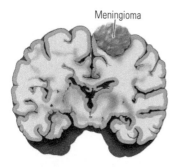

Figure 26.5 ▲

Encapsulated Tumor
Frontal section showing a meningioma arising in the dura mater and compressing the right cerebral hemisphere. Notice that the tumor has not infiltrated the brain.

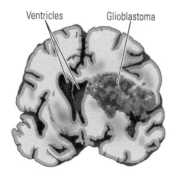

Figure 26.6 ▲

Infiltrating Tumor Frontal section showing a glioblastoma (a malignant type of glia-derived tumor) in the right cerebral hemisphere. Note the displacement of the ventricular system and the invasion of brain tissue (dark area).

tumors grow varies widely, depending on the type of cell that gave rise to them. Tumors account for a relatively high proportion of neurological disease compared with other causes; after the uterus, tumors are most commonly found in the brain.

Benign tumors are not likely to recur after removal, whereas *malignant* tumors are often progressive and threaten life. Although there are good reasons for distinguishing between benign and malignant tumors, the benign tumor may be as serious as the malignant one because benign brain tumors are often inaccessible to the surgeon. Many types of tumors affect the brain, and no brain region is immune to tumor formation.

A brain tumor may develop as a distinct entity, or *encapsulated tumor*, and put pressure on the other parts of the brain (**Figure 26.5**). Some encapsulated tumors are also cystic: they produce a fluid-filled cavity in the brain, usually lined with tumor cells. Because the skull is fixed in size, any increase in its contents compresses the brain, resulting in dysfunctions. In contrast, so-called *infiltrating tumors* are not clearly distinct from the surrounding tissue (**Figure 26.6**). An infiltrating tumor may either destroy healthy cells and occupy their place or surround existing cells (both neurons and glia) and interfere with their functioning.

Tumors can affect behavior in numerous ways. General symptoms result from increased intracranial pressure, including headache, vomiting, swelling of the optic disc (papilledema), slowing of the heart rate (bradycardia), mental dullness, double vision (diplopia), and, finally, convulsions, as well as functional impairments due to damage to the brain where the tumor is located. Brain tumors are distinguished on the basis of where they originate:

- **Glioma** is a general term for the roughly 45 percent of brain tumors that arise from glial cells and infiltrate the brain substance. Gliomas, ranging from the relatively benign to the highly malignant, vary considerably in responsiveness to treatment.

- **Meningiomas** are growths attached to the meninges, the brain's protective outer layer. They grow entirely outside the brain, are well encapsulated, and are the most benign of all brain tumors (see Figure 26.5). But even though meningiomas do not invade the brain, they are often multiple and disturb brain function by putting pressure on the brain, often producing seizures as a symptom. Although most meningiomas lie over the hemispheres, some develop between them and are therefore more difficult to remove. If meningiomas are removed completely, they tend not to recur. When they are present, however, it is not uncommon for these tumors to erode the overlying skull bone.

- A **metastatic tumor** in the brain has become established by a transfer of tumor cells from some other region of the body, most often a lung or a breast. (*Metastasis* is the transfer of disease from one organ or body part to another that is not directly connected.) Indeed, it is not uncommon for evidence of a brain tumor to be the first indication of lung cancer. Metastases to the brain are usually multiple, making treatment complicated and prognosis poor.

The most straightforward treatment of brain tumors is surgery, which is also the only way to make a definite histological diagnosis. If feasible, brain tumors are removed, but as with tumors elsewhere in the body, success depends on early diagnosis. Radiation therapy is a useful treatment for certain types of brain tumors. Chemotherapy has not yet been very successful in treating brain tumors, partly because of the difficulty of getting drugs to pass the blood–brain barrier and enter the tumor.

26.6 Headache

Rare indeed is the person who has never had a headache. Headache may constitute a neurological disorder in itself, as in migraine; it may be secondary to neurological disease such as tumor or infection; or it may result from psychological factors, especially stress, as in tension headaches. The pain-sensitive structures within the skull that can produce headache include the dura mater; the large arteries of the brain; the venous sinuses; and the branches of the fifth, ninth, and tenth cranial nerves and the first and third cervical nerves (see Figures 3.12 and 3.14). Pain can be elicited in these structures by pressure, displacement, or inflammation.

Types of Headache

Specific kinds of headache include migraine, headache associated with neurological disease, muscle-contraction headache, and nonmigrainous vascular headache.

Migraine

Perhaps the most common neurological disorder, migraine (derived from the Greek *hemi* and *kranion*, meaning "half of skull") afflicts some 5 percent to 20 percent of any population at some time in their lives. The World Federation of Neurology defines migraine as a "familial disorder characterized by recurrent attacks of headache widely variable in intensity, frequency, and duration. Attacks are commonly unilateral and are usually associated with anorexia, nausea, and vomiting. In some cases they are preceded by, or associated with, neurological and mood disturbances." Among the several types of migraine are classic migraine, common migraine, cluster headache, and hemiplegic and ophthalmologic migraine.

Classic migraine, occurring in about 12 percent of migraine sufferers, begins with an aura that usually lasts for 20 to 40 minutes. Karl Lashley (1941), arguably the first neuropsychologist, had classic migraine and carefully described his visual aura, which turned out to be common to many migraine sufferers (**Figure 26.7**). The aura is thought to occur because *vasoconstriction* (narrowing)

Figure 26.7 ▼

Development of a Migraine Scotoma As a migraine scotoma develops, a person looking at the small white "x" in the photo at far left would first see a small patch of lines. This striped area spreads progressively outward, leaving an opaque area (scotoma) where the stripes were before, almost completely blocking the visual field within 15 to 20 minutes (photo at far right). Normal vision returns shortly thereafter. (Tyler Olson/Shutterstock.)

X = Fixation point

of one or more cerebral arteries has produced ischemia of the occipital cortex. The results of PET studies have shown that during the aura, blood flow in the posterior cortex is reduced, and this reduction spreads at the rate of about 2 millimeters per minute without regard to its location with respect to major blood vessels. Why the reduction in blood flow should spread independently of the major vessels is not known, but it suggests that the vascular changes are secondary to changes in neural function.

The actual headache begins as the vasoconstriction reverses (ending the neurological disturbance) and vasodilation takes place. The headache is experienced as an intense pain localized in one side of the head, although it often spreads on that side and sometimes extends to the opposite side as well. A severe headache can be accompanied by nausea and vomiting, and it may last for hours or even days. A significant number of people considered to have classic migraine never have the headache but do experience the aura.

Common migraine is the most frequent type, occurring in more than 80 percent of migraine sufferers. There is no clear aura as there is in classic migraine, but a gastrointestinal or other "signal" may presage an attack. **Cluster headache** is a unilateral pain in the head or face that rarely lasts longer than 2 hours but recurs repeatedly for a period of weeks or even months before disappearing. Sometimes long periods pass between one series of cluster headaches and the next. The remaining two types of migraine, **hemiplegic migraine** and **ophthalmologic migraine**, are relatively rare and include loss of movement on one side of the body or of the eyes, respectively.

The frequency of migraine attacks varies from as often as once a week to as seldom as once in a lifetime. Where migraine is frequent, the occurrence generally decreases with age and usually ceases in middle age. Migraine was generally believed to be rare before adolescence, but now is recognized to afflict children as well. The actual incidence in this population is uncertain.

Headache Associated with Neurological Disease

Headache is a symptom of many nervous system disorders, usually resulting from the distortion of pain-sensitive structures. Common disorders producing headache include tumor, head trauma, infection, vascular malformations, and severe hypertension. The characteristics and locations of these headaches vary according to the underlying cause. For example, headache from a brain tumor is almost always located on the same side of the head as the tumor, particularly in the early stages of tumor growth. Headaches induced by brain tumors have no characteristic severity; they may vary from mild to excruciating. Likewise, hypertension headache, although it is nearly always located in the occipital region, is highly variable in severity.

Muscle-Contraction Headache

The most common headaches are **muscle-contraction headaches**, also known as *tension* or *nervous headaches*. They result from sustained contraction in the muscles of the scalp and neck caused by constant stress and tension, especially if poor posture is maintained for any length of time. Patients describe their pain as steady, nonpulsing, tight, squeezing, or pressing, or as the feeling of having their head in a vise. Some patients complain of a crawling sensation. Anxiety, dizziness, and bright spots appearing before the eyes may accompany these headaches. Caffeine may exacerbate muscle-contraction headache in some people, presumably because it is a general stimulant and also exacerbates anxiety.

Nonmigrainous Vascular Headaches

Headache associated with dilation of the cranial arteries can be induced by a wide variety of diseases and conditions. The most common causes are fever, *anoxia*, anemia, high altitude, physical effort, hypoglycemia (low blood sugar), foods, and chemical agents. Headache also may result from congestion and edema of the nasal membranes, often termed *vasomotor rhinitis*, and assumed to be a localized vascular reaction to stress.

◎ Treating Headache

Migraine is treated by specific drugs at the time of an attack and by preventive measures between attacks. In an acute attack, **ergotamine** compounds, often given in conjunction with caffeine, are useful in alleviating the headache, probably because they constrict the cerebral arteries, thus reducing dilation, the source of the pain. Most migraine sufferers find that their headache is reduced in a totally dark room. Nevertheless, a range of drug treatments for headache may be effective for different individuals, and behavioral therapy and lifestyle changes can be effective.

The most obvious treatment for headache arising from neurological disease is to treat the disease itself. Sources of relief for tension headaches include muscle-relaxant drugs, minor tranquilizers, application of heat to the affected muscles, and improved posture. When headaches are persistent, biofeedback that promotes relaxation can bring relief. Finally, avoiding the life situations that give rise to stress also can prevent headache.

26.7 Infections

Infection is the invasion of the body by disease-producing (pathogenic) microorganisms and the reaction of the tissues to their presence and to the toxins they generate. Because the CNS can be invaded by a wide variety of infectious agents—including viruses, bacteria, fungi, and metazoan parasites—diagnosing and treating infection are important components of clinical neurology. Although nervous system infections usually spread from infection elsewhere in the body—especially the ears, nose, and throat—they also may be introduced directly into the brain as a result of head trauma, skull fracture, or surgery. Nervous system infections are particularly serious because the affected neurons and glia usually die, leaving permanent lesions.

Infections kill neural cells via several processes:

- Interfering with the neuronal blood supply to produce thrombosis, hemorrhaging of capillaries, or even complete choking off of larger blood vessels.

- Disturbing glucose or oxygen metabolism in brain cells severely enough to kill them.

- Altering the characteristics of neural-cell membranes, thus changing the neurons' electrical properties or interfering with their basic enzymatic processes, producing an array of abnormal conditions.

- Leading to the formation of *pus*, a by-product of the body's defense against infection. Pus is a fluid composed basically of white blood cells, their by-products, by-products of the infectious microorganisms, and a thin fluid called *liquor puris*. Pus impairs neuronal functioning in at least two ways: it changes the composition of the extracellular fluids surrounding a neuron, thus altering neuronal function, and its presence increases pressure on the brain, disturbing normal functioning.

- Causing edema, which leads to compression of the brain tissues, resulting in dysfunction.

Nervous system infections that are secondary to infections elsewhere in the body are accompanied by symptoms of those other infections, including lowered blood pressure and other changes in blood circulation, fever, general malaise, headache, and delirium. In addition, symptoms of cerebral infections include both generalized symptoms of increased intracranial pressure—such as headache, vertigo, nausea, convulsions, and mental confusion—and symptoms specifically associated with the disturbance of particular brain functions.

Diagnostic tests for infection include analyses of the cerebrospinal fluid in addition to conventional methods of infection identification, such as smear and culture studies. CT and other brain scans may be used to diagnose and locate some infectious nervous system disorders.

Types of CNS Infection

Four sorts of infection can affect the CNS: viral, bacterial, mycotic (fungal), and parasitic.

Viral Infections

A virus is an encapsulated aggregate of nucleic acid that may be made of either DNA or RNA, characterized by a lack of independent metabolism and by the ability to replicate only within living host cells. Some viruses, such as those causing poliomyelitis and rabies, are neurotropic: they have a special affinity for CNS cells. In contrast, pantropic viruses (such as those that cause mumps and herpes simplex) attack other body tissues in addition to the CNS. Within the nervous system, most viral infections produce nonspecific lesions affecting widespread brain regions, such as lesions due to St. Louis encephalitis, rabies, and poliomyelitis.

Optimal habitats for mosquitoes are expanding along with changing climates. As a result, mosquito-borne infections likewise are expanding. One, West Nile virus, was first identified in Uganda in the 1930s, appeared in New York in 1999, and has now spread throughout North America and Europe. About 80 percent of infected humans show no symptoms. For the remaining 20 percent, the threat of **viral meningitis**, inflammation of the brain's triple-layered protective covering caused by infection, can threaten to infect the brain itself and produce neurological impairment, which for some people can be severe and long-lasting, and sometimes fatal.

Bacterial Infections

Bacterium is a loose generic name for any microorganism (typically one-celled) that has no chlorophyll and multiplies by simple cell division. Bacterial infections of the CNS result from an infestation of these organisms, usually through the bloodstream. The most common neurological disorders resulting from bacterial infection are meningitis and brain abscess.

In **bacterial meningitis**, the triple-layered meninges that encase the CNS are infected by any of a variety of bacteria and inflamed. **Brain abscesses** also are produced by a variety of bacteria, secondary to infection elsewhere in the body. An abscess begins as a small focus of purulent (pus-producing) bacteria that cause necrosis (death) of cells in the affected region. As the bacteria multiply and destroy more brain cells, the abscess behaves like an expanding mass (often hollow in the center), producing increasing intracranial pressure.

▲ Pus is visible over the anterior surface of this brain infected with bacterial meningitis. (Biophoto Associates/Science Source.)

Mycotic Infections

Invasion of the nervous system by a fungus is a **mycotic infection**. A fungus is any member of a large group of lower plants (in some taxonomic schemes), including yeasts, molds, and mushrooms, that lack chlorophyll and subsist on living or dead organic matter. Ordinarily, the CNS is highly resistant to mycotic infections, but fungi may invade a brain whose resistance has been reduced by diseases such as cancer or tuberculosis.

Parasitic Infestations

A **parasite** is an organism that lives on or within another living organism—the host—at the host's expense. Several kinds of parasites can invade the CNS and produce disease. **Amebiasis** (*amebic dysentery*), caused by an infestation of the protozoan *Entamoeba histolytica* (protozoa are one-celled animals), results in encephalitis and brain abscesses. **Malaria** is caused by protozoa of the genus *Plasmodium*, transmitted by the bites of infected mosquitoes. Cerebral malaria arises when the plasmodia infect the brain's capillaries, producing local hemorrhages and subsequent neuronal degeneration.

◎ Treating CNS Infection

Treatment varies with the type of infection. Viral infections are extremely difficult to treat because no specific antidotes exist. Although many antiviral drugs are being developed in conjunction with intense research efforts to treat HIV and AIDS, viral infections remain difficult to treat. The usual option is to let the disease run its course. Sedatives are sometimes administered to make the patient more comfortable. The exception to this general rule is rabies treatment. When a person has had contact with a rabid animal, antirabies vaccine is administered over a period of 2 to 4 weeks to produce immunity before the disease actually develops. When the disease does develop, rabies is fatal.

Bacterial cerebral infections have become less common with the introduction of antibiotic drugs. In some cases, it may be necessary to drain abscesses to relieve intracranial pressure or perform spinal taps to remove cerebrospinal fluid and thus reduce the pressure of edema or a buildup of pus. Overuse of antibiotic drugs, including in industrial farming operations, has spawned antibiotic-resistant bacteria, or "superbugs." Research on new antibiotic drugs is hard-pressed to keep pace with bacterial resistance. Neither mycotic nor parasitic infections can be treated satisfactorily, although antibiotics are often used to treat associated disorders.

26.8 Disorders of Motor Neurons and the Spinal Cord

Several movement disorders result from damage either to the spinal cord or to cortical projections to the spinal cord, including *myasthenia gravis*, *poliomyelitis*, *multiple sclerosis*, *paraplegia*, *Brown-Séquard syndrome*, and *hemiplegia*. **Table 26.4** lists medical terms commonly used in describing movement disorders. Section 27.7 reviews behavioral symptoms of such motor disorders as Parkinson's disease, Tourette's syndrome, and Huntington's disease.

Myasthenia Gravis

Myasthenia gravis (severe muscle weakness), a disorder of the muscle receptors, is characterized by muscular fatigue in the wake of very little exercise. It may be apparent after a short exercise or work period, toward the end of a long conversation, or sometimes even after a few repetitions of a movement. Rest brings a feeling of recovery.

The rapid onset of weakness distinguishes myasthenia gravis from other disorders such as depression or general fatigue. There are no visible signs of muscle pathology. Although myasthenia can affect people of any age, it is most likely to begin in the third decade of life and is more common in women than in men.

All the muscles of the body may be affected, but those innervated by the cranial nerves are usually affected first. In this case, the initial symptoms are *diplopia* (double vision), *ptosis* (drooping of the eyelid), weakness of voice, and difficulty

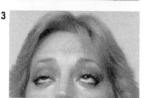

▲ When asked to look up (1) a myasthenia gravis patient's eyelids quickly become fatigued and droop (2 and 3). Her eyelids open normally after a few minutes of rest (4). (Courtesy of Y. Harati, M.D., Baylor College of Medicine, Houston, Texas.)

Table 26.4 **Terms commonly used to describe movement disorders**

Apraxia. Inability, in the absence of paralysis or other motor or sensory impairments, to make or copy voluntary movements. Usually follows damage to the neocortex.

Ataxia. Failure of muscular coordination or irregularity of muscular action. Commonly follows cerebellar damage.

Athetosis. Ceaseless slow, sinuous, writhing movements, especially in the hands, due to abnormal function of the extrapyramidal system.

Catalepsy. Muscular rigidity in which voluntary movements are reduced or absent but posture is maintained. A feature of Parkinson's disease, due to dopamine loss.

Cataplexy. Complete loss of movement and posture during which muscle tone is absent but consciousness is spared.

Chorea. Literally, "to dance"; refers a wide variety of ceaseless, jerky movements that appear well-coordinated but are performed involuntarily.

Hemiplegia. Complete or partial paralysis to one half of the body. Usually follows damage to the contralateral motor cortex.

Palsy. Usually refers to persisting movement disorders due to brain damage acquired perinatally.

Paralysis. Complete loss of movement (more commonly) or sensation in a part of the body. Usually permanent after damage to motor neurons; temporary after damage to motor cortex (area 4).

Paraplegia. Paralysis or paresis of the lower torso and legs following spinal-cord damage.

Spasticity. Increased tone in certain muscle groups that maintain posture against the force of gravity. If the limb is moved against the rigidity, resistance will initially increase, then tone will suddenly melt (clasp-knife reflex). Thought to be produced by damage to the extrapyramidal motor fibers.

Tardive dyskinesia. Slow, persistent movements, particularly of the mouth and tongue. Usually follows long-term treatment with antipsychotic drugs.

chewing and swallowing or holding up the head. In some people, only the limbs are affected. Usually the symptoms are most apparent at the end of the day and are relieved after sleep. The severity of myasthenia gravis varies from a mild unilateral ptosis in some people to an incapacitating generalized weakness, threatening death by respiratory paralysis in others.

Muscular weakness is caused by a failure of standard muscular neurotransmission due to a paucity of muscle receptors for acetylcholine. These receptors may have been attacked by antibodies from the patient's own immune system. Treatment for myasthenia gravis has two objectives. First, acetylcholine therapy is used to relieve the symptoms. Second, thymectomy (surgical removal of the thymus to reduce antibody formation) and immunosuppressive drug treatment are used in the hope of arresting the disease's further progress. With these advances in treatment, mortality is currently very low.

Poliomyelitis

A disorder of the motor-neuron cell bodies, **poliomyelitis** is an acute infectious disease caused by a virus with a special affinity for spinal cord motor neurons and sometimes for the motor neurons of the cranial nerves. Motor neuron loss causes paralysis and muscle wasting. If the motor neurons of the respiratory centers are attacked, death can result from asphyxia.

The occurrence of poliomyelitis was sometimes sporadic and sometimes epidemic in North America until the Salk and Sabin vaccines were developed in the 1950s and 1960s. Since then, the disease has been well-controlled. Why the virus has a special affinity for motor neurons remains a scientific question. One possibility is that it interferes with acetylcholine synthesis. People who have recovered from polio or who displayed only mild symptoms initially may begin to display symptoms of fatigue and weakness many years later, a condition called *postpolio syndrome*.

Multiple Sclerosis

Multiple sclerosis (MS; *sclerosis*, from the Greek, meaning "hardness"), a disorder of myelinated motor fibers, is characterized by loss of myelin, largely in motor tracts but also in sensory tracts. The myelin loss is not uniform; rather, it is lost in patches—small, hard, circumscribed scars, called *sclerotic plaques*, in which the myelin sheath and sometimes the axons are destroyed (see the Snapshot on page 108).

MS produces strange symptoms that usually appear first in adulthood. The initial symptoms may be loss of sensation in the face, limbs, or body; blurring of vision; or loss of sensation and control in one or more limbs. Often, these early symptoms go into remission, after which they may not appear again for years. In some forms, however, the disease may progress rapidly in just a few years until an affected person is limited to bed care.

The cause of MS remains unknown. Proposed causes include bacterial infection, a virus, environmental factors, and an immune response of the CNS. Often, multiple cases will be seen in a single family, suggesting that MS is related to a genetic predisposition. MS is most prevalent in northern Europe, somewhat less prevalent in North America, and rare in Japan and in more southerly or tropical countries. Where MS is prevalent, its incidence of 50 per 100,000 makes it one of the most common structural nervous system diseases. Only Parkinson's disease is equally common.

Multiple sclerosis has a female-to-male ratio of about 3:2, and its progress is often more rapid in females than in males. The prevalence of MS at northern latitudes has raised the question of its possible relation to vitamin D deficiency. Vitamin D is obtained from sunlight and oily fish; access to both sources is reduced at northern latitudes. According to Duan and colleagues (2014), vitamin D may be important for myelin development in childhood and for its maintenance in adulthood. Yet vitamin D plays many roles in the nervous system, so it remains uncertain what, if any, role vitamin D deficiency plays in MS.

A new drug treatment, alemtuzumab (Lemtrada), which destroys a class of immune cells that attack healthy body tissue, shows promise for treating MS. Advances in brain–computer interface (BCI) technology likewise hold promise for aiding mobility in people with rapidly progressing multiple sclerosis.

Paraplegia

In **paraplegia** (from the Greek *para*, "alongside of," and *plegia*, "stroke"), caused by complete transection of the spinal cord, both lower limbs are paralyzed; **quadriplegia** is the paralysis of all four extremities. Immediately after the cord has been severed, all activity ceases in the part distal to the cut, and all movement, sensation, and reflexes distal to the cut disappear. Owing to the loss of reflex activity, thermoregulatory control is absent (ending perspiration and leaving the skin cool and dry), as is bladder control (necessitating drainage of the bladder to prevent urinary retention). This condition, called *spinal shock*, lasts for 4 days to about 6 weeks.

Gradually, some spinal reflexes return until, after a year or so, a stabilized condition is reached. A pinprick, for example, may again elicit a withdrawal reflex such as the *triple response*—flexion of the hip, knee, and ankle. No sensations, voluntary movements, or thermoregulatory control ever reappears below the lesion. Eventually, extensor activity may become sufficiently strong so that weight can be supported briefly, but spinal circuits are too dependent on brain facilitation to permit prolonged standing in its absence.

Brown-Séquard Syndrome

Brown-Séquard syndrome refers to the consequences of a unilateral transection through the spinal cord (**Figure 26.8**). Because some ascending and descending pathways cross the spinal cord and others do not, different symptoms appear on the two sides of the body below the cut. Contralateral to the side of the section, there is a loss of pain and te perature sensation because these pathways cross where they enter the cord. Sensations of fine touch and pressure are preserved there, however, because their pathways do not cross until they reach the caudal medulla. Fine touch and pressure sensation, but not pain and temperature sensation, is lost ipsilateral to the section, as are sensation and voluntary movements of distal musculature. Walking ability is recovered within 2 to 3 days because this activity is controlled bilaterally.

Figure 26.8 ▼

Spinal Hemitransection

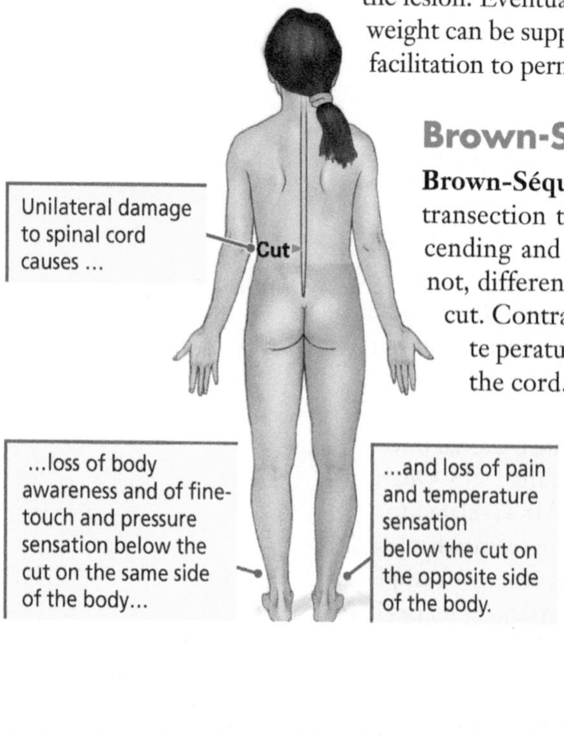

Unilateral damage to spinal cord causes ...

Cut

...loss of body awareness and of fine-touch and pressure sensation below the cut on the same side of the body...

...and loss of pain and temperature sensation below the cut on the opposite side of the body.

Hemiplegia

The characteristics of **hemiplegia** are loss of voluntary movements on one side of the body and changes in postural tone and in the status of various reflexes. Hemiplegia results from damage to the neocortex and basal ganglia contra-lateral to the motor symptoms. In infancy, such damage may result from birth injury, epilepsy, or fever. (Infant hemiplegia is usually discussed under the um-brella of cerebral palsy; see Section 24.3.) In young adults, hemiplegia is usually caused by rupture of a congenital aneurysm or by an embolism, tumor, or head injury. Most cases of hemiplegia, however, are found in middle-aged to elderly people and are usually due to hemorrhaging as a consequence of high blood pressure and degeneration of the blood vessels.

The damage that produces hemiplegia also affects a number of diagnosti-cally important reflexes. In healthy people, scratching the sole of the foot with a dull object produces a downward flexion of all toes. A person with hemiplegia, in contrast, responds with an upward flexion, especially of the big toe, and an outward fanning of the toes (**Figure 26.9**).

This response, called the **Babinski sign** or **extensor plantar response**, is caused by the activation of extensor muscles and is often accompanied by leg flexion at the knee and hip. It is one of a family of abnormal flexion responses subsequent to motor-cortex or pyramidal-tract damage. Two reflexes are ab-sent in hemiplegia: the **abdominal reflex**, which in healthy people causes the abdominal muscles to retract when stroked, and the **cremasteric reflex**, which in healthy males causes retraction of the testicles when the inner thigh is stroked.

The extent of recovery after hemiplegia varies widely, and treatment may have one or a combination of objectives. A patient may be trained to use the unaffected side, to use the affected side as much as spasticity and residual abili-ties allow, or to make movements that lessen spasticity and maximize voluntary control. The last strategy, described in detail by Berta Bobath (1970), is based on the fact that the strength of spasticity is related to posture. Bending over lessens spasticity, and if the arm is extended and the head is turned toward the arm, flexion spasticity is lessened. Such knowledge may enable some patients to make considerable use of their affected limbs.

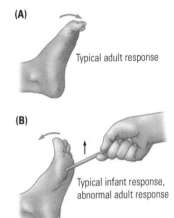

(A) Typical adult response

(B) Typical infant response, abnormal adult response

Figure 26.9 ▲

Hemiplegia Effect (A) The typical adult response to stimu-lation of the lateral plantar surface of the left foot. (B) The typical infant and abnormal adult response, known as the Babinski sign.

◎ 26.9 Sleep Disorders

The need for sleep varies considerably from one person to another, as well as in the same person at different stages of life. We have all been told that we need 8 hours of sleep each night for good health. In fact, there are both long and short sleepers. Some people reportedly stay healthy on as little as an hour of sleep per day, whereas others sleep as much as 10 to 12 hours. The definition of what constitutes adequate sleep must be decided within the context of a person's sleep history. Not surprisingly, because sleep may take up one-third of a person's life, it is also associated with a number of disorders.

People with sleep-related disorders are usually examined in a sleep labora-tory for 1 to 2 days (**Figure 26.10**). A computerized *polygraph* records their brain waves to produce an EEG (Figure 26.10A); an **electromyogram**, or EMG, records muscle activity (Figure 26.10B); an **electrooculogram**, or EOG,

(A) EEG

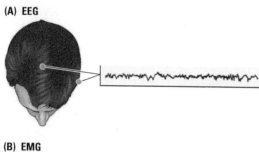

(B) EMG

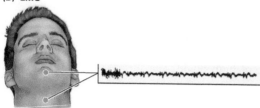

(C) EOG

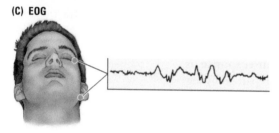

Figure 26.10 ▲

Sleep-Laboratory Protocol Readouts from electrodes attached to a sleeping subject record (A) brain-wave activity, (B) muscle activity, and (C) eye movements. (HANK MORGAN/Science Source/Getty Images.)

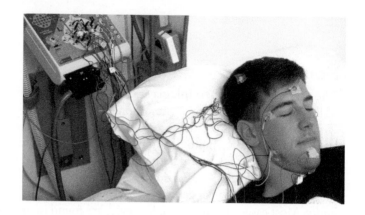

records eye movements (Figure 26.10C); and a thermometer measures body temperature during sleep. Together, these recordings provide a comprehensive and reliable description of sleep–wake behavior. Because all of these recording procedures can be miniaturized, a smartphone can monitor sleep at home. The advent of wearable electronics promises similar convenience.

The EEG recording traces distinct patterns of brain-wave activity and is the primary measure of sleep states. Sleep consists of at least two states that alternate periodically in the course of a complete sleep session. One state is characterized by vivid dreaming, during which the subjects display rapid eye movements, or REMs. This state is **REM sleep**, and by default the other is **non-REM (NREM) sleep**. Both states feature numerous subcategories.

Figure 26.11 summarizes the brain activity of a healthy person recorded during a typical night's sleep. Part A displays the EEG patterns associated with waking and with the four stages of sleep. The main change characterizing a sleeper's progression from stage 1 through stage 4 sleep is that that EEG waves become larger and slower. The numbering of these stages assumes that the sleeper moves from relatively shallow sleep in stage 1 to deep sleep in stage 4. Notice that the EEG of REM sleep resembles that of waking.

Figure 26.11 ▶

Sleep Cycles (A) EEG patterns associated with waking, with the four NREM sleep stages, and with REM sleep. (B) In a typical night's sleep, a person undergoes a number of sleep-state cycles in periods roughly 90 minutes in length. NREM sleep dominates the early periods, and REM sleep dominates later sleep. The duration of each sleep stage is reflected in the thickness of each bar, which is color-coded to the corresponding stage in part A. The depth of each stage is graphed as the relative length of the bar. (Information from Kelley, D. D. Sleep and Dreaming. In E. R. Kandel, H. H. Schwartz, and T. M. Jessell, Eds., *Principles of Neural Science*. New York: McGraw-Hill, 2000, p. 938.)

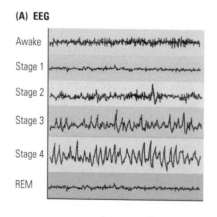

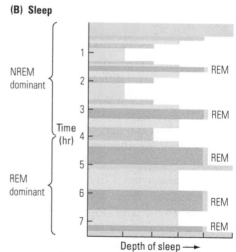

Figure 26.11B shows the sleeper cycling from one sleep stage to another as the night progresses. Depth of sleep is shown by steps indicating when the person descends and ascends through the four sleep stages and how long each stage lasts. All of the stages, including REM sleep, are periodic. Notice that earlier sleep cycles are dominated by stage 4 sleep, and REM sleep dominates later cycles.

Typically, centers in the brainstem produce muscular paralysis during REM sleep, so apart from REMs and short bursts of twitches in the fingers, toes, and other body parts, the body remains largely motionless. Even so, EEGs taken during dreams resemble the patterns seen when participants are awake. NREM sleep is characterized by large movements, such as tossing and turning, and by a slow-wave EEG of various amplitudes.

Sleep disorders are generally divided into two major groups: (1) **Narcolepsy**, characterized by excessive sleep or brief, inappropriate sleep episodes including REM sleep, often is associated with other symptoms. (2) **Insomnia**, characterized by inadequate sleep, is an inability to fall asleep or frequent arousals from sleep. In addition to these two groups of disorders, other behaviors during sleep can disturb the afflicted person. Among them are night terrors, sleepwalking, grinding of the teeth, and myoclonic jerks (sudden vigorous movements). They are usually too transitory, too infrequent, or not sufficiently disruptive to classify as sleep disorders.

Narcolepsy

In narcolepsy, the affected person has an overwhelming impulse to fall asleep or simply collapses into sleep at inconvenient times. Attacks may be infrequent or occur many times a day. Narcolepsy disorders are surprisingly common; estimates suggest that as much as 0.02 percent of the population may have them. Males and females seem equally affected. The incidence of narcolepsy in the families of afflicted persons is high. Genetic mutations related to narcolepsy have been identified in both mouse and dog models, and evidence points to a genetic basis for narcolepsy in humans.

One form of narcolepsy is associated with the loss of hypothalamus neurons that make the peptide neurotransmitter hypocretin (orexin). An allele of the *HLA-DQB1* gene on chromosome 6, which is important for immune system function, has been linked to some narcolepsy cases. Investigators propose that narcolepsy can arise as an autoimmune disorder in which the immune system, which usually attacks foreign substances, kills hypocretin neurons in the hypothalamus (Mignot, 2014). The precise relation of *HLA-DQB1* to narcolepsy is unclear: the gene is common, yet not all carriers become narcoleptic. Symptoms usually appear between the ages of 10 and 20, and once sleep attacks develop, they continue throughout life. Amphetaminelike stimulants and tricyclic antidepressants have been found to be useful in treating narcolepsy.

Varieties of narcolepsy include sleep attacks, cataplexy, sleep paralysis, and hypnagogic hallucinations. Although all these disorders do not generally exist at the same time or in the same person, they occur together often enough to be considered interrelated.

- **Sleep attacks** are brief, often irresistible, sleep episodes—probably slow-wave, NREM, naplike sleep—that last about 15 minutes and can occur at any time. Their approach is sometimes recognizable, but they can also occur without warning. Episodes are most apt to occur in times of boredom or after meals, but they can also occur during such activities as sexual intercourse, scuba diving, or baseball games. After a brief sleep attack, the affected person may awaken completely alert and remain attack free for several hours.

- **Cataplexy** (from the Greek *cata*, meaning "down," and *plexy*, meaning "strike") is a complete loss of muscle tone or a sudden paralysis that results in buckling of the knees or complete collapse. The attack may be so sudden that the fall results in injury, particularly because the loss of muscle tone and reflexes prevents an affected person from making any motion to break the fall. During the attack, the person remains conscious and, if the eyelids stay open or are opened, can recall seeing events that took place during the attack. In contrast with sleep attacks, cataplexic attacks usually occur at times of emotional excitement, such as when a person is laughing or angry. If emotions are held under tight control, the attacks can be prevented. Cataplexy is probably an attack of REM, or dream, sleep.

- **Sleep paralysis** occurs in the transition between wakefulness and sleep. The episode is usually brief but can last as long as 20 minutes. Sleep paralysis has been experienced by half of all people, if classroom surveys are a true indication of its frequency. In contrast with cataplexy, the sleep-paralyzed person can be easily aroused by being touched or called by name and if experienced with the attacks, can terminate them by grunting or using some other strategy that shakes off sleep. What may happen in sleep paralysis is that the person wakes up but is still in the paralytic state associated with dream sleep.

- **Hypnagogic hallucinations** (from the Greek *hypnos*, meaning "sleep," and *gogic* meaning "enter into") are episodes of auditory, visual, or tactile hallucination during sleep paralysis as an affected person is falling asleep or waking up. The hallucinations are generally frightening; the person may feel that a monster or something equally terrifying is lurking nearby. Similar hallucinations can occur during cataplexic episodes. A curious feature is that the hallucinating person is conscious and often aware of what is actually happening, making the hallucinations even more bizarre, because they can become intermixed with real events. Hypnagogic hallucinations may actually be dreams that a person is having while conscious.

Insomnia

Results from studies of people who claim that they do not sleep, do not sleep well, or wake up frequently from sleep show that insomnia can have many causes. Nevertheless, systematic EEG recordings from poor sleepers before and during sleep show that they exaggerated the length of time it took them to get to sleep. But poor sleepers do have decreased dream sleep, move more during sleep, and go through more transitions between sleep stages than healthy sleepers do. Moreover, when awakened from slow-wave sleep, they claim that they have not been sleeping. In rare cases, *prion disease*, in which proteins display abnormal folding, can result in chronic insomnia that is ultimately fatal (Blasé et al., 2014).

Even though, by EEG criteria, poor sleepers do sleep, they do not seem to benefit completely from sleep's restorative properties. Surveys suggest that as many as 14 percent of people claim to have insomnia, but the causes are diverse and include general factors such as anxiety, depression, fear of sleeping, environmental disturbances, and jet lag. Insomnia may be associated with nightmares and night terrors, sleep apnea (arrested breathing during sleep), *restless legs syndrome* (RLS, described in the Snapshot), myoclonus (involuntary muscle contraction), the use of certain kinds of drugs, and certain kinds of brain damage.

SNAPSHOT | Restless Legs Syndrome

RLS, also called *Willis-Ekbom disease*, is a sleep disorder in which a person experiences unpleasant sensations as creeping, crawling, tingling, pulling, or pain in the legs. These sensations usually occur in the calf area but may be felt anywhere from thigh to ankle. One or both legs may be affected; for some people, the sensations are also felt in the arms. About 15 percent of sufferers display the condition in only one leg (Garcia-Borreguero and Williams, 2014).

RLS can affect as many as 5 of every 100 people, and the propensity may be inherited. Other causes include iron deficiency and Parkinson's disease, anemia, kidney failure, diabetes, and peripheral neuropathy. RLS has been associated with vitamin D deficiency but has been reported to have a higher incidence in the summer, when vitamin D levels should be high. Some pregnant women experience RLS, especially in their last trimester. For most of these women, symptoms usually disappear within 4 weeks after giving birth.

Measures of oxygen levels in the legs suggest that peripheral hypoxia (lack of oxygen) can be associated with RLS. Certain medications, including anti-nausea drugs (prochlorperazine or metoclopramide), anti-seizure drugs (phenytoin or droperidol), antipsychotic drugs (haloperidol or phenothiazine derivatives), and some cold and allergy medications, may aggravate symptoms. Although RLS is common, the number of people requiring medication for the condition is uncertain.

People with RLS describe an irresistible urge to move the legs when sensations occur. Many have a related sleep disorder called *periodic limb movement in sleep* (PLMS), characterized by involuntary jerking or bending leg movements

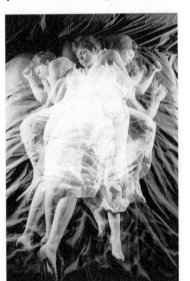

B. W. Hoffmann/Envision

that typically occur every 10 to 60 seconds. Some people experience hundreds of such movements per night, which can wake them, disturb their sleep, and annoy bed partners. People who have these disorders get less sleep at night and may feel sleepy during the day.

RLS affects both sexes, and symptoms can begin at any age but are more severe among older people. Young people who experience symptoms are sometimes thought to have "growing pains" or may be considered hyperactive because they cannot easily sit still in school.

There is no laboratory test for RLS, and a doctor cannot detect anything abnormal in a physical examination. The disorder is likely of CNS origin because the syndrome has been reported in a patient who had no legs. A direct cause of the symptoms may be low levels of dopamine in the nigrostriatal pathway, but the brain changes accompanying leg movements are widespread.

Because iron participates in the synthesis and the use of dopamine, some people find improvement with iron supplements. For those who are not responsive to iron, L-dopa, a drug used to increase dopamine and thus treat Parkinson's disease, has proved useful, as have dopamine-receptor agonists such as pramipexole (Mirapex and Sifrol). Symptomatic treatment for RLS includes massage, exercise, stretching, and hot baths. Patients can also restrict their caffeine intake or take benzodiazepines or both to help them get to sleep.

Garcia-Borreguero, D., and A. M. Williams. An update on restless legs syndrome (Willis-Ekbom disease): Clinical features, pathogenesis and treatment. *Current Opinion in Neurology* 27:493–501, 2014.

Nightmares are intense, frightening dreams that lead to waking. Less common are *night terrors*, attempts to fight or flee accompanied by panic and screams or similar utterances. Nightmares occur during dream sleep, but night terrors occur during NREM sleep. Night terrors are usually brief (1 or 2 minutes) and are usually forgotten on waking. Both phenomena are more common in children than in adults, perhaps because adults have had more experience with disturbing dreams and so are less easily awakened by them. Both can be sufficiently disturbing to disrupt sleep and lead to insomnia.

Sleep apnea (from the Greek for "not breathing") is an inability to breathe during sleep: the brain fails to signal the muscles to breathe, so a person has to wake up to do so. A periodic cessation of respiration in sleep, ranging in length from about 10 seconds to 3 minutes, is of two types:

Obstructive sleep apnea occurs mainly in the course of dreaming and seems to be caused by a collapse of the oropharynx during the paralysis of dream sleep. Patients invariably have a history of loud snoring—sounds produced as a consequence of difficulty breathing through the constricted air passage. The obstruction can be reduced through surgical intervention or various wearable devices that aid in keeping the airways open.

Central sleep apnea stems from a CNS disorder. It primarily affects males and is characterized by a failure of the diaphragm and accessory muscles to move. (For more information on sleep apnea and its possible relation to sudden infant death syndrome—SIDS—see the Snapshot on page 136.)

Sleep apnea can be caused or aggravated by obesity, which contributes to narrowing of the air passage and is associated with many other symptoms of metabolic syndrome, including high blood pressure and diabetes. All-night recording sessions are requisite for detecting and diagnosing sleep apneas of both types. Both interrupt sleep because an affected person is awakened partly or fully by oxygen deprivation. According to Caterina Tonon and colleagues (2007), oxygen deprivation incurred in sleep apnea can lead to neuronal loss in the brain. Accordingly, sleep apnea should be a suspected cause of daytime sleepiness, is easily diagnosed, and can be treated both by weight loss and wearable devices that produce negative airway pressure during sleep and so improve sleep.

Most psychoactive drugs, whether stimulants or sedatives, eventually lead to insomnia. Hypnotics and sedatives may promote sleep at first, but only until habituation sets in. Furthermore, when drugs do induce sleep, it is not dream sleep, and so the user continues to feel sleep-deprived. Stimulants directly reduce sleep, but they may have their greatest effect in reducing slow-wave sleep. Withdrawal from the drug usually puts an end to drug-induced insomnia.

SUMMARY

26.1 The Neurological Examination

A neurologist is a medical specialist who gives patients a nervous system examination, takes their personal history, assesses their condition, and recommends treatment. Although they specialize in diagnosing and treating nervous system damage caused by overt brain trauma and disease, neurologists also examine conditions such as PTSD, which for some people results in brain damage.

26.2 Cerebral Vascular Disorders

Vascular disorders entailing constriction of blood vessels or bleeding in the brain are the most common cause of disability and death. Treatments include lifestyle changes to reduce metabolic syndromes that damage blood vessels and medications that control metabolic disease, including reducing blood pressure.

26.3 Traumatic Brain Injuries

Brain traumas include open head injuries, in which the skull and brain are penetrated, and closed head injuries, in which the brain is bruised by a blow. TBI occurs most commonly in the very young and very old and can occur with very mild insults, such as concussions encountered in sports.

26.4 Epilepsy

Epilepsy includes several varieties of seizure, abnormal discharges of brain neurons that occur spontaneously as a result of scarring from injury, infections, or tumors. Treatments for epilepsy include treating those primary causes; pharmacological therapies; and in intractable cases, deep brain stimulation and elective brain surgery.

26.5 Tumors

The varieties of brain tumors include glioma, meningioma, and metastatic tumors. Treatments include brain surgery to remove the tumor and drug treatments as well as therapy to treat tumor symptoms.

26.6 Headache

Headaches include those associated with neurological diseases such as stroke, tumors, and brain infections; migraine; muscle contraction; and nonmigrainous vascular headache. Behavioral and pharmacological treatments are directed to primary causes.

26.7 Infections

Infections—viral, bacterial, mycotic, and parasitic—may affect the brain. Because the blood–brain barrier blocks easy access to CNS tissue, infections are difficult to treat with drugs. New treatment options are ongoing areas of research such as those directed toward antibiotic-resistant bacteria and prompted by research on viruses.

26.8 Disorders of Motor Neurons and the Spinal Cord

Motor neuron and spinal cord disorders include myasthenia gravis, poliomyelitis, multiple sclerosis, and injuries that transect the spinal cord partly or completely. Treatments for motor disorders include physical therapy, pharmacological treatments, and brain–computer interfaces.

26.9 Sleep Disorders

Sleep disorders include insomnia, an inability to sleep, and narcolepsy, excessive sleep. These disorders can have a CNS origin but also include sleep apnea, failure to breathe while asleep, and disorders related to drug use. Miniaturization and development of wearable computers promise to allow individualized sleep monitoring and improved diagnosis and treatment of sleep disorders.

References

Blasé, J. L., L. Cracco, L. B. Schonberger, R. A. Maddox, Y. Cohen, I. Cali, and E. D. Belay. Sporadic fatal insomnia in an adolescent. *Pediatrics* 133(3):e766–770, 2014. doi:10.1542/peds.2013-1396.Epub February 2, 2014.

Bobath, B. *Adult Hemiplegia: Evaluation and Treatment.* London: Heinemann Medical Books, 1970.

Costanzo, M. E., Y. Y. Chou, S. Leaman, D. L. Pham, D. Keyser, D. E. Nathan, M. Coughlin, P. Rapp, and M. J. Roy. Connecting combat-related mild traumatic brain injury with posttraumatic stress disorder symptoms through brain imaging. *Neuroscience Letters* 577C:11–15. doi:10.1016/j.neulet.2014.05.054.June 4, 2014.

Duan, S., Z. Lv, and X. Fan. Vitamin D status and the risk of multiple sclerosis: A systematic review and meta-analysis *Neuroscience Letters* 570:108–113, 2014.

Förstl, H., C. Haass, and B. Hemmer. Boxing—acute complications and late sequelae from concussion to dementia. *Deutsches Arzteblatt International* 107:835-U18, 2010.

Ghobrial, G. M., P. S. Amenta, and M. Maltenfort. Longitudinal incidence and concurrence rates for traumatic brain injury and spine injury—A twenty year analysis. *Clinical Neurology and Neurosurgery* 123:174–180, 2014.

Giffords G., M. Kelly, and J. Zaslow. *Gabby: A Story of Courage and Hope.* Scribner: New York, 2011.

Gonçalves, R., A. L. Pedrozo, E. L. Coutinho, I. Figueira, and P. Ventura. Efficacy of virtual reality exposure therapy in the treatment of PTSD: A systematic review. *PLoS ONE* 7(12):e48469.doi:10.1371/journal.pone.0048469, 2012.

Gregorio, G. W., K. R. Gould, and G. Spitz. Changes in self-reported pre- to postinjury coping styles in the first 3 years after traumatic brain injury and the effects on psychosocial and emotional functioning and quality of life. *Journal of Head Trauma and Rehabilitation* 29:43–53, 2014.

Kaba, F., P. Diamond, and A. Haque. Traumatic brain injury among newly admitted adolescents in the New York City jail system. *Journal of Adolescent Health* 54:615–617, 2014.

Karr, J. E., C. N. Areshenkoff, and M. A. Garcia-Barrera. The neuropsychological outcomes of concussion: a systematic review of meta-analyses on the cognitive sequelae of mild traumatic brain injury. *Neuropsychology*, 28(3):321–336, 2014.

Kersten, P., A. McCambridge, M. Kayes, A. Theadom, and K. M. McPherson. Bridging the gap between goal intentions and actions: A systematic review in patient populations. *Disability and Rehabilitation* 7:1–8, 2014.

Knox, D. B., M. J. Lanspa, C. M. Pratt, K. G. Kuttler, J. P. Jones, and S. M. Brown. Glasgow Coma Scale score dominates the association between admission Sequential Organ Failure Assessment score and 30-day mortality in a mixed intensive care unit population. *Journal of Critical Care* 29:780–785, 2014.

Lashley, K. S. Patterns of cerebral integration indicated by the scotomas of migraine. *Archives of Neurology and Psychiatry* 46:331–339, 1941.

Lezak, M. D., D. B. Howiesen, E. D. Bigler, and D. Tranel. *Neuropsychological Assessment*, 5th ed. New York: Oxford University Press, 2012.

Luria, A. R. *The Working Brain*. New York: Penguin, 1973.

Mignot, E. J. M. History of narcolepsy at Stanford University. *Immunologic Research* 58:325–339, 2014.

Newcombe, F. *Missile Wounds of the Brain*. London: Oxford University Press, 1969.

Pincus, J. H., and G. J. Tucker. *Behavioral Neurology*. New York: Oxford University Press, 2003.

Rizzo, A., T. D. Parsons, B. Lange, P. Kenny, J. G. Buckwalter, B. Rothbaum, J. Difede, J. Frazier, B. Newman, J. Williams, and G. Reger. Virtual reality goes to war: A brief review of the future of military behavioral healthcare. *Clinical and Psychological Medical Settings* 18:176–187, 2011.

Selassie, A. W., D. A. Wilson, and E. E. Pickelsimer. Incidence of sport-related traumatic brain injury and risk factors of severity: A population-based epidemiologic study. *Annals of Epidemiology* 23:750–756, 2013.

Solomon, G. S., and A. Kuhn. Relationship between concussion history and neurocognitive test performance in National Football League draft picks. *American Journal of Sports Medicine* 42:934–939, 2014.

Sprengers, M., K. Vonck, E. Carrette, A. G. Marson, and P. Boon. Deep brain and cortical stimulation for epilepsy. *Cochrane Database Systematic Reviews* 6:CD008497. doi:10.1002/14651858.CD008497.pub2.June 17, 2014.

Tartaglia, M. C., L.-N. Hazrati, K. D. Davis, R. E. A. Green, R. Wennberg, D. Mikulis, L. J. Ezerins, M. Keightley, and C. Tator. Chronic traumatic encephalopathy and other neurodegenerative proteinopathies. *Frontiers in Human Neuroscience* 8: 8–30, 2014.

Teasdale, G., and B. Jennett. *The Glasgow Coma Scale. Lancet* 2:81–84, 1974.

Teuber, H.-L., W. S. Battersby, and M. B. Bender. *Visual Field Defects after Penetrating Wounds of the Brain*. Cambridge, Mass.: Harvard University Press, 1960.

Tonon, C., R. Vetrugno, R. Lodi, R. Gallassi, F. Provini, S. Iotti, G. Plazzi, P. Montagna, E. Lugaresi, and B. Barbiroli. Proton magnetic resonance spectroscopy study of brain metabolism in obstructive sleep apnea syndrome before and after continuous positive airway pressure treatment. *Sleep* 30:305–311, 2007.

van Zuiden, M., A. Kavelaars, and E. Geuze. Predicting PTSD: Pre-existing vulnerabilities in glucocorticoid-signaling and implications for preventive interventions. *Brain Behavior and Immunity* 30:305–311, 2013.

Wingenfeld, K., and O. T. Wolf. Stress, memory, and the hippocampus. *Frontiers in Neurological Neuroscience*.34:109–120. doi:10.1159/000356423.Epub April 16, 2014.

27

Psychiatric and Related Disorders

| PORTRAIT | Losing Touch with Reality |

When Mrs. T. was 16 years old, she began to experience her first symptom of schizophrenia: a profound feeling that people were staring at her. These bouts of self-consciousness soon forced her to end her public piano performances. Her self-consciousness led to withdrawal, then to fearful delusions that others were speaking of her, and finally to suspicions that they were plotting to harm her. At first Mrs. T.'s illness was intermittent, and the return of her intelligence, warmth, and ambition between episodes allowed her to complete several years of college, to marry, and to rear three children. She had to enter a [psychiatric] hospital for the first time at 28, after the birth of her third child, when she began to hallucinate.

Now, at 45, Mrs. T. is never entirely well. She has seen dinosaurs on the street and live animals in her refrigerator. While hallucinating, she speaks and

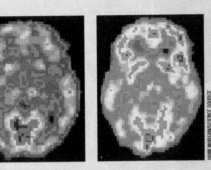

HANK MORGAN/SCIENCE SOURCE

writes in an incoherent, but almost poetic, way. At other times, she is more lucid, but even then her voices sometimes lead her to do dangerous things, such as driving very fast down the highway in the middle of the night, dressed only in a nightgown. . . . At other times and without any apparent stimulus, Mrs. T. has bizarre visual hallucinations. For example, she saw cherubs in the grocery store. These experiences leave her preoccupied, confused, and frightened, unable to perform such everyday tasks as cooking or playing the piano (Gershon and Rieder, 1992, p. 127)

The PET scan at left reveals the metabolic changes that accompany schizophrenia, characterized by abnormally low blood flow in the prefrontal cortex (top of scan). By contrast, the scan on the right shows the brain of a healthy person who does not have schizophrenia.

This chapter focuses on behavioral disorders—those characterized by dramatic abnormalities in cognitive functioning absent obvious lesions to the brain. We begin with the disorders commonly regarded as mental illness—schizophrenia, affective disorders, and anxiety disorders—then consider psychiatric symptoms that can result from vascular disease. A brief history of psychosurgery precedes a survey of the physical and mental aspects of motor disorders, such as Parkinson's disease. A discussion of dementias, particularly those related to aging, follows. We conclude by discussing the role micronutrients may play in behavior.

27.1 The Brain and Behavior

Throughout the centuries since René Descartes first posed the mind–body problem, the contrast between psychological and biological views of mental disorders has mirrored the debate between dualists and monists. Like these polar philosophical views, described in Section 1.2, the mind–body problem is with us still.

Religion and poetry have viewed madness as an affliction of the spirit. Madness is central to classic as well as contemporary fiction. Think of Shakespeare's *Macbeth* and *Othello* or *The Idiot* by Dostoyevsky. Historically, by contrast, medicine has explained madness as a disorder of various bodily humors and organs, although in most cases, without much evidence or success.

In the past 4 decades, it has become clear that psychiatric, or behavioral, disorders have biochemical, anatomical, experiential, and genetic bases. It has also become clear that the distinction between behavioral disorders often referred to as "mental illness," such as schizophrenia, and those called "motor disorders," such as Parkinson's disease, is not as clear-cut as it once seemed.

One challenge to understanding psychiatric disorders lies in diagnosing them. When the American Psychiatric Association published the *Diagnostic and Statistical Manual-III* (DSM-III) in 1980, it was widely believed that listing objective categories for disorders would provide a working draft that research would refine. Unfortunately, this did not occur: DSM-III diagnoses were largely unquestioned and unvalidated.

Subsequent revisions up to the current DSM-5 are plagued by similar problems. Steven Hyman (2012), former director of the U.S. National Institute of Mental Health (NIMH), has emphasized that disorders recognized by the DSM should be clustered according to the best available data. Among likely candidates are those related to the growing data on the normal and abnormal human **connectome**, a comprehensive map of the structural connectivity (the physical wiring) of an organism's nervous system. For example, Hyman notes that high levels of comorbidity and twin studies suggest clustering of fear-based anxiety disorders and depression. NIMH is actively encouraging this approach and launched the Research Domain Criteria (RDoC) project in 2013 to transform diagnosis by incorporating data from a variety of sources including imaging, genetics, and cognitive neuroscience. RDoC is currently a research framework and not yet a clinical tool. It is expected to be a decade-long project with the goal of using the best available evidence to inform how to diagnose and treat mental disorders.

27.2 Schizophrenia

Schizophrenia is extraordinary. It has always been easier to identify schizophrenic behavior than to define schizophrenia. Perhaps the one universally accepted criterion for diagnosing schizophrenia is elimination of the presence of other neurological disturbances or affective disorders—a definition by default.

The DSM-5 lists five symptoms of schizophrenia, all displayed by Mrs. T. as described in the Portrait:

1. **Delusions**, beliefs that distort reality. Mrs. T. harbored suspicions that people were plotting against her.

2. **Hallucinations**, altered perceptions such as hearing voices—or for Mrs. T., seeing dinosaurs in the street—for which there are no appropriate external stimuli.

3. **Disorganized speech**, such as incoherent statements or senseless rhyming. Mrs. T.'s speech and writing were incoherent yet had a poetic quality.

4. **Disorganized or excessively agitated behavior**, exemplified by Mrs. T.'s dangerous late-night drives.

5. **Other symptoms that cause social or occupational dysfunction.** Mrs. T.'s disturbing experiences left her unable to play the piano or even prepare a meal.

Not all patients will exhibit all symptoms; rather, the symptoms observed in different patients are heterogeneous, which suggests that their biological correlates also will be heterogeneous. The DSM-5 specifies that at least two symptoms must be present for 6 months and include at least 1 month of active symptoms.

An alternative method of classifying schizophrenia's symptoms is to categorize them as type I or type II. Type I, referred to as *positive symptoms*, is characterized by delusions, hallucinations, and/or disorganized or bizarre behavior. Type II is characterized by *negative symptoms* such as flat affect, social withdrawal, and poverty of speech.

Although schizophrenia was once seen as characterized by a progressively deteriorating course with a dismal final outcome, this view is probably incorrect. Most patients appear to stay at a fairly stable level after the first few years, with little evidence of declining neuropsychological functioning. The symptoms come and go, much as in Mrs. T.'s case, but their severity is relatively constant after the first few years.

Structural Abnormalities in Schizophrenic Brains

Numerous studies have looked at the gross morphology of the brains of people with schizophrenia, both in tissue obtained at autopsy and in MRI and CT scans. Although the results are variable, most researchers agree that the brains of those with schizophrenia weigh less than healthy brains and that the ventricles are enlarged. Brains of those with schizophrenia have also been suggested to have smaller frontal lobes or at least a reduction in the number of neurons in the prefrontal cortex, as well as thinner parahippocampal gyri.

Results of studies of cellular structure have shown abnormalities in both the prefrontal cortex and the hippocampus. Dorsolateral prefrontal cells have a simple dendritic organization, indicating fewer synapses than typical. Pyramidal neurons in the hippocampus, illustrated in **Figure 27.1A**, show

(A)

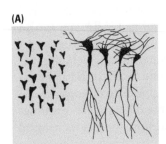

Organized (healthy) pyramidal neurons

(B)

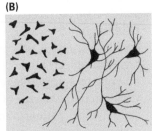

Disorganized (schizophrenic) pyramidal neurons

Figure 27.1 ◀

Suspect Brain Structure Examples of pyramidal-cell orientation from the hippocampus of (A) a normal (organized) brain and (B) a schizophrenic (disorganized) brain. Note the haphazard orientations of these cells. (Research from Kovelman, J. A., and A. B. Scheibel. A neurohistologic correlate of schizophrenia. *Biological Psychiatry* 19:1601–1621, 1984, Fig. 5, p. 1613.)

haphazard orientations, as in Figure 27.1B. Another intriguing cellular abnormality in the brains of people with schizophrenia is found in the DLPFC (dorsolateral prefrontal cortex), where a subpopulation of GABA neurons shows a reduced GABA synthesis associated with poor working memory (see review by Lewis et al., 2005). (GABA is the main inhibitory transmitter in the forebrain.)

Investigators use neuroimaging to study brain activation in those with schizophrenia while they perform tasks such as the Wisconsin Card-Sorting Test (see Figure 16.10). For example, the results of experiments by Daniel Weinberger and his colleagues (1992) show that controls exhibit significant prefrontal cortex activation when performing card-sorting. Patients with schizophrenia do not. In one intriguing report, Karen Berman and Daniel Weinberger (1992) studied identical twins who were discordant for schizophrenia (that is, only one was schizophrenic). PET scans showed differences between the twins during resting or control conditions, but during card-sorting, the brains of every twin with schizophrenia was hypofrontal compared with that of the well twin. This result is consistent with the hypothesis that the prefrontal cortex of patients with schizophrenia is abnormal in both structure and function.

Biochemical Abnormalities in the Brains of People with Schizophrenia

An important pathway for the prefrontal cortex is its mesolimbic dopaminergic input from the midbrain tegmental area. Interference with dopaminergic function disturbs laboratory animals' performance on cognitive tasks, so a reasonable inference is that an abnormality in dopamine activity in the frontal lobes could be responsible for at least some schizophrenia symptoms.

Perhaps the strongest evidence favoring a role for dopamine in schizophrenia comes from studies of the action of **antipsychotic drugs** (also called **neuroleptic drugs** or **major tranquilizers**) that principally affect psychomotor activity, generally without hypnotic effects. These drugs act on the dopamine synapse, and dopamine agonists (such as cocaine, amphetamine, and L-dopa) that enhance dopamine action can induce psychotic symptoms almost indistinguishable from those of classic paranoid schizophrenia. Moreover, schizophrenia symptoms are heightened if a person with schizophrenia takes amphetamine.

Table 27.1 summarizes some major neurochemical changes associated with schizophrenia. In particular, added to abnormalities in dopamine and dopamine receptors are abnormalities in glutamate and glutamate receptors and in GABA and GABA binding sites. Newer *atypical antipsychotic* drugs target a wider variety of neurotransmitters, including antagonistic effects on serotonin (5-HT$_2$) and alpha adrenergic receptors. There appears to be considerable variation in the degree of the different abnormalities in individual patients, and how the neurochemical variations might be related to specific symptoms is not yet known.

▼ Mesolimbic dopamine pathway.

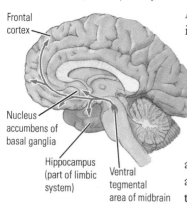

Frontal cortex

Nucleus accumbens of basal ganglia

Hippocampus (part of limbic system)

Ventral tegmental area of midbrain

Table 27.1 **Biochemical changes in schizophrenia**

Decreased dopamine metabolites in cerebrospinal fluid

Increased striatal D$_2$ receptors

Decreased expression of D$_3$ and D$_4$ mRNA in specific cortical regions

Decreased cortical glutamate

Increased cortical glutamate receptors

Decreased glutamate uptake sites in cingulate cortex

Decreased mRNA for the synthesis of GABA in prefrontal cortex

Increased GABA$_A$-binding sites in cingulate cortex

Abbreviations: D, dopamine; GABA, gamma-aminobutyric acid.

Source: *The Neurobiology of Mental Illness*, edited by Charney, Nestler, and Bunney (1999). Table 19.1 from chapter "The Neurochemistry of Schizophrenia," by Byne, Kemegther, Jones, Harouthunian, and Davis, p. 238 © 1999 by Oxford University Press, Inc. By permission of Oxford University Press, USA.

⊚ Schizophrenia as a Neurodevelopmental Disorder

Schizophrenia symptoms typically develop in late adolescence, and schizophrenia has long been seen as a neurodevelopmental disorder. David Lewis and Pat Levitt (2002) conclude that people who develop schizophrenia are much more likely to have experienced a combination of potentially adverse events in prenatal or perinatal life, including poor maternal nutrition, maternal infection, and obstetrical complications. Analyses of home movies of people who later developed schizophrenia have shown subtle but reliable disturbances in a variety of behaviors (motor, cognitive, social) many years before clinical symptoms of schizophrenia appear. In addition, there is evidence of a slow emergence of brain abnormalities, especially in the frontal lobe, during adolescence.

The idea emerging is that schizophrenia reflects an epigenetic change related to a combination of genetic predisposition and environmental insults, which establish a developmental trajectory that eventually leads to the clinical syndrome. No single gene is implicated, and the extent to which early environmental insults might trigger changes in gene expression that contribute to any epigenetic basis for schizophrenia is unknown.

Barbara Lipska, Daniel Weinberger, and their colleagues (2001) proposed that early hippocampal abnormality, such as that illustrated in Figure 27.1B, may be at least partly responsible for abnormalities in the structure and function of the prefrontal cortex in schizophrenia. They developed an intriguing animal model in which rats with perinatal hippocampal injuries develop abnormal dopaminergic organization in prefrontal cortex. Not only do the animals have symptoms of prefrontal dysfunction but, like patients with schizophrenia, the rats also have reduced synaptic space in dorsolateral prefrontal pyramidal cells. Surprisingly, however, the rats have increased synaptic space in orbitofrontal neurons.

⊚ Cognitive Symptoms in Schizophrenia

Although the general tendency is to point to hallucinations and delusions (positive symptoms) and the poverty of affect and speech (negative symptoms) in schizophrenia, by far the most debilitating symptoms are cognitive. Cognitive function in schizophrenia may be the most important determinant of quality of life and functioning.

People with schizophrenia can have deficits in a diverse range of abilities, including working memory, episodic memory, language, executive function, attention, and sensory processing (see review by Deanna Barch and Alan Ceaser, 2012). Since 2000, researchers have tended to focus on deficits in working memory in relation to the abnormalities in the prefrontal cortex, but the diverse cognitive symptoms may be tied together by a dysfunctioning DLPFC that disrupts networks involving both parietal and medial temporal regions. Thus, the abnormalities in dopamine, GABA, and glutamate inputs to the prefrontal cortex lead to a disruption in the circuitry and activity in networks with significant prefrontal involvement.

But Barch and Ceaser note that the diverse cognitive deficits displayed in schizophrenia can be viewed in at least two ways. The unifying mechanism may be psychological (**Figure 27.2**, left), involving a core cognitive deficit, which

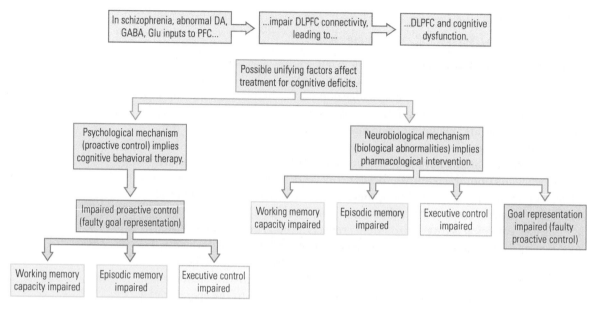

Figure 27.2 ▲

Cognitive Dysfunction in Schizophrenia Two potential pathways may link deficits in DLPFC function, goal representation, and other cognitive impairments in schizophrenia (charted at top). (Left) In a proposed psychological mechanism, biological abnormalities impair a core deficit, proactive control. This faulty goal representation in turn leads to other cognitive deficits. (Right) In a proposed neurobiological mechanism, biological abnormalities directly influence multiple cognitive functions, including goal representation. (Information from Barch, D. M., and A. Ceaser, Cognition in schizophrenia: Core psychological and neural mechanisms. *Trends in Cognitive Sciences* 16:27–34, 2012, Figure 3.)

Barch and Ceaser label *proactive control*. Or the unifying mechanism may be neurobiological (Figure 27.2, right), in which biological abnormalities lead directly to cognitive abnormalities. This difference is important because the neurobiological view implies a need for direct pharmacological intervention, whereas the psychological view implies that cognitive therapies may be effective.

Neurobiological interventions include antipsychotic medications, the mainstay of current treatments (Minzenberg and Carter, 2012). These drugs are effective in reducing positive symptoms, but even the newer atypical antipsychotics, with fewer motor side effects than the original neuroleptic drugs, have limited effects on deficits in cognitive functioning. Another neurobiological treatment uses either transcranial magnetic stimulation (TMS) or direct cortical stimulation to the scalp. The jury is still out on the usefulness of these treatments, especially for cognitive symptoms.

Cognitive training procedures, however, show promise in remediating cognitive functions in schizophrenia. **Cognitive behavioral therapy** (CBT) employs problem-focused, action-oriented, structured treatments for eliminating dysfunctional thoughts and maladaptive behaviors (e.g., Morrison, 2009). This includes developing enhanced coping strategies for positive symptoms such as hallucinations or delusions as well as learning to schedule activities and to develop social skills training for negative symptoms such as lost motivation and social withdrawal. Another type of behavioral therapy flows from the experience of training people with brain injury by employing cognitive training software packages targeting various cognitive functions such as memory and prefrontal functions. A review by Michael Minzenberg and Cameron Carter (2012) concludes that cognitive training procedures show great promise for improving cognitive functions in people with schizophrenia.

27.3 Mood Disorders

Although the DSM-5 identifies mood disorders of many types, depression and mania, which represent the extremes on a continuum of affect, are our principal focus here. The main symptoms of **major**, or **clinical**, **depression** are prolonged feelings of worthlessness and guilt, disruption of normal eating habits, sleep disturbances, a general slowing of behavior, and frequent thoughts of suicide. **Mania**, by contrast, is a mental state of extreme excitement characterized by excessive euphoria. An affected person often formulates grandiose plans and behaves with uncontrollable hyperactivity. In **bipolar disorder**, periods of mania may switch, sometimes abruptly, into periods of depression and back again, or may alternate with periods of regular behavior.

Neurochemical Aspects of Depression

The observation that patients given reserpine for high blood pressure often became severely depressed was a source of insight into the neurobiological basis of depression. Reserpine depletes monoamine neurotransmitters, including norepinephrine, dopamine, and serotonin, which led to the idea that monoamines might be reduced in depression. Postmortem studies of suicide victims supported this hypothesis.

Research in the past two decades has complicated the picture because it is now clear that many different receptors exist for each monoamine and that specific monoamine receptors may be disrupted in depression. An added complication is that no clear unifying theory accounts for the action of antidepressant medications to treat depression. For example, *neurotrophic* (that is, growth-supporting) factors may play a role in the action of antidepressants. Brain-derived neurotrophic factor (BDNF) is upregulated by antidepressant medication and downregulated by stress. Given that BDNF acts to enhance the growth and survival of neurons and synapses, BDNF dysfunction may adversely affect monoamine systems through the loss of either neurons or synapses.

▲ Physical activity, in combination with other therapies, improves well-being and can counteract the effects of depression because it boosts dopamine levels and increases production of neurotrophic factors such as BNDF. (GreatStock/Masterfile.)

The possible role of stress in lowering BDNF production is important because, as has become increasingly clear, monoamines modulate hormone production and secretion via the hypothalamic–pituitary–adrenal circuit, or **HPA axis** illustrated in **Figure 27.3**. The best-established abnormality is oversecretion of hydrocortisone (cortisol). Cortisol, a hormone secreted by the adrenal glands, is associated with stress reactions.

As diagrammed in Figure 6.21, when you are stressed, the hypothalamus secretes corticotropin-releasing hormone, which stimulates the pituitary to

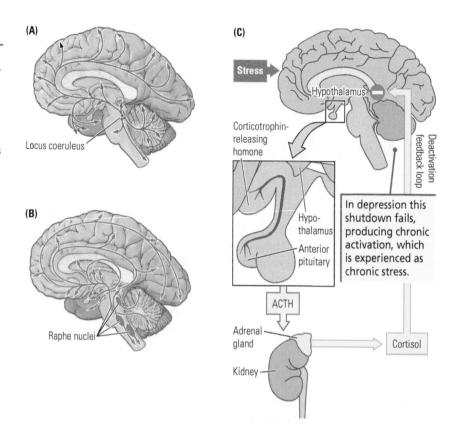

◉ Figure 27.3 ▶

The HPA Axis (A) Medial view of the right hemisphere illustrating the brain stress system. Neurons containing norepinephrine have their cell bodies in the locus coeruleus; neurons containing corticotrophin-releasing hormone are in the hypothalamus; and neurons containing dopamine have their cell bodies in the ventral tegmentum. (B) Medial view illustrating the serotonin cell bodies in the raphe nuclei and their projections to the rest of the brain. (C) When activated, this system affects mood, thought, and, indirectly, the secretion of cortisol by the adrenal glands. Deactivation normally begins when cortisol binds to hypothalamic receptors.

produce adrenocorticotropin (ACTH). ACTH circulates through the blood and stimulates the adrenal gland to produce cortisol. The hypothalamic neurons that begin this cascade are regulated by norepinephrine neurons in the locus coeruleus. The possibility that the body's stress reaction is abnormal in depression has important implications because stress-related hormones and transmitters have widespread influence on cerebral functioning.

The development of fluoxetine (Prozac) as a major drug for treating depression has an interesting relation to neurotrophic factors. Fluoxetine is a *selective serotonin reuptake inhibitor* (SSRI); it effectively increases serotonin in the cortex. But fluoxetine may also act in ways that are important to the hippocampus, independent of serotonin. The sustained elevation of stress-related hormones, the glucocorticoids, results in the death of hippocampal granule cells (described in Section 18.2). This cell death could be a result of the lowered BDNF production. Fluoxetine stimulates both BDNF production and neurogenesis in the hippocampus, resulting in a net increase in the number of granule cells. The effects of fluoxetine on depression may therefore tell us a great deal about the relation between the HPA axis and behavior.

Neuropathological and Blood-Flow Abnormalities in Depression

The general symptoms of depression might lead us to predict a diffuse reduction in cerebral activity, which was the general finding in early PET studies. Striking regional differences in the brains of people experiencing depression have become clear, however, especially within the prefrontal cortex and associated structures.

SNAPSHOT Cortical Metabolic and Anatomical Abnormalities in Mood Disorders

Disorders of mood may follow either a "unipolar" course consisting only of depression or a "bipolar" course in which typical affect alternates with episodes of both depression and mania.

Wayne Drevets and his colleagues (1997) collected PET images of cerebral blood flow from unmedicated unipolar and bipolar subjects (both groups were in a depressive phase and had a familial history of mood disorder) and from controls. The brain area exhibiting the largest

Medial section   **Cross section**

Location of
section at right
        Corpus callosum

C.C.

Subgenual prefrontal cortex

Reduced activation in depression imaged by PET, specifically an area of reduced metabolism and blood flow in a region just below the corpus callosum (subgenual prefrontal cortex). (Drevets, W. C., J. L. Price, J. R. Simpson, R. D. Todd, T. Reich, M. Vannier, and M. E. Raichle. Subgenual prefrontal cortex abnormalities in mood disorders. *Nature* 386:826, 1997. Figure 2.)

difference between control and depressive groups was the medial frontal region lying immediately below the *genu*, the most anterior region of the corpus callosum and referred to as *subgenual prefrontal cortex*. This region showed about a 12 percent decrease in blood flow, as shown in the PET images.

In a follow-up series, the researchers compared controls with bipolar subjects in a manic phase and found a significant increase in activity in the same subgenual area. One bipolar patient had decreased blood flow in the depressive phase and increased blood flow in the manic phase.

Because the decreased blood flow in depressive patients could be due to changes either in synaptic activity or in tissue volume, the investigators collected MRI images in mood-disordered subjects and controls in a parallel set of studies. The gray-matter volume of the left subgenual prefrontal cortex was reduced by about 39 percent in both the unipolar and the bipolar groups. This reduced volume was present regardless of the mood state.

The Drevets group concludes that the reduction in gray-matter volume in mood disorders could correspond either to an abnormality of brain development related to the tendency to develop mood episodes or to a degenerative change resulting from the illness.

Drevets, W. C., J. L. Price, J. R. Simpson, R. D. Todd, T. Reich, M. Vannier, and M. E. Raichle. Subgenual prefrontal cortex abnormalities in mood disorders. *Nature* 386:824–827, 1997.

Both postmortem and structural MRI studies have found similar abnormalities, including reduced gray matter or thickness of anterior cingulate cortex, posterior orbitofrontal cortex (OFC), nucleus accumbens, and hippocampus, in both depression and bipolar disorder (e.g., Price and Drevets, 2012). In addition, imaging reveals a loss of glia (largely oligodendrocytes) and synapses in anterior cingulate cortex (ACC), DLPFC, and amygdala. These changes reflect abnormalities in the amygdala network illustrated in Figure 20.12B and the prefrontal default network shown in Figure 16.6.

Neuroimaging studies have shown that depression severity correlates with decreased blood flow and metabolism in ACC and ventromedial prefrontal cortex (see the Snapshot above). Blood-flow increases in these regions in remitted depressed patients. Raymond Dolan and his colleagues (1994) suggest that the lowered activity relates to the reduced memory and attentional processing in depression.

Figure 27.4 ▼

Brain Atrophy in Bipolar Disorder This series of MRI scans shows regions of gray-matter loss (yellow areas) in bipolar subjects. (Moorhead, T. W., J. McKirdy, J. E. Sussmann, J. Hall, S. M. Lawrie, E. C. Johnston, and A. M. McIntosh. Progressive gray matter loss in patients with bipolar disorder. *Biological Psychiatry* 62(8):894–900, 2007. © Elsevier.)

Left   Right

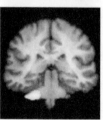
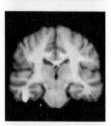
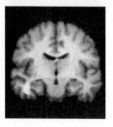

PET studies also have shown an abnormal increase in glucose metabolism in the amygdala that correlates with the severity of depressive symptoms. The amygdala assigns emotional significance to stimuli (see Section 20.3). Amygdala activity stimulates cortisol release, suggesting that this may increase HPA-axis activity in depression. The increased activity in the orbital cortex could correspond to an attempt to modulate or inhibit amygdala activity.

One common symptom of depressed individuals is a sense of "unease" or "dread." It is hypothesized that this results from an overactivation of a somatic marker (see Section 20.4) provided by visceral activation that normally assists nonconscious cognitive processes (e.g., Bechera et al., 2005). In depression, the prefrontal–anterior cingulate abnormalities are thought to be responsible for the increased visceral experiences. The prefrontal cortex has extensive connections with a variety of subcortical regions involved in visceral experiences, including the amygdala, hypothalamus, periaqueductal gray, locus coeruleus, raphe, and brainstem autonomic regions.

Progress in understanding neuropathological and blood-flow abnormalities in depression makes clear that mood disorders have a neurobiological basis. Consistent with the heterogeneity of symptoms in depression, however, it is unlikely that all depressed people have exactly the same abnormalities.

Neurobiological Aspects of Bipolar Disorder

Consistent changes have been much harder to find in the brains of people with bipolar disorder than in those with depressive disorder. When positive results have been found, the effects are typically similar to those observed in depression, although there appears to be less consistency across patients with bipolar disorder. Robert Post and Susan Weiss (1999) hypothesize that psychosocial stressors precipitate many mood-disorder episodes initially, but the episodes begin to recur spontaneously, unrelated to external stressors in predisposed individuals.

These episodes can escalate rapidly, with cycling occurring daily. Bipolar episodes may also be triggered by pharmacological agents, such as antidepressants or in postpartum manic and depressive episodes, and then develop an autonomous course unrelated to external events. When this happens, medication appears to become less and less effective.

William Moorhead and his colleagues (2007) performed MRI scans at each end of a 4-year period, in the course of which each patient had at least one bipolar episode and some as many as six. All patients showed decreased gray matter in the temporal lobe (fusiform gyrus and hippocampus) and cerebellum, relative to the controls (**Figure 27.4**). Importantly, the investigators found a positive relation between the number of episodes and the amount of gray-matter and cognitive loss. These findings suggest that bipolar disorder has a progressive neurodegenerative aspect.

What causes the autonomous recurrence of bipolar episodes? One possibility is that the bipolar patient's brain is especially sensitive to the effects of stressors or drugs and that episodes of mood disorder actually change the brain. One model of such change is drug- or stress-induced sensitization, which we consider briefly next. (For a more extensive discussion, see Post and Weiss, 1999.)

If animals are subjected to stress or are given psychomotor stimulants repeatedly, behavioral responsivity progressively increases. This increased responsivity is correlated with changes in both neurochemistry and neuronal morphology in dopamine-recipient regions—especially the prefrontal cortex. Terry Robinson and Bryan Kolb (2004) discovered that drugs of abuse have different effects on the medial and orbital prefrontal regions, a finding reminiscent of the differences in blood flow and metabolism found in homologous areas in humans displaying depression. Thus, in predisposed people, an episode of some kind may sensitize the brain and produce changes in brain morphology.

Three factors make this **sensitization model** intriguing for understanding bipolar disorder:

1. **Large individual differences appear in the degree of sensitization and drug effects in laboratory animals and people.** Genetically predisposed individuals may be especially sensitive and produce faster and likely larger neuronal changes in response to stressors.

2. **Abuse of psychomotor stimulants such as cocaine is associated with full-blown manic episodes.** This suggests a link between psychomotor-stimulant–induced neuronal change and mania.

3. **Individuals who are bipolar are at high risk for substance abuse.** This suggests that they are especially sensitive to drug effects.

The sensitization model is still largely hypothetical, but it does explain bipolar disorder, which has proved difficult to understand and to treat. A challenge for researchers is to find a treatment that can effectively reverse the effects of sensitization.

◎ 27.4 Anxiety Disorders

We all become anxious at times, especially in times of danger. Anxiety disorders, however, are characterized by intense fear or anxiety inappropriate to the circumstances. The DSM-5 lists many separate anxiety disorders that together affect an estimated 4 in 10 people at some point in their lives. Among the most common are:

1. **Panic disorder**, recurrent attacks of intense terror that arise without warning and without any apparent relation to external circumstances.

2. **Posttraumatic stress disorder** (PTSD), characterized by physiological arousal stemming from recurring memories and dreams related to a traumatic event for months or years after the event.

3. **Generalized anxiety disorder**, a sustained worrying state associated with at least three anxiety symptoms, including restlessness, decreased energy, concentration difficulties, irritability, muscle tension, and sleep disturbance.

4. **Obsessive-compulsive disorder** (OCD), characterized by compulsively repeated acts (such as hand washing) and repetitive, often unpleasant thoughts (obsessions).

5. Specific **phobias**, which entail fear of a clearly defined object or situation. Panic disorder often links into phobias. Examples include *social anxiety disorder* (*social phobia*), avoidance of social situations owing to fear of negative

evaluation, and *agoraphobia*, fear of public places or situations with no opportunity for escape or help.

A common thread woven through these anxiety disorders is fear. Neural network models have emphasized the roles of the ACC, medial prefrontal cortex, OFC, and hippocampus in controlling fear reactions generated by the amygdala (see Figure 20.13). The somatic symptoms of fear are thought to arise from the anterior insula and its connections with the amygdala and OFC (see review by Mathew et al., 2008).

Structural MRI studies have shown reduced hippocampal volume and thinning of DLPFC in combat soldiers with PTSD (e.g., Geuze et al., 2008; see Figure 26.1). The cortical thinning correlates with memory measures, suggesting that functional abnormalities are related to the cortical thinning and hippocampal atrophy. There is also evidence that abnormalities in the HPA axis may characterize some anxiety disorders, with an increase in corticotropin-releasing factor (CRF) concentrations in blood.

Treatment for anxiety disorders has focused on pharmacological interventions, but although **anxiolytics**—drugs (e.g., Valium, Ativan) that reduce anxiety—minor tranquilizers, benzodiazepines, sedative-hypnotic agents, and SSRIs may reduce symptoms, they are probably not directed to the root causes of these disorders. Sanjay Mathew and colleagues (2008) reviewed trends in pharmacological treatments of anxiety disorders and suggest the use of CRF-receptor antagonists and glutamate-receptor antagonists. Both may have potent anxiolytic effects.

The variable effectiveness of drug therapies has spurred many other treatment strategies, including deep brain stimulation (DBS), TMS, and vagus nerve stimulation. Yet to date, cognitive-behavioral therapies have proved at least as effective as all other treatments for anxiety, including drug therapy. The success of CBT lends credence to the idea that most anxiety disorders are learned, and the neurobiological correlates of anxiety reflect the way that the learning has altered the functional circuits. Treatment generally includes some type of *extinction training*, or graded exposure to the fear-inducing objects or contexts. *Virtual-reality exposure therapy* for PTSD is one example (see Chapter 26 Portrait). For a review of treatments, see Ressler and Mayberg (2007).

▲ Systematic desensitization, a form of CBT, helps people overcome phobias. Here, a woman with arachnophobia is learning to tolerate an imitation spider placed on her hand. Up to 90 percent of people with animal phobias overcome their fears in a single extinction training session that lasts for 2 to 3 hours. (Lea Paterson/Science Source.)

27.5 Psychiatric Symptoms of Cerebral Vascular Disease

Vascular diseases, such as stroke, which affect the central nervous system, have long been associated with depression. Estimates of the incidence of poststroke depression range from 25 percent to 50 percent, and treating stroke patients with antidepressants is commonplace in the United States. Less studied is the prevalence of other psychiatric disorders following stroke.

The relation between depression and mania might lead you to expect that some patients would show poststroke mania, but the incidence is very low (about 0.5 percent or less). In view of the involvement of medial temporal regions in mania noted in Section 27.3, stroke would likely have to include this region to lead to mania.

About 25 percent of stroke patients have poststroke anxiety—typically, generalized anxiety disorder—and those with left-hemisphere stroke often experience depression as well (see review by Chemerinski and Levine, 2006). The preferred treatment appears to be SSRIs because elderly patients, the population most likely to have strokes, do not tolerate anxiolytics well.

Two other disorders associated with stroke are the *catastrophic reaction*, discussed in Sections 20.4 and 20.5, and *pathological affect*, characterized by uncontrollable laughing or crying. Estimates of incidence among poststroke patients range from 11 percent to 50 percent.

27.6 Psychosurgery

Before drugs were developed to treat schizophrenia and affective and anxiety disorders, few treatments were available. One that emerged in the 1930s was surgical. Although no longer commonly used, surgical treatment is worth reviewing here in the context of schizophrenia and depression. For excellent discussions, we recommend two books by Eliot Valenstein: *The Psychosurgery Debate* (1980) and *Great and Desperate Cures* (1986).

Psychosurgery is the destruction of some brain region to alleviate severe and otherwise intractable psychiatric disorders or to alter behavior. To distinguish current psychosurgical techniques from earlier, cruder *lobotomy* procedures, the term *psychiatric surgery* has been suggested as a substitute. **Neurosurgery**, brain surgery intended to repair damage to and alleviate symptoms resulting from known neurological disease, is not considered psychosurgery, even if the patient has severe behavioral and emotional symptoms. Brain surgery to alleviate intractable pain is typically considered psychosurgery because the operations are performed on healthy brain tissue and because serious emotional disturbances often accompany chronic pain.

The belief that mental aberrations are related to disturbances of brain function dates to prehistoric times. The practice of opening the skull (*trephining*) for magical–medical purposes was apparently performed extensively, dating at least to 2000 B.C.E. (see Figure 1.13A). Modern psychosurgery is usually traced to Portuguese neurologist Egas Moniz, who first instituted prefrontal procedures in 1935.

Later modifications were made in the United States by Walter Freeman and James Watts, including the Freeman–Watts procedure of drilling holes in the temples and Freeman's lateral transorbital procedure (**Figure 27.5**A). An accurate estimate of how many psychosurgical procedures were performed worldwide is impossible, although Valenstein (1986) thinks that the best estimate for the United States between 1936 and 1978 is 35,000.

The introduction of antipsychotic drugs in the mid-1950s led to a sharp reduction in the number of psychosurgical operations, but those drugs did not help a significant number of psychiatric patients. Thus, interest in surgical intervention to change behavior has continued, but since the 1960s, the psychosurgical procedures employed have changed, in part because of advances in the neurosciences. There are currently about 13 targets of psychosurgical

Figure 27.5 ▶

Targets for Psychosurgery (A) In the procedure for a transorbital leukotomy, a special surgical knife (leukotome) is inserted through the bone of the eye socket above the eyeball, disconnecting the inferior frontal cortex from the rest of the brain. (B) Approximate targets of psychosurgical operations currently in use. *Frontal-lobe procedures*: (1) bimedial leukotomy; (2) yttrium lesions in subcortical white matter; (3) orbital undercutting; (4) bifrontal stereotaxic subcaudate tractotomy; (5) anterior capsulotomy (destruction of fibers of internal capsule); (6) mesoloviotomy (similar to rostral cingulotomy, but lesion invades the genu, or "knee," of the corpus callosum). *Cingulotomies*: (7) anterior cingulotomy; (8) mid cingulotomy; (9) posterior cingulotomy. *Amygdalectomy*: (10) amygdalectomy or amygdalotomy. *Thalamotomies*: (11) thalamotomy of the dorsomedial, centromedian, or parafascicular nuclei; (12) anterior thalamotomy. *Hypothalamotomy*: (13) section of the posterior, ventromedial, or lateral hypothalamus. (Part B: information from Valenstein, 1980.)

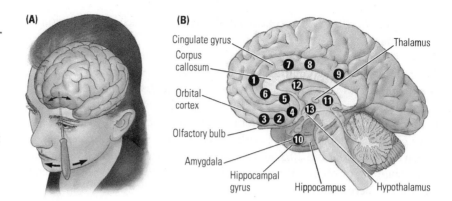

operations, which are summarized in Figure 27.5B. These procedures generally produce smaller lesions than did the original lobotomy-type procedures and are rarely performed.

The development of new generations of psychiatric drugs has meant that virtually everybody is responsive to some form of psychoactive medication. We note, parenthetically, that the most common form of psychosurgery—namely, frontal leukotomy—disconnected regions of the prefrontal cortex from the rest of the brain, and we have seen that abnormalities there are associated with both schizophrenia and depression. The difficulty with psychosurgery is that although the abnormal activity of the prefrontal regions was removed, it was not replaced by normal activity. The goal of drug treatment is to do just that.

27.7 Motor Disorders

The group of diseases comprising motor disorders has clinical symptoms marked by abnormalities in movement and posture referable to dysfunctions of the basal ganglia. Although the most obvious symptom is the motor affliction, all produce cognitive changes as well, changes that become especially marked as motor disorders progress. Indeed, many patients develop symptoms similar to those of schizophrenia. Thus, although motor disorders could be discussed among the neurological disorders in Chapter 26, the nature of the nonmotor behavioral symptoms warrants including them here.

Clinically, two groups of motor symptoms are distinguished: (1) loss of movement, referred to as a *hypokinetic-rigid syndrome* (for example, Parkinson's disease); and (2) increased motor activity, known as a *hyperkinetic-dystonic syndrome* (for example, Tourette's syndrome).

⬚ Hyperkinetic Disorders

The earliest descriptions of hyperkinetic disorders, dating to the nineteenth century, focused on women afflicted with either Huntington's disease or Tourette's syndrome and dwelt on increased motor activity as a symptom of hysteria.

Huntington's Disease

Late in the 1850s, 8-year-old George Huntington was riding with his father in his native New York when they came upon two tall, thin women who were twisting and grimacing. The sight of these women left such a profound impression on young George that he studied their disease when, following in his father's and grandfather's footsteps, he became a physician. In 1872, when he was 22 years old, Huntington wrote the first complete description of "that disease," as it was called then.

Its history in the United States can be traced to the village of Bures in England in 1630. Whole families in Bures and its vicinity were branded and tried as witches at that time. Some family members sailed to America among the 700 passengers of John Winthrop's fleet in 1630. In 1653, Ellin Wilkie (name fictitious), who had arrived with Winthrop, apparently had developed the disorder, because she was tried and hanged for witchcraft. Her granddaughter was later tried and pardoned in 1692.

Huntington's disease results in intellectual deterioration and personality changes as well as abnormal movements called *choreas* (from the Greek for "dance"). The first symptoms usually appear in people 30 to 50 years of age but can occur earlier. The first involuntary movements usually appear within a year of the onset of the behavioral symptoms. The movements are initially slight and consist of little more than continual fidgeting but slowly increase until they are almost incessant, irregular, and follow no set pattern.

Behavioral symptoms include impairment of recent memory, defective ability to manipulate acquired knowledge, and slowed information processing. Emotional changes include anxiety, depression, mania, and schizophrenialike psychoses. Suicide is not uncommon in younger-onset patients, whose disease progresses faster than those older at onset. On average after disease onset, patients live for 12 years.

Huntington's disease is rare, with death rates of 1.6 per million people per year, worldwide. It most commonly affects white Europeans and their descendants and is rare among Asian and African racial groups. Huntington's is transmitted genetically as an autosomal dominant allele with complete penetrance, meaning that half of the offspring of an affected person will develop the disease, which likely is on the decline as a result of advances in genetic counseling (see Figure 2.9B). The approximate location of the gene is now known, and a marker can be used before symptoms appear (even in utero) to determine whether a family member will develop Huntington's (Gusella et al., 1993).

At autopsy, the brains of people with Huntington's show cortical shrinkage and thinning. The basal ganglia are grossly atrophied and show marked neuronal loss. A dominant explanation of the disease is an imbalance among the various neurotransmitter systems of the basal ganglia. A simplified model of these transmitter systems is shown in **Figure 27.6A**, including:

1. A glutamate projection from the cortex to the basal ganglia.

2. A GABA projection from the basal ganglia to the *substantia nigra*, a nucleus in the midbrain involved in initiating movement.

3. A dopamine projection from the substantia nigra to the basal ganglia.

4. Acetylcholine (ACh) neurons in the basal ganglia.

As shown in Figure 27.6B, researchers postulate that the intrinsic (GABA and ACh) neurons of the basal ganglia die in the course of the disease, leaving

▲ Woody Guthrie, whose folk songs inspired farm workers during the Great Depression of the 1930s and countless others since, struggled with the symptoms of Huntington's disease in the years before he died in 1967. Two of Guthrie's five children developed the disease, and his mother had died of similar symptoms, although her illness was never diagnosed. His unpublished lyrics and artwork are archived at woodyguthrie.org. (Woody Guthrie, 1943. Photograph by Robin Carson. Courtesy of Woody Guthrie Publications, Inc.)

(A) Healthy transmitter system

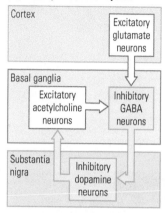

(B) Huntington's disease

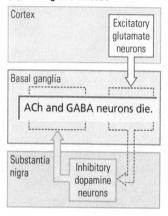

Figure 27.6 ▲

Neurochemical Progress of Huntington's Disease ACh and GABA neurons in the basal ganglia are thought to die, and, as a result, dopamine cells are released from GABA inhibition and become hyperactive, thus producing abnormal movements. The death of GABA cells may be caused by excessive activity of the glutamate pathway.

a largely intact nigrostriatal dopamine pathway. Decreased inhibition of dopamine cells by the GABA pathway results in increased dopamine release in the basal ganglia. The dopamine system hyperactivity is believed to produce the characteristic choreas, although exactly how is not clear.

Results of extensive neuropsychological studies show that patients with Huntington's disease are impaired in a broad range of memory and perceptual tests (see Fedio et al., 1979, and Wexler, 1979). Patients are especially poor at performing various frontal-lobe tests (for example, the Chicago Word-Fluency Test and the stylus–maze test). People who have at least one parent with the disease, and it can thus be considered at risk, appear to perform poorly only on the frontal-lobe tests, suggesting their possible usefulness as predictors of the disease.

Tourette's Syndrome

Georges Gilles de la Tourette described **Tourette's syndrome** in 1885. In most important ways, his description is still remarkably good. Until his review, this syndrome was seen either as an undifferentiated chorea or as a symptom of hysteria, and it had gained a variety of names, depending on where it had been observed.

The symptoms tend to evolve and to become more elaborate with age. Gilles de la Tourette described three stages. In the first, the only symptoms are multiple tics (twitches of the face, limbs, or the whole body). In the second stage, inarticulate cries accompany the multiple tics. In the third stage, the emission of articulate words with **echolalia** (repeating what others have said, as well as repeating actions) and **coprolalia** (from the Greek *copro*, meaning "dung," but its current meaning is "obscene" or "lewd," and *lalia*, meaning "speech") join the multiple tics and inarticulate cries.

Georges Gilles de la Tourette reported the following case history, which illustrates most of the major features of the syndrome:

> Miss X., 15 years old, spent several months at the Longchamps hydrotherapy institution at Bordeaux in the winter of 1883, where she was treated for convulsive attacks of chorea and ejaculations of loud vulgar and obscene words. Miss X. was very intelligent, she learned the lessons given her by her teacher with the greatest ease, and she played the piano well. She was tall and largely built. She was not well disciplined.
>
> When 9, Miss X. began having violent and irregular choreiform tics of the face, arms, and legs. At the same time she occasionally uttered a few vulgar words. After a few months the attacks disappeared. A year later they came back again. The tics first reappeared in the shoulders, then in the arms, and then in the face, where they were accompanied by loud guttural sounds. These indistinct sounds became very clearly articulated when she was 13. At that time her most frequent words were "get away, go away, imbecile." A little later her words became more frequent and much clearer, and were rough and lewd. She remained that way until the present.
>
> Miss X. belonged to an upper-class family. Her education was excellent. She never left her mother, who surrounded her in continuous, tender loving care. One had to wonder how and where she picked up the words she continually uttered: for example, "In God's name,

fuck, shit, et cetera." When she is in her calm, normal state such words never pass her lips. (Gilles de la Tourette, 1885, pp. 41–42; translated by Lorna Whishaw)

Gilles de la Tourette recognized that people with the syndrome could be intelligent and productive and were not neurotic or psychotic. He also noted that the syndrome, or parts of it, ran in families and thus seemed hereditary. He pointed out that although the symptoms lessened or disappeared during fevers, there was no treatment, so the symptoms were likely to be with the person for life.

Through the years, many patients with Tourette's syndrome have been misdiagnosed as troublemakers, hysterics, schizophrenics, and more—no doubt because they seem intelligent yet display bizarre behavior. Renewed interest in Tourette's syndrome resulted largely through the work of the Tourette Society in North America, and interest in trying to understand the disorder's cause in relation to brain function has grown.

According to a 2012 study by the U.S. Centers for Disease Control, the incidence of Tourette's syndrome has risen over the past decades to about 1 in 360 persons (Bitsko et al., 2014). The average age of onset ranges between 2 and 15 years, with a median of 7 years; by 11 years of age, symptoms have appeared in 97 percent of cases. The most frequent symptoms are tics of the eye, head, or face (97 percent), upper limbs (81 percent), and lower limbs and body (55 percent). Complex movements including touching, hitting, and jumping appear in 30 percent to 40 percent of cases. Coprolalia may develop in as many as 60 percent of cases and then disappear in one-third of them.

Tourette's syndrome is presumed to have a subcortical origin, likely in the basal ganglia, although abnormalities appear in the frontoparietal circuitry (**Figure 27.7**). Few autopsy examinations of the brains of people with Tourette's syndrome have been conducted, and of those that have been done, only one reports an excessive number of small cells in the basal ganglia; others report that the cells there are normal. To date, the most consistent improvements are obtained with antidopaminergic agents such as haloperidol, which points to some abnormality in the basal ganglia dopamine system. Clonidine, a norepinephrine-receptor agonist, also is reportedly effective in some cases.

In general, the results of neuropsychological studies suggest abnormalities in some cognitive functions usually supported by the right hemisphere. For example, Robert Sutherland and his colleagues (1982) gave a composite test battery to a large sample of children and adults with Tourette's syndrome and found that the patients were especially bad at drawing and remembering complex geometric figures. The poor performance of these patients on the Rey Complex-Figure Test was particularly striking because even patients with superior verbal IQ scores performed very poorly compared with control children or patients with schizophrenia. The visuospatial difficulties observed in the Rey figure may have a real-world analogue as well: many patients with Tourette's syndrome complain of having difficulty in remembering the locations of things in their daily lives.

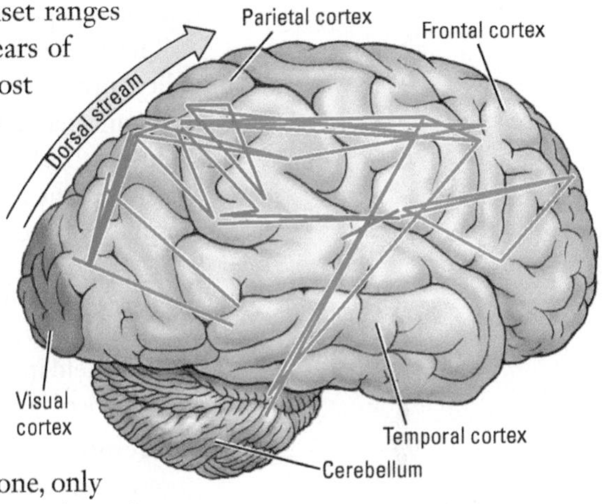

Figure 27.7 ▲

Cortical Changes Associated with Tourette's Syndrome Brain areas that show enhanced connectivity (green) or decreased connectivity (red) in fMRI analysis of young adults with Tourette's syndrome suggest abnormalities in dorsal-stream structures linking the parietal cortex to the frontal cortex. (Information from Church, J. A., D. A. Fair, N. U. Dosenbach, A. L. Cohen, F. M. Miezen, S. E. Petersen, and B. L. Schlaggar. Control networks in paediatric Tourette syndrome show immature and anomalous patterns of functional connectivity. *Brain* 132(Pt. 1): 225–238, 2009, Fig. 4A, p. 233.)

Hypokinetic Disorders

In 1817, James Parkinson, a London physician, published an essay in which he argued that several different motor symptoms could be considered together as a group forming a distinctive condition that he referred to as "the shaking palsy" (Parkinson, 1955). His observations are interesting not only because his conclusion was correct but also because he made his observations in part at a distance, by watching the movements of affected people in the streets of London. French neurologist Jean-Martin Charcot suggested that the shaking palsy be renamed to honor James Parkinson's recognition of its essential nature.

Parkinson's disease is fairly common; incidence estimates vary from 0.1 percent to 1 percent of the population worldwide, and the incidence rises sharply in old age. Among about 10 million patients with Parkinson's worldwide, incidence is higher in countries with longer life expectancies. For example, about 1 million people in the United States have Parkinson's disease. In view of the increasingly aging population in Western Europe and North America, the incidence is certain to rise in the coming decades. In the United States and Canada one person is diagnosed every 9 minutes.

The four major symptoms of Parkinson's disease are tremor, muscular rigidity, involuntary movement, and postural disturbance; each symptom may be manifested in different body parts in different combinations. Because some symptoms reflect the acquisition of abnormal behaviors (positive symptoms) and others the loss of normal behaviors (negative symptoms), we consider Parkinson's symptoms within these two major categories.

Positive Symptoms

Because positive symptoms are common in Parkinson's disease, they are presumably held in check (inhibited) in healthy people but released from inhibition in the process of the disease. The most common positive symptoms:

1. **Tremor at rest.** Alternating movements of the limbs when they are at rest stop during voluntary movements or during sleep. Hand tremors often have a "pill-rolling" quality, as if a pill were being rolled between the thumb and forefinger.

2. **Muscular rigidity.** Simultaneously increased muscle tone in both extensor and flexor muscles is particularly evident when the limbs are moved passively at a joint. Movement is resisted, but with sufficient force the muscles yield for a short distance and then resist movement again. Thus, complete passive flexion or extension of a joint occurs in a series of steps, giving rise to the term *cogwheel rigidity*.

3. **Involuntary movements.** These may consist of continual changes in posture, sometimes to relieve tremor and sometimes to relieve stiffness, but often for no apparent reason. These small movements or posture changes, sometimes referred to as **akathesia** or *cruel restlessness*, may be concurrent with general inactivity. Other involuntary movements are distortions of posture, such as those during *oculogyric crisis* (involuntary turns of the head and eyes to one side), which last for periods of minutes to hours.

Negative Symptoms

After detailed analysis of the most common negative symptoms, James Purdon Martin (1967) divided patients severely affected with Parkinson's disease into five groups, those with:

1. **Postural disorders.** A *disorder of fixation* consists of an inability to maintain or difficulty in maintaining a body part (head, limbs, and so forth) in its normal position in relation to other body parts. Thus, a person's head may droop forward or a standing person may gradually bend forward until he or she ends up on the knees. *Disorders of equilibrium* consist of difficulties in standing or even sitting unsupported. In less-severe cases, patients may have difficulty standing on one leg, or if pushed lightly on the shoulders, they may fall passively without taking corrective steps or attempting to catch themselves.

2. **Righting disorders.** Patients have difficulty standing from a supine position. Many patients with advanced disease have difficulty even in rolling over, which is problematic in bed.

3. **Locomotive disorders.** Normal locomotion requires supporting the body against gravity, stepping, balancing while body weight is transferred from one limb to another, and pushing forward. Patients with Parkinson's disease have difficulty initiating stepping. When they do walk, they shuffle with short footsteps on a fairly wide base of support because they have trouble maintaining equilibrium when shifting weight from one limb to the other. Often, patients who have begun to walk demonstrate **festination**: they take faster and faster steps and end up running forward.

4. **Speech disturbances.** A symptom most noticeable to relatives is the almost complete absence of tone (prosody) in the speaker's voice.

5. **Akinesia.** A poverty or slowness of movement may also manifest itself in a blank facial expression or lack of blinking, swinging the arms when walking, spontaneous speech, or typical fidgeting movements. Akinesia also manifests in difficulty making repetitive movements, such as tapping, even in the absence of rigidity. People who sit motionless for hours demonstrate akinesia in its most striking manifestation.

Genetic Risk Factors for Parkinson's Disease

Most Parkinson's cases are not likely inherited, but about 25 percent of people with Parkinson's do have a living relative with the disease. A vast array of individual researchers and research organizations analyzed over 13,000 Parkinson's cases and nearly 100,000 controls, all of European ancestry, and identified more than two dozen genome-wide variations (Nalls et al., 2014). The results show that the more variants a person has, the greater the risk of developing the disease.

Progression of Parkinsonism

Positive and negative symptoms of Parkinson's disease begin insidiously, often with a tremor in one hand and slight stiffness in the distal parts of the limbs. Movements may then slow, the face becoming masklike with loss of eye-blinking and poverty of emotional expression. Thereafter, the body may become stooped, the gait a shuffle, with the arms hanging motionless at the sides. Speech may slow and become monotonous in tone. Difficulty in swallowing saliva may result in drooling.

Although the disease is progressive, the rate at which symptoms worsen is variable. Only rarely is progression so rapid that a person becomes disabled within 5 years; usually 10 to 20 years elapse before symptoms cause incapacity. One man less severely afflicted by muscular rigidity was moved to comment to us, "The slowness of movement is conscious but not willed. That is, I form a plan in my mind; for instance, I wish to uncork that bottle. Then I deliberately invoke the effort that sets the muscles in motion. I'm aware of the slowness of the process; I'm unable to increase [its speed], but I always get the bottle open."

A most curious aspect of Parkinson's disease is its on-again–off-again quality: symptoms may appear suddenly and disappear just as suddenly. Partial remission may also occur in response to interesting or stimulating situations. Oliver Sacks (1973) recounted an incident in which a patient with Parkinson's disease leaped from his wheelchair at the seaside and rushed into the breakers to save a drowning man, only to fall back into his chair immediately afterward and become inactive again. Although remission of some symptoms in activating situations is common, remission is not usually as dramatic as in this case.

Causes of Parkinsonism

The three major types of Parkinson's disease are idiopathic, postencephalitic, and drug-induced. Parkinson's disease may also result from arteriosclerosis, syphilis, tumor development, carbon monoxide poisoning, or manganese intoxication.

As its name suggests, the cause of *idiopathic* Parkinson's disease is unknown. Its origin may be familial, or it may be part of the aging process, but it is also widely thought to have a viral origin. The idiopathic type most often develops in people older than 50 years of age.

The *postencephalitic* form originated in the sleeping sickness (*encephalitis lethargica*) that appeared in the winter of 1916–1917 and vanished by 1927. Although the array of symptoms was so bewilderingly varied that hardly any two patients seemed alike, Constantin von Economo (1931) demonstrated a unique pattern of brain damage—namely, the death of cells in the substantia nigra. Although many people seemed to recover completely from the encephalitis, most subsequently developed neurological or psychiatric disorders and parkinsonism. The latency between the initial occurrence of the sleeping sickness and subsequent occurrences of the disease has never been adequately explained. Specific searches for viral particles or virus-specific products in Parkinson patients without encephalitis have revealed no evidence of viral cause, although it is still believed to be likely.

Drug-induced Parkinson's disease developed most recently and is associated with ingesting various drugs, particularly major tranquilizers, including reserpine and several phenothiazine and butyrophenone derivatives. The symptoms are usually reversible but are difficult to distinguish from those of the genuine disorder.

External agents can cause Parkinson's symptoms quite rapidly. J. William Langston and his coworkers (1983, 2008) reported that a contaminant, MPTP, of synthetic heroin is converted to MPP+, which is extremely toxic to dopamine cells. A number of young drug users were found to display a complete parkinsonian syndrome shortly after using contaminated drugs (see Chapter 6 Portrait). This finding suggests that other substances might cause similar effects. The results of later demographic studies of patient admission in the cities of Vancouver, Canada, and Helsinki, Finland, show an increased incidence of patients contracting Parkinson's disease at ages younger than 40. This finding suggests that water and air might contain environmental toxins that work in a fashion similar to MPTP.

The cells of the substantia nigra are the point of origin of fibers that extend into the frontal cortex and basal ganglia and to the spinal cord. The neurotransmitter at the synapses of these projections is dopamine. Bioassay of the brains of deceased individuals who had Parkinson's disease and analysis of the major metabolite of dopamine—homovanillic acid, which is excreted in the urine—demonstrate that the amount of dopamine in the brain is reduced by more than 90 percent and often to undetectable amounts. Thus, the cause of Parkinson's disease has been identified with some certainty as a lack of dopamine or, in drug-induced cases, as a lack of dopamine action. Dopamine depletion may not account for the whole problem in some people, however, because decreases in norepinephrine have been recorded, and numerous results show that cells in some basal ganglia nuclei may degenerate as well.

Treating Parkinson's Disease

No known cure for Parkinson's disease exists, and none will be in sight until the factors that produce the progressive deterioration of the substantia nigra are known. Thus, treatment is symptomatic and directed toward support and comfort. Psychological factors influence the major symptoms of parkinsonism, and a person's outcome is strongly affected by how well he or she copes with the disability. As a result, patients should be counseled early regarding the meaning of symptoms, the nature of the disease, and the potential for most of them to lead long and productive lives. Physical therapy should consist of simple measures such as heat and massage to alleviate painful muscle cramps and training and exercise to cope with the debilitating changes in movement.

Pharmacological treatment has two main objectives: first, increase the activity in whatever dopamine synapses remain; and second, suppress the activity in structures that show heightened activity in the absence of adequate dopamine action. Drugs such as L-dopa, which is converted into dopamine in the brain; amantadine; amphetamine; monoamine oxidase (MAO) inhibitors; and tricyclic antidepressants enhance effective dopamine transmission. Naturally occurring anticholinergic drugs, such as atropine and scopolamine, and synthetic anticholinergics, such as

▼ For patients with Parkinson's disease, rhythmic movement apparently helps to restore the balance between neural excitation and inhibition—between the loss and the release of behavior. Patients who attend dance classes report that moving to music helps them regain muscle control. Exercise and music are helpful additions to treatments directed toward replacing depleted dopamine. (Copyright Katsuyoshi Tanaka, courtesy Mark Morris Dance Group.)

benztropine (Cogentin), and trihexyphenidyl (Artane), block the cholinergic activating systems that seem to show heightened activity in the absence of adequate dopamine activity.

One promising treatment is trying to increase the number of dopamine-producing cells. The simplest way to do so is to transplant embryonic dopamine cells into the basal ganglia; in the 1980s and 1990s, this treatment was used with varying degrees of success. A newer course of treatment proposes to increase the number of dopamine cells either by transplanting fetal stem cells, which could then be induced to adopt a dopaminergic phenotype, or by stimulating endogenous stem cells to be produced and migrate to the basal ganglia. Both treatments are still highly experimental, although a report by Ole Isacson and colleagues (Hallett et al., 2014) found that five patients who had tiny bits of liquefied fetal dopamine cells implanted into the striatum were still producing dopamine 14 years after implantation.

Finally, the development of deep brain stimulation for treating Parkinson's is detailed in Section 7.2. Electrodes applied to several brainstem regions can lessen both tremor and akinesia, but not without risk. Nevertheless, the combination of drug and DBS therapies may prove the most effective treatment.

⊚ Psychological Aspects of Parkinson's Disease

Psychological symptoms in patients with Parkinson's disease are as variable as the motor symptoms. Nonetheless, a significant percentage of patients have cognitive symptoms that mirror their motor symptoms. Oliver Sacks (1973), for example, reported the negative effects of the disease on cognitive function: an impoverishment of feeling, libido, motive, and attention; people may sit for hours, apparently lacking the will to enter or continue any course of activity. In our experience, thinking seems generally to be slowed and is easily confused with dementia because patients do not appear to be processing the content of conversations. In fact, they are simply processing very slowly.

The results of neuropsychological studies confirm that patients with Parkinson's disease often show cognitive symptoms similar to those shown by people with frontal-lobe or basal-ganglia lesions—deficits on the Wisconsin Card-Sorting Test, for example. This association is not surprising, because the functions of the basal ganglia and the frontal cortex are closely related and because dopamine projections into the frontal cortex might be expected to degenerate in the same way as those of the basal ganglia degenerate. Test performance is not noticeably improved by drug therapy.

Cognitive slowing displayed by patients with Parkinson's disease has some parallels to changes seen in Alzheimer's disease, and findings in postmortem studies show clear evidence of Alzheimerlike abnormalities in most patients, even if they had no obvious signs of dementia (**Figure 27.8**). Neuropsychological investigations of other populations confirm the possibility of a general cognitive deterioration in patients with Parkinson's disease. For example, in their extensive study, Francis Pirozzolo and his coworkers (1982) found such patients significantly impaired—relative to age-matched controls—on several subtests of the Wechsler Adult Intelligence Scale, including information, digit span, digit symbol, and block design, and on measures of verbal memory (logical

Figure 27.8 ▼

Midbrain Lewy Body The best-studied similarity between Parkinson's and Alzheimer's diseases is the Lewy body (arrow), found most often in the substantia nigra. Such circular, fibrous structures form within neurons and are thought to signal abnormal neurofilament metabolism. (Biophoto Associates/Science Source.)

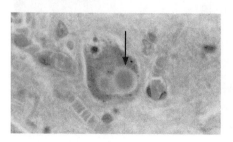

stories and paired associates). Finally, François Boller and his colleagues (1984) found patients with Parkinson's disease impaired on a wide array of visuospatial tests, independent of intellectual impairment.

27.8 Dementias

The demographics now developing in North America and Europe are unique in recorded history. In 1900, about 4 percent of the population had attained 65 years of age. By 2030, about 20 percent of the population will be older than 65—about 60 million people in the United States alone. Dementias affect between 5 percent and 7 percent of the population older than 65 and between 25 percent and 50 percent of those older than 80 years of age. Furthermore, for every person with dementia, several others have cognitive impairments that affect their quality of life (see Hebert et al., 2003; Prince et al., 2013).

An estimated one in three seniors in the United States dies with some form of dementia, with 5.2 million cases estimated in 2014. Within the next 2 decades, projections warn that between 10 million and 20 million elderly people in the United States will endure mild to severe cognitive impairments. When this projection is extended to the rest of the developed world, the social and economic costs are staggering. Not every person who becomes old also becomes depressed, forgetful, or demented. Many people live to very old age and enjoy active, healthy, productive lives. The challenge is how to ensure that we are in this group. The best current advice suggests daily exercise, such as walking, and an engaged, active social life.

Dementia is an acquired and persistent syndrome of intellectual impairment. The DSM-5 gathers all dementia diagnoses into two categories as either *major neurocognitive disorder* (NCD) or *mild neurocognitive disorder* (mild NCD).

NCD is defined as "evidence of substantial cognitive decline from a previous level of performance based upon the concerns of the individual, a knowledgeable informant or the clinician; and a decline in neurocognitive performance, typically involving test performance in the range of two or more standard deviations below appropriate norms on formal testing or equivalent clinical evaluation" (DSM-5). The cognitive deficits must be sufficient to interfere with independent functioning and must not be attributable to another mental disorder (for example, major depressive disorder). Mild NCD is defined similarly, but the DSM-5 stresses a modest cognitive decline from a previous performance level, a decline in neurocognitive test performance in the range between one and two standard deviations, and that cognitive deficits do not interfere with functioning independently.

Dementias can also be divided by suspected cause, as summarized in **Table 27.2**. Causes include the accumulation of defective proteins (tau or alphasynuclein); vascular problems; or other conditions, including chronic traumatic encephalopathy (see Chapter 25 Portrait). The most prevalent form of dementia is **Alzheimer's disease**, which accounts for about 65 percent of all dementias

▲ Engaging in cognitively stimulating activities—these ladies play bridge regularly—can help to keep neural networks and general cognitive function from declining with age. (Sandy Huffaker/*The New York Times*/Redux.)

Table 27.2 **Types of Dementias**

Tauopathies: accumulation of tau proteins inside neurons
Alzheimer's disease: tau forms amyloid and tangles in neurons
Corticobasal degeneration: neuron loss and shrinkage in cortex and basal ganglia
Frontotemporal disorders (FTD): neuron loss in frontal and temporal lobes
Progressive supranuclear palsy (PSP): neuron loss in upper brainstem

Synucleinopathies: accumulation of alpha-synuclein protein in neurons
Lewy body dementia: causes Lewy bodies to form in neurons
Parkinson's disease dementia

Vascular Dementias and Vascular Cognitive Impairment: injuries to cerebral blood vessels
Multi-infarct dementia
Subcortical vascular dementia (Binswanger's disease)

Mixed Dementias
Combinations of disorders such as Alzheimer's and vascular symptoms

Other Dementias
Prion-related dementias, e.g., Creutzfeld–Jakob disease
Huntington's disease
Secondary dementias, e.g., Wilson's disease, multiple sclerosis, encephalitis
Head injury: chronic traumatic encephalopathy from repeated brain trauma
Infectious dementias, e.g., AIDS dementia, syphilis
Drug-related dementias: chronic alcohol or psychotropic drugs such as ecstasy

in people over 65 and is named for German physician Alois Alzheimer, who published a case study in 1906. The patient was a 51-year-old woman for whom Alzheimer described a set of clinical and neuropathological findings.

Anatomical Correlates of Alzheimer's Disease

Until the 1990s, the only way to identify and to study Alzheimer's disease was to study postmortem pathology. This approach was less than ideal, however, because it was impossible to determine which changes came early in the disease and which followed as a result of those early changes. Nonetheless, it became clear that widespread changes occur in the neocortex and paralimbic cortex as well as associated changes in several neurotransmitter systems, none of which alone can be correlated simply with the clinical symptoms. Interestingly, most of the brainstem, cerebellum, and spinal cord are spared Alzheimer's major ravages.

Neuritic (Amyloid) Plaques

Neuritic plaques, also known as senile plaques, are found chiefly in the cerebral cortex and result from the accumulation of tau protein. Their increased concentration in the cortex has been correlated with the magnitude of cognitive deterioration. Neuritic plaques consist of a central core of homogeneous protein material known as *amyloid*, surrounded by degenerative cellular fragments (**Figure 27.9**). These fragments include axonal and dendritic processes and other components of neural cells. Neuritic plaques are generally considered

Figure 27.9 ▼

Neuritic Plaque Often found in the cerebral cortices of patients with Alzheimer's disease, the amyloid core of the plaque (dark spot in the center) is surrounded by the residue of degenerate cells. (Dr. Cecil H. Fox/Science Source.)

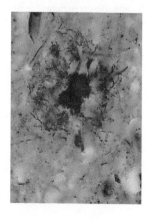

(A) Healthy Brain

(B) Brain with Alzheimer's

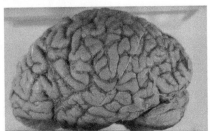
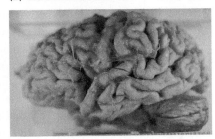

◄ Contrast between (A) brain of a healthy elderly adult and (B) brain of an elderly adult, shriveled by cell shrinkage characteristic of Alzheimer's disease. (Courtesy of the Nun Study, University of Minnesota.)

nonspecific phenomena in that they can be found in non-Alzheimer patients and in dementias caused by other known events.

Paired Helical Filaments

Also known as *neurofibrillary tangles*, paired helical filaments are found in both the cerebral cortex and the hippocampus and are believed to be related to the tau protein. The posterior half of the hippocampus is affected more severely than the anterior half. Light-microscopic examination has shown that the filaments have a double-helical configuration. They have been described mainly in human tissue and have been observed not only in patients with Alzheimer's disease but also in patients with Down syndrome, Parkinson's disease, and other dementias.

Neocortical Changes

The neocortical changes are not uniform. Although the cortex shrinks, or atrophies, losing as much as one-third of its volume as the disease progresses (compare photos A and B above), some areas are relatively spared. **Figure 27.10** shows lateral and medial views of the human brain; shading indicates the areas of degeneration. The darker the red, the more severe the degeneration.

Note in Figure 27.10A that the primary sensory and motor areas of the cortex, especially the visual cortex and the sensorimotor cortex, are spared. The frontal lobes are less affected than the posterior cortex, where the areas of most extensive change are in the posterior parietal, inferior temporal, and limbic cortices.

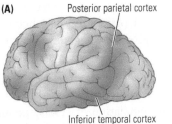

(A) Posterior parietal cortex

Inferior temporal cortex

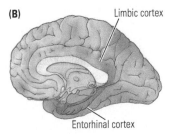

(B) Limbic cortex

Entorhinal cortex

Figure 27.10 ▲

Cortical Atrophy

Distribution and severity of degeneration on (A) lateral and (B) medial aspects of the brain in an average Alzheimer case. The darker the area, the more pronounced the degeneration. White areas are spared, with only basic change discernible. (Research from Brun, 1983.)

Paralimbic Cortex Changes

The limbic system undergoes the most severe degenerative changes in Alzheimer's disease, and of the limbic structures, the entorhinal cortex is affected earliest and most severely (Figure 27.10B). A number of investigators agree that the entorhinal cortex shows the clearest evidence of cell loss, and this has important implications for understanding some disease symptoms. The entorhinal cortex is the major relay through which information from the neocortex gets to the hippocampus and related structures and is then sent back to the neocortex (charted in Figure 18.8B). Damage to the entorhinal cortex is associated with memory loss, and given that memory loss is an early and enduring symptom of the disease, it is most likely caused by the degenerative changes that take place in this limbic area.

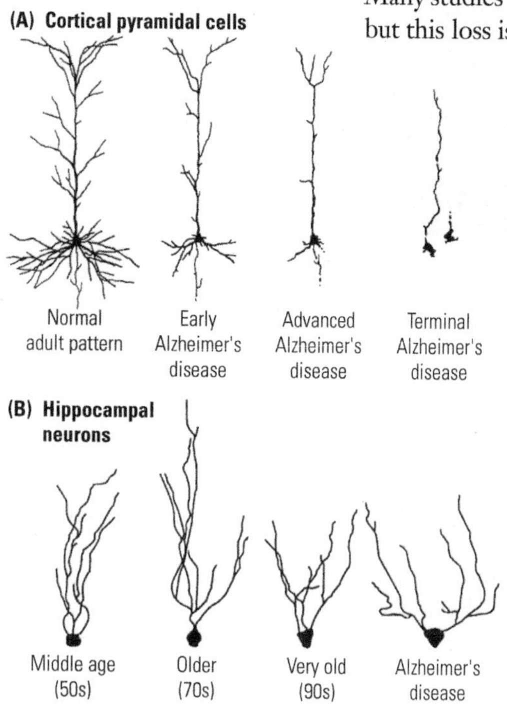

Cell Changes

Many studies describe cell loss in the cortices of patients with Alzheimer's disease, but this loss is disputed. There seems to be a substantial reduction in large neurons, but these cells may shrink rather than disappear. The more widespread cause of cortical atrophy, however, appears to be a loss of dendritic arborization, as illustrated in **Figure 27.11**A.

The cause of these changes is not known. Note in Figure 27.11B, however, that degradation in hippocampal neurons is not simply typical of aging. Healthy people actually show increased dendritic length and branching between their fifties and seventies (see Coleman and Flood, 1987). Only in very old age does the pattern of degeneration begin to look like neural cells typical of Alzheimer's disease.

(A) Cortical pyramidal cells

Normal adult pattern / Early Alzheimer's disease / Advanced Alzheimer's disease / Terminal Alzheimer's disease

(B) Hippocampal neurons

Middle age (50s) / Older (70s) / Very old (90s) / Alzheimer's disease

Figure 27.11 ▲

Neuronal Pathology in Alzheimer's Disease
(A) Early stages of disease are marked in cortical pyramidal cells by patchy spine loss and thinning out of the dendritic tree, especially horizontal branches. Advanced stages show almost complete loss of basilar dendrites, continuing into the terminal stage. (B) The average length of hippocampal dendrites in healthy adults increases from middle age into old age, decreasing only in late old age. Dendrites in brains with Alzheimer's disease do not show the age-related growth. (Part A: drawn from Golgi-stained sections of human prefrontal cortex; information from Scheibel, 1983. Part B: information from Selkoe, 1992.)

Neurotransmitter Changes

In the 1970s, researchers sought a treatment for Alzheimer's to parallel L-dopa treatment for Parkinson's disease. The prime candidate neurotransmitter was ACh. Unfortunately, the disease has proved far more complex, because transmitters other than ACh are clearly changed in Alzheimer's as well. Noradrenaline, dopamine, and serotonin are reduced, as are the NMDA (N-methyl-D-aspartate) and AMPA (α-amino-3-hydroxy-5-methylisoazole-4-proprionic acid) receptors for glutamate.

The most interesting feature of these neurotransmitter changes is not their absolute decreases in any individual patient but rather the pattern of decreases. Although age-matched controls also show reductions in transmitter levels, when the pattern of reductions in all transmitter substances is plotted, patients with Alzheimer's disease distinguish themselves from the control groups by showing greater reductions in two or more neurotransmitters.

Putative Causes of Alzheimer's Disease

The cause or causes of Alzheimer's disease remain unknown. Given the increasing population of elderly people and thus of those with Alzheimer's disease, copious research is being directed toward several possible causes, summarized in the following sections.

Genetic Susceptibility and Protein Abnormalities

The frequency of Alzheimer's disease increases in families that have had a member with Alzheimer's disease. The risk increases to 3.8 percent if a sibling has had the disease and to 10 percent if a parent has had the disease.

The application of molecular genetic methods has led to the discovery of three Alzheimer-disease-susceptibility genes; they encode β-amyloid precursor protein (B-APP), and transmembrane proteins presenilin 1 and presenilin 2. These susceptibilities were discovered by examining families with an unusually high incidence of Alzheimer's disease. The B-APP gene maps on chromosome 21, the chromosome found to be abnormal in Down syndrome. People with Down syndrome almost invariably develop dementia by age 40.

How an abnormality in the gene for B-APP produces dementia is not known, but it is believed to cause the formation of amyloid plaques and neurofibrillary tangles. The two proposed causes are related to protein abnormalities. In one proposal, the tau protein, which is found naturally in neurons and functions to stabilize microtubules, becomes defective, leading to abnormalities in microtubule function. The tau abnormality is believed to result from a disturbance in the MAPT gene on chromosome 16. In a second proposed cause, found in the presenilin proteins, mutations of genes producing these transmembrane proteins have been found in patients with early-onset Alzheimer's.

Trace Metals

Early studies with animals identified neurofibrillary degeneration, similar to that in Alzheimer's disease, after the animals were given aluminum salts. Research that followed up on this hint found increases ranging from 10 to 30 times the normal concentration of aluminum in the brains of patients' with Alzheimer's disease. At present, the reason for the accumulation is not known; whether taking action to reduce the accumulation would be helpful also is unknown.

Immune Reactions

Some researchers think that in old age the immune system loses its ability to recognize a person's own body. As a result, it develops antibrain antibodies that cause neuronal degeneration. In other words, the body actually begins to kill its own neurons, which leads to dementia.

Blood Flow

Historically, Alzheimer's disease was attributed to poor circulation. The results of PET studies confirm an extreme reduction in the amount of blood delivered to the brain and the amount of glucose extracted from the blood by neural tissue.

In healthy people, blood flow to the brain declines by more than 20 percent between the ages of 30 and 60, but the brain compensates by more-efficient oxygen uptake. In Alzheimer's disease, the decline is enhanced, but there are no compensatory mechanisms. The greatest decreases in blood flow are found in those brain areas in which the most degenerative change is seen (see Figure 27.10). What is not known is whether the declines in blood flow and glucose metabolism are causal or secondary to degenerative brain changes.

◎ Clinical Symptoms and the Progression of Alzheimer's Disease

Alzheimer's slow onset and steady progress are its most insidious features, gradually robbing a person first of recent memory, then of more remote memory, and finally of the abilities to recognize family members and to function independently. Disease progress is gradual: patients spend months to years in each of several progressive stages ranging from mild to severe impairment. Impairments span five measures of cognitive function: concentration, recent and past memory, orientation, social functioning, and self-care (see, e.g., Reisberg, 1983).

In view of the distinctive pattern of anatomical changes in Alzheimer's disease, one might expect a distinctive pattern of cognitive changes. Finding such a pattern would be important because the symptoms displayed by patients with Alzheimer's disease are often confused with those seen in other disorders, such

Healthy pyramidal neuron

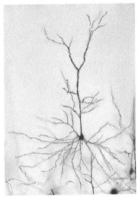

Damaged neuron

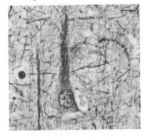

▲ **Deteriorating Neurons in Dementia** Pathological changes in neurons are associated with Alzheimer's disease. (Part A: Courtesy Bryan Kolb. Part B: SPL/ Science Source.

as depression or multi-infarct dementia. In view of the distinctly different approaches to managing patients with depression and those with Alzheimer's disease, differential diagnosis would be very useful.

Neuropsychological Testing for Alzheimer's

IQ subtest scales from the Wechsler Adult Intelligence Scale can be used to distinguish the impairment patterns of Alzheimer's disease from those produced by cerebrovascular disease (see Fuld, 1983). Patients with Alzheimer's disease are marked by the striking deficits that they show on digit symbol and block design, with successively milder impairments on object assembly, similarities and digit span, and information and vocabulary. Other Alzheimer-sensitive tests include backward digits, telling the time on clocks without numbers, and object naming. Additionally, patients with Alzheimer's disease typically show deficits on tests of both left- and right-hemisphere function, and the impairments are not marked by sudden onset.

Perhaps the most striking impairment in patients with Alzheimer's disease is related to memory performance. Virtually every neuropsychological test of memory reveals impairments relative to age-matched controls. Patients with Alzheimer's disease are particularly prone to difficulties in producing the names of objects and in distinguishing among objects within a category.

F. Jacob Huff and his colleagues (1986) concluded that the anomia deficit is characterized by a loss of information about specific objects and their names rather than by a simple difficulty in retrieving information. The difficulties in naming are unlikely due simply to difficulties with memory because patients with Alzheimer's disease have a variety of language impairments that become most obvious as the complexity of the cognitive processing required increases. Thus, when engaging in simple conversations about the weather and so on, patients' language functioning appears typical, but if they are required to engage in more-complex discussions, their language difficulty becomes more apparent.

Considering Age at Onset

Although Alzheimer's disease is usually seen as a single disorder, emerging evidence suggests that the age at onset may predict different cognitive and anatomical changes. Giovani Frisoni and colleagues (2007) compared the MRI scans of patients with early-onset (before age 65) Alzheimer's disease and late-onset (age 65 and older) Alzheimer's disease and found that the early-onset patients had more diffuse atrophy across the cerebral hemispheres but less atrophy in the hippocampus than did the late-onset patients. There thus appear to be different patterns of brain atrophy, depending on age at onset, suggesting different predisposing or etiological factors.

⊚ 27.9 Micronutrients and Behavior

As long ago as the 1920s, scattered sources suggested that mood disorders might be linked to dietary vitamins and minerals. The idea that poor nutrition can be related to behavioral disorders seems sensible on the surface. Considerable skepticism has persisted, however, because no one has offered a reasonable conceptual explanation for how *micronutrients*, including the minerals and vitamins our bodies require in trace amounts, can influence mood.

Most studies have investigated one micronutrient at a time—folate (folic acid), zinc, vitamin D_3, vitamin B_{12} among them—but in an extensive review, Julia Rucklidge and Bonnie Kaplan (2013) argue that the "one-disease–one-nutrient" idea is outdated because humans evolved to utilize many nutrients together and in balance. Given the complexity of brain metabolism, they emphasize the need for studies using micronutrient combinations.

It seems more likely that nutrient combinations, rather than individual nutrients, will influence brain function. Rucklidge and Kaplan summarize about 60 studies focusing on participants with mood disorders (depression or bipolar), ADHD, substance abuse and dependence, autism, or antisocial behavior. Although not all of these were randomized trials, the overwhelming consensus is that broad-spectrum micronutrient treatments were beneficial. The investigators conclude that studies on mood disorders show significant impact on behavior and justify moving to vigorous trials in large clinical samples. In a parallel review, Popper (2014) reached a similar conclusion.

Rucklidge and Kaplan conclude as well that data on the efficacy of micronutrients for reducing violent offenses in forensic populations are sufficiently consistent to warrant including micronutrient supplements as an intervention for reducing offenses within prison populations. Although the data from studies of autism and ADHD are encouraging, the great variability in micronutrient ingredients and outcomes suggests that more research with effective supplements should be undertaken. Micronutrients have also been shown to reduce stress, in particular using high doses of B vitamins.

Bonnie Kaplan and her colleagues (2007) collected evidence of a clear link between mood and micronutrients. In a thoughtful review, they propose that symptoms of mood disorders may reflect the following:

1. Inborn errors in metabolism

2. Alterations in gene expression

3. Epigenetic alterations by environmental interactions related to abnormal gene methylation; that is, changes in gene regulation that take place without a change in the DNA sequence (see Figure 4.8)

4. Long-latency effects of nutritional abnormalities—analogous to cardiovascular disease being a slow-developing disorder

Research on a multi-micronutrient approach to treating behavioral symptoms is just beginning. At first glance, it appears surprising and even implausible that such an approach might have an effect across a wide range of psychiatric symptoms, but growing evidence reveals that both prenatal diet and gut bacteria can influence gene expression. Paula Dominguez-Salas and her colleagues (2014), for example, showed that maternal nutrition at conception modulates gene expression in newborns (see Figure 23.13). They compared DNA methylation in babies conceived in the wet or rainy seasons in Gambia. Maternal diet varies considerably in the two seasons, leading to the different patterns of gene expression.

Many studies show that differential patterns of gene expression are related to differences in brain development and behavior. Similarly, evidence shows that bacterial organisms in the gut can alter both brain and behavior (for reviews see Cryan and Dinan, 2012; Dinan et al., 2013). Given that gut bacteria influence absorption of nutrients, a link between gut and brain–behavior connections is likely. For example, specific groups of gut bacteria could be related to reduced levels of micronutrients that in turn are related to behavioral syndromes such as mood disorders. This line of reasoning has led to the idea that supplements of specific gut bacteria, a class of compounds known as *psychobiotics*, can be used to treat behavioral disorders. Vigorous research and debate await the topics of micronutrients and psychobiotics in the coming decade.

SUMMARY

27.1 The Brain and Behavior

Historically, psychiatry and neurology were one field, and while the two specialties are separate today, for many patients, the distinction is arbitrary. Brain diseases, the realm of neurology, can produce severe psychological disturbances, traditionally psychiatry's territory. Investigators are only beginning to understand the relationships between disturbance and disease.

27.2 Schizophrenia

Schizophrenia, a disease that emerges in the course of development, usually late in adolescence, is associated especially with abnormalities in the structure and function of the DLPFC and medial temporal region. The most debilitating symptoms are cognitive. Schizophrenia is likely not a single disorder but rather a continuum of positive and negative symptoms that vary by degrees. Treatments have largely been pharmacological in the past 30 years, but interest in behavioral treatments alone or in combination with drugs is increasing.

27.3 Mood Disorders

The primary disorders of mood are depression and bipolar disorder, in which depression alternates with episodes of mania. Both are related to abnormalities in the brain's response to stress through the HPA axis. Depression is associated with abnormally high activity in the OFC, amygdala, and insula, and low activity in DLPFC. Antidepressants reduce amygdala activity, likely by increasing monoamine levels. Bipolar disorder may result from an oversensitive brain response to stressors, including drugs. The response in turn alters neuronal chemistry and morphology, especially in the orbital cortex or the amygdala or both. Repeated bipolar episodes are associated with atrophy of the hippocampus and fusiform gyrus.

27.4 Anxiety Disorders

As the most common class of psychiatric disorders, many categories and subtypes of anxiety disorders exist. The thread tying them together is increased fear stemming from enhanced activity in the amygdala. Neural network models emphasize the roles played by the anterior cingulate cortex, medial prefrontal cortex, orbitofrontal cortex, and

hippocampus in controlling fear reactions generated by the amygdala. Anxiolytics and cognitive-behavioral therapy have proved equally effective as treatments.

27.5 Psychiatric Symptoms of Cerebral Vascular Disease

The most common poststroke psychiatric symptoms include depression, generalized anxiety, catastrophic reactions, and pathological affect.

27.6 Psychosurgery

Surgical treatments for schizophrenia and depression—rare today—were developed in the 1930s. The best-known psychosurgery, frontal lobotomy, was commonly used to treat schizophrenia until the late 1950s, when drug treatments came into wide use.

27.7 Motor Disorders

Traditionally, motor disorders, both hyperkinetic and hypokinetic, have been considered neurological, but they can produce significant psychological abnormalities, likely owing to an imbalance in neurotransmitter systems, especially the catecholamines and ACh. These chemical changes appear to have significant effects on frontal- and temporal-lobe function, leading to a variety of behavioral disturbances prominent in disorders such as Tourette's syndrome and Parkinson's disease. Treatments are pharmacological, but for progressive disorders such as Parkinson's disease and Huntington's disease, they do not stop the disease progression.

27.8 Dementias

Dementias are an increasing problem for society, owing mainly to changing demographics but also to an understanding of multiple causes including repeated brain trauma leading to chronic traumatic encephalitis. By far the most common dementia is Alzheimer's disease, which is associated with a variety of pathological changes in the forebrain. The cause or causes are not known, although research in molecular genetics has identified at least three genes that predispose people to the disease.

27.9 Micronutrients and Behavior

Diet has long been known to affect behavior. Accumulating evidence supports the idea that micronutrients are critical to healthy brain functioning, especially relevant in understanding mood disorders. Regimens of micronutrients for treating mood and stress-related disorders appear especially encouraging. A growing body of research results indicates that supplements of specific gut bacteria (psychobiotics) can treat behavioral disorders.

References

American Psychiatric Association. *Diagnostic and Statistical Manual of Mental Disorders-Fifth Edition* (DSM-5). Arlington, VA: American Psychiatric Association, 2013.

Barch, D. M., and A. Ceaser. Cognition in schizophrenia: Core psychological and neural mechanisms. *Trends in Cognitive Sciences* 16:27–34, 2012.

Bechara, A., H. Damasio, D. Tranel, and A. R. Damasio. The Iowa Gambling Task and the somatic marker hypothesis: Some questions and answers. *Trends in Cognitive Sciences* 9:159–164, 2005.

Berman, K. F., and D. R. Weinberger. Regional cerebral blood flow in monozygotic twins concordant and discordant for schizophrenia. *Archives of General Psychiatry* 49:927–934, 1992.

Bitsko, R. H., J. R. Holbrook, S. N. Visser, J. W. Mink, S. H. Zinner, R. M. Ghandour, and S. J. Blumberg. A national profile of Tourette syndrome, 2011–2012. *Journal of Developmental and Behavioral Pediatrics* 35:317–322, 2014.

Boller, F., D. Passafiume, M. C. Keefe, K. Rogers, L. Morrow, and Y. Kim. Visuospatial impairment in Parkinson's disease: Role of perceptual and motor factors. *Archives of Neurology* 41:485–490, 1984.

Brun, A. An overview of light and electron microscopic changes. In B. Reisberg, Ed. *Alzheimer's Disease, the standard reference*. New York: The Free Press, 1983.

Byne, W., E. Kemegther, L. Jones, V. Harouthunian, and K. L. Davis. The neurochemistry of schizophrenia. In D. S. Charney, E. J. Nestler, and B. S. Bunney, Eds. *The Neurobiology of Mental Illness*, pp. 236–245. New York: Oxford University Press, 1999.

Charney, D. S., E. J. Nestler, and B. S. Bunney, Eds. *The Neurobiology of Mental Illness*. New York: Oxford University Press, 1999.

Chemerinski, E., and S. R. Levine. Neuropsychiatric disorders following vascular brain injury. *The Mount Sinai Journal of Medicine* 76:1006–1014, 2006.

Coleman, P. D., and D. G. Flood. Neuron numbers and dendritic extent in normal aging and Alzheimer's disease. *Neurobiology of Aging* 8:521–545, 1987.

Cryan, J. F., and T. G. Dinan. Mind-altering microorganisms: The impact of the gut microbiota on brain and behavior. *Nature Reviews Neuroscience* 13: 701–712, 2012.

Dinan, T.G., C. Stanton, and J. F. Cryan. Psychobiotics: A novel class of psychotropic. *Biological Psychiatry* 74:720–726, 2013.

Dolan, R. J., C. J. Bench, R. G. Brown, L. C. Scott, and R. S. J. Frackowiak. Neuropsychological dysfunction in depression: The relationship to regional cerebral blood flow. *Psychological Medicine* 24:849–857, 1994.

Dominguez-Salas, P., S. E. Moore, M. S. Baker, A. W. Bergen, S. E. Cox, R. A. Dyer, A. J. Fulford, Y. Guan, E. Laritsky,

M. J. Silver, G. E. Swan, S. H. Zeisel, S. M. Innis, R. A. Waterland, A. M. Prentice, and B. J. Hennig. Maternal nutrition at conception modulates DNA methylation of human metastable epialleles. *Nature Communications* 5:3746. doi:10.1038/ncomms4746, 2014.

Fedio, P., C. S. Cox, A. Neophytides, G. Canal Frederick, and T. N. Chase. Neuropsychological profile of Huntington's disease: Patients and those at risk. *Advances in Neurology* 23:239–256, 1979.

Frisoni, G. B., M. Pievai, C. Testa, F. Sabattoli, L. Bresciani, M. Bonetti, A. Beltramello, K. M. Hayashi, A. W. Toga, and P. M. Thompson. The topography of grey matter involvement in early and late onset Alzheimer's disease. *Brain* 130:720–730, 2007.

Fuld, P. A. Psychometric differentiation of the dementias: An overview. In B. Reisberg, Ed. *Alzheimer's Disease*. New York: The Free Press, 1983.

Gershon, E. S., and R. O. Rieder. Major disorders of mind and brain. *Scientific American* 267(3):126–133, 1992.

Geuze, E., H. G. M. Westenberg, A. Heinecke, C. S. de Koet, R. Goebel, and E. Vermetten. Thinner prefrontal cortex in veterans with posttraumatic stress disorder. *NeuroImage* 41:675–681, 2008.

Gilles de la Tourette, G. Étude sur un affection, nerveuse caractérisée par l'incoordination motrice accompagnée d'écholalie et de copralalie (jumping, latah, myriachit). *Archives of Neurology* 9:19–42, 158–200, 1885.

Gusella, J. F., M. E. MacDonald, C. M. Ambrose, and M. P. Duyao. Molecular genetics of Huntington's disease (Review). *Archives of Neurology* 50:1157–1163, 1993.

Hallett, P. J., O. Cooper, D. Sadi, H. Robertson, I. Mendez, and O. Isacson. Long-term health of dopaminergic neuron transplants in Parkinson's disease patients. *Cell Reports* 7:1755–1761, 2014.

Hebert, L. E., P. A. Scherr, J. L. Bienias, D. A. Bennett, and D. A. Evans. Alzheimer disease in the U.S. population: Prevalence estimates using the 2000 census. *Archives of Neurology* 60:1119–1122, 2003.

Huff, F. J., S. Corkin, and J. H. Growdon. Semantic impairment and anomia in Alzheimer's disease. *Brain and Language* 28:235–249, 1986.

Hyman, S. E. Interview with Steve Hyman. *Trends in Cognitive Sciences* 16:3–5, 2012.

Kaplan, B. J., S. G. Crawford, C. J. Field, and J. S. A. Simpson. Vitamins, minerals, and mood. *Psychological Bulletin* 133:747–760, 2007.

Kovelman, J. A., and A. B. Scheibel. A neurohistologic correlate of schizophrenia. *Biological Psychiatry* 19:1601–1621, 1984.

Langston, J. W. *The Case of the Frozen Addicts*. New York: Pantheon, 2008.

Langston, J. W., P. Ballard, J. W. Tegrud, and I. Irwin. Chronic parkinsonism in humans due to a product of meperidine-analog synthesis. *Science* 219:979–980, 1983.

Lewis, D. A., T. Hashimoto, and D. W. Volk. Cortical inhibitory neurons and schizophrenia. *Nature Reviews Neuroscience* 6:312–324, 2005.

Lewis, D. A., and P. Levitt. Schizophrenia as a disorder of development. *Annual Review of Neuroscience* 25:409–432, 2002.

Lipska, B. K., Z. Z. Khaing, C. S. Weickert, and D. R. Weinberger. BDNF mRNA expression in rat hippocampus and prefrontal cortex: Effects of neonatal ventral hippocampal damage and antipsychotic drugs. *European Journal of Neuroscience* 14:135–144, 2001.

Martin, J. P. *The Basal Ganglia and Posture*. London: Ritman Medical Publishing, 1967.

Mathew, S. J., R. B. Price, and D. S. Charney. Recent advances in the neurobiology of anxiety disorders: Implications for novel therapies. *American Journal of Medical Genetics* 148C:89–98, 2008.

Minzenberg, M. J., and C. S. Carter. Developing treatments for impaired cognition in schizophrenia. *Trends in Cognitive Sciences* 16:35–42, 2012.

Moorhead, T. W., J. McKirdy, J. E. Sussmann, J. Hall, S. M. Lawrie, E. C. Johnstone, and A. M. McIntosh. Progressive gray matter loss in patients with bipolar disorder. *Biological Psychiatry* 62:894–900, 2007.

Morrison A. K. Cognitive behavior therapy for people with schizophrenia. *Psychiatry* 6: 32–39, 2009.

Nalls, M. A., N. Pankratz, C. M. Lill, C. B. Do, D. G. Hernandez, M. Saad, A. L. DeStefano, E. Kara, J. Bras, M. Sharma, C. Schulte, M. F. Keller, S. Arepalli, C. Letson, C. Edsall, H. Stefansson, X. Liu, H. Pliner, J. H. Lee, R. Cheng; International Parkinson's Disease Genomics Consortium (IPDGC); Parkinson's Study Group (PSG); Parkinson's Research: The Organized GENetics Initiative (PROGENI); 23andMe; GenePD; NeuroGenetics Research Consortium (NGRC); Hussman Institute of Human Genomics (HIHG); The Ashkenazi Jewish Dataset Investigator; Cohorts for Health and Aging Research in Genetic Epidemiology (CHARGE); North American Brain Expression Consortium (NABEC); United Kingdom Brain Expression Consortium (UKBEC); Greek Parkinson's Disease Consortium; Alzheimer Genetic Analysis Group, M. A. Ikram, J. P. Ioannidis, G. M. Hadjigeorgiou, J. C. Bis, M. Martinez, J. S. Perlmutter, A. Goate, K. Marder, B. Fiske, M. Sutherland, G. Xiromerisiou, R. H. Myers, L. N. Clark, K. Stefansson, J. A. Hardy, P. Heutink, H. Chen, N. W. Wood, H. Houlden, H. Payami, A. Brice, W. K. Scott, T. Gasser, L. Bertram, N. Eriksson, T. Foroud, and A. B. Singleton. Large-scale meta-analysis of genome-wide association data identifies six new risk loci for Parkinson's disease. *Nature Genetics* 46:989–993, 2014.

Parkinson, J. Essay on the shaking palsy. Reprinted in M. Critchley, Ed. *James Parkinson*. London: Macmillan, 1955.

Pirozzolo, F. J., E. C. Hansch, J. A. Mortimer, D. D. Webster, and M. A. Kuskowski. Dementia in Parkinson's disease: A neuropsychological analysis. *Brain and Cognition* 1:71–83, 1982.

Popper, C. W. Single-micronutrient and broad-spectrum micronutrient approaches for treating mood disorders in youth and adults. *Child Adolescent Psychiatry Clinics of North America* 23:591–672, 2014.

Post, R. M., and S. R. B. Weiss. Neurobiological models of recurrence in mood disorder. In D. S. Charney, E. J. Nestler, and B. S. Bunney, Eds. *The Neurobiology of Mental Illness*, pp. 365–384. New York: Oxford University Press, 1999.

Price, J. L., and W. C. Drevets. Neural circuits underlying the pathophysiology of mood disorders. *Trends in Cognitive Sciences* 16:61–71, 2012.

Prince, M., R. Bryce, E. Albanese, A. Wimo, W. Ribeiro, and C. P. Ferri. The global prevalence of dementia: A systematic review and metaanalysis. *Alzheimer's Dementia* 9:63–75, 2013.

Reisberg, B. Clinical presentation, diagnosis, and symptomatology of age-associated cognitive decline and Alzheimer's disease. In B. Reisberg, Ed. *Alzheimer's Disease*. New York: The Free Press, 1983.

Ressler, K. J., and H. S. Mayberg. Targeting abnormal neural circuits in mood and anxiety disorders: From the laboratory to the clinic. *Nature Neuroscience* 10:1116–1142, 2007.

Robinson, T. E., and B. Kolb. Structural plasticity associated with drugs of abuse. *Neuropharmacology* 47(Suppl. 1):33–46, 2004.

Rucklidge, J. J., and B. J. Kaplan. Broad-spectrum micronutrient formulas for the treatment of psychiatric symptoms: A systematic review. *Expert Reviews in Neurotherapeutics* 13:49–73, 2013.

Sacks, O. *Awakenings*. New York: Doubleday, 1973.

Scheibel, A. B. Dendritic changes. In B. Reisberg, Ed. *Alzheimer's Disease*. New York: The Free Press, 1983.

Selkoe, D. J. Aging brain, aging mind. *Scientific American* 267(3):135–142, 1992.

Sutherland, R. J., B. Kolb, W. M. Schoel, I. Q. Whishaw, and D. Davies. Neuropsychological assessment of children and adults with Tourette's syndrome: A comparison with learning disabilities and schizophrenia. *Advances in Neurology* 35:311–322, 1982.

Valenstein, E. S., Ed. *The Psychosurgery Debate*. San Francisco: W. H. Freeman and Company, 1980.

Valenstein, E. S. *Great and Desperate Cures*. New York: Basic Books, 1986.

Von Economo, C. *Encephalitis Lethargica: Its Sequelae and Treatment*. London: Oxford University Press, 1931.

Weinberger, D. R., K. F. Berman, R. L. Suddath, and E. F. Torrey. Evidence for dysfunction of a prefrontal-limbic network in schizophrenia: An MRI and regional cerebral blood flow study of discordant monozygotic twins. *American Journal of Psychiatry* 149:890–897, 1992.

Wexler, N. S. Perceptual-motor, cognitive, and emotional characteristics of persons at risk for Huntington's disease. *Advances in Neurology* 23:257–272, 1979.

28 Neuropsychological Assessment

PORTRAIT   Lingering Effects of Brain Trauma

Driving home from work one afternoon, R.L., a 32-year-old nurse and mother of four, stopped at a red light. The vehicle traveling behind rear-ended her car. R.L.'s head snapped back and struck the headrest, then the side window as she bounced forward. She blacked out for a few minutes, but by the time the emergency vehicles arrived, she was conscious—albeit disoriented and dysphasic—and experiencing severe pain in her back and neck from the whiplash. Several vertebrae were damaged.

R.L. spent about a week in the hospital. Neither a CT nor an MRI scan identified any cerebral injury. Nonetheless, evidence of closed-head trauma (diagrammed in Figure 26.4) was abundant. An accomplished musician, R.L. could still play the piano well from memory, but she could no longer read music. Her oral language skills remained impaired, and she was completely unable to read.

R.L.'s difficulties did not abate, and she had spells of apraxia. For example, she often found herself unable to figure out how to put on her makeup; she would stare at her lipstick with no idea how to use it. When she came to us a year after the accident, R.L. was depressed because the neurologists could find no reason for her continuing impairments.

As described in Section 16.3, perhaps the most commonly observed trait of frontal-lobe patients is difficulty

in using environmental feedback to regulate or change their behavior. One manifestation is *response inhibition*: patients with frontal-lobe lesions consistently perseverate on responses in various test situations, particularly those in which the solution demands change. The Wisconsin Card-Sorting Test exemplifies the predicament of a patient with frontal damage.

A subject is given a deck of cards containing multiple copies of those represented here. Presented with a row of four cards selected from among them, the subject's task is to place each card from the deck in front of the appropriate card in the row, sorting by one of three possible categories: color, number of elements, or shape. Subjects are not told the correct sorting category but only whether their responses are correct or incorrect. When a subject selects the correct category ten consecutive times, the correct solution changes unexpectedly.

Shifting response strategies is particularly difficult for people with frontal damage. R.L. eventually performed the card-sorting task, but with great difficulty. Our neuropsychological evaluation revealed a woman of above-average intelligence with a significant loss of verbal fluency and verbal memory as well as severe dyslexia even a year after the accident. Nearly 20 years later, R.L. is still unable to read music and reads text only with great difficulty.

People with closed-head traumatic brain injuries often show little or no visible sign of cerebral injury on neuroimaging but still have significant cognitive deficits, often so severe that they cannot resume their preinjury lifestyles. For many, the extent of neurological disorder becomes clear only from the results of neuropsychological tests.

This fundamentally diagnostic role of neuropsychological assessment has changed radically since its heyday in the 1980s, when clinically trained neuropsychologists and neuropsychological evaluation were regarded as essential in neurological assessment. In this chapter, we describe this changing role and the opportunities it presents, consider the rationale behind neuropsychological assessment and its goals, explain the problem of effort in testing subjects, and summarize three actual case assessments.

28.1 The Changing Face of Neuropsychological Assessment

Neuropsychological assessment is rooted in neurology and psychiatry. One of its pioneers was Kurt Goldstein, a clinician who was expert in neurology, psychology, and psychiatry. After World War II, Goldstein and others pushed the development of psychological assessments for neurological patients, and especially returning veterans, leading to a divergence of psychological assessment from traditional medicine by the late 1940s. The first neuropsychological tests were designed to identify people with cerebral dysfunction attributable to organic disease processes (brain pathology), rather than to "functional disorders" linked to behavior.

Although test designers originally believed that a single test for brain damage could be constructed, with a cutoff point that separated the brain-damaged from the non–brain-damaged patient, the task proved impossible. Gradually, more-sophisticated testing procedures were developed, largely by teams working in a few far-flung locations, from Europe and North America to Australia, and headed by Oliver Zangwill (Cambridge), Freda Newcombe (Oxford), Alexander Luria (Moscow), Brenda Milner and Laughlin Taylor (Montreal), Edith Kaplan and Hans-Leukas Teuber (Boston), Arthur Benton (Iowa City), and Kevin Walsh (Melbourne).

By the early 1980s, neuropsychology was no longer confined to a few elite laboratories focused on research, and the new field of clinical neuropsychology blossomed in clinics and hospitals. Since that time, three factors have enhanced the rate of change in neuropsychological assessment: functional brain imaging, cognitive neuroscience, and managed health care. We consider each briefly.

Functional Brain Imaging

We emphasize the importance of functional imaging in the Snapshots throughout the preceding chapters. Whereas in earlier eras the effects of cerebral injury or disease often had to be inferred from behavioral symptoms, neuroimaging allows investigators to identify changes in cerebral functioning in a wide variety of disorders, including most of the neurological, developmental, and behavioral disorders discussed in Chapters 23 through 27.

With the advent of functional neuroimaging, the clinical neuropsychologist's main role has changed from diagnostician to participant in rehabilitation, especially in cases of chronic disease such as stroke and head trauma. As charted in **Figure 28.1,** by the early 2000s neuropsychologists were seeing about 3 in 10 patients for rehabilitation and another 4 in 10 as medical referrals. The most common question relates to general cognitive functioning.

◉ **Figure 28.1 ▼**

Presenting Problems
Fully 70 percent of all patients undergoing neuropsychological assessment are referred either for rehabilitation or in connection with medical or psychiatric problems. (Information from Zillmer and Spiers, 2001.)

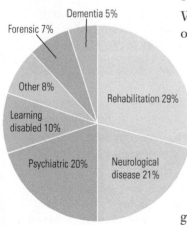

Even the most sophisticated functional-imaging techniques often do not predict the extent of behavioral disturbance observed in people with certain types of brain injury, especially head trauma, as R.L.'s case illustrates. And as the Portrait recounts, for people with closed-head injury, often the only way to document the nature and extent of disability is by a thorough neuropsychological assessment (see Christensen and Uzzell, 2000; Zillmer, 2004; Zillmer et al., 2008). This is where experience in assessment can make a significant difference, for neurology as well as for neuropsychology, and ultimately, for the patient.

In his presidential address to the National Academy of Neuropsychology on "The Future of Neuropsychology," Eric Zillmer (2004) argues that neuropsychology is *the* primary method for studying the brain by examining its behavioral product. Although certainly useful as a complementary assessment tool, neuroimaging measures *structure*, not *function*. Neurologist Allan Ropper and Brian Burrell (2014) argue that clinicians and physicians experienced in using their eyes and ears and brains can diagnose neurological problems as effectively as those using complex technology. The advantage of neuropsychological assessment for cognitive function is that its measures are quantified objectively, whereas imaged-based neurology measures are qualitative and subjective.

Cognitive Neuroscience

The growth of clinical neuropsychology promoted a diversification of methods used by individual practitioners. The choice of tests varies with the disorder being investigated and the question being asked. From the early 1950s through the early 1990s, batteries of tests were developed, each with a different focus (**Table 28.1**). Many, such as the Halstead–Reitan Battery, retain the concept of **cutoff scores**, although performance below a particular level cannot always be taken as indicative of brain damage.

Among the difficulties with cutoff scores is cerebral organization, which varies with such factors as sex, handedness, age, education, culture, and life experience. Another is problem-solving strategy: test problems can be solved by using different strategies and can thus entail different cortical regions. Symptoms of cortical injury can be highly specific (see the case of J.I., the color-blind painter,

Table 28.1 **Overview of neuropsychological test batteries**

Test Battery	Type	Basic Reference
Benton's neuropsychological investigation	Composite	Benton et al., 1983
Boston Process Approach	Composite	Kaplan, 1988
Oxford neuropsychological procedures	Composite	Newcombe, 1969
Montreal Neurological Institute approach	Composite	Taylor, 1979
Frontal-lobe assessment	Composite	Stuss and Levine, 2002
Western Ontario procedures	Composite	Kimura and McGlone, 1983
Halstead–Reitan Battery	Standardized	Reitan and Davison, 1974
Luria's neuropsychological investigation	Standardized	Christensen, 1975
Luria–Nebraska Battery	Standardized	Golden, 1981
CANTAB	Computerized	Robbins et al., 1998

described in Section 13.4). Finally, because many tests require various kinds of problem solving, we might expect task performance to vary with intelligence. All these factors make the use of cutoff scores difficult to justify.

A serious handicap in developing test batteries was the absence of neurological theory in test construction or use. Knowledge of brain function was based largely on clinical observation, and few clinicians other than Alexander Luria had tried to formulate a general theory of how the brain functions to produce cognition (shown in Figure 10.17).

The emergence of cognitive neuroscience in the 1990s brought a dramatic change in the theoretical understanding of brain and cognition. Case studies once again became popular, each directed by sophisticated cognitive theory and assisted by structural- and functional-imaging technologies (see Shallice, 1988). These more-cognitive approaches also use multivariate statistical methods, such as structural equation modeling, to attempt to understand how the neural networks and the connectome are disrupted, both in individual cases and in groups. Test design now incorporates this knowledge, and the cognitive approach will continue to change neuropsychological assessment in the future.

Perhaps the greatest influence of cognitive neuroscience is in clarifying the functions of the right frontal lobe (see a review by Stuss and Levine, 2002). Historically, the right frontal lobe proved remarkably unresponsive to neuropsychological assessment. The combination of functional imaging and neuropsychological test development has now led to an understanding of the right frontal lobe's role in formerly inaccessible functions such as *social cognition* (see Section 20.6).

Managed Care

Economics is perhaps the greatest challenge faced by practicing psychologists in recent decades (see Zillmer, 2004). With the high cost of medical care, clinicians often face pressure to reduce the time and money spent on neuropsychological services, which are time consuming and expensive. In particular, the perception that medical imaging can provide faster and more accurate assessments of cerebral dysfunction sometimes fosters unreasonable pressure to reduce the number of neuropsychological tests given to individual patients.

Clearly, imaging has changed the way in which neuropsychological assessment will be used, but in head-trauma cases, as R.L. and the many examples of TBI throughout this book demonstrate, neuropsychological assessment is often the *only* way to document cognitive disturbances. Gary Groth-Marnat (1999) suggests that psychologists must develop and promote assessment procedures that:

- Focus on diagnostic matters most clearly linked to treatment choice and outcomes

- Identify conditions likely to result in cost savings

- Are time efficient

- Integrate treatment planning, progress monitoring, and outcome evaluation

Clearly, clinical assessment has to adapt if it is to survive the challenge of health care costs. But we emphasize once more that many diagnoses remain invisible to neuroimaging and can be reached only by careful observation. Improving patient outcomes thus requires teamwork—a combination of medical tests, from blood work to neuroimaging, and neuropsychological assessment—along with a collaborative effort among practitioners expert in medical, psychological, and administrative specialties.

28.2 Rationale Behind Neuropsychological Assessment

By the 1990s, neuropsychologists had an impressive choice among tests, as summarized in Table 28.1. At one end of the spectrum are **standardized test batteries** with fixed criteria for **organicity**, atypical behavior assumed to have a biological (organic) basis. Thus, organicity criteria are used to distinguish behavioral symptoms from those not directly related to brain pathology. These tests have in common the advantage of straightforward administration, scoring, and interpretation. There is little need to understand the theoretical bases of the tests or the nuances of cerebral organization to administer them. Such understanding is necessary for interpretation, however. Examples include the Halstead–Reitan Battery and the Luria–Nebraska Battery.

More recently, Trevor Robbins and his colleagues at the University of Cambridge devised a computerized version of a standardized battery, the Cambridge Neuropsychological Test Automated Battery (CANTAB), that has the advantage of being administered in a highly structured manner (e.g., Robbins et al., 1994; 1998). CANTAB has been used extensively for research and increasingly in clinical practice. At last count, over 600 publications were using the CANTAB, although to date it has not been directly compared to older comprehensive test batteries (see Smith et al., 2013, for a discussion).

At the other end of the testing spectrum are **individualized test batteries** that require particular theoretical knowledge to administer and interpret. These assessments are more qualitative than quantitative. The testing of each patient is tailored both to that person's etiology and to the qualitative nature of his or her performance on each test. An example is Luria's neurological approach, which is not really so much a test battery as a strategy for examining patients. (The Luria–Nebraska Battery was an attempt to make Luria's procedure more structured and quantitative, but the process made the battery into a completely different analysis.)

Composite test batteries occupy a middle ground between the standardized and individualized batteries. Each test is administered in a formalized way and may have comparison norms, but qualitative performance and the pattern of test results are considered. An example is the Boston Process Approach (**Table 28.2**). Arthur Benton and his colleagues (Benton et al., 1983; Benton, 1994) have described other composite batteries that can be tailored to individuals, as have Muriel Lezak et al. (2012), Pat McKenna and Elizabeth Warrington (1986), William Milberg and his colleagues (1986), Freda Newcombe (1969), Aaron Smith (1981), Laughlin Taylor (1979), and Kevin Walsh (1991).

Across this spectrum, each battery is constantly changing in response to test revisions and developments as well as to the clinical population being evaluated. One constraint on the choice of any test, however, is the clinical neuropsychologists' training. The use of tests based on theory requires an understanding of the theory of cerebral organization.

Table 28.2 Representative tests used in the Boston Process Approach battery

Intellectual and Conceptual Functions
Wechsler Adult Intelligence Scale IV
Raven's Standard Progressive Matrices
Shipley Institute of Living Scale
Wisconsin Card-Sorting Test
Proverbs test

Memory Functions
Wechsler Memory Scale IV
Rey Auditory Verbal Learning Test
Rey Complex-Figure Test
Benton Visual-Recognition Test
Consonant trigrams test
Cowboy Story-Reading Memory Test

Language Functions
Narrative writing sample
Tests of verbal fluency
Visual-perceptual functions
Cow-and-circle experimental test
Automobile puzzle
Parietal-lobe battery
Hooper Visual Organization Test

Academic Skills
Wide Range Achievement Test

Self-Control and Motor Functions
Proteus Maze Test
Stroop Color-Word Interference Test
Luria Three-Step Motor Program
Finger tapping

Factors Affecting Test Choice

Throughout this book, you have seen that circumscribed lesions in different cortical regions can produce discrete behavioral changes. Working backward from this knowledge to localize unknown brain damage seems reasonable. That is, given a particular behavioral change, we should be able to predict the site or sites of the disturbance most likely to be causing the change.

Problems emerge in working backward in such a manner, however. Research patients are often chosen for specific reasons. For example, whereas patients with rapidly expanding tumors would not be chosen for research because their results are so difficult to interpret, neurosurgical patients are neuropsychologists' ideal research subjects because the extent of their damage is known. Therefore, we might expect differences in the neurological disorder's etiology to make assessment difficult. Indeed, people with diffuse dysfunction, as in head trauma, likely would perform very differently from people with surgical removals.

Even after the practitioner has chosen tests appropriate for a specific etiology, significant questions must be resolved. First, how sensitive are the tests? If a large brain region is dysfunctional, the assessment test need not be particularly sensitive to demonstrate the dysfunction. If the lesion is small, on the other hand, the behavioral effect may be rather specific. For example, a lesion in the right somatosensory representation of the face may produce very subtle sensory changes, and unless specific tests of nonverbal fluency are used (see, for example, Figure 16.9), the cognitive changes may go unnoticed, even with dozens of tests.

A related problem is that various factors may interact with brain pathology to make interpreting test results difficult. Both age and ethnic or cultural background can influence test performance. Therefore, as noted in Section 28.1, test scores with strict cutoff criteria cannot be interpreted.

Intelligence also alters an investigator's expectations of test performance: someone with an IQ score of 130 may be relatively impaired on a test of verbal memory but may appear typical compared with someone with an IQ score of 90. Thus, unlike standard, quantitative psychometric assessment, neuropsychological assessment must be flexible. This flexibility makes interpretation difficult and requires extensive training in fundamental neuropsychology and neurology as well as in neuropsychological assessment. (For an interesting legal discussion related to flexible batteries, see Bigler, 2008.)

Finally, significant differences in test performance are related to factors such as sex and handedness, both detailed in Chapter 12. In addition, test performance is often biased by demographics. For example, in one three-city study of the effects of head trauma, investigators found that healthy participants in one city performed as poorly as brain-damaged subjects in another. Significant demographic differences influenced test performance and thus had to be considered in interpreting test results.

Goals of Neuropsychological Assessment

The goal of assessment in general clinical psychology is diagnosing a disorder for the purpose of changing behavior. For example, to aid in teaching, intelligence and achievement tests may be given to schoolchildren with the goal of identifying particular problem areas (poor short-term memory, for example, or slow reading). Similarly, personality tests are used with an eye toward defining and curing a behavioral disorder, such as generalized anxiety.

The goals of clinical neuropsychology are different in some respects. Neuropsychological assessment:

- **Aims to determine a person's general level of cerebral functioning and to identify cerebral dysfunction and localize it where possible.** In doing so, the assessment attempts to provide an accurate and unbiased estimate of a person's cognitive capacity.

- **Facilitates patient care and rehabilitation.** Serial assessments can provide information about the rate of recovery and the potential for resuming a former lifestyle.

- **Identifies mild disturbances when other diagnostic studies have produced equivocal results.** Examples are the effects of head trauma or the early symptoms of a degenerative disease.

- **Identifies unusual brain organization that may exist in left-handers or in people who have had a childhood brain injury.** This information is particularly valuable to surgeons, who would not want, for example, to remove primary speech zones inadvertently while performing surgery. Such information is likely to be obtained only from behavioral measures.

- **Corroborates an abnormal EEG in disorders such as focal epilepsy.** Indeed, the primary evidence may emerge from behavioral assessment, because radiological procedures, including noninvasive imaging, can fail to identify specifically the abnormal brain tissue giving rise to the seizures.

- **Documents recovery of function after brain injury.** Because some recovery may be expected, documentation aids not only in planning for rehabilitation but also in determining the effectiveness of medical treatment, particularly for neoplasms (tumors) or vascular abnormalities.

- **Promotes realistic outcomes.** Assisting a patient and the patient's family in understanding the patient's possible residual deficits facilitates setting realistic life goals and planning rehabilitation programs.

Intelligence Testing in Neuropsychological Assessment

Most neuropsychological assessments begin with a measure of general intelligence, most often one of the Wechsler scales, which have proved invaluable in determining a base level of cognitive functioning. The most recent version, released in 2008, is the Wechsler Adult Intelligence Scale—Fourth Edition (WAIS-IV), which is normed on people aged 16 to 90. The WAIS-IV has 10 core subtests and 5 supplemental subtests.

The 10 core subtests comprise the Full Scale IQ (FSIQ). Earlier editions of the Wechsler Scale (Wechsler-Bellevue, WAIS-R, and WAIS-III) used separate scales to establish a verbal and a performance IQ score. In the WAIS-IV, these two scales have been replaced by five index scores: General Ability Index (GAI), Verbal Comprehension Index (VCI), Perceptual Reasoning Index (PRI),

Working Memory Index (WMI), and Processing Speed Index (PSI). The FSIQ has a mean of 100 and a standard deviation of 15, and the manual states that for clinical decision making, the VCI and PRI indexes now substitute for the Verbal and Performance IQ scores (Hartman, 2009).

An advantage of the WAIS-IV is that it can be given more quickly than the WAIS-III (about 70 versus 80 or more minutes, respectively), an important improvement for testing patients who might fatigue easily. A briefer test can be given by using only the GAI, which yields a composite score based on three VCI subtests and three PRI subtests. The GAI correlates at 0.97 with the FSIQ and may provide a "purer" estimate of intelligence in older or disabled adults with compromised memory and/or motor function (Hartman, 2009).

Sufficient studies have not as yet been conducted to determine the usefulness of the five WAIS-IV indexes in neuropsychological assessment, although there are hints that they might prove useful. For example, adults with ADHD show significant decrements in WMI and PRI relative to matched controls (Theilling & Petermann, 2014). Similarly, TBI patients show a specific decrement in processing speed relative to neurologically healthy controls (Donders & Strong, 2014).

Although the verbal and performance scales of earlier WAIS versions were not designed to measure left- and right-hemisphere functions, respectively, the FSIQ core subtests have proved useful as a rough measure. FSIQ scores obtained on both the VCI and PRI have a mean of 100 and a standard deviation of 15. A difference of more than 10 points between the verbal comprehension and the perceptual reasoning index scores is usually taken as clinically significant, although statistically this interpretation is liberal.

The results of numerous studies on earlier editions of the Weschler Scales demonstrate that well-defined left-hemisphere lesions produce a relatively low verbal IQ score compared with performance score, whereas well-defined right-hemisphere lesions produce a relatively low performance score. Diffuse damage, on the other hand, tends to produce a low performance score, leading to the erroneous belief that the verbal–performance IQ difference was not diagnostically useful. Although a reduced performance score was not definitive, study results reveal that obtaining a relatively low verbal IQ was rare and that its appearance should not be ignored.

Elizabeth Warrington and her colleagues (1986) evaluated the WAIS-R subscales and IQ values in a retrospective study of 656 unselected patients with unilateral brain damage. Overall, their results showed that left-hemisphere lesions depress verbal IQ scores, whereas right-hemisphere lesions depress performance IQs. The exception in both cases is occipital lesions.

However, the verbal–performance discrepancy score was fewer than 10 points in 53 percent of left-hemisphere cases and in 43 percent of right-hemisphere cases. A small number of patients had discrepancy scores greater than 10 points in the opposite direction: 6 percent of those with left-hemisphere lesions and 3 percent with right-hemisphere lesions. (It is curious that the patients with left parietal or temporoparietal lesions did not show a large drop in IQ score, considering, presumably, that they would be dysphasic. Because language skills were not mentioned in the Warrington study, her analysis could have excluded aphasic subjects. In our experience, dysphasic patients have very depressed verbal IQ scores, as would be expected.)

Warrington also analyzed a subset of WAIS-R subtests, including four verbal instruments (arithmetic, similarities, digit span, and vocabulary) and three performance (nonverbal) tests (picture completion, block design, and picture arrangement). Overall, the performance of left-hemisphere frontal, temporal, and parietal patients was significantly poorer on the four verbal tests. No differences appeared between these left-hemisphere groups on the tests, however. The performance tests were less predictive of lesion side because only the right parietal patients were significantly poorer on block design and picture arrangement. These conclusions will likely prove true of the WAIS-IV as well.

Postinjury intelligence testing is useless without a premorbid estimate of intellectual level. A relatively low IQ score cannot be ascribed to a brain injury unless there is some idea of what the score was before the injury. Such estimates usually are informal and based on a patient's education, occupation, and socioeconomic background. Robert Wilson and his colleagues (1979) describe a statistical procedure for estimating premorbid IQ scores.

Other related Wechsler scales are the Wechsler Memory Scale (WMS-IV) and Wechsler Intelligence Scale for Children (WISC-IV). Although the WMS-IV and WAIS-IV both measure memory, each measures distinct memory functions and should be seen as complementary (e.g., Lepach et al., 2013).

Categories of Neuropsychological Assessment

Eric Zillmer and Mary Spiers (2001) reviewed a survey of 2000 neuropsychologists and identified the 10 most frequently used categories of neuropsychological assessment tests, summarized in **Table 28.3**. Several volumes catalogue the range of neuropsychological tests available, the two most extensive being those by Muriel Lezak and her colleagues (2012) and by Otfried Spreen and Esther Strauss (1991).

Deborah Waber and her colleagues (2007) published a landmark longitudinal study of neuropsychological performance in children aged 6 to 18 years in which normative data are presented for a wide range of measures. For many measures, raw scores improved steeply from 6 to 10 years of age before decelerating during adolescence. Household income predicted IQ and achievement

Table 28.3 **Ten commonly assessed neuropsychological categories**

Abstract reasoning and conceptualization (e.g., problem solving, executive functions)
Attention (e.g., selective, sustained, shifting, or neglect)
Daily activities (e.g., toileting, dressing, eating)
Emotional or psychological distress (e.g., depression, impulsivity)
Language (e.g., receptive or expressive speech, aphasia)
Memory (e.g., verbal, visual, working)
Motor (e.g., dexterity, speed, strength)
Orientation (e.g., awareness of place, time)
Sensation and perception (e.g., visual acuity, taste/smell, tactile)
Visuospatial (e.g., construction, route finding, facial recognition)

Data from Zillmer and Spiers, 2001.

scores but not other test performance. The neuropsychological scores are linked to an MRI developmental database.

Sports medicine is a growing area for neuropsychological assessment. Of particular interest is tracking athletes with concussions. Alison Cernich and colleagues (2007) describe a test battery (the Automated Neuropsychological Assessment Metrics Sports Medicine Battery, ASMB) specifically designed for use in concussion surveillance and management. The ASMB is currently being refined with the development of appropriate norms and with the goal of pre-testing athletes in sports with high incidence of concussion (for example, U.S. football and ice hockey). This type of battery has a clear utility, given the number of athletes in professional football and university hockey who experience lingering effects from head injuries (see Chapter 25 Portrait and Section 26.3).

28.3 Neuropsychological Tests and Brain Activity

Neuropsychological tests have been developed to identify cerebral dysfunction under the presumption that they actually measure the activity of specific cerebral regions. However, cognitive processes correspond to the activity of widely distributed neural networks (see Section 19.3 for examples in language processing). One means for examining the question of what brain regions are active during specific tests employs noninvasive imaging as control participants perform one or more tests.

The most common studies focus on brain activation during frontal-lobe tests such as the Wisconsin Card-Sorting Task. Julie Alvarez and Eugene Emory's meta-analysis (2006) of such studies reveals clearly reliable activation of frontal regions when subjects perform tasks such as the Wisconsin Card-Sorting Test, Stroop Test, and Chicago Word-Fluency Test (see Section 16.3 for test details). But activation always appears in other cerebral regions too, even when studies use subtraction methods (see Figure 7.15) to reduce general activity related to noncognitive functions such as sensory processing. This more extended activation presumably occurs because the frontal cortex participates in several extended brain networks. Preceding chapters illustrate a wide range, for example in Figures 16.17, 17.3, and 20.12.

Such results suggest that the interpretation of neuropsychological test performance should move away from the historical anatomical localization approach, in which anatomy and function are inseparable, to an approach more consistent with the developing view of connectivity and extended neural networks. Indeed, we have seen dozens of cases in which patients with verified localized brain injuries fail to show symptoms that we would expect on the basis of our experience and cases that may actually show some symptoms that we would not predict.

Neuropsychologists must remain cognizant of the facts: considerable inter-subject variation exists in brain organization; the effects of education and specific experiences (for example, playing video games or not) are great; and large individual differences emerge in how cognitively engaged aging people remain. All of these factors will influence both test performance and the specificity of brain activation.

28.4 The Problem of Effort

A major challenge for neuropsychologists is determining whether subjects are performing tests as requested or are malingering, typically by exaggerating their cognitive deficits. The American Psychiatric Association's DSM-5 (2013) defines malingering as "the intentional production of false or grossly exaggerated physical or psychological symptoms, motivated by external incentives such as avoiding work, obtaining financial compensation, evading criminal prosecution, or obtaining drugs."

Paul Green and his colleagues (2001) gave 904 consecutive patients a battery of neuropsychological tests, including a test of effort. Suboptimal effort suppressed the overall test-battery performance four and a half times as much as moderate to severe brain injury did. Their conclusion: effort has a greater effect on test performance than brain damage. In a follow-up study, Green (2007) also found that poor performance on tests of effort not only affects memory performance but actually influences performance across the entire test battery.

Although we would like to hope that expert clinicians would be able to detect malingering, the consensus is that clinical judgment is not impressive. The only valid method of assessing a lack of effort appears to be the use of specific tests of effort. Among the variety of tests published over the years, the most sensitive is consistently found to be the Forced Choice Digit Memory Test devised by Merille Hiscock (see, for example, Guilmette et al., 1994).

The test is extremely simple: subjects are shown a number (for example, 56093) and are then immediately shown two numbers, including the first one and a novel one (for example, 56093 and 82104) and asked which of the two they have already seen. Jeanette McGlone at Dalhousie University has shown that even severely amnesic patients usually score nearly perfectly on a series of 32 trials, provided that they are not distracted (McGlone, 2007). People faking memory problems may score as low as chance, indicating a lack of effort and invalidating the entire assessment. A cutoff of no lower than 90 percent correct is generally used in scoring the Forced Choice Digit Memory Test.

Although the actual incidence of malingering is unknown, at least 20 percent of people with head traumas or alleged exposure to toxic substances are likely to exert low effort intentionally. Such estimates emphasize the need to employ testing measures such as the Forced Choice Digit Memory Test in any assessment in which an advantage accrues to the test subject, such as in cases involving potential financial compensation.

The question of motivation in test performance is perhaps most clearly shown in a comparison of neuropsychological test performance between people with mild head injury seeking compensation from the Workers' Compensation Board and people ordered by a court to undergo a parenting assessment. The former group gains financially by doing poorly and the latter group by doing well: they retain custody of their children. Lloyd Flaro and his colleagues (2007) found that the group seeking compensation was 23 times as likely to fail a test of effort as those in the parenting group. In fact, the mild TBI group was twice as likely to fail the test as the more severe TBI group. Such effects cannot be explained by differences in cognitive skills, but they are explainable by differences in external incentives.

28.5 Case Histories

Having surveyed the basic principles of neuropsychological theory and assessment, we now apply the tests and the theory in considering the case histories and test results of three patients. This sampling of clinical problems illustrates the use of neuropsychological tests in neuropsychological assessment.

Because of our affiliation with the Montreal Neurological Institute, our composite assessment battery is based on tests derived from the study of neurosurgical patients by Brenda Milner, Laughlin Taylor, and their colleagues. Most of the tests have been discussed elsewhere in the text, especially in Chapters 14 through 16 in relation to neuropsychological assessment of parietal-, temporal-, and frontal-lobe function.

Case 1: Epilepsy Caused by Left-Hemisphere Tumor

This 33-year-old man had a history of seizures beginning 4 years before his admission to the hospital. His neurological examination on admission was negative, but his seizures were increasingly frequent and characterized by his head and eyes turning to the right, a pattern that suggests supplementary motor cortex involvement. The results of radiological and EEG studies suggested a left-frontal-lobe lesion (**Figure 28.2** at left), which was confirmed at surgery when a poorly differentiated astrocytoma was removed.

The only difficulty that the patient experienced before surgery was in doing the Wisconsin Card-Sorting Test, where he made numerous perseverative errors and sorted only one category correctly. Two weeks after surgery, all of the intelligence ratings, memory quotients, and delayed verbal-recall scores decreased, but they remained in essentially the same ratio to one another. Other tests were unchanged, the only significantly low score again being on the card-sorting test.

Figure 28.2 ▼

Neuropsychological Test Results Before and After Surgery in Two Cases

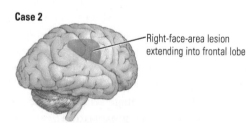

Case 1   Left-frontal-lobe lesion

Case 2   Right-face-area lesion extending into frontal lobe

	Preop	Postop
Full-scale IQ	115	102
Verbal IQ	111	103
Performance IQ	117	99
Memory quotient	118	108
Verbal recall	20	14
Nonverbal recall	10.5	10
Card sorting	1 category*	1 category*
Finger-position sense	Left Right 60/60 60/60	Left Right 60/60 60/60
Drawings: Copy	36/36	35/36
Recall	21/36	24/36

* Significantly low score.

	Preop	Postop
Full-scale IQ	97	97
Verbal IQ	100	106
Performance IQ	94	88*
Memory quotient	94	92
Verbal recall	13.5	14.0
Nonverbal recall	3.5*	7.0
Card sorting	0 category*	1 category*
Finger-position sense	Left Right 55/60* 59/60	Left Right 54/60* 60/60
Drawings: Copy	28/36*	26.5/36*
Recall	4/36*	9.5/36*

* Significantly low score.

If this patient was like other patients with similar lesions, on follow-up a year after surgery, his intelligence ratings and memory scores would likely have returned to the preoperative level. His card sorting, however, would be unlikely to show any improvement.

Case 2: Epilepsy Caused by Right-Hemisphere Infection

This 26-year-old man had an 8-year history of seizures dating to an episode of meningitis in which he was thought to have an intracerebral abscess. Subsequently, he developed seizures beginning in the left side of his face and left hand. He was referred as a candidate for surgery because his seizures were uncontrolled by medication.

Before surgery, the patient scored within normal limits on tests of intelligence and general memory, although he did have difficulty with delayed recall of verbal material. He had slight defects of finger-position sense on the left hand, which, together with some weakness in the left arm and leg, pointed to damage in the right central area of the cortex. In addition, he had difficulty copying and recalling the Rey Complex Figure and was unable to perform the Wisconsin Card-Sorting Test, suggesting that his lesion might extend into the frontal and temporal areas as well.

The right facial area and a region extending into the right frontal lobe were removed at surgery (Figure 28.2 at right). Afterward, some residual epileptiform abnormality in both the frontal lobe and the superior temporal gyrus remained. Postoperative testing showed improvement in both verbal IQ score and long-term verbal memory, but the patient had persistent difficulties on the card-sorting test, with finger-position sense on the left hand, and on the copy and recall of the Rey Complex Figure. His performance (perceptual reasoning index) IQ score also declined.

The difficulty with finger position would be expected in such a case, but the continuing difficulties with card sorting and the Rey Complex Figure imply that areas in his right hemisphere remain dysfunctional. This dysfunction is seen in residual abnormalities in the EEG recordings from the frontal and temporal regions.

Case 3: Rehabilitation

This 37-year-old man had been in a traffic accident some 15 years earlier. He was in a coma for 6 weeks and had secondary injury from brain infection. At the time of his accident, he was a student in a graduate program in journalism, having previously obtained a bachelor's degree with honors in English literature.

When we first met him, he had severe motor problems, used canes to walk, and was both apraxic and ataxic. He had great difficulty in pronouncing words, especially when hurried or stressed, but careful language testing on the Token Test revealed no aphasic symptoms; his language problems were entirely due to a difficulty in coordinating the muscles of the mouth (*anarthria*).

Since the time of his accident, this man had lived at home with his parents and had not learned the social skills necessary to cope with his handicap. In short, he was being treated as though he were intellectually disabled and was being completely looked after by his family. Indeed, the patient believed himself to be intellectually disabled and was very reluctant to attempt rehabilitation.

At his family's urging, we administered a thorough assessment to evaluate his intellectual potential. The results were surprising, even to us. His intellect was superior (WAIS verbal IQ score of 127) and although he had deficits on some tests, especially those requiring motor skills, his performance on most tests was average or above average. Despite his obvious motor handicaps, this man clearly was not intellectually disabled.

One significant cognitive loss, however, was his nonverbal memory, which was very poor. Armed with our test results, we were able to show him—and his family—that he could look after himself and should seek occupational therapy. He is now a chartered accountant in Canada, equivalent to a certified public accountant (CPA) in the United States.

SUMMARY

28.1 The Changing Face of Neuropsychological Assessment

Developments in functional and structural brain imaging have had a significant impact on the fields of neurology and clinical neuropsychology. Whereas neuropsychological assessment had promised a way to localize focal cerebral injury, medical imaging techniques now have largely replaced this function. But imaging cannot detect all neurological dysfunction. Rather, the most sensitive measure of cerebral integrity is behavior, and behavioral analysis using neuropsychological assessment can identify dysfunction invisible to MRI or CT, especially in cases of TBI, epilepsy, and mild stroke.

The tests used in neuropsychological assessment and the use of test results have changed, owing in part to the continuing development of cognitive neuroscience and enhanced neuroimaging. Tests remain useful for diagnosis and have expanded to become integral to rehabilitation. This changing role has economic implications as managed health care challenges the cost of extensive neuropsychological evaluations, especially when adequate imaging data are available, regardless of its effectiveness.

28.2 Rationale Behind Neuropsychological Assessment

A wide range of clinical neuropsychological assessment tools is now available, the factors affecting test choice and the goals

of assessment varying with the particular clinical question being asked. Analysis of test results must consider a range of variables including age, sex, handedness, cultural background, IQ score, and life experience.

28.3 Neuropsychological Tests and Brain Activity

One way to validate neuropsychological tests is to measure brain activity as subjects perform them. Although activity in the expected regions is usually enhanced, activity elsewhere in the brain increases as well, corresponding to the widespread neural networks within the connectome that underlie cognition. Such results remind us that test performance does not necessarily equate to focal neural anatomy.

28.4 The Problem of Effort

Lack of effort poses a serious problem for assessing people who might benefit from doing poorly on neuropsychological tests. If subjects are seeking compensation of some sort, for instance, lack of effort invalidates the entire assessment. Several tests that are simple to administer can detect a lack of effort.

28.5 Case Histories

Despite technological advances, case histories demonstrate that neuropsychological assessment remains an important tool for demonstrating functional localization after discrete functional injury and for assisting in planning for rehabilitation.

References

Alvarez, J. A., and E. Emory. Executive function and the frontal lobes: A meta-analytic review. *Neuropsychology Review* 16:17–42, 2006.

American Psychiatric Association. *Diagnostic and Statistical Manual of Mental Disorders*, 5th ed. Washington, D.C.: American Psychiatric Association, 2013.

Benton, A. L. Neuropsychological assessment. *Annual Review of Psychology* 45:1–23, 1994.

Benton, A. L., D. de S. Hamsher, N. R. Varney, and O. Spreen. *Contributions to Neuropsychological Assessment: A Clinical Manual.* New York: Oxford University Press, 1983.

Bigler, E. D. Response to Russell's (2007) and Hom's (2008) commentary on "A motion to exclude and the 'fixed' versus 'flexible' battery in 'forensic' neuropsychology." *Archives of Clinical Neuropsychology* 23:755–761, 2008.

Cernich, A., D. Reeves, W. Sun, and J. Bleiberg. Automated neuropsychological assessment metrics sports medicine battery. *Archives of Clinical Neuropsychology* 22:S101–S114, 2007.

Christensen, A.-L. *Luria's Neuropsychological Investigation.* New York: Spectrum, 1975.

Christensen, A.-L., and B. P. Uzzell. *International Handbook of Neuropsychological Rehabilitation.* New York: Plenum, 2000.

Donders, J., and C. A. Strong. Clinical utility of the Wechsler Adult Intelligence Scale-Fourth Edition after traumatic brain injury. *Assessment*, in press, 2014.

Flaro, L., P. Green, and E. Robertson. Word memory test failure 23 times higher in mild brain injury than in parents seeking custody: The power of external incentives. *Brain Injury* 21:373–383, 2007.

Golden, C. J. A standardized version of Luria's neuropsychological tests. In S. Filskov and T. J. Boll, Eds. *Handbook of Clinical Neuropsychology.* New York: Wiley-Interscience, 1981.

Green, P. The pervasive effect of effort on neuropsychological tests. *Archives of Clincial Neuropsychology* 18:43–68, 2007.

Green, P., M. L. Rohling, P. R. Lees-Haley, and L. M. Allen. Effort has a greater effect on test scores than severe brain injury in compensation claimants. *Brain Injury* 15:1045–1060, 2001.

Groth-Marnat, G. Financial efficacy of clinical assessment: Rationale guidelines and issues for future research. *Journal of Clinical Psychology* 55:813–824, 1999.

Guilmette, T. J., W. Whelihan, F. R. Sparadeo, and G. Buongiorno. Validity of neuropsychological test results in disability evaluations. *Perceptual Motor Skills* 78:1179–1186, 1994.

Hartman, D. E. Wechsler Adult Intelligence Scale IV (WAIS-IV): Return of the gold standard. *Applied Neuropsychology* 16:85–87, 2009.

Kaplan, E. A process approach to neuropsychological assessment. In T. Boll and B. K. Bryant, Eds. *Clinical Neuropsychology and Brain Function: Research, Development, and Practice,* pp. 129–167. Washington, D.C.: American Psychological Association, 1988.

Kimura, D., and J. McGlone. *Neuropsychology Test Procedures.* Manual used at the University Hospital, London, Ontario, Canada, 1983.

Lepach, A. C., M. Daseking, F. Petermann, and H. C. Waldmann. The relationships of intelligence and memory assessed using the WAIS-IV and the WMS-IV (article in German). *Gesundheitswesen* 75:775–781, 2013.

Lezak, M. D., D. B. Howieson, B. Diane, E. D. Bigler, and D. Tranel. *Neuropsychological Assessment,* 5th ed. New York: Oxford University Press, 2012.

McGlone, J. Personal communication, August 2007.

McKenna, P., and E. K. Warrington. The analytical approach to neuropsychological assessment. In I. Grant and K. M. Adams, Eds. *Assessment of Neuropsychiatric Disorders.* New York: Oxford University Press, 1986.

Milberg, W. P., N. Hebben, and E. Kaplan. The Boston Process Approach to neuropsychological assessment. In I. Grant and K. M. Adams, Eds. *Assessment of Neuropsychiatric Disorders.* New York: Oxford University Press, 1986.

Newcombe, F. *Missile Wounds of the Brain.* London: Oxford University Press, 1969.

Reitan, R. M., and L. A. Davison. *Clinical Neuropsychology: Current Status and Application.* New York: Wiley, 1974.

Robbins, T. W., M. James, A. M. Owen, B. J. Sahakian, A. D. Lawrence, L. McInnes, and P. M. Rabbitt. A study of performance on tests from the CANTAB battery sensitive to frontal lobe dysfunction in a large sample of normal volunteers: Implications for theories of executive functioning and cognitive aging. Cambridge Neuropsychological Test Automated Battery. *Journal of the International Neuropsychology Society* 4:474–490, 1998.

Robbins, T. W., M. James, A. M. Owen, B. J. Sahakian, L. McInnes, and P. M. Rabbit. Cambridge Neuropsychological Test Automated Battery (CANTAB): A factor analytic study of a large sample of normal elderly volunteers. *Dementia* 5:266–281, 1994.

Ropper, A. H., and B. D. Burrell. *Reaching Down the Rabbit Hole.* New York: St. Martin's Press, 2014.

Shallice, T. *From Neuropsychology to Mental Structure.* Cambridge, U.K.: Cambridge University Press, 1988.

Smith, A. Principles underlying human brain functions in neuropsychological sequelae of different neuropathological processes. In S. B. Filskov and T. J. Boll, Eds. *Handbook of Clinical Neuropsychology.* New York: Wiley-Interscience, 1981.

Smith, P. J., A. C. Need, E. T. Cirulli, O. Chiba-Falek, and D. K. Attix. A comparison of the Cambridge Automated Neuropsychological Test Battery (CANTAB) with "traditional" neuropsychological testing instruments. *Journal of Clinical and Experimental Neuropsychology* 35:319–328, 2013.

Spreen, O., and E. Strauss. *A Compendium of Neuropsychological Tests.* New York: Oxford University Press, 1991.

Stuss, D. T., and B. Levine. Adult clinical neuropsychology: Lessons from studies of the frontal lobes. *Annual Review of Psychology* 53:401–433, 2002.

Taylor, L. B. Psychological assessment of neurosurgical patients. In T. Rasmussen and R. Marino, Eds. *Functional Neurosurgery.* New York: Raven Press, 1979.

Theiling, J., and F. Petermann. Neuropsychological profiles on the WAIS-IV of ADHD adults. *Journal of Attention Disorders* in press, 2014.

Waber, D. P., C. De Moor, P. W. Forbes, R. Almli, K. N. Botteron, G. Leonard, D. Milovan, T. Paus, and J. Rumsey. The NIH MRI study of normal brain development: Performance of a population based sample of healthy children aged 6 to 18 years. *Journal of the International Neuropsychological Society* 13:1–18, 2007.

Walsh, K. W. *Understanding Brain Damage*, 2nd ed. London: Churchill Livingstone, 1991.

Warrington, E. K., M. James, and C. Maciejewski. The WAIS as a lateralizing and localizing diagnostic instrument: A study of 656 patients with unilateral cerebral excisions. *Neuropsychologia* 24:223–239, 1986.

Wilson, R. S., G. Rosenbaum, and G. Brown. The problem of premorbid intelligence in neuropsychological assessment. *Journal of Clinical Neuropsychology* 1:49–56, 1979.

Zillmer, E. A. National Academy of Neuropsychology: President's address. The future of neuropsychology. *Archives of Clinical Neuropsychology* 19:713–724, 2004.

Zillmer, E. A., and M. V. Spiers. *Principles of Neuropsychology*. Belmont, CA: Wadsworth, 2001.

Zillmer, E. A., M. V. Spiers, and W. C. Culbertson. *Principles of Neuropsychology*, 2nd ed. Belmont, CA: Wadsworth, 2008.

GLOSSARY

abdominal reflex. Contraction of the abdominal muscles in response to stroking the abdomen.

ablation. Intentional destruction or removal of parts of the brain or spinal cord; brain lesion.

absolutely refractory. Period in an action potential during which a new action potential cannot be elicited.

acalculia. Inability to perform mathematical operations.

acetylcholine (ACh). First neurotransmitter discovered in the peripheral and central nervous systems; activates skeletal muscles in the somatic nervous system and may either excite or inhibit internal organs in the autonomic system.

achromatopsia. Inability to distinguish different hues despite the presence of normally pigmented cells in the retina. Sometimes called *cortical color blindness*.

acopia. Inability to copy a geometric design.

acquired dyslexia. Inability to read caused by brain damage in a person who could read formerly; distinguished from **developmental dyslexia**, which is a failure to learn to read.

action potential. Large, brief reversal in the polarity of an axon; results from brief changes in the membrane's permeability to potassium and sodium ions.

activating system. Neural pathways that coordinate brain activity through a single neurotransmitter; cell bodies are located in a nucleus in the brainstem and axons are distributed through a wide region of the brain.

active-transport system. Protein pump specialized to transport a particular substance across a membrane. *See also* **transporter**.

addiction. Desire for a drug manifested by its frequent use, leading to development of physical dependence in addition to abuse; often associated with tolerance and unpleasant, sometimes dangerous, withdrawal symptoms on cessation of drug use. Also called *substance dependence*.

adenosine triphosphate (ATP). Molecule important to cellular energy metabolism. The conversion of ATP into ADP (adenosine diphosphate) liberates energy. ATP can also be converted into cyclic AMP (adenosine monophosphate), which serves as an intermediate messenger in the production of postsynaptic potentials by some neurotransmitters and in the mediation of the effects of polypeptide hormones.

affect. Conscious, subjective feeling about a stimulus, independent of where or what it is. Affective behavior is internal and subjective.

afference theory. Theory that all behavior is driven by sensory events. Compare **efference theory**.

afferent. Conducting toward a central nervous system area.

afferent paresis. Loss of kinesthetic feedback that results from lesions to the postcentral gyrus (areas 3-1-2) and produces clumsy movements.

agenesis of the corpus callosum. Condition in which the corpus callosum fails to develop.

agnosia. Partial or complete inability to recognize sensory stimuli, unexplainable by a defect in elementary sensation or by a reduced level of alertness.

agonist. Substance that enhances the function of a synapse.

agrammatism. Impairment in the ability to use verbs and to produce appropriate grammar.

agraphia. Decline in or loss of the ability to write.

akathesia. Condition of motor restlessness, ranging from a feeling of inner disquiet to an inability to sit or lie quietly.

akinesia. Absence or poverty of movement.

akinetic seizure. Seizure producing temporary paralysis of muscles, characterized by a sudden collapse without warning; most common in children.

alcohol. Any organic compound containing a hydroxyl group.

alcohol myopia. "Nearsighted" behavior displayed under the influence of alcohol: local and immediate cues become prominent; remote cues and consequences are ignored.

alexia. Inability to read.

allele. Alternative form of a gene; a gene pair contains two alleles.

allesthesia. Stage of recovery from contralateral neglect characterized by a person's beginning to respond to stimuli on the neglected side as if the stimuli were on the unlesioned side.

allocentric space. Object location relative to another object, independent of the observer's perspective and usually at a distance. Compare **egocentric space**.

alpha rhythm. Regular (approximately 10 Hz) wave pattern in an electroencephalogram; found in most people when they are relaxed with eyes closed.

Alzheimer's disease. Degenerative brain disorder related to aging that first appears as progressive memory loss and later develops into generalized dementia.

amativeness. Inclination to love; localized by the phrenologists in the nape of the neck.

amblyopia. Deficit of vision without obvious impairment of the eye itself.

amebiasis. Also known as amebic dysentery, an infection due to amebas, especially *Entamoeba histolytica*, that results in encephalitis and brain abscesses.

amino acids. Class of biologically active compounds containing an NH_2 chemical group.

Ammon's horn. Region of the hippocampal formation named for the mythological horn of plenty.

amnesia. Partial or total loss of memory.

amnesic aphasia. Aphasic syndrome characterized by the inability to name objects and by the production of unintended syllables, words, or phrases while speaking. Also called **anomic aphasia**.

amphetamine. Drug that releases dopamine into its synapse and, like cocaine, blocks dopamine reuptake.

amusia. Tone deafness: inability to produce (motor) or to comprehend (sensory) musical sounds.

amygdala. Almond-shaped collection of nuclei in the base of the temporal lobe; the part of the limbic system that participates in emotional and species-typical behaviors.

anabolic steroid. A class of synthetic hormones related to testosterone that have both muscle-building (anabolic) and masculinizing (androgenic) effects. Also called *andabolic-androgenic steroid*.

anandamide. From the Sanskrit meaning "joy" or "bliss," chemical neurotransmitter that acts on a THC receptor that naturally inhibits adenyl cyclase, part of a second-messenger system active in sensitization.

anarthria. Paralysis or incoordination of the musculature of the mouth.

anastomosis. Connection between parallel blood vessels that allows them to communicate their blood flows.

aneurysm. Vascular dilation resulting from a localized defect in a vessel's elasticity. A sac is formed by the dilation of the walls of an artery or a vein and is filled with blood and prone to rupture.

angiography. Radiographic imaging of blood vessels filled with a contrast medium.

angioma. Collections of abnormal blood vessels, including capillary, venous, and arteriovenous malformations, resulting in abnormal blood flow.

angular gyrus. Gyrus in the parietal lobe corresponding roughly to Brodmann's area 39; important in language functions.

anion. Negatively charged ion.

anomia. Difficulty in finding words, especially those naming objects.

anomic aphasia. Inability to name objects; also called **amnesic aphasia**.

anopia. Loss of vision.

anorexia nervosa. Exaggerated concern with being overweight that leads to inadequate food intake and often excessive exercising; can lead to severe weight loss and even starvation.

anosmia. Absence of the sense of smell.

anosodiaphoria. Indifference to illness.

anosognosia. Loss of ability to recognize or to acknowledge an illness or bodily defect; usually associated with right parietal lesions.

antagonist. Substance that blocks the function of a neurotransmitter.

anterior cerebral artery (ACA). Vessel originating from the carotid artery to irrigate the medial and dorsal parts of the cortex, including the orbitofrontal and dorsolateral frontal regions, anterior cingulate cortex, corpus callosum, and striatum.

anterior cingulate cortex (ACC). Medial region containing von Economo neurons that makes extensive, bidirectional connections with motor, premotor, and prefrontal cortex as well as the insula.

anterior commissure. Fiber tract that connects the left and right temporal lobes.

anterior corticospinal tract. Pathway carrying instructions from the cortex to the spinal cord for the movement of the trunk; does not cross over to the opposite side of the brainstem at the pyramidal protrusion.

anterior root. Nerve composed of fibers carrying motor information from the anterior part of the human spinal cord. Compare **ventral root**.

anterograde amnesia. Inability to acquire new memories subsequent to a disturbance such as head injury, electroconvulsive shock, or certain degenerative diseases. Compare **retrograde amnesia**.

anterograde disorientation. Impairment in spatial orientation that persists after a brain injury.

anterograde transport. Transport by a neuron, usually along axons, of substances in a direction that is away from the cell body.

antianxiety agent. See **anxiolytic**.

antianxiety site. Site that accepts benzodiazepines and enhances the binding of gamma-aminobutryic acid (GABA) to its receptors, which means that the availability of GABA determines the potency of an antianxiety drug.

antipsychotic drug. Drug that acts on the dopamine synapse and affects psychomotor activity, generally without hyponotic effects. Also called **neuroleptic** or **major tranquilizer**.

anvil. The middle of the three ossicles of the ear. In turn with the stapes and malleus, the anvil conducts vibrations from the tympanic membrane to the inner ear. Also called the *incus*.

anxiolytic. Drug (e.g., Valium, Ativan) that reduces anxiety; includes minor tranquilizers, benzodiazepines, and sedative-hypnotic agents.

aphagia. Inability to eat or chew.

aphasia. Inability to speak or comprehend language despite the presence of normal comprehension and intact vocal mechanisms.

apoptosis. Genetically programmed cell death.

apotemnophilia. Disorder in which an individual desires to have a limb amputated.

apperceptive agnosia. Broad category of visual agnosias in which elementary sensory functions appear intact but a perceptual deficit prevents object recognition.

apraxia. Inability, in the absence of paralysis or other motor or sensory impairment, to make or copy voluntary movements, especially an inability to make proper use of an object.

aprosodia. Condition in which there is a loss of production or comprehension of the meaning of different tones of voice.

arachnoid. Thin sheet of delicate collagenous connective tissue that follows the contours of the brain.

arcuate fasciculus. Long bundle of fibers connecting Wernicke's and Broca's areas.

area postrema. Brainstem nucleus sensitive to blood-borne toxins; causes vomiting.

Argyll-Robertson pupil. Constriction of the pupil of the eye to accommodation but not to light; used to diagnose damage to the midbrain relays of the third cranial (oculomotor) nerve.

arteriovenous malformation (AVM). Abnormality of both the arterial and the venous blood flow, which often appears as a mass of vessels that are intertwined and lie on the surface of the cortex.

asomatognosia. Loss of knowledge or sensory awareness of one's own body and bodily condition; may be on one or both sides of the body; most commonly results from damage to the right parietal lobe.

Asperger's syndrome. Autism spectrum disorder in which a person has relatively good verbal communication but difficulty with social communication. Sometimes called *high-functioning autism*.

aspiny neurons. Class of inhibitory neurons that do not have dendritic spines.

association area. Cortical regions that receive projections from secondary areas or send projections to them; encompasses all cortex not specialized for sensory or motor function and mediates complex activities such as language, planning, memory, and attention. *See also* **prefrontal cortex** and **tertiary area**.

association cell layers. Layers II and III of the cerebral cortex.

associative agnosia. Inability to recognize or identify an object despite its apparent perception.

associative learning. Form of learning in which two or more unrelated stimuli become associated with one another so that any one of them can elicit the same behavioral response.

astereognosis. Inability to recognize the nature of an object by touch.

astrocyte. Star-shaped glial cell that provides structural support to neurons in the central nervous system and transports substances between neurons and blood vessels.

astrocytoma. Slow-growing brain tumor resulting from the growth of astrocytes.

asymbolia. Inability to employ a conventional sign to stand for another object or event.

asymbolia for pain. Inability to understand the meaning of or react to pain.

ataxia. Failure of muscular coordination; any of various irregularities of muscular action.

athetosis. Motor disorder marked by involuntary movements or slow writhing movements, especially in the hands.

attention. Narrowing or focusing awareness selectively, to part of the sensory environment or to a class of stimuli.

attention-deficit/hyperactivity disorder (ADHD). Developmental disorder characterized by core behavioral symptoms of impulsivity, hyperactivity, and/or inattention.

attentional dyslexia. Disorder in which naming a letter is more difficult when it is accompanied by a second letter.

auditory agnosia. Impaired capacity to identify nonverbal acoustical stimuli.

auditory flow. Change in sound heard as a person moves past a sound source or as a sound source moves past a person.

aura. Subjective sensation, perceptual experience, or motor phenomenon that precedes and marks the onset of an epileptic seizure or migraine.

autism spectrum disorder (ASD). Range of cognitive symptoms, from mild to severe, that characterize autism; severe symptoms include greatly impaired social interaction, a bizarre and narrow range of interests, marked abnormalities in language and communication, and fixed, repetitive movements.

autobiographic (episodic) memory. Memory of life experiences centered on the person him- or herself; a person's recall of singular events that enables human beings to remember personal experiences.

autoimmune disease. Immune reaction directed against one's own body.

automatic behaviors. Stereotyped units of behavior linked in a fixed sequence—for example, grooming and chewing. Also called reflexive, consummatory, or respondent behaviors. *See also* **automatism**.

automatic movement. Unit of stereotyped behavior linked in a sequence, such as grooming, chewing food, and lapping water. Spontaneous or involuntary movement.

automatism. Performance of nonreflex acts without conscious volition. Also called **automatic behavior**.

autonoetic awareness. Awareness of one's self, or self-knowledge.

autonomic nervous system (ANS). Division of the peripheral nervous system that regulates the functioning of the body's internal organs and glands.

autopagnosia. Inability to localize and name the parts of one's own body—for example, *finger agnosia*.

autoradiography. Process by which radiolabeled substances are injected into the bloodstream, incorporated into cells, and transported along the cells' processes. When the tissue is exposed to a photographic film, it "takes its own picture" and reveals the route taken by the radiolabeled substance.

autoreceptor. A "self-receptor" in a neural membrane that responds to the transmitter released by that neuron.

axoaxonic synapse. Synapse between two axons.

axodendritic synapse. Synapse between an axon and a dendrite.

axoextracellular synapse. Synapse that releases its neurotransmitter chemical into the extracellular space.

axomuscular synapse. Synapse between an axon and a muscle.

axon. "Root," or single fiber, of a neuron that carries messages to other neurons (or to muscles or glands).

axon collateral. Major branch of an axon.

axon hillock. Juncture of soma and axon where the action potential begins.

axosecretory synapse. Synapse between an axon and a blood vessel in which the transmitter substance is passed into the bloodstream as a hormone.

axosomatic synapse. Synapse between an axon and the cell body of a neuron.

axosynaptic synapse. Synapse between an axon and another synapse.

Babinski sign. Abnormal response to stimulation on the sole of the foot in which there is an upward, extensor movement of the big toe; indicative of a corticospinal-tract lesion. Also called **extensor plantar response.**

back propagation. Reverse movement of an action potential into the dendritic field of a neuron; postulated to play a role in plastic changes that underlie learning.

bacterial meningitis. Inflammation of the brain's triple-layered protective covering by a bacterial infection.

bacterium. Generic name for any microorganism (typically one-celled) that has no chlorophyll and multiplies by simple cell division.

Bálint's syndrome. Agnosic syndrome that results from large bilateral parietal lesions and is composed of three deficits: (1) paralysis of eye fixation with inability to look voluntarily into the peripheral visual field, (2) optic ataxia, and (3) disturbance of visual attention such that the peripheral field is neglected.

balloonist theories. Notion that muscles move as they are filled with a substance such as a fluid from nerves.

barbiturates. Drugs used for their hypnotic and sedative effects; main therapeutic use is to induce anesthesia.

basal ganglia. Subcortical forebrain nuclei (caudate nucleus, putamen, globus pallidus) that connect to the thalamus and midbrain and coordinate voluntary movements of the limbs and body.

basilar membrane. Receptor surface in the cochlea that transduces sound waves into neural activity.

behavioral compensation. Mechanism of recovery from brain injury in which behavior is modified to compensate for lost functions. Neither the recovered behavior nor the area that mediates recovery is the same as those that are lost.

Bell–Magendie law. Principle that the dorsal or posterior roots in the spinal cord are sensory and the ventral or anterior roots in the spinal cord are motor.

benzodiazepine. Any of a group of minor tranquilizers having a common molecular structure and similar pharmacological activities, such as antianxiety, muscle-relaxing, and sedative and hypnotic effects.

beta-endorphin. Meaning "endogenous morphine"; peptide neurotransmitter that has actions similar to those of ingested opium.

beta (β) rhythm. Fast brain-wave activity pattern associated with an alert state, or waking EEG.

bilateral. Applying to both sides of the body.

binding problem. Philosophical question focused on how the brain ties single and varied sensory and motor events together into a unified perception or behavior.

binocular deprivation. Removal of visual stimulation from both eyes by raising an animal in the dark, bandaging the eyes, or a similar technique.

biochemical techniques. Techniques that measure biologically relevant chemicals in tissue, including various types of assay procedures for determining the presence or concentration of different compounds.

biogenic amines. Group of neurotransmitters that includes *norepinephrine*, *dopamine*, and *serotonin*.

bipolar cells. Neurons with processes at both poles; characteristic especially of retinal cells.

bipolar disorder. Mood disorder characterized by periods of depression alternating with periods of regular behavior and periods of *mania* (intense excitation and euphoria).

birthday effect. Influence of birth date on subsequent success at sports or school, where some entrants are older and others are younger than average, producing differential advantages due to age.

bitemporal hemianopia. Loss of vision in both temporal fields due to damage to the medial region of the optic chiasm that severs the crossing fibers.

black widow spider venom. Poison produced by the black widow spider that promotes the release of acetylcholine from the synapse.

blast. Immature neuron or glial cell.

blindsight. Ability of patients with visual-field defects to identify at better-than-chance levels the nature of visual stimuli that are not consciously perceived. Also called *cortical blindness*.

blood–brain barrier. Tight junctions between capillary cells that block entry of an array of substances, including toxins, into the brain.

BOLD contrast. Acronym for blood oxygen level–dependent contrast, a measure used in fMRI; provides an index of the brain's relative activity level.

botulinum toxin (botulin). Poisonous bacterial agent that blocks the release of acetylcholine from the synapse; used clinically to block unwanted activity in muscles.

boundary expansion. Phenomenon displayed in a test of spatial performance: amnesic patients draw framed objects accurately relative to the size of the frame, whereas controls draw the object in a reduced size relative to the frame, thus expanding the space between an object and its frame (boundary); obtained in various sensory modalities.

brain. The encephalon—forebrain, midbrain, and hindbrain—developed from the anterior part of the embryonic neural tube and the part of the central nervous system contained within the cranium.

brain abscess. Localized collection of pus in the brain; formed from tissues that have disintegrated as a result of infection.

brain plasticity. *See* **neuroplasticity.**

brain scan. Any procedure of imaging the structure and function of the living brain. *See also* **radioisotope scan.**

brainstem. Hypothalamus, midbrain, and hindbrain. (Some authorities also include the thalamus and basal ganglia.)

brain stimulation. Method that induces changes in the electrical activity of the brain.

brain theory. Principle that the brain produces behavior.

Broca's aphasia. Inability to speak fluently despite the presence of normal comprehension and intact vocal mechanisms; results from a lesion to Broca's area. Also called **expressive,** or **nonfluent, aphasia.**

Broca's area. Anterior speech area in the left hemisphere (frontal operculum) that functions with the motor cortex to produce movements needed for speaking. Damage to this area results in Broca's aphasia.

Brodmann's map. Map of the cerebral cortex devised by Korbinian Brodmann circa 1905 and based on cytoarchitec-tonic structure with anatomical areas identified by number; conforms remarkably closely to functional areas identified by the results of later lesion and recording studies.

Brown-Séquard syndrome. Condition of unilateral paralysis, loss of joint sensation, and contralateral loss of pain and temperature sensation caused by unilateral damage to the spinal cord.

butyrophenones. One class of drugs that block dopamine receptors.

caffeine. Central nervous system stimulant. Coffee and tea contain caffeine.

calcification. Accumulation of calcium in various brain regions after brain damage.

callosal agenesis. Congenitally reduced or absent interhemispheric connections: lack of a corpus callosum as a result of a developmental abnormality.

calmodulin. Protein that, on stimulation by Ca^{2+}, plays a role in undocking vesicles containing a neurotransmitter so that the neurotransmitter can be released into the synaptic cleft.

carbon monoxide (CO). Gas that acts as a neurotransmitter in the activation of cellular metabolism.

cataplexy. Condition in which a person collapses owing to the loss of all muscle activity or tone; often triggered by an emotional stimulus such as mirth, anger, or fear, among others, and often associated with narcolepsy.

catecholamines. Class of neurotransmitters that includes *epinephrine*, *norepinephrine*. and *dopamine*.

cation. Positively charged ion.

caudate putamen. Large cluster of nuclei located beneath the frontal cortex; prominent structure of the basal ganglia.

cell assembly. Hypothetical group of neurons that become functionally connected because they receive the same sensory inputs; proposed by Donald Hebb to be the basis of perception, memory, and thought.

cell body. Core region of the cell containing the nucleus and other organelles for making proteins. Also called the **soma.**

cellular tolerance. Adjustments in neuronal activities that minimize the effects of alcohol in the blood, lowering the behavioral signs of intoxication despite a high blood-alcohol level.

central nervous system (CNS). The brain and spinal cord that are encased in bone—the skull and vertebrae, respectively—and cannot regrow after damage.

central sleep apnea. Sleep disturbance stemming from a CNS disorder that primarily affects males and is characterized by a failure of the diaphragm and accessory muscles to move.

central sulcus. Fissure running from the dorsal border of each hemisphere near its midpoint and obliquely downward and forward until it nearly meets the lateral fissure, dividing the frontal and parietal lobes. Also called **fissure of Rolando.**

cerebellum. Major structure of the hindbrain specialized for learning and coordinating skilled movements. In large-brained animals, may also participate in coordinating other mental processes.

cerebral aqueduct. Connection between the third and fourth ventricles; drains cerebrospinal fluid from the fourth ventricle into the circulatory system at the base of the brainstem.

cerebral arteriosclerosis. Condition marked by loss of elasticity in and thickening and hardening of the arteries; eventually results in dementia. *See also* **cerebral vascular insufficiency** and **transient ischemia**.

cerebral compression. Contraction of the brain substance due to an injury that has caused hemorrhage and the development of a hematoma.

cerebral contusion. Vascular injury resulting in bruising and edema and in hemorrhaging of capillaries.

cerebral cortex. Outer layer of gray matter on the surface of the cerebral hemispheres and composed of neurons and their synaptic connections that forms six sublayers. *See also* **cortex, neocortex**; compare **cingulate cortex**.

cerebral hemorrhage. Bleeding into the brain.

cerebral hypoxia. Deficiency in the amount of oxygen getting into the brain through the bloodstream.

cerebral ischemia. Deficiency in the amount of blood getting to the brain; may be restricted to limited regions and may be caused by an obstruction or constriction of cerebral arteries.

cerebral laceration. Contusion severe enough to breach the brain substance.

cerebral palsy (CP). Category of incurable disabilities due to nonprogressive brain abnormalities and often amenable to therapy and training and to environmental modifications that aid the affected individual.

cerebral trauma. Injury to the brain, usually resulting from a blow to the head.

cerebral vascular accident (CVA). *See* **stroke**.

cerebral vascular insufficiency. Deficiency in the amount of blood getting to the brain.

cerebrospinal fluid (CSF). Clear solution of sodium chloride and other salts that cushions the brain and may play a role in removing metabolic waste. CSF fills the ventricles inside the brain and circulates around the brain beneath the arachnoid layer in the subarachnoid space.

channel. Any passageway across the neuron membrane that allows the passage of different ions, which subsequently influence the membrane potential; different channels are opened by different ions or by voltage changes in the membrane.

chemical synapse. Junction at which messenger molecules are released when stimulated by an action potential. Contrast **gap junction**.

childhood amnesia. Inability to remember events from infancy or early childhood.

cholinergic neuron. Neuron that uses acetylcholine as its main neurotransmitter. The term *cholinergic* applies to any neuron that uses ACh as its main transmitter.

choroid plexus. Tissue that lines the cerebral ventricles and produces cerebrospinal fluid.

chromatolysis. Loss of protein in a damaged cell, resulting in the loss of the cell's ability to absorb stain; literally, the breakdown of its ability to be colored.

chromosome. DNA- and protein-containing structure in the nucleus of each cell. DNA contains the genes that determine the traits and function of each individual organism.

chronic traumatic encephalopathy (CTE). Progressive degenerative disease caused by multiple concussions and other closed-head injuries; characterized by neurofibrillary tangles, plaques, and cerebral atrophy and expanded ventricles due to cell loss.

cingulate cortex. Strip of three- to four-layered limbic cortex lying just above the corpus callosum along the medial walls of the cerebral hemispheres.

cingulate sulcus. Cortical sulcus located on the medial wall of the cerebral hemisphere just above the corpus callosum.

cladogram. Phylogenetic tree that branches repeatedly, suggesting a classification of organisms based on the time sequence in which evolutionary branches arise.

class-common behaviors. Behaviors and behavioral capacities common to all members of a phylogenetic class.

classical (Pavlovian) conditioning. Form of nonconscious learning in which a neutral stimulus is paired with a stimulus that evokes behavior.

classic migraine. Symptom complex of periodic headaches preceded by a visual aura thought to occur with vasoconstriction of one or more cerebral arteries that produces ischemia of the occipital cortex; headache commences with the vasodilation that follows; usually temporal and unilateral, often accompanied by irritability, nausea, vomiting, constipation or diarrhea, and photophobia. *See also* **common migraine**.

claustrum. Thin sheet of gray matter that, in the human brain, lies below the general region of the insula. Its connectivity is unique in that it receives input from virtually all regions of the cortex and projects back to almost all regions of the cortex.

clinical depression. *See* **major depression**.

clinical trial. Consensual experiment directed toward developing a treatment.

cluster headache. Migrainelike disorder marked by unilateral intense pain in the head or face; rarely lasts longer than 2 hours but recurs repeatedly over weeks or even months.

cocaine. Alkaloid obtained from the leaves of various species of *Erytroxylon* (coca plants) or produced synthetically; primary clinical use is as a local anesthetic.

cochlea. Inner-ear structure that contains the auditory receptor cells; the essential organ of hearing.

codeine. Alkaloid obtained from opium or prepared from morphine by methylation; used as a narcotic analgesic and as an antitussive agent.

cognition. General term for the processes of thinking; acquiring knowledge.

cognitive behavioral therapy (CBT). Problem-focused, action-oriented, structured treatment for eliminating dysfunctional thoughts and maladaptive behaviors. *See also* **virtual-reality (VR) exposure therapy**.

cognitive enhancement. Brain-function enhancement by pharmacological, physiological, or surgical manipulation.

cognitive map. Neural representation of a cognitive process such as spatial localization.

cognitive set. Tendency to approach a problem with a particular bias in thought; for example, the gestalt bias stresses the whole, whereas the analytical bias stresses individual components.

cognitive space. Space or time about which a person has knowledge.

coherence theory. Proposal that, rather than brain activity consisting of a number of conscious "states," a continuum-of-state exists, from high coherence (the brain is idling) to low coherence (the brain is actively processing information).

collaterals. Side branches of axons or blood vessels.

color agnosia. Inability to associate particular colors with objects or objects with colors.

color amnesia. Inability to remember the colors of common objects.

color anomia. Inability to name colors; generally associated with other aphasic symptoms. Also called *color aphasia*.

color constancy. Phenomenon whereby the perceived color of an object tends to remain constant relative to other colors, regardless of illumination.

column. Hypothetical unit of cortical organization believed to represent vertically organized, intracortical connectivity and assumed to be a single functional unit. Sometimes used as a synonym for a *module*.

coma. State of deep unconsciousness due to brain injury or disease.

commissure. Bundle of fibers connecting corresponding points on the two sides of the central nervous system.

commissurotomy. Surgical disconnection of the two hemispheres by cutting the corpus callosum.

common migraine. Most frequent type, occurring in more than 80% of migraine sufferers, with no clear aura preceding but rather a gastrointestinal or other signal. *See also* **classic migraine**.

comparative approach. Method of study in which similarities and differences in morphology or behavior across different species are emphasized as a means to understanding the organization of the brain and behavior.

competitive inhibitor. Drug such as nalorphine and naloxone that acts quickly to block the actions of opioids by competing with them for binding sites; used to treat opioid addiction.

complex partial seizure. Focal seizure that most commonly originates in the temporal lobe; characterized by subjective feelings (e.g., forced, repetitive thoughts, sudden alterations in mood, feelings of déjà vu, or hallucinations), automatisms, and motor symptoms. Sometimes referred to as a *temporal-lobe seizure*.

composite test battery. Set of neuropsychological tests administered in a formalized way, and which may have comparison norms, but also considers qualitative performance and the pattern of test results.

computed tomography (CT). X-ray technique that produces a static, three-dimensional image of the brain in cross section—a *CT scan*.

concentration gradient. Difference in the concentrations of an ion on the two sides of a membrane.

concussion. Common term for *mild traumatic brain injury (mTBI)*.

conduction aphasia. Type of *fluent aphasia* resulting from severing fiber connections between anterior and posterior speech zones; speech sounds and movements are retained, but speech is impaired because it cannot be conducted from one region to the other.

cone. Photoreceptor cell specialized for color and high visual acuity.

confabulation. Creating imaginary but plausible experiences to fill gaps in memory.

conjunction search. Concept in attentional theory that assumes the existence of a mechanism with which the sensory system searches for particular combinations of sensory information.

connectome. A comprehensive map of the structural connectivity (the physical wiring) of an organism's nervous system.

consciousness. The state of being awake; responsiveness of the mind to impressions made by the senses.

consolidation theory. *See* **system consolidation theory**.

constraint-induced movement therapy. Procedure in which restraint of a healthy limb forces a patient to use an impaired limb to enhance recovery of function.

constructional apraxia. Visuomotor disorder in which spatial organization is disturbed.

continuity theory. Proposal that language evolved gradually: similarities in the genes and behaviors of ancestral species, when uniquely modified in modern humans, produced language. Contrast **discontinuity theory**.

contralateral. Residing in the side of the body opposite the reference point.

contralateral neglect. Neglect of part of the body or space contralateral to a lesion; also called *neglect*.

contrast X-ray. Radiographic procedure using the injection of radiopaque dye or air into the ventricles or of dye into the arteries for purposes of diagnosis.

contrecoup. Brain injury caused when a blow to the head impels the brain to strike the skull opposite the primary blow.

conventional radiography. X-ray procedure.

convergent thinking. A search for a single answer to a question (for example, 2 + 2 = ?), in contrast with *divergent thinking*, in which multiple solutions are sought.

conversion reaction. Formerly called hysteria in reference to paralysis, changes in sensory ability such as loss of vision, and a variety of other illnesses that seemingly could not be explained as physical ailments.

coprolalia. The utterance of obscene or lewd words (from the Greek *copro*, meaning "dung").

corollary discharge. Signal from the frontal lobe to the parietal and temporal association cortex that presets the sensory system to anticipate a motor act; thus, the sensory system can interpret changes in the external world in light of information about voluntary movement. Also known as *reafference*.

corpus callosum. Commissure (fiber system) that connects homotopic areas in the two hemispheres. A **split-brain** patient is one whose corpus callosum has been severed.

cortex. Six-layered external surface of the brain; in this book, synonymous with **neocortex**.

cortical blindness. *See* **blindsight**.

cortical quotient (CQ). Measure of the relative size of the cortex; analogous to *encephalization quotient* but applied only to the cortex.

corticobulbar tract. Descending tracts from the neocortex to the lower brainstem that innervate facial motor neurons.

corticospinal tracts. Descending tracts from the neocortex originating in layer V of the cerebral cortex and ending in the spinal cord. Also called **pyramidal tracts**.

coup. Bruise (contusion) at the site of a blow to the head incurred where the brain has been compacted by the skull bone pushing inward.

cranial nerves. Set of 12 pairs of nerves conveying sensory and motor signals to and from the head.

cranioscopy. Technique of measuring the skull to determine the location of bumps and depressions for phrenological analysis.

cremasteric reflex. Retraction of testicles in response to stroking the inner thigh.

Creutzfeldt-Jakob disease. Prion-related dementia in which there is generalized cortical atrophy.

critical period. Developmental window during which some event has a long-lasting influence on the individual; also called *sensitive period*.

crossed aphasia. Aphasia that results from damage to the right hemisphere.

cross-modal matching. Ability to match sensory characteristics of objects across sensory modalities—for example, the ability to visually recognize an object that was previously perceived by touch.

cross-tolerance. Reduced response to a novel drug because of tolerance developed in response to a chemically related drug.

crystallized intelligence. Ability to retain and use knowledge acquired through prior learning and experience; compare **fluid intelligence**.

CT scan. *See* **computed tomography (CT)**.

cue response. Navigational behavior in which an animal moves to a position on the basis of its location relative to a single cue. Distinguished from *place response* or *position response*.

culture. Complex learned behaviors passed from generation to generation through teaching and experience.

curare. Poison extracted from seeds of a South American plant; blocks acetylcholine receptors.

cutoff score. Arbitrary demarcation point; in neuropsychological assessment, level below which a testing subject's performance is considered to indicate dysfunction.

cytoarchitectonic map. Cortical map based on *cytology*, the organization, structure, and distribution of cells.

cytochrome oxidase. Enzyme made in mitochondria. Increased enzyme activity is thought to correspond to heightened neural activity; tissue can be stained for this enzyme to estimate which areas of the brain display high levels of activity.

D$_2$ receptor. Receptor for the neurotransmitter dopamine; target for major tranquilizers.

dead reckoning. Navigational ability to monitor one's movement using cues generated by the movement.

deafferentation. Loss of sensory input usually due to damage to sensory fibers; also loss of any afferent input to a structure or region of the nervous system.

decerebrate. To eliminate cerebral function by transecting the brainstem just above the superior colliculi; an animal so prepared is said to be decerebrate.

decerebrate rigidity. Excessive tone in all muscles, producing extension of the limbs and dorsoflexion of the head because antigravity musculature overpowers other muscles; caused by brainstem or cerebellar lesions.

decerebration. Disconnection of the cerebral hemispheres from the brainstem, resulting in the deprivation of sensory input and the ability to affect behavior.

declarative memory. Type of memory illustrated by the ability to recount the details of events, including time, place, and circumstances, compared with the ability to perform some act or behavior. Literally, it refers to the ability to recount what one knows, which is lost in many types of amnesia.

decortication. Removal of the neocortex of the brain.

decussation. A band of fibers crossing from one side of the brain to the other.

deep brain stimulation (DBS). Neurosurgery in which electrodes implanted in the brain stimulate a targeted area with a low-voltage electrical current to facilitate behavior.

deep dyslexia. Reading impairment characterized by semantic errors.

default network. Linked brain regions active in participants who are resting rather than engaged in specific cognitive tasks and also active during such directed tasks as thinking about one's past (autobiographical memory), thinking about the future, or when the mind is wandering; compare **salience network**.

degeneration. Death of neurons or neuronal processes in response to injury in the degenerating neuron or, in some cases, in other neurons.

delayed non-matching-to-sample task. Behavioral task in which a subject is presented with a sample stimulus and then, after some delay, is presented with the same stimulus and a novel stimulus. The subject's task is to choose the novel stimulus to obtain reward.

delayed-response task. Behavioral task in which a subject observes a reward being placed under a plaque, in a well. The subject's view is blocked for a few seconds then it is allowed to retrieve the reward.

delta (δ) wave. Slow brain-wave activity pattern associated with deep sleep.

delusion. Belief opposed to reality but firmly held despite evidence of its falsity; characteristic of some types of psychotic disorders.

dementia. Organic loss of intellectual function.

dendrite. Branching extension of a neuron's cell membrane that greatly increases the surface area of the cell and collects information from other cells.

dendritic spine. Protrusion from a dendrite that greatly increases its surface area and is the usual point of contact with the axons of other cells.

dendrodendritic synapse. Synapse between two dendrites.

denervation supersensitivity. Condition of increased susceptibility to drugs, resulting from the proliferation of receptors after denervation (removal of terminations) of an area.

dentate gyrus. Region of the hippocampal formation.

2-deoxyglucose. Sugar that interferes with the metabolism of glucose. It is used to measure metabolic activity in the brain: a radioactive marker (such as ^{14}C) can be attached to 2-deoxyglucose; when this compound is taken up by the blood, it is transported to the brain and will stay in the brain regions that have been most active.

deoxyribonucleic acid (DNA). Long, complex macromolecule consisting of two interconnected helical strands; contains an organism's genetic information.

dependence. State in which doses of a drug are required to prevent the onset of abstinence (that is, withdrawal) symptoms.

dependence hypothesis. Drug-addiction hypothesis that drug use is maintained to prevent withdrawal symptoms.

depolarization. Inward transfer of positive ions, erasing a difference of potential between the inside and the outside of a neuron.

depression. *See* **major depression**.

depth-of-processing effect. Improvement in subsequent recall of an object that a person has given thought to, for example, its meaning or shape.

depth perception. Ability to perceive three-dimensionality in visual stimuli.

dermatome. Body segment corresponding to a segment of the spinal cord.

desynchronization. Change in electroencephalographic activity from a high-amplitude slow pattern to a low-amplitude fast pattern.

developmental approach. Method of study in which changes in the brain and behavior across different ages are used as a way to understand relations between the brain and behavior.

developmental dyslexia. Inability to learn adequate reading skills even when opportunity and appropriate instruction are given; contrast to **acquired dyslexia**.

developmental topographic disorientation (DTD). Cognitive disorder characterized by selective spatial and navigational disabilities that likely derive from abnormalities in dorsal stream projections; often runs in families and persists throughout life.

diaschisis. Shock subsequent to brain damage in which areas connected to the damaged area show a transitory arrest of function.

dichaptic test. Somatosensory procedure for simultaneously presenting different objects to each hand to determine which is more effective at identifying the objects.

dichotic-listening test. Auditory procedure for simultaneously presenting different auditory input to each ear through stereophonic earphones.

diencephalic animal. Animal in which the diencephalon is the highest-functioning region.

diencephalon. Region of the brain that includes the hypothalamus, thalamus, and epithalamus.

diffusion. Process of becoming diffused, or widely spread.

diffusion tensor imaging (DTI). Magnetic resonance imaging method that, by detecting the directional movements of water molecules, can image fiber pathways in the brain. *DTI tractography* maps the brain's pathways and connectivity.

diplopia. Perception of two images of a single object; double vision.

disconnection. Severing, by damage or by surgery, of the fibers that connect two areas of the brain such that the two areas can no longer communicate; the condition that results.

disconnection syndrome. Behavioral syndrome resulting from the disconnection of two or more brain regions rather than from damage to a specific brain region.

discontinuity theory. Proposal that language evolved rapidly and appeared suddenly in modern humans, within the last 200,000 years or so. Contrast **continuity theory**.

discourse. Highest level of language processing, in which sentences are strung together to form a meaningful narrative.

disengagement. Process by which attention is shifted from one stimulus to another.

disinhibition. Removal of inhibition from a system.

disinhibition theory. Explanation holding that alcohol has a selective depressant effect on the cortex, the brain region that controls judgment, while sparing subcortical structures responsible for more primitive instincts, such as desire.

disorientation. Loss of proper bearings, or a state of mental confusion concerning time, place, or identity.

dissociative anesthetic. Anesthetic agent belonging to a group of sedative-hypnotics that produce altered states of consciousness and hallucinations; group includes gamma-hydroxybutyric acid, flunitrazepam, and ketamine. Also known as "date rape" or "drug-assisted sexual assault" drugs, dissociative anesthetics are soluble in alcohol, act quickly, and impair memory for recent events.

dissolution. A conceptual notion in which disease or damage in the highest levels of the brain would produce a repertory of simpler behaviors seen in animals that have not evolved that particular brain structure.

distal. Distant from some point.

distributed hierarchy. Theory stating that widespread networks of neurons represent behavior, with some networks responsible for more complex behaviors than others.

distributed systems. Mediation of behavior by neurons and connections between neurons that are located in different areas of the brain.

divergent thinking. A search for multiple solutions to a problem (for example, how many ways to use a pen), in contrast with *convergent thinking*, in which a single answer is sought.

dopamine (DA). Amine neurotransmitter that plays a role in coordinating movement, in attention and learning, and in reinforcing behaviors.

dopamine hypothesis of schizophrenia. Idea that schizophrenia symptoms are due to excess activity of the neurotransmitter dopamine.

dorsal column. Cells in the dorsal spinal cord, which, in upright humans, can be thought of as forming a column from the bottom to the top of the spinal cord, in contrast with ventral column.

dorsal root. Nerve composed of fibers carrying sensory information that enters each segment of the dorsal (posterior in humans) spinal cord.

dorsal-root ganglion. Protuberance produced by the aggregation of cell bodies of the sensory fibers, which are located adjacent to the part of the spinal cord into which their axons enter.

dorsal stream. Visual processing pathway from the primary visual cortex to the parietal lobe; guides movements relative to objects.

dorsolateral prefrontal cortex (DLPFC). Cortex comprising Brodmann areas 9 and 46; makes reciprocal connections with posterior parietal cortex and the superior temporal sulcus; responsible for selecting behavior and movement with respect to temporal memory.

dorsomedial thalamus. Thalamic nucleus providing a major afferent input to the prefrontal cortex; degenerates in Korsakoff's syndrome, leading to a severe amnesic syndrome.

double dissociation. Experimental technique by which two neocortical areas are functionally dissociated by two behavioral tests; performance on each test is affected by a lesion in one zone but not in the other.

Down syndrome. Chromosomal abnormality resulting in intellectual disability and other deficits, usually caused by an extra chromosome 21.

dream sleep. Stage of sleep in which muscles are paralyzed, sensory input to the brain is blocked, and the brain shows a waking state of activity, during which vivid dreaming takes place. *See also* **REM (rapid eye movement) sleep**.

drug. Any medicinal substance.

dualism. Philosophical position that two distinct entities underlie human consciousness: one is mind (or soul), the other is the body.

dual-route theory. Idea that reading written language is accomplished by using two distinct but interactive procedures: the lexical and the nonlexical routes.

dura mater. Tough double layer of collagenous fiber enclosing the brain in a kind of loose sac.

dynamic form. The shape of objects in motion.

dynamic imaging. Recording and manipulating ongoing changes in brain activity, including electrical activity of cells, biochemical events, differences in glucose consumption, and blood flow to various regions.

dysarthria. Difficulty in speech production caused by incoordination of the speech apparatus.

dyscalculia. Difficulty in performing arithmetical operations.

dyskinesia. Any disturbance of movement.

dyslexia. Difficulty in reading.

dysphasia. Impairment of speech caused by damage to the central nervous system.

dystonia. Imbalance in muscle tone, usually excessive muscle tone.

echolalia. Condition in which a person repeats words or noises that others have said as well as repeating actions.

echolocation. Ability to identify and locate an object by bouncing sound waves off it.

edema. An abnormal accumulation of fluid in intercellular spaces of the body.

effect size. Process for quantifying how well statistical significance measures behavioral differences over a range of contexts by calculating the difference between the mean of an experimental group and a control group as a proportion of a standard deviation in performance.

efference theory. Idea that the sensations produced by an act provide the conscious perception of the act.

efferent. Conducting away from central nervous system area and toward muscle or gland.

egocentric disorientation. Difficulty in determining one's location in space.

egocentric space. Spatial location relative to an individual's perspective. Compare **allocentric space.**

electrical recording. Recording that detects changes in the electrical activity of neurons.

electrical synapse. *See* **gap junction.**

electroconvulsive therapy (ECT). The first electrical brain-stimulation treatment, originally used for otherwise untreatable depression; can impair memory and is used only rarely with the advent of noninvasive treatments such as transcranial magnetic stimulation (TMS).

electroencephalogram (EEG). Graph that records electrical activity through the skull or from the brain and represents graded potentials of many neurons.

electromyogram (EMG). Recording of electrical activity of the muscles as well as the electrical response of the peripheral nerves.

electron microscope. Microscope that produces images of very small objects by bouncing electrons off an object and detecting the object's resistance to the electrons.

electrooculogram (EOG). Electroencephalographic tracings made while a person moves his or her eyes a constant distance between two fixation points.

electrostatic gradient. Gradient between an area of low electrical charge and an area of high electrical charge; develops across the membrane of a cell or between two parts of the same cell.

embolism. Blood clot or other plug (bubble of air, fat deposit, or small mass of cells) brought through the blood from a larger vessel and forced into a smaller one, where it obstructs circulation.

emotion. Cognitive interpretation of subjective feelings.

emotional memory. Memory for the affective properties of stimuli or events that is arousing, vivid, and available on prompting.

empathy. Ability to see others' points of view.

encephalitis. Inflammation of the central nervous system as a result of infection.

encephalization. Process by which higher structures, such as the cerebral cortex, take over the functions of lower centers; may imply either a phylogenetic or an ontogenetic shift of function. Also called *encorticalization.*

encephalization quotient (EQ). Ratio of actual brain size to expected brain size for a typical mammal of a particular body size.

encephalomalacia. Softening of the brain, resulting from vascular disorders caused by inadequate blood flow.

encephalon. *See* **brain.**

encephalopathy. Chemical, physical, allergic, or toxic inflammation of the central nervous system.

encorticalization. *See* **encephalization.**

end foot. Terminal part of an axon; conveys information to other neurons. Also called a *terminal button.*

endoplasmic reticulum (ER). Extensive internal membrane system in the cytoplasm. Ribosomes attach to part of the ER to form what is known as the rough ER.

endorphin. Shortened from "endogenous morphine"; peptide hormone that acts on a neurotransmitter and may be associated with feelings of pain or pleasure; mimicked by opioid drugs such as morphine, heroin, opium, and codeine.

endothelial cells. Thin, flat cells occurring in a single layer; form blood vessels.

enhancement. *See* **long-term enhancement (LTE).**

entorhinal cortex. Cortex on the medial surface of the temporal lobe that provides a major route for neocortical input to the hippocampal formation; often shows degeneration in Alzheimer's disease.

ependymal cells. Glial cells that make and secrete cerebrospinal fluid and form the lining of the ventricles.

epigenetics. Differences in gene expression related to environment and experience.

epilepsy. Condition caused by spontaneous, abnormal discharges of brain neurons as a result of scarring from injury, infections, or tumors, and characterized by recurrent seizures associated with a disturbance of consciousness.

epinephrine (EP, or adrenaline). Chemical messenger that acts as a hormone to mobilize the body for fight or flight during times of stress and as a neurotransmitter in the central nervous system.

episodic (autobiographic) memory. Memory of life experiences centered on the person him- or herself; a person's recall of singular events that enables human beings to remember past personal experiences.

epithalamus. Collection of nuclei that forms the phylogenetically most primitive region of the thalamus; includes the pineal gland, which secretes the hormone melatonin that influences daily and seasonal body rhythms.

equipotentiality. Hypothesis that each part of a given area of the brain is able to encode or produce the behavior normally controlled by the entire area.

ergotamine. Drug used to treat migraine and tension headaches; acts by constricting cerebral arteries to relieve pain.

ethology. Study of the natural behavior of animals.

Euclidean space. Real space, with three dimensions, according to the laws of Euclid.

event-related potential (ERP). Complex electroencephalographic waveform related in time to a specific sensory event.

evoked potential. Short train of large, slow waves recorded from the scalp and corresponding to dendritic activity.

excitatory neurotransmitter. Transmitter substance that decreases a cell's membrane potential and increases the likelihood that the cell will fire.

excitatory postsynaptic potential (EPSP). Small change in the membrane potential of a cell that leads to depolarization and increased likelihood that the cell will fire.

exocytosis. Discharge from a cell of particles that are too large to diffuse through the wall.

explicit memory. Memory in which a participant can retrieve an item and indicate that he or she knows the item (that is, conscious memory). Conscious, intentional remembering of events, facts, and personal experiences (*episodic memories*) that depends on conceptually driven, top-down processing in which a person reorganizes the data to store it. Compare **implicit memory**.

expressive aphasia. Nonfluent aphasia involving a severe deficit in producing language. Also called **Broca's aphasia**.

extension. Reflex by which a limb is straightened.

extensor muscle. Muscle that acts to straighten a limb.

extensor plantar response. Extensor movement of the foot toward a surface that the foot touches.

extensor reflex. Advancement of a limb to contact a stimulus in response to tactile stimuli that activate fine touch and pressure receptors. The response is mediated by a multisynaptic spinal reflex circuit.

external imagery. Third-person imagery in which a person engaging in an act imagines that it is another person doing so.

exteroceptive receptor. Receptor that functions to identify events that take place outside the body. Compare **interoceptive receptor**.

extinction. Term used in learning theory for the decreased probability that a behavior will occur if reinforcement is withheld. Somatoperceptual disorder most commonly associated with damage to the secondary somatic cortex (areas PE and PF), especially in the right parietal lobe; failure to report one of two stimuli presented together.

extracellular fluid. Fluid and its contents that surround a neuron or glial cell.

face amnesia. Inability to remember faces. Contrast **prosopagnosia**.

factor analysis. Statistical procedure designed to determine if the variability in scores can be related to one or more factors that are reliably influencing performance.

fasciculation. Small local contraction of muscles, visible through the skin, representing a spontaneous discharge of a number of fibers innervated by a single motor-nerve filament.

fear conditioning. Form of learning in which a noxious stimulus is paired with a neutral stimulus to elicit an emotional response.

feature search. Cognitive strategy in which sensory stimuli are scanned for a specific feature, such as color.

festination. Tendency to engage in behavior at faster and faster speeds; usually refers to walking but can include other behaviors such as talking and thinking.

fetal alcohol spectrum disorder (FASD). Range of physical and intellectual impairments observed in some children born to alcoholic mothers.

fimbria-fornix. Pathway that connects the hippocampus to the thalamus, prefrontal cortex, basal ganglia, and hypothalamus.

finger agnosia. Inability to distinguish fingers; most common form of **autopagnosia**.

fissure. Cleft, produced by folds of the neocortex, that extends to the ventricles.

flexion. Reflex that brings a limb toward the body.

flexor muscle. Muscle that acts to bend a limb at a joint.

flocculus. Small lobe projecting from the ventral surface of the cerebellum that receives projections from the vestibular system and so takes part in controlling balance.

fluent aphasia. Speech disorder in which a person articulates words in a languagelike fashion, but what is said actually makes little sense; usually results from damage to the left posterior cortex. *See also* **Wernicke's aphasia**.

fluid intelligence. Ability to see abstract relationships and draw logical inferences; contrast **crystallized intelligence**.

fMRI. *See* **functional magnetic resonance imaging**.

focal seizure. Seizure that begins locally and then spreads—for example, from one finger to the whole body.

folia. Narrow folds of the cerebellum.

forebrain. Cerebral hemispheres, basal ganglia, thalamus, amygdala, hippocampus, and septum.

formant. Group of sound waves specific to each vowel sound.

fovea. Region at the center of the retina that is specialized for high acuity; its receptive fields are at the center of the eye's visual field.

fragile-X syndrome. Most common inherited cause of mental impairment and autism spectrum disorder; caused by an abnormality in the FMR1 gene on the X chromosome.

frontal lobes. All the neocortex and connections forward of the central sulcus.

frontal operculum. Upper region of the inferior frontal gyrus.

fugue state. Sudden, usually transient, memory loss of personal history accompanied by abrupt departure from home and assumption of a new identity.

functional analysis. Analysis of brain organization based on studying the effects of brain damage, stimulating areas of the brain chemically or electrically, or recording the activity of cells in relation to behavior.

functional magnetic resonance imaging (fMRI). Magnetic resonance imaging in which changes in elements such as iron or oxygen are measured during the performance of a specific behavior; used to measure cerebral blood flow during rest or behavior. *See also* **magnetic resonance imaging (MRI)**.

functional map. Map of the cortex constructed by stimulating areas of the brain electrically and noting elicited behavior or by recording electrical activity during certain behaviors; relates specific behaviors to brain areas.

functional near-infrared spectroscopy (fNIRS). Non-invasive dynamic technique that gathers light transmitted through cortical tissue to image blood–oxygen consumption; form of optical tomography.

functional validation. Theory that a neural system requires sensory stimulation to become fully functional.

GABA$_A$ receptor. Gamma-aminobutyric acid receptor on which sedative hypnotics and antianxiety drugs act.

gamma-aminobutyric acid (GABA). Amino acid neurotransmitter that inhibits neurons.

ganglion (pl. ganglia). Collection of nerve cells that function somewhat like a brain.

ganglion cells. Cells of the retina that give rise to the optic nerve.

gap junction. Fused prejunction and postjunction cell membrane in which connected ion channels form a pore that allows ions to pass directly from one neuron to the next. Also **electrical synapse**.

gated channel. Membrane channel that allows the passage of specific ions when the gate is open and prevents such passage when the gate is closed.

gating. Inhibition of sensory information produced by descending signals from the cortex; for example, descending messages from the brain can gate transmission of a pain stimulus from the spinal cord to the brain.

gene. DNA segment that encodes the synthesis of a particular protein.

gene (DNA) methylation. Process in which a methyl group attaches to the DNA sequence, suppressing gene expression.

generalized anxiety disorder. Sustained worrying state associated with at least three anxiety symptoms, among which are restlessness, decreased energy, concentration difficulties, irritability, muscle tension, and sleep disturbance.

generalized seizure. Bilaterally symmetrical seizure without focal onset that can be characterized by loss of consciousness and by stereotyped motor activity; typified by three stages: tonic, clonic, and *postictal depression*.

generator. Part of a neuron that produces a signal in response to changing inputs; also called a *signal generator*.

geniculostriate pathway. Projections from the eye to the lateral geniculate nucleus of the thalamus to the visual cortex (areas 17, 18, and 19), then to areas 20 and 21; controls perception of form, color, and pattern.

genome. The full set of a species' genes.

genotype. An individual's genetic makeup.

genu. Bulbous part of the anterior part of the corpus callosum.

germinal cells. Cells from which particular tissues are formed in the course of development.

Gerstmann syndrome. Collection of symptoms due to left parietal lesion; alleged to include finger agnosia, right–left confusion, acalculia, and agraphia (a source of some controversy).

gestalt. Unified and coherent whole.

gestural theory. Theory of language evolution stating that language developed from gestures used for communication.

glia. Nervous-system cells that provide insulation, nutrients, and support and aid in repairing neurons and eliminating waste products. Also called *glial cells*.

glioblast. Progenitor cell that gives rise to various types of glial cells.

glioma. Any brain tumor that arises from glial cells.

gliosis. Migration and proliferation of glial cells in areas of neural tissue that have undergone damage. Their presence serves as a sign of tissue damage.

glucocorticoid. One of a group of steroid hormones, such as cortisol and corticosterone, secreted in times of stress; important in protein and carbohydrate metabolism.

glutamate (Glu). Amino acid neurotransmitter that excites neurons.

glycine (Gly). Amino acid neurotransmitter that inhibits neurons in the brainstem and spinal cord, where it acts within the Renshaw loop, for example.

glycoprotein. A protein with an attached carbohydrate group.

Golgi apparatus. Complex of parallel membranes in the cytoplasm that wraps the product of a secretory cell or a protein manufactured by a nerve cell.

Golgi body. Membrane in neurons that covers proteins made in neurons.

gonadal (sex) hormones. One of a group of hormones, such as testosterone, that control reproductive functions and bestow sexual appearance and identity as male or female.

G protein. Guanyl-nucleotide-binding protein coupled to a metabotropic receptor that, when activated, binds to other proteins.

graded potential. Electrical potential in a neuron or receptor cell that changes with the intensity of the stimulus. Also known as a *generator potential.*

granule cells. Sensory cells of the hippocampus; neurons that are round in appearance, in contrast with *pyramidal cells,* which have pyramid-shaped cell bodies.

granulovacuolar bodies. Abnormal structures in the brain characterized by granules (small beadlike masses of tissue) and vacuoles (small cavities in the protoplasm of cells).

grapheme. The pictorial qualities of a written word that permit it to be understood without being sounded out; a group of letters that conveys a meaning.

graphemic reading. Reading in which the memorized meaning of a word is derived from the image (grapheme) it makes as a whole rather than by sounding out the syllables. Also called *lexical* or *whole-word reading.*

graphesthesia. Ability to identify numbers or letters traced on the skin with a blunt object.

gray level index (GLI). Computer-generated shading pattern that calculates brightness differences among the cell bodies and the neuropil.

gray matter. Any brain area composed predominantly of cell bodies and capillaries.

grid cell. Type of neuron in the hippocampal formation; grid cells fire at regularly spaced nodes that appear to divide an environment into a grid.

growth spurt. Sudden growth in development that lasts for a relatively short time.

guanyl nucleotide-binding protein (G protein). Protein that carries a message from a metabotropic receptor to other receptors or to second messengers.

gyrus (pl. gyri). Convolution (bump) in the neocortex produced by folding.

habituation. Learning behavior in which a response to a stimulus weakens with repeated stimulus presentations.

hair cells. Auditory sensory receptors in the cochlea.

hallucination. Perception for which there is no appropriate external stimulus; characteristic of some types of psychotic disorders.

hammer. Ossicle in the middle ear.

hapsis. Perceptual ability to discriminate objects on the basis of touch.

head-direction (HD) cell. Neuron in the hippocampal formation that discharges when an animal faces in a particular direction.

heading disorientation. Inability to move or guide one's movements in a direction appropriate to the perceived cues.

hedonic hypothesis. Proposal that people abuse drugs because the drugs make them feel good.

hematoma. Local swelling or tumor filled with effused blood.

heme group. Nonprotein, insoluble iron protoporphyrin constituent of hemoglobin, a constituent of blood.

hemianopia. Loss of pattern vision in either the left or the right visual field.

hemiballism. Motor disorder characterized by sudden involuntary movements of a single limb.

hemiparesis. Muscular weakness affecting one side of the body.

hemiplegia. Paralysis on the side of the body contralateral to a brain injury.

hemiplegic migraine. Migraine that leads to paralysis of one side of the body.

hemisphere. On the left and right sides of the cerebrum and cerebellum, either of the pair of structures constituting the telencephalon.

hemispherectomy. Removal of a cerebral hemisphere.

hemorrhagic stroke. Severe stroke that results from a burst vessel bleeding into the brain.

heroin. Diacetylmorphine, a highly addictive morphine derivative.

Heschl's gyrus. Gyrus of the human temporal lobe that is roughly equivalent to auditory area I. Also known as the *transverse temporal gyrus.*

heterozygous. Having two different alleles for the same trait.

hierarchical organization. Principle of cerebral organization in which information is processed serially, with each level of processing assumed to represent the elaboration of some hypothetical process.

high decerebrate. Condition in which an injury separates the diencephalon from the midbrain, resulting in an intact midbrain, hindbrain, spinal cord, and higher-order areas. *See also* **decerebrate** and **decerebration**.

high decerebration. Injury to the brainstem in which the highest intact functioning structure is the midbrain.

higher-order area. Brain area that is of more recent evolutionary origin and receives its inputs from older (lower) areas.

hindbrain. Brain region that consists primarily of the cerebellum, medulla oblongata, pons, and fourth ventricle.

hippocampus. Distinctive limbic-system structure lying in the anterior medial region of the temporal lobe; participates in species-specific behaviors, memory, and spatial navigation and is vulnerable to the effects of stress.

histamine (H). Amino acid neurotransmitter that controls arousal and waking; can cause the constriction of smooth muscles and so, when activated in allergic reactions, contributes to asthma, a constriction of the airways.

histochemical techniques. Various techniques that rely on chemical reactions in cells to mark features of a cell for microscopic visualization.

histofluorescent technique. Literally, cell fluorescence, a technique in which a fluorescent compound is used to label cells.

homeostasis. Maintenance of a chemically and physically constant internal environment.

homeostatic hormone. One of a group of hormones that maintain internal metabolic balance and regulate physiological systems in an organism.

hominid. General term referring to primates that walk upright, including all forms of humans, living and extinct.

homonymous hemianopia. Blindness of an entire visual field due to complete cuts of the optic tract, lateral geniculate body, or area 17 (V1).

homotopic. At the same place on the body.

homotopic areas. Corresponding, identical points in the two cerebral hemispheres that are related to the body's midline.

homozygous. Having two identical alleles for a trait.

homunculus. Representation of the human body in the sensory or motor cortex; any topographic representation of the body by a neural area.

horseradish peroxidase (HRP). Compound that, when introduced into a cell, is then distributed to all its parts, allowing the cell to be visualized.

HPA axis. The hypothalamic–pituitary–adrenal circuit; controls production and release of hormones related to stress.

Huntington's disease. Hereditary disorder characterized by chorea (ceaseless, involuntary, jerky movements) and progressive dementia, ending in death.

hydrocephalus. Buildup of pressure in the brain and, in infants, swelling of the head, caused by blockage in the flow of cerebrospinal fluid; can result in intellectual disabilities.

6-hydroxydopamine (6-OHDA). Chemical selectively taken up by axons and terminals of norepinephrinergic or dopaminergic neurons; acts as a poison, damaging or killing the neurons.

hyperactive-child syndrome. Behavioral syndrome characterized by low attention span and poor impulse control, which results in disruptive behavior.

hyperactivity. More activity than normally expected, usually applied to children.

hyperkinesia. Condition in which movements of part or all of the body increase.

hyperkinetic symptom. Involuntary excessive movements; symptom of brain damage. Compare **hypokinetic symptom**.

hyperlexia. Condition in which a person is given to excessive reading or is a precocious reader, often without understanding the meaning of what is read.

hypermetamorphosis. Tendency to attend and react to every visual stimulus, leading to mental distraction and confusion.

hyperpolarization. Process by which a nerve membrane becomes more resistant to the passage of sodium ions and consequently more difficult to excite with adequate stimulation; during hyperpolarization, the electrical charge on the inside of the membrane relative to that on the outside becomes more negative.

hypnagogic hallucination. Episodes of auditory, visual, or tactile hallucination during sleep paralysis as an affected person is falling asleep or waking up.

hypokinetic symptom. Difficulty in making movements; symptom of brain damage. Compare **hyperkinetic symptom**.

hypothalamus. Collection of nuclei located below the thalamus in the diencephalon; controls behavior including movement, feeding, sexual activity, sleeping, emotional expression, temperature regulation, and endocrine regulation.

ideational apraxia. Vague term used to describe a disorder of gestural behavior in which the overall conception of how a movement is carried out is lost; emerges when a person is required to manipulate objects.

ideomotor apraxia. Inability to use and understand nonverbal communication such as gesture and pantomime or to copy movement sequences.

idiopathic seizure. Seizure that appears to arise spontaneously and in the absence of other central nervous system diseases.

idiothetic cue. Derives from the self; a cue generated by one's own movement.

illusion. False or misinterpreted sensory impression of a real sensory image.

immunohistochemical staining. Antibody-based label that, when applied to tissue postmortem, reveals the presence of a specific molecule or close relatives of that molecule.

implicit memory. Nonconscious and nonintentional memory of learned skills, conditioned reactions, and events. Compare **explicit memory**.

incentive salience. Desire to seek drugs triggered by cues associated with them.

incentive-sensitization theory. Holds that, when a drug has been used in association with certain cues, the cues themselves will elicit desire for the drug.

individualized test battery. Set of neuropsychological tests tailored both to a person's etiology and to the qualitative nature of his or her performance on each test.

infantile amnesia. *See* **childhood amnesia**.

infarct. Area of dead or dying tissue resulting from an obstruction of the blood vessels normally supplying the area.

infection. Invasion and multiplication of pathogenic microorganisms in body tissues and the reaction of the tissues to their presence and to the toxins they generate.

inferior colliculi. Nuclei of the midbrain tectum that receive auditory projections and mediate orientation to auditory stimuli.

inferotemporal cortex. Area TE in von Economo's designation; visual regions of the temporal cortex.

inhibitory neurotransmitter. Neurotransmitter that increases the membrane polarity of a cell, making an action potential less likely.

inhibitory postsynaptic potential (IPSP). Small localized change that increases a membrane's potential, making an action potential less likely.

input cell layers. Layers of tissue that receive inputs, such as layer IV in the cerebral cortex.

insomnia. Inability to fall asleep or frequent arousals from sleep.

insula. Tissue in the lateral (Sylvian) fissure; includes gustatory and auditory association cortices.

intelligence quotient (IQ). Defined originally as the ratio of mental age to chronological age multiplied by 100. On contemporary intelligence tests, the average performance for a given age is assigned a value of 100 and a person's IQ score is expressed relative to 100.

intermediate zone. Layer of cells in the spinal cord that lies immediately above the motor neurons of the ventral horn.

internal carotid artery. Branch of the carotid artery that is a major source of blood to the brain.

internal imagery. First-person imagery in which a person imagines that it is himself or herself who engages in an act.

interneuron. Any neuron lying between a sensory neuron and a motor neuron.

interoceptive receptor. Receptor that responds to information originating inside the body. Compare **exteroceptive receptor**.

intracellular fluid. Fluid and its contents found within neurons and glial cells.

invariance hypothesis. Idea that the structure of each cerebral hemisphere ensures that the hemisphere will develop a set of specialized functions; for example, the left hemisphere is specialized at birth for language.

ion. Positively or negatively charged atom or molecule.

ionotropic receptor. Embedded membrane protein that acts as (1) a binding site for a neurotransmitter and (2) a pore that regulates ion flow to directly and rapidly change membrane voltage.

ipsilateral. Residing in the same side of the body as the point of reference.

ischemia. Deficient blood flow to the brain due to functional constriction or actual obstruction of a blood vessel by a clot.

isolation syndrome. *See* **transcortical aphasia**.

Jacksonian focal seizure. Seizure that has consistent sensory or motor symptoms such as a twitching in the face or hand.

Kennard principle. Idea that early brain damage produces less-severe behavioral effects than does brain damage incurred later in life; coined after Margaret Kennard reported this phenomenon in a series of papers on the study of neonatally brain-damaged monkeys.

kindling. Development of persistent seizure activity after repeated exposure to an initially subconvulsant stimulus.

kinesthesis (also **kinesthesia**). Perception of movement or position of the limbs and body; commonly used to refer to the perception of changes in the angles of joints.

Klüver–Bucy syndrome. Group of symptoms resulting from bilateral damage to the temporal lobes; characterized especially by hypersexuality, excessive oral behavior, and visual agnosia.

Korsakoff's syndrome. Group of symptoms resulting from degeneration of thalamic nuclei and produced by chronic alcoholism; metabolic disorder of the central nervous system due to a lack of Vitamin B_1 (thiamine) and often associated with chronic alcoholism.

landmark agnosia. Loss of the ability to know one's location or guide one's movement in relation to a building or landmark that had once been familiar.

landmark test. Behavioral test in which the subject must learn the association between a specific cue (the landmark) and the location of reward.

larynx. "Voice box," the organ of voice; the air passage between the lower pharynx and trachea, containing the vocal cords and formed by nine cartilages: the thyroid, cricoid, and epiglottis and the paired arytenoid, corniculate, and cuneiform cartilages.

lateral corticospinal tract. Pathway in the lateral spinal cord that carries information instructing movement; crosses over to the opposite side of the brainstem at the pyramidal protrusion.

lateral fissure. Deep cleft in the cortical surface of the brain that separates the temporal and parietal lobes. Also called *Sylvian fissure.*

laterality. Refers to the side of the brain that controls a given function. Hence, studies of laterality are undertaken to determine which side of the brain controls various functions.

lateralization. Process by which functions become located primarily on one side of the brain.

learned-behavior theory. Theory that behavior under the influence of alcohol changes from one context to another because of learning; contradicts the idea that alcohol lowers inhibitions.

learned tolerance. Experience in performing a behavior under the influence of a drug results in improved performance of the behavior when subsequently under the influence of the drug.

learning. Relatively permanent change in behavior that results from experience.

learning disability. *See* **neurodevelopmental disorder**.

lesion. Any damage to the nervous system.

letter-by-letter reading. Reading in which the meaning of a text is determined by extracting information from each letter, one letter at a time.

leu-enkephalin. Peptide neurotransmitter that produces some of the effects of opioid drugs.

lexicon. Memory store that contains words and their meanings.

light microscope. Microscope that relies on shining light through tissue to visualize that tissue through an eyepiece.

limbic system. Disparate forebrain structures lying between the neocortex and the brainstem that form a functional system controlling affective and motivated behaviors and certain forms of memory; includes cingulate (limbic) cortex, amygdala, hippocampus, and hypothalamus, among other structures. Also, *reptilian brain*; formerly, *limbic lobe.*

localization of function. Theory that different brain regions have different functions.

longitudinal fissure. Deep cleft that divides the brain's two hemispheres. Also known as the *sagittal fissure.*

long-term enhancement (LTE). *See* **long-term potentiation (LTP)**.

long-term memory. Explicit memory, including episodic memory, related to personal experiences, and semantic memory, related to facts and implicit memory, such as motor skills; each type is supported by different brain pathways.

long-term potentiation (LTP). Long-lasting change in the postsynaptic response of a cell resulting from previous experience with a high-frequency stimulation. Also known as *long-term enhancement (LTE).*

low decerebrate. Condition in which the hindbrain and spinal cord remain connected after an injury but both are disconnected from the rest of the brain. *See also* **decerebrate** and **decerebration**.

lysergic acid diethylamide (LSD). Drug that produces visual hallucinations, presumably by influencing the serotonin system.

lysosome. Small body containing digestive enzymes seen with the use of an electron microscope in many types of cells.

macular sparing. Condition occurring only after unilateral lesions to the visual cortex in which the central region of the visual field is not lost, even though temporal or nasal visual fields are lost.

magnetic resonance imaging (MRI). Technique that produces a static, three-dimensional brain image by passing a strong magnetic field through the brain, followed by a radio wave, then measuring the radiation emitted from hydrogen atoms. *See also* **functional magnetic resonance imaging (fMRI)**.

magnetic resonance spectroscopy (MRS). Modification of MRI to identify changes in specific markers of neuronal function, including all macromolecules (DNA, RNA, most proteins, and phospholipids); cell membranes; organelles (such as mitochondria); and glial cells, not imaged by *magnetic resonance imaging.*

magnetoencephalogram (MEG). Magnetic potentials recorded from detectors placed outside the skull.

magnocellular layer. Layer of neurons composed of large cells.

major depression. Mood disorder characterized by prolonged feelings of worthlessness and guilt, disruption of normal eating habits, sleep disturbances, general slowing of behavior, and frequent thoughts of suicide. Also called **clinical depression**.

major tranquilizer. Drug that blocks the dopamine 2 (D_2) receptor; used mainly for treating schizophrenia. Also called a **neuroleptic** or **antipsychotic drug**.

malaria. Infectious febrile disease caused by protozoa of the genus *Plasmodium*, which are parasitic in red blood cells; transmitted by the bites of infected mosquitoes. Cerebral malaria arises when the plasmodia infect the brain's capillaries, producing local hemorrhages and subsequent degeneration of neurons.

mania. Disordered mental state of extreme excitement characterized by excessive euphoria.

mass-action hypothesis. Proposal that the entire neocortex participates in every behavior.

massa intermedia. An area of gray matter (cells) that connects the left and right sides of the thalamus across the midline.

materialism. Philosophical position that holds that behavior can be explained as a function of the nervous system without explanatory recourse to the mind.

maturation hypothesis. Argument that both hemispheres initially have roles in language but the left hemisphere gradually becomes more specialized for language control.

maturational-lag hypothesis. Explains a disability by suggesting that a system is not yet mature or is maturing slowly.

MDMA (3,4-methylenedioxymethamphetamine). Synthetic psychoactive drug chemically similar to the stimulant methamphetamine and the hallucinogen mescaline.

medial longitudinal fissure. Fissure that separates the two hemispheres.

median eminence. Pathway connecting the two sides of the thalamus.

medulla oblongata. Part of the hindbrain immediately rostral to the spinal cord.

medulloblastoma. Highly malignant brain tumor found almost exclusively in the cerebellum of children; results from the growth of germinal cells that infiltrate the cerebellum.

meme. An idea, behavior, or style that spreads from person to person within a culture.

memory consolidation. Process through which short-term memories are converted into long-term memories.

Ménière's disease. Disorder of the middle ear resulting in vertigo and loss of balance.

meninges. Three layers of protective tissue—dura mater, arachnoid, and pia mater—that encase the brain and spinal cord.

meningioma. Encapsulated brain tumor growing from the meninges.

meningitis. Inflammation of the brain's triple-layered protective covering by a bacterial or viral infection.

mental level. Measure of intelligence in which ability is expressed as a level of performance that is average for a given age.

mental rotation. Ability to make a mental image of an object and imagine it in a new location relative to its background.

mescaline. Alkaloid from the flowering heads of a Mexican cactus; produces an intoxication with delusions of color and sound.

mesencephalon. Middle brain; one of the three primary embryonic vesicles, which in the embryonic mammalian brain subsequently comprises the tectum and tegmentum; in adult fish, amphibians, and reptiles, the seat of vision and hearing.

mesolimbic dopamine system. Dopamine neurons in the midbrain that project to the nucleus accumbens and to medial parts of the basal ganglia, limbic system, and neocortex.

messenger RNA (mRNA). Type of ribonucleic acid synthesized from DNA (deoxyribonucleic acid); attaches to ribosomes to specify the sequences of amino acids that form proteins.

metabolic syndrome. A combination of medical disorders, including obesity and insulin abnormalities, that collectively increases the risk of developing cardiovascular disease and diabetes.

metabolic tolerance. Increase in enzymes that break down alcohol in the liver, blood, and brain resulting in the body metabolizing alcohol more quickly and reducing blood-alcohol levels.

metabotropic receptor. Receptor-embedded membrane protein that can affect other receptors or act with second messengers to affect other cellular processes; receptor has a neurotransmitter binding site but no pore and is linked to a G protein (guanyl nuleotide-binding protein).

metastasis. Transfer of a disease from one part of the body to another; common characteristic of *malignant tumors*.

metastatic tumor. Tumor that arises through the transfer of tumor cells from elsewhere in the body.

metencephalon. Anterior part of the mammalian rhombencephalon; composed of the cerebellum and pons.

met-enkephalin. Peptide neurotransmitter that produces some of the effects of opioid drugs.

mGluR4. Receptor on the tongue; sensitive to glutamate.

microfilaments. Small tubelike processes in cells that function to control the shape, movement, or fluidity of the cytoplasm or substances within the cell.

microglia. Glial cells that originate in the blood, aid in cell repair, and scavenge debris in the nervous system.

micrometer (μm). One-millionth of a meter or one-thousandth of a millimeter. The neurons of most animals, including humans, are very tiny, on the order of 1 to 20 micrometers.

microtubules. Fiberlike substances in the soma and processes of nerve cells; transport substances from the soma to the distal elements of the cell or from distal parts of the cell to the soma.

midbrain. Short segment between the forebrain and hindbrain, including the tectum and tegmentum.

middle cerebral artery (MCA). Runs along the length of the lateral (Sylvian) fissure to irrigate the lateral surface of the cortex, including the ventral part of the frontal lobe, most of the parietal lobe, and the temporal lobe.

migraine. From the Greek word meaning "one half of the head"; a headache characterized by an aching, throbbing pain, often unilateral; may be preceded by a visual aura presumed to result from ischemia of the occipital cortex induced by vasoconstriction of cerebral arteries. Variants include classic migraine, common migraine, cluster headache, and hemiplegic and ophthalmologic migraine.

migraine stroke. Transient ischemic attack with a variety of neurological symptoms, including impaired sensory function (especially vision), numbness of the skin (especially in the arms), difficulties in moving, and aphasia

millisecond (ms). One-thousandth of a second.

millivolt (mV). One-thousandth of a volt.

mind. The psyche; the faculty, or brain function, by which one is aware of one's surroundings and by which one experiences feeling, emotions, and desires and is able to attend, reason, and make decisions.

mind–body problem. Quandary of explaining how a nonmaterial mind and a material body interact.

miniature postsynaptic potential (MPP). Small excitatory or inhibitory graded potential, the amplitude of which is related to the number of quanta of neurotransmitter released at the synapse.

minimally conscious state (MCS). Condition in which a person can display some rudimentary behaviors but is otherwise not conscious.

minor tranquilizers. Class of drugs used to treat anxiety. *See also* **benzodiazepines**.

mirror system neurons. Cells in the primate premotor cortex that fire when an individual observes a specific action taken by another individual. The *core mirror neuron system* is transitive, responding to a wide range of actions that might be used to obtain a goal; the *distributed mirror neuron system* responds to intransitive actions, movements in which a goal is not present.

mitochondrion. Complex cellular organelle that produces most of a cell's energy through a number of processes.

module. Hypothetical unit of cortical organization believed to represent a vertically organized, intracortical connectivity; assumed to correspond to a single functional unit. Sometimes used as a synonym for *column*.

monist. Person who believes that the mind and body are one.

monoamine oxidase (MAO) inhibitor. Antidepressant drug that blocks the enzyme monoamine oxidase from degrading neurotransmitters such as dopamine, noradrenaline, and serotonin.

monoamines. Group of neurotransmitters, including norepinephrine and dopamine, that have an amine (NH_2) group.

monoclonal antibody. Antibody that is cloned or derived from a single cell.

monocular blindness. Blindness in one eye caused by the destruction of its retina or optic nerve.

monocular deprivation. Removal of visual stimulation to one eye by closure or bandaging.

mood stabilizer. Drug such as lithium or valproate used to treat bipolar disorder; typically mutes the intensity of one pole of the disorder, thus making the other pole less likely to recur.

morpheme. Smallest meaningful unit of speech.

morphine. Principal and most active alkaloid of opium. Its hydrochloride and sulfate salts are used as narcotic analgesics.

morphological reconstruction. Reconstruction of the body of an animal, often from only skeletal remains.

motifs. Recurring elements formed in waves of cortical activity, indicating functional connectivity (inherent functional relationships) among cortical systems.

motoneuron. Charles Scott Sherrington's term for the unit formed by motor neurons and the muscle fiber to which their axon terminations are connected.

motor aphasia. Disorder in which an affected person is unable to make the correct movements of the mouth and tongue to form words, in contrast with *Wernicke's aphasia* (*sensory aphasia*), in which speech is fluent but without content; a form of *nonfluent aphasia*.

motor apraxia. Inability, in the absence of paralysis, to execute the voluntary movements needed to perform a goal-oriented action.

motor cortex (M1). Area 4 of the frontal cortex; produces muscle movements.

motor neuron. Neuron that carries information from the brain and spinal cord to make muscles contract.

motor pathway. Nerve fibers that connect the brain and spinal cord to the body's muscles through the somatic nervous system.

motor program. Hypothetical neural circuit so arranged that it produces a certain type of movement—for example, walking.

movement. Act of moving; motion.

multimodal (polymodal) cortex. Cortex that presumably functions to combine characteristics of stimuli across different sensory modalities—for example, vision and audition.

multiple sclerosis (MS). Disorder, largely of myelinated motor fibers but also of sensory tracts, that results from the loss of myelin.

multiple-trace theory. Postulates both multiple kinds of amnesia, differentially susceptible to temporal-lobe injury, and of memory (*autobiographic* and *factual* and *general semantic*), and changes in memory over time.

muscarine receptor. An acetylcholine receptor acted on by acetylcholine psychedelic drugs. Muscarine is a chemical obtained from *Amanita muscaria*, a mushroom that affects the parasympathetic system but does not cross the blood–brain barrier.

muscle-contraction headache. Tension or nervous headache that results from sustained contraction of the muscles of the scalp and neck caused by constant stress and tension, especially if poor posture is maintained for any length of time.

mutation. Alteration of an allele that yields a different version of the allele.

myasthenia gravis. Condition of fatigue and weakness of the muscular system without sensory disturbance or atrophy; results from a reduction in acetylcholine available at the synapse.

mycotic infection. Invasion of the nervous system by a fungus.

myelencephalon. Spinal brain; posterior part of the mammalian rhombencephalon, including the medulla oblongata and fourth ventricle.

myelin. Lipid substance forming an insulating sheath around certain nerve fibers; formed by oligodendroglia in the central nervous system and by Schwann cells in the peripheral nervous system.

myelin sheath. *See* **myelin**.

myelin stains. Dyes that stain glial cells, particularly those that wrap themselves around axons.

myelination. Formation of myelin on axons; sometimes used as an index of maturation.

myoclonic spasm. Massive seizure consisting of sudden flexions or extensions of the body and often beginning with a cry.

nalorphine. Semisynthetic congener of morphine; used as an antagonist to morphine and related opioids and in the diagnosis of opioid addiction.

naloxone. Narcotic antagonist structurally related to oxymorphone; used as an antidote to opioid overdosage.

narcolepsy. Condition in which a person is overcome by excessive sleep or inappropriate, recurrent, brief sleep episodes that include REM sleep.

narcotic analgesic. *See* **opioid analgesic**.

nasal hemianopia. Loss of vision of one nasal visual field due to damage to the lateral region of the optic chiasm.

natural selection. Darwin's theory for explaining how new species evolve and how existing species change over time. Differential success in the reproduction of characteristics (phenotypes) results from the interaction of organisms with their environment.

necrosis. Tissue death, usually as individual cells, groups of cells, or in small, localized areas.

negative symptoms. The absence of behaviors; contrasts with *positive symptoms*, which indicate the presence of abnormal behaviors.

neglect dyslexia. Misreading errors usually confined to a single half of a word.

neocortex. Newest layer of the brain, forming the outer layer, or "new bark"; has four to six layers of cells; in this book, synonymous with **cortex**.

neostriatum. The caudate nucleus plus putamen of the basal ganglia; also called the **striatum**.

neotony. Process derived from the observation that newly evolved species resemble the young of their common ancestors.

nerve. Large collection of axons (nerve fibers) coursing together outside the central nervous system.

nerve fiber. As part of a neuron, a long process that carries information from the neuron to other neurons; also a collection of nerve fibers.

nerve growth factor (NGF). Protein that plays a role in maintaining the growth of a cell.

nerve impulse. Movement or propagation of an action potential along the length of an axon; begins at a point close to the cell body and travels away from it.

nerve-net hypothesis. Idea that the brain is composed of a continuous network of interconnected fibers.

neural stem cell. Self-renewing, multipotential cell that gives rise to any of the different types of neurons and glia in the nervous system.

neural tube. Structure in the early stage of brain development from which the brain and spinal cord develop.

neuritic plaques. Areas of incomplete necrosis that are often seen in the cortices of people with senile dementias such as Alzheimer's disease.

neuroblast. Any progenitor cell that develops into a neuron.

neurodevelopmental disorder. Disorder generally defined by performance in a specific school subject that falls significantly below average and seemingly has its origin in abnormal brain development but encompassing disorders of attention, social behavior, and general intellectual functioning as well as learning. Also called *learning disability*.

neuroeconomics. Interdisciplinary field that seeks to understand how the brain makes decisions.

neuroendocrine. Of the interaction of the neural and endocrine (hormonal) systems.

neurofibril. Any of numerous fibrils making up part of the internal structure of a neuron; may be active in transporting precursor chemicals for the synthesis of neurotransmitters.

neurohumoral. In general, of the action of hormones on the brain.

neuroleptic drug. Drug that has an antipsychotic action principally affecting psychomotor activity and that is generally without hypnotic effects. Also called **antipsychotic drug** or **major tranquilizer**.

neurologist. Physician specializing in the treatment of nervous system disorders, brain injury, or dysfunction.

neurology. Branch of medical science dealing with the nervous system, both normal and diseased.

neuron. A nerve cell that transmits and stores information: the basic unit of the nervous system; includes the cell body (soma), many processes (dendrites), and an axon.

neuron theory. Principle that the unit of brain structure and function is the neuron.

neuropeptide. Multifunctional chain of amino acids that acts as a neurotransmitter; synthesized from mRNA on instructions from the cell's DNA. Peptide neurotransmitters can act as hormones and may contribute to learning.

neuropil. Any area in the nervous system composed of mostly unmyelinated axons, dendrites, and glial cell processes that forms a synaptically dense region containing a relatively low number of cell bodies.

neuroplasticity. The nervous system's potential for physical or chemical change that enhances its adaptability to environmental change and its ability to compensate for injury. Also called *plasticity* or *brain plasticity*.

neuroprosthetics. Field that develops computer-assisted devices to replace lost biological function.

neuropsychology. Study of the relations between brain function and behavior.

neurosurgery. Brain surgery intended to repair damage to alleviate symptoms resulting from known neurological disease. Contrast **psychosurgery**.

neurotoxin. Any substance that is poisonous or destructive to nerve tissue; for example, 6-hydroxydopamine, placed in the ventricles of the brain, will selectively destroy the norepinephrine and dopamine systems.

neurotransmitter. Chemical released by a neuron onto a target with an excitatory or inhibitory effect.

neurotrophic factors. Class of nourishing compounds that support growth and differentiation in developing neurons and may act to keep certain neurons alive in adulthood.

neurotropic viruses. Viruses having a strong affinity for cells of the central nervous system. *See also* **pantropic viruses**.

nicotine. Poisonous alkaloid obtained from tobacco or produced synthetically.

nicotinic receptor. Cholinergic receptor at the neuromuscular junction.

nightmares. Terrifying dreams.

Nissl stain. Dye used to stain neurons for microscopic examination.

Nissl substance. Large granular body that stains with basic dyes; collectively forms the substance of the reticulum of the cytoplasm of a nerve cell.

nitric oxide (NO). Gas that acts as a chemical neurotransmitter, for example, to dilate blood vessels, aid digestion, and activate cellular metabolism.

nocioception. Perception of pain, temperature, and itch.

node of Ranvier. Space separating the Schwann cells that form the covering (or myelin) on a nerve axon; richly endowed with voltage-sensitive ion channels. Nodes of Ranvier accelerate the propagation of nerve impulses.

nonfluent aphasia. Impairment of speech subsequent to brain damage, particularly to the frontal part of the hemisphere dominant for speech; characterized by difficulty in articulating words.

non-REM (NREM) sleep. All segments of sleep excluding REM sleep.

nonspecific afferents. Neuronal projections that presumably serve general functions, such as maintaining a level of activity or arousal so that the cortex can process information; terminate diffusely over large regions of the cortex. Compare **specific afferents**.

noradrenergic neuron. From adrenaline, Latin for "epinephrine"; a neuron containing norepinephrine.

norepinephrine (NE, or noradrenaline). Neurotransmitter found in the brain and in the sympathetic division of the autonomic nervous system; accelerates heart rate in mammals.

norepinephrinergic neuron. Neuron that contains norepinephrine in its synapses or uses norepinephrine as its neurotransmitter.

nuclear magnetic resonance (NMR). *See* **magnetic resonance imaging (MRI)**.

nuclear membrane. Membrane surrounding the nucleus of a cell.

nucleus (pl. nuclei). Spherical structure in the soma of a cell; contains DNA and is essential to cell function; also, a cluster of cells that can be identified histologically and has specific functions in mediating behavior.

nystagmus. Constant, tiny involuntary eye movements that have a variety of causes.

object agnosia. *See* **apperceptive agnosia** and **associative agnosia**.

object constancy. Perceptual experience in which objects are identified as being the same regardless of the angle of view.

object recognition. Ability to identify the characteristics of objects, including their names and functions.

obsessive–compulsive disorder (OCD). Behavioral condition characterized by compulsively repeated acts (such as hand washing) and repetitive, often unpleasant, thoughts (obsessions).

obstructive sleep apnea. Constriction of the breathing apparatus that results in loss of breath, mainly during REM sleep; thought to be caused by a collapse of the oropharynx during the paralysis of dream sleep.

occipital horns. Most-posterior projections of the lateral ventricles that protrude into the occipital lobe.

occipital lobe. General area of the cortex lying in the back part of the head.

olfaction. Sense of smell or the act of smelling.

oligodendrocytes. Glial cells in the central nervous system that myelinate axons.

ophthalmologic migraine. Migraine affecting vision.

opioid analgesic. Drug like morphine, with sleep-inducing (narcotic) and pain-relieving (analgesic) properties; originally *narcotic analgesic*.

opium. Crude resinous extract from the opium poppy.

optic ataxia. Deficit in visually guided hand movements that cannot be ascribed to motor, somatosensory, or visual-field or -acuity deficits.

optic chiasm. Point at which the optic nerve from one eye partly crosses to join the other, forming a junction at the base of the brain.

optic flow. Streaming of visual stimuli that accompanies an observer's forward movement through space.

optogenetics. Transgenic technique that combines genetics and light to control targeted cells in living tissue.

orbitofrontal cortex (OFC). Cortex comprising Brodmann areas 47 and lateral parts of 11, 12, and 13; gains input from all sensory modalities; projections influence autonomic nervous system physiological changes important for decision making related to emotion and reward.

organ of Corti. Organ lying against the basilar membrane in the cochlear duct; contains special sensory receptors for hearing and consists of neuroepithelial hair cells and several types of supporting cells.

organic brain syndrome. General term for behavioral disorders that result from brain malfunction attributable to known or unknown causes.

organicity. General term referring to atypical behavior assumed to have a biological (organic) basis.

organizational hypothesis. Proposal that actions of hormones in development alter tissue differentiation; for example, testosterone masculinizes the brain.

organophosphate. Extremely toxic compound used to manufacture insecticides, herbicides, and chemical weapons including sarin gas.

orientation. Direction.

orienting reaction. Process by which an animal's attention is engaged by a novel stimulus.

oscilloscope. Instrument that displays a visual representation of electrical variations on the fluorescent screen of a cathode-ray tube.

ossicles. Bones of the middle ear: malleus (hammer), incus (anvil), and stapes (stirrup).

otolith organs. Bodies in the inner ear that provide vestibular information.

output cell. Cell that conveys information away from a circuit; motor neuron that conveys information to a muscle.

output cell layers. Cell layers that send efferent connections to other parts of the nervous system; layers 5 and 6 in the cerebral cortex.

oval window. Region in the inner ear where the ossicles amplify and convey vibrations that subsequently stimulate the basilar membrane.

pain gate. Hypothetical neural circuit in which activity in fine-touch and pressure pathways diminishes the activity in pain and temperature pathways.

paired helical filaments. Two spiral filaments made of chains of amino acids.

paleocortex. Part of the cerebral cortex forming the pyriform cortex and parahippocampal gyrus. Also called the paleopallium.

panic disorder. Recurrent attacks of intense terror that arise without warning and without any apparent relation to external circumstances.

pantropic viruses. Viruses that attack any body tissue. *See also* **neurotropic viruses**.

papilledema. Swelling of the optic disc caused by increased pressure from cerebrospinal fluid; used as a diagnostic indicator of tumors or other swellings in the brain.

paragraphia. Writing of incorrect words or perseveration in writing the same word.

paralimbic cortex. Area of three-layered cortex adjacent to the classically defined limbic cortex and directly connected with the limbic cortex—for example, the *cingulate cortex*.

parallel-development hypothesis. Idea that both hemispheres, by virtue of their anatomy, play special roles, one for language and one for space.

paraphasia. Production of unintended syllables, words, or phrases during speech.

paraplegia. Paralysis of the legs due to complete transection spinal-cord damage.

paraplegic. Of persons whose spinal cord has been cut, making them unable to have control over their legs.

parasite. Plant or animal that lives on or within another living organism at whose expense it obtains some advantage.

parasympathetic nerves. Calming nerves of the autonomic nervous system that enable the body to "rest and digest." Compare **sympathetic nerves**.

paresis. General term for loss of physical and mental ability due to brain disease, particularly from syphilitic infection; a term for slight or incomplete paralysis.

parietal lobe. General region of the brain lying behind the frontal lobe, beneath the parietal bone.

parietal occipital sulcus. Sulcus in the occipital cortex.

Parkinson's disease. Disorder of the motor system correlated with a loss of dopamine in the brain and characterized by tremors, muscular rigidity, involuntary movements (*akathesia*), and changes in emotion and memory.

pars opercularis. Part of the inferior frontal lobe adjacent to the parietal lobe and overhanging the insula.

partial seizure. Abnormal electrical discharges restricted to only one or a few brain regions.

parvocellular layer. Layer of neurons containing small cells.

Pavlovian (classical) conditioning. Form of *associative learning*.

peptide. Any member of a class of compounds of low molecular weight that yield two or more amino acids on hydrolysis. Peptides form the consistent parts of proteins.

peptide hormone. Chemical messenger synthesized by cellular DNA that acts to affect the target cell's physiology.

perception. Subjective interpretation of sensations by the brain.

perforant pathway. Connects ("perforates") the hippocampus to medial temporal (limbic) regions; when disrupted, results in major hippocampal dysfunction.

periaqueductal gray matter (PAG). Nuclei in the midbrain that surround the cerebral aqueduct; PAG contains circuits for species-typical behaviors and play an important role in modulating pain.

peripheral nerves. Nerves that lie outside the spinal cord and the brain.

peripheral nervous system (PNS). Collective name for all the neurons in the body that are located outside the brain and spinal cord and can regrow after damage.

perseveration. Tendency to emit repeatedly the same verbal or motor response to varied stimuli.

persistent vegetative state (PVS). Condition in which a person is alive but unable to communicate or to function independently at even the most basic level.

pervasive developmental disorder not otherwise specified (PDD-NOS). A form of autism spectrum disorder that does not meet specific DSM-5 criteria.

phagocytes. Cells that engulf microorganisms, other cells, and foreign particles as part of the lymphatic system's defenses.

phenothiazines. Group of major tranquilizers (for example, chlorpromazine) that are similar in molecular structure to the compound phenothiazine.

phenotype. Individual characteristics that can be seen or measured.

phenotypic plasticity. An individual's capacity to develop into more than one phenotype.

pheromone. Odorant biochemical released by one individual that acts as a chemosignal and can affect the physiology or behavior of another animal of the same species.

phobia. Fear of a clearly defined object or situation.

phoneme. Unit of sound that forms a word or part of a word.

phonological dyslexia. Reading disorder characterized by an inability to read nonwords aloud; reading otherwise may be nearly flawless.

phonological reading. Reading that relies on sounding out the parts of words to decode their meanings.

phospholipid. Molecule having a "head" that contains phosphorus and two tails that are lipid, or fat. Phospholipids constitute the membrane bilayer, a double-layered cell membrane.

phrenology. Long-discredited study of the relation between mental faculties and the skull's surface features.

physical dependence. Physical need for a drug; indicated by the display of withdrawal symptoms on cessation of drug use.

physostigmine. Drug, toxic in large doses, that acts as an acetylcholine agonist by inhibiting acetylcholinesterase, the enzyme that breaks down acetylcholine.

pia mater. Moderately tough connective tissue that clings to the surface of the brain.

piloerection. Erection of the hair.

pineal gland. Gland in the hypothalamus; source of hormones that influence daily and seasonal biorhythms.

pinna. External structure of the outer ear.

pituitary gland. Collection of neurons at the base of the hypothalamus.

place cell. Type of neuron in the hippocampal formation maximally responsive to specific locations in the world; *place-by-direction cells* encode not only location but also direction and speed of movement.

place response. Navigational behavior in which an animal moves to a position on the basis of its location relative to two or more cues. Compare **cue response** and **position response**.

place task. Task in which an animal must find a place that it cannot see by using the relation between two or more cues in its surroundings.

planum temporale. Area comprising the anterior and posterior superior temporal planes (aSTP and pSTP), together with the auditory cortex (Heschl's gyrus) within the lateral (Sylvian) fissure.

Plasmodium. Genus of a sporozoan parasite in the red blood cells of animals and humans; causative agent of malaria.

plasticity. *See* **neuroplasticity**.

pneumoencephalography. Invasive X-ray technique in which cerebrospinal fluid is replaced by air introduced through a lumbar puncture.

poliomyelitis. Disorder of motor-neuron cell bodies caused by an acute, infectious viral disease; loss of motor neurons causes paralysis and muscle wasting, and if motor neurons of the respiratory centers are attacked, death can result from asphyxia.

polygraph. Apparatus for simultaneously recording blood pressure, pulse, and respiration, as well as variations in electrical resistance of the skin; popularly known as a lie detector.

polymodal (multimodal) cortex. Cortex that receives sensory inputs from more than one sensory modality—for example, vision and audition.

polypeptide chain. Peptide containing more than two amino acids linked by peptide bonds.

polyribosome. Structure formed by the combination of mRNA and ribosomes that serves as the site for protein synthesis.

polysensory neuron. Neuron within multimodal cortex that is responsive to both visual and auditory or both visual and somatosensory input.

pons. Part of the hindbrain; composed mostly of motor-fiber tracts going to such areas as the cerebellum and spinal cord.

position response. Navigational behavior in which an animal uses its previous movements as a cue—that is, movements (for example, left or right) previously made to arrive at the same location. Compare **cue response** and **place response**.

positive symptoms. Occurrence of abnormal behaviors. Compare **negative symptoms**.

positron-emission tomography (PET). Imaging technique that detects changes in blood flow by measuring changes in the uptake of compounds such as oxygen or glucose; used to analyze the metabolic activity of neurons.

posterior cerebral artery (PCA). Vessel that irrigates the ventral and posterior surfaces of the cortex, including the occipital lobe and hippocampal formation.

posterior cortex. Neocortex posterior to the central fissure; specifies movement goals and sends sensory information from vision, touch, and hearing into the frontal regions via multiple routes.

posterior parietal cortex. Parietal areas PE, PF, and PG lying posterior to the primary somatosensory areas.

posterior root. Nerve composed of fibers carrying sensory information that enters each segment of the posterior spinal cord. Compare **dorsal root**.

postictal depression. State of reduced affect and confusion subsequent to a seizure.

postsynaptic membrane. Membrane on the transmitter-input side of a synapse (dendritic spine).

posttraumatic stress disorder (PTSD). Syndrome characterized by physiological arousal stemming from recurring memories and dreams related to a traumatic event for months or years after the event.

praxis. Action, movement, or series of movements.

preadaption. Behavior that evolves for one purpose but then becomes useful for another purpose.

precentral gyrus. Gyrus lying in front of the central sulcus; also called **M1** or **primary motor cortex**.

precession. Comparatively slow gyration of the rotation axis of a spinning body about another line intersecting it, describing a cone shape.

preferred cognitive mode. Use of one type of thought process in preference to another—for example, visuospatial instead of verbal; sometimes attributed to the assumed superior function of one hemisphere over the other.

prefrontal cortex (PFC). Large frontal-lobe area anterior to the motor, premotor, and cingulate cortex, including dorsolateral, ventromedial, and orbitofrontal regions that receive projections from the dorsomedial nucleus of the thalamus; plays a key role in controlling functions such as planning and strategizing and in emotional behaviors.

premotor cortex (PMC). Frontal lobe areas 6, 8, and 44, lying immediately anterior to the motor cortex; houses a movement repertoire (lexicon) that recognizes others' movements and selects similar or different actions.

presynaptic membrane. Membrane on the transmitter-output side of a synapse (axon terminal).

primary areas. Neocortical regions that receive projections from the major sensory systems or send projections to the muscles.

primary motor cortex (M1). Neocortical area corresponding to Brodmann's area 4; a major source of the corticospinal tract.

primary projection area. *See* **primary areas**.

primary sensory cortex. Neocortical area that receives the projections of the principal thalamic regions for each sensory modality; corresponds to Brodmann's areas 17 (vision), 41 (audition), and 3-1-2 (somatosensation).

primary zones. *See* **primary areas**.

priming. Experimental technique using a stimulus to sensitize the nervous system to a later presentation of the same or a similar stimulus.

proactive interference. Interference of something already experienced with the learning of new information.

procedural memory. Memory for certain ways of doing things or for certain movements; this memory system is thought to be independent of declarative memory (that is, memory used to "tell about" some event).

progenitor cell. Precursor cell derived from a stem cell; it migrates and produces a neuron or glial cell.

projection map. Map of the cortex made by tracing axons from the sensory systems into the brain and from the neocortex to the motor systems of the brainstem and spinal cord.

proprioception. Perception of the position and movement of the body, limbs, and head.

proprioceptive. Of sensory stimuli coming from the muscles and tendons.

prosencephalon. Front brain, the most anterior part of the embryonic mammalian brain; in adult fish, amphibians, and reptiles, responsible for olfaction.

prosody. Tone of voice: variation in stress, pitch, and rhythm of speech that conveys different shades of meaning.

prosopagnosia. Facial-recognition deficit not explained by defective acuity or reduced consciousness or alertness; rare in pure form and thought to be secondary to right parietal lesions or bilateral lesions.

protein. Any of a group of complex organic compounds containing carbon, hydrogen, oxygen, nitrogen, and, in some cases, sulfur. Proteins, the principal constituents of the protoplasm of all cells, are of high molecular weight and consist of amino acids connected by peptide linkages.

proximal. Close to some point.

pseudodepression. Personality change subsequent to frontal-lobe lesion in which apathy, indifference, and loss of initiative are apparent symptoms but are not accompanied by a patient's sense of being dejected or dispirited.

pseudopsychopathy. Personality change subsequent to frontal-lobe lesion in which immature behavior, lack of tact and restraint, and other behaviors symptomatic of psychopathology are apparent but are not accompanied by the equivalent mental or emotional components of psychopathology.

psilocybin. Psychedelic drug obtained from the mushroom *Psilocybe mexicana.*

psychedelic drug. Drug that can alter sensation and perception; examples are lysergic acid diethylamide, mescaline, and psilocybin.

psychoactive drug. Substance that acts to alter mood, thought, or behavior; is used to manage neuropsychological illness; or is abused.

psychology. Science dealing with the mind and mental processes, especially in relation to human and animal behavior.

psychometrics. Science of measuring human abilities.

psychomotor activation. Increased behavioral and cognitive activity; at certain levels of drug consumption, the user feels energetic and in control.

psychopharmacology. Study of how drugs affect the nervous system and behavior.

psychosis. Major mental disorder of organic or emotional origin in which a person's ability to think, respond emotionally, remember, communicate, interpret reality, and behave appropriately is sufficiently impaired that the ordinary demands of life cannot be met; applicable to conditions having a wide range of severity and duration—for example, schizophrenia or depression.

psychosurgery. Surgical destruction of some brain region to alleviate severe and otherwise intractable psychiatric disorders or to alter behavior. Contrast **neurosurgery**.

ptosis. Drooping of the upper eyelid from paralysis of the third nerve (oculomotor).

pulvinar. Thalamic nucleus that receives projections from the visual cortex and superior colliculus and sends connections to the secondary and tertiary temporal and parietal cortex.

pump. Protein in the cell membrane that actively transports a substance across the membrane. Also called a **transporter**.

punctate evolution. Evolution that appears to occur suddenly, rather than in gradual steps; sometimes referred to as *punctuated evolution*.

punctuated evolution. *See* **punctate evolution**.

pure aphasia. Aphasia in the absence of other language disorders such as *alexia* or *agraphia*.

putative transmitters. Chemicals strongly suspected of being neurotransmitters but not conclusively proved to be so.

pyramid. Pointed or cone-shaped structure or part; refers to protrusion of corticospinal tract on the ventral surface of the brainstem.

pyramidal cells. Nerve cells with pyramid-shaped cell bodies that usually send information from one region of the cortex to some other area in the central nervous system.

pyramidal tract. Corticospinal tract; pathway from the neocortex to the spinal cord that crosses after the pyramids in the brainstem.

pyramidalis area. Brodmann's area 4.

pyriform cortex. Old cortex; subserves olfactory functions.

quadrantanopia. Defective vision or blindness in one-fourth of the fovea (visual field).

quadriplegia. Paralysis of the legs and arms due to spinal-cord damage or transection.

quantum (pl. quanta). Amount of neurotransmitter, equivalent to the contents of a single synaptic vesicle, that produces a just observable change in postsynaptic electric potential.

quasi-evolutionary sequence. Hypothetical sequence of animals that represent consecutive stages in evolutionary history; ancestral lineage of a contemporary species comprising currently living species that most closely resemble those ancestors.

radial glial cells. Cells that form miniature "highways" provide pathways for migrating neurons to follow to their appropriate destinations.

rapidly adapting receptor. Somatosensory receptor that responds briefly to the onset of a stimulus on the body.

rate-limiting factor. Any enzyme that is in limited supply, thus restricting the pace at which a chemical can be synthesized.

readiness potential. Event-related potential that occurs just before a movement.

reafference. Confirmation by one part of the nervous system of the activity in another. *See also* **corollary discharge**.

reafference theory. *See* **corollary-discharge theory**.

real space. Space that one sees around oneself; three-dimensional space.

recency memory. *See* **short-term memory, temporal memory, working memory.**

receptive field. Area from which a stimulus can activate a sensory receptor.

receptor. Protein on a cell membrane to which another molecule can attach.

reciprocal inhibition. Activation of one muscle group with inhibition of its antagonists.

reconsolidated memory. Memory that enters a labile phase when recalled and is then restored as a new memory.

reconsolidation theory. Proposal that memories rarely consist of a single trace or neural substrate but are revised each time they are recalled or shared or elaborated on with others.

red nucleus. Nucleus in the anterior part of the tegmentum that is the source of a major motor projection.

reentry. Interactive mechanism by which any cortical area can influence the area from which it receives input; proposed as a mechanism for solving the *binding problem*.

referred pain. Pain felt on the surface of the body that is actually due to pain in an internal body organ.

reflex. Specific movement dependent only on a simple spinal-cord circuit and elicited by specific forms of sensory stimulation.

regeneration. Process by which neurons damaged by trauma regrow connections to the area that they innervated before the trauma.

relatively refractory period. The later phase of an action potential during which increased electrical current is required to produce another action potential; a phase during which potassium channels are still open.

REM (rapid eye movement) sleep. Period of sleep during which rapid eye movements occur; associated with loss of muscle tone and vivid dreams.

Renshaw loop. Circular set of connections in which the axon collateral of motor-neuron axon leaving the spinal cord synapses on a nearby CNS interneuron, which synapses back on the motor neuron's cell body.

resting potential. Normal voltage across a nerve-cell membrane; varies between 60 and 90 mV in the cells of various animals.

resting-state fMRI (rs-fMRI). Functional magnetic resonance imaging method that measures changes in elements such as iron or oxygen when the individual is resting (not engaged in a specific task).

reticular formation. Mixture of nuclei and fibers that runs through the center of the brainstem, extending from the spinal cord to the thalamus; associated with sleep–wake behavior and behavioral arousal. Also known as the *reticular activating system (RAS)*.

reticular matter. Any nervous system area composed of intermixed cell bodies and axons; has a mottled gray and white, or netlike, appearance.

retinal ganglion cell (RGC). One of a group of retinal neurons with axons that give rise to the optic nerve.

retrograde amnesia. Inability to remember events that took place before the onset of amnesia; compare **anterograde amnesia**.

retrograde degeneration. Degeneration of a nerve cell between the site of damage and the cell body, including the cell body and all its remaining processes.

retrograde transport. Transport of material by a neuron from its axon back to the cell body. Labels or dyes can be placed at the termination of an axon, picked up by the axonal arborization, and transported to the cell body, which makes it possible to trace pathways.

reuptake. Deactivation of a neurotransmitter when membrane transporter proteins bring it back into the presynaptic axon terminal for subsequent reuse.

rhombencephalon. Posterior chamber of the embryonic mammalian brain, which divides into the *metencephalon* and *myelencephalon*; in adult fish, amphibians, and reptiles, controls movement and balance.

ribonucleic acid (RNA). Complex macromolecule composed of a sequence of nucleotide bases attached to a sugar–phosphate backbone. Messenger RNA delivers genetic information from DNA to a ribosome (containing ribosomal RNA), where the appropriate molecules of transfer RNA assemble the appropriate amino acids to produce the polypeptide encoded by the DNA.

ribosome. Large complex of enzymes and ribosomal RNA molecules that catalyzes reactions in the formation of proteins.

righting reflex. Behavior by which an animal placed in an inverted posture returns to upright; survives low decerebration.

rod. Photoreceptor cells that contain rhodopsin specialized for functioning at low light levels.

saccade. Series of involuntary, abrupt, and rapid small movements or jerks of both eyes simultaneously in changing the point of fixation.

saccule. One of two vestibular receptors of the middle ear; stimulated when the head is oriented normally; maintains head and body in an upright position.

salience network. Correlated activity among the anterior cingulate cortex, supplementary motor cortex, and anterior insular cortex that operates to modulate other brain networks' activities and is most active when a behavioral change is needed; compare **default network**.

saltatory conduction. Propagation of a nerve impulse on a myelinated axon; characterized by its leaping from one node of Ranvier to another.

savant syndrome. Condition characterized by various degrees of neurodevelopmental disorder, along with some special, sometimes supranormal, skill.

scanning electron microscope. Electron microscope that can produce three-dimensional images of an object.

scene construction theory. Hypothesis that, for information to be biologically useful, it has to be "packaged" as a composite of past experience, present context, and future prospects.

schizophrenia. Behavioral disorder characterized by delusions, hallucinations, disorganized speech, blunted emotion, agitation or immobility, and a host of associated symptoms.

Schwann cells. Glial cells in the peripheral nervous system that myelinate sensory and motor axons.

sclera. Tough white outer coat of the eyeball.

sclerotic plaque. Hardened or inflamed connective tissue or blood vessels. Sclerotic plaques are often seen in the brains of people with Alzheimer's disease.

scotoma. Small blind spot in the visual field caused by small lesions, an epileptic focus, or migraines of the occipital lobe.

secondary area. Cortical region that receives inputs from the primary areas and is thought to participate in more-complex sensory and perceptual or motor functions.

secondary projection area. Area of the cortex that receives projections from a *primary projection area* or sends projections to it.

second-generation antidepressant. Drug whose action is similar to that of tricyclics (first-generation antidepressants) but more selective in its action on serotonin reuptake transporters; also called *atypical antidepressant.*

second messenger. Chemical that carries a message to initiate a biochemical process when activated by a neurotransmitter (the first messenger).

sedative-hypnotic. Any drug that acts to depress neural activity (and behavior) by either decreasing noradrenergic activity or increasing GABAergic activity.

selective serotonin reuptake inhibitor (SSRI). Tricyclic antidepressant drug that blocks the reuptake of serotonin into the presynaptic terminal.

semantic memory. Memory of world knowledge stored independently of the time and place at which it was acquired.

semantics. Study of meaning in language.

semicircular canals. Structures in the middle ear that are open on one side and act as part of the receptor unit for balance.

sensation. Registration by the sensory systems of physical or chemical energy from the environment and its transduction into nervous-system activity.

sensitization. Increased responsiveness to equal doses of a drug; learned behavior in which the response to a stimulus strengthens with repeated presentations because the stimulus is novel or is stronger than normal—for example, after habituation has occurred.

sensitization model. Model for bipolar illness; proposes that the brain of the bipolar patient is especially sensitive to the effects of stressors or drugs and that episodes of mood disorder actually change the brain.

sensorimotor transformation. Neural calculations that integrate the movements of different body parts (eyes, body, arm, and so forth) with the sensory feedback of what movements are actually being made and the plans to make the movements. Sensorimotor transformation depends on both movement-related and sensory-related signals produced by cells in the posterior parietal cortex.

sensory aphasia. *See* **Wernicke's aphasia.**

sensory neglect. Condition in which an organism does not respond to sensory stimulation.

sensory pathway. Nerve fibers that convey sensory information to the brain.

sensory receptor. Cell that transduces sensory information into nervous system activity.

septum. Nucleus in the limbic system that, when lesioned in rats, produces sham rage and abolishes the theta EEG waveform.

serial lesion effect. Effect in which slowly acquired lesions or lesions acquired in stages tend to have less-severe symptoms than those of lesions of equivalent size that are acquired at one time.

serotonin (5-HT). Amine neurotransmitter that plays a role in regulating mood and aggression, appetite and arousal, pain perception, and respiration.

sex-related differences. Behavioral differences between males and females that are related to experience, genes, or hormones, or some combination of them.

sexual selection. Mechanism of evolution in which the processes of determining who mates with whom also determine the characteristics of the offspring that will be produced.

short-term memory. System for holding a neural record of recent events and their order used to recall sensory events; movements; and cognitive information such as digits, words, names, or other items for a brief period. *See also* **recency memory, temporal memory, working memory.**

simultagnosia. Agnosia symptom in which a person is unable to perceive more than one object at a time.

simultaneous extinction. Somatoperceptual disorder in which two stimuli would be reported if applied singly, but only one would be reported if both were applied together; second stage of recovery from contralateral neglect characterized by response to stimuli on the neglected side as if there were a simultaneous stimulation on the contralateral side.

single-photon emission computed tomography (SPECT). Imaging technique in which a subject is given a radioactively labeled compound such as glucose, which is metabolized by the brain. The radioactivity is later recorded by a special detector.

skull. The cranium; the bony framework of the head, composed of the cranial and facial bones.

sleep apnea. Inability to breathe during sleep: the brain fails to signal the muscles to breathe, so a person has to wake up to do so.

sleep attack. Brief, often irresistible sleep episodes—probably slow-wave, NREM, naplike sleep that may occur with or without warning.

sleep paralysis. Inability to move on awakening from sleep. *See also* **hypnogogic hallucination**.

slowly adapting receptor. Body sensory receptor that responds as long as a sensory stimulus is on the body.

slow-wave sleep. Stage of sleep characterized by an electroencephalogram dominated by large-amplitude slow waves.

small-molecule transmitter. Quick-acting neurotransmitters synthesized in the axon terminal from products derived from the diet.

social cognition. Perceptual categorizing that enables a person to develop hypotheses about other people's intentions. Also referred to as **theory of mind**.

social neuroscience. Interdisciplinary field that seeks to understand how the brain mediates social interactions.

sodium–potassium (Na⁺–K⁺) pump. Pumplike mechanism that shunts sodium out of the cell and potassium into it.

soma. *See* **cell body**.

somasomatic. Cell body to cell body connections on gap junctions that allow neighboring neurons to synchronize their signals and glial cells to function.

somatic nervous system (SNS). Nerve fibers that are extensively connected to sensory receptors on the body's surface and to muscles and that carry information to the CNS. Subdivision of the *peripheral nervous system*.

somatosensory neuron. Neuron that projects from the body's sensory receptors into the spinal cord; the dendrite and axon are connected, which speeds information conduction because messages do not have to pass through the cell body.

somatosensory system. Neural system pertaining to the tactile senses, including touch, kinesthesia, pain, and proprioception.

somatosensory threshold. Threshold for detecting tactile sensations.

somatosensory zone. Any region of the brain responsible for analyzing sensations of fine touch and pressure and possibly of pain and temperature.

somnolence. Sleepiness; excessive drowsiness.

sparing. Phenomenon by which some brain functions are saved from disruption after the occurrence of a lesion early in life, usually before the particular function has developed.

spatial learning. Learning spatial information such as the location of a goal object; also called *spatial memory*.

spatial summation. Tendency of two adjacent events to add. Hence, two adjacent postsynaptic potentials add or subtract.

species. Group of organisms that can interbreed.

species-typical behavior. Behavior characteristic of all members of a species.

specific afferents. Neuronal projections that bring information (sensory information, for example) to an area of the cortex and terminate in relatively discrete cortical regions, usually in only one or two layers. Compare **nonspecific afferents**.

specifically reading retarded. Refers to people who have adequate intelligence to be able to read but cannot read.

spinal animal. Animal in which an injury severs the spinal cord from the rest of the central nervous system.

spinal cord. Part of the central nervous system enclosed within the vertebral column.

spinal reflex. Response obtained when only the spinal cord is functioning.

spiny neurons. Class of mostly excitatory neurons that have dendritic spines.

splenium. Generally, a bandlike structure; used in reference to the posterior rounded end of the corpus callosum.

split brain. Brain in which the two hemispheres are isolated.

spongioblasts. Immature cells that develop into glial cells.

spreading depression. Condition in which a wave of depolarization spreads across the cortical surface, leading to a period in which the tissue is functionally blocked.

sprouting. Phenomenon subsequent to partial damage in which the remaining neurons or parts of a neuron sprout terminations to connect to the previously innervated area.

standardized test battery. Set of neuropsychological tests with fixed criteria for *organicity*, which is used to distinguish behavioral symptoms from those not directly related to brain pathology.

stellate cell. Nerve cell characterized by a star-shaped cell body. Such cells serve largely as association cells whose processes remain within the region of the brain in which the cell body is located.

stem cell. Cell capable of producing daughter cells that differentiate into other more specialized cells.

stereognosis. Tactile perception: recognition of objects through the sense of touch.

steroid hormone. Lipid-soluble chemical messenger synthesized from cholesterol.

stimulation. Act of applying a stimulus or an irritant to something.

stimulus. Irritant or event that causes a change in action of some brain area.

stimulus gradient. Gradient along which the intensity of a cue increases or decreases—for example, an odor becomes stronger as its source is approached.

stirrup. One of the ossicle bones of the middle ear. Also known as the stapes.

storage granule. Membranous compartment that holds several vesicles containing a neurotransmitter.

stretch reflex. Contraction of a muscle to resist stretching; mediated through a muscle spindle, a special sensory-receptor system in the muscle.

striate cortex. Primary visual cortex (area 17, V1) in the occipital lobe; has a striped appearance when stained.

striatum. The caudate nucleus plus putamen of the basal ganglia; also called the **neostriatum**.

stroke. Sudden appearance of neurological symptoms as a result of severe interruption of blood flow.

study–test modality shift. Process by which people, when presented with information in one modality (reading) and tested in another modality (aurally), display poorer performance than when they are instructed and tested in the same modality.

subarachnoid space. Space between the arachnoid layer and the pia mater of the meninges.

subcortical loop. Reciprocal cortical–subcortical connections or feedback loops.

substance abuse. Use of a drug for the psychological and behavioral changes it produces aside from its possible therapeutic effects.

substance dependence. *See* **addiction**.

substantia gelatinosa. Gelatinous-appearing cap forming the dorsal part of the posterior horn of the spinal cord.

substantia nigra. Nuclei in the midbrain containing the cell bodies of dopamine-containing axons that connect to the forebrain and are important in rewarding behaviors. In freshly prepared human tissue, the region appears black; hence the name (Latin for "black substance").

subventricular zone. Lining of neural stem cells surrounding the ventricles in adults.

sudden infant death syndrome (SIDS). Sudden, unexplained death of a seemingly healthy infant less than 1 year old.

sulcus (pl. sulci). Cleft in the cortex produced by folding.

superior colliculi. Bilateral nuclei of the midbrain tectum that receive projections from the retina of the eye and mediate visually related behavior.

superior temporal sulcus (STS). Furrow separating the superior and middle temporal gyri; part of the multimodal cortex characterized by *polysensory neurons* responsive to both visual and auditory or both visual and somatosensory input; the third stream of visual processing originates from structures associated with both the parietal and the temporal pathways and flows to a region buried in the STS.

surface dyslexia. Ability to read by using phonological, or sounding-out, procedures but inability to read words on the basis of their pictographic or graphemic representations. Common in children who have difficulty learning to read.

Sylvian fissure. *See* **lateral fissure**.

sympathetic nerves. Arousing nerves of the autonomic nervous system that enable the body to "fight or flee" or engage in vigorous activity. Compare **parasympathetic nerves**.

symptomatic seizures. Seizures identified with a specific cause, such as infection, trauma, tumor, vascular malformation, toxic chemicals, very high fever, or other neurological disorder.

synapse. Junction that forms the information-transfer site between an axon terminal and another cell

synaptic cleft. Gap that separates the presynaptic membrane from the postsynaptic membrane.

synaptic vesicle. Organelle consisting of a membrane structure that encloses a quantum of neurotransmitter.

synesthesia. Sensory mixing: the ability to perceive a stimulus of one sense as the sensation of a different sense; literally, "feeling together."

syntax. Ways in which words are put together, following the rules of grammar, to form phrases, clauses, or sentences; proposed as a unique characteristic of human language.

synthetic biology. Design and construction of biological devices and systems for useful purposes, focusing on engineering biology and biotechnology.

system consolidation theory. Idea that the hippocampus consolidates new memories, a process that makes them permanent then stores them in a new location, in the neocortex.

tachistoscope. Mechanical apparatus consisting of projector, viewer, and screen by which visual stimuli can be presented to selective parts of the visual field.

tactile. Of the sense of touch.

tactile form recognition. Recognition of the shape of an object by touch.

tardive dyskinesia. Slow, abnormal limb or body-part movements.

tau protein. Protein abundant in the CNS that stabilizes microtubules within neurons. High levels in fluid bathing the brain are linked to poor recovery after head trauma; accumulation in brain tissue is a sign of *dementia*.

Tay-Sachs disease. Inherited birth defect caused by the loss of genes that encode the enzyme necessary for breaking down certain fatty substances; appears 4 to 6 months after birth and results in seizures, blindness, degenerating motor and mental abilities, and death by about age 5.

tectopulvinar pathway. Projections from the retina to the superior colliculus (tectum) to the pulvinar (thalamus) to the parietal and temporal visual areas; functions to locate visual stimuli.

tectum. Roof of the midbrain; located above the cerebral aqueduct; consists of the superior and inferior colliculi, which mediate whole-body responses to visual and auditory stimuli, respectively, and the production of orienting movements.

tegmentum. Floor of the midbrain; located below the cerebral aqueduct; contains a collection of sensory and motor tracts and nuclei with movement-related, species-specific, and pain-perception functions.

telencephalon. Endbrain; includes the mammalian cerebral cortex, basal ganglia, limbic system, and olfactory bulbs.

teleodendria. Fine terminal branches of an axon.

temporal lobe. Area of the cortex and connections below the lateral fissure, adjacent to the temporal bones.

temporal memory. Memory for the order of events in time. Also **working memory**, **short-term memory**, **recency memory**.

temporal summation. Tendency of two events related in time to add. Hence, two temporally related postsynaptic potentials add or subtract.

temporoparietal junction (TPJ). Region where the temporal and parietal lobes meet at the end of the Sylvian fissure.

terminal button. *See* **end foot**.

terminal degeneration. Degeneration of the terminals of neurons; can be detected by selective tissue staining.

tertiary areas. Cortical regions that receive projections from secondary areas or send projections to them; encompasses all cortex not specialized for sensory or motor function and mediates complex activities such as language, planning, memory, and attention. Also **association cortex**.

tesla. Unit for measuring the strength of a magnetic field.

testosterone. Sex hormone secreted by the testes and responsible for the distinguishing characteristics of the male.

tetrahydrocannabinol (THC). Active ingredient in marijuana; obtained from the female hemp plant *Cannabis sativa*.

thalamus. Group of nuclei in the diencephalon that integrates information from all sensory systems and projects it into the appropriate cortical regions.

theory of mind. Ability to predict what others are thinking or planning to do. Also called **social cognition**.

thermoregulation. Ability to regulate body temperature.

theta rhythm. Brain rhythm with a frequency of 4 to 7 Hz.

threshold. Point at which a stimulus produces a response.

threshold potential. Voltage level of a neural membrane at which an action potential is triggered by the opening of sodium and potassium voltage-sensitive channels; about −50 mV.

thrombosis. Plug or clot in a blood vessel, formed by the coagulation of blood, that remains at the place of its formation.

tight junction. Connection between cells when their membranes are fused. Normally, cells are separated by a small space. *See* **gap junction**.

time-dependent retrograde amnesia. Amnesia typically induced by traumatic brain injury, the severity of which determines how far back in time the amnesia extends, extending from the present to the more-distant past, and generally shrinking over time, often leaving a residual amnesia of only a few seconds to a minute for events immediately preceding the injury.

tissue plasminogen activator (t-PA). Drug for treating ischemic stroke; breaks up clots and allows the return of normal blood flow to the affected region if administered within 3 hours.

tolerance. Decline in response to repeated administration of a drug over time.

tonotopic representation. Property of audition in which sound waves are processed in a systematic fashion from lower to higher frequencies.

topographic disorientation. Following brain injury, gross disability in finding one's way in relation to salient environmental cues; likely due to topographic agnosia or amnesia.

topographic map. Spatially organized neural representation of the external world.

topographic memory. Memory for the organization of the world.

topographic organization. Neural–spatial representation of the body or areas of the sensory world a sensory organ detects.

topographic representation. Representation of the auditory world in which sounds are located in a systematic fashion in a progression from lower to higher frequencies.

Tourette's syndrome. Disorder of the basal ganglia characterized by tics; involuntary vocalizations (including curse words and animal sounds); and odd, involuntary movements of the body, especially of the face and head.

tract. Large collection of axons coursing together within the central nervous system; also **fiber pathway**.

transcortical aphasia. Disorder in which an affected person can repeat and understand words and name objects but cannot speak spontaneously or can repeat words but cannot comprehend them. Also called **isolation syndrome**.

transcranial magnetic stimulation (TMS). Noninvasive procedure in which a magnetic coil is placed over the skull to stimulate the underlying brain; can be used either to induce behavior or to disrupt ongoing behavior.

transcranially. Across the skull.

transcription. Synthesis of RNA from a DNA template, catalyzed by RNA polymerase. The base sequences of the RNA and DNA are complementary.

transformation hypothesis. Idea that memory is recoded with use and thus changes from one type to another.

transgenic animal. Product of technology in which numbers of genes or a single gene from one species is introduced into the genome of another species, passed along, and expressed in subsequent generations.

transient global amnesia. Short-lived memory impairment with a sudden onset, usually a short course, and described as loss of old memories and inability to form new memories; may result from transient episodes of ischemia.

transient ischemia. Short-lived condition of inadequate supply of blood to a brain area.

translation. Synthesis of a polypeptide with the use of messenger RNA as a template.

transmitter-activated receptor. Protein that has a binding site for a specific neurotransmitter and is embedded in the cell membrane.

transmitter substance. Chemical that allows neurons to communicate with one another and with glands, muscles, and other body organs.

transneuronal degeneration. Degeneration of a cell that synapses with a damaged cell or a cell onto which a damaged cell synapses; for example, sectioning of optic tracts results in the degeneration of lateral geniculate body cells.

transporter. Protein in the cell membrane that actively pumps a substance across the membrane. Also called a **pump**.

traumatic brain injury (TBI). Wound to the brain that results from a blow to the head. *See also* **concussion**.

traumatic encephalopathy. Degenerative disease of the brain brought on by a head trauma; compare **chronic traumatic encephalopathy**.

trephining. Removing a disc of bone, chiefly from the skull.

tricyclic antidepressant. First-generation antidepressant drug with a chemical structure characterized by three rings that block the serotonin reuptake transporter.

tubules. Variety of kinds of thin rods of material in cells that provide structure, aid in movement, and serve as pathways for the transport of material within a cell.

tumor. A *neoplasm*, or mass of new tissue that persists and grows independently, surrounds healthy tissue, and has no physiological use.

Turner's syndrome. Genetic condition in which a female has only a single X chromosome. Women with Turner's syndrome have severe spatial deficits.

two-point sensitivity. Ability to discriminate two individual points on the skin. The threshold is the minimum distance apart that two points must be placed to be perceived as two points rather than one point. Also called **two-point discrimination**.

uncinate fasciculus. Fiber pathway connecting temporal and frontal cortices; a hooked or curved tract.

unconscious inference. Processes outside of awareness and learned by experience whereby observers use knowledge to perceive and make decisions.

unilateral visual neglect. Neglect of all sensory events of one or more modalities of stimulation when the stimulation is restricted to one half of the world as defined by the central axis of the body.

unit activity. Electrical potential of a single cell.

utricle. Largest of the subdivisions of the labyrinth of the middle ear; major organ of the vestibular system, which provides information about the position of the head.

ventral root. Nerve composed of fibers carrying motor information from the ventral (in humans, anterior) part of an animal's spinal cord.

ventral stream. Visual processing pathway from the primary visual cortex to the temporal cortex for object identification and perceiving related movements.

ventricle. Cavity of the brain that contains cerebrospinal fluid.

ventriculography. X-ray technique by which the contours of the ventricles are highlighted with the use of an opaque medium introduced into the ventricle through a cannula inserted through the skull.

ventromedial prefrontal cortex (VMPFC). Comprises Brodmann areas 10, 14, 25 and medial parts of areas 11, 12, and 13 plus anterior area 32. Connects subcortically with structures capable of emotional behavior bodywide; responsible for selecting behavior with respect to context, based either on current circumstance or previous knowledge, including self-knowledge.

vertebral artery. Major artery supplying blood to the hindbrain and spinal cord.

vesicle. Small bladder or sac containing liquid.

vestibular system. Somatosensory system comprising a set of receptors in each inner ear that respond to body position and movement of the head.

viral meningitis. Inflammation of the brain's triple-layered protective covering by a viral infection.

virtual-reality (VR) exposure therapy. Controlled virtual-immersion environment that, by allowing individuals to relive traumatic events, gradually desensitizes them to stress. *See* **cognitive behavioral therapy**.

virus. Encapsulated aggregate of nucleic acid made of either DNA or RNA and characterized by a lack of independent metabolism and by the ability to replicate only within living host cells.

visual ataxia. Inability to recognize where objects are located.

visual-form agnosia. Inability to see the shapes of objects, to recognize objects or drawings of them.

visual localization. Identification of a place in visual space.

visualization. Ability to form a mental image of an object.

vocal cords. Folds of mucous membrane in the larynx that are attached to the vocal muscles; also, *vocal folds*.

voltage. Strength of a charged electrical current.

voltage gradient. Difference in voltage between two regions that allows a flow of current if the two regions are connected.

voltage-sensitive channel. Narrow passageway across the neuron membrane that is opened and closed in response to changes in the voltage across the membrane.

voltage-sensitive potassium channel. Voltage-sensitive channel that allows the passage of potassium ions.

voltage-sensitive sodium channel. Voltage-sensitive channel that allows the passage of sodium ions.

volume conducted. Descriptor for electrical potential recorded in tissue at some distance from its source.

volume-conducted wave. Wave recorded through the brain and through the skull—conducted in the manner that waves travel through water.

voluntary movement. Any movement that takes an animal from one place to another to accomplish some adaptive purpose. Also called appetitive, instrumental, purposive, or operant movement.

voxel. Area from which a measurement is taken, thus defining the resolution of a brain-imaging method.

wanting-and-liking theory. Theory that, when a drug has been used in association with certain cues, the cues themselves will elicit desire for the drug. Also called **incentive-sensitization theory**.

Wernicke–Geschwind model. Theoretical model of the neurological organization of language involving a serial passage of information from the auditory cortex to the posterior speech zone to the anterior speech zone.

Wernicke's aphasia. Inability to comprehend or to produce meaningful speech even though the production of words remains intact. Also called **sensory aphasia**. *See also* **fluent aphasia**.

Wernicke's area. Secondary auditory cortex (part of the planum temporale, roughly equivalent to Brodmann's area 22), that regulates language comprehension; also called *posterior speech zone*.

white matter. Areas of the nervous system rich in fat-sheathed neural axons that form the connections between brain cells.

wild type. Allele most common in a populaton.

Wilson's disease. Genetic disease characterized by the failure to metabolize copper, which is concentrated in the brain.

withdrawal reflex. Withdrawal of a limb in response to applied stimuli that activate pain and temperature fibers. The reflex is mediated by a multisynaptic pathway in the spinal cord.

withdrawal symptom. Physical and psychological behavior displayed by an addicted user when drug use ends.

word salad. Fluent aphasia in which a person produces intelligible words that appear to be strung together randomly.

working memory. *See* **short-term memory**.

X-ray imaging. Imaging methods sensitive to the density of different parts of the brain, the ventricles, nuclei, and pathways.

NAME INDEX

SUBJECT INDEX

Note: Page numbers followed by f indicate figures; those followed by t indicate tables.

interconnections among, 272–275,
272f–274f. *See also* Connectome;
Cortical connections
Association cortex, 77, 77f
Association fibers, 464
Associative agnosia, 369
Associative learning, 433–434, 445–446,
446f
frontal lobe in, 445–446, 446f
Astereognosis, 385, 385f
Astroglia, 61, 61t
Asymbolia for pain, 386
Asymmetry, 284–313. *See also*
Cerebral organization; Laterality/
lateralization
anatomical, 284–289, 285f, 287t
in animals, 343–345
in auditory system, 299–300, 299f,
300f, 300t
behavioral, 298–304
in birds, 344
of body parts, 330
cultural factors in, 338–340
deafness and, 340
development and, 342–343, 343f
environmental factors in, 338–340
of facial expressions, 563–564, 563f
of facial structure, 409–411, 411f
of fingerprints, 330, 330f
of frontal lobe, 435
genetic factors in, 288–289
handedness and, 301–302, 316–323,
345. *See also* Handedness
hemispheric encoding and retrieval
and, 496–497
in hominids, 287
in homosexuals, 330–331
imaging studies and, 304–306
interaction models of, 308–309
lateralized lesions and, 289–290
of lesion-related deficits, 332–333
mapping of, 286, 286f
in motor system, 301–303, 302f
neurodevelopmental disorders and,
693–694, 694f
neuronal, 288, 288f
in nonhuman primates, 344–345
of occipital lobe, 368
ontogeny of, 342–343, 343f
of parietal lobe, 375, 394, 394t
of planum temporale, 693, 694f
sensory deficits and, 340–341
sex differences in, 329–330, 329f,
330f
sexual orientation and, 330–331
in somatosensory system, 300–301,
300f
specialization models of, 306–308
in split-brain patients, 470–471
of temporal lobe, 415–416
testosterone and, 693–694

variations in, 316–346
in visual system, 298, 368
Ataxia, 750t
optic, 367, 387, 582
visual, 17, 213, 387, 582
Athetosis, 641, 750t
Athletes, neuropsychological
assessment of, 802
Atlases, brain-imaging, 199, 199f
Attention, 607–625
alerting network in, 619
auditory, 420
candidate structures in, 615–618,
616f
in consciousness, 628
deficits in, 622–625
definition of, 608
disengagement and, 393
divided/shifting, 613, 615–618, 616f,
617f
drug effects on, 619
dual executive networks in, 620
effort and, 613, 614f
evolutionary changes in, 608
fear and, 611
frontal lobe in, 625
imaging studies of, 615–618, 616f
mechanisms of, 621–622
to negative stimuli, 611, 611f, 612f
neural basis of, 621–622, 621f
neural networks for, 618–621, 619f
neuropsychological evidence for,
612–614, 612f, 614f
orienting network in, 619–620
parallel processing and, 615
parietal lobe in, 392–393, 613, 616f,
617, 618, 623–624
parietotemporal cortex in, 608–609,
624
Posner-Petersen model of, 620,
621–622, 621f
in reading, 676
in searching, 610–611, 610f–612f
selective, 393, 420, 608, 613–614,
617–618, 617f
self-control and, 620–621
spatial, 392–393
synchronous processing in, 621–622,
621f
temporal lobe in, 420
visual, 357, 420, 610–611, 610f,
611f
vs. automatic processing, 609–611,
626–627
vs. consciousness, 609
Attentional blink, 623
Attentional dyslexia, 543
Attention-deficit/hyperactivity disorder,
157, 158, 681–683
adult outcome in, 695–696
brain abnormalities in, 646

Atypical antipsychotics, 764
Audition. *See* Hearing
Auditory cortex, 217, 217f, 400, 401,
402f, 404. *See also* Cortex
multiple representations in, 210f
Auditory flow, 206
Auditory hallucinations, 417
Auditory maps, 271
Auditory nerve, 68f, 68t, 217, 217f
Auditory pathways, 217, 217f
Auditory processing. *See also* Hearing
brain organization and, 340
disconnection and, 474
in dyslexia, 676–677
lateralization in, 299–300, 299f, 300f
in reading, 675
selective, 420
sound localization in, 214
specialization models of, 306–308
Auditory receptors, 204, 214
Auditory system, 214–217
asymmetry in, 299–300, 299f, 300f,
300t
Aura
in epilepsy, 742
in migraine, 745–746, 745f
Australopithecus, 31, 31f, 33. *See also*
Hominids
Autism spectrum disorders, 281,
686–689, 688f
anatomic correlates of, 687–689,
688f
Asperger's syndrome in, 510,
686–687
brain size in, 37
causes of, 687–689
genetic factors in, 689
memory deficits in, 687
mirror neurons and, 243
savant syndrome and, 687
viral infections and, 689
Autobiographical memory. *See* Episodic
memory
Automatic movements, 257f, 258, 258f,
260–261, 263
Automatic processing, 609–611
vs. consciousness, 626–627
Automatisms, 743
Autonoetic awareness, 434–435, 577
episodic memory and, 487–488
Autonomic nervous system, 4, 69–70,
69f, 116–117, 117f
Autopagnosia, 386
Autoreceptors, 121
Autosomes, 43
Aversive childhood experiences,
developmental effects of, 651
Axoaxonic synapse, 122, 123f
Axodendritic synapse, 122, 123f
Axoextracellular synapse, 122, 123f
Axomuscular synapse, 122